GUIDE TO THE [illegible] TRE

Cases and Materials on EU Law is accompanied by a free Online Resource Centre which contains a range of resources designed to support you throughout your EU law module

www.oxfordtextbooks.co.uk/orc/weatherill12e/

Get started . . .

If you're studying EU law for the first time the Online Resource Centre provides a range of resources to help build your understanding and prepare you for your first lectures including:

- Interactive map of the EU with key facts on each Member State
- Interactive timeline of the development of the EU
- Video clips of key moments in the EU's development

Prepare for exams . . .

The Online Resource Centre includes a range of tools designed to help with your revision including:

- Flashcard glossary of key EU law terminology
- Guide to further web resources to help you pursue areas of interest

Stay up to date . . .

The Online Resource Centre provides updates from the authors on key developments in EU law as well as links to the latest EU law blogs and the European Commission's YouTube channel

And for lecturers . . .

There is guidance on using the book which provides useful tips on how to make the best use of the casebook when teaching

Cases and Materials on EU Law

12th Edition

Stephen Weatherill

OXFORD
UNIVERSITY PRESS

Great Clarendon Street, Oxford, OX2 6DP,
United Kingdom

Oxford University Press is a department of the University of Oxford.
It furthers the University's objective of excellence in research, scholarship,
and education by publishing worldwide. Oxford is a registered trade mark of
Oxford University Press in the UK and in certain other countries

Ninth edition 2010
Tenth edition 2012
Eleventh edition 2014

Impression: 1

Published in the United States of America by Oxford University Press
198 Madison Avenue, New York, NY 10016, United States of America

British Library Cataloguing in Publication Data
Data available

Library of Congress Control Number: 2016938696

ISBN 978–0–19–874880–9

Printed in Great Britain by
Bell & Bain Ltd., Glasgow

OUTLINE CONTENTS

DETAILED CONTENTS

PREFACE

It may seem perverse to begin a Preface explaining what a book is *not* about, but in the case of the law of the European Union I think it is justified. The subject has grown at such a pace over recent years that it is no longer possible to aspire to write a book which is truly comprehensive. The best that one can do is to select areas for examination which seem particularly important and then to use those areas as illustrations to draw out the themes and principles on which the law is based. In this way, one can encourage the student to develop an intellectually appropriate approach which will permit him or her to tackle substantive areas beyond the scope of this book. So, although it is easy to explain away a failure to cover the full extent of the law of the European Union simply by pointing out how much there is of it, I hope that this book has adopted a coherent principle in deciding what to include and what to exclude.

The book is *not* about English law and its reaction to membership of the Union. There is no deep exploration of Parliamentary Sovereignty, the European Communities Act 1972, or the European Union Act 2011. This is a European law book. Nevertheless, the development of the European Community legal order, and lately a European Union legal order, has not occurred in isolation and is in part dependent on action and reaction at national level. In depicting this process, I have tended to draw on the example of the British experience of the impact of membership of the EU. However, the *Cohn Bendit* decision (p. 121) will provide an example of practice in another Member State and the student should always be prepared to look beyond domestic law. Most of all, the attitudes of German courts cannot be ignored, and I have included the *Brunner* decision relating to ratification of the Maastricht Treaty (p. 591), the *Bananas* decision concerning the protection of fundamental rights (p. 594), the *Lisbon* decision concerning ratification of that Treaty (p. 596) and the rumbles of the *Gauweiler* ('OMT') saga (p. 605).

I have touched relatively little on matters of external competence. There is, for example, passing reference only to the Common Customs Tariff, the Common Commercial Policy, and Treaty-making competence generally. The growth of a Common Foreign and Security Policy is located in the context of the three-pillar Union edifice constructed at Maastricht (p. 9) and abandoned at Lisbon (p. 19), but not examined in detail. I have adopted this primarily internal focus with regret, aware that it smacks of an unappealing 'Fortress Europe' attitude. But I think that my choice is in this respect in accordance with most British University degree courses in EU law.

The Treaty of Lisbon entered into force on 1 December 2009. Chapter 1 begins by explaining how and why this Treaty matters (pp. 19–22) and this deserves the student's immediate attention. There are, since the Lisbon Treaty entered into force on 1 December 2009, two governing Treaties, the Treaty on European Union (TEU) and the Treaty on the Functioning of the European Union (TFEU). The TFEU is the successor to the EC Treaty, and it is the main concern of this book. Chapter 1 also explains that Lisbon makes numerical changes to Articles throughout the Treaty, and the reader will be reminded of this (frustrating but unavoidable) detail time and again, chapter by chapter.

In previous editions, essential updating apart, my approach to amendment has always been to prefer to leave material untouched in cases of doubt rather than fiddle with it. I stick to that cautious approach in this new edition in the belief that it helps users. The structure of this twelfth edition is that of the eleventh edition: there are three parts to the book, covering first the constitutional law of the EU, second, trade law and policy – the law of the internal market, including assessment of the status of European citizenship – and third, policy-making, governance, and the constitutional debate. The book has of course been updated and in places freshened up but I have changed nothing merely for the sake of it. I aim at consistency.

As in the previous editions of the book, my concern remains to depict the dynamic process of evolution in the European Union. I have maintained the range of material used in the previous editions, while making some adjustment in the particular sources used. I use lawyers, practising and academic, but also economists, political scientists, and journalists. My aim remains to encourage the student to appreciate how the legal order has been developed (and is still in the process of being developed) in response to sometimes conflicting economic, social, and political pressures.

I continue to owe countless debts of gratitude. Thank you to everyone who has helped. But above all I thank Catherine Redgwell, without whom this book would have been written in a much less happy frame of mind.

The law described is that in force on 1 December 2015.

Stephen Weatherill
December 2015

NEW TO THIS EDITION

The book remains faithful to its long-standing structure but it has been revised and fully updated to give a clear account of the law at the end of 2015. Additions for this new edition include material relevant to the rising prominence of the Charter of Fundamental Rights, including the Court's highly significant rulings in *Digital Rights* and *Schrems* in which EU measures were found to be invalid. Attention is also devoted to Opinion 2/13, in which the Court, anxious to preserve the 'autonomy' of the EU legal order, refused to accept that the EU could accede to the ECHR on the terms negotiated. Chapter 15 deals with the Court's burgeoning case law on Citizenship, including decisions which challenge the need for a cross-border element as an essential trigger to the invocation of EU law, while the ruling in *Dano*, concerning the migrant who is not economically active, proves that the Court is not remorselessly concerned to curtail national autonomy. Chapter 18 pays attention to current trends associated with subsidiarity and enhanced co-operation: both, in different ways, reveal increasing discomfort with old-style narratives about ever closer Union. Chapter 19 includes *Gauweiler* ('OMT') as the latest example of indirect judicial dialogue in the EU.

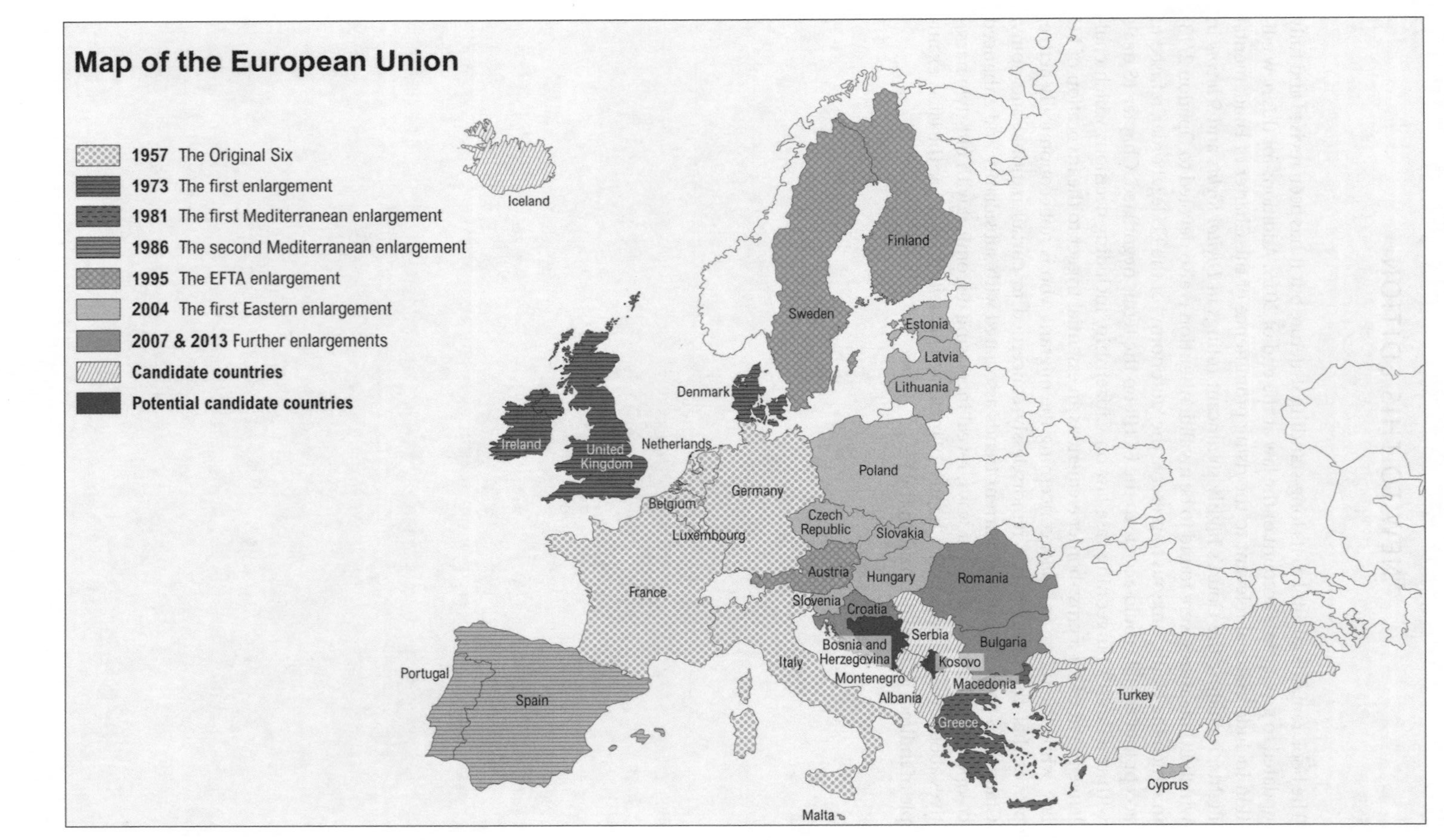
Map of the European Union
1957 The Original Six
1973 The first enlargement
1981 The first Mediterranean enlargement
1986 The second Mediterranean enlargement
1995 The EFTA enlargement
2004 The first Eastern enlargement
2007 & 2013 Further enlargements
Candidate countries
Potential candidate countries
Iceland
Finland
Sweden
Estonia
Latvia
Lithuania
Denmark
Ireland
United Kingdom
Netherlands
Poland
Germany
Belgium
Czech Republic
Slovakia
Luxembourg
Austria
Hungary
Romania
France
Slovenia
Croatia
Serbia
Bosnia and Herzegovina
Bulgaria
Italy
Kosovo
Portugal
Montenegro
Macedonia
Spain
Albania
Turkey
Greece
Cyprus
Malta

ACKNOWLEDGEMENTS

The permission of the following authors and publishers, who have kindly agreed to allow the use of material in this book, is gratefully acknowledged:

Extracts from the following articles published in the *Common Market Law Review* (e Kluwer Academic Publishers):

O. Brouwer, 'Free Movement of Foodstuffs and Quality Requirements: Has the Commission Got it Wrong?' (1988) 25 CML Rev 237.

F. Mancini, 'The Making of a Constitution for Europe', (1989) 26 CML Rev 595.

Extracts from the following article published in the *Journal of Consumer Policy* (Kluwer Academic Publishers): N. Reich, 'Protection of Diffuse Interests in the EEC and the Perspective of Progressively Establishing an Internal Market' (1988) 11 JCP 395.

Extracts from the following articles published in the *Journal of Common Market Studies* (Basil Blackwell, Oxford): J. Pelkmans, 'The New Approach to Technical Harmonization and Standardization' (1986–87) JCMS 249; D. Hodson and I. Maher, 'The Open Method as a new Mode of Governance' (2001) 39 JCMS 719.

Extracts from the following article published in *Legal Issues of European Integration* (Kluwer Academic Publishers): R. Dehousse, '1992 and Beyond: the Institutional Dimension of the Internal Market Programme' [1989/1] LIEI 109.

Extract from the following article published in the *Northern Ireland Legal Quarterly* (SLS Legal Publications): R. Harmsen, 'A European Union of Variable Geometry: Problems and Perspectives' (1994) 45 NILQ 109.

Extract from the following article published in the *Modern Law Review* (Blackwell Publishers, Oxford): F. Snyder, 'The Effectiveness of European Community Law: Institutions, Processes, Tools and Techniques' (1993) 56 MLR 19.

Extract from the *Common Market Law Reports* (reproduced with the permission of Sweet and Maxwell Ltd): '*Minister of the Interior* v *Cohn Bendit*' [1980] 1 CMLR 543.

Extracts from *The European Union: Economics and Policies*, 9th ed. A. M. El-Agraa (2011). Extracts reprinted with the permission of Cambridge University Press.

Extracts from *1992: One European Market?*, eds R. Bieber, R. Dehousse, J. Pinder and J. Weiler (1988, Nomos Verlagsgesellschaft, Baden Baden).

Extracts from P. Cecchini, *The European Challenge: 1992, the Benefits of a Single Market* (1988, Wildwood House/Gower Publishing). Permission of the EC Commission is also gratefully acknowledged.

Extracts from *The European Community and the Challenge of the Future*, ed. J. Lodge (1990 and 2nd ed., 1993, Pinter Publishers Ltd, London). All rights reserved.

Extracts from J. Pinder, *European Community: The Building of a Union* (3rd ed., 1998, Oxford University Press). Copyright J. Pinder.

Extracts from R. Merkin, *A Guide to the Consumer Protection Act 1987* (1987, Financial Training Publications Ltd, London).

Extracts from M. Wilke and H. Wallace, *Subsidiarity: Approaches to Power-Sharing in the European Community* (1990, Royal Institute of International Affairs, London). Published as RIIA Discussion Paper 27.

Extract from *The Guardian* of 13 March 1987.

For the use of material from the *European Court Reports*, the Court of Justice of the European Union.

For the use of Community source material, the Commission of the European Union.

Extract from *The Court of Justice after Maastricht* in D. O'Keeffe and P. Twomey (eds), *Legal Issues of the Maastricht Treaty* (Chancery, 1994); permission granted by the author, William Robinson.

Extract from the following article published in the *Cambridge Law Journal*: R. Caranta, 'Government Liability after Francovich' (1993) 52 CLJ 272, permission kindly granted by both journal and author.

Extracts from the following articles published in *Aussenwirtschaft* (published by Verlag Rüegger AG/ The Swiss Institute for Research into International Economic Relations, Economic Structures and Regional Science at St Gallen): H. Hauser and A. Müller, 'Legitimacy: the Missing Link for Explaining EU-Institution Building' (1995) 50 *Aussenwirtschaft* 17 and D. Curtin, 'The Shaping of a European Constitution and the 1996 IGC' (1995) 50 *Aussenwirtschaft* 237.

Extracts from H.U. Jessurun D'Oliveira, 'Union Citizenship: Pie in the Sky?' in A. Rosas and E. Antola (eds), *A Citizens' Europe* (1995, Sage Publications, London).

Extract from Miguel Poiares Maduro, 'Europe and the Constitution: *What if This is as Good as it Gets?*', Constitutionalism Web-Papers (University of Manchester).

Extracts from A. Menon and S. Weatherill, 'Legitimacy, Accountability and Delegation in the European Union' in A. Arnull and D. Wincott (eds), *Accountability and Legitimacy in the European Union* (OUP, 2002).

Extracts from T. Kostakopoulou, 'Democracy-talk in the European Union: the Need for a Reflexive Approach', (2003) 9(3) *Columbia Journal of European Law* 411.

Extract from V. Heiskanen and K. Kulovesi, *Function and Future of European Law* (Publications of the Faculty of Law, University of Helsinki).

Extracts from the following articles printed in the European Law Journal (published by Basil Blackwell, Oxford): J. Habermas, 'Remarks on Dieter Grimm's "Does Europe Need a Constitution?" ' (1995) 1 ELJ 303; and from J. Scott and D. Trubek, 'Mind the Gap' (2002) 8 ELJ 1. Extract from M. Höpner and A. Schäfer, 'A New Phase of European Integration: Organized Capitalisms in Post-Ricardian Europe' MPifG Discussion Paper 07/4 Max-Planck-Institut für Gesellschaftsforschung, Köln, 2007.

Extract from W. Kerber and R. Van den Bergh, 'Unmasking Mutual Recognition: Current Inconsistencies and Future Chances' Marburg Papers on Economics, No 11–2207 (2007).

Extract from C. Schweiger, 'Beyond Growth and Jobs? Perspectives for the EU Single Market Policy Framework' (2009) 5 Journal of Contemporary European Research 521.

TABLE OF CASES

*Cases and page references in **bold** indicate extracted material*

Alphabetical

Chronological

TABLE OF LEGISLATION

*Page references in **bold** indicate extracted material*

Directives

Regulations

Decisions

UK Statutes

Foreign Statutes

LISBON TABLES OF EQUIVALENCES

Treaty on European Union

Original numbering of the Treaty on European Union	Post-Amsterdam numbering of the Treaty on European Union	Current numbering of the Treaty on European Union (as amended by the Treaty of Lisbon)
Title I	**Title I**	**Title I**
Article A	Article 1	Article 1
		Article 2
Article B	Article 2	Article 3
Article C	Article 3 (repealed)[1]	Article 4
		Article 5[2]
Article D	Article 4 (repealed)[3]	
Article E	Article 5 (repealed)[4]	
Article F	Article 6	Article 6
Article F.1[*]	Article 7	Article 7
		Article 8
Title II	**Title II**	**Title II**
Article G	Article 8 (repealed)[5]	Article 9
	Article 10[6]	
		Article 11
		Article 12
Title III	**Title III**	**Title III**
Article H	Article 9 (repealed)[7]	Article 13
		Article 14[8]
		Article 15[9]
		Article 16[10]
		Article 17[11]
		Article 18
		Article 19[12]
Title IV	**Title IV**	**Title IV**
Article I	Article 10 (repealed)[13]	Article 20 [14]
	Articles 27a to 27e (replaced)	
	Articles 40 to 40b (replaced)	
	Articles 43 to 45 (replaced)	
Title V[***]	**Title V**	**Title V**
		Chapter 1 — General provisions on the Union's external action
		Article 21
		Article 22
		Chapter 2 — Specific provisions on the common foreign and security policy
		Section 1 — common provisions

Original numbering of the Treaty on European Union	Post-Amsterdam numbering of the Treaty on European Union	Current numbering of the Treaty on European Union (as amended by the Treaty of Lisbon)
		Article 23
Article J.1	Article 11	Article 24
Article J.2	Article 12	Article 25
Article J.3	Article 13	Article 26
		Article 27
Article J.4	Article 14	Article 28
Article J.5	Article 15	Article 29
	Article 22 (moved)	Article 30
	Article 23 (moved)	Article 31
Article J.6	Article 16	Article 32
Article J.7	Article 17 (moved)	Article 42
Article J.8	Article 18	Article 33
Article J.9	Article 19	Article 34
Article J.10	Article 20	Article 35
Article J.11	Article 21	Article 36
Article J.12	Article 22 (moved)	*Article 30*
Article J.13	Article 23 (moved)	*Article 31*
Article J.14	Article 24	Article 37
Article J.15	Article 25	Article 38
		Article 39
	Article 47 (moved)	Article 40
Article J.16	Article 26 (repealed)	
Article J.17	Article 27 (replealed)	
	Article 27a (replaced)[(15)]	*Article 20*
	Article 27b (replaced)[(15)]	*Article 20*
	Article 27c (replaced)[(15)]	*Article 20*
	Article 27d (replaced)[(15)]	*Article 20*
	Article 27e (replaced)[(15)]	*Article 20*
Article J.18	Article 28	Article 41
		Section 2 — Provisions on the common security and defence policy
Article J.7	*Article 17 (moved)*	Article 42
		Article 43
		Article 44
		Article 45
		Article 46
Title VI[(***)]	**Title VI(16)**	
Article K.1	Article 29 (replaced)[(17)]	
Article K.2	Article 30 (replaced)[(18)]	
Article K.3	Article 31 (replaced)[(19)]	
Article K.4	Article 32 (replaced)[(20)]	
Article K.5	Article 33 (replaced)[(21)]	
Article K.6	Article 34 (repealed)	

Original numbering of the Treaty on European Union	Post-Amsterdam numbering of the Treaty on European Union	Current numbering of the Treaty on European Union (as amended by the Treaty of Lisbon)
Article K.7	Article 35 (repealed)	
Article K.8	Article 36 (replaced)[22]	
Article K.9	Article 37 (repealed)	
Article K.10	Article 38 (repealed)	
Article K.11	Article 39 (repealed)	
Article K.12	Article 40 (replaced)[23]	*Article 20*
	Article 40 A (replaced)[23]	*Article 20*
	Article 40 B (replaced)[23]	*Article 20*
Article K.13	Article 41 (repealed)	
Article K.14	Article 42 (repealed)	
Title VIa[**]	**Title VII(24)**	**Title VII**
Article K.15[*]	Article 43 (replaced)[24]	*Article 20*
	Article 43 A (replaced)[24]	*Article 20*
	Article 43 B (replaced)[24]	*Article 20*
	Article 44[24]	*Article 20*
Article K.16[*]	Article 44 A (replaced)[24]	*Article 20*
Article K.17[*]	Article 45 (replaced)[24]	*Article 20*
Title VII	**Title VIII**	**Title VIII**
Article L	Article 46	
		Article 47
Article M	Article 47 (replaced)	*Article 40*
Article N	Article 48	Article 48
Article O	Article 49	Article 49
		Article 50
		Article 51
		Article 52
Article P	Article 50 (repealed)	
Article Q	Article 51	Article 53
Article R	Article 52	Article 54
Article S	Article 53	Article 55

(*) New Article introduced by the Treaty of Amsterdam.

(**) New Title introduced by the Treaty of Amsterdam.

(***) Title restructured by the Treaty of Amsterdam.

(1) Replaced, in substance, by Article 7 of the Treaty on the Functioning of the European Union ('TFEU') and by Articles 13(1) and 21, paragraph 3, second subparagraph of the Treaty on European Union ('TEU').

(2) Replaces Article 5 of the Treaty establishing the European Community ('TEC').

(3) Replaced, in substance, by Article 15.

(4) Replaced, in substance, by Article 13, paragraph 2.

(5) Article 8 TEU, which was in force until the entry into force of the Treaty of Lisbon (hereinafter 'current'), amended the TEC. Those amendments are incorporated into the latter Treaty and Article 8 is repealed. Its number is used to insert a new provision.

(6) Paragraph 4 replaces, in substance, the first subparagraph of Article 191 TEC.
9.5.2008 EN Official Journal of the European Union C 115/361
(1) Tables of equivalences as referred to in Article 5 of the Treaty of Lisbon. The original centre column, which set out the intermediate numbering as used in that Treaty, has been omitted.

(7) The current Article 9 TEU amended the Treaty establishing the European Coal and Steel Community. This latter expired on 23 July 2002. Article 9 is repealed and the number thereof is used to insert another provision.

(8) — Paragraphs 1 and 2 replace, in substance, Article 189 TEC;
— paragraphs 1 to 3 replace, in substance, paragraphs 1 to 3 of Article 190 TEC;
— paragraph 1 replaces, in substance, the first subparagraph of Article 192 TEC;
— paragraph 4 replaces, in substance, the first subparagraph of Article 197 TEC.

(9) Replaces, in substance, Article 4.

(10) — Paragraph 1 replaces, in substance, the first and second indents of Article 202 TEC;
— paragraphs 2 and 9 replace, in substance, Article 203 TEC;
— paragraphs 4 and 5 replace, in substance, paragraphs 2 and 4 of Article 205 TEC.

(11) — Paragraph 1 replaces, in substance, Article 211 TEC;
— paragraphs 3 and 7 replace, in substance, Article 214 TEC.
— paragraph 6 replaces, in substance, paragraphs 1, 3 and 4 of Article 217 TEC.

(12) — Replaces, in substance, Article 220 TEC.
— the second subparagraph of paragraph 2 replaces, in substance, the first subparagraph of Article 221 TEC.

(13) The current Article 10 TEU amended the Treaty establishing the European Atomic Energy Community. Those amendments are incorporated into the Treaty of Lisbon. Article 10 is repealed and the number thereof is used to insert another provision.

(14) Also replaces Articles 11 and 11a TEC.

(15) The current Articles 27a to 27e, on enhanced cooperation, are also replaced by Articles 326 to 334 TFEU.

(16) The current provisions of Title VI of the TEU, on police and judicial cooperation in criminal matters, are replaced by the provisions of Chapters 1, 5 and 5 of Title IV of Part Three of the TFEU.

(17) Replaced by Article 67 TFEU.

(18) Replaced by Articles 87 and 88 TFEU.

(19) Replaced by Articles 82, 83 and 85 TFEU.

(20) Replaced by Article 89 TFEU.

(21) Replaced by Article 72 TFEU.

(22) Replaced by Article 71 TFEU.

(23) The current Articles 40 to 40 B TEU, on enhanced cooperation, are also replaced by Articles 326 to 334 TFEU.

(24) The current Articles 43 to 45 and Title VII of the TEU, on enhanced cooperation, are also replaced by Articles 326 to 334 TFEU.

Treaty on the Functioning of the European Union

Original numbering of the Treaty on European Union	Post-Amsterdam numbering of the Treaty on European Union	Current numbering of the Treaty on European Union (as amended by the Treaty of Lisbon)
PART ONE	PART ONE — PRINCIPLES	PART ONE — PRINCIPLES
Article 1	Article 1 (repealed)	
		Article 1
Article 2	Article 2 (repealed)(25)	
		Title I — Categories and areas of union competence
		Article 2
		Article 3
		Article 4
		Article 5
		Article 6
		Title II — Provisions having general application
		Article 7
Article 3	Article 3, paragraph 1 (repealed)(26)	
Article 3	Article 3, paragraph 2	Article 8
Article 3a	Article 4 (moved)	*Article 119*
Article 3b	Article 5 (replaced)(27)	
		Article 9
		Article 10
Article 3c(*)	Article 6	Article 11
	Article 153, paragraph 2 (moved)	Article 12
		Article 13(28)
Article 4	Article 7 (repealed)(29)	
Article 4a	Article 8 (repealed)(30)	
Article 4b	Article 9 (repealed)	
Article 5	Article 10 (repealed)(31)	
Article 5a(*)	Article 11 (replaced)(32)	*Articles 326 to 334*
	Article 11a (replaced)(32)	*Articles 326 to 334*
Article 6	Article 12 (repealed)	*Article 18*
Article 6a(*)	Article 13 (moved)	*Article 19*
Article 7 (repealed)		
Article 7a	Article 14 (moved)	*Article 26*
Article 7b (repealed)		
Article 7c	Article 15 (moved)	*Article 27*
Article 7d(*)	Article 16	Article 14
	Article 255 (moved)	Article 15
	Article 286 (moved)	Article 16
		Article 17
PART TWO	PART TWO — CITIZENSHIP OF THE UNION	PART TWO — NON-DISCRIMINATION AND CITIZENSHIP OF THE UNION
	Article 12 (moved)	Article 18

Original numbering of the Treaty on European Union	Post-Amsterdam numbering of the Treaty on European Union	Current numbering of the Treaty on European Union (as amended by the Treaty of Lisbon)
	Article 13 (moved)	Article 19
Article 8	Article 17	Article 20
Article 8a	Article 18	Article 21
Article 8b	Article 19	Article 22
Article 8c	Article 20	Article 23
Article 8d	Article 21	Article 24
Article 8e	Article 22	Article 25
PART THREE	PART THREE — COMMUNITY POLICIES	PART THREE — POLICIES AND INTERNAL ACTIONS OF THE UNION
		Title I — The internal market
	Article 14 (moved)	Article 26
	Article 15 (moved)	Article 27
Title 1	Title I — Free movement of goods	Title II — Free movement of goods
Article 9	Article 23	Article 28
Article 10	Article 24	Article 29
Article 11 (repealed)		
Chapter 1	Chapter 1 — The customs union	Chapter 1 — The customs union
Section 1 (deleted)		
Article 12	Article 25	Article 30
Articles 13–26 (repealed)		
Article 27 (repealed)	Article 26	Article 31
Article 28	Article 27	Article 32
	Part Three, Title X, Customs cooperation (moved)	Chapter 2 — Customs cooperation
Article 29	*Article 135 (moved)*	Article 33
	Chapter 2 — Prohibition of quantitative restrictions between Member States	Chapter 3 — Prohibition of quantitative restrictions between Member States
Article 30	Article 28	Article 34
Articles 31–33 (repealed)		
Article 34	Article 29	Article 35
Article 35		
Article 36	Article 30	Article 36
Article 37	Article 31	Article 37
Title II	Title II — Agriculture	Title III — Agriculture and fisheries
Article 38	Article 32	Article 38
Article 39	Article 33	Article 39
Article 40	Article 34	Article 40
Article 41	Article 35	Article 41
Article 42	Article 36	Article 42
Article 43	Article 37	Article 43
Articles 44–45 (repealed)		

Original numbering of the Treaty on European Union	Post-Amsterdam numbering of the Treaty on European Union	Current numbering of the Treaty on European Union (as amended by the Treaty of Lisbon)
Article 46	Article 38	Article 44
Article 47 repealed		
Title II	Title III — Free movement of persons, services and capital	Title IV — Free movement of persons, services and capital
Chapter 1	Chapter 1 — Workers	Chapter 1 — Workers
Article 48	Article 39	Article 45
Article 49	Article 40	Article 46
Article 50	Article 41	Article 47
Article 51	Article 42	Article 48
Chapter 2	Chapter 2 — Right of establishment	Chapter 2 — Right of establishment
Article 52	Article 43	Article 49
Article 53 (repealed)		
Article 54	Article 44	Article 50
Article 55	Article 45	Article 51
Article 56	Article 46	Article 52
Article 57	Article 47	Article 53
Article 58	Article 48	Article 54
	Article 294 (moved)	Article 55
Chapter 3	Chapter 3 — Services	Chapter 3 — Services
Article 59	Article 49	Article 56
Article 60	Article 50	Article 57
Article 61	Article 51	Article 58
Article 62 (repealed)		
Article 63	Article 52	Article 59
Article 64	Article 53	Article 60
Article 65	Article 54	Article 61
Article 66	Article 55	Article 62
Chapter 4	Chapter 4 — Capital and payments	Chapter 4 — Capital and payments
Articles 67–73a (repealed)		
Article 73b	Article 56	Article 63
Article 73c	Article 57	Article 64
Article 73d	Article 58	Article 65
Article 73e (repealed)		
Article 73f	Article 59	Article 66
Article 73h (repealed)		
	Article 60 (moved)	*Article 75*
Title IIIa[(**)]	Title IV — Visas, asylum, immigration and other policies related to free movement of persons	Title V — Area of freedom, security and justice
		Chapter 1 — General provisions
Article 73i[(*)]	Article 61	Article 67[(33)]
		Article 68
		Article 69

Original numbering of the Treaty on European Union	Post-Amsterdam numbering of the Treaty on European Union	Current numbering of the Treaty on European Union (as amended by the Treaty of Lisbon)
		Article 70
		Article 71[34]
	Article 64, paragraph 1 (replaced)	Article 72[35]
		Article 73
	Article 66 (replaced)	Article 74
	Article 60 (moved)	Article 75
		Article 76
		Chapter 2 — Policies on border checks, asylum and immigration
Article 73j(*)	Article 62	Article 77
Article 73k(*)	Article 63, points 1 et 2, and Article 64, paragraph 2[36]	Article 78
Article 73k(*)	Article 63, points 3 and 4	Article 79
		Article 80
Article 73l(*)	Article 64, paragraph 1 (replaced)	*Article 72*
		Chapter 3 — Judicial cooperation in civil matters
Article 73m(*)	Article 65	Article 81
Article 73n(*)	Article 66 (replaced)	Article 74
Article 73o(*)	Article 67 (repealed)	
Article 73p(*)	Article 68 (repealed)	
Article 73q (*)	Article 69 (repealed)	
		Chapter 4 — Judicial cooperation in criminal matters
		Article 82[37]
		Article 83[37]
		Article 84
		Article 85[37]
		Article 86
		Chapter 5 — Police cooperation
		Article 87[38]
		Article 88[38]
		Article 89[39]
Title IV	Title V — Transport	Title VI — Transport
Article 74	Article 70	Article 90
Article 75	Article 71	Article 91
Article 76	Article 72	Article 92
Article 77	Article 73	Article 93
Article 78	Article 74	Article 94
Article 79	Article 75	Article 95
Article 80	Article 76	Article 96
Article 81	Article 77	Article 97
Article 82	Article 78	Article 98
Article 83	Article 79	Article 99
Article 84	Article 80	Article 100

Original numbering of the Treaty on European Union	Post-Amsterdam numbering of the Treaty on European Union	Current numbering of the Treaty on European Union (as amended by the Treaty of Lisbon)
Title V	Title VI — Common rules on competition, taxation and approximation of laws	Title VII — Common rules on competition, taxation and approximation of laws
Chapter 1	Chapter 1 — Rules on competition	Chapter 1 — Rules on competition
Section 1	Section 1 — Rules applying to undertakings	Section 1 — Rules applying to undertakings
Article 85	Article 81	Article 101
Article 86	Article 82	Article 102
Article 87	Article 83	Article 103
Article 88	Article 84	Article 104
Article 89	Article 85	Article 105
Article 90	Article 86	Article 106
Section 2 (deleted)		
Article 91 (repealed)		
Section 3	Section 2 — Aids granted by States	Section 2 — Aids granted by States
Article 92	Article 87	Article 107
Article 93	Article 88	Article 108
Article 94	Article 89	Article 109
	Chapter 2 — Tax provisions	Chapter 2 — Tax provisions
Article 95	Article 90	Article 110
Article 96	Article 91	Article 111
Article 97 (repealed)		
Article 98	Article 92	Article 112
Article 99	Article 93	Article 113
	Chapter 3 — Approximation of laws	Chapter 3 — Approximation of laws
Article 100a	*Article 95 (moved)*	Article 114
Article 100	*Article 94 (moved)*	Article 115
Articles 100b-d (repealed)		
Article 101	Article 96	Article 116
Article 102	Article 97	Article 117
		Article 118
	Title VII — Economic and monetary policy	Title VIII — Economic and monetary policy
	Article 4 (moved)	Article 119
	Chapter 1 — Economic policy	Chapter 1 — Economic policy
Article 102a	Article 98	Article 120
Article 103	Article 99	Article 121
Article 103a	Article 100	Article 122
Article 104	Article 101	Article 123
Article 104a	Article 102	Article 124
Article 104b	Article 103	Article 125
Article 104c	Article 104	Article 126

Original numbering of the Treaty on European Union	Post-Amsterdam numbering of the Treaty on European Union	Current numbering of the Treaty on European Union (as amended by the Treaty of Lisbon)
Chapter 2	Chapter 2 — monetary policy	Chapter 2 — monetary policy
Article 105	Article 105	Article 127
Article 105a	Article 106	Article 128
Article 106	Article 107	Article 128
Article 107	Article 108	Article 130
Article 108	Article 109	Article 131
Article 108a	Article 110	Article 132
Article 109	Article 111, paragraphs 1 to 3 and 5 (moved)	*Article 219*
Article 109	Article 111, paragraph 4 (moved)	*Article 138*
		Article 133
Chapter 3	Chapter 3 — Institutional provisions	Chapter 3 — Institutional provisions
Article 109a	Article 112 (moved)	Article 283
Article 109b	Article 113 (moved)	Article 284
Article 109c	Article 114	Article 134
Article 109d	Article 115	Article 135
		Chapter 4 — Provisions specific to Member States whose currency is the euro
		Article 136
		Article 137
	Article 111, paragraph 4 (moved)	Article 138
	Chapter 4 — Transitional provisions	Chapter 5 — Transitional provisions
Article 109e	Article 116 (repealed)	Article 139
Article 109f	Article 117, paragraphs 1, 2, sixth indent, and 3 to 9 (repealed)	
Article 109f	Article 117, paragraph 2, first five indents (moved)	*Article 141, paragraph 2*
	Article 121, paragraph 1 (moved)	
	Article 122, paragraph 2, second sentence (moved)	
	Article 123, paragraph 5 (moved)	Article 140[40]
Article 109g	Article 118 (repealed)	
	Article 123, paragraph 3 (moved)	
	Article 117, paragraph 2, first five indents (moved)	Article 141[41]
	Article 124, paragraph 1 (moved)	Article 142
Article 109h	Article 119	Article 143
Article 109i	Article 120	Article 144
Article 109j	Article 121, paragraph 1 (moved)	*Article 140, paragraph 1*

Original numbering of the Treaty on European Union	Post-Amsterdam numbering of the Treaty on European Union	Current numbering of the Treaty on European Union (as amended by the Treaty of Lisbon)
Article 109j	Article 121, paragraphs 2 to 4 (repealed)	
Article 109k	Article 122, paragraphs 1, 2, first sentence, 3, 4, 5 and 6 (repealed)	
Article 109k	Article 122, paragraph 2, second sentence (moved)	*Article 140, paragraph 2, first subparagraph*
Article 109l	Article 123, paragraphs 1, 2 and 4 (repealed)	
Article 109l	Article 123, paragraph 3 (moved)	*Article 141, paragraph 1*
Article 109l	Article 123, paragraph 5 (moved)	*Article 140, paragraph 3*
Article 109m	Article 124, paragraph 1 (moved)	Article 142
Article 109m	Article 124, paragraph 2 (repealed)	
Title VIa(**)	Title VIII — Employment	Title IX — Employment
Article 109n(*)	Article 125	Article 145
Article 109o(*)	Article 126	Article 146
Article 109p(*)	Article 127	Article 147
Article 109q(*)	Article 128	Article 148
Article 109r(*)	Article 129	Article 149
Article 109s(*)	Article 130	Article 150
Title VIII	Title IX — Common commercial policy (moved)	Part Five, Title II, -common commercial policy
Article 110	Article 131 (moved)	*Article 206*
Article 111 (repealed)		
Article 112	Article 132 (repealed)	
	Article 133 (moved)	Article 207
	Article 134 (repealed)	
Title VIIa(**)	Title X — Customs cooperation (moved)	Part Three, Title II, Chapter 2, Customs cooperation
Article 116(*)	Article 135 (moved)	Article 33
Title VIII	Title XI — Social policy, education, vocational training and youth	Title X — Social policy
Chapter 1(***)	Chapter 1 — social provisions (repealed)	
Article 117	Article 136	Article 151
		Article 152
Article 118	Article 137	Article 153
Article 118a	Article 138	Article 154
Article 118b	Article 139	Article 155
Article 118c	Article 140	Article 156
Article 119	Article 141	Article 157
Article 119a	Article 142	Article 158

Original numbering of the Treaty on European Union	Post-Amsterdam numbering of the Treaty on European Union	Current numbering of the Treaty on European Union (as amended by the Treaty of Lisbon)
Article 120	Article 143	Article 159
Article 121	Article 144	Article 160
Article 122	Article 145	Article 161
Chapter 2	Chapter 2 — The European Social Fund	Title XI — The European Social Fund
Article 123	Article 146	Article 162
Article 124	Article 147	Article 163
Article 125	Article 148	Article 164
Chapter 3	Chapter 3 — Education, vocational training and youth	Title XII — Education, vocational training, youth and sport
Article 126	Article 149	Article 165
Article 127	Article 150	Article 166
Title IX	Title XII — Culture	Title XIII — Culture
Article 128	Article 151	Article 167
Title X	Title XIII — Public health	XIV — Public health
Article 129	Article 152	Article 168
Title XI	Title XIV — Consumer protection	Title XV — Consumer protection
Article 129a	Article 153, paragraphs 1, 3, 4 and 5	Article 169
	Article 153, paragraph 2 (moved)	*Article 12*
Title XII	Title XV — Trans European networks	
	Title XVI — Trans-European networks	
Article 129b	Article 154	Article 170
Article 129c	Article 155	Article 171
Article 129d	Article 156	Article 172
Title XIII	Title XVI — Industry	
	Title XVII — Industry	
Article 130	Article 157	Article 173
Title XIV	Title XVII — Economic and social cohesion	Title XVIII — Economic, social and territorial cohesion
Article 130a	Article 158	Article 174
Article 130b	Article 159	Article 175
Article 130c	Article 160	Article 176
Article 130d	Article 161	Article 177
Article 130e	Article 162	Article 178
Title XV	Title XVIII — Research and technological development	Title XIX — Research and technological development and space
Article 130f	Article 163	Article 179
Article 130g	Article 164	Article 180
Article 130h	Article 165	Article 181

Original numbering of the Treaty on European Union	Post-Amsterdam numbering of the Treaty on European Union	Current numbering of the Treaty on European Union (as amended by the Treaty of Lisbon)
Article 130i	Article 166	Article 182
Article 130j	Article 167	Article 183
Article 130k	Article 168	Article 184
Article 130l	Article 169	Article 185
Article 130m	Article 170	Article 186
Article 130n	Article 171	Article 187
Article 130o	Article 172	Article 188
		Article 189
Article 130p	Article 173	Article 190
Article 130q (repealed)		
Title XVI	Title XIX — Environment	Title XX — Environment
Article 130r	Article 174	Article 191
Article 130s	Article 175	Article 192
Article 130t	Article 176	Article 193
		Title XXI — Energy
		Article 194
		Title XXII — Tourism
		Article 195
		Title XXIII — Civil-protection
		Article 196
		Title XXIV — Administrative cooperation
		Article 197
Title XVII	Title XX — Development cooperation (moved)	Part Five, Title III, Chapter 1, Development cooperation
Article 130u	Article 177 (moved)	*Article 208*
Article 130v	Article 178 (repealed)[42]	
Article 130w	Article 179 (moved)	*Article 209*
Article 130x	Article 180 (moved)	*Article 210*
Article 130y	Article 181 (moved)	*Article 211*
	Title XXI — Economic, financial and technical cooperation with third countries (moved)	*Part Five, Title III, Chapter 2, Economic, financial and technical cooperation with third countries*
	Article 181a (moved)	*Article 212*
PART FOUR	**PART FOUR — ASSOCIATION OF THE OVERSEAS COUNTRIES AND TERRITORIES**	**PART FOUR — ASSOCIATION OF THE OVERSEAS COUNTRIES AND TERRITORIES**
Article 131	Article 182	Article 198
Article 132	Article 183	Article 199
Article 133	Article 184	Article 200
Article 134	Article 185	Article 201
Article 135	Article 186	Article 202
Article 136	Article 187	Article 203
Article 136a	Article 188	Article 204

Original numbering of the Treaty on European Union	Post-Amsterdam numbering of the Treaty on European Union	Current numbering of the Treaty on European Union (as amended by the Treaty of Lisbon)
		PART FIVE — EXTERNAL ACTION BY THE UNION
		Title I —General provisions on the union's external action
		Article 205
	Part Three, Title IX, Common commercial policy (moved)	Title II —Common commercial policy
	Article 131 (moved)	Article 206
	Article 133 (moved)	Article 207
		Title III — Cooperation with third countries and humanitarian aid
	Part Three, Title XX, Development cooperation (moved)	Chapter 1 — development cooperation
	Article 177 (moved)	Article 208[(43)]
	Article 179 (moved)	Article 209
	Article 180 (moved)	Article 210
	Article 181 (moved)	Article 211
	Part Three, Title XXI, Economic, financial and technical cooperation with third countries (moved)	Chapter 2 — Economic, financial and technical cooperation with third countries
	Article 181a (moved)	Article 212
		Article 213
		Chapter 3 — Humanitarian aid
		Article 214
		Title IV — Restrictive measures
	Article 301 (replaced)	Article 215
		Title V — International agreements
		Article 216
	Article 310 (moved)	Article 217
	Article 300 (replaced)	Article 218
	Article 111, paragraphs 1 to 3 and 5 (moved)	Article 219
		Title VI — The Union's relations with international organisations and third countries and the Union delegations
	Articles 302 to 304 (replaced)	Article 220
		Article 221
		Title VII — Solidarity clause
		Article 222
PART FIVE	**PART FIVE — INSTITUTIONS OF THE COMMUNITY**	**PART SIX — INSTITUTIONAL AND FINANCIAL PROVISIONS**
Title I	Title I — Institutional provisions	Title I — Institutional provisions
Chapter 1	Chapter 1 — The institutions	Chapter 1 — The institutions

Original numbering of the Treaty on European Union	Post-Amsterdam numbering of the Treaty on European Union	Current numbering of the Treaty on European Union (as amended by the Treaty of Lisbon)
Section 1	Section 1 — The European Parliament	Section 1 — The European Parliament
Article 137	Article 189 (repealed)[44]	
Article 138	Article 190, paragraphs 1 to 3 (repealed)[45]	
Article 138	Article 190, paragraphs 4 and 5	Article 223
Article 138a	Article 191, first paragraph (repealed)[46]	
Article 138a	Article 191, second paragraph	Article 224
Article 138b	Article 192, first paragraph (repealed)[47]	
Article 138b	Article 192, second paragraph	Article 225
Article 138c	Article 193	Article 226
Article 138d	Article 194	Article 227
Article 138e	Article 195	Article 228
Article 139	Article 196 Article 229	Article 229
Article 140	Article 197, first paragraph (repealed)[48]	
Article 140	Article 197, second, third and fourth paragraphs	Article 230
Article 141	Article 198	Article 231
Article 142	Article 199	Article 232
Article 143	Article 200	Article 233
Article 144	Article 201	Article 234
		Section 2 — The European Council
		Article 235
		Article 236
Section 2	Section 2 — The Council	Section 3 — The Council
Article 145	Article 202 (repealed)[49]	
Article 146	Article 203 (repealed)[50]	
Article 147	Article 204 Article 237	
Article 148	Article 205, paragraphs 2 and 4 (repealed)[51]	
Article 148	Article 205, paragraphs 1 and 3	Article 238
Article 149 (repealed)		
Article 150	Article 206	Article 239
Article 151	Article 207	Article 240
Article 152	Article 208	Article 241
Article 153	Article 209	Article 242
Article 154	Article 210	Article 243
Section 3	Section 3 — The Commission	Section 4 — The Commission
Article 155	Article 211 (repealed)[53]	
		Article 244
Article 156	Article 212 (moved)	*Article 249, paragraph 2*

Original numbering of the Treaty on European Union	Post-Amsterdam numbering of the Treaty on European Union	Current numbering of the Treaty on European Union (as amended by the Treaty of Lisbon)
Article 157	Article 213	Article 245
Article 158	Article 214 (repealed)[(55)]	
Article 159	Article 215	Article 246
Article 160	Article 216	Article 247
Article 161	Article 217, paragraphs 1, 3 and 4 (repealed)[(56)]	
Article 161	Article 217, paragraph 2	Article 248
Article 162	Article 218, paragraph 1 (repealed)[(57)]	
Article 162	Article 218, paragraph 2	Article 249
Article 163	Article 219	Article 250
Section 4	Section 4 — The Court of Justice	Section 5 — The Court of Justice of the European Union
Article 164	Article 220 (repealed)[(58)]	
Article 165	Article 221, first paragraph (repealed)[(59)]	
Article 165	Article 221, second and third paragraphs Article 251	
Article 166	Article 222	Article 252
Article 167	Article 223	Article 253
Article 168	Article 224[(60)]	Article 254
		Article 255
Article 168a	Article 225	Article 256
	Article 225a	Article 257
Article 169	Article 226	Article 258
Article 170	Article 227	Article 259
Article 171	Article 228	Article 260
Article 172	Article 229	Article 261
	Article 229a	Article 262
Article 173	Article 230	Article 263
Article 174	Article 231	Article 264
Article 175	Article 232	Article 265
Article 176	Article 233	Article 266
Article 177	Article 234	Article 267
Article 178	Article 235	Article 268
		Article 269
Article 179	Article 236	Article 270
Article 180	Article 237	Article 271
Article 181	Article 238	Article 272
Article 182	Article 239	Article 273
Article 183	Article 240	Article 274
		Article 275
		Article 276
Article 184	Article 241	Article 277
Article 185	Article 242	Article 278
Article 186	Article 243	Article 279

Original numbering of the Treaty on European Union	Post-Amsterdam numbering of the Treaty on European Union	Current numbering of the Treaty on European Union (as amended by the Treaty of Lisbon)
Article 187	Article 244	Article 280
Article 188	Article 245	Article 281
		Section 6 — The European Central Bank
		Article 282
	Article 112 (moved)	Article 283
	Article 113 (moved)	Article 284
Section 5	Section 5 — The Court of Auditors	Section 7 — The Court of Auditors
Article 188a	Article 246	Article 285
Article 188b	Article 247	Article 286
Article 188c	Article 248	Article 287
Chapter 2	Chapter 2 — Provisions common to several institutions	Chapter 2 — Legal acts of the Union, adoption procedures and other provisions
		Section 1 — The legal acts of the Union
Article 189	Article 249	Article 288
		Article 289
		Article 290[61]
		Article 291[61]
		Article 292
		Section 2 — Procedures for the adoption of acts and other provisions
Article 189a	Article 250	Article 293
Article 189b	Article 251	Article 294
Article 189c	Article 252 (repealed)	
		Article 295
Article 190	Article 253	Article 296
Article 191	Article 254	Article 297
		Article 298
Article 191a[*]	Article 255 (moved)	*Article 15*
Article 192	Article 256	Article 299
		Chapter 3 — The Union's advisory bodies
		Article 300
Chapter 3	Chapter 3 — The Economic and Social Committee	Section 1 — The Economic and Social Committee
Article 193	Article 257 (repealed)[62]	
Article 194	Article 258, first, second and fourth paragraphs	Article 301
Article 195	Article 258, third paragraph (repealed)[63]	
Article 196	Article 259	Article 302
Article 197	Article 260	Article 303

Original numbering of the Treaty on European Union	Post-Amsterdam numbering of the Treaty on European Union	Current numbering of the Treaty on European Union (as amended by the Treaty of Lisbon)
Article 198	Article 261 (repealed)	
	Article 262	Article 304
Chapter 4	Chapter 4 — The Committee of the Regions	Section 2 — The Committee of the Regions
Article 198a	Article 263, first and fifth paragraphs (repealed)[(64)]	
Article 198a	Article 263, second to fourth paragraphs	Article 305
Article 198b	Article 264	Article 306
Article 198c	Article 265	Article 307
Chapter 5	Chapter 5 — The European Investment Bank	Chapter 4 — The European Investment Bank
Article 198d	Article 266	Article 308
Article 198e	Article 267	Article 309
Title II	Title II — Financial provisions	Title II — Financial provisions
Article 199	Article 268	Article 310
Article 200 (repealed)		
		Chapter 1 — The Union's own resources
Article 201	Article 269	Article 311
Article 201a	Article 270 (repealed)[(65)]	
		Chapter 2 — The multiannual financial framework
		Article 312
		Chapter 3 — The Union's annual budget
Article 203	*Article 272, paragraph 1 (moved)*	Article 313
Article 202	Article 271 (moved)	*Article 316*
Article 203	Article 272, paragraph 1 (moved)	*Article 313*
Article 203	Article 272, paragraphs 2 to 10	Article 314
Article 204	Article 273	Article 315
Article 202	*Article 271 (moved)*	Article 316
		Chapter 4 — Implementation of the budget and discharge
Article 205	Article 274	Article 317
Article 205a	Article 275	Article 318
Article 206	Article 276	Article 319
Article 206a (repealed)		
		Chapter 5 — Common provisions
Article 207	Article 277	Article 320
Article 208	Article 278	Article 321
Article 209	Article 279	Article 322
		Article 323
		Article 324
		Chapter 6 — Combating fraud
Article 209a	Article 280	Article 325

Original numbering of the Treaty on European Union	Post-Amsterdam numbering of the Treaty on European Union	Current numbering of the Treaty on European Union (as amended by the Treaty of Lisbon)
		Title III — Enhanced cooperation
	Articles 11 and 11a (replaced)	Article 326[66]
	Articles 11 and 11a (replaced)	Article 327[66]
	Articles 11 and 11a (replaced)	Article 328[66]
	Articles 11 and 11a (replaced)	Article 329[66]
	Articles 11 and 11a (replaced)	Article 330[66]
	Articles 11 and 11a (replaced)	Article 331[66]
	Articles 11 and 11a (replaced)	Article 332[66]
	Articles 11 and 11a (replaced)	Article 333[66]
	Articles 11 and 11a (replaced)	Article 334[66]
PART SIX	PART SIX — GENERAL AND FINAL PROVISIONS	PART SEVEN — GENERAL AND FINAL PROVISIONS
Article 210	Article 281 (repealed)[67]	
Article 211	Article 282	Article 335
Article 212[*]	Article 283	Article 336
Article 213	Article 284	Article 337
Article 213a[*]	Article 285	Article 285
Article 213b[*]	Article 286 (replaced)	*Article 16*
Article 214	Article 287	Article 339
Article 215	Article 288	Article 340
Article 216	Article 289	Article 341
Article 217	Article 290	Article 342
Article 218[*]	Article 291	Article 343
Artilce 219	Article 292	Article 344
Article 220	Article 293 (repealed)	
Article 221	Article 294 (moved)	Article 55
Article 222	Article 295	Article 345
Article 223	Article 296	Article 346
Article 224	Article 297	Article 347
Article 225	Article 298	Article 348
Article 226 (repealed)		
Article 227	Article 299, paragraph 1 (repealed)[68]	
Article 227	Article 299, paragraph 2, second, third and fourth subparagraphs	Article 349
Article 227	Article 299, paragraph 2, first subparagraph, and paragraphs 3 to 6 (moved)	*Article 355*
Article 228	Article 300 (replaced)	*Article 218*
Article 228a	Article 301 (replaced)	*Article 215*
Article 229	Article 302 (replaced)	*Article 220*
Article 230	Article 303 (replaced)	*Article 220*
Article 231	Article 304 (replaced)	*Article 220*
Article 232	Article 305 (repealed)	
Article 233	Article 306	Article 350
Article 234	Article 307	Article 351

Original numbering of the Treaty on European Union	Post-Amsterdam numbering of the Treaty on European Union	Current numbering of the Treaty on European Union (as amended by the Treaty of Lisbon)
Article 235	Article 308	Article 352
		Article 353
Article 236(*)	Article 309	Article 354
Article 237 (repealed)		
Article 238	Article 310 (moved)	Article 217
Article 239	Article 311 (repealed)(69)	
	Article 299, paragraph 2, first subparagraph, and – paragraphs 3 to 6 (moved)	Article 355
Article 240	Article 312 Article 356	
Articles 241–246 (repealed)		
Final Provisions	Final Provisions	
Article 247	Article 313	Article 357
		Article 358
Article 248	Article 314 (repealed)(70)	

(*) New Article introduced by the Treaty of Amsterdam.
(**) New Title introduced by the Treaty of Amsterdam.
(***) Chapter 1 restructured by the Treaty of Amsterdam.
(25) Replaced, in substance, by Article 3 TEU.
(26) Replaced, in substance, by Articles 3 to 6 TFEU.
(27) Replaced, in substance, by Article 5 TEU.
(28) Insertion of the operative part of the protocol on protection and welfare of animals.
(29) Replaced, in substance, by Article 13 TEU.
(30) Replaced, in substance, by Article 13 TEU and Article 282, paragraph 1, TFEU.
(31) Replaced, in substance, by Article 4, paragraph 3, TEU.
(32) Also replaced by Article 20 TEU.
(33) Also replaces the current Article 29 TEU.
(34) Also replaces the current Article 36 TEU.
(35) Also replaces the current Article 33 TEU.
(36) Points 1 and 2 of Article 63 EC are replaced by paragraphs 1 and 2 of Article 78 TFEU, and paragraph 2 of Article 64 is replaced by paragraph 3 of Article 78 TFEU.
(37) Replaces the current Article 31 TEU.
(38) Replaces the current Article 30 TEU.
(39) Replaces the current Article 32 TEU.
(40) — Article 140, paragraph 1 takes over the wording of paragraph 1 of Article 121.
— Article 140, paragraph 2 takes over the second sentence of paragraph 2 of Article 122.
— Article 140, paragraph 3 takes over paragraph 5 of Article 123.
(41) — Article 141, paragraph 1 takes over paragraph 3 of Article 123.
— Article 141, paragraph 2 takes over the first five indents of paragraph 2 of Article 117.
(42) Replaced, in substance, by the second sentence of the second subparagraph of paragraph 1 of Article 208 TFUE.
(43) The second sentence of the second subparagraph of paragraph 1 replaces, in substance, Article 178 TEC.
(44) Replaced, in substance, by Article 14, paragraphs 1 and 2, TEU.
(45) Replaced, in substance, by Article 14, paragraphs 1 to 3, TEU.
(46) Replaced, in substance, by Article 11, paragraph 4, TEU.
(47) Replaced, in substance, by Article 14, paragraph 1, TEU.
(48) Replaced, in substance, by Article 14, paragraph 4, TEU.
(49) Replaced, in substance, by Article 16, paragraph 1, TEU and by Articles 290 and 291 TFEU.
(50) Replaced, in substance, by Article 16, paragraphs 2 and 9 TEU.
(51) Replaced, in substance, by Article 16, paragraphs 4 and 5 TEU.
(53) Replaced, in substance, by Article 17, paragraph 1 TEU.

(55) Replaced, in substance, by Article 17, paragraphs 3 and 7 TEU.
(56) Replaced, in substance, by Article 17, paragraph 6, TEU.
(57) Replaced, in substance, by Article 295 TFEU.
(58) Replaced, in substance, by Article 19 TEU.
(59) Replaced, in substance, by Article 19, paragraph 2, first subparagraph, of the TEU.
(60) The first sentence of the first subparagraph is replaced, in substance, by Article 19, paragraph 2, second subparagraph of the TEU.
(61) Replaces, in substance, the third indent of Article 202 TEC.
(62) Replaced, in substance, by Article 300, paragraph 2 of the TFEU.
(63) Replaced, in substance, by Article 300, paragraph 4 of the TFEU.
(64) Replaced, in substance, by Article 300, paragraphs 3 and 4, TFEU.
(65) Replaced, in substance, by Article 310, paragraph 4, TFEU.
(66) Also replaces the current Articles 27a to 27e, 40 to 40b, and 43 to 45 TEU.
(66) Also replaces the current Articles 27a to 27e, 40 to 40b, and 43 to 45 TEU.
(67) Replaced, in substance, by Article 47 TEU.
(68) Replaced, in substance by Article 52 TEU.
(69) Replaced, in substance by Article 51 TEU.
(70) Replaced, in substance by Article 55 TEU.

ABBREVIATIONS

AC	Appeal Cases
AJCL	American Journal of Comparative Law
All ER	All England (Law) Reports
CA	Court of Appeal (England)
CDE	Cahiers de Droit Européen
CEE	Charges having equivalent effect
Ch	Chancery Reports
CLJ	Cambridge Law Journal
CMLR	Common Market Law Reports
CML Rev	Common Market Law Review
Cmnd.	Command Paper
Crim LR	Criminal Law Review
EBLR	European Business Law Review
EC (ECs)	European Community (-ies)
ECB	European Central Bank
ECLJ	European Consumer Law Journal
ECLR	European Competition Law Review
ECR	European Court Reports
ECSC	European Coal and Steel Community
EEC	European Economic Community
EEIG	European Economic Interest Grouping
EIPR	European Intellectual Property Review
EJIL	European Journal of International Law
EL Rev	European Law Review
ERPL	European Review of Private Law
EU	European Union
EuL R	European Law Reports
EuR	Europarecht
EURATOM	European Atomic Energy Community
GATT	General Agreement on Tariffs and Trade
HL	House of Lords (UK)
IBL	International Business Lawyer
ICLQ	International and Comparative Law Quarterly
ILJ	Industrial Law Journal
IRLR	Industrial Relations Law Reports
JBL	Journal of Business Law
JCMS	Journal of Common Market Studies
JCP	Journal of Consumer Policy
JEL	Journal of Environmental Law
JEPP	Journal of European Public Policy
J Law and Econ	Journal of Law and Economics
JSWFL	Journal of Social Welfare and Family Law
LIEI	Legal Issues of European Integration
LQR	Law Quarterly Review
MEQR	Measures having equivalent effect to a quantitative restriction
MJ	Maastricht Journal of European & Comparative Law
MLR	Modern Law Review
NILQ	Northern Ireland Legal Quarterly

OJ	Official Journal (of the ECs)
OJLS	Oxford Journal of Legal Studies
QB	Queen's Bench
RTDE	Revue Trimistrelle de Droit Européen
SEA	Single European Act
SI	Statutory Instrument
TEU	Treaty on European Union
TFEU	Treaty of the Functioning of the European Union
WLR	Weekly Law Reports
WTO	World Trade Organization
YEL	Yearbook of European Law

PART I

The Constitutional Law of the EU

1

The Evolution of the European Union

The Treaty of Lisbon entered into force on 1 December 2009, over fifty years since the entry into force of the first of the Treaties that shaped the modern European Union. The student is entitled to ask: 'Do I really need to know anything about what happened before December 2009? Can't I just start with the Lisbon Treaty and look forward in my studies, not back?'

It's a very fair question, and in writing this book I have done everything I possibly can to abandon the clutter of what has become merely historically interesting. Just because we old hands have stored up a pile of knowledge about the twists and turns of the EU's development does not mean we should inflict it on the student. But the answer to the question the student is entitled to ask is nevertheless – 'no! You can't just start with the Lisbon Treaty, and yes! You do need to know something about what has gone before'.

In part that is because the Lisbon Treaty is, on its own, utterly incomprehensible. It is an *amending* Treaty. Like its predecessors – the Nice Treaty (which entered into force in 2003), the Amsterdam Treaty (1999), the Maastricht Treaty (1993), and the Single European Act (1987) – it is not designed to be read in isolation. Rather, it amends the original texts, most significantly that of the Treaty of Rome which established from 1958 the most important of the original European Communities, the European Economic Community. The text that you will in practice need to learn to work with is the *consolidated text* of the European Union Treaties – that means, the text that absorbs all the amendments made over the years and sets out the true – comprehensible – picture. It was first made available at http://eurlex.europa.eu/JOHtml.do?uri=OJ:C:2008:115:SOM:EN:HTML. And there are two Treaties, the Treaty on European Union (TEU) and the Treaty on the Functioning of the European Union (TFEU). Most of the nuts and bolts are contained in the TFEU, and that will be our major preoccupation in this book.

So in the 1950s there was created a European Economic Community (EEC), but it was renamed the European Community (EC) by the amendments of the Maastricht Treaty with effect from 1993, when the EC became part of a wider, but oddly shaped, European Union (EU). Since 1 December 2009, the date of entry into force of the Lisbon Treaty, the European Community is no more, and the structure has been pulled under a single roof, that of the European Union. So the correct label now is the European Union, and it is European Union (or EU) law which we deal with today.

The majority of the material contained in this book – legislation, case law, academic comment – pre-dates the entry into force of the amendments crafted by the Lisbon Treaty. So it does not always use the precise wording of the current texts. You will see regular references to the European Community and to Community law, even though both were transformed in December 2009 into the European Union and Union law respectively. More awkward still, older material does not use the current numbers of the Articles of the Treaty. In fact the Amsterdam Treaty altered the numbering of the provisions of the Treaties, and the Lisbon Treaty did so once again. So, for example, the original Article 30 EEC became, after Amsterdam, Article 28 EC, and now it is

Article 34 TFEU. A table of equivalence(s) is provided at pp. xxxix–lviii. These numerical headaches are now unavoidable, and the shift from Article xyx 'EC' to Article abc 'TFEU' is just something that we have to get used to, but I have written this book in such a way as to avoid making a meal of it. I aim simply to remind you of the mundane but frustrating changes in numbering whenever we come across older material. A lot of the time the alterations are merely cosmetic and older material is as relevant today as it ever was, even though we now live 'after Lisbon' in a European Union, not a European Community. To a large extent, Lisbon matters little when we look at the core issues of EU law. And in this book I do not take any time with dry explanation of what the law *was* – my concern is only to draw out where there are changes, and to reflect on why, in explaining what the law is today. In that sense, you sometimes need to know what the situation was before Lisbon in order to understand why things are as they are today. And, of course, the more you know about past patterns of European integration, the better equipped you are to understand what may lie in the future. But in this book I avoid telling you how things were simply for the sake of it.

The purpose of this introductory chapter is to provide the historical and institutional background. What are the motivations underlying the European Union? How has it acquired its present shape? So we shall return to Lisbon at the end of this chapter, for it is the most recent episode in the EU's construction project.

For students in British law schools, EU law has long held a well-deserved reputation for being extremely difficult to come to grips with. Yet at the end of the course most students tend to look back on it as a subject which they have found more interesting than most of the others which they have studied. There are good reasons for this apparent paradox. European Union law is initially difficult, because it represents an adventure into a new legal system. When a student starts the study of a new English or Scots law subject, he or she comes to it with an accumulated fund of knowledge and expectation about the basic principles of the legal order. It is possible immediately to approach the substance of the subject. Not so with European Union law. Indeed, nothing could be worse than to try to leap into the study of this new legal order equipped with domestic preconceptions about what judges do and about how law should be interpreted and applied. EU law is simply different, and it is necessary to learn to walk before one can run. For the law student who had thought that he or she had already picked up a spanking pace in legal education, this return to basic constitutional law can be a dispiriting experience. However, once the essentials of the subject are mastered, EU law is likely to prove a rewarding race to have run. It is a subject which enjoys internal coherence. Its themes and principles are consistent and can be understood and applied relatively easily. There are themes in the substantive law, such as the objective of establishing an internal market, and there are principles in the constitutional law, such as the supremacy and direct effect of EU law. The approach of the judges of the Court of Justice of the European Union may initially seem odd, but it too displays a certain thematic consistency which can quickly be appreciated. There is even consistency in the difficulties and tensions which beset the development of EU law. The problems of integrating the features of the EU legal order with the traditions of domestic legal systems will be observed on many occasions.

As an academic lawyer with a particular interest in European Union law, I hope that it will one day be possible to abandon these cautionary notes. Most Law Schools are aware of the need to integrate the key elements of the study of EU law into their degree programmes from the earliest possible stage, so that it does not present to the student this initially forbidding prospect. Those who teach substantive European Union law courses remain aware that this task is by no means complete.

Part I of this book deals with the constitutional law of the EU. This covers the sources of Union law in Chapter 2, and then examines in Chapters 3 to 8 the fundamental ground rules of the legal order. The most prominent of these essential principles are the doctrines of supremacy and of direct effect, and the preliminary reference procedure.

However, given these comments, is it right to start with Part I? I have already mentioned that the early weeks of study are difficult, even intimidating. True, in examining a legal system, there is an obvious logic in beginning with its sources. But there is an equally strong argument for starting by acquiring a knowledge of the purpose of the system. This broader perspective can help the subject to come alive more quickly. Chapter 9, in Part II, therefore deserves the student's examination at an early stage. So too do Chapters 17–19, which comprise Part III of the book and which help to illustrate what the Union actually does, while also drawing out some bigger questions about its nature and its relationship with the Member States. Equally, once the student has grasped the substantive law of the Union it would be helpful to refer back once again to the earlier constitutional law chapters. They will make more sense in the broader context.

It would be ill-advised to approach the study of EU law as a purely legal undertaking. Narrowness of focus is damaging in any branch of the law, but perhaps especially so in European law, where economic, political, and social objectives are close to the surface and exert a profound formative influence on the law. From this perspective, then, the student about to read Part I of this book might be well advised to equip him- or herself in advance with a basic understanding of modern European history. Such introductory material may be found in the opening chapter or chapters of the major textbooks listed in the Selected Bibliography. Other more general sources of information, which do not offer a specifically legal focus, are also mentioned there and deserve the student's attention.

However, the following extracts provide a short but valuable introductory overview of some of the elements of the past, present, and future, which will be glimpsed, but not studied directly, in the course of this book. The opportunity is also taken to clarify terminology – there was a European Community, then there was a European Community within a wider European Union, now, since December 2009, there is only a European Union.

J. Pinder, *The Building of the European Union*

(3rd ed., Oxford: OUP, 1998), pp. 3–8 [Reproduced by permission of Oxford University Press]

(Footnotes omitted.)

1 CREATING THE COMMUNITY AND THE UNION: NATION-STATE AND FEDERAL IDEA

The [. . .] European Union is a remarkable innovation in relations among states. Its institutions are more powerful than those of conventional international organisations, and offer more scope for development. Much of their specific character was determined in a few weeks in the summer of 1950, when representatives of the six founder members, France, the German Federal Republic, Italy, Belgium, the Netherlands, and Luxembourg, agreed on the outline of the Treaty to establish the European Coal and Steel Community. The initiative had been taken by Robert Schuman, the French foreign minister, who explained the gist of his proposal with these words:

. . . the French government proposes to take action immediately on one limited but decisive point . . . to place Franco-German production of coal and steel under a common High Authority, within the framework of an organisation open to the participation of the other countries of Europe . . . The solidarity in production thus established will make it plain that any war between France and Germany becomes not merely unthinkable, but materially impossible . . . this proposal will build the first concrete foundation of a European federation which is indispensable to the preservation of peace . . .

World War II, national sovereignty, the federal idea

World War II was a catastrophe that discredited the previous international order and, for many Europeans, the basic element in that order: the absolutely sovereign nation-state. In the Europe of such states, France and Germany had been at war three times in less than a century, twice at the centre of terrible world wars. Autarky and protection, fragmenting Europe's economy, had caused economic malaise and political antagonism. Fascist glorification of the nation-state had been revealed as a monstrosity; and many felt that insistence on its sovereignty, even without fascist excess, distorted and ossified the political perspective.

This critique pointed towards the limitation of national sovereignty. It was accepted by many people of the anti-fascist resistance, in Germany and Italy as well as the occupied countries. While the idea of limiting sovereignty in a united Europe was widespread, some influential figures were more precise. They envisaged a federal constitution for Europe, giving powers over trade, money, security, and related taxation, to a federal parliament, government, and court, leaving all other powers to be exercised by the institutions of the member states.

Such ideas evoked a ready echo from those Europeans who asked themselves why the war had occurred and what could be done to ensure a better future; and they were encouraged by Winston Churchill who, in a speech in Zurich in September 1946, suggested that France should lead Germany into a United States of Europe. Not everybody noticed that he was reticent about the part that Britain should play in such a union; and many, impressed by the magnanimous vision of the wartime leader with his immense prestige, did not realise how hard it would be to accomplish. For despite the popularity of the federal idea in Continental countries, the structures of the states were gathering strength again and were to prove resistant to radical federal reform.

Some of this resistance stemmed from the principle of national sovereignty as a basic political value. General de Gaulle was to be the most powerful and eloquent exponent of this view; and Mrs Thatcher was a subsequent protagonist. But most of the resisters were more pragmatic. Many bureaucrats, central bankers, and politicians would allow that sovereignty could in principle be shared on the right terms and at the right time: but the right terms were not on offer and the right time would be later.

Two main strategies were devised to overcome the reluctance of governments. One, promoted by the Italian federalist leader, Altiero Spinelli, was to mobilise popular support for a constituent assembly, in which the people's representatives would draw up a European constitution. But this idea bore little fruit until, with the direct elections to the European Parliament in 1979, Spinelli persuaded the people's newly elected representatives to design and approve a Draft Treaty to constitute a European Union. The other strategy, devised by Jean Monnet, was to identify a 'limited but decisive point', as Schuman's declaration put it, on which governments could be persuaded to agree and which, without going the whole way, would mark a significant step towards federation. With this idea, Monnet was to secure an early and spectacular success.

Founding the Community: the ECSC

Monnet's 'limited but decisive point' was the need for a new structure to contain the resurgent heavy industries of the Ruhr, the traditional economic basis for Germany's military might, which had been laid low as a result of the war. It was clear by 1950 that industry in West Germany must develop if Germans were to pay their way in the world and help the West in its rivalry with the Soviet Union, and that this required the revival of German steel production. Of the western Allies then responsible for West Germany, the United States and Britain were increasingly insistent on this. France, through history and geography more sensitive to the potential danger of German power, insisted that the Ruhr's heavy industries should be kept under control. But France lacked the means to restrain the Americans and British; and there were Frenchmen in key positions who realised that the perpetuation of an international Ruhr authority such as had been set up in 1948 to exert control over the Germans, apart from being unacceptable to the two Allies, would be an unstable arrangement, apt to be overturned by Germany at the first opportunity. Hence the idea of a common structure to govern the coal and steel industries, not only of the Ruhr but also of France and other European countries.

This idea was not the invention of Monnet alone. Officials in the French foreign ministry were also working on it. But they would surely have created a conventional international organisation, governed by committees of ministers, whereas Monnet was determined that the new institutions should have a political life independent of the existing governments: that they should be 'the first concrete foundation of a European federation'.

It is the theme of this book that the concept of European institutions which go beyond a conventional system of intergovernmental co-operation, however imperfectly realised so far, has given the Community, and now the Union, its special character: its stability, capacity for achievement, and promise for the future. It is of course possible to argue that the Community is, on the contrary, essentially an intergovernmental organisation to secure free trade and economic co-operation, and that the rest is frills and rhetoric. This book sets out a case for seeing it as more than that.

Monnet, from his vantage point as head of the French Commissariat du Plan, persuaded Schuman to adopt the more radical project; and he did it at the moment when the French government was most apt to accept, because a solution to the problem of German steel could no longer be delayed. Monnet's solution had the merit of meeting not only the French national interest in the control of German steel but also a wider interest in the development of European political institutions. The proposal was immediately welcomed by the governments of West Germany, Italy, Belgium, the Netherlands, and Luxembourg; and it was enthusiastically received by the wide sectors of opinion in those countries and in France that could be called broadly federalist, in the sense of supporting steps towards a federal end, even if not all would be precise in defining this. The project also received strong and steady support from the United States.

Support for the federal idea had mushroomed in Britain too in 1939 and the first half of 1940, culminating with the Churchill government's proposal for union with France. But after the fall of France in June 1940, with Nazi domination of the Continent, British interest in European union ebbed. For more than a decade after the war, British governments wanted to confine their relationship with the Continent to no more than a loose association. They were not ready to accept the federal implications of Monnet's proposal. So the six founder members negotiated the Treaty establishing the European Coal and Steel Community (ECSC) without Britain or the other West European countries that took the same view.

As chairman of the intergovernmental conference that drew up the ECSC Treaty, Monnet was well placed to ensure that his basic idea was followed through. The High Authority was to be the executive responsible for policy relating to the coal and steel industries in the member countries, and its decisions were to apply directly to the economic agents in each country, without requiring the approval of its government. The policies envisaged in the Treaty bore the mark of French planning ideas. Investment in the two industries was to be influenced by the High Authority, though not subject to much control. Prices and production could be regulated, but only if there were crises of shortage or overproduction. Policies for training, housing, and redeployment were to cater for workers' needs. Competition was at the same time to be stimulated by rules on price transparency, as well as by antitrust laws on American lines.

Monnet insisted on the principle of the High Authority's independence from the member states' governments because his experience as an international civil servant had convinced him that it would be hamstrung if they controlled it too directly. But that raised the question of the High Authority's accountability. Monnet, in his inaugural speech as the first President of the High Authority in August 1952, was to explain the Treaty's answer like this. The High Authority was responsible to an Assembly (now called the European Parliament), which would eventually be directly elected, and which had the power to dismiss it. There was recourse to the European Court of Justice in cases that concerned the High Authority's acts. In short, the powers defined by the Treaty would be exercised by institutions with federal characteristics, sovereign within the limits of their competences. The policy of the High Authority and those of the member states would be 'harmonised' by a Council of ministers, voting by majority 'save in exceptional cases'. Monnet ensured that the federal elements in the Community would be clearly explained by employing Spinelli's help in drafting the speech.

Monnet's idea was that the European federation would be built over the years on this 'first concrete foundation' as new sectors of activity were brought within the scope of the pre-federal institutions; and the establishment of the European Economic Community and Euratom in 1958 lent remarkable support to this view. But he does not appear to have foreseen how much the Council would come to dominate the politics of the Community, as the political structures of member states came to assert themselves against the realisation of the federal idea. This reaction led to a long-drawn-out conflict within the Community, which began with a major assault by General de Gaulle as President of France and continued up to the 1990s, with Britain succeeding de Gaulle as champion of national sovereignty . . .

NOTE: The Treaties of Rome, signed in 1957 and creating the EEC and EURATOM in 1958, led to a deepening of the process. The EEC envisaged the creation of a common market and was not limited to particular sectors of the economy. Its institutions followed the pattern of the ECSC. The EEC had a Commission, where the ECSC has a High Authority. (From 1967 the two functioned as one under the title 'Commission', until 2002 when the ECSC's functions were formally taken over by the EC.) The EEC also had three other institutions – Council, Parliament, and Court. The system is rooted in international Treaties agreed between States, but it represents a much more institutionally sophisticated and intricate model of co-operation than can be found in the orthodox type of 'intergovernmental co-operation' to which Treaty-making is dedicated. Admittedly the roots remain deep and each time the Treaty is revised the process of ratification by States offers a reminder of their foundational role. But there is much more to it than mere intergovernmental co-operation. The dynamic process of institutional interplay *within* the system endows it with a momentum that is not capable of crude control by Member State political elites. It operates as a layer of governance for Europe that is driven by motives that are distinct from, though certainly influenced by, those dear to individual Member States. To this extent the system is *not only* intergovernmental *but also* quasi-federal.

Questions about political accountability and institutional development demand the attention of anyone with an interest in the European Union. If the institutions of the Union are to develop autonomous policy-making competence, it is necessary to provide the appropriate democratic safeguards. The evolution of the Union is increasingly characterized by controversial debates about how best to subject the institutions to political and legal control. It is impossible for this book to explore these issues in detail. The next extract covers some specific points which will not yet be familiar, but the themes which it introduces are already valuable. It depicts the Community in the wake of subjection to its first major process of formal Treaty revision. This was effected by the *Single European Act*, which entered into force in 1987, and which took as a major objective the renovation of the institutional and constitutional system in order to improve its capacity to deliver the political objective of completing the internal market by the end of 1992.

R. Dehousse, '1992 and Beyond: The Institutional Dimension of the Internal Market Programme'
[1989/1] LIEI 109, 133–6

(Footnotes omitted.)

The evolution of the Community in the last few years teaches us a series of lessons on what might be called the politics of institutional reform. The first conclusion to be drawn from this experience is that institutional reform is easier to arrive at when it is not pursued for its own sake, but emerges as a logical implication of other political choices. Once the general idea of completing the internal market by 1992 had been accepted, it proved possible to convince even the most reluctant Member States that a shift towards more majority voting was necessary. Had the objective itself not met with consensus, the change would not have been possible. The same logic is apparent in the Single Act's provisions on economic and social cohesion, on research and technological development or on the environment. In all these sectors, unanimous agreement is needed in order to define the objectives to be pursued at Community level; it is only at a second stage that resort to majority voting can be envisaged. The rationale of all these provisions is the same: when a decision of principle is to be taken, Member States must be able to preserve what they regard as their essential interests but, precisely because they have been given this guarantee, no vital interest to be harmed at the implementation stage; the 'Community interest' – and in particular the necessity of an efficient decision-making system – can therefore be given precedence.

Thus, most of the developments which have taken place in these years find their origin in the Commission's capacity to capitalise on the political pressures exerted by the Parliament and to define a 'new frontier' which would be acceptable to all Member States. But the way in which the institutional reform was accomplished also deserves attention. The main feature of the process was certainly its piecemeal character, which is often the case with compromises achieved in decentralised systems. As is known, the Single European Act was not the result of an inspired exercise in constitution-making, but the product of strenuous international negotiation. This cumbersome process had a direct incidence on the final result, which reflects the various aspirations and fears of more or less all Member States. In a typical quid pro quo exercise, France and Germany secured the adoption of provisions on political cooperation, and the backward countries a general commitment in favour of the reinforcement of economic and social cohesion within the Community, while several countries managed to limit the Community's capacity to act autonomously as far as the environment is concerned. Several of the institutional problems mentioned above are linked to the complexity of the structure which eventually emerged. The lengthy discussions on the subject of legal basis offer good examples of difficulties connected with the ambiguity of the compromises made at the time of drafting the Single Act.

With the White Paper on the internal market, questions which were previously considered as essentially technical gained the status of major political objectives. This change was paralleled by an evolution in the decision-making process: the creation of an internal market Council, with its induced effects at national level, has made it easier to coordinate national and Community action in this sphere. The introduction of majority voting has had a similar effect. Even if it is not systematically used, the possibility of a vote reinforces the weight of political decision-makers over that of specialised departments, which are to a large extent deprived of the veto right they had in the past.

> In spite of all the difficulties which can be foreseen, it is clear that the Community has now embarked on an era of dynamism which few expected a couple of years ago. Part of this dynamism finds its origin in external factors like the economic growth experienced in recent years; but it is equally clear that the momentum generated by the White Paper would not have been possible without its healthy institutional pragmatism. Not only did this approach make possible advances generally regarded as beyond reach not so long ago; but it might lead to even further-reaching results. For whether it is achieved by 1992 or only later, completion of the internal market could well generate its own dynamic. It has, for instance, often been argued that the liberalisation of capital movements in a Community with stable exchange rates will make it more difficult for Member States to pursue autonomous macro-economic policies. If at some stage two thirds of the economic and social legislation will have to be adopted at the Community level, as President Delors recently hinted, Community citizens and interest groups might press for a stronger voice in the decision-making process. At the same time, Member States might also realise that more systematic resort to voting, or a stronger involvement of Parliament in the legislative process, do not necessarily mean unbearable threats to their national interests. . .

NOTE: Even before the deadline for the completion of the internal market, the end of 1992, both the dynamism and the taste for ambiguous compromises noted by Dehousse in this extract were redeployed. In December 1991 agreement was reached at Maastricht on the next step forward – the Treaty on European Union. The Treaty was signed at Maastricht on 7 February 1992. However, only on 1 November 1993 did the Treaty finally come into force following hard-fought campaigns surrounding the ratification process in several Member States. The Danish people voted narrowly against ratification in a referendum in 1992 before voting in favour by a slightly larger margin in a second referendum in 1993. Germany was the last of the 12 Member States to ratify and could do so only after its Constitutional Court had ruled in October 1993 that ratification was not incompatible with the German Constitution ([1994] 1 CMLR 57: see further Chapter 19, p. 9).

The basic structure instituted by the Maastricht Treaty on European Union, and abandoned only as late as December 2009 on the entry into force of the Lisbon Treaty, is best presented in diagrammatic form.

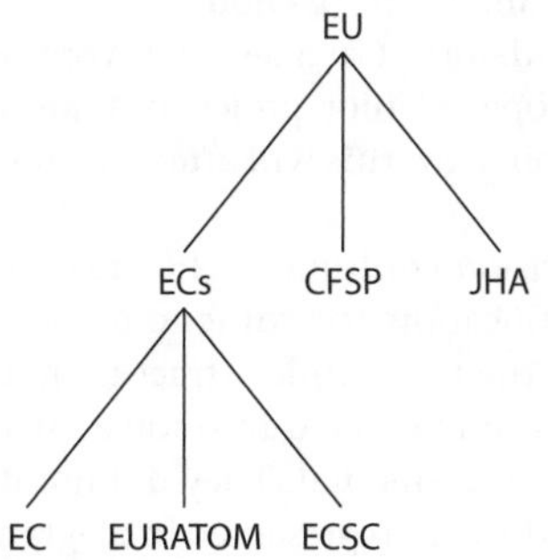

The Treaty on European Union declared that 'The Union shall be founded on the European Communities'. Be that as it may, the Union structure fashioned at Maastricht was built on three pillars and the European Communities were only one of those three pillars. Two of the pillars, those relating to a Common Foreign and Security Policy (the 'second pillar') and Cooperation in the Fields of Justice and Home Affairs (the 'third pillar'), existed outside the traditional, developed EC structure and were much more overtly intergovernmental in nature. Meanwhile, the three European Communities remained in existence as components of what is commonly termed the European Community pillar, or the 'first pillar'. So there was an EC – but it was not co-terminous with the EU. It was a part of the EU. In fact, the most important of the three Communities, the EEC, was formally renamed the EC by the Maastricht Treaty. It was also amended in a number of more substantial respects, such as the inclusion of new Titles enhancing competences, the creation of the status of Citizenship of the Union, and adjustments to the legislative procedure which enhanced the position of the Parliament. Perhaps the centrepiece of the Treaty is the insertion into the EC Treaty of detailed provisions designed to lead to Economic and Monetary Union. These provisions carry immense constitutional significance. The Treaty timetable was adhered to and the third stage of economic and monetary union was launched on 1 January 1999, when 11 Member States adopted the euro as their common currency. Greece joined in 2001, Slovenia in 2007, Cyprus and Malta in 2008, Slovakia in 2009, Estonia in 2011, Latvia in 2014 and Lithuania in 2015, bringing the tally to 19 Member States (out of 28). Euro banknotes and coins have circulated validly since 1 January 2002. EMU is further discussed, albeit briefly, at p. 264.

There is a disjointed facade to the European Union created at Maastricht. The nature of each of the three pillars is different. The Council seems to be the only institution which is in any significant sense an institution of the whole Union. In November 1993, it accordingly chose to rename itself the Council of the European Union. The impression of a disjointed structure is heightened when one appreciates that even within the EC there were emerging tendencies towards fragmentation. A flavour of the debate at the time can be acquired from Deirdre Curtin's famous expressions of concern about the growth of a 'Europe of Bits and Pieces' (Curtin, D., 'The Constitutional Structure of the Union: A Europe of Bits and Pieces' (1993) 30 CML Rev 17), and there will be further discussion in Chapter 18. The picture was complicated yet further by the coming into existence of the European Economic Area (EEA) at the start of 1994, which extended a mass of rules relevant to free trade more widely into Europe. The EEA structure established further institutions, most prominently the EEA Council. The accession of Austria, Finland, and Sweden to the Union at the start of 1995 greatly reduced the practical importance of the non-EU part of the EEA, which today comprises only Norway, Iceland, and Liechtenstein.

It has been astutely commented that 'the success of the internal market programme lay in its apparent lack of ambition' (Dehousse, Joerges, Majone, and Snyder (eds), 'Europe after 1992: New Regulatory Strategies', EUI Working Paper Law 92/31, Florence). In sharp contrast, as the European Union project unfolds, what is increasingly apparent is the breadth of the ambition. How this will affect the prospects for success dominates the European agenda.

The process of Treaty revision continued. The Treaty of Amsterdam was signed in October 1997. It secured ratification according to domestic constitutional procedures in the 15 Member States of the time while attracting noticeably less opposition than the Maastricht Treaty and it duly entered into force on 1 May 1999. The Amsterdam changes to the Treaties were incremental. They did not disturb the basic existence of the three-pillar structure of the Union presented in diagrammatic form at p. 9. However, the Amsterdam Treaty moved material between the pillars. Of greatest significance was the transfer of material relevant to the free movement of people within the Union from the third pillar to the first pillar, the EC. A new Title was inserted into the EC Treaty on 'Visas, asylum, immigration and other policies related to free movement of persons' dedicated to the progressive establishment of 'an area of freedom, security and justice'. The Title was built around a five-year timetable for dismantling internal borders, although special provision was made in Protocols to the Treaty for Denmark, the United Kingdom, and Ireland. This Title in the EC Treaty was home to modified versions of material that had been allocated to the 'third pillar' by the Maastricht Treaty on European Union. So the first pillar, the EC, gained ground at the expense of the third, formerly dealing with Justice and Home Affairs but now re-worked and restyled *Provisions on Police and Judicial Co-operation in Criminal Matters*. However, the new Title, although part of the EC Treaty, was marked by some institutional aspects alien to the EC system.

As is true of every process of Treaty revision, the Amsterdam changes meant that there was EU law 'pre-Amsterdam' and EU law 'post-Amsterdam', and this must be taken into account when reading older legislative materials and judicial pronouncements. But the pre-Amsterdam legal world is also numerically distinct from the post-Amsterdam. The Amsterdam Treaty's most immediately visible feature was the re-numbering from start to finish of the whole EC Treaty and of the EU Treaty (pursuant to Article 12 of the Treaty of Amsterdam). This cleaned out the unwieldy insertions made by the Single European Act and the Maastricht Treaty, but the obvious disadvantage of this spring-clean lies in the need to become accustomed to the replacement of familiar numbers for Articles of the Treaty with new numbers. And it is an obstacle that is doubled in height with effect from 1 December 2009 and the entry into force of the Lisbon Treaty, which effects a yet further round of re-numbering for the TFEU (successor to the EC Treaty) and the TEU. These changes will always have to be borne in mind when reading pre-Amsterdam texts and texts from the period between Amsterdam (1999) and Lisbon (2009), including legislation and court judgments, and in fact the EU lawyer will need to become adept at this form of 'currency conversion'. Pages xxxix-lviii of this book contain the Table of Equivalence between the pre-Lisbon and the new numbering which is annexed to the Lisbon Treaty, and the reader will find frequent resort to that table invaluable while he or she is making the necessary mental adjustments. Moreover (see Preface, p. xi), references to the numerical changes are made in introducing key Treaty provisions throughout the book.

Michel Petite, The Treaty of Amsterdam

(1998), published as a Harvard Jean Monnet Chair Working Paper, 2/98 available at http://jeanmonnetprogram.org/papers/

The Amsterdam Treaty is by no means the last word on European integration. Like its predecessors it marks a further stage in the process. However one views it, it probably represents the most that the Member States were prepared to agree among themselves at a given moment.

... Two simple remarks suggest cause for both humility and perseverance:

— first, all of the delegations asserted their commitment to maintaining the institutional balance (yet this balance is constantly shifting, as exemplified by the increased role of the European Parliament); this commitment means that everyone wants to build on the foundations of the achievements of forty years of European integration – and will continue to do so for the foreseeable future. There will be no tabula rasa on which radically new institutional formulas will be rebuilt;

— secondly, there is no magic formula that can confound the mathematics: the organisation will inevitably be more difficult for a group of 21, 26 or 30 than one of 6 or even 15. Enlargement has certain inherent consequences.

What this amounts to is that the reforms to be undertaken in response to the demands of enlargement cannot be achieved by new constitutional formulas so much as by a less headline-grabbing series of changes to the way our institutions operate. Most of these reforms are a question of fine-tuning, and many rightfully belong in the internal rules of procedure rather than in the Treaty itself.

NOTE: For good or ill (*cf* p. 10), the Amsterdam Treaty seemed bereft of any 'big idea'. For J. Weiler, finding 'no shared agenda and no mobilising force behind the exercise', this was 'an Intergovernmental Conference which should never have started'; and in the light of the complexity of the unresolved issues, 'it was, too, an Intergovernmental Conference which should never have ended'. The product was 'an inconclusive Treaty leaving all hard issues for tomorrow' ((1997) 3 ELJ, Editorial, 309, 310).

Tomorrow always comes, and unfinished business needed to be addressed. Some institutional and constitutional questions, relating most of all to Council voting and the composition of the Commission, were left unresolved by the Amsterdam Treaty. These had to be settled in order to re-shape the Union's institutional architecture in anticipation of the pressures imposed by impending enlargement into Central and Eastern Europe. A fresh intergovernmental conference concluded in December 2000 at Nice, where a new amending Treaty was agreed. The broad purpose of the Nice Treaty was to perform surgery designed to improve the efficiency of the EU's institutions without delaying enlargement.

The Nice Treaty, like the Amsterdam Treaty before it, maintained the three-pillar structure of the Union, while making detailed adjustments to each of the pillars. The Nice Treaty too is essentially incremental in its impact. It was agreed in December 2000, but – like the Maastricht Treaty, and unlike the Amsterdam Treaty – it gathered a considerable amount of opposition when put to the test of domestic ratification. The people of Denmark had been the 'problem' in the Maastricht process; now it was the people of Ireland who asserted their right to choose in a referendum held in 2001. The Nice Treaty was rejected in a popular referendum. It was frankly difficult to identify any particular provision of the Nice Treaty to which the Irish objected. It altered arcane matters such as voting rules in Council and the number of seats allocated to each State in the European Parliament. But the Nice Treaty's absence of defining features was perhaps precisely the point; the alienated people of Ireland had little understanding of what they being asked to vote on. A patient campaign of information by the Irish government prepared the ground for a second referendum and in Autumn 2002 the Irish once again followed the example of the Danish approach to Maastricht and, second time round, voted 'yes'. Duly ratified by all 15 Member States, the Nice Treaty entered into force on 1 February 2003.

The accession of new Member States in Central and Eastern Europe was planned to proceed according to a timetable agreed at the December 2002 European Council in Copenhagen. Treaties of accession were duly agreed and ratified, and ten more countries joined the Union from 1 May 2004: Cyprus, the Czech Republic, Estonia, Hungary, Latvia, Lithuania, Malta, Poland, Slovakia, and Slovenia. On 1 January 2007 Bulgaria and Romania joined the club. Croatia followed on 1 July 2013. The EU comprises 28 Member States.

There is much discussion about the nature of the entity into which the European Union is evolving. Although not itself a State, it possesses an institutional and constitutional sophistication which marks it out from normal intergovernmental associations. Moreover, the creature has developed not only through the formal process of periodic Treaty revision, but also (as will be traced in this book) through wide-ranging legislative action and through the remarkable activism of its Court. So the Union is not a State, but it displays some State-like features and it profoundly affects the nature of the States that are members of it. The concluding chapter of this book will devote further attention to these broader questions, once the reader has acquired a fuller understanding of constitutional and substantive law. This chapter is concerned only to trace the trajectory of the process. But Nice was intended to be the last Treaty to respect the pattern for the European Union cautiously mapped at Maastricht. A political preference gradually emerged to eliminate the constitutionally and institutionally distinct 'three pillars', and to replace them with a single trunk. More ambitiously, the aspiration developed to encourage deeper and wider participation by the peoples of Europe in the planning of their destinies. A strong political impetus to dispel the alienation of citizens from the project of European integration urged that it be made more comprehensible, in the (far from uncontroversial) expectation that this will make it more appealing. This quest for *legitimacy* propelled the EU along the rocky road that eventually led to the next round of revision of the Treaties, the Treaty of Lisbon which entered into force on 1 December 2009.

From a formal perspective the legitimacy of the process of European integration is guaranteed by the requirement that Treaty revision be conducted with respect for the domestic constitutional arrangements of each Member State and with the support of all of them. The procedure is mapped out in Article 48 TEU. Some Member States are obliged to hold or choose to hold a referendum before proceeding to ratification. This caused awkwardness in the process of ratification of both the Maastricht Treaty (to which the Danes voted first 'no', and only subsequently 'yes') and the Nice Treaty (which generated a similar 'first no, then yes' pattern in Ireland). Other Member States prefer to confine discussion of ratification to Parliamentary processes. This has been true of the UK, which has never held a referendum on ratification (although it did hold a referendum on the question of continued membership in 1975 and will hold another of this type before the end of 2017). But the key point is that from a formal perspective the Treaty can be revised, and the EU's powers extended, only provided each Member State agrees. The nature of the legal order as a creature of international law is most vividly demonstrated at times of Treaty revision.

But legitimacy has dimensions that stretch beyond the formal. Do the peoples of Europe treat the European Union as a legitimate source of authority? This is a matter of social observation, not a matter of formal legal authority. The intergovernmental conference is, on the one hand, the means of conferring formal State approval on the shaping of the Union, but it is, on the other hand, a powerful statement to citizens that the Union is remote from their concerns, the plaything of political élites – that it is, in short, none of their business.

Efforts were increasingly devoted to investing the Union with a greater degree of social legitimacy. Relevant devices included the proclamation in 2000 of a non-binding EU Charter of Fundamental Rights (Chapter 2), the creation of the status of Citizenship of the Union (Chapter 15) and the irresistible rise of the principle of subsidiarity (Chapter 18).

The European Council meeting in Nice in December 2000 adopted a Declaration on the Future of the Union. The aim was to initiate a debate about the nature and purpose of the EU and within that debate to emphasize the engagement of citizens.

DECLARATION ON THE FUTURE OF THE UNION
(adopted by the Conference at Nice)

1. Important reforms have been decided in Nice. The Conference welcomes the successful conclusion of the Conference of Representatives of the Governments of the Member States and commits the Member States to pursue the early ratification of the Treaty of Nice.

2. It agrees that the conclusion of the Conference of Representatives of the Governments of the Member States opens the way for enlargement of the European Union and underlines that, with ratification of the Treaty of Nice, the European Union will have completed the institutional changes necessary for the accession of new Member States.

3. Having thus opened the way to enlargement, the Conference calls for a deeper and wider debate about the future of the European Union. In 2001, the Swedish and Belgian Presidencies, in cooperation with the Commission and involving the European Parliament, will encourage wide-ranging discussions with all interested parties: representatives of national parliaments and all those reflecting public opinion, namely political, economic and university circles, representatives of civil society, etc. The candidate States will be associated with this process in ways to be defined.

4. Following a report to be drawn up for the European Council in Göteborg in June 2001, the European Council, at its meeting in Laeken/Brussels in December 2001, will agree on a declaration containing appropriate initiatives for the continuation of this process.

5. The process should address, *inter alia*, the following questions:
- how to establish and monitor a more precise delimitation of powers between the European Union and the Member States, reflecting the principle of subsidiarity;
- the status of the Charter of Fundamental Rights of the European Union, proclaimed in Nice, in accordance with the conclusions of the European Council in Cologne;
- a simplification of the Treaties with a view to making them clearer and better understood without changing their meaning;
- the role of national parliaments in the European architecture.

6. Addressing the abovementioned issues, the Conference recognises the need to improve and to monitor the democratic legitimacy and transparency of the Union and its institutions, in order to bring them closer to the citizens of the Member States.

7. After these preparatory steps, the Conference agrees that a new Conference of the Representatives of the Governments of the Member States will be convened in 2004, to address the abovementioned items with a view to making corresponding changes to the Treaties.

8. The Conference of Member States will not constitute any form of obstacle or precondition to the enlargement process. Moreover, those candidate States which have concluded accession negotiations with the Union will be invited to participate in the Conference. Those candidate States which have not concluded their accession negotiations shall be invited as observers.

NOTE: As envisaged in para 4 of this Declaration the European Council met in Laeken (Belgium) in December 2001 and agreed to convene a Convention on the 'Future of Europe'. This was designed to pave the way for the next Intergovernmental Conference, to be convened in 2004 (according to para 7 of this Declaration). The Laeken Declaration picks up the four matters to which specific attention is drawn in para 5 of this Declaration, but it goes much further. It attempts to set in motion a process of deliberation that will do justice to the grand aspirations contained in para 6. And the model of a more broadly representative 'Convention', distinct from intergovernmental orthodoxy, was considered sufficiently to have proved its worth in the drafting of the Charter of Fundamental Rights to deserve redeployment in the search for a blueprint for the 'Future of Europe'. The questions raised by the Laeken Declaration are of enduring structural and intellectual importance and the document remains well worth reading.

THE LAEKEN DECLARATION

I. EUROPE AT A CROSSROADS

For centuries, peoples and states have taken up arms and waged war to win control of the European continent. The debilitating effects of two bloody wars and the weakening of Europe's position in the world brought a growing realisation that only peace and concerted action could make the dream of a strong, unified Europe come true. In order to banish once and for all the demons of the past, a start was made with a coal and steel community. Other economic activities, such as agriculture, were subsequently added in. A genuine single market was eventually established for goods, persons, services and capital, and a single currency was added in 1999. On 1 January 2002 the euro is to become a day-to-day reality for 300 million European citizens.

The European Union has thus gradually come into being. In the beginning, it was more of an economic and technical collaboration. Twenty years ago, with the first direct elections to the European Parliament, the Community's democratic legitimacy, which until then had lain with the Council alone, was considerably strengthened. Over the last ten years, construction of a political union has begun and cooperation been established on social policy, employment, asylum, immigration, police, justice, foreign policy and a common security and defence policy.

The European Union is a success story. For over half a century now, Europe has been at peace. Along with North America and Japan, the Union forms one of the three most prosperous parts of the world. As a result of mutual solidarity and fair distribution of the benefits of economic development, moreover, the standard of living in the Union's weaker regions has increased enormously and they have made good much of the disadvantage they were at.

Fifty years on, however, the Union stands at a crossroads, a defining moment in its existence. The unification of Europe is near. The Union is about to expand to bring in more than ten new Member States, predominantly

Central and Eastern European, thereby finally closing one of the darkest chapters in European history: the Second World War and the ensuing artificial division of Europe. At long last, Europe is on its way to becoming one big family, without bloodshed, a real transformation clearly calling for a different approach from fifty years ago, when six countries first took the lead.

The democratic challenge facing Europe

At the same time, the Union faces twin challenges, one within and the other beyond its borders.

Within the Union, the European institutions must be brought closer to its citizens. Citizens undoubtedly support the Union's broad aims, but they do not always see a connection between those goals and the Union's everyday action. They want the European institutions to be less unwieldy and rigid and, above all, more efficient and open. Many also feel that the Union should involve itself more with their particular concerns, instead of intervening, in every detail, in matters by their nature better left to Member States' and regions' elected representatives. This is even perceived by some as a threat to their identity. More importantly, however, they feel that deals are all too often cut out of their sight and they want better democratic scrutiny.

Europe's new role in a globalised world

Beyond its borders, in turn, the European Union is confronted with a fast-changing, globalised world. Following the fall of the Berlin Wall, it looked briefly as though we would for a long while be living in a stable world order, free from conflict, founded upon human rights. Just a few years later, however, there is no such certainty. The eleventh of September has brought a rude awakening. The opposing forces have not gone away: religious fanaticism, ethnic nationalism, racism and terrorism are on the increase, and regional conflicts, poverty and underdevelopment still provide a constant seedbed for them.

What is Europe's role in this changed world? Does Europe not, now that is finally unified, have a leading role to play in a new world order, that of a power able both to play a stabilising role worldwide and to point the way ahead for many countries and peoples? Europe as the continent of humane values, the Magna Carta, the Bill of Rights, the French Revolution and the fall of the Berlin Wall; the continent of liberty, solidarity and above all diversity, meaning respect for others' languages, cultures and traditions. The European Union's one boundary is democracy and human rights. The Union is open only to countries which uphold basic values such as free elections, respect for minorities and respect for the rule of law.

Now that the Cold War is over and we are living in a globalised, yet also highly fragmented world, Europe needs to shoulder its responsibilities in the governance of globalisation. The role it has to play is that of a power resolutely doing battle against all violence, all terror and all fanaticism, but which also does not turn a blind eye to the world's heartrending injustices. In short, a power wanting to change the course of world affairs in such a way as to benefit not just the rich countries but also the poorest. A power seeking to set globalisation within a moral framework, in other words to anchor it in solidarity and sustainable development.

The expectations of Europe's citizens

The image of a democratic and globally engaged Europe admirably matches citizens' wishes. There have been frequent public calls for a greater EU role in justice and security, action against cross-border crime, control of migration flows and reception of asylum seekers and refugees from far-flung war zones. Citizens also want results in the fields of employment and combating poverty and social exclusion, as well as in the field of economic and social cohesion. They want a common approach on environmental pollution, climate change and food safety, in short, all transnational issues which they instinctively sense can only be tackled by working together. Just as they also want to see Europe more involved in foreign affairs, security and defence, in other words, greater and better coordinated action to deal with trouble spots in and around Europe and in the rest of the world.

At the same time, citizens also feel that the Union is behaving too bureaucratically in numerous other areas. In coordinating the economic, financial and fiscal environment, the basic issue should continue to be proper operation of the internal market and the single currency, without this jeopardising Member States' individuality. National and regional differences frequently stem from history or tradition. They can be enriching. In other words, what citizens understand by 'good governance' is opening up fresh opportunities, not imposing further red tape. What they expect is more results, better responses to practical issues and not a European superstate or European institutions inveigling their way into every nook and cranny of life.

In short, citizens are calling for a clear, open, effective, democratically controlled Community approach, developing a Europe which points the way ahead for the world. An approach that provides concrete results in terms of more jobs, better quality of life, less crime, decent education and better health care. There can be no doubt that this will require Europe to undergo renewal and reform.

II. CHALLENGES AND REFORMS IN A RENEWED UNION

The Union needs to become more democratic, more transparent and more efficient. It also has to resolve three basic challenges: how to bring citizens, and primarily the young, closer to the European design and the European institutions, how to organise politics and the European political area in an enlarged Union and how to develop the Union into a stabilising factor and a model in the new, multipolar world. In order to address them a number of specific questions need to be put.

A better division and definition of competence in the European Union

Citizens often hold expectations of the European Union that are not always fulfilled. And vice versa – they sometimes have the impression that the Union takes on too much in areas where its involvement is not always essential. Thus the important thing is to clarify, simplify and adjust the division of competence between the Union and the Member States in the light of the new challenges facing the Union. This can lead both to restoring tasks to the Member States and to assigning new missions to the Union, or to the extension of existing powers, while constantly bearing in mind the equality of the Member States and their mutual solidarity.

A first series of questions that needs to be put concerns how the division of competence can be made more transparent. Can we thus make a clearer distinction between three types of competence: the exclusive competence of the Union, the competence of the Member States and the shared competence of the Union and the Member States? At what level is competence exercised in the most efficient way? How is the principle of subsidiarity to be applied here? And should we not make it clear that any powers not assigned by the Treaties to the Union fall within the exclusive sphere of competence of the Member States? And what would be the consequences of this?

The next series of questions should aim, within this new framework and while respecting the 'acquis communautaire', to determine whether there needs to be any reorganization of competence. How can citizens' expectations be taken as a guide here? What missions would this produce for the Union? And, vice versa, what tasks could better be left to the Member States? What amendments should be made to the Treaty on the various policies? How, for example, should a more coherent common foreign policy and defence policy be developed? Should the Petersberg tasks be updated? Do we want to adopt a more integrated approach to police and criminal law cooperation? How can economic-policy coordination be stepped up? How can we intensify cooperation in the field of social inclusion, the environment, health and food safety? But then, should not the day-to-day administration and implementation of the Union's policy be left more emphatically to the Member States and, where their constitutions so provide, to the regions? Should they not be provided with guarantees that their spheres of competence will not be affected?

Lastly, there is the question of how to ensure that a redefined division of competence does not lead to a creeping expansion of the competence of the Union or to encroachment upon the exclusive areas of competence of the Member States and, where there is provision for this, regions. How are we to ensure at the same time that the European dynamic does not come to a halt? In the future as well the Union must continue to be able to react to fresh challenges and developments and must be able to explore new policy areas. Should Articles 95 and 308 of the Treaty be reviewed for this purpose in the light of the 'acquis jurisprudentiel'?

Simplification of the Union's instruments

Who does what is not the only important question; the nature of the Union's action and what instruments it should use are equally important. Successive amendments to the Treaty have on each occasion resulted in a proliferation of instruments, and directives have gradually evolved towards more and more detailed legislation. The key question is therefore whether the Union's various instruments should not be better defined and whether their number should not be reduced.

In other words, should a distinction be introduced between legislative and executive measures? Should the number of legislative instruments be reduced: directly applicable rules, framework legislation and non-enforceable instruments (opinions, recommendations, open coordination)? Is it or is it not desirable to have more frequent recourse to framework legislation, which affords the Member States more room for manoeuvre in achieving policy objectives? For which areas of competence are open coordination and mutual recognition the most appropriate instruments? Is the principle of proportionality to remain the point of departure?

More democracy, transparency and efficiency in the European Union

The European Union derives its legitimacy from the democratic values it projects, the aims it pursues and the powers and instruments it possesses. However, the European project also derives its legitimacy from democratic, transparent and efficient institutions. The national parliaments also contribute towards the legitimacy of the European project. The declaration on the future of the Union, annexed to the Treaty of Nice, stressed the need to examine their role in European integration. More generally, the question arises as to what initiatives we can take to develop a European public area.

The first question is thus how we can increase the democratic legitimacy and transparency of the present institutions, a question which is valid for the three institutions.

How can the authority and efficiency of the European Commission be enhanced? How should the President of the Commission be appointed: by the European Council, by the European Parliament or should he be directly elected by the citizens? Should the role of the European Parliament be strengthened? Should we extend the right of co-decision or not? Should the way in which we elect the members of the European Parliament be reviewed? Should a European electoral constituency be created, or should constituencies continue to be determined nationally? Can the two systems be combined? Should the role of the Council be strengthened? Should the Council act in the same manner in its legislative and its executive capacities? With a view to greater transparency, should the meetings of the Council, at least in its legislative capacity, be public? Should citizens have more access to Council documents? How, finally, should the balance and reciprocal control between the institutions be ensured?

A second question, which also relates to democratic legitimacy, involves the role of national parliaments. Should they be represented in a new institution, alongside the Council and the European Parliament? Should they have a role in areas of European action in which the European Parliament has no competence? Should they focus on the division of competence between Union and Member States, for example through preliminary checking of compliance with the principle of subsidiarity?

The third question concerns how we can improve the efficiency of decision-making and the workings of the institutions in a Union of some thirty Member States. How could the Union set its objectives and priorities more effectively and ensure better implementation? Is there a need for more decisions by a qualified majority? How is the co-decision procedure between the Council and the European Parliament to be simplified and speeded up? What of the six-monthly rotation of the Presidency of the Union? What is the future role of the European Parliament? What of the future role and structure of the various Council formations? How should the coherence of European foreign policy be enhanced? How is synergy between the High Representative and the competent Commissioner to be reinforced? Should the external representation of the Union in international fora be extended further?

Towards a Constitution for European citizens

The European Union currently has four Treaties. The objectives, powers and policy instruments of the Union are currently spread across those Treaties. If we are to have greater transparency, simplification is essential.

Four sets of questions arise in this connection. The first concerns simplifying the existing Treaties without changing their content. Should the distinction between the Union and the Communities be reviewed? What of the division into three pillars?

Questions then arise as to the possible reorganisation of the Treaties. Should a distinction be made between a basic treaty and the other treaty provisions? Should this distinction involve separating the texts? Could this lead to a distinction between the amendment and ratification procedures for the basic treaty and for the other treaty provisions?

Thought would also have to be given to whether the Charter of Fundamental Rights should be included in the basic treaty and to whether the European Community should accede to the European Convention on Human Rights.

The question ultimately arises as to whether this simplification and reorganization might not lead in the long run to the adoption of a constitutional text in the Union. What might the basic features of such a constitution be? The values which the Union cherishes, the fundamental rights and obligations of its citizens, the relationship between Member States in the Union?

III. CONVENING OF A CONVENTION ON THE FUTURE OF EUROPE

In order to pave the way for the next Intergovernmental Conference as broadly and openly as possible, the European Council has decided to convene a Convention composed of the main parties involved in the debate on the future of the Union. In the light of the foregoing, it will be the task of that Convention to consider the key issues arising for the Union's future development and try to identify the various possible responses.

The European Council has appointed Mr V. Giscard d'Estaing as Chairman of the Convention and Mr G. Amato and Mr J.L. Dehaene as Vice-Chairmen.

Composition

In addition to its Chairman and Vice-Chairmen, the Convention will be composed of 15 representatives of the Heads of State or government of the Member States (one from each Member State), 30 members of national parliaments (two from each Member State), 16 members of the European Parliament and two Commission representatives. The accession candidate countries will be fully involved in the Convention's proceedings. They will be represented in the same way as the current Member States (one government representative and two national parliament members) and will be able to take part in the proceedings without, however, being able to prevent any consensus which may emerge among the Member States...

NOTE: And the Convention was duly established. It held its inaugural session under the Chairmanship of Valery Giscard d'Estaing in February 2002. Representatives of heads of State and government were joined by representatives of the Parliament and the Commission and of national Parliaments. Representatives from candidate accession countries were also included.

Eleven working groups were established to delve into the range of relevant material, and by early 2003 each had submitted a Final Report. The 11 areas covered by the explorations of the working groups were: I Subsidiarity; II Charter/European Convention on Human Rights; III Legal Personality; IV National Parliaments; V Complementary Competencies; VI Economic Governance; VII External Action; VIII Defence; IX Simplification; X Freedom, Security and Justice; and XI Social Europe.

A complete draft Treaty establishing a Constitution for Europe was finally submitted to the Presidency of the European Council in Rome on 18 July 2003 and the Convention on the Future of Europe was closed. A 'Rome Declaration' of 18 July 2003 submitted by Valery Giscard d'Estaing encouraged political leaders to take the text as it stood, but momentum in favour of securing its adoption in an unamended condition by the Member States proved insufficiently strong. Ultimately any proposed amendment to the EU's constituent Treaties must itself take the legal form of a Treaty and must be supported by and ratified by all the Member States. In December 2003 agreement proved impossible to reach. However, after the astute Irish Presidency that occupied the first half of 2004, a breakthrough was achieved in June 2004, and a Treaty establishing a Constitution for Europe was agreed by the Heads of State and government. Notwithstanding modest adjustments made during the 2004 political endgame, the framework of the agreed Treaty remained visibly that proposed by the Convention on the Future of Europe in 2003. A definitive final text was signed by the Member States in Rome on 29 October 2004. Under the Treaty establishing a Constitution, the pre-existing three-pillar structure of the European Union would have been replaced by a single Treaty establishing a single Constitution for Europe. So there would have been an EU, and no longer an EC within a wider EU, although deep within the newly minted unified EU there remained some sector specific institutionally distinctive treatment, in particular of common foreign and security policy. Much of what was at stake concerned improving the presentation of what was already done in the name of the EU, and not in effecting radical change. The principal concern was to improve transparency – to make the whole enterprise more intelligible. So the taste for institutional and constitutional continuity identified in the Treaty of Amsterdam by Petite (p. 11) was again prominent in the Treaty establishing a Constitution.

But late 2004 proved to be the high watermark of the constitutional project. Some Member States were required to hold a referendum, others chose to do so, while others were able to ratify without resort to the electorate. In France and the Netherlands 'no' votes were recorded in referenda in 2005. The device of putting the matter to a second referendum, a ploy in the past used successfully in Denmark (Maastricht) and Ireland (Nice), was judged inadvisable. The European Council, meeting in June 2005, announced a so-called 'period of reflection', which appeared at bottom to have involved avoidance of any overt political discussion of how to cope.

There remained a political desire to complete the process of revision initiated with the Laeken Declaration of December 2001 (p. 14) and to tackle some of the problems which the Treaty establishing a Constitution had been intended to address. There was, in this sense, a momentum in favour of agreeing a new Treaty which the pair of negative referendums had braked but had been insufficient to bring to a halt. However, a consensus prevailed that decisive rejection in two referendums had sealed the fate of the Treaty establishing a Constitution. Re-presenting exactly what had already been rejected by the French and Dutch was not politically possible. And, it became increasingly plain, the aim was to agree a text that could be ratified with the minimum of fuss, and, best of all, as far as possible without reference to the direct expression of will by troublesome voters in the Member States.

So was born the Lisbon Treaty.

Crafted in the summer of 2007 it initially went under the label of the 'Reform Treaty'. It would seek to improve the current system – much as the Treaty establishing a Constitution was designed to achieve. It would be different from the Treaty establishing a Constitution so that it could be ratified quickly and without resort to a referendum in all but a minority of Member States – though *how* different it would be remains a matter of persisting controversy. And, most of all, it would bring to an end the constitutional experiment launched by the Laeken Declaration.

The Treaty was signed in Lisbon in December 2007. Member States proceeded to ratify it in 2008, and only one, Ireland, felt it necessary to seek approval for ratification by staging a referendum. This was held in the summer of 2008. And once again the result was – no!

So the Lisbon Treaty, like the Treaty establishing a Constitution before it, was put on hold. On this occasion the device of a second referendum was redeployed. A package of promises and safeguards was made by the Heads of State or government of the Member States which were designed to lure a majority of Irish voters into supporting ratification: for a useful explanation and discussion, see Kingston (2009) 34 EL Rev 455. A second referendum was held in Ireland on 2 October 2009. As with the Nice Treaty (p. 12), so with the Lisbon Treaty: the outcome was positive. Other obstacles were also cleared, including the need for approval of ratification by constitutional courts in some Member States, most notably in Germany (Chapter 19, p. 596) and the Czech Republic, the final State to ratify. The Lisbon Treaty duly entered into force on 1 December 2009.

The Treaty of Lisbon amends both the Treaty on European Union and the Treaty establishing the European Community. The European Union loses the three pillars crafted for it at Maastricht (p. 9). But there is not a single EU Treaty, as had been envisaged by the Treaty establishing a Constitution. There remains the EU Treaty (TEU), duly amended, and there is also the Treaty on the Functioning of the European Union (TFEU), which is the amended and re-named EC Treaty.

The first and third pillars of the pre-Lisbon EU are in effect merged into a single system, governed principally by the TFEU, which replaces the EC Treaty. The second pillar, governing a common foreign and security policy (CFSP), retains a visibly separate identity within the EU Treaty (and such matters are after all typically handled differently in most States). The TEU structure is institutionally distinct – displaying heavier emphasis on intergovernmental cooperation and action by unanimity among the States than one finds in the TFEU – and here too the Court's jurisdiction is largely excluded.

It is stated in the Lisbon Treaty that the European Union is founded on the two Treaties, which have the same legal value (Article 1 of both the EU Treaty and the TFEU). And in this vein Article 40 EU provides *both* that the implementation of the CFSP shall not affect the operation of the TFEU *and* that the implementation of the policies set out in the TFEU shall not affect the operation of the CFSP. The 'EC' and 'EC law' have not existed since 1 December 2009. It is correct to refer only to the EU and to EU law. But there are still two principal Treaties, the EU Treaty and the TFEU, and, on detailed inspection, the TFEU is readily recognizable as the old EC Treaty, even if the numbering of the Articles has been changed (see Table of Equivalence, pp. xxxix–lviii). It is the TFEU, not the TEU, which provides most of the subject matter of this book.

The Lisbon Treaty makes some significant changes and some cosmetic changes to the EU, while leaving a great deal of the substance of EU law unaffected.

Article 19 TEU provides for the basic institutional arrangements governing the Court. There shall be the Court of Justice, the 'General Court' (the successor to the Court of First Instance) and 'specialized courts'. Article 19(1) TEU states that the Court 'shall ensure that in the interpretation and application of the Treaties the law is observed' and also that 'Member States shall provide remedies sufficient to ensure effective legal protection in the field covered by Union law' (for the role of national courts see Chapter 4, p. 104, and in the particular context of judicial review, Chapter 8, p. 217). Broadly, however, there are no significant changes in the tasks entrusted to the Court by the Treaties. And although the Treaty establishing a Constitution would have brought the principle of supremacy into the text of the Treaty, the Lisbon Treaty does not (Chapter 3, p. 77).

The place of fundamental rights protection in the EU is covered at p. 54 of Chapter 2. As will be explained, the Lisbon Treaty makes changes here, both by converting the Charter of Fundamental Rights into a legally binding document and by providing for the EU's accession to the European Convention.

The Lisbon Treaty also makes major presentational and minor substantive changes to the treatment of the competences of the Union. This is explained more fully in Chapter 2, p. 29.

The driving force in institutional reform is a concern to make the system work more *effectively*. Radical overhaul of the pattern of involvement of the political (Council, Commission, Parliament) and judicial (Court) institutions was never on the agenda. The detailed institutional provisions are located in Title III of the EU Treaty, which begins with Article 13 EU and runs to Article 19 EU. The exclusive right of legislative initiative held by the Commission since the 1950s is preserved in the TFEU, excepting only in relation to activity concerning the area of freedom, security, and justice (Chapter 15: this is a lingering remnant of the 'old' three-pillar structure). Article 289 TFEU provides that the ordinary legislative procedure 'shall consist in the joint adoption by the Parliament and the Council of a regulation, directive or decision on a proposal from the Commission', and Article 294 TFEU sets out the detail. This 'ordinary legislative procedure' now dominates EU practice even more than previously, thereby maintaining the theme of recent Treaty revisions which have cemented its primacy. Here the place of both people(s) and States is recognized as central to the EU's functioning: the Parliament, directly elected by the peoples of Europe, and the Member States, represented in the Council, 'co-decide' under the ordinary legislative procedure. The Council votes according to qualified majority under this procedure, and Lisbon goes a considerable way to making the applicable rules transparent and intelligible. From April 2017 a qualified majority in Council will be defined as at least 55% of the members of the Council comprising at least 15 of them and representing Member States comprising at least 65% of the population of the Union. So: both States and people are relevant. In addition: a successful 'blocking minority' must include at least four members of the Council. Until April 2017 there are transitional arrangements: this is covered by Article 238 TFEU and a Protocol on transitional provisions, supported by a Declaration.

Article 16(3) EU provides that the Council shall vote by Qualified Majority unless the Treaties provide otherwise, and the few exceptions are areas of *particular* sensitivity, where the advantages of quicker decision-making do not override the political need to retain a veto: for example, taxation and, partially, social policy and defence.

Page 18 mentions that 'the taste for institutional and constitutional continuity identified in the Treaty of Amsterdam by Petite (p. 11) is again prominent in the Treaty establishing a Constitution'. The Lisbon Treaty generally sticks to this trend.

The most newsworthy changes made by the Lisbon Treaty involved the three most high-profile jobs in the EU. Jose Manuel Barroso, Herman Van Rompuy, and Catherine Ashton were appointed in late 2009 as respectively the President of the Commission, the President of the European Council, and the High Representative of the Union for Foreign Affairs and Security Policy. They were replaced from 2014 by Jean-Claude Juncker, Donald Tusk, and Federica Mogherini respectively. The President of the Commission is nothing new. The post of President of the European Council is by contrast an innovation. The European Council is composed of the Heads of State or Government of the Member States plus its President and the President of the Commission. Pre-Lisbon the Presidency of the European Council was held by each Member State by rotation for a six-month period. Equitable perhaps, but hardly conducive to consistency or to effective leadership. The Lisbon Treaty created the post of President which will be filled for a two-and-a-half-year term, open to renewal once (Art. 15(5) EU). The detailed job description is found in Art. 15(6) EU but the general intention is that greater coherence and consistency will be provided by virtue of the fact that the individual will not be confined to a six-month tenure. The post of High Representative of the Union for Foreign Affairs and Security Policy is also a new creation. The idea is to provide a sharper focus and a clearer identity for the Union's external face. Article 18 EU sets out the detail, while further elaboration of the envisaged functions of the role is found in the relevant Chapter later in the EU Treaty (especially Article 27 EU et seq). The mandate comes from the Council and the High Representative shall preside over the Foreign Affairs Council. But he or she shall be a member of the Commission. There is therefore a rather dramatic denial of the institutional separation between the intergovernmental and the supranational elements of the Union, which is foundational across much of the EU's operation. CFSP truly is *different*.

The changes to substantive EU law made by the Lisbon Treaty are very few, beyond the awkward cosmetic issue of re-numbering of the Articles of the Treaty. The heartland of the law of the internal market studied in Part Two of this book is little affected by the Lisbon Treaty. Separate consideration will have to be given in Chapter 15 to Title IV of the TFEU, which is entitled *Area of Freedom, Security and Justice*. It is here that the consolidation of the former pre-Lisbon third pillar with the first pillar treatment of matters pertaining to persons is housed. Page 9 explains the initial choice at Maastricht to establish three pillars for the European Union and page 10 explains how at Amsterdam a certain rapprochement between the pillars was effected. Now, after Lisbon, the pillars are formally removed.

Article 50 TEU is entirely new and arranges a procedure according to which a Member State may choose to withdraw from the Union.

The question whether the Lisbon Treaty is the same as the Treaty establishing a Constitution generated a great deal of argument in and after 2007, particularly from those who believed that once a referendum had been held (as in France and the Netherlands) or promised (as in the UK) on the latter, the same should have applied to the former. Passage of time has taken much of the heat out of the debate. It is, in short, clear that the Lisbon Treaty is *not* the same as the Treaty establishing a Constitution. Lisbon does not re-make the system under a single Treaty, as would have the Treaty establishing a Constitution; Lisbon makes detailed adjustments to the workings of the EU's institutions which display a degree of divergence from those envisaged by the Treaty establishing a Constitution. But it is *similar* – in many respects it is very similar. Lisbon is another incremental – and regrettably intransparent – round of Treaty reform whereas the Treaty establishing a Constitution would have made a presentationally fresh start by re-making the system under a single Treaty, but this tells us nothing about the *content* of the reforms. And here although Lisbon makes detailed adjustments to the workings of the EU's institutions which display an admitted degree of divergence from those envisaged by the Treaty establishing a Constitution, many of the divergences are minor, for example eight weeks, not six, during which the national Parliaments may raise defined objections to legislative acts (Chapter 2, p. 32, Chapter 18, p. 568); the addition of the UK/Polish Protocol on the Charter (Chapter 2, p. 63) or even merely cosmetic (e.g. the Union Minister becomes the High Representative). The core of the reform effected by the Lisbon Treaty is recognizably the core of that envisaged by the Treaty establishing a Constitution – even if it is not the *same*. Moreover large parts of EU law and policy remain wholly unchanged in their substance by Lisbon as they would have been left untouched by the Treaty establishing a Constitution. The legal order 'constitutionalized' by the Court lives on (Part One of the book); so too the basics of EU trade law (Part Two of the book).

Perhaps the best argument that the two documents are different in materially significant ways insists that Lisbon abandons constitutional trappings such as a motto, a flag, and an anthem favoured by the Treaty establishing a Constitution. This is of no significance in strict legal terms but of great significance in so far as one may have wished – or feared – that such adornments would have propelled the Union towards a more State-like character. After all such emblems have real symbolic force in some national Constitutions and consequently their elimination probably offers the strongest argument to those who would contend that the Lisbon Treaty is *qualitatively* different from the ill-fated Treaty establishing a Constitution. Still, the undoubted similarities between the two documents fuelled much anger that the Treaty establishing a Constitution was placed before the people of several Member States for approval and denied it by two of them while the Lisbon Treaty was calculatedly sheltered from a popular verdict (except in Ireland).

The story also suggests that the Member States will be hesitant to pursue further revision of the Treaties unless left with no choice.

■ QUESTION

To what extent is the process of ratification of the Lisbon Treaty consistent with the Laeken Declaration's concern that the EU 'must be brought closer to its citizens' who 'feel that deals are all too often cut out of their sight and. . .[who] want better democratic scrutiny' (p. 14)? Is this a proper source of concern?

FURTHER READING

Be aware that much of the debate on such fast-moving issues is today conducted electronically, rather than in academic journals. Sites that deserve your attention for their inclusion of topical material, although their intellectual interest is not confined to the process of Treaty revision, include:

Centre for European Studies, University of Oslo: www.sv.uio.no/arena/english/

European Constitutional Law Network: www.ecln.net/

European Integration online papers: http://eiop.or.at/eiop/

The Federal Trust: www.fedtrust.co.uk

Centre for European Policy Studies, Brussels: www.ceps.eu/publications

And do not neglect more conventional forms of publication:

On the Treaty of Lisbon:

Craig, P., 'The Lisbon Treaty: Process, Architecture and Substance' (2008) 33 EL Rev 137.

Dougan, M., 'The Treaty of Lisbon 2007: Winning Minds, not Hearts' (2008) 45 CML Rev 617.

Jacque, J.-P., 'Le traité de Lisbonne: une vue cavalière' (2008) 44 RTDE 439.

Scicluna, N., 'When Failure isn't Failure: European Union Constitutionalism after the Lisbon Treaty' (2012) 50 JCMS 441.

Snell, J., 'European Constitutional Settlement, an Ever-Closer Union and the Treaty of Lisbon: Democracy or Relevance?' (2008) 33 EL Rev 619.

On the (failed) Treaty establishing a Constitution:

Follesdal, A. 'Towards a Stable Finalité with Federal Features? The Balancing Acts of the Constitutional Treaty for Europe' (2005) 12 JEPP 572.

Halberstam, D. 'The Bride of Messina: Constitutionalism and Democracy in Europe' (2005) 30 EL Rev 775.

NOTE: Discussion of the process leading up to the Treaty of Lisbon's entry into force in December 2009 and also its aftermath will be resumed in the wider context of the legitimacy of the European Union as a uniquely sophisticated transnational organization in Chapter 19. By that time the reader will be better equipped to reflect on the detailed implications of the exercise of power by the European Union. This book now turns to a more detailed exploration of the way the EU system works.

NOTE: For additional material and resources see the Online Resource Centre at: www.oxfordtextbooks.co.uk/orc/weatherill12e.

2

The Sources of the Law

The three major sources of the law of the European Union are examined in this chapter. Section 1 discusses the founding Treaties; Section 2 explains the nature and method of adoption of legislation; Section 3 examines the general legal principles which have been shaped by the Court of Justice of the European Union (and in some cases subsequently absorbed by the Treaties). Another basis for making this three-fold classification is to view Section 1, the Treaties, as the product of the Member States, Section 2, legislation, as the product of the system's autonomous political institutions acting as a legislature, and Section 3, general principles, as the contribution of the judicial institution.

In *A Guide to European Union Law* Professor Mathijsen declares that 'the Union legal order grew and developed mainly at the hands of the Union judges' (p. 67, 11th ed.). The Court's creativity will be introduced in Section 3 of this chapter, but it also exerts an important influence over the sources in Sections 1 and 2 by virtue of its interpretative function. The activism of the judges will be observed throughout this book in many aspects of the Union's constitutional and institutional law. Two questions in particular will be addressed. First, to what extent is such judicial activism appropriate? This raises the general jurisprudential issue of the respective roles of courts and legislators. The second, more modern, more specifically European, question is the extent to which such judicial initiative is still forthcoming. Some observers have identified a more cautious, 'minimalist' approach by the European Court; see T. Koopmans (then a judge of the Court) (1986) 35 ICLQ 925, while in other aspects the Court's work is sometimes lacking consistency. See the *Further Reading* list at the end of this chapter.

SECTION 1: THE TREATIES

In the 1950s three founding Treaties were agreed. The Treaty of Paris came into force in 1952 and established the European Coal and Steel Community (ECSC). The two Treaties of Rome came into force in 1958 and established EURATOM, The European Atomic Energy Community, and the EEC, the European Economic Community. The six original parties were France, Germany, Luxembourg, Belgium, the Netherlands, and Italy.

The first major formal Treaty revision which the original Treaties underwent was the Single European Act 1986 (SEA). This adjusted several aspects of the structure and brought about a modest extension in competence. The SEA was chiefly motivated by the plan to complete the internal market by the end of 1992 (see further Chapter 9).

The Treaties shared common principles. The two Treaties of Rome were closely analogous in their specific provisions. The Treaty of Paris contained certain distinct features, but the European Coal and Steel Community, unlike EURATOM and the EEC, was limited to a span of only 50 years and so in July 2002 it reached the end of its natural life and control of the coal and steel sectors was brought under the umbrella of the EC. The primary focus of this book is on the current state of the most important of the three original Communities – what was the EEC, becoming the EC, the 'European Community' proper, on the entry into force of the Maastricht Treaty on 1 November 1993.

The alteration in name – EEC to EC – represented just a small piece of the Maastricht Treaty reforms. Effective from 1 November 1993 that Treaty created a 'European Union'. The original Treaties from the 1950s remained in force under the European Union umbrella. The EC Treaty was amended significantly, most notably through the insertion of detailed provisions for the establishment of Economic and Monetary Union.

The Amsterdam Treaty, which entered into force on 1 May 1999 (p. 10), retained the overall three-pillar structure of the Union, though it moved some matters from the third pillar into the first pillar, the EC (see Chapter 15). It also amended a substantial number of provisions of the EC Treaty. The Nice Treaty, which entered into force on 1 February 2003 (p. 12), also respected the three-pillar structure of the Union, while amending a number of detailed provisions.

Since the entry into force of the Treaty of Lisbon on 1 December 2009 the three-pillar structure was abandoned, and the 'EC' was no more, just as there is longer any such thing as 'EC law'. Now there is only the EU, and EU law. As explained in Chapter 1 (p. 19), the European Union post-Lisbon is based on two Treaties, which are of equal legal value (Article 1 of both the EU Treaty and the TFEU). The first is the *Treaty on European Union*, duly amended – the 'TEU'. The TEU contains some general provisions which will be considered where appropriate – pertaining to competence, fundamental rights, institutional arrangements and enhanced cooperation – and it also includes the detailed rules governing the conduct of the common foreign and security policy, which is touched on only briefly in this book. The second is the Treaty establishing the European Community, which is not only amended, it is also renamed, becoming the *Treaty on the Functioning of the European Union* (TFEU). The first and third pillars of the pre-Lisbon EU have in effect been merged into a single system, governed by the TFEU. This book is largely concerned with the legal system under the TFEU.

The creation of an integrated economy which transcends national frontiers is the most prominent of the tasks undertaken by this Treaty-based system. The substantive legal provisions in the TFEU which are examined in this book are primarily concerned to eliminate barriers to trade between Member States and to establish an internal market. The constitutional principles too are shaped in accordance with this central objective. However, it is important to appreciate that the original European Community and now the European Union are about more than economics. This is plain even from a superficial understanding of the tensions in post-war Europe from which the original Communities emerged. It is wise to begin by reading the Preambles to the Treaties in order to appreciate that the Union is based on a vision rather less tangible, but, to many, more inspiring, than Gross Domestic Product.

TREATY OF ROME ESTABLISHING THE EUROPEAN ECONOMIC COMMUNITY 1957 PREAMBLE

His Majesty The King of the Belgians, the President of the Federal Republic of Germany, the President of the French Republic, the President of the Italian Republic, Her Royal Highness the Grand Duchess of Luxembourg, Her Majesty The Queen of the Netherlands,

Determined to lay the foundations of an ever closer union among the peoples of Europe,

Resolved to ensure the economic and social progress of their countries by common action to eliminate the barriers which divide Europe,

Affirming as the essential objective of their efforts the constant improvement of the living and working conditions of their peoples,

Recognising that the removal of existing obstacles calls for concerted action in order to guarantee steady expansion, balanced trade and fair competition,

Anxious to strengthen the unity of their economies and to ensure their harmonious development by reducing the differences existing between the various regions and the backwardness of the less favoured regions,

Desiring to contribute, by means of a common commercial policy, to the progressive abolition of restrictions on international trade,

Intending to confirm the solidarity which binds Europe and the overseas countries and desiring to ensure the development of their prosperity, in accordance with the principles of the Charter of the United Nations,

Resolved by thus pooling their resources to preserve and strengthen peace and liberty, and calling upon the other peoples of Europe who share their ideal to join in their efforts,

Have decided to create a European Economic Community. . .

CONSOLIDATED VERSION OF THE TREATY ON EUROPEAN UNION (effective from 1 December 2009)

. . .

Resolved to mark a new stage in the process of European integration undertaken with the establishment of the European Communities,

Drawing inspiration from the cultural, religious and humanist inheritance of Europe, from which have developed the universal values of the inviolable and inalienable rights of the human person, freedom, democracy, equality and the rule of law,

Recalling the historic importance of the ending of the division of the European continent and the need to create firm bases for the construction of the future Europe,

Confirming their attachment to the principles of liberty, democracy and respect for human rights and fundamental freedoms and of the rule of law,

Confirming their attachment to fundamental social rights as defined in the European Social Charter signed at Turin on 18 October 1961 and in the 1989 Community Charter of the Fundamental Social Rights of Workers,

Desiring to deepen the solidarity between their peoples while respecting their history, their culture and their traditions,

Desiring to enhance further the democratic and efficient functioning of the institutions so as to enable them better to carry out, within a single institutional framework, the tasks entrusted to them,

Resolved to achieve the strengthening and the convergence of their economies and to establish an economic and monetary union including, in accordance with the provisions of this Treaty and of the Treaty on the Functioning of the European Union, a single and stable currency,

Determined to promote economic and social progress for their peoples, taking into account the principle of sustainable development and within the context of the accomplishment of the internal market and of reinforced cohesion and environmental protection, and to implement policies ensuring that advances in economic integration are accompanied by parallel progress in other fields,

Resolved to establish a citizenship common to nationals of their countries,

Resolved to implement a common foreign and security policy including the progressive framing of a common defence policy, which might lead to a common defence in accordance with the provisions of Article 42, thereby reinforcing the European identity and its independence in order to promote peace, security and progress in Europe and in the world,

Resolved to facilitate the free movement of persons, while ensuring the safety and security of their peoples, by establishing an area of freedom, security and justice, in accordance with the provisions of this Treaty and of the Treaty on the Functioning of the European Union,

Resolved to continue the process of creating an ever closer union among the peoples of Europe, in which decisions are taken as closely as possible to the citizen in accordance with the principle of subsidiarity,

In view of further steps to be taken in order to advance European integration,

Have decided to establish a European Union . . .

NOTE: These sentiments must be taken to influence the more specific provisions of the Treaty which are examined in the course of this book.

SECTION 2: LEGISLATION

A: Legislation in the European Union

The Treaties are *traité cadre*: frameworks which set out an overall design, but which require more specific amplification. That task belongs to the political and judicial institutions of the Union. The creative role of the Court of Justice of the European Union (the Court) is considered below, but it is the other three principal institutions, the Council, the Commission, and the Parliament, which are responsible for the adoption of legislation. As far as the TFEU is concerned, the 'ordinary legislative procedure' contained in Article 289 TFEU is the normal, though not exclusive, method for adopting legislation. As introduced in Chapter 1 (p. 20) Article 289 TFEU provides that the ordinary legislative procedure 'shall consist in the joint adoption by the Parliament and the Council of a regulation, directive or decision on a proposal from the Commission'. The available measures are set out in Article 288 TFEU:

ARTICLE 288 TFEU

To exercise the Union's competences, the institutions shall adopt regulations, directives, decisions, recommendations and opinions.

A regulation shall have general application. It shall be binding in its entirety and directly applicable in all Member States.

A directive shall be binding, as to the result to be achieved, upon each Member State to which it is addressed, but shall leave to the national authorities the choice of form and methods.

A decision shall be binding in its entirety. A decision which specifies those to whom it is addressed shall be binding only on them.

Recommendations and opinions shall have no binding force.

NOTE: Article 288 TFEU was Article 249 EC pre-Lisbon, and the text has been lightly amended. The provision was Article 189 pre-Amsterdam.

The Court has insisted that the different acts available to the institutions are distinguishable on the basis of their nature, not their form. A label is not conclusive. In *International Fruit Company* v *Commission* (Cases 41–44/70) [1971] ECR 411, a measure was labelled a Regulation. The applicant company argued that in reality it was a set of Decisions. The Court's examination of the substance of the measure led it to agree with the applicant:

International Fruit Company v *Commission* (Cases 41–44/70)

[1971] ECR 411, Court of Justice of the European Communities

[21] Consequently, Article 1 of Regulation No 983/70 is not a provision of general application within the meaning of the second paragraph of Article 189 of the Treaty, but must be regarded as a conglomeration of individual decisions taken by the Commission under the guise of a regulation pursuant to Article 2(2) of Regulation No 459/70, each of which decisions affects the legal position of each author of an application for a licence.

NOTE: The primary significance which flows from classifying a measure under one Article 288 pigeonhole rather than another relates to the individual's opportunity to challenge its validity. Showing a measure to be a Decision, rather than a Regulation, greatly increased the likelihood that an applicant can get the chance to persuade the Court to hold the legislation invalid. Classification is, however, of reduced significance since the entry into force of the Treaty of Lisbon. Judicial review of Union legislation will be examined in more depth in Chapter 8. To return to the task of identifying the types of legislation which exist, the Court held in the next case that the list of measures in (what is now) Article 288 is not exhaustive. The EU's institutions are capable of adopting other acts of legal significance.

Commission v *Council* (Case 22/70)

[1971] ECR 263, Court of Justice of the European Communities

The Member States acting together in Council had adopted a Resolution on 20 March 1970, in which they agreed to coordinate their approaches in negotiations for the conclusion of a European Road Transport Agreement (ERTA/AETR). The question of the Resolution's legal status arose when the Commission brought proceedings under Article 173 of the EC Treaty (now, after amendment, Article 263 TFEU), which provides for judicial review of EU acts. Was the Resolution an act? The Council observed that it did not fit into any of the categories in Article 189 of the EC Treaty (now Article 288 TFEU). The Court, however, was more concerned to identify whether the Resolution had legal effects. That possibility could not be excluded simply because the resolution was not within the list now found in Article 288 TFEU.

[44] In the course of the meeting on 20 March 1970, the Council, after an exchange of views between its members and the representative of the Commission, reached a number of 'conclusions' on the attitude to be taken by the Governments of the Member States in the decisive negotiations on the AETR.

[45] These proceedings were concerned partly with the objective of the negotiations and partly with negotiating procedure.

[46] As regards the objective to be pursued, the Council settled on a negotiating position aimed at having the AETR adapted to the provisions of the Community system, apart from the concession of certain derogations from that system which would have to be accepted by the Community.

[47] Having regard to the objective thus established, the Council invited the Commission to put forward, at the appropriate time and in accordance with the provisions of Article 75 of the Treaty, the necessary proposals with a view to amending Regulation No 543/69.

[48] As regards negotiating, the Council decided, in accordance with the course of action decided upon at its previous meetings, that the negotiations should be carried on and concluded by the six Member States, which would become contracting parties to the AETR.

[49] Throughout the negotiations and at the conclusion of the agreement, the States would act in common and would constantly coordinate their positions according to the usual procedure in close association with the Community institutions, the delegation of the Member State currently occupying the Presidency of the Council acting as spokesman.

[50] It does not appear from the minutes that the Commission raised any objections to the definition by the Council of the objective of the negotiations.

[51] On the other hand, it did lodge an express reservation regarding the negotiating procedure, declaring that it considered that the position adopted by the Council was not in accordance with the Treaty, and more particularly with Article 228.

[52] It follows from the foregoing that the Council's proceedings dealt with a matter falling within the power of the Community, and that the Member States could not therefore act outside the framework of the common institutions.

[53] It thus seems that in so far as they concerned the objective of the negotiations as defined by the Council, the proceedings of 20 March 1970 could not have been simply the expression or the recognition of a voluntary coordination, but were designed to lay down a course of action binding on both the institutions and the Member States, and destined ultimately to be reflected in the tenor of the regulation.

[54] In the part of its conclusions relating to the negotiating procedure, the Council adopted provisions which were capable of derogating in certain circumstances from the procedure laid down by the Treaty regarding negotiations with third countries and the conclusion of agreements.

[55] Hence, the proceedings of 20 March 1970 had definite legal effects both on relations between the Community and the Member States and on the relationship between institutions.

NOTES

1. The significance of finding that the Council's act, although not mentioned in Article 189 of the EC Treaty (now Article 288 TFEU), nevertheless had legal effects, was that its validity could be challenged by the Commission before the Court. As in the *International Fruit Company* case, the task of identifying a legal act occurred in the context of a challenge to it. *Commission* v *Council* (Case 22/70) will be considered again in Chapter 8 which examines challenges to Union acts.
2. Union law has become increasingly multi-dimensional. An increasingly wide range of acts may carry direct or indirect legal implications. In Case C-322/88 *Grimaldi* v *Fonds des Malaises Professionelles* [1989] ECR 4407 the Court held that a recommendation, though not legally binding, may carry significance in the interpretation of texts.
3. This book focuses on the TFEU. The procedures governing the conduct of the Common Foreign and Security Policy are found in Title V of the TEU, and they are quite different from those discussed here.

B: The principle of conferral

The Union has neither a general legislative competence nor a single uniform legislative procedure. This means, first, that any proposed legislation must fall within the scope of the Treaty. This, the 'principle of conferral', is the subject of this sub-section. It also means, second, that even if proposed legislation falls within the scope of the Treaty, it may be necessary to select between legal bases granted by the Treaty in so far as applicable legislative procedures vary. This is examined in the next sub-section.

Article 5 TEU is constitutionally fundamental.

ARTICLES 5(1) AND 5(2) TEU

1. The limits of Union competences are governed by the principle of conferral. The use of Union competences is governed by the principles of subsidiarity and proportionality.

2. Under the principle of conferral, the Union shall act only within the limits of the competences conferred upon it by the Member States in the Treaties to attain the objectives set out therein. Competences not conferred upon the Union in the Treaties remain with the Member States.

Articles 5(3) and 5(4) TEU amplify the dictates of the principles of subsidiarity and of proportionality respectively and these are considered more fully elsewhere (pp. 557, 48 respectively). The core of the principle of conferral contained in Articles 5(1) and 5(2) TEU holds that there are *limits* on what may be done under the EU Treaty – *limits* defined by the Member States in agreeing the Treaties and beyond which, as the final sentence of Article 5(2) TEU makes clear and is echoed in Article 4(1) TEU, the Member States retain their own competences. On several occasions in this chapter it will be possible to observe a thematic nervousness about the risk that these limits be transgressed.

Prior to the entry into force of the Lisbon Treaty it would have been necessary to hunt through the Treaties to track down the areas in which a legislative competence is conferred, and to identify the applicable legislative procedures. However, the Lisbon Treaty goes some way to making the matter more transparent. It introduced what is now Title I of Part One of the TFEU:

CATEGORIES AND AREAS OF UNION COMPETENCE

ARTICLE 2 TFEU

1. When the Treaties confer on the Union exclusive competence in a specific area, only the Union may legislate and adopt legally binding acts, the Member States being able to do so themselves only if so empowered by the Union or for the implementation of Union acts.

2. When the Treaties confer on the Union a competence shared with the Member States in a specific area, the Union and the Member States may legislate and adopt legally binding acts in that area. The Member States shall exercise their competence to the extent that the Union has not exercised its competence. The Member States shall again exercise their competence to the extent that the Union has decided to cease exercising its competence.

3. The Member States shall coordinate their economic and employment policies within arrangements as determined by this Treaty, which the Union shall have competence to provide.

4. The Union shall have competence, in accordance with the provisions of the Treaty on European Union, to define and implement a common foreign and security policy, including the progressive framing of a common defence policy.

5. In certain areas and under the conditions laid down in the Treaties, the Union shall have competence to carry out actions to support, coordinate or supplement the actions of the Member States, without thereby superseding their competence in these areas.

Legally binding acts of the Union adopted on the basis of the provisions of the Treaties relating to these areas shall not entail harmonisation of Member States' laws or regulations.

6. The scope of and arrangements for exercising the Union's competences shall be determined by the provisions of the Treaties relating to each area.

ARTICLE 3 TFEU

1. The Union shall have exclusive competence in the following areas:
   (a) customs union;
   (b) the establishing of the competition rules necessary for the functioning of the internal market;
   (c) monetary policy for the Member States whose currency is the euro;
   (d) the conservation of marine biological resources under the common fisheries policy;
   (e) common commercial policy.

2. The Union shall also have exclusive competence for the conclusion of an international agreement when its conclusion is provided for in a legislative act of the Union or is necessary to enable the Union to exercise its internal competence, or insofar as its conclusion may affect common rules or alter their scope.

ARTICLE 4 TFEU

1. The Union shall share competence with the Member States where the Treaties confer on it a competence which does not relate to the areas referred to in Articles 2 B and 2 E.

2. Shared competence between the Union and the Member States applies in the following principal areas:
   (a) internal market;
   (b) social policy, for the aspects defined in this Treaty;
   (c) economic, social and territorial cohesion;
   (d) agriculture and fisheries, excluding the conservation of marine biological resources;
   (e) environment;
   (f) consumer protection;
   (g) transport;
   (h) trans-European networks;
   (i) energy;
   (j) area of freedom, security and justice;
   (k) common safety concerns in public health matters, for the aspects defined in this Treaty.

3. In the areas of research, technological development and space, the Union shall have competence to carry out activities, in particular to define and implement programmes; however, the exercise of that competence shall not result in Member States being prevented from exercising theirs.

4. In the areas of development cooperation and humanitarian aid, the Union shall have competence to carry out activities and conduct a common policy; however, the exercise of that competence shall not result in Member States being prevented from exercising theirs.

ARTICLE 5 TFEU

1. The Member States shall coordinate their economic policies within the Union. To this end, the Council shall adopt measures, in particular broad guidelines for these policies.
   Specific provisions shall apply to those Member States whose currency is the euro.

2. The Union shall take measures to ensure coordination of the employment policies of the Member States, in particular by defining guidelines for these policies.

3. The Union may take initiatives to ensure coordination of Member States' social policies.

ARTICLE 6 TFEU

The Union shall have competence to carry out actions to support, coordinate or supplement the actions of the Member States. The areas of such action shall, at European level, be:

(a) protection and improvement of human health;
(b) industry;
(c) culture;
(d) tourism;
(e) education, vocational training, youth and sport;
(f) civil protection;
(g) administrative cooperation.

NOTE: These provisions supply a digestible impression of the areas in which the EU is competent to adopt legislation, and they also show that there are three main types of legislative competence – exclusive, shared and supporting. Then, as Article 2(6) TFEU makes clear, it is necessary to find the relevant provision in the TFEU in order to grasp the scope of and arrangements for exercising the competence in question. The place to go is Part Three of the TFEU, entitled *Union Policies and Internal Actions*. It contains 24 Titles and stretches from Article 26 to Article 197 TFEU. Here are the nuts and bolts of what the EU is competent to do, with what aims and through which procedures. Some provisions are sector-specific and relatively detailed. For example, the EU may adopt legislation dealing with environmental protection within the parameters set by Articles 191–193 TFEU; agricultural and fisheries policy are subject to legislative development pursuant to Articles 38–44 TFEU. However, two provisions of the TFEU confer a particularly broad legislative competence on the EU. These are Articles 352 TFEU and 114 TFEU. It is not in the gift of the EU legislature to override the limits set by the principle of conferral. Only Treaty revision, and due confirmation through national constitutional processes leading to Treaty ratification, can change the settlement. But these two provisions strain in practice the promise of a *limited* legislative competence made by Article 5 TEU.

ARTICLE 352 TFEU

1. If action by the Union should prove necessary, within the framework of the policies defined in the Treaties, to attain one of the objectives set out in the Treaties, and the Treaties have not provided the necessary powers, the Council, acting unanimously on a proposal from the Commission and after obtaining the consent of the European Parliament, shall adopt the appropriate measures. Where the measures in question are adopted by the Council in accordance with a special legislative procedure, it shall also act unanimously on a proposal from the Commission and after obtaining the consent of the European Parliament.

2. Using the procedure for monitoring the subsidiarity principle referred to in Article 5(3) of the Treaty on European Union, the Commission shall draw national Parliaments' attention to proposals based on this Article.

3. Measures based on this Article shall not entail harmonisation of Member States' laws or regulations in cases where the Treaties exclude such harmonisation.

4. This Article cannot serve as a basis for attaining objectives pertaining to the common foreign and security policy and any acts adopted pursuant to this Article shall respect the limits set out in Article 40, second paragraph, of the Treaty on European Union.

This is an amplified version of what was Article 308 EC before the entry into force of the Lisbon Treaty (and it was Article 235 before the Amsterdam re-numbering). Article 352(2) reflects the Lisbon innovation of drawing national Parliaments into review of the EU law-making process (see further p. 569), while paragraphs (3) and (4) both in different ways reflect a concern not to allow Article 352 to be used to overturn limits on EU action found elsewhere in the Treaties. The first paragraph of Article 352, however, is clearly potentially very broad in its scope of application.

The Court has been given the opportunity to explain that Article 352 (or, strictly, its predecessors) is broad in scope but not unlimited. This is in conformity with the principle of conferral found in Article 5 TEU.

In Case 45/86 *Commission* v *Council* [1987] ECR 1493 it decided that a *specific* legal base for legislation, if available in the Treaty, must be preferred over the more *general* base now found in Article 352 TFEU. The Court has never deviated from this view. The increase in the availability of specific legal bases as a result of periodic Treaty revision has consequently in principle reduced the role of Article 352 TFEU. The Lisbon Treaty, by adding new competences in fields such as energy and intellectual property, has extended this trend – for examination see T. Konstadinides, 'Drawing the Line between Circumvention and Gap-Filling: An Exploration of the Conceptual Limits of the Treaty's Flexibility Clause' (2012) 31 YEL 227. However, even in the absence of a specific legal base elsewhere in the Treaty, Article 352 may not be used unless its preconditions are met.

Accession by the Community to the European Convention for the Protection of Human Rights and Fundamental Freedoms (Opinion 2/94)

[1996] ECR I-1759, Court of Justice of the European Communities

The Court was asked for an Opinion pursuant to what is now Article 218 TFEU whether the EC's accession to the European Convention for the Protection of Human Rights and Fundamental Freedoms would be compatible with the Treaty.

[29] Article 235 [*predecessor to the current Article 352 TFEU*] is designed to fill the gap where no specific provisions of the Treaty confer on the Community institutions express or implied powers to act, if such powers appear none the less to be necessary to enable the Community to carry out its functions with a view to attaining one of the objectives laid down by the Treaty.

[30] That provision, being an integral part of an institutional system based on the principle of conferred powers, cannot serve as a basis for widening the scope of Community powers beyond the general framework created by the provisions of the Treaty as a whole and, in particular, by those that define the tasks and the activities of the Community. On any view, Article 235 cannot be used as a basis for the adoption of provisions whose effect would, in substance, be to amend the Treaty without following the procedure which it provides for that purpose.

NOTE: The Court therefore draws a line between permissibly broad reliance on (what is now) Article 352 TFEU as a basis for legislation and impermissible revision of the Treaty by legislative act. And the proposed accession would be a step too far.

[34] Respect for human rights is therefore a condition of the lawfulness of Community acts. Accession to the Convention would, however, entail a substantial change in the present Community system for the protection of human rights in that it would entail the entry of the Community into a distinct international institutional system as well as integration of all the provisions of the Convention into the Community legal order.

[35] Such a modification of the system for the protection of human rights in the Community, with equally fundamental institutional implications for the Community and for the Member States, would be of constitutional significance and would therefore be such as to go beyond the scope of Article 235. It could be brought about only by way of Treaty amendment.

NOTE: One of the innovations of the Lisbon Treaty is to amend the Treaty to provide the necessary competence to accede to the ECHR which was previously lacking: Article 6(2) TEU, p. 58.

Article 352 TFEU is broad but not unlimited, and the same is true of the other provision in the Treaty which most conspicuously confers a legislative competence which is not sector-specific. This is Article 114 TFEU.

ARTICLE 114 TFEU

1. Save where otherwise provided in the Treaties, the following provisions shall apply for the achievement of the objectives set out in Article 26. The European Parliament and the Council shall, acting in accordance with the ordinary legislative procedure and after consulting the Economic and Social Committee, adopt the measures for the approximation of the provisions laid down by law, regulation or administrative action in Member States which have as their object the establishment and functioning of the internal market.

2. Paragraph 1 shall not apply to fiscal provisions, to those relating to the free movement of persons nor to those relating to the rights and interests of employed persons.

3. The Commission, in its proposals envisaged in paragraph 1 concerning health, safety, environmental protection and consumer protection, will take as a base a high level of protection, taking account in particular of any new development based on scientific facts. Within their respective powers, the European Parliament and the Council will also seek to achieve this objective.

NOTE: Article 114 TFEU is an amended version of what was, before the entry into force of the Lisbon Treaty, Article 95 EC (and it was Article 100a before the Amsterdam re-numbering, p. 11). It provides a competence to 'approximate' or to harmonize national laws. But such approximation or harmonization must have as its object the establishment and functioning of the internal market. The internal market, according to Article 26 TFEU, 'shall comprise an area without internal frontiers in which the free movement of goods, persons, services, and capital is ensured in accordance with the provisions of this Treaty'. Case C-155/91 *Commission* v *Council* [1993] ECR I-939 established that recourse to this provision is not justified where the measure has only the incidental effect of harmonizing market conditions within the Community. Case C-84/94 *UK* v *Council* [1996] ECR I-5755 concluded that the legal base authorizing harmonization could not have constituted the appropriate legal basis for the adoption of the 'Working Time' Directive since its 'principal objective' (para 45) was the protection of the health and safety of workers. In each case other Treaty provisions took the strain – what is now (after amendment) Article 192 TFEU on environmental protection in Case C-155/91, and what is now (after amendment) Article 153 TFEU in Case C-84/94. In the next case it is harmonization or nothing. And the Court, in the famous 'Tobacco Advertising' judgment of October 2000, finds that constitutionally the answer is nothing – the Treaty does not confer a competence to adopt the contested measure.

Germany v *European Parliament and Council of the European Union* (Case C-376/98)

[2000] ECR I-8419, Court of Justice of the European Communities

Directives based on Article 100a, predecessor to the current Article 114 TFEU, prohibited the sale of oral snuff and high tar cigarettes (Directives 89/622 [1989] OJ L359/1, and 92/41 [1992] OJ L158/30). In 1998 a third measure of harmonization was added to the package of Directives governing tobacco products. This was Directive 98/43 [1998] OJ L213/9 imposing severe restrictions on the advertising of tobacco products. It too was based on Article 100a (and also Articles 57(2) and 66, governing the services sector). These provisions required then, as Article 114 TFEU requires now, only a qualified majority in Council and the Directive had been adopted despite German opposition. Germany brought an action pursuant to Article 173 (now, after amendment, Article 263 TFEU) to challenge the validity of the Directive. The German objections covered a number of matters, but the core of the application, which succeeded before the Court, attacked the 'Tobacco Advertising' Directive as being inadequately closely connected to the process of market-making to which the Treaty provisions on harmonization were then and still are dedicated. Germany was, in short, alleging that a qualified majority of States in Council allied with the Parliament had trespassed into an area lying beyond the scope of action authorized by the Treaty.

Advocate-General Fennelly's Opinion charted a route to which the Court subsequently adhered. In his Opinion he stated:

> [83] . . . the internal market is not a value-free synonym for general economic governance. . . the conferral of competence to pursue its establishment and functioning, under both Article 100A and more specific provisions such as Article 57(2), cannot, in my view, be equated with creation of a general Community regulatory power. These competences are conferred either to facilitate the exercise of the four freedoms or to equalize the conditions of competition.
>
> [89] . . . the pursuit of equal conditions of competition does not give *carte blanche* to the Community legislator to harmonize any national rules that meet the eye, be it in a liberalizing or restrictive fashion. . . I would say that it would risk transferring general Member State regulatory competence to the Community if recourse to Article 100A to adopt harmonising measures in the interests of undistorted competition were not subject to some test of the reality of the link between such measures and internal market objectives. The silence of Articles 7A and 100A of the Treaty regarding equal conditions of competition furnishes an additional reason to avoid turning Article 100A into an instrument of general economic governance on this ground.

This is the detailed manifestation of a much broader constitutional anxiety about the need to police legislative excesses perpetrated by the EU legislature at the expense of other interests and actors in the political process. Mr Fennelly had introduced his inquiry in the following terms:

> [4] The legal basis invoked by the Advertising Directive relates to the internal market. The Community's internal market competence is not limited, a priori, by any reserved domain of Member State power. It is a horizontal competence, whose exercise displaces national regulatory competence in the field addressed. Judicial review of the exercise of such a competence is a delicate and complex matter. On the one hand, unduly restrained judicial review might permit the Community institutions to enjoy, in effect, general or unlimited legislative power, contrary to the principle that the Community only enjoys those limited competences, however extensive, which have been conferred on it by the Treaty with a view to the attainment of specified objectives. This could permit the Community to encroach impermissibly on the powers of the Member States. On the other hand, the Court cannot, in principle, restrict the legitimate performance by the Community legislator of its task of removing barriers and distortions to trade in goods and services. It is the task of the Court, as the repository of the trust and confidence of the Community institutions, the Member States and the citizens of the Union, to perform this difficult function of upholding the constitutional division of powers between the Community and the Member States on the basis of objective criteria.

The Court was playing for high constitutional stakes, not least because of the risk that if it was perceived to apply a soft standard of review when invited to police the margins of the competence conferred by the Treaty, it might risk triggering rebellion among national judiciaries anxious to protect the reserved domain of State power. This judicial interplay is examined further in Chapter 19. In 'Tobacco Advertising' the Court devoted close analysis to the scope of the Treaty-conferred competence to harmonize national laws – and it is an analysis which is equally applicable to the post-Lisbon texts.

> [76] The Directive is concerned with the approximation of laws, regulations and administrative provisions of the Member States relating to the advertising and sponsorship of tobacco products. The national measures affected are to a large extent inspired by public health policy objectives.
>
> [77] The first indent of Article 129(4) of the Treaty excludes any harmonization of laws and regulations of the Member States designed to protect and improve human health.
>
> [78] But that provision does not mean that harmonizing measures adopted on the basis of other provisions of the Treaty cannot have any impact on the protection of human health. Indeed, the third paragraph of Article 129(1) provides that health requirements are to form a constituent part of the Community's other policies.

[79] Other articles of the Treaty may not, however, be used as a legal basis in order to circumvent the express exclusion of harmonization laid down in Article 129(4) of the Treaty.

This explains the observation made that this case, unlike earlier cases, involved harmonization or nothing. If the Directive, which severely restricted tobacco advertising, albeit on a common EU-wide basis, was treated as a public health measure, then it appeared to fall beyond the scope of the conferred legislative competence. Public health is a competence conferred by the Treaty, but Article 129(4) EC (now 168(5) TFEU) explicitly excludes harmonization of laws under that Title. So the Directive would be ruled invalid and unsalvageable unless it properly took the Treaty provisions governing harmonization as its bases.

[81] Article 100a(1) of the Treaty empowers the Council, acting in accordance with the procedure referred to in Article 189b (now, after amendment, Article 251 EC) and after consulting the Economic and Social Committee, to adopt measures for the approximation of the provisions laid down by law, regulation or administrative action in Member States which have as their object the establishment and functioning of the internal market.

[82] Under Article 3(c) of the EC Treaty (now, after amendment, Article 3(1)(c) EC), the internal market is characterized by the abolition, as between Member States, of all obstacles to the free movement of goods, persons, services and capital. Article 7a of the EC Treaty (now, after amendment, Article 14 EC), which provides for the measures to be taken with a view to establishing the internal market, states in paragraph 2 that that market is to comprise an area without internal frontiers in which the free movement of goods, persons, services and capital is ensured in accordance with the provisions of the Treaty.

[83] Those provisions, read together, make it clear that the measures referred to in Article 100a(1) of the Treaty are intended to improve the conditions for the establishment and functioning of the internal market. To construe that article as meaning that it vests in the Community legislature a general power to regulate the internal market would not only be contrary to the express wording of the provisions cited above but would also be incompatible with the principle embodied in Article 3b of the EC Treaty (now Article 5 EC) that the powers of the Community are limited to those specifically conferred on it.

[84] Moreover, a measure adopted on the basis of Article 100a of the Treaty must genuinely have as its object the improvement of the conditions for the establishment and functioning of the internal market. If a mere finding of disparities between national rules and of the abstract risk of obstacles to the exercise of fundamental freedoms or of distortions of competition liable to result therefrom were sufficient to justify the choice of Article 100a as a legal basis, judicial review of compliance with the proper legal basis might be rendered nugatory. The Court would then be prevented from discharging the function entrusted to it by Article 164 of the EC Treaty (now Article 220 EC) of ensuring that the law is observed in the interpretation and application of the Treaty.

[85] So, in considering whether Article 100a was the proper legal basis, the Court must verify whether the measure whose validity is at issue in fact pursues the objectives stated by the Community legislature (see, in particular, *Spain* v *Council*, cited above [Case C-350/92], paragraphs 25 to 41, and Case C-233/94 *Germany* v *Parliament and Council* [1997] ECR I-2405, paragraphs 10 to 21).

[86] It is true, as the Court observed in paragraph 35 of its judgment in *Spain* v *Council*, cited above, that recourse to Article 100a as a legal basis is possible if the aim is to prevent the emergence of future obstacles to trade resulting from multifarious development of national laws. However, the emergence of such obstacles must be likely and the measure in question must be designed to prevent them.

[87] The foregoing considerations apply to interpretation of Article 57(2) of the Treaty, read in conjunction with Article 66 thereof, which expressly refers to measures intended to make it easier for persons to take up and pursue activities by way of services. Those provisions are also intended to confer on the Community legislature specific power to adopt measures intended to improve the functioning of the internal market.

[88] Furthermore, provided that the conditions for recourse to Articles 100a, 57(2) and 66 as a legal basis are fulfilled, the Community legislature cannot be prevented from relying on that legal basis on the ground that public health protection is a decisive factor in the choices to be made. On the contrary, the third paragraph of Article 129(1) provides that health requirements are to form a constituent part of the Community's other policies and Article 100a(3) expressly requires that, in the process of harmonization, a high level of human health protection is to be ensured.

[89] It is therefore necessary to verify whether, in the light of the foregoing, it was permissible for the Directive to be adopted on the basis of Articles 100a, 57(2) and 66 of the Treaty.

The Directive

[90] In the first recital in the preamble to the Directive, the Community legislature notes that differences exist between national laws on the advertising and sponsorship of tobacco products and observes that, as a result of such advertising and sponsorship transcending the borders of the Member States, the differences in question are likely to give rise to barriers to the movement of the products which serve as the media for such activities and the exercise of freedom to provide services in that area, as well as to distortions of competition, thereby impeding the functioning of the internal market.

[91] According to the second recital, it is necessary to eliminate such barriers, and, to that end, approximate the rules relating to the advertising and sponsorship of tobacco products, whilst leaving Member States the possibility of introducing, under certain conditions, such requirements as they consider necessary in order to guarantee protection of the health of individuals.

[92] Article 3(1) of the Directive prohibits all forms of advertising and sponsorship of tobacco products and Article 3(4) prohibits any free distribution having the purpose or the effect of promoting such products. However, its scope does not extend to communications between professionals in the tobacco trade, advertising in sales outlets or in publications published and printed in third countries which are not principally intended for the Community market (Article 3(5)).

[93] The Directive also prohibits the use of the same names both for tobacco products and for other products and services as from 30 July 1998, except for products and services marketed before that date under a name also used for a tobacco product, whose use is authorized under certain conditions (Article 3(2)). With effect from 30 July 2001, tobacco products must not bear the brand name, trademark, emblem or other distinctive feature of any other product or service, unless the tobacco product has already been traded under that brand name, trade-mark, emblem or other distinctive feature before that date (Article 3(3)(a)).

[94] Pursuant to Article 5, the Directive is not to preclude Member States from laying down, in accordance with the Treaty, such stricter requirements concerning the advertising or sponsorship of tobacco products as they deem necessary to guarantee the health protection of individuals.

[95] It is therefore necessary to verify whether the Directive actually contributes to eliminating obstacles to the free movement of goods and to the freedom to provide services, and to removing distortions of competition.

Elimination of Obstacles to The Free Movement of Goods and the Freedom to Provide Services

[96] It is clear that, as a result of disparities between national laws on the advertising of tobacco products, obstacles to the free movement of goods or the freedom to provide services exist or may well arise.

[97] In the case, for example, of periodicals, magazines and newspapers which contain advertising for tobacco products, it is true, as the applicant has demonstrated, that no obstacle exists at present to their importation into Member States which prohibit such advertising. However, in view of the trend in national legislation towards ever greater restrictions on advertising of tobacco products, reflecting the belief that such advertising gives rise to an appreciable increase in tobacco consumption, it is probable that obstacles to the free movement of press products will arise in the future.

[98] In principle, therefore, a Directive prohibiting the advertising of tobacco products in periodicals, magazines and newspapers could be adopted on the basis of Article 100a of the Treaty with a view to ensuring the free movement of press products, on the lines of Directive 89/552, Article 13 of which prohibits television advertising of tobacco products in order to promote the free broadcasting of television programmes.

[99] However, for numerous types of advertising of tobacco products, the prohibition under Article 3(1) of the Directive cannot be justified by the need to eliminate obstacles to the free movement of advertising media or the freedom to provide services in the field of advertising. That applies, in particular, to the prohibition of advertising on posters, parasols, ashtrays and other articles used in hotels, restaurants and cafés, and the prohibition of advertising spots in cinemas, prohibitions which in no way help to facilitate trade in the products concerned.

[100] Admittedly, a measure adopted on the basis of Articles 100a, 57(2) and 66 of the Treaty may incorporate provisions which do not contribute to the elimination of obstacles to exercise of the fundamental freedoms

provided that they are necessary to ensure that certain prohibitions imposed in pursuit of that purpose are not circumvented. It is, however, quite clear that the prohibitions mentioned in the previous paragraph do not fall into that category.

[101] Moreover, the Directive does not ensure free movement of products which are in conformity with its provisions.

[102] Contrary to the contentions of the Parliament and Council, Article 3(2) of the Directive, relating to diversification products, cannot be construed as meaning that, where the conditions laid down in the Directive are fulfilled, products of that kind in which trade is allowed in one Member State may move freely in the other Member States, including those where such products are prohibited.

[103] Under Article 5 of the Directive, Member States retain the right to lay down, in accordance with the Treaty, such stricter requirements concerning the advertising or sponsorship of tobacco products as they deem necessary to guarantee the health protection of individuals.

[104] Furthermore, the Directive contains no provision ensuring the free movement of products which conform to its provisions, in contrast to other directives allowing Member States to adopt stricter measures for the protection of a general interest (see, in particular, Article 7(1) of Council Directive 90/239/EEC of 17 May 1990 on the approximation of the laws, regulations and administrative provisions of the Member States concerning the maximum tar yield of cigarettes (OJ 1990L 137, p. 36) and Article 8(1) of Council Directive 89/622/EEC of 13 November 1989 on the approximation of the laws, regulations and administrative provisions of the Member States concerning the labelling of tobacco products (OJ 1989L 359, p. 1).

[105] In those circumstances, it must be held that the Community legislature cannot rely on the need to eliminate obstacles to the free movement of advertising media and the freedom to provide services in order to adopt the Directive on the basis of Articles 100a, 57(2) and 66 of Treaty.

Elimination of Distortion of Competition

[106] In examining the lawfulness of a directive adopted on the basis of Article 100a of the Treaty, the Court is required to verify whether the distortion of competition which the measure purports to eliminate is appreciable (*Titanium Dioxide*, cited above [Case C-300/89], paragraph 23).

[107] In the absence of such a requirement, the powers of the Community legislature would be practically unlimited. National laws often differ regarding the conditions under which the activities they regulate may be carried on, and this impacts directly or indirectly on the conditions of competition for the undertakings concerned. It follows that to interpret Articles 100a, 57(2) and 66 of the Treaty as meaning that the Community legislature may rely on those articles with a view to eliminating the smallest distortions of competition would be incompatible with the principle, already referred to in paragraph 83 of this judgment, that the powers of the Community are those specifically conferred on it.

[108] It is therefore necessary to verify whether the Directive actually contributes to eliminating appreciable distortions of competition.

[109] First, as regards advertising agencies and producers of advertising media, undertakings established in Member States which impose fewer restrictions on tobacco advertising are unquestionably at an advantage in terms of economies of scale and increase in profits. The effects of such advantages on competition are, however, remote and indirect and do not constitute distortions which could be described as appreciable. They are not comparable to the distortions of competition caused by differences in production costs, such as those which, in particular, prompted the Community legislature to adopt Council Directive 89/428/EEC of 21 June 1989 on procedures for harmonizing the programmes for the reduction and eventual elimination of pollution caused by waste from the titanium dioxide industry (OJ 1989L 201, p. 56).

[110] It is true that the differences between certain regulations on tobacco advertising may give rise to appreciable distortions of competition. As the Commission and the Finnish and United Kingdom Governments have submitted, the fact that sponsorship is prohibited in some Member States and authorized in others gives rise, in particular, to certain sports events being relocated, with considerable repercussions on the conditions of competition for undertakings associated with such events.

[111] However, such distortions, which could be a basis for recourse to Article 100a of the Treaty in order to prohibit certain forms of sponsorship, are not such as to justify the use of that legal basis for an outright prohibition of advertising of the kind imposed by the Directive.

[112] Second, as regards distortions of competition in the market for tobacco products, irrespective of the applicant's contention that such distortions are not covered by the Directive, it is clear that, in that sector, the Directive is likewise not apt to eliminate appreciable distortions of competition.

[113] Admittedly, as the Commission has stated, producers and sellers of tobacco products are obliged to resort to price competition to influence their market share in Member States which have restrictive legislation. However, that does not constitute a distortion of competition but rather a restriction of forms of competition which applies to all economic operators in those Member States. By imposing a wide-ranging prohibition on the advertising of tobacco products, the Directive would in the future generalize that restriction of forms of competition by limiting, in all the Member States, the means available for economic operators to enter or remain in the market.

[114] In those circumstances, it must be held that the Community legislature cannot rely on the need to eliminate distortions of competition, either in the advertising sector or in the tobacco products sector, in order to adopt the Directive on the basis of Articles 100a, 57(2) and 66 of the Treaty.

[115] In view of all the foregoing considerations, a measure such as the directive cannot be adopted on the basis of Articles 100a, 57(2) and 66 of the Treaty.

NOTE: The Court had no need to consider other pleas advanced by Germany, which included breach of the principles of subsidiarity, proportionality, and freedom of expression (although these issues are addressed in the Opinion of Advocate-General Fennelly). It annulled the Directive.

The Court makes it quite clear that it is *not* denying that public health concerns may play a part in the shaping of harmonization legislation (paras 78, 88). Nor is it holding it impermissible to ban particular practices in pursuit of the internal market (paras 98, 110–11). But it is insistent that harmonization must be tied to market-making. Were harmonization a competence *per se* the EU would in practice enjoy open-ended competence (paras 83–84, 107). That is not what the Treaty stipulates – see Article 5(1) TEU's principle of conferral, p. 29. A Directive must actually contribute to eliminating obstacles to the free movement of goods or to the freedom to provide services, or to removing distortions of competition. The challenged Directive did not.

As 'Tobacco Advertising' (Case C-376/98) reveals, the rise of qualified majority voting in Council increases the likelihood of dissentient States outvoted in Council but willing to pursue the matter before the Court. But challenges to the validity of EU acts may also be advanced before national courts, who have available the Article 267 preliminary reference procedure as a means for bringing the matter before the Court in Luxembourg (see p. 217). This is how the next case reached the Court and it supplied an opportunity to revisit the kernel of 'Tobacco Advertising'.

R v *Secretary of State for Health, ex parte British American Tobacco (Investments) Ltd and Imperial Tobacco Ltd* (Case C-491/01)

[2002] ECR I-1154 3, Court of Justice of the European Communities

Health Warning: Don't mix up your Tobacco Directives! Directive 98/43 was annulled in Case C-376/98. It concerned advertising. This case concerns Directive 2001/37. It amended and extended common rules governing tar yields and warnings on tobacco product packaging. It was based on Article 95 EC, predecessor to the current Article 114 TFEU, and, in view of its impact on external trade, Article 133 EC, predecessor to the current Article 207 TFEU. Directive 2001/37 was put to the test. Unlike Directive 98/43 which was at stake in 'Tobacco Advertising' (Case C-376/98), it survived.

[64] . . . national rules laying down the requirements to be met by products, in particular those relating to their designation, composition or packaging, are in themselves liable, in the absence of harmonization at Community level, to constitute obstacles to the free movement of goods (see, to that effect, Joined Cases C-267/91 and C-268/91 *Keck and Mithouard* [1993] ECR I-6097, paragraph 15).

[65] Notwithstanding the Community harmonization measures already adopted, namely, Directive 89/622 concerning the labelling of tobacco products and Directive 90/239 concerning the maximum tar yield of cigarettes, differences between the Member States' laws, regulations and administrative provisions on the manufacture, presentation and sale of tobacco products, which create obstacles to trade, had already emerged, or were likely to emerge, by the time the Directive was adopted.

The vital 'market-making' connection was therefore established.

[75] It follows that the Directive genuinely has as its object the improvement of the conditions for the functioning of the internal market and that it was, therefore, possible for it to be adopted on the basis of Article 95 EC, and it is no bar that the protection of public health was a decisive factor in the choices involved in the harmonizing measures which it defines.

[76] That conclusion is not called into question by the argument that, since the Community legislature had established a fully harmonized regime applicable to the tar yields of cigarettes, it could not legislate afresh on the basis of Article 95 EC in order to settle that matter or, in any event, could do so only on the basis of new scientific facts.

[77] The fact is that since the Community legislature made exhaustive provision in Directive 90/239 over the question of fixing the maximum tar yield of cigarettes, the Member States no longer had the power to enact individual rules in that area. As the Advocate-General has observed in paragraph 124 of his Opinion, the Community legislature can properly carry out its task of safeguarding the general interests recognized by the Treaty, such as public health, only if it has the freedom to amend the relevant Community legislation so as to take account of any change in perceptions or circumstances.

[78] It follows that, even where a provision of Community law guarantees the removal of all obstacles to trade in the area it harmonizes, that fact cannot make it impossible for the Community legislature to adapt that provision in step with other considerations.

[79] With regard in particular to the protection of public health, it follows from Article 95(3) EC that the Community legislature, in harmonizing the legislation, must guarantee a high level of protection, taking particular account of any new development based on scientific facts.

[80] Progress in scientific knowledge is not, however, the only ground on which the Community legislature can decide to adapt Community legislation since it must, in exercising the discretion it possesses in that area, also take into account other considerations, such as the increased importance given to the social and political aspects of the anti-smoking campaign.

The approach taken in Case C-491/01 is followed in the next case. It also concerns a challenge to provisions of Directive 2001/37 – specifically Article 8 which requires that Member States prohibit the marketing of tobacco for oral use. Sweden enjoys a derogation from this prohibition and the litigation arose from an attempt by a Swedish firm to export such products to the United Kingdom, where they were banned in compliance with the Directive. So the validity of the Directive's requirement of a ban was at issue.

_R_ v _Secretary of State for Health, ex parte Swedish Match AB_ (Case C-210/03)

[2004] ECR I-11893, Court of Justice of the European Communities

The Court, citing both Case C-376/98 and Case C-491/01, ruled that the presence of public health considerations as a 'decisive factor' in the shaping of the regime did not deprive it of a valid basis in Article 95 EC where conditions for recourse to that Article were satisfied. They were.

[37] It is common ground that for those products ... there were differences, at the time of adoption of that directive, between the laws, regulations and administrative provisions of the Member States. Two of them had already prohibited the marketing of such products and a third had adopted provisions which, while not yet in force, had the same object. Those provisions were intended, according to their authors, to stop the expansion of consumption of products harmful to health which were new to the markets of the Member States and were thought to be especially attractive to young people.

[38] As the market in tobacco products is one in which trade between Member States represents a relatively large part (see *British American Tobacco (Investments) and Imperial Tobacco*, paragraph 64), those prohibitions of marketing contributed to a heterogeneous development of that market and were therefore such as to constitute obstacles to the free movement of goods.

[39] Having regard also to the public's growing awareness of the dangers to health of the consumption of tobacco products, it was likely that obstacles to the free movement of those products would arise by reason of the adoption by the Member States of new rules reflecting that development and intended more effectively to discourage consumption of those products (*British American Tobacco (Investments) and Imperial Tobacco*, paragraph 67).

[41] Action by the Community legislature on the basis of Article 95 EC was therefore justified with respect to tobacco products for oral use.

NOTE: The Court plainly allows a margin of discretion to the legislature in choosing the level of intensity at which to pitch its harmonized measures of market regulation and the harmonized rule may be a product ban – *provided* the threshold that the measures be 'intended to improve the conditions for the establishment and functioning of the internal market and must genuinely have that object, actually contributing to the elimination of obstacles to the free movement of goods or to the freedom to provide services, or to the removal of distortions of competition' is crossed. In Case C-376/98 it was not. In Case C-491/01 and Case C-210/03 it was. And in fact the threshold has been crossed in almost all the cases in which 'Tobacco Advertising' has provided the framework for analysis of the validity of EU measures. Applications for annulment failed in e.g. Cases C-154/04 and C-155/04 *Alliance for Natural Health* [2005] ECR I-6451; Case C-66/04 *UK* v *Parliament and Council* [2005] ECR I-10553; Case C-217/04 *UK* v *Parliament and Council* [2006] ECR I-3771; Case C-301/06 *Ireland* v *Parliament and Council* [2009] ECR I-593; Case C-58/08 *Vodafone, O2 et al.* [2010] ECR I-4999; Case C-398/13P *Inuit Tapiriit Kanatami* judgment of 3 September 2015. In the next case the Court reviews the Directive adopted to replace the Directive annulled in 'Tobacco Advertising' itself. On this occasion the measure survives.

Germany v *Parliament and Council* (Case C-380/03)

[2006] ECR I-11573, Court of Justice of the European Communities

The Tobacco Advertising Directive annulled in Case C-376/98 (p. 33) was replaced by Directive 2003/33 ([2003] OJ L152/16). This was more narrowly drawn, focusing in particular on obstacles to free movement resulting from differences in national rules governing tobacco advertising in the press and distortions of competition arising from sponsorship of sporting events. Replacement Directive 2003/33 too was challenged but the Court found it valid. It set out the legal test in the following terms.

[37] While a mere finding of disparities between national rules is not sufficient to justify having recourse to Article 95 EC, it is otherwise where there are differences between the laws, regulations or administrative provisions of the Member States which are such as to obstruct the fundamental freedoms and thus have a direct effect on the functioning of the internal market (see, to this effect, the tobacco advertising judgment, paragraphs 84 and 95; Case C-491/01 *British American Tobacco (Investments) and Imperial Tobacco* [2002] ECR I-11453, paragraph 60; Case C-434/02 *Arnold André* [2004] ECR I-11825, paragraph 30; Case C-210/03 *Swedish Match* [2004] ECR I-11893, paragraph 29; and Joined Cases C-154/04 and C-155/04 *Alliance for Natural Health and Others* [2005] ECR I-6451, paragraph 28).

[38] It is also settled case-law that, although recourse to Article 95 EC as a legal basis is possible if the aim is to prevent the emergence of future obstacles to trade resulting from multifarious development of national laws, the emergence of such obstacles must be likely and the measure in question must be designed to prevent them (Case C-350/92 *Spain* v *Council* [1995] ECR I-1985, paragraph 35; Case C-377/98 *Netherlands* v *Parliament and Council* [2001] ECR I-7079, paragraph 15; *British American Tobacco (Investments) and Imperial Tobacco*, paragraph 61; *Arnold André*, paragraph 31; *Swedish Match*, paragraph 30; and *Alliance for Natural Health and Others*, paragraph 29).

[39] The Court has also held that, provided that the conditions for recourse to Article 95 EC as a legal basis are fulfilled, the Community legislature cannot be prevented from relying on that legal basis on the ground that public health protection is a decisive factor in the choices to be made (*British American Tobacco (Investments) and Imperial Tobacco*, paragraph 62; *Arnold André*, paragraph 32; *Swedish Match*, paragraph 31; and *Alliance for Natural Health and Others*, paragraph 30).

[40] It should be noted that the first subparagraph of Article 152(1) EC provides that a high level of human health protection is to be ensured in the definition and implementation of all Community policies and activities, and that Article 95(3) EC explicitly requires that, in achieving harmonization, a high level of protection of human health should be guaranteed (*British American Tobacco (Investments) and Imperial Tobacco*, paragraph 62; *Arnold André*, paragraph 33; *Swedish Match*, paragraph 32; and *Alliance for Natural Health and Others*, paragraph 31).

[41] It follows from the foregoing that when there are obstacles to trade, or it is likely that such obstacles will emerge in the future, because the Member States have taken, or are about to take, divergent measures with respect to a product or a class of products, which bring about different levels of protection and thereby prevent the product or products concerned from moving freely within the Community, Article 95 EC authorizes the Community legislature to intervene by adopting appropriate measures, in compliance with Article 95(3) EC and with the legal principles mentioned in the EC Treaty or identified in the case-law, in particular the principle of proportionality (*Arnold André*, paragraph 34; *Swedish Match*, paragraph 33; and *Alliance for Natural Health and Others*, paragraph 32).

[42] It is also to be observed that, by using the words 'measures for the approximation' in Article 95 EC, the authors of the Treaty intended to confer on the Community legislature a discretion, depending on the general context and the specific circumstances of the matter to be harmonized, as regards the method of approximation most appropriate for achieving the desired result, in particular in fields with complex technical features (see Case C-66/04 *United Kingdom* v *Parliament and Council* [2005] ECR I-10553, paragraph 45, and Case C-217/04 *United Kingdom* v *Parliament and Council* [2006] ECR I-3771, paragraph 43).

[43] Depending on the circumstances, those measures may consist in requiring all the Member States to authorize the marketing of the product or products concerned, subjecting such an obligation of authorization to certain conditions, or even provisionally or definitively prohibiting the marketing of a product or products (*Arnold André*, paragraph 35; *Swedish Match*, paragraph 34; and *Alliance for Natural Health and Others*, paragraph 33).

The measure passed the test. Article 95 EC, predecessor to the current Article 114 TFEU, was validly used to support a harmonized ban, albeit a narrower ban than was imposed by the original – and annulled – Tobacco Advertising Directive. In its judgment the Court referred explicitly to paras 97 and 98 of the judgment in Case C-376/98 (p. 33) in which it had mapped out the permissible limits of harmonization of rules affecting tobacco advertising. This was constitutionally sensitive advice which had clearly been taken to heart by the legislature in adopting the more narrowly drawn replacement Directive 2003/33.

■ QUESTION

According to para 41 of Case C-380/03 *Germany* v *Parliament and Council* harmonization of laws is validly pursued under the Treaty when it is likely that obstacles to trade will emerge in the future because of diverse national legislative practice. If it is not likely, the EU lacks competence. How does one judge what is 'likely' for these purposes? A similar type of question, which asks whether the limits of EU legislative competence can be reliably monitored, may be directed at the use of the word 'appreciable' in para 106 of Case C-376/98 (p. 133).

C: The choice of legal base

The Lisbon Treaty consecrated the 'ordinary legislative procedure' contained in Article 289 TFEU as the normal method for adopting legislation in the EU. As introduced in Chapter 1 (p. 20) Article 289 TFEU provides that the ordinary legislative procedure 'shall consist in the joint adoption by the Parliament and the Council of a regulation, directive or decision on a proposal from the Commission'.

If the 'ordinary legislative procedure' were the *only* method for adopting legislation envisaged by the Treaty then choosing between different potential legal bases for the adoption of legislation would not matter. However, things are not quite so simple – though they are much simpler than they used to be before the Lisbon Treaty propelled the ordinary legislative procedure to its current position of dominance. The need to make a choice between competing legal bases in the Treaty arises where, exceptionally, they engage different procedures. This may arise where the qualified majority voting that is normal in Council under the ordinary legislative procedure is displaced by the need for unanimity or where the Parliament's right of co-decision under the ordinary legislative procedure is downgraded to a less influential role (e.g. Articles 113, 192(2) TFEU); or where the type of competence envisaged by legal bases is different (see Articles 2–6 TFEU, p. 30). One simple example has already been encountered at p. 31: Article 352 TFEU cannot be used where a more specific legal base is available, and this *matters* because Article 352 requires the unusually burdensome requirement of unanimity in Council.

The next extract captures the *constitutional* significance attached to choosing the applicable legal base.

Commission v *Council* (Case C-370/07)

[2009] ECR I-8917, Court of Justice of the European Communities

[47] In that regard, the Court has already held that the choice of the appropriate legal basis has constitutional significance, since, having only conferred powers, the Community must tie the contested decision to a Treaty provision which empowers it to approve such a measure (see, to that effect, Opinion 2/00, paragraph 5).

[48] The indication of the legal basis also has particular importance for preserving the prerogatives of the Community institutions concerned by the procedure for the adoption of a measure. Thus, in the present case, such an indication is liable to have an effect on the powers of the Parliament, given that Articles 133 EC, 175 EC, and 300(2) EC do not confer on it the same degree of involvement in the adoption of a measure. In the same way, an indication of the legal basis is necessary in order to determine the voting procedure within the Council. In that regard, the first subparagraph of Article 300(2) EC provides that the Council is to act by qualified majority except, first, when the agreement covers a field for which unanimity is required for the adoption of internal rules and, second, for the agreements referred to in Article 310 EC.

[49] Furthermore, the indication of the legal basis determines the division of powers between the Community and the Member States. In the present case, the application of Article 175 EC or Article 133 EC alone would not have had the same implications for the division of powers between the Community and the Member States as a combined application of those two provisions, since Article 133 EC confers powers exclusive to the Community, whereas Article 175 EC provides for powers shared between the Community and the Member States. The failure to indicate a legal basis may thus give rise to confusion as to the nature of the Community's powers and is liable to weaken the Community in the defence of its position in international negotiations.

NOTE: A heap of case law has addressed these awkward issues over recent years. Happily, most of it, including this decision, is now irrelevant in its *detail*, because Treaty revision has changed the points of friction. Moreover, the dominance of the ordinary legislative procedure post-Lisbon means that there is less friction. But the Court's pre-Lisbon approach will on occasion retain relevance, and it is here summarized.

In the first instance the Court has consistently stated that the choice of legal base must be determined according to objective factors. It is defined by the Treaty and is not a matter of political discretion. The Court asserts a concern to protect the 'principle of institutional balance' mapped out by the Treaty (Case C-133/06 *Parliament* v *Council* [2008] ECR I-3189 para 54: neither the political sensitivity of the matter nor the effectiveness of decision-making can justify disregard for the procedures established by the Treaty). Where an institution's power is based on two provisions of the Treaty, it is bound to adopt the relevant measures on the basis of the two relevant provisions (e.g., Case 165/87 *Commission* v *Council* [1988] ECR 5545). Failure to do so will result in the annulment of the act, unless the error constitutes a purely formal defect giving rise to no irregularity in the procedure for adoption (e.g., Case C-491/01 *R* v *Secretary of State, ex parte BAT and Imperial Tobacco* [2002] ECR I-11435). However, the question arises *when* the use of two provisions will be appropriate and when instead a choice between competing legal bases is required.

***Commission* v *Council* (Case C-94/03)**

[2006] ECR I-1, Court of Justice of the European Communities

[34] It must be borne in mind at the outset that, according to settled case-law, the choice of the legal basis for a Community measure. . . must be based on objective factors which are amenable to judicial review and include in particular the aim and content of the measure (see Case 45/86 *Commission* v *Council*, cited above, paragraph 11; Case C-300/89 *Commission* v *Council* (the '*Titanium dioxide* case') [1991] ECR I-2867, paragraph 10; Case C-268/94 *Portugal* v *Council* [1996] ECR I-6177, paragraph 22; Opinion 2/00, cited above, paragraph 22; and Case C-176/03 *Commission* v *Council* [2005] ECR I-7879, paragraph 45).

[35] If examination of a Community measure reveals that it pursues a twofold purpose or that it has a twofold component and if one of those is identifiable as the main or predominant purpose or component, whereas the other is merely incidental, the act must be based on a single legal basis, namely that required by the main or predominant purpose or component (see Case C-36/98 *Spain* v *Council* [2001] ECR I-779, paragraph 59; Case C-211/01 *Commission* v *Council* [2003] ECR I-8913, paragraph 39; and Case C-338/01 *Commission* v *Council* [2004] ECR I-4829, paragraph 55).

[36] Exceptionally, if on the other hand it is established that the act simultaneously pursues a number of objectives or has several components that are indissociably linked, without one being secondary and indirect in relation to the other, such an act will have to be founded on the various corresponding legal bases (see, to that effect, Case C-336/00 *Huber* [2002] ECR I-7699, paragraph 31; C-281/01 *Commission* v *Council*, cited above, paragraph 35; and Case C-211/01 *Commission* v *Council*, cited above, paragraph 40).

In Case C-94/03 itself the Court, applying this test, annulled Council Decision 2003/106/EC concerning approval of the Rotterdam Convention on the Prior Informed Consent Procedure for certain hazardous chemicals and pesticides. The Council had adopted the measure as a measure of environmental protection alone, but the Court concluded that the measure's environmental and commercial features were 'two indissociably linked components'. By contrast in Case C-42/97 *Parliament* v *Council* [1999] ECR I-869 an application for annulment of Council Decision 96/664/EC on the adoption of a multiannual programme to promote linguistic diversity failed. It had been adopted solely on the basis of the Title on Industry but the Parliament argued that the Title on Culture should also have been used. Not so. Culture was not an essential component of the contested decision, but rather only incidentally affected. The main aim was to ensure that undertakings did not suffer damage to their competitiveness as a result of communications costs caused by linguistic diversity. The Parliament's application for annulment therefore failed.

■ **QUESTION**

How realistic is the Court's 'main or predominant purpose' test, given that public regulation of the market is inevitably multi-functional? And how can the 'main or predominant purpose' test be reconciled with the assertion of linkage between different policy areas made by horizontal clauses having general application in the Treaty such as Articles 8–14 TFEU?

The Lisbon Treaty, as mentioned, affects and reduces the detailed incentives to pursue such litigation (though it does not eliminate them entirely: e.g. Case C-377/12 *Commission v Council* judgment of 11 June 2014). Lisbon also causes a gratifying reduction in so-called inter-pillar disputes. Under the three-pillar structure of the EU that existed prior to Lisbon (p. 9) the Court was forced to decide which pillar was the true home for proposed legislation. It resolved the disputes as far as possible by reference to a now deleted provision, Article 47 EU, which asserted a primacy for the EC 'first' pillar over the second and third pillars. In effect, if legislation *could* be adopted via the EC, then it *should* be.

Things are different now. Disputes between the first and third pillar are transformed by the Lisbon Treaty into disputes that are internal to the TFEU. The TFEU provisions on the area of freedom, security, and justice, the successors to the pre-Lisbon 'third pillar', are atypical (Chapter 15) and may generate friction with legal bases under the TFEU that are more orthodox, but probably the Court will handle any such dispute by relying on its 'predominant purpose' test. There remains scope for a lingering flavour of the inter-pillar dispute in so far as CFSP matters handled under the TEU may rub up against matters allocated to the TFEU. Article 40 TEU provides *both* that the implementation of the CFSP shall not affect the operation of the TFEU *and* that the implementation of the policies set out in the TFEU shall not affect the operation of the CFSP. So the primacy granted to the EC by the now deleted Article 47 EU is suppressed post-Lisbon and probably here too, in TEU versus TFEU disputes, the Court will rely on its 'predominant purpose' test.

NOTES

1. The broad question of how to exercise 'control' over perceived legislative expansionism in the EU has been increasingly prominent on the political and legal agendas in recent years. 'Subsidiarity' has been an all-embracing label covering a range of concerns associated with the perceived need to protect Member States from excessive encroachment by EU intervention. But subsidiarity was not dealt with at all by the Court in the 'Tobacco Advertising' case (Case C-376/98 p. 33). In fact the Court's decision in that case demonstrates logical precision. It analysed the matter from the perspective of whether a valid legislative competence existed. It did not, and therefore subsidiarity simply did not come into play. This is also clear from Article 5 TEU, p. 29. However, subsidiarity is clearly relevant to decisions about whether and, if so, how to exercise a legislative competence once it is shown to exist in principle. It will be explored in its full legal and political context in Chapter 18 as part of a broader investigation of strategies for regulation and governance in the functionally and geographically expanded European Union.
2. The Laeken Declaration of December 2001 contributed to setting the agenda for the Convention (p. 14). It includes the observation that many citizens 'feel that the Union should involve itself more with their particular concerns, instead of intervening, in every detail, in matters by their nature better left to Member States' and regions' elected representatives. This is even perceived by some as a threat to their identity.' It continues: 'In coordinating the economic, financial and fiscal environment, the basic issue should continue to be proper operation of the internal market and the single currency, without this jeopardizing Member States' individuality.' So what is to be done? The Laeken Declaration continues: '. . . the important thing is to clarify, simplify and adjust the division of competence between the Union and the Member States . . . there is the question of how to ensure that a redefined division of competence does not lead to a creeping

expansion of the competence of the Union or to encroachment upon the exclusive areas of competence of the Member States and, where there is provision for this, regions. How are we to ensure at the same time that the European dynamic does not come to a halt? In the future as well the Union must continue to be able to react to fresh challenges and developments and must be able to explore new policy areas. Should Articles 95 and 308 of the Treaty be reviewed for this purpose in the light of the *acquis jurisprudentiel*?'

■ QUESTION

Why are Articles 95 and 308 (alone of all the provisions of the Treaty) picked out in the Laeken Declaration as ripe for review? Are they today, as Articles 114 and 352 TFEU, more or less of a source of the anxieties expressed?

FURTHER READING

Azoulai, L. *The Question of Competence in the European Union* (Oxford: OUP, 2014).

Garben, S., 'Confronting the Competence Conundrum: Democratising the European Union through an Expansion of its Legislative Powers' (2015) 35 Ox JLS 55.

Tridimas, T., 'Competence after Lisbon: The Elusive Search for Bright Lines' in Ashiagbor, D., Countouris, N., and Lianos, I., (eds), *The European Union after the Treaty of Lisbon* (Cambridge: CUP, 2012).

Weatherill, S., 'The Limits of Legislative Harmonisation Ten Years After *Tobacco Advertising*: How the Court's Case Law Has Become a *Drafting Guide*' (2011) 12 *German Law Journal* 827. (www.germanlawjournal.com/index.php?pageID=11&artID=1344).

Wyatt, D., 'Community Competence to Regulate the Internal Market', in Dougan, M. and Currie, S., *Fifty Years of the European Treaties: Looking Back and Thinking Forward* (Oxford: Hart, 2009).

■ QUESTION

What reforms would you advocate for the Union's legislative procedure in order to improve:

(i) the efficacy of judicial control; and

(ii) democratic accountability?

D: Reasoning

The second paragraph of Article 296 TFEU declares that EU legal acts must be reasoned.

ARTICLE 296 TFEU

... Legal acts shall state the reasons on which they are based and shall refer to any proposals, initiatives, recommendations, requests or opinions required by the Treaties.

NOTES

1. Article 296 TFEU is an amended version of Article 253 EC pre-Lisbon (and it was Article 190 pre-Amsterdam).
2. In an early decision, the Court explained the objective and scope of the requirement to give reasons in the following terms:

Germany v *Commission* (Case 24/62)

[1963] ECR 63, Court of Justice of the European Communities

In imposing upon the Commission the obligation to state reasons for its decisions, Article 190 is not taking mere formal considerations into account but seeks to give an opportunity to the parties of defending their rights, to the Court of exercising its supervisory functions and to Member States and to all interested nationals of ascertaining the circumstances in which the Commission has applied the Treaty. To attain these objectives, it is sufficient for the Decision to set out, in a concise but clear and relevant manner, the principal issues of law and of fact upon which it is based and which are necessary in order that the reasoning which has led the Commission to its Decision may be understood. . ..

Applying this test, the Court proceeded to consider whether the Commission had supplied sufficient information to support a Decision which granted Germany a wine tariff quota far below that for which it had submitted a request:

. . . [T]he Commission has been content to rely upon 'the information collected', without specifying any of it, in order to reach a conclusion 'that the production of the wines in question is amply sufficient'.

This elliptical reasoning is all the more objectionable because the Commission gave no indication, as it did belatedly before the Court, of the evolution and size of the surpluses, but only repeated, without expanding the reasons for it, the same statement 'that there was no indication that the existing market situation within the Community did not allow these branches of the industry in the German Federal Republic a supply which is adequate in quantity and in quality'. On the other hand, although it maintained that the production of the Community was sufficient, the Commission restricted itself to 'deducing from this' that 'the grant of a tariff quota of the volume requested might therefore lead to serious disturbances of the market in the products in question', but these disturbances were not specified. Thus it neither described the risk involved in this case, nor did it disclose what it considered to be the necessary and sufficient connexion in the present case between the two concepts which it links one with the other by a simple deduction. However, by granting a restricted quota notwithstanding its description of production as 'amply sufficient', and thereby admitting that Article 25(3) applied, the Commission thus conceded that this factor was not enough to make it possible 'to deduce from it' the risk of serious disturbance.

Thus the statement of reasons expressed appears on this point to be contradictory, since in spite of its statement with regard to an adequate supply and of the automatic conclusion to be drawn therefrom the Commission grants a quota and thereby implies that it would not cause any serious disturbance. Moreover, several, of the recitals in the German text, which is authentic, lack the necessary clarity.

It follows from these factors that the inadequacy, the vagueness and the inconsistency of the statement of reasons for the Decision, both in respect of the refusal of the quota requested and of the concession of the quota, granted, do not satisfy the requirements of Article 190.

Those parts of the Decision which have been submitted to the Court must therefore be annulled.

NOTE: The extent of the detail which must be provided in support of a measure will vary according to the circumstances.

Schwarze v *Einfuhrund Vorratsstelle Getreide* (Case 16/65)

[1965] ECR 877, Court of Justice of the European Communities

The challenged Decision fixed prices for cereals. It referred back to an earlier Decision without explicitly setting out the reasons contained therein. The Court accepted that given the manner in which one measure built on the other in the administration of the policy, it was permissible for the Commission simply to refer back in this way. But were the reasons in the original Decision, thus incorporated, themselves sufficient?

The degree of precision of the statement of reasons for such a decision must be weighed against practical realities and the time and technical facilities available for making such a decision. A specific statement of reasons for each individual decision fixing a free-at-frontier price as envisaged by the Finanzgericht would mean the publication and technical evaluation of all the facts submitted by the exporting Member State or gathered by the

Commission's staff for several hundreds of prices requiring to be fixed. In view, first, of the time available for the issue of the decisions and, secondly, of the number of prices to be fixed, the requirement of such a specific statement of reasons would be incompatible with the proper functioning of the machinery provided for in Regulation No 19 of the Council and Regulation No 89 of the Commission. The preparation and drafting of this kind of statement of reasons would take up so much time that the determination of prices would run the risk of being, to some extent, out of date by the time it was issued.

Moreover a comparison of the free-at-frontier prices as fixed with the general criteria published is sufficient to inform persons with a legitimate interest of the character of the data on the basis of which the decision was taken and of the conclusions to be drawn therefrom. The need to protect the parties to whom the decision is addressed and nationals of Member States affected by the decision, as also the need for proper judicial review, is sufficiently met as long as the Commission, as here, puts at the disposal of the parties the technical data used by it in fixing the free-at-frontier prices whenever the decision is challenged before a court having the appropriate jurisdiction.

For these reasons it must be concluded that the Commission was entitled to confine itself to setting out in a general form the essential factors to and the procedure which formed the background to its evaluation of the facts without its being necessary to specify the facts themselves.

NOTES

1. The Court is concerned with the balance between protecting the rights of the individual and imposing unreasonable burdens on administrative authorities in complicated, rapidly moving areas of market regulation.
2. See *Commission* v *Council* (Case 45/86) (p. 32). The Court held that the measures were adopted on the wrong legal basis. It also found them flawed for inadequate reasoning on this point:

Commission v *Council* (Case 45/86)

[1987] ECR 1493, Court of Justice of the European Communities

[7] ... the Council contends that, although the indication of the legal basis is not precise, the recitals in the preambles to the regulations, taken as a whole, provide sufficient alternative information as to the aims pursued by the Council, that is to say both commercial aims and aims of development-aid policy.

[8] However, those indications are not sufficient to identify the legal basis by virtue of which the Council acted. Although the recitals in the preambles to the regulations do refer to improving access for developing countries to the markets of the preference-giving countries, they merely state that adaptations to the Community system of generalized preferences have proved to be necessary in the light of experience in the first 15 years. Moreover, according to information given the Court by the Council itself, the wording 'Having regard to the Treaty' was adopted as a result of differences of opinion about the choice of the appropriate legal basis. Consequently, the wording chosen was designed precisely to leave the legal basis of the regulations in question vague.

[9] Admittedly, failure to refer to a precise provision of the Treaty need not necessarily constitute an infringement of essential procedural requirements when the legal basis for the measure may be determined from other parts of the measure. However, such explicit reference is indispensable where, in its absence, the parties concerned and the Court are left uncertain as to the precise legal basis.

NOTE: Similarly the measure attacked in Case C-370/07 *Commission* v *Council*, p. 42, was annulled for want of clarity as to the correct legal base.

SECTION 3: GENERAL PRINCIPLES OF UNION LAW

The substance of EU law concerns market integration, market regulation, the establishment of an internal market and an increasing pattern of social regulation. These provisions are examined in Part Two of this book. Because these rules of law, which permit regulation of the economy, directly affect individuals, the procedures must respect the position of the individual. EU law accordingly contains important principles protecting the individual. The legislative and administrative tasks performed by the EU institutions are subject to review on the basis of these principles.

The Treaty contains some explicit principles which protect the individual. Article 18 TFEU, for example, imposes a requirement that there shall be no discrimination on grounds of nationality within the scope of application of the Treaty. However, the Court has proved vigorous in developing a substantial body of principles independently of explicit Treaty support. These principles are important in themselves. More generally, the Court's influence in this area reveals its concern to develop a broadly based EU legal system. Some of these principles are now considered. For an extended analysis see T. Tridimas, *The General Principles of EU Law* (Oxford: OUP, 3rd ed., 2014); P. Craig, *EU Administrative Law* (Oxford: OUP, 2nd ed., 2012).

A: Proportionality

Article 5(4) TEU contains a version of the principle of proportionality.

> Under the principle of proportionality, the content and form of Union action shall not exceed what is necessary to achieve the objectives of the Treaties.
>
> The institutions of the Union shall apply the principle of proportionality as laid down in the Protocol on the application of the principles of subsidiarity and proportionality.

This provision, a Lisbon innovation, for the first time explicitly embraces the proportionality principle in the Treaty. It appears elsewhere too post-Lisbon in its application to EU institutions: e.g. Article 296(1) TFEU. The Protocol is not new, and it amplifies the application of the principles of subsidiarity and proportionality, albeit that admittedly it is more concerned to elucidate the former principle than the latter. (See Chapter 18 on subsidiarity.) However, the Court had long before already developed proportionality as a basis for checking the exercise of public power in the Union. So Article 5(4) TEU clearly establishes the shape of the principle of proportionality, but it is the Court's case law that amplifies what is at stake in its application.

The following case arose before English courts. It reached Luxembourg *via* the preliminary reference procedure which allows national courts to cooperate with the Court of Justice and is discussed in Chapter 7. The Court of Justice took the opportunity in this case to insist that legislation must conform to the principle of proportionality.

R v Intervention Board, ex parte Man (Sugar) Ltd (Case 181/84)

[1985] ECR 2889, Court of Justice of the European Communities

The case involved the sugar market, which is regulated by EU legislation administered at national level. Man, a British sugar trader, submitted to the Intervention Board, the regulatory agency, tenders for the export of sugar to States outside the EU. It lodged securities with a bank. Under relevant legislation, Man ought to have applied for export licences by noon on 2 August 1983. It was nearly four hours late, because of its own internal staff difficulties. The Board, acting pursuant to Community Regulation 1880/83, declared the security forfeit. This amounted to £1,670,370 lost by Man. Man claimed that this penalty was disproportionate; a small error resulted in a severe sanction. It accordingly instituted judicial review proceedings before the English courts in respect of the Board's action and argued that the authorizing EC legislation was invalid because of its disproportionate effect. The matter was referred to the Court of Justice under the preliminary reference procedure. Man's submission was explained by the Court as follows:

[16] . . . Man Sugar maintains that, even if it is accepted that the obligation to apply for an export licence is justifiable, the forfeiture of the entire security for failure to comply with that obligation infringes the principle of proportionality, in particular for the following reasons: the contested regulation unlawfully imposes the same penalty for failure to comply with a secondary obligation – namely, the obligation to apply for an export licence – as for failure to comply with the primary obligation to export the sugar. The obligation to apply for an export licence could be enforced by other, less drastic means than the forfeiture of the entire security and therefore the burden imposed is not necessary for the achievement of the aims of the legislation. The severity of the penalty bears no relation to the nature of the default, which may, as in the present case, be only minimal and purely technical.

The Court held:

[20] It should be noted that, as the Court held in its judgments of 20 February 1979 (Case 122/78, *Buitoni* v *FORMA*, [1979] ECR 677) and of 23 February 1983 (Case 66/82, *Fromançais SA* v *FORMA*, [1983] ECR 395), in order to establish whether a provision of Community law is in conformity with the principle of proportionality it is necessary to ascertain whether the means which it employs are appropriate and necessary to attain the objective sought. Where Community legislation makes a distinction between a primary obligation, compliance with which is necessary in order to attain the objective sought, and a secondary obligation, essentially of an administrative nature, it cannot, without breaching the principle of proportionality, penalize failure to comply with the secondary obligation as severely as failure to comply with the primary obligation.

[21] It is clear from the wording of the above mentioned Council and Commission regulations concerning standing invitations to tender for exports of white sugar, from an analysis of the preambles thereto and from the statements made by the Commission in the proceedings before the Court that the system of securities is intended above all to ensure that the undertaking, voluntarily entered into by the trader, to export the quantities of sugar in respect of which tenders have been accepted is fulfilled. The trader's obligation to export is therefore undoubtedly a primary obligation, compliance with which is ensured by the initial lodging of a security of 9 ECU per 100 kilograms of sugar.

[22] The Commission considers, however, that the obligation to apply for an export licence within a short period, and to comply with that time-limit strictly, is also a primary obligation and as such is comparable to the obligation to export; indeed, it is that obligation alone which guarantees the proper management of the sugar market. In consequence, according to the Commission, failure to comply with that obligation, and in particular failure to comply with the time-limit, even where that failure is minimal and unintentional, justifies the forfeiture of the entire security, just as much as the total failure to comply with the primary obligation to export justifies such a penalty.

[23] In that respect the Commission contended, both during the written procedure and in the oral argument presented before the Court, that export licences fulfil four separate and important functions:

(i) They make it possible to control the release onto the market of sugar.
(ii) They serve to prevent speculation.
(iii) They provide information for the relevant Commission departments.
(iv) They establish the system of monetary compensatory amounts chosen by the exporter.

[24] As regards the use of export licences to control the release onto the world market of exported sugar, it must be noted that the traders concerned have a period of five months within which to export the sugar and no Community provision requires them to export it at regular, staggered intervals. They may therefore release all their sugar onto the market over a very short period. In those circumstances export licences cannot be said to have the controlling effect postulated by the Commission. That effect is guaranteed, though only in part, simply by staggering the invitations to tender.

[25] The Commission considers, secondly, that the forfeiture of the entire security for failure to comply with the time-limit for applying for an export licence makes it possible to prevent traders from engaging in speculation with regard to fluctuations in the price of sugar and in exchange rates and accordingly delaying the submission of their applications for export licences.

[26] Even if it is assumed that there is a real risk of such speculation, it must be noted that Article 12(c) of Regulation No 1880/83 requires the successful tenderer to pay the additional security provided for in Article 13(3)

of the same regulation. The Commission itself recognised at the hearing that that additional security removes any risk of speculation by traders. It is true that at the hearing the Commission expressed doubts about the applicability of Article 13(3) before export licences have been issued. However, even if those doubts are well founded, the fact remains that a simple amendment of the rules regarding the payment of an additional security, requiring for example that, in an appropriate case, the additional security should be paid during the tendering procedure, in other words, even before the export licence has been issued, would make it possible to attain the objective sought by means which would be much less drastic for the traders concerned. The argument that the fight against speculation justifies the contested provision of Regulation No 1880/83 cannot therefore be accepted.

[27] With regard to the last two functions attributed by the Commission to export licences, it is true that those licences make it possible for the Commission to monitor accurately exports of Community sugar to non-member countries, although they do not provide it with important new information not contained in the tenders and do not, in themselves, guarantee that the export will actually take place. It is also true that the export licence makes it possible for the exporter to state whether he wishes the monetary compensatory amounts to be fixed in advance.

[28] However, although it is clear from the foregoing that the obligation to obtain export licences performs a useful administrative function from the Commission's point of view, it cannot be accepted that that obligation is as important as the obligation to export, which remains the essential aim of the Community legislation in question.

[29] It follows that the automatic forfeiture of the entire security, in the event of an infringement significantly less serious than the failure to fulfil the primary obligation, which the security itself is intended to guarantee, must be considered too drastic a penalty in relation to the export licence's function of ensuring the sound management of the market in question.

[30] Although the Commission was entitled, in the interests of sound administration, to impose a time-limit for the submission of applications for export licences, the penalty imposed for failure to comply with that time-limit should have been significantly less severe for the traders concerned than forfeiture of the entire security and it should have been more consonant with the practical effects of such a failure.

[31] The reply to the question submitted must therefore be that Article 6(3) of Regulation No 1880/83 is invalid inasmuch as it prescribes forfeiture of the entire security as the penalty for failure to comply with the time-limit imposed for the submission of applications for export licences.

NOTE: A key element in the practical expression of the principle of proportionality is the need to show a link between the nature and scope of the measures taken and the object in view. The next extract is taken from a case in which a firm sought to show that a measure affected it disproportionately and that it was accordingly invalid. The issue arose in the coal and steel sector, and therefore the provisions in question were found in the ECSC Treaty, which has now expired. However, the Court explained the nature of the principle of proportionality in terms of general application.

Valsabbia v *Commission* (Case 154/78)

[1980] ECR 907, Court of Justice of the European Communities

[117] It is now necessary to examine whether in view of the omissions established the obligations imposed upon the undertakings cast disproportionate burdens upon the applicants which would constitute an infringement of the principle of proportionality. In reply to the applicants' allegations on this matter, the Commission states that the validity of a general decision cannot depend on the existence or absence of other formally independent decisions.

[118] That argument is not relevant in this case and the Court must inquire whether the defects established imposed disproportionate burdens upon the applicants, having regard to the objectives laid down by Decision No 962/77. But the Court has already recognized in its judgment of 24 October 1973 in Case 5/73, *Balkan-Import-Export* v *Hauptzollamt Berlin-Packhof* [1973] ECR 1091, that 'In exercising their powers, the Institutions must ensure that the amounts which commercial operators are charged are no greater than is required to achieve the aim which the authorities are to accomplish; however, it does not necessarily follow

that that obligation must be measured in relation to the individual situation of any one particular group of operators'.

[119] It appears that, on the whole, the system established by Decision No 962/77 worked despite the omissions disclosed and in the end attained the objectives pursued by that decision. Although it is true that the burden of the sacrifices required of the applicants may have been aggravated by the omissions in the system, that does not alter the fact that that decision did not constitute a disproportionate and intolerable measure with regard to the aim pursued.

[120] In those circumstances, and taking into consideration the fact that the objective laid down by Decision No 962/77 is in accordance with the Commission's duty to act in the common interest, and that a necessary consequence of the very nature of Article 61 of the ECSC Treaty is that certain undertakings must, by virtue of European solidarity, accept greater sacrifices than others, the Commission cannot be accused of having imposed disproportionate burdens upon the applicants.

NOTE: The nature of the Court's scrutiny is influenced by the type of act subject to challenge. (See, for example, Arai-Takahashi, 'Scrupulous but Dynamic' (2005) 24 YEL 27; Special Issue, (2008) 3 of Legal Issues of Economic Integration.) Notice that in Case 181/84 (p. 48) Man Sugar was not complaining about a broad legislative choice. The matter was more specific to its circumstances. By contrast the principle of proportionality, though flexible and therefore a tempting addition to any challenge to the validity of a legislative act, is only infrequently held to have been violated where broad legislative choices are impugned. This is well illustrated by revisiting a ruling already considered.

R v *Secretary of State for Health, ex parte British American Tobacco (Investments) Ltd and Imperial Tobacco Ltd* (Case C-491/01)

[2002] ECR I-11543, Court of Justice of the European Communities

The validity of Directive 2001/37, which amended and extended common rules governing tar yields and warnings on tobacco product packaging, was challenged in this case. As explained (at p. 38), the Court was not persuaded that an incorrect legal base had been chosen. The applicant fared no better by alleging the measure violated the principle of proportionality.

[122] ... the principle of proportionality, which is one of the general principles of Community law, requires that measures implemented through Community provisions should be appropriate for attaining the objective pursued and must not go beyond what is necessary to achieve it ...

[123] With regard to judicial review of the conditions referred to in the previous paragraph, the Community legislature must be allowed a broad discretion in an area such as that involved in the present case, which entails political, economic and social choices on its part, and in which it is called upon to undertake complex assessments. Consequently, the legality of a measure adopted in that sphere can be affected only if the measure is manifestly inappropriate having regard to the objective which the competent institution is seeking to pursue (see, to that effect, Case C-84/94 *United Kingdom* v *Council* [1996] ECR I-5755, paragraph 58; Case C-233/94 *Germany* v *Parliament and Council* [1997] ECR I-2405, paragraphs 55 and 56, and Case C-157/96 *National Farmers' Union and Others* [1998] ECR I-2211, paragraph 61).

[124] With regard to the Directive, the first, second and third recitals in the preamble thereto make it clear that its objective is, by approximating the rules applicable in this area, to eliminate the barriers raised by differences which, notwithstanding the harmonization measures already adopted, still exist between the Member States' laws, regulations and administrative provisions on the manufacture, presentation and sale of tobacco products and impede the functioning of the internal market. In addition, it is apparent from the fourth recital that, in the attaining of that objective, the Directive takes as a basis a high level of health protection, in accordance with Article 95(3) of the Treaty.

[125] During the procedure various arguments have been put forward in order to challenge the compatibility of the Directive with the principle of proportionality, particularly so far as Articles 3, 5 and 7 are concerned.

[126] It must first be stated that the prohibition laid down in Article 3 of the Directive on releasing for free circulation or marketing within the Community cigarettes that do not comply with the maximum levels of tar, nicotine and carbon monoxide, together with the obligation imposed on the Member States to authorise the import, sale and consumption of cigarettes which do comply with those levels, in accordance with Article 13(1) of the Directive, is a measure appropriate for the purpose of attaining the objective pursued by the Directive and one which, having regard to the duty of the Community legislature to ensure a high level of health protection, does not go beyond what is necessary to attain that objective.

[127] Secondly, as pointed out in paragraph 85 above, the purpose of the prohibition, also laid down in Article 3 of the Directive, on manufacturing cigarettes which do not comply with the maximum levels fixed by that provision is to avoid the undermining of the internal market provisions in the tobacco products sector which might be caused by illicit reimports into the Community or by deflections of trade within the Community affecting products which do not comply with the requirements of Article 3(1).

[128] The proportionality of that ban on manufacture has been called into question on the ground that it is not a measure for the purpose of attaining its objective and that it goes beyond what is necessary to attain it since, in particular, an alternative measure, such as reinforcing inspections of imports from non-member countries, would have been sufficient.

[129] It must here be stated that, while the prohibition at issue does not of itself make it possible to prevent the development of the illegal trade in cigarettes in the Community, having particular regard to the fact that cigarettes which do not comply with the requirements of Article 3(1) of the Directive may also be placed illegally on the Community market after being manufactured in non-member countries, the Community legislature did not overstep the bounds of its discretion when it considered that such a prohibition nevertheless constitutes a measure likely to make an effective contribution to limiting the risk of growth in the illegal trafficking of cigarettes and to preventing the consequent undermining of the internal market.

[130] Nor has it been established that reinforcing controls would in the circumstances be enough to attain the objective pursued by the contested provision. It must be observed that the prohibition on manufacture at issue is especially appropriate for preventing at source deflections in trade affecting cigarettes manufactured in the Community for export to non-member countries, deflections which amount to a form of fraud which, *ex hypothesi*, it is not possible to combat as efficiently by means of an alternative measure such as reinforcing controls on the Community's frontiers.

[131] As regards Article 5 of the Directive, the obligation to show information on cigarette packets as to the tar, nicotine and carbon monoxide levels and to print on the unit packets of tobacco products warnings concerning the risks to health posed by those products are appropriate measures for attaining a high level of health protection when the barriers raised by national laws on labelling are removed. Those obligations in fact constitute a recognised means of encouraging consumers to reduce their consumption of tobacco products or of guiding them towards such of those products as pose less risk to health.

[132] Accordingly, by requiring in Article 5 of the Directive an increase in the percentage of the surface area on certain sides of the unit packet of tobacco products to be given over to those indications and warnings, in a proportion which leaves sufficient space for the manufacturers of those products to be able to affix other material, in particular concerning their trade marks, the Community legislature has not overstepped the bounds of the discretion which it enjoys in this area.

[133] Article 7 of the Directive calls for the following observations.

[134] The purpose of that provision is explained in the 27th recital in the preamble to the Directive, which makes it clear that the reason for the ban on the use on tobacco product packaging of certain texts, such as 'low-tar', 'light', 'ultra-light', names, pictures and figurative or other signs is the fear that consumers may be misled into the belief that such products are less harmful, giving rise to changes in consumption. That recital states in this connection that the level of inhaled substances is determined not only by the quantities of certain substances contained in the product before consumption, but also by smoking behaviour and addiction, which fact is not reflected in the use of such terms and so may undermine the labelling requirements set out in the Directive.

[135] Read in the light of the 27th recital in the preamble, Article 7 of the Directive has the purpose therefore of ensuring that consumers are given objective information concerning the toxicity of tobacco products.

[136] Such a requirement to supply information is appropriate for attaining a high level of health protection on the harmonization of the provisions applicable to the description of tobacco products.

[137] It was possible for the Community legislature to take the view, without overstepping the bounds of its discretion, that stating those tar, nicotine and carbon monoxide levels in accordance with Article 5(1) of the Directive ensured that consumers would be given objective information concerning the toxicity of tobacco products connected to those substances, whereas the use of descriptors such as those referred to in Article 7 of the Directive did not ensure that consumers would be given objective information.

[138] As the Advocate-General has pointed out in paragraphs 241 to 248 of his Opinion, those descriptors are liable to mislead consumers. In the first place, they might, like the word 'mild', for example, indicate a sensation of taste, without any connection with the product's level of noxious substances. In the second place, terms such as 'low-tar', 'light', 'ultra-light', do not, in the absence of rules governing the use of those terms, refer to specific quantitative limits. In the third place, even if the product in question is lower in tar, nicotine and carbon monoxide than other products, the fact remains that the amount of those substances actually inhaled by consumers depends on their manner of smoking and that that product may contain other harmful substances. In the fourth place, the use of descriptions which suggest that consumption of a certain tobacco product is beneficial to health, compared with other tobacco products, is liable to encourage smoking.

[139] Furthermore, it was possible for the Community legislature to take the view, without going beyond the bounds of the discretion which it enjoys in this area, that the prohibition laid down in Article 7 of the Directive was necessary in order to ensure that consumers be given objective information concerning the toxicity of tobacco products and that, specifically, there was no alternative measure which could have attained that objective as efficiently while being less restrictive of the rights of the manufacturers of tobacco products.

[140] It is not clear that merely regulating the use of the descriptions referred to in Article 7, as proposed by the claimants in the main proceedings and by the German, Greek and Luxembourg Governments, or saying on the tobacco products' packaging, as proposed by Japan Tobacco, that the amounts of noxious substances inhaled depend also on the user's smoking behaviour would have ensured that consumers received objective information, having regard to the fact that those descriptions are in any event likely, by their very nature, to encourage smoking.

[141] It follows from the preceding considerations concerning Question 1(c) that the Directive is not invalid by reason of infringement of the principle of proportionality.

_R_ v _Secretary of State for Health, ex parte Swedish Match AB_ (Case C-210/03)

[2004] ECR I-11893, Court of Justice of the European Communities

This is the decision (encountered at p. 39), in which the Court found that Directive 2001/37's ban on the marketing of tobacco for oral use was validly based on Article 95 EC, predecessor to Article 114 TFEU. Faced with the submission that the measure was nonetheless invalid for violation of the proportionality principle, the Court made an explicit connection with the direction in Article 95(3), now Article 114(3) TFEU (p. 33), that the legislature shall take as a base a high level of health protection in setting harmonized standards.

[56] To satisfy its obligation to take as a base a high level of protection in health matters, in accordance with Article 95(3) EC, the Community legislature was thus able, without exceeding the limits of its discretion in the matter, to consider that a prohibition of the marketing of tobacco products for oral use was necessary, and in particular that there was no alternative measure which allowed that objective to be achieved as effectively.

[57] As the Advocate General observes in points 116 to 119 of his Opinion, no other measures aimed at imposing technical standards on manufacturers in order to reduce the harmful effects of the product, or at regulating the labelling of packagings of the product and its conditions of sale, in particular to minors, would have the same preventive effect in terms of the protection of health, inasmuch as they would let a product which is in any event harmful gain a place in the market.

[58] It follows from the above considerations that, with respect both to the objective of ensuring a high level of protection of human health given to the Community legislature by Article 95(3) EC and to its obligation to comply with the principle of proportionality, the contested prohibition cannot be regarded as manifestly inappropriate.

The applicant in Case C-380/03 *Germany* v *Parliament and Council* (p. 40) was similarly luckless in seeking to rely on the proportionality principle as a ground for annulment of the Directive.

NOTE: The principle of proportionality applies not only to EU legislation, but also arises in the application of substantive Treaty provisions. It will be examined further in several of the chapters in Part Two of this book.

B: Fundamental rights

The protection of fundamental rights in the EU has lately become a high-profile part of the process of Treaty revision. The Lisbon Treaty made significant adjustments to the pattern. But before 1993, and the entry into force of the Maastricht Treaty (p. 9), it was the Court that led the way on a solo mission. Its case law has been so influential that it deserves consideration before attention turns to the current state of the Treaties.

The absence of explicit protection of fundamental rights in the Treaty of Rome was in part due to the impossibility of predicting in 1957 how deeply the legal order would intrude into the social sphere and the field of individual rights. However, once that development had occurred it would have been unacceptable for the (then) European Community to fail to show respect for the protection of fundamental rights. The Court began to plug the gap.

The Court made a hesitant start; a terse start. The preliminary reference to the European Court by a German court in *Stauder* v *Ulm* (Case 29/69) arose out of concern that a Commission Decision infringed fundamental rights.

Stauder v *Ulm* (Case 29/69)

[1969] ECR 419, Court of Justice of the European Communities

[7] ... the provision at issue contains nothing capable of prejudicing the fundamental human rights enshrined in the general principles of Community law and protected by the Court.

NOTE: The next case constituted a much more serious judicial commitment to the protection of fundamental rights as part of the developing legal order.

Nold v *Commission* (Case 4/73)

[1974] ECR 491, Court of Justice of the European Communities

Nold, a wholesale coal and construction materials dealer, sought annulment of a Commission Decision. The Decision had authorized Nold's supplier, Ruhrkohle AG, to sell coal only subject to onerous conditions which Nold could not fulfil. Nold therefore suffered damage to its business due to the Decision, because it could no longer buy direct from its supplier. The Court first considered Nold's submissions relating to discrimination and inadequate reasoning:

[9] In the reasoning given in its Decision the Commission emphasized that it was aware that the introduction of the new terms of business would mean that a number of dealers would lose their entitlement to buy direct from the producer, due to their inability to undertake the obligations specified above.

It justifies this measure by the need for Ruhrkohle AG, in view of the major decline in coal sales, to rationalize its marketing system in such a way as to limit direct business association to dealers operating on a sufficient scale.

The requirement that dealers contract for an annual minimum quantity is in fact intended to ensure that the collieries can market their products on a regular basis and in quantities suited to their production capacity.

[10] It emerges from the explanations given by the Commission and the interveners that the imposition of the criteria indicated above can be justified on the grounds not only of the technical conditions appertaining to coal mining but also of the particular economic difficulties created by the recession in coal production.

It therefore appears that these criteria, established by an administrative act of general application, cannot be considered discriminatory and, for the purposes of law, were sufficiently well-reasoned in the Decision of 21 December 1972.

As regards the application of these criteria, it is not alleged that the applicant is treated differently from other undertakings which, having failed to meet the requirements laid down under the new rules, have likewise lost the advantage of their entitlement to purchase direct from the producer.

[11] These submissions must therefore be dismissed.

The Court then examined the status of fundamental rights:

[12] The applicant asserts finally that certain of its fundamental rights have been violated, in that the restrictions introduced by the new trading rules authorized by the Commission have the effect, by depriving it of direct supplies, of jeopardizing both the profitability of the undertaking and the free development of its business activity, to the point of endangering its very existence.

In this way, the Decision is said to violate, in respect of the applicant, a right akin to a proprietary right, as well as its right to the free pursuit of business activity, as protected by the Grundgesetz of the Federal Republic of Germany and by the Constitutions of other Member States and various international treaties, including in particular the Convention for the Protection of Human Rights and Fundamental Freedoms of 4 November 1950 and the Protocol to that Convention of 20 March 1952.

[13] As the Court has already stated, fundamental rights form an integral part of the general principles of law, the observance of which it ensures.

In safeguarding these rights, the Court is bound to draw inspiration from constitutional traditions common to the Member States, and it cannot therefore uphold measures which are incompatible with fundamental rights recognized and protected by the Constitutions of those States.

Similarly, international treaties for the protection of human rights on which the Member States have collaborated or of which they are signatories, can supply guidelines which should be followed within the framework of Community law.

The submissions of the applicant must be examined in the light of these principles.

[14] If rights of ownership are protected by the constitutional laws of all the Member States and if similar guarantees are given in respect of their right freely to choose and practice their trade or profession, the rights thereby guaranteed, far from constituting unfettered prerogatives, must be viewed in the light of the social function of the property and activities protected thereunder.

For this reason, rights of this nature are protected by law subject always to limitations laid down in accordance with the public interest.

Within the Community legal order it likewise seems legitimate that these rights should, if necessary be subject to certain limits justified by the overall objectives pursued by the Community, on condition that the substance of these rights is left untouched.

As regards the guarantees accorded to a particular undertaking, they can in no respect be extended to protect mere commercial interests or opportunities, the uncertainties of which are part of the very essence of economic activity.

[15] The disadvantages claimed by the applicant are in fact the result of economic change and not of the contested Decision.

It was for the applicant, confronted by the economic changes brought about by the recession in coal production, to acknowledge the situation and itself carry out the necessary adaptations.

[16] This submission must be dismissed for all the reasons outlined above.

NOTES

1. This is a 'give and take' judgment. Nold fails on the facts; its rights must yield. However, of more long-term importance, the Court explicitly acknowledges the importance of fundamental rights within the legal order. Paragraph 13 is ringingly resonant: its influence lives on today in Article 6(3) TEU, p. 58.

2. In *Hoechst* v *Commission* (Case 46/87) [1989] ECR 2859 the Court insisted that the exercise of the Commission's powers of investigation under the Treaty competition law regime must respect fundamental rights. This case is mentioned in its substantive context at p. 510, but in its constitutional aspects it belongs here as a demonstration of the link between constitutional principles and the substantive law of market integration and regulation. The next case also concerns the application of the Treaty competition rules.

Roquette Frères SA v *Directeur général de la concurrence, de la consommation et de la répression des frauds* (Case C-94/00)

[2002] ECR I-9011, Court of Justice of the European Communities

This preliminary reference concerned the scope of legal protection of business premises subject to search. The Court emphasizes that the absence at the time of an organic link between the EU legal order and that of the ECHR did not preclude it, sitting in Luxembourg, from explicit recognition of decisions taken by the European Court of Human Rights in Strasbourg.

[29] For the purposes of determining the scope of that principle in relation to the protection of business premises, regard must be had to the case law of the European Court of Human Rights subsequent to the judgment in *Hoechst.* According to that caselaw, first, the protection of the home provided for in Article 8 of the ECHR may in certain circumstances be extended to cover such premises (see, in particular, the judgment of 16 April 2002 in *Colas Est and Others v France*, not yet published in the *Reports of Judgments and Decisions*, § 41) and, second, the right of interference established by Article 8(2) of the ECHR 'might well be more far-reaching where professional or business activities or premises were involved than would otherwise be the case' (*Niemietz v Germany*, cited above, § 31).

NOTE: The Court knows that it will earn (and deserve) the confidence of national constitutional courts only if it demonstrates that the EU observes fundamental rights. Without such a guarantee one could expect that national courts would deny the legitimacy and autonomy of EU law by testing it against national fundamental constitutional principles. This prospect seems to motivate the Court's observations in the next case.

Hauer v *Rheinland-Pfalz* (Case 44/79)

[1979] ECR 3727, Court of Justice of the European Communities

The case was a preliminary reference from a German court and concerned the validity of a Regulation. The first paragraph details the anxiety of the national court. The *Grundgesetz* is the Federal Republic's Basic Law, established immediately after the war, and understandably much cherished. The Court responds by delicately but firmly re-writing the question.

[13] In its order making the reference, the Verwaltungsgericht states that if Regulation No 1162/76 must be interpreted as meaning that it lays down a prohibition of general application, so as to include even land appropriate for wine growing, that provision might have to be considered inapplicable in the Federal Republic of Germany owing to doubts existing with regard to its compatibility with the fundamental rights guaranteed by Articles 14 and 12 of the Grundgesetz concerning, respectively, the right to property and the right freely to pursue trade and professional activities.

[14] As the Court declared in its judgment of 17 December 1970, *Internationale Handelsgesellschaft* [1970] ECR 1125, the question of a possible infringement of fundamental rights by a measure of the Community institutions can only be judged in the light of Community law itself. The introduction of special criteria for assessment stemming from the legislation or constitutional law of a particular Member State would, by damaging the substantive unity and efficacy of Community law, lead inevitably to the destruction of the unity of the Common Market and the jeopardizing of the cohesion of the Community.

[15] The Court also emphasized in the judgment cited, and later in the judgment of 14 May 1974, *Nold* [1974] ECR 491, that fundamental rights form an integral part of the general principles of the law, the observance of which it ensures; that in safeguarding those rights, the Court is bound to draw inspiration from constitutional traditions common to the Member States, so that measures which are incompatible with the fundamental rights recognized by the constitutions of those States are unacceptable in the Community; and that, similarly, international treaties

for the protection of human rights on which the Member States have collaborated or of which they are signatories, can supply guidelines which should be followed within the framework of Community law. That conception was later recognised by the joint declaration of the European Parliament, the Council and the Commission of 5 April 1977, which, after recalling the case law of the Court, refers on the one hand to the rights guaranteed by the constitutions of the Member States and on the other hand to the European Convention for the Protection of Human Rights and Fundamental Freedoms of 4 November 1950 (Official Journal C 103, 1977, p. 1).

[16] In these circumstances, the doubts evinced by the Verwaltungsgericht as to the compatibility of the provisions of Regulation No 1162/76 with the rules concerning the protection of fundamental rights must be understood as questioning the validity of the regulation in the light of Community law. In this regard, it is necessary to distinguish between, on the one hand, a possible infringement of the right to property and, on the other hand, a possible limitation upon the freedom to pursue a trade or profession.

The Court then proceeded to examine the nature of the right to property:

[17] The right to property is guaranteed in the Community legal order in accordance with the ideas common to the constitutions of the Member States, which are also reflected in the first Protocol to the European Convention for the Protection of Human Rights.

[18] Article 1 of the Protocol provides as follows:

'Every natural or legal person is entitled to the peaceful enjoyment of his possessions. No one shall be deprived of his possessions except in the public interest and subject to the conditions provided for by law and by the general principles of international law.

The preceding provisions shall not, however, in any way impair the right of a State to enforce such laws as it deems necessary to control the use of property in accordance with the general interest or to secure the payment of taxes or other contributions or penalties.'

[19] Having declared that persons are entitled to the peaceful enjoyment of their property, that provision envisages two ways in which the rights of a property owner may be impaired, according as the impairment is intended to deprive the owner of his right or to restrict the exercise thereof. In this case it is incontestable that the prohibition on new planting cannot be considered to be an act depriving the owner of his property, since he remains free to dispose of it or to put it to other uses which are not prohibited. On the other hand, there is no doubt that that prohibition restricts the use of the property. In this regard, the second paragraph of Article 1 of the Protocol provides an important indication in so far as it recognizes the right of a State 'to enforce such laws as it deems necessary to control the use of property in accordance with the general interest'. Thus the Protocol accepts in principle the legality of restrictions upon the use of property, whilst at the same time limiting those restrictions to the extent to which they are deemed 'necessary' by a State for the protection of the 'general interest'. However, that provision does not enable a sufficiently precise answer to be given to the question submitted by the Verwaltungsgericht.

[20] Therefore, in order to be able to answer that question, it is necessary to consider also the indications provided by the constitutional rules and practices of the nine Member States. One of the first points to emerge in this regard is that those rules and practices permit the legislature to control the use of private property in accordance with the general interest. Thus some constitutions refer to the obligations arising out of the ownership of property (German Grundgesetz, Article 14(2), first sentence), to its social function (Italian constitution, Article 42(2)), to the subordination of its use to the requirements of the common good (German Grundgesetz, Article 14(2), second sentence, and the Irish constitution, Article 43.2.2), or of social justice (Irish constitution, Article 43.2.1). In all the Member States, numerous legislative measures have given concrete expression to that social function of the right to property. Thus in all the Member States there is legislation on agriculture and forestry, the water supply, the protection of the environment and town and country planning, which imposes restrictions, sometimes appreciable, on the use of real property.

[21] More particularly, all the wine-producing countries of the Community have restrictive legislation, albeit of differing severity, concerning the planting of vines, the selection of varieties and the methods of cultivation. In none of the countries concerned are those provisions considered to be incompatible in principle with the regard due to the right to property.

[22] Thus it may be stated, taking into account the constitutional precepts common to the Member States and consistent legislative practices, in widely varying spheres, that the fact that Regulation No 1162/76 imposed restrictions on the new planting of vines cannot be challenged in principle. It is a type of restriction which is known and accepted as lawful, in identical or similar forms, in the constitutional structure of all the Member States.

NOTE: The Court's analysis led it to the conclusion that there was no violation of the substance of the right to property recognized by EC law and, citing *Nold* (Case 4/73), the Court also concluded that there was no breach of the freedom to pursue a trade or profession.

In *Wunsche Handelsgesellschaft* [1987] 3 CMLR 225, the German Federal Constitutional Court, the *Bundesverfassungsgericht*, declared it would not test legislation of the (then) EC against the requirements of the German Constitution, because it was satisfied that the EC legal order offered adequate protection against violation of fundamental rights. The EC legal order has thus been shaped in the context of litigation at national level and in response to national constitutional concerns. This matter will be examined further in Chapter 3, for it impinges on the doctrine of the supremacy of EU law. A distinct but connected concern surrounds the question of whether a national court may invalidate an EU act as lying beyond the competence conferred by the Treaty. The Court of Justice's view is perfectly clear – only it possesses this jurisdiction. National courts do not all agree. This too has generated a form of indirect judicial dialogue between national (especially German) and European courts: see Chapter 19.

As mentioned (at p. 54), it was only on the entry into force of the Maastricht Treaty in 1993 that fundamental rights became subject to express reference within the Treaties. Since the entry into force of the Lisbon Treaty in 2009, there are four distinct elements to the Treaty-based commitment to fundamental rights.

The first locates the matter at the heart of the project. Respect for human rights is a foundational value of the EU, according to Article 2 TEU, and Article 6(3) TEU provides that 'Fundamental rights, as guaranteed by the European Convention for the Protection of Human Rights and Fundamental Freedoms and as they result from the constitutional traditions common to the Member States, shall constitute general principles of the Union's law.' The inspiration provided by the Court's pioneering case law is plain. Furthermore, respect for human rights shall also guide the EU's external action (Articles 3(5), 21 TEU).

Connected to this is the second element in the Treaty's scheme of fundamental rights protection, the possibility provided by Article 7 TEU to take action against a Member State in serious breach of the Union's values. This procedure was inserted into the Treaty at Amsterdam with effect from 1999. Gratifyingly it has not (yet) been used against a Member State.

The two remaining elements of the EU Treaty's architecture for the protection of fundamental rights are Lisbon innovations. The Court's cautious Opinion 2/94 on Accession to the ECHR was mentioned (at p. 32): it denied a legislative competence to accede to the ECHR under the Treaty as then constituted. Article 6(2) TEU now fills that gap. It provides that 'The Union shall accede to the European Convention for the Protection of Human Rights and Fundamental Freedoms.' A persisting anxiety among at least some Member States is that infusing the EU with deeper commitments to human rights might generate unforeseen extension in the scope of its competence. This anxiety is reflected in a second sentence added to Article 6(2) TEU: 'Such accession shall not affect the Union's competences as defined in the Treaties.' Moreover, a supplementary Protocol relating to Article 6(2) TEU states that accession is to 'make provision for preserving the specific characteristics of the Union and Union law'. And it is to be ensured that accession 'shall not affect the competences of the Union or the powers of its institutions'. These provisos led to the Court refusing to authorize accession on the terms that had been negotiated in Opinion 2/13 of 18 December 2014, considered on page 65, so accession is on hold.

The fourth and final element in the mosaic of fundamental rights protection is provided by the Charter of Fundamental Rights. And here too there is a narrative of suspicion about the propensity of human rights discourse to extend the scope of EU competence. The Charter was solemnly proclaimed at Nice in December 2001. On its face it constitutes a powerful assertion of the importance of weaving the protection of fundamental rights deep into the very fabric of the Union's wide sweep of activities. But the Charter, when agreed at Nice, was carefully arranged so as *not* to be legally binding.

The Court was initially reluctant to draw on the Charter at all, even as an aid to interpretation. It scrupulously avoided referring to the non-binding Charter in its judgments until 2006, when, for the first time, it referred briefly to the document (Case C-540/03 *Parliament* v *Council* [2006] ECR I-5769). Resistance crumbled, and the Court began to draw more heavily on the Charter as a source of interpretation, albeit typically simply to confirm decisions taken on the basis of other grounds (e.g. Case C-275/06 *Promusciae* [2008] ECR I-271, Case C-244/06 *Dynamic Medien* [2008] ECR I-505, Joined Cases C-402/05P & C-415/05P *Kadi and Al Barakaat* v *Council* [2008] ECR I-6351).

Now, since the entry into force of the Lisbon Treaty, Article 6 TEU provides that the Union 'recognises the rights, freedoms and principles set out in the Charter'; and that it 'shall have the same legal value as the Treaties'. The Charter has become legally binding, a point which the Grand Chamber of the Court made as soon as it had the chance after the entry into force of the Lisbon Treaty even though the relevant litigation pre-dated that landmark (Case C-555/07 *Seda Kücükdeveci* [2010] ECR I-365, para 22). It is cautiously provided in Article 6 TEU that the Charter 'shall not extend in any way the competences of the Union as defined in the Treaties'; and that the Charter shall be interpreted in accordance with the general principles contained in the Charter's own Title VII governing its interpretation and application and also with due regard to the explanations referred to in the Charter. This reveals a concern on the part of the Member States as far as possible to fix the scope and impact of the Charter in advance, and in particular to forestall unanticipated extension of its impact as a result of creative judicial interpretation. So Article 51 covers *Field of Application*:

1. The provisions of this Charter are addressed to the institutions, bodies, offices and agencies of the Union with due regard for the principle of subsidiarity and to the Member States only when they are implementing Union law. They shall therefore respect the rights, observe the principles and promote the application thereof in accordance with their respective powers and respecting the limits of the powers of the Union as conferred on it in the Treaties.

2. The Charter does not extend the field of application of Union law beyond the powers of the Union or establish any new power or task for the Union, or modify powers and tasks as defined in the Treaties.

NOTE: The concern to put a leash on the Court is evident. But it quickly showed determination not to treat the Charter as having *reduced* the scope of EU fundamental rights by interpreting the notion that Member States are bound only when 'implementing' EU law in the same generous way it had always done: Case C-617/10 *Åkerberg Fransson* judgment of 26 February 2013.

Article 52 of the Charter deals with *Scope and interpretation of rights and principles*. Article 52(5) is especially significant:

The provisions of this Charter which contain principles may be implemented by legislative and executive acts taken by institutions, bodies, offices and agencies of the Union, and by acts of Member States when they are implementing Union law, in the exercise of their respective powers. They shall be judicially cognisable only in the interpretation of such acts and in the ruling on their legality.

NOTE: Principles – as opposed to rights – are to be confined in their effect and influence. And the 'Explanations' attached to the Charter ([2007] OJ C303/17) set out the view that principles do not provide a basis for a direct claim by an individual for positive action by the institutions of the EU or by the authorities of the Member States. These provisions reveal a willingness to accept a binding Charter of Fundamental Right within the EU legal order coupled to an anxiety about the use that may be made of such an instrument by the Court to extend the impact of such a document beyond the Member States' basically cautious view of its proper role. There is, however, clear ambiguity surrounding these provisions. The *political* concern to signal to the Court (but not only the Court) that the Charter should not be interpreted in an extensive manner is not matched by *legal* precision (*cf* J. Krommendijk, 'Principed silence or mere silence on principles?' (2015) 11 Euro Const Law Rev 321, tracking the case law so far). There is slack in the leash that the Court might choose to exploit.

In particular, the anxiety to confine the legal effect of principles under the Charter, visible in Article 52(5), may be effective with regard to litigation based squarely on the Charter but of no relevance to litigation in which the general principles of EU law are engaged. However, the indications so far are that the Court has chosen to place the Charter, now granted formal binding effect by the Member States, at the forefront of its examination of fundamental rights in preference to the potentially wider sweep of general principles which the Court itself has so actively nurtured. The Charter tends increasingly to provide the Court's starting point, and sometimes it looks no further for sources on which to rely: for example, Case C-199/11 *Otis NV* judgment of 6 November 2012, paras 46–47, Case C-396/11 *Ciprian Radu* judgment of 29 January 2013, para 32). In the next case the Court found a provision in a Directive to be unlawful when tested against the Charter.

***Association Belge des Consommateurs Test-Achats* (C-236/09)**

[2011] ECR I-773, Court of Justice of the European Union

Directive 2004/113 implements the principle of equal treatment between men and women in the access to and supply of goods and services. Its Article 5(2) allowed Member States to permit differences relating to sex in the calculation of insurance premiums and benefits. The Court was asked in a preliminary reference whether this complied with the principle of equal treatment for men and women.

[16] Article 6(2) EU, to which the national court refers in its questions and which is mentioned in recital 1 to Directive 2004/113, provides that the European Union is to respect fundamental rights as guaranteed by the European Convention for the Protection of Human Rights and Fundamental Freedoms and as they result from the constitutional traditions common to the Member States, as general principles of Community law. Those fundamental rights are incorporated in the Charter, which, with effect from 1 December 2009, has the same legal status as the Treaties.

[17] Articles 21 and 23 of the Charter state, respectively, that any discrimination based on sex is prohibited and that equality between men and women must be ensured in all areas. Since recital 4 to Directive 2004/113 expressly refers to Articles 21 and 23 of the Charter, the validity of Article 5(2) of that directive must be assessed in the light of those provisions (see, to that effect, Joined Cases C-92/09 and C-93/09 *Volker und Markus Schecke and Eifert* [2010] ECR I-0000, paragraph 46).

[18] The right to equal treatment for men and women is the subject of provisions in the FEU Treaty. First, under Article 157(1) TFEU, each Member State must ensure that the principle of equal pay for men and women for equal work or work of equal value is applied. Secondly, Article 19(1) TFEU provides that, after obtaining the consent of the European Parliament, the Council may take appropriate action to combat discrimination based on sex, racial or ethnic origin, religion or belief, disability, age or sexual orientation.

[19] While Article 157(1) TFEU establishes the principle of equal treatment for men and women in a specific area, Article 19(1) TFEU confers on the Council competence which it must exercise in accordance, *inter alia*, with the second subparagraph of Article 3(3) TEU, which provides that the European Union is to combat social exclusion and discrimination and to promote social justice and protection, equality between men and women, solidarity between generations and protection of the rights of the child, and with Article 8 TFEU, under which, in all its activities, the European Union is to aim to eliminate inequalities, and to promote equality, between men and women.

[20] In the progressive achievement of that equality, it is the EU legislature which, in the light of the task conferred on the European Union by the second subparagraph of Article 3(3) TEU and Article 8 TFEU, determines

when it will take action, having regard to the development of economic and social conditions within the European Union.

[21] However, when such action is decided upon, it must contribute, in a coherent manner, to the achievement of the intended objective, without prejudice to the possibility of providing for transitional periods or derogations of limited scope.

The Court found Article 5(2) of the Directive invalid for violation of the principle of equal treatment contained in the Charter and which is also the stated purpose of Directive 2004/113 (albeit that a five-year transitional period of validity was accepted, expiring in December 2012).

The *Schecke* judgment, mentioned by the Court in para 17, opens a window on a likely future source of much litigation: the need to reconcile conflicting provisions of the Charter.

***Volker und Markus Schecke and Eifert* (Joined Cases C-92/09 and C-93/09)**

[2010] ECR I-11063, Court of Justice of the European Union

[75] It is not disputed that the publication on the internet of data by name relating to the beneficiaries concerned and the precise amounts received by them from the EAGF [European Agricultural Guarantee Fund] and the EAFRD [European Agricultural Fund for Rural Development] is liable to increase transparency with respect to the use of the agricultural aid concerned. Such information made available to citizens reinforces public control of the use to which that money is put and contributes to the best use of public funds.

[76] As to whether the measure is necessary, it must be recalled that the objective of the publication at issue may not be pursued without having regard to the fact that that objective must be reconciled with the fundamental rights set forth in Articles 7 and 8 of the Charter (see, to that effect, Case C-73/07 *Satakunnan Markkinapörssi and Satamedia* [2008] ECR I-9831, paragraph 53).

[77] It is thus necessary to determine whether the Council of the European Union and the Commission balanced the European Union's interest in guaranteeing the transparency of its acts and ensuring the best use of public funds against the interference with the right of the beneficiaries concerned to respect for their private life in general and to the protection of their personal data in particular. The Court has held in this respect that derogations and limitations in relation to the protection of personal data must apply only in so far as is strictly necessary. . . .

On the facts the Court found the legislative 'balance' to be misplaced and consequently it held provisions of the challenged Regulations to be invalid.

Charter-based challenges to EU legislation are a growth area, albeit that most so far have, unlike the two cases discussed (*Association Belge des Consommateurs Test-Achats* (C-236/09) and *Volker und Markus Schecke and Eifert* (Joined Cases C-92/09 and C-93/09)), proved unsuccessful (e.g. C-544/10 *Deutsches Weintor eG* v *Land Rheinland-Pfalz* judgment of 6 September 2012; Case C-396/11 *Ciprian Radu* judgment of 29 January 2013; Case C-611/12P *Giordano v Commission* judgment of 14 October 2014). The matter is plainly of pressing concern in the shaping of EU legislation – Commissioner Reding declared that 'All EU law must be fundamental rights proof' (cited in I. De Jesus Butler, 'Ensuring Compliance with the Charter of Fundamental Rights in Legislative Drafting: the Practice of the European Commission' (2012) 37 EL Rev 397).

The concerns about privacy that animated the Court's ruling in *Schecke* resurfaced in the next case, in which the Court found that the EU's Data Protection Directive (2006/24) was incompatible with the Charter. The Court did not dispute that concerns about security might justify restrictions on privacy, but it objected to the depth of intrusion made by the Charter.

Digital Rights Ireland (Joined Cases C-293/12 and C-594/12)

Judgment of 8 April 2014, Court of Justice of the European Union

58 Directive 2006/24 affects, in a comprehensive manner, all persons using electronic communications services, but without the persons whose data are retained being, even indirectly, in a situation which is liable to give rise to criminal prosecutions. It therefore applies even to persons for whom there is no evidence capable of suggesting that their conduct might have a link, even an indirect or remote one, with serious crime. Furthermore, it does not provide for any exception, with the result that it applies even to persons whose communications are subject, according to rules of national law, to the obligation of professional secrecy.

59 Moreover, whilst seeking to contribute to the fight against serious crime, Directive 2006/24 does not require any relationship between the data whose retention is provided for and a threat to public security and, in particular, it is not restricted to a retention in relation (i) to data pertaining to a particular time period and/or a particular geographical zone and/or to a circle of particular persons likely to be involved, in one way or another, in a serious crime, or (ii) to persons who could, for other reasons, contribute, by the retention of their data, to the prevention, detection or prosecution of serious offences.

60 Secondly, not only is there a general absence of limits in Directive 2006/24 but Directive 2006/24 also fails to lay down any objective criterion by which to determine the limits of the access of the competent national authorities to the data and their subsequent use for the purposes of prevention, detection or criminal prosecutions concerning offences that, in view of the extent and seriousness of the interference with the fundamental rights enshrined in Articles 7 and 8 of the Charter, may be considered to be sufficiently serious to justify such an interference. On the contrary, Directive 2006/24 simply refers, in Article 1(1), in a general manner to serious crime, as defined by each Member State in its national law.

61 Furthermore, Directive 2006/24 does not contain substantive and procedural conditions relating to the access of the competent national authorities to the data and to their subsequent use. Article 4 of the directive, which governs the access of those authorities to the data retained, does not expressly provide that that access and the subsequent use of the data in question must be strictly restricted to the purpose of preventing and detecting precisely defined serious offences or of conducting criminal prosecutions relating thereto; it merely provides that each Member State is to define the procedures to be followed and the conditions to be fulfilled in order to gain access to the retained data in accordance with necessity and proportionality requirements.

62 In particular, Directive 2006/24 does not lay down any objective criterion by which the number of persons authorised to access and subsequently use the data retained is limited to what is strictly necessary in the light of the objective pursued. Above all, the access by the competent national authorities to the data retained is not made dependent on a prior review carried out by a court or by an independent administrative body whose decision seeks to limit access to the data and their use to what is strictly necessary for the purpose of attaining the objective pursued and which intervenes following a reasoned request of those authorities submitted within the framework of procedures of prevention, detection or criminal prosecutions. Nor does it lay down a specific obligation on Member States designed to establish such limits.

63 Thirdly, so far as concerns the data retention period, Article 6 of Directive 2006/24 requires that those data be retained for a period of at least six months, without any distinction being made between the categories of data set out in Article 5 of that directive on the basis of their possible usefulness for the purposes of the objective pursued or according to the persons concerned.

64 Furthermore, that period is set at between a minimum of 6 months and a maximum of 24 months, but it is not stated that the determination of the period of retention must be based on objective criteria in order to ensure that it is limited to what is strictly necessary.

65 It follows from the above that Directive 2006/24 does not lay down clear and precise rules governing the extent of the interference with the fundamental rights enshrined in Articles 7 and 8 of the Charter. It must therefore be held that Directive 2006/24 entails a wide-ranging and particularly serious interference with those fundamental rights in the legal order of the EU, without such an interference being precisely circumscribed by provisions to ensure that it is actually limited to what is strictly necessary.

In C-362/14 *Maximillian Schrems* judgment of 6 October 2015 the Court took a similarly negative view of Decision 2000/520 on the transfer of data to the US under the so-called 'safe harbour' arrangements. It was unlawful for non-compliance with privacy rights guaranteed by the Charter.

Even the thicket of caveats about the scope of the Charter (and reinforced by legally non-binding Declarations) was not enough for two Member States. First the UK, joined by Poland, sought extra protection from the Charter. The result is a Protocol, applicable to the two States alone. The Protocol provides that the Charter is to be applied by the courts of Poland and the UK as it is by the courts of all the other Member States. But it is provided in Article 1 of the Protocol that:

> The Charter does not extend the ability of the Court of Justice of the European Union, or any court or tribunal of Poland or of the United Kingdom, to find that the laws, regulations or administrative provisions, practices or action of Poland or of the United Kingdom are inconsistent with the fundamental rights, freedoms and principles that it reaffirms. In particular, and for the avoidance of doubt, nothing in Title IV of the Charter creates justiciable rights applicable to Poland or the United Kingdom except in so far as Poland or the United Kingdom has provided for such rights in its national law.

Then Article 2 adds that:

> To the extent that a provision of the Charter refers to national laws and practices, it shall only apply to Poland or the United Kingdom to the extent that the rights or principles that it contains are recognised in the law or practices of Poland or of the United Kingdom.

The *political* intent is plain enough, and has two elements from the UK perspective. First, the addition of this Protocol formed part of the government's case, based infamously on 'red lines', that the Lisbon Treaty differs from the Treaty establishing a Constitution, and that accordingly the original promise of a referendum in the UK could be legitimately withdrawn. With regard to its substance, the Protocol is designed to reflect and allay fears that expansionist case law fed by the Charter might upset particular features of British (and Polish) social and economic life. Title IV of the Charter, mentioned in Article 1 of the Protocol, concerns social and labour interests.

Legally the matter is much less clear. One extreme is to suppose that there will develop two streams of fundamental rights protection in the EU: the creative and dynamic pattern applicable to 26 Member States and a dammed set of rules applying to the UK and Poland alone, remaining unalterable. That seems inconsistent with any notion of equality between citizens of the Union – but the Protocol cannot be ignored.

Indeed it cannot be ignored – but nor can it be treated as unambiguous. It is possible to take a very different interpretation – one that would effectively read the supposed special position of Poland and the UK out of existence. One could argue that what is provided for in the case of the UK and Poland is in fact no more than a statement of what anyway applies now and in the future to all the Member States. So the Protocol begins by stating that it does not *extend* judicial powers – arguably Article 6(1) EU already ensures this. Moreover, the Protocol (in Articles 1(2) and 2) seems to assume there is a settled and static content to rights and principles contained in UK law – which is far from convincing.

Plainly then the Protocol is not an opt-out from the Charter – a point made with force by the Court in Case C-411/10 *N.S.* 21 December 2011 (the facts did not involve Title IV of the Charter). The Protocol offers an interpretation of the impact of the Charter which is ambiguous in its effect – including whether it really does conserve a special position for the UK and Poland. Litigation will doubtless eventually tease out these conundrums. This is hardly consistent with the UK government's expressed concern in negotiating the Protocol to provide security for UK business.

The Court has played – and will continue to play – such an influential role in driving the EU's commitment to fundamental rights protection that it seems appropriate to allow it to have the last word. In autumn 2008 it delivered perhaps its most stirring assertion so far of the existential importance it attributes to fundamental rights protection in the EU legal order.

Kadi and Al Barakaat v _Council_ (Joined Cases C-402/05P & C-415/05P)

[2008] ECR I-6351, Court of Justice of the European Communities.

EC legislative measures 'freezing' individuals' assets pursuant to action taken at the level of the United Nations Security Council were challenged for violation of fundamental rights standards, in particular for want of regard for the right to be heard, the right to effective legal protection, and the right to property.

> [284] It is ... clear from the case-law that respect for human rights is a condition of the lawfulness of Community acts (Opinion 2/94, paragraph 34) and that measures incompatible with respect for human rights are not acceptable in the Community (Case C-112/00 *Schmidberger* [2003] ECR I-5659, paragraph 73 and case-law cited).

Crucially, this could not be altered in the view of the Court by the fact that the acts in question constituted the implementation in the EU of measures binding under international law. It chose to *defend* the EU legal order:

> [302] It is true also that Article 297 EC implicitly permits obstacles to the operation of the common market when they are caused by measures taken by a Member State to carry out the international obligations it has accepted for the purpose of maintaining international peace and security.
>
> [303] Those provisions cannot, however, be understood to authorise any derogation from the principles of liberty, democracy and respect for human rights and fundamental freedoms enshrined in Article 6(1) EU as a foundation of the Union.
>
> [304] Article 307 EC may in no circumstances permit any challenge to the principles that form part of the very foundations of the Community legal order, one of which is the protection of fundamental rights, including the review by the Community judicature of the lawfulness of Community measures as regards their consistency with those fundamental rights. . . .
>
> . . . [316] . . . the review by the Court of the validity of any Community measure in the light of fundamental rights must be considered to be the expression, in a community based on the rule of law, of a constitutional guarantee stemming from the EC Treaty as an autonomous legal system which is not to be prejudiced by an international agreement.

NOTE: The Court annulled the Regulation, though exceptionally it held it should be maintained in force for 3 months to permit political re-consideration. Regular litigation is inevitable in this area – for '*Kadi II*', and examination of the appropriate level of judicial scrutiny of reasons provided by the public authorities, see Joined Cases C-584/10P, C-593/10P and C595/10P *Commission and Others* v *Kadi* judgment of 18 July 2013.

The ruling in *Kadi* was welcomed as a promotion of fundamental rights in the EU in defiance of an attempt to lower them from 'outside' (C. Gearty, 'In Praise of Awkwardness: *Kadi* in the CJEU' (2014) 10 Euro Const LR 15). But the structurally similar concern of the Court to protect EU law and its own jurisdiction from review pursued by the European Court of Human Rights based in Strasbourg has been less warmly received.

In December 2014 the Court, to general surprise, refused to accept that the EU could accede to the European Convention for the Protection of Human Rights (ECHR), as mandated by Article 6(2) TEU, under the terms that had been negotiated.

The Opinion was delivered pursuant to a request made to the Court by the Commission under Article 218(11) TFEU. This envisages that the Court shall in effect check the compatibility of a planned international agreement with EU law. The Court's verdict in the case of the arrangements for accession to the ECHR was negative. The Opinion contains several detailed objections which could feasibly be the subject of re-negotiation but at its core is a deeper existential claim about the nature of the EU legal order and the Court's place within it which will be very difficult to address satisfactorily.

Opinion 2/13 of 18 December 2014,

Court of Justice of the European Union

The Court emphasised that, as noted earlier (p. 58), the Treaty basis for accession is not unconditional. In particular the supporting Protocol stipulates the need to preserve the specific characteristics of EU law. But what were these 'specific characteristics'?

165. It should be borne in mind that these characteristics include those relating to the constitutional structure of the EU, which is seen in the principle of conferral of powers referred to in Articles 4(1) TEU and 5(1) and (2) TEU, and in the institutional framework established in Articles 13 TEU to 19 TEU.

166. To these must be added the specific characteristics arising from the very nature of EU law. In particular, as the Court of Justice has noted many times, EU law is characterised by the fact that it stems from an independent source of law, the Treaties, by its primacy over the laws of the Member States (see, to that effect, judgments in *Costa*, EU:C:1964:66, p. 594, and *Internationale Handelsgesellschaft*, EU:C:1970:114, paragraph 3; Opinions 1/91, EU:C:1991:490, paragraph 21, and 1/09, EU:C:2011:123, paragraph 65; and judgment in *Melloni*, C-399/11, EU:C:2013:107, paragraph 59), and by the direct effect of a whole series of provisions which are applicable to their nationals and to the Member States themselves (judgment in *van Gend & Loos*, EU:C:1963:1, p. 12, and Opinion 1/09, EU:C:2011:123, paragraph 65).

167. These essential characteristics of EU law have given rise to a structured network of principles, rules and mutually interdependent legal relations linking the EU and its Member States, and its Member States with each other, which are now engaged, as is recalled in the second paragraph of Article 1 TEU, in a 'process of creating an ever closer union among the peoples of Europe'.

168. This legal structure is based on the fundamental premiss that each Member State shares with all the other Member States, and recognises that they share with it, a set of common values on which the EU is founded, as stated in Article 2 TEU. That premiss implies and justifies the existence of mutual trust between the Member States that those values will be recognised and, therefore, that the law of the EU that implements them will be respected.

169. Also at the heart of that legal structure are the fundamental rights recognised by the Charter (which, under Article 6(1) TEU, has the same legal value as the Treaties), respect for those rights being a condition of the lawfulness of EU acts, so that measures incompatible with those rights are not acceptable in the EU (see judgments in *ERT*, C-260/89, EU:C:1991:254, paragraph 41; *Kremzow*, C-299/95, EU:C:1997:254, paragraph 14; *Schmidberger*, C-112/00, EU:C:2003:333, paragraph 73; and *Kadi and Al Barakaat International Foundation* v *Council and Commission*, EU:C:2008:461, paragraphs 283 and 284).

170. The autonomy enjoyed by EU law in relation to the laws of the Member States and in relation to international law requires that the interpretation of those fundamental rights be ensured within the framework of the structure and objectives of the EU (see, to that effect, judgments in *Internationale Handelsgesellschaft*, EU:C:1970:114, paragraph 4, and *Kadi and Al Barakaat International Foundation* v *Council and Commission*, EU:C:2008:461, paragraphs 281 to 285).

171. As regards the structure of the EU, it must be emphasised that not only are the institutions, bodies, offices and agencies of the EU required to respect the Charter but so too are the Member States when they are implementing EU law (see, to that effect, judgment in *Åkerberg Fransson*, C-617/10, EU:C:2013:105, paragraphs 17 to 21).

172. The pursuit of the EU's objectives, as set out in Article 3 TEU, is entrusted to a series of fundamental provisions, such as those providing for the free movement of goods, services, capital and persons, citizenship of

the Union, the area of freedom, security and justice, and competition policy. Those provisions, which are part of the framework of a system that is specific to the EU, are structured in such a way as to contribute — each within its specific field and with its own particular characteristics — to the implementation of the process of integration that is the *raison d'être* of the EU itself.

173. Similarly, the Member States are obliged, by reason, inter alia, of the principle of sincere cooperation set out in the first subparagraph of Article 4(3) TEU, to ensure, in their respective territories, the application of and respect for EU law. In addition, pursuant to the second subparagraph of Article 4(3) TEU, the Member States are to take any appropriate measure, general or particular, to ensure fulfilment of the obligations arising out of the Treaties or resulting from the acts of the institutions of the EU (Opinion 1/09, EU:C:2011:123, paragraph 68 and the case-law cited).

174. In order to ensure that the specific characteristics and the autonomy of that legal order are preserved, the Treaties have established a judicial system intended to ensure consistency and uniformity in the interpretation of EU law.

175. In that context, it is for the national courts and tribunals and for the Court of Justice to ensure the full application of EU law in all Member States and to ensure judicial protection of an individual's rights under that law (Opinion 1/09, EU:C:2011:123, paragraph 68 and the case-law cited).

176. In particular, the judicial system as thus conceived has as its keystone the preliminary ruling procedure provided for in Article 267 TFEU, which, by setting up a dialogue between one court and another, specifically between the Court of Justice and the courts and tribunals of the Member States, has the object of securing uniform interpretation of EU law (see, to that effect, judgment in *van Gend & Loos*, EU:C:1963:1, p. 12), thereby serving to ensure its consistency, its full effect and its autonomy as well as, ultimately, the particular nature of the law established by the Treaties (see, to that effect, Opinion 1/09, EU:C:2011:123, paragraphs 67 and 83).

Once the Court had made this claim to preserve the 'autonomy' of EU law, it followed that accession to the ECHR could proceed only if autonomy were not threatened. But, in the estimation of the Court, it was. Accession would, by virtue of Article 216(2) TFEU, mean that the ECHR would be binding upon the EU and would form an integral part of EU law. The EU would be subject to external control: the Court would be subject to the control mechanisms provided for by the ECHR, including the decisions of the ECtHR.

183. . . . the Court of Justice has . . . declared that an international agreement may affect its own powers only if the indispensable conditions for safeguarding the essential character of those powers are satisfied and, consequently, there is no adverse effect on the autonomy of the EU legal order (see Opinions 1/00, EU:C:2002:231, paragraphs 21, 23 and 26, and 1/09, EU:C:2011:123, paragraph 76; see also, to that effect, judgment in *Kadi and Al Barakaat International Foundation* v *Council and Commission*, EU:C:2008:461, paragraph 282).

184. In particular, any action by the bodies given decision-making powers by the ECHR, as provided for in the agreement envisaged, must not have the effect of binding the EU and its institutions, in the exercise of their internal powers, to a particular interpretation of the rules of EU law (see Opinions 1/91, EU:C:1991:490, paragraphs 30 to 35, and 1/00, EU:C:2002:231, paragraph 13).

185. It is admittedly inherent in the very concept of external control that, on the one hand, the interpretation of the ECHR provided by the ECtHR would, under international law, be binding on the EU and its institutions, including the Court of Justice, and that, on the other, the interpretation by the Court of Justice of a right recognised by the ECHR would not be binding on the control mechanisms provided for by the ECHR, particularly the ECtHR, as Article 3(6) of the draft agreement provides and as is stated in paragraph 68 of the draft explanatory report.

186. The same would not apply, however, with regard to the interpretation by the Court of Justice of EU law, including the Charter. In particular, it should not be possible for the ECtHR to call into question the Court's findings in relation to the scope *ratione materiae* of EU law, for the purposes, in particular, of determining whether a Member State is bound by fundamental rights of the EU.

The Court concluded that the planned arrangements cut across its understanding of the nature of EU law and so they were liable adversely to affect the specific characteristics of EU law and its autonomy.

It is therefore plain that assessing the quality of the Court's fidelity to fundamental rights is especially important because it claims a type of *exclusive* review of the compatibility of EU rules with such standards.

■ **QUESTION**

Is it desirable to establish a control over the Court of Justice by putting it in turn under the supervision of the European Court of Human Rights, as is envisaged by the Lisbon Treaty? How might the Court's objections in Opinion 2/13 be overcome?

■ **FURTHER READING**

The development of fundamental rights

Alston, P., (ed.), *The EU and Human Rights* (Oxford: OUP, 1999 – a collection of 28 essays).

Smismans, S., 'The European Union's Fundamental Rights Myth' (2010) 48 JCMS 45.

The Charter of Fundamental Rights (and beyond)

de Burca, G., 'After the EU Charter of Fundamental Rights: The Court of Justice as a Human Rights Adjudicator?' (2013) 20 MJ 168.

Douglas-Scott, S., 'The EU and Human Rights after the Treaty of Lisbon' (2011) 11 *Human Rights Law Review* 645.

Krisch, N., 'The Open Architecture of European Human Rights Law' (2008) 71 MLR 183.

Leczykiewicz, D., 'Horizontal Application of the Charter of Fundamental Rights' (2013) 38 EL Rev 479.

Sarmiento, D., 'Who's Afraid of the Charter? The Court of Justice, National Courts and the New Framework of Fundamental Rights Protection in Europe' (2013) 50 CML Rev 1267.

Schütze, R., 'Three Bills of Rights for the European Union' (2011) 30 YEL 131.

Opinion 2/13 (and beyond)

De Witte, B. and Imamović, S., 'Opinion 2/13 on Accession to the ECHR: Defending the EU Legal Order against a Foreign Human Rights Court' (2015) 40 ELRev 683.

Spaventa, E., 'A Very Fearful Court? The Protection of Fundamental Rights in the European Union after Opinion 2/13' 22 MJ 1 (2015) 35.

Special Section: Opinion 2/13 (2015) 16 German Law Journal Issue 1, 105–222.

C: Technique

The Court's technique in realizing the elaboration of the principles of Union law is of more general interest beyond the content of those principles. Article 340 TFEU, examined in Chapter 8, requires the Court to construct a principle of non-contractual liability, 'in accordance with the general principles common to the laws of the Member States'. It has become increasingly apparent that Article 340 is a statement of a broader principle of legal technique. The Court develops Union law by building from the foundations of national law. As the case law on proportionality and the fundamental rights case law shows, this is an incremental process. National law spills over into Union law and *vice versa*. The Union legal order is potentially broadened and replenished by the comparative approach. In 'European Public Law: Reality and Prospects' [1991] *Public Law* 53, at p. 58, T. Koopmans, a former judge of the Court, refers to general principles 'defined and developed at the Community level. . . [which] tend to extend their influence to the application of purely national law. They are discovered, by the Court of Justice, on the basis of the existing national legal systems, but they then "travel back" to these same systems with a kind of added force.' Our examination of fundamental rights shows that sources such as the European Convention on Human Rights are also heavily influential, even though organically independent of the Union structure. Moreover, the wider the scope of the Union's activities – and it has increasingly affected private law as well as public law – the richer this legal cross-fertilization becomes. Aspects of EU law can be understood as an exercise in applied comparative law: K. Lenaerts, 'Interlocking Legal Orders in the European Union and Comparative Law' (2003) 52 ICLQ 873.

It is notable that these principles are developed both in Article 263 judicial review actions and in Article 267 preliminary reference procedures. There is more than one context in which the Court of Justice is offered the opportunity to develop the Union's legal order.

In *The Community Legal Order*, J.-V. Louis points out that the Court, in shaping the principles of EU law, must 'determine the solution that appears most appropriate having regard to the requirements of the Community [now Union] legal order'. However, he warns that 'it may not... usurp the role of the Community [now Union] legislator if the deficiency could be filled by legislation . . . In applying the general principles common to the laws of the Member States it must exercise self-restraint' (pp. 98–9). Has it? The most notable proponent of the view that the Court lacks such due inhibition is H. Rasmussen. In *On Law and Policy in the ECJ*, he comments (at p. 508) that 'The Court of Justice's law making activities, defiant of much European tradition in that respect, were regularly preceded by deep involvements in making choices between competing public policies for which the available sources of law did not offer the Court judicially applicable guidelines.'

Rasmussen's more recent views may be explored in *European Court of Justice* (Copenhagen: Gadjura, 1998), although this is explicitly *not* designed as a 2nd edition of *On Law and Policy in the ECJ*.

'Judicial activism' is a phrase commonly, though troublingly imprecisely, used to describe the approach of the Court. There will be much more discussion of this issue later in the book, but do not expect the Court of Justice to follow the methods of an English court. Many of the Treaty obligations are loosely worded, which has given the Court great latitude in developing the shape of the law. It is expected to be creative in pursuit of broad general objectives in an overt manner unfamiliar to the English judiciary. Clearly, however, the relationship between the three sources of law considered in this chapter is not static. This book contains many examples of remarkably ambitious 'activist' decisions issued by the Court of Justice. Many, though by no means all, pre-date the entry into force of the Single European Act in 1987. That was the first major formal revision of the founding Treaties, the subject of examination in Section 1 of this chapter, but since then there were three further significant revisions (Maastricht, Amsterdam, and Nice) before the Lisbon reforms of 2009. Moreover, the nature and method of adoption of legislation, covered in Section 2 of this chapter, has been altered by those Treaties, *inter alia* by expanding the fields in which the EU is competent to legislate and, eventually, by establishing the 'ordinary legislative procedure' under Article 289 TFEU as the dominant legislative procedure. So the environment within which the Court develops general principles – Section 3 of this chapter – has changed, both because of the correspondingly broader application of those principles and the realization that today the Court takes its place as a lawmaker alongside a process of Treaty revision and legislation which is much more dynamic than it was in the first 30 years of the system's life cycle. Awareness of this changed institutional context is plain in the next case. It is chosen less for its substantive importance than for its value in putting the reader on notice that an enduring question, to be kept in mind in traversing the material contained in this book, is how far the Court *should* go in renovating the legal order. This is a question about the nature and legitimacy of legal reasoning and it is obviously not unique to the EU's constitutional order.

***Lisa Jacqueline Grant* v *South-West Trains Ltd* (Case C-249/96)**

[1998] ECR I-621, Court of Justice of the European Communities

The applicant, Ms Grant, had been denied travel benefits for her female partner by her employer, South-West Trains (SWT). SWT granted such benefits to an unmarried partner only if of the opposite sex to the employee. Discrimination based on sex was addressed explicitly by EC law at the time, but discrimination based on sexual orientation, of which Ms Grant had fallen victim, was not. The Court, in receipt of a preliminary reference made by an Industrial Tribunal in Southampton, was pressed to interpret the existing EC rules to accommodate a prohibition against discrimination based on sexual orientation. Two years earlier, in Case C-13/94 *P* v *S and Cornwall County Council* [1996] ECR I-2143, it had agreed that the principle of equality, which it treated as one of the fundamental principles of the legal order, favoured a broad interpretation of the scope of the provisions combating discrimination and it held them applicable to a case of discrimination based on the worker's gender reassignment. Ms Grant was not so fortunate before the Court.

[29] . . . the Court must consider whether, with respect to the application of a condition such as that in issue in the main proceedings, persons who have a stable relationship with a partner of the same sex are in the same situation as those who are married or have a stable relationship outside marriage with a partner of the opposite sex.

[30] Ms Grant submits in particular that the laws of the Member States, as well as those of the Community and other international organisations, increasingly treat the two situations as equivalent.

[31] While the European Parliament, as Ms Grant observes, has indeed declared that it deplores all forms of discrimination based on an individual's sexual orientation, it is nevertheless the case that the Community has not as yet adopted rules providing for such equivalence.

[32] As for the laws of the Member States, while in some of them cohabitation by two persons of the same sex is treated as equivalent to marriage, although not completely, in most of them it is treated as equivalent to a stable heterosexual relationship outside marriage only with respect to a limited number of rights, or else is not recognised in any particular way.

[33] The European Commission of Human Rights for its part considers that despite the modern evolution of attitudes towards homosexuality, stable homosexual relationships do not fall within the scope of the right to respect for family life under Article 8 of the Convention (see in particular the decisions in application No 9369/81, *X. and Y.* v *the United Kingdom*, 3 May 1983, *Decisions and Reports* 32, p. 220; application No 11716/85, *S.* v *the United Kingdom*, 14 May 1986, D.R. 47, p. 274, paragraph 2; and application No 15666/89, *Kerkhoven and Hinke* v *the Netherlands*, 19 May 1992, unpublished, paragraph 1), and that national provisions which, for the purpose of protecting the family, accord more favourable treatment to married persons and persons of opposite sex living together as man and wife than to persons of the same sex in a stable relationship are not contrary to Article 14 of the Convention, which prohibits *inter alia* discrimination on the ground of sex (see the decisions in *S.* v *the United Kingdom*, paragraph 7; application No 14753/89, *C. and L.M.* v *the United Kingdom*, 9 October 1989, unpublished, paragraph 2; and application No 16106/90, *B.* v *the United Kingdom*, 10 February 1990, D.R. 64, p. 278, paragraph 2).

[34] In another context, the European Court of Human Rights has interpreted Article 12 of the Convention as applying only to the traditional marriage between two persons of opposite biological sex (see the *Rees* judgment of 17 October 1986, Series A no. 106, p. 19, § 49, and the *Cossey* judgment of 27 September 1990, Series A no. 184, p. 17, § 43).

[35] It follows that, in the present state of the law within the Community, stable relationships between two persons of the same sex are not regarded as equivalent to marriages or stable relationships outside marriage between persons of opposite sex. Consequently, an employer is not required by Community law to treat the situation of a person who has a stable relationship with a partner of the same sex as equivalent to that of a person who is married to or has a stable relationship outside marriage with a partner of the opposite sex.

[36] In those circumstances, it is for the legislature alone to adopt, if appropriate, measures which may affect that position.

[37] Finally, Ms Grant submits that it follows from *P* v *S* that differences of treatment based on sexual orientation are included in the 'discrimination based on sex' prohibited by Article 119 of the Treaty.

[38] In *P* v *S* the Court was asked whether a dismissal based on the change of sex of the worker concerned was to be regarded as 'discrimination on grounds of sex' within the meaning of Directive 76/207.

[39] The national court was uncertain whether the scope of that directive was wider than that of the Sex Discrimination Act 1975, which it had to apply and which in its view applied only to discrimination based on the worker's belonging to one or other of the sexes.

[40] In their observations to the Court the United Kingdom Government and the Commission submitted that the directive prohibited only discrimination based on the fact that the worker concerned belonged to one sex or the other, not discrimination based on the worker's gender reassignment.

[41] In reply to that argument, the Court stated that the provisions of the directive prohibiting discrimination between men and women were simply the expression, in their limited field of application, of the principle of equality, which is one of the fundamental principles of Community law. It considered that that circumstance argued against a restrictive interpretation of the scope of those provisions and in favour of applying them to discrimination based on the worker's gender reassignment.

[42] The Court considered that such discrimination was in fact based, essentially if not exclusively, on the sex of the person concerned. That reasoning, which leads to the conclusion that such discrimination is to be prohibited just as is discrimination based on the fact that a person belongs to a particular sex, is limited to the case of a worker's gender reassignment and does not therefore apply to differences of treatment based on a person's sexual orientation.

[43] Ms Grant submits, however, that, like certain provisions of national law or of international conventions, the Community provisions on equal treatment of men and women should be interpreted as covering discrimination based on sexual orientation. She refers in particular to the International Covenant on Civil and Political Rights of 19 December 1966 (*United Nations Treaty Series*, Vol. 999, p. 171), in which, in the view of the Human Rights Committee established under Article 28 of the Covenant, the term 'sex' is to be taken as including sexual orientation (communication No 488/1992, *Toonen* v *Australia*, views adopted on 31 March 1994, 50th session, point 8.7).

[44] The Covenant is one of the international instruments relating to the protection of human rights of which the Court takes account in applying the fundamental principles of Community law (see, for example, Case 374/87 *Orkem* v *Commission* [1989] ECR 3283, paragraph 31, and Joined Cases C-297/88 and C-197/89 *Dzodzi* v *Belgian State* [1990] ECR I-3763, paragraph 68).

[45] However, although respect for the fundamental rights which form an integral part of those general principles of law is a condition of the legality of Community acts, those rights cannot in themselves have the effect of extending the scope of the Treaty provisions beyond the competences of the Community (see, *inter alia*, on the scope of Article 235 of the EC Treaty as regards respect for human rights, Opinion 2/94 [1996] ECR I-1759, paragraphs 34 and 35).

[46] Furthermore, in the communication referred to by Ms Grant, the Human Rights Committee, which is not a judicial institution and whose findings have no binding force in law, confined itself, as it stated itself without giving specific reasons, to 'noting... that in its view the reference to "sex" in Articles 2, paragraph 1, and 26 is to be taken as including sexual orientation'.

[47] Such an observation, which does not in any event appear to reflect the interpretation so far generally accepted of the concept of discrimination based on sex which appears in various international instruments concerning the protection of fundamental rights, cannot in any case constitute a basis for the Court to extend the scope of Article 119 of the Treaty. That being so, the scope of that article, as of any provision of Community law, is to be determined only by having regard to its wording and purpose, its place in the scheme of the Treaty and its legal context. It follows from the considerations set out above that Community law as it stands at present does not cover discrimination based on sexual orientation, such as that in issue in the main proceedings.

[48] It should be observed, however, that the Treaty of Amsterdam amending the Treaty on European Union, the Treaties establishing the European Communities and certain related acts, signed on 2 October 1997, provides for the insertion in the EC Treaty of an Article 6a which, once the Treaty of Amsterdam has entered into force, will allow the Council under certain conditions (a unanimous vote on a proposal from the Commission after consulting the European Parliament) to take appropriate action to eliminate various forms of discrimination, including discrimination based on sexual orientation.

NOTE: Notice that the Court refers to a number of sources of law that lie outwith the formal bounds of the EU legal order. This resembles the approach taken in the fundamental rights cases. But in *Grant* the Court places limits on the porous nature of the legal order. 'The principle of equality, which is one of the fundamental principles of Community law' (para 41) cannot help the applicant, for the Court is unprepared to interpret the existing law in a manner that brings the discriminatory conduct within the ambit of EU law's protection. It is striking that the Treaty provision authorizing legislation to which the Court refers in the concluding paragraph was at the time of the judgment not even in force. It is now. Legislation designed to provide a basis for attacking *inter alia* discrimination based on sexual orientation in employment has now been adopted: see Directive 2000/78 [2000] OJ L303/16. And the relevant legal base since the entry into force of the Lisbon Treaty is Article 19 TFEU. But even this by no means exhausts the debate about how far the EU reaches in establishing legal rules governing equality – and how far the Court should propel it. In Case C-144/04 *Mangold* [2005] ECR I-9981 the Court identified the principle of non-discrimination on grounds of age as a general principle of EU law. Categorizing the principle in this way enabled the applicant to evade limits on the application of unimplemented Directives, *in casu* Directive 2000/78, before national courts (examined more fully in Chapter 5). Subsequently, in Case C-13/05 *Sonia Chacon Navas* [2006] ECR I-6467 the Court delivered a ruling more reminiscent of *Grant*. It ruled that discrimination on grounds of sickness is covered by neither Article 13 EC, predecessor to Article 19 TFEU, nor Directive 2000/78. There is no reference in the judgment to *Mangold* at all, while in his Opinion Advocate General Geelhoed warns that an ever broader reading of equality law cuts deeply into the powers left in the hands of the Member States under the Treaty. Subsequently Advocate General Sharpston agreed that there is a general EU law principle of non-discrimination on grounds of age, observing that principles 'evolve with society' (para 46), but carefully outlined the limits of its application under the Treaty, whereas the Court kept its ruling unhelpfully brief, simply observing the fact pattern to be different from that arising in *Mangold* (Case C-427/06 *Bartsch* [2008] ECR I-7245). Then, in cautious vein, the Court in Case C-354/13 *Fag og Arbejde* judgment of 18 December 2014 decided there is no general principle of EU law forbidding discrimination on the basis of obesity (albeit that obesity may count as a disability within the meaning of Directive 2000/78).

The *detailed* development of EU equality law is at stake in these cases. But so too is the *general* question of judicial technique and, in particular, the division of function between the Court and the legislature, both of which are bound by Article 5 TEU's principle of conferral, met at p. 29 and mentioned by implication in para 45 of the *Grant* judgment. In the background stands the power of the Member States to revise the scope of the Treaty, which is itself a reason for cautioning restraint practised by the institutions operating *within* the EU Treaty system.

■ QUESTIONS

1. It is striking that both proportionality and fundamental rights were first developed as legal principles by the Court, and only later embraced within the body of the Treaty. To what extent does the rise of regular Treaty revision dampen the likelihood of future judicial willingness to elaborate principles of law that exert control over the exercise of legislative and administrative discretion? Is the Charter of Fundamental Rights properly seen as an inhibition on future improvements rather than as a new stage in the process of rights protection?
2. In the light of your knowledge of techniques of judicial reasoning in the EU and more generally, do you think the Court's deferral to other forms of law making (paras 36, 48 of the *Grant* judgment) is justified? How does one measure 'justification'?

NOTE: The Court contends that the 'Treaty, albeit concluded in the form of an international agreement, nonetheless constitutes the constitutional charter of a Community based on the rule of law' (Opinion 1/91 [1991] ECR I-6079). Beyond Treaty sources and secondary legislation, there are general principles which permeate the fabric of the law. The EU offers both a Constitution for economic integration and a Constitution for the protection of the individual. This twin purpose of EU law will be observed in many manifestations throughout this book. And in fact tracing this process of 'constitutionalization' of what began as, and in formal terms still is, a legal order founded on an international Treaty holds the key to understanding the remarkable evolution of the EU legal order. Moreover, it raises fascinating yet deeply sensitive questions about how sustainable the Court's vision of the nature of the legal order over which it presides truly is. The Court's 'constitutionalization' of the Treaty has attracted increasing attention as one part of a broader inquiry into the nature of the Union and its impact on the constitutional structures of the Member States. These are matters to which to return. We shall do so at several places in Part One of this book, including at the very end of Part One (p. 230), and then, more broadly, in Chapter 19, when attention will be focused on what it may mean to advance the case for a formal 'Constitution' for the European Union. This allows the book to connect Chapter 1's introductory descriptions of the pattern of Treaty revision with Chapter 19's investigation of the normative claims associated with EU Constitution-making.

FURTHER READING

Adams, A., de Waele, H., Meeusen, J., and Straetmans, G. (eds), *Judging Europe's Judges: The Legitimacy of the Case Law of the European Court of Justice* (Oxford: Hart, 2013).

Bengoetxea, J., MacCormick, N., and Moral Soriano, I., 'Integration and Integrity in the Legal Reasoning of the European Court of Justice', Ch. 3 in de Búrca, G. and Weiler, J.H.H., *The European Court of Justice* (Oxford: OUP, 2001).

Bengoetxea, J., 'Text and Telos in the European Court of Justice' (2015) 11 Euro Const Law Rev 184.

Besselink, L., Pennings, F., and Prechal, S., *The Eclipse of the Legality Principle in the European Union* (Alphen aan den Rijn: Wolters Kluwer, 2011).

Mestmäcker, E.-J., 'On the Legitimacy of European Law' (1994) 58 Rabels Z 615.

Micklitz, H.-W. and de Witte, B. (eds), *The European Court of Justice and the Autonomy of the Member States* (Antwerp: Intersentia, 2012).

Weiler, J., 'The Transformation of Europe' (1991) 100 Yale LJ 2403.

Wilhelmsson, T., 'Jack-in-the-Box Theory of European Community Law', in Krämer, L., *et al.* (eds), *Law and Diffuse Interests in the European Legal Order* (Baden-Baden: Nomos, 1997), p. 177.

NOTE: For additional material and resources see the Online Resource Centre at: www.oxfordtextbooks.co.uk/orc/weatherill12e.

3

The Nature of Union Law: Supremacy

The Court's development of the key notions of *supremacy* and of *direct effect* represents a classic exercise of the teleological interpretative function favoured by the Court. Nowhere in the body of the Treaty is it possible to find an explicit commitment to the idea that Union law shall be supreme, nor to the notion that it shall be directly effective. Yet the Court has deduced the existence of both these fundamental principles from the *object* of the Treaty. It would be impossible to create the structure envisaged by the Treaties *unless* the law is supreme and directly effective. So, reasoned the Court, the Treaty impliedly contains the principles of supremacy and direct effect. This chapter examines supremacy and its consequences; the next chapter studies direct effect.

SECTION 1: SUPREMACY

The case of *Costa* v *ENEL* (Case 6/64) provided the Court with one of its earliest opportunities to explain the nature of the legal order established by the Treaty of Rome. (Naturally, the references to Treaty Articles use the 'old', i.e., pre-Amsterdam, numbering – see p. 10.)

Costa v *ENEL* (Case 6/64)

[1964] ECR 585, Court of Justice of the European Communities

By contrast with ordinary international treaties, the EEC Treaty has created its own legal system which, on the entry into force of the Treaty, became an integral part of the legal systems of the Member States and which their courts are bound to apply.

By creating a Community of unlimited duration, having its own institutions, its own personality, its own legal capacity and capacity of representation on the international plane and, more particularly, real powers stemming from a limitation of sovereignty or a transfer of powers from the States to the Community, the Member States have limited their sovereign rights, albeit within limited fields, and have thus created a body of law which binds both their nationals and themselves.

The integration into the laws of each Member State of provisions which derive from the Community, and more generally the terms and the spirit of the Treaty, make it impossible for the States, as a corollary, to accord precedence to a unilateral and subsequent measure over a legal system accepted by them on a basis of reciprocity. Such a measure cannot therefore be inconsistent with that legal system. The executive force of Community law cannot vary from one State to another in deference to subsequent domestic laws, without jeopardizing the attainment of the objectives of the Treaty set out in Article 5(2) and giving rise to the discrimination prohibited by Article 7.

The obligations undertaken under the Treaty establishing the Community would not be unconditional, but merely contingent, if they could be called in question by subsequent legislative acts of the signatories. Wherever the Treaty grants the States the right to act unilaterally, it does this by clear and precise provisions (for example, Articles 15, 93(3), 223, 224 and 225). Applications, by Member States for authority to derogate from the Treaty are subject to a special authorization procedure (for example, Articles 8(4), 17(4), 25, 26, 73, the third subparagraph of

Article 93(2), and 226) which would lose their purpose if the Member States could renounce their obligations by means of an ordinary law.

The precedence of Community law is confirmed by Article 189, whereby a regulation 'shall be binding' and 'directly applicable in all Member States'. This provision, which is subject to no reservation, would be quite meaningless if a State could unilaterally nullify its effects by means of a legislative measure which could prevail over Community law.

It follows from all these observations that the law stemming from the Treaty, an independent source of law, could not, because of its special and original nature, be overridden by domestic legal provisions, however framed, without being deprived of its character as Community law and without the legal basis of the Community itself being called into question.

The transfer by the States from their domestic legal system to the Community legal system of the rights and obligations arising under the Treaty carries with it a permanent limitation of their sovereign rights, against which a subsequent unilateral act incompatible with the concept of the Community cannot prevail . . .

In paragraph 14 of Case 44/79 *Hauer*, met at p. 56 in Chapter 2, the Court cited its own ruling in Case 11/70 *Internationale Handelsgesellschaft* [1970] ECR 1125, in which it applied the logic of supremacy to claim that EU law must prevail over even national *constitutional* law in order to protect the unity and efficacy of EC law. Lately, in a ruling dealing with EU law since the entry into force of the Lisbon Treaty, it confirmed that hierarchy decisively.

Stefano Melloni (Case C-399/11)

Judgment of 26 February 2013, Court of Justice of the EU

The Court was asked whether a national court could maintain stricter standards of protection guaranteed by its national (Spanish) constitution than those envisaged by Framework Decision 2002/584 on the European arrest warrant. This was pertinent because Article 53 of the Charter on Fundamental Rights, granted binding status by the Lisbon Treaty with effect from 2009 (p. 59), states that nothing in the Charter shall be interpreted as restricting human rights and fundamental freedoms recognized by Union law, international law, and by the Member States' constitutions. But the Court swatted aside this apparent attack on its long-standing assumptions of EU law's supremacy (or 'primacy').

[56] The interpretation envisaged by the national court at the outset is that Article 53 of the Charter gives general authorisation to a Member State to apply the standard of protection of fundamental rights guaranteed by its constitution when that standard is higher than that deriving from the Charter and, where necessary, to give it priority over the application of provisions of EU law. Such an interpretation would, in particular, allow a Member State to make the execution of a European arrest warrant issued for the purposes of executing a sentence rendered *in absentia* subject to conditions intended to avoid an interpretation which restricts or adversely affects fundamental rights recognised by its constitution, even though the application of such conditions is not allowed under Article 4a(1) of Framework Decision 2002/584.

[57] Such an interpretation of Article 53 of the Charter cannot be accepted.

[58] That interpretation of Article 53 of the Charter would undermine the principle of the primacy of EU law inasmuch as it would allow a Member State to disapply EU legal rules which are fully in compliance with the Charter where they infringe the fundamental rights guaranteed by that State's constitution.

[59] It is settled case-law that, by virtue of the principle of primacy of EU law, which is an essential feature of the EU legal order (see Opinion 1/91 [1991] ECR I-6079, paragraph 21, and Opinion 1/09 [2011] ECR I-1137, paragraph 65), rules of national law, even of a constitutional order, cannot be allowed to undermine the effectiveness of EU law on the territory of that State (see, to that effect, inter alia, Case 11/70 *Internationale Handelsgesellschaft* [1970] ECR 1125, paragraph 3, and Case C-409/06 *Winner Wetten* [2010] ECR I-8015, paragraph 61).

[60] It is true that Article 53 of the Charter confirms that, where an EU legal act calls for national implementing measures, national authorities and courts remain free to apply national standards of protection of fundamental rights, provided that the level of protection provided for by the Charter, as interpreted by the Court, and the primacy, unity and effectiveness of EU law are not thereby compromised.

Scrutiny according to stricter national standards was excluded and, after inspection, the measure was found to comply with EU fundamental rights.

In reflecting on EU law's supremacy, the cases dealing with fundamental rights in Chapter 2 should be recalled. It was precisely the aspiration to supremacy that led to concern at national level about respect for fundamental rights at EU level. That, in turn, motivated the Court to develop the content of what was then EC law to meet such concerns. So was built the legal order established by the Treaties. It remains a developing project. As emphasized in Chapter 2, the Charter is now in the forefront, and accordingly the Court's interpretation of the Charter is significant in determining both the pattern of EU fundamental rights protection and the national reaction to supremacy (which will be considered more fully in Chapter 19). The point in *Melloni* is that in order to protect the 'unity and effectiveness of EU law' the EU's protection of fundamental rights is a ceiling – Member States may not go higher.

NOTE: In the next case the Court made plain its view of the implications of (what was then) EC law before national courts asked to rule on a conflict between EC law and domestic law.

***Amministrazione delle Finanze* v *Simmenthal* (Case 106/77)**

[1978] ECR 629, Court of Justice of the European Communities

[14] ... [R]ules of Community law must be fully and uniformly applied in all the Member States from the date of their entry into force and for so long as they continue in force.

[15] These provisions are therefore a direct source of rights and duties for all those affected thereby, whether Member States or individuals, who are parties to legal relationships under Community law.

[16] This consequence also concerns any national court whose task it is as an organ of a Member State to protect, in a case within its jurisdiction, the rights conferred upon individuals by Community law.

[17] Furthermore, in accordance with the principle of the precedence of Community law, the relationship between provisions of the Treaty and directly applicable measures of the institutions on the one hand and the national law of the Member States on the other is such that those provisions and measures not only by their entry into force render automatically inapplicable any conflicting provision of current national law but – in so far as they are an integral part of, and take precedence in, the legal order applicable in the territory of each of the Member States – also preclude the valid adoption of new national legislative measures to the extent to which they would be incompatible with Community provisions.

[18] Indeed any recognition that national legislative measures which encroach upon the field within which the Community exercises its legislative power or which are otherwise incompatible with the provisions of Community law had any legal effect would amount to a corresponding denial of the effectiveness of obligations undertaken unconditionally and irrevocably by Member States pursuant to the Treaty and would thus imperil the very foundations of the Community.

[19] The same conclusion emerges from the structure of Article 177 of the Treaty which provides that any court or tribunal of a Member State is entitled to make a reference to the Court whenever it considers that a preliminary ruling on a question of interpretation or validity relating to Community law is necessary to enable it to give judgment.

[20] The effectiveness of that provision would be impaired if the national court were prevented from forthwith applying Community law in accordance with the decision or the case law of the Court.

[21] It follows from the foregoing that every national court must, in a case within its jurisdiction, apply Community law in its entirety and protect rights which the latter confers on individuals and must accordingly set aside any provision of national law which may conflict with it, whether prior or subsequent to the Community rule.

[22] Accordingly any provision of a national legal system and any legislative, administrative or judicial practice which might impair the effectiveness of Community law by withholding from the national court having jurisdiction to apply such law the power to do everything necessary at the moment of its application to set aside national legislative provisions which might prevent Community rules from having full force and effect are incompatible with those requirements which are the very essence of Community law.

[23] This would be the case in the event of a conflict between a provision of Community law and a subsequent national law if the solution of the conflict were to be reserved for an authority with a discretion of its own, other than the court called upon to apply Community law, even if such an impediment to the full effectiveness of Community law were only temporary.

[24] The first question should therefore be answered to the effect that a national court which is called upon, within the limits of its jurisdiction, to apply provisions of Community law is under a duty to give full effect to those provisions, if necessary refusing of its own motion to apply any conflicting provision of national legislation, even if adopted subsequently, and it is not necessary for the court to request or await the prior setting aside of such provision by legislative or other constitutional means.

[25] The essential point of the *second question* is whether – assuming it to be accepted that the protection of rights conferred by provisions of Community law can be suspended until any national provisions which might conflict with them have been in fact set aside by the competent national authorities – such setting aside must in every case have unrestricted retroactive effect so as to prevent the rights in question from being in any way adversely affected.

[26] It follows from the answer to the first question that national courts must protect rights conferred by provisions of the Community legal order and that it is not necessary for such courts to request or await the actual setting aside by the national authorities empowered so to act of any national measures which might impede the direct and immediate application of Community rules.

[27] The second question therefore appears to have no purpose.

The Court's ruling in response to the questions referred was:

A national court which is called upon, within the limits of its jurisdiction, to apply provisions of Community law is under a duty to give full effect to those provisions, if necessary refusing of its own motion to apply any conflicting provision of national legislation, even if adopted subsequently, and it is not necessary for the court to request or await the prior setting aside of such provisions by legislative or other constitutional means.

In the next case the Court returned to the duties of national courts called upon to deal with national law that is inconsistent with EU law.

Ministero delle Finanze v *IN.CO.GE'90 Srl and others* (Joined Cases C-10/97 to C-22/97)

[1998] ECR I-6307, Court of Justice of the European Communities

[20] In *Simmenthal*, the issue facing the Court related in particular to the consequences of the direct applicability of a provision of Community law where that provision was incompatible with a subsequently adopted provision of national law. The Court had already stressed, in its previous decisions (see, in particular, Case 6/64 *Costa* v *ENEL* [1964] ECR 585), that it was impossible for a Member State to accord precedence to a national rule over a conflicting rule of Community law, but did not draw any distinction between pre-existing and subsequently adopted national law. So, in *Simmenthal*, the Court held that every national court must, in a case within its jurisdiction, apply Community law in its entirety and protect rights which the latter confers on individuals, setting aside any provision of national law which may conflict with it, whether prior or subsequent to the Community rule (*Simmenthal*, paragraphs 21 and 24). That case-law has been reaffirmed on numerous occasions (see, in particular, *Debus*, cited above [Joined Cases C-13/91 & C-113/91], paragraph 32; Case C-158/91 *Levy* [1993] ECRI-4287, paragraph 9; and Case C-347/96 *Solred* v *Administración General del Estado* [1998] ECR I-937, paragraph 30).

[21] It cannot therefore, contrary to the Commission's contention, be inferred from the judgment in *Simmenthal* that the incompatibility with Community law of a subsequently adopted rule of national law has the effect of rendering that rule of national law non-existent. Faced with such a situation, the national court is, however, obliged to disapply that rule, provided always that this obligation does not restrict the power of the competent national courts to apply, from among the various procedures available under national law, those which are appropriate for protecting the individual rights conferred by Community law (see Case 34/67 *Lück v Hauptzollamt Köln-Rheinau* [1968] ECR 245).

NOTE: In similar vein on the job of national courts see Case C-314/08 *KrzysztofFilipczak* [2009] ECRI-11049; Case C-409/06 *Winner Wetten GmbH* [2010] ECR I-8015.

The Treaty establishing a Constitution for Europe would have brought the principle of supremacy within the text of the Treaty for the first time, albeit using the term 'primacy' instead of supremacy.

ARTICLE I-6 OF THE TREATY ESTABLISHING A CONSTITUTION, UNION LAW

The Constitution and law adopted by the institutions of the Union in exercising competences conferred on it shall have primacy over the law of the Member States.

But the Treaty establishing a Constitution failed (p. 18). The Lisbon Treaty rejects this step. In line with its general intent to soften the constitutional force and profile of the reforms made when compared with the rejected Treaty establishing a Constitution, Lisbon merely adds a Declaration – an instrument which lacks binding legal force – which recalls the Court's case law on supremacy (or primacy). Attached as an annex to the Declaration is an opinion of the Council Legal Service on primacy, stating that:

The fact that the principle of primacy will not be included in the future treaty shall not in any way change the existence of the principle and the existing case-law of the Court of Justice.

The basic amendments of the Lisbon Treaty mean that it is now EU law, not simply EC law, which is supreme.

■ QUESTION

Would the Treaty establishing a Constitution have changed anything? Does the Lisbon Treaty change anything? Should anything be changed? You might return to these questions later, after reading Chapter 19, when the attitude of national courts to the European Court's depiction of the supreme nature of the legal order established by the Treaty will be tracked.

The next case examines the scope of the obligation on Member States to ensure that the influence of EU law, which is supreme, is not obstructed. (Once again, it should be borne in mind that the vintage of the case means that pre-Amsterdam Treaty numbering is used.)

Commission v *France* (Case 167/73)

[1974] ECR 359, Court of Justice of the European Communities

The French *Code du Travail Maritime* required the crew of merchant ships to comprise at least three French for every non-French sailor. This is in principle unlawful discrimination on grounds of nationality, forbidden by EU law. However, the French authorities were prepared in practice to allow nationals of other Member States to count as French for these purposes. It was argued that because it was proper to focus on the application of the law in practice, not its terms in the abstract, France had not violated the Treaty.

[41] ... [A]lthough the objective legal position is clear, namely, that Article 48 and Regulation No 1612/68 are directly applicable in the territory of the French Republic, nevertheless the maintenance in these circumstances of the wording of the Code du Travail Maritime gives rise to an ambiguous State of affairs by maintaining, as regards those subject to the law who are concerned, a State of uncertainty as to the possibilities available to them of relying on Community law.

[42] This uncertainty can only be reinforced by the internal and verbal character of the purely administrative directions to waive the application of the national law.

[43] The free movement of persons, and in particular workers, constitutes, as appears both from Article 3(c) of the Treaty and from the place of Articles 48 to 51 in Part Two of the Treaty, one of the foundations of the Community.

[44] According to Article 48(2) it entails the abolition of any discrimination based on nationality, whatever be its nature or extent, between workers of the Member States as regards employment, remuneration and other conditions of work and employment.

[45] The absolute nature of this prohibition, moreover, has the effect of not only allowing in each State equal access to employment to the nationals of other Member States, but also, in accordance with the aim of Article 177 of the Treaty, of guaranteeing to the State's own nationals that they shall not suffer the unfavourable consequences which could result from the offer or acceptance by nationals of other Member States of conditions of employment or remuneration less advantageous than those obtaining under national law, since such acceptance is prohibited.

[46] It thus follows from the general character of the prohibition on discrimination in Article 48 and the objective pursued by the abolition of discrimination that discrimination is prohibited even if it constitutes only an obstacle of secondary importance as regards the equality of access to employment and other conditions of work and employment.

[47] The uncertainty created by the maintenance unamended of the wording of Article 3 of the Code du Travail Maritime constitutes such an obstacle.

[48] It follows that in maintaining unamended, in these circumstances, the provisions of Article 3(2) of the Code du Travail Maritime as regards the nationals of other Member States, the French Republic has failed to fulfil its obligations under Article 48 of the Treaty and Article 4 of Regulation No 1612/68 of the Council of 15 October 1968.

SECTION 2: DIRECT APPLICABILITY

The attribute of *direct applicability,* referred to in *Simmenthal* (Case 106/77) at p. 75, is linked to the doctrine of supremacy. Article 288 TFEU declares Regulations to be directly applicable in the national legal order. This means that they are automatically law in all the Member States when made under the EU legislative procedure. In principle it is not open to Member States to interfere with the direct application of the Regulation in the national legal order. Only exceptionally will a Regulation require implementation at national level.

Variola v *Amministrazione delle Finanze* (Case 34/73)

[1973] ECR 981, Court of Justice of the European Communities

[9] In the fourth and fifth questions, the Court is, in effect, asked to determine whether the disputed provisions of the Regulations can be introduced into the legal order of Member States by internal measures reproducing the contents of Community provisions in such a way that the subject-matter is brought under national law, and the jurisdiction of the Court is thereby affected.

[10] The direct application of a Regulation means that its entry unto force and its application in favour of or against those subject to it are independent of any measure of reception into national law.

By virtue of the obligations arising from the Treaty and assumed on ratification, Member States are under a duty not to obstruct the direct applicability inherent in Regulations and other rules of Community law.

Strict compliance with this obligation is an indispensable condition of simultaneous and uniform application of Community Regulations throughout the Community.

[11] More particularly, Member States are under an obligation not to introduce any measure which might affect the jurisdiction of the Court to pronounce on any question involving the interpretation of Community law or the validity of an act of the institutions of the Community, which means that no procedure is permissible whereby the Community nature of a legal rule is concealed from those subject to it.

Under Article 177 of the Treaty in particular, the jurisdiction of the Court is unaffected by any provisions of national legislation which purport to convert a rule of Community law into national law.

...

[15] A legislative provision of internal law could not be set up against the direct effect, in the legal order of Member States, of Regulations of the Community and other provisions of Community law, including the prohibition, under Articles 9 *et seq.* of the Treaty, of charges having equivalent effect to customs duties, without compromising the essential character of Community rules as such and the fundamental principle that the Community legal system is supreme.

This is particularly true as regards the date from which the Community rule becomes operative and creates rights in favour of private parties.

The freedom of each Member State to vary, in relation to itself and without express authority, the date on which a Community rule comes into force is excluded by reason of the need to ensure uniform and simultaneous application of Community law throughout the Community.

SECTION 3: EXCLUSIVITY AND PRE-EMPTION

A further aspect of the nature of the Union legal order is that in some fields the competence of the Union is exclusive. In order to maintain integrity and uniformity in the application of the legal order, Member States are held to have lost the power to act independently in particular areas.

As set out in Chapter 2, p. 30, Article 2(1) TFEU provides that:

When the Treaties confer on the Union exclusive competence in a specific area, only the Union may legislate and adopt legally binding acts, the Member States being able to do so themselves only if so empowered by the Union or for the implementation of Union acts.

NOTE: Article 3(1) TFEU (p. 30) lists as areas in which the Union enjoys exclusive competence: customs union, the establishing of the competition rules necessary for the functioning of the internal market, monetary policy for the Member States whose currency is the euro, the conservation of marine biological resources under the common fisheries policy and common commercial policy. The Union also has exclusive competence pursuant to Article 3(2) TFEU for the conclusion of an international agreement when its conclusion is provided for in a legislative act of the Union or is necessary to enable the Union to exercise its internal competence, or insofar as its conclusion may affect common rules or alter their scope.

This list is an innovation of the Lisbon Treaty but it is based on the case law of the Court which has been speaking the language of exclusive competence for many years.

Commission v *Council* (Case 22/70) was examined in Chapter 2 as an instance of an act, a Council Resolution, falling outside the list in Article 189 of the EC Treaty (now Article 288 TFEU), which was held nevertheless to have legal effects. Of interest here is exactly what that act related to – its substance.

Commission v *Council* (Case 22/70)

[1971] ECR 263, Court of Justice of the European Communities

The Resolution adopted by the States relating to negotiation of the European Road Transport Agreement (the common acronym 'AETR' reflects the French version of this name) was based on the assumption that it was for the Member States to participate independently in the conclusion of the Agreement. The ostensible purpose of the Commission's challenge was to show that it was for the Community to participate, and that it had replaced the Member States as the competent actor in the field. The Court embarked on a close examination of the Treaty in order to determine the correct allocation of competence.

[12] In the absence of specific provisions of the Treaty relating to the negotiation and conclusion of international agreements in the sphere of transport policy – a category into which, essentially, the AETR falls – one must turn to the general system of Community law in the sphere of relations with third countries.

[13] Article 210 provides that 'The Community shall have legal personality'.

[14] This provision, placed at the head of Part Six of the Treaty, devoted to 'General and Final Provisions', means that in its external relations the Community enjoys the capacity to establish contractual links with third countries over the whole field of objectives defined in Part One of the Treaty, which Part Six supplements.

[15] To determine in a particular case the Community's authority to enter into international agreements, regard must be had to the whole scheme of the Treaty no less than to its substantive provisions.

[16] Such authority arises not only from an express conferment by the Treaty – as is the case with Articles 113 and 114 for tariff and trade agreements and with Article 238 for association agreements – but may equally flow from other provisions of the Treaty and from measures adopted, within the framework of those provisions, by the Community institutions.

[17] In particular, each time the Community, with a view to implementing a common policy envisaged by the Treaty, adopts provisions laying down common rules, whatever form these may take, the Member States no longer have the right, acting individually or even collectively, to undertake obligations with third countries which affect those rules.

[18] As and when such common rules come into being, the Community alone is in a position to assume and carry out contractual obligations towards third countries affecting the whole sphere of application of the Community legal system.

[19] With regard to the implementation of the provisions of the Treaty the system of internal Community measures may not therefore be separated from that of external relations.

[20] Under Article 3(e), the adoption of a common policy in the sphere of transport is specially mentioned amongst the objectives of the Community.

[21] Under Article 5, the Member States are required on the one hand to take all appropriate measures to ensure fulfilment of the obligations arising out of the Treaty or resulting from action taken by the institutions and, on the other hand, to abstain from any measure which might jeopardize the attainment of the objectives of the Treaty.

[22] If these two provisions are read in conjunction, it follows that to the extent to which Community rules are promulgated for the attainment of the objectives of the Treaty, the Member States cannot, outside the framework of the Community institutions, assume obligations which might affect those rules or alter their scope.

[23] According to Article 74, the objectives of the Treaty in matters of transport are to be pursued within the framework of a common policy.

[24] With this in view, Article 75(1) directs the Council to lay down common rules and, in addition, 'any other appropriate provisions'.

[25] By the terms of subparagraph (a) of the same provision, those common rules are applicable 'to international transport to or from the territory of a Member State or passing across the territory of one or more Member States'.

[26] This provision is equally concerned with transport from or to third countries, as regards that part of the journey which takes place on Community territory.

[27] It thus assumes that the powers of the Community extend to relationships arising from international law, and hence involve the need in the sphere in question for agreements with the third countries concerned.

[28] Although it is true that Articles 74 and 75 do not expressly confer on the Community authority to enter into international agreements, nevertheless the bringing into force, on 25 March 1969, of Regulation No 543/69 of the Council on the harmonization of certain social legislation relating to road transport (OJ L 77, p. 49) necessarily vested in the Community power to enter into any agreements with third countries relating to the subject-matter governed by that regulation.

[29] This grant of power is moreover expressly recognized by Article 3 of the said regulation which prescribes that: 'The Community shall enter into any negotiations with third countries which may prove necessary for the purpose of implementing this regulation'.

[30] Since the subject-matter of the AETR falls within the scope of Regulation No 543/69, the Community has been empowered to negotiate and conclude the agreement in question since the entry into force of the said regulation.

[31] These Community powers exclude the possibility of concurrent powers on the part of Member States, since any steps taken outside the framework of the Community institutions would be incompatible with the unity of the Common Market and the uniform application of Community law.

NOTES

1. It is clearly apparent from the final paragraph of this extract that the ruling is based on the nature of the legal order established by the Treaty. However, despite this ruling in principle in favour of the Community (as it then was) at the expense of the Member States acting independently, the Commission's application was rejected on the facts. Given the long history of negotiations on the Agreement, the Community had not yet fully assumed competence in this particular matter. The resolution was not invalid.
2. See also *Kramer* (Case 3/76) [1976] ECR 1279, in which the Court was still firmer in its insistence on pre-emption. Some of these issues have already been explored in part in Chapter 2. A more recent significant ruling on the allocation of competences between Community (as it then was) and Member States in external relations is Opinion 1/94 [1994] ECR I-5267. The Court found that some aspects of the World Trade Organization Agreement fell within the EC's exclusive competence, while others fell outside the scope of exclusive competence. The case law was duly revisited in the context of external competence in the air transport sector in a group of cases decided by the Court on 5 November 2002: Case C-467/98 *Commission* v *Denmark*, Case C-468/98 *Commission* v *Sweden*, Case C-471/98 *Commission* v *Belgium*, Case C-472/98 *Commission* v *Luxembourg*, Case C-475/98 *Commission* v *Austria*, Case C-476/98 *Commission* v *Germany*, and the following ruling involving Finland.

Commission v *Finland* (Case 469/98)

[2002] ECR I-9627, Court of Justice of the European Communities

[75] ... whilst Article 84(2) of the Treaty does not establish an external Community competence in the field of air transport, it does make provision for a Community power of action in that area, albeit one that is dependent on there being a prior decision by the Council.

[76] It was, moreover, by taking that provision as a legal basis that the Council adopted the 'third package' of legislation in the field of air transport.

[77] The Court has already held, in paragraphs 16 to 18 and 22 of the *AETR* judgment, that the Community's competence to conclude international agreements arises not only from an express conferment by the Treaty but may equally flow from other provisions of the Treaty and from measures adopted, within the framework of those provisions, by the Community institutions; that, in particular, each time the Community, with a view to implementing a common policy envisaged by the Treaty, adopts provisions laying down common rules,

whatever form these may take, the Member States no longer have the right, acting individually or even collectively, to undertake obligations towards non-member countries which affect those rules or distort their scope; and that, as and when such common rules come into being, the Community alone is in a position to assume and carry out contractual obligations towards non-member countries affecting the whole sphere of application of the Community legal system.

[78] Since those findings imply recognition of an exclusive external competence for the Community in consequence of the adoption of internal measures, it is appropriate to ask whether they also apply in the context of a provision such as Article 84(2) of the Treaty, which confers upon the Council the power to decide 'whether, to what extent and by what procedure appropriate provisions may be laid down' for air transport, including, therefore, for its external aspect.

[79] If the Member States were free to enter into international commitments affecting the common rules adopted on the basis of Article 84(2) of the Treaty, that would jeopardise the attainment of the objective pursued by those rules and would thus prevent the Community from fulfilling its task in the defence of the common interest.

[80] It follows that the findings of the Court in the *AETR* judgment also apply where, as in this case, the Council has adopted common rules on the basis of Article 84(2) of the Treaty.

[81] It must next be determined under what circumstances the scope of the common rules maybe affected or distorted by the international commitments at issue and, therefore, under what circumstances the Community acquires an external competence by reason of the exercise of its internal competence.

[82] According to the Court's case law, that is the case where the international commitments fall within the scope of the common rules (*AETR* judgment, paragraph 30), or in any event within an area which is already largely covered by such rules (Opinion 2/91, [1993] ECR I-1061], paragraph 25). In the latter case, the Court has held that Member States may not enter into international commitments outside the framework of the Community institutions, even if there is no contradiction between those commitments and the common rules (Opinion 2/91, paragraphs 25 and 26).

[83] Thus it is that, whenever the Community has included in its internal legislative acts provisions relating to the treatment of nationals of non-member countries or expressly conferred on its institutions powers to negotiate with non-member countries, it acquires an exclusive external competence in the spheres covered by those acts (Opinion 1/94, paragraph 95; Opinion 2/92, [1995] ECR I-521, paragraph 33).

[84] The same applies, even in the absence of any express provision authorising its institutions to negotiate with non-member countries, where the Community has achieved complete harmonisation in a given area, because the common rules thus adopted could be affected within the meaning of the *AETR* judgment if the Member States retained freedom to negotiate with non-member countries (Opinion 1/94, paragraph 96; Opinion 2/92, paragraph 33).

[85] On the other hand, it follows from the reasoning in paragraphs 78 and 79 of Opinion 1/94 that any distortions in the flow of services in the internal market which might arise from bilateral 'open skies' agreements concluded by Member States with non-member countries do not in themselves affect the common rules adopted in that area and are thus not capable of establishing an external competence of the Community.

[86] There is nothing in the Treaty to prevent the institutions arranging, in the common rules laid down by them, concerted action in relation to non-member countries or to prevent them prescribing the approach to be taken by the Member States in their external dealings (Opinion 1/94, paragraph 79).

[87] It is in the light of those considerations that it falls to be determined whether the common rules relied on by the Commission in the present action are capable of being affected by the international commitments entered into by the Republic of Finland.

Examining the matter, the Court concluded that the common rules were capable of being affected by the international commitments concerning air fares and rates entered into by Finland. This constituted an unlawful intrusion into an area of exclusive external competence contrary to Article 10 EC (predecessor to the current and amended Article 4(3) TEU).

■ QUESTION

To what extent does the distillation of the Court's case law concerning the scope of exclusive competence into what is now Article 3 TFEU (p. 30) adequately capture its nuances?

NOTES

1. The Treaty has always provided the EC with the legal personality necessary to conclude such international agreements. On the entry into force of the Lisbon Treaty and the demise of the EC (p. 19) legal personality was logically conferred on the EU: Article 47 TEU. A Declaration annexed to the Treaty (No 24) adds that this does not authorize action beyond the competences conferred by the Treaties – which is obvious as a matter of law but complies with the Lisbon Treaty's thematic presentational concern to broadcast the *limits* of EU competences more aggressively.
2. Comparable issues of competence-allocation arise in the EU's internal legal order. So where the EU legislates, for example, in the area of health inspections for animals, Member States may be precluded from adopting different legislation in that area. Here too anxiety to protect 'the unity of the Common Market and the uniform application of Community [now Union] law' mentioned in para 31 of Case 22/70 is prominent. This is examined in Chapter 12 in relation to the free movement of goods under Articles 34–36 TFEU. Broader questions relating to the respective competences of the Union and the Member States are addressed in Chapter 17.

NOTE: For additional material and resources see the Online Resource Centre at: www.oxfordtextbooks.co.uk/orc/weatherill12e.

4

The Enforcement of Union Law: 'Dual Vigilance'

SECTION 1: DUAL VIGILANCE

A Member State in breach of the Treaty may be brought before the Court of Justice by the Commission in the context of the Article 258 infringement procedure (Article 226 pre-Lisbon, Article 169 pre-Amsterdam), or, less common, by another Member State in reliance on Article 259 (Article 227 pre-Lisbon, Article 170 pre-Amsterdam). However, the State may also be challenged at national level by litigants relying on the direct effect of EU law. It is then for national courts to grant appropriate remedies against the State in breach, if necessary after seeking the assistance of the Court of Justice in matters of interpretation of EU law *via* an Article 267 preliminary reference (see Chapter 7).

According to this model of enforcement there are two routes for protecting rights arising under EU law; that means, two routes for tackling action that is contrary to the Treaty. The first, the 'European-level' infringement procedure under Articles 258 and 259 TFEU, was clearly marked out in the Treaty from the day of its entry into force in 1958. The second, the 'national-level' control, was not set out in the Treaty. It is the child of creative jurisprudence. 'Direct effect' is one of the Court's most remarkable achievements and it addressed the matter at an early stage in the development of what was then the European Community.

No decision is more important in the development of EU law than the following:

***Van Gend en Loos* v *Nederlandse Administratie der Belastingen* (Case 26/62)**

[1963] ECR 1, Court of Justice of the European Communities

Van Gend en Loos had imported ureaformaldehyde from Germany into the Netherlands. It had been charged a customs duty. This violated the principle of the free movement of goods between Member States – specifically Article 12 of the Treaty of Rome (which is now Article 30 TFEU post-Lisbon, see further Chapter 10). Van Gend en Loos claimed reimbursement of the sum before the Dutch courts. The Dutch court made a preliminary reference to the European Court under Article 177 (which is now Article 267 TFEU post-Lisbon) in order to discover whether Article 12 of the Treaty (now 30) could assist a private litigant before a national court.

> The first question of the Tariefcommissie is whether Article 12 of the Treaty has direct application in national law in the sense that nationals of Member States may on the basis of this Article lay claim to rights which the national court must protect.
>
> To ascertain whether the provisions of an international treaty extend so far in their effects it is necessary to consider the spirit, the general scheme and the wording of those provisions.
>
> The objective of the EEC Treaty, which is to establish a Common Market, the functioning of which is of direct concern to interested parties in the Community, implies that this Treaty is more than an agreement which merely creates mutual obligations between the contracting states. This view is confirmed by the preamble to the Treaty which refers not only to governments but to peoples. It is also confirmed more specifically by the establishment of institutions endowed with sovereign rights, the exercise of which affects Member States and also their citizens.

Furthermore, it must be noted that the nationals of the states brought together in the Community are called upon to cooperate in the functioning of this Community through the intermediary of the European Parliament and the Economic and Social Committee.

In addition the task assigned to the Court of Justice under Article 177, the object of which is to secure uniform interpretation of the Treaty by national courts and tribunals, confirms that the states have acknowledged that Community law has an authority which can be invoked by their nationals before those courts and tribunals.

The conclusion to be drawn from this is that the Community constitutes a new legal order of international law for the benefit of which the states have limited their sovereign rights, albeit within limited fields, and the subjects of which comprise not only Member States but also their nationals.

Independently of the legislation of Member States, Community law therefore not only imposes obligations on individuals but is also intended to confer upon them rights which become part of their legal heritage. These rights arise not only where they are expressly granted by the Treaty, but also by reason of obligations which the Treaty imposes in a clearly defined way upon individuals as well as upon the Member States and upon the institutions of the Community.

The Court then addressed the objection that Articles 169 and 170 (now 258 and 259) of the Treaty had already created a system for exercising supervision of alleged violations of the Treaty by Member States, and that enforcement before national courts should therefore be excluded.

In addition the argument based on Articles 169 and 170 of the Treaty put forward by the three Governments which have submitted observations to the Court in their statements of case is misconceived. The fact that these Articles of the Treaty enable the Commission and the Member States to bring before the Court a State which has not fulfilled its obligations does not mean that individuals cannot plead these obligations, should the occasion arise, before a national court, any more than the fact that the Treaty places at the disposal of the Commission ways of ensuring that obligations imposed upon those subject to the Treaty are observed, precludes the possibility, in actions between individuals before a national court, of pleading infringements of these obligations.

A restriction of the guarantees against an infringement of Article 12 by Member States to the procedures under Article 169 and 170 would remove all direct legal protection of the individual rights of their nationals. There is the risk that recourse to the procedure under these Articles would be ineffective if it were to occur after the implementation of a national decision taken contrary to the provisions of the Treaty.

The vigilance of individuals concerned to protect their rights amounts to an effective supervision in addition to the supervision entrusted by Articles 169 and 170 to the diligence of the Commission and of the Member States.

NOTE: The final sentence of this extract provides the source of the title of this chapter – the 'vigilance of individuals' supplements that of the Commission and (albeit rarely) Member States in securing the enforcement of EU. This is a system of 'dual vigilance'. The Court shows itself in this judgment determined carefully to justify its discovery of the key principle of direct effect from the point of view of the purpose of the Treaty. The inclusion of individuals as those capable of benefiting from and being subject to the law immeasurably deepens its impact. It also makes it more likely to be observed. Breach of EU law may be challenged at EU level and also at national level. The two routes are now examined in turn.

SECTION 2: CONTROL AT EU LEVEL

ARTICLES 258 AND 259 TFEU

ARTICLE 258 TFEU

If the Commission considers that a Member State has failed to fulfil an obligation under the Treaties, it shall deliver a reasoned opinion on the matter after giving the State concerned the opportunity to submit its observations.

If the State concerned does not comply with the opinion within the period laid down by the Commission, the latter may bring the matter before the Court of Justice of the European Union.

ARTICLE 259 TFEU

A Member State which considers that another Member State has failed to fulfil an obligation under the Treaties may bring the matter before the Court of Justice of the European Union.

Before a Member State brings an action against another Member State for an alleged infringement of an obligation under the Treaties, it shall bring the matter before the Commission.

The Commission shall deliver a reasoned opinion after each of the States concerned has been given the opportunity to submit its own case and its observations on the other party's case both orally and in writing.

If the Commission has not delivered an opinion within three months of the date on which the matter was brought before it, the absence of such opinion shall not prevent the matter from being brought before the Court.

NOTE: Article 259 is plainly politically sensitive and has been little used (but see e.g. *France* v *UK* (Case 141/78) [1979] ECR 2923; *Belgium* v *Spain* (Case C-388/95) [2000] ECR I-3123; and *Hungary* v *Slovakia* (Case C-364/10) judgment of 16 October 2012).

A: The nature of Article 258 TFEU

R. White and A. Dashwood, 'Enforcement Actions under Articles 169 and 170 EEC' [now 258 and 259 TFEU]

(1989) 14 EL Rev 388, 388–9

(Footnotes omitted; numbering altered to reflect the post-Lisbon Treaty.)

THE NATURE OF ARTICLES 258 AND 259 TFEU

. . . Under both Article [258] and Article [259] the procedure falls into two distinct phases. In a first 'administrative' phase, the Commission receives observations on the allegation of non-compliance from the Member State (or in proceedings under Article [259], the Member States) concerned and defines its own position in a reasoned opinion. An attempt is made to reach a satisfactory settlement without resorting to litigation, and in the great majority of cases this has proved possible. Where it is not, an action is brought by the Commission or by the complaining Member State in the European Court. The aim of the action is to obtain a declaration by the European Court that the defendant Member State has failed in a specified manner to fulfil its obligation under specified provisions of Community law. The Member State will be bound under Article [260] to take the necessary measures to comply with the judgment.

The procedure under Article [258] represents a considerable advance on the rules that normally apply in public international law where a State fails to fulfil its obligations under a treaty. In the first place, a right to prosecute infringements is given to the Commission, an institution specifically charged with protecting and promoting the interests of the Community as a whole. This makes it much more likely that effective action will be taken than if the Decision depended exclusively on Member State's estimation as to what would best serve their particular interests. Secondly, by virtue of their adherence to the EEC Treaty, Member States accept the compulsory jurisdiction of the European Court. No express declaration of acceptance is required; and no reservations or time limit may be imposed. These special features of the procedure are explained by the vital role the Member States are called upon to play in the concrete implementation of Community policies and rules.

NOTE: A State may be liable even for violations committed by bodies which are constitutionally independent.

Commission v *Belgium* (Case 77/69)

[1970] ECR 237, Court of Justice of the European Communities

The action arose out of a discriminatory tax on wood imposed by Belgium. This was a violation of Article 95 of the EC Treaty (now Article 110 TFEU) (see Chapter 10).

[11] The defendant does not dispute the existence of discrimination resulting from the provisions which form the subject-matter of the proceedings.

[12] Following a series of steps taken by the Commission the first of which dates back to 1963, the Belgian government has shown its willingness to take the necessary measures with a view to eliminating the discrimination complained of.

[13] A draft law intended to make possible a revision of the disputed scheme was put before Parliament in 1967 and provisions were later adopted in order to revive this draft law which had lapsed owing to the dissolution of the Belgian Parliament in the meanwhile.

[14] In these circumstances the Belgian government considers that the delay in enacting the law amounts as far as it is concerned to a 'case of *force majeure*'.

[15] The obligations arising from Article 95 of the Treaty devolve upon States as such and the liability of a Member State under Article 169 arises whatever the agency of the State whose action or inaction is the cause of the failure to fulfil its obligations, even in the case of a constitutionally independent institution.

[16] The objection raised by the defendant cannot therefore be sustained.

[17] In these circumstances, by applying a duty at the same rate, as laid down by Article 31–14 of the Royal Decree of 3 March 1927 as amended, to home-grown wood transferred standing or felled and to imported wood calculated on its value at the time of the declaration of entry for home use, the Kingdom of Belgium has failed to fulfil its obligations under Article 95 of the Treaty.

***Commission* v *Belgium* (Case 1/86)**

[1987] ECR 2797, Court of Justice of the European Communities

Belgium had failed to implement in time Directive 80/68, a measure designed to combat water pollution.

[8] The Belgian government has explained that the delay in transposing the Directive in respect of the entire country is due to the fact that, as a result of the institutional reforms of 8 August 1980, the national government's powers in regard to the environment have been transferred to the regions, which involved the creation and organization of new institutions, such as the Brussels region, established in 1985. Furthermore, it has pointed out that a draft decree has been approved by the Walloon Executive for the purpose of implementing the Directive in the Walloon region and is shortly to be submitted to the Conseil d'État (State Council) before being submitted to the Conseil régional wallon (Walloon Regional Council), and that for the Brussels region a draft royal decree is in preparation.

[9] It must be stated that the fact that the procedure for the adoption of implementing measures has been initiated in respect of the Walloon region and the Brussels region does not put an end to the failure to fulfil obligations. Furthermore, according to settled case law, a Member State may not plead provisions, practices or circumstances existing in its internal legal system in order to justify a failure to comply with obligations resulting from Community Directives.

[10] Accordingly, it must be held that, by failing to adopt within the prescribed period all the measures necessary to comply with Council Directive 80/68 of 17 December 1979, the Kingdom of Belgium has failed to fulfil its obligations under the EEC Treaty.

NOTE: **Practical difficulties are no excuse for infringement of Treaty obligations.**

***Commission* v *UK* (Case 128/78)**

[1979] ECR 419, Court of Justice of the European Communities

The UK failed to introduce legislation requiring the use of recording equipment in road transport – tachographs.

[6] It is not denied that provision for the installation and use of the recording equipment has been made by the British legislation only on an optional and voluntary basis as regards both vehicles engaged in intra-Community transport and those engaged in national transport. On the other hand, the British legislation

has maintained in force the obligations relating to the keeping of an individual control book which were abolished by the said Regulation.

[7] The defendant claims that this arrangement is sufficient to meet the objectives of promoting road safety, of social progress for workers and of the harmonization of conditions of competition. It maintains that the implementation of Regulation No 1463/70 on its territory is best achieved by the installation and use of the recording equipment on a voluntary basis, though this may be made compulsory at an appropriate time. It adds that implementation of the Regulation involving compulsory measures would meet with active resistance from the sectors concerned, in particular the trade unions, which would result in strikes in the transport sector and would therefore seriously damage the whole economy of the country.

[8] It contends that since, in the case of the United Kingdom, the objectives of the Community policy in this field can be achieved just as satisfactorily by the maintenance of the system of the individual control book as by the compulsory introduction of recording equipment, the alleged failure to fulfil an obligation is of a purely technical nature and, in view of the difficulties referred to, should not be taken into account. Moreover the installation and use of recording equipment is in practice already guaranteed in respect of intra-Community transport by the fact that the other Member States have made it compulsory.

[9] Article 189 of the Treaty provides that a Regulation shall be binding 'in its entirety' in the Member States. As the Court has already stated in its judgment of 7 February 1973 (Case 39/72 *Commission* v *Italian Republic* [1973] ECR 101) it cannot therefore be accepted that a Member State should apply in an incomplete or selective manner provisions of a Community Regulation so as to render abortive certain aspects of Community legislation which it has opposed or which it considers contrary to its national interests. In particular, as regards the putting into effect of a general rule intended to eliminate certain abuses to which workers are subject and which in addition involve a threat to road safety, a Member State which omits to take, within the requisite period and simultaneously with the other Member States, the measures which it ought to take, undermines Community solidarity by imposing, in particular as regards intra-Community transport, on the other Member States the necessity of remedying the effects of its own omissions, while at the same time taking an undue advantage to the detriment of its partners.

[10] As the Court said in the same judgment, practical difficulties which appear at the stage when a Community measure is put into effect cannot permit a Member State unilaterally to opt out of fulfilling its obligations. The Community institutional system provides the Member State concerned with the necessary means to ensure that its difficulties be given due consideration, subject to compliance with the principles of the common market and the legitimate interests of the other Member States.

[11] In these circumstances, the possible difficulties of implementation alleged by the defendant cannot be accepted as a justification.

[12] Further, as the Court said in the case mentioned above, in permitting Member States to profit from the advantages of the Community, the Treaty imposes on them also the obligation to respect its rules. For a State unilaterally to break, according to its own conception of national interest, the equilibrium between the advantages and obligations flowing from its adherence to the Community brings into question the equality of Member States before Community law and creates discrimination at the expense of their nationals. This failure in the duty of solidarity accepted by Member States by the fact of their adherence to the Community strikes at the very root of the Community legal order.

[13] It appears therefore that, in deliberately refusing to give effect on its territory to the provisions of Regulation No 1463/70, the United Kingdom has markedly failed to fulfil the obligation which it has assumed by virtue of its membership of the European Economic Community.

B: The effectiveness of Article 258 TFEU

The procedure under Article 258 occupies two phases – the administrative and the judicial. As the extract from White and Dashwood observes (p. 86), most cases are resolved to mutual satisfaction as a result of dialogue within (or even before) the first phase.

Some, a minority, are brought before the Court. The Commission enjoys a discretion in choosing how to deal with a suspected infringement of EU law, and its hand cannot be forced.

Star Fruit Co. v *Commission* (Case 247/87)

[1989] ECR 291, Court of Justice of the European Communities

Star Fruit, a Belgian banana trader, felt itself prejudiced by French banana market regulation which it believed to be contrary to the Treaty. It considered that the Commission's failure to institute infringement proceedings against France constituted a failure to act, which it was entitled to challenge under Article 175 of the EC Treaty (now, after amendment, Article 265 TFEU: see Chapter 8, p. 208).

[10] In so far as it is based on the third paragraph of Article 175 of the Treaty, the purpose of the application is to obtain a declaration that in not commencing against the French Republic proceedings to establish its breach of obligations the Commission infringed the Treaty by failing to take a decision.

[11] However, it is clear from the scheme of Article 169 of the Treaty [now Article 258 TFEU] that the Commission is not bound to commence the proceedings provided for in that provision but in this regard has a discretion which excludes the right for individuals to require that institution to adopt a specific position.

[12] It is only if it considers that the Member State in question has failed to fulfil one of its obligations that the Commission delivers a reasoned opinion. Furthermore, in the event that the State does not comply with the opinion within the period allowed, the institution has in any event the right, but not the duty, to apply to the Court of Justice for a declaration that the alleged breach of obligations has occurred

The next extracts provide, first, a summary of the Commission's view of the role of the infringement procedure and, second, a statistical flavour of Commission practice. A preference for informal resolution of disputes is motivated by a strong desire on the part of the Commission for cost-effective, non-litigious rule enforcement.

Report from the Commission on Monitoring the Application of Community Law (2005), Overall Position, 23rd Annual Report

COM (2006) 416, 24 July 2006, pp. 3–4, available *via* http://ec.europa.eu/atwork/applying-eu-law/infringements-proceedings/annual-reports/index_en.htm

1.1 INTRODUCTION

In exercising its exclusive function as guardian of the Treaties, the Commission ensures and monitors the uniform application of Community law by the Member States . . .

The White Paper on European Governance [European Governance – a White Paper (COM (2001) 428)] published by the Commission in 2001 emphasises that the primary responsibility for applying Community law lies with national administrations and courts in the Member States. The primary objective of infringement proceedings is to encourage the Member States to comply voluntarily with Community law as quickly as possible. Furthermore, the Commission has aimed to boost cooperation with the Member States by means of complementary or alternative methods to resolve problems.

The undertaking of monitoring the application of Community law is vital in terms of the rule of law generally, but it also helps to make the principle of a Community based on the rule of law a tangible reality for Europe's citizens and economic operators. The numerous complaints received from citizens of the Member States constitute a vital means of detecting infringements of Community law.

NOTE: The White Paper on European Governance, mentioned in the second paragraph of this extract, is discussed further in Chapter 18, p. 585.

Report from the Commission on Monitoring the Application of EU Law (2014), Overall Position, 32nd Annual Report

COM (2015) 329, 9 July 2015, pp. 14–15, Available *via* http://ec.europa.eu/atwork/applying-eu-law/infringements-proceedings/annual-reports/index_en.htm

At the end of 2014, **1347** infringement cases remained open. While in 2014 the number of open infringement cases increased slightly, overall the figure has fallen since 2010. . . .

The dialogue between the Member State and the Commission continues during the formal procedure, in order to seek compliance. Statistics confirm that Member

States make serious efforts to settle their infringements before the Court hands down its ruling. In 2014, the Commission closed:

- 580 infringements after sending a letter of formal notice;
- 190 cases after sending reasoned opinions to the Member State; and
- 11 cases after deciding to refer the case before the Court but befor submitting the application. In addition, the Commission has withdrawn 16 cases from the Court before it handed down its ruling.

The Court delivered 38 judgments under Article 258 TFEU in 2014, of which 35 (92%) were in favour of the Commission.

NOTE: Although the Commission brings alleged infringements before the Court in only a minority of cases, there are two important elements in furthering the effectiveness of Article 258 which depend on recourse to the Court. The first is the Court's ability to make interim orders against defaulting States; the second is the power to impose fines. The power to make interim orders is conferred by Article 279, which states: 'The Court of Justice of the European Union may in any cases before it prescribe any necessary interim measures.'

This is a flexible provision, but the Court has imposed relatively strict conditions on its own capacity to make interim orders. This runs parallel to its attitude to the grant of interim relief against acts of the EU institutions discussed subsequently in Chapter 8, at p. 207.

Commission v *UK* (Case C-246/89R)

[1989] ECR 3125, Court of Justice of the European Communities

The Commission's action related to the UK's Merchant Shipping Act 1988. The Commission took the view that the Act violated Treaty rules forbidding discrimination on grounds of nationality. Under the arrangements governing the accession of Spain to the (then) European Community, the volume of catches which Spanish fishing vessels could make in Community waters was regulated. Many Spanish fishing vessels were re-registered by their owners as British and fished under the British flag, thereby taking advantage of enhanced access to Community waters, but continued to land catches in Spain and to earn profits for Spanish nationals. At the start of January 1986, the UK introduced new licensing requirements for British fishing vessels. These were supplemented by the Merchant Shipping Act 1988. The thrust of the requirements was the demand that a genuine economic link with the UK be shown beyond the mere fact of registration. British ownership and management was required. In challenging the 1988 Act, the Commission argued that its provisions contravened the Treaty rules prohibiting discrimination on grounds of nationality. It initiated an action under Article 169 of the EC Treaty (now Article 258 TFEU), but it also asked the Court to make an interim order against the UK under Article 186 of the Treaty (now Article 279 TFEU).

[20] Under Article 186 of the EEC Treaty the Court may in any cases before it prescribe any necessary interim measures.

[21] Under Article 83(2) of the Rules of Procedure, interim measures such as those requested may not be ordered unless there are circumstances giving rise to urgency and factual and legal grounds establishing a prima-facie case for the measures applied for.

[22] It must be considered whether these conditions are satisfied in this case.

[23] As regards first of all the condition of existence of a prima-facie case, the Commission points out that it is contesting solely the nationality requirements laid down by section 14 of the Merchant Shipping Act 1988. These requirements prohibit nationals of the other Member States from acquiring, through a company, a British fishing vessel and from managing a company operating such a vessel under the same conditions as British nationals. This constitutes direct discrimination, in flagrant breach of the prohibition of discrimination on grounds of nationality, which cannot be justified either by the Community rules on fishing quotas or by the United Kingdom's obligations under international law.

[24] For its part, the United Kingdom considers that the national provisions contested by the Commission do not infringe Community law. Any Member State is at liberty to lay down the conditions for registration of ships and for flying its flag. International law requires the United Kingdom to lay down these conditions in such a way that the ship has a genuine link with the United Kingdom, enabling that country to exercise effectively its jurisdiction and control over the ship. The conditions contained in the Merchant Shipping Act 1988 correspond to those imposed by other Member States for flying their flag.

[25] The United Kingdom further considers that the nationality requirements introduced by the 1988 Act are justified by the present Community legislation on fisheries; that legislation, although it establishes a common system, is based on a principle of nationality for the purposes of the distribution of fishing quotas. Under Article 5(2) of Council Regulation 170/83 it is for the Member States to determine the detailed rules for the utilization of the quotas allocated to them and thus to lay down the conditions which the vessels authorized to fish from these quotas must satisfy.

[26] It must be observed that the system of national quotas established by Council Regulation 170/83 constitutes, as the United Kingdom contends, a derogation from the principle of equal access for Community fishermen to fishing grounds and to the exploitation thereof in waters coming within the jurisdiction of the Member States, which is itself a specific expression of the principle of non-discrimination laid down in Article 40(3) of the EEC Treaty.

[27] That derogation is justified, according to the recitals in the preamble to Regulation No 170/83, by the need, in a situation where there is a dearth of fishery resources, to ensure a relative stability in regard to fishing activities in order to safeguard the particular needs of regions where local populations are especially dependent on fisheries and related industries.

[28] The possibility cannot therefore be excluded that in their legislation concerning in particular the registration of fishing vessels and access to fishing activities the Member States may be led to introduce requirements whose compatibility with Community law can be justified only by the necessity to attain the objectives of the Community system of fishing quotas. As the Commission itself has admitted in these proceedings, such requirements may be necessary in order to ensure that there is a genuine link with the fishing industry of the Member State against whose quota the vessel may fish.

[29] However there is nothing which would prima facie warrant the conclusion that such requirements may derogate from the prohibition of discrimination on grounds of nationality contained in Articles 52 and 221 of the EEC Treaty regarding, respectively, the right of establishment and the right to participate in the capital of companies or firms within the meaning of Article 58.

[30] The rights deriving from the abovementioned provisions of the Treaty include not only the rights of establishment and of participation in the capital of companies or firms but also the right to pursue an economic activity, as the case may be through a company, under the conditions laid down by the legislation of the country of establishment for its own nationals.

[31] These rights prima facie also include the right to incorporate and manage a company whose object is to operate a fishing vessel registered in the State of establishment under the same conditions as a company controlled by nationals of that State.

[32] As regards the United Kingdom's first submission based on its obligations under international law, it is sufficient to note, at this stage, that in this respect nothing has been put forward which at first sight could necessitate any derogation from the abovementioned rights under Community law in order to ensure the effective exercise of British jurisdiction and control over the vessels in question.

[33] It must therefore be held that, at the stage of these proceedings for the grant of interim relief, the application in the main proceedings does not appear to be without foundation and that the requirement of a prima-facie case is thus satisfied.

[34] As regards, next, the condition relating to urgency, it should be borne in mind that the urgency of an application for interim measures must be assessed in relation to the necessity for an order granting interim relief in order to prevent serious and irreparable damage.

[35] The Commission makes the observation that the establishment of the new register of British fishing vessels has had the effect of forcing the entire 'Anglo-Spanish' fleet to remain idle. According to its information the registration in that register of a number of those vessels is precluded solely by reason of the nationality requirements at issue, since the vessels in question could satisfy the other requirements under section 14 of the Merchant Shipping Act 1988, in particular that relating to management and control from the United Kingdom. The owners of the vessels in question are suffering heavy losses as a result of the vessels' remaining idle and will in the short term be forced to sell them under very adverse conditions. Under British civil law these losses cannot later be recovered by means of actions brought against the British authorities.

[36] The United Kingdom contends that the interim measures applied for would in practice be ineffectual. Leaving aside the nationality requirements, the United Kingdom denies that the vessels forced to remain idle would be able to satisfy the requirements for registration, in particular those relating to residence in the United Kingdom and the management of the vessel from the United Kingdom. The suspension of the application of the nationality requirements, requested by the Commission, could not, therefore, prevent the damage alleged and there is accordingly no urgency. The United Kingdom stresses moreover that the interest which the Commission may have in obtaining these interim measures must be weighed against the United Kingdom's interest in achieving a lasting settlement of the problems caused by the 'Anglo-Spanish' vessels for the British fishing industry. The measures adopted to that end by the British authorities in 1983 and 1986 remained ineffective and only the introduction of requirements that are clear and easy to administer makes it possible to resolve these problems.

[37] It must be held in the first place that for fishing vessels which until 31 March 1989 were flying the British flag and fishing under a British fishing licence the loss of the flag and the cessation of their activities entail serious damage. There is no ground for believing that, pending delivery of the judgment in the main proceedings, these vessels can be operated in the pursuit of alternative fishing activities. The aforesaid damage must also, should the application in the main proceedings be granted, be regarded as irreparable.

[38] It is true that, for there to be urgency, it is necessary that the interim measures requested should be of a nature to prevent the alleged damage. At the present stage of the proceedings the possibility cannot however be excluded that a number of the vessels in question may, as the Commission maintains, satisfy the registration requirements if the application of the nationality requirement is suspended.

[39] Finally, as regards the balance of interests, it is not established that the interim measures applied for may jeopardize the objective pursued by the British legislation at issue, namely to ensure the existence of a genuine link between the vessels fishing against the British quotas and the British fishing industry.

[40] It appears prima facie that the registration requirements laid down by the new legislation, other than those relating to nationality, and the measures adopted by the United Kingdom authorities in 1983 and 1986 would be sufficient to ensure the existence of such a link. The United Kingdom itself considers that the 'Anglo-Spanish' vessels, which do not have that link with the United Kingdom, will not be able to satisfy the aforesaid requirements.

[41] It is true that the nationality requirements would be easier to administer than the requirements relating to the actual operation of a vessel. A Member State may not however plead administrative difficulties in order not to comply with the obligations laid on it by Community law.

[42] It follows that the condition relating to urgency is also satisfied. The interim measures applied for must therefore be ordered.

On those grounds, THE PRESIDENT hereby orders:

(1) Pending delivery of the judgment in the main proceedings, the United Kingdom shall suspend the application of the nationality requirements laid down in section 14(1)(a) and (c) of the Merchant Shipping Act 1988, read in conjunction with paragraphs (2) and (7) of that section, as regards the nationals of other Member States and in respect of fishing vessels which, until 31 March 1989, were pursuing a fishing activity under the British flag and under a British fishing licence.

(2) The costs, including those relating to the intervention, are reserved.

NOTE: In October 1991, the full Court ruled that the UK was indeed in breach of its Treaty obligations ([1991] ECR I-4585). The substance of this case will be readdressed (p. 111, for challenge to the Act was also initiated before the English courts.

A power to impose financial sanctions is obviously helpful in inducing improved State compliance with the Treaty. The Maastricht Treaty added such a procedure with effect from 1993, which is now found in amended form in Article 260 TFEU.

ARTICLE 260 TFEU

1. If the Court of Justice of the European Union finds that a Member State has failed to fulfil an obligation under the Treaties, the State shall be required to take the necessary measures to comply with the judgment of the Court.

2. If the Commission considers that the Member State concerned has not taken the necessary measures to comply with the judgment of the Court, it may bring the case before the Court after giving that State the opportunity to submit its observations. It shall specify the amount of the lump sum or penalty payment to be paid by the Member State concerned which it considers appropriate in the circumstances.

If the Court finds that the Member State concerned has not complied with its judgment it may impose a lump sum or penalty payment on it.

This procedure shall be without prejudice to Article 259.

3. When the Commission brings a case before the Court pursuant to Article 258 on the grounds that the Member State concerned has failed to fulfil its obligation to notify measures transposing a Directive adopted under a legislative procedure, it may, when it deems appropriate, specify the amount of the lump sum or penalty payment to be paid by the Member State concerned which it considers appropriate in the circumstances.

If the Court finds that there is an infringement it may impose a lump sum or penalty payment on the Member State concerned not exceeding the amount specified by the Commission. The payment obligation shall take effect on the date set by the Court in its judgment.

NOTES

1. The Lisbon Treaty removed an intervening stage, whereby the Commission was forced to issue a reasoned opinion before bringing the matter before the Court, and therefore the procedure has been made speedier with effect from December 2009. Moreover, the third paragraph of Article 260 is a Lisbon innovation, also designed to make control of infractions more effective (see Communication, OJ 2011 C12/1).
2. Lump sum fines and/or penalty payments, introduced by the Maastricht Treaty, have been threatened relatively infrequently, but this procedure has not proved to be a dead letter. A penalty payment was first confirmed by the Court in Case C-387/97 *Commission* v *Greece* [2000] ECR I-5047, and several other such judgments have followed. In the next case the Court makes clear its role in the procedure.

Commission v *France* (Case C-304/02)

[2005] ECR I-6263, Court of Justice of the European Communities

The Commission's case was that France had failed to comply with a judgment of the Court delivered in 1991 (Case C-64/88 *Commission* v *France* [1991] ECR I-2727) to the effect that France had not secured the application of rules governing fisheries conservation on its territory. The Court agreed and accordingly found a violation of Article 228 EC, predecessor to Article 260 TFEU. It then explained the nature of its jurisdiction.

[103] ... while it is clear that a penalty payment is likely to encourage the defaulting Member State to put an end as soon as possible to the breach that has been established (Case C-278/01 *Commission* v *Spain*, paragraph 42), it should be remembered that the Commission's suggestions cannot bind the Court and are only a useful point of reference (Case C-387/97 *Commission* v *Greece*, paragraph 89). In exercising its discretion, it is for the Court to set the penalty payment so that it is appropriate to the circumstances and proportionate both to

the breach that has been established and to the ability to pay of the Member State concerned (see, to this effect, Case C-387/97 *Commission* v *Greece*, paragraph 90, and Case C-278/01 *Commission* v *Spain*, paragraph 41).

[104] In that light, and as the Commission has suggested in its communication of 28 February 1997, the basic criteria which must be taken into account in order to ensure that penalty payments have coercive force and Community law is applied uniformly and effectively are, in principle, the duration of the infringement, its degree of seriousness and the ability of the Member State to pay. In applying those criteria, regard should be had in particular to the effects of failure to comply on private and public interests and to the urgency of getting the Member State concerned to fulfil its obligations (Case C-387/97 *Commission* v *Greece*, paragraph 92).

In this case the Court decided for the first time to impose both the lump sum and the penalty payment foreseen by the Treaty on the defaulting Member State.

[80] The procedure laid down in Article 228(2) EC has the objective of inducing a defaulting Member State to comply with a judgment establishing a breach of obligations and thereby of ensuring that Community law is in fact applied. The measures provided for by that provision, namely a lump sum and a penalty payment, are both intended to achieve this objective.

[81] Application of each of those measures depends on their respective ability to meet the objective pursued according to the circumstances of the case. While the imposition of a penalty payment seems particularly suited to inducing a Member State to put an end as soon as possible to a breach of obligations which, in the absence of such a measure, would tend to persist, the imposition of a lump sum is based more on assessment of the effects on public and private interests of the failure of the Member State concerned to comply with its obligations, in particular where the breach has persisted for a long period since the judgment which initially established it.

[82] That being so, recourse to both types of penalty provided for in Article 228(2) EC is not precluded, in particular where the breach of obligations both has continued for a long period and is inclined to persist.

Once the Court had made its calculations based on ability to pay and the seriousness and duration of the infringement, it required France to pay 57,761,250 euros for each period of six months in which she remained in breach of the 1991 judgment and supplemented that with liability to pay a lump sum of 20,000,000 euros.

The ruling demonstrates the potential power of this provision even if it has not been used aggressively (see in this vein I. Kilbey, 'The Interpretation of Article 260 TFEU' (2010) 35 EL Rev 370; S. Peers, 'Sanctions for Infringement of EU Law After the Treaty of Lisbon' (2012) 18 *Euro Public Law* 33; and P. Wennerås, 'Sanctions against Member States under Article 260 TFEU: Still Alive but not Kicking?' (2012) 49 CML Rev 145). The Commission responded to the judgment by issuing a communication in 2005 which replaced that referred to by the Court in para 104. It is available in its updated 2015 version at http://ec.europa.eu/atwork/applying-eu-law/infringements-proceedings/financial-sanctions/index_en.htm. It sets out the structure according to which the Commission calculates the sums it asks the Court to extract from defaulting Member States. However, the decision ultimately belongs with the Court. This is vividly illustrated by the ruling in another costly case for France, Case C-177/04 *Commission* v *France* [2006] ECR I-2461. The Court, in determining 'the degree of persuasion which appears to it to be needed' (para 63), concluded that the Commission's proposed penalty payment was based on an underestimate of the duration of the infringement. It imposed a daily penalty payment on France of 31,650 euros – more than double that favoured by the Commission.

NOTE: In assessing the likely impact of Article 260 TFEU on the incidence of default by Member States, you should also take account of the Court's ruling in *Francovich* (Cases C-6/90 and C-9/90, p. 143) that Member States may be liable to individuals in damages in proceedings brought before *national* courts, elaborated in the package of rulings of March 1996 including '*Factortame III*' (Case C-48/93), p. 151. Remember 'dual vigilance' at p. 85.

C: Complaining to the Commission

R. White and A. Dashwood, 'Enforcement Actions under Articles 169 and 170 EEC' [now 258 and 259 TFEU]

(1989) 14 EL Rev 388, 388–9

. . . However, the procedure does not go so far as to allow an action to be brought in the European Court by individuals or firms whose interests have been harmed by a Member State's failure to fulfil an obligation under the EEC Treaty. Two courses are open to a private party in such circumstances. One would be to lodge a complaint with the Commission, which might lead to the initiation of proceedings under Article [258]. The other would be to bring proceedings in the courts of the Member State concerned, assuming the Community provision in question is a directly effective one, and an appropriate national remedy is available. To help establish the infringement, it may be necessary to ask the national court to make a reference to the European Court under Article [267] for a preliminary ruling on the interpretation of the Community provision.

The Court's ruling in *Star Fruit Co.* v *Commission* (Case 247/87, p. 89) confirms the inability of the complainant to *require* the Commission to initiate proceedings under Article 258. However, complaints frequently provide the Commission with valuable information on malpractice. So the Commission is sometimes prepared to act on complaints and open an investigation. In 2014 complaints accounted for over a third of new dossiers opened (32nd Annual Report, p. 11) and the Commission makes available an on-line form for complaints (available *via* http://ec.europa.eu/your-rights/help/individuals/index_en.htm).

Effective and fair complaint handling is also the subject of a Commission communication to the European Parliament and the European Ombudsman on relations with the complainant, [2002] OJ C244/5. The notice was the result of the European Ombudsman's own-initiative enquiry and the Commission's subsequent undertaking to comply with certain administrative formalities, and in particular to inform the complainant in advance of any decision to close a case. The Commission takes care in this Communication to insist on its 'discretionary power in deciding whether or not to commence infringement proceedings and to refer a case to the Court', recognized by the Court. For discussion of the several interests at stake in the management of complaints by the Commission, see R. Rawlings, 'Engaged Elites: Citizen Action and Institutional Attitudes in Commission Enforcement' (2000) 6 ELJ 4, which locates the matter in the broader context of enforcement in the public interest. Also worth reading for contextual analysis are C. Harlow and R. Rawlings, 'Accountability and Law Enforcement: the Centralised EU Infringements Procedure' (2006) 31 EL Rev 447; and L. Prete and B. Smulders, 'The Coming of Age of Infringement Proceedings' (2010) 47 CML Rev 9.

NOTE: The fact that a State puts an end to its violation before the Court has the opportunity to rule on the matter does not automatically lead to the proceedings being dropped by the Commission.

In the next case the Court refers to the value such an action may have from the perspective of parties affected by the (discontinued) infringement of EU law, which may include complainants.

Commission v *Greece* (Case 240/86)

[1988] ECR 1835, Court of Justice of the European Communities

The Commission's action related to obstacles to cereal imports which it considered incompatible with *inter alia* Article 30 of the EC Treaty (now, after amendment, Article 34 TFEU: see Chapter 12). When the matter reached the stage of a hearing before the Court, the Greek government contested the case's admissibility.

[12] The Greek government considers that since the barriers to cereal imports were lifted before the action was commenced it is devoid of purpose.

[13] At the hearing the Commission acknowledged that the failure to fulfil obligations had been remedied but nevertheless asserted that it had an interest in obtaining a ruling in respect of measures adopted by the Hellenic Republic in the past.

[14] As the Court has consistently held. . . the subject-matter of an action brought under Article 169 [now 226] is established by the Commission's reasoned opinion and even where the default has been remedied after the period laid down pursuant to the second paragraph of that article has elapsed, an interest still subsists in pursuing the action. That interest may consist in establishing the basis for a liability which a Member State may incur, by reason of its failure to fulfil its obligations, towards those to whom rights accrue as a result of that failure.

[15] Since the Hellenic Republic did not comply with the reasoned opinion of 25 November 1985 within the period stipulated by the Commission the action is admissible in so far as it concerns the subject matter of the dispute as defined by that opinion.

SECTION 3: CONTROL AT NATIONAL LEVEL

The Court's ruling in *Commission* v *Greece* (Case 240/86) leads logically into the next stage of the discussion; control at national level. The Court mentions the possibility of liability arising out of the State's violation of obligations arising under the Treaty (final sentence of para 14). A State in violation of EU law may be challenged before its own national courts. The principles of direct effect, supremacy, and the Article 267 preliminary reference procedure all come into play. A complainant unable to persuade the Commission to investigate the matter may be able to resort to this second limb of 'dual vigilance', national-level control. Even a complainant able to provoke a Commission investigation under Article 258 may in addition choose to bring proceedings at national level in so far as that may offer legal protection unavailable at EU level: this will be the case in particular if the applicant seeks compensation for loss suffered as a result of State violation of EU law (Chapter 6).

The structure also permits private parties to challenge at national level acts of other private parties in violation of EU law. This is illustrated by many cases connected with the competition rules, the enforcement of which is considered separately in Chapter 16. It also applies to other provisions of the Treaty that are capable of application directly against private parties such as the rule requiring equal pay for equal work between the sexes, now found in Article 157 TFEU (e.g., *Defrenne* v *SABENA* (Case 43/75) [1976] ECR 455) and the Treaty provisions concerning freedom of movement of persons (*Roman Angonese* (Case C-281/98) [2000] ECR I-4139; see Chapter 13). However, the first limb of 'dual vigilance' is deficient here: Article 258 proceedings may not be brought against private parties.

A: The criteria governing direct effect

Van Gend en Loos (Case 26/62) was encountered at p. 84. It is the seminal case concerning direct effect, which the Court identifies as flowing from the objectives of the Treaty, if not from its explicit terms. Once the Court had established the point of principle that provisions of the Treaty are capable of direct effect, the Court then considered Article 12 of the Treaty itself (now, remember, Article 30 TFEU post-Lisbon). Provisions of the Treaty *can* be directly effective before a national court; but is Article 12?

Van Gend en Loos v *Nederlandse Administratie der Belastingen* (Case 26/62)

[1963] ECR 1, Court of Justice of the European Communities

The wording of Article 12 contains a clear and unconditional prohibition which is not a positive but a negative obligation. This obligation, moreover, is not qualified by any reservation on the part of states which would make its implementation conditional upon a positive legislative measure enacted under national law. The very nature of this prohibition makes it ideally adapted to produce direct effects in the legal relationship between Member States and their subjects.

The implementation of Article 12 does not require any legislative intervention on the part of the states. The fact that under this Article it is the Member States who are made the subject of the negative obligation does not imply that their nationals cannot benefit from this obligation . . .

It follows from the foregoing considerations that, according to the spirit, the general scheme and the wording of the Treaty, Article 12 must be interpreted as producing direct effects and creating individual rights which national courts must protect.

NOTE: In the next two cases the Court repeats its views of the nature and purpose of the direct effect doctrine. It also explains further the conditions which must be satisfied before a provision will be held directly effective. The test is one which will more readily be fulfilled than might initially have been expected. Direct effect, it seems, is the rule rather than the exception.

Van Duyn v *Home Office* (Case 41/74)

[1974] ECR 1337, Court of Justice of the European Communities

Van Duyn, a Dutch woman, had been refused leave to enter the UK, where she wished to take up employment with the Church of Scientology. Her action against the Home Office was based on Article 48 of the EEC Treaty (today, after amendment, Article 45 TFEU). Chapter 13 of this book examines the free movement of workers. There is a basic right to travel from Member State A to Member State B to take up work, subject to exceptions based on, *inter alia*, public policy. The UK sought to exclude Van Duyn on the basis of the exceptions, claiming the Church of Scientology to be socially undesirable. The High Court made a preliminary reference to the Court of Justice to seek clarification of the issues involved. The first two questions concerned the enforceability of (what were then) EC law provisions before national courts – direct effect.

[4] By the first question, the Court is asked to say whether Article 48 of the EEC Treaty is directly applicable so as to confer on individuals rights enforceable by them in the courts of a Member State.

[5] It is provided, in Article 48(1) and (2), that freedom of movement for workers shall be secured by the end of the transitional period and that such freedom shall entail 'the abolition of any discrimination based on nationality between workers of Member States as regards employment, remuneration and other conditions of work and employment'.

[6] These provisions impose on Member States a precise obligation which does not require the adoption of any further measure on the part either of the Community institutions or of the Member States and which leaves them, in relation to its implementation, no discretionary power.

[7] Paragraph 3, which defines the rights implied by the principle of freedom of movement for workers, subjects them to limitations justified on grounds of public policy, public security or public health. The application of these limitations is, however, subject to judicial control, so that a Member State's right to invoke the limitations does not prevent the provisions of Article 48, which enshrine the principle of freedom of movement for workers, from conferring on individuals rights which are enforceable by them and which the national courts must protect.

[8] The reply to the first question must therefore be in the affirmative.

Second Question

[9] The second question asks the Court to say whether Council Directive No 64/221 of 25 February 1964 on the co-ordination of special measures concerning the movement and residence of foreign nationals which are justified on grounds of public policy, public security or public health is directly applicable so as to confer on individuals rights enforceable by them in the courts of a Member State.

[10] It emerges from the order making the reference that the only provision of the Directive which is relevant is that contained in Article 3(1) which provides that 'measures taken on grounds of public policy or public security shall be based exclusively on the personal conduct of the individual concerned'.

[11] The United Kingdom observes that, since Article 189 of the Treaty distinguishes between the effects ascribed to regulations, directives and decisions, it must therefore be presumed that the Council, in issuing a directive rather than making a regulation, must have intended that the directive should have an effect other than that of a regulation and accordingly that the former should not be directly applicable.

[12] If, however, by virtue of the provisions of Article 189 regulations are directly applicable and, consequently, may by their very nature have direct effects, it does not follow from this that other categories of acts mentioned in that Article can never have similar effects. It would be incompatible with the binding effect attributed to a directive by Article 189 to exclude, in principle, the possibility that the obligation which it imposes may be invoked by those concerned. In particular, where the Community authorities have, by directive, imposed on Member States the obligation to pursue a particular course of conduct, the useful effect of such an act would be weakened if individuals were prevented from relying on it before their national courts and if the latter were prevented from taking it into consideration as an element of Community law. Article 177, which empowers national courts to refer to the Court questions concerning the validity and interpretation of all acts of the Community institutions, without distinction, implies furthermore that these acts may be invoked by individuals in the national courts. It is necessary to examine, in every case, whether the nature, general scheme and wording of the provision in question are capable of having direct effects on the relations between Member States and individuals.

[13] By providing that measures taken on grounds of public policy shall be based exclusively on the personal conduct of the individual concerned, Article 3(1) of Directive No 64/221 is intended to limit the discretionary power which national laws generally confer on the authorities responsible for the entry and expulsion of foreign nationals. First, the provision lays down an obligation which is not subject to any exception or condition and which, by its very nature, does not require the intervention of any act on the part either of the institutions of the Community or of Member States. Secondly, because Member States are thereby obliged, in implementing a clause which derogates from one of the fundamental principles of the Treaty in favour of individuals, not to take account of factors extraneous to personal conduct, legal certainty for the persons concerned requires that they should be able to rely on this obligation even though it has been laid down in a legislative act which has no automatic direct effect in its entirety.

[14] If the meaning and exact scope of the provision raise questions of interpretation, these questions can be resolved by the courts, taking into account also the procedure under Article 177 of the Treaty.

[15] Accordingly, in reply to the second question, Article 3(1) of Council Directive No 64/221 of 25 February 1964 confers on individuals rights which are enforceable by them in the courts of a Member State and which the national courts must protect.

Defrenne v *SABENA* (Case 43/75)

[1976] ECR 455, Court of Justice of the European Communities

This was a preliminary reference from a Brussels court. It concerned Article 119 EEC, which contained the principle of equal pay for equal work. The current version of this provision is Article 157 TFEU, though, as explained in Chapter 18, the Treaty provisions on social policy have been much altered along the way. It is the Treaty's major provision in the field of sex discrimination. Defrenne, an air hostess, was seeking compensation from SABENA, her employer, for low pay she had received in comparison with male workers. But could she rely on the Treaty provision before a national court?

[16] Under the terms of the first paragraph of Article 119, the Member States are bound to ensure and maintain 'the application of the principle that men and women should receive equal pay for equal work'.

[17] The second and third paragraphs of the same article add a certain number of details concerning the concepts of pay and work referred to in the first paragraph.

[18] For the purposes of the implementation of these provisions a distinction must be drawn within the whole area of application of Article 119 between, first, direct and overt discrimination which may be identified solely with the aid of the criteria based on equal work and equal pay referred to by the article in question and, secondly, indirect and disguised discrimination which can only be identified by reference to more explicit implementing provisions of a Community or national character.

[19] It is impossible not to recognise that the complete implementation of the aim pursued by Article 119, by means of the elimination of all discrimination, direct or indirect, between men and women workers, not only as regards individual undertakings but also entire branches of industry and even of the economic system as a whole, may in certain cases involve the elaboration of criteria whose implementation necessitates the taking of appropriate measures at Community and national level.

[20] This view is all the more essential in the light of the fact that the Community measures on this question, to which reference will be made in answer to the second question, implement Article 119 from the point of view of extending the narrow criterion of 'equal work', in accordance in particular with the provisions of Convention No 100 on equal pay concluded by the International Labour Organization in 1951, Article 2 of which establishes the principle of equal pay for work 'of equal value'.

[21] Among the forms of direct discrimination which may be identified solely by reference to the criteria laid down by Article 119 must be included in particular those which have their origin in legislative provisions or in collective labour agreements and which may be detected on the basis of a purely legal analysis of the situation.

[22] This applies even more in cases where men and women receive unequal pay for equal work carried out in the same establishment or service, whether public or private.

[23] As is shown by the very findings of the judgment making the reference, in such a situation the court is in a position to establish all the facts which enable it to decide whether a woman worker is receiving lower pay than a male worker performing the same tasks.

[24] In such situation, at least, Article 119 is directly applicable and may thus give rise to individual rights which the courts must protect.

[25] Furthermore, as regards equal work, as a general rule, the national legislative provisions adopted for the implementation of the principle of equal pay as a rule merely reproduce the substance of the terms of Article 119 as regards the direct forms of discrimination.

[26] Belgian legislation provides a particularly apposite illustration of this point, since Article 14 of Royal Decree No 40 of 24 October 1967 on the employment of women merely sets out the right of any female worker to institute proceedings before the relevant court for the application of the principle of equal pay set out in Article 119 and simply refers to that article.

[27] The terms of Article 119 cannot be relied on to invalidate this conclusion.

[28] First of all, it is impossible to put forward an argument against its direct effect based on the use in this article of the word 'principle', since, in the language of the Treaty, this term is specifically used in order to indicate the fundamental nature of certain provisions, as is shown, for example, by the heading of the first part of the Treaty which is devoted to 'Principles' and by Article 113, according to which the commercial policy of the Community is to be based on 'uniform principles'.

[29] If this concept were to be attenuated to the point of reducing it to the level of a vague declaration, the very foundations of the Community and the coherence of its external relations would be indirectly affected.

[30] It is also impossible to put forward arguments based on the fact that Article 119 only refers expressly to 'Member States'.

[31] Indeed, as the Court has already found in other contexts, the fact that certain provisions of the Treaty are formally addressed to the Member States does not prevent rights from being conferred at the same time on any individual who has an interest in the performance of the duties thus laid down.

[32] The very wording of Article 119 shows that it imposes on States a duty to bring about a specific result to be mandatorily achieved within a fixed period.

[33] The effectiveness of this provision cannot be affected by the fact that the duty imposed by the Treaty has not been discharged by certain Member States and that the joint institutions have not reacted sufficiently energetically against this failure to act.

[34] To accept the contrary view would be to risk raising the violation of the right to the status of a principle of interpretation, a position the adoption of which would not be consistent with the task assigned to the Court by Article 164 of the Treaty.

[35] Finally, in its reference to 'Member States', Article 119 is alluding to those States in the exercise of all those of their functions which may usefully contribute to the implementation of the principle of equal pay.

[36] Thus, contrary to the statements made in the course of the proceedings this provision is far from merely referring the matter to the powers of the national legislative authorities.

[37] Therefore, the reference to 'Member States' in Article 119 cannot be interpreted as excluding the intervention of the courts in direct application of the Treaty.

[38] Furthermore it is not possible to sustain any objection that the application by national courts of the principle of equal pay would amount to modifying independent agreements concluded privately or in the sphere of industrial relations such as individual contracts and collective labour agreements.

[39] In fact, since Article 119 is mandatory in nature, the prohibition on discrimination between men and women applies not only to the action of public authorities, but also extends to all agreements which are intended to regulate paid labour collectively, as well as to contracts between individuals.

[40] The reply to the first question must therefore be that the principle of equal pay contained in Article 119 may be relied upon before the national courts and that these courts have a duty to ensure the protection of the rights which this provision vests in individuals, in particular as regards those types of discrimination arising directly from legislative provisions or collective labour agreements, as well as in cases in which men and women receive unequal pay for equal work which is carried out in the same establishment or service, whether private or public.

NOTES

1. In *Van Duyn* v *Home Office* (Case 41/74), the Court found the provisions directly effective despite the existence of derogations available to Member States; in *Defrenne* v *SABENA* (Case 43/75), direct effect was upheld despite the very broad, underdeveloped terms of the provision in question.
2. Two particular aspects of *Defrenne* v *SABENA* (Case 43/75) should not be overlooked. First, the Treaty provision was held directly effective against a private party, the employer (para 39). Treaty provisions, then, are capable of binding not only the State, as in *Van Gend en Loos* and *Van Duyn* (so-called vertical direct effect), but also private parties (horizontal direct effect). This was mentioned at p. 96. The same is true of provisions of the Charter of Fundamental Rights, albeit that the Court has only just begun to make clear which provisions have this capacity (Case C-555/07 *Kücükdeveci* [2010] ECR I-365; Case C-176/12 *Association de médiation sociale* judgment of 15 January 2014). The second aspect of the *Defrenne* ruling that is worthy of attention is that the Court decided to restrict the implications of its ruling:

Defrenne v *SABENA* (Case 43/75)

[1976] ECR 455, Court of Justice of the European Communities

[69] The Governments of Ireland and the United Kingdom have drawn the Court's attention to the possible economic consequences of attributing direct effect to the provisions of Article 119, on the ground that such a decision might, in many branches of economic life, result in the introduction of claims dating back to the time at which such effect came into existence.

[70] In view of the large number of people concerned such claims, which undertakings could not have foreseen, might seriously affect the financial situation of such undertakings and even drive some of them to bankruptcy.

[71] Although the practical consequences of any judicial decision must be carefully taken into account, it would be impossible to go so far as to diminish the objectivity of the law and compromise its future application on the ground of the possible repercussions which might result, as regards the past, from such a judicial decision.

[72] However, in the light of the conduct of several of the Member States and the views adopted by the Commission and repeatedly brought to the notice of the circles concerned, it is appropriate to take exceptionally into account the fact that, over a prolonged period, the parties concerned have been led to continue with practices which were contrary to Article 119, although not yet prohibited under their national law.

[73] The fact that, in spite of the warnings given, the Commission did not initiate proceedings under Article 169 against the Member States concerned on grounds of failure to fulfil an obligation was likely to consolidate the incorrect impression as to the effects of Article 119.

[74] In these circumstances, it is appropriate to determine that, as the general level at which pay would have been fixed cannot be known, important considerations of legal certainty affecting all the interests involved, both public and private, make it impossible in principle to reopen the question as regards the past.

[75] Therefore, the direct effect of Article 119 cannot be relied on in order to support claims concerning pay periods prior to the date of this judgment, except as regards those workers who have already brought legal proceedings or made an equivalent claim.

NOTE: The Court has subsequently insisted that it alone can declare that a directly effective provision may not be relied on retrospectively. This power does not belong to a national court; see *Blaizot* v *University of Liège* (Case 24/86) [1988] ECR 379; *Barra* v *Belgium* (Case 309/85) [1988] ECR 355; and *Evangelischer Krankenhausverein Wien* (Case C-437/97) [2000] ECR I-1157.

B: Direct effect as a policy choice

The Court has made a conscious policy choice in asserting the central significance of direct effect in the EU legal order. Most of the key substantive provisions of law studied in Part Two of this book are directly effective and therefore susceptible to enforcement by private individuals before national courts.

To get a feel for the key choices made many years ago, read particularly P. Pescatore, 'The Doctrine of Direct Effect: an infant disease of Community law' (1983) 8 EL Rev 155. At p. 157 he observes that, 'the reasoning of the Court shows that the judges had "une certaine ideé de l'Europe" of their own and that it is this idea which has been decisive and not arguments based on the legal technicalities of the matter'.

Read also R. Lecourt, *L'Europe des Juges* (Brussels: Bruylant, 1976). At p. 248 he explains that:

En effet, ou bien la Communauté est, pour les particuliers, une séduisante mais lointaine abstraction intéressant seulement les gouvernements qui leur en appliquent discrétionnairement les règles; ou bien elle est pour eux une réalité effective et par conséquence créatrice de droits.

The vigour of directly effective law is a key constitutional feature of the EU legal order. The following extract provides an elegantly written overview of the course pursued by the Court in shaping the constitutional principles of the Community legal order (becoming, post-Lisbon, the Union legal order). The author is not impartial. He was a judge of the Court from 1988 until his death in 1999.

F. Mancini, 'The Making of a Constitution for Europe' (1989) 26 CML Rev 595

(Some footnotes omitted.)

1. For educated observers of European affairs, whether friends or foes of a strong Community, the magnitude of the contribution made by the Court of Justice to the integration of Europe has almost become a by-word. It is unnecessary to quote the friends, which in any event, since they tend to be enthusiastic, would be somewhat embarrassing for a member of the Court. Far more interesting are the enemies or the less than lukewarm supporters of a united Europe. In England politicians who openly criticise judges are frowned upon; Mrs Thatcher, a barrister, is aware of this rule and cannot therefore be quoted, though her private reactions to judgments encroaching on British sovereign rights and interests are easy to visualise. But that old, unredeemed Gaullist, the former Prime Minister Michel Debré, is eminently quotable: 'J'accuse la Cour de Justice' – he said as late as 1979 – 'de megalomania maladive', by which, of course, he meant insufficient deference to the sovereign rights and interests of France.

If one were asked to synthetise the direction in which the case law produced in Luxembourg has moved since 1957, one would have to say that it coincides with the making of a constitution for Europe. Unlike the United States, the EC was born as a peculiar form of international organisation. Its peculiarity resided in the unique institutional structure and the unprecedented law-making and judicial powers it was given. But these features – admittedly reminiscent of a federal State – should not overshadow two essential facts. First: while the American Declaration of Independence spoke of 'one people' dissolving the bonds which connected them with *'another people'*, the preamble of the Rome Treaty recites that the contracting parties are 'determined to lay the foundations of an ever closer union among the *peoples* of Europe'. Second and more important: the instrument giving rise to the Community was a traditional multilateral *treaty*.

Treaties are basically different from constitutions. In many countries (and 'many' includes even some of the founding States of the EC) they do not enjoy the status of higher law. The interpretation of treaties is subject to canons unlike all others (such as, for example, the presumption that States do not lose their sovereignty). As a rule, treaties devise systems of checks and balances whose main function is to keep under control the powers of the organisation which they set up. In the case of the Rome Treaty these differences are emphasised by two highly significant characteristics. The Treaty does not safeguard the fundamental rights of the individuals affected by its application, nor does it recognise, even in an embryonic form, a constitutional right to European citizenship. Europe cannot confer citizenship; this remains the prerogative of the Member States. By the same token, individual citizens of a Member State are entitled to move from their State to another Member State exclusively by virtue of their being workers, self-employed persons or providers of services, that is *qua* units of a production factor.

The main endeavour of the Court of Justice has precisely been to remove or reduce the differences just mentioned. In other words, the Court has sought to 'constitutionalise' the Treaty, that is to fashion a constitutional framework for a federal-type structure in Europe. Whether this effort was always inspired by a clear and consistent philosophy is arguable, but that is not really important. What really matters are its achievements – and they are patent to all.

To be sure, the Court has been helped by favourable circumstances. The combination of being, as it were, out of sight and out of mind by virtue of its location in the fairy-tale Grand Duchy of Luxembourg and the benign neglect of the media has certainly contributed to its ability to create a sense of belonging on the part of its independent-minded members and, where necessary, to convert them into confirmed Europeans. Furthermore, the judges and advocates general have usually been middle-aged and at least half of them have been academics. As a group, therefore, they have never met the three conditions of Lord Diplock's famous verdict: 'by training, temperament and age judges are too averse to change to be entrusted with the development of rules of conduct for a brave new world'.

Nevertheless, these circumstances do not explain the whole story. The Court would have been far less successful had it not been assisted by two mighty allies: the national courts and the Commission. The institutional position of the former will be clarified below. It is sufficient to mention here that by referring to Luxembourg sensitive questions of interpretation of Community law they have been indirectly responsible for the boldest judgments the Court has made. Moreover, by adhering to these judgments in deciding the cases before them, and therefore by lending them the credibility which national judges usually enjoy in their own countries, they have rendered the case law of the Court both effective and respected throughout the Community.

As to the Commission, the founding fathers and especially Jean Monnet conceived it as a sort of 'Platonic embodiment of Communitarian spirit, with Gallic élan, self-confidence and expertise'. As the executive-political branch of the Community, the Commission may not have always lived up to those expectations, but as 'watchdog of the Treaty', that is both as the prosecutor of Member State infractions and as an *amicus curiae* in cases referred by the national courts, it has undoubtedly played a positive rôle. In other words, the Commission has led the Court – particularly by assuaging the concern some of the judges may have felt regarding the acceptability of their rulings – on the path toward further integration and increased Community power.

On the other hand, the Parliament and the Council are not natural allies of the Court. The Parliament evinced great sympathy for the Court in the 1960s and the 1970s, but then its function was simply that of a debating forum. More recently, however, the Parliament has been involved in a permanent trial of strength with the Council: the stake is a new allocation of power in the budgetary and legislative areas. The Court is a victim of this (in itself entirely legitimate) turbulence. The reason is obvious. Luxembourg is more and more encumbered by increasingly political and emotion-loaded intra-Community controversies: hence a visibility and an exposure to scrutiny by the media that are in sharp contrast with the conditions under which progress was made in the past.

The Council, the Community legislative body, is bound not to be an ally of the Court. Although formally an institution with supranational characteristics like the others, it was drawn by its very composition – a gathering of national Ministers – into resembling an intergovernmental round table often characterised by all the warmth of a love match in a snake-pit. In other words, its members regularly speak, and no doubt think, in terms of negotiating with their partners much as they would do in any other international context. The observation that 'decisionally, the Community is closer to the United Nations than it is to the United States' is therefore particularly telling.

This situation is heightened by the weight acquired in the area of law-making by COREPER (the Committee of Permanent Representatives of the Member States) and its many subcommittees. The permanent representatives are ambassadors and the subcommittees are composed of national officials. While a minister may occasionally be expected to deal with a given problem in a supranational spirit, it would be naïve to expect an ambassador or a national bureaucrat, whatever his leanings, to assist willfully in the process of the wasting away of Member State power, thereby blighting his own career.

2. It was noted above that, unlike federal constitutions, the treaties creating international organisations do not usually enjoy higher-law status with regard to the laws of the contracting powers. Article VI of the American Constitution reads: 'the laws of the United States... shall be the supreme law of the land; and the judges in every state shall be bound thereby; any thing in the constitution or laws of any state to the contrary notwithstanding'. In the same vein section 109 of the Australian Constitution provides that 'When a law of a State is inconsistent with the law of the Commonwealth the latter shall prevail and the former shall be... invalid', and the German Fundamental Law stipulates just as clearly that *Bundesrecht bricht Landesrecht*. On the contrary, the Rome Treaty, while including some hortatory provisions to the same effect (Article 5 [now 4(3) TEU]), fails to state squarely whether Community law is pre-eminent *vis-à-vis* prior and subsequent Member State law.

The now undisputed existence of a supremacy clause in the Community framework is therefore a product of judicial creativeness. In *Costa* v *Enel*, a case which arose in the early 1960s before a *giudice conciliatore* (local magistrate) in Milan, a shareholder of a nationalised power company challenged as being contrary to the Treaty the Italian law nationalising the electric industry. The Italian Government claimed before the Court of Justice that the Court had no business to deal with the matter: the magistrate, it said, should apply the nationalisation law as the most current indication of parliamentary intention and could not avail of the reference procedure provided for by the Treaty. But the Court ruled that 'by creating a Community of unlimited duration, having its own institutions, its own personality... and, more particularly, real powers stemming from a limitation of sovereignty or a transfer of powers from the States to the Community, the Member States have limited their sovereign rights ... and have thus created a body of law which binds both their nationals and themselves'.

Is this line of reasoning entirely cogent? Some legal writers doubt it and a few have regarded Costa V Enel as an example of judicial activism 'running wild'.[10] Yet, the Court's supremacy doctrine was accepted by the judiciaries and the administrations of both the original and the new Member States, with the exception of some grumblings by the *French Conseil d'Etat*, the Italian *Corte costituzionale* and a couple of English law lords. Lord Denning, a majestic but irritable elderly gentleman, was caught intimating that 'once a bill is passed by Parliament, that will dispose of all this discussion about the Treaty'.[11] A few years later, however, Lord Diplock admitted that even subsequent acts of Parliament must be interpreted in line with Community law, no matter how far-fetched the interpretation.[12] Lord Diplock, and many other national judges before him, obviously realised that the alternative to the supremacy clause would have been a rapid erosion of the Community; and this was a possibility that nobody really envisaged, not even the most intransigent custodians of national sovereignty. Actually, the 'or else' argument, though not fully spelled out, was used by the Court, and it was this argument, much more than the one I have quoted, that led to a ready reception of the doctrine in *Costa* v *Enel*.

10 Rasmussen, *On Law and Policy in the European Court of Justice: A Comparative Study in Judicial Policy-making* (Dordrecht-Boston-Lancaster: Martinus Nijhoff, 1986). [cf p. 68]

11 *Felixstowe Dock and Ry Co.* v *British Transport Docks Board* [1976] 2 CMLR 655.

12 *Garland* v *British Rail Engineering* [1982] 2 All ER 402.

But the recognition of Community pre-eminence was not only an indispensable development, it was also a logical development. It is self-evident that in a federal or quasi-federal context the issue of supremacy will arise only if federal norms are to apply directly, that is to bear upon the federation's citizens without any need of intervention by the Member States. Article 189 [now 288 TFEU] of the Rome Treaty identifies a category of Community norms that do not require national implementing measures but are binding on the States and their citizens as soon as they enter into force: the founding fathers called them 'regulations' and provided them principally for those areas where the Treaty itself merely defines the thrust of Community policy and leaves its elaboration to later decisions of the Council and the Commission. One year before *Costa* v *Enel*, however, the Court had enormously extended the Community power to deal directly with the public by ruling in *Van Gend en Loos* that even Treaty provisions may be relied upon by private individuals if they expressly grant them rights and impose on the Member States an obligation so precise and unconditional that it can be fulfilled without the necessity of further measures.

■ QUESTION

How persuasive is the *or else* argument, set out in the final sentence of the penultimate paragraph of this extract?

C: Procedure and remedies

EU law establishes substantive rights. It also establishes the constitutional principles which allow a private individual to rely on those rights at national level to defeat conflicting national law – direct effect, plus supremacy, plus the preliminary reference under Article 267 TFEU. However, EU law also exerts an impact on the national law of procedure and remedies. National autonomy is in principle respected, but subjected to overriding requirements imposed by EU law. Since the entry into force of the Lisbon Treaty, Article 19(1) TEU provides that 'Member States shall provide remedies sufficient to ensure effective legal protection in the fields covered by Union law', but this spare sentence reveals little. It is, in fact, a summary of an intricate and nuanced adventure undertaken by the Court of Justice. This is now examined.

The Court's first clear explanation of the division of function between EU law and national law was supplied in the next case.

Comet v *Produktschap* (Case 45/76)

[1976] ECR 2043, Court of Justice of the European Communities

Comet argued before Dutch courts that it had paid sums to Produktschap on the export of plants and bulbs which were incompatible with (what was then) Article 16 (Chapter 10; Article 16 was a transitional provision deleted by the Treaty of Amsterdam). It sought reimbursement. The defendant argued that the claim could not succeed because it had been lodged after the expiry of the limitation period for such actions under Dutch law. A Treaty-conferred right; but national procedures. The issue was referred to the Court of Justice. In the following extract, the Court first explains the nature of Comet's argument designed to defeat Dutch procedural law, and then disposes of the case.

[9] The applicant in the main action contends, on the other hand, that the primacy of Community law means that it overrules any decision which constitutes an infringement of it and that, before the national courts, which are bound to protect the rights conferred on it by Article 16, it possesses, in consequence, an independent right of action which is unaffected by limitations provided for under national law which are liable to weaken the impact of the direct effect of that article in the legal order of the Member States.

[10] Thus, the question referred seeks to establish whether the procedural rules for proceedings designed to ensure the protection of the rights which individuals acquire as a result of the direct effect of a Community provision, in the present case Article 16 of the Treaty and Article 10 of Regulation No 234/68, especially the rules concerning the period within which an action must be brought are governed by the national law of the Member State where the action is brought or whether, on the other hand, they are independent and fall to be determined only by Community law itself.

[11] The prohibition laid down in Article 16 of the Treaty and that contained in Article 10 of Regulation No 234/68 have direct effect and confer on individuals rights which the national courts must protect.

[12] Thus, in application of the principle of cooperation laid down in Article 5 [now 4(3) TEU] of the Treaty, the national courts are entrusted with ensuring the legal protection conferred on individuals by the direct effect of the provisions of Community law.

[13] Consequently, in the absence of any relevant Community rules, it is for the national legal order of each Member State to designate the competent courts and to lay down the procedural rules for proceedings designed to ensure the protection of the rights which individuals acquire through the direct effect of Community law, provided that such rules are not less favourable than those governing the same right of action on an internal matter.

[14] Articles 100 to 102 [now 114–115, 117 TFEU] and 235 [now 352 TFEU] of the Treaty enable the appropriate steps to be taken as necessary, to eliminate differences between the provisions laid down in such matters by law, regulation or administrative action in Member States if these differences are found to be such as to cause distortion or to affect the functioning of the common market.

[15] In default of such harmonization measures, the rights conferred by Community law must be exercised before the national courts in accordance with the rules of procedure laid down by national law.

[16] The position would be different only if those rules and time-limits made it impossible in practice to exercise rights which the national courts have a duty to protect.

[17] This does not apply to the fixing of a reasonable period of limitation within which an action must be brought.

[18] The fixing, as regards fiscal proceedings, of such a period is in fact an application of a fundamental principle of legal certainty which protects both the authority concerned and the party from whom payment is claimed.

[19] The answer must therefore be that, in the case of a litigant who is challenging before the national courts a decision of a national body for incompatibility with Community law, that law, in its present state, does not prevent the expiry of the period within which proceedings must be brought under national law from being raised against him, provided that the procedural rules applicable to his case are not less favourable than those governing the same right of action on an internal matter.

NOTE: At first glance, then, the applicant able to show a violation of EU law is dependent on existing national procedures, which may thwart the claim. Procedural law varies from State to State, with the result that in practice the means of enforcement of EU law are not uniform State by State. (See J. Bridge, 'Procedural Aspects of the Enforcement of EC Law through the Legal Systems of the Member States' (1984) 9 EL Rev 28.) Paragraph 14 of *Comet* (Case 45/76) hints at the way to resolve such disunity, but little legislative progress has been made (except in the special case of public procurement).

However, the judgment in *Comet* (Case 45/76) does not confer absolute autonomy on the national system. In the concluding words of para 13, and in para 16, it offers two EU law qualifications to the approach which a national court may adopt in providing remedies for a litigant which has suffered loss as a result of violation of obligations arising under the Treaty. These have become commonly known as the 'the principle of equivalence' and the 'principle of effectiveness' respectively.

The 'principle of equivalence' was discussed by the Court in the next case.

Shirley Preston and Others v *Wolverhampton NHS Healthcare Trust and Others* (Case C-78/98)

[2000] ECR I-3201, Court of Justice of the European Communities

This was a sex equality claim based on the Equal Pay Act 1970 which in turn constituted the UK's implementation of Article 119 of the EEC Treaty (see now, after much amendment, Article 157 TFEU). The applicant claimed to be subject to procedures that were less favourable than those applying to similar domestic claims under the Sex Discrimination Act 1975 and the Race Relations Act 1976. The Court began with a statement of principle:

> [31] First, it should be borne in mind that, according to settled case law, in the absence of relevant Community rules, it is for the national legal order of each Member State to designate the competent courts and to lay down the procedural rules for proceedings designed to ensure the protection of the rights which individuals acquire through the direct effect of Community law, provided that such rules are not less favourable than those governing similar domestic actions (principle of equivalence) and are not framed in such a way as to render impossible in practice the exercise of rights conferred by Community law (principle of effectiveness).

It proceeded to conduct a more specific examination:

> [49] In order to verify whether the principle of equivalence has been complied with in the present case, it is for the national court, which alone has direct knowledge of the procedural rules governing actions in the field of domestic law, to verify whether the procedural rules intended to ensure that the rights derived by individuals from Community law are safeguarded under domestic law comply with that principle and to consider both the purpose and the essential characteristics of allegedly similar domestic actions (see Case C-326/96 *Levez* [1998] ECR I-7835, paragraphs 39 and 43).
>
> [50] However, with a view to the appraisal to be carried out by the national court, the Court may provide guidance for the interpretation of Community law.
>
> [51] It must be borne in mind that the Court held, in paragraph 46 of *Levez*, a judgment delivered after the House of Lords sought a ruling in this case, that the EPA was the domestic legislation which gave effect to the Community principle of non-discrimination on grounds of sex in relation to pay, pursuant to Article 119 of the Treaty and Council Directive 75/117/EEC of 10 February 1975 on the approximation of the laws of the Member States relating to the application of the principle of equal pay for men and women (OJ 1975 L 45, p. 19). In paragraph 47 of the same judgment, the Court stated that the fact that the same procedural rules applied to two comparable claims, one relying on a right conferred by Community law, the other on a right acquired under domestic law, was not enough to ensure compliance with the principle of equivalence, since one and the same form of action was involved.
>
> [52] Since, following the accession of the United Kingdom to the Communities, the EPA constituted the legislation by means of which the United Kingdom discharged its obligations under Article 119 of the Treaty and, subsequently, under Directive 75/117, the Court concluded that the EPA could not provide an appropriate ground of comparison against which to measure compliance with the principle of equivalence (*Levez* paragraph 48).
>
> [53] The answer to the first part of the second question must therefore be that an action alleging infringement of a statute such as the EPA does not constitute a domestic action similar to an action alleging infringement of Article 119 of the Treaty.
>
> [54] By the second part of its second question the House of Lords seeks to ascertain the Community law criteria for identifying a similar action in domestic law.
>
> [55] The principle of equivalence requires that the rule at issue be applied without distinction, whether the infringement alleged is of Community law or national law, where the purpose and cause of action are similar (*Levez*, paragraph 41).
>
> [56] In order to determine whether the principle of equivalence has been complied with in the present case, the national court – which alone has direct knowledge of the procedural rules governing actions in the field of employment law – must consider both the purpose and the essential characteristics of allegedly similar domestic actions (*Levez*, paragraph 43).

[57] In view of the foregoing, the answer to the second part of the second question must be that, in order to determine whether a right of action available under domestic law is a domestic action similar to proceedings to give effect to rights conferred by Article 119 of the Treaty, the national court must consider whether the actions concerned are similar as regards their purpose, cause of action and essential characteristics.

[58] By the third part of its second question, the House of Lords seeks to ascertain what are the relevant criteria for determining whether the procedural rules governing any claim which it may have identified as being similar are more favourable than the procedural rules which govern the enforcement of rights conferred by Article 119 of the Treaty.

[59] For the purposes of the appraisal to be undertaken by the national court, regard must be had to the relevant guidance as to the interpretation of Community law given in Levez.

[60] Thus, in paragraph 51, the Court stated that the principle of equivalence would be infringed if a person relying on a right conferred by Community law were forced to incur additional costs and delay by comparison with a claimant whose action was based solely on domestic law.

[61] More generally, it observed that whenever it fell to be determined whether a procedural provision of national law was less favourable than those governing similar domestic actions, the national court must take into account the role played by that provision in the procedure as a whole, as well as the operation and any special features of that procedure before the different national courts (*Levez*, paragraph 44).

[62] It follows that the various aspects of the procedural rules cannot be examined in isolation but must be placed in their general context. Moreover, such an examination may not be carried out subjectively by reference to circumstances of fact but must involve an objective comparison, in the abstract, of the procedural rules at issue.

[63] In view of the foregoing, the answer to the third part of the second question must be that, in order to decide whether procedural rules are equivalent, the national court must verify objectively, in the abstract, whether the rules at issue are similar taking into account the role played by those rules in the procedure as a whole, as well as the operation of that procedure and any special features of those rules.

NOTE: Recognition that the national court alone has direct knowledge of the relevant procedural rules (para 56) justifies caution on the part of the Court of Justice when invited to intrude on national procedural autonomy. However, turning from the 'principle of equivalence' to the 'principle of effectiveness' (a modern rewriting of para 16 of the judgment in *Comet* (Case 45/76)) the Court of Justice has been increasingly prepared to make specific the nature of the obligation cast on national judges by EU law. In defence of legal certainty all legal systems impose time limits. Such limits imposed by national law have proved a particular favourite target of litigants basing their action on EU law. *Comet* (Case 45/76, p. 104) was a case of this nature. In the next case a time limit complied with the 'principle of equivalence' but fell foul of the 'principle of effectiveness'.

***Marks and Spencer plc* v *Commissioners of Customs and Excise* (Case C-62/00)**

[2002] ECR I-6325, Court of Justice of the European Communities

The UK was in breach of the Sixth VAT Directive, Directive 77/388. The relevant provisions had direct effect, so Marks and Spencer could rely on them before the English courts to seek recovery of money wrongly paid to the tax authorities. But the company was faced by rules that retroactively curtailed the period within which repayment of sums could be sought.

[34] It should be recalled at the outset that in the absence of Community rules on the repayment of national charges wrongly levied it is for the domestic legal system of each Member State to designate the courts and tribunals having jurisdiction and to lay down the detailed procedural rules governing actions for safeguarding rights which individuals derive from Community law, provided, first, that such rules are not less favourable than those governing similar domestic actions (the principle of equivalence) and, second, that they do not render virtually impossible or excessively difficult the exercise of rights conferred by Community law (the principle of effectiveness) . . .

[35] As regards the latter principle, the Court has held that in the interests of legal certainty, which protects both the taxpayer and the administration, it is compatible with Community law to lay down reasonable time-limits for bringing proceedings. . .. Such time-limits are not liable to render virtually impossible or excessively difficult the exercise of the rights conferred by Community law. In that context, a national limitation period of three years which runs from the date of the contested payment appears to be reasonable . . .

[36] Moreover . . . national legislation curtailing the period within which recovery may be sought of sums charged in breach of Community law is, subject to certain conditions, compatible with Community law. First, it must not be intended specifically to limit the consequences of a judgment of the Court to the effect that national legislation concerning a specific tax is incompatible with Community law. Secondly, the time set for its application must be sufficient to ensure that the right to repayment is effective. In that connection, the Court has held that legislation which is not in fact retrospective in scope complies with that condition.

[37] It is plain, however, that that condition is not satisfied by national legislation such as that at issue in the main proceedings which reduces from six to three years the period within which repayment may be sought of VAT wrongly paid, by providing that the new time-limit is to apply immediately to all claims made after the date of enactment of that legislation and to claims made between that date and an earlier date, being that of the entry into force of the legislation, as well as to claims for repayment made before the date of entry into force which are still pending on that date.

[38] Whilst national legislation reducing the period within which repayment of sums collected in breach of Community law may be sought is not incompatible with the principle of effectiveness, it is subject to the condition not only that the new limitation period is reasonable but also that the new legislation includes transitional arrangements allowing an adequate period after the enactment of the legislation for lodging the claims for repayment which persons were entitled to submit under the original legislation. Such transitional arrangements are necessary where the immediate application to those claims of a limitation period shorter than that which was previously in force would have the effect of retroactively depriving some individuals of their right to repayment, or of allowing them too short a period for asserting that right.

[39] In that connection it should be noted that Member States are required as a matter of principle to repay taxes collected in breach of Community law. . ., and whilst the Court has acknowledged that, by way of exception to that principle, fixing a reasonable period for claiming repayment is compatible with Community law, that is in the interests of legal certainty, as was noted in paragraph 35 hereof. However, in order to serve their purpose of ensuring legal certainty limitation periods must be fixed in advance . . .

[40] Accordingly, legislation such as that at issue in the main proceedings, the retroactive effect of which deprives individuals of any possibility of exercising a right which they previously enjoyed with regard to repayment of VAT collected in breach of provisions of the Sixth Directive with direct effect must be held to be incompatible with the principle of effectiveness.

[41] That applies notwithstanding the argument of the United Kingdom Government to the effect that the enactment of the legislation at issue in the main proceedings was motivated by the legitimate purpose of striking a due balance between the individual and the collective interest and of enabling the State to plan income and expenditure without the disruption caused by major unforeseen liabilities.

[42] Whilst such a purpose may serve to justify fixing reasonable limitation periods for bringing claims, as was noted in paragraph 35, it cannot permit them to be so applied that rights conferred on individuals by Community law are no longer safeguarded.

NOTE: It is plain that the 'principle of effectiveness' has potency before national courts. It offers litigants an EU means to try to lever open settled provisions of national law governing procedure and remedies. The cases dealing with time-limits reveal the Court's awareness that preserving finality in adjudication may be a reason for curtailing the vigour of the principle of effectiveness. In Case C-234/04 *Rosmarie Kapferer* v *Schlank & Schick* [2006] ECR I-2585 the Court accepted that an appellate court is not required to intervene even if there has been a misapplication of EU law in the lower court. And in Case C-392/04 & C-422/04 i-21 *Germany and Arcor* v *Germany* [2006] ECR I-8559 it held that EU law does *not* require that administrative bodies be placed under an obligation to re-open a decision which has become final upon expiry of reasonable time-limits for legal remedies or by exhaustion of those remedies. So concern to preserve legal certainty, to which the Court referred at paras 35 and 39 of *Marks and Spencer* (Case C-62/00), may be enough to defeat an argument that proceedings should be re-opened, although in the case itself the Court reminds the national court of the 'principle of equivalence'. In so far as German law would allow the procedure to be re-opened in a domestic case, at least the same concession must be made in a claim based on EU law. It is, however, important to grasp that context matters. The Court's receptiveness to the preservation of legal certainty and the insulation of national procedures from intervention is noticeably weaker where consumers wishing to rely on EU law find themselves prejudiced by national procedural law, as the next extract reveals.

Elisa María Mostaza Claro v *Centro Móvil Milenium SL* (Case C-168/05)

[2006] ECR I-10421, Court of Justice of the European Communities

Directive 93/13 provides that unfair terms in consumer contracts shall be unenforceable. It is a harmonization Directive (Chapter 2, p. 33). In this litigation a consumer had failed to argue that an arbitration clause was unfair during the course of the arbitration. She raised the matter only in subsequent proceedings contesting the (adverse) arbitral finding. As a matter of Spanish law this was too late. The Spanish court asked the Court of Justice whether the application of Directive 93/13 required that the closure under Spanish law be levered open. Which interest should prevail?

[33] Móvil and the German Government submit that, if the national court were allowed to determine whether an arbitration agreement is void where the consumer did not raise such an objection during the arbitration proceedings, this would seriously undermine the effectiveness of arbitration awards.

[34] It follows from that argument that it is in the interest of efficient arbitration proceedings that review of arbitration awards should be limited in scope and that annulment of or refusal to recognise an award should be possible only in exceptional circumstances (Case C-126/97 *Eco Swiss* [1999] ECR I-3055, paragraph 35).

[35] However, the Court has already ruled that, where its domestic rules of procedure require a national court to grant an application for annulment of an arbitration award where such an application is founded on failure to observe national rules of public policy, it must also grant such an application where it is founded on failure to comply with Community rules of this type (see, to that effect, *Eco Swiss*, paragraph 37).

[36] The importance of consumer protection has in particular led the Community legislature to lay down, in Article 6(1) of the Directive, that unfair terms used in a contract concluded with a consumer by a seller or supplier 'shall... not be binding on the consumer'. This is a mandatory provision which, taking into account the weaker position of one of the parties to the contract, aims to replace the formal balance which the latter establishes between the rights and obligations of the parties with an effective balance which re-establishes equality between them.

[37] Moreover, as the aim of the Directive is to strengthen consumer protection, it constitutes, according to Article 3(1)(t) EC, a measure which is essential to the accomplishment of the tasks entrusted to the Community and, in particular, to raising the standard of living and the quality of life in its territory (see, by analogy, concerning Article 81 EC, *Eco Swiss*, paragraph 36).

[38] The nature and importance of the public interest underlying the protection which the Directive confers on consumers justify, moreover, the national court being required to assess of its own motion whether a contractual term is unfair, compensating in this way for the imbalance which exists between the consumer and the seller or supplier.

[39] Having regard to the foregoing, the answer to the question referred must be that the Directive must be interpreted as meaning that a national court seised of an action for annulment of an arbitration award must determine whether the arbitration agreement is void and annul that award where that agreement contains an unfair term, even though the consumer has not pleaded that invalidity in the course of the arbitration proceedings, but only in that of the action for annulment.

NOTE: But consumers must not remain passive. In *Asturcom Telecomunicaciones SL* v *Maria Cristina Rodriguez Noguiera* (Case C-40/08) [2009] ECR I-9579 the consumer had by contrast failed even to challenge the arbitral award within the time limit. It had therefore become final under Spanish law. The Court of Justice accepted the importance of ensuring the sound administration of justice and it therefore seems the rule of finality would apply unaffected by the demands of 'effectiveness'—though it would be set aside if the principle of equivalence were breached, which required a comparison with national law to be carried out by the national court.

It is plain that the scope of application of the principle of effectiveness as a basis to set aside national procedures involves drawing some fine lines. A vivid example is provided by Case C-618/10 *Banco Español de Crédito* v *Joaquín Calderón Camino* judgment of 14 June 2012. The Court found that EU law did *not* allow the application of a Spanish rule precluding a court before which an application for repayment of a loan has been made against a consumer from assessing whether a term concerning interest on late payments is unfair, where the consumer has not lodged an objection. EU law therefore empowers Spanish courts to intervene when they could not do so under Spanish law. But it really is a fine line – in contrast, A.G. Trstenjak had proposed the Court find *no* breach of the effectiveness principle and her Opinion stresses the virtue of the rule's contribution to ensuring the speedy administration of civil justice.

■ QUESTION

Reviewing aspects of this accumulated case law Angela Ward has concluded that 'All of this is too confusing', adding that the Court should 'place primary reliance on the principle of equivalence, rather than the principle of effectiveness, in assessing the compatibility of national procedural rules with Community law. Once this test has been satisfied, procedural rules will be compatible with Community law, provided that they do not strike at the essence of right of access to a court, pursue a legitimate aim, and are proportionate' ((2008) 33 EL Rev 739, 753, 754). Do you think the Court has intervened too deeply into national procedures? Would Ward's formula offer a better balance? To what extent should Article 19(1) TEU, an innovation of the Lisbon Treaty which provides that 'Member States shall provide remedies sufficient to ensure effective legal protection in the fields covered by Union law' (p. 104), affect the Court's approach, if at all?

NOTE: Other decisions that are of illustrative value include Case C-2/06 *Willy Kempter* [2008] ECR I-411; Case C-2/08 *Fallimento Olimiclub Srl* [2009] ECR I-7501; Case C-445/06 *Danske Slagterier* [2009] ECR I-2119; Case C-89/10 *Q-Beef* [2011] ECR I-7819; Case C-249/11 *Byankov* judgment of 4 October 2012; Case C-213/13 *Impresa Pizzarotti* judgment of 10 July 2014. The rich, even eccentric, variety in the case law combined with the intrusive character of EU law is well captured by the title of an article by A. Arnull: 'The Principle of Effective Judicial Protection in EU law: An Unruly Horse?' (2011) 36 EL Rev 51. And scepticism that the procedural autonomy promised by *Comet* (Case 45/76 p.000 above) survives is clear on the face of Bobek, M., 'Why There is no Principle of Procedural Autonomy of the Member States' in B. de Witte and H. Micklitz (eds), *The European Court of Justice and Autonomy of the Member States* (Intersentia, 2011).

Consider *Commission* v *UK* (Case C-246/89R), at p. 91. Re-read the summary of the facts. While the Commission was pursuing the UK at EU level, private parties were acting before English courts to protect their interests. Factortame was one of several Spanish fishing undertakings holding a British registration which alleged that it had been discriminated against on grounds of nationality contrary to the Treaty. It saw the imminent prospect of severe curtailment of its fishing operations. Factortame wished to challenge the UK's Merchant Shipping Act 1988, which it did by an application for judicial review of the decision of the Secretary of State for Transport which brought particular provisions of the Act into force. This raised fundamental issues of constitutional law in the UK relating to Parliamentary Sovereignty. The *Factortame* litigation provides an extremely important indication of modern British judicial thinking about the constitutional implications of membership of the Community, as it then was. However, in the present context the tale deserves attention for the Court's view of the application of national remedies and procedures in such litigation.

***R* v *Secretary of State for Transport, ex parte Factortame* (Case C-213/89)**

[1990] ECR I-2433, [1990] 3 WLR 852, Court of Justice of the European Communities

Factortame's claim that the Act violated Treaty rules prohibiting discrimination was initially treated in straightforward fashion; a reference was made by the High Court to the Court of Justice requesting assistance in the interpretation of relevant points of law ([1989] 2 CMLR 353, Case C-221/89 – eventually, in July 1991, the Court ruled in terms favourable to Factortame – [1991] ECR I-3905.) But what should happen pending that ruling? Should the Act apply, or should it be suspended? The House of Lords ruled that as a matter of English law it had no power to make the award of interim relief against the application of the statute which Factortame had sought (*Factortame* v *Secretary of State for Transport* (No 1) [1989] 3 CMLR 1, [1990] 2 AC 85). However, the House of Lords referred to the Court of Justice the following questions relating to the impact of (what was then) Community law on available remedies:

1. Where:
   (i) a party before the national court claims to be entitled to rights under Community law having direct effect in national law ('the rights claimed'),
   (ii) a national measure in clear terms will, if applied, automatically deprive that party of the rights claimed,
   (iii) there are serious arguments both for and against the existence of the rights claimed and the national court has sought a preliminary ruling under Article 177 [now 234] as to whether or not the rights claimed exist,
   (iv) the national law presumes the national measure in question to be compatible with Community law unless and until it is declared incompatible,
   (v) the national court has no power to give interim protection to the rights claimed by suspending the application of the national measure pending the preliminary ruling,
   (vi) if the preliminary ruling is in the event in favour of the rights claimed, the party entitled to those rights is likely to have suffered irremediable damage unless given such interim protection, does Community law either
      (a) oblige the national court to grant such interim protection of the rights claimed; or
      (b) give the Court power to grant such interim protection of the rights claimed?

2. If Question 1(a) is answered in the negative and Question 1(b) in the affirmative, what are the criteria to be applied in deciding whether or not to grant such interim protection of the rights claimed?

The Court of Justice ruled within 13 months in June 1990.

[17] It is clear from the information before the Court, and in particular from the judgment making the reference and, as described above, the course taken by the proceedings in the national courts before which the case came at first and second instance, that the preliminary question raised by the House of Lords seeks essentially to ascertain whether a national court which, in a case before it concerning Community law, considers that the sole obstacle which precludes it from granting interim relief is a rule of national law, must disapply that rule.

[18] For the purpose of replying to that question, it is necessary to point out that in its judgment of 9 March 1978 in Case 106/77 (*Amministrazione delle Finanzedello Stato* v *Simmenthal SpA* [1978] ECR 629) the Court held that directly applicable rules of Community law 'must be fully and uniformly applied in all the Member States from the date of their entry into force and for so long as they continue in force' (paragraph 14) and that 'in accordance with the principle of the precedence of Community law, the relationship between provisions of the Treaty and directly applicable measures of the institutions on the one hand and the national law of the Member States on the other is such that those provisions and measures... by their entry into force render automatically inapplicable any conflicting provision of... national law' (paragraph 17).

[19] In accordance with the case-law of the Court, it is for the national courts, in application of the principle of co-operation laid down in Article 5 of the EEC Treaty [now Article 4(3) TFEU], to ensure the legal protection which persons derive from the direct effect of provisions of Community law (see, most recently, the judgments of 10 July 1980 in Case 811/79 *Ariete SpA* v *Amministrazione delle Finanzedello Stato* [1980] ECR 2545 and *MIRECO SaS* v *Amministrazione delle Finanzedello Stato* [1980] ECR 2559).

[20] The Court has also held that any provision of a national legal system and any legislative, administrative or judicial practice which might impair the effectiveness of Community law by withholding from the national court having jurisdiction to apply such law the power to do everything necessary at the moment of its application to set aside national legislative provisions which might prevent, even temporarily, Community rules from having full force and effect are incompatible with those requirements, which are the very essence of Community law (judgment of 9 March 1978 in *Simmenthal*, cited above, at paragraphs 22 and 23).

[21] It must be added that the full effectiveness of Community law would be just as much impaired if a rule of national law could prevent a court seised of a dispute governed by Community law from granting interim relief in order to ensure the full effectiveness of the judgment to be given on the existence of the rights claimed under Community law. It follows that a court which in those circumstances would grant interim relief, if it were not for a rule of national law, is obliged to set aside that rule.

[22] That interpretation is reinforced by the system established by Article 177 of the EEC Treaty [now Article 268 TFEU] whose effectiveness would be impaired if a national court, having stayed proceedings pending the reply by the Court of Justice to the question referred to it for a preliminary ruling, were not able to grant interim relief until it delivered its judgment following the reply given by the Court of Justice.

[23] Consequently, the reply to the question raised should be that Community law must be interpreted as meaning that a national court which, in a case before it concerning Community law, considers that the sole obstacle which precludes it from granting interim relief is a rule of national law must set aside that rule.

NOTE: The Court's brisk reformulation of the question causes it to be rather dismissive of the view advanced by the UK that *Simmenthal* (Case 106/77, p. 75) was not directly in point because the rights under Community law in that case had been firmly established and were not, as in *Factortame*, merely claimed. Advocate-General Tesauro was rather fuller in his treatment of the role of interim protection in a system of effective remedies.

***R* v *Secretary of State for Transport, ex parte Factortame* (Case C-213/89)**

[1990] ECR I-2433, [1990] 3 WLR 852, Court of Justice of the European Communities

ADVOCATE-GENERAL TESAURO:. . . Sometimes the right's existence is established too late for the right claimed to be fully and usefully exercised, which is the more likely to be the case the more structured and complex, and the more probably rich in safeguards, is the procedure culminating in the definitive establishment of the right. The result is that in such a case the utility as well as the effectiveness of judicial protection may be lost and there could be a betrayal of the principle, long established in jurisprudence, according to which the need to have recourse to legal proceedings to enforce a right should not occasion damage to the party in the right.

Interim protection has precisely that objective purpose, namely to ensure that the time needed to establish the existence of the right does not in the end have the effect of irremediably depriving the right of substance, by eliminating any possibility of exercising it; in brief, the purpose of interim protection is to achieve that fundamental objective of every legal system, the effectiveness of judicial protection. Interim protection is intended to prevent so far as possible the damage occasioned by the fact that the establishment and the existence of the right are not fully contemporaneous from prejudicing the effectiveness and the very purpose of establishing the right, which was also specifically affirmed by the Court when it linked interim protection to a requirement that, when delivered, the judgment will be fully effective; or to the need to 'preserve the existing position pending a decision on the substance of the case'.

Now that the function of interim protection has been brought into focus, such protection can be seen to be a fundamental and indispensable instrument of any judicial system, which seeks to achieve, in the particular case and always in an effective manner, the objective of determining the existence of a right and more generally of giving effect to the relevant legal provision, whenever the duration of the proceedings is likely to prejudice the attainment of this objective and therefore to nullify the effectiveness of the judgment.

The requirement for interim protection, moreover, as has already been noted, arises in the same terms, both where the establishment of the right's existence involves the facts and, consequently, the determination of the correct provision to be applied, that is to say where the uncertainty as to the outcome of the application involves – although the expression is not perhaps a happy one – 'the facts', and where it is a question of choosing between two or more provisions which may be applicable (for example, a classification problem), irrespective of whether both are presumed to be valid or whether one is presumed to be incompatible with the other, which is of a higher order or in any event has precedence.

In particular, where, as in the case now before the Court, the determination as to the existence of the right not only involves a choice between two or more provisions which may be applicable but also involves a prior review of the validity or compatibility of one provision vis-à-vis another of a higher order or in any event having precedence, the difference is merely one of appearance, particularly when that review is entrusted to a court on which special jurisdiction has been conferred for the purpose. This situation, too, is fully covered by the typical function of judicial proceedings, which seek to establish the existence of and hence to give effect to the right, so that the requirement that the individual's position be protected on a provisional basis remains the same, inasmuch as it is a question of determining, interpreting and applying to the case in question the relevant (and valid) legal rules.

It follows that what is commonly called the presumption of validity, which attaches to laws or administrative acts no less than it does to Community acts, until such time as it is established by judicial determination that the measure in question is incompatible with a rule of law of a higher order or in any event having precedence, *to the extent that such a procedure is provided for*, does not constitute a formal obstacle to the interim protection of enforceable legal rights. In fact, precisely because what is concerned is a presumption, which as such may be rebutted by the final determination, it remains necessary to provide a remedy to compensate for the fact that the final ruling establishing the existence of the right may come too late and therefore be of no use to the successful party.

In fact, it is certain and undeniable that a provision, whether it is contained in an Act of Parliament or a Community act, or in an administrative act, must be presumed to be valid. But that cannot and must not mean that the courts are precluded from temporarily paralyzing its effects with regard to the concrete case before them where, pending a final determination on its validity *vis-à-vis* or compatibility with a provision of a higher order or having precedence, one or other of the legal rights in question is likely to be irremediably impaired and there is a suspicion (the degree of which must be established) that the final determination may entail a finding that the statute or administrative act in question is invalid.

In brief, the presumption that a law or an administrative act is valid may not and must not mean that the very possibility of interim protection is precluded *where the measure in question may form the subject of a final judicial review of its validity.*

Far from running counter to the principle of the validity of laws or administrative acts, which finds expression in a presumption that may always be rebutted by a final determination, interim protection in fact removes the risk that that presumption may lead to the perverse result, certainly not desired by any legal system, negating the function of judicial review and, in particular, of the review of the validity of laws. To take a different view would amount to radically denying the possibility of interim protection, not only in relation to laws, but absolutely, given that any act of a public authority, whether it is a rule-making instrument properly so-called or an individual decision, is presumed to be valid until the outcome of the judicial review of its validity.

NOTE: It was then for the House of Lords, equipped with the ruling that it possessed the power to grant interim relief, to decide whether to exercise that power on the facts of the case before it.

Their Lordships considered the case appropriate for the grant of relief in favour of Factortame, pending the final ruling ([1991] 1 All ER 70, [1990] 3 CMLR 375). Lord Bridge was moved by some well-publicized denunciations of the Court of Justice's alleged intrusion on the sovereignty of the UK (see especially Hansard, HC Debs, vol. 174, 20 June 1990) to remark that:

there is nothing in any way novel in according supremacy to rules of Community law in those areas to which they apply and to insist that, in the protection of rights under Community law, national courts must not be inhibited by rules of national law from granting interim relief in appropriate cases is no more than a logical recognition of that supremacy.

FURTHER READING

Bengoetxea, J., 'Is Direct Effect a General Principle of European Law?' Ch 1 in Bernitz, U., Nergelius, J., and Cardner, A., (eds), *General Principles of EC Law in a Process of Development* (The Hague: Kluwer, 2008).

Chalmers, D. and Barroso, L., 'What *Van Gend en Loos* stands for' (2014) 12 Int Jnl Const Law 105.

Dougan, M., 'The Vicissitudes of Life at the Coalface: Remedies and Procedures for Enforcing Union Law Before the National Courts' Ch 14 in P. Craig and G. de Búrca, *The Evolution of EU Law* (Oxford: OUP, 2nd ed., 2011).

Eliantonio, M., 'The Influence of the ECJ's Case Law on Time Limits in the Italian, German and English Administrative Legal Systems: A Comparative Analysis' (2009) 15 European Public Law 615.

Havelka, L., 'Escaping the Trap: The Simplified Application of EU Law' (2014) 10 Croatian Ybk ELP 131.

Lenaerts, K., 'The Rule of Law and the Coherence of the Judicial System of the European Union' (2007) 44 CML Rev 1625.

NOTE: For additional material and resources see the Online Resource Centre at: www.oxfordtextbooks.co.uk/orc/weatherill12e.

5

The Direct Effect of Directives

SECTION 1: ESTABLISHING THE PRINCIPLE

The most difficult area relating to 'direct effect' arises in the application of the notion to EU *Directives*. Although the rest of this chapter concentrates on this area, it is important not to develop an inflated notion of the importance of the problem of the direct effect of Directives. Directives are after all only one source of Union law. However, the issue deserves examination in some depth, not least because Directives play a major role in elaborating the detailed scope of Union policy-making in respect of which the Treaty provides a mere framework. Moreover, Directives are a rather peculiar type of act – Union law but implemented at national level. An examination of this area, then, should reveal much about the general problem of the interrelation of national law with the EU legal order.

The starting point is Article 288 TFEU, formerly Article 249 EC, and before that Article 189 EEC, set out at p. 27. This suggests that a Directive, in contrast to a Regulation, would *not* be directly effective. Regulations are directly applicable, and if they meet the *Van Gend en Loos* (Case 26/62) test for direct effect they are directly effective too. They are law in the Member States (direct applicability) and they may confer legally enforceable rights on individuals (direct effect). Directives, in marked contrast, are clearly dependent on implementation by each State, according to Article 288 TFEU. When made at EU level, they are not designed to be law in that form at national level. Nor are they designed directly to affect the individual. Yet in *Van Duyn* (Case 41/74), at p. 97, the Court held that a Directive might be relied on by an individual before a national court. In the next case, *Pubblico Ministero* v *Ratti* (Case 148/78), the Court of Justice explains how, when and why Directives can produce direct effects (or, at least, effects analogous thereto) at national level.

Pubblico Ministero v *Ratti* (Case 148/78)

[1979] ECR 1629, Court of Justice of the European Communities

Directive 73/173 required Member States to introduce into their domestic legal orders rules governing the packaging and labelling of solvents. This had to be done by December 1974. Italy had failed to implement the Directive and maintained in force a different national regime. Ratti produced his solvents in accordance with the Directive, not the Italian law. In 1978 he found himself the subject of criminal proceedings in Milan for non-compliance with Italian law. Could he rely on the Directive which Italy had left unimplemented?

[18] This question raises the general problem of the legal nature of the provisions of a directive adopted under Article 189 of the Treaty [now Article 288 TFEU].

[19] In this regard the settled case law of the Court, last reaffirmed by the judgment of 1 February 1977 in Case 51/76 *Nederlandse Ondernemingen* [1977] 1 ECR 126, lays down that, whilst under Article 189 regulations

are directly applicable and, consequently, by their nature capable of producing direct effects, that does not mean that other categories of acts covered by that article can never produce similar effects.

[20] It would be incompatible with the binding effect which Article 189 ascribes to directives to exclude on principle the possibility of the obligations imposed by them being relied on by persons concerned.

[21] Particularly in cases in which the Community authorities have, by means of directive, placed Member States under a duty to adopt a certain course of action, the effectiveness of such an act would be weakened if persons were prevented from relying on it in legal proceedings and national courts prevented from taking it into consideration as an element of Community law.

[22] Consequently a Member State which has not adopted the implementing measures required by the directive in the prescribed periods may not rely, as against individuals, on its own failure to perform the obligations which the directive entails.

[23] It follows that a national court requested by a person who has complied with the provisions of a directive not to apply a national provision incompatible with the directive not incorporated into the internal legal order of a defaulting Member State, must uphold that request if the obligation in question is unconditional and sufficiently precise.

[24] Therefore the answer to the first question must be that after the expiration of the period fixed for the implementation of a directive a Member State may not apply its internal law – even if it is provided with penal sanctions – which has not yet been adapted in compliance with the directive, to a person who has complied with the requirements of the directive.

NOTE: Directive 77/728 applied a similar regime to varnishes. But here Ratti had jumped the gun. The deadline for implementation was November 1979. Yet in 1978 his varnishes were already being made according to the Directive, not Italian law. In the criminal prosecution for breach of Italian law he sought to rely on this Directive too. He argued that he had a legitimate expectation that compliance with the Directive prior to its deadline for implementation would be permissible:

Pubblico Ministero v *Ratti* (Case 148/78)

[1979] ECR 1629, Court of Justice of the European Communities

[43] It follows that, for the reasons expounded in the grounds of the answer to the national court's first question, it is only at the end of the prescribed period and in the event of the Member State's default that the directive – and in particular Article 9 thereof – will be able to have the effects described in the answer to the first question.

[44] Until that date is reached the Member States remain free in that field.

[45] If one Member State has incorporated the provisions of a directive into its internal legal order before the end of the period prescribed therein, that fact cannot produce any effect with regard to other Member States.

[46] In conclusion, since a directive by its nature imposes obligations only on Member States, it is not possible for an individual to plead the principle of 'legitimate expectation' before the expiry of the period prescribed for its implementation.

[47] Therefore the answer to the fifth question must be that Directive No 77/728 of the Council of the European Communities of 7 November 1977, in particular Article 9 thereof, cannot bring about with respect to any individual who has complied with the provisions of the said directive before the expiration of the adaptation period prescribed for the Member State any effect capable of being taken into consideration by national courts.

Note: A small indentation into the Court's insistence that the expiry of the period prescribed for a Directive's implementation is the vital trigger for its relevance in law before national courts was made in Case C-129/96 *Inter-Environnement Wallonie ASBL* v *Région Wallone* [1997] ECRI-7411. In advance of the deadline, Member States are obliged 'to refrain . . . from adopting measures liable seriously to compromise the result prescribed' by the Directive. This applies 'whether or not the rule of domestic law in question, adopted after the directive entered into force, is concerned with the transposition of the directive' (Case C-144/04 *Mangold* [2005] ECR I-9981). A violation was established in Case C-14/02 *ATRAL* [2003] ECR I-4431. In normal circumstances, however, it is the expiry of the prescribed deadline which converts an unimplemented (and sufficiently unconditional) Directive into a provision on which an individual may rely before a national court.

■ QUESTION

Why did the Court of Justice decide to uphold Ratti's ability to rely on the unimplemented 1973 solvents Directive in the face of the apparently conflicting wording of the Treaty (Article 189, now 288)? One may return to Judge Mancini for one explanation:

F. Mancini, 'The Making of a Constitution for Europe'

(1989) 26 CML Rev 595

(Footnotes omitted.)

3. *Costa* v *Enel* may be therefore regarded as a sequel of *Van Gend en Loos*. It is not the only sequel, however. Eleven years after *Van Gend en Loos*, the Court took in *Van Duyn* v *Home Office* a further step forward by attributing direct effect to provisions of Directives not transposed into the laws of the Member States within the prescribed time limit, so long as they met the conditions laid down in *Van Gend en Loos*. In order to appreciate fully the scope of this development it should be borne in mind that while the principal subjects governed by Regulations are agriculture, transport, customs and the social security of migrant workers, Community authorities resort to Directives when they intend to harmonise national laws on such matters as taxes, banking, equality of the sexes, protection of the environment, employment contracts and organisation of companies. Plain cooking and haute cuisine, in other words. The hope of seeing Europe grow institutionally, in matters of social relationships and in terms of quality of life rests to a large extent on the adoption and the implementation of Directives.

Making Directives immediately enforceable poses, however, a formidable problem. Unlike Regulations and the Treaty provisions dealt with by *Van Gend en Loos*, Directives resemble international treaties, in so far as they are binding only on the States and only as to the result to be achieved. It is understandable therefore that, whereas the *Van Gend en Loos* doctrine established itself within a relatively short time, its extension to Directives met with bitter opposition in many quarters. For example, the French Conseil d'État and the German Bundesfinanzhof bluntly refused to abide by it and Professor Rasmussen, in a most un-Danish fit of temper, went so far as to condemn it as a case of 'revolting judicial behaviour'.

Understandable criticism is not necessarily justifiable. It is mistaken to believe that in attributing direct effect to Directives not yet complied with by the Member States, the Court was only guided by political considerations, such as the intention of by-passing the States in a strategic area of law making. Non-compliance with Directives is the most typical and most frequent form of Member State infraction; moreover, the Community authorities often turn a blind eye to it and, even when the Commission institutes proceedings against the defaulting State under Article 169 of the Treaty, the Court cannot impose any penalty on that State. [It can now! See Article 260 TFEU, a Maastricht innovation, p. 93.] This gives the Directives a dangerously elastic quality: Italy, Greece or Belgium may agree to accept the enactment of a Directive with which it is uncomfortable knowing that the price to pay for possible failure to transpose it is non-existent or minimal.

Given these circumstances, it is sometimes submitted that the *Van Duyn* doctrine was essentially concerned with assuring respect for the rule of law. The Court's main purpose, in other words, was 'to ensure that neither level of government can rely upon its malfeasance – the Member State's failure to comply, the Community's failure or even inability to enforce compliance', with a view to frustrating the legitimate expectation of the Community citizens on whom the Directive confers rights. Indeed, 'if a Court is forced to condone wholesale violation of a norm, that norm can no longer be termed law'; nobody will deny that 'Directives are intended to have the force of law under the Treaty'.

Doubtless, in arriving at its judgment in *Van Duyn*, the Court may also have considered that by reducing the advantages Member States derived from non-compliance, its judgment would have strengthened the 'federal' reach of the Community power to legislate and it may even have welcomed such a consequence. But does that warrant the revolt staged by the Conseil d'État or the Bundesfinanzhof? The present author doubts it; and so did the German Constitutional Court, which sharply scolded the Bundesfinanzhof for its rejection of the *Van Duyn* doctrine. This went a long way towards restoring whatever legitimacy the Court of Justice had lost in the eyes of some observers following *Van Duyn*. The wound, one might say, is healed and the scars it has left are scarcely visible.

■ QUESTION

Do you agree with Mancini that the Court's work in this area is 'essentially concerned with assuring respect for the rule of law'? See also N. Green, 'Directives, Equity and the Protection of Individual Rights' (1984) 9 EL Rev 295.

Note: Difficult constitutional questions arise at EU level and at national level in relation to the direct effect of Directives. You will quickly notice that many of the issues have arisen in the context of cases about sex discrimination. This has happened because equality between the sexes constitutes an area of EU competence which is given shape by a string of important Directives, often inadequately implemented at national level.

SECTION 2: CURTAILING THE PRINCIPLE

The next case allowed the Court to refine its approach to the direct effect of Directives.

Marshall v *Southampton Area Health Authority* (Case 152/84)

[1986] ECR 723, Court of Justice of the European Communities

Ms Marshall was dismissed by her employers, the Health Authority, when she reached the age of 62. A man would not have been dismissed at that age. This was discrimination on grounds of sex. But was there a remedy in law? Apparently not under the UK's Sex Discrimination Act 1975, because of a provision excluding discrimination arising out of treatment in relation to retirement. Directive 76/207, requiring equal treatment between the sexes, did appear to envisage a legal remedy for such discrimination, but that Directive had not been implemented in the UK, even though the deadline was past. So could Ms Marshall base a claim on the unimplemented Directive before an English court? The Court of Justice was asked this question in a preliminary reference by the Court of Appeal.

The Court of Justice first held that Ms Marshall's situation was an instance of discrimination on grounds of sex contrary to the Directive. It continued:

[39] ... it is necessary to consider whether Article 5(1) of Directive No 76/207 may be relied upon by an individual before national courts and tribunals.

[40] The appellant and the Commission consider that that question must be answered in the affirmative. They contend in particular, with regard to Articles 2(1) and 5(1) of Directive No 76/207, that those provisions are sufficiently clear to enable national courts to apply them without legislative intervention by the Member States, at least so far as overt discrimination is concerned.

[41] In support of that view, the appellant points out that directives are capable of conferring rights on individuals which may be relied upon directly before the courts of the Member States; national courts are obliged by virtue of the binding nature of a directive, in conjunction with Article 5 of the EEC Treaty, to give effect to the provisions of directives where possible, in particular when construing or applying relevant provisions of national law (judgment of 10 April 1984 in Case 14/83 *von Colson and Kamann* v *Land Nordrhein-Westfalen* [1984] ECR 1891). Where there is any inconsistency between national law and Community law which cannot be removed by means of such a construction, the appellant submits that a national court is obliged to declare that the provision of national law which is inconsistent with the directive is inapplicable.

[42] The Commission is of the opinion that the provisions of Article 5(1) of Directive No 76/207 are sufficiently clear and unconditional to be relied upon before a national court. They may therefore be set up against section 6(4) of the Sex Discrimination Act, which, according to the decisions of the Court of Appeal, has been extended to the question of compulsory retirement and has therefore become ineffective to prevent dismissals based upon the difference in retirement ages for men and for women.

[43] The respondent and the United Kingdom propose, conversely, that the second question should be answered in the negative. They admit that a directive may, in certain specific circumstances, have direct effect as against a Member State in so far as the latter may not rely on its failure to perform its obligations under the directive. However, they maintain that a directive can never impose obligations directly on individuals and that it can only have direct effect against a Member State qua public authority and not against a Member State qua employer. As an employer a State is no different from a private employer. It would not therefore be proper to put persons employed by the State in a better position than those who are employed by a private employer.

[44] With regard to the legal position of the respondent's employees the United Kingdom states that they are in the same position as the employees of a private employer. Although according to United Kingdom constitutional law the health authorities, created by the National Health Service Act 1977, as amended by the Health Services Act 1980 and other legislation, are Crown bodies and their employees are Crown servants, nevertheless the administration of the National Health Service by the health authorities is regarded as being separate from the government's central administration and its employees are not regarded as civil servants.

[45] Finally, both the respondent and the United Kingdom take the view that the provisions of Directive No 76/207 are neither unconditional nor sufficiently clear and precise to give rise to direct effect. The directive provides for a number of possible exceptions, the details of which are to be laid down by the Member States. Furthermore, the wording of Article 5 is quite imprecise and requires the adoption of measures for its implementation.

[46] It is necessary to recall that, according to a long line of decisions of the Court (in particular its judgment of 19 January 1982 in Case 8/81 *Becker* v *Finanzamt Münster-Innenstadt* [1982] ECR 53), wherever the provisions of a directive appear, as far as their subject-matter is concerned, to be unconditional and sufficiently precise, those provisions may be relied upon by an individual against the State where that State fails to implement the directive in national law by the end of the period prescribed or where it fails to implement the directive correctly.

[47] That view is based on the consideration that it would be incompatible with the binding nature which Article 189 confers on the directive to hold as a matter of principle that the obligation imposed thereby cannot be relied on by those concerned. From that the Court deduced that a Member State which has not adopted the implementing measures required by the directive within the prescribed period may not plead, as against individuals, its own failure to perform the obligations which the directive entails.

[48] With regard to the argument that a directive may not be relied upon against an individual, it must be emphasised that according to Article 189 of the EEC Treaty the binding nature of a directive, which constitutes the basis for the possibility of relying on the directive before a national court, exists only in relation to 'each Member State to which it is addressed'. It follows that a directive may not of itself impose obligations on an individual and that a provision of a directive may not be relied upon as such against such a person. It must therefore be examined whether, in this case, the respondent must be regarded as having acted as an individual.

[49] In that respect it must be pointed out that where a person involved in legal proceedings is able to rely on a directive as against the State he may do so regardless of the capacity in which the latter is acting, whether employer or public authority. In either case it is necessary to prevent the State from taking advantage of its own failure to comply with Community law.

[50] It is for the national court to apply those considerations to the circumstances of each case; the Court of Appeal has, however, stated in the order for reference that the respondent, Southampton and South West Hampshire Area Health Authority (Teaching), is a public authority.

[51] The argument submitted by the United Kingdom that the possibility of relying on provisions of the directive against the respondent qua organ of the State would give rise to an arbitrary and unfair distinction between the rights of State employees and those of private employees does not justify any other conclusion.

Such a distinction may easily be avoided if the Member State concerned has correctly implemented the directive in national law.

[52] Finally, with regard to the question whether the provision contained in Article 5(1) of Directive No 76/207, which implements the principle of equality of treatment set out in Article 2(1) of the directive, may be considered, as far as its contents are concerned, to be unconditional and sufficiently precise to be relied upon by an individual as against the State, it must be stated that the provision, taken by itself, prohibits any discrimination on grounds of sex with regard to working conditions, including the conditions governing dismissal, in a general manner and in unequivocal terms. The provision is therefore sufficiently precise to be relied on by an individual and to be applied by the national courts.

[53] It is necessary to consider next whether the prohibition of discrimination laid down by the directive may be regarded as unconditional, in the light of the exceptions contained therein and of the fact that according to Article 5(2) thereof the Member States are to take the measures necessary to ensure the application of the principle of equality of treatment in the context of national law.

[54] With regard, in the first place, to the reservation contained in Article 1(2) of Directive No 76/207 concerning the application of the principle of equality of treatment in matters of social security, it must be observed that, although the reservation limits the scope of the directive ratione materiae, it does not lay down any condition on the application of that principle in its field of operation and in particular in relation to Article 5 of the directive. Similarly, the exceptions to Directive No 76/207 provided for in Article 2 thereof are not relevant to this case.

[55] It follows that Article 5 of the Directive No 76/207 does not confer on the Member States the right to limit the application of the principle of equality of treatment in its field of operation or to subject it to conditions and that that provision is sufficiently precise and unconditional to be capable of being relied upon by an individual before a national court in order to avoid the application of any national provision which does not conform to Article 5(1).

[56] Consequently, the answer to the second question must be that Article 5(1) of Council Directive No 76/207 of 9 February 1976, which prohibits any discrimination on grounds of sex with regard to working conditions, including the conditions governing dismissal, may be relied upon as against a State authority acting in its capacity as employer, in order to avoid the application of any national provision which does not conform to Article 5(1).

NOTES

1. Ms Marshall was able to rely on the Directive because she was employed by the State. Her subsequent quest for compensation took her back to Luxembourg, where it was made clear that national limits on compensatory awards should not be applied in so far as they impede an effective remedy (Case C-271/91 [1993] ECR I-4367). However, had she been employed by a private firm she would have been unable to rely on the direct effect of the Directive. So, as far as direct effect is concerned, there are requirements which always apply – those explained in *Van Gend en Loos* (Case 26/62) (p. 84). But for Directives there are extra requirements: first, that the implementation date has passed; and, second, that the State is the party against which enforcement is claimed. Directives may be vertically directly effective, but not horizontally directly effective. This is why it was so helpful to the applicant in Case C-144/04 *Mangold* [2005] ECR I-9981, encountered in Chapter 2 (p. 71), to show that the principle of non-discrimination on grounds of age was a general principle of EU law, for he would have been unable to rely on a mere Directive to secure legal protection before national courts against such maltreatment perpetrated by a private employer. This approach was confirmed in Case C-555/07 *Seda Kücükdeveci* [2010] ECR I-365, which drew also on the Charter. But many applicants will not be lucky enough to find such a general principle: *cf* Case C-13/05 *Sonia Chacon Navas* [2006] ECR I-6467, also encountered in Chapter 2 (p. 71).
2. In rejecting the horizontal direct effect of Directives, the Court in fact made a choice between competing rationales for the direct effect of Directives. In its early decisions the Court laid emphasis on the need to extend direct effect in this area in order to secure the 'useful effect' of measures left unimplemented by defaulting States. Consider para 12 of *Van Duyn* (Case 41/74) (p. 97); and, for example, in *Nederlandse Ondernemingen* (Case 51/76) [1977] ECR 113, the Court observed (at para 23) that:

> where the Community authorities have, by Directive, imposed on Member States the obligation to pursue a particular course of conduct, the useful effect of such an act would be weakened if individuals were prevented from relying on it before their national courts and if the latter were prevented from taking it into consideration as an element of Community law.

This dictum came in the context of a case against the State, but this logic would lead a bold court to hold an unimplemented Directive enforceable against a private party too, in order to improve its useful effect. However, in *Ratti* (Case 148/78) (p. 115) and in *Marshall* (Case 152/84) (p. 118), the Court appears to switch its stance away from the idea of 'useful effect' to a type of 'estoppel' as the (narrower) legal rationale for holding Directives capable of direct effect. See para 49 of the judgment in *Marshall* (Case 152/84).

3. The Court's curtailment of the impact of Directives before national courts may also be seen as a manifestation of judicial minimalism, mentioned at p. 24. The realist would examine the awareness of the Court that in this area it risks assaulting national sensitivities if it insists on deepening the impact of EU law in the national legal order. The next case was mentioned in passing by Judge Mancini (p. 117), but the decision deserves further attention.

Minister of the Interior v *Cohn Bendit*

[1980] 1 CMLR 543, Conseil d'État

The matter concerned the exclusion from France of Cohn Bendit, a noted political radical (who subsequently became a Member of the European Parliament!). He relied on Treaty rules governing free movement to challenge the exclusion. The Conseil d'État, the highest court in France dealing with administrative law, addressed itself to the utility of a Directive in Cohn Bendit's action before the French courts.

> According to Article 56 of the Treaty instituting the European Economic Community of 25 March 1957, no requirement of which empowers an organ of the European Communities to issue, in matters of *ordre public*, regulations which are directly applicable in the member-States, the co-ordination of statute and of subordinate legislation (*dispositions législatives et réglementaires*) 'providing for special treatment for foreign nationals on grounds of public policy (*ordre public*), public security or public health' shall be the subject of Council directives, enacted on a proposal from the Commission and after consultation with the European Assembly. It follows clearly from Article 189 of the Treaty of 25 March 1957 that while these directives bind the member-States 'as to the result to be achieved' and while, to attain the aims set out in them, the national authorities are required to adapt the statute law and subordinate legislation and administrative practice of the member-States to the directives which are addressed to them, those authorities alone retain the power to decide on the form to be given to the implementation of the directives and to fix themselves, under the control of the national courts, the means appropriate to cause them to produce effect in national law. Thus, whatever the detail that they contain for the eyes of the member-States, directives may not be invoked by the nationals of such States in support of an action brought against an individual administrative act. It follows that M. Cohn-Bendit could not effectively maintain, in requesting the Tribunal Administratif of Paris to annul the decision of the Minister of the Interior of 2 February 1976, that that decision infringed the provisions of the directive enacted on 25 February 1964 by the Council of the European Communities with a view to coordinating, in the circumstances laid down in Article 56 of the EEC Treaty, special measures concerning the movement and residence of foreign nationals which are justified on grounds of public policy, public security or public health. Therefore, in the absence of any dispute on the legality of the administrative measures taken by the French Government to comply with the directives enacted by the Council of the European Communities, the solution to be given to the action brought by M. Cohn-Bendit may not in any case be made subject to the interpretation of the directive of 25 February 1964. Consequently, without it being necessary to examine the grounds of the appeal, the Minister of the Interior substantiates his argument that the Tribunal Administratif of Paris was wrong when in its judgment under appeal of 21 December 1977 it referred to the Court of Justice of the European Communities questions relating to the interpretation of that directive and stayed proceedings until the decision of the European Court.
>
> In the circumstances the case should be referred back to the Tribunal Administratif of Paris to decide as may be the action of M. Cohn-Bendit.

NOTE: See, similarly, the *Bundesfinanzhof* (German federal tax court) in *VAT Directives* [1982] 1 CMLR 527.

As D. Anderson observed in the wake of the Court's rejection in *Marshall* (Case 152/84) of the enforceability of unimplemented Directives against private parties, '[t]he present concern of the Court is to consolidate the advances of the 1970s rather than face the legal complexities and political risks of attempting to extend the doctrine [of direct effect] further' (*Boston College International & Comparative Law Review* (1988) XI 91, 100). This implies that the Court might have been expected to return to the matter. This proved correct. In 1993 and 1994 three Advocates-General pressed the Court to reconsider its rejection of the horizontal direct effect of Directives: Van Gerven in '*Marshall 2*' (Case C-271/91) [1993] ECR I-4367; Jacobs in *Vaneetveld* v *SA Le Foyer* (Case C-316/93) [1994] ECR I-763 and Lenz in *Paola Faccini Dori* v *Recreb Srl* (Case C-91/92) [1994] ECR I-3325. Advocate-General Lenz insisted that the Citizen of the Union was entitled to expect equality before the law throughout the territory of the Union and observed that, in the absence of horizontal direct effect, such equality was compromised by State failure to implement Directives. Advocate-General Jacobs thought that the effectiveness principle militated against drawing distinctions based on the status of a defendant. All three believed that the pursuit of coherence in the law dictated acceptance of the horizontal direct effect of Directives. Only in the third of these cases, *Faccini Dori* v *Recreb*, was the Court of Justice unable to avoid addressing the issue directly.

Paola Faccini Dori v *Recreb Srl* (Case C-91/92)

[1994] ECR I-3325, Court of Justice of the European Communities

Ms Dori had concluded a contract at Milan Railway Station to buy an English language correspondence course. By virtue of Directive 85/577, which harmonizes laws governing the protection of consumers in respect of contracts negotiated away from business premises, the so-called 'Doorstep Selling Directive' (today replaced by Directive 2011/83 on Consumer Rights), she ought to have been entitled to a 'cooling-off' period of at least seven days within which she could exercise a right to withdraw from the contract. However, she found herself unable to exercise that right under Italian law because Italy had not implemented the Directive. She therefore sought to rely on the Directive to defeat the claim brought against her by the private party with which she had contracted. The ruling in *Marshall* (Case 152/84) appeared to preclude reliance on the Directive. The Court despite the promptings of Advocate-General Lenz, *refused* to overrule *Marshall*. It maintained that Directives are incapable of horizontal direct effect.

[23] It would be unacceptable if a State, when required by the Community legislature to adopt certain rules intended to govern the State's relations – or those of State entities – with individuals and to confer certain rights on individuals, were able to rely on its own failure to discharge its obligations so as to deprive individuals of the benefits of those rights. Thus the Court has recognised that certain provisions of directives on conclusion of public works contracts and of directives on harmonisation of turnover taxes may be relied on against the State (or State entities) (see the judgment in Case 103/88 *Fratelli Costanzo* v *Comune di Milano* [1989] ECR 1839 and the judgment in Case 8/81 *Becker* v *Finanzamt Münster-Innenstadt* [1982] ECR 53).

[24] The effect of extending that case law to the sphere of relations between individuals would be to recognise a power in the Community to enact obligations for individuals with immediate effect, whereas it has competence to do so only where it is empowered to adopt regulations.

[25] It follows that, in the absence of measures transposing the directive within the prescribed time-limit, consumers cannot derive from the directive itself a right of cancellation as against traders with whom they have concluded a contract or enforce such a right in a national court.

NOTE: Paragraph 48 of the ruling in *Marshall* expresses comparable sentiments to those expressed in para 24 of the *Dori* ruling, but the emphasis in the latter on the limits of Treaty conferred competence (specifically under Article 189 – now 288) is noticeably firmer. Although the Court did not consider that Ms Dori was wholly barred from relying on the Directive (see p. 135 on 'indirect' effect and p. 144 on a claim against the defaulting State), it nevertheless refused to allow a Directive to exert direct effect in relations between private individuals. In rulings subsequent to *Dori*, the Court has consistently repeated its rejection of the horizontal direct effect of Directives: e.g., Case C-192/94 *El Corte Inglés* v *Cristina Blasquez Rivero* [1996] ECR I-1281; Case C-80/06 *Carp Snc v Ecorad* [2007] ECR I-4473 Case C-508/14 *Česky telekomunikačni* judgment of 6 October 2015. The reader is invited to consider whether, just as the Conseil d'État's ruling in *Cohn Bendit* (p. 121) may have prompted the Court of Justice's caution in *Marshall*, so too national judicial anxieties, expressed with particular force by the *Bundesverfassungsgericht*, about Treaty amendment in the guise of judicial interpretation may have prompted the Court in *Dori* to emblazon its fidelity to the text of the Treaty by declining to extend legislative competence to include the enactment of obligations for individuals with immediate effect. Chapter 19 will examine this judicial interaction in more depth, but it is important to grasp that this is a two-way process. Not only might one expect a degree of sensitivity in Luxembourg to anxieties expressed in national courts, so too national courts do not maintain a stubbornly static position. It took 30 years but eventually the Conseil d'Etat abandoned its stance in *Cohn-Bendit* and in 2009 it accepted the Court of Justice's position that Directives, though not 'horizontally directly effective', are capable of application by national courts against *public* authorities: *Madame Perreux* [2009] RFDA p. 1125 (noted by C. Charpy (2010) 6 Euro Const Law Rev 123).

SECTION 3: THE SCOPE OF THE PRINCIPLE: THE STATE

Whatever one's view of the Court's motivations in ruling against the horizontal direct effect of Directives in *Marshall* (Case 152/84), confirmed in *Dori* (Case C-91/92) and subsequently, the decision left many questions unanswered. First, what is the 'State'? The more widely this is interpreted, the more impact the unimplemented Directive will have.

Foster v *British Gas* (Case C-188/89)

[1990] ECR I-3133, Court of Justice of the European Communities

The applicant wished to rely on the Equal Treatment Directive 76/207 against her employer before English courts. She and other applicants had been compulsorily retired at an age earlier than male employees. This raised the familiar issue of the enforceability of Directives before national courts where national law is inadequate. The Court examined the nature of the defendant (the British Gas Corporation: BGC).

[3] By virtue of the Gas Act 1972, which governed the BGC at the material time, the BGC was a statutory corporation responsible for developing and maintaining a system of gas supply in Great Britain, and had a monopoly of the supply of gas.

[4] The members of the BGC were appointed by the competent Secretary of State. He also had the power to give the BGC directions of a general character in relation to matters affecting the national interest and instructions concerning its management.

[5] The BGC was obliged to submit to the Secretary of State periodic reports on the exercise of its functions, its management and its programmes. Those reports were then laid before both Houses of Parliament. Under the Gas Act 1972 the BGC also had the right, with the consent of the Secretary of State, to submit proposed legislation to Parliament.

[6] The BGC was required to run a balanced budget over two successive financial years. The Secretary of State could order it to pay certain funds over to him or to allocate funds to specified purposes.

It then proceeded to explain the legal approach to defining the 'State' for these purposes:

[13] Before considering the question referred by the House of Lords, it must first be observed as a preliminary point that the United Kingdom has submitted that it is not a matter for the Court of Justice but for the national courts to determine, in the context of the national legal system, whether the provisions of a directive may be relied upon against a body such as the BGC.

[14] The question what effects measures adopted by Community institutions have and in particular whether those measures may be relied on against certain categories of persons necessarily involves interpretation of the articles of the Treaty concerning measures adopted by the institutions and the Community measure in issue.

[15] It follows that the Court of Justice has jurisdiction in proceedings for a preliminary ruling to determine the categories of persons against whom the provisions of a directive may be relied on. It is for the national courts, on the other hand, to decide whether a party to proceedings before them falls within one of the categories so defined.

The Court then disposed of the question referred:

[16] As the Court has consistently held (see the judgment of 19 January 1982 in Case 8/81, *Becker* v *Hauptzollamt Münster-Innenstadt*, [1982] ECR 53 at paragraphs 23 to 25), where the Community authorities have, by means of a directive, placed Member States under a duty to adopt a certain course of action, the effectiveness of such a measure would be diminished if persons were prevented from relying upon it in proceedings before a court and national courts were prevented from taking it into consideration as an element of Community law. Consequently, a Member State which has not adopted the implementing measures required by the directive within the prescribed period may not plead, as against individuals, its own failure to perform the obligations which the directive entails. Thus, wherever the provisions of a directive appear, as far as their subject-matter is concerned, to be unconditional and sufficiently precise, those provisions may, in the absence of implementing measures adopted within the prescribed period, be relied upon as against any national provision which is incompatible with the directive or in so far as the provisions define rights which individuals are able to assert against the State.

[17] The Court further held in its judgment of 26 February 1986 in Case 152/84 (*Marshall*, at paragraph 49) that where a person is able to rely on a directive as against the State he may do so regardless of the capacity in which the latter is acting, whether as employer or as public authority. In either case it is necessary to prevent the State from taking advantage of its own failure to comply with Community law.

[18] On the basis of those considerations, the Court has held in a series of cases that unconditional and sufficiently precise provisions of a directive could be relied on against organizations or bodies which were subject to the authority or control of the State or had special powers beyond those which result from the normal rules applicable to relations between individuals.

[19] The Court has accordingly held that provisions of a directive could be relied on against tax authorities (the judgments of 19 January 1982 in Case 8/81, *Becker*, cited above, and of 22 February 1990 in Case C-22188, *ECSC* v *Acciaierie e Ferriere Busseni (in liquidation)*), local or regional authorities (judgment of 22 June 1989 in Case 103/88, *Fratelli Costanzo* v *Comune di Milano*), constitutionally independent authorities responsible for the maintenance of public order and safety (judgment of 15 May 1986 in Case 222/84, *Johnston* v *Chief Constable of the Royal Ulster Constabulary*, [1986] ECR 1651), and public authorities providing public health services (judgment of 26 February 1986 in Case 152/84, *Marshall*, cited above).

[20] It follows from the foregoing that a body, whatever its legal form, which has been made responsible, pursuant to a measure adopted by the State, for providing a public service under the control of the State and has for that purpose special powers beyond those which result from the normal rules applicable in relations between individuals is included in any event among the bodies against which the provisions of a directive capable of having direct effect may be relied upon.

NOTE: The case has been widely commented upon; see, e.g., N. Grief, (1991) 16 EL Rev 136; E. Szyszczak, (1990) 27 CML Rev 859. For a full examination of the policy issues, see D. Curtin, 'The Province of Government' (1990) 15 EL Rev 195. For another case discussing the reach of unimplemented Directives in this vein see Case C-157/02 *Rieser International Transport* ([2004] ECR I-1477).

■ QUESTION

The case arose before British Gas was 'privatized' under the Gas Act 1986 (sold to the private sector). What difference would this sale make to the application of the Court's test?

NOTE: The notion of the 'State' embraces local authorities.

Fratelli Costanzo v *Milano* (Case 103/88)

[1989] ECR 1839, Court of Justice of the European Communities

The case arose out of the alleged failure of the municipal authorities in Milan to respect *inter alia* a Directive in awarding contracts for the construction of a football stadium for the 1990 World Cup. Could a disappointed contractor rely on the unimplemented Directive before Italian courts against the municipal authorities? The matter reached the Court of Justice by way of a preliminary reference.

[28] In the fourth question the national court asks whether administrative authorities, including municipal authorities, are under the same obligation as a national court to apply the provisions of Article 29(5) of Council Directive 71/305 and to refrain from applying provisions of national law which conflict with them.

[29] In its judgments of 19 January 1982 in Case 8/81 *Becker* v *Finanzamt Münster-Innenstadt* [1982] ECR 53, at p. 71 and 26 February 1986 in Case 152/84 *Marshall* v *Southampton and South-West Hampshire Area Health Authority* [1986] ECR 723, at p. 748, the Court held that wherever the provisions of a directive appear, as far as their subject-matter is concerned, to be unconditional and sufficiently precise, those provisions may be relied upon by an individual against the State where that State has failed to implement the directive in national law by the end of the period prescribed or where it has failed to implement the Directive correctly.

[30] It is important to note that the reason for which an individual may, in the circumstances described above, rely on the provisions of a directive in proceedings before the national courts is that the obligations arising under those provisions are binding upon all the authorities of the Member States.

[31] It would, moreover, be contradictory to rule that an individual may rely upon the provisions of a directive which fulfil the conditions defined above in proceedings before the national courts seeking an order against the administrative authorities, and yet to hold that those authorities are under no obligation to apply the provisions of the directive and refrain from applying provisions of national law which conflict with them. It follows that when the conditions under which the Court has held that individuals may rely on the provisions of a directive before the national courts are met, all organs of the administration, including decentralized authorities such as municipalities, are obliged to apply those provisions.

[32] With specific regard to Article 29(5) of Directive 71/305, it is apparent from the discussion of the first question that it is unconditional and sufficiently precise to be relied upon by an individual against the State. An individual may therefore plead that provision before the national courts and, as is clear from the foregoing, all organs of the administration, including decentralized authorities such as municipalities, are obliged to apply it.

SECTION 4: 'INCIDENTAL EFFECT'

It has been shown that Directives are incapable of application against private individuals before national courts. In other words, there is no 'horizontal direct effect' of Directives. It is only when the State has fulfilled its Treaty obligation of implementation pursuant to Article 288 TFEU that the Directive, duly transformed, becomes 'live' for the purposes of imposing obligations on private parties.

But this is not to say that an unimplemented Directive will never exert an effect before a national court that is prejudicial to a private party. Without abandoning its stance against horizontal direct affect the Court has nevertheless chosen to recognize circumstances in which the State's default may incidentally affect the position of a private individual. The status of a Directive in national legal proceedings is a complex phenomenon.

Case C-201/94 *R* v *The Medicines Control Agency, ex parte Smith & Nephew Pharmaceuticals Ltd* and *Primecrown Ltd* v *The Medicine Control Agency* [1996] ECR I-5819 concerned Article 3 of Directive 65/65. This provided that no proprietary medicinal product could be placed on the market in a Member State unless a prior authorization had been issued by the competent authority of that Member State – the Medicines Control Agency (MCA) in the UK. The UK's MCA had issued to Primecrown a licence to import a proprietary medicinal product of Belgian origin bearing the same name, and manufactured under an agreement with the same (American) licensor, as a product for which Smith & Nephew already held a marketing authorization in the United Kingdom. But the MCA decided it was in error and it withdrew the authorization. Both Primecrown and Smith & Nephew initiated proceedings before the English courts and, in a preliminary reference, the Court of Justice was asked to provide an interpretation of the Directive's rules governing authorization. But it was also asked whether Smith & Nephew, as the holder of the original authorization issued under the normal procedure referred to in Directive 65/65, could rely on the Directive in proceedings before a national court in which it contested the validity of a marketing authorization granted by a competent public authority to one of its competitors. The Court decided that it could. The consequence is that Primecrown's position could be detrimentally affected by a competitor's reliance on a Directive in proceedings against the public authorities. True, Smith & Nephew did not rely on the Directive in an action against Primecrown. This is *not* horizontal direct effect of the type painstakingly excluded by the Court in *Dori* (Case C-91/92, p. 122). But it is a case in which the application of a Directive by a national court *incidentally* affected the legal position of a private party.

The Court has developed this case law further. Without any direct challenge to its dogged resistance to the horizontal direct effect of Directives, it has nevertheless extended the *incidental* effect of Directives on private parties in national proceedings.

Council Directive 83/189/EEC provided for Member States to give advance notice to the Commission and other Member States of plans to introduce new product specifications. The amendments were consolidated in Directive 98/34 [1998] OJ L204/37, itself amended by Directive 98/48 [1998] OJ L217/18. The purpose of this notification system is to avoid the introduction of new measures having equivalent effect to quantitative restrictions on trade in the internal market (and to supply the Commission with a possible basis for developing its harmonization programme). It is an 'early warning system' (see Chapter 9 more generally on 'market management').

In the next case the Court decided that non-notification of a draft technical regulation (as defined by the Directive) affected the enforceability of that measure before the courts of the defaulting Member State.

***CIA Security International SA* v *Signalson SA and Securitel Sprl* (Case C-194/94)**

[1996] ECR I-2201, Court of Justice of the European Communities

Signalson and Securitel sought a court order from a Belgian court requiring that their competitor CIA Security cease marketing a burglar alarm. The alarm was not compatible with Belgian technical standards. But the Belgian technical standards had not been notified to the Commission, as was required by Directive 83/189. Did this State default have any effect in the national proceedings involving two private parties? The Directive did not address the matter. This did not deter the Court.

[42] It is settled law that, wherever provisions of a directive appear to be, from the point of view of their content, unconditional and sufficiently precise, they may be relied on against any national provision which is not in accordance with the directive (see the judgment in Case 8/81 *Becker* [1982] ECR 53 and the judgment in Joined Cases C-6/90 and C-9/90 *Francovich and Others* [1991] ECR I-5357).

[43] The United Kingdom considers that the provisions of Directive 83/189 do not satisfy those criteria on the ground, in particular, that the notification procedure contains a number of elements that are imprecise.

[44] That view cannot be adopted. Articles 8 and 9 of Directive 83/189 lay down a precise obligation on Member States to notify draft technical regulations to the Commission before they are adopted. Being, accordingly, unconditional and sufficiently precise in terms of their content, those articles may be relied on by individuals before national courts.

[45] It remains to examine the legal consequences to be drawn from a breach by Member States of their obligation to notify and, more precisely, whether Directive 83/189 is to be interpreted as meaning that a breach of the obligation to notify, constituting a procedural defect in the adoption of the technical regulations concerned, renders such technical regulations inapplicable so that they may not be enforced against individuals.

[46] The German and Netherlands Governments and the United Kingdom consider that Directive 83/189 is solely concerned with relations between the Member States and the Commission, that it merely creates procedural obligations which the Member States must observe when adopting technical regulations, their competence to adopt the regulations in question after expiry of the suspension period being, however, unaffected, and, finally, that it contains no express provision relating to any effects attaching to non-compliance with those procedural obligations.

[47] The Court observes first of all in this context that none of those factors prevents non-compliance with Directive 83/189 from rendering the technical regulations in question inapplicable.

[48] For such a consequence to arise from a breach of the obligations laid down by Directive 83/189, an express provision to this effect is not required. As pointed out above, it is undisputed that the aim of the directive is to protect freedom of movement for goods by means of preventive control and that the obligation to notify is essential for achieving such Community control. The effectiveness of Community control will be that much greater if the directive is interpreted as meaning that breach of the obligation to notify constitutes a substantial procedural defect such as to render the technical regulations in question inapplicable to individuals.

[49] That interpretation of the directive is in accordance with the judgment given in Case 380/87 *Enichem Base and Others* v *Comune di Cinisello Balsamo* [1989] ECR 2491, paragraphs 19 to 24. In that judgment, in which the Court ruled on the obligation for Member States to communicate to the Commission national draft rules falling within the scope of an article of Council Directive 75/442/EEC of 15 July 1975 on waste (OJ 1975 L 194, p. XXX), the Court held that neither the wording nor the purpose of the provision in question provided any support for the view that failure by the Member States to observe their obligation to give notice in itself rendered unlawful the rules thus adopted. In this regard, the Court expressly considered that the provision in question was confined to imposing an obligation to give prior notice which did not make entry into force of the envisaged rules subject to the Commission' s agreement or lack of opposition and which did not lay down the procedure for Community control of the drafts in question. The Court therefore concluded that the provision under examination concerned relations between the Member States and the Commission but that it did not afford individuals any right capable of being infringed in the event of breach by a Member State of its obligation to give prior notice of its draft regulations to the Commission.

[50] In the present case, however, the aim of the directive is not simply to inform the Commission. As already found in paragraph 41 of this judgment, the directive has, precisely, a more general aim of eliminating or restricting obstacles to trade, to inform other States of technical regulations envisaged by a State, to give the Commission and the other Member States time to react and to propose amendments for lessening restrictions to the free movement of goods arising from the envisaged measure and to afford the Commission time to propose a harmonising directive. Moreover, the wording of Articles 8 and 9 of Directive 83/189 is clear in that those articles provide for a procedure for Community control of draft national regulations and the date of their entry into force is made subject to the Commission' s agreement or lack of opposition.

NOTE: The *effectiveness* rationale contained in para 48 is remarkably far-reaching. It was also encountered in *Ratti* (Case 148/78 para 21, p. 115). But the reasoning in *Ratti* was treated more circumspectly by the Court subsequently in *Marshall* (Case 152/84, p. 118), and the approach taken in *CIA Security* has also been curtailed in the light of the salutary experience provided by litigation.

Johannes Martinus Lemmens (Case C-226/97)

[1998] ECR I-3711, Court of Justice of the European Communities

Lemmens was charged with driving while under the influence of alcohol. He argued that the breathalyser was made according to a technical standard that had not been notified to the Commission and that accordingly, following *CIA Security*, it was incompatible with the Directive to rely on such evidence before national (criminal) courts.

Para 12 of the judgment records Mr Lemmens' disingenuous but ingenious idea:

> It is apparent from the order for reference that, in the course of the criminal proceedings instituted against him, Mr Lemmens said 'I understand from the press that there are difficulties regarding the breath-analysis apparatus. I maintain that this apparatus has not been notified to Brussels and wonder what the consequences of this could be for my case'.

The Court concluded that the Dutch Regulation governing breathalyser kits constituted a technical regulation which should, prior to its adoption, have been notified to the Commission in accordance with Article 8 of the Directive. But with what consequence in proceedings before a national court?

> [32] . . .it should be noted that, in paragraph 40 of its judgment in *CIA Security International*, cited above, the Court emphasised that the Directive is designed to protect, by means of preventive control, freedom of movement for goods, which is one of the foundations of the Community. This control serves a useful purpose in that technical regulations covered by the Directive may constitute obstacles to trade in goods between Member States, such obstacles being permissible only if they are necessary to satisfy compelling requirements relating to the public interest.
>
> [33] In paragraphs 48 and 54 of that judgment, the Court pointed out that the obligation to notify is essential for achieving such Community control and went on to State that the effectiveness of such control will be that much greater if the Directive is interpreted as meaning that breach of the obligation to notify constitutes a substantial procedural defect such as to render the technical regulations in question inapplicable, and thus unenforceable against individuals.
>
> [34] In criminal proceedings such as those in the main action, the regulations applied to the accused are those which, on the one hand, prohibit and penalise driving while under the influence of alcohol and, on the other, require a driver to exhale his breath into an apparatus designed to measure the alcohol content, the result of that test constituting evidence in criminal proceedings. Such regulations differ from those which, not having been notified to the Commission in accordance with the Directive, are unenforceable against individuals.
>
> [35] While failure to notify technical regulations, which constitutes a procedural defect in their adoption, renders such regulations inapplicable inasmuch as they hinder the use or marketing of a product which is not in conformity therewith, it does not have the effect of rendering unlawful any use of a product which is in conformity with regulations which have not been notified.
>
> [36] The use of the product by the public authorities, in a case such as this, is not liable to create an obstacle to trade which could have been avoided if the notification procedure had been followed.
>
> [37] The answer to the first question must therefore be that the Directive is to be interpreted as meaning that breach of the obligation imposed by Article 8 thereof to notify a technical regulation on breath-analysis apparatus does not have the effect of making it impossible for evidence obtained by means of such apparatus, authorised in accordance with regulations which have not been notified, to be relied upon against an individual charged with driving while under the influence of alcohol.

Paragraph 35 of *Lemmens* provides a re-focusing of the test applied in *CIA Security*. Paragraph 36 constitutes a narrower reading of the *effectiveness* rationale. In the next case the Court explicitly adopts the reasoning advanced in *Lemmens* but accepts the application of the notification Directive in litigation between two contracting parties in which, at first glance, the State had no involvement.

Unilever Italia SpA v *Central Food SpA* (Case C-443/98)

[2000] ECR I-7535, Court of Justice of the European Communities

Unilever had supplied Central Food with a quantity of virgin olive oil. Central Food rejected the goods on the basis that they were not labelled in accordance with a relevant Italian law. This law had been notified to the Commission but Italy had not observed the Directive's 'standstill' obligation, which required it to wait a defined period before bringing the law into force. The Court treated breach of the 'standstill' obligation as indistinguishable for these purposes from outright failure to notify (which was the nature of the default in both *CIA Security* and *Lemmens*). Unilever submitted that the law should not be applied and sued Central Food under the contract for the price of the goods.

[46] . . .in civil proceedings of that nature, application of technical regulations adopted in breach of Article 9 of Directive 83/189 may have the effect of hindering the use or marketing of a product which does not conform to those regulations.

[47] That is the case in the main proceedings, since application of the Italian rules is liable to hinder Unilever in marketing the extra virgin olive oil which it offers for sale.

[48] Next, it must be borne in mind that, in *CIA Security*, the finding of inapplicability as a legal consequence of breach of the obligation of notification was made in response to a request for a preliminary ruling arising from proceedings between competing undertakings based on national provisions prohibiting unfair trading.

[49] Thus, it follows from the case law of the Court that the inapplicability of a technical regulation which has not been notified in accordance with Article 8 of Directive 83/189 can be invoked in proceedings between individuals for the reasons set out in paragraphs 40 to 43 of this judgment. The same applies to non-compliance with the obligations laid down by Article 9 of the same directive, and there is no reason, in that connection, to treat disputes between individuals relating to unfair competition, as in the *CIA Security* case, differently from disputes between individuals concerning contractual rights and obligations, as in the main proceedings.

[50] Whilst it is true, as observed by the Italian and Danish Governments, that a directive cannot of itself impose obligations on an individual and cannot therefore be relied on as such against an individual (see Case C-91/92 *Faccini Dori* [1994] ECR I-3325, paragraph 20), that case-law does not apply where noncompliance with Article 8 or Article 9 of Directive 83/189, which constitutes a substantial procedural defect, renders a technical regulation adopted in breach of either of those articles inapplicable.

[51] In such circumstances, and unlike the case of non-transposition of directives with which the case-law cited by those two Governments is concerned, Directive 83/189 does not in any way define the substantive scope of the legal rule on the basis of which the national court must decide the case before it. It creates neither rights nor obligations for individuals.

[52] In view of all the foregoing considerations, the answer to the question submitted must be that a national court is required, in civil proceedings between individuals concerning contractual rights and obligations, to refuse to apply a national technical regulation which was adopted during a period of postponement of adoption prescribed in Article 9 of Directive 83/189.

NOTE: This is *not* horizontal direct effect. The Directive did not impose an obligation on Central Food. The contract with Unilever imposed the obligation. This seems to be the Court's point in para 51. But the invocation of the Directive completely changed the legal position that had appeared to prevail between the two parties under the contract. It transplanted the commercial risk.

Advocate-General Jacobs had argued vigorously in his Opinion in *Unilever* that legal certainty would be damaged by a finding that the notification Directive be relevant to the status of the contractual claim between private parties.

ADVOCATE-GENERAL JACOBS

[99] ... The fact that a Member State did not comply with the procedural requirements of the directive as such should not, in my view, entail detrimental effects for individuals.

[100] That is, first, because such effects would be difficult to justify in the light of the principle of legal certainty. For the day-to-day conduct of trade, technical regulations which apply to the sale of goods must be clearly and readily identifiable as enforceable or as unenforceable. Although the present dispute concerns a relatively small quantity of bottled olive oil of a value which may not affect the finances of either Unilever or Central Food to any drastic extent, it is easy to imagine an exactly comparable case involving highly perishable goods and sums of money which represent the difference between prosperity and ruin for one or other of the parties concerned. In order to avoid difficulties in his contractual relations, an individual trader would have to be aware of the existence of Directive 83/189, to know the judgment in *CIA Security*, to identify a technical regulation as such, and to establish with certainty whether or not the Member State in question had complied with all the procedural requirements of the directive. The last element in particular might prove to be extremely difficult because of the lack of publicity of the procedure under the directive. There is no obligation on the Commission to publish the fact that a Member State has notified or failed to notify a given draft technical regulation. In respect of the standstill periods under Article 9 of the directive, there is no way for individuals to know that other Member States have triggered the six-month standstill period by delivering detailed opinions to the Commission. Similarly, the Commission is also not required to publish the fact that it has informed a Member State of intended or pending Community legislation.

[101] The second problem is possible injustice. If failure to notify were to render a technical regulation unenforceable in private proceedings an individual would lose a case in which such a regulation was in issue, not because of his own failure to comply with an obligation deriving from Community law, but because of a Member State's behaviour. The economic survival of a firm might be threatened merely for the sake of the effectiveness of a mechanism designed to control Member States' regulatory activities. That would be so independently of whether the technical regulation in question constituted an obstacle to trade, a measure with neutral effects on trade, or even a rule furthering trade. The only redress for a trader in such a situation would be to bring *ex post* a hazardous and costly action for damages against a Member State. Nor is there any reason for the other party to the proceedings to profit, entirely fortuitously, from a Member State's failure to comply with the directive.

[102] It follows, in my view, that the correct solution in proceedings between individuals is a substantive solution. The applicability of a technical regulation in proceedings between individuals should depend only on its compatibility with Article 30 [now Article 34 TFEU: Chapter 11 of this book] of the Treaty. If in the present case Italian Law No 313 complies with Article 30, I can see no reason why Central Food, which understandably relied on the rules laid down in the Italian statute book, should lose the case before the national court. If, however, Italian Law No 313 infringes Article 30 then the national court should be obliged to set the Law aside on that ground.

[103] I accordingly conclude that as against an individual another individual should not be able to rely on a Member State's failure to comply with the requirements of Directive 83/189 in order to set aside a technical regulation.

NOTE: Plainly these anxieties did not move the Court in *Unilever*. It did not follow the Advocate-General and it did not limit the matter to resolution under Article 30 EC, now Article 34 TFEU, concerning the free movement of goods. It accepted the incidental effect of the notification Directive on the contractual claim. This thrusts the law of market integration deep into national contract law in so far as private compliance with technical standards is at stake. In the next case the Court nonetheless adopts an additional line of reasoning which may be capable of providing a basis for softening some of the harsh commercial uncertainty likely to flow from the principle that technical standards may be treated as unenforceable by national courts if the requirements of the notification Directive are not observed by the State.

Sapod Audic v *Eco-Emballages SA* (Case C-159/00)

[2002] ECR I-5031, Court of Justice of the European Communities

[49] . . . it should be observed, first, that according to settled case law Directive 83/189 must be interpreted as meaning that a failure to observe the obligation to notify laid down in Article 8 of that directive constitutes a substantial procedural defect such as to render the technical regulations in question inapplicable and thus unenforceable against individuals (see, in particular, *CIA Security International*, paragraphs 48 and 54, and *Lemmens*, paragraph 33).

[50] Second, it should be borne in mind that according to the case law of the Court the inapplicability of a technical regulation which has not been notified to the Commission in accordance with Article 8 of Directive 83/189 may be invoked in legal proceedings between individuals concerning, *inter alia*, contractual rights and duties (see *Unilever*, paragraph 49).

[51] Accordingly, if the national court were to interpret the second paragraph of Article 4 of Decree No 92-377 as establishing an obligation to apply a mark or label and, hence, as constituting a technical regulation within the meaning of Directive 83/189, it would be incumbent on that court to refuse to apply that provision in the main proceedings.

[52] It should, however, be observed that the question of the conclusions to be drawn in the main proceedings from the inapplicability of the second paragraph of Article 4 of Decree No 92-377 as regards the severity of the sanction under the applicable national law, such as nullity or unenforceability of the contract between Sapod and Eco-Emballages, is a question governed by national law, in particular as regards the rules and principles of contract law which limit or adjust that sanction in order to render its severity proportionate to the particular defect found. However, those rules and principles may not be less favourable than those governing similar domestic actions (principle of equivalence) and may not be framed in such a way as to render impossible in practice the exercise of rights conferred by Community law (principle of effectiveness) (see, *inter alia*, Case 33/76 *Rewe* v *Landwirtschaftskammer für das Saarland* [1976] ECR 1989, paragraph 5, and Joined Cases C-52/99 and C-53/99 *Camorotto and Vignone* [2001] ECR I-1395, paragraph 21).

NOTE: The principles of equivalence and effectiveness, mentioned in para 52, were examined in Chapter 4, p. 107. With reference to relevant national rules on remedies with which you are familiar, consider what they may mean in the context sketched by the Court in para 52 of *Sapod Audic*.

In conclusion, none of these decisions on 'incidental' effect overturns the Court's longstanding exclusion of the horizontal direct effect of Directives. After all in none of these cases did a Directive impose an obligation directly on a private party. However, these decisions do demonstrate that the legal position of private parties may be prejudicially affected by the lurking presence of an unimplemented Directive of which they may be perfectly unaware.

■ QUESTION

The Court's case law places a sharp distinction between the horizontal direct effect of Directives (which is not allowed) and the 'incidental' effect of Directives on private parties (which is allowed). Is this distinction fair?

FURTHER READING

Dougan, M., 'Annotation of *Sapod Audic*' (2003) 40 CML Rev 193.

Skouris, V., '*Effet utile* versus Legal Certainty: the Case Law of the Court of Justice on the Direct Effect of Directives' (2006) 17/2 *European Business Law Review* 241.

Weatherill, S., 'Breach of Directives and Breach of Contract' (2001) 26 EL Rev 177.

SECTION 5: THE PRINCIPLE OF INDIRECT EFFECT, OR THE OBLIGATION OF 'CONFORM-INTERPRETATION'

The previous section questioned the extent to which the rejected notion that Directives may exert horizontal direct effect can be rationally sealed off from the phenomenon of incidental effect. But however one chooses to categorize the horizontal direct effect/ incidental effect case law, and however one defines the 'State' for the purposes of fixing the outer limits of 'vertical' direct effect (Case 152/84 *Marshall*, p. 118), an unavoidable anomaly taints the law governing the scope of the direct effect of Directives. Consider the sex discrimination Directives. If a State has failed to implement a Directive properly, then, provided that the standard *Van Gend en Loos* (Case 26/62) 'test' for direct effect is met by the provision in question, a State employee can rely on the direct effect of the Directive (vertical direct effect). A private employee cannot (horizontal direct effect). So, in the UK, where Directive 76/207 on Equal Treatment of the Sexes was not properly implemented in time, Ms Marshall, a State employee, succeeded in relying on the Directive, whereas Ms Duke (*Duke* v *GEC Reliance* [1988] 2 WLR 359, [1988] 1 All ER 626), who was making the same complaint, failed, for she happened to be a private sector employee.

The UK had made this point in *Marshall* (Case 152/84) as a reason for *withholding* direct effect, but its objections were swept aside by the Court in para 51 of the judgment (p. 118). Yet the anomaly is real, even if the Court's refusal to permit a recalcitrant State to benefit from pointing it out is understandable. Submissions in *Dori* (Case C-91/92, p. 122) urged the Court to eliminate the anomaly by *extending* direct effect, but these were not successful.

The Court of Justice's contribution to the resolution of this anomaly first began to take shape in *Von Colson and Kamann* v *Land Nordrhein-Westfalen* (Case 14/83) and *Harz* v *Deutsche Tradax* (Case 79/83). Mention is made of Case 14/83 in para 41 of the judgment in *Marshall* at p. 118, but the Court's approach in the case deserves careful separate attention.

Von Colson and Kamann v *Land Nordrhein-Westfalen* (Case 14/83)

[1984] ECR 1891, [1986] 2 CMLR 430, Court of Justice of the European Communities

The case was a preliminary reference from Germany, and concerned that fertile source of litigation, the Equal Treatment Directive 76/207. The issue was described by the Court as follows:

> [2] Those questions were raised in the course of proceedings between two qualified social workers, Sabine von Colson and Elisabeth Kamann, and the Land Nordrhein-Westfalen. It appears from the grounds of the order for reference that Werl prison, which caters exclusively for male prisoners and which is administered by the Land Nordrhein-Westfalen, refused to engage the plaintiffs in the main proceedings for reasons relating to their sex. The officials responsible for recruitment justified their refusal to engage the plaintiffs by citing the problems and risks connected with the appointment of female candidates and for those reasons appointed instead male candidates who were however less well-qualified.
>
> [3] The Arbeitsgericht Hamm held that there had been discrimination and took the view that under German law the only sanction for discrimination in recruitment is compensation for 'Vertrauensschaden', namely the loss incurred by candidates who are victims of discrimination as a result of their belief that there would be no discrimination in the establishment of the employment relationship. Such compensation is provided for under Paragraph 611a(2) of the Bürgerliches Gesetzbuch.
>
> [4] Under that provision, in the event of discrimination regarding access to employment, the employer is liable for 'damages in respect of the loss incurred by the worker as a result of his reliance on the expectation

that the establishment of the employment relationship would not be precluded by such a breach [of the principle of equal treatment]'. That provision purports to implement Council Directive No 76/207.

[5] Consequently the Arbeitsgericht found that, under German law, it could order the reimbursement only of the travel expenses incurred by the plaintiff von Colson in pursuing her application for the post (DM 7.20) and that it could not allow the plaintiffs' other claims.

Von Colson's objection centred on Article 6 of the Directive:

[18] Article 6 requires Member States to introduce into their national legal systems such measures as are necessary to enable all persons who consider themselves wronged by discrimination 'to pursue their claims by judicial process'. It follows from the provision that Member States are required to adopt measures which are sufficiently effective to achieve the objective of the directive and to ensure that those measures may in fact be relied on before the national courts by the persons concerned. Such measures may include, for example, provisions requiring the employer to offer a post to the candidate discriminated against or giving the candidate adequate financial compensation, backed up where necessary by a system of fines. However the directive does not prescribe a specific sanction; it leaves Member States free to choose between the different solutions suitable for achieving its objective.

Was this adhered to in the German legal order? The Court's approach was markedly different from standard 'direct effect' analysis:

[22] It is impossible to establish real equality of opportunity without an appropriate system of sanctions. That follows not only from the actual purpose of the directive but more specifically from Article 6 thereof which, by granting applicants for a post who have been discriminated against recourse to the courts, acknowledges that those candidates have rights of which they may avail themselves before the courts.

[23] Although, as has been stated in the reply to Question 1, full implementation of the directive does not require any specific form of sanction for unlawful discrimination, it does entail that that sanction be such as to guarantee real and effective judicial protection. Moreover it must also have a real deterrent effect on the employer. It follows that where a Member State chooses to penalize the breach of the prohibition of discrimination by the award of compensation, that compensation must in any event be adequate in relation to the damage sustained.

[24] In consequence it appears that national provisions limiting the right to compensation of persons who have been discriminated against as regards access to employment to a purely nominal amount, such as, for example, the reimbursement of expenses incurred by them in submitting their application, would not satisfy the requirements of an effective transposition of the directive.

[25] The nature of the sanctions provided for in the Federal Republic of Germany in respect of discrimination regarding access to employment and in particular the question whether the rule in Paragraph 611a(2) of the Bürgerliches Gesetzbuch excludes the possibility of compensation on the basis of the general rules of law were the subject of lengthy discussion before the Court. The German Government maintained in the oral procedure that that provision did not necessarily exclude the application of the general rules of law regarding compensation. It is for the national court alone to rule on that question concerning the interpretation of its national law.

[26] However, the Member States' obligation arising from a directive to achieve the result envisaged by the directive and their duty under Article 5 of the Treaty [now in amended form Article 4(3) TEU] to take all appropriate measures, whether general or particular, to ensure the fulfilment of that obligation, is binding on all the authorities of Member States including, for matters within their jurisdiction, the courts. It follows that, in applying the national law and in particular the provisions of a national law specifically introduced in order to implement Directive No 76/207, national courts are required to interpret their national law in the light of the wording and the purpose of the directive in order to achieve the result referred to in the third paragraph of Article 189.

[27] On the other hand, as the above considerations show, the directive does not include any unconditional and sufficiently precise obligation as regards sanctions for discrimination which, in the absence of implementing measures adopted in good time may be relied on by individuals in order to obtain specific compensation under the directive, where that is not provided for or permitted under national law.

[28] It should, however, be pointed out to the national court that although Directive No 76/207/EEC, for the purpose of imposing a sanction for the breach of the prohibition of discrimination, leaves the Member States free to choose between the different solutions suitable for achieving its objective, it nevertheless requires that if a Member State chooses to penalize breaches of that prohibition by the award of compensation, then in order to ensure that it is effective and that it has a deterrent effect, that compensation must in any event be adequate in relation to the damage sustained and must therefore amount to more than purely nominal compensation such as, for example, the reimbursement only of the expenses incurred in connection with the application. It is for the national court to interpret and apply the legislation adopted for the implementation of the directive in conformity with the requirements of Community law, in so far as it is given discretion to do so under national law.

NOTE: J. Steiner, (1985) 101 LQR 491, observed that the decision marks 'a subtle but significant change of direction' in the European Court's approach to the enforceability of EEC Directives before national courts'. P. Morris, (1989) JBL 233, at p. 241, suggested that 'if national judiciaries respond positively to this exhortation [in *Von Colson*] something approaching horizontal direct effect may be achieved by a circuitous route'. B. Fitzpatrick, (1989) 9 OJLS 336, at p. 346, refers to *Von Colson* having established a principle of 'indirect effect' and suggests that 'it may effectively bridge the gap between vertical and horizontal direct effect'. In any event the Court is developing something different from the orthodox principle of direct effect, thereby deepening the penetration of national law by provisions of EU law.

■ QUESTION

To what extent do you think the *Von Colson* approach offers a route for resolving the anomalies of the horizontal/vertical direct effect distinction which emerges from the Court's ruling in *Marshall* (Case 152/84)?

NOTE: In the *Von Colson* (Case 14/83) judgment itself, one can pick out important contradictions in respect of the national court's task of 'conform-interpretation' (para 28). Compare the second sentence of para 26 with the more qualified statement in the concluding sentence of the Court's ruling in answer to the question. The next two cases are both worthy of examination from the perspective of clarifying the ambit of *Von Colson* (Case 14/83).

Officier van Justitie v *Kolpinghuis Nijmegen* (Case 80/86)

[1987] ECR 3969, Court of Justice of the European Communities

A criminal prosecution was brought against a café owner for stocking mineral water which was in fact simply fizzy tap water. The Dutch authorities sought to supplement the basis of the prosecution by relying on definitions of mineral water detrimental to the defendant which were contained in a Directive which had not been implemented in the Netherlands. A preliminary reference was made to the Court of Justice.

The Court ruled that 'a national authority may not rely, as against an individual, upon a provision of a Directive whose necessary implementation in national law has not yet taken place'. It then turned to the third question referred to it:

[11] The third question is designed to ascertain how far the national court may or must take account of a directive as an aid to the interpretation of a rule of national law.

[12] As the Court stated in its judgment of 10 April 1984 in Case 14/83 *Von Colson and Kamann* v *Land Nordrhein-Westfalen* [1984] ECR 1891, the Member States' obligation arising from a directive to achieve the result envisaged by the directive and their duty under Article 5 of the Treaty to take all appropriate measures, whether general or particular, to ensure the fulfilment of that obligation, is binding on all the authorities of Member States including, for matters within their jurisdiction, the courts. It follows that, in applying the national law and in particular the provisions of a national law specifically introduced in order to implement the directive, national courts are required to interpret their national law in the light of the wording and the purpose of the directive in order to achieve the result referred to in the third paragraph of Article 189 of the Treaty.

[13] However, that obligation on the national court to refer to the content of the directive when interpreting the relevant rules of its national law is limited by the general principles of law which form part of Community law and in particular the principles of legal certainty and non-retroactivity. Thus the Court ruled in its judgment of 11 June 1987 in Case 14/86 *Pretore di Salò* v *X* [1987] ECR 2545 that a directive cannot, of itself and independently of a national law adopted by a Member State for its implementation, have the effect of determining or aggravating the liability in criminal law of persons who act in contravention of the provisions of that directive.

[14] The answer to the third question should therefore be that in applying its national legislation a court of a Member State is required to interpret that legislation in the light of the wording and the purpose of the directive in order to achieve the result referred to in the third paragraph of Article 189 of the Treaty, but a directive cannot, of itself and independently of a law adopted for its implementation, have the effect of determining or aggravating the liability in criminal law of persons who act in contravention of the provisions of that directive.

NOTE: The Court is anxious to emphasize the importance of preserving legal certainty and protecting reasonable expectations, which carry special weight in the field of criminal law in which this case arose. See also Joined Cases C-387/02, C-391/02, and C-403/02 *Silvio Berlusconi et al.* [2005] ECR I-3565.

***Marleasing SA* v *La Comercial Internacional de Alimentación SA* (Case C-106/89)**

[1990] ECR I-4135, Court of Justice of the European Communities

The case arose out of a conflict between the Spanish Civil Code and a company law Directive (68/151) which was unimplemented in Spain. The litigation was between private parties, which, following *Marshall* (Case 152/84), ruled out the direct effect of the Directive. The European Court explained the national court's duty of interpretation in the following terms:

[8] . . . [T]he Member States' obligation arising from a directive to achieve the result envisaged by the directive and their duty under Article 5 of the Treaty to take all appropriate measures, whether general or particular, to ensure the fulfilment of that obligation, is binding on all the authorities of Member States including, for matters within their jurisdiction, the courts. It follows that, in applying national law, whether the provisions in question were adopted before or after the directive, the national court called upon to interpret it is required to do so, as far as possible, in the light of the wording and the purpose of the directive in order to achieve the result pursued by the latter and thereby comply with the third paragraph of Article 189 of the Treaty.

NOTE: The obligation imposed on national courts in *Marleasing* (Case C-106/89) has a firmer feel than that in *Von Colson* (Case 14/83, p. 132). See J. Stuyck and P. Wytinck, (1991) 28 CML Rev 205.

As is clear from the extract, the Court locates the source of this obligation of sympathetic interpretation that is cast on national courts in Article 5 EC, which was adjusted post-Amsterdam (p. 11) as Article 10 EC, and which is now found in amended form in Article 4(3) TEU. It confirmed this approach in its ruling in *Paola Faccini Dori* (Case C-91/92). Even though Ms Dori was not able to rely directly on the unimplemented Directive in proceedings involving another private party (p. 122), she was entitled to expect that the national court would not simply ignore the Directive in applying national law.

***Paola Faccini Dori* v *Recreb Srl* (Case C-91/92)**

[1994] ECR I-3325, Court of Justice of the European Communities

[26] It must also be borne in mind that, as the Court has consistently held since its judgment in Case 14/83 *Von Colson and Kamann* v *Land Nordrhein-Westfalen* [1984] ECR 1891, paragraph 26, the Member States' obligation arising from a directive to achieve the result envisaged by the directive and their duty under Article 5 of the Treaty to take all appropriate measures, whether general or particular, is binding on all the

authorities of Member States, including, for matters within their jurisdiction, the courts. The judgments of the Court in Case C-106/89 *Marleasing* v *La Comercial Internacional de Alimentación* [1990] ECR I-4135, paragraph 8, and Case C-334/92 *Wagner Miret* v *Fondo de Garantia Salarial* [1993] ECR I-6911, paragraph 20, make it clear that, when applying national law, whether adopted before or after the directive, the national court that has to interpret that law must do so, as far as possible, in the light of the wording and the purpose of the directive so as to achieve the result it has in view and thereby comply with the third paragraph of Article 189 of the Treaty.

NOTE: The logic of this reasoning leads to the conclusion that the legal obligations pertaining to the absorption of a Directive into the national legal order are enduring, and do not come to an end on the Directive's transposition 'on paper' into national law. This is made clear in the next case.

Marks and Spencer plc v *Commissioners of Customs and Excise* (C-62/00)

[2002] ECR I-6325, Court of Justice of the European Communities

[24] . . .it should be remembered, first, that the Member States' obligation under a directive to achieve the result envisaged by the directive and their duty under Article 5 of the EC Treaty (now Article 10 EC) to take all appropriate measures, whether general or particular, to ensure fulfilment of that obligation are binding on all the authorities of the Member States, including, for matters within their jurisdiction, the courts (see, *inter alia*, Case C-168/95 *Arcaro* [1996] ECR I-4705, paragraph 41). It follows that in applying domestic law the national court called upon to interpret that law is required to do so, as far as possible, in the light of the wording and purpose of the directive, in order to achieve the purpose of the directive and thereby comply with the third paragraph of Article 189 of the EC Treaty (now the third paragraph of Article 249 EC) (see, in particular, Case C-106/89 *Marleasing* [1990] ECR I-4135, paragraph 8, and Case C-334/92 *Wagner Miret* [1993] ECR I-6911, paragraph 20).

[25] Second, as the Court has consistently held, whenever the provisions of a directive appear, so far as their subject-matter is concerned, to be unconditional and sufficiently precise, they may be relied upon before the national courts by individuals against the State where the latter has failed to implement the directive in domestic law by the end of the period prescribed or where it has failed to implement the directive correctly (see, *inter alia*, Case 8/81 *Becker* [1982] ECR 53, paragraph 25; Case 103/88 *Fratelli Costanzo* [1989] ECR 1839, paragraph 29; and Case C-319/97 *Kortas* [1999] ECR I-3143, paragraph 21).

[26] Third, it has been consistently held that implementation of a directive must be such as to ensure its application in full (see to that effect, in particular, Case C-217/97 *Commission* v *Germany* [1999] ECR I-5087, paragraph 31, and Case C-214/98 *Commission* v *Greece* [2000] ECR I-9601, paragraph 49).

[27] Consequently, the adoption of national measures correctly implementing a directive does not exhaust the effects of the directive. Member States remain bound actually to ensure full application of the directive even after the adoption of those measures. Individuals are therefore entitled to rely before national courts, against the State, on the provisions of a directive which appear, so far as their subject-matter is concerned, to be unconditional and sufficiently precise whenever the full application of the directive is not in fact secured, that is to say, not only where the directive has not been implemented or has been implemented incorrectly, but also where the national measures correctly implementing the directive are not being applied in such a way as to achieve the result sought by it.

[28] As the Advocate General noted in point 40 of his Opinion, it would be inconsistent with the Community legal order for individuals to be able to rely on a directive where it has been implemented incorrectly but not to be able to do so where the national authorities apply the national measures implementing the directive in a manner incompatible with it.

NOTE: The scope of the obligation to interpret national law in conformity with a Directive was taken a step further in the next case. However, the Court did not help to stabilize and clarify the state of the law by introducing textual anomalies into its ruling.

Centrosteel Srl v _Adipol GmbH_ (Case C-456/98)

[2000] ECR I-6007, Court of Justice of the European Communities

[15] It is true that, according to settled case law of the Court, in the absence of proper transposition into national law, a directive cannot of itself impose obligations on individuals (Case 152/84 *Marshall* v *Southampton and South-West Hampshire Health Authority* [1986] ECR 723, paragraph 48, and Case C-91/92 *Faccini Dori* v *Recreb* [1994] ECR I-3325, paragraph 20).

[16] However, it is also apparent from the case law of the Court (Case C-106/89 *Marleasing* v *La Comercial Internacional de Alimentación* [1990] ECR I-4135, paragraph 8; Case C-334/92 *Wagner* v *Fondo de Garantía Salarial* [1993] ECR I-6911, paragraph 20; *Faccini Dori*, paragraph 26; and Joined Cases C-240/98 to C-244/98 *Océano Grupo Editorial* v *Salvat Editores* [2000] ECR I-4941, paragraph 30) that, when applying national law, whether adopted before or after the directive, the national court that has to interpret that law must do so, as far as possible, in the light of the wording and the purpose of the directive so as to achieve the result it has in view and thereby comply with the third paragraph of Article 189 of the EC Treaty (now the third paragraph of Article 249 EC).

[17] Where it is seised of a dispute falling within the scope of the Directive and arising from facts postdating the expiry of the period for transposing the Directive, the national court, in applying provisions of domestic law or settled domestic case law, as seems to be the case in the main proceedings, must therefore interpret that law in such a way that it is applied in conformity with the aims of the Directive . . .

The reference in para 17 to the application of 'settled domestic case law' in conformity with the aims of the Directive is striking. However, this phrase is missing from the formal ruling.

Council Directive 86/653/EEC of 18 December 1986 on the coordination of the laws of the Member States relating to self-employed commercial agents precludes national legislation which makes the validity of an agency contract conditional upon the commercial agent being entered in the appropriate register. The national court is bound, when applying provisions of domestic law predating or postdating the said Directive, to interpret those provisions, so far as possible, in the light of the wording and purpose of the Directive, so that those provisions are applied in a manner consistent with the result pursued by the Directive.

NOTE: In its subsequent ruling in *AXA Royal Belge* (Case C-386/00 [2002] ECR I-2209) the Court referred explicitly to its own ruling in *Centrosteel* (Case C-456/98), but cited only paragraphs 15 and 16, not 17!

This peculiarity was not addressed directly by the Court in the next case, but the Court did take the opportunity to refer to *Centrosteel* and to revisit its view of the nature of the obligation imposed on national judges.

Bernhard Pfeiffer v _Deutsches Rotes Kreuz_ (Joined Cases C-397/01 to C-403/01)

[2004] ECR I-8835, Court of Justice of the European Communities

The litigation, originating before German labour courts, concerned matters falling within the scope of Directive 89/391 on health and safety at work and Directive 93/104 on the organization of working time. After confirming its long-standing refusal to accept that Directives are capable of application in litigation before national courts exclusively involving private parties – that is, no horizontal direct effect – the Court insisted:

[111] It is the responsibility of the national courts in particular to provide the legal protection which individuals derive from the rules of Community law and to ensure that those rules are fully effective.

[112] That is *a fortiori* the case when the national court is seised of a dispute concerning the application of domestic provisions which, as here, have been specifically enacted for the purpose of transposing a directive

intended to confer rights on individuals. The national court must, in the light of the third paragraph of Article 249 EC, presume that the Member State, following its exercise of the discretion afforded it under that provision, had the intention of fulfilling entirely the obligations arising from the directive concerned (see Case C-334/92 *Wagner Miret* [1993] ECR I-6911, paragraph 20).

[113] Thus, when it applies domestic law, and in particular legislative provisions specifically adopted for the purpose of implementing the requirements of a directive, the national court is bound to interpret national law, so far as possible, in the light of the wording and the purpose of the directive concerned in order to achieve the result sought by the directive and consequently comply with the third paragraph of Article 249 EC (see to that effect, inter alia, the judgments cited above in *Von Colson and Kamann*, paragraph 26; *Marleasing*, paragraph 8, and *Faccini Dori*, paragraph 26; see also Case C-63/97 *BMW* [1999] ECR I-905, paragraph 22; Joined Cases C-240/98 to C-244/98 *Oceano Grupo Editorial and Salvat Editores* [2000] ECR I-4941, paragraph 30; and Case C-408/01 *Adidas-Salomon and Adidas Benelux* [2003] ECR I-0000, paragraph 21).

[114] The requirement for national law to be interpreted in conformity with Community law is inherent in the system of the Treaty, since it permits the national court, for the matters within its jurisdiction, to ensure the full effectiveness of Community law when it determines the dispute before it (see, to that effect, Case C-160/01 *Mau* [2003] ECR I-4791, paragraph 34).

[115] Although the principle that national law must be interpreted in conformity with Community law concerns chiefly domestic provisions enacted in order to implement the directive in question, it does not entail an interpretation merely of those provisions but requires the national court to consider national law as a whole in order to assess to what extent it may be applied so as not to produce a result contrary to that sought by the directive (see, to that effect, *Carbonari* [Case C-131/97], paragraphs 49 and 50).

[116] In that context, if the application of interpretative methods recognised by national law enables, in certain circumstances, a provision of domestic law to be construed in such a way as to avoid conflict with another rule of domestic law or the scope of that provision to be restricted to that end by applying it only in so far as it is compatible with the rule concerned, the national court is bound to use those methods in order to achieve the result sought by the directive.

[117] In such circumstances, the national court, when hearing cases which, like the present proceedings, fall within the scope of Directive 93/104 and derive from facts postdating expiry of the period for implementing the directive, must, when applying the provisions of national law specifically intended to implement the directive, interpret those provisions so far as possible in such a way that they are applied in conformity with the objectives of the directive (see, to that effect, the judgment in Case C-456/98 *Centrosteel* [2000] ECR I-6007, paragraphs 16 and 17).

[118] In this instance, the principle of interpretation in conformity with Community law thus requires the referring court to do whatever lies within its jurisdiction, having regard to the whole body of rules of national law, to ensure that Directive 93/104 is fully effective, in order to prevent the maximum weekly working time laid down in Article 6(2) of the directive from being exceeded (see, to that effect, *Marleasing*, paragraphs 7 and 13).

[119] Accordingly, it must be concluded that, when hearing a case between individuals, a national court is required, when applying the provisions of domestic law adopted for the purpose of transposing obligations laid down by a directive, to consider the whole body of rules of national law and to interpret them, so far as possible, in the light of the wording and purpose of the directive in order to achieve an outcome consistent with the objective pursued by the directive. In the main proceedings, the national court must thus do whatever lies within its jurisdiction to ensure that the maximum period of weekly working time, which is set at 48 hours by Article 6(2) of Directive 93/104, is not exceeded.

The assertion in para 114 that the principle of conform-interpretation is 'inherent in the system of the Treaty' was repeated in Case C-212/04 *Adeneler* [2006] ECR I-6057 and in Case C-268/06 *Impact* [2008] ECR I-2483, and updated as 'inherent in the system of the TFEU' in Case C-306/12 *Spedition Welter* judgment of 10 October 2013. It is strikingly bold. As mentioned, previous case law had rooted the obligation of national courts in a specific Treaty provision – Article 5, which became Article 10 and is now, in amended version, Article 4(3) TEU. Drawing on what is 'inherent in the system of the Treaty' is a deeper claim. However, this cements a direct connection between this principle and the Court's finding in *Francovich* (Cases C-6/90 and C-9/90) that a State may be liable for damage caused to individuals as a result of breach of EU law. That judgment too locates the principle as 'inherent in the system of the Treaty' (para 35 of the judgment in *Francovich*, p. 143).

If the obligation cast on national courts is inherent in the system of the Treaty it is not to be confined to the impact of Directives. A Regulation is directly applicable but may in some circumstances leave room for necessary national implementation (for example in fixing penalties in the event of infringement). In Case C-60/02 *Rolex* [2004] ECR I-651 the Court transposed the principle of 'conform-interpretation' from the sphere of Directives to the context of a Regulation of this type. It stated that 'National courts are required to interpret their national law within the limits set by Community law, in order to achieve the result intended by the Community rule in question', referring to Case C-106/89 *Marleasing* [1990] ECR I-4135 (para 59 of the ruling in *Rolex*). However, the Court accepted the relevance of principles of legal certainty and of non-retroactivity in criminal matters, which preclude an EU act from determining or aggravating the liability in criminal law of persons who act in contravention of its provisions, mentioned at p. 134.

By way of concluding comment, an enduring tension lies embedded within this line of case law. On the one hand, there is a concern to enhance the 'full effectiveness' of EU law, which is promoted by requiring national judiciaries to adapt national provisions in order to achieve the objectives set out by the Treaty and legislation adopted thereunder. On the other hand, there is a concern that such adaptation, which in some circumstances may fall little short of judicial re-writing of national law which does not conform to EU law, generates uncertainty and unpredictability in the law and inflicts potential unfairness on private parties who happen to find apparently reliable rules of national law set aside by a court, not the legislature. A similar tension afflicts the approach to incidental direct effect of Directives (p. 125) and it is also visible in the general case law governing the application of the 'principle of effectiveness' to national law of remedies and procedures outwith the special case of Directives (Chapter 4). In some circumstances – for example, the use of an unimplemented Directive to aggravate criminal liability under national law – the Court has clearly ruled out the aggressive application of the principle of effectiveness. Nor is *contra legem* interpretation of national law expected. And on occasion the Court spells out what a national court may refuse to do on the basis that it is being asked to interpret *contra legem*. The next extract provides an illustration.

Impact **(Case C-268/06)**

[2008] ECR I-2483, Court of Justice of the European Communities.

This is another case concerning equal treatment. The Court rules that clause 4(1) of the Framework Agreement annexed to Directive 1999/70 is apt for application by a national court. Then the job of interpretation is addressed.

[99] The requirement that national law be interpreted in conformity with Community law is inherent in the system of the EC Treaty, since it permits national courts, for the matters within their jurisdiction, to ensure the full effectiveness of Community law when they determine the disputes before them (see, inter alia, *Pfeiffer and Others*, paragraph 114, and *Adeneler and Others*, paragraph 109).

[100] However, the obligation on a national court to refer to the content of a directive when interpreting and applying the relevant rules of domestic law is limited by general principles of law, particularly those of legal certainty and non-retroactivity, and that obligation cannot serve as the basis for an interpretation of national

law *contra legem* (see Case 80/86 *Kolpinghuis Nijmegen* [1987] ECR 3969, paragraph 13, and *Adeneler and Others*, paragraph 110; see also, by analogy, Case C-105/03 *Pupino* [2005] ECR I-5285, paragraphs 44 and 47).

[101] The principle that national law must be interpreted in conformity with Community law none the less requires national courts to do whatever lies within their jurisdiction, taking the whole body of domestic law into consideration and applying the interpretative methods recognised by domestic law, with a view to ensuring that the directive in question is fully effective and achieving an outcome consistent with the objective pursued by it (see *Pfeiffer and Others*, paragraphs 115, 116, 118 and 119, and *Adeneler and Others*, paragraph 111).

[102] In the present case, since, according to the information given in the order for reference, domestic law appears to include a rule that precludes the retrospective application of legislation unless there is a clear and unambiguous indication to the contrary, it is for the referring court to ascertain whether there is a provision in that legislation, in particular in the 2003 Act, which contains such an indication capable of giving retrospective effect to section 6 of the 2003 Act.

[103] In the absence of such a provision, Community law – in particular the requirement for national law to be interpreted in conformity with Community law – cannot be interpreted as requiring the referring court to give section 6 of the 2003 Act retrospective effect to the date by which Directive 1999/70 should have been transposed, as the referring court would otherwise be constrained to interpret national law *contra legem*.

NOTE: The Court did something similar in Case C-176/12 *Association de médiation sociale* judgment of 15 January 2014. However, this level of precision is uncommon in the Court's case law. Although the principle of legal certainty is unequivocally part of EU law and serves to protect private parties, it will often be difficult for a national court to determine how much momentum it carries when it collides with the principle of conform-interpretation to which national judges are subject. The Court of Justice frequently seems concerned to avoid clarifying in concrete terms what limits on creative judicial interpretation are envisaged by the proviso that interpretation be conducted 'so far as possible' located (*inter alia*) in para 24 of *Marks and Spencer* (Case C-62/00) and para 119 of *Pfeiffer* (Joined Cases C-397/01–403/01). This is in part attributable to the nature of the preliminary reference procedure as a basis for judicial co-operation: see further Chapter 7.

■ QUESTIONS

1. *Marleasing* seems clearly to require interpretation of pre-existing national legislation in the light of a subsequent Directive and this is confirmed in the subsequent case law. This is by no means uncontroversial. The late Lord Slynn, who served as both Advocate-General and judge in Luxembourg before assuming the role of a Law Lord, has observed extra-judicially that:

   > I find it difficult to say that a statute of 1870 must be interpreted in the light of a 1991 directive. If the former is in conflict with the latter, it is not for judges to strain language but for Governments to introduce new legislation. (Introducing a European Legal Order, Stevens/Sweet and Maxwell, 1992, p. 124; see also 'Looking at European Community Texts' (1993) 14/1 Statute L Rev 12)

   What are the limits of 'interpretation'? Do you think the Court of Justice is improperly asking national courts to perform tasks which belong with national legislatures?
2. How might the EU legal order rid itself of the complexities engendered by the extension of the notion of direct effect to Directives?

FURTHER READING (COVERING MOST OR ALL ASPECTS OF THIS CHAPTER)

Craig, P., 'The Legal Effect of Directives: Policy, Rules and Exceptions' (2009) 34 EL Rev 349.

Dickson, J., 'Directives in EU Legal Systems: Whose Norms Are They Anyway?' (2011) 17 ELJ 190.

Dougan, M., 'When Worlds Collide! Competing Visions of the Relationship between Direct Effect and Supremacy' (2007) 44 CML Rev 931.

Drake, S. 'Twenty Years after *Von Colson*: the Impact of 'Indirect Effect' on the Protection of the Individual's Community Rights' (2005) 30 EL Rev 329.

Dubout, E., 'L'invocabilité d'éviction des directives dans les litiges horizontaux' RTDE 46(2) 277 (2010).

Mörsdorf, J., 'Unmittelbare Anwendung von EG-Richtlinienzwischen Privaten in der Rechtsprechung des EuGH' 2009/2 *Europarecht* 219.

Prechal, S. 'Direct effect, Indirect Effect, Supremacy and the Evolving Constitution of the European Union' Ch 3 in C. Barnard (ed.), *The Fundamentals of EU Law Revisited: Assessing the Impact of the Constitutional Debate* (Oxford: OUP, 2007).

Ross, M. 'Effectiveness in the European Legal Order(s): Beyond Supremacy to Constitutional Proportionality?' (2006) 31 EL Rev 476.

NOTE: For additional material and resources see the Online Resource Centre at: www.oxfordtextbooks.co.uk/orc/weatherill12e.

6

State Liability

Chapter 5 explained that Directives are capable of direct effect – but only against the State. The unimplemented Directive is barred from application against private parties, although it may exert an incidental effect on private parties. Chapter 5 concluded with examination of the obligation imposed on national courts to interpret national rules in order to conform with relevant Directives. This represents an ingenious strategy for embedding Directives within national legal orders even where the State authorities have failed to effect the legal transplant from EU to national level envisaged by Article 288 TFEU. However, there are enduring difficulties in defining the proper scope of the obligation of judicial interpretation. And those difficulties are in effect multiplied by 28, since courts in all the Member States are forced to grapple with the issue. One may doubt whether the notion of 'indirect effect' or 'conform-interpretation' is a fully satisfactory method of securing the application at national level of unimplemented EU measures.

In any event even if the national court is willing and able to carry out the interpretative function, there remains a persisting concern about its consequences. Where national courts actively interpret national law in the light of unimplemented Directives, interference with the legitimate expectations of private parties may result. Private parties may find themselves bound by obligations drawn by interpretation from Directives of which they are quite unaware. That concern seems to motivate the Court's reluctance to sanction 'indirect effect' in *Kolpinghuis Nijmegen* (Case 80/86, p. 134) where the State would be the beneficiary. In cases involving private parties alone, it might be possible to contend that this interpretative approach is justified as a means of protecting the expectations of the intended beneficiary of rights under an unimplemented Directive. In that sense, the issue is a choice between two deserving private parties, one of which must ultimately be prejudiced. Moreover, in the 'incidental effect' cases the Court seems to have been carefree in imposing unexpected burdens on private parties *via* the medium of unimplemented Directives. Yet at bottom the problem is that this route fails to impose a burden on the party responsible for the gap in legal protection – the *Member State* which has failed to implement the Directive. There is a strong case for holding that the primary target for the individual who has suffered loss through non-implementation of a Directive should be the public authorities. This was a point astutely made by commentators (N. Green, (1984) 9 EL Rev 295, 321–4; J. Usher, (1989) 10 Statute Law Rev 95, 102; D. Curtin, (1990) 27 CML Rev 709, 729). The Court took the chance to develop its jurisprudence in the direction of State liability in Cases C-6/90 and C-9/90 *Francovich and Others* v *Italian State* [1991] ECR I-5357. In shaping our understanding of the application of EU law by national courts and tribunals *Francovich* is a landmark case of a stature comparable to *Van Gend en Loos* (Case 26/62, p. 84).

Directive 80/987 required Member States to set up guarantee funds to compensate workers in the event of employer insolvency. Italy failed to implement the Directive. That Treaty violation had already been recorded in a Court ruling – Case 22/87, *Commission* v *Italy* [1989] ECR 143. Italian workers, among them Andrea Francovich, believed themselves denied the protection envisaged by the Directive but not transposed into Italian law. Proceedings before the Italian courts yielded a preliminary reference to the Court of Justice.

The Court determined that the workers could claim no directly effective rights, for the relevant provisions of the Directive lacked sufficient unconditionality. The provider of the guarantee could not be identified. The Court then turned to the question of the liability of the State to make good loss suffered by individuals as a result of the failure to implement. The Court considered that this was an issue which fell to be considered in the light of the general system of the Treaty and its fundamental principles:

Francovich and Others v *Italian State* (Cases C-6/90 and C-9/90)

[1991] ECR I-5357, Court of Justice of the European Communities

(a) The existence of State liability as a matter of principle

[31] It should be borne in mind at the outset that the EEC Treaty has created its own legal system, which is integrated into the legal systems of the Member States and which their courts are bound to apply. The subjects of that legal system are not only the Member States but also their nationals. Just as it imposes burdens on individuals, Community law is also intended to give rise to rights which become part of their legal patrimony. Those rights arise not only where they are expressly granted by the Treaty but also by virtue of obligations which the Treaty imposes in a clearly defined manner both on individuals and on the Member States and the Community institutions (see the judgments in Case 26/62 *Van Gend en Loos* [1963] ECR 1 and Case 6/64 *Costa* v *ENEL* [1964] ECR 585).

[32] Furthermore, it has been consistently held that the national courts whose task it is to apply the provisions of Community law in areas within their jurisdiction must ensure that those rules take full effect and must protect the rights which they confer on individuals (see in particular the judgments in Case 106/77 *Amministrazione delle Finanze dello Stato* v *Simmenthal* [1978] ECR 629, paragraph 16, and Case C-213/89 *Factortame* [1990] ECR I-2433, paragraph 19).

[33] The full effectiveness of Community rules would be impaired and the protection of the rights which they grant would be weakened if individuals were unable to obtain redress when their rights are infringed by a breach of Community law for which a Member State can be held responsible.

[34] The possibility of obtaining redress from the Member State is particularly indispensable where, as in this case, the full effectiveness of Community rules is subject to prior action on the part of the State and where, consequently, in the absence of such action, individuals cannot enforce before the national courts the rights conferred upon them by Community law.

[35] It follows that the principle whereby a State must be liable for loss and damage caused to individuals as a result of breaches of Community law for which the State can be held responsible is inherent in the system of the Treaty.

[36] A further basis for the obligation of Member States to make good such loss and damage is to be found in Article 5 of the Treaty, under which the Member States are required to take all appropriate measures, whether general or particular, to ensure fulfilment of their obligations under Community law. Among these is the obligation to nullify the unlawful consequences of a breach of Community law. . .

[37] It follows from all the foregoing that it is a principle of Community law that the Member States are obliged to make good loss and damage caused to individuals by breaches of Community law for which they can be held responsible.

(b) The conditions for State liability

[38] Although State liability is thus required by Community law, the conditions under which that liability gives rise to a right to reparation depend on the nature of the breach of Community law giving rise to the loss and damage.

[39] Where, as in this case, a Member State fails to fulfil its obligation under the third paragraph of Article 189 of the Treaty to take all the measures necessary to achieve the result prescribed by a directive, the full effectiveness of that rule of Community law requires that there should be a right to reparation provided that three conditions are fulfilled.

[40] The first of those conditions is that the result prescribed by the directive should entail the grant of rights to individuals. The second condition is that it should be possible to identify the content of those rights on the

basis of the provisions of the directive. Finally, the third condition is the existence of a causal link between the breach of the State's obligation and the loss and damage suffered by the injured parties.

[41] Those conditions are sufficient to give rise to a right on the part of individuals to obtain reparation, a right founded directly on Community law.

[42] Subject to that reservation, it is on the basis of the rules of national law on liability that the State must make reparation for the consequences of the loss and damage caused. In the absence of Community legislation, it is for the internal legal order of each Member State to designate the competent courts and lay down the detailed procedural rules for legal proceedings intended fully to safeguard the rights which individuals derive from Community law (see the judgments in Case 60/75 *Russo* v *AIMA* [1976] ECR 45, Case 33/76 *Rewe* v *Landwirtschaftskammer Saarland* [1976] ECR 1989 and Case 158/80 *Rewe* v *Hauptzollamt Kiel* [1981] ECR 1805).

[43] Further, the substantive and procedural conditions for reparation of loss and damage laid down by the national law of the Member States must not be less favourable than those relating to similar domestic claims and must not be so framed as to make it virtually impossible or excessively difficult to obtain reparation (see, in relation to the analogous issue of the repayment of taxes levied in breach of Community law, *inter alia* the judgment in Case 199/82 *Amministrazione delle Finanze dello Stato* v *San Giorgio* [1983] ECR 3595).

[44] In this case, the breach of Community law by a Member State by virtue of its failure to transpose Directive 80/987 within the prescribed period has been confirmed by a judgment of the Court. The result required by that directive entails the grant to employees of a right to a guarantee of payment of their unpaid wage claims. As is clear from the examination of the first part of the first question, the content of that right can be identified on the basis of the provisions of the directive.

[45] Consequently, the national court must, in accordance with the national rules on liability, uphold the right of employees to obtain reparation of loss and damage caused to them as a result of failure to transpose the directive.

[46] The answer to be given to the national court must therefore be that a Member State is required to make good loss and damage caused to individuals by failure to transpose Directive 80/987.

NOTE: Article 19(1) TEU, encountered in Chapter 4 (p. 104) provides that 'Member States shall provide remedies sufficient to ensure effective legal protection in the fields covered by Union law', but this is an innovation of the Lisbon Treaty. Already in *Francovich* almost twenty years earlier the Court had been more concrete in the demands it placed on national legal orders.

The Court repeated its formulation in *Dori* (Case C-91/92). Having denied Ms Dori the possibility of relying on the Directive as such to defeat the claim against her by a private supplier (p. 122), the Court proceeded to rule that the Italian court was subject to the obligation of interpretation ('indirect effect' or 'conform-interpretation', p. 132). It then directed Ms Dori to a different target – the defaulting State.

***Paola Faccini Dori* v *Recreb Srl* (Case C-91/92)**

[1994] ECR I-3325, Court of Justice of the European Communities

[27] If the result prescribed by the directive cannot be achieved by way of interpretation, it should also be borne in mind that, in terms of the judgment in Joined Cases C-6/90 and C-9/90 *Francovich and Others* v *Italy* [1991] ECR I-5357, paragraph 39, Community law requires the Member States to make good damage caused to individuals through failure to transpose a directive, provided that three conditions are fulfilled. First, the purpose of the directive must be to grant rights to individuals. Second, it must be possible to identify the content of those rights on the basis of the provisions of the directive. Finally, there must be a causal link between the breach of the State's obligation and the damage suffered.

[28] The directive on contracts negotiated away from business premises is undeniably intended to confer rights on individuals and it is equally certain that the minimum content of those rights can be identified by reference to the provisions of the directive alone (see paragraph 17 above).

[29] Where damage has been suffered and that damage is due to a breach by the State of its obligation, it is for the national court to uphold the right of aggrieved consumers to obtain reparation in accordance with national law on liability.

■ QUESTION

To what extent do the techniques of, first, 'indirect effect'/'conform-interpretation' and, second, State liability under *Francovich* provide an adequate protection for the individual deprived of rights against a private party that are envisaged under an unimplemented Directive? (See, in particular, the Opinion of Advocate-General Jacobs in *Vaneetveld* v *SA Le Foyer* (Case C-316/93) [1994] ECR I-763.) Has the Court repaired the damage done to individual protection by its refusal in *Marshall* and *Dori* to accept that Directives are capable of horizontal direct effect?

NOTE: National authorities, including the judiciary, are required actively to support EU law and if necessary to adjust their 'normal' approach under domestic law. 'The principle of effectiveness' was examined in Chapter 4 in its application to national courts charged with the mission to apply EU law. It also underlies the obligations which the Court of Justice has imposed on national courts to give effect to unimplemented Directives. *Francovich*, like *Factortame*, examined in Chapter 4 (p. 111), demands that national courts adjust their domestic law of remedies where this is required in order to provide effective protection to EU law rights. *Francovich*, like *Factortame*, envisages a minimum level of protection which must be available to the EU law litigant in the national system. *Francovich*, like *Marleasing* (Case C-106/89), makes an important contribution to the vigour of EU law at national level *even in circumstances where direct effect is lacking.*

The *Francovich* focus on State liability appears to be acquiring an increasing priority within the system governing effective judicial protection at national level, at the expense of other devices for addressing the consequences of State failures to implement Directives in accordance with Article 288 TFEU. Chapter 4 included discussion of the impact of EU law on time-limits in national proceedings brought to secure repayment of charges levied, or payment of sums not made, in breach of a Directive that has not been properly implemented. The 'principle of effectiveness' may be invoked to challenge such restrictions, but the Court of Justice has accepted that restrictions on backdating claims may be imposed under national law; and that reasonable time limits may be applied in the interests of preserving legal certainty. So these procedural rules may be permissible even though they may serve to shelter the State from the full consequences of its unlawful failure to implement unless, exceptionally, the Member State has made the exercise of rights excessively difficult (*cf* Case C-62/00 *Marks and Spencer*, p. 107, and similarly Case C-445/06 *Danske Slagterier* [2009] ECR I-2199; Case C-89/10 *Q-Beef* [2011] ECR I-7819).

Advocate-General Jacobs in *Fantask* (Case C-188/95 [1997] ECR I-6783) argued strongly in favour of the contribution to legal security made by the application of time-limits even in cases involving unimplemented Directives and suggested that a *Francovich* claim was the appropriate method of protecting an individual suffering loss in such circumstances. This approach to the protection of the individual would place great emphasis on the significance of the defaulting State's culpability as an element in the criteria governing *Francovich* liability.

More broadly still, H. Schermers has argued that in the wake of rulings such as *Francovich* and *Faccini Dori* 'we do not need direct effect for directives any more. When Member States do not fulfil their obligations under a directive, the affected individuals will be able to claim damages' ('No Direct Effect for Directives' (1997) 3 Euro Public Law 527, 539). He observes that the abandonment of the capacity of Directives to exert direct effect in favour of emphasis on *Francovich* claims against the defaulting State would expel from the EU legal order the current imbalance, which lends direct effect to

Directives only in *some* circumstances (individual versus State). Does this provocative suggestion appeal to you?

It is, however, important to appreciate that the increasing tendency of *Francovich* to take centre stage in the pattern of individual protection developed by the Court of Justice has not been universally welcomed. C. Harlow ('Francovich and the Problem of the Disobedient State' (1996) 2 ELJ 199), for example, finds the theoretical underpinnings for State liability in the EU to be weak, and fears that the intermingling of EU law with national liability systems may corrupt both. One may certainly question the *practical* feasibility of pursuing a *Francovich* claim other than in instances involving very wealthy applicants; yet EU law is supposed to confer rights on a wider range of interest groups than large commercial concerns.

The judgment in *Francovich* nevertheless counts as one of the Court of Justice's most remarkable. It has created a remedy defined by criteria under EU law which must be absorbed into the national legal order. *Francovich* represents a statement of the Court of Justice's readiness to appeal to the 'system of the Treaty' (para 35) as a basis for establishing a system of judicial remedies that will further the cause of effective protection of EU law rights. That systemic source has also come to the fore in the Court's treatment of the obligation of judicial 'conform-interpretation' as a means to ensure the full effectiveness of EU law (Joined Cases C-397/01 to C-403/01 *Pfeiffer* p. 137). At a more general level, the Court is presiding over the development of a type of EU 'common law'. The next extract traces the Court's development of the notion of effective judicial protection (at national level), already introduced in Chapter 4, before concluding with observations in this wider context.

R. Caranta, 'Government Liability after Francovich'

(1993) 52 *Cambridge Law Journal* 272, 279–82

. . . The ground upon which the *Francovich* case was decided is the principle of effective protection of individuals.

The case law concerning this principle has evolved remarkably during the past ten years, the court having moved from an initial position which amounted to almost complete indifference to the remedial aspect of the rights conferred on individuals by Community law, to an ever greater involvement in questions concerning the conditions under which the protection of such rights is ensured by the judiciary of the Member States.

The initial position was the result of a widespread belief that Community law in general was only interested in substantive aspects of law, the procedural aspects having been left to the competence of the Member States. In the *Rewe*[42] and *Comet*[43] cases, for example, the court ruled that it was for each national legal system to determine the procedural aspects of actions claiming the protection of individual rights provided by Community law. There were two qualifications, namely that the domestic remedies had to be no less favourable than those established for comparable national rights, and that in any case the remedies conferred had to be effective, but the actual incidence of Community law on procedure was virtually non-existent.

The *Francovich* decision does maintain the traditional rule whereby procedures to ensure the execution of Community law are left to national legal systems, but with a small, and not so innocent, change; the competence of Member States ceases to be the governing principle, and becomes the rule only in the absence of relevant Community provisions.[44]

These qualifications of the principle of the competence of Member States in procedural matters acquired relevance long before *Francovich*. In the *Simmenthal* case, notably, the principle of the effectiveness of judicial protection ceased to be a mere obiter dictum and began to bite. In that case another Italian judge of first instance, the *Pretore* of Susa, had asked the Court of Justice whether it was consistent with Community law for a national system of judicial review of legislation to make it the duty of every judge, before excluding the operation of a national

42 Case 33/76, [1976] ECR 1997, cons. 5.

43 Case 45/76, [1976] ECR 2053, cons. 12–17.

44 But for a traditional reading of the rule see G. de Búrca, 'Giving Effect to European Community Directives' (1992) 55 MLR 215, at p. 238.

legal provision in conflict with Community law, to request a preliminary ruling by the country's Constitutional Court. The European Court, as is well known, held that:[45]

> any provision of a national legal system and any legislative, administrative or judicial practice which might impair the effectiveness of Community law by withholding from the national court having jurisdiction to apply such law the power to do everything necessary at the moment of its application to set aside national legal provisions which might prevent Community rules from having full force and effect are incompatible with those requirements which are the very essence of Community law.

On this ground the Court held that a system of centralised judicial review such as the one existing in Italy which delayed the final decision by requiring the matter to be referred to the Constitutional Court was not compatible with the principle of the effective protection of individual rights which was based upon Community law, and for this reason had to be set aside by every judge in the Member State.

Even in *Simmenthal*, however, it could be thought that the real issue was not just the effective protection of individuals; what was actually at stake in that case was which court was to have the last word when national law conflicted with Community law. If every national judge had to make a reference to the Constitutional Court, it would be that Court which determined the consistency of the national law with Community law, without even consulting the Court of Justice, because the Italian Constitutional Court in practice never made a reference under article 177 of the EEC Treaty. On the other hand, if every judge was left free to decide the conflict between national and Community law on his own, he would probably resort to the European Court to have Community law interpreted and the question of compatibility assessed. It was a contest for power, the Court of Justice against the Italian Constitutional Court, and the latter finally bowed to the supremacy of Community law and of its court.[46]

More relevant to the protection of individuals were the decisions concerning the repayment of wrongly paid taxes. On references by some Italian courts, the Court of Justice in the *San Giorgio* case[47] held it to be inconsistent with Community law for a national provision to subject the right to restitution of sums paid pursuant to a national tax law contrary to Community law to proof that the charge had not been transferred to the final consumer of the goods; the court thought it contrary to the principle of effective judicial protection to impose on citizens invoking their Community law rights an onus of proof which it was almost impossible to discharge.

There can be no doubt that *Factortame*[48] is the most important decision so far concerning the consequences of the principle of the effectiveness of judicial protection of individuals; its impact upon the respective roles of the Community and Member States in the creation of remedies for infringements of Community law rights seriously undermines the position according to which procedure is a matter to be left to Member States.

The facts which constitute the background to, and the legal questions involved in, the *Factortame* decision are widely known on the Continent as well as in Britain.[49] It is sufficient to recall that some Spanish owners of fishing vessels had challenged the conformity with Community law of a British statute and regulations designed to ensure that ships flying the Union Jack were owned and operated by British citizens or corporations.

Fearing that irrecoverable damage could accrue pending the judgment, the plaintiffs had asked for an interim injunction, but this was refused by the Court of Appeal[50] which held that courts had no authority under the law to suspend the application of a legal provision which had not yet been judicially determined to be in conflict with Community law. The House of Lords,[51] having come to the same conclusion on the point of English law as the Court of Appeal, thought it necessary to ask the Court of Justice for a preliminary ruling under article 177 whether, in relation to the grant of interim protection in the circumstances of the case,

45 Case 106/77, [1978] ECR 629, para 22.

46 Corte cost, 8 giugno 1984 n. 170, in *Giurisprudenza constituzionale* 1984, I, 1098: for a commentary see J-V. Louis, 'Droit communautaire et loi postérieure: un revirement de la Cour constitutionelle italienne', in *Cah. dr. europ*, 1986, 194.

47 Case 199/82, [1983] ECR 3595.

48 *R* v *Secretary of State for Transport, ex parte Factortame Ltd No 2* [1991] 1 AC 603; see the commentaries by D. Oliver, 'Fishing on the Incoming Tide' (1991) 54 MLR 442, and A.G. Toth (1990) 27 CML Rev 574; see also H.W.R. Wade, 'What has Happened to the Sovereignty of Parliament?' (1991) 107 LQR 1; *Id.*, 'Injunctive Relief against the Crown and Ministers' *ibidem*, 4; N.P. Gravells, 'Disapplying an Act of Parliament Pending Ruling: Constitutional Enormity or Community Law Right?' [1989] PL 568; A. Barav, 'Enforcement of Community Rights in the National Courts: The Case for Jurisdiction to Grant an Interim Relief' (1989) 26 CML Rev 369 ff.

49 See R.R. Churchill, '"Quota hopping": The Common Fisheries Policy Wrongfooted?' (1990) 27 CML Rev 209, and the commentary by the same author in (1992) 29 CML Rev 415.

50 [1989] 2 CMLR 353.

51 [1990] 2 AC 85.

Community law overrode English law.[52] The Court of Justice, following the learned conclusions of Advocate General Tesauro, held that:[53]

> Community law must be interpreted as meaning that a national court which, in a case before it concerning Community law, considers that the sole obstacle which precludes it from granting interim relief is a rule of national law must set aside that rule.

Decisive to the outcome of the *Factortame* case was, according to the Court of Justice which laid great emphasis on its previous decision in the *Simmenthal* case,[54] the consideration that:[55]

> the full effectiveness of Community law would be . . . much impaired if a rule of national law could prevent a court seised of a dispute governed by Community law from granting interim relief in order to ensure the full effectiveness of the judgment to be given on the existence of the rights claimed under Community law.

Just as in *Factortame* it was from the principle of the effectiveness of Community law that the Court of Justice deduced the necessity for interim protection, so in *Francovich* it distilled the necessity for an entitlement to damages when Community law is infringed.

These decisions, it is submitted, mark the definitive departure by the Court of Justice from the model, recalled above, according to which Community law was confined to the substantive aspects of law, to the definition of rights and duties, while the rules governing the actual enforcement of such rights and duties depended entirely on the possibly different legal rules in force in the various Member States.

The new approach is not limited to the case law. It is sufficient to mention two EEC directives, namely directive 89/665[56] and the more recent 92/13,[57] both designed to promote uniformity of national remedies for violation of Community rules applicable to public works and procurement contracts.[58]

From a comparative point of view it is clear that, under the mounting pressure exerted by the case law of the Court of Justice and also by the legislator, Community law has increasingly begun to 'fasten upon remedies', in this way introducing at a continental level a style of legal thinking which was characteristic of common law rather than civil law systems.

The author concludes his examination in the following terms (pp. 296–7):

. . . The *Francovich* decision has a relevance which goes beyond the field of governmental liability. It marks the birth of a 'jus commune', of a law common to all the Member States and to the Community itself, in the field of the judicial protection of individuals against public powers.[107]

In *Factortame* and to a larger degree in *Zuckerfabrik Süderdithmarschen*[108] the Court of Justice laid down the rules to be applied by domestic courts when granting interim relief in Community law cases. The rules were the same as those applied by the European Court itself in proceedings under articles 185 and 186 of the EEC Treaty, the first of which was explicitly referred to by the court.[109]

In *Francovich* the Court of Justice applied to actions of the Member States inconsistent with Community law the same rules which had been elaborated by the court itself in relation to non-contractual liability for invalid acts of Community organs – but with a qualification: it forgot that in Community law the breach has to be 'sufficiently serious'. But qualifications are inconsistent with a 'jus commune'; they destroy its inherent condition, namely, to be common . . . .

---

52 [1990] 2 AC 85 at 152, *per* Lord Bridge of Harwich, with whom all the other Law Lords concurred.

53 [1991] 1 AC 603, 644.

54 [1991] 1 AC 603, 643–4.

55 [1991] 1 AC 603, 644.

56 OJEC 1989, No L. 395/34.

57 OJEC 1992, No L. 76/14.

58 See M. Bronckers, 'Private Enforcement of 1992: Do Trade and Industry Stand a Chance against Member States?' (1989) 26 CML Rev 528.

107 See more generally J. Schwarze, 'Tendencies towards a Common Administrative Law in Europe' (1991) 16 EL Rev 3; J. Rivero, 'Vers un droit commun européen: nouvelles perspectives en droit administratif', in *Pages de doctrine* (Paris 1980), p. 489 *et. seq.*; M.P. Chiti, 'I signori del diritto communitario: la Corte di giustizia e lo sviluppo del diritto amministrativo europeo', in *Rivista trimestrale di diritto pubblico* 1991, 796.

108 Joint Cases C-143/88 and C-92/89, [1991] 1 ECR 415; the decision was considered by Lord Goff of Chieveley in *Kirklees Metropolitan Borough Council v Wickes Building Supplies Ltd* [1992] 3 WLR 170, 187.

109 See cons. 27.

The next extract locates these rulings in the context of a process of the judicial harmonization of national remedies and invites consideration of the wider role played by the Court.

F. Snyder, 'The Effectiveness of European Community Law: Institutions, Processes, Tools and Techniques'

(1993) 56 MLR 19, 45–7

In *Francovich*, the Court of Justice recalled that, in the absence of Community provisions, it was for national legal systems to lay down the procedural steps for legal action to ensure the full protection of Community rights.[156] These 'conditions of substance and form' were not to be less favourable than those governing national remedies, and they were not to make the enforcement of Community rights impossible.[157] While thus recognising that Community rights are to be enforced primarily in national courts,[158] the Court's jurisprudence has nonetheless impinged increasingly on national legal remedies. At the same time as national administrative law is being influenced considerably by general principles of Community law, such as proportionality,[159] the Court of Justice is beginning to contribute to the restructuring of national procedural systems.[160]

In the celebrated *Factortame*[161] case, the Court of Justice set aside the rule of English constitutional law that an injunction cannot be granted against the Crown, at least where the rule prevents the enforcement of a right conferred by Community law. In *Emmott* it declared that, where an individual wishes to rely as against a Member State on rights contained in a directly effective directive, time does not begin to run, and therefore the individual cannot be time-barred even under the normal domestic rules on limitations on actions, until such time as the directive has been properly transposed into national law.[162] More recently, in *Zuckerfabrik*,[163] the Court held that interim measures should be available when the legality of Community law was being questioned before a national court, and a national court has a duty to consider granting such relief if requested by a party to do so.[164] These steps towards the gradual reshaping of national remedies can be viewed as a fourth element in the Community judicial liability system.

The four elements in this system need to be appreciated as a whole from two different perspectives. Seen from the bottom up, they help to provide judicial protection for the individual. Seen from the top down, they perform an essentially political function of social control.[165] These two perspectives are complementary, one representing the view of individual actors or organisations, and the other representing a conception of the Community legal system as a whole. Both perspectives are essential in order to understand the contribution and the limits of the judicial liability system in ensuring the effectiveness of Community law.

Seen from the second perspective, the judicial liability system embodies a type of structural reform, not by administrative negotiation but by adjudication. In the United States, constitutional lawyers have focused on the Supreme Court. In the late 1970s, they identified a new kind of public law litigation, 'institutional litigation', which

156 [Joined cases C-6/90 and C-9/90 *Francovich and Bonifaci* v *Italy*, para 42 of the judgment].

157 See Case 45/76, *Comet* v *Produktschap voor Siergewassen* [1976] ECR 2043.

158 See Green and Barav, 'Damages in the National Courts for Breach of Community Law' (1986) 6 YEL 55; Oliver, 'Enforcing Community Rights in English Courts' (1987) 50 MLR 881; Steiner, 'How to Make the Action Suit the Case: Domestic Remedies for Breach of EEC Law' (1987) 12 EL Rev 102; Ward, 'Government Liability in the United Kingdom for Breach of Individual Rights in European Community Law' (1990) 19 *Anglo-American Law Review* 1.

159 See Schwarze, *European Administrative Law* (London: Sweet and Maxwell, 1992).

160 See Duffy, [(1992) 17 EL Rev 133], pp. 137–8.

161 See Duffy, [(1992) 17 EL Rev 133], pp. 137–8.

162 Including where the directive has been implemented but in terms which vary from the directive such that the implementing measure does not fully represent the rights contained in the directive: Case C208/90, *Emmott* v *Minister for Social Welfare* [1991] 3 CMLR 894, 916 (para 23).

163 Joined Cases C-143/88 and C-92/89, *Zuckerfabrik Süderdithmarschen et Zuckerfabrik Soest* v *Hauptzollamt Itzehoe* [1991] *Recueil*-415, nyr in English, noted Schermers (1992) 29 CML Rev 133.

164 In addition, the conditions for suspending community acts could not vary from one Member State to another. See further Oliver, 'Interim Measures: Some Recent Developments' (1992) 27 CML Rev 7, 24–5; Barav, 'Enforcement of Community Rights in the National Courts: The Case for Jurisdiction to Grant Interim Relief' (1989) 26 CML Rev 369.

165 This point is argued forcefully with regard to appeal courts in general: Shapiro, 'Appeal' (1980) 14 *Law and Society Review* 629. Note that a similar dual role in the Community legal order is played by the concept of institutional balance: see the Opinion by Advocate-General Van Gerven in Case 70/88, *European Parliament* v *Council* [1990] ECRI-2041. Whether such a duality of function is characteristic of other basic concepts of Community constitutional and administrative law remains to be seen.

typically requires the courts to scrutinize the operation of large public institutions. The suits are generally brought by persons subject to the control of the institutions who seek as relief some relatively elaborate rearrangement of the institution's mode of operation.[166]

Views have differed as to the novelty of institutional litigation.[167] All agree, however, that in institutional litigation, '[l]itigation inevitably becomes an explicitly political forum and the court a visible arm of the political process'.[168]

It is tempting to apply these observations to the Court of Justice. After all, in the Community, as in the United States, the institutional vacuum resulting from executive and legislative inaction led to an increased role for the judiciary. In both systems, the appropriateness of such a judicial response has been the subject of intense controversy.[169]

It is suggested, however, that the precise analogy is misplaced. First, the Court of Justice is activated by individuals and organisations who, in contrast to plaintiffs in American institutional litigation, are not inmates of institutions in any specific sense. Second, the judicial liability system in the Community has been developed by the Court of Justice mainly through the Article 177 [now 234] procedure: the reach of the Court into the operation of national public institutions, including administrations, is restricted by the fact that its jurisdiction is limited in principle to interpreting (or ruling on the validity of) Community law. Third, and consequently, Community litigation does not involve the negotiation by the Court of Justice with defendant institutional parties of detailed rules regarding the internal organisation of national institutions.

In the United States, it has been argued that:

> The demands of structural reform have magnified the explicitly political dimensions of litigation. Parties have used litigation less as a method for authoritative resolution of conflict than as a means of reallocation of power. Rather than an isolated, self-contained transaction, the lawsuit becomes a component of the continuous political bargaining process that determines the shape and content of public policy. This transformation in the character of litigation necessarily transforms the judge's role as well.[170]

In the Community, it is suggested, the role of 'political powerbroker'[171] in this strong sense has been resisted thus far by the Court of Justice. Nonetheless, there are common features and this brief comparison with the United States Supreme Court is instructive. It enables us to begin to situate Community law litigation in the political process, at both the Community and the national levels, and it illuminates the political dimension of the Community judicial liability system. By elaborating the elements of this system, rather than by institutional litigation in the American sense, the Court of Justice has played a central role in organising and reshaping relations among Community institutions and between the Community and the Member States.

NOTE: It is apparent that the issue of effective protection extends far beyond the question of the application of Directives alone and beyond questions of a remedy in damages alone. *Francovich* is part of a wider phenomenon. The Court of Justice is building a notion of effective protection as a general principle of the legal order established by the Treaties. This was already plain from the *Factortame* saga, mentioned by Caranta and Snyder and examined at p. 111.

The one sure consequence of *Francovich* was that the Court would be invited to clarify the scope of liability. The Court's rulings in March 1996, including a further episode in the *Factortame* saga, '*Factortame III*' (Case C-48/93), are crucial. These are relevant beyond the specific issue of unimplemented Directives.

---

166 Eisenberg and Yeazell, 'The Ordinary and the Extraordinary in Institutional Litigation' (1980) 93 *Harvard Law Review* 465, 467–8. See also, e.g., Chayes, 'The Role of the Judge in Public Law Litigation' (1976) 89 *Harvard Law Review* 1281; Cox, 'The New Dimensions of Constitutional Litigation' (1976) 51 *Washington Law Review* 791; Diver, 'The Judge as Political Powerbroker: Superintending Structural Change in Public Institutions' (1979) 65 *Virginia Law Review* 43.

167 Chayes and Cox argue that its procedures and remedies depart significantly from the model of traditional litigation: see Chayes, *op cit* n 166; Cox, *op cit* n 166. In contrast, Eisenberg and Yeazell, *op cit* n 166, suggest that the only new features are its substance, especially new rights, and its power.

168 Chayes, *op cit* n 166, p. 1304; Diver, [(1979) 65 *Virginia Law Review* 43], p. 65.

169 With regard to the Community, see Pescatore, 'La carence du législateur et le devoir du juge' in *Rechtsverglechung, Europarecht und Staateninegration, Gedachtnisschrift für L.-J. Constantinesco* (Saarbrucken: Europa Institute, 1983) and Rasmussen, *On Law and Policy in the European Court of Justice* (Dordrecht: Martinus Nijhoff, 1986).

170 Diver, [(1979) 65 *Virginia Law Review* 43], p. 45.

171 *ibid.*

***Brasserie du Pêcheur SA* v *Germany and R* v *Secretary of State for Transport, ex parte Factortame Ltd and Others* (Joined Cases C-46/93 and C-48/93)**

[1996] ECR I-1029, [1996] 1 CMLR 889, Court of Justice of the European Communities

Factortame was not content with its success in establishing the availability of interim protection against a domestic statute (p. 90), or with the final ruling that the UK had acted in violation of its Treaty obligations (p. 111). Factortame sought compensation for loss suffered as a result of action in 1989 by the UK authorities that had been shown to be incompatible with the Treaty. This raised questions about the application of *Francovich* liability to violations of primary Treaty provisions, rather than in the specific instance of failure to implement a Directive. Questions of the culpability required to ground liability, which (as R. Caranta observes in the extract at p. 146) had not been addressed in *Francovich*, were also raised. A preliminary reference was made by the High Court in the UK. This was joined to a reference made by the *Bundesgerichtshof*, the German Federal Court of Justice, which arose out of a complaint by a French company based in Alsace which claimed that it had suffered loss as a result of German restrictions on trade in beer which had been shown to be incompatible with Article 30 of the EC Treaty (now Article 34 TFEU): see the 'Beer Purity' case, *Commission* v *Germany* (Case 178/84, p. 324). Here too the national court was in search of elaboration of the scope of State liability in damages for loss caused by violation of the Treaty.

The Court first traced the nature and scope of the principle of State liability for acts and omissions of the national legislature contrary to what was then Community law:

[16] By their first questions, each of the two national courts essentially seeks to establish whether the principle that Member States are obliged to make good damage caused to individuals by breaches of Community law attributable to the State is applicable where the national legislature was responsible for the infringement in question.

[17] In joined Cases C-6/90 and C-9/90 *Francovich and Others* [1991] ECR I-5357, paragraph 37, the Court held that it is a principle of Community law that Member States are obliged to make good loss and damage caused to individuals by breaches of Community law for which they can be held responsible.

[18] The German, Irish and Netherlands Governments contend that Member States are required to make good loss or damage caused to individuals only where the provisions breached are not directly effective: in *Francovich and Others* the Court simply sought to fill a lacuna in the system for safeguarding rights of individuals. In so far as national law affords individuals a right of action enabling them to assert their rights under directly effective provisions of Community law, it is unnecessary, where such provisions are breached, also to grant them a right to reparation founded directly on Community law.

[19] That argument cannot be accepted.

[20] The Court has consistently held that the right of individuals to rely on the directly effective provisions of the Treaty before national courts is only a minimum guarantee and is not sufficient in itself to ensure the full and complete implementation of the Treaty (see, in particular, Case 168/85 *Commission* v *Italy* [1986] ECR 2945, paragraph 11, Case C-120/88 *Commission* v *Italy* [1991] ECR I-621, paragraph 10, and C-119/89 *Commission* v *Spain* [1991] ECR I-641, paragraph 9). The purpose of that right is to ensure that provisions of Community law prevail over national provisions. It cannot, in every case, secure for individuals the benefit of the rights conferred on them by Community law and, in particular, avoid their sustaining damage as a result of a breach of Community law attributable to a Member State. As appears from paragraph 33 of the judgment in *Francovich and Others*, the full effectiveness of Community law would be impaired if individuals were unable to obtain redress when their rights were infringed by a breach of Community law.

[21] This will be so where an individual who is a victim of the non-transposition of a directive and is precluded from relying on certain of its provisions directly before the national court because they are insufficiently precise and unconditional, brings an action for damages against the defaulting Member State for breach of the third paragraph of Article 189 [now 288] of the Treaty. In such circumstances, which obtained in the case of *Francovich and Others*, the purpose of reparation is to redress the injurious consequences of a Member State's failure to transpose a directive as far as beneficiaries of that directive are concerned.

[22] It is all the more so in the event of infringement of a right directly conferred by a Community provision upon which individuals are entitled to rely before the national courts. In that event, the right to reparation is the necessary corollary of the direct effect of the Community provision whose breach caused the damage sustained.

[23] In this case, it is undisputed that the Community provisions at issue, namely Article 30 [now 34] of the Treaty in Case C-46/93 and Article 52 [now 49] in Case C-48/93, have direct effect in the sense that they confer on individuals a right upon which they are entitled to rely directly before the national courts. Breach of such provisions may give rise to reparation.

[24] The German Government further submits that a general right to reparation for individuals could be created only by legislation and that for such a right to be recognised by judicial decision would be incompatible with the allocation of powers as between the Community institutions and the Member States and with the institutional balance established by the Treaty.

[25] It must, however, be stressed that the existence and extent of State liability for damage ensuing as a result of a breach of obligations incumbent on the State by virtue of Community law are questions of Treaty interpretation which fall within the jurisdiction of the Court.

[26] In this case, as in *Francovich and Others*, those questions of interpretation have been referred to the Court by national courts pursuant to Article 177 [now 267] of the Treaty.

[27] Since the Treaty contains no provision expressly and specifically governing the consequences of breaches of Community law by Member States, it is for the Court, in pursuance of the task conferred on it by Article 164 [now 220] of the Treaty of ensuring that in the interpretation and application of the Treaty the law is observed, to rule on such a question in accordance with generally accepted methods of interpretation, in particular by reference to the fundamental principles of the Community legal system and, where necessary, general principles common to the legal systems of the Member States.

[28] Indeed, it is to the general principles common to the laws of the Member States that the second paragraph of Article 215 [now 340] of the Treaty refers as the basis of the non-contractual liability of the Community for damage caused by its institutions or by its servants in the performance of their duties.

[29] The principle of the non-contractual liability of the Community expressly laid down in Article 215 [now 340] of the Treaty is simply an expression of the general principle familiar to the legal systems of the Member States that an unlawful act or omission gives rise to an obligation to make good the damage caused. That provision also reflects the obligation on public authorities to make good damage caused in the performance of their duties.

[30] In any event, in many national legal systems the essentials of the legal rules governing State liability have been developed by the courts.

[31] In view of the foregoing considerations, the Court held in *Francovich and Others*, at paragraph 35, that the principle of State liability for loss and damage caused to individuals as a result of breaches of Community law for which it can be held responsible is inherent in the system of the Treaty.

[32] It follows that that principle holds good for any case in which a Member State breaches Community law, whatever be the organ of the State whose act or omission was responsible for the breach.

[33] In addition, in view of the fundamental requirement of the Community legal order that Community law be uniformly applied (see, in particular, Joined Cases C-143/88 and C-92/89 *Zuckerfabrik Süderdithmarschen and Zuckerfabrik Soest* [1991] ECR I-415, paragraph 26), the obligation to make good damage caused to individuals by breaches of Community law cannot depend on domestic rules as to the division of powers between constitutional authorities.

[34] As the Advocate General points out in paragraph 38 of his Opinion, in international law a State whose liability for breach of an international commitment is in issue will be viewed as a single entity, irrespective of whether the breach which gave rise to the damage is attributable to the legislature, judiciary or the executive. This must apply *a fortiori* in the Community legal order since all State authorities, including the legislature, are bound in performing their tasks to comply with the rules laid down by Community law directly governing the situation of individuals.

[35] The fact that, according to national rules, the breach complained of is attributable to the legislature cannot affect the requirements inherent in the protection of the rights of individuals who rely on Community law and, in this instance, the right to obtain redress in the national courts for damage caused by that breach.

[36] Consequently, the reply to the national courts must be that the principle that Member States are obliged to make good damage caused to individuals by breaches of Community law attributable to the State is applicable where the national legislature was responsible for the breach in question.

The Court then turned to the conditions under which the State may incur liability:

[37] By these questions, the national courts ask the Court to specify the conditions under which a right to reparation of loss or damage caused to individuals by breaches of Community law attributable to a Member State is, in the particular circumstances, guaranteed by Community law.

[38] Although Community law imposes State liability, the conditions under which that liability gives rise to a right to reparation depend on the nature of the breach of Community law giving rise to the loss and damage (*Francovich and Others*, paragraph 38).

[39] In order to determine those conditions, account should first be taken of the principles inherent in the Community legal order which form the basis for State liability, namely, first, the full effectiveness of Community rules and the effective protection of the rights which they confer and, second, the obligation to cooperate imposed on Member States by Article 5 [now 4(3) TEU] of the Treaty (*Francovich and Others*, paragraphs 31 to 36).

[40] In addition, as the Commission and the several governments which submitted observations have emphasised, it is pertinent to refer to the Court's case-law on non-contractual liability on the part of the Community.

[41] First, the second paragraph of Article 215 [now 340] of the Treaty refers, as regards the non-contractual liability of the Community, to the general principles common to the laws of the Member States, from which, in the absence of written rules, the Court also draws inspiration in other areas of Community law.

[42] Second, the conditions under which the State may incur liability for damage caused to individuals by a breach of Community law cannot, in the absence of particular justification, differ from those governing the liability of the Community in like circumstances. The protection of the rights which individuals derive from Community law cannot vary depending on whether a national authority or a Community authority is responsible for the damage.

[43] The system of rules which the Court has worked out with regard to Article 215 [now 340] of the Treaty, particularly in relation to liability for legislative measures, takes into account, *inter alia*, the complexity of the situations to be regulated, difficulties in the application or interpretation of the texts and, more particularly, the margin of discretion available to the author of the act in question.

[44] Thus, in developing its case law on the non-contractual liability of the Community, in particular as regards legislative measures involving choices of economic policy, the Court has had regard to the wide discretion available to the institutions in implementing Community policies.

[45] The strict approach taken towards the liability of the Community in the exercise of its legislative activities is due to two considerations. First, even where the legality of measures is subject to judicial review, exercise of the legislative function must not be hindered by the prospect of actions for damages whenever the general interest of the Community requires legislative measures to be adopted which may adversely affect individual interests. Second, in a legislative context characterised by the exercise of a wide discretion, which is essential for implementing a Community policy, the Community cannot incur liability unless the institution concerned has manifestly and gravely disregarded the limits on the exercise of its powers (Joined Cases 83/76, 94/76, 4/77 and 40/77, 15/77 *HNL and Others* v *Council and Commission* [1978] ECR 1209, paragraphs 5 and 6).

[46] That said, the national legislature – like the Community institutions – does not systematically have a wide discretion when it acts in a field governed by Community law. Community law may impose upon it obligations to achieve a particular result or obligations to act or refrain from acting which reduce its margin of discretion, sometimes to a considerable degree. This is so, for instance, where, as in the circumstances to which the judgment in *Francovich and Others* relates, Article 189 [now 288] of the Treaty places the Member

State under an obligation to take, within a given period, all the measures needed in order to achieve the result required by a directive. In such a case, the fact that it is for the national legislature to take the necessary measures has no bearing on the Member State's liability for failing to transpose the directive.

[47] In contrast, where a Member State acts in a field where it has a wide discretion, comparable to that of the Community institutions in implementing Community policies, the conditions under which it may incur liability must, in principle, be the same as those under which the Community institutions incur liability in a comparable situation.

[48] In the case which gave rise to the reference in Case C-46/93, the German legislature had legislated in the field of foodstuffs, specifically beer. In the absence of Community harmonisation, the national legislature had a wide discretion in that sphere in laying down rules on the quality of beer put on the market.

[49] As regards the facts of Case C-48/93, the United Kingdom legislature also had a wide discretion. The legislation at issue was concerned, first, with the registration of vessels, a field which, in view of the State of development of Community law, falls within the jurisdiction of the Member States and, secondly, with regulating fishing, a sector in which implementation of the common fisheries policy leaves a margin of discretion to the Member States.

[50] Consequently, in each case the German and United Kingdom legislatures were faced with situations involving choices comparable to those made by the Community institutions when they adopt legislative measures pursuant to a Community policy.

[51] In such circumstances, Community law confers a right to reparation where three conditions are met: the rule of law infringed must be intended to confer rights on individuals; the breach must be sufficiently serious; and there must be a direct causal link between the breach of the obligation resting on the State and the damage sustained by the injured parties.

[52] Firstly, those conditions satisfy the requirements of the full effectiveness of the rules of Community law and of the effective protection of the rights which those rules confer.

[53] Secondly, those conditions correspond in substance to those defined by the Court in relation to Article 215 [now 340] in its case-law on liability of the Community for damage caused to individuals by unlawful legislative measures adopted by its institutions.

[54] The first condition is manifestly satisfied in the case of Article 30 [now 34] of the Treaty, the relevant provision in Case C-46/93, and in the case of Article 52 [now 49], the relevant provision in Case C-48/93. Whilst Article 30 imposes a prohibition on Member States, it nevertheless gives rise to rights for individuals which the national courts must protect (Case 74/76 *Iannelli & Volpi* v *Meroni* [1977] ECR 557, paragraph 13). Likewise, the essence of Article 52 is to confer rights on individuals (Case 2/74 *Reyners* [1974] ECR 631, paragraph 25).

[55] As to the second condition, as regards both Community liability under Article 215 [now 340] and Member State liability for breaches of Community law, the decisive test for finding that a breach of Community law is sufficiently serious is whether the Member State or the Community institution concerned manifestly and gravely disregarded the limits on its discretion.

[56] The factors which the competent court may take into consideration include the clarity and precision of the rule breached, the measure of discretion left by that rule to the national or Community authorities, whether the infringement and the damage caused was intentional or involuntary, whether any error of law was excusable or inexcusable, the fact that the position taken by a Community institution may have contributed towards the omission, and the adoption or retention of national measures or practices contrary to Community law.

[57] On any view, a breach of Community law will clearly be sufficiently serious if it has persisted despite a judgment finding the infringement in question to be established, or a preliminary ruling or settled case-law of the Court on the matter from which it is clear that the conduct in question constituted an infringement.

[58] While, in the present cases, the Court cannot substitute its assessment for that of the national courts, which have sole jurisdiction to find the facts in the main proceedings and decide how to characterise the breaches of Community law at issue, it will be helpful to indicate a number of circumstances which the national courts might take into account.

[59] In Case C-46/93 a distinction should be drawn between the question of the German legislature's having maintained in force provisions of the Biersteuergesetz concerning the purity of beer prohibiting the marketing under the designation 'Bier' of beers imported from other Member States which were lawfully produced in conformity with different rules, and the question of the retention of the provisions of that same law prohibiting the import of beers containing additives. As regards the provisions of the German legislation relating to the designation of the product marketed, it would be difficult to regard the breach of Article 30 by that legislation as an excusable error, since the incompatibility of such rules with Article 30 was manifest in the light of earlier decisions of the Court, in particular Case 120/78 *Rewe-Zentral* [1979] ECR 649 ('Cassis de Dijon') and Case 193/80 *Commission* v *Italy* [1981] ECR 3019 ('vinegar'). In contrast, having regard to the relevant case law, the criteria available to the national legislature to determine whether the prohibition of the use of additives was contrary to Community law were significantly less conclusive until the Court's judgment of 12 March 1987 in *Commission* v *Germany*, cited above, in which the Court held that prohibition to be incompatible with Article 30.

[60] A number of observations may likewise be made about the national legislation at issue in Case C-48/93.

[61] The decision of the United Kingdom legislature to introduce in the Merchant Shipping Act 1988 provisions relating to the conditions for the registration of fishing vessels has to be assessed differently in the case of the provisions making registration subject to a nationality condition, which constitute direct discrimination manifestly contrary to Community law, and in the case of the provisions laying down residence and domicile conditions for vessel owners and operators.

[62] The latter conditions are prima facie incompatible with Article 52 of the Treaty in particular, but the United Kingdom sought to justify them in terms of the objectives of the common fisheries policy. In the judgment in *Factortame II*, cited above, the Court rejected that justification.

[63] In order to determine whether the breach of Article 52 thus committed by the United Kingdom was sufficiently serious, the national court might take into account, *inter alia*, the legal disputes relating to particular features of the common fisheries policy, the attitude of the Commission, which made its position known to the United Kingdom in good time, and the assessments as to the state of certainty of Community law made by the national courts in the interim proceedings brought by individuals affected by the Merchant Shipping Act.

[64] Lastly, consideration should be given to the assertion made by Rawlings (Trawling) Ltd, the 37th claimant in Case C-48/93, that the United Kingdom failed to adopt immediately the measures needed to comply with the Order of the President of the Court of 10 October 1989 in *Commission* v *United Kingdom*, cited above, and that this needlessly increased the loss it sustained. If this allegation – which was certainly contested by the United Kingdom at the hearing – should prove correct, it should be regarded by the national court as constituting in itself a manifest and, therefore, sufficiently serious breach of Community law.

[65] As for the third condition, it is for the national courts to determine whether there is a direct causal link between the breach of the obligation borne by the State and the damage sustained by the injured parties.

[66] The aforementioned three conditions are necessary and sufficient to found a right in individuals to obtain redress, although this does not mean that the State cannot incur liability under less strict conditions on the basis of national law.

[67] As appears from paragraphs 41, 42 and 43 of *Francovich and Others*, cited above, subject to the right to reparation which flows directly from Community law where the conditions referred to in the preceding paragraph are satisfied, the State must make reparation for the consequences of the loss and damage caused in accordance with the domestic rules on liability, provided that the conditions for reparation of loss and damage laid down by national law must not be less favourable than those relating to similar domestic claims and must not be such as in practice to make it impossible or excessively difficult to obtain reparation (see also Case 199/82 *Amministrazione delle Finanze dello Stato* v *San Giorgio* [1983] ECR 3595).

[68] In that regard, restrictions that exist in domestic legal systems as to the non-contractual liability of the State in the exercise of its legislative function may be such as to make it impossible in practice or excessively difficult for individuals to exercise their right to reparation, as guaranteed by Community law, of loss or damage resulting from the breach of Community law.

[69] In Case C-46/93 the national court asks in particular whether national law may subject any right to compensation to the same restrictions as apply where a law is in breach of higher-ranking national provisions, for instance, where an ordinary Federal law infringes the Grundgesetz of the Federal Republic of Germany.

[70] While the imposition of such restrictions may be consistent with the requirement that the conditions laid down should not be less favourable than those relating to similar domestic claims, it is still to be considered whether such restrictions are not such as in practice to make it impossible or excessively difficult to obtain reparation.

[71] The condition imposed by German law where a law is in breach of higher-ranking national provisions, which makes reparation dependent upon the legislature's act or omission being referable to an individual situation, would in practice make it impossible or extremely difficult to obtain effective reparation for loss or damage resulting from a breach of Community law, since the tasks falling to the national legislature relate, in principle, to the public at large and not to identifiable persons or classes of person.

[72] Since such a condition stands in the way of the obligation on national courts to ensure the full effectiveness of Community law by guaranteeing effective protection for the rights of individuals, it must be set aside where an infringement of Community law is attributable to the national legislature.

[73] Likewise, any condition that may be imposed by English law on State liability requiring proof of misfeasance in public office, such an abuse of power being inconceivable in the case of the legislature, is also such as in practice to make it impossible or extremely difficult to obtain effective reparation for loss or damage resulting from a breach of Community law where the breach is attributable to the national legislature.

The Court proceeded to deal with three further, related questions, and provided the following answers to the questions referred:

1. The principle that Member States are obliged to make good damage caused to individuals by breaches of Community law attributable to the State is applicable where the national legislature was responsible for the breach in question.

2. Where a breach of Community law by a Member State is attributable to the national legislature acting in a field in which it has a wide discretion to make legislative choices, individuals suffering loss or injury thereby are entitled to reparation where the rule of Community law breached is intended to confer rights upon them, the breach is sufficiently serious and there is a direct causal link between the breach and the damage sustained by the individuals. Subject to that reservation, the State must make good the consequences of the loss or damage caused by the breach of Community law attributable to it, in accordance with its national law on liability. However, the conditions laid down by the applicable national laws must not be less favourable than those relating to similar domestic claims or framed in such a way as in practice to make it impossible or excessively difficult to obtain reparation.

3. Pursuant to the national legislation which it applies, reparation of loss or damage cannot be made conditional upon fault (intentional or negligent) on the part of the organ of the State responsible for the breach, going beyond that of a sufficiently serious breach of Community law.

4. Reparation by Member States of loss or damage which they have caused to individuals as a result of breaches of Community law must be commensurate with the loss or damage sustained. In the absence of relevant Community provisions, it is for the domestic legal system of each Member State to set the criteria for determining the extent of reparation. However, those criteria must not be less favourable than those applying to similar claims or actions based on domestic law and must not be such as in practice to make it impossible or excessively difficult to obtain reparation. National legislation which generally limits the damage for which reparation may be granted to damage done to certain, specifically protected individual interests not including loss of profit by individuals is not compatible with Community law. Moreover, it must be possible to award specific damages, such as the exemplary damages provided for by English law, pursuant to claims or actions founded on Community law, if such damages may be awarded pursuant to similar claims or actions founded on domestic law.

5. The obligation for Member States to make good loss or damage caused to individuals by breaches of Community law attributable to the State cannot be limited to damage sustained after the delivery of a judgment of the Court finding the infringement in question.

■ **QUESTION**

Do you think the Court dealt convincingly with the constitutional objections of the German Government recorded at para 24 of the judgment? Would Article 19(1) TEU, inserted by the Lisbon Treaty with effect from 2009, affect the force of such objections, were they to be advanced today?

NOTE: The Question invites reflection on the legitimacy of the Court's boldness. Whatever one's view of that matter, the *practical* edge of the Court's approach is sharp. Eventually a settlement of some £55 million in favour of the applicants was agreed (in the House of Lords, see *Factortame* [2000] Eu LR 40: and for a survey of the *Factortame* litigation see D. Vaughan, '*Factortame* and After: a Fishy Story' [2005] EBLR 16.) The Court has clearly taken the scope of *Francovich* liability beyond the specific issue of non-implementation of Directives and it has established an approach which places emphasis on the context of particular infractions. As para 46 of the ruling indicates, the issue of non-implementation of Directives itself could lead to liability in circumstances as clear cut as those prevailing in *Francovich* itself, but not in others. This was made plain in a ruling delivered just three weeks later.

***R* v *H.M. Treasury, ex parte British Telecommunications* (Case C-392/93)**

[1996] ECR I-1631, Court of Justice of the European Communities

The litigation arose out of the UK's implementation of Article 8(1) of Directive 90/531, in the field of public procurement. The Court ruled that the UK had not implemented the Directive correctly. It was asked to consider the scope of State liability in a case of incorrect implementation.

[40] . . .A restrictive approach to State liability is justified in such a situation, for the reasons already given by the Court to justify the strict approach to non-contractual liability of Community institutions or Member States when exercising legislative functions in areas covered by Community law where the institution or State has a wide discretion – in particular, the concern to ensure that the exercise of legislative functions is not hindered by the prospect of actions for damages whenever the general interest requires the institutions or Member States to adopt measures which may adversely affect individual interests (see, in particular, the judgments in Joined Cases 83/76, 94/76, 4/77, 15/77 and 40/77 *HNL and Others* v *Council and Commission* [1978] ECR 1209, paragraphs 5 and 6, and in *Brasserie du Pêcheur and Factortame*, paragraph 45).

[41] Whilst it is in principle for the national courts to verify whether or not the conditions governing State liability for a breach of Community law are fulfilled, in the present case the Court has all the necessary information to assess whether the facts amount to a sufficiently serious breach of Community law.

[42] According to the case-law of the Court, a breach is sufficiently serious where, in the exercise of its legislative powers, an institution or a Member State has manifestly and gravely disregarded the limits on the exercise of its powers (judgments in *HNL and Others* v *Council and Commission*, cited above, paragraph 6, and in *Brasserie du Pêcheur and Factortame*, paragraph 55). Factors which the competent court may take into consideration include the clarity and precision of the rule breached (judgment in *Brasserie du Pêcheur and Factortame*, paragraph 56).

[43] In the present case, Article 8(1) is imprecisely worded and was reasonably capable of bearing, as well as the construction applied to it by the Court in this judgment, the interpretation given to it by the United Kingdom in good faith and on the basis of arguments which are not entirely devoid of substance (see paragraphs 20 to 22 above). That interpretation, which was also shared by other Member States, was not manifestly contrary to the wording of the directive or to the objective pursued by it.

[44] Moreover, no guidance was available to the United Kingdom from case law of the Court as to the interpretation of the provision at issue, nor did the Commission raise the matter when the 1992 Regulations were adopted.

[45] In those circumstances, the fact that a Member State, when transposing the directive into national law, thought it necessary itself to determine which services were to be excluded from its scope in implementation of Article 8, albeit in breach of that provision, cannot be regarded as a sufficiently serious breach of Community law of the kind intended by the Court in its judgment in *Brasserie du Pêcheur and Factortame*.

A comparably compassionate approach to the liability of a defaulting Member State may be observed in Case C-470/04 *N* [2006] ECR I-7409. The Court found that Dutch rules establishing a system for taxing increases in value in the case of a taxpayer's transferring his residence outside the Netherlands violated Article 43 EC (now Article 49 TFEU: Chapter 14). However, when the Dutch tax system entered into force, the Court had not given a ruling dealing directly with the point at issue. It seems plain that the referring national court is thereby offered scope to find *against* a compensation claim for want of legal clarity at the material time. It follows that the clearer the Court's existing case law (and the clearer the view of the Commission: see para 56 of *Brassserie du Pêcheur*), the more likely that the breach will be treated as 'sufficiently serious' for the purposes of a compensation claim. So in Case C-398/11 *Hogan* v *Minister for Social and Family Affairs* judgment of 25 April 2013 it was held that from the moment that the Court had made clear the nature of the protection envisaged by Directive 2008/94 – the Directive on insolvency which is the successor to the measure at stake in *Francovich* – Ireland, by maintaining incompatible provisions, was committing a sufficiently serious breach.

Could a State incur liability as a result of errors made in the application of EU law by its *judiciary*? It is hard to see any reason in principle why not, although one would expect the relevant conditions to acknowledge the peculiar sensitivity of such a possibility: see H. Toner, 'Thinking the Unthinkable? State Liability for Judicial Acts' (1997) 17 YEL 165. Eventually the Court was provided with the possibility to confirm both limbs of this prognosis.

***Gerhard Köbler* (Case C-224/01)**

[2003] ECR I-10239, Court of Justice of the European Communities

[51] As to the conditions to be satisfied for a Member State to be required to make reparation for loss and damage caused to individuals as a result of breaches of Community law for which the State is responsible, the Court has held that these are threefold: the rule of law infringed must be intended to confer rights on individuals; the breach must be sufficiently serious; and there must be a direct causal link between the breach of the obligation incumbent on the State and the loss or damage sustained by the injured parties (*Haim*, cited above [Case C-424/97], paragraph 36).

[52] State liability for loss or damage caused by a decision of a national court adjudicating at last instance which infringes a rule of Community law is governed by the same conditions.

[53] With regard more particularly to the second of those conditions and its application with a view to establishing possible State liability owing to a decision of a national court adjudicating at last instance, regard must be had to the specific nature of the judicial function and to the legitimate requirements of legal certainty, as the Member States which submitted observations in this case have also contended. State liability for an infringement of Community law by a decision of a national court adjudicating at last instance can be incurred only in the exceptional case where the court has manifestly infringed the applicable law.

[54] In order to determine whether that condition is satisfied, the national court hearing a claim for reparation must take account of all the factors which characterise the situation put before it.

[55] Those factors include, in particular, the degree of clarity and precision of the rule infringed, whether the infringement was intentional, whether the error of law was excusable or inexcusable, the position taken, where applicable, by a Community institution and non-compliance by the court in question with its obligation to make a reference for a preliminary ruling under the third paragraph of Article 234 EC [now 267 TFEU].

[56] In any event, an infringement of Community law will be sufficiently serious where the decision concerned was made in manifest breach of the case-law of the Court in the matter (see to that effect *Brasserie du Pêcheur and Factortame*, cited above, paragraph 57).

[57] The three conditions mentioned at paragraph 51 hereof are necessary and sufficient to found a right in favour of individuals to obtain redress, although this does not mean that the State cannot incur liability under less strict conditions on the basis of national law (see *Brasserie du Pêcheur and Factortame*, cited above, paragraph 66).

[58] Subject to the existence of a right to obtain reparation which is founded directly on Community law where the conditions mentioned above are met, it is on the basis of rules of national law on liability that the State must make reparation for the consequences of the loss and damage caused, with the proviso that the conditions for reparation of loss and damage laid down by the national legislation must not be less favourable than those relating to similar domestic claims and must not be so framed as to make it in practice impossible or excessively difficult to obtain reparation (*Francovich and Others*, paragraphs 41 to 43 and *Norbrook Laboratories*, [Case C-127/95] paragraph 111).

[59] In the light of all the foregoing, the reply to the first and second questions must be that the principle that Member States are obliged to make good damage caused to individuals by infringements of Community law for which they are responsible is also applicable where the alleged infringement stems from a decision of a court adjudicating at last instance where the rule of Community law infringed is intended to confer rights on individuals, the breach is sufficiently serious and there is a direct causal link between that breach and the loss or damage sustained by the injured parties. In order to determine whether the infringement is sufficiently serious when the infringement at issue stems from such a decision, the competent national court, taking into account the specific nature of the judicial function, must determine whether that infringement is manifest. It is for the legal system of each Member State to designate the court competent to determine disputes relating to that reparation.

In Case C-173/03 *Traghetti del Mediterraneo* [2006] ECR I-5177 the Court found limits placed on State liability under Italian law in cases of judicial misfeasance to be too strict and incompatible with *Gerhard Köbler*. The Court's concern was explicitly not to allow *Gerhard Köbler* to be deprived of all practical effect. Discussion in 2009 found no cases in which compensation has been awarded: B. Beutler, 'State Liability for Breaches of Community Law by National Courts' (2009) 46 CML Rev 773. This may change. In Case C-160/14 *Ferreira da Silva e Brito and others* 9 September 2015 the Court decided that the Portuguese Supreme Court had misapplied Directive 2001/23 on transfer of undertakings and that it had improperly failed to make a preliminary reference. Whether damages are due now falls to be decided by the Portuguese courts.

■ QUESTION

To what extent does the ruling in *Gerhard Köbler* threaten the finality of decisions taken by national courts of last instance?

NOTES

1. In relation to all breaches of EU law, not simply those arising out of the process of implementation of Directives, it appears that an assessment of the gravity of the breach is required in determining the availability of compensation. This is a condition the fulfilment of which seems hard to predict in advance. For further examples involving exploration of the seriousness of the breach for these purposes, see *R* v *Ministry of Agriculture, Fisheries and Food, ex parte Hedley Lomas (Ireland) Ltd* (Case C-5/94) [1996] ECR I-2553; *Dillenkofer* v *Germany* (Joined Cases C-178 *et al.*) [1996] ECR I-4845; *ex parte Synthon* (Case C-452/06) [2008] ECR I-7681; Case C-429/09 *Günter Fuss v Stadt Halle* [2010] ECR I-12167. It seems, however, that awards of damages by national courts are rare: see e.g. T. Lock, 'Is Private Enforcement of EU law through State Liability a Myth? An Assessment 20 Years after Francovich' (2012) 49 CML Rev 1675.
2. The Court has brought the rules on State liability for breach of EU law into alignment with the rules governing the liability of the EU's institutions for unlawful conduct. The latter system is envisaged by the Treaty. It is set out in Articles 268 and 340(2) TFEU, which are examined in Chapter 8, p. xxx. The former is by contrast the product of the Court's ingenuity. This correspondence means that the case law arising in recent years in one branch is helpful in

understanding the case law in the other. See for example *Commission* v *Camar and Others* (Case C-312/00P), p. 214. See also C. Hilson, 'The Role of Discretion in EC law on Non-Contractual Liability' (2005) 42 CML Rev 677.

3. The Commission tracks application at national level of the rulings in *Francovich* and *Brasserie du Pêcheur/Factortame* and refers to them routinely in its Annual Reports on monitoring the application of Union law (currently available *via* http://ec.europa.eu/atwork/applying-eu-law/infringements-proceedings/annual-reports/index_en.htm). This reflects the significance of these legal principles in improving the policing of State compliance with the Treaty.
4. And not only *State* compliance! In Case C-453/99 *Courage Ltd v Crehan* [2001] ECR I-6297 the Court ruled that in the enforcement of the Treaty competition rules actions for damages may be pursued against *private* parties (see Chapter 16, p. 515).

FURTHER READING

Barav, A., 'State Liability in Damages for Breach of Community Law in the National Courts' (1996) 16 YEL 87.

Bernitz, U. and Reich, N., 'Annotation' (2011) 48 CML Rev 603 (covers an award of damages in Sweden).

Dougan, M., 'The Vicissitudes of Life at the Coalface: Remedies and Procedures for Enforcing Union Law Before the National Courts' Ch 14 in P. Craig and G. de Búrca, *The Evolution of EU Law* (Oxford: OUP, 2nd ed., 2011).

Havu, K., 'Horizontal Liability for Damages in EU Law: the Changing Relationship of EU and National law' (2012) 18 ELJ 407.

Künnecke, M., 'Divergence and the *Francovich* Remedy in German and English Courts', Ch 10 in S. Prechal and B. van Roermund, *The Coherence of EU Law: the Search for Unity in Divergent Concepts* (Oxford: OUP, 2008).

Martinez Lage, S. and Brokelmann, H., 'The Liability of the Spanish State for Breach of EC Law' (2004) 29 EL Rev 530 (covers an award of damages in Spain).

■ QUESTIONS

1. To what extent are public authorities entitled to expect protection under the law where an honest but mistaken attempt to meet legal obligations may result in liability to an indeterminate class for an indeterminate time and in an indeterminate amount? To what extent has the Court of Justice responded to such concerns?
2. To what extent do the Court's judgments in this area display a willingness to perform a task of harmonization of EU and national rules relating to interim protection and liability in damages which ought to be the preserve of the legislature, not the courts?
3. (Imaginary) Directive 1/2013 provides that from January 2016, all workers shall be entitled to bring a claim that they have been unfairly dismissed before a national tribunal, provided they have been employed for at least one year prior to dismissal. A UK Statutory Instrument made in 1999 provides that the relevant qualifying period for an unfair dismissal claim in the UK is two years. The UK has not implemented the Directive. It ought to have done so by 1 July 2014, but the Government has been unable to introduce implementing measures because of protests by the opposition parties and some of its own backbench MPs. At the start of 2015, Alice took up a post with British Stodge plc, a firm which supplies catering services to National Health Service hospitals. It is June 2016 and she has just been dismissed. Advise Alice of any assistance she may derive from EU law.

NOTE: For additional material and resources see the Online Resource Centre at: www.oxfordtextbooks.co.uk/orc/weatherill12e.

7

Article 267: The Preliminary Reference Procedure

Article 267 TFEU

The Court of Justice of the European Union shall have jurisdiction to give preliminary rulings concerning:

(a) the interpretation of the Treaties;
(b) the validity and interpretation of acts of the institutions, bodies, offices or agencies of the Union;

Where such a question is raised before any court or tribunal of a Member State, that court or tribunal may, if it considers that a decision on the question is necessary to enable it to give judgment, request the Court to give a ruling thereon.

Where any such question is raised in a case pending before a court or tribunal of a Member State, against whose decisions there is no judicial remedy under national law, that court or tribunal shall bring the matter before the Court.

If such a question is raised in a case pending before a court or tribunal of a Member State with regard to a person in custody, the Court of Justice of the European Union shall act with the minimum of delay.

NOTE: The preliminary reference procedure was originally contained in Article 177 EEC and then, as a result of the Amsterdam re-numbering, it became Article 234 EC. Clearly this numerical adjustment must be borne in mind when reading older documents, including judgments of the Court. The Treaty of Lisbon re-numbered it as Article 267 TFEU and made small cosmetic changes, but also made one significant addition. The final paragraph, concerning proceedings involving a person in custody, is entirely new, and reflects the extension of the Court's jurisdiction consequent on the absorption of the provisions governing the EU's area of freedom, security, and justice into the TFEU (Chapter 15). The expedited procedure, the so-called 'PPU', is put in context at p. 183.

SECTION 1: THE PURPOSE OF ARTICLE 267

The purpose of Article 267 can be traced directly to the need to secure uniformity in the EU legal order throughout the Member States. The introduction delivered by Advocate-General Lagrange over 50 years ago in his Opinion in *Bosch* v *de Geus* (Case 13/61), can hardly be bettered:

***Bosch* v *de Geus* (Case 13/61)**

[1962] ECR 45, Court of Justice of the European Communities

ADVOCATE-GENERAL LAGRANGE: *MR PRESIDENT, MEMBERS OF THE COURT,*

This case – the first submitted to you under the provisions of Article 177 of the Treaty [now 267] establishing the European Economic Community – is of importance under that head alone, since it involves the working of a procedure for the submission of preliminary questions which is apparently designed to play a central part in the application of the Treaty. The progressive integration of the Treaty into the legal, social and economic life of the Member States must involve more and more frequently the application and, when the occasion arises, the interpretation of the Treaty in municipal litigation, whether public or private, and not only the provisions of the Treaty itself but also those of the Regulations adopted for its implementation will give rise to questions of interpretation and indeed of legality. Applied judiciously – one is tempted to say loyally – the provisions of Article 177 must lead to a real and fruitful collaboration between the municipal courts and the Court of Justice of the Communities with mutual regard for their respective jurisdictions. It is in this spirit that each side must solve the sometimes delicate problems which may arise in all systems of preliminary procedure, and which are necessarily made more difficult in this case by the differences in the legal systems of the Member States as regards this type of procedure.

Rheinmühlen-Düsseldorf v *Einfuhr- und Vorratsstelle für Getreide und Futtermittel* (No 1) (Case 166/73)

[1974] ECR 33, Court of Justice of the European Communities

Article 177 is essential for the preservation of the Community character of the law established by the Treaty and has the object of ensuring that in all circumstances the law is the same in all States of the Community.

NOTE: *Stauder* v *Ulm* (Case 29/69) was examined at p. 54 in connection with the protection of fundamental rights. The case was also illuminating for its use of the preliminary reference procedure to secure uniform interpretation of EU texts:

Stauder v *Ulm* (Case 29/69)

[1969] ECR 419, Court of Justice of the European Communities

[2] . . . Article 4 of Decision No 69/71 stipulates in two of its versions, one being the German version, that the States must take all necessary measures to ensure that beneficiaries can only purchase the product in question on presentation of a 'coupon indicating their names', whilst in the other versions, however, it is only stated that a 'coupon referring to the person concerned' must be shown, thus making it possible to employ other methods of checking in addition to naming the beneficiary. It is therefore necessary in the first place to ascertain exactly what methods the provision at issue prescribes.

[3] When a single decision is addressed to all the Member States the necessity for uniform application and accordingly for uniform interpretation makes it impossible to consider one version of the text in isolation but requires that it be interpreted on the basis of both the real intention of its author and the aim he seeks to achieve, in the light in particular of the versions in all four languages.

NOTES

1. It will be recalled from p. 54, that the Court's interpretation led it to reject the contention that the rules infringed fundamental rights.
2. The preliminary reference procedure's role in securing authoritative interpretation of the law places it alongside the principles of supremacy and direct effect and the notion of effective judicial protection (which, as illustrated in *Francovich* (Cases C-6 and C-9/90, p. 143), extends beyond direct effect) as one of the pillars of the EU legal order. Its deepening significance may be appreciated when one realizes that the four official languages to which the Court refers in *Stauder* have now increased to 24.

Opinion 2/13 on accession to the ECHR, 18 December 2014,

Court of Justice of the European Union

[176] . . . the judicial system as thus conceived has as its keystone the preliminary ruling procedure provided for in Article 267 TFEU, which, by setting up a dialogue between one court and another, specifically between the Court of Justice and the courts and tribunals of the Member States, has the object of securing uniform interpretation of EU law (see, to that effect, judgment in *van Gend & Loos*, EU:C:1963:1, p. 12), thereby serving to ensure its consistency, its full effect and its autonomy as well as, ultimately, the particular nature of the law established by the Treaties.

SECTION 2: THE SEPARATION OF FUNCTIONS

The preliminary reference procedure under Article 267 TFEU is based on a separation of functions. It does not elevate the Court of Justice to an appellate status. The Court may not rule on the validity of national law. This was made clear in *Van Gend en Loos* (Case 26/62), which was examined at p. 84 for its explanation of the nature of direct effect. It will be recalled that the substance of the case concerned the compatibility of a Dutch levy with the Treaty.

Van Gend en Loos v *Nederlandse Administratie der Belastingen* (Case 26/62)

[1963] ECR 1, Court of Justice of the European Communities

According to the observations of the Belgian and Netherlands Governments, the wording of this question appears to require, before it can be answered, an examination by the Court of the tariff classification of urea-formaldehyde imported into the Netherlands, a classification on which Van Gend & Loos and the Inspector of Customs and Excise at Zaandam hold different opinions with regard to the 'Tariefbesluit' of 1947. The question clearly does not call for an interpretation of the Treaty but concerns the application of Netherlands customs legislation to the classification of aminoplasts, which is outside the jurisdiction conferred upon the Court of Justice of the European Communities by subparagraph (a) of the first paragraph of Article 177.

The Court has therefore no jurisdiction to consider the reference made by the Tariefcommissie.

However, the real meaning of the question put by the Tariefcommissie is whether, in law, an effective increase in customs duties charged on a given product as a result not of an increase in the rate but of a new classification of the product arising from a change of its tariff description contravenes the prohibition in Article 12 of the Treaty.

Viewed in this way the question put is concerned with an interpretation of this provision of the Treaty and more particularly of the meaning which should be given to the concept of duties applied before the Treaty entered into force.

Therefore the Court has jurisdiction to give a ruling on this question.

As to whether the facts of the case disclosed a violation of Article 12, which is today Article 30 TFEU, the Court concluded:

The Court has no jurisdiction to check the validity of the conflicting views on this subject which have been submitted to it during the proceedings but must leave them to be determined by the national courts.

NOTE: The same approach may be observed in *Costa* v *ENEL* (Case 6/64), examined at p. 73 in relation to the doctrine of supremacy.

Costa v *ENEL* (Case 6/64)

[1964] ECR 585, Court of Justice of the European Communities

The complaint is made that the intention behind the question posed was to obtain, by means of Article 177, a ruling on the compatibility of a national law with the Treaty.

By the terms of this Article, however, national courts against whose decisions, as in the present case, there is no judicial remedy, must refer the matter to the Court of Justice so that a preliminary ruling may be given upon the 'interpretation of the Treaty' whenever a question of interpretation is raised before them. This provision gives the Court no jurisdiction either to apply the Treaty to a specific case or to decide upon the validity of a provision of domestic law in relation to the Treaty, as it would be possible for it to do under Article 169.

Nevertheless, the Court has power to extract from a question imperfectly formulated by the national court those questions which alone pertain to the interpretation of the Treaty. Consequently a decision should be given by the Court not upon the validity of an Italian law in relation to the Treaty, but only upon the interpretation of the abovementioned Articles in the context of the points of law stated by the Giudice Conciliatore.

NOTE: However, the Court's inability to rule on the validity of national law is not as absolute as it first seems. In *Walter Rau* v *de Smedt* (Case 261/81), the Court was asked to interpret Article 30 of the EC Treaty (now, after amendment, Article 34 TFEU; see Chapter 11). The case concerned a challenge to Belgian rules requiring the packaging of margarine in cubes. The Court's response was rather more full and direct than mere interpretation of the relevant Treaty provision.

Walter Rau v *de Smedt* (Case 261/81)

[1982] ECR 3961, Court of Justice of the European Communities

The application in one Member State to margarine imported from another Member State and lawfully produced and marketed in that State of legislation prohibiting the marketing of margarine or edible fats where each block or its external packaging does not have a particular shape, for example the shape of a cube, in circumstances in which the consumer may be protected and informed by means which hinder the free movement of goods to a lesser degree constitutes a measure having an effect equivalent to a quantitative restriction within the meaning of Article 30 of the Treaty.

NOTES

1. Look out for other examples of the Court adopting an approach beyond mere interpretation in its answers to questions referred.
2. The Court typically expands its answers when it is eager to ensure that an important principle is fully understood; *Van Gend en Loos* (Case 26/62) (p. 84) stands as a classic example of this. In fact, it would be rather unrealistic to expect the Court to adhere to the abstract in its answers. The flavour was prettily captured by Advocate General Ruiz-Jarabo Colomer in his Opinion in *Gintec International* (Case C-374/05) [2007] ECR I-9517: 'While the national courts take primary responsibility for the dish, the Court of Justice merely provides them with the all-important Community seasoning, without interfering in matters which do not concern it. Nevertheless, the European and national elements frequently become mixed up and, to allow them to perform their functions, each must absorb and refine the flavours of the other.' In this way the preliminary reference procedure is capable of exerting a much wider and deeper influence on judicial and political preferences than an unduly narrow focus on its role in providing abstract interpretation alone may suggest. See L. Conant, *Justice Contained: Law and Politics in the European Union* (Ithaca: Cornell UP, 2004); H. Micklitz, *The Politics of Judicial Co-operation in the EU* (Cambridge: CUP, 2005); and for a helpful classification of rulings according to their degree of specificity – 'outcome', 'guidance', or 'deference' – see T. Tridimas, 'Constitutional Review of Member State Action: The Virtues and Vices of an Incomplete Jurisdiction' (2011) 9 Intl Jnl Constitutional Law 737.
3. Since the Court of Justice's formal role under the preliminary reference procedure relates to EU law only, it should not question the national court's decision in the case before it to make a reference. Whether it is necessary to obtain a decision on a question is a matter for the national court. This stems from the separation of functions between national courts and the Court of Justice.

Van Gend en Loos v *Nederlandse Administratie der Belastingen* (Case 26/62)

[1963] ECR 1, Court of Justice of the European Communities

The Belgian Government further argues that the Court has no jurisdiction on the ground that no answer which the Court could give to the first question of the Tariefcommissie would have any bearing on the result of the proceedings brought in that court.

However, in order to confer jurisdiction on the Court in the present case it is necessary only that the question raised should clearly be concerned with the interpretation of the Treaty. The considerations which may have led a national court or tribunal to its choice of questions as well as the relevance which it attributes to such questions in the context of a case before it are excluded from review by the Court of Justice.

It appears from the wording of the questions referred that they relate to the interpretation of the Treaty. The Court therefore has the jurisdiction to answer them.

Costa v *ENEL* (Case 6/64)

[1964] ECR 585, Court of Justice of the European Communities

The complaint is made that the Milan court has requested an interpretation of the Treaty which was not necessary for the solution of the dispute before it.

Since, however, Article 177 is based upon a clear separation of functions between national courts and the Court of Justice, it cannot empower the latter either to investigate the facts of the case or to criticize the grounds and purpose of the request for interpretation.

Irish Creamery Milk Suppliers v *Government of Ireland* (Case 36/80)

[1981] ECR 735, Court of Justice of the European Communities

[4] The first question raised by the High Court of Ireland is worded as follows:

> 'Was the decision by the High Court, at this stage of the hearing, to refer to the European Court under Article 177 of the Treaty the question set out in paragraph 2 below a correct exercise on the part of the High Court of its discretion pursuant to the said article?'

[5] Before an answer is given to that question it should be recalled that Article 177 of the Treaty establishes a framework for close co-operation between the national courts and the Court of Justice based on the assignment to each of different functions. The second paragraph of that article makes it clear that it is for the national court to decide at what stage in the proceedings it is appropriate for that court to refer a question to the Court of Justice for a preliminary ruling.

[6] The need to provide an interpretation of Community law which will be of use to the national court makes it essential, as the Court has already stated in its judgment of 12 July 1979 (Union Laitière Normande, Case 244/78 [1979] ECR 2663) to define the legal context in which the interpretation requested should be placed. From that aspect it might be convenient, if circumstances permit, for the facts in the case to be established and for questions of purely national law to be settled at the time the reference is made to the Court of Justice so as to enable the latter to take cognizance of all the features of fact and of law which may be relevant to the interpretation of Community law which it is called upon to give.

[7] However, those considerations do not in any way restrict the discretion of the national court, which alone has a direct knowledge of the facts of the case and of the arguments of the parties, which will have to take responsibility for giving judgment in the case and which is therefore in the best position to appreciate at what stage in the proceedings it requires a preliminary ruling from the Court of Justice.

[8] Hence it is clear that the national court's decision when to make a reference under Article 177 must be dictated by considerations of procedural organization and efficiency to be weighed by that court.

[9] The reply to the first question which has been raised should therefore be that under Article 177 the decision at what stage in proceedings before it a national court should refer a question to the Court of Justice for a preliminary ruling is a matter for the discretion of the national court.

NOTES

1. It is perfectly permissible to refer in interim proceedings, although this will not be normal; *Hoffman la Roche* v *Centrafarm* (Case 107/76) [1977] ECR 957.
2. An outstanding exception to the receptiveness of the Court to references made by national courts is found in the two *Foglia* v *Novello* cases (Cases 104/79 and 244/80).

Foglia v *Novello* (No 1) (Case 104/79)

[1980] ECR 745, Court of Justice of the European Communities

Foglia, an Italian wine dealer, dispatched goods to Novello in France. The contract stipulated that Novello would not be liable for any charges levied by the French or Italian authorities which were incompatible with what was then Community law. A tax then levied by the French authorities formed the basis of the litigation. Novello refused to bear the cost. Foglia sued Novello before the Italian courts; Novello's defence was based on the incompatibility of the charge with Article 95 of the EC Treaty (now Article 110 TFEU: Chapter 10). A reference was made by the Italian judge, the Pretura di Bra.

[8] The parties to the main action submitted a certain number of documents to the Pretura which enabled it to investigate the French legislation concerning the taxation of liqueur wines and other comparable products. The court concluded from its investigation that such legislation created a 'serious discrimination' against Italian liqueur wines and natural wines having a high degree of alcoholic strength by means of special arrangements made for French liqueur wines termed 'natural sweet wines' and preferential tax treatment accorded certain French natural wines with a high degree of alcoholic strength and bearing a designation of origin. On the basis of that conclusion the court formulated the questions which it has submitted to the Court of Justice.

[9] In their written observations submitted to the Court of Justice the two parties to the main action have provided an essentially identical description of the tax discrimination which is a feature of the French legislation concerning the taxation of liqueur wines; the two parties consider that that legislation is incompatible with Community law. In the course of the oral procedure before the Court Foglia stated that he was participating in the procedure before the Court in view of the interest of his undertaking as such and as an undertaking belonging to a certain category of Italian traders in the outcome of the legal issues involved in the dispute.

[10] It thus appears that the parties to the main action are concerned to obtain a ruling that the French tax system is invalid for liqueur wines by the expedient of proceedings before an Italian court between two private individuals who are in agreement as to the result to be attained and who have inserted a clause in their contract in order to induce the Italian court to give a ruling on the point. The artificial nature of this expedient is underlined by the fact that Danzas [the carrier] did not exercise its rights under French law to institute proceedings over the consumption tax although it undoubtedly had an interest in doing so in view of the clause in the contract by which it was also bound and moreover of the fact that Foglia paid without protest that undertaking's bill which included a sum paid in respect of that tax.

[11] The duty of the Court of Justice under Article 177 of the EEC Treaty is to supply all courts in the Community with the information on the interpretation of Community law which is necessary to enable them to settle genuine disputes which are brought before them. A situation in which the Court was obliged by the expedient of arrangements like those described above to give rulings would jeopardize the whole system of legal remedies available to private individuals to enable them to protect themselves against tax provisions which are contrary to the Treaty.

[12] This means that the questions asked by the national court, having regard to the circumstances of this case, do not fall within the framework of the duties of the Court of Justice under Article 177 of the Treaty.

[13] The Court of Justice accordingly has no jurisdiction to give a ruling on the questions asked by the national court.

NOTE: The judge was evidently perplexed that the Court seemed to have abandoned its policy of non-interference with the decision of the referring judge, and referred further questions in the second *Foglia* v *Novello* case.

Foglia v *Novello* (No 2) (Case 244/80)

[1981] ECR 3045, Court of Justice of the European Communities

[17] In order that the Court of Justice may perform its task in accordance with the Treaty it is essential for national courts to explain, when the reasons do not emerge beyond any doubt from the file, why they consider that a reply to their questions is necessary to enable them to give judgment.

[18] It must in fact be emphasised that the duty assigned to the Court by Article 177 is not that of delivering advisory opinions on general or hypothetical questions but of assisting in the administration of justice in the Member States. It accordingly does not have jurisdiction to reply to questions of interpretation which are submitted to it within the framework of procedural devices arranged by the parties in order to induce the Court to give its views on certain problems of Community law which do not correspond to an objective requirement inherent in the resolution of a dispute. A declaration by the Court that it has no jurisdiction in such circumstances does not in any way trespass upon the prerogatives of the national court but makes it possible to prevent the application of the procedure under Article 177 for purposes other than those appropriate for it.

[19] Furthermore, it should be pointed out that, whilst the Court of Justice must be able to place as much reliance as possible upon the assessment by the national court of the extent to which the questions submitted are essential, it must be in a position to make any assessment inherent in the performance of its own duties in particular in order to check, as all courts must, whether it has jurisdiction. Thus the Court, taking into account the repercussions of its decisions in this matter, must have regard, in exercising the jurisdiction conferred upon it by Article 177, not only to the interests of the parties to the proceedings but also to those of the Community and of the Member States. Accordingly it cannot, without disregarding the duties assigned to it, remain indifferent to the assessments made by the courts of the Member States in the exceptional cases in which such assessments may affect the proper working of the procedure laid down by Article 177.

[20] Whilst the spirit of co-operation which must govern the performance of the duties assigned by Article 177 to the national courts on the one hand and the Court of Justice on the other requires the latter to have regard to the national court's proper responsibilities, it implies at the same time that the national court, in the use which it makes of the facilities provided by Article 177, should have regard to the proper function of the Court of Justice in this field.

[21] The reply to the first question must accordingly be that whilst, according to the intended role of Article 177, an assessment of the need to obtain an answer to the questions of interpretation raised, regard being had to the circumstances of fact and of law involved in the main action, is a matter for the national court it is nevertheless for the Court of Justice, in order to confirm its own jurisdiction, to examine, where necessary, the conditions in which the case has been referred to it by the national court.

The Court then observed:

[25] The reply to the fourth question must accordingly be that in the case of preliminary questions intended to permit the national court to determine whether provisions laid down by law or regulation in another Member State are in accordance with Community law the degree of legal protection may not differ according to whether such questions are raised in proceedings between individuals or in an action to which the State whose legislation is called in question is a party, but that in the first case the Court of Justice must take special care to ensure that the procedure under Article 177 is not employed for purposes which were not intended by the Treaty.

NOTES

1. In the result, the Court did not significantly modify the stance which it had taken in the first *Foglia* v *Novello* case (Case 104/79). There are sound arguments both for and against the Court's stance. See, e.g., discussion by A. Barav, (1980) 5 EL Rev 443; D. Wyatt, (1982) 7 EL Rev 186; and G. Bebr, (1982) 19 CML Rev 421.
2. However, contrary to the impression left by these two judgments, subsequent case law confirms that the Court had *not* chosen to embark on a new policy of inquiry into the national court's decision to refer. It is striking that in the main the Court has routinely declined subsequent invitations to repeat the *Foglia* v *Novello* approach. In *Walter Rau* (Case 261/81), mentioned at p. 164, the Court was curt when presented with objections to its jurisdiction:

Walter Rau v *de Smedt* (Case 261/81)

[1982] ECR 3961, Court of Justice of the European Communities

[8] The Belgian Government points out that the importation of margarine into Belgium by the defendant in the main action is already the subject of criminal proceedings in Belgium and that the Court should therefore inquire whether the dispute which gave rise to the request for a preliminary ruling is a genuine dispute. In this regard the Belgian Government recalls the judgment of the Court of 16 December 1981 in Case 244/80 *Foglia* [1981] ECR 3045.

[9] In this instance there is nothing in the file on the case which provides grounds for doubting that the dispute is genuine. Therefore there is no reason for concluding that the Court has no jurisdiction.

NOTE: In *Parfumerie-Fabrik* v *Provide* (Case C-150/88), the Court confirmed that it will not lightly infer an absence of a genuine dispute.

***Parfumerie-Fabrik* v *Provide* (Case C-150/88)**

[1989] ECR 3891, Court of Justice of the European Communities

[11] The Italian Government notes that the preliminary questions arose in the context of a dispute between individuals, the genuineness of which is open to doubt, and that they are intended to permit a court in one Member State to determine whether the rules of another Member State are compatible with Community law. Referring to the Court's judgment of 16 December 1981 in Case 244/80 *Foglia* v *Novello* [1981] ECR 3045, the Italian Government therefore expresses its doubts as to the propriety of the request for a preliminary ruling. It further maintains that the Court has no jurisdiction under Article 177 to rule on the compatibility of national legislation with Community law.

[12] Those objections must be dismissed. First, the documents before the Court do not allow any doubt as to the genuineness of the dispute in the main proceedings or, therefore, the propriety of the request for a preliminary ruling. Secondly, the Court has consistently held (see, in particular, its judgment of 9 October 1984 in Joined Cases 91 and 127/83 Heineken *Brouwerijen BV* v *Inspecteurs der Vennootschapsbelasting, Amsterdam and Utrecht* [1984] ECR 3435) that, when ruling on questions intended to permit the national court to determine whether national provisions are in accordance with Community law, the Court may provide the criteria for the interpretation of Community law which will enable the national court to solve the legal problem with which it is faced. The same is true when it is to be determined whether the provisions of a Member State other than that of the court requesting the ruling are compatible with Community law.

NOTE: It is pertinent to recall that the fact that the parties to litigation may be in agreement about the desired result does not necessarily eliminate the existence of a real dispute calling for a ruling by the Court of Justice. The Court made this point in *Société d'Importation Édouard Leclerc-Siplec* v *TFI Publicité SA & M6 Publicité SA* (Case C-412/93) [1995] ECR I-179 and expanded on it in the next case.

***Cura Anlagen GmbH* v *Auto Service Leasing GmbH* (Case C-451/99)**

[2002] ECR I-3193, Court of Justice of the European Communities

Cura Anlagen, an Austrian company, rented a German-registered car from Auto Service Leasing, a company based in Germany. But Cura Anlagen could not use the car because Austrian rules prevented the driving of a vehicle with foreign plates in Austria for more than three days. In an action on the contract brought before a court in Vienna the question of the compatibility of the Austrian rules with the Treaty's free movement provisions was raised and duly referred to Luxembourg under the preliminary reference procedure contained at the time in Article 234 EC. But was it admissible?

[16] According to settled case law, it is solely for the national court before which the dispute has been brought, and which must assume responsibility for the subsequent judicial decision, to determine in the light of the particular circumstances of the case both the need for a preliminary ruling in order to enable it to deliver judgment and the relevance of the questions which it submits to the Court. Nevertheless, the Court has held that it cannot give a preliminary ruling on a question submitted by a national court where it is quite obvious that the ruling sought by that court on the interpretation or validity of Community law bears no relation to the actual facts of the main action or its purpose, where the problem is hypothetical, or where the Court does not have before it the factual or legal material necessary to give a useful answer to the questions submitted to it. . . .

[21] The Austrian Government . . . argues that the dispute in the main proceedings concerns the interpretation and performance of a private law contract which bears no relation to the question referred.

[22] It should be noted in that respect that, pursuant to Article 234 EC, where a question on the interpretation of the Treaty or of subordinate acts of the institutions of the Community is raised before any court or tribunal of a Member State, that court or tribunal may, if it considers that a decision on the question is necessary to enable it to give judgment, request the Court of Justice to give a ruling thereon (see, in particular, Case C-412/93 *Leclerc-Siplec* [1995] ECR I-179, paragraph 9).

[23] In the context of that procedure for making a reference, the national court, which alone has direct knowledge of the facts of the case, is in the best position to assess, with full knowledge of the matter before it, the need for a preliminary ruling to enable it to give judgment (see, in particular, *Leclerc-Siplec*, paragraph 10).

[24] Moreover, as the Advocate General has pointed out in paragraph 23 of his Opinion, it is important for a court which is asked to order the enforcement or annulment of a contract to know whether the national provisions which appear to hinder its performance are compatible with Community law or not. The question therefore appears to be relevant.

[25] Finally, the Austrian Government challenges the genuineness of the dispute in the main proceedings, which it claims is to a large extent contrived.

[26] In that respect, the Court of Justice has held that, in order to determine whether it has jurisdiction, it must examine the conditions in which the case has been referred to it by the national court. The spirit of cooperation which must prevail in the preliminary ruling procedure requires the national court to have regard to the function entrusted to the Court of Justice, which is to assist in the administration of justice in the Member States and not to deliver advisory opinions on general or hypothetical questions (Case 149/82 *Robards* [1983] ECR 171, paragraph 19; Case C-83/91 *Meilicke* [1992] ECR I-4871, paragraph 25).

[27] In this case, even if some of the information on the file might give rise to a suspicion that the situation underlying the main proceedings was contrived with a view to obtaining a decision from the Court of Justice on a question of Community law of general interest, it cannot be denied that there is a genuine contract the performance or annulment of which undeniably depends on a question of Community law.

NOTE: The question was therefore treated as admissible. This judgment strengthens the impression that *Foglia* v *Novello* continues to be treated as an exception to a general rule of receptivity to preliminary references. But, though an exception, it is not dead, as the next case demonstrates.

***Bacardi-Martini SAS, Cellier des Dauhpins* v *Newcastle United* (Case C-318/00)**

[2003] ECR I-905, Court of Justice of the European Communities

Newcastle United permitted the broadcasting of football matches from their home ground, at which advertisements for alcoholic drinks were displayed. This was compatible with English law but in conflict with the highly restrictive French Loi Évin governing advertising of alcohol. After a match against Metz was transmitted on French television, litigation was commenced between the companies whose products had been advertised and the club. The possible application of the Treaty rules governing the free movement of services (then Article 49 EC, now Article 56 TFEU: Chapter 14) was raised and the High Court in London referred questions to Luxembourg under what was then Article 234 EC, now Article 267 TFEU. But they were held inadmissible.

[42] . . .The spirit of cooperation which must prevail in preliminary ruling proceedings requires the national court for its part to have regard to the function entrusted to the Court of Justice, which is to contribute to the administration of justice in the Member States and not to give opinions on general or hypothetical questions. . .

[43] Thus the Court has held that it has no jurisdiction to give a preliminary ruling on a question submitted by a national court where it is quite obvious that the interpretation or the assessment of the validity of a provision of Community law sought by that court bears no relation to the actual facts of the main action or its purpose, or where the problem is hypothetical, or where the Court does not have before it the factual or legal material necessary to give a useful answer to the questions submitted to it (see Bosman, paragraph 61; Case C-437/97 *EKW and Wein & Co* [2000] ECR I-1157, paragraph 52. . .

[44] In order that the Court may perform its task in accordance with the Treaty, it is essential for national courts to explain, when the reasons do not emerge beyond any doubt from the file, why they consider that a reply to their questions is necessary to enable them to give judgment (Case 244/80 Foglia [1981] ECR 3045, paragraph 17). Thus the Court has held that it is essential that the national court should give at the very least

some explanation of the reasons for the choice of the Community provisions which it requires to be interpreted and of the link it establishes between those provisions and the national legislation applicable to the dispute (order in Case C-116/00 *Laguillaumie* [2000] ECR I-4979, paragraph 16).

[45] Moreover, the Court must display special vigilance when, in the course of proceedings between individuals, a question is referred to it with a view to permitting the national court to decide whether the legislation of another Member State is in accordance with Community law (*Foglia*, paragraph 30).

[46] In the present case, as the questions referred are intended to enable the national court to assess the compatibility with Community law of the legislation of another Member State, the Court must be informed in some detail of that court's reasons for considering that an answer to the questions is necessary to enable it to give judgment.

[47] It appears from the High Court's account of the legal context that it has to apply English law in the main proceedings. It nevertheless considers that 'the issue of the legality of the Loi Évin provisions is central to resolution of the proceedings before [it]'. It does not, however, state positively that an answer to that question is necessary to enable it to give judgment.

[48] On being requested by the Court to explain more fully the basis on which Newcastle could rely on the Loi Évin, the High Court has essentially confined itself to repeating the defendant's argument that it could reasonably anticipate that a failure to give instructions to remove the advertisements in the stadium would result in a breach of French law.

[49] On the other hand, the High Court has not said whether it itself considered that Newcastle could reasonably suppose that it was obliged to comply with the French legislation, and there is nothing else to that effect before the Court.

These deficiencies led the Court to conclude that it did not have the material before it to show that it was 'necessary to rule on the compatibility with the Treaty of legislation of a Member State other than that of the court making the reference'. The questions were therefore inadmissible.

The compatibility of the Loi Évin with Article 49 EC, now Article 56 TFEU, was subsequently directly addressed by the Court in Case C-262/02 *Commission* v *France* and Case C-429/02 *Bacardi* v *TF1* [2004] ECR I-6569, I-6613 (see further Chapter 14).

NOTE: In *Wienand Meilicke* v *ADV/ORGA FA Meyer AG* (Case C-83/91) [1992] ECR I-4871, mentioned in paragraph 26 of *Cura Anlagen* (Case C-451/99, p. 168), the Court declined to answer questions referred to it by a German court because it considered it was being asked to rule on a purely hypothetical general problem. It had not had made available to it information necessary to enable it to provide a useful reply. In *Telemarsicabruzzo* v *Circostel* (Cases C-320–322/90) [1993] ECR I-393, the Court refused to give a ruling where it had been supplied with inadequate background information. The rulings, in conjunction with *Newcastle United* (Case C-318/00), may be taken in part as an encouragement to a referring court to take more care in the preparation of relevant documentation (see *Further Reading* at the end of this chapter). In this vein the Court in the next case was ready to pick and choose the questions in respect of which it had jurisdiction, while offering fuller explanation of why it does not leave the door unconditionally open:

Jyri Lehtonen, Castors Canada Dry Namur-Braine ASBL v *Fédération Royale Belge des Sociétés de Basket-ball ASBL* (FRBSB) (Case C-176/96)

[2000] ECR I-2681, Court of Justice of the European Communities

[22] According to settled case-law, the need to provide an interpretation of Community law which will be of use to the national court makes it necessary that the national court define the factual and legal context of the questions it is asking or, at the very least, explain the factual circumstances on which those questions are based. Those requirements are of particular importance in certain areas, such as that of competition, where the factual and legal situations are often complex (see, in particular, Joined Cases C-320/90 to C-322/90 *Telemarsicabruzzo and Others* [1993] ECR I-393, paragraphs 6 and 7, CaseC-67/96 *Albany International* v *Stichting*

Bedrijfspensioenfonds Textielindustrie [1999] ECR I-5751, paragraph 39, and Joined Cases C-115/97 to C-117/97 *Brentjens' Handelsonderneming* v *Stichting Bedrijfspensioenfonds voor de Handel in Bouwmaterialen* [1999] ECR I-6025, paragraph 38).

[23] The information provided in decisions making references must not only enable the Court to reply usefully but also give the governments of the Member States and other interested parties the opportunity to submit observations pursuant to Article 20 of the EC Statute of the Court of Justice. It is the Court's duty to ensure that that opportunity is safeguarded, bearing in mind that, by virtue of the abovementioned provision, only the decisions making references are notified to the interested parties...

[24] In the main proceedings, it appears, first, from the observations submitted by the parties, the Governments of the Member States and the Commission pursuant to Article 20 of the EC Statute of the Court of Justice that the information in the order for reference enabled them properly to state their position on the question put to the Court, in so far as it concerns the Treaty rules on freedom of movement for workers.

However, this was only part of the reference submitted by the Belgian court. The Court continued:

[28] In so far as the question put concerns the competition rules applicable to undertakings, on the other hand, the Court considers that it does not have enough information to give guidance as to the definition of the market or markets at issue in the main proceedings. Nor does the order for reference show clearly the character and number of undertakings operating on that market or markets. In addition, the information provided by the national court does not enable the Court to make meaningful findings as to the existence and volume of trade between Member States or as to the possibility of that trade being affected by the rules on transfers of players.

[29] The order for reference therefore does not contain sufficient information to satisfy the requirements described in paragraphs 22 and 23 above, as far as the competition rules are concerned.

[30] Accordingly, the Court should answer the question referred in so far as it relates to the interpretation of the Treaty rules on the principle of the prohibition of discrimination on grounds of nationality and on freedom of movement for workers. The question is inadmissible, however, in so far as it relates to the interpretation of the competition rules applicable to undertakings.

NOTE: For further examples of cases in which the Court inspected the documentation provided by the referring court but felt itself unable to provide a 'useful answer', see *Christina Bellamy* (Case C-123/00) [2001] ECR I-2795, Case C-380/05 *Centro Europa 7 Srl* [2008] ECR I-349 and Case C-299/15 *Daniele Striani* order of 16 July 2015. Nonetheless this outcome remains unusual. In the absence of exceptional circumstances, the Court of Justice's readiness to adhere to a 'spirit of cooperation' and to answer questions of interpretation which a national court chooses to refer seems likely to continue. In *Landesgrundverkehrsreferent der Tiroler Landesregierung* v *Beck, Bergdorf Wohnbau* (Case C-355/97) [1999] ECR I-4977, for example, questions posed by an Austrian court were answered despite submissions by the Austrian Government and the Commission that answers could be of no value whatsoever in resolving the dispute. The 'presumption of relevance' attaching to questions referred was not rebutted on the facts. In *Wiener* (Case C-338/95) [1997] ECR I-6495, the Court coolly ignored Advocate-General Jacobs' plea for more self-restraint by both national courts and the Court of Justice. That does not rule out the possibility that national courts may refer fewer cases to Luxembourg as they gain confidence in their ability to handle EU law materials. However, in recent years the number of referrals has tended to creep upwards. The figures are 385 in 2010, 423 in 2011, 404 in 2012, 450 in 2013, the highest ever figure, and 428 in 2014. In each of these five years, German courts made the highest number of referrals (71, 83, 68, 97, and 87 respectively), with Italian, Belgian, French, and Dutch courts the next most prolific. Courts in the UK made 29 references to Luxembourg in 2010, 26 in 2011, 16 in 2012, 14 in 2013, and 12 in 2014. The average time taken over a preliminary ruling varies year-by-year but has lately been reduced from over two years to 15 months in 2014 (this information is available *via* the Court's website, http://curia.europa.eu). It was mentioned (p. 161) that the text of Article 267 TFEU was amended by the Lisbon Treaty to take account of the impact of references on a person in custody, and, in connection with this adjustment, an urgent preliminary reference procedure applicable to Title V of Part Three TFEU (see Chapter 15) has been in place since March 2008. This is the 'PPU': the acronym derives from the

French language version. The first use made of the procedure was in Case C-195/08 *Rinau*, a reference concerning child abduction made by the Supreme Court of Lithuania, received by the Court on 14 May 2008 and dealt with by a ruling on 11 July 2008 ([2008] ECR I-5271). Six requests to use this procedure were made in 2014, four of which were accepted, and the average time taken to deliver a ruling was 2.2 months.

Looking into the future, it is plausible that the weight of preliminary references transmitted to the Court will increase, under pressures caused by *inter alia* enlargement of the Union and the modestly enhanced jurisdiction conferred on the Court by the Lisbon Treaty. The heavier the Court's workload, the more intense becomes the pressure for reform of the system. The Treaty of Nice made a relatively modest contribution by providing for the possibility of equipping the Court of First Instance with jurisdiction to deliver preliminary rulings in specific areas. The Court of First Instance was re-named the General Court by the Lisbon Treaty and the procedure is now found in Article 256(3) TFEU:

> The General Court shall have jurisdiction to hear and determine questions referred for a preliminary ruling under Article 267, in specific areas laid down by the Statute. Where the General Court considers that the case requires a decision of principle likely to affect the unity or consistency of Union law, it may refer the case to the Court of Justice for a ruling. Decisions given by the General Court on questions referred for a preliminary ruling may exceptionally be subject to review by the Court of Justice, under the conditions and within the limits laid down by the Statute, where there is a serious risk of the unity or consistency of Union law being affected.

No such 'specific areas' have yet been laid down.

■ QUESTION

F. Mancini has compared the structure of the preliminary reference procedure with 'a fully-fledged dual system of federal courts as can be found in the US', and found it 'legally frailer, but politically more faithful to the federal ethos' ((1989) 26 CML Rev 595, 605; see also D. Edward (also at the time a judge at the Court) (1995) 20 EL Rev 539, 546–7). Discuss. What alterations to the Article 267 division of function might improve the procedure?

SECTION 3: THE EFFECT OF AN ARTICLE 267 RULING

ICC v *Amministrazione delle Finanze* (Case 66/80)

[1981] ECR 1191, Court of Justice of the European Communities

> [11] The main purpose of the powers accorded to the Court by Article 177 [now 267 TFEU] is to ensure that Community law is applied uniformly by national courts. Uniform application of Community law is imperative not only when a national court is faced with a rule of Community law the meaning and scope of which need to be defined; it is just as imperative when the Court is confronted by a dispute as to the validity of an act of the institutions.
>
> [12] When the Court is moved under Article 177 to declare an act of one of the institutions to be void there are particularly imperative requirements concerning legal certainty in addition to those concerning the uniform application of Community law. It follows from the very nature of such a declaration that a national court may not apply the act declared to be void without once more creating serious uncertainty as to the Community law applicable.
>
> [13] It follows therefrom that although a judgment of the Court given under Article 177 of the Treaty declaring an act of an institution, in particular a Council or Commission regulation, to be void is directly addressed only to the national court which brought the matter before the Court, it is sufficient reason for any other national court to regard that act as void for the purposes of a judgment which it has to give.
>
> [14] That assertion does not however mean that national courts are deprived of the power given to them by Article 177 of the Treaty and it rests with those courts to decide whether there is a need to raise once again

a question which has already been settled by the Court where the Court has previously declared an act of a Community institution to be void. There may be such a need in particular if questions arise as to the grounds, the scope and possibly the consequences of the invalidity established earlier.

[15] If that is not the case national courts are entirely justified in determining the effect on the cases brought before them of a judgment declaring an act void given by the Court in an action between other parties.

NOTES

1. Case 66/80 concerned a reference relating to the validity of Union (then Community) legislation. A comparable approach should be taken in relation to the effect of preliminary rulings on the interpretation of Union law.
2. The point that a preliminary ruling exerts an impact beyond the case in which it is delivered may affect the way in which the Court handles a request for a reference. In the current (2013) version of the Court's *Rules of Procedure* (available at http://curia.europa.eu) Article 99 states that where the question referred is identical to one on which the Court has already ruled, where the answer may be clearly deduced from existing case law or where the answer admits of no reasonable doubt the Court may simply issue a reasoned order rather than proceeding to judgment.
3. The Court has the competence to restrict the temporal effects of its rulings; see, e.g., in relation to a ruling on interpretation (*Defrenne* (Case 43/75)) and the other cases mentioned at p. 101. These issues will be re-addressed in the next chapter. The Court is determined to construct a comprehensive system of remedies which is coherent. It accordingly draws inspiration in interpreting Article 267 from other Treaty provisions, notably Article 263 (e.g., *Société de Produits de Maïs* v *Administration des Douanes* (Case 112/83), at p. 228).

SECTION 4: BODIES COMPETENT TO REFER

Broeckmeulen v *Huisarts Registratie Commissie* (Case 246/80)

[1981] ECR 2311, Court of Justice of the European Communities

Broeckmeulen was refused registration as (the equivalent of) a General Practitioner in the Netherlands by the defendant *Commissie*. He held a Belgian medical qualification and sought to rely on rules governing the free movement of professionals between Member States. The first issue for the Court of Justice to consider was whether the Appeals Committee was competent to refer questions under Article 177 – now Article 267 TFEU – which refers only to a 'court or tribunal of a Member State'.

[10] According to the internal rules of the Society, the Appeals Committee, appointed for a period of five years, is composed of three members appointed by the Netherlands medical faculties, three members appointed by the Board of the Society and three members, including the chairman (preferably a high-ranking judge), who are appointed by the ministers responsible for higher education and health respectively. It may therefore be seen that the composition of the Appeals Committee entails a significant degree of involvement on the part of the Netherlands public authorities.

[11] Pursuant to those rules, the Appeals Committee determines disputes on the adversarial principle, that is to say having heard the Registration Committee and the doctor concerned, as well as his adviser or lawyer, if necessary.

[12] The Netherlands Government stated that, in its opinion, the Appeals Committee cannot be considered a court or tribunal under Netherlands law. However, it pointed out that that fact is not decisive for the interpretation of Article 177 of the Treaty and suggested that the question whether a body such as the Appeals Committee is entitled to refer a case to the Court under that provision should be determined in the light of the function performed by that body within the system of remedies available to those who consider that their rights under Community law have been infringed.

[13] In this regard, the order for reference mentions a Royal Decree of 1966, the decree concerning benefits ('Verstreckingenbesluit'), adopted under the Sickness Fund Law; for the purposes of that decree the term 'general practitioner' refers exclusively to a doctor enrolled on the register of general practitioners maintained by the Society. The practice of a doctor who is not enrolled on the register would thus not be recognized by the sickness insurance schemes. Under those circumstances a doctor who is not enrolled on the register is unable to treat, as a general practitioner, patients covered by the social security system. In fact, private practice is likewise made impossible by the fact that private insurers also define the term 'general practitioner' in their policies in the same way as the provisions of the decree concerning benefits.

[14] A study of the Netherlands legislation and of the statutes and internal rules of the Society shows that a doctor who intends to establish himself in the Netherlands may not in fact practise either as a specialist, or as an expert in social medicine, or as a general practitioner, without being recognized and registered by the organs of the Society. In the same way it may be seen that the system thus established is the result of close cooperation between doctors who are members of the Society, the medical faculties and the departments of State responsible for higher education and health.

[15] It is thus clear that both in the sector covered by the social security system and in the field of private medicine the Netherlands system of public health operates on the basis of the status accorded to doctors by the Society and that registration as a general practitioner is essential to every doctor wishing to establish himself in the Netherlands as a general practitioner.

[16] Therefore a general practitioner who avails himself of the right of establishment and the freedom to provide services conferred upon him by Community law is faced with the necessity of applying to the Registration Committee established by the Society, and, in the event of his application's being refused, must appeal to the Appeals Committee. The Netherlands Government expressed the opinion that a doctor who is not a member of the Society would have the right to appeal against such a refusal to the ordinary courts, but stated that the point had never been decided by the Netherlands courts. Indeed all doctors, whether members of the Society or not, whose application to be registered as a general practitioner is refused, appeal to the Appeals Committee, whose decisions to the knowledge of the Netherlands Government, have never been challenged in the ordinary courts.

[17] In order to deal with the question of the applicability in the present case of Article 177 of the Treaty, it should be noted that it is incumbent upon Member States to take the necessary steps to ensure that within their own territory the provisions adopted by the Community institutions are implemented in their entirety. If, under the legal system of a Member State, the task of implementing such provisions is assigned to a professional body acting under a degree of governmental supervision, and if that body, in conjunction with the public authorities concerned, creates appeal procedures which may affect the exercise of rights granted by Community law, it is imperative, in order to ensure the proper functioning of Community law, that the Court should have an opportunity of ruling on issues of interpretation and validity arising out of such proceedings.

[18] As a result of all the foregoing considerations and in the absence, in practice, of any right of appeal to the ordinary courts, the Appeals Committee, which operates with the consent of the public authorities and with their cooperation, and which, after an adversarial procedure, delivers decisions which are in fact recognized as final, must, in a matter involving the application of Community law, be considered as a court or tribunal of a Member State within the meaning of Article 177 of the Treaty. Therefore, the Court has jurisdiction to reply to the question asked.

NOTE: The Court thus felt itself able to proceed to examine the substance of the case.

***Nordsee* v *Reederei Mond* (Case 102/81)**

[1982] ECR 1095, Court of Justice of the European Communities

This was a reference by an arbitrator in a dispute between three German firms.

[7] Since the arbitration tribunal which referred the matter to the Court for a preliminary ruling was established pursuant to a contract between private individuals the question arises whether it may be considered as a court or tribunal of one of the Member States within the meaning of Article 177 of the Treaty.

[8] The first question put by the arbitrator concerns that problem. It is worded as follows:

'Is a German arbitration court, which must decide not according to equity but according to law, and whose decision has the same effects as regards the parties as a definitive judgment of a court of law (Article 1040 of the Zivilprozeßordnung [rules of civil procedure]) authorized to make a reference to the Court of Justice of the European Communities for a preliminary ruling pursuant to the second paragraph of Article 177 of the EEC Treaty?'

[9] It must be noted that, as the question indicates, the jurisdiction of the Court to rule on questions referred to it depends on the nature of the arbitration in question.

[10] It is true, as the arbitrator noted in his question, that there are certain similarities between the activities of the arbitration tribunal in question and those of an ordinary court or tribunal inasmuch as the arbitration is provided for within the framework of the law, the arbitrator must decide according to law and his award has, as between the parties, the force of *res judicata*, and may be enforceable if leave to issue execution is obtained. However, those characteristics are not sufficient to give the arbitrator the status of a 'court or tribunal of a Member State' within the meaning of Article 177 of the Treaty.

[11] The first important point to note is that when the contract was entered into in 1973 the parties were free to leave their disputes to be resolved by the ordinary courts or to opt for arbitration by inserting a clause to that effect in the contract. From the facts of the case it appears that the parties were under no obligation, whether in law or in fact, to refer their disputes to arbitration.

[12] The second point to be noted is that the German public authorities are not involved in the decision to opt for arbitration nor are they called upon to intervene automatically in the proceedings before the arbitrator. The Federal Republic of Germany, as a Member State of the Community responsible for the performance of obligations arising from Community law within its territory pursuant to Article 5 and Articles 169 to 171 of the Treaty, has not entrusted or left to private individuals the duty of ensuring that such obligations are complied with in the sphere in question in this case.

[13] It follows from these considerations that the link between the arbitration procedure in this instance and the organization of legal remedies through the courts in the Member State in question is not sufficiently close for the arbitrator to be considered as a 'court or tribunal of a Member State' within the meaning of Article 177.

***Doris Saltzmann* (Case C-178/99)**

[2001] ECR I-4421, Court of Justice of the European Communities

[13] In order to determine whether a referring body is a court or tribunal within the meaning of Article 177 of the Treaty, which is a question governed by Community law alone, the Court takes account of a number of factors, such as whether the body is established by law, whether it is permanent, whether its jurisdiction is compulsory, whether its procedure is *inter partes*, whether it applies rules of law and whether it is independent (see, in particular, Case C-54/96 *Dorsch Consult* [1997] ECR I-4961, paragraph 23, and the case law cited therein, and in Joined Cases C-110/98 to C-147/98 *Gabalfrisa and Others* [2000] ECR I-1577, paragraph 33).

NOTE: For further illustrations of the Court's approach to the determination of whether a referring body is a court or tribunal for these purposes, see Case C-111/94 *Job Centre Coop. arl* [1995] ECR I-3361 (referral by administrative body performing a non-judicial function inadmissible, though an appeal to a court against the decision of the administrative body prompted an admissible reference in Case C-55/96 *Job Centre Coop. arl* [1997] ECR I-7119); Case C-516/99 *Walter Schmid* [2002] ECR I-4573 (body's absence of independence from the tax administration fatal – referral inadmissible); Case C-125/04 *Denuit, Cordenier* [2005] ECR I-923 (referral by arbitration board to which the parties had agreed to submit a dispute – inadmissible); Case C-14/08 *Roda Golf and Beach Resort* [2009] ECR I-5439 (reference by an adjudicative body exercising judicial functions, so admissible); Case C-394/11 *Belov* judgment of 31 January 2013 (inadmissible because the referring body could make only an administrative, not a judicial, decision). See G. Anagnostaras, 'Preliminary Problems and Jurisdiction Uncertainties: the Admissibility of Questions Referred by Bodies Performing Quasi-judicial Functions' (2005) 30 EL Rev 878.

SECTION 5: THE OBLIGATION TO REFER AND THE DOCTRINE OF *ACTE CLAIR*

Article 267 makes a distinction in paragraphs 2 and 3 between courts which can refer and those which must. The obligation to refer latter category covers highest courts. Its function was explained by the Court as follows:

***Hoffmann la Roche* v *Centrafarm* (Case 107/76)**

[1977] ECR 957, Court of Justice of the European Communities

[5] In the context of Article 177, whose purpose is to ensure that Community law is interpreted and applied in a uniform manner in all the Member States, the particular objective of the third paragraph is to prevent a body of national case law not in accord with the rules of Community law from coming into existence in any Member State . . .

NOTE: A question arises as to which courts are subject to this obligation to refer. The highest courts within Member States are obviously covered by the obligation. But what of a court whose decisions will be examined by a superior court only if that superior court declares an appeal to be admissible?

***Kenny Roland Lyckeskog* (Case C-99/00)**

[2002] ECR I-4839, Court of Justice of the European Communities

[14] The obligation on national courts against whose decisions there is no judicial remedy to refer a question to the Court for a preliminary ruling has its basis in the cooperation established, in order to ensure the proper application and uniform interpretation of Community law in all the Member States, between national courts, as courts responsible for applying Community law, and the Court. That obligation is in particular designed to prevent a body of national case law that is not in accordance with the rules of Community law from coming into existence in any Member State (see, *inter alia, Hoffmann-La Roche*, cited above, paragraph 5, and Case C-337/95 *Parfums Christian Dior* [1997] ECR I-6013, paragraph 25).

[15] That objective is secured when, subject to the limits accepted by the Court of Justice (CILFIT), supreme courts are bound by this obligation to refer (*Parfums Christian Dior*, cited above) as is any other national court or tribunal against whose decisions there is no judicial remedy under national law (Joined Cases 28/62, 29/62 and 30/62 *Da Costa en Schaake* [1963] ECR 31).

[16] Decisions of a national appellate court which can be challenged by the parties before a supreme court are not decisions of a 'court or tribunal of a Member State against whose decisions there is no judicial remedy under national law' within the meaning of Article 234 EC. The fact that examination of the merits of such appeals is subject to a prior declaration of admissibility by the supreme court does not have the effect of depriving the parties of a judicial remedy.

[17] That is so under the Swedish system. The parties always have the right to appeal to the Högstadomstol against the judgment of a hovrätt, which cannot therefore be classified as a court delivering a decision against which there is no judicial remedy. Under Paragraph 10 of Chapter 54 of the Rättegångsbalk, the Högstadomstol may issue a declaration of admissibility if it is important for guidance as to the application of the law that the appeal be examined by that court. Thus, uncertainty as to the interpretation of the law applicable, including Community law, may give rise to review, at last instance, by the supreme court.

[18] If a question arises as to the interpretation or validity of a rule of Community law, the supreme court will be under an obligation, pursuant to the third paragraph of Article 234 EC, to refer a question to the Court of Justice for a preliminary ruling either at the stage of the examination of admissibility or at a later stage.

[19] The answer to the first question must therefore be that, where the decisions of a national court or tribunal can be appealed to the supreme court under conditions such as those that apply to decisions of the referring court in the present case, that court or tribunal is not under the obligation referred to in the third paragraph of Article 234 EC.

NOTE: But even highest courts, so defined, need not refer if the doctrine of *acte clair* applies. The Court of Justice carefully explained the nature of this doctrine in the following case.

CILFIT (Case 283/81)

[1982] ECR 3415, Court of Justice of the European Communities

The Italian Ministry of Health took the view that the answer to a question concerning the interpretation of a Regulation was so obvious as to rule out the possibility of there being any interpretative doubt, thus lifting the obligation to refer imposed on the Italian Corte Suprema di Cassazione, against whose decisions there was no judicial remedy under national law.

[4] Faced with those conflicting arguments, the Corte Suprema di Cassazione referred to the Court the following question for a preliminary ruling:

> 'Does the third paragraph of Article 177 of the EEC Treaty, which provides that where any question of the same kind as those listed in the first paragraph of that article is raised in a case pending before a national court or tribunal against whose decisions there is no judicial remedy under national law that court or tribunal must bring the matter before the Court of Justice, lay down an obligation so to submit the case which precludes the national court from determining whether the question raised is justified or does it, and if so within what limits, make that obligation conditional on the prior finding of a reasonable interpretative doubt?'

[5] In order to answer that question it is necessary to take account of the system established by Article State 177, which confers jurisdiction on the Court of Justice to give preliminary rulings on, *inter alia*, the interpretation of the Treaty and the measures adopted by the institutions of the Community.

[6] The second paragraph of that article provides that any court or tribunal of a Member State may, if it considers that a decision on a question of interpretation is necessary to enable it to give judgment, request the Court of Justice to give a ruling thereon. The third paragraph of that article provides that, where a question of interpretation is raised in a case pending before a court or tribunal of a Member State against whose decisions there is no judicial remedy under national law, that court or tribunal shall bring the matter before the Court of Justice.

[7] That obligation to refer a matter to the Court of Justice is based on cooperation, established with a view to ensuring the proper application and uniform interpretation of Community law in all the Member States, between national courts, in their capacity as courts responsible for the application of Community law, and the Court of Justice. More particularly, the third paragraph of Article 177 seeks to prevent the occurrence within the Community of divergences in judicial decisions on questions of Community law. The scope of that obligation must therefore be assessed, in view of those objectives, by reference to the powers of the national courts, on the one hand, and those of the Court of Justice, on the other, where such a question of interpretation is raised within the meaning of Article 177.

[8] In this connection, it is necessary to define the meaning for the purposes of Community law of the expression 'where any such question is raised' in order to determine the circumstances in which a national court or tribunal against whose decisions there is no judicial remedy under national law is obliged to bring a matter before the Court of Justice.

[9] In this regard, it must in the first place be pointed out that Article 177 does not constitute a means of redress available to the parties to a case pending before a national court or tribunal. Therefore the mere fact that a party contends that the dispute gives rise to a question concerning the interpretation of Community law does not mean that the court or tribunal concerned is compelled to consider that a question has been raised within the meaning of Article 177. On the other hand, a national court or tribunal may, in an appropriate case, refer a matter to the Court of Justice of its own motion.

[10] Secondly, it follows from the relationship between the second and third paragraphs of Article 177 that the courts or tribunals referred to in the third paragraph have the same discretion as any other national court or tribunal to ascertain whether a decision on a question of Community law is necessary to enable them to give judgment. Accordingly, those courts or tribunals are not obliged to refer to the Court of Justice a question

concerning the interpretation of Community law raised before them if that question is not relevant, that is to say, if the answer to that question, regardless of what it may be, can in no way affect the outcome of the case.

[11] If, however, those courts or tribunals consider that recourse to Community law is necessary to enable them to decide a case, Article 177 imposes an obligation on them to refer to the Court of Justice any question of interpretation which may arise.

[12] The question submitted by the Corte di Cassazione seeks to ascertain whether, in certain circumstances, the obligation laid down by the third paragraph of Article 177 might none the less be subject to certain restrictions.

[13] It must be remembered in this connection that in its judgment of 27 March 1963 in Joined Cases 28 to 30/62 (*Da Costa* v *Nederlandse Belastingadministratie* [1963] ECR 31) the Court ruled that: 'Although the third paragraph of Article 177 unreservedly requires courts or tribunals of a Member State against whose decisions there is no judicial remedy under national law. . .to refer to the Court every question of interpretation raised before them, the authority of an interpretation under Article 177 already given by the Court may deprive the obligation of its purpose and thus empty it of its substance. Such is the case especially when the question raised is materially identical with a question which has already been the subject of a preliminary ruling in a similar case.'

[14] The same effect, as regards the limits set to the obligation laid down by the third paragraph of Article 177, may be produced where previous decisions of the Court have already dealt with the point of law in question, irrespective of the nature of the proceedings which led to those decisions, even though the questions at issue are not strictly identical.

[15] However, it must not be forgotten that in all such circumstances national courts and tribunals, including those referred to in the third paragraph of Article 177, remain entirely at liberty to bring a matter before the Court of Justice if they consider it appropriate to do so.

[16] Finally, the correct application of Community law may be so obvious as to leave no scope for any reasonable doubt as to the manner in which the question raised is to be resolved. Before it comes to the conclusion that such is the case, the national court or tribunal must be convinced that the matter is equally obvious to the courts of the other Member States and to the Court of Justice. Only if those conditions are satisfied, may the national court or tribunal refrain from submitting the question to the Court of Justice and take upon itself the responsibility for resolving it.

[17] However, the existence of such a possibility must be assessed on the basis of the characteristic features of Community law and the particular difficulties to which its interpretation gives rise.

[18] To begin with, it must be borne in mind that Community legislation is drafted in several languages and that the different language versions are all equally authentic. An interpretation of a provision of Community law thus involves a comparison of the different language versions.

[19] It must also be borne in mind, even where the different language versions are entirely in accord with one another, that Community law uses terminology which is peculiar to it. Furthermore, it must be emphasised that legal concepts do not necessarily have the same meaning in Community law and in the law of the various Member States.

[20] Finally, every provision of Community law must be placed in its context and interpreted in the light of the provisions of Community law as a whole, regard being had to the objectives thereof and to its state of evolution at the date on which the provision in question is to be applied.

[21] In the light of all those considerations, the answer to the question submitted by the Corte Suprema di Cassazione must be that the third paragraph of Article 177 of the EEC Treaty is to be interpreted as meaning that a court or tribunal against whose decisions there is no judicial remedy under national law is required, where a question of Community law is raised before it, to comply with its obligation to bring the matter before the Court of Justice, unless it has established that the question raised is irrelevant or that the Community provision in question has already been interpreted by the Court or that the correct application of Community law is so obvious as to leave no scope for any reasonable doubt. The existence of such a possibility must be assessed in the light of the specific characteristics of Community law, the particular difficulties to which its interpretation gives rise and the risk of divergences in judicial decisions within the Community.

■ QUESTION

'The real strategy of *CILFIT* is not to incorporate an *acte clair* concept into Community law. It is to call the national judiciaries to circumspection when they are faced with problems of interpretation and application of Community law' (H. Rasmussen (1984) 9 EL Rev 242). Discuss. To what extent might this circumspection be intensified by the possibility that the State may incur liability for judicial misapplication of EU law (Case C-224/01 *Gerhard Köbler*, p. 158)?

NOTE: The Court explored these realms in the unusual context of the Benelux Court in Case C-337/95 *Parfums Christian Dior SA and Parfums Christian Dior BV* v *Evora BV* [1997] ECR I-6013, a reference made by the Dutch Hoge Raad (Supreme Court) and cited in the extract from the judgment in *Lyckeskog* (Case C-99/00). The Benelux Court was established by a 1965 Treaty between Belgium, Luxembourg, and the Netherlands. Given that the Benelux Court interprets EU rules in the performance of its functions, it was treated by the Court of Justice in *Dior* as capable of making preliminary references in order to ensure the uniform interpretation of the law. Subsequently, by contrast, in Case C-196/09 *Paul Miles* [2011] ECR I-5105 the Court found that the Complaints Board of the European Schools was not able to make a reference because it was established by an international organization, formally distinct from the EU and its Member States – even though it wished faithfully to apply EU law. In *Dior* the Court, citing *CILFIT*, then added that in so far as no appeal lies against its decisions, the Benelux Court may be *obliged* to make a reference. However, the authority of an interpretation provided by the Court under the procedure may deprive that obligation of its purpose and thus empty it of its substance. In the Benelux context, this may arise where, prior to making a reference to the Benelux Court, a national court has already made use of its power to submit the question raised to Luxembourg. The obligation imposed by the third paragraph of Article 267 TFEU loses its purpose when the question raised is 'substantially the same' as a question already the subject of a preliminary ruling in the same national proceedings.

SECTION 6: THE POWER TO REFER

When should a lower court exercise its Article 267(2) discretion to make a reference?

NOTES

1. The Court of Justice's approach is distinctly flexible. In acknowledging 'considerations of procedural organization and efficiency to be weighed by [the national] court', the ruling in *Irish Creamery Milk Suppliers* (Case 36/80, at p. 165) shows an openness on the part of the Court of Justice and a concern not to raise technical obstacles to referral. Remember also how in *CILFIT* (Case 283/81) the Court pointed out the perils of non-referral (p. 177).
2. In the English courts, the notoriously mechanistic attitude expounded by Lord Denning MR in *Bulmer* v *Bollinger SA* [1974] 3 WLR 202 has been superseded by a more flexible, *communautaire* approach. In *Customs and Excise Commissioners* v *Samex* [1983] 1 All ER 1042, Bingham J (as he then was) made a reference to Luxembourg after conceding:

> the advantages enjoyed by the Court of Justice. It has a panoramic view of the Community and its institutions, a detailed knowledge of the treaties and of much subordinate legislation made under them, and an intimate familiarity with the functioning of the Community market which no national judge denied the collective experience of the Court of Justice could hope to achieve.

3. In one respect, however, the Court of Justice has decided to abandon its flexible approach to the power to refer. This is where the *validity* of EU measures is at stake. In the next case it takes to itself an important jurisdiction, thus insisting on referral in so far as questions of validity arise before national courts.

***Firma Foto Frost* v *HZA Lubeck Ost* (Case 314/85)**

[1987] ECR 4199, Court of Justice of the European Communities

Foto Frost instituted proceedings before the German courts in order to secure the annulment of a demand by the customs authorities for payment of duties on imported binoculars. The basis for the customs authorities' demand was a Commission Decision addressed to Germany. The basis of Foto Frost's application was that the Commission Decision was invalid. The referring court (*Finanzgericht*) addresses in its first question the important jurisdictional point.

[11] In its first question the Finanzgericht asks whether it itself is competent to declare invalid a Commission decision such as the decision of 6 May 1983. It casts doubt on the validity of that decision on the ground that all the requirements laid down by Article 5(2) of Regulation No 1697/79 for taking no action for the post-clearance recovery of duty seem to be fulfilled in this case. However, it considers that in view of the division of jurisdiction between the Court of Justice and the national courts set out in Article 177 of the EEC Treaty only the Court of Justice is competent to declare invalid acts of the Community institutions.

[12] Article 177 confers on the Court jurisdiction to give preliminary rulings on the interpretation of the Treaty and of acts of the Community institutions and on the validity of such acts. The second paragraph of that article provides that national courts may refer such questions to the Court and the third paragraph of that article puts them under an obligation to do so where there is no judicial remedy under national law against their decisions.

[13] In enabling national courts, against those decisions where there is a judicial remedy under national law, to refer to the Court for a preliminary ruling questions on interpretation or validity, Article 177 did not settle the question whether those courts themselves may declare that acts of Community institutions are invalid.

[14] Those courts may consider the validity of a Community act and, if they consider that the grounds put forward before them by the parties in support of invalidity are unfounded, they may reject them, concluding that the measure is completely valid. By taking that action they are not calling into question the existence of the Community measure.

[15] On the other hand, those courts do not have the power to declare acts of the Community institutions invalid. As the Court emphasised in the judgment of 13 May 1981 in Case 66/80 *International Chemical Corporation* v *Amministrazione delle Finanze* [1981] ECR 1191, the main purpose of the powers accorded to the Court by Article 177 is to ensure that Community law is applied uniformly by national courts. That requirement of uniformity is particularly imperative when the validity of a Community act is in question. Divergences between courts in the Member States as to the validity of Community acts would be liable to place in jeopardy the very unity of the Community legal order and detract from the fundamental requirement of legal certainty.

[16] The same conclusion is dictated by consideration of the necessary coherence of the system of judicial protection established by the Treaty. In that regard it must be observed that requests for preliminary rulings, like actions for annulment, constitute means for reviewing the legality of acts of the Community institutions. As the Court pointed out in its judgment of 23 April 1986 in Case 294/83 *Partiécologiste 'les Verts'* v *European Parliament* [1986] ECR 1339), 'in Articles 173 and 184, on the one hand, and in Article 177, on the other, the Treaty established a complete system of legal remedies and procedures designed to permit the Court of Justice to review the legality of measures adopted by the institutions'.

[17] Since Article 173 [now 263 TFEU: see Chapter 8] gives the Court exclusive jurisdiction to declare void an act of a Community institution, the coherence of the system requires that where the validity of a Community act is challenged before a national court the power to declare the act invalid must also be reserved to the Court of Justice.

[18] It must also be emphasised that the Court of Justice is in the best position to decide on the validity of Community acts. Under Article 20 of the Protocol on the Statute of the Court of Justice of the EEC, Community institutions whose acts are challenged are entitled to participate in the proceedings in order to defend the validity of the acts in question. Furthermore, under the second paragraph of Article 21 of that Protocol the Court may require the Member States and institutions which are not participating in the proceedings to supply all information which it considers necessary for the purposes of the case before it.

[19] It should be added that the rule that national courts may not themselves declare Community acts invalid may have to be qualified in certain circumstances in the case of proceedings relating to an application for interim measures; however, that case is not referred to in the national court's question.

[20] The answer to the first question must therefore be that the national courts have no jurisdiction themselves to declare that acts of Community institutions are invalid.

The Court proceeded to hold the contested Commission Decision invalid.

■ QUESTION

Why did the Court deny national courts competence to declare EU acts invalid? Read G. Bebr, (1988) 25 CML Rev 667.

NOTES

1. *Foto-Frost* (Case 314/85) involved a challenge to the validity of a provision before a national court, which duly sparked a preliminary reference. The next chapter examines in more depth the ways in which Article 267 can be used as a device to support such an indirect challenge to the legality of EU legislation. The matter of interim protection, referred to in paragraph 19 of *Foto-Frost*, has now been elucidated in subsequent case law (p. 223). The matter is also touched on in the next sub-section of this chapter.
2. The case law considered at p. 167 concerning the inadmissibility of irrelevant or hypothetical questions is in principle equally applicable to references concerning the validity of EU acts. But it is in any circumstances exceptional for the Court to reject a reference and in *R* v *Secretary of State, ex parte BAT and Imperial Tobacco* (Case C-491/01) [2002] ECR I-11543 the Court, faced with objections, nonetheless found that a reference concerning validity was admissible.
3. There are intriguing general questions about the nature of the relationship between national courts and the Court of Justice under this procedure. The logic of the Court's reasoning in *Foto-Frost* (Case 314/85) appears to be that it would assert its own exclusive jurisdiction in all cases where the validity of EU acts is challenged, including those involving alleged interference with areas of exclusive national competence. Such litigation would be a great deal more constitutionally sensitive than the relatively technical matters at stake in *Foto-Frost* itself. The Court's approach in *Foto-Frost* offers a perfectly clear statement of what was then EC law, now EU law, but the willingness of national courts to accept with due deference the Court's claim to exclusive competence in the matter of the validity of EU acts is a question to which to return later, once the challenges to the Court's approach that have lately emerged among the national judiciaries who are expected to absorb and apply these rulings have been explored: of particular interest will be the stance of the German *Bundesverfassungsgericht*, p. 594.

SECTION 7: THE COURT'S RECOMMENDATIONS ON REFERENCES

In 1996 the Court issued guidelines on the use of what was then Article 177 EC, now Article 267 TFEU. These have been periodically published in updated form. The current version of these *Recommendations* was published in 2012 at [2012] OJ C338/1. They are also available at the Court's website, http://curia.europa.eu. Beginning with the stirring assertion that 'The reference for a preliminary ruling is a fundamental mechanism of European Union law aimed at enabling the courts and tribunals of the Member States to ensure uniform interpretation and application of that law within the European Union', they serve as a useful distillation of the principles of law and the practice explained in the course of this chapter.

SECTION 8: REFORMING THE COURT SYSTEM

Institutional reform was the *leitmotif* of the intergovernmental conference that commenced in 2000 and ultimately generated the Treaty of Nice (Chapter 1, p. 12). The structure of the Court was on the agenda. The preliminary reference procedure was one of the main points for consideration in the Report of the Working Party on the Future of the European Communities' Court System established by the Commission under the Chairmanship of Ole Due, former President of the Court, which was published in January 2000. On this report was based the Commission's contribution to the Intergovernmental Conference on reform of the Community courts. The success of the preliminary reference procedure was trumpeted, but adjustment proposed.

This extract must be read with awareness that, first, the Lisbon Treaty has converted the EC into the EU, the CFI into the General Court and Article 234 (ex 177) into Article 267 TFEU, and, second, that – as this chapter has shown – none of these radical options were in fact accepted in either the Nice or the Lisbon Treaty. But it remains worthwhile to conclude study of the preliminary reference procedure by considering how, if at all, it could usefully be reformed in future.

Reform of the Community Courts (additional Commission contribution to the Intergovernmental Conference on institutional reform)

COM (2000) 109, 1 March 2000

A. PRELIMINARY RULINGS

(i) Jurisdiction of the Court of Justice

The preliminary ruling procedure is undoubtedly the keystone of the Community's legal order. Forty years' experience have shown that it is the most effective means of securing the uniform application of Community law throughout the Union and that it is an exceptional factor for integration owing to the simple, direct dialogue which it establishes with national courts. The Commission considers that this regulating function, which is essential to the Community legal order, must therefore in principle be the exclusive responsibility of the Court of Justice.

The Working Party shares this opinion. But it proposes that the last sentence of Article 225(1) of the EC Treaty [now 256 TFEU] be deleted to give the CFI exceptional jurisdiction to give preliminary rulings in very specialised areas of Community law.[5] The Working Party considers that special categories of case, including preliminary questions in such areas, should be entrusted as a whole to the CFI and that the Court of Justice, as the supreme court of the Union, should become involved where appropriate only in appeals on points of law lodged by the Commission.[6]

This proposal will have to be examined in connection with any specific changes to jurisdiction that will have to be provided for in certain categories of special case, such as intellectual property proceedings.

(ii) Clarification of the roles of the Court of Justice and the national courts

To preserve the effectiveness of the preliminary ruling procedure, it is essential that the Court of Justice should be able to concentrate on genuinely new questions and give its judgments considerably sooner. To this end, the Commission believes it is necessary to amend Article 234 (ex Article 177) of the Treaty in order to clarify the distribution of jurisdiction between the Court of Justice and national courts.

1. The first amendment proposed seeks to give national courts greater responsibility as courts of ordinary law in Community matters. At present, this function is not expressly laid down in the Treaty. It can only be inferred from reading Articles 234 and 240 together. It is therefore essential to correct this omission by spelling out the introductory provision in Article 234, clearly stating that it is for the national courts in the first place to apply Community law to the cases before them and that they may consult the Court of Justice when faced with a specific problem of interpretation.

5 E.g. intellectual property (trademarks, patents, and industrial designs, etc.).

6 As provided by, for instance, Article 68(3) of the Treaty.

2. In similar vein, it could be worthwhile amending the second paragraph of Article 234, so as to invite national courts other than those of final instance to specify why they have doubts as to the meaning of the rule of Community law applicable in the case before them and why they feel the need to put a question to the Court of Justice. This provision could be accompanied by the requisite corollary changes to the Rules of Procedure.

3. As part of this clarification exercise, it is necessary, lastly, to insert in Article 234 the rule established in case-law whereby, in cases of doubt as to the validity of a Community act, all national courts must consult the Court of Justice since the latter has the monopoly of the review of Community legality.The Commission does not feel it would be right to give flexibility to the obligation on courts of final instance to refer preliminary questions, currently laid down in the third paragraph of Article 234, requiring them to consult the Court of Justice only if the question were sufficiently important for Community law and if, after examination by the lower courts, there were still reasonable doubts as to the reply. The Commission considers that the advantages of such flexibility as far as the Court's workload is concerned are very slight and that there are real dangers for the uniform application of Community law, especially with enlargement on the horizon. It therefore thinks it is essential to stick with the current wording of the third paragraph of Article 234. Naturally, the flexibility introduced by case-law would continue to apply.

Proposed new wording
Article 234

1. Subject to the provisions of this Article, the courts and tribunals of the Member States shall rule on the questions of Community law which they encounter in exercise of their national jurisdiction.

2. The Court of Justice shall have jurisdiction to give preliminary rulings concerning:
   (a) the interpretation of this Treaty,
   (b) the validity and interpretation of acts of the institutions of the Community and of the ECB;
   (c) the interpretation of the statutes of bodies established by an act of the Council, where those statutes so provide.

3. Where such a question is raised before any national court or tribunal, that court or tribunal may, if it considers that a decision on the question is necessary to enable it to give a judgement, request the Court of Justice to give a ruling thereon. In that event, it shall specify why the validity or interpretation of the rule of Community law raises difficulties in the case before it.

4. Where any such question is raised in a case pending before a national court or tribunal against whose decisions there is no judicial remedy under national law, that court or tribunal shall bring the matter before the Court of Justice.

5. A national court or tribunal must consult the Court of Justice where it proposes not to apply an act of Community law on the grounds that the latter is invalid.

■ QUESTION

Consider the strengths and weaknesses of this (rejected) proposed new wording. Were the Nice Treaty and the Lisbon Treaty too conservative?

■ GENERAL QUESTIONS RELATING TO THE MATERIAL COVERED IN THIS CHAPTER

1. 'Preliminary rulings should be replaced by post hoc and selective review by the Court of Justice of national court decisions' (P. Allott, 'Preliminary Rulings – Another Infant Disease' (2000) 25 EL Rev 538). Discuss.

2. Read the following decisions. Comment critically on their application of what was Article 234 of the EC Treaty, now Article 267 TFEU. What do the decisions tell you about the strengths and weaknesses of the preliminary reference procedure? Would the proposals for reform, if adopted at some time in the future, make any difference to the way in which such cases would be dealt with by national courts?

   R v *Henn and Darby*; contrast the Court of Appeal [1978] 1 WLR 1031 with the House of Lords [1981] AC 850, [1980] 2 WLR 597;

Minister of the Interior v *Cohn Bendit* [1980] 1 CMLR 543 (p. 121);

Procurator Fiscal, Stranraer v *Marshall* [1988] 1 CMLR 657 (this case eventually reached the Court as Case 370/88 *via* the High Court in Edinburgh, and the Court's decision is reported at [1990] ECR I-4071);

Arsenal Football Club v *Reed* ([2002] EWHC 2695, High Court, [2003] EWCA Civ 96, [2003] 3 All ER 865, Court of Appeal, available *via* www.courtservice.gov.uk, noted by Snell, J., (2004) 29 EL Rev 178.

Office of Fair Trading v *Abbey National plc* [2009] UKSC 6, available via www.supremecourt.gov.uk/decided-cases/docs/UKSC_2009_0070_Judgment.pdf., noted by Whittaker (2011) 74 MLR 106; Kenny [2011] Euro Rev Private Law 43.

3. 'Two somewhat contradictory principles – the effectiveness of Community law and the procedural autonomy of the State – must be reconciled. The result is that the direct effect of Community law is to some extent restricted while national autonomy must sometimes yield to the requirements of Community law.' (R. Kovar, *Thirty Years of Community Law* (Luxembourg: Office for Official Publications of the ECs, 1983), p. 146). Discuss.

FURTHER READING

Bobek, M., 'Learning to Talk: Preliminary Rulings, the Courts of the new Member States and the Court of Justice' (2008) 45 CML Rev 1611.

Broberg, M. 'Acte Clair Revisited' (2008) 45 CML Rev 1383.

Broberg, M., and Fenger, N., 'Variations in Member States' Preliminary References to the Court of Justice – are Structural Factors (Part of) the Explanation? (2013) 19 ELJ 488.

Davies, G., 'Abstractness and Concreteness in the Preliminary Reference Procedure: Implications for the Division of Powers and Effective Market Regulation' Ch 8 in N. Nic Shuibhne, *Regulating the Internal Market* (Cheltenham: Edward Elgar, 2006).

Johnston, A., 'Judicial Reform and the Treaty of Nice' (2001) 38 CML Rev 499.

Komarek, J., 'In the Court(s) We Trust? On the Need for Hierarchy and Differentiation in the Preliminary Ruling Procedure' (2007) 32 EL Rev 467.

Sarmiento, D., 'Half a Case at a Time: Dealing with Judicial Minimalism at the European Court of Justice' Ch 1 in M. Claes, M. De Visser, P. Popelier, and C. Van de Heyning (eds), *Constitutional Conversations in Europe: Actors, Topics and Procedures* (Cambridge: Intersentia, 2012).

Tridimas, G. and Tridimas, T., 'National Courts and the European Court of Justice: a Public Choice Analysis of the Preliminary Reference Procedure' (2004) 24 Int'l Rev of Law and Economics 125.

NOTE: For additional material and resources see the Online Resource Centre at: www.oxfordtextbooks.co.uk/orc/weatherill12e.

8

Judicial Control of the Institutions of the EU

SECTION 1: INTRODUCTION

All legal systems contain administrative law and a law of remedies in some form. The substance of the EU's system therefore deserves attention, but it should neither be considered unique nor be viewed in isolation. Its study can be enriched by drawing comparisons with other national and international systems. However, what is of especial interest is the pattern of development of the EU legal order. This has occurred in a fashion which *is* peculiar to the EU. The original structure established by the Treaty of Rome with effect from 1958 owed a great deal to French administrative law traditions. The EU legal order still retains many of these features but has increasingly developed a life of its own, drawing on diverse national traditions. Under the influence of the Court, it has evolved along distinctive lines in response to the needs of the institutional and constitutional structures of the maturing Community which has now become a Union.

Article 19 TEU sets out the basic rules governing the Court and its jurisdiction.

1. The Court of Justice of the European Union shall include the Court of Justice, the General Court and specialised courts. It shall ensure that in the interpretation and application of the Treaties the law is observed. Member States shall provide remedies sufficient to ensure effective legal protection in the fields covered by Union law.

2. The Court of Justice shall consist of one judge from each Member State. It shall be assisted by Advocates-General.

The General Court shall include at least one judge per Member State.

The Judges and the Advocates-General of the Court of Justice and the Judges of the General Court shall be chosen from persons whose independence is beyond doubt and who satisfy the conditions set out in Articles 253 and 254 of the Treaty on the Functioning of the European Union. They shall be appointed by common accord of the governments of the Member States for six years. Retiring Judges and Advocates-General may be reappointed.

3. The Court of Justice of the European Union shall, in accordance with the Treaties:
   (a) rule on actions brought by a Member State, an institution or a natural or legal person;
   (b) give preliminary rulings, at the request of courts or tribunals of the Member States, on the interpretation of Union law or the validity of acts adopted by the institutions;
   (c) rule in other cases provided for in the Treaties.

NOTE: Some of the terminology was altered by the Lisbon Treaty. The two principal courts within the structure are the Court of Justice, which sits at the apex, and the subsidiary General Court; the latter, established in 1989, was known pre-Lisbon as the Court of First Instance (CFI). Article 19(3) TEU contains the basic statement of the Court's jurisdiction to supervise acts of the EU institutions, but it is to the TFEU that one must turn to grasp the details of what is involved in these procedures. Articles 251–281 TFEU provide extensive detail, and this forms the subject matter of this chapter. There is also a Protocol on the Statute of the Court of Justice attached to the TFEU which deals with matters of detailed practice. The Court's jurisdiction was expanded by the Lisbon Treaty, most obviously by the collapse of the old 'third pillar' into the TFEU (Chapter 1, p. 19, Chapter 15) and the binding force granted to the Charter on Fundamental Rights (p. 58), but the basic pattern is long-standing and consequently much of the material covered in this chapter, though dating from before the entry into force of the Lisbon Treaty, remains of enduring relevance.

Article 263 TFEU (Article 230 EC pre-Lisbon and Article 173 pre-Amsterdam) provides an action to annul EU acts. Article 265 TFEU (Article 232 EC pre-Lisbon and Article 175 pre-Amsterdam) provides a complementary action aimed at controlling failure to act. Article 277 TFEU (Article 241 EC pre-Lisbon and Article 184 pre-Amsterdam) allows a measure to be challenged indirectly in an action brought against another measure. Articles 268 and 340 TFEU (Articles 235 and 288 EC pre- Lisbon and Articles 178 and 215 pre-Amsterdam respectively) allow claims to be brought against the EU institutions for compensation for loss suffered as a result of unlawful action. In some circumstances, however, it will be possible to challenge the validity of EU acts without the need to institute a direct challenge before the Court in Luxembourg. It may be possible to claim before a national tribunal that a relevant EU act is unlawful. Typically, this will arise where national authorities are responsible for the implementation of EU legislation. A challenge at national level to the national authorities' acts will involve a plea that the legal basis for the act, EU legislation, is invalid. Where enforcement before a national court is in issue, the bridge between the action at national level and proceedings at EU level is the Article 267 procedure. It will be recalled from the previous chapter that Article 267 ensures that points of EU law raised at national level are interpreted authoritatively at EU level. This is essential in order to preserve the uniformity and integrity of the EU legal order.

The entry into force of the Lisbon Treaty happily cleared away many of the oddities whereby the Court's jurisdiction was different under each of the three (now abandoned) 'pillars' (Chapter 1, p. 19). Vestiges linger, however. Article 275 TFEU largely excludes the Court's jurisdiction in the area of CFSP under the TEU, while Article 276 TFEU places a smaller limitation on jurisdiction pertaining to law and order and internal security under Title V of Part Three TFEU (the area of freedom, security, and justice: see Chapter 15).

The inter-relationship between the remedies envisaged by the TEU and TFEU may seem complicated, but the central point is that the Court has consistently endeavoured to treat the several strands as contributions to a coherent whole. There is a complete system of remedies.

Parti Ecologiste 'Les Verts' v *Parliament* (Case 294/83)

[1986] ECR 1339, Court of Justice of the European Communities

[23] It must first be emphasised in this regard that the European Economic Community is a Community based on the rule of law, inasmuch as neither its Member States nor its institutions can avoid a review of the question whether the measures adopted by them are in conformity with the basic constitutional charter, the Treaty. In particular, in Articles 173 [now 263] and 184 [now 277], on the one hand, and in Article 177 [now 267], on the other, the Treaty established a complete system of legal remedies and procedures designed to permit the Court of Justice to review the legality of measures adopted by the institutions. Natural and legal persons are thus protected against the application to them of general measures which they cannot contest directly before the Court by reason of the special conditions of admissibility laid down in the second paragraph of Article 173 [now the fourth paragraph of Article 263] of the Treaty. Where the Community institutions are responsible for the administrative implementation of such measures, natural or legal persons may bring a direct action before the Court against implementing measures which are addressed to them or which are of direct and individual concern to them and, in support of such an action, plead the illegality of the general measure on which they are based. Where implementation is a matter for the national authorities, such persons may plead the invalidity of general measures before the national courts and cause the latter to request the Court of Justice for a preliminary ruling.

R v *Secretary of State, ex parte BAT and Imperial Tobacco* (Case C-491/01)

[2002] ECR I-11543, Court of Justice of the European Communities

[39] . . . in the complete system of legal remedies and procedures established by the EC Treaty with a view to ensuring judicial review of the legality of acts of the institutions, where natural or legal persons cannot, by reason of the conditions for admissibility laid down in the fourth paragraph of that article [Article 263], directly challenge Community measures of general application, they are able, depending on the case, either indirectly to plead the invalidity of such acts before the Community judicature under Article 277 EC or to do so before the national courts and ask them, since they have no jurisdiction themselves to declare those measures invalid, to make a reference to the Court of Justice for a preliminary ruling on validity . . .

NOTE: This quest for a 'complete system' of remedies within a Union based on the rule of law governs the Court's approach to the interpretation of each relevant Treaty provision. Fixing the scope of one source of judicial protection may be influenced by the possibilities and limitations under another.

SECTION 2: ARTICLE 263

Article 263 TFEU provides a procedure whereby EU acts may be annulled by the Court. What is now Article 263 TFEU was Article 230 EC before the entry into force of the Lisbon Treaty (and Article 173 pre-Amsterdam, p. 10), and so older texts need to be read with this conversion in mind. However, Lisbon has effected important changes that go beyond mere numerical juggling, as will be explained.

ARTICLE 263 TFEU

The Court of Justice of the European Union shall review the legality of legislative acts, of acts of the Council, of the Commission and of the European Central Bank, other than recommendations and opinions, and of acts of the European Parliament and of the European Council intended to produce legal effects *vis-à-vis* third parties. It shall also review the legality of acts of bodies, offices or agencies of the Union intended to produce legal effects *vis-à-vis* third parties.

It shall for this purpose have jurisdiction in actions brought by a Member State, the European Parliament, the Council or the Commission on grounds of lack of competence, infringement of an essential procedural requirement, infringement of the Treaties or of any rule of law relating to their application, or misuse of powers.

The Court shall have jurisdiction under the same conditions in actions brought by the Court of Auditors, by the European Central Bank and by the Committee of the Regions for the purpose of protecting their prerogatives.

Any natural or legal person may, under the conditions laid down in the first and second paragraphs, institute proceedings against an act addressed to that person or which is of direct and individual concern to them, and against a regulatory act which is of direct concern to them and does not entail implementing measures.

Acts setting up bodies, offices and agencies of the Union may lay down specific conditions and arrangements concerning actions brought by natural or legal persons against acts of these bodies, offices or agencies intended to produce legal effects in relation to them.

The proceedings provided for in this Article shall be instituted within two months of the publication of the measure, or of its notification to the plaintiff, or, in the absence thereof, of the day on which it came to the knowledge of the latter, as the case may be.

Article 264 specifies the consequences and offers the Court some flexibility in its rulings.

ARTICLE 264 EC

If the action is well founded, the Court of Justice of the European Union shall declare the act concerned to be void.

However, the Court shall, if it considers this necessary, state which of the effects of the act which it has declared void shall be considered as definitive.

NOTE: The case law which has arisen under this procedure for judicial review is vast, and this selection is designed merely to draw out the main principles. However, perhaps the most useful starting point is the general observation that most applications for the annulment of acts of the institutions of the EU fail. This is especially striking in relation to the fourth paragraph of Article 263, which contains restrictive standing rules which must be satisfied before the merits of an application for annulment will be heard.

A: Article 263, first to third paragraphs

It is useful first to return to a case already considered in Chapter 2, in order to appreciate the nature of acts susceptible to review by the Court under this procedure.

***Commission* v *Council* (Case 22/70)**

[1971] ECR 263, Court of Justice of the European Communities

The Member States had participated in the conclusion of the AETR/ERTA (European Road Transport Agreement). They had expressed agreement to coordinate their approach to the ERTA in a resolution adopted at an EEC Council meeting on 20 March 1970. The Commission formed the view that the matter fell within the competence of what was then the Community, not the individual Member States. In order to test its view of the correct allocation of competence in this field, it brought proceedings to annul the Council resolution. However, the resolution was not a Regulation, a Directive, or a Decision, acts mentioned in Article 189 of the EC Treaty (now Article 288 TFEU) which are clearly reviewable by the Court under Article 173 of the EC Treaty (now, after amendment, Article 263 TFEU). Was the resolution susceptible to review?

[34] The Council considers that the proceedings of 20 March 1970 do not constitute an act, within the meaning of the first sentence of the first paragraph of Article 173, the legality of which is open to review.

[35] Neither by their form nor by their subject-matter or content, it is argued, were these proceedings a regulation, a decision or a directive within the meaning of Article 189.

[36] They were really nothing more than a coordination of policies amongst Member States within the framework of the Council, and as such created no rights, imposed no obligations and did not modify any legal position.

[37] This is said to be the case more particularly because in the event of a dispute between the institutions admissibility has to be appraised with particular rigour.

[38] Under Article 173, the Court has a duty to review the legality 'of acts of the Council. . .other than recommendations or opinions'.

[39] Since the only matters excluded from the scope of the action for annulment open to the Member States and the institutions are 'recommendations or opinions' – which by the final paragraph of Article 189 are declared to have no binding force – Article 173 treats as acts open to review by the Court all measures adopted by the institutions which are intended to have legal force.

[40] The objective of this review is to ensure, as required by Article 164, observance of the law in the interpretation and application of the Treaty.

[41] It would be inconsistent with this objective to interpret the conditions under which the action is admissible so restrictively as to limit the availability of this procedure merely to the categories of measures referred to by Article 189.

[42] An action for annulment must therefore be available in the case of all measures adopted by the institutions, whatever their nature or form, which are intended to have legal effects.

NOTE: The Court then proceeded to determine that the resolution was of this character (see the extract at p. 28). Note also the Court's willingness to review (and annul) a Commission 'communication' in Case C-57/95 *France* v *Commission* [1997] ECR I-1627, p. 303. An action for annulment may be directed at 'measures the legal effects of which are binding on, and capable of affecting the interests of, the applicant by bringing about a distinct change in its legal position' (e.g. Case C-477/11P *Sepracor* v *Commission* judgment of 14 April 2012 para 51). But the scope of review under Article 263 TFEU may not be pushed wider, and the rise of 'softer' forms of governance in the EU, tracked in Chapter 18, raises intriguing questions about subjection to orthodox forms of review and enforcement.

We here now appreciate the full significance of designating the resolution a legal 'act'; it was therefore susceptible to review. Several of the constitutional cases discussed in Part One of this book will be seen in this chapter in the broader context of judicial review.

The second paragraph of Article 263 makes it clear that the Parliament is a 'privileged applicant' occupying the same status as the Council, Commission, or a Member State. It may bring an action without a need to show any particular interest in the matter. It has not always been so well equipped. This is an improvement brought about by the Nice Treaty. Prior to Nice the Parliament was marooned in the third paragraph of Article 263, while prior to Maastricht it was completely absent from the list of privileged applicants and had to take its chances in the same way as other non-privileged applicants. The Lisbon Treaty added to the dynamic narrative of adjustment: the references in the first paragraph to the European Council and bodies, offices, and agencies of the Union and in the third paragraph to the Committee of the Regions are new and effective only from 1 December 2009.

B: Article 263, non-privileged applicants

Whereas the first three paragraphs of Article 263 confer a special status on privileged applicants, most applicants for annulment must use the non-privileged route found in Article 263(4). The efficacy of this route is qualified by the standing rules which carefully confine the ability of non-privileged applicants, commonly private parties, to bring their challenge before the Court in Luxembourg. If the applicant lacks standing to bring the case, the merits of the challenge to the validity of the EU act are not even considered by the Court.

Since the entry into force of the Lisbon Treaty there are three distinct types of action available to the natural and legal person under Article 263(4) TFEU (p. 187). One, a challenge to an act addressed to the applicant. Two, a challenge to an act which is of direct and individual concern to the applicant. Three, a challenge to a regulatory act which is of direct concern to the applicant and does not entail implementing measures. The underlying point throughout is that if an applicant is *not* able to fit him- or herself within one of these categories then he or she does not have standing to seek the act's annulment before the Court in Luxembourg – though he or she may be able instead to rely on proceedings before a *national* court coupled to use of the Article 267 preliminary reference procedure (p. 217). The three types of action foreseen by Article 263 will now be examined in turn. The first, the challenge to an act addressed to the applicant, is not new and perfectly straightforward. Plenty of examples will be found in Chapter 16, for Commission Decisions in the field of competition law are regularly challenged by their addressees. It needs no further discussion in this chapter. The second, a challenge to an act which is of direct and individual concern to the applicant, is in part new and subject to some interpretative difficulty. First direct concern, and then individual concern, are considered in the next two sub-sections. The third, a challenge to a regulatory act which is of direct concern to the applicant and does not entail implementing measures, is a wholly new Lisbon insertion and troublingly ambiguous in its scope. It is examined in sub-section E (p. 200).

Case law elucidates the nature of the standing rules and accordingly, in reading older texts, numerical confusion must be resolutely avoided. What is now Article 263(4) TFEU was Article 230(4) EC after the entry into force of the Amsterdam Treaty in 1999 and before the entry into force of the Lisbon Treaty in 2009; it was Article 173(4) from Maastricht (1993) until Amsterdam (1999); and before Maastricht it was Article 173(2). It should also be added at this point that since 1994 jurisdiction to hear applications brought by natural or legal persons has belonged with the Court of First Instance, which has been called the General Court since the entry into force of the Lisbon Treaty in December 2009.

C: Direct concern

Under Article 263(4) showing 'direct concern' is a pre-condition in showing standing to challenge two distinct types of act: the act which is of direct and individual concern to the applicant and the regulatory act which is of direct concern to the applicant and does not entail implementing measures. What is at stake is showing the existence of a direct causal link between the challenged EU act and the impact on the applicant. There now follows pre-Lisbon case law which interprets the meaning of 'direct concern': the concept is to be understood post-Lisbon in the same way it was understood pre-Lisbon (Case C-583/11P *Inuit Tapiriit Kanatami* judgment of 3 October 2013 paras 54–56, 70).

International Fruit Company v *Commission* (Cases 41–44/70)

[1971] ECR 411, Court of Justice of the European Communities

[23] . . .it is clear from the system introduced by Regulation No 459/70, and particularly from Article 2(2) thereof, that the Decision on the grant of import licences is a matter for the Commission.

[24] According to this provision, the Commission alone is competent to assess the economic situation in the light of which the grant of import licences must be justified.

[25] Article 1(2) of Regulation No 459/70, by providing that 'the Member States shall in accordance with the conditions laid down in Article 2, issue the licence to any interested party applying for it', makes it clear that the national authorities do not enjoy any discretion in the matter of the issue of licences and the conditions on which applications by the parties concerned should be granted.

[26] The duty of such authorities is merely to collect the data necessary in order that the Commission may take its Decision in accordance with Article 2(2) of that Regulation, and subsequently adopt the national measures needed to give effect to that Decision.

[27] In these circumstances as far as the interested parties are concerned, the issue of or refusal to issue the import licences must be bound up with this Decision.

[28] The measure whereby the Commission decides on the issues of the import licences thus directly affects the legal position of the parties concerned.

[29] The applications thus fulfil the requirements of the second paragraph of Article 173 of the Treaty [now Article 263(4) TFEU], and are therefore admissible.

NOTE: Typically, the insertion of a discretionary power vested by EU legislation in national authorities will preclude a direct challenge to the EU act lying in the background which establishes the general system.

Municipality of Differdange v *Commission* (Case 222/83)

[1984] ECR 2889, Court of Justice of the European Communities

The contested act was addressed by the Commission to Luxembourg. It authorized Luxembourg to grant aids to steel firms, provided they undertook reductions in capacity. The applicant municipality argued it was directly (and individually) concerned by the Commission's Decision on the following grounds:

[5] . . .Although the contested decision is addressed to the Grand Duchy of Luxembourg it is, from two points of view, of direct and individual concern to the applicants within the meaning of the second paragraph of Article 173 of the EEC Treaty [now Article 263(4) TFEU]. In the first place the reduction of production capacity and the closure of factories located in their municipal territory results, they claim, in a reduction of the yield from local taxes. In the second place, they contend that according to a principle of administrative law known to several Member States, which also applies in Community law, the interests of the inhabitants of a municipality and the interests of the undertakings established in the municipal territory must be regarded as the municipalities' own interests.

The Court found the applicant had no standing under the ECSC Treaty and turned to the EEC rules as they applied at the time:

[9] With regard, secondly, to the admissibility of the action under the EEC Treaty it must be recalled that the second paragraph of Article 173 of the Treaty makes the admissibility of an action brought by a natural or legal person other than the person to whom a Council or Commission Decision is addressed, for a declaration that the measure in question is void, subject to the requirement that the contested Decision is of direct and individual concern to him. The purpose of that provision is to ensure that legal protection is also available to a person who, whilst not the person to whom the contested measure is addressed, is in fact affected by it in the same way as is the addressee.

[10] In this case the contested measure, which is addressed to the Grand Duchy of Luxembourg, authorises it to grant certain aids to the undertakings named therein provided that they reduce their production capacity by a specified amount. However, it neither identifies the establishments in which the production must be reduced or terminated nor the factories which must be closed as a result of the termination of production. In addition, the Decision states that the Commission was to be notified of the closure dates only by 31 January 1984 so that the undertakings affected were free until that date to fix, where necessary with the agreement of the Luxembourg Government, the detailed rules for the restructuring necessary to comply with the conditions laid down in the Decision.

[11] That conclusion is, moreover, confirmed by Article 2 of the Decision according to which the capacity reductions may also be carried out by other undertakings.

[12] It follows that the contested Decision left to the national authorities and undertakings concerned such a margin of discretion with regard to the manner of its implementation and in particular with regard to the choice of the factories to be closed, that the Decision cannot be regarded as being of direct and individual concern to the municipalities with which the undertakings affected, by virtue of the location of their factories, are connected.

[13] Since the action is therefore inadmissible also to the extent to which it is based on the provisions of the EEC Treaty, it must be dismissed.

NOTE: Notice that where the intervention of the national authorities prevents a direct action against the EU act under what is now Article 263 TFEU, it may instead be possible to challenge the acts of the national authorities at national level, p. 217. Indirectly this may permit a challenge to the EU act. Here, then, is a further example of the construction of a complete system of remedies through the interrelation of the several Treaty provisions. This structure will become clearer once the material in this chapter is fully understood.

D: Individual concern

The phrase 'individual concern' is already familiar from the extract from *Municipality of Differdange* (Case 222/83). It forms the second pre-condition confronting the applicant wishing to attack an act 'of direct and individual concern' pursuant to Article 263(4) TFEU. The requirement of individual concern has always been a pre-condition for an application for annulment brought by a private party. Pre-Lisbon there were also rules governing the type of act that could be challenged: in particular, a Decision or a Decision in the form of a Regulation could be attacked, but not a true Regulation. This requirement is now abandoned. Post-Lisbon any 'act' that is of direct and individual concern is open to challenge. So the pre-Lisbon case law deals with a differently worded test. The older case law still helps to appreciate how 'individual concern' was used to filter out applicants judged to have an inadequate interest in the measure under attack, and the Court has no intention to adjust its approach to identifying 'individual concern' post-Lisbon (Case C-583/11P *Inuit Tapiriit Kanatami* judgment of 3 October 2013 paras 54–56, 70). The problem of defining 'individual concern' has long been addressed in a string of cases arising out of *general* market regulation which adversely affects *individual* firms.

Plaumann v *Commission* (Case 25/62)

[1963] ECR 95, Court of Justice of the European Communities

Plaumann was a German importer of clementines. In importing clementines from third world countries outside the Community (as it then was), it had to pay a customs duty of 13 per cent. This sum was due under the Common Customs Tariff, part of the uniform trade policy which the EU presents to the wider world. The German Government asked the Commission to authorize it to levy only 10 per cent duty. The Commission refused. That refusal became the act challenged by Plaumann. No doubt Plaumann was prejudiced by it. But could it challenge it before the Court given the limitations contained in what was then Article 173(2) EEC, now Article 263(4) TFEU?

ADMISSIBILITY

Under the second paragraph of Article 173 of the EEC Treaty 'any natural or legal person may . . . institute proceedings against a decision . . . which, although in the form of . . . a decision addressed to another person, is of direct and individual concern to the former'. The defendant contends that the words 'other person' in this paragraph do not refer to Member States in their capacity as sovereign authorities and that individuals may not therefore bring an action for annulment against the decisions of the Commission or of the Council addressed to Member States.

However the second paragraph of Article 173 does allow an individual to bring an action against decisions addressed to 'another person' which are of direct and individual concern to the former, but this Article neither defines nor limits the scope of these words. The words and the natural meaning of this provision justify the broadest interpretation. Moreover provisions of the Treaty regarding the right of interested parties to bring an action must not be interpreted restrictively. Therefore, the Treaty being silent on the point, a limitation in this respect may not be presumed.

It follows that the defendant's argument cannot be regarded as well founded.

The defendant further contends that the contested decision is by its very nature a regulation in the form of an individual decision and therefore action against it is no more available to individuals than in the case of legislative measures of general application.

It follows however from Articles 189 and 191 of the EEC Treaty that decisions are characterized by the limited number of persons to whom they are addressed. In order to determine whether or not a measure constitutes a decision one must enquire whether that measure concerns specific persons. The contested Decision was addressed to the government of the Federal Republic of Germany and refuses to grant it authorisation for the partial suspension of customs duties on certain products imported from third countries. Therefore the contested measure must be regarded as a decision referring to a particular person and binding that person alone.

Under the second paragraph of Article 173 of the Treaty private individuals may institute proceedings for annulment against decisions which, although addressed to another person, are of direct and individual concern to them, but in the present case the defendant denies that the contested decision is of direct and individual concern to the applicant.

It is appropriate in the first place to examine whether the second requirement of admissibility is fulfilled because, if the applicant is not individually concerned by the decision, it becomes unnecessary to enquire whether he is directly concerned.

Persons other than those to whom a decision is addressed may only claim to be individually concerned if that decision affects them by reason of certain attributes which are peculiar to them or by reason of circumstances in which they are differentiated from all other persons and by virtue of these factors distinguishes them individually just as in the case of the person addressed. In the present case the applicant is affected by the disputed Decision as an importer of clementines, that is to say, by reason of a commercial activity which may at any time be practised by any person and is not therefore such as to distinguish the applicant in relation to the contested Decision as in the case of the addressee.

For these reasons the present action for annulment must be declared inadmissible.

NOTE: A string of cases have been decided in similar fashion, to the detriment of the applicant.

***Calpak SpA* v *Commission* (Cases 789 and 790/79)**

[1980] ECR 1949, Court of Justice of the European Communities

The applicant, an Italian firm, sought annulment under Article 173 of the EC Treaty (now, after amendment, Article 263 TFEU) of Regulations governing the grant of production aid for Williams pears preserved in syrup. It observed that an identifiable class of producers, including the applicant itself, was affected by the measure. It added that, even within that group it was especially prejudiced, because the Commission's aid was fixed according to production in 1978/79 when Italian production was unusually low. *Plaumann* was a Decision addressed to another; here is a prima facie Regulation. The issue, however, is the same, and post-Lisbon it is in any event the sole issue; does the applicant have individual concern in the matter? The Court first explains the Commission's view and then disposes of the application.

[6] The Commission's main contention is that as the disputed provisions were adopted in the form of regulations their annulment may only be sought if their content shows them to be, in fact, decisions. But in the Commission's view the provisions in question, which lay down rules of general application, are truly in the nature of regulations within the meaning of Article 189 of the Treaty. By selecting the 1978/79 marketing year as the reference period the Commission's intention was to limit and stabilize production at a level as low as that of that year. It is said to be possible, but certainly not indefensible that such a restriction has a greater incidence upon marginal producers such as the applicants than, for example, upon co-operatives, but that does not mean that the applicants are individually concerned within the meaning of the second paragraph of Article 173, which hypothesis the Commission denies in any case.

[7] The second paragraph of Article 173 empowers individuals to contest, *inter alia*, any decision which, although in the form of a regulation, is of direct and individual concern to them. The objective of that provision is in particular to prevent the Community institutions from being in a position, merely by choosing the form of a regulation, to exclude an application by an individual against a decision which concerns him directly and individually; it therefore stipulates that the choice of form cannot change the nature of the measure.

[8] By virtue of the second paragraph of Article 189 of the Treaty the criterion for distinguishing between a regulation and a decision is whether the measure at issue is of general application or not. As the amendment to Regulation No 1530/78 made by Article 1(3) of Regulation No 1732/79 concerning the information to be submitted in support of the application for aid is merely the natural consequence of the limitation imposed by Article 1 of Regulation No 1731/79, consideration need only be given to the nature of the latter provision.

[9] A provision which limits the granting of production aid for all producers in respect of a particular product to a uniform percentage of the quantity produced by them during a uniform preceding period is by nature a

measure of general application within the meaning of Article 189 of the Treaty. In fact the measure applies to objectively determined situations and produces legal effects with regard to categories of persons described in a generalized and abstract manner. The nature of the measure as a regulation is not called in question by the mere fact that it is possible to determine the number or even the identity of the producers to be granted the aid which is limited thereby.

[10] Nor is the fact that the choice of reference period is particularly important for the applicants, whose production is subject to considerable variation from one marketing year to another as a result of their own programme of production, sufficient to entitle them to an individual remedy. Moreover, the applicants have not established the existence of circumstances such as to justify describing that choice – the conformity of which with the Council's regulations, and especially with the basic regulation, is only relevant to the substantive issues of the case – as a decision adopted specifically in relation to them and, as such, entitling them to institute proceedings under the second paragraph of Article 173.

[11] It follows that the objection raised by the Commission must be accepted as regards the applications for the annulment of the provisions in the two regulations in question.

The action was dismissed as inadmissible.

***Union Deutsche Lebensmittelwerke* v *Commission* (Case 97/85)**

[1987] ECR 2265, Court of Justice of the European Communities

By a Decision addressed to Germany, the Commission authorized a scheme for selling cheap butter for a short period on the West Berlin market. The object was market research into consumer demand for butter. However, promoting butter hurt sales of margarine. The applicant was a German margarine producer active on the Berlin market. It sought annulment of the Decision addressed to Germany.

[9] It should be noted that, according to the second paragraph of Article 173 of the EEC Treaty, proceedings instituted by a natural or legal person against a decision addressed to another person are admissible only if that decision is of direct and individual concern to the applicant.

[10] The Court has consistently held, since its judgment of 15 July 1963 in Case 25/62 *Plaumann* [1963] ECR 95, that a decision addressed to a Member State is of direct and individual concern to natural or legal persons only if that decision affects them by reason of certain attributes which are peculiar to them, or by reason of circumstances in which they are differentiated from all other persons, and by virtue of these factors distinguishes them individually just as in the case of the person addressed.

[11] In this case it must be stated that the contested decision does not apply to a closed circle of persons who were known at the time of its adoption and whose rights the Commission intended to regulate. Although the contested decision affects the applicants, that is only because of the effects it produces on their position on the market. In that regard, the decision is of concern to the applicants just as it was to any other person supplying margarine on the West Berlin market while the contested operation was in progress, and it is not therefore of individual concern to them for the purposes of the second paragraph of Article 173 of the EEC Treaty.

[12] The applicants' argument to the effect that this application should be declared admissible so as to enable them to enjoy full legal protection must be rejected. It must be pointed out that, in support of an action challenging a national measure implementing a Community decision, the applicant may plead the illegality of that decision and thereby require the national court to adjudicate on all the allegations formulated in that respect, if necessary after making a reference to the Court of Justice for a ruling on the validity of the decision in question. The fact that the national court is empowered to determine which questions it intends to submit to the Court is an inherent feature of the system of means of redress established by the Treaty and is not therefore an argument which is capable of justifying a broad interpretation of the conditions of admissibility laid down in the second paragraph of Article 173 of the EEC Treaty.

NOTE: Paragraph 12 of the judgment indicates that this was not the only avenue of redress open to the applicant. The telling of the tale of the Berlin butter will be resumed later in this chapter. It provides a fine illustration of the pattern of interrelation of the remedies in the system of judicial protection, mentioned in the introduction to this chapter.

Note that the Court never even reaches the merits of the challenge to the contested act in these cases.

These decisions indicate that the issue of individual concern and the issue whether the measure is a true Regulation or in reality a Decision are conceptually similar. From December 2009, the entry into force of the Lisbon Treaty, it is the former that matters to the exclusion of the latter.

The next case arose from the enforcement of the competition rules. They will be examined in Chapter 16. It clearly involves a Decision addressed to a person other than the applicant, and the Court focuses on the problem of individual concern.

***Metro-SB-Grossmärkte GmbH & Co. KG* v *Commission* (Case 26/76)**

[1977] ECR 1875, Court of Justice of the European Communities

Metro complained to the Commission under Article 3(2) of Regulation 17/62 about SABA's distributorship network. (This has been replaced by Regulation 1/2003 but the system of complaint is retained by Article 7 Reg 1/2003, Chapter 16): Metro had been excluded from it, and suggested that SABA was acting in violation of the Treaty competition rules. Contrary to Metro's hopes, the Commission ruled that some terms of SABA's system did not violate Article 85(1) of the EC Treaty (now Article 101(1) TFEU); others were exemptable under Article 85(3) (now Article 101(3) TFEU, see Chapter 16).) That ruling became the contested act. Metro wished to challenge the Decision addressed to SABA giving it a clean bill of health.

> ... [T]he contested decision was adopted in particular as the result of a complaint submitted by Metro and that it relates to the provisions of SABA's distribution system, on which SABA relied and continues to rely as against Metro in order to justify its refusal to sell to the latter or to appoint it as a wholesaler, and which the applicant had for this reason impugned in its complaint.
>
> It is in the interests of a satisfactory administration of justice and of the proper application of Articles 85 and 86 that natural or legal persons who are entitled, pursuant to Article 3(2)(b) of Regulation No 17, to request the Commission to find an infringement of Articles 85 and 86 should be able, if their request is not complied with either wholly or in part, to institute proceedings in order to protect their legitimate interests.
>
> In those circumstances the applicant must be considered to be directly and individually concerned, within the meaning of the second paragraph of Article 173 [now 263(4) TFEU], by the contested decision and the application is accordingly admissible.

NOTE: There is a long-standing debate about whether the Court's interpretation of 'individual concern' is too restrictive. That debate lives on after the entry into force of the Lisbon Treaty, which retains the requirement as a filter. But well in advance of Lisbon the Court hinted at a more liberal approach, at least in relation to some manifestations of general market regulation.

***Codorniu SA* v *Council* (Case C-309/89)**

[1994] ECR I-1853, Court of Justice of the European Communities

Codorniu, a Spanish producer of sparkling wines, sought to annul a provision in Council Regulation 2045/89, amending Regulation 3309/85, laying down general rules for the description and presentation of sparkling wines. The measure reserved the term *crémant* for certain quality sparkling wines manufactured in France and Luxembourg. It was explained in the recitals to the Regulation that this protected traditional descriptions used in those two countries. Codorniu had held and, since 1924, had used the Spanish trade mark *Gran Crémant de Codorniu* to designate one of its wines. It wished to challenge the Regulation. The Council objected to the admissibility of the application.

> [14] In support of its objection of inadmissibility the Council states that it did not adopt the contested provision on the basis of the circumstances peculiar to certain producers but on the basis of a choice of wine-marketing policy in relation to a particular product. The contested provision reserves the use of the term

'crémant' to quality sparkling wines psr manufactured under specific conditions in certain Member States. It thus constitutes a measure applicable to an objectively determined situation which has legal effects in respect of categories of persons considered in a general and abstract manner.

[15] According to the Council, Codorniu is concerned by the contested provision only in its capacity as a producer of quality sparkling wine psr using the term 'crémant', like any other producer in an identical situation. Even if when that provision was adopted the number or identity of producers of sparkling wines using the term 'crémant' could theoretically be determined, the measure in question remains essentially a regulation inasmuch as it applies on the basis of an objective situation of law or fact defined by the measure in relation to its objective.

[16] Codorniu alleges that the contested provision is in reality a decision adopted in the guise of a regulation. It has no general scope but affects a well-determined class of producers which cannot be altered. Such producers are those who on 1 September 1989 traditionally designated their sparkling wines with the term 'crémant'. For that class the contested provision has no general scope. Furthermore, the direct result of the contested provision will be to prevent Codorniu from using the term 'Gran Cremant' which will involve a loss of 38% of its turnover. The effect of that damage is to distinguish it, within the meaning of the second paragraph of Article 173 of the Treaty, from any other trader. Codorniu alleges that the Court has already recognized the admissibility of an action for annulment brought by a natural or legal person against a regulation in such circumstances (see the judgment in Case C-358/89 *Extramet Industrie* v *Council* [1991] ECR I-2501).

[17] Under the second paragraph of Article 173 of the Treaty the institution of proceedings by a natural or legal person for a declaration that a regulation is void is subject to the condition that the provisions of the regulation at issue in the proceedings constitute in reality a decision of direct and individual concern to that person.

[18] As the Court has already held, the general applicability, and thus the legislative nature, of a measure is not called in question by the fact that it is possible to determine more or less exactly the number or even the identity of the persons to whom it applies at any given time, as long as it is established that it applies to them by virtue of an objective legal or factual situation defined by the measure in question in relation to its purpose (see most recently the judgment in Case C-298/89 *Gibraltar* v *Council* [1993] ECR I-3605, paragraph 17).

[19] Although it is true that according to the criteria in the second paragraph of Article 173 of the Treaty the contested provision is, by nature and by virtue of its sphere of application, of a legislative nature in that it applies to the traders concerned in general, that does not prevent it from being of individual concern to some of them.

[20] Natural or legal persons may claim that a contested provision is of individual concern to them only if it affects them by reason of certain attributes which are peculiar to them or by reason of circumstances in which they are differentiated from all other persons (see the judgment in Case 25/62 *Plaumann* v *Commission* [1963] ECR 95).

[21] Codorniu registered the graphic trade mark 'Gran Cremant de Codorniu' in Spain in 1924 and traditionally used that mark both before and after registration. By reserving the right to use the term 'crémant' to French and Luxembourg producers, the contested provision prevents Codorniu from using its graphic trade mark.

[22] It follows that Codorniu has established the existence of a situation which from the point of view of the contested provision differentiates it from all other traders.

[23] It follows that the objection of inadmissibility put forward by the Council must be dismissed.

NOTE: The Court proceeded to determine that the measure's discrimination between producers from different countries lacked objective justification. The contested provision was accordingly declared void.

The important statement at para 19 of the ruling in *Codorniu*, that a measure may be 'of a legislative nature in that it applies to the traders concerned in general' yet simultaneously of 'individual concern to some of them', is to an extent a precursor to the Lisbon Treaty's reforms to Article 263(4) TFEU. The nature of the act, Regulation or Decision, no longer matters post-Lisbon: but this was already the direction taken by this case law. What *does* matter is whether the act is of individual concern to the applicant. In *Codorniu* there were special factors affecting the applicant's position, most notably its property right in the trade mark, which were capable of being used as a basis for limiting the decision's contribution to a potential liberalization of the approach taken to finding 'individual concern'. After *Codorniu* the development of the law shifted initially to the Court of First Instance (today, the General Court) to which jurisdiction to hear such cases had been transferred (p. 190). Its rulings regularly cited para 19 of *Codorniu*, to the effect that a measure may be 'of a legislative nature in that it applies to the traders concerned in general' yet simultaneously of 'individual concern to some of them', yet applicants consistently found it difficult to succeed in bringing their situation within the charmed circle of 'individual concern'.

Terres Rouges v *Commission* (Case T-47/95)

[1997] ECR II-481, Court of First Instance of the European Communities

Challenge was directed at Regulation 3224/94, which amended Regulation 404/93 and in doing so significantly reduced the tariff quota entitlement for non-traditional ACP (African, Caribbean, and Pacific) bananas from Côte d'Ivoire (Ivory Coast). The applicants submitted that they, as importers into the EU of 70 per cent of the banana production of Côte d'Ivoire, would be prejudiced by the downwards adjustment of the figure and that they were therefore directly and individually concerned.

[41] In this case the contested regulation does not have any features which would enable it to be classed as a decision taken in the form of a regulation. It is drafted in general and abstract terms and is applicable in all the Member States, without any regard being had to the situation of individual producers. It is designed to amend the arrangements for the import of bananas laid down by Regulation No 404/93 in order to adapt them to the changes introduced by the Framework Agreement entered into with the Latin American countries concerned.

[42] It follows that the contested regulation applies to situations which have been determined objectively and has legal effects with respect to a category of persons viewed in a general and abstract manner.

[43] As regards the question whether the applicants are individually concerned by the contested regulation, it is settled law that, in certain circumstances, even a legislative measure applying to the traders concerned in general may concern some of them individually (judgments in Case C-358/89 *Extramet Industrie* v *Council* [1991] ECR I-2501, paragraph 13, and Case C-309/89 *Codorniu* v *Council* [1994] ECR I-1853, paragraph 19. . . . In such circumstances, a Community measure could be of a legislative nature and, at the same time, in the nature of a decision *vis-à-vis* some of the traders concerned . . .

[44] However, the possibility of determining more or less precisely the number or even the identity of the persons to whom a measure applies by no means implies that it must be regarded as being of individual concern to them (Case 123/77 *UNICME* v *Council* [1978] ECR 845, paragraph 16).

[45] In that regard, the legislative provisions relevant to this dispute should be borne in mind. Article 19 of Regulation No 404/93 provides that the tariff quota is to be opened as to 66.5% for the category of operators who marketed third-country and/or non-traditional ACP bananas (category A); as to 30% for the category of operators who marketed Community and/or traditional ACP bananas (category B); and as to 3.5% for the category of operators established in the Community who started marketing bananas other than Community and/or traditional ACP bananas from 1992 (category C). Supplementary criteria to be met by operators are to be laid down in accordance with the procedure provided for in Article 27 of the regulation. Operators who satisfy those conditions and who are granted import licences by the competent authorities of the relevant Member State may import third-country or non-traditional ACP bananas within the tariff quota, whatever category of importer they fall within.

[46] In addition, the Court of Justice has held that the purpose of Articles 18 and 19 of Regulation No 404/93 is to establish arrangements for trade in bananas with third countries and a mechanism for the allocation of the tariff quota between categories of traders defined according to objective criteria. Those provisions accordingly apply to situations which have been determined objectively and have legal effects as regards categories of persons viewed in a general and abstract manner. It follows that the contested measure is of concern to the applicants only in their objective capacity as traders engaged in the marketing of bananas from third countries in the same way as any other trader in an identical position (order of 21 June 1993 in Case C-276/93 *Chiquita Banana Company and Others* v *Council* [1993] ECR I-3345, paragraphs 10, 11 and 12).

[47] Regulation No 3224/94 admittedly restricted the quantity of non-traditional ACP bananas that Côte d'Ivoire could export within the tariff quota. However, under Regulation No 404/93 (see paragraph 45 of this judgment), all importers in categories A, B and C are entitled to import bananas from Côte d'Ivoire. Regulation No 3224/94 thus affects every importer wishing to import bananas from Côte d'Ivoire and the fact that the applicants currently import a large proportion of Côte d'Ivoire's bananas does not amount to circumstances differentiating them from other importers.

[48] The applicants' argument that Regulation No 3224/94 fundamentally altered the rights conferred by Regulation No 404/93 must be rejected.

[49] It is based on the premise that, before Regulation No 3224/94 was adopted, Côte d'Ivoire could have placed approximately 50,000 tonnes of non-traditional ACP bananas on the Community market in addition to the 155,000 tonnes of traditional ACP bananas allocated to it by Regulation No 404/93 (see paragraphs 34 to 38 of this judgment).

[50] First, Regulation No 3224/94 does not in any way preclude the applicants from importing into the Community traditional ACP bananas from Côte d'Ivoire. They can still import 70%, or even more, of the 155,000 tonnes of traditional ACP bananas allocated to that country.

[51] Secondly, as the Commission stated at the hearing and the applicants did not dispute, the total amount of traditional ACP and non-traditional ACP bananas exported from Côte d'Ivoire in 1993 and 1994 after the new arrangements had been established by Regulation No 404/93 did not exceed 160,000 tonnes per year. Those exports did not therefore exceed the quantity of 162,500 tonnes constituted by the reserve of 155,000 tonnes of traditional ACP bananas and the share of 7,500 tonnes of non-traditional ACP bananas reserved for Côte d'Ivoire by Regulation No 3224/94. The truth is that the figure of 50,000 tonnes quoted by the applicants is only an estimate of the potential production of Côte d'Ivoire's plantations and does not refer to current exports. Contrary to the applicants' submissions, therefore, their position has not in actual fact been affected by the adoption of Regulation No 3224/94.

The Court of First Instance concluded that Regulation 3224/94 concerned the applicants only in their objective capacity as importers of third-country bananas, and that their legal position was not affected by circumstances in which they were differentiated from the other traders in the same position. It was therefore not of individual concern to them. It added that under Regulation 404/93 importers of third-country bananas must obtain an import licence from the authorities of a Member State, and that only decisions on whether or not to grant a licence affect the applicants directly. The quota allocated by Regulation 3224/94 was therefore not capable of affecting the applicants' legal position directly, as was required under Article 173(4) of the EC Treaty (now, after amendment, Article 263(4) TFEU)). The Court dismissed the application as inadmissible after commenting:

[59] Nor have the applicants established that in appropriate circumstances it would be impossible for them to challenge the validity of Regulation No 3224/94 before a national court, for example in an action brought against a refusal by the competent national authorities to issue them with import licences for non-traditional ACP bananas from Côte d'Ivoire, and to request the national court to seek a preliminary ruling in that regard from the Court of Justice pursuant to Article 177 [now 267] of the Treaty.

NOTE: See similarly Case T-138/98 *ACAV* v *Council* [2000] ECR II-341. The next case also offered no joy to the private applicants.

Stichting Greenpeace Council (Greenpeace International) and Others v *Commission* (Case C-321/95 P)

[1998] ECR I-1651, Court of Justice of the European Communities

In Case T-585/93 *Greenpeace and Others* v *Commission* [1995] ECR II-2205, the CFI (now, post-Lisbon, the General Court) held inadmissible an action for the annulment of a Commission decision to allocate funds to Spain within the framework of the European

Regional Development Fund for the construction of two power stations in the Canary Islands. It was alleged that EU rules on environmental protection had been neglected, but the CFI adhered to existing case law and treated the applicants, who included associations concerned with the protection of the environment, as lacking any distinct interest in the matter of the type necessary to establish 'individual concern' within the meaning of Article 173 of the EC Treaty (now, after amendment, Article 263 TFEU). On appeal to the Court of Justice, the applicants observed *inter alia* that the CFI's approach 'creates a legal vacuum in ensuring compliance with Community environmental legislation, since in this area the interests are, by their very nature, common and shared, and the rights relating to those interests are liable to be held by a potentially large number of individuals so that there could never be a closed class of applicants satisfying the criteria adopted by the Court of First Instance'. The Court of Justice was then pressed to take the lead in relaxing the strict approach. The Court's 'Findings' occupy no more than nine short paragraphs.

FINDINGS OF THE COURT

27. The interpretation of the fourth paragraph of Article 173 of the Treaty that the Court of First Instance applied in concluding that the appellants did not have *locus standi* is consonant with the settled case law of the Court of Justice.

28. As far as natural persons are concerned, it follows from the case-law, cited at both paragraph 48 of the contested order and at paragraph 7 of this judgment, that where, as in the present case, the specific situation of the applicant was not taken into consideration in the adoption of the act, which concerns him in a general and abstract fashion and, in fact, like any other person in the same situation, the applicant is not individually concerned by the act.

29. The same applies to associations which claim to have *locus standi* on the basis of the fact that the persons whom they represent are individually concerned by the contested decision. For the reasons given in the preceding paragraph, that is not the case.

30. In appraising the appellants' arguments purporting to demonstrate that the case-law of the Court of Justice, as applied by the Court of First Instance, takes no account of the nature and specific characteristics of the environmental interests underpinning their action, it should be emphasised that it is the decision to build the two power stations in question which is liable to affect the environmental rights arising under Directive 85/337 that the appellants seek to invoke.

31. In those circumstances, the contested decision, which concerns the Community financing of those power stations, can affect those rights only indirectly.

32. As regards the appellants' argument that application of the Court's case-law would mean that, in the present case, the rights which they derive from Directive 85/337 would have no effective judicial protection at all, it must be noted that, as is clear from the fi le, Greenpeace brought proceedings before the national courts challenging the administrative authorizations issued to Unelco concerning the construction of those power stations. TEA and CIC also lodged appeals against CUMAC's declaration of environmental impact relating to the two construction projects (see paragraphs 6 and 7 of the contested order, reproduced at paragraph 2 of this judgment).

33. Although the subject-matter of those proceedings and of the action brought before the Court of First Instance is different, both actions are based on the same rights afforded to individuals by Directive 85/337, so that in the circumstances of the present case those rights are fully protected by the national courts which may, if need be, refer a question to this Court for a preliminary ruling under Article 177 of the Treaty [now 267].

34. The Court of First Instance did not therefore err in law in determining the question of the appellants' *locus standi* in the light of the criteria developed by the Court of Justice in the case law set out at paragraph 7 of this judgment.

35. In those circumstances the appeal must be dismissed.

NOTE: Although the applicants in *Greenpeace* referred to *Codorniu* in urging that a restrictive interpretation of Article 173 EC (now, after amendment, Article 263 TFEU) be eschewed, it will be noted that the Court made no direct mention of it, or any other decision, in these 'Findings'. Moreover, although environmental cases may in principle be decided according to generally applicable rules of law, the dispersed impact of acts affecting the environment creates special problems in determining standing (especially where, as in *Greenpeace*, both national and EU acts are involved). Consequently, the outcome of such cases may not be indicative of trends in the wider arena of challenge to forms of economic regulation. However, even with those *caveats*, *Greenpeace*, in its style and brevity, offered no encouragement to those seeking a hint that the Court of Justice might be inclined to issue any corrective to the CFI's doggedly restrictive reading of *Codorniu*.

■ **QUESTION**

Could decisions by EU institutions affecting the environment ever be of individual concern to individuals or groups concerned to secure protection of the environment?

NOTE: The model developed by the Court envisages two principal routes for the judicial protection of parties whose interests are prejudiced by the adoption of EU acts which they wish to challenge as unlawful. The first takes an applicant to Luxembourg, and it is the application for annulment created by Article 263 TFEU. The second is located in the ordinary courts of the Member States, where a challenge may be brought to a national act within which the question of the validity of a parent EU act may be raised. A national court may not rule the EU act invalid, but rather must follow the route to Luxembourg created by the Article 267 preliminary reference procedure, considered more fully in this context at p. 217. Accordingly one may interpret this model as a recognition by the Court that although the standing rules under Article 263 impose severe restrictions on the access of private parties to the courts in Luxembourg, the availability of an action at national level supplemented by the Article 267 preliminary reference procedure offers compensation. The latter secures judicial protection in circumstances where it is denied under the former. In this vein, it is notable that in *Terres Rouges* (Case T-47/95, p. 197) and in *Greenpeace* (Case C-321/95P, p. 198) a finding of inadmissibility under Article 263(4) was accompanied by comment on the availability of judicial protection before national courts able to make preliminary references.

This seems neat. However, as the next sub-section explores, there is a flaw in this system. And it has been addressed – albeit perhaps not satisfactorily – by the Lisbon Treaty.

E. Challenging a 'regulatory act'

The third of the three types of act which may be attacked by the non-privileged applicant pursuant to Article 263(4), set out at p. 187, is the regulatory act which is of direct concern to the applicant and does not entail implementing measures. This type of act is entirely novel as a target of judicial review. It is an innovation of the Lisbon Treaty. The condition of 'direct concern' is well understood, and was examined at p. 190. But the 'regulatory act' on which this basis for review depends is – extraordinarily – not defined anywhere in the Treaty. To understand what it may cover, and to grasp why this extension was made, it is necessary briefly to identify the gap in legal protection that was supposed to exist prior to the entry into force of the Lisbon Treaty.

The classic problem case is the following. An EU Regulation prejudices the individual's position. He or she cannot challenge its validity directly by resort to Article 263 TFEU because it is not addressed to him or her, nor is it of direct and individual concern. But nor can he or she challenge the act indirectly by bringing proceedings against implementing measures adopted at national level because it is characteristic of a Regulation that *there are no implementing measures at national level* (Chapter 3, p. 78). So here the neat collaborative role involving Articles 263 and 267 TFEU sketched in the final paragraph of the previous sub-section breaks down. The individual appears to be subject to the EU act, yet has no access to a court to contest its validity.

The question of principle about how this apparent gap in judicial protection should be filled, and by whom, was addressed in two vigorously discussed cases decided in the first half of the last decade. The CFI (today, the General Court) put forward an aggressive agenda of reform. In *Jégo-Quéré et Cie SA* v *Commission* (Case T-177/01) [2002] ECR II-2365 it found that the right to an effective remedy, drawn *inter alia* from the Charter of Fundamental Rights (Chapter 2, p. 58), was inadequately protected by the model of judicial protection developed over decades since *Plaumann* (Case 25/62 p. 192). Referring to the Treaty having established a complete system of legal remedies and procedures designed to permit review of the legality of measures adopted by the EU's institutions, it chose to find that this particular problem case of the unimplemented Regulation should after all be treated as engaging the 'individual concern' of the applicant. It was reviewable. But the Court of Justice was not persuaded. Shortly afterwards in *Uniónde Pequeños Agricultores ('UPA')* v *Council of the European Union* (Case C-50/00P) [2002] ECR I-6677 the Court of Justice too recited the importance of the complete system of legal remedies and procedures designed to ensure judicial review of the legality of acts of the institutions. But as far as protection available initially at national level was concerned it found that it was for the Member States to establish a system of legal remedies and procedures which would ensure respect for the right to effective judicial protection. At EU level the Court could not do more: in particular, ignoring the Charter, it felt that although one could envisage a system of judicial review different from that established by the Treaty, it rested with the Member States to reform the system by amending the Treaty. Its own approach to the meaning of 'individual concern' was irrevocably fixed and it excluded finding that it existed in these particular circumstances. Accordingly – and unsurprisingly – it subsequently granted an appeal against the CFI's ambitious ruling in *Jégo-Quéré*, finding that application was after all unreviewable (*Commission* v *Jégo-Quéré* (Case C-263/02P) [2004] ECR I-3425). Subsequently the CFI was obliged to follow the lead set by the Court. It therefore refused to embrace submissions encouraging it to widen the notion of 'individual concern' by relying on the quest for effective judicial protection (e.g. in both Case T-94/04 *EEB et al.* v *Commission* [2005] ECR II-4919 and Case T-95/06 *Federacion de Cooperativas* [2008] ECR II-31 the applicants were found to have no individual concern).

Neither Court appeared entirely happy with the prevailing state of the direct action for annulment of EU acts. But whereas the Court of First Instance felt it had room to interpret 'individual concern' more generously than has been past practice in order to upgrade judicial protection, the Court of Justice felt it had no such room for manoeuvre. Improvements in the scope of protection at EU level would have to be delivered by the process of Treaty revision. And inadequacies in protection available through national procedures would have to be remedied at national level.

The reforms introduced by the Lisbon Treaty picked up both elements. Article 19(1) TEU provides that 'Member States shall provide remedies sufficient to ensure effective legal protection in the fields covered by Union law'. This is confirmation rather than innovation (see further Chapter 4, p. 104). But the addition to Article 263(4) TFEU, which provides for review of a regulatory act which is of direct concern to the applicant and does not entail implementing measures, is clearly something new. In this instance the requirement of 'individual concern' is absent. So, is the problem solved?

Perhaps. In 2010 a Commission Decision removed triclosan from the list of additives which may be used in the manufacture of plastic materials pursuant to a Directive, 2002/72. In consequence Microban, a private company, was no longer able to use triclosan in its manufacturing processes. In Case T-262/10 *Microban* v *Commission* ([2011] ECR II-7697) the General Court found admissible a challenge to that Commission

Decision (and annulled it). It found that the Commission Decision was a 'regulatory act' of direct concern to the applicant and for which there were no implementing measures. The Commission Decision would appear *not* to have been of individual concern to the applicant because the exclusion of triclosan affected all traders in the sector. So *Microban* is a case showing how the Lisbon reforms have extended the scope of judicial protection under EU law.

But there may yet be a gap in that judicial protection. Since the entry into force of the Lisbon Treaty a distinction is drawn between the legislative and the non-legislative act: legal acts adopted by legislative procedure shall constitute legislative acts (Article 289(3) TFEU). The 'regulatory act' envisaged by Article 263(4) TFEU is left undefined. If the 'regulatory act' is interpreted to mean any act of general application with legal consequences for the individual then the perceived weaknesses of the system pre-Lisbon would seem to be largely addressed (in favour, Balthasar (2010) 35 EL Rev 542). If, however, the 'regulatory act' were to be assimilated to the 'non-legislative act' then an enduring gap in legal protection even post-Lisbon would yawn, because the legislative act which is of direct concern to the applicant and which does not entail implementing measures would be immune from challenge (unless it is addressed, or of direct and individual concern, to the applicant). However, that latter interpretation is the one which has been chosen by the Court.

***Inuit Tapiriit Kanatami* v *Parliament and Council* (Case C-583/11P)**

Judgment of the Court of Justice, 3 October 2013

This was a series of applications brought by private traders for the annulment of Regulation 1007/2009 on trade in seal products (OJ 2009 L 286/36), the purpose of which was to establish harmonized (and very restrictive) rules concerning the placing on the market of seal products.

The General Court concluded that the 'regulatory act' covered all acts of general application *apart from* legislative acts (Case T-18/10 *Inuit Tapiriit Kanatami* v *Parliament and Council* [2011] ECR II-5599). The Court agreed.

[57] ... by means of the Treaty of Lisbon, there was added to the fourth paragraph of Article 263 TFEU a third limb which relaxed the conditions of admissibility of actions for annulment brought by natural and legal persons. Since the effect of that limb is that the admissibility of actions for annulment brought by natural and legal persons is not subject to the condition of individual concern, it renders possible such legal actions against 'regulatory acts' which do not entail implementing measures and are of direct concern to the applicant.

[58] As regards the concept of 'regulatory act', it is apparent from the third limb of the fourth paragraph of Article 263 TFEU that its scope is more restricted than that of the concept of 'acts' used in the first and second limbs of the fourth paragraph of Article 263 TFEU, in respect of the characterisation of the other types of measures which natural and legal persons may seek to have annulled. The former concept cannot, as the General Court held correctly in paragraph 43 of the order under appeal, refer to all acts of general application but relates to a more restricted category of such acts. To adopt an interpretation to the contrary would amount to nullifying the distinction made between the term 'acts' and 'regulatory acts' by the second and third limbs of the fourth paragraph of Article 263 TFEU.

[59] Further, it must be observed that the fourth paragraph of Article 263 TFEU reproduced in identical terms the content of Article III-365(4) of the proposed treaty establishing a Constitution for Europe. It is clear from the *travaux préparatoires* relating to that provision that while the alteration of the fourth paragraph of Article 230 EC was intended to extend the conditions of admissibility of actions for annulment in respect of natural and legal persons, the conditions of admissibility laid down in the fourth paragraph of Article 230 EC relating to legislative acts were not however to be altered. Accordingly, the use of the term 'regulatory act' in the draft amendment of that provision made it possible to identify the category of acts which might thereafter be the subject of an action for annulment under conditions less stringent than previously, while maintaining

'a restrictive approach in relation to actions by individuals against legislative acts (for which the "of direct and individual concern" condition remains applicable)' (see, inter alia, Secretariat of the European Convention, Final report of the discussion circle on the Court of Justice of 25 March 2003, CONV 636/03, paragraph 22, and Cover note from the Praesidium to the Convention of 12 May 2003, CONV 734/03, p. 20).

[60] In those circumstances, it must be held that that the purpose of the alteration to the right of natural and legal persons to institute legal proceedings, laid down in the fourth paragraph of Article 230 EC, was to enable those persons to bring, under less stringent conditions, actions for annulment of acts of general application other than legislative acts.

[61] The General Court was therefore correct to conclude that the concept of 'regulatory act' provided for in the fourth paragraph of Article 263 TFEU does not encompass legislative acts.

So this Regulation was *not* a 'regulatory act'. This interpretative reliance on the Convention and the Treaty establishing a Constitution, which was laid to rest after the French and Dutch 'no' votes in in 2005 (p. 18), will deepen the dismay of those who protested that the Lisbon Treaty was no more than a re-packaging of the Treaty establishing a constitution designed to evade the need for national referendums (except in Ireland, twice: Ch. 1): and it was repeated in Case C-274/12P *Telefónica SA v Commission* judgment of 19 December 2013. The Court then agreed with the General Court that the contested Regulation was not of direct and individual concern to the applicant. It confirmed the relevance of the pre-Lisbon case law, citing inter alia *Plaumann* (Case 25/62 p. 192). The applicants relied on Article 47 of the EU Charter of Fundamental Rights and Articles 6 and 13 of the ECHR in claiming that the General Court's approach was unlawful. But this did not impress the Court at all.

[89] . . . the appellants claim, in essence, that the interpretation adopted by the General Court of the fourth paragraph of Article 263 TFEU is in breach of Article 47 of the Charter in that it enables natural and legal persons to bring actions for annulment of European Union legislative acts solely where those acts are of direct and individual concern to them, within the meaning of the fourth paragraph of Article 263 TFEU.

[90] First, it must be recalled that judicial review of compliance with the European Union legal order is ensured, as can be seen from Article 19(1) TEU, by the Court of Justice and the courts and tribunals of the Member States (see, to that effect, Opinion of the Court 1/09 [2011] ECR I-1137, paragraph 66).

[91] Further, the European Union is a union based on the rule of law in which the acts of its institutions are subject to review of their compatibility with, in particular, the Treaties, the general principles of law and fundamental rights (see, to that effect, Case C-550/09 *E and F* [2010] ECR I-6213, paragraph 44).

[92] To that end, the FEU Treaty has established, by Articles 263 and 277, on the one hand, and Article 267, on the other, a complete system of legal remedies and procedures designed to ensure judicial review of the legality of European Union acts, and has entrusted such review to the Courts of the European Union (see Case 294/83 *Les Verts* v *Parliament* [1986] ECR 1339, paragraph 23; *Unión de Pequeños Agricultores* v *Council*, paragraph 40; *Reynolds Tobacco and Others* v *Commission*, paragraph 80; and Case C-59/11 *Association Kokopelli* [2012] ECR I-0000, paragraph 34).

[93] Accordingly, natural or legal persons who cannot, by reason of the conditions of admissibility stated in the fourth paragraph of Article 263 TFEU, challenge directly European Union acts of general application do have protection against the application to them of those acts. Where responsibility for the implementation of those acts lies with the European Union institutions, those persons are entitled to bring a direct action before the Courts of the European Union against the implementing measures under the conditions stated in the fourth paragraph of Article 263 TFEU, and to plead, pursuant to Article 277 TFEU, in support of that action, the illegality of the general act at issue. Where that implementation is a matter for the Member States, such persons may plead the invalidity of the European Union act at issue before the national courts and tribunals and cause the latter to request a preliminary ruling from the Court of Justice, pursuant to Article 267 TFEU (see, to that effect, *Les Verts* v *Parliament*, paragraph 23).

[94] In that context, it must be emphasised that, in proceedings before the national courts, individual parties have the right to challenge before the courts the legality of any decision or other national measure relative to the application to them of a European Union act of general application, by pleading the invalidity of such an act (see, to that effect, *Unión de Pequeños Agricultores* v *Council*, paragraph 42, and *E and F*, paragraph 45).

[95] It follows that requests for preliminary rulings which seek to ascertain the validity of a measure constitute, like actions for annulment, means for reviewing the legality of European Union acts (see Joined Cases C-143/88 and C-92/89 *Zuckerfabrik Süderdithmarschen and Zuckerfabrik Soest* [1991] ECR I-415, paragraph 18, and Joined Cases C-453/03, C-11/04, C-12/04 and C-194/04 *ABNA and Others* [2005] ECR I-10423, paragraph 103).

[96] In that regard, it must be borne in mind that where a national court or tribunal considers that one or more arguments for invalidity of a European Union act, put forward by the parties or, as the case may be, raised by it of its own motion, are well founded, it is incumbent upon it to stay proceedings and to make a reference to the Court for a preliminary ruling on the act's validity, the Court alone having jurisdiction to declare a European Union act invalid (Case C-344/04 *IATA and ELFAA* [2006] ECR I-403, paragraphs 27 and 30 and the case-law cited).

[97] Having regard to the protection conferred by Article 47 of the Charter, it must be observed that that article is not intended to change the system of judicial review laid down by the Treaties, and particularly the rules relating to the admissibility of direct actions brought before the Courts of the European Union, as is apparent also from the Explanation on Article 47 of the Charter, which must, in accordance with the third subparagraph of Articles 6(1) TEU and Article 52(7) of the Charter, be taken into consideration for the interpretation of the Charter (see the judgment of 22 January 2013 in Case C-283/11 *Sky Österreich* [2013] ECR I-0000, paragraph 42, and the judgment of 18 July 2013 in Case C 426/11 *Alemo-Herron and Others* [2013] ECR I-0000, paragraph 32).

[98] Accordingly, the conditions of admissibility laid down in the fourth paragraph of Article 263 TFEU must be interpreted in the light of the fundamental right to effective judicial protection, but such an interpretation cannot have the effect of setting aside the conditions expressly laid down in that Treaty (see, to that effect, *Unión de Pequeños Agricultores* v *Council*, paragraph 44, and *Commission* v *Jégo-Quéré*, paragraph 36).

[99] As regards the role of the national courts and tribunals, referred to in paragraph 90 of this judgment, it must be recalled that the national courts and tribunals, in collaboration with the Court of Justice, fulfil a duty entrusted to them both of ensuring that in the interpretation and application of the Treaties the law is observed (Opinion of the Court 1/09, paragraph 69).

[100] It is therefore for the Member States to establish a system of legal remedies and procedures which ensure respect for the fundamental right to effective judicial protection (*Unión de Pequeños Agricultores* v *Council*, paragraph 41, and *Commission* v *Jégo-Quéré*, paragraph 31).

[101] That obligation on the Member States was reaffirmed by the second subparagraph of Article 19(1) TEU, which states that Member States 'shall provide remedies sufficient to ensure effective judicial protection in the fields covered by European Union law'.

[102] In that regard, in the absence of European Union rules governing the matter, it is for the domestic legal system of each Member State to designate, with due observance of the requirements stemming from paragraphs 100 and 101 of this judgment and the principles of effectiveness and equivalence, the courts and tribunals with jurisdiction and to lay down the detailed procedural rules governing actions brought to safeguard rights which individuals derive from European Union law (see, to that effect, inter alia, Case C-268/06 *Impact* [2008] ECR I-2483, paragraph 44 and the case-law cited; Case C-118/08 *Transportes Urbanos y Servicios Generales* [2010] ECR I-635, paragraph 31; and Joined Cases C-317/08 to C-320/08 *Alassini and Others* [2010] ECR I-2213, paragraphs 47 and 61).

[103] As regards the remedies which Member States must provide, while the FEU Treaty has made it possible in a number of instances for natural and legal persons to bring a direct action, where appropriate, before the Courts of the European Union, neither the FEU Treaty nor Article 19 TEU intended to create new remedies before the national courts to ensure the observance of European Union law other than those already laid down by national law (Case C-432/05 *Unibet* [2007] ECR I-2271, paragraph 40).

> [104] The position would be otherwise only if the structure of the domestic legal system concerned were such that there was no remedy making it possible, even indirectly, to ensure respect for the rights which individuals derive from European Union law, or again if the sole means of access to a court was available to parties who were compelled to act unlawfully (see, to that effect, *Unibet*, paragraphs 41 and 64 and the case-law cited).
>
> [105] As regards the appellants' argument that the interpretation adopted by the General Court of the concept of 'regulatory act', provided for in the fourth paragraph of Article 263 TFEU, creates a gap in judicial protection, and is incompatible with Article 47 of the Charter in that its effect is that any legislative act is virtually immune to judicial review, it must be stated that the protection conferred by Article 47 of the Charter does not require that an individual should have an unconditional entitlement to bring an action for annulment of European Union legislative acts directly before the Courts of the European Union.
>
> [106] Last, neither that fundamental right nor the second subparagraph of Article 19(1) TEU require that an individual should be entitled to bring actions against such acts, as their primary subject matter, before the national courts or tribunals.

Paragraph 92 re-asserts the 'complete system' of remedies which was met in the first section of this chapter, and this extract carefully sets out the Court's current understanding of what this entails, before the Court in Luxembourg and before national courts. Note, however, that paragraphs 105–106 accept that a complete system of remedies does not mean that any and every legal act shall be open to judicial review initiated by a private party.

Judicial protection is missing where an individual is shown to be prejudiced by a legislative act which is of direct concern to them and which does not entail implementing measures. The individual must seek to influence the legislative process instead.

There are further aspects of Article 263(4) TFEU that will require judicial attention. Exactly what 'implementing measures' means is not entirely clear and will require elucidation – there are many different types of administrative procedure structured at EU level in policy terms and then in some way executed by national authorities. The point is that where the EU's regulatory act *does* entail implementing measures, the applicant may not attack it directly using Article 263 TFEU (unless it is addressed, or of direct and individual concern, to him or her). This seems to require the Court to examine national administrative practice and procedural law – which pre-Lisbon the Court regarded as beyond its jurisdiction (*UPA* Case C-50/00P para 43) and which will certainly not be easy.

F: Grounds for annulment

Having established sufficient standing, the applicant must show the measure is flawed in order to win annulment. The grounds for review are made clear in the Article itself:

> . . . lack of competence, infringement of an essential procedural requirement, infringement of the Treaties or of any rule of law relating to their application, or misuse of powers.

These grounds seem broad. Of particular interest is 'any rule of law relating to [the Treaties'] application'. It is here that the significance of the Court's development of the general principles of Union law referred to in Chapter 2 becomes apparent. The validity of EU acts can be tested against these principles. Indeed, many of the principles have been developed by the Court in the context of direct applications for the annulment of EU acts.

International Fruit Company v *Commission* (Cases 41–44/70)

[1971] ECR 411, Court of Justice of the European Communities

The Court, having held the application admissible (p. 190), proceeded to examine the merits. It held the application unfounded. The next extract explains the Court's rejection of one of the grounds of complaint.

[66] . . . [T]he applicants claim that Regulations Nos 565/70 and 686/70 are void or at least are not applicable to them, inasmuch as they establish a system of import licences which is in conflict with Articles 3(f), 85 and 96 of the Treaty.

[67] Moreover, these regulations are said to be insufficiently supported by reasons, inasmuch as the grounds on which the system was necessary or at least permissible under the said articles and under Article 39 of the Treaty are not stated.

[68] Article 3 of the Treaty lists several general objectives, towards the attainment and harmonization of which the Commission has to direct its activities.

[69] Amongst these objectives Article 3 specifies not only 'the institution of a system ensuring that competition in the common market is not distorted', but also (subparagraph (d)) 'the adoption of a common policy in the sphere of agriculture'.

[70] The Treaty attaches very great importance to the attainment of this latter objective in the sphere of agriculture, devoting Article 39 to it and providing, in the first paragraph of Article 42, that the provisions relating to competition shall apply to agricultural products only to the extent determined by the Council, account being taken of the objectives set out in Article 39.

[71] It follows from this that the application of protective measures in the form of a restriction of imports from third countries might in the present case prove to be necessary with a view to preventing, in the market in the products in question, serious disturbances capable of endangering the objectives of Article 39.

[72] In these circumstances an explicit statement of the reasons for the measures in question, in relation to Articles 85 and 86 of the Treaty, was not indispensable.

[73] It may well be that the grant of import licences according to the criterion of a reference quantity led in the present case to a crystallization of the previously existing trade relations with third countries. Yet, on the other hand, the laying down of objective criteria for calculating the quantities of which import was permitted made it possible to avoid discrimination among those who received licences on the basis of previously existing trade relations with third countries.

[74] This system was the one best adapted to distort competition to the smallest possible extent.

[75] For these reasons, the submissions directed against Regulations Nos 459/70, 565/70 and 686/70 must be rejected.

NOTE: In *Kadi and Al Barakaat* v *Council* (Joined Cases C-402/05P & C-415/05P), [2008] ECR I-6351 (p. 64) the Court insisted that respect for human rights is a condition of the lawfulness of Union acts, and consequently annulled a Regulation that fell short of the required standard. Allegations of violation of the Charter of Fundamental Rights are increasingly common: its Article 47 was invoked (unsuccessfully) in Case C-583/11P *Inuit Tapiriit Kanatami* (p. 202), its Articles 7 and 8 were invoked (successfully) in Joined Cases C-293/12 and C-594/12 *Digital Rights Ireland* (p. 62). In *R* v *Secretary of State for Health, ex parte British American Tobacco (Investments) Ltd and Imperial Tobacco Ltd* (Case C-491/01) [2002] ECR I-11543 (p. 51) the Court reviewed the proportionality of a Directive harmonizing rules governing aspects of tobacco products, but found no violation of EU law. The EU legislature 'must be allowed a broad discretion in an area such as that involved in the present case, which entails political, economic and social choices on its part, and in which it is called upon to undertake complex assessments' (para 123). This is a familiar formula in the Court's case law. It entails that even in cases where the standing rules applicable to challenge to EU acts are satisfied – rare where a direct action brought by a private applicant is at stake – the EU act is likely to survive judicial review in all but extraordinary cases. Legislative discretion is prized – the political process is respected.

G: Interim measures

ARTICLES 278 AND 279 TFEU

ARTICLE 278

Actions brought before the Court of Justice of the European Union shall not have suspensory effect. The Court may, however, if it considers that circumstances so require, order that application of the contested act be suspended.

ARTICLE 279

The Court of Justice of the European Union may in any cases before it prescribe any necessary interim measures.

These provisions confer a wide discretion on the Court. It has generally been slow to grant interim relief from EU acts. Here, however, is a successful interim application made in respect of anti-dumping duties imposed on Japanese ball bearings under Regulation 1778/77.

NTN Toyo Bearing Co. v *Council* (Case 113/77R)

[1977] ECR 1721, Court of Justice of the European Communities

[4] . . . The Council has not contested that the competent British, French and German customs authorities are insisting that the payments required under Article 3 of Regulation No 1778/77 shall be made forthwith. Nor has it contested that the NTN Group will incur the additional charges referred to by NTN in the event of the dismissal of the latter's application for the adoption of interim measures.

[5] It has not been possible to establish conclusively within the context of the present proceedings whether, in the event of NTN's being successful in the main action, this expenditure would be wholly recouped.

[6] Having regard to the probable duration of the procedure in the main action, charges at the rate quoted by the applicant cannot be regarded as negligible.

[7] On the other hand the Council has not been able to demonstrate that the adoption of the interim measures applied for would cause appreciable detriment to the European Economic Community if the NTN Group were to maintain the existing bank guarantees in the sums to be paid in accordance with Article 3 of Regulation No 1778/77 and if NTN were to be unsuccessful in the main action.

[8] NTN has thus substantiated the circumstances giving rise to urgency and the factual and legal grounds establishing a *prima facie* case for the suspension of the application, as far as the NTN Group is concerned, of the abovementioned Article 3 (Article 83(2) of the Rules of Procedure of the Court of Justice).

[9] To that extent therefore the application of the said Article must be suspended until the final judgment in the case of *NTN* v *Council* (Case 113/77) on condition that and for so long as the NTN Group continues to provide security for the performance of its obligation in the amounts which it is required to pay in pursuance of Article 3 of Regulation No 1778/77.

NOTE: Case 113/77 subsequently reached full trial: Case 113/77 *NTN Toyo Bearing Co.* v *Council* [1979] ECR 1185.

■ QUESTION

Compare and contrast the EU's rules on judicial review, especially those relating to standing, with those of any other administrative law system with which you are familiar. To what extent should judicial review show respect for the exercise of (i) legislative and (ii) administrative discretion?

SECTION 3: ARTICLE 265

ARTICLE 265 TFEU

Should the European Parliament, the European Council, the Council, the Commission or the European Central Bank, in infringement of the Treaties, fail to act, the Member States and the other institutions of the Union may bring an action before the Court of Justice of the European Union to have the infringement established. This Article shall apply, under the same conditions, to bodies, offices and agencies of the Union which fail to act.

The action shall be admissible only if the institution, body, office or agency concerned has first been called upon to act. If, within two months of being so called upon, the institution, body, office or agency concerned has not defined its position, the action may be brought within a further period of two months.

Any natural or legal person may, under the conditions laid down in the preceding paragraphs, complain to the Court that an institution, body, office or agency of the Union has failed to address to that person any act other than a recommendation or an opinion.

Whereas Article 263 concerns challenges to acts, Article 265 concerns challenges to omissions. It complements Article 263. Article 265 was Article 232 pre-Lisbon (and Article 175 pre-Amsterdam). In the next case the Parliament obtained a ruling that the Council had unlawfully remained inactive.

Parliament v *Council* (Case 13/83)

[1985] ECR 1513, Court of Justice of the European Communities

The matter concerned the Council's alleged failure to ensure freedom to provide services in the sphere of international transport, and to lay down the conditions under which non-resident carriers may operate transport services in a Member State.

[64] . . . the Parliament, the Commission and the Netherlands Government have rightly contended that the obligations imposed on the Council by Article 75(1)(a) and (b) include the introduction of freedom to provide services in relation to transport, and that the scope of that obligation is clearly defined by the Treaty. Pursuant to Articles 59 and 60 the requirements of freedom to provide services include, as the Court held in its judgment of 17 December 1981 (Case 279/80 *Webb* [1981] ECR 3305), the removal of any discrimination against the person providing services based on his nationality or the fact that he is established in a Member State other than that where the services are to be provided.

[65] It follows that in that respect the Council does not have the discretion on which it may rely in other areas of the common transport policy. Since the result to be achieved is determined by the combined effect of Articles 59, 60, 61 and 75(1)(a) and (b), the exercise of a certain measure of discretion is allowed only as regards the means employed to obtain that result, bearing in mind, as required by Article 75, those features which are special to transport.

[66] In so far as the obligations laid down in Article 75(1)(a) and (b) relate to freedom to provide services, therefore, they are sufficiently well-defined for disregard of them to be the subject of a finding of failure to act pursuant to Article 175.

[67] The Council was required to extend freedom to provide services to the transport sector before the expiry of the transitional period, pursuant to Article 75(1)(a) and (2), in so far as the extension related to international transport to or from the territory of a Member State or across the territory of one or more Member States and, within the framework of freedom to provide services in the transport sector, to lay down, pursuant to Article 75(1)(b) and (2), the conditions under which non-resident carriers may operate transport services within a Member State. It is common ground that the necessary measures for that purpose have not yet been adopted.

[68] On that point the Court must therefore hold that the Council has failed to act since it has failed to adopt measures which ought to have been adopted before the expiry of the transitional period and whose subject-matter and nature may be determined with a sufficient degree of precision.

NOTE: The case is a good illustration of the nature and purpose of Article 265. It might also be noted as an example of inter-institutional wrangling in the quest to develop policymaking in an important sector.

The next case demonstrates that although Article 265 complements Article 263, it does not offer a method of outflanking the limitations to Article 263. An applicant may find one available, but not both.

Societá 'Eridania' Zuccherifici Nazionali v *Commission* (Cases 10 and 18/68)

[1969] ECR 459, Court of Justice of the European Communities

The application for annulment of Commission Decisions had failed to clear the standing hurdles in Article 173 of the EC Treaty (now, after amendment, Article 263 TFEU). It was then argued that the Commission's failure to revoke the Decisions despite the applicant's requests was challengeable under Article 175 of the EC Treaty (now, after amendment, Article 265 TFEU) as a failure to act. On admissibility, the Court held as follows:

> [16] The action provided for in Article 175 is intended to establish an illegal omission as appears from that article, which refers to a failure to act 'in infringement of this Treaty' and from Article 176 which refers to a failure to act declared to be 'contrary to this Treaty'.
>
> Without stating under which provision of Community law the Commission was required to annul or to revoke the said decisions, the applicants have confined themselves to alleging that those decisions were adopted in infringement of the Treaty and that this fact alone would thus suffice to make the Commission's failure to act subject to the provisions of Article 175.
>
> [17] The Treaty provides, however, particularly in Article 173, other methods of recourse by which an allegedly illegal Community measure may be disputed and if necessary annulled on the application of a duly qualified party.
>
> To admit, as the applicants wish to do, that the parties concerned could ask the institution from which the measure came to revoke it and, in the event of the Commission's failing to act, refer such failure to the Court as an illegal omission to deal with the matter would amount to providing them with a method of recourse parallel to that of Article 173, which would not be subject to the conditions laid down by the Treaty.
>
> [18] This application does not therefore satisfy the requirements of Article 175 of the Treaty and must thus be held to be inadmissible.

SECTION 4: ARTICLE 277

Article 277 TFEU

> Notwithstanding the expiry of the period laid down in Article 263, sixth paragraph, any party may, in proceedings in which an act of general application adopted by an institution, body, office or agency of the Union is at issue, plead the grounds specified in Article 263, second paragraph, in order to invoke before the Court of Justice of the European Union the inapplicability of that act.

Article 277 TFEU was lightly amended and re-numbered from Article 241 EC on the entry into force of the Treaty of Lisbon (and it was Article 184 before the Amsterdam re-numbering in 1999). The nature and purpose of Article 277 would be immediately apparent to a lawyer familiar with French administrative law, which contains the similar *exception d'illegalité*. Article 277 is, however, initially peculiar to British eyes. It is commonly referred to as the 'plea of illegality', which hardly invites instant recognition of its function. The following extract from *'Les Verts'* v *Parliament* (Case 294/83) (mentioned at p. 187) provides an explanation of the place of Article 277 in the system of judicial remedies instituted by the Treaty.

***Parti Ecologiste 'Les Verts'* v *Parliament* (Case 294/83)**

[1986] ECR 1339, Court of Justice of the European Communities

[23] . . . Natural and legal persons are . . . protected against the application to them of general measures which they cannot contest directly before the Court by reason of the special conditions of admissibility laid down in the second paragraph of Article 173 [now the fourth paragraph of Article 263] of the Treaty. Where the Community institutions are responsible for the administrative implementation of such measures, natural or legal persons may bring a direct action before the Court against implementing measures which are addressed to them or which are of direct and individual concern to them and, in support of such an action, plead the illegality of the general measure on which they are based. . . .

NOTE: This, then, is the plea of illegality – Article 277. It is a form of indirect challenge to a measure which the applicant is unable to challenge directly.

Article 277's operation may be illustrated with reference to the next case.

***Simmenthal SpA* v *Commission* (Case 92/78)**

[1979] ECR 777, Court of Justice of the European Communities

The applicant sought annulment of a February 1978 Decision. The basis of the challenge was the alleged invalidity of several earlier Regulations and Notices from which that Decision of February 1978 derived. The limitations in Article 173 of the EC Treaty (now, after amendment, Article 263 TFEU), relating to standing and time limits, impeded direct challenge to those 'parent' measures. This application challenged those measures indirectly *via* a direct challenge to the February 1978 measure which stemmed from them. The Court explained the nature of Article 184 of the EC Treaty (now Article 277 TFEU) in these circumstances.

[36] There is no doubt that this provision enables the applicant to challenge indirectly during the proceedings, with a view to obtaining the annulment of the contested Decision, the validity of the measures laid down by Regulation which form the legal basis of the latter. . ..

[41] [it] provide[s] those persons who are precluded by the second paragraph of Article 173 [now the fourth paragraph of Article 263] from instituting proceedings directly in respect of general acts with the benefit of a judicial review of them at the time when they are affected by implementing Decisions which are of direct and individual concern to them.

[42] The notices of invitations to tender of 13 January 1978 in respect of which the applicant was unable to initiate proceedings are a case in point, seeing that only the Decision taken in consequence of the tender which it had submitted in answer to a specific invitation to tender could be of direct and individual concern to it.

[43] There are therefore good grounds for declaring that the applicant's challenge during the proceedings under Article 184, which relates not only to the above-mentioned Regulations but also to the notices of invitations to tender of 13 January 1978, is admissible, although the latter are not in the strict sense measures laid down by Regulation.

NOTE: On the merits the application succeeded. The grounds for review under Article 277 are the same as those applicable to Article 263 (see p. 187).

SECTION 5: ARTICLES 268 AND 340

ARTICLES 268 AND 340 TFEU

ARTICLE 268

The Court of Justice of the European Union shall have jurisdiction in disputes relating to the compensation for damage provided for in the second and third paragraphs of Article 340.

ARTICLE 340

The contractual liability of the Union shall be governed by the law applicable to the contract in question.

In the case of non-contractual liability, the Union shall, in accordance with the general principles common to the laws of the Member States, make good any damage caused by its institutions or by its servants in the performance of their duties.

Notwithstanding the second paragraph, the European Central Bank shall, in accordance with the general principles common to the laws of the Member States, make good any damage caused by it or by its servants in the performance of their duties.

The personal liability of its servants towards the Union shall be governed by the provisions laid down in their Staff Regulations or in the Conditions of Employment applicable to them.

Articles 268 and 340 TFEU were Articles 235 and 288 EC respectively prior to the entry into force of the Treaty of Lisbon (and pre-Amsterdam they were Articles 178 and 215).

The early development of the case law was marked by a very restrictive approach to the imposition of non-contractual liability on the institutions of the Community (as it then was).

Aktien-Zuckerfabrik Schöppenstedt v *Council* (Case 5/71)

[1971] ECR 975, Court of Justice of the European Communities

[2] The Council contests the admissibility of the application contending in the first place that it is aimed in fact not at compensation for damage due to its wrongful act or omission but to the removal of the legal effects arising from the contested measure. To recognize the admissibility of the application would frustrate the contentious system provided for by the Treaty in particular in the second paragraph of Article 173 [now Article 263(4) TFEU, p. 186], under which individuals are not entitled to bring applications for annulment of regulations.

[3] The action for damages provided for by Articles 178 and 215, paragraph 2, of the Treaty [now Articles 268 and 340 TFEU] was introduced as an autonomous form of action, with a particular purpose to fulfil within the system of actions and subject to conditions on its use dictated by its specific nature. It differs from an application for annulment in that its end is not the abolition of a particular measure, but compensation for damage caused by an institution in the performance of its duties.

[4] The Council further contends that the principal conclusions are inadmissible in that they involve the substitution of new rules, in accordance with the criteria described by the applicant, for the rules in question, a substitution which the Court has not the power to order.

[5] The principal conclusions seek only an award of damages and, therefore, a benefit intended solely to produce effects in the case of the applicant. Therefore this submission must be dismissed.

NOTE: This remains good law, and represents an authoritative statement of the function of the action for damages as 'an autonomous form of action' (para 3). The Court then proceeded to examine the nature of the violation required to generate a liability to compensate.

[11] In the present case the non-contractual liability of the Community pre-supposes at the very least the unlawful nature of the act alleged to be the cause of the damage. Where legislative action involving measures of economic policy is concerned, the Community does not incur noncontractual liability for damage suffered

by individuals as a consequence of that action, by virtue of the provisions contained in Article 215, second paragraph, of the Treaty [now Article 340 TFEU], unless a sufficiently flagrant violation of a superior rule of law for the protection of the individual has occurred. For that reason the Court, in the present case, must first consider whether such a violation has occurred.

NOTE: Such a violation had not occurred. The Court's test in para 11 of the judgment appears extremely difficult to satisfy. This was borne out by subsequent case law in which claims for compensation were regularly rejected. There were only occasional successes; see, e.g., *Mulder et al.* v *Council & Commission* (Cases C-104/89 and C-37/90) [1992] ECR I-3061 and, on assessing compensation, [2000] ECR I-203. The case law has more recently taken a new turn. Principles of liability under Article 340 TFEU applicable to *Union* institutions cannot rationally be developed in isolation from those developed under EU law applicable to *national* institutions. Chapter 6 explored the Court's reliance on the inherent system of the Treaty to craft a system of liability applicable to national institutions accused of infringing Union law rights. The landmark case was *Francovich* (Cases C-6 and C-9/90, p. 143). The principle was elucidated and its scope of application expanded in *Brasserie du Pêcheur and Factortame* (Joined Cases C-46/93 and C-48/93, p. 151). The pressure to bring the principles of liability into alignment irrespective of the national or Union origin of the challenged institution convinced the Court to depart from the *Schöppenstedt* formula.

Laboratoires Pharmaceutiques Bergaderm SA and Jean-Jacques Goupil v *Commission* (Case C-352/98P)

[2000] ECR I-5291, Court of Justice of the European Communities

This was an appeal against the decision of the Court of First Instance (now the General Court, p. 183) in Case T-199/96 *Laboratoires Pharmaceutiques Bergaderm and Goupil* v *Commission* [1998] ECR II-2805. Bergaderm had applied for compensation for damage which they claimed to have suffered as a result of the adoption of Directive 95/34/EC, adapting the regime governing cosmetic products. This measure had the effect of preventing the sale of one of Bergaderm's sun oil products by introducing restrictions on permissible ingredients on scientific grounds associated with perceived risks to health. The Court of First Instance dismissed the application.

On appeal, the Court began by setting out the basis for the Court of First Instance's decision which was now being challenged before it.

[13] In the contested judgment, the Court of First Instance recalled that, as regards liability arising from legislative measures, the conduct with which the Community is charged must constitute a breach of a higher-ranking rule of law for the protection of individuals (paragraph 48). It held that the Adaptation Directive was a measure of general application (paragraph 50) and concluded that it was necessary therefore to determine whether the Commission had disregarded a higher-ranking rule of law for the protection of individuals (paragraph 51).

[14] Without deeming it necessary to determine whether the provisions governing the procedure for the adoption of the Adaptation Directive contained higher-ranking rules of law for the protection of individuals, the Court of First Instance concluded that the Commission had not infringed those provisions (paragraph 56). It stated that they did not provide for the protection of certain rights of the defence (paragraph 59) and that, in any event, the appellants had had the opportunity to express their views before the adoption of the Adaptation Directive (paragraph 60).

[15] As regards the plea alleging manifest error of assessment and breach of the principle of proportionality, the Court of First Instance held that, in the light of the evidence before the Court, the Commission's conduct and the measure adopted by it could not be regarded as vitiated by a manifest error of assessment or as disproportionate (paragraph 67).

[16] Finally, as regards the plea alleging misuse of powers, the Court of First Instance held that the appellants had failed to provide evidence such as to show that the Adaptation Directive had been adopted with the exclusive or main purpose of achieving an end other than that stated (paragraphs 69 and 70).

The appeal was based on three grounds: (i) that the Court of First Instance erred in law in declaring that the Adaptation Directive was a legislative measure, (ii) that the Court of First Instance committed a manifest error in assessing the Commission's exercise of its powers, and (iii) in the alternative, that there was a breach of higher-ranking rules of law. The Court took the first two grounds of appeal together.

[38] By their first two grounds of appeal, the appellants essentially claim that, in the light of the nature of the measure adopted by the Commission, the Court of First Instance erred in law in concluding, in paragraph 67 of the contested judgment, that the Commission's conduct and the measure adopted by it to restrict to 1 mg/kg the maximum level of psoralens in sun protection products cannot be regarded as vitiated by a manifest error of assessment or as disproportionate.

[39] The second paragraph of Article 215 of the Treaty [now Article 340] provides that, in the case of non-contractual liability, the Community is, in accordance with the general principles common to the laws of the Member States, to make good any damage caused by its institutions or by its servants in the performance of their duties.

[40] The system of rules which the Court has worked out with regard to that provision takes into account, *inter alia*, the complexity of the situations to be regulated, difficulties in the application or interpretation of the texts and, more particularly, the margin of discretion available to the author of the act in question (Joined Cases C-46/93 and C-48/93 *Brasserie du Pêcheur and Factortame* [1996] ECR I-1029, paragraph 43).

[41] The Court has stated that the conditions under which the State may incur liability for damage caused to individuals by a breach of Community law cannot, in the absence of particular justification, differ from those governing the liability of the Community in like circumstances. The protection of the rights which individuals derive from Community law cannot vary depending on whether a national authority or a Community authority is responsible for the damage (*Brasserie du Pêcheur and Factortame*, paragraph 42).

[42] As regards Member State liability for damage caused to individuals, the Court has held that Community law confers a right to reparation where three conditions are met: the rule of law infringed must be intended to confer rights on individuals; the breach must be sufficiently serious; and there must be a direct causal link between the breach of the obligation resting on the State and the damage sustained by the injured parties (*Brasserie du Pêcheur and Factortame*, paragraph 51).

[43] As to the second condition, as regards both Community liability under Article 215 of the Treaty and Member State liability for breaches of Community law, the decisive test for finding that a breach of Community law is sufficiently serious is whether the Member State or the Community institution concerned manifestly and gravely disregarded the limits on its discretion (*Brasserie du Pêcheurand Factortame*, paragraph 55; and Joined Cases C-178/94, C-179/94, C-188/94, C-189/94, C-190/94 *Dillenkofer and Others* v *Germany* [1996] ECR I-4845, paragraph 25).

[44] Where the Member State or the institution in question has only considerably reduced, or even no, discretion, the mere infringement of Community law may be sufficient to establish the existence of a sufficiently serious breach (see, to that effect, Case C-5/94 *Hedley Lomas* [1996] ECR I-2553, paragraph 28).

[45] It is therefore necessary to examine whether, in the present case, as the appellants assert, the Court of First Instance erred in law in its examination of the way in which the Commission exercised its discretion when it adopted the Adaptation Directive.

[46] In that regard, the Court finds that the general or individual nature of a measure taken by an institution is not a decisive criterion for identifying the limits of the discretion enjoyed by the institution in question.

[47] It follows that the first ground of appeal, which is based exclusively on the categorisation of the Adaptation Directive as an individual measure, has in any event no bearing on the issue and must be rejected.

[48] By the first limb of the second ground of appeal, the appellants challenge the finding, by the Court of First Instance, that there existed disputed scientific studies and data as regards the risk for human health caused by the use of furocoumarines present in natural essences, even when associated with sun filters.

[49] Article 168a of the Treaty and Article 51 of the EC Statute of the Court of Justice state that an appeal is to be limited to points of law and, therefore, the Court of First Instance has exclusive jurisdiction, first, to establish the facts except where the substantive inaccuracy of its findings is apparent from the documents submitted

> to it and, second, to assess those facts (Case C-7/95 P *Deere* v *Commission* [1998] ECR I-3111, paragraphs 18 and 21).
>
> [50] Before the Court, the appellants have not shown either by their arguments or by the documents they have submitted that the Court of First Instance distorted the nature of the evidence submitted to it by holding, in paragraph 63 of the contested judgment, that 'there is nothing in the documents before the Court to support the conclusion that the Commission misunderstood the scientific arguments'.
>
> [51] Therefore, since the first limb of the second ground of appeal contests a finding of fact, without showing that the facts were distorted, it must be declared inadmissible.
>
> [52] By the second limb of that ground of appeal, the appellants dispute the reference to the precautionary principle in paragraph 66 of the contested judgment.
>
> [53] However, paragraph 66 of the contested judgment, which begins with the word 'furthermore', is a statement of reasons added for completeness, since the Court of First Instance had already concluded its reasoning in paragraph 65 by stating that the Commission could not be criticised for placing the matter before the Scientific Committee or for complying with that body's opinion, which was drawn up on the basis of a large number of meetings, visits and specialist reports.
>
> [54] It follows that the second limb of the second ground of appeal is irrelevant and must be rejected.

The third ground of appeal based on breach of higher-ranking rules of law was reinterpreted by the Court:

> [62] Having regard to the conditions, set out in paragraphs 41 and 42 above, that must be met for Community liability to be incurred, the third ground of appeal must be interpreted as alleging that the Court of First Instance misinterpreted the legislation in considering that the Commission did not infringe a rule of law intended to confer rights on individuals.

But this too failed to persuade, and the appeal was dismissed.

Having made the key statement of principle in para 41 of the judgment in *Bergaderm*, the Court is now adept at weaving together the case law concerning the liability of Union institutions pursuant to what are now Articles 268 and 340(2) TFEU and the liability of national authorities pursuant to the *Francovich* and *Brasserie du Pêcheur/ Factortame* case law developed on the basis of the inherent system of the Treaty. (For analysis see C. Hilson, 'The Role of Discretion in EC law on Non-Contractual Liability' (2005) 42 CML Rev 677; K. Gutman, 'The Evolution of the Action for Damages against the EU and its Place in the System of Judicial Protection' (2011) 48 CML Rev 695.) This is a single stream of legal principle.

Commission v *Camar and Others* (Case C-312/00P)

[2002] ECR I-11355, Court of Justice of the European Communities

> [52] ... the system of rules which the Court has worked out in relation to the non-contractual liability of the Community takes into account, *inter alia*, the complexity of the situations to be regulated, difficulties in the application or interpretation of the texts and, more particularly, the margin of discretion available to the author of the act in question (see Joined Cases C-46/93 and C-48/93 *Brasserie du Pêcheur and Factortame* [1996] ECR I-1029, paragraph 43, and *Bergaderm and Goupil* v *Commission*, cited above, paragraph 40).
>
> [53] It is appropriate to point out also that, Community law confers a right to reparation where three conditions are met: the rule of law infringed must be intended to confer rights on individuals; the breach must be sufficiently serious; and there must be a direct causal link between the breach of the obligation resting on the author of the act and the damage sustained by the injured parties (see the judgments cited above *Brasserie du Pêcheur and Factortame*, paragraph 51, and *Bergaderm and Goupil* v *Commission*, paragraphs 41 and 42).
>
> [54] As to the second condition, the decisive test for finding that a breach of Community law is sufficiently serious is whether the Community institution concerned manifestly and gravely disregarded the limits on its

discretion (see the judgments cited above *Brasserie du Pêcheur and Factortame*, paragraph 55, and *Bergaderm and Goupil* v *Commission*, paragraph 43). Where that institution has only considerably reduced, or even no, discretion, the mere infringement of Community law may be sufficient to establish the existence of a sufficiently serious breach (Case C-5/94 *Hedley Lomas* [1996] ECR I-2553, paragraph 28; Joined Cases C-178/94, C-179/94 and C-188/94 to C-190/94 *Dillenkofer and Others* [1996] ECR I-4845, paragraph 25; Case C-127/95 *Norbrook Laboratories* [1998] ECR I-1531, paragraph 109; Case C-424/97 *Haim* [2000] ECR I-5123, paragraph 38, and *Bergaderm and Goupil* v *Commission*, cited above, paragraph 44).

[55] It follows from the foregoing that the decisive test for determining whether there has been such an infringement is not the individual nature of the act in question, but the discretion available to the institution when it was adopted.

NOTE: Outside the field of economic policymaking which was at issue in these cases, the Court seems a little more receptive to claims for compensation. The next case, which involves 'administrative illegality' rather than 'legislative illegality', tells a tragic tale. It is thankfully outside the mainstream of practice, but deserves attention as an example of how the Court can adopt a flexible approach to these rules.

Adams v *Commission* (No 1) (Case 145/83)

[1985] ECR 3539, Court of Justice of the European Communities

Stanley Adams sought compensation for damage he claimed to have suffered as a result of wrongful acts on the part of the Commission. Adams, an employee of the Swiss firm Hoffman-La Roche, had 'leaked' to the Commission documents which showed that Roche had been acting contrary to the Treaty competition rules. He requested the Commission to keep his identity secret. In the course of the inquiry, which culminated in the imposition of a fine on Roche, the Commission had let the firm see documents which indicated its participation in unlawful practices. Roche was able to deduce from the documents that the Commission's informant was Adams. Adams was charged with economic espionage under the Swiss Penal Code. He had left Roche and moved to Italy, but in 1974 he was arrested as he crossed the Swiss/Italian border. He was held in solitary confinement. He was not allowed to communicate with his family. His wife committed suicide. He received a one-year suspended prison sentence.

In the following extract from the judgment the Court examines breaches of the duty of confidentiality and the duty to warn Adams as the basis for the Commission's liability to him.

[34] As regards the existence of a duty of confidentiality it must be pointed out that Article 214 of the EEC Treaty [now Article 339 TFEU] lays down an obligation, in particular for the members and the servants of the institutions of the Community 'not to disclose information of the kind covered by the obligation of professional secrecy, in particular information about undertakings, their business relations or their cost components'. Although that provision primarily refers to information gathered from undertakings, the expression 'in particular' shows that the principle in question is a general one which applies also to information supplied by natural persons, if that information is 'of the kind' that is confidential. That is particularly so in the case of information supplied on a purely voluntary basis but accompanied by a request for confidentiality in order to protect the informant's anonymity. An institution which accepts such information is bound to comply with such a condition.

[35] As regards the case before the Court, it is quite clear from the applicant's letter of 25 February 1973 that he requested the Commission not to reveal his identity. It cannot therefore be denied that the Commission was bound by a duty of confidentiality towards the applicant in that respect. In fact the parties disagree not so much as to the existence of such a duty but as to whether the Commission was bound by a duty of confidentiality after the applicant had left his employment with Roche.

[36] In that respect it must be pointed out that the applicant did not qualify his request by indicating a period upon the expiry of which the Commission would be released from its duty of confidentiality regarding the

identity of its informant. No such indication can be inferred from the fact that the applicant was prepared to appear before any court after he had left Roche. The giving of evidence before a court implies that the witness has been duly summoned, that he is under a duty to answer the questions put to him, and is, in return, entitled to all the guarantees provided by a judicial procedure. The applicant's offer to confirm the accuracy of his information under such conditions cannot therefore be interpreted as a general statement releasing the Commission from its duty of confidentiality. Nor can any such intention be inferred from the applicant's subsequent conduct.

[37] It must therefore be stated that the Commission was under a duty to keep the applicant's identity secret even after he had left his employer.

[38] Of the events mentioned by the applicant, the only occasion on which the Commission directly revealed the identity of its informant was the telephone conversation between Mr Schlieder and Dr Alder at the beginning of February 1975. However, that conversation took place after the applicant had caused an anonymous letter to be sent to the Commission informing it of his detention and seeking its help. It is difficult to see how the Commission could have acted on that request without confirming, at least by implication, that the applicant was indeed its informant. Moreover, it transpired subsequently that at that time the applicant had already admitted to the Swiss police that he had given information, at least orally, to the Commission and it is clear from the decisions of the Swiss courts that the confirmation of that fact by Mr Schlieder did not have a decisive bearing on the applicant's conviction. The disclosure of the applicant's identity at that time and in those circumstances cannot be regarded as constituting a breach of the duty of confidentiality which could give rise to the Commission's liability *vis-à-vis* the applicant.

[39] On the other hand, it is clear that the handing over of the edited photocopies to members of the staff of the Roche subsidiaries enabled Roche to identify the applicant as the main suspect in the complaint which it lodged with the Swiss Public Prosecutor's Office. It was therefore that handing over of the documents which led to the applicant's arrest and which in addition supplied the police and the Swiss courts with substantial evidence against him.

[40] It appears from the documents before the Court that the Commission was fully aware of the risk that the handing over to Roche of the photocopies supplied by the applicant might reveal the informant's identity to the company. For that reason the Commission officials first attempted to obtain other copies of the documents in question from the Roche subsidiaries in Paris and Brussels. When that attempt failed, the Commission prepared new copies of the documents which it considered were the least likely to lead to the discovery of the applicant's identity and it took care to remove from those copies any indication which it considered might reveal the source of the documents. However, since it was not familiar with Roche's practices regarding the distribution of the documents in question within the company, the Commission could not be sure that those precautions were sufficient to eliminate all risk of the applicant's being identified by means of the copies handed over to Roche. The Commission was therefore, in any event, imprudent in handing over those copies to Roche without having consulted the applicant.

[41] It is not however necessary to decide whether, in view of the situation at the time and in particular of the information in the Commission's possession, the handing over of the documents is sufficient to give rise to the Commission's liability regarding the consequences of the applicant's being identified as the informant. Although the Commission was not necessarily aware, when those documents were handed over, of the gravity of the risk to which it was exposing the applicant, Dr Alder's visit on 8 November 1974, on the other hand, provided it with all the necessary information in that respect. Following that visit the Commission knew that Roche was determined to discover how the Commission had come into possession of the documents in question and that it was preparing to lay a complaint against the informant under Article 273 of the Swiss Penal Code, the contents of which Dr Alder even took care to explain. The Commission also knew that there was a possibility of obtaining from Roche, in return for the disclosure of the informant's identity, an undertaking not to take action against him. It could not however pursue that possibility without the applicant's consent.

[42] In those circumstances it was not at all sufficient for the Commission merely to take the view that it was unlikely that the applicant would be identified, that he was probably never going to return to Switzerland and that, in any event, the Swiss authorities did not intend to institute criminal proceedings against him. On the contrary, the Commission was under a duty to take every possible step to warn the applicant, thereby enabling him to make his own arrangements in the light of the information given by Dr Alder, and to consult him as to the approach to be adopted in relation to Dr Alder's proposals.

The Court then rejected the Commission's submission that the action was time barred. In what may seem a cruel concluding twist, it awarded Adams compensation, but halved the sum payable on the following basis:

> [53] It must therefore be concluded that in principle the Community is bound to make good the damage resulting from the discovery of the applicant's identity by means of the documents handed over to Roche by the Commission. It must however be recognized that the extent of the Commission's liability is diminished by reason of the applicant's own negligence. The applicant failed to inform the Commission that it was possible to infer his identity as the informant from the documents themselves, although he was in the best position to appreciate and to avert that risk. Nor did he ask the Commission to keep him informed of the progress of the investigation of Roche, and in particular of any use that might be made of the documents for that purpose. Lastly, he went back to Switzerland without attempting to make any inquiries in that respect, although he must have been aware of the risks to which his conduct towards his former employer had exposed him with regard to Swiss legislation.
>
> [54] Consequently, the applicant himself contributed significantly to the damage which he suffered. In assessing the conduct of the Commission on the one hand and that of the applicant on the other, the Court considers it equitable to apportion responsibility for that damage equally between the two parties.

NOTE: On this case read J. Meade, (1986) 37 NILQ 370; N. March Hunnings, (1987) 24 CML Rev 65.

SECTION 6: THE ARTICLE 267 PRELIMINARY REFERENCE PROCEDURE

A: The function of the Article 267 preliminary reference procedure in judicial review

The restrictive standing rules under the fourth paragraph of Article 263 and the time limit in its sixth paragraph (p. 187) conspire to diminish the efficacy of direct challenge to EU legislation before the Court. However, the existence of the Article 267 preliminary reference procedure allows indirect challenge to be brought before national courts. In practice, this is of immense value to the private litigant.

R v *Intervention Board, ex parte Man (Sugar) Ltd* (Case 181/84) was examined in Chapter 2 and deserves re-reading (p. 48). It is an example of an action instituted at national level in which the validity of (what was then) Community legislation is called into question. The preliminary reference made by the national court allows the Court of Justice to rule on the measure's validity. So, once EU legislation finds expression in national implementing legislation, a challenge to the validity of the EU legislation may be achieved *via* a challenge at national level to the national implementing acts.

Universität Hamburg v _HZA Hamburg-Kehrwieder_ (Case 216/82)

[1983] ECR 2771, Court of Justice of the European Communities

The dispute between the University and the German customs authorities related to the levy due on a Spectrometer imported from the USA for use in laboratory experiments on animals. A Commission Decision addressed to all Member States indicated an outcome unfavourable to the University, and the German authorities confirmed this. The University then brought proceedings at national level against the German authorities. The Finance Court in Hamburg made a preliminary reference questioning the lawfulness of the Commission Decision, but first it asked whether Article 177 of the EC Treaty (now Article 267 TFEU) could be used in this fashion. After all, the University had failed to use Article 173 of the EC Treaty (now, after amendment, Article 263 TFEU) directly to challenge the Commission's Decision before the Court of Justice.

[7] The Decision adopted by the Commission is addressed to all the Member States. By virtue of Article 191 of the Treaty it must therefore be notified to the Member States and it takes effect upon such notification. However, it does not have to be notified to the person applying for exemption from customs duty and it is not one of the measures which the Treaty requires to be published. Even if in practice the Decision is in fact published in the *Official Journal of the European Communities*, its wording does not necessarily enable the applicant to ascertain whether it was adopted in relation to the procedure which he initiated.

[8] Since the Decision is binding on the Member States, the national authority must reject the application for duty-free admission in the event of a negative Decision on the part of the Commission; however, Community law does not require it to refer to the Commission's Decision in its own Decision rejecting the application. Furthermore, as this case demonstrates, the national authority's Decision may be adopted some time after the notification of the Commission's Decision.

[9] Finally, as the Finanzgericht rightly points out, for the purpose of bringing an action under the second paragraph of Article 173 of the Treaty against the Commission's Decision, the scientific establishment in question must demonstrate that the Decision is of direct and individual concern to it.

[10] In those circumstances the rejection by the national authority of the scientific establishment's application is the only measure which is directly addressed to it, of which it has necessarily been informed in good time and which the establishment may challenge in the courts without encountering any difficulty in demonstrating its interest in bringing proceedings. According to a general principle of law which finds its expression in Article 184 of the EEC Treaty, in proceedings brought under national law against the rejection of his application the applicant must be able to plead the illegality of the Commission's Decision on which the national Decision adopted in his regard is based.

[11] That statement is sufficient to provide an answer capable of dispelling the doubts expressed by the national court without there being any need to consider the wider issue of the general relationship between Articles 173 and 177 of the Treaty or to give a separate answer to the first question.

[12] The answer to the first two questions of the Finanzgericht should therefore be that the person or persons concerned by a Decision adopted by the Commission pursuant to Article 4 of Regulation No 3195/75 may plead the illegality of the Decision before the national court in proceedings against the fixing of customs duty and that the question of the validity of the Decision may therefore be referred to the Court in proceedings for a preliminary ruling.

On the merits, however, the Court found no reason to impugn the validity of the Decision.

***Walter Rau* v *BALM* (Case 133/85)**

[1987] ECR 2289, Court of Justice of the European Communities

The Community (as it then was) instituted a scheme whereby cheap butter was sold on the West Berlin market in order to test consumer reaction. German margarine producers challenged the scheme before German courts arguing that the German implementing measures were unlawful because their source, the Community scheme, was unlawful. The national court was immediately concerned whether this line of argument could properly be advanced before it, given the existence of the direct action to challenge acts before the Court.

[11] It must be emphasized that there is nothing in Community law to prevent an action from being brought before a national court against a measure implementing a Decision adopted by a Community institution where the conditions laid down by national law are satisfied. When such an action is brought, if the outcome of the dispute depends on the validity of that Decision the national court may submit questions to the Court of Justice by way of a reference for a preliminary ruling, without there being any need to ascertain whether or not the plaintiff in the main proceedings has the possibility of challenging the Decision directly before the Court.

[12] The answer to the first question must therefore be that the possibility of bringing a direct action under the second paragraph of Article 173 of the EEC Treaty against a Decision adopted by a Community institution does not preclude the possibility of bringing an action in a national court against a measure adopted by a national authority for the implementation of that Decision on the ground that the latter Decision is unlawful.

However, the Court held that none of several submissions provided a basis for holding the scheme invalid. On the issue of proportionality, for example, the Court held:

[33] In its eighth question the national court asks whether the Decision of 25 February 1985 is compatible with the principle of proportionality in so far as the expansion of the markets or the search for new outlets may be achieved by action which has less impact on the workings of the market.

[34] By way of explanation, the national court states that rules which interfere with the fundamental right to exercise a trade or profession are justified only if they are dictated by objectives in the general interest which are of such overriding importance that they deserve to take precedence over that fundamental right. The national court considers that that is not the case in this instance. If, on the one hand, the purpose of the operation was to reduce public stocks by 900 tonnes of butter, it could have been achieved by measures which had a less serious effect on the position of competitors protected by fundamental rights. Thus the 900 tonnes of butter could have been distributed over a longer period or over a wider area. If, on the other hand, the purpose of the operation was the search for new outlets, the national court doubts whether the operation is capable of yielding useful results. A measure which is such as to interfere with fundamental rights but not such as to help achieve the aim pursued can never be justified by overriding considerations pertaining to the general interest.

[35] It follows from those considerations that the question raised by the national court was, more precisely, whether the principle of proportionality had been contravened on the ground that the aim of reducing public stocks by 900 tonnes of butter was attainable by methods which had a serious effect on the position of competitors and that it was doubtful whether a test market such as West Berlin was capable of yielding useful results.

[36] It must be remembered in the first place that, as the Court stated in reply to the third question, the operation did not have as its purpose to reduce intervention stocks by 900 tonnes of butter and did not conflict with the principle of freedom to pursue a trade or profession, the principle of general freedom to pursue any lawful activity and the principle of freedom of competition.

[37] Next, it must be emphasized that the operation constituted, as it was intended to, the basis of a scientific survey from which the Commission was able to derive useful information. Furthermore, the Commission chose the West Berlin market because of its isolated geographical location and the possibility of carrying out there, in view of its limited size, an operation at relatively low cost. In so doing, the Commission would not appear to have exceeded the discretion conferred upon it by the Council in Article 4 of Regulation No 1079/77.

[38] Accordingly, the answer to the eighth question must be that consideration of the decision of 25 February 1985 has not disclosed any evidence of a breach of the principle of proportionality.

NOTE: The value of the preliminary reference procedure to the applicant is clear when it is appreciated that the applicant's direct action was doomed to fail as inadmissible without any examination of the merits of the claim; it was *Union Deutsche Lebensmittelwerke* (Case 97/85) (p. 194), and this is the promised next episode in the saga of the Berlin butter.

B: The limitations of Article 267 in judicial review

Resort to the Article 267 'indirect' route for challenging EU acts has real attractions for the individual confronted by the high hurdles governing standing under Article 263. Moreover, the process emphasizes the role of national courts acting for these purposes as ordinary courts of EU law. It has a flavour of subsidiarity. The availability of Article 267 in addition to Article 263 gives the individual flexibility in acting to secure protection of interests affected by EU acts, although the value of Article 267 is limited *inter alia* by the individual's inability to *require* that a referral be made. Nevertheless, the next ruling amounts to a sharp rejection of any notion that an individual is entitled to choose to surrender an opportunity to sue directly under Article 263 and subsequently await reliance on Article 267.

TWD Textilwerke Deggendorf GmbH v *Germany* (Case C-188/92)

[1994] ECR I-833, Court of Justice of the European Communities

A Commission Decision addressed to Germany declared that aid paid to TWD Textilwerke Deggendorf GmbH, a Bavarian producer of polyamide and polyester yarn, was incompatible with the rules on State aid, Articles 92–94 of the EC Treaty (now, after amendment, Articles 107–109 TFEU). Germany was required to recover the aid. No direct action before the Court of Justice was initiated by either Germany or the firm, TWD, even though TWD had received a copy of the Commission Decision from the relevant German Ministry, which had also informed TWD that it could employ Article 173 of the EC Treaty (now, after amendment, Article 263 TFEU) to challenge the Decision (circumstances which were emphasized by the referring court). Subsequently in national proceedings to recover the aid, TWD raised challenges to the validity of the Commission Decision on which the national action was based. This led to a preliminary reference relating to the validity of the Commission Decision. But the Court of Justice focused on TWD's tactics in selecting remedies.

[14] The undertaking in receipt of individual aid which is the subject-matter of a Commission decision adopted on the basis of Article 93 of the Treaty has the right to bring an action for annulment under the second paragraph of Article 173 of the Treaty even if the decision is addressed to a Member State (judgment in Case 730/79 *Philip Morris* v *Commission* [1980] ECR 2671). By virtue of the third paragraph of that article, the expiry of the time-limit laid down in that provision has the same time-barring effect vis-à-vis such an undertaking as it does *vis-à-vis* the Member State which is the addressee of the decision.

[15] It is settled law that a Member State may no longer call in question the validity of a decision addressed to it on the basis of Article 93(2) of the Treaty once the time-limit laid down in the third paragraph of Article 173 of the Treaty has expired (see the judgments in Case 156/77 *Commission* v *Belgium* [1978] ECR 1881 and Case C-183/91 *Commission* v *Greece* [1993] ECR I-3131).

[16] That case law, according to which it is impossible for a Member State which is the addressee of a decision taken under the first paragraph of Article 93(2) of the Treaty to call in question the validity of the decision in the proceedings for non-compliance provided for in the second paragraph of that provision, is based in particular on the consideration that the periods within which applications must be lodged are intended to safeguard legal certainty by preventing Community measures which involve legal effects from being called in question indefinitely.

[17] It follows from the same requirements of legal certainty that it is not possible for a recipient of aid, forming the subject-matter of a Commission decision adopted on the basis of Article 93 of the Treaty, who could have challenged that decision and who allowed the mandatory time-limit laid down in this regard by the third paragraph of Article 173 of the Treaty to expire, to call in question the lawfulness of that decision before the national courts in an action brought against the measures taken by the national authorities for implementing that decision.

[18] To accept that in such circumstances the person concerned could challenge the implementation of the decision in proceedings before the national court on the ground that the decision was unlawful would in effect enable the person concerned to overcome the definitive nature which the decision assumes as against that person once the time-limit for bringing an action has expired.

[19] It is true that in its judgment in Joined Cases 133 to 136/85 *Rau* v *BALM* [1987] ECR 2289, on which the French Government relies in its observations, the Court held that the possibility of bringing a direct action under the second paragraph of Article 173 of the EEC Treaty against a decision adopted by a Community institution did not preclude the possibility of bringing an action in a national court against a measure adopted

by a national authority for the implementation of that decision, on the ground that the latter decision was unlawful.

[20] However, as is clear from the Report for the Hearing in those cases, each of the plaintiffs in the main proceedings had brought an action before the Court of Justice for the annulment of the decision in question. The Court did not therefore rule, and did not have to rule, in that judgment on the time barring effects of the expiry of time-limits. It is precisely that issue with which the question referred by the national court in this case is concerned.

[21] This case is also distinguishable from Case 216/82 *Universität Hamburg* v *Hauptzollamt Hamburg-Kehrwieder* [1983] ECR 2771.

[22] In the judgment in that case the Court held that a plaintiff whose application for duty-free admission had been rejected by a decision of a national authority taken on the basis of a decision of the Commission addressed to all the Member States had to be able to plead, in proceedings brought under national law against the rejection of his application, the illegality of the Commission's decision on which the national decision adopted in his regard was based.

[23] In that judgment the Court took into account the fact that the rejection of the application by the national authority was the only measure directly addressed to the person concerned of which it had necessarily been informed in good time and which it could challenge in the courts without encountering any difficulty in demonstrating its interest in bringing proceedings. It held that in those circumstances the possibility of pleading the unlawfulness of the Commission's decision derived from a general principle of law which found its expression in Article 184 of the EEC Treaty, namely the principle which confers upon any party to proceedings the right to challenge, for the purpose of obtaining the annulment of a decision of direct and individual concern to that party, the validity of previous acts of the institutions which form the legal basis of the decision which is being attacked, if that party was not entitled under Article 173 of the Treaty to bring a direct action challenging those acts by which it was thus affected without having been in a position to ask that they be declared void (see the judgment in Case 92/78 *Simmenthal* v *Commission* [1979] ECR 777).

[24] In the present case, it is common ground that the applicant in the main proceedings was fully aware of the Commission's decision and of the fact that it could without any doubt have challenged it under Article 173 of the Treaty.

[25] It follows from the foregoing that, in factual and legal circumstances such as those of the main proceedings in this case, the definitive nature of the decision taken by the Commission pursuant to Article 93 of the Treaty *vis-à-vis* the undertaking in receipt of the aid binds the national court by virtue of the principle of legal certainty.

[26] The reply to be given to the first question must therefore be that the national court is bound by a Commission decision adopted under Article 93(2) of the Treaty where, in view of the implementation of that decision by the national authorities, the recipient of the aid to which the implementation measures are addressed brings before it an action in which it pleads the unlawfulness of the Commission's decision and where that recipient of aid, although informed in writing by the Member State of the Commission's decision, did not bring an action against that decision under the second paragraph of Article 173 of the Treaty, or did not do so within the period prescribed.

NOTE: See also the analogy drawn in *TWD Textilwerke Deggendorf GmbH* v *Commission* (Cases T-244/93 and T-486/93) [1995] ECR II-2265, where the Court of First Instance (now the General Court) limited access to Article 184 of the EC Treaty (now Article 277 TFEU) (p. 209) where an available action under Article 173 of the EC Treaty (now, after amendment, Article 263 TFEU) had not been initiated. In the ruling the Court is careful to make plain that it does not intend to overturn its pre-existing receptivity to the use of the preliminary reference procedure as a means of indirect challenge to EU acts. Rather, it considers that it is dealing with a special situation in which a firm declining to pursue the available routes of the direct action should not subsequently be able to rely on the preliminary reference procedure. By contrast, in *Eurotunnel SA and Others* v *SeaFrance* (Case C-408/95) [1997] ECR I-6315, challenge to the validity of Directives 91/680 and 92/12 establishing transitional arrangements for 'duty free' shops failed on the merits, but was treated as permissibly advanced *via* proceedings at national level involving a preliminary reference even though the applicant had not attempted to pursue a direct action, for it was not obvious that the applicant would have had individual concern for the purposes of a direct action and clearly would not have had direct concern. Similarly, in Joined Cases C-346/03 & C-529/03 *Atenzi, Scalas and Lilliu* [2006] ECR I-1875 the Court found that standing to bring an application for annulment under what is now Article 263 TFEU would not have been 'self-evident' (para 34), 'unlike' in *TWD Textilwerke Deggendorf*, so the preliminary reference under what is now Article 267 TFEU was admissible. The message is that a firm immediately affected by an EU act must decide its litigation strategy with an eye to the two-month time-limit contained in the final paragraph of Article 263.

■ QUESTIONS

1. *In principle* do you accept the Court's concern in Case C-188/92 that legal certainty would be compromised were a party in the applicant's position permitted to avail itself of national proceedings supplemented by Article 267 TFEU in order to contest EU acts?
2. *In practice*, in the light of your examination in this chapter of the twists and turns of the Court's approach to standing under Article 263 TFEU as well as the new ambiguities introduced by the Lisbon Treaty, do you consider that the Court's reference to the ability *without any doubt* (para 24 of the ruling in Case C-188/92) of the applicant to make use of Article 263 represents a workable criterion for lawyers who in future must advise clients as to when they should invest time and money in pursuing a direct Article 263 challenge, in order to preclude the subsequent unpleasant discovery that the Article 267 route is barred? Consider in this vein also Case C-241/01 *NFU* v *Secretariat général du gouvernement* [2002] ECR I-9079 (a recipient who 'could undoubtedly have challenged that decision' under Article 263 may not call its lawfulness into question before a national court, para 35 of the judgment) and, in connection with the analogous question whether the availability of Article 277 depends on recourse to Article 263, Case C-11/00 *Commission* v *ECB* [2003] ECR I-7147.

C: Article 267 and the validity of Union acts

The next case was an important milestone in the Court's development of the preliminary reference procedure as a tool of judicial review of EU legislation. It has already been discussed at p. 180, but the core of the judgment bears repetition here.

***Foto Frost* v *HZA Lubeck Ost* (Case 314/85)**

[1987] ECR 4199, Court of Justice of the European Communities

[15] ... [T]he main purpose of the powers accorded to the Court by Article 177 [now 267] is to ensure that Community law is applied uniformly by national courts. That requirement of uniformity is particularly imperative when the validity of a Community act is in question. Divergences between courts in the Member States as to the validity of Community acts would be liable to place in jeopardy the very unity of the Community legal order and detract from the fundamental requirement of legal certainty.

...

[17] Since Article 173 [now 263] gives the Court exclusive jurisdiction to declare void an act of a Community institution, the coherence of the system requires that where the validity of a Community act is challenged before a national court the power to declare the act invalid must also be reserved to the Court of Justice.

. . .

[19] It should be added that the rule that national courts may not themselves declare Community acts invalid may have to be qualified in certain circumstances in the case of proceedings relating to an application for interim measures; however, that case is not referred to in the national court's question.

[20] The answer to the first question must therefore be that the national courts have no jurisdiction themselves to declare that acts of Community institutions are invalid.

The Commission Decision was held invalid.

NOTE: Once this case is placed in the general context of the EU's judicial review procedures, it is perhaps easier to appreciate why the Court was eager to deny the competence of national courts to hold EU legislation unlawful (*cf* p. 180). The proposition that the Court of Justice is indeed properly treated as 'the ultimate umpire of the system' is carefully defended by J. Weiler and U. Haltern in 'The Autonomy of the Community Legal Order – Through the Looking Glass' (1996) 37 Harvard Intl L Jnl 411. The stance of national courts on judicial competence to fix the outer limits of EU competence has the potential to cause tension in the light of the Court of Justice's perception that its own exclusive jurisdiction is essential to the very unity of the EU legal order. This relationship between EU and national attitudes is considered more fully in Chapter 19.

***Zuckerfabrik Süderdithmarschen* v HZA Itzehoe (Case C-143/88); *Zuckerfabrik Soest* v *HZA Paderborn* (Case C-92/89)**

[1991] ECR I-415, Court of Justice of the European Communities

These cases involved two separate disputes between firms and German customs offices concerning demands for the payment of levies. The firms challenged the national administrative measures before German courts; the basis of the challenge was the validity of the legislation adopted by (what was then) the Community setting up the structure. The questions referred to Luxembourg concerned, first, the circumstances in which the national court could grant interim relief against the contested measures, it being clear from *Foto Frost* that the final decision on validity belongs with the Court of Justice; and, secondly, questions about the validity of the challenged Regulation itself.

The Court insisted that in order to ensure that the preliminary reference procedure under Article 177 of the EC Treaty (now Article 267 TFEU) works effectively, it must be possible for a national court to grant interim relief suspending the operation of a national measure based on impugned Community legislation, pending the Court's final ruling on validity. It pointed out that it had already ruled that interim relief must be available before a national court asked to rule on the compatibility of national law with Community law (*Factortame*, p. 111), and added that no different solution should apply where the dispute was about the compatibility of secondary Community law with Community law. The Court then went on to explain the circumstances in which such interim relief should be granted by a national court.

[23] It must first of all be noted that interim measures suspending enforcement of a contested measure may be adopted only if the factual and legal circumstances relied on by the applicants are such as to persuade the national court that serious doubts exist as to the validity of the Community regulation on which the contested administrative measure is based. Only the possibility of a finding of invalidity, a matter which is reserved to the court, can justify the granting of suspensory measures.

[24] It should next be pointed out that suspension of enforcement must retain the character of an interim measure. The national court to which the application for interim relief is made may therefore grant a suspension only until such time as the Court has delivered its ruling on the question of validity. Consequently, it is for the national court, should the question not yet have been referred to the Court of Justice, to refer that question itself, setting out the reasons for which it believes that the regulation must be held to be invalid.

[25] As regards the other conditions concerning the suspension of enforcement of administrative measures, it must be observed that the rules of procedure of the courts are determined by national law and that those conditions differ according to the national law governing them, which may jeopardize the uniform application of Community law.

[26] Such uniform application is a fundamental requirement of the Community legal order. It therefore follows that the suspension of enforcement of administrative measures based on a Community regulation, whilst it is governed by national procedural law, in particular as regards the making and examination of the application, must in all the Member States be subject, at the very least, to conditions which are uniform so far as the granting of such relief is concerned.

[27] Since the power of national courts to grant such a suspension corresponds to the jurisdiction reserved to the Court of Justice by Article 185 in the context of actions brought under Article 173, those courts may grant such relief only on the conditions which must be satisfied for the Court of Justice to allow an application to it for interim measures.

[28] In this regard, the Court has consistently held that measures suspending the operation of a contested act may be granted only in the event of urgency, in other words, if it is necessary for them to be adopted and to take effect before the decision on the substance of a case, in order to avoid serious and irreparable damage to the party seeking them.

[29] With regard to the question of urgency, it should be pointed out that damage invoked by the applicant must be liable to materialize before the Court of Justice has been able to rule on the validity of the contested Community measure. With regard to the nature of the damage, purely financial damage cannot, as the Court has held on numerous occasions, be regarded in principle as irreparable. However, it is for the national court hearing the application for interim relief to examine the circumstances particular to the case before it. It must in this connection consider whether immediate enforcement of the measure which is the subject of the application for interim relief would be likely to result in irreversible damage to the applicant which could not be made good if the Community act were to be declared invalid.

[30] It should also be added that a national court called upon to apply, within the limits of its jurisdiction, the provisions of Community law is under an obligation to ensure that full effect is given to Community law and, consequently, where there is doubt as to the validity of Community regulations, to take account of the interest of the Community, namely that such regulations should not be set aside without proper guarantees.

[31] In order to comply with that obligation, a national court seised of an application for suspension must first examine whether the Community measure in question would be deprived of all effectiveness if not immediately implemented.

[32] If suspension of enforcement is liable to involve a financial risk for the Community, the national court must also be in a position to require the applicant to provide adequate guarantees, such as the deposit of money or other security.

[33] It follows from the foregoing that the reply to the second part of the first question put to the Court by the Finanzgericht Hamburg must be that suspension of enforcement of a national measure adopted in implementation of a Community regulation may be granted by a national court only:

(i) if that court entertains serious doubts as to the validity of the Community measure and, should the question of the validity of the contested measure not already have been brought before the Court, itself refers that question to the Court;
(ii) if there is urgency and a threat of serious and irreparable damage to the applicant;
(iii) and if the national court takes due account of the Community's interests.

NOTE: There is a sure indication that the Court was aware in the *Zuckerfabrik* cases that it was establishing an important principle. The decision is against the applicants; the legislation is held valid. Yet the Court had not dealt with the matter in brief, as it could have done. It took time to explain the applicable principles of law.

In the next case the Court added a further, fourth criterion. There seems little doubt that the addition reflects the Court's concern to sustain uniformity in the application of EU law. The decision is a preliminary ruling on questions referred from a German court, the *Verwaltungsgericht* of Frankfurt-am-Main.

Atlanta Fruchthandelsgesellschaft mbH and Others v *Bundesamt für Ernährung und Forstwirtschaft* (Case C-465/93)

[1995] ECR I-3761, Court of Justice of the European Communities

The challenged act was Council Regulation 404/93 on the common organization of the market in bananas, establishing a common import regime. The applicants, traditional importers of bananas, found themselves with import quotas which they viewed as insufficient. Among other strategies to challenge the system, they brought proceedings before the German courts to attack measures associated with the implementation of the EU regime. The Court of Justice was asked questions on the national court's power to order interim measures disapplying a Regulation pending a preliminary ruling by the Court on its validity. The Court stated that the case afforded it 'an opportunity to clarify' the conditions established in *Zuckerfabrik* (Cases C-143/88, C-92/89), p. 223.

[35] In *Zuckerfabrik* (paragraph 23) the Court held that interim measures may be adopted only if the factual and legal circumstances relied on by the applicants are such as to persuade the national court that serious doubts exist as to the validity of the Community regulation on which the contested administrative measure is based. Only the possibility of a finding of invalidity, a matter which is reserved to the Court, can justify the grant of interim relief.

[36] That requirement means that the national court cannot restrict itself to referring the question of the validity of the regulation to the Court for a preliminary ruling, but must set out, when making the interim order, the reasons for which it considers that the Court should find the regulation to be invalid.

[37] The national court must take into account here the extent of the discretion which, having regard to the Court's case-law, the Community institutions must be allowed in the sectors concerned.

[38] The Court further held in *Zuckerfabrik* (paragraph 24) that the grant of relief must retain the character of an interim measure. The national court to which the application for interim relief is made may therefore order interim measures and maintain them only for so long as the Court has not ruled that consideration of the questions referred for a preliminary ruling has disclosed no factor of such a kind as to affect the validity of the regulation in question.

[39] Since the power of national courts to order interim relief corresponds to the jurisdiction reserved to the Court of Justice by Article 186 in the context of actions brought under Article 173 of the Treaty, those national courts may grant such relief only on the same conditions as apply when the Court of Justice is dealing with an application for interim measures (*Zuckerfabrik*, paragraph 27).

[40] In that respect the Court held in *Zuckerfabrik* (paragraph 28), on the basis of settled case law, that interim measures may be ordered only where they are urgent, that is to say, where it is necessary for them to be adopted and take effect before the decision on the substance of the case, in order to avoid serious and irreparable damage to the party seeking them.

[41] As to urgency, the damage relied on by the applicant must be such as to materialise before the Court of Justice has been able to rule on the validity of the contested Community act. As to the nature of the damage, purely financial damage cannot, as the Court has held on numerous occasions, be regarded in principle as irreparable. However, it is for the national court hearing the application for interim relief to examine the circumstances particular to the case before it. It must in this connection consider whether immediate enforcement of the measure with respect to which the application for interim relief is made would be likely to result in irreversible damage to the applicant which could not be made good if the Community act were to be declared invalid (*Zuckerfabrik*, paragraph 29).

[42] Furthermore, a national court called upon to apply, within the limits of its jurisdiction, the provisions of Community law is under an obligation to ensure that full effect is given to Community law and, consequently, where there is doubt as to the validity of Community regulations, to take account of the interest of the Community, namely that such regulations should not be set aside without proper guarantees (*Zuckerfabrik*, paragraph 30).

[43] In order to comply with that obligation, the national court to which an application for interim relief has been made must first examine whether the Community act in question would be deprived of all effectiveness if not immediately implemented (*Zuckerfabrik*, paragraph 31).

[44] In that respect the national court must take account of the damage which the interim measure may cause the legal regime established by that regulation for the Community as a whole. It must consider, on the one hand, the cumulative effect which would arise if a large number of courts were also to adopt interim measures for similar reasons and, on the other, those special features of the applicant's situation which distinguish him from the other operators concerned.

[45] If the grant of interim relief represents a financial risk for the Community, the national court must also be in a position to require the applicant to provide adequate guarantees, such as the deposit of money or other security (*Zuckerfabrik*, paragraph 32).

[46] When assessing the conditions for the grant of interim relief, the national court is obliged under Article 5 [now 4(3) TEU] of the Treaty to respect what the Community court has decided on the questions at issue before it. Thus if the Court of Justice has dismissed on the merits an action for annulment of the regulation in question or has held, in the context of a reference for a preliminary ruling on validity, that the reference disclosed nothing to affect the validity of that regulation, the national court can no longer order interim measures or must revoke existing measures, unless the grounds of illegality put forward before it differ from the pleas in law or grounds of illegality rejected by the Court in its judgment. The same applies if the Court of First Instance, in a judgment which has become final and binding, has dismissed on the merits an action for annulment of the regulation or a plea of illegality.

[47] In the present case the Court, adjudicating on the same factual situation as that which gave rise to the proceedings before the national court, has held that the Member States which bring an action for annulment of the regulation, being responsible for the interests, in particular those of an economic and social nature, which are regarded as general interests at national level, are entitled to take judicial proceedings to defend such interests. They may therefore invoke damage affecting a whole sector of their economy, in particular when the contested Community measure may entail unfavourable repercussions on the level of employment and the cost of living (order in *Germany* v *Council*, cited above [Case C-280/93 R [1993] ECR I-3667], paragraph 27).

[48] The national court, when called upon to protect the rights of individuals, may indeed assess the extent to which refusal to order an interim measure may be liable to have a serious and irreparable effect on important individual interests.

[49] However, if an applicant is unable to show a specific situation which distinguishes him from other operators in the relevant sector, the national court must accept any findings already made by the Court of Justice concerning the serious and irreparable nature of the damage.

[50] The national court's obligation to respect a decision of the Court of Justice applies in particular to the Court's assessment of the Community interest and the balance between that interest and that of the economic sector concerned.

[51] Accordingly, the answer to the second question put to the Court by the Verwaltungsgericht Frankfurt am Main must be that interim relief, with respect to a national administrative measure adopted in implementation of a Community regulation, can be granted by a national court only if:

(1) that court entertains serious doubts as to the validity of the Community act and, if the validity of the contested act is not already in issue before the Court of Justice, itself refers the question to the Court of Justice;
(2) there is urgency, in that the interim relief is necessary to avoid serious and irreparable damage being caused to the party seeking the relief;
(3) the court takes due account of the Community interest; and
(4) in its assessment of all those conditions, it respects any decisions of the Court of Justice or the Court of First Instance ruling on the lawfulness of the regulation or on an application for interim measures seeking similar interim relief at Community level.

NOTE: On the very same day the Court answered questions relating to the validity of the same Regulation, 404/93, referred to it by the same court in litigation between the same parties: *Atlanta Fruchthandelsgesellschaft mbH and Others* v *Bundesamt für Ernährung und Forstwirtschaft* (Case C-466/93)

[1995] ECR I-3799. The Court observed that an action for annulment of the Regulation brought by Germany, based on comparable pleas to those covered by the questions referred, had already been dismissed as unfounded (*Germany* v *Council* (Case C-280/93) [1994] ECR I-4973). The Court of Justice had there found no violation of principles of law including that of undistorted competition, nor of fundamental rights including the right to property; neither had the Court in Case C-280/93 been prepared to test the Regulation against the standards of the GATT which it viewed as too 'flexible' to be apt for application in the context of a direct action for annulment (the Court has subsequently transplanted this reluctance to the incorporation of the Standards of the WTO, which has replaced the GATT: Case C-149/96 *Portugal* v *Council* [1999] ECR I-8395, and for elucidation of the applicable principles, see Case C-366/10 *Air Transport Association of America* judgment of 21 December 2011). Nothing new had been advanced in the preliminary reference to alter the Court's findings in Case C-280/93, excepting only a submission based on lack of reasons within the meaning of Article 190 of the EC Treaty (now Article 296 TFEU) (p. 45) which the Court did not accept. The Court therefore found no basis to impugn the validity of the Regulation. Subsequently, a claim for damages was unsuccessful; Case T-521/93 *Atlanta AG and Others* v *Council and Commission* [1996] ECR II-1707, from which an appeal failed in substance in Case C-104/97P *Atlanta AG and Others* v *Council and Commission* [1999] ECR I-6983. (On some of the background tensions in the 'banana cases', see N. Reich, (1996) 7 EJIL 103; S. Peers, (1999) 4 Euro Foreign Affairs Rev 195; and the *Bundesverfassungsgericht* ruling in *Bananas* is set out in Chapter 19, p. 594.)

Whereas *Atlanta* (Case C-465/93) explores the criteria according to which the application of national measures adopted pursuant to a Union act may exceptionally be suspended in national proceedings in which the validity of the EU act is impugned, the next case in this saga, also involving the disputed bananas regime founded on Regulation 404/93, saw the Court unwilling further to extend the powers of national courts.

T. Port GmbH v *Bundesanstalt für Landwirtschaft und Ernährung* (Case C-68/95)

[1996] ECR I-6065, [1997] 1 CMLR 1, Court of Justice of the European Communities

The applicant company's aim was to secure an increased quota of bananas. Proceedings were initiated before a German court, which made a preliminary reference asking for guidance on the powers of a national court to grant interim relief to traders pending a Commission determination on a request for an increased quota; specifically, could the national court make an interim order granting an increase? This goes beyond that which the Court accepted was within the competence of a national court in *Zuckerfabrik* and *Atlanta*, and in *T. Port* the Court, having referred to those cases, was not prepared to make that extension. Traders must seek judicial protection before the Court of Justice of the EU in such circumstances.

[52] However, the situation now raised by the national court is different from the situation at issue in those cases. The present case is not about granting interim measures in the context of the implementation of a Community regulation whose validity is being contested, in order to ensure interim protection of rights which individuals derive from the Community legal system, but about granting traders interim judicial protection in a situation where, by virtue of a Community regulation, the existence and scope of traders' rights must be established by a Commission measure which the Commission has not yet adopted.

[53] The Treaty makes no provision for a reference for a preliminary ruling by which a national court asks the Court of Justice to rule that an institution has failed to act. Consequently, national courts have no jurisdiction to order interim measures pending action on the part of the institution. Judicial review of alleged failure to act can be exercised only by the Community judicature.

[54] In a situation such as that in the present case, only the Court of Justice or the Court of First Instance, as the case may be, can ensure judicial protection for the persons concerned.

[55] It is to be remembered that, under the procedure provided for in Article 27 of the Regulation, the Commission is to adopt transitional measures following an opinion of the Management Committee before which the matter is brought by a representative of the Commission or of a Member State.

[56] In circumstances such as those in the main proceedings, it is for the relevant Member State, urged if necessary by the trader concerned, to request initiation of the Management Committee procedure, should this be necessary.

[57] Having regard to the hardship which the applicant in the main proceedings claims to be suffering, the applicant may also approach the Commission directly and request it to adopt, in accordance with the Article 27 procedure, the specific measures which its situation requires.

[58] Where the Community institution fails to act, the Member State may bring an action for failure to act before the Court of Justice. Likewise, the trader concerned, who would be the addressee of the measure which the Commission is alleged to have failed to adopt, or at least directly and individually concerned by it, could bring such an action before the Court of First Instance . . .

NOTE: Notice in these cases the Court's concern to build through analogies between EU level and national level. The Treaty provisions governing remedies are singularly incomplete, and the Court here shows itself bent on developing the system. What is particularly interesting in this area is the extent to which the Court of Justice is presiding over the development of a coherent legal order governing remedies. These cases concern interim relief at national level from Union acts. *Factortame* (Case C-213/89) concerns interim relief at national level from Member State practices allegedly incompatible with Union law; p. 111. Interim relief at Union level is examined at p. 203 in relation to Union acts, at p. 90 in relation to Member State practices. It is interesting and important to assess the extent to which the Court is bringing all these procedures into line. The process is far from complete, and naturally lacks the comprehensive coverage of legislation, but the Court appears gradually to be building the Union legal order through jurisprudence in linked but not identical areas.

D: The effect of an Article 267 ruling

ICC v *Amministrazione delle Finanze* (Case 66/80)

[1981] ECR 1191, Court of Justice of the European Communities

The case has already been encountered at p. 172. The Court held:

. . . [A]lthough a judgment of the Court given under Article 177 [now 234] of the Treaty declaring an act of an institution, in particular a Council or Commission Regulation, to be void is directly addressed only to the national court which brought the matter before the Court, it is sufficient reason for any other national court to regard that act as void for the purposes of a judgment which it has to give.

NOTE: Accordingly, a finding in Article 267 proceedings that Union legislation is invalid should be respected by other national courts. In practice, the effects of an Article 267 ruling of invalidity may not be significantly different from the impact of an Article 263 ruling, which according to Article 264 renders the act 'void'.

The Court has also claimed the power under Article 267 to rule on the validity of Union legislation in a nuanced manner. Validity need not be all or nothing.

Société de Produits de Maïs v *Administration des Douanes* (Case 112/83)

[1985] ECR 719, Court of Justice of the European Communities

This was a preliminary reference from a French court relating to the validity of Commission Regulation 652/76.

[16] It should in the first place be recalled that the Court has already held in its judgment of 13 May 1981 (Case 66/80 *International Chemical Corporation* [1981] ECR 1191) that although a judgment of the Court given under Article 177 of the Treaty declaring an act of an institution, in particular a Council or Commission Regulation,

to be void is directly addressed only to the national court which brought the matter before the Court, it is sufficient reason for any other national court to regard that act as void for the purposes of a judgment which it has to give.

[17] Secondly, it must be emphasized that the Court's power to impose temporal limits on the effects of a declaration that a legislative act is invalid, in the context of preliminary rulings under indent (b) of the first paragraph of Article 177, is justified by the interpretation of Article 174 [now 264] of the Treaty having regard to the necessary consistency between the preliminary ruling procedure and the action for annulment provided for in Articles 173, 174 and 176 of the Treaty, which are two mechanisms provided by the Treaty for reviewing the legality of acts of the Community institutions. The possibility of imposing temporal limits on the effects of the invalidity of a Community Regulation, whether under Article 173 or Article 177, is a power conferred on the Court by the Treaty in the interest of the uniform application of Community law throughout the Community. In the particular case of the judgment of 15 October 1980, referred to by the Tribunal [Case 145/79], the use of the possibility provided for in the second paragraph of Article 174 was based on reasons of legal certainty more fully explained in paragraph 52 of that judgment.

[18] It must be pointed out that where it is justified by overriding considerations the second paragraph of Article 174 [now 264] gives the Court discretion to decide, in each particular case, which specific effects of a Regulation which has been declared void must be maintained. It is therefore for the Court, where it makes use of the possibility of limiting the effect on past events of a declaration in proceedings under Article 177 [now 267] that a measure is void, to decide whether an exception to that temporal limitation of the effect of its judgment may be made in favour of the party which brought the action before the national court or of any other trader which took similar steps before the declaration of invalidity or whether, conversely, a declaration of invalidity applicable only to the future constitutes an adequate remedy even for traders who took action at the appropriate time with a view to protecting their rights.

NOTE: *Cf* the second paragraph of Article 264, at p. 188. Notice once again the Court's interest in bringing about coherence between the different routes for challenging Union acts.

The Court's approach in this case to the validity of Union legislation also finds a parallel in its approach to the interpretation of Union law. In *Defrenne* v *SABENA* (Case 43/75), at p. 101, it insisted that it alone has the competence to limit the implications of its ruling at national level.

SECTION 7: THE INTERRELATION OF THE SEVERAL REMEDIES

It should now be plain that although Article 263 constitutes the major direct means of challenging Union acts before the Court, other avenues of redress may be open to applicants. These include other avenues before the Court, as well as procedures at national level involving the use of the Article 267 preliminary reference procedure.

An extract from para 23 of *'Les Verts'* (Case 294/83) was set out at p. 210 to demonstrate how at Union level Article 277 may allow the applicant to circumvent the hurdles which guard the Article 263 direct action. Here now is the full text of para 23, which confirms how in addition Article 267 may serve that purpose *via* the action at national level.

***Parti Ecologiste 'Les Verts'* v *Parliament* (Case 294/83)**

[1986] ECR 1339, Court of Justice of the European Communities

[23] It must first be emphasised in this regard that the European Economic Community is a Community based on the rule of law, inasmuch as neither its Member States nor its institutions can avoid a review of the question whether the measures adopted by them are in conformity with the basic constitutional charter, the Treaty.

> In particular, in Articles 173 [now 263] and 184 [now 277], on the one hand, and in Article 177 [now 267], on the other, the Treaty established a complete system of legal remedies and procedures designed to permit the Court of Justice to review the legality of measures adopted by the institutions. Natural and legal persons are thus protected against the application to them of general measures which they cannot contest directly before the Court by reason of the special conditions of admissibility laid down in the second paragraph of Article 173 [now the fourth paragraph of Article 263] of the Treaty. Where the Community institutions are responsible for the administrative implementation of such measures, natural or legal persons may bring a direct action before the Court against implementing measures which are addressed to them or which are of direct and individual concern to them and, in support of such an action, plead the illegality of the general measure on which they are based. Where implementation is a matter for the national authorities, such persons may plead the invalidity of general measures before the national courts and cause the latter to request the Court of Justice for a preliminary ruling.

NOTE: And, as a result of the Lisbon amendments, we can add that natural or legal persons may also bring a direct action against a regulatory act which is of direct concern and does not entail implementing measures (p. 200).

In this chapter there have been many examples of the Court's concern to draw analogies between different levels of enforcement and remedies in order to ensure the structure displays an internal coherence. See the *Zuckerfabrik* cases at p. 223; and read para 10 of the judgment in *Universität Hamburg* (Case 216/82), at p. 217; para 17, *Foto Frost* (Case 314/85), at p. 222; para 39, *Atlanta* (Case 465/93), at p. 225; para 17, *Société de Produits de Maïs* (Case 112/83), at p. 228. This is part of the Court's process of 'constitutionalizing' the Treaty.

FURTHER READING

Albors-Llorens, A., 'Remedies Against the EU Institutions after Lisbon: An Era of Opportunity?' (2012) 71 CLJ 507.

De Sadeleer, N. and Poncelet C., 'Protection Against Acts Harmful to Human Health and the Environment Adopted by the EU Institutions' (2012) 14 Camb Ybk Euro Legal Studies 177.

Van Malleghem, P. and Baeten, N., 'Before the law stands a gatekeeper – or, what is a regulatory act in Article 263(4) TFEU?' (2014) 51 CMLRev 1187.

■ QUESTIONS

1. In *Plaumann* v *Commission* (Case 25/62) (p. 192) the Court commented that 'provisions of the Treaty regarding the right of interested parties to bring an action must not be interpreted restrictively'. Has the Court adhered to this view in its treatment of applications for annulment of the acts of the EU institutions? Should it?
2. 'It is ill-advised to consider whether natural and legal persons should enjoy more generous rules on standing in order to enhance their capacity to control acts of EU institutions in isolation from questions about the adequacy of the systems of accountability to citizens to which EU institutions are subject and the propensity of those systems for securing representative and responsive governance in the Union.' Discuss.

SECTION 8: THE NARRATIVE OF CONSTITUTIONALISM

The concluding sentence of the previous section identified the Court's quest to ensure a complete system of legal remedies and procedures as 'part of the Court's process of "constitutionalizing" the Treaty'. In bringing to an end Part I of this book's inquiry into *The Constitutional Law of the EU* it is appropriate to situate this trend in the wider context of the material covered in these eight chapters.

'The Court has sought to "constitutionalize" the Treaty, that is to fashion a constitutional framework for a federal-type structure in Europe.' These words were written in 1989 by Mancini and are set out in the extract at p. 102. The shaping of inter-State relations according to EU law has at least as much, and perhaps more, in common with the modes of internal distribution of power within a federal State than it does with the structuring of an international organization established by a Treaty. The principles of supremacy and direct effect are central to this claim that the EU legal regime operates in many respects *as if* it were organizing the internal governance of a (federal) State. This reveals that 'constitutionalism' has equipped the EU with a working method that allows it to avoid choices about whether it is 'really' international law or 'really' State law. It is both; it is neither; it doesn't matter (in practice).

C. Timmermans, 'The Constitutionalization of the European Union'

(2002) 21 *Yearbook of European Law* 1, extracts at pp. 1 and 2.

> What do we mean by saying that the European Union is in a process of being constitutionalized? In a way the founding instruments, and speaking in this context, the founding Treaty or Treaties of an international organization could always be referred to as the 'Constitution' of the organisation (as has been done, for instance, in the founding Treaty of the International Labour Organization). That is not what we have in mind, of course, when referring to constitutionalization. . . . when we refer to 'a constitution', we mean more than a technical instrument embodying the organizational chart for a state spelling out who should do what and in doing so be controlled by whom. The term constitution, at least to me, implies values of a more fundamental nature; values that should underpin and penetrate the institutional structuring of the state system and its functioning. That is why it is possible to have a Constitution without a written text and why we can use the term constitutionalization. These values which are the guarantees for a proper organisation and exercise of State power, and also constitute to some extent the basic objectives to be pursued by State action, are more particularly expressed in terms of protection of fundamental rights, democracy and the rule of law.

'Constitutionalization' provides an insight into the deeper mission of European integration. Joerges and Sand describe constitutionalism 'as a metaphor for the challenges that the emerging transnational governance presents to the notion of democratic legitimacy' ('Constitutionalism and transnational governance', unpublished paper). It is vital to escape imprisonment in thinking that assumes the rise of transfrontier markets generates a need for geographically bigger States. Economic structures migrate in ways that do not have to be followed and frequently cannot be followed by political institutions. The EU is part of the necessary leap of imagination in the direction of an understanding of governance that transcends the State, either acting alone or in constructing inter-State bargains. The 'constitutionalized' legal order serves to bind together national and transnational actors within a system that does not require choices to be made about where to locate ultimate political and legal authority, nor to require the wholesale transfer of authority from a State to a 'Euro-State'. A more subtle network of governance is envisaged. The debate about the EU's legitimacy will be rejoined in Chapter 19 but it suffices for present purposes to observe that from this perspective, criticism of the EU as lacking the democratic credentials that are characteristic of a State is not to take as given that which is contested. It is to take as given that which is denied. The EU is not a State nor is it to become one.

■ **QUESTION**

At the beginning of Chapter 2 it was declared that 'Some observers have identified a more cautious, "minimalist" approach by the Court of Justice; see T. Koopmans (then a judge of the Court) (1986) 35 ICLQ 925' (p. 24). Thirty years on, and now, at the end of Chapter 8, equipped with a panoramic view of the constitutionalization of the legal order, you are asked to what extent you now find minimalism an appropriate description of the Court of Justice's technique? Should the Court aspire to be minimalist? Should any court?

Once one assembles the several pieces of the jigsaw examined in Part One of this book – autonomy, supremacy, direct effect, effective judicial protection, preliminary rulings, judicial review – Union law has functional resemblances to a Constitution for a federal-type State. In particular, supremacy appears to dictate a hierarchical relationship between the two levels of law-making, placing the (quasi-)federal rules on top. There is much more to the claim to constitutionalization. Beyond Treaty sources and secondary legislation, there are general principles which permeate the fabric of the law, in some instances without explicit textual support in the Treaty; and the Treaty establishes institutionally relatively sophisticated forms of law making which reflect forms of representative democracy at both national and European level, in the shape of the Council and the Parliament respectively. So it functions as a constitution in the 'thin' sense that it is constitutive of the system that is the EU legal order. But the Court is rhetorically bolder. *Parti Ecologiste 'Les Verts'* v *Parliament* (Case 294/83) is important enough to have been extracted three times in this chapter (pp. 187, 210, and 229). In that ruling the Court described 'a Community based on the rule of law, inasmuch as neither its Member States nor its institutions can avoid a review of the question whether the measures adopted by them are in conformity with the basic constitutional charter, the Treaty . . .' (see similarly Opinion 1/91 on the draft EEA Agreement [1991] ECR I-6079). The Lisbon Treaty pushes further, in that the Community, riven by its 'three pillars' (p. 9), is replaced by the Union. Accordingly Pech finds that 'By providing greater judicial protection against a broader set of Union measures . . . the Lisbon Treaty substantially strengthens compliance with the principle of the rule of law as far as the Union's constitutional framework is concerned' ('A Union founded on the Rule of Law' (2010) Euro Const Law Rev 359, 396). What seems to be at stake here is a constitution that is characterized by an assumption of the subjection of the exercise of public power to judicial control even in circumstances where this is not explicitly foreseen in the governing texts. The legal control of the institutions of the EU itself, which is what was in dispute in *Parti Ecologiste 'Les Verts'*, was deepened by the Court's readiness to extend its powers of review beyond those explicitly conferred by the Treaty. This tends towards a stronger and thicker kind of constitution, of a type that might not be readily associated with an organization existing beyond the State. The EU offers both a Constitution for economic integration and a Constitution for the protection of the individual. This twin purpose of EU law has been and will be observed in many manifestations throughout this book. And in fact tracing this process of 'constitutionalization' of what began as, and in formal terms still is, a legal order founded on an international Treaty holds the key to understanding the remarkable evolution of the EU legal order. Moreover, it raises fascinating yet deeply sensitive questions about how sustainable the Court's vision of the nature of the legal order over which it presides truly is – and how sustainable it should be. It is a debate that will be re-joined in Part III of this book, especially Chapter 19.

NOTE: For additional material and resources see the Online Resource Centre at: www.oxfordtextbooks.co.uk/orc/weatherill12e.

PART II

Union Trade Law and Policy

9

Law and the Economic Objectives of the Union

SECTION 1: INTRODUCTION

This part of the book examines the major provisions of EU substantive law. These are the provisions which are designed to eliminate barriers to trade between Member States and to suppress distortions in the competitive structure of the market. These provisions are the instruments for transforming the territory of the Union into an integrated single market.

Chapter 9 provides an introduction to the subject of EU trade law. It explains basic economic theory. It shows why an integrated market is economically advantageous and discusses the shortcomings of the process hitherto. It also examines the project which in the late 1980s and early 1990s reinvigorated what was then the European Community – the completion of the single (or internal) market by the end of 1992. It shows how this is a dynamic process, reverberating long after the 1992 deadline has passed. Chapter 9 concludes with a brief introduction to the pursuit of the objective of Economic and Monetary Union which was first elaborated in the (Maastricht) Treaty on European Union.

Thereafter Chapters 10–16 examine the legal provisions which permit the opening up of the market and which contribute to the regulation of that single economic space. This is achieved in part by prohibiting States from imposing barriers to the free movement of the factors of production (goods, persons, services, capital) between Member States. Chapters 10–12 examine the legal instruments for securing the free movement of goods; Chapters 13 and 14 examine the free movement of persons and services. These provisions are 'negative' in the sense that they involve prohibitions on State action. Chapter 15 looks at the broadening of the project of integration in the shape of the creation of European Citizenship and the quest to establish an 'area of freedom, security and justice'. These notions operate at a grander and more constitutionally demanding level than the pursuit of market integration and have injected some serious controversy into the nature and scope of European-level policy-making. Chapter 16 then surveys the competition law of the EU, which in part serves to align control of private practices antagonistic to inter-State trade with the control over State practices exerted by the free movement provisions, but which also extends more broadly to supervise potentially anti-competitive practices pursued by private parties.

SECTION 2: ECONOMIC INTEGRATION IN CONTEXT

ARTICLE 2 EU, THE UNION'S VALUES

The Union is founded on the values of respect for human dignity, freedom, democracy, equality, the rule of law and respect for human rights, including the rights of persons belonging to minorities. These values are common to the Member States in a society in which pluralism, non-discrimination, tolerance, justice, solidarity and equality between men and women prevail.

There is no mention of economics here! However, economic integration has been and remains central to the project pursued today by the EU, albeit that, as emphasized in Chapter 1 of this book, economic integration has always been a means to grander political ends in the EU. Article 3(2) TEU provides that 'The Union shall offer its citizens an area of freedom, security and justice without internal frontiers.' Article 3(3) TEU deserves to be set out in full:

ARTICLE 3(3) TEU

The Union shall establish an internal market. It shall work for the sustainable development of Europe based on balanced economic growth and price stability, a highly competitive social market economy, aiming at full employment and social progress, and a high level of protection and improvement of the quality of the environment. It shall promote scientific and technological advance.

It shall combat social exclusion and discrimination, and shall promote social justice and protection, equality between women and men, solidarity between generations and protection of the rights of the child.

It shall promote economic, social and territorial cohesion, and solidarity among Member States.

It shall respect its rich cultural and linguistic diversity, and shall ensure that Europe's cultural heritage is safeguarded and enhanced.

NOTE: Article 3(4) TEU then adds that 'The Union shall establish an economic and monetary union whose currency is the euro.' So economic integration is part of this 'mission statement' – only a part, but an important part. From its very inception the Treaty placed emphasis on the establishment of a *common market*, and this existed alongside a commitment to create an *internal market* from the entry into force of the Single European Act in 1987. There was probably no difference, at least in practice, between the 'common market' and the 'internal market' but with effect from 1 December 2009 the position has been clarified. The phrase 'common market' was removed by the Lisbon Treaty, and all references are to the 'internal market' alone. So, Article 3(3) TEU begins by stating that 'The Union shall establish an internal market', and the concept of the internal market is defined in Article 26(2) TFEU as an 'area without internal frontiers in which the free movement of goods, persons, services and capital is ensured in accordance with the provisions of this Treaty'.

A: What are the different types of economic integration that are available to States?

A. M. El-Agraa (ed.), *The European Union: Economics and Policies*
(9th ed., Cambridge: CUP, 2011), pp. 1–2

IEI [international economic integration] is one aspect of 'international economics' which has been growing in importance since the middle of the twentieth century. The term itself has quite a short history; indeed, Machlup [*A History of Thought on Economic Integration* (Macmillan, 1977)] was unable to find a single instance of its use prior to 1942. Since then the term has been used at various times to refer to practically any area of international economic relations. By 1950, however, the term had been given a specific definition by international trade specialists to denote *a state of affairs or a process which involves the amalgamation of separate economies into larger free trading regions.* It is in this more limited sense that the term is used today. However, one should hasten to add that recently the term has been used to mean simply increasing economic interdependence between nations, now glamorized as globalization.

More specifically, economic integration (also referred to as 'regional integration', regional trading agreements ('RTAs'), 'preferential trading agreements' ('PTAs') and trading blocs) is concerned with (a) the discriminatory removal of all trade impediments between at least two participating nations, and with (b) the establishment of certain elements of cooperation and coordination between them. The latter depends entirely on the actual form that IEI takes. Different forms of IEI can be envisaged and many have actually been implemented (see Table 1.1 for schematic presentation):

1. In *Free trade areas* (FTAs or PTAs), the member nations (MNs) remove tariffs among themselves but retain their freedom to determine their own policies *vis-à-vis* the outside world (the non-participants). Recently, the trend has been to extend this treatment to investment.
2. *Customs unions* (CUs) are very similar to FTAs/PTAs, except that MNs must conduct and pursue common external commercial relations – for instance, they must adopt common external tariffs (CETs) on imports from the non-participants.
3. *Common markets* (CMs) are CUs that allow also for free factor mobility across MN' frontiers – that is, capital, labour, technology and enterprises should move unhindered between MNs.
4. *Complete economic unions*, or economic unions (EcUs), are CMs plus the complete unification of monetary and fiscal policies – that is, MNs must introduce a central authority to exercise control over these matters so that MNs effectively become regions of the same nation.
5. In *complete political unions* (PUs), MNs literally become one nation – that is, the central authority needed in EcUs should be paralleled by a common parliament and other institutions needed to guarantee the sovereignty of one state.

Table 9.1 Schematic presentation of economic integration schemes

Scheme	Free intrascheme trade	Common commercial policy (CCP)	Free factor mobility	Common monetary and fiscal policy	One Government
Free trade area (FTA)	Yes	No	No	No	No
Customs union (CU)	Yes	Yes	No	No	No
Common market (CM)	Yes	Yes	Yes	No	No
Economic union (EcU)	Yes	Yes	Yes	Yes	No
Political union (PU)	Yes	Yes	Yes	Yes	Yes

However, one should hasten to add that political integration need not be, and in the majority of cases will never be, part of this list. Nevertheless, it can of course be introduced as a form of unity and for no economic reason whatsoever, as was the case with the two Germanys in 1990, and as is the case with the pursuit of the unification of the Korean Peninsula, although we should naturally be interested in its economic consequences (see below). More generally, we should stress that each of these forms of IEI can be introduced in its own right; hence they should not be confused with stages in a process which eventually leads to complete economic or political union.

It should also be noted that there may be sectoral integration, as distinct from general across-the-board IEI, in particular areas of the economy as was the case with the European Coal and Steel Community (ECSC), created in 1951, but sectoral integration is considered to be only a form of cooperation because it is inconsistent with the accepted definition of IEI, and also because it may contravene the rules of the General Agreement on Tariffs and Trade (GATT), which began to be run by the WTO in 1995. . . . Sectoral integration may also occur within any of the mentioned schemes, as is the case with the EU's Common Agricultural Policy (CAP), but then it is nothing more than a 'policy'.

It has been claimed that IEI can be *negative* or *positive*. The term 'negative IEI' was coined by Tinbergen (*International Economic Integration* (Elsevier, 1954)) to refer to the simple act of the removal of impediments on trade between MNs. The term 'positive integration' relates to the modification of existing instruments and institutions and, more importantly, to the creation of new ones so as to enable the market of the integrated area to function properly and effectively and also to promote other broader policy aims of the scheme. Hence, at the risk of oversimplification, according to this classification, it can be stated that sectoral integration and FTAs/PTAs are forms of IEI which require only negative integration, while the remaining types require positive integration, since, as a minimum, they need the positive act of adopting common external trade and investment relations. However, in reality this distinction is over simplistic, not only because practically all existing types of IEI have found it essential to introduce some elements of positive integration, but also because theoretical considerations clearly indicate that no scheme of IEI is viable without certain elements of positive integration.

NOTE: The EU is just one example of what El-Agraa labels 'IEI' – but it has what he calls the 'deepest scheme' of IEI in the world (p. 4), in particular the scheme within the 'eurozone' of 18 Member States (p. 261). The aim is economic efficiency, to be achieved through greater specialization ('comparative advantage'), the release of economies of scale, intensification of competition, as well as an improved bargaining position on the international plane. Economists separate these advantages into static gains consequent on improved resource reallocation and long-term or dynamic effects.

However, the European Union is a response to the post-war devastation of the continent of Europe, and grew in part because of the perceived failure of the nation State as an international actor. The Union encompasses aspirations beyond economics. This should already have become clear from your reading of the material in Chapter 1 of this book.

What, then, is the role of law in achieving these goals?

In Chapter 2 it was explained that the Lisbon Treaty introduced what is now Title I of Part One of the TFEU. It is set out at p. 30. Entitled 'Categories and Areas of Union Competence' it comprises Articles 2–6 TFEU. It provides a list of the areas in which the Union is competent. Here we find the areas of activity which make up the law of the internal market – and beyond. Of particular relevance to economic integration are:

The customs union; the establishing of the competition rules necessary for the functioning of the internal market; monetary policy for the Member States whose currency is the euro; and the common commercial policy. These are all competences *exclusive* to the Union according to Article 3 TFEU.

The internal market; social policy (for the aspects defined in the TFEU); economic, social and territorial cohesion; environment; consumer protection; transport; energy; and the area of freedom, security and justice. These are all areas of competences *shared* between the Union and the Member States according to Article 4 TFEU.

Article 2(6) TFEU states that 'The scope of and arrangements for exercising the Union's competences shall be determined by the provisions of the Treaties relating to each area.' Therefore, it is necessary to find the relevant provision in the TFEU in order to grasp the scope of and arrangements for exercising the competence in question. They are located in Part Three of the TFEU, entitled *Union Policies and Internal Actions*. This, in fact, is very large. It contains 24 Titles and stretches from Article 26 to Article 197 TFEU. These provisions, taken together, comprise the EU's working methods, and of particular relevance to Part II of this book they contain the detailed rules for establishing and maintaining the internal market.

It is conventionally understood that there are both negative and positive aspects to EU trade law – as already introduced in the extract by El-Agraa. The law is negative in the sense that it is designed to eliminate national laws which act as obstacles to trade within the internal market. This is especially apparent in relation to the so-called four fundamental freedoms of the Treaty, the free movement of goods, persons, services and capital. 'Negative' law controls obstacles to cross-border trading freedom. EU trade law is positive in the sense that it implies regulation of that wider market through EU legislation. Sometimes positive EU policy-making may be seen as a means of breaking down remaining barriers to trade which are lawful under EU law. This will be observed in the chapters that follow (in particular, Chapter 10, p. 279, Chapter 11, p. 318, and

Chapter 14, p. 414). It is also examined more broadly in Chapter 17. On other occasions Union policies may be designed more to cope with the consequences of free movement rather than simply to bring it about. Some of the material in Chapters 13 and 15 may be usefully addressed from this perspective, but the discussion in Chapters 18 and 19 takes the inquiry onto a broader plane. The substantive provisions of EU law which are studied in the chapters that follow are essentially the provisions which are designed to achieve the internal market which is to be established according to Article 3(3) TEU and which is defined in Article 26(2) TFEU.

The changes to substantive EU law made with effect from 2009 by the Lisbon Treaty were very few, beyond the unavoidable curse of having to get to grips with the re-numbering of the Articles of the Treaty (p. 19). A change that is *probably* only cosmetic is concealed. As mentioned, Article 3(3) TEU states that 'The Union shall establish an internal market.' The newcomer would not grasp the significance of this deceptive phrase. However, the pre-Lisbon Article 3(l)(g) EC provided that the activities of the EC shall include 'a system ensuring that competition in the internal market is not distorted'. This is now lost from the text of the Treaty proper. This concession was apparently extracted during the Treaty negotiations in 2007 by the French, where part of the reason for voter dissatisfaction appears to have been disquiet over a perceived hard-edged pro-competition philosophy. A Protocol on the Internal Market and Competition attached to both the EU Treaty and the TFEU states that the internal market referred to in Article 2 EU 'includes a system ensuring that competition is not distorted'. And in formal terms Protocols carry the same legal force as the Treaty itself. So perhaps the concession extracted by the French is of no practical or constitutional significance. But it cannot be excluded that the Court might conclude that the prominence of the Union's commitment to undistorted competition has been reduced and that it accordingly carries less weight than it has done hitherto when pitched against other concerns such as social cohesion or targeted industrial policy. After all, in a case such as *Albany International* (C-67/96, p. 476) the Court explicitly drew on Article 3(1)(g) as the source of opposition to distortion of competition in the internal market and in *Courage* v *Crehan* (C-453/99, p. 515) it referred to Article 3(1)(g) in describing (what was then) Article 81 as fundamental in nature. No longer does the early part of the Treaty provide explicit nourishment for such strong claims about the centrality of ensuring undistorted competition in the Union's internal market. One could certainly expect public authorities wishing, for example, to grant aid in circumstances where there are objections rooted in consequent competitive distortion to the market to argue that the balance of priorities has been shifted away from that aim by the Lisbon Treaty. The Commission may reject any such adjustment; the Court may too. But if the Court does conclude that the system is now less heavily weighted in favour of undistorted competition and interprets EU law accordingly, the Member States will have only themselves to blame. Accordingly, in assessing the law's role in securing achievement of the economic objectives of the Union, one must retain a background awareness that there is at least a whisper of an argument that the Lisbon Treaty has unbalanced the long-standing assumptions underpinning the Union's economic project.

■ **QUESTION**

To what extent are the *substantive* rules of the internal market achievable only through the development of the *constitutional* principles examined in Chapters 2–7? Could an internal market be achieved without a legal system which is supreme and directly effective; or without a procedure under which authoritative uniform interpretation of the law can be supplied?

SECTION 3: THE INTERNAL MARKET: 1992

A: The background

Why does the internal market referred to in Article 3(3) TEU not exist? Economic barriers to trade proved enduring in the early years of the EU. Moreover, the institutional and legislative apparatus of what was then the European Community also proved inadequate to secure the advancement of the economic project. There was a marked weakening in political will. Difficult decisions were stifled by the effect of the requirement in practice of unanimity in voting in Council. Violation of the law became more common. The Community was in a state of stagnation by the early 1980s. Loss of confidence in its prospects reduced cross-border investment. The plan to complete the internal market by the end of 1992 was a response.

Leon Brittan, EC Commissioner, Annual General Meeting of Justice

London, 7 July 1989

> ... [W]hy [was] the 1992 process ... necessary in the first place. Really, in a way, it was necessary because of the recognition that the prescriptions of the Treaty of Rome had not been fully fulfilled. The idea of a single European market in which there would be freedom of goods and services had manifestly not been created by the early 1980s, and although there was freedom of physical goods, the unseen barriers to trade were so substantial that you could not say that we had created a single Common Market. That perception was allied with the further perception that in order to achieve that progress towards a genuine single market, it was necessary for there to be constitutional change in the Community, because as long as all decisions had to be taken by unanimity, in practice, if not in strict theory, it was impossible to remove the non-tariff barriers, whether in public procurement, whether through the abuse of standards, whatever their nature, towards the creation of a genuine single market. And so, alongside the programmes of 1992, went the Single European Act and the constitutional changes, giving greater power to the European Parliament, and the ability for decisions to be taken in many, if not all, areas by qualified majority vote. It was that that provided the impetus to 1992.

NOTE: For a collection of essays, see D. Swann (ed.), *The Single European Market and Beyond* (London: Routledge, 1992).

Thus, the 1992 project is properly seen as an attempt to secure reinvigoration. It was the New Impetus, without which the Community would at best have remained marginalized and at worst have collapsed.

The blueprint for the 1992 programme was provided by COM (85) 310 – the Commission White Paper on Completing the Internal Market. This declared that 'A well developed free trade area offers significant advantages .... but it would fail and fail dismally to release the energies of the people of Europe; it would fail to deploy Europe's immense economic resources to the maximum advantage; and it would fail to satisfy the aspirations of the people of Europe' (para 220). The White Paper provided a policy agenda of some 300 measures which needed to be adopted by the end of 1992 in order to make the internal market a reality. The legal propulsion to give the plan the might to succeed was provided by the Single European Act, which came into force on 1 July 1987. That Treaty amended the Treaty of Rome in certain important respects; most notably for present purposes it shifted voting procedures in relation to 1992 measures towards qualified majority voting in Council, instead of unanimous voting (contrast Article 100a, introduced by the SEA, with the original Treaty's Article 100 – becoming Articles 95 and 94 respectively post-Amsterdam, and now, inverted by the Lisbon Treaty, Articles 114 and 115 TFEU). More generally, the Member States had committed themselves to a new wave of European integration through an explicit political act.

H. Schmitt von Sydow, 'Basic Strategies of the Commission's White Paper', in R. Bieber, R. Dehousse, J. Pinder, J. Weiler (eds), *1992: One European Market?*
(Baden-Baden: Nomos Verlagsgesellschaft, 1988), pp. 79, 86–92

(Footnotes omitted.)

THE IDEA

A successful politician does not always need to have brilliant ideas, but he must be aware of existing problems and possible solutions and, most of all, he needs a sense of good timing, knowing when an ambitious idea is ripe to be pushed with vigour.

When the Delors Commission took office in January 1985, the Commissioners – 14 out of 17 were newcomers – looked for a motto, for a major goal to be achieved during the next four or eight years, the lifetime of one or two Commissions.

There were about five topics to choose from. Two concerned the reform of the agricultural policy and of the budget. These were significant tasks and, no doubt, they had to be fulfilled. But were they sufficient to give a positive trade mark to the Commission? Repairing the errors of the past was important, but a quantum leap forward was even more so.

Institutional reform and progress towards political union were overdue, but would they be sufficient to reach the citizens of Europe? The man on the street would not be convinced of the usefulness of Community institutions as long as, crossing the borders between Member States, he met the same old customs officials and had to take along the same whole set of different currencies in order to pay the local taxi driver. Commissioners were influenced by the disappointing results of the 1984 election to the European Parliament where the campaigns had focused on national policies and where voters had snubbed the polling stations not only because the Parliament was lacking powers, but also because the whole Community did not seem able to solve citizens' problems.

These problems concern employment and economic prosperity, and they need a regenerative impetus of which the European countries are intrinsically capable if they overcome the fragmentation of their economies and their markets. The instruments for this kind of integration are Economic and Monetary Union and the Internal Market.

Economic and Monetary Union was certainly an attractive goal, especially to the five Commissioners who previously had been Ministers of Finance in their national governments; and there was no doubt that it should be pursued vigourously. But Member States' fears regarding its political and financial impact made it difficult to draft a realistic timetable.

So the choice became the Internal Market. Indeed this file was ripe for a decisive breakthrough.

First of all, since 1983, a new momentum in the right direction had been taking shape, which just needed a determined push and a precise perspective. Never before had there been such a promising basis for removing all visible and most of the invisible barriers to free movement inside the Community.

Second, there was a clear political will. Since the early 1980s, Heads of State and Government, as well as Parliament and Commission, had repeatedly committed themselves to achieve the goals – already enshrined in the Treaty – of the internal market. Even down in the Council's expert groups, there was no fundamental opposition, neither from economic, regional nor sectoral interests, to the completion of the internal market. Delays were mainly due to procedural difficulties such as quarrels about legal base, reluctance to delegate powers of implementation, conflicting priorities, and lack of flexibility fostered by the practice of unanimity. These difficulties within the institutions were supposed to vanish once the global vision of the immense economic advantages of an integrated market became consolidated by a binding overall programme.

Third, the completion of the internal market required no additional spending from national or Community budgets. On the contrary, it would set free gains several times superior to the Community budget. The European Parliament had just given widespread publicity to the calculations of Messrs. Albert and Ball demonstrating that money lost by the fragmentation of public markets and by the delays encountered by barriers at intra-Community borders was equal to two years' Community budgets. And these were only two items on the costs of Non-Europe bill; if one added the expenses for the infrastructure of intra-Community borders and the potential prosperity resulting, directly and indirectly, from the increased competitiveness of industry in a home market of continental dimensions, then it became increasingly surprising that Heads of State and Government had personally, for years and years, wasted time and energy on trying to adjust percentages of national contributions to the Community budget, neglecting the internal market with its much greater, intrinsic benefits. As was stated in the House of Lords, the cost of just one single barrier to trade, namely the discriminatory element of tax levied from 1978 to 1981 on Scotch Whisky, was four times as much as the British annual net contribution to the Community budget.

THE FORMULATION

The Commission lost no time. Only one week after he took office, President Delors went to the Parliament and announced the new Commission's intention to ask the European Council to pledge itself to completion of a fully unified internal market by 1992, to be achieved with the help of a programme comprising a realistic and binding timetable. This intention was repeated in the overall 'Programme of the Commission for 1985'.

The members of the Parliament and the Heads of State and Government could not help but approve the target and the procedure. In its meeting of 29 and 30 March, the European Council identified as its first priority 'action to achieve a single large market by 1992 thereby creating a more favourable environment for stimulating enterprise, competition and trade'; it called upon the Commission to draw up a detailed programme with a specific timetable before its next meeting.

The Commission's White Paper in response to this invitation was rapid, bold and radical. The document was written in seven weeks. It covered a vast series of topics and left no stone unturned. Seldom before had a single paper required such detailed inter-service discussions with so many Commission departments necessitating the redefinition of so many policies. It took seventeen drafts before Lord Cockfield, the Vice-President responsible for internal market, could present the Paper to the public on Saturday, 15 June 1985. He was aware that the strategy proposed in the White Paper implied a profound change in the habits and traditional ways of thinking; but he also knew the pledge of the Heads of State and Government to the target of 1992. 'They asked for it', he calmly said, 'they have got it'.

THE CONTENTS

The White Paper does not propose the target of 1992, nor does it rehearse the arguments in favour of that target. Instead the Commission, given the European Council's clear commitment to the target, just spells out the logical consequences of the commitment, together with an action programme for achieving the objective.

Consequently, the fields of action proposed by the White Paper have not been chosen because of their feasibility, but because of their necessity. The question to be answered was not: 'What can be realistically done by 1992?', but: 'What must be done in order to achieve the internal market and how could one squeeze it into the 1992 timetable?' Paradoxically, this 'unrealistic' approach has largely contributed to the Paper's credibility, since the global vision of what has to be done – with no jack-in-the-box-barriers hidden – helps to make the overall efforts measurable and to scale the 'unfeasible' actions down to their real political and economic proportions. During the drafting of the White Paper, all Commission departments had been warned that afterwards they would not be allowed to raise additional problems, and they responded to the challenge as if they – and not national administrations – were personally responsible for the emergence of new barriers to the free movement.

Identifying all problems without exception, the White Paper did not hesitate to tackle sensitive areas where no realistic immediate solution was at hand, e.g., commercial policy *vis-à-vis* third countries, nor to deal with policies for which no clear Community competence could be established, e.g. the right of asylum or the fight against terrorism. Whatever the underlying reason giving rise to a physical or technical barrier is, the White Paper spells it out and examines how justified interests can be taken care of without disturbing free movement inside the Community.

On the other hand, there are numerous other policies, such as regional, social, environmental, consumer, transport, research, competition, economic and monetary policies, which are closely linked to the internal market and the integration of economies; but they are touched by the White Paper only where they have a direct bearing on the abolition of physical and technical barriers. While progress on these policies becomes even more important because of the completion of the internal market, and indeed has been positively enhanced by the verve of the White Paper and the perspective of the great 'rendez-vous' of 1992, they must not constitute a precondition to completing the internal market. The White Paper mentions them only for the record refraining from offering any recipe.

Similarly, institutional reforms are not explicitly called for in the White Paper. Its main merit is not to have presented detailed solutions, but to have identified the problems. Of course, where problems had been tackled for a long time and where formal Commission proposals were already on the table, the White Paper refers, in many cases, to those proposals. But in cases where the problems had not been tackled at Community level before or where rapid but realistic solutions were difficult to define, such as asylum or commercial policy, the White Paper just sketches the responsibilities and possible ways of solution, maintaining nevertheless the pressure stemming from the time schedule.

Comprehensive as the White Paper's strategy is, its fields of action form a single entity. One cannot extract individual files which seem to have a higher priority or to be easier, and postpone the decision on other files, without jeopardising the objective of complete abolition of all border controls.

This objective has been confirmed by the Single European Act which defines the internal market as 'an area without internal frontiers in which the free movement of goods, persons, services and capital is ensured'. A Europe without internal frontiers – not a Europe with fewer or simpler controls, but one with no such divisive frontier controls at all.

THE STRUCTURE

In line with this comprehensive character, the chapters of the White Paper do not follow the legal categories of the Treaty (goods, persons, services, capital) but the types of barriers which are met in practice; hence the division of the Paper in three parts dealing with physical, technical and fiscal barriers.

The physical barriers at the customs posts are the most obvious and glaring manifestation of the continued fragmentation of the Community; they must be removed for both economic and political reasons. It should be noted that the White Paper understands the notion of 'border' not in a geographical, but in a practical sense. Physical barriers are to be abolished not only where they are carried out at the very frontier of Member States, but also where they are carried out, thanks for example to the Community Transit Procedure, inside the Member States' territory at the premises of consignors and consignees of goods. In this sense, physical barriers are those barriers which are triggered by the fact of crossing a border; which are discriminatory insofar as they are opposed only to goods, persons, services and capital coming from abroad and are not identical to, and an integrated part of, internal controls.

The technical barriers result from national legislation which, in practice, hampers free movement even if, from a legal point of view, it does not refer to border crossings, and which is indistinctly applied to foreign and indigenous goods, persons, services and capital. Again, the White Paper's definition goes beyond the traditional notion of technical barriers: It is not limited to goods but intentionally includes services, capital movements, public procurement, industrial property and other national policies insofar as they risk to obstruct free movement and to annihilate the benefits of the removal of physical barriers.

The fiscal barriers appear in both forms, as physical and as technical barriers. The White Paper devotes a special chapter to them because they are the most important single group of impediments; their abolition had fallen a long way behind the advances made in other fields of integration, and they required a particularly radical change of strategy.

The Annex to the White Paper contains a detailed timetable for approximately 300 Commission proposals and Council decisions in order to implement the Commission's proposed programme . . .

R. Bieber, R. Dehousse, J. Pinder, J. Weiler, 'Back to the Future: Policy, Strategy and Tactics of the White Paper on the Creation of a Single European Market', in R. Bieber et al. (eds), *1992: One European Market*

(Baden-Baden: Nomos Verlagsgesellschaft, 1988), pp. 13–16

(Footnotes omitted.)

THE AIM AND METHOD

If you want to attract support for a big political project, you do well to explain in half a dozen words what it is all about. The Cockfield White Paper selected the words 'action to achieve a single market by 1992'. At a time when the EC member governments disagreed about most major issues, it was possible to focus their minds and secure their agreement on making a priority of this apparently simple aim. . .

Yet the apparent simplicity of the aim and the definition conceal the enormous complexity of the undertaking . . . it involves the most intricate adjustment of regulations, taxes and laws. Completing a single market among advanced industrial economies is an exercise not of laissez-faire but of *Ordnungspolitik*; and *Ordnungspolitik* has become immensely more complicated since the idea of the social market economy was developed nearly half a century ago. In the terms of integration theory, negative integration, or the removal of barriers to transactions across the frontiers of different states, implies also the more exacting effort to achieve positive integration, or common policies with aims going beyond the straightforward removal of discrimination, when the barriers are not just tariffs and quotas, but differing regulations, taxes or laws. The White Paper gives rise, indeed, to some large and complex political, social and even ideological problems . . .

VIRTUES AND LIMITS OF AN INDUCTIVE METHOD

What we have learnt in the intervening thirty years is a healthy disrespect of programmes which are not linked to specific executory commitments and to adequate institutional arrangements.

The White Paper presents a striking difference from other ambitious attempts to reform the Community in depth. Unlike the Draft Treaty Establishing the European Union adopted by the European Parliament which invited theological debates about the nature of Community governance, the White Paper is essentially inductive. It spells out in detail over 300 specific measures which will have to be adopted to complete the internal market; it even sets a proximate goal which, while it may fall short of a fully-formed single market, is at least unambiguous: to do away with frontier controls in their entirety by the end of 1992.

NOTE: The 'internal market' was defined with reference to the aim of securing its completion by the end of 1992 by Treaty provisions which changed their number bewilderingly frequently – Article 8a became Article 7a, then 14. The relevant provision now, finally shorn by the Lisbon Treaty of outdated references to the year 1992, is Article 26 TFEU:

ARTICLE 26

1. The Union shall adopt measures with the aim of establishing or ensuring the functioning of the internal market, in accordance with the relevant provisions of the Treaties.

2. The internal market shall comprise an area without internal frontiers in which the free movement of goods, persons, services and capital is ensured in accordance with the provisions of the Treaties.

3. The Council, on a proposal from the Commission, shall determine the guidelines and conditions necessary to ensure balanced progress in all the sectors concerned.

NOTE: Lord Cockfield was the Commissioner responsible from 1985 to 1989 for the development of the 1992 strategy. Speaking in London on 22 February 1988, he confirmed the uncompromising nature of the objective: '[it is] *not* an area where frontier controls have merely been simplified or are retained for this reason or that: but an area *without* internal frontiers' (Lord Cockfield reflects on the project in *The European Union* (Chichester: Wiley Chancery Law, 1994)).

B: The anticipated benefits of the completion of the internal market

The Commission supported its campaign to have adopted the medium-term objective of completing the internal market by funding an extensive survey of the economic benefits of increased integration. This was 'The Costs of Non-Europe' – the Cecchini Report.

An immensely optimistic picture is painted by the following summary of the survey's conclusions:

P. Cecchini, *The European Challenge: 1992, the Benefits of a Single Market*

(Aldershot: Wildwood House/Gower Publishing, 1988), pp. xvii–xxi

(Endnotes omitted.)

THE RESEARCH

The outlook emerges from an unprecedented research programme, launched in 1986 by EC Commission vice-president Lord Cockfield. Its purpose was to provide a solid body of scientifically-assembled evidence as a means of judging the extent of the market fragmentation confronting European business and Community policy-makers alike. In the process, the research has thrown up a vivid illustration and rigorous analysis of the costs imposed on Europeans by the mosaic of non-tariff barriers which – 30 years after the Community's birth – continue to mock the term 'common market'. The findings of this research into the 'costs of non-Europe', are outlined in their essential detail in the pages of this book. ...

They estimate the size of the costs and thus a potential for gains exceeding Ecu 200 billions. This basic benefit, which could be magnified by modestly positive economic policies, is the reward for removing the barriers targeted by the 1992 legislative programme set out in the EC's 1985 White Paper *Completing the Internal Market*. Thus when EC political decisions are taken and the business community has fully adjusted to the new competitive environment, gains of this order of magnitude would be acquired once and for all, meaning that the European economy would be lifted onto a higher plane of overall performance.

The barriers – like border controls and customs red-tape, divergent standards and technical regulations, conflicting business laws and protectionist procurement practice – are well enough known by name. But not until now has their impact, and that of their removal, been charted and costed. These results, the product of the extensive field-work and subsequent analysis, are outlined in Part I, together with illustrations of the workings of non-Europe in a broad range of industries and services.

Likewise, the White Paper's legislative programme for removing market barriers, reinforced since mid-1987 by the Single European Act, is also well known. But what has not been estimated until now is the value of the ultimate prize which Community governments could, by enacting it in full, deliver to Europe's citizens, its companies – and to themselves. ...

THE SHOCK AND THE PROSPECT

For all the complexities, the essential mechanism is simple. The starting point of the whole process of economic gain is the removal of non-tariff barriers.

The release of these constraints will trigger a supply-side shock to the Community economy as a whole. The name of the shock is European market integration. Costs will come down. Prices will follow as business, under the pressure of new rivals on previously protected markets, is forced to develop fresh responses to a novel and permanently changing situation. Ever-present competition will ensure the completion of a self-sustaining virtuous circle. The downward pressure on prices will in turn stimulate demand, giving companies the opportunity to increase output, to exploit resources better and to scale them up for European, and global, competition.

However, the effect of the shock is to be gauged not just in terms of the market, and of the companies and consumers who buy and sell there. Its waves will ripple out into the economy at large. By its very size, the shock will have reverberations on general economic management. Over time, creation of a European home market will unbind the macro-economic constraints which have chronically fettered the prospects of sustained growth in Europe for the best part of twenty years.

Public deficits will be eased, under the dual impact of open public procurement and the economy's regeneration. Inflation, traditionally growth's ugly sister, will be cooled down by the drop in prices provoked by open markets. The jolt so imparted to Europe's competitivity should ensure that growth is achieved without damage to the Community's external trade position.

But, perhaps most important of all, is the medium-term impact of market integration on employment. With its injection of inflation-free growth, coupled with a loosening of the constraints on public exchequers in the Community's member states, the European home market of the 1990s raises the prospect, for the first time since the early 1970s, of very substantial job creation. The added financial elbow-room given to governments should, in addition, enable any unevenness in the rewards distributed by market integration to be compensated.

This medium-term prospect of substantial growth is not just a boon for Europe. The world economy of the late 1980s and early 1990s, overshadowed by American deficits, a fickle dollar and the spectre of a US recession, needs to take confidence where it can. The expectation may be that a dynamic European market, trading with the world on a footing of revamped competitivity, will provide a much-needed shot in the arm for other markets and economies in less buoyant shape.

In return, EC governments will have the right to expect appropriate responses from the Community's economic partners abroad, notably the US and Japan. If the fruits of the European home market are to be shared internationally, there must also be a fair share-out of the burdens of global economic responsibility, with market opening measures extended internationally on a firm basis of clear reciprocity.

THE ACTORS AND THE OPPORTUNITY

The European home market will not materialize at the wave of a wand. 1992 will not come by whispering words of mysterious Eurospeak into a receding future, or the future will return the compliment by staying conveniently out of reach. For business and government, the two main actors, the road to market integration will be paved with tough adjustments and the need for new strategies.

For business, removing protective barriers creates a permanent opportunity, but signals a definitive end to national soft options. Cost reductions will be good news, but market opening means also the permanent threat, actual or potential, of competition. This is also good news for the company which is gearing up to capitalize on the enlarged market's enhanced opportunities for innovation and economies of scale. But profits which derive from cashing in on monopoly or protected positions will tend to be squeezed. The situation will be one of constant competitive renewal.

Managing change will mean changing management – or rather the focus of its business strategy. There is already widespread evidence that this is happening, as companies – ahead of 1992 and often way ahead of the politicians – are adjusting both their management goals and business structures in readiness for new patterns of competition. But opportunities must continue to be seized – merely to neglect them will create a threat. One thing is certain. Firms from outside the EC, who are already positioning themselves in Community markets in anticipation of the White Paper programme's success, will not miss opportunities overlooked by their indigenous rivals.

Governments, already being watched closely by business, will be expected to give clear signs of their commitment to the 1992 goal. The credibility of the European market as an operational environment for business depends in the first instance on the legislator persuading companies of the seriousness of its intentions. There is only one way of doing this. EC governments must enact the White Paper programme fully and on schedule. In so doing, they will release the costs, outlined in this book, which presently inhibit Europe's market and economic expansion.

This means a further role for companies. Business cannot afford to sit passively by, idly expecting governments to keep to long-term legislative commitments, unaided. There is a need of more active political involvement, in the sense of constructive input to policy, orchestrated at Community level but targeted above all at the seats of national political power.

But governments must do more than achieve the European home market. They must maintain it – and, once again, give companies tangible proof that they are committed to doing so.

No great insight is needed to see that maintaining market integration will in turn pose the Community with some ineluctable choices. The business managers of the European market of the 1990s cannot be indefinitely divorced from the political managers of the Community economy.

Attempting to sustain this unserviceable dichotomy would be to invite disaster. Market integration, for example, particularly in its early stages, is likely to accentuate pressures on exchange rates and thus the need for firm currency management and for a stronger European monetary system. Without an institutional framework to deal effectively with these and other problems inherent in the success of the 1992 programme, the European home market will soon be put in jeopardy. The tensions that will be created will not be susceptible of management in an institutional vacuum. In short, for Europe to meet its market challenge, it must also, sooner rather than later, review the overall structure of its economic organisation.

NOTE: *Cecchini* was evidently significant in adjusting the political debate in favour of the Commission's project, although its economic analysis was unavoidably in part speculative. It should be apparent from this analysis that these issues did not suddenly drop from view after the end of 1992. Market integration is a continuing process. Building and maintaining an internal market, and proceeding to an economic and monetary union, demands a long-term agenda.

SECTION 4: MEASURING THE IMPACT OF '1992'

A: Measurement in 1996

Roughly a decade after providing the impetus needed to pursue completion of the internal market by the end of 1992, the Commission sponsored a research programme designed to discover what economic benefits had actually accrued. The fruits were published in a set of 38 sector-specific volumes, divided into six sub-sets: impact on manufacturing; impact on services; dismantling of barriers; impact on trade and investment; impact on competition and scale effects; and aggregate and regional impact. These volumes were co-published in 1997 by the Commission and Kogan Page. Naturally, the inquiry is not straightforward, for, sector by sector, it is difficult to demarcate advantages accruing from the '1992' initiative and those that would have occurred in any event or which are attributable to other factors such as global trade liberalization. Moreover, the essence of the internal market programme is that benefits will be felt not only in the short term, but also in the long term, and accordingly measurement cannot yet be decisive. However, the Commission, presenting a Communication to the Parliament and Council on 30 October 1996, summarized the results of its research in the following broadly positive terms.

Summary – The Impact and Effectiveness of the Single Market

(available *via* http://ec.europa.eu/internal_market/economic-reports/docs/single_en.pdf

1. Jobs and sustainable growth are at the top of the Union's agenda. The Commission's Confidence Pact, 'Action for Employment in Europe', identified the Single Market as the launching pad for attaining higher levels of job creation and sustainable growth. The Commission now has solid evidence of the positive effects of the Single Market, based on a first exhaustive survey of its economic impact and effectiveness conducted over the past two years.

2. In terms of economic impact the news is encouraging. It is still too early for many Single Market measures to have taken full effect but there are clear signs of significant change in the European economy. We now have evidence of the following positive, albeit preliminary effects of the Single Market in triggering the expected reinforcement of integration, competition, economic performance and benefits for consumers:
— growing competition between companies in both manufacturing and services;
— an accelerated pace of industrial restructuring, with the resultant benefits in terms of greater competitiveness;
— a wider range of products and services available to public sector, industrial and domestic consumers at lower prices, particularly in newly liberalised service sectors such as transport, financial services, telecommunications and broadcasting;
— faster and cheaper cross-frontier deliveries resulting from the absence of border controls on goods;
— greater mobility between Member States for both workers and those not economically active (including students and retired people).

3. Calculations of the overall economic effects of these changes suggest that the SMP has resulted in:
— between 300,000 and 900,000 more jobs than would have existed in the absence of the Single Market;
— an extra increase in EU income of 1.1–1.5% over the period 1987–93;
— inflation rates which are 1.0–1.5% lower than they would be in the absence of the SMP;
— economic convergence and cohesion between different EU regions.

4. These benefits have been gained without any reduction in safety standards for consumers or workers. In many areas standards of protection for the citizen have in fact increased. Citizens of the Union also enjoy more personal freedom and have more choice than ever before. The Commission's survey confirms that Community legislation in the Single Market area has, taken as a whole, created the basic conditions for free movement and economic efficiency. The situation in today's Single Market is in sharp contrast to that of the mid-1980s when:
— all goods were stopped and subject to checks at frontiers;
— most products had to comply with different laws in each Member State;
— services such as transport, telecommunications, banking and broadcasting were not subject to competition; and
— citizens who were not employed could be subject to restrictions on residence and risk losing social security rights in another Member State.

5. It is up to economic operators to make the most of the Single Market. The role of public authorities at national and Community level is confined to creating appropriate economic and institutional conditions. In the context of a more favourable economic climate, operators will be better placed to exploit to the full the opportunities that are now available. This report shows that where these opportunities are taken the benefits are significant.

6. The Commission's analysis suggests that these opportunities would have been even greater if Member States had been more diligent in putting in place the Single Market measures already agreed and applying the principles of the Community law on which they are based. Delays in applying and enforcing Single Market rules at national level continue to limit the Single Market's positive contribution to growth, competitiveness and more employment.

B: Measurement in 2002

The tenth anniversary of 'deadline 2002' prompted the Commission to return to the quest to measure the gains achieved through the programme. Once again it was confronted by the unavoidable absence of reliable data on what would have occurred had the internal market *not* been pursued in the chosen manner, but it made the following assessment.

The Macroeconomic Effects of the Single Market Programme after Ten Years

http://ec.europa.eu/growth/single-market/index_en.htm

At the end of 1992, the single market programme (SMP) came into force in Europe. It was aimed at eliminating the remaining barriers to trade among member countries. The expected consequences were increases in competition, industrial restructuring and reallocation of economic activities. In turn, these consequences were intended to induce three categories of gain. Allocative efficiency gain: when producers have market power, prices deviate substantially and persistently from marginal costs. Thus the structure of consumption is distorted and total output is kept below its socially optimal level. Productive efficiency gain: while firms produce at lowest cost under conditions of competition, they begin to operate inefficiently (through overstaffing, higher wages, lack of response to new opportunities, poor management) in situations of poor competition. Dynamic efficiency gain: fostering product and process innovations and, hence, speeding up the move to the modern technology frontier, which is a major source of growth. Recent empirical studies have tried to assess the allocative and productive efficiency gains from trade liberalization focusing on industries. Although similar gains are expected in services, no study provides a quantitative assessment.

A recent study by Salgado (2002) investigates the impact of trade, domestic product market and domestic labor market reforms on productivity performance. The analysis is based on panel data for 20 OECD countries over the period 1965–1998. The results suggest that trade and domestic product market reforms explain the trend in productivity growth. Their impact on total factor productivity growth is weak in the short run but substantial in the long run (i.e. between 0.2 and 0.3 percentage points a year). This is, however, an average estimate over OECD countries. Given the difference in the coverage and speed of reforms across these countries, the estimate may not be a reliable measure of the impact of the SMP. Notaro (2002) focused on the impact of the SMP on industrial productivity in a panel of 6 European countries and 30 industries. Using Buigues et al. (1990) methodology, these industries are classified as non-sensitive, moderately sensitive and highly sensitive to the SMP. The econometric evidence provided strong support to the positive impact of the SMP on industrial productivity in the last category of industries. In 1992 and 1993 the productivity in the high and medium sensitive sector increased by around 2%.

Allen et al. (1998) studied the impact of the SMP distinguishing among its effect on patterns of production and trade and its effects on price-cost margins and industrial restructuring. They also classified the industries according to their sensitivity to the SMP. The results showed that the SMP was mainly trade creating: the domestic production share of demand has fallen by 5.4 percentage point on average while the shares of both intra-European trade and extra-European trade have increased by 2.95 and 2.45 percentage point respectively. With respect to price, the result suggested that price competition has increased: on the average, price-cost margins have fallen by 3.6 percentage points in the high and medium sensitive industries. Bottasso and Sembenelli (2001) examined the impact of the SMP on market power of a large sample of Italian firms using a similar industry split. They found that in the most sensitive industries, firms' market power decreased by around 10 percentage points during the implementation of the SMP.

The results of these studies point to a consistent positive (negative) impact of the SMP on productivity (mark-up) in the high and medium sensitive industries. However, no clear pattern emerged in the other industries. The high and medium sensitive industries represent around 25% of the EU GDP. To get an estimate of the impact of the SMP on mark-up and productivity at the EU economy as a whole, we take the estimates by Notaro (2002) and Allen et al. (1998) and weight them by the share of the high and medium sensitive industries in the EU GDP. This implies an average decrease of mark-up by around 0.9 percentage points and an increase of productivity by around 0.5%. The evidence on services is not clear yet and there exists no study which provides a quantitative assessment of the Internal Market effect on services. There are, however some results from network industries (telecom, electricity and transportation) which have been used for our macro assessment. Nevertheless, our results should be considered as a 'lower bound' to the overall impact of the SMP on the EU economy.

Ranges of these estimates are also computed using the standard deviation provided in the respective papers. These ranges give a lower bound of 0.45 and an upper bound of 1.35 percentage points for mark-up decrease. The bounds for productivity increase are respectively 0.25% and 0.75%.

The Commission's QUEST II model is used to assess the macroeconomic effect of these two shocks. The following question is asked in this exercise: What would have been the level of GDP and employment in 2002, 2012 and 2022 if the single market programme would not have been implemented? Various simulations are performed depending on whether average, upper or lower bounds of the SMP impact on productivity and mark-up are considered. Moreover, three scenarios are envisaged concerning the time it takes for the full realization of the TFP increase and the mark-up reduction: 3, 5 and 7 years. The results emanating from the manufacturing sector and the network industries separately have been calculated separately. A table at the end of the note gives the total results.

MACROECONOMIC EFFECTS OF LIBERALIZING MANUFACTURING

The simulation results suggest that real GDP would have been 1.4% lower (with a lower and upper of 0.76 and 2.05) in 2002 without the internal market programme. Small additional gains are to be expected in this and the next decade, with an additional GDP effect of.4% until 2012 and 0.5 in 2022. Similarly the level of employment would have been.86% lower (with a lower bound of 0.43 and an upper bound of 1.3%) compared to its actual current level in 2002 without the single market programme. However, according to the simulation results no further employment gains should be expected. Both the increase in efficiency of production and increased competition contribute about equally to the GDP gain, while about 80% of the increase in employment is due to the removal of restrictions impeding competition.

MACROECONOMIC EFFECTS OF LIBERALIZING NETWORK INDUSTRIES

Not much empirical work has so far been undertaken in assessing the effects of liberalization in network industries. Some preliminary evidence for the electricity sector (Roeger and Warzynski, 2002) suggest a decline in the price cost margin from 25% to 19%. Given that the price decline in the telecom sector (relative to the consumer price deflator) has been more significant, namely about 23% relative to 9% in the electricity sector since 1996, profit margins have most likely been reduced more strongly in that sector. This would also be consistent with the more advanced state of liberalization in telecommunication. Taking into account the relative GDP weights and making the cautious assumption that mark-ups in the telecom sector have only decreased by 50% more compared to electricity would yield an aggregate mark-up decline of about 0.5%.

In the forthcoming European Economy Review 2002, the GDP and employment effects from the more recent liberalization of network industries, in particular electricity and telecom markets, are estimated to be 0.4% and 0.6% respectively after 4 years already and GDP will increase by 0.6% after 10 years. These effects are somewhat stronger than the internal market effects because in these simulations it is assumed that deregulation also has an effect on rent sharing between workers and firms. Thus the decline in price cost mark-ups is associated with a decline in the mark-up of wages over the reservation wage.

The following table provides absolute GDP and employment figures from the SMP and the liberalization of network industries.

Table 9.2 Simulation Results of the Total Effect

Scenario	Additional GDP (Bio of Euros) in			Additional Employment (1000 of persons) in		
	2002	2012	2022	2002	2012	2022
Average	164.5	203.1	214.0	2450.6	2463.8	2463.8
Lower Bound	105.6	127.5	158.4	1733.9	1741.5	1741.5
Upper Bound	223.2	264.2	273.3	3189.2	3202.3	3202.3

REFERENCES

Allen, C., Gasiorek, M. and Smith, A. (1998), 'European Single Market: How the programme has fostered competition', *Economic Policy*, 441–486.

Buigues, P., Ilzkovitz, F. and Lebrun, J.F. (1990), 'The impact of the internal market by industrial sector: The challenge for the Member States', *European Economy*, special edition.

Bottasso, A. and Sembenelli, A. (2001), 'Market power, productivity and the EU Single Market Programme: Evidence from a panel of Italian firms', *European Economic Review*, vol. 45, 167–186.

Notaro, G. (2002), 'European Integration and Productivity: Exploring the Gains of the Single Market', London Economics, Working Paper.

Roeger, W and F. Warzynski (2002), 'A Joint Estimation of Price-Cost Margins and the Importance of Fixed Costs in the European Electricity sector using Firm Level data', work in progress.

Salgado, R. (2002), 'Impact of structural reforms on productivity growth in industrial countries', IMF Working Paper, January.

C: The Single Market Review

As the twentieth anniversary of the '1992' project loomed, the Commission launched a review of the Single Market. The contested nature of the economic project is well captured in the following extract, authored by Commission officials. The rhetoric is more sober than *Cecchini*.

F. Ilzkovitz, A. Dierx, V. Kovacs and N. Sousa, *Steps Towards a Deeper Economic Integration: The Internal Market in the 21st Century: A Contribution to the Single Market Review*
January 2007

http://ec.europa.eu/economy_finance/publications/publication_summary788_en.htm

The European Internal Market project, which was initiated in the mid-1980s with the publication of the White Paper on the Single Market Programme, opened up perspectives for restoring confidence of European business and for improving the performance of European companies through the formation of a better integrated, more competitive and innovative market place. While the Internal Market has contributed to promote integration and to a lesser extent competition within the EU, its potential has not been fully exploited. The contribution of the Internal Market to the transformation of the EU into a more dynamic, innovative and competitive economy at world level was insufficient because: (i) existing instrument to remove non-tariff barriers to cross-border transactions and factor movements are not fully adequate; (ii) some markets remain fragmented; and (iii) the Internal Market has failed to fully adapt to a changing environment. The Single Market Review provides an opportunity to sketch a new vision for the Internal Market in the 21st century and to give it new impetus.

NOTE: The 'Monti report' of May 2010 – *A New Strategy for the Single Market: at the service of Europe's Economy and Society* – explained the risk that 'economic nationalism' and plain fatigue may undermine the single market, and argued it still needs efforts to secure its completion. 'The single market today is less popular than ever while Europe needs it more than ever' (p. 6).

The timing of the Commission's Single Market Review was not good and, by contrast with the 1985 White Paper's political centrality, in 2010 political attention was largely focused on 'fire fighting' in the banking sector and the Eurozone, not on the Review.

The Single Market Act was published in April 2011.

European Commission, 'Single Market Act: Twelve Levers to Boost Growth and Strengthen Confidence, Working Together to Create New Growth' (COM (2011) 206)

http://ec.europa.eu/internal_market/smact/docs/20110413-communication_en.pdf

(Footnotes omitted, all – baffling – points of emphasis as in the original)

At the heart of the European project since its inception, the common market – which has now become the *internal market – has for over 50 years woven strands of solidarity between the men and women of Europe, whilst opening up new opportunities for growth for more than 21 million European businesses.* An area of free movement for goods, people, services and capital, the internal market has been further developed since 1993 by the consolidation of economic integration, the Euro and solidarity and cohesion policies. Today more than ever *it has become a part of people's everyday life* in their professional and private activities and as consumers. It is the *real growth engine within the European economy.*

Nevertheless, *the internal market has shortcomings*, which were highlighted by Mario Monti in his report *'A New Strategy for the Single Market'* . . .

AN ACTION PLAN TO RELAUNCH GROWTH AND STRENGTHEN CONFIDENCE

To *remedy these shortcomings* we must *give the single market the opportunity to develop its full potential.* To this end, *a proactive and cross-cutting strategy* should be developed. This *means putting an end to market fragmentation and eliminating barriers and obstacles to the movement of services, innovation and creativity.* It means *strengthening citizens' confidence in their internal market and ensuring that its benefits are passed on to consumers.* A better integrated market which fully plays its role as a *platform* on which to build European competitiveness for its peoples, businesses and regions, including the remotest and least developed. There is an *urgent need to act.*

NOTE: 'Twelve levers' to boost growth and strengthen confidence were proposed: Access to finance for SMEs, mobility for citizens, intellectual property rights, consumer empowerment, services, networks, the digital single market, social entrepreneurship, taxation, social cohesion, business environment, and public procurement. The document explains the significance of each lever and then attaches to each one a 'key action'. The Commission urges the Council and Parliament to act to ensure each 'key action' is adopted by the end of 2012 at the latest, so as to re-launch the single market: and the Commission will then take stock and plan the next stage (pp. 5, 22).

Fixing a deadline is plainly a strategy copied from the 1985 White Paper's identification of 1992 as the deadline for completing the internal market.

The follow-up appeared almost 18 months later, and confessed that 11 of the key actions had not (yet) been agreed.

Communication from the Commission to the European Parliament, the Council, the European Economic and Social Committee and the Committee of the Regions

Single Market Act II: Together for New Growth (COM (2012) 573 final)

1. INTRODUCTION

This year marks the 20th anniversary of the Single Market. A lot has been achieved: from 1992 to 2008 the Single Market has generated an extra 2.77 million jobs in the EU and an additional 2.13% in GDP.[1] For European consumers the Single Market means more choice at lower prices – a 70% reduction in mobile phone costs is but one example. For citizens, the Single Market has given them the capacity to travel freely, to settle and work where they wish. For young people it has opened up the opportunity to study abroad – more than 2.5 million students have seized this opportunity in the last 25 years. For the 23 million companies in the EU the Single Market has opened access to 500 million consumers. The message is clear, the evidence is there: a strong, deep and integrated Single Market creates growth, generates jobs and offers opportunities for European citizens which were not there 20 years ago.

The development of the Single Market is a continuous exercise. The Single Market must respond to a constantly changing world where social and demographic challenges, new technology and imperatives, and pressure on natural resources and climate change must be incorporated into policy thinking.

The economic and financial crisis has generated additional challenges and has emphasised the need for fundamental structural reforms. With persistent high unemployment, in particular among young people, and a part of the European population living in poverty, the economic crisis is also a social crisis. We need to address this crisis with urgency, ambition and resolve. Failure to do so would increase the risk of Europe and its Member States turning inward and could undermine the confidence in the European project.

The Single Market is a key tool to achieve our long-term vision of a highly competitive social market economy. It enhances Europe's competitiveness in the global market place. Consistency and complementarity between internal and external policies will foster trade and growth.

1 European Commission calculations using the macroeconomic model QUEST II. For more details on the model, please consult http://ec.europa.eu/economy_finance/publications/publication1719_en.pdf.

More than ever, we need a Single Market that supports reforms for more growth and jobs, strengthens the confidence of citizens and businesses and delivers concrete day-to-day benefits to them. It will require our continuous attention and focus.

NOTE: The Single Market Act II offers a second set of priority actions, which the document proclaims, 'are designed to generate real effects on the ground and make citizens and businesses confident to use the Single Market to their advantage' (p. 5). There are four 'drivers for new growth': 1. Developing fully integrated networks in the Single Market; 2. Fostering mobility of citizens and businesses across borders; 3. Supporting the digital economy across Europe; 4. Strengthening social entrepreneurship, cohesion, and consumer confidence. These are then connected to 12 levers and key actions, which concern rail transport, maritime transport, air transport, energy, mobility of citizens, access to finance, business environment, services, a digital single market, electronic invoicing in public procurement, consumers and social cohesion, and social entrepreneurship.

The document's concluding paragraph (p. 17) has a hint of desperation, and its final sentence may readily be compared with the final sentence in the extract (p. 251) from the first Single Market Act:

If implemented swiftly, the Single Market Act II, together with the delivery of the Single Market Act I, will open new paths towards growth, employment and social cohesion for 500 million Europeans. It will show the determination of Europe to create new growth through a common agenda to exit the crisis. Together we need to act quickly and with ambition. We have no time to lose.

The most recent document in this series was published by the Commission in October 2015. It betrays a similar sense of mild desperation and follows the model of targeting a mixed bag of (11) 'Actions'.

Communication: Upgrading the Single Market: more opportunities for people and business

COM (2015) 550 http://ec.europa.eu/growth/single-market/index_en.html pp. 1, 11

1. UPGRADING THE SINGLE MARKET

The Single Market is one of Europe's great achievements. In the past 50 years, it has generated new opportunities and economies of scale for European companies that have strengthened industrial competitiveness, it has created jobs and offered greater choice at lower prices for consumers and it has enabled people to live, study and work where they want. It has contributed to better integrating EU firms into international value chains and strengthening the global competitiveness of European companies.

But the EU and the Single Market need to adapt to a changing environment. Europe is facing economic and social challenges. The economic and financial crisis has tested our economies and created immense social costs. Unemployment remains stubbornly high across Europe, particularly among the young people who should be the heart of Europe's vitality. Low levels of growth have affected people's confidence in Europe. Inadequate levels of investment and obstacles in product and services markets have hampered productivity and the competitiveness of the European economy. Businesses often feel stifled by outdated and excessively burdensome regulations and unable to find the information that they need.

At the same time, innovation and global value chains are generating major new opportunities. Digital technologies are transforming many industrial sectors, leading to more efficient production and new, innovative business models. Manufacturing and services are increasingly being merged into smart and clean business offers that provide greater value added for customers. But this innovation is also challenging traditional business models and established relationships between consumers and business operators. ...

5. CONCLUSION

The Commission set out to create a deeper and fairer Single Market with a strengthened industrial base. To achieve this objective, we need to upgrade our Single Market in line with today's economic realities of increased digitalisation, new business models and increasing links between manufacturing and services in today's global value chains. The Single Market Strategy proposes a concrete and ambitious set of actions to remove economically significant barriers that hold back Europe's jobs, growth and investment agenda. The Commission counts on the European Parliament and the Council, as well as on all stakeholders, to strongly support this ambitious and urgently needed programme and help make a significant step forward in the interests of citizens and businesses across Europe. Most importantly, it is essential for this programme to be carried forward by the Member States at national, regional and local level, for there can only be a Single Market with their support and commitment.

The actions envisaged in this Strategy will be launched in 2016 and 2017. By the end of 2017, the Commission will review progress on its implementation and, on the basis of comprehensive economic analysis, consider whether additional action is needed to meet its objective of a deeper and fairer EU Single Market.

NOTE: Regular reports are made available at http://ec.europa.eu/dgs/internal_market/studies/economic-reports_en.htm.

D: The business response

The assumption must be that the opportunities presented by the completion of the internal market will be seized by business. As the Commission insists in the extracts, it is essentially private commercial interests, not governments, that will make the project of economic integration a visible reality. Business, then, must plan ahead. More: it must *keep* planning!

R. Dudley, *1992: Strategies for the Single Market*
(London: Kogan Page, 1990), pp. 74–5
[Reproduced by permission of Kogan Page]

THE EFFECTS OF COMPETITION ON INDUSTRY STRUCTURES

The intensification of business activity triggered by the creation of the Single Market will have a number of effects on the shaping of industry structures across the community. The main elements will be:

— the exit of a number of firms due to competitive intensity;
— the relocation of production by companies needing to produce more competitive products in recognised centres of excellence or needing to find lower-cost production centres;
— the acquisition by predatory companies of firms located within Community markets to provide or strengthen their marketing and manufacturing dispositions in target markets or to acquire essential technology;
— acquisition of smaller companies which may in themselves be at a competitive disadvantage but are attractive enough for them to successfully offer themselves to larger firms;
— acquisitions by external Community firms as a means of creating an indigenous presence;
— acquisition and mergers for vertical integration reasons to control upstream and downstream elements of their industry's value system; and
— mergers and joint ventures to reinforce the strength and position of companies in the face of the need to scale up activities, collaborate on distribution, meet R & D needs etc.

It is these potential changes to industry structures which will affect the competitive conditions under which both suppliers and customers will have to operate. It is vital, therefore, that managers look more closely at the risks of change and the impact they will bring to their individual firms.

NOTE: The effect of the internal market varies according to the sector of the economy under review, but no sector escapes unaffected. A firm planning its internal market strategy must consider a range of factors touching, for example, its production, marketing, and distribution strategies, opportunities for structural growth through takeovers and research and development policy.

In addition to decisions about responding to the nature of the market, business must become accustomed to dealing with the EU's regulatory authorities.

R. Dudley, *1992: Strategies for the Single Market*
(London: Kogan Page, 1990), pp. 60–1

(Footnote omitted.)

... a new feature of company strategy development will be the need to become adept at the political level. The European Community recognises the need for companies to become involved in the development of a number of legal areas. It encourages their participation in the processes of eliminating discriminatory anti-competitive activity. It provides forums for the views of industry to be heard. It provides the machinery for firms to involve themselves with product standards and so on ...

Companies need, therefore, to put a political strategy somewhere towards the top of their agenda. They will need to understand the political motivations of the different member states within the Community and the workings of the Community's executive and legislative. Competition is no longer a mere market phenomenon, it is exercised at the political level. Companies, therefore, not having their views and interests represented will have to accept what is handed out to them whether or not it is in their interests.

■ **QUESTIONS**

1. This extract insists on the need for a 'political strategy'. To what extent is the increasing power of the EU authorities matched by increased responsibility (e.g., to electors)? How, if at all, would you like to see the institutional framework of the EU adjusted in order to improve democratic accountability for the decisions which are presently being taken?
2. The EU is firmly on the national political agenda in a way which would have seemed scarcely credible 35 years ago. As an advertising campaign slogan, '1992' proved a remarkable success.

   'As a mobilising theme, as an impulse for innovation and restructuring, as a justification and sometimes as an alibi for unpopular decisions, the myth of 1992 has had a deep influence which we have every reason to be satisfied with and must congratulate those who conceived it.' (Mertens de Wilmars [1989/1] LIEI 1 (Editorial))

   Who do you think make up the 'we' who have every reason to be satisfied?

SECTION 5: MANAGING THE INTERNAL MARKET

The end of 1992 plainly had major significance for the Commission, but it signified a shift in its internal market strategy rather than a termination of it. It was true that most of the major measures had been prepared by the Commission and agreed by the Member States by the end of 1992 (although some matters remained outstanding, not least those concerning persons), but there then arose questions of monitoring compliance. The summary at p. 247 highlights the central role of proper application of the rules of the internal market in ensuring full realization of its economic advantages. The Commission produces an annual report on the monitoring of the application of Union law, which provides information on *inter alia* the progress of implementation of Directives. They are available at http://ec.europa.eu/atwork/applying-eu-law/infringements-proceedings/annual-reports/index_en.htm. These reports have typically told of an accelerating pace of implementation by the Member States, but there remain many gaps between the law on paper and the law in practice.

The reports have contained 'league tables' which reveal in percentage terms the success of each Member State in complying with its obligation to notify its transposition measures to the Commission. In order to sharpen this statistical spur to the Member States to respond to the obligations agreed in Directives, the Commission established an 'Internal Market Scoreboard' in 1997. The relevant website may be entered *via* http://ec.europa.eu/index_en.htm (it is currently at http://ec.europa.eu/internal_market/score/index_en.htm); the site also carries a great deal of up-to-date information on broader policy direction. The first published scoreboard revealed that on 1 November 1997, over 25 per cent of internal market Directives were not implemented in all Member States. Particular problem areas were the transport and public procurement sectors, where over 50 per cent of Directives were unimplemented in one or more States. The Second Implementation Report of the Internal Market Strategy for 2003–2006 published in January 2005, tells a tale of persisting flaws.

Second Implementation Report of the Internal Market Strategy for 2003–2006

January 2005, pp. 16–17

http://ec.europa.eu/internal_market/score/index_en.htm

(Footnotes omitted.)

ANNEX 1: IMPLEMENTATION REPORT SCOREBOARD

1. Transposition by Member States of Internal Market rules into national law

Member States persistently fail to transpose Internal Market rules correctly and on time. The transposition deficit for the EU has got significantly worse and now stands at 3.6%. This is a long way from the 1.5% interim target set by successive European Councils. And the real target is, of course, 0% because timely and correct transposition is a legal obligation.

The deficit for the EU 15 Member States is 2.9%, which represents a very significant step backwards after their progress in reducing the deficit since the Lisbon summit in 2000. When all 25 Member States are included in the calculation, the deficit rises to 3.6% – too high, but still considerably better than the 7.1% deficit at enlargement thanks to the sustained notification efforts of the new Member States. Concretely, this means that the Commission is still awaiting 1428 notifications of national implementing measures.

Of all Internal Market directives, over a quarter (27% or 427 directives) have not been fully transposed in at least one Member State. This figure is much higher than before – and its rise is in large part due to enlargement, as many of the directives still to be transposed by each of the EU 10 Member States are not the same. Member States' failure is not only a breach of their legal obligations – it also deprives businesses and citizens in practice of their rights and undermines the day-to-day working of the Internal Market.

In 2007 the target was shifted from 1.5 per cent down to 1 per cent. And by July 2009, when the Commission published Internal Market Scoreboard 19, revealing the position in May 2009, it was able to paint a more optimistic picture.

Internal Market Scoreboard No 19

July 2009, p. 7 http://ec.europa.eu/internal_market/score/index_en.htm

TRANSPOSITION

For the third consecutive time the EU average transposition deficit is at 1%. The consistent good result suggests that Member States have put in place structural improvements to ensure timely transposition.

In total, 18 out of 27 Member States are in line with the 1% target: Once again, Denmark and Malta are the overall best performers both with only 3 directives away from a perfect score. A further 2 Member States (United Kingdom and Belgium) are close to reaching the 1% target: At the other end of the spectrum, Greece, Poland, Portugal, the Czech Republic, Italy, Luxembourg and Estonia are far off the target. The transposition deficit in 6 out of these 9 Member States has increased even further compared to half a year ago. This is a serious source of concern. Only Belgium and Luxembourg managed to reduce their deficits.

NOTE: The Single Market Act of April 2011 (p. 24) proposed shifting the target downwards from 1 per cent to 0.5 per cent. The February 2013 Scoreboard retains an optimistic tone.

Internal Market Scoreboard No 26
February 2013
http://ec.europa.eu/internal_market/score/index_en.htm
(Footnotes omitted.)

. . . the average transposition deficit in the EU has fallen again below the target agreed by the European Heads of State and Government to 0.6 %, which is the best result ever since the Internal Market Scoreboard has been published. Due to the improvement, the number of Member States achieving the 1 % target went up from sixteen to twenty-three. In total, twelve Member States achieved or equalled their best result ever. This illustrates the high priority given by those Member States to timely transposition. For the second time, a Member State has reached the perfect score (0.0 %): Ireland, the best transposition performer in this edition of the Scoreboard, has transposed all due directives on time. Only Bulgaria had previously ever reached this result, in May 2008. Moreover, three Member States are only one or two directives away from this goal (Estonia, Malta and Sweden). Italy, Cyprus and Romania show the biggest improvements in reducing the number of outstanding directives. The Czech Republic continues the positive results seen in May 2012. Nevertheless, this encouraging result in the first challenge ('achieving the 1% target') goes hand in hand with a worsening result for other challenges highlighted in the Scoreboard, such as reducing the number of directives for which transposition is overdue by two years or more (second challenge, 'meeting the zero tolerance target') and shortening transposition delays (third challenge). Eight directives have not been transposed two years or more after their transposition deadline by one or more Member States. In total, five Member States have not achieved the 'zero tolerance' target. Moreover, Member States take an average of almost ten extra months to transpose EU directives after their transposition deadline. In response to the fourth challenge ('improving the conformity of national legislation'), Member States have succeeded in further reducing the number of incorrectly transposed directives. The average compliance deficit has fallen from 0.7 % six months ago to 0.6 % today, coming closer to the 0.5 % compliance deficit proposed in the Single Market Act. Incompleteness of the Single Market due to lack of transposition, i.e. a failure by one or more Member States to transpose directives in full, remains at 5 %, which corresponds to seventy-three directives not producing their full effect in the EU. For almost one third of these directives, this is due to the failure of just one Member State to transpose them. The most fragmented areas remain financial services, the environment and transport.

NOTE: The Commission has recently opened an on-line version of the Scoreboard, which is available at http://ec.europa.eu/internal_market/scoreboard/ and which continues to show a relatively uneven but generally improving pattern of compliance.

These statistics relate only to legislative measures concerned with the internal market. And patterns vary by sector: public procurement remains a special problem.

In its Internal Market Scoreboard No 11, published in November 2002, the Commission confessed that 'The Internal Market will never be "completed". The effort to maximise its performance is a process, not an event.' The dynamic nature of the process of market-building and market-management, which makes enduring demands of the Commission's capacities, is captured in the next extract, taken from a major survey of the evolving political, institutional, and legal implications of a 'post-1992' Community.

K. Armstrong and S. Bulmer, *The Governance of the Single European Market*
(Manchester: Manchester University Press, 1998), pp. 307–8

In procedural terms there are serious concerns about the 'holy trinity' of transposition, enforcement and redress. Although the Commission report states that the transposition rate for the White Paper measures was on average 90% for the EU-15, it notes that 'fifty-six per cent . . . have been transposed in every Member State' ([COM (96) 520]). That yields a rather different picture and one which is arguably more pertinent to those firms conducting business across the SEM. The comparability of enabling legislation also remains a concern. Enforcement is more complex still because the relevant agencies may be national, regional or local, thus making it extremely difficult to monitor the impact of the SEM 'on the ground' to ensure equivalence across the EU. The Commission's resources simply do not permit sufficient oversight of this dimension . . . Finally, the ability of private parties to secure redress through the courts is complex and variable because of differences in national legal systems.

A final issue worthy of mention here concerns over-zealous regulation: where national transposition introduces costs over and above those necessitated by the relevant EC Directive. This phenomenon, known in the UK as 'gold-plating', lies behind the recent emphasis in SEM policy on reducing the regulatory burden . . .

Despite the legislation to open up public procurement in the utilities . . ., the results in this area of activity have been much more limited. Although a major area of economic activity – 11.5 per cent of EU GDP in 1994 – the achievements have been limited, with only 10 per cent import penetration of import markets. A major explanation for this situation is 'the substantial delay in incorporating the 11 procurement Directives into national legislation and enforcing them effectively' ([COM (96) 520]). The 1996 Florence European Council underlined the importance of accelerating national transposition in this area. Finally, it is worth mentioning that the general impact of the single market upon small and medium-sized enterprises has been rather limited.

NOTE: The Commission is aware that it requires a more sophisticated strategy than mere publication of figures and establishment of timetables. In order to foster a 'compliance culture' among the Member States, it has placed an increasing emphasis on administrative co-operation as a basis for managing the internal market. The Commission, energized by Mario Monti, the Commissioner who held responsibility for the internal market until 1999, prepared an *Action Plan for the Single Market*, which was published in June 1997. It was submitted to the European Council in Amsterdam in that month, where it was firmly endorsed as a basis for renewed effort to eliminate remaining obstacles to realization of the full benefits of the single market programme. The *Action Plan* picked out four priority areas ripe for action designed to improve the functioning of the internal market.

Action Plan for the Single Market, Communication of the Commission to the European Council

CSE(97)1, final, 4 June 1997

FOUR STRATEGIC TARGETS

The Action Plan follows the Commission's report on the Impact and Effectiveness of the Single Market. It sets priorities to give a clear and strategic vision of what is now needed. Four Strategic Targets have been set. They are of equal importance and must be pursued in parallel:

1. Making the rules more effective: The Single Market is based on confidence. Proper enforcement of common rules is the only way to achieve this goal. Simplification of rules at Community and national level is also essential to reduce the burden on business and create more jobs.
2. Dealing with key market distortions: There is general agreement that tax barriers and anti-competitive behaviour constitute distortions that need to be tackled.
3. Removing sectoral obstacles to market integration: The Single Market will only deliver its full potential if barriers that remain – and, of course, any new ones that emerge – are removed. This may require legislative action to fill gaps in the Single Market framework, but it also calls for a significant change in national administrations' attitudes towards the Single Market.
4. Delivering a Single Market for the benefit of all citizens: The Single Market generates employment, increases personal freedom and benefits consumers, while ensuring high levels of both health and safety and environmental protection. But further steps are needed, including steps to enhance the social dimension of the Single Market. And to enjoy their Single Market rights to the full, citizens must be aware of them and be able to obtain speedy redress.

NOTE: In December 2002 the Commission released a Communication aimed at better 'monitoring' of the application of the law.

Commission Communication, Better Monitoring of the Application of Community Law

COM (2002) 725, 11 December 2002

To ensure that Community policies are effectively implemented and have the desired effect, thereby gaining the public's confidence, the institutions must now try not just to improve the quality of legislation but also to ensure further downstream that its application is efficiently monitored. In this regard, the discussion on the *White Paper on European Governance*, focuses on the quality of Community legislation and the improvement of monitoring. The two issues are clearly linked.

The White Paper on European Governance is explored in Chapter 18. In it the Commission comments that 'Late transposition, bad transposition and weak enforcement all contribute to the public impression of a Union which is not delivering' (COM (01) 428 p. 25). In its December 2002 Communication, the Commission proceeds to develop the notion of administrative co-operation as a basis for generating the required public confidence in the viability of the internal market.
(Footnotes omitted.)

2.1. IMPROVING COOPERATION BETWEEN THE COMMISSION AND THE MEMBER STATES IN THE FIELD OF PREVENTION

Preventive action to enforce Community law begins with selecting the best instrument. But once a selection has been made, it continues with cooperation on the implementation of the legislation. A variety of practical cooperation instruments have already been tried out with a view to preventing infringements. These include:

(1) Interpretative communications on a specific matter of Community law (both the Treaty and secondary legislation).
(2) The obligation to notify the Commission of draft technical regulations arising from Directives 98/34/EC (goods) and 98/48/EC (information society services) in the nonharmonised sector of the internal market.
(3) The regular publication of statistics by the Commission in the internal market scoreboard; the annual report on monitoring the application of Community law which aims to promote peer pressure between the Member States by creating a form of mutual monitoring of efforts to apply European legislation. Commission reports on the application of directives provided for by certain of them play a similar role.
(4) Anticipation of major events, linked, for example, to infrastructure projects: experience shows that when investments have to be made on a national scale the national authorities involved are occasionally inclined to take insufficient account of Community regulations. This approach has been followed in the field of public procurement, in the case of both the Treaty and secondary legislation, and could usefully be extended to the prevention of infringements in the area of the environment and, if appropriate to other sectors.
(5) Training, information and transparency campaigns intended for national administrations and judges, along the lines of the Grotius II civil and criminal programmes, or, in connection with enlargement, twinning arrangements between national administrations.
(6) For the purposes of the exchange of information and good practice, regarding both the Treaty and secondary legislation, the use of expert committees and networks to assist the Commission, or the setting up of *ad hoc* groups of experts in particular fields.

NOTE: The first of these points, interpretative communications designed to clarify internal market law, may be illustrated by the Commission communication on facilitating the access of products to the markets of other Member States: the practical application of mutual recognition, OJ 2003 C265/2, considered in Chapter 12. The second of these points, the obligation to notify draft technical regulations, has already been encountered in its constitutional context. The Court's rulings in Case C-194/94 *CIA Security International SA* v *Signalson SA and Securitel SPRL* [1996] ECR I-2201 were examined in Chapter 5, pp. 126–31, and they concerned this 'early warning' procedure. In *CIA Security* the Court was vigorous in interpreting the consequences before national courts of breach of the Directive in the light of the demands of effective market-management. Here one can observe a community of interest between the Court and the Commission in strengthening the incentives for States to adhere to the system of notification. The Commission was pleased. In 1986, in Communication 86/C 245/05 [1986] OJ C245/4 it had argued for the outcome reached in *CIA Security*; and indeed the Court cited this Communication in para 36 of *CIA Security*. The Commission in turn routinely cites this judgment with pride when it publishes notified technical rules in the Official Journal – see for example [2001] OJ C152/4, [2006] OJ C220/13.

■ QUESTION

Is concern for effective market management a sufficient justification for the Court's willingness to tweak the principle of direct effect to exert an 'incidental' effect prejudicial to private parties in cases where the State has failed to comply with this Directive? How does *Unilever* (Case C-443/98, p. 129) help?

In 2003 the Commission published its Internal Market Strategy for 2003–2006.

Communication from the Commission to the Council, the European Parliament, the European Economic and Social Committee and the Committee of the Regions, Internal Market Strategy Priorities 2003–2006

COM (2003) 238, 7 May 2003, pp. 5–6

(Footnotes omitted.)

2. WHY A NEW STRATEGY NOW?

The Commission sees three main reasons why the EU needs to make a determined push now to improve the Internal Market:–

— The sub-optimal performance of the Internal Market is one of the challenges that stands between the EU and the realisation of the ambitious objective it set itself at Lisbon in 2000. It is necessary to take decisive action quickly. We know that it can take several years before adopted measures produce real impacts on the ground. In order for the EU to become the most competitive and dynamic knowledge based economy in the world by 2010, the measures needed to create a genuinely unified and integrated market must be adopted very soon.

— It is urgent to develop an effective strategy to strengthen the Internal Market, because enlargement is only a year away. Enlargement offers unprecedented opportunities for both existing and new Member States, but it is not without risks. The Internal Market is perpetually vulnerable to fragmentation and enlargement will be a moment of heightened vulnerability, unless we strengthen all our key policy instruments and concepts so that they continue to work well, or better, in a Union of 25 countries. Only then can the potential gains which enlargement offers be realised.

— The EU, in common with other parts of the world, is currently facing a slowdown in economic growth and job creation. This makes it all the more essential to press ahead with structural reforms in order to increase the capacity of our economies to grow. Removing the bottlenecks in the Internal Market will put Europe in a much better position to face up to the ever stiffer competition from emerging economies. It will also leave the Union better protected against future fluctuations in the economic cycle and provide it with a stronger economic basis to deal with the huge challenges of an ageing population.

In November 2007 the Commission published a Communication entitled *A single market for 21st century Europe* (COM (2007) 724). This calls for 'new working methods and the use of a diverse set of instruments'; implementation and enforcement of the rules will be prioritized, in line with the broader agenda of 'Better Regulation' in the EU (p. 4). This 'requires a commitment well beyond "Brussels" '. The Review 'does not include a classic legislative action programme. Its aim is rather to foster flexibility and adaptability while maintaining the legal and regulatory certainty to preserve a well-functioning single market' (p. 4). Page 5 of the paper on *Instruments for a modernised single market policy* asserts the need to move beyond 'integration though law'.

However, the adoption of binding rules was not completely excluded. Legislative requirements to notify the Commission of practices hostile to the internal market were increased by Regulation 764/2008 laying down procedures relating to the application of certain national technical rules to products lawfully marketed in another Member State (OJ 2008 L218/21), which concerns the application of a (notified) technical regulation to exclude a product lawfully marketed in another Member State. Regulation 764/2008 also requires Member States to establish 'Product Contact Points' (Articles 9–11), which conforms to the thematic concern to create an administrative infrastructure which is adequate to make the internal market a practical reality.

The 'Monti Report' of 2010 was mentioned at p. 257 – its author is the self-same Mario Monti who was previously the Commissioner responsible for the Internal Market. The Report focuses on three broad sets of initiatives: initiatives to build a stronger single market; initiatives to build consensus on a stronger single market; initiatives to deliver a stronger single market. In relation to the third of these, familiar themes concerning the need for effective 'market management' and a scepticism about the value of yet more 'top-down' EU rule-making may be traced.

Commission, *A New Strategy for the Single Market: at the service of Europe's Economy and Society* pp. 93, 95–7

http://ec.europa.eu/internal_market/strategy/docs/monti_report_final_10_05_2010_en.pdf

Today, the *acquis communautaire* comprises 1521 directives and 976 regulations related to the various single market policy areas. An action to deepen the single market is therefore unlikely to require a new wave of regulations and directives, as it was the case with the 1985 White Paper. Furthermore, the EU Better regulation agenda sets out strict requirements on how new legislation should be designed. However, this does not exempt from addressing the issue of what modes of regulation and policy making methods are the most appropriate to regulate the single market.

Currently, 80% of the single market rules are set out through directives. These have the advantage of allowing for an adjustment of rules to local preferences and situations. The downsides are the time-lag between adoption at EU level and implementation on the ground and the risks of non implementation or goldplating at national level. The recent debate on regulation in the financial services area has shown the merits of having a single European rule book. There is thus a growing case for choosing regulations rather than directives as the preferred legal technique for regulating the single market. Regulation brings the advantages of clarity, predictability and effectiveness. It establishes a level playing field for citizens and business and carries a greater potential for private enforcement. However, the use of regulation is not a panacea. Regulations are appropriate instruments only when determined legal and substantial preconditions are satisfied. They may not even result in greater efficiency, if the discussion that would have taken place at national level at the time of transposition is shifted to the European level at the time of adoption by the Council and Parliament.

Harmonisation through regulations can be most appropriate when regulating new sectors from scratch and easier when the areas concerned allow for limited interaction between EU rules and national systems. In other instances, where upfront harmonisation is not the solution, it is worthwhile exploring the idea of a 28th regime, a EU framework alternative to but not replacing national rules. . . .

. . . The single market is a construct based on law. Thus, it is crucial that Member States take seriously their obligation to timely transpose and correctly apply the rules they agreed to . . . .

The single market remains highly fragmented. At the end of 2009, 74 single market directives had not yet produced their full effects in the EU due to lack of national transposition measures in one or more Member States. In other words, the single market is an engine that works at around 95% of its potential. Member States also have quite a relaxed attitude towards transposition deadlines. On average, they grant themselves an extra 9 months to adopt the implementing legislation after the deadline expires . . . . The law on the ground often turns out to be very different from the law in the Single rule-book. This 'regulatory patchwork' is a serious threat to the credibility and reputation of the single market.

. . . The hard truth is that the decentralised system in which Member States are responsible for the implementation of EU law and the Commission monitors their action presents many advantages but cannot ensure total and homogeneous compliance. Private enforcement is a complementary tool, but it has limitations as well. At the same time, it is neither possible nor desirable to police the single market only from Brussels. To get out of this sub-optimal compliance trap, it is necessary to strengthen central enforcement through the infringement procedure and grass-root private enforcement. At the same time, it is crucial to explore with determination how to apply a new approach based on network-based governance and partnership. This new approach would best be applied to alternative dispute resolution and to cooperation between the Commission and national administrations. The ultimate objective would be to design a coherent enforcement system in which infringement procedures, informal problem solving mechanisms and private enforcement through national courts form a seamless web of remedies against breaches of EU law.

For Monti, 'Transparency, peer pressure and administrative cooperation are the silver bullets in this area' (pp. 98–9). The Commission's Single Market Act of 2011, mentioned at p. 251, also stresses the need for better enforcement of the rules of the single market game and the Single Market Act II (p. 252) insists at p. 5 that 'the transposition and day-to-day implementation of Single Market rules by authorities in Member States is of paramount importance'. Clearly, however, there are limits on the usefulness of EU legislation in forcing such change – it is (also) a question of improving administrative culture within the Member States, and facilitating co-operation between the Commission and public authorities in the Member States. The Commission's 2015 Communication 'Upgrading the Single market: more opportunities for people and business', mentioned earlier (p. 252) as the latest in this series of documents, fully endorses the need for 'better integration of evaluation and enforcement aspects in policy design, better assistance and guidance to Member States in the implementation of Single Market rules and a more consistent and efficient enforcement policy aimed at improving overall compliance with Single Market rules and EU law in general' (p. 16). An insight into how hard this is to achieve is provided by the confession that despite Regulation 764/2008, designed to improve practical application of the rules (p. 259), '[n]ational authorities often require specific proof of lawful marketing or simply refuse access to their national market (p. 18).

The last word is helpfully given to a Commission Recommendation (which, remember, is a non-binding act: Article 288 TFEU, p. 27) which brings together many of the enduring challenges that confront those engaged in ensuring the internal market is and remains capable of delivering the intended and loudly advertised economic benefits.

Commission Recommendation of 29 June 2009 on measures to improve the functioning of the single market

(2009/524/EC) OJ 2009 L176/17

THE COMMISSION . . . HEREBY RECOMMENDS THAT THE MEMBER STATES:

1. Ensure and strengthen a single market coordination function, to promote efficient coordination within and between authorities responsible for single market issues at national, regional and local level, and to act as a reference point for the single market within the administration.

2. Facilitate active cooperation between administrative authorities responsible for single market issues in different Member States, and with the Commission, through the allocation of sufficient resources.

3. Take all necessary measures to improve the transposition of Directives affecting the single market.

4. Support the Commission's work on market monitoring and related data collection by actively contributing to the exercise at the Community level, and, if relevant, by considering similar exercises at national level.

5. Ensure that national authorities and officials have sufficient knowledge of Community law in general and of single market rules in particular to efficiently apply single market rules and where relevant, take these rules into account when preparing and introducing new national legislation.

6. Facilitate and encourage a quick and efficient resolution of problems encountered by citizens and businesses in exercising their single market rights by in general, taking measures to improve the enforcement of single market rules, and in particular, by ensuring that the judiciary has sufficient knowledge of Community law including single market rules, and by providing sufficient support to problem-solving mechanisms.

7. Carry out regular evaluation and assessment of national legislation to ensure full compliance with single market rules and in so doing keep under review any use of exemptions or derogations provided for in existing single market rules.

8. Enhance the provision of practical information on single market issues to businesses and citizens.

9. Examine the measures and practices set out in the Annex and, having regard to their national institutional traditions, adopt those practices that will, or can be expected to, lead to an improvement in the functioning of the single market and are best suited to implement this Recommendation.

10. Cooperate with the Commission and other Member States in monitoring the implementation of this Recommendation, inform the Commission of actions taken in implementing this Recommendation on a regular basis and provide a final report to the Commission three years after the publication of this Recommendation in the Official Journal.

FURTHER READING ON 'MARKET MANAGEMENT'

Engsig Sørensen, K., 'Non-Harmonized Technical Regulations and the Free Movement of Goods' [2012] Euro Business Law Rev 163

Kaeding, M., 'In Search of Better Quality of EU Regulations for Prompt Transposition: the Brussels Perspective' (2008) 14 ELJ 583.

Kovar, R., 'Le législateur communautaire encadre le régime de la mises des produits dans le marché intérieur' 44(2) RTDE 2008, p. 289.

Lafarge, E., 'Administrative Cooperation between Member States and Implementation of EU Law' (2010) 16 Euro Public Law 597.

Mastenbroek, E. 'EU Compliance: Still a Black Hole?' (2005) 12 JEPP 1103.

Munoz, R., 'The Monitoring of the application of Community Law: a Need to Improve the Current Tools and an Obligation to Innovate' (2006) 25 YEL 395.

Pelkmans J. and Correia de Brito, A., 'Enforcement in the EU Single Market' (Brussels: CEPS, 2012, *via* www.ceps.be/book/enforcement-eu-single-market).

For a report that is generally supportive of the Commission's approach to the single market, emphasising the importance of better regulation, better implementation and better problem solving, see House of Lords EU Committee, 5th Report of Session 2007/08, *The Single Market: Wallflower or Dancing Partner? Inquiry into the European Commission's Review of the Single Market* (HL Paper 36-I, 2008), available *via* www.publications.parliament.uk/pa/ld200708/ldselect/ldeucom/36/36.pdf.

■ QUESTION

To what extent can identified failings in the internal market be remedied purely by the adoption of legal rules? What more is needed in order to ensure effective management of the internal market? Will it ever be complete?

NOTE: For commerce too, as well as for the institutions of the EU, it should be apparent from much of the material in this chapter that the significance of the 'legal deadline' of 31 December 1992 was never to be accorded undue weight. Important though the end of 1992 was, the development of the internal market is an evolving process – legally, politically and commercially. The Cecchini Report (p. 244) is based on the perception that the benefits of integration persist over time – they are not obtained once and for all. Equally, the debate about how extensive the benefits of the internal market will really prove to be, presented through the foregoing extracts, continues as integration evolves. Moreover, as the more recent extracts reveal, internal market-making is just one component in the EU's wider strategy for economic reform and growth. For commerce, the process involves questions about how best to restructure operations which will persist for many years yet.

Integration also poses questions about the patterns of supporting legal regulation. This issue was visible in 1988 as the internal market programme began to take shape.

R. Bieber, R. Dehousse, J. Pinder, J. Weiler, *1992: One European Market?*
(Baden-Baden: Nomos Verlagsgesellschaft, 1988), pp. 30–1

Despite the beguiling simplicity of the ideas of completing the single market and abolishing the frontier controls, it is not hard to see that the project outlined by the White Paper is a complex one: a vast exercise in harmonising laws, regulations and practices, presenting a tough challenge to the Community's political and institutional capacity. That is hardly contestable. More open to judgment, but nevertheless plausible, are the propositions that the process of completion carries with it pressures for related policies in fields such as the environment, competition, industry, cohesion, monetary integration and macro economic management. These in turn would not only require the creation of new common policy instruments, but also imply the strengthening of Community institutions, in matters such as majority voting in the Council, codecision with the Parliament, and enhancing the Community's juridical capacity and the Commission's role. All this would not only develop the Community internally, but would also strengthen its international position and bargaining power, not only in trade policy but also in the fields of money and of technological development.

In so far as this is accepted, the White Paper should be viewed not in the minimalist perspective of a Community which emphasises free trade at the expense of other values, but as a bold initiative to impel the Community forward where agreement among all the member governments was possible, which, if it succeeds, will imply also a major effort of policy integration in related fields and development of the Community institutions.

NOTE: This perception has much in common with the fruits of a more recent investigation into the way in which the process of market-building and market-management has made deep demands of the institutional capacity of the Community, now Union.

M. Egan, *Constructing a European Market*
(Oxford: OUP, 2001), p. 260

(Footnotes omitted.)

The governance of the market has inspired considerable debate. Part of that discussion has focused on the relationship between states and markets, and their effectiveness as alternative mechanisms for coordinating economic activity, setting parameters, and simplifying and stabilizing conditions of choice. While the pendulum appears to have shifted towards markets, many neoliberal reforms, often touted as a means of 'rolling back the state', contain elements that actually strengthen the state in some ways. In fact, the divorce of markets from states is untenable, and markets are absolutely dependent on public authority. The market-oriented reforms enacted by the European Union are particularly striking in this regard since the effort to create 'freer markets' has resulted in 'more rules' and strengthened the authority of the European Union in exercising market governance.

The analysis of market integration in this book has sought to explain this puzzle by demonstrating that the regulatory agenda of the EU has come to dominate the regulatory agenda of the member states, as the supply of and demand for European regulations has produced thousands of regulations in a host of policy areas. As the EU increasingly recognised the need to tackle the growing number of national regulations and standards, since these could threaten market integration, the central task facing the EU seemed to be finding the most efficient way to achieve its public policy goals and objectives. In trying to find an effective mechanism to bridge the gap between different regulatory traditions, European governments grapple with a double challenge. They have to reduce obstacles to trade to promote competition and find more efficient ways to regulate, while also protecting important welfare policy goals. In the end, however, there is more at stake in the discussion of regulation than the question of an efficient choice of instruments.

'Free markets'. . . 'more rules'. This is a crisp catchphrase for the conundrum of European integration.

SECTION 6: ECONOMIC AND MONETARY UNION

The questions raised in the penultimate extract of the preceding sub-section remain high on the agenda. Cecchini (p. 244) identified the single currency as a potential major element in the integrative process. This next step of policy integration was initiated by the Maastricht Treaty, which entered into force in 1993 (p. 9). Thus was launched the process of Economic and Monetary Union.

Article 119 TFEU provides an outline for the plan.

ARTICLE 119 TFEU

1. For the purposes set out in Article 3 of the Treaty on European Union, the activities of the Member States and the Union shall include, as provided in the Treaties, the adoption of an economic policy which is based on the close coordination of Member States' economic policies, on the internal market and on the definition of common objectives, and conducted in accordance with the principle of an open market economy with free competition.

2. Concurrently with the foregoing, and as provided in the Treaties and in accordance with the procedures set out therein, these activities shall include a single currency, the euro, and the definition and conduct of a single monetary policy and exchange-rate policy the primary objective of both of which shall be to maintain price stability and, without prejudice to this objective, to support the general economic policies in the Union, in accordance with the principle of an open market economy with free competition.

3. These activities of the Member States and the Union shall entail compliance with the following guiding principles: stable prices, sound public finances and monetary conditions and a sustainable balance of payment.

NOTE: Title VIII of Part Three of the TFEU, 'Economic and Monetary Policy', which occupies Articles 119–144 TFEU, provides elaboration of the plan. The economic convergence criteria on which the entry into being of the single currency is predicated are found in Article 140 TFEU:

— the achievement of a high degree of price stability; this will be apparent from a rate of inflation which is close to that of, at most, the three best performing Member States in terms of price stability;
— the sustainability of the government financial position; this will be apparent from having achieved a government budgetary position without a deficit that is excessive as determined in accordance with Article 126(6);
— the observance of the normal fluctuation margins provided for by the exchange-rate mechanism of the European Monetary System, for at least two years, without devaluing against the euro;
— the durability of convergence achieved by the Member State with a derogation and of its participation in the exchange-rate mechanism being reflected in the long-term interest-rate levels.

After conformity with these criteria was (in some instances, controversially) confirmed in accordance with the Treaty (see Decision 98/317, [1998] OJ L139/30), the third stage of economic and monetary union began on 1 January 1999, with 11 participants: Belgium, Germany, Spain, France, Ireland, Italy, Luxembourg, the Netherlands, Austria, Portugal, and Finland. Coins and banknotes of the euro have been physically available from 1 January 2002, and, after a brief period of overlap, national currencies of the participants were withdrawn. Lithuania became the 19th participant State in 2014. The UK has an opt-out from the third stage, secured at the time of the Maastricht negotiations, and its currency remains outside the 'eurozone' and therefore continues to fluctuate against the euro. Economic, political, and legal perspectives converge in acknowledging that the significance of economic and monetary union is profound. One rather central question asks: will it prove a success?

D. Dinan, *Ever Closer Union: an Introduction to European Integration*
(London: Macmillan Press, 1999), p. 477

WILL EMU WORK

The short answer to the question 'Will EMU work?' is yes, it *will* work because a majority of Europeans have decided that it *must* work. During the transition stages, member states displayed a determination to make it happen; new and existing administrative bodies demonstrated the necessary expertise to bring it about; and public opinion showed surprising compliance with it. Having concluded during the transition stages not only that EMU was feasible but also that the political and economic costs of failure were greater than the costs of success, politicians, technocrats, and ordinary Europeans alike were bound to conclude after the launch of Stage III that the costs of maintaining the single currency are considerably less than the costs of its collapse.

NOTE: The phenomenon of EMU deserves no more than a brief introduction, or else a profound exploration of its economic, institutional, and constitutional consequences. This book is compelled to take the first option. But the interested reader is encouraged to read more widely. This is a project on a dauntingly ambitious scale. Over 25 years ago the Cecchini Report observed that 'The business managers of the European market of the 1990s cannot be indefinitely divorced from the political managers of the Community economy' (p. 244), and amid contemporary turbulence in the 'Eurozone' (and with effects beyond it) key questions must be faced about the political implications of this ambitious economic project. As outlined by El-Agraa in sketching patterns of 'IEI' (p. 236), further steps towards unification of fiscal, economic, and monetary policies demand that choices be made about the nature of the rules and the presiding central authority. As the story unfolds it reveals a mixed menu, comprising binding rules on economic governance adopted under the TFEU (Articles 136 and 121(6)), 'softer' forms of co-ordination such as the 'European Semester', a cycle within which Member States' planned economic and structural reforms are assessed by the Commission with a view to the adoption by the Council of country-specific recommendations on budgetary options, and initiatives that are formally placed outwith the EU structure altogether. Most prominent among this third type are the Treaty on Stability, Co-Ordination and Governance (which entered into force in 2013) and the European Stability Mechanism (ESM) Treaty (2012). Constitutional limits and political blockages, including the intransigence of the UK, prevented these arrangements being struck under the EU's roof and they are instead orthodox international Treaties, to which most but not all EU Member States are party. The ESM Treaty had to survive a challenge that it prejudiced pre-existing obligations under EU law but it did so in *Pringle* (Case C-370/12 judgment of 27 November 2012). The constitutional anxiety about fracture of the EU's orthodox method in the face of the Eurozone's travails is sharply captured by the very title of B. Crum's article at (2013) 51 JCMS 614: 'Saving the Euro at the Cost of Democracy?'. (See also A. Hinarejos, *The Euro Area Crisis in Constitutional Perspective* (OUP, 2015).

Analysis now turns over the following chapters contained in Part Two of this book to the substantive legal rules which serve to eliminate national rules which act as impediments to trade between Member States. The concern, then, is initially with the negative aspect of the creation of the internal market. Chapters 10–12 and Chapters 13–15 examine 'Opening up the Market', first in relation to the free movement of goods, then in relation to the free movement of persons and services. Chapter 16 supplements this with an explanation of the Treaty competition rules.

As the maintenance of border controls declines, in part as a result of legal prohibition but also because of the irrelevance of border controls to supervision of technologically advanced economic activity, so the question for negative Union law has become more one of coping with regulatory diversity between the Member States rather than physical frontiers or discriminatory practices. In many fields it is the simple fact of differences between non-discriminatory regulatory standards State by State that impedes traders from constructing an integrated strategy for the territory of the whole Union. Where States tax products at different rates, the trader in a low-taxing state will face a demand for extra payment when he or she tries to sell the product in the high-taxing state. Where States make different demands with regard to the composition of, say, foodstuffs, the trader in a State which allows use of ingredient *alpha* will be unable to gain access to the market of a State which forbids use of *alpha*. And where States apply different standards of professional qualification, a lawyer trained in State X may be refused the opportunity of working, establishing him- or herself, or providing services in State Y simply because State Y has a different training regime.

Were these cases based on overt discrimination against out-of-State providers, then they would be rather easy to resolve in favour of free trade. But there is no discrimination in such cases; all products are highly taxed irrespective of origin in the first example, all products are denied use of ingredient *alpha* in the second example, and all lawyers must meet the host State's requirements in the third. The rules are different, but this tends to lead to protection of home State producers who naturally comply with their own State's rules. The rules restrict cross-border trade. The validity of such rules comes into sharper focus as the integrative process evolves and such less-than-obvious technical barriers to trade are revealed. In the EU, the three examples given would be considered under different Treaty provisions – Article 110 (tax, Chapter 10), Article 34 (goods, Chapters 11 and 12), and Articles 45, 48, and 56 (persons, Chapter 13, services, Chapter 14) respectively. They would not be dealt with in precisely the same way; but they raise the same policy issue – the compatibility with EU trade law of regulatory diversity between the States in so far as that diversity acts as an impediment to integration.

The Court of Justice has developed principles for judging the acceptable limits of regulatory diversity where trade restriction is caused. The roots of this case law pre-date '1992' by over a decade (*Cassis de Dijon*, p. 319), which emphasizes once again that the construction of the EU's internal market was and remains a dynamic process, constructed on already well-established principles that are of continuing significance; but the management of regulatory diversity is a quintessentially post-1992, post-border control issue.

***Reinhard Gebhard* v *Consiglio dell'Ordine degli Avvocati e Procuratori di Milano* (Case C-55/94)**

[1995] ECR I-4165, [1996] 1 CMLR 603, Court of Justice of the European Communities

Gebhard, a German national and a member of the Bar of Stuttgart, was resident in Italy. He had worked as a lawyer in Milan, but found himself the subject of disciplinary proceedings by the Milan Bar Council on the ground that he had infringed Italian law by pursuing a professional activity in Italy on a permanent basis using the title *avvocato*. The Court rejected the view of the Milan Bar Council that Gebhard could not be regarded for the purposes of the Treaty as 'established' in Italy unless he belonged to the professional body, or at least pursued his activity in collaboration or in association with persons belonging to that body. The Court conceded that the pursuit of certain self-employed activities may be conditional on complying with certain provisions justified by 'the general good', such as rules relating to organization, qualification, professional ethics, supervision, and liability. It added that where the pursuit of a specific activity is subject to such conditions in the host State, a national of another Member State intending to pursue that activity must in principle comply with them. This concedes regulatory diversity, and the Court referred to the role of secondary legislation governing recognition of professional qualifications (especially Directive 89/48, p. 414). It then stated:

> [37] It follows, however, from the Court's case-law that national measures liable to hinder or make less attractive the exercise of fundamental freedoms guaranteed by the Treaty must fulfil four conditions: they must be applied in a non-discriminatory manner; they must be justified by imperative requirements in the general interest; they must be suitable for securing the attainment of the objective which they pursue; and they must not go beyond what is necessary in order to attain it . . .

NOTE: The *Gebhard* case concerned the free movement of persons, but the principle stated is capable of application in the context of Article 34 TFEU, which deals with the free movement of goods (though not, it would seem, to Article 110 TFEU where the Court's control of non-discriminatory regulatory diversity is less assertive, Chapter 10). This is part of an emerging, though (as will be seen) not entirely consistent, pattern of EU trade law applicable to all national rules that impede the exercise of economic freedoms. The principles expressed by the Court in this ruling will be traced through the chapters on negative trade law that follow.

It is plain that the Court envisages that States may justify rules against standards recognized under EU law (e.g., environmental and consumer protection) even where there is a restrictive effect on cross-border trade. How, then, can integration be achieved? As already suggested in connection with *Gebhard*, the classic answer is to move beyond negative law to positive law – to harmonize the diverse national laws so that a common Union-wide rule is put in place. The Union measure governs the interests that underpinned national intervention but achieves protection of those interests at Union level. Traders may then plan integrated strategies according to this common rule which applies throughout the EU's territory.

Areas in which a positive contribution from EU law is required may be observed on several occasions, and accordingly the themes set out in this chapter will be seen to underlie the substantive rules. This becomes more explicit in the remaining chapters of this book. Part Three of the book takes the discussion on to a broader plane. Chapter 17 considers harmonization and common policy-making, where several of the themes introduced in the present chapter are reassessed in the light of the substantive law examined in Chapters 10–16. Chapter 18 looks more broadly still at questions of subsidiarity, flexibility, and new forms of governance. It will be seen that the beguiling notion of common rules for a common market is under strain. In part this is attributable to the geographic and functional expansion of the EU which renders agreement increasingly hard to achieve. The range of interests at stake in the EU cannot readily be reduced to a single agreed norm. More fundamentally, there is an increasingly voiced case against harmonization. Better, it is said by some sources, to allow traders access to the markets of all Member States subject only to compliance with the rules of their home State. The host State could retain a regulatory regime different from other States, but could not use those regulatory differences as a basis for denying access to an out-of-State trader. This would be a system of mutual recognition of national rules. Firms could then choose where to locate in order to supply the whole market, and their choice would be informed by prevailing regulatory strategies. Firms – the market – would select which regulatory regime suited them best. It can readily be appreciated that this approach not only downplays the need for harmonization and a level playing field, it also portrays harmonization as an undesirable suppression of a market in which regulators compete for customers. The debate is not only directed at the internal aspects of EU policy; it is also argued that externally the EU will lose its competitive position if it locks itself into a single standard.

This is an inevitably superficial summary of a key philosophical debate about the future of the Union. This preference for 'competition between regulators' over the 'level playing field' is most closely associated with the long-ousted Thatcher/Major administrations in the UK, although it is a debate with global resonances. The debate is being conducted in many sectors. Social policy was the most high-profile example at Maastricht. The United Kingdom then fought against provisions permitting a deepening of regulation; unable to win that argument, it then successfully argued that it should be insulated from the regulations that other Member States wished to introduce. The United Kingdom thus competed in social policy standards against the other 11, then 14, in the area covered by the Protocol-plus-Agreement. This is touched on in Chapter 18 (p. 571) although, *via* the Amsterdam Treaty, the UK's exclusion was brought to an end by the Labour Government which took office in May 1997. Shadows of this debate have been cast once again by the UK's insistence that it be granted a degree of special protection from the impact of the Charter of Fundamental Rights, in part because of a fear that the Charter might be interpreted in such a way as to exert a deepening impact on social policy and labour rights. This is recorded in a special Protocol to the Lisbon Treaty, and affects the UK and Poland alone (Chapter 2, p. 58). Lately some voices in the UK Conservative party have been raised in favour of seeking 'repatriation' of some powers in the field of (especially but not only) social policy: this is another echo of the preference for regulatory competition over common rule-making. At a more general level, the reader should consider whether the EU is adjusting to new patterns of growth to which all members need not necessarily subscribe, or whether these patterns of fragmentation are fatal to its survival. Enlargement to 28 Member States has served to sharpen the debate. Chapter 18 contains relevant material. This is variable geometry – and it challenges many of the assumptions about the role of positive law beyond negative law. It is nothing new. Variable geometry has already been touched on in this chapter in the case of economic and monetary union (p. 264), but, as the EU pursues its path of geographic and functional expansion marked by periodic intergovernmental conferences, the debate about how far to move beyond deregulation and market liberalization towards patterns of substantive and institutional re-regulation (in common or not) is becoming increasingly acute. The Treaty provisions on 'enhanced cooperation' constitute an intriguing manifestation. They are examined in Chapter 18. Chapter 18 also investigates new forms of governance which assume a less rigid form than orthodox patterns of EU rule-making and rule-application. Chapter 19 concludes the book by placing this debate in the context of that which will shape the 'Future of Europe' beyond the Treaty of Lisbon, which is the latest stage in the EU's evolution and in no sense a 'solution' to these several conundrums. But it is time now to usher the reader towards closer study of the relevant patterns of substantive EU law.

NOTE: For additional material and resources see the Online Resource Centre at: www.oxfordtextbooks.co.uk/orc/weatherill12e.

10

Fiscal Barriers to Trade: Articles 30 and 110 TFEU

NOTE: The customs union is a matter of exclusive Union competence (Article 3(1)(a) TFEU, p. 31). Article 28 of the TFEU commits the Union to the creation of a customs union.

ARTICLE 28 TFEU

The Union shall comprise a customs union which shall cover all trade in goods and which shall involve the prohibition between Member States of customs duties on imports and exports and of all charges having equivalent effect, and the adoption of a common customs tariff in their relations with third countries.

NOTE: Article 31 TFEU empowers the Council acting on a proposal from the Commission to fix common customs tariff duties. It is the internal aspects of the customs union which form the focus of this chapter.

ARTICLE 30 TFEU

Customs duties on imports and exports and charges having equivalent effect shall be prohibited between Member States. This prohibition shall also apply to customs duties of a fiscal nature.

NOTE: The elimination of customs duties on trade between Member States is essential as part of the process of market integration, but it is not enough on its own to secure origin neutrality in fiscal law. Consequently the provisions which prohibit customs duties are supplemented by provisions directed at the internal taxation systems of the Member States. Article 110 TFEU forbids discrimination against imported goods in the State's internal system of taxation.

ARTICLE 110 TFEU

No Member State shall impose, directly or indirectly, on the products of other Member States any internal taxation of any kind in excess of that imposed directly or indirectly on similar domestic products.

Furthermore, no Member State shall impose on the products of other Member States any internal taxation of such a nature as to afford indirect protection to other products.

NOTES

1. These are fundamentally important provisions. Both plainly connect with Article 26 TFEU's commitment to establishing an internal market, examined in the previous chapter. The wording was not affected by the Lisbon Treaty, but the numbering was. What is now Article 30 TFEU was, pre-Lisbon, Article 25 EC (and pre-Amsterdam it was, in lightly amended form, Article 12); what is now Article 110 TFEU was, pre-Lisbon, Article 90 EC (and pre-Amsterdam it was, in lightly amended form, Article 95). This must be kept in mind when reading earlier case law and comment.

2. It has become axiomatic that Article 30 and Article 110 are *complementary but mutually exclusive*. Both are directed at the abolition of fiscal barriers to trade; but a charge is controlled by one or the other, not both. There is no overlap. (See *Commission* v *Italy* (Case 24/68), p. 271 and more recently Case C-254/13 *Orgacom* judgment of 2 October 2014.)
3. The nature of the control exercised over domestic competence to levy tax is distinct. Article 30 TFEU forbids customs duties and charges having equivalent effect. Article 110 TFEU does not forbid internal taxation; it merely forbids discrimination according to nationality. States remain otherwise free to levy taxation as they see fit.

SECTION 1: ARTICLE 30 TFEU

The Court has used the prohibition on customs duties and charges having equivalent effect to challenge a range of levies imposed on goods which cross a frontier. The Court is concerned with the restrictive *effect* on trade, not the purpose of the charge. The following cases, both infringement proceedings against Italy (see Chapter 4), illustrate the Court's application of the Article 30 TFEU prohibition (which, at the time the cases were decided, was contained in Article 12).

Commission v *Italy* (Case 7/68)

[1968] ECR 423, Court of Justice of the European Communities

The case concerned an Italian tax on the export of artistic, historical, and archaeological articles.

1. The scope of the disputed tax

By basing its action on Article 16 of the Treaty, the Commission considers that articles of an artistic, historic, archaeological or ethnographic nature, which are the subject of the Italian Law of 1 June 1939, No 1089, fall under the provisions relating to the customs union. This point of view is disputed by the defendant, which considers that the articles in question cannot be assimilated to 'consumer goods or articles of general use' and are not therefore subject to the provisions of the Treaty which apply to 'ordinary merchandise'; for that reason they are excluded from the application of Article 16 of the Treaty.

Under Article 9 of the Treaty the Community is based on a customs union 'which shall cover all trade in goods' [now Article 28 TFEU, p. 267]. By goods, within the meaning of that provision, there must be understood products which can be valued in money and which are capable, as such, of forming the subject of commercial transactions.

The articles covered by the Italian Law, whatever may be the characteristics which distinguish them from other types of merchandise, nevertheless resemble the latter, inasmuch as they can be valued in money and so be the subject of commercial transactions. That view corresponds with the scheme of the Italian Law itself, which fixes the tax in question in proportion to the value of the articles concerned.

It follows from the above that the rules of the Common Market apply to these goods subject only to the exceptions expressly provided by the Treaty.

2. The classification of the disputed tax having regard to Article 16 of the Treaty

In the opinion of the Commission the tax in dispute constitutes a tax having an effect equivalent to a customs duty on exports and therefore the tax should have been abolished, under Article 16 of the Treaty, no later than the end of the first stage of the common market, that is to say, from 1 January 1962. The defendant argues that the disputed tax does not come within the category, as it has its own particular purpose which is to ensure the protection and safety of the artistic, historic and archaeological heritage which exists in the national territory. Consequently, the tax does not in any respect have a fiscal nature, and its contribution to the budget is insignificant.

Article 16 of the Treaty prohibits the collection in dealings between Member States of any customs duty on exports and of any charge having an equivalent effect, that is to say, any charge which, by altering the price of an article exported, has the same restrictive effect on the free circulation of that article as a customs duty. This provision makes no distinction based on the purpose of the duties and charges the abolition of which it requires.

It is not necessary to analyse the concept of the nature of fiscal systems on which the defendant bases its argument upon this point, for the provisions of the section of the Treaty concerning the elimination of customs duties between the Member States exclude the retention of customs duties and charges having equivalent effect without distinguishing in that respect between those which are and those which are not of a fiscal nature.

The disputed tax falls within Article 16 by reason of the fact that export trade in the goods in question is hindered by the pecuniary burden which it imposes on the price of the exported articles.

NOTE: The Court went on to reject Italian arguments of justification based on what is now Article 36 TFEU. Article 36 is available only in respect of physical and technical barriers to trade caught by Article 34, and is unavailable in the field of fiscal barriers to trade. Chapter 11 examines Articles 34–36 TFEU.

***Commission* v *Italy* (Case 24/68)**

[1969] ECR 193, Court of Justice of the European Communities

Italy collected a levy on goods exported to other Member States in order to fund the compilation of statistical data relating to trade patterns. The Court began by examining the nature of the Article 30 (then Article 12) prohibition before proceeding to find the charge incompatible with the Treaty.

[6] . . . the purpose of the abolition of customs barriers is not merely to eliminate their protective nature, as the Treaty sought on the contrary to give general scope and effect to the rule on the elimination of customs duties and charges having equivalent effect, in order to ensure the free movement of goods.

[7] It follows from the system as a whole and from the general and absolute nature of the prohibition of any customs duty applicable to goods moving between Member States that customs duties are prohibited independently of any consideration of the purpose for which they were introduced and the destination of the revenue obtained therefrom.

The justification for this prohibition is based on the fact that any pecuniary charge, however small, imposed on goods by reason of the fact that they cross a frontier constitutes an obstacle to the movement of such goods.

[8] The extension of the prohibition of customs duties to charges having equivalent effect is intended to supplement the prohibition against obstacles to trade created by such duties by increasing its efficiency.

The use of these two complementary concepts thus tends, in trade between Member States, to avoid the imposition of any pecuniary charge on goods circulating within the Community by virtue of the fact that they cross a national frontier.

[9] Thus, in order to ascribe to a charge an effect equivalent to a customs duty, it is important to consider this effect in the light of the objectives of the Treaty, in the Parts, Titles and Chapters in which Articles 9, 12, 13 and 16 are to be found, particularly in relation to the free movement of goods.

Consequently, any pecuniary charge, however small and whatever its designation and mode of application, which is imposed unilaterally on domestic or foreign goods by reason of the fact that they cross a frontier, and which is not a customs duty in the strict sense, constitutes a charge having equivalent effect within the meaning of Articles 9, 12, 13 and 16 of the Treaty, even if it is not imposed for the benefit of the State, is not discriminatory or protective in effect and if the product on which the charge is imposed is not in competition with any domestic product.

[10] It follows from all the provisions referred to and from their relationship with the other provisions of the Treaty that the prohibition of new customs duties or charges having equivalent effect, linked to the principle of the free movement of goods, constitutes a fundamental rule which, without prejudice to the other provisions of the Treaty, does not permit of any exceptions.

. . .

[15] The Italian Government further maintains that the disputed charge constitutes the consideration for a service rendered and as such cannot be designated as a charge having equivalent effect.

According to the Italian Government the object of the statistics in question is to determine precisely the actual movements of goods and, consequently, changes the state of the market. It claims that the exactness of the information thus supplied affords importers a better competitive position in the Italian market whilst exporters enjoy a similar advantage abroad and that the special advantages which dealers obtain from the survey justifies their paying for this public service and moreover demonstrates that the disputed charge is in the nature of a *quid pro quo.*

[16] The statistical information in question is beneficial to the economy as a whole and *inter alia* to the relevant administrative authorities.

Even if the competitive position of importers and exporters were to be particularly improved as a result, the statistics still constitute an advantage so general, and so difficult to assess, that the disputed charge cannot be regarded as the consideration for a specific benefit actually conferred.

[17] It appears from the abovementioned considerations that in so far as the disputed charge is levied on exports it is contrary to Article 16 of the Treaty.

NOTES

1. Paragraph 9 of the judgment constitutes the Court's definition of the scope of the prohibition; a formula which has proved enduring through subsequent case law.
2. See also, on the Court's approach, e.g., *Sociaal Fonds voor de Diamantarbeiders* v *Brachfeld* (Cases 2 and 3/69) [1969] ECR 211.
3. The Court accepts that a State is permitted to levy a fee for services provided to an importer. Such a charge is demanded as part of a commercial transaction, not because of the passage of the goods across a frontier. The charge is accordingly not caught by Article 30 TFEU. However, the risk that States may use this approach as a device for imposing charges on importers for unwanted services which impede free trade has led the Court to scrutinize with great care arguments of this nature. In paras 15 and 16 of its judgment in *Commission* v *Italy* (Case 24/68), the Court rejected submissions along these lines by the Italian Government. It took a similar approach in *Bresciani* v *Amministrazione Italiana delle Finanze* (Case 87/75).

***Bresciani* v *Amministrazione Italiana delle Finanze* (Case 87/75)**

[1976] ECR 129, Court of Justice of the European Communities

The case involved the imposition of a charge for compulsory veterinary and public health inspections carried out on the importation of raw cowhides. The Court was asked by a court in Genoa to consider whether such a levy constitutes a charge having equivalent effect to a customs duty on imports.

[9] ... [A]ny pecuniary charge, whatever its designation and mode of application, which is unilaterally imposed on goods imported from another Member State by reason of the fact that they cross a frontier, constitutes a charge having an effect equivalent to a customs duty. In appraising a duty of the type at issue it is... of no importance that it is proportionate to the quantity of the imported goods and not to their value.

[10] Nor, in determining the effects of the duty on the free movement of goods, is it of any importance that a duty of the type at issue is proportionate to the costs of a compulsory public health inspection carried out on entry of the goods. The activity of the administration of the State intended to maintain a public health inspection system imposed in the general interest cannot be regarded as a service rendered to the importer such as to justify the imposition of a pecuniary charge. If, accordingly, public health inspections are still justified at the end of the transitional period, the costs which they occasion must be met by the general public which, as a whole, benefits from the free movement of Community goods.

[11] The fact that the domestic production is, through other charges, subjected to a similar burden matters little unless those charges and the duty in question are applied according to the same criteria and at the same stage of production, thus making it possible for them to be regarded as falling within a general system of internal taxation applying systematically and in the same way to domestic and imported products.

NOTE: Arguments of fee-for-service also failed in, e.g., *Cadsky* v *ICE* (Case 63/74) [1975] ECR 281. See *Commission* v *Belgium* (Case 132/82) [1983] ECR 1649 for discussion of circumstances in which a fee might legitimately be demanded; the case was nonetheless still decided against the charging State.

However, where the inspection is carried out under mandatory provisions of Union law, then a charge may be lawful.

Commission v *Germany* (Case 18/87)

[1988] ECR 5427, Court of Justice of the European Communities

German *Länder* (regions) charged fees on the importation of live animals to cover costs of inspections undertaken under Directive 81/389. The Court adopted a step-by-step approach in ruling on the compatibility of the system with (what was then) Community law.

[5] It should be observed in the first place that, as the Court has held on a number of occasions, the justification for the prohibition of customs duties and any charges having an equivalent effect lies in the fact that any pecuniary charge, however small, imposed on goods by reason of the fact that they cross a frontier, constitutes an obstacle to the movement of goods which is aggravated by the resulting administrative formalities. It follows that any pecuniary charge, whatever its designation and mode of application, which is imposed unilaterally on goods by reason of the fact that they cross a frontier and is not a customs duty in the strict sense constitutes a charge having an equivalent effect to a customs duty within the meaning of Articles 9, 12, 13 and 16 of the Treaty.

[6] However, the Court has held that such a charge escapes that classification if it relates to a general system of internal dues applied systematically and in accordance with the same criteria to domestic products and imported products alike (judgment of 31 May 1979 in Case 132/78 *Denkavit* v *France* [1979] ECR 1923), if it constitutes payment for a service in fact rendered to the economic operator of a sum in proportion to the service (judgment of 9 November 1983 in Case 158/82 *Commission* v *Denmark* [1983] ECR 3573), or again, subject to certain conditions, if it attaches to inspections carried out to fulfil obligations imposed by Community law (judgment of 25 January 1977 in Case 46/76 *Bauhuis* v *Netherlands* [1977] ECR 5).

[7] The contested fee, which is payable on importation and transit, cannot be regarded as relating to a general system of internal dues. Nor does it constitute payment for a service rendered to the operator, because this condition is satisfied only if the operator in question obtains a definite specific benefit (see judgment of 1 July 1969 in Case 24/68 *Commission* v *Italy* [1969] ECR 193), which is not the case if the inspection serves to guarantee, in the public interest, the health and life of animals in international transport (see judgment of 20 March 1984 in Case 314/82 *Commission* v *Belgium* [1984] ECR 1543).

[8] Since the contested fee was charged in connection with inspections carried out pursuant to a Community provision, it should be noted that according to the case-law of the Court (judgment of 25 January 1977 in Bauhuis, cited above; judgment of 12 July 1977 *Commission* v *Netherlands* [1977] ECR 1355; judgment of 31 January 1984 in Case 1/83 *IFG* v *Freistaat Bayern* [1984] ECR 349) such fees may not be classified as charges having an effect equivalent to a customs duty if the following conditions are satisfied:

(a) they do not exceed the actual costs of the inspections in connection with which they are charged;
(b) the inspections in question are obligatory and uniform for all the products concerned in the Community;
(c) they are prescribed by Community law in the general interest of the Community;
(d) they promote the free movement of goods, in particular by neutralizing obstacles which could arise from unilateral measures of inspection adopted in accordance with Article 36 of the Treaty.

[9] In this instance these conditions are satisfied by the contested fee . . .

NOTE: The Court appears prepared to accept in such a case that in so far as the European Union as a whole obtains a benefit from the facilitation of free trade secured through a harmonized system of health inspections, the State is permitted to pass on the costs to individual traders. It has adopted the same view in respect of inspections mandatory under international conventions to which all Member States are party; *Commission* v *Netherlands* (Case 89/76) [1977] ECR 1355.

It should however be noted that where EU law does no more than permit the inspection, any fee levied to cover costs is incompatible with Article 30 TFEU; *Commission* v *Belgium* (Case 314/82) [1984] ECR 1543.

SECTION 2: ARTICLE 110 TFEU

A charge may fall to be considered in the light of Article 110 (text at p. 269) where it is imposed not on an importer as such, but instead on all traders irrespective of origin. If the State can show that the charge 'relates to a general system of internal dues applied systematically and in accordance with the same criteria to domestic products and imported products alike' (para 6 of *Commission* v *Germany* (Case 18/87 at p. 273)), then the charge is lawful, provided only that the non-discrimination requirements of Article 110 are complied with.

The next case shows the application of Article 110 to an internal system of taxation which was held to favour the domestic trader over the importer. Remember that pre-Amsterdam the current Article 110 TFEU was numbered Article 95.

Schottle v *Finanzamt Freudenstadt* (Case 20/76)

[1977] ECR 247, Court of Justice of the European Communities

The case arose out of German taxation of carriage of goods by road. Long-distance road transport was taxed as part of a policy to encourage use of rail and waterways instead, but no tax was imposed on short-distance road transport. The definition of 'short distance' included special arrangements for importers. The net result was that a short journey might be exempt if purely internal to Germany, but subject to tax if it crossed a border.

[20] The first paragraph of Article 95 is infringed where the taxation on the imported product and that on the similar domestic product are calculated in a different manner on the basis of different criteria which lead, if only in certain cases, to higher taxation being imposed on the imported product.

[21] Higher taxation of the imported product exists when the conditions under which the carrier is subject to tax are different with regard to international transport and purely domestic transport so that in comparable situations the product moving within the Member State is not subject to the tax to which an imported product is subject. Indeed in order to compare the tax on goods moving within the national territory with that on the imported product for the purposes of the application of Article 95, account must be taken of both the basis of assessment of the tax and the advantages or exemptions which each tax carries with it. For the taxation of the imported product to be higher it is sufficient that in certain circumstances the national product may be transported without being subject to tax for the same distance within the Member State while the imported product is subject to the tax solely because the border was crossed. In this respect it is for the national judge to compare in specific cases the situations which may arise.

[22] The information supplied by the national court shows that a real obstacle to free movement of goods may sometimes result from the application of different conditions for the imposition of taxation with regard to both international transport and domestic transport. The minor and incidental nature of the obstacle created by a national tax and the fact that it could only have been avoided in practice by abolishing the tax are not sufficient to prevent Article 95 from being applicable. Title IV of Part Two of the Treaty concerning the common transport policy enables Member States to resolve problems of competition between means of transport without however adversely affecting the free movement of goods. However the lack of such a policy is no justification for a derogation from Article 95 of the Treaty.

NOTE: The tax system lacked origin neutrality. However, States are commonly more devious. It is possible to avoid direct discrimination on grounds of nationality (the problem in *Schottle*), but to achieve a similar result by instead basing a taxation system on criteria which indirectly prejudice the imported product. In the following case the Court decided that such indirect discrimination on grounds of nationality is also capable of falling foul of Article 110.

***Humblot* v *Directeur des Services Fiscaux* (Case 112/84)**

[1985] ECR 1367, Court of Justice of the European Communities

France imposed two different types of annual car tax. The key threshold between the two was 16 CV, a power rating. Below that level the tax increased gradually in proportion to the car's power, up to a maximum of 1,100 francs. Above 16 CV a flat rate of 5,000 francs was imposed. No French car was rated above 16 CV, so only imported vehicles were burdened by the high flat rate. M. Humblot, charged 5,000 francs tax on his 36 CV imported car, claimed the tax violated what was then Article 95, now Article 110, and sought a refund. The French court in Belfort referred questions under Article 177 (Article 267 TFEU post-Lisbon: see Chapter 7).

[12] It is appropriate in the first place to stress that as Community law stands at present the Member States are at liberty to subject products such as cars to a system of road tax which increases progressively in amount depending on an objective criterion, such as the power rating for tax purposes, which may be determined in various ways.

[13] Such a system of domestic taxation is, however, compatible with Article 95 only in so far as it is free from any discriminatory or protective effect.

[14] That is not true of a system like the one at issue in the main proceedings. Under that system there are two distinct taxes: a differential tax which increases progressively and is charged on cars not exceeding a given power rating for tax purposes and a fixed tax on cars exceeding that rating which is almost five times as high as the highest rate of the differential tax. Although the system embodies no formal distinction based on the origin of products it manifestly exhibits discriminatory or protective features contrary to Article 95, since the power rating determining liability to the special tax has been fixed at a level such that only imported cars, in particular from other Member States, are subject to the special tax whereas all cars of domestic manufacture are liable to the distinctly more advantageous differential tax.

[15] In the absence of considerations relating to the amount of the special tax, consumers seeking comparable cars as regards such matters as size, comfort, actual power, maintenance costs, durability, fuel consumption and price would naturally choose from among cars above and below the critical power rating laid down by French law. However, liability to the special tax entails a much larger increase in taxation than passing from one category of car to another in a system of progressive taxation embodying balanced differentials like the system on which the differential tax is based. The resultant additional taxation is liable to cancel out the advantages which certain cars imported from other Member States might have in consumers' eyes over comparable cars of domestic manufacture, particularly since the special tax continues to be payable for several years. In that respect the special tax reduces the amount of competition to which cars of domestic manufacture are subject and hence is contrary to the principle of neutrality with which domestic taxation must comply.

[16] In the light of the foregoing considerations the question raised by the national court for a preliminary ruling should be answered as follows: Article 95 of the EEC Treaty prohibits the charging on cars exceeding a given power rating for tax purposes of a special fixed tax the amount of which is several times the highest amount of the progressive tax payable on cars of less than the said power rating for tax purposes, where the only cars subject to the special tax are imported, in particular from other Member States.

NOTES

1. An amended French car tax system was also found incompatible with Article 95 (now Article 110 TFEU) in *Feldain* (Case 433/85) [1987] ECR 3536.
2. However, the establishment of a taxation system based on a criterion which indirectly affects imported goods more severely than domestic products is not automatically unlawful. It is open to the State to show that there is an objective justification for the use of that criterion which is not connected with nationality. The tax may then be accepted as compatible with Article 110.

***Chemial Farmaceutici* v *DAF* (Case 140/79)**

[1981] ECR 1, Court of Justice of the European Communities

Italian taxation of denatured synthetic ethyl alcohol was higher than taxation of denatured ethyl alcohol obtained by fermentation, although the products were interchangeable in use. Italy produced little of the more heavily taxed synthetic version of the product. The Court explained that the facts and the result were distinguishable from *Humblot* (Case 112/84).

[13] . . . the different taxation of synthetic alcohol and of alcohol produced by fermentation in Italy is the result of an economic policy decision to favour the manufacture of alcohol from agricultural products and, correspondingly, to restrain the processing into alcohol of ethylene, a derivative of petroleum, in order to reserve that raw material for other more important economic uses. It accordingly constitutes a legitimate choice of economic policy to which effect is given by fiscal means. The implementation of that policy does not lead to any discrimination since although it results in discouraging imports of synthetic alcohol into Italy, it also has the consequence of hampering the development in Italy itself of production of alcohol from ethylene, that production being technically perfectly possible.

[14] As the Court has stated on many occasions, particularly in the judgments cited by the Italian Government, in its present stage of development Community law does not restrict the freedom of each Member State to lay down tax arrangements which differentiate between certain products on the basis of objective criteria, such as the nature of the raw materials used or the production processes employed. Such differentiation is compatible with Community law if it pursues economic policy objectives which are themselves compatible with the requirements of the Treaty and its secondary law and if the detailed rules are such as to avoid any form of discrimination, direct or indirect, in regard to imports from other Member States or any form of protection of competing domestic products.

[15] Differential taxation such as that which exists in Italy for denatured synthetic alcohol on the one hand and denatured alcohol obtained by fermentation on the other satisfies these requirements. It appears in fact that that system of taxation pursues an objective of legitimate industrial policy in that it is such as to promote the distillation of agricultural products as against the manufacture of alcohol from petroleum derivatives. That choice does not conflict with the rules of Community law or the requirements of a policy decided within the framework of the Community.

[16] The detailed provisions of the legislation at issue before the national court cannot be considered as discriminatory since, on the one hand, it is not disputed that imports from other Member States of alcohol obtained by fermentation qualify for the same tax treatment as Italian alcohol produced by fermentation and, on the other hand, although the rate of tax prescribed for synthetic alcohol results in restraining the importation of synthetic alcohol originating in other Member States, it has an equivalent economic effect in the national territory in that it also hampers the establishment of profitable production of the same product by Italian industry.

NOTE: Notice that it is only indirect discrimination on grounds of nationality which may be justified in this way; never direct discrimination. Concessions must be made available to all products meeting the criteria, even if in practice few imports conform. See, e.g., *Commission* v *Italy* (Case 213/79) [1980] ECR 1.

■ QUESTION

Advise a State which has several regions which suffer from abnormally high rainfall and which wishes to introduce a tax which favours production of goods typical of high-rainfall areas in order to confer economic support on the farmers of such areas.
See *Commission* v *France* (Case 196/85) [1987] ECR 1597.

NOTES

1. The second paragraph of Article 110 (p. 269) broadens the scope of the provisions beyond tax equality for similar products to equality for competing products. This involves an economic assessment of the relationship of products in order to reveal whether the State is engaged in conferring protection on its domestic producers by imposing undue burdens on competing imports.

2. The Court explained the nature of the control exercised by the first and second paragraphs of what was then Article 95, now Article 110 TFEU, in the 'Spirits' cases, a series of cases concerned to challenge taxation laws relating to alcohol alleged to favour domestic products.

Commission v *France* (Case 168/78)

[1980] ECR 347, Court of Justice of the European Communities

[4] As the Commission has correctly stated, Article 95 must guarantee the complete neutrality of internal taxation as regards competition between domestic products and imported products.

[5] The first paragraph of Article 95, which is based on a comparison of the tax burdens imposed on domestic products and on imported products which may be classified as 'similar', is the basic rule in this respect. This provision, as the Court has had occasion to emphasize in its judgment of 10 October 1978 in Case 148/77, H. Hansen jun. & O.C. *Balle GmbH & Co.* v *Hauptzollamt Flensburg* [1978] ECR 1787, must be interpreted widely so as to cover all taxation procedures which conflict with the principle of the equality of treatment of domestic products and imported products; it is therefore necessary to interpret the concept of 'similar products' with sufficient flexibility. The Court specified in the judgment of 17 February 1976 in the REWE case (Case 45/75 [1976] ECR 181) that it is necessary to consider as similar products which 'have similar characteristics and meet the same needs from the point of view of consumers'. It is therefore necessary to determine the scope of the first paragraph of Article 95 on the basis not of the criterion of the strictly identical nature of the products but on that of their similar and comparable use.

[6] The function of the second paragraph of Article 95 is to cover, in addition, all forms of indirect tax protection in the case of products which, without being similar within the meaning of the first paragraph, are nevertheless in competition, even partial, indirect or potential, with certain products of the importing country. The Court has already emphasized certain aspects of that provision in its judgment of 4 April 1978 in Case 27/77, *Firma Fink-Frucht GmbH* v *Hauptzollamt Munchen-Landsbergerstrasse* [1978] ECR 223, in which it stated that for the purposes of the application of the first paragraph of Article 95 it is sufficient for the imported product to be in competition with the protected domestic production by reason of one or several economic uses to which it may be put, even though the condition of similarity for the purposes of the first paragraph of Article 95 is not fulfilled.

[7] Whilst the criterion indicated in the first paragraph of Article 95 consists in the comparison of tax burdens, whether in terms of the rate, the mode of assessment or other detailed rules for the application thereof, in view of the difficulty of making sufficiently precise comparisons between the products in question, the second paragraph of that article is based upon a more general criterion, in other words the protective nature of the system of internal taxation.

NOTE: Most of the 'Spirits' cases, including *Commission* v *France* (Case 168/78), were decided on the basis that the Treaty prohibition was plainly infringed, and without detailed examination of the two paragraphs separately. This was not possible in the most difficult of the cases, *Commission* v *UK* (Case 170/78), which involved tax differentials between wine and beer. These products are not similar within Article 110(1), and therefore argument centred on the possible application of Article 110(2) (then, of course, Article 95(2)). So complex were the economic calculations that the Court declined to give final judgment at the same time as it upheld the Commission's complaints in the other 'Spirits' cases ([1980] ECR 417). Eventually, however, after deeper investigation had been presented to the Court, the UK was held in breach of the Treaty.

Commission v *UK* (Case 170/78)

[1983] ECR 2263, Court of Justice of the European Communities

The Court first explored the nature of the competitive relationship between wine and beer, and built on its initial findings three years earlier.

[8] As regards the question of competition between wine and beer, the Court considered that, to a certain extent at least, the two beverages in question were capable of meeting identical needs, so that it had to be acknowledged that there was a degree of substitution for one another. It pointed out that, for the purpose of measuring the possible degree of substitution, attention should not be confined to consumer habits in a Member State or in a given region. Those habits, which were essentially variable in time and space, could not be considered to be immutable; the tax policy of a Member State must not therefore crystallize given consumer habits so as to consolidate an advantage acquired by national industries concerned to respond to them.

[9] The Court nonetheless recognized that, in view of the substantial differences between wine and beer, it was difficult to compare the manufacturing processes and the natural properties of those beverages, as the Government of the United Kingdom had rightly observed. For that reason, the Court requested the parties to provide additional information with a view to dispelling the doubts which existed concerning the nature of the competitive relationship between the two products.

. . .

[11] The Italian Government contended in that connection that it was inappropriate to compare beer with wines of average alcoholic strength or, a fortiori, with wines of greater alcoholic strength. In its opinion, it was the lightest wines with an alcoholic strength in the region of 9, that is to say the most popular and cheapest wines, which were genuinely in competition with beer. It therefore took the view that those wines should be chosen for purposes of comparison where it was a question of measuring the incidence of taxation on the basis of either alcoholic strength or the price of the products.

[12] The Court considers that observation by the Italian Government to be pertinent. In view of the substantial differences in the quality and, therefore, in the price of wines, the decisive competitive relationship between beer, a popular and widely consumed beverage, and wine must be established by reference to those wines which are the most accessible to the public at large, that is to say, generally speaking, the lightest and cheapest varieties. Accordingly, that is the appropriate basis for making fiscal comparisons by reference to the alcoholic strength or to the price of the two beverages in question.

Having established a competitive relationship between the products, the Court then examined the effect of the taxation system:

[26] After considering the information provided by the parties, the Court has come to the conclusion that, if a comparison is made on the basis of those wines which are cheaper than the types of wine selected by the United Kingdom and of which several varieties are sold in significant quantities on the United Kingdom market, it becomes apparent that precisely those wines which, in view of their price, are most directly in competition with domestic beer production are subject to a considerably higher tax burden.

[27] It is clear, therefore, following the detailed inquiry conducted by the Court – whatever criterion for comparison is used, there being no need to express a preference for one or the other – that the United Kingdom's tax system has the effect of subjecting wine imported from other Member States to an additional tax burden so as to afford protection to domestic beer production, inasmuch as beer production constitutes the most relevant reference criterion from the point of view of competition. Since such protection is most marked in the case of the most popular wines, the effect of the United Kingdom tax system is to stamp wine with the hallmarks of a luxury product which, in view of the tax burden which it bears, can scarcely constitute in the eyes of the consumer a genuine alternative to the typical domestically produced beverage.

NOTES

1. For analysis of the Court's approach see A.J. Easson, (1984) 6 EL Rev 57.
2. Cases under this provision are rarities lately, but for a recent example of discussion of internal taxation and Case 170/78 *Commission* v *UK* see Case C-167/05 *Commission* v *Sweden* [2008] ECR I-2127, where the Court concluded the Commission was wrong to accuse Sweden of taxing wine in such a way as to afford protection to beer.

3. A product which is available entirely or mainly only as an import can be subject to taxation, provided the tax on that product falls within the general scheme of internal taxation. A State which wishes to tax, for example, an exotic fruit or a raw material of which it has no supplies of its own, will have to demonstrate that the tax is simply an aspect of its broader tax regime for fruit or raw materials of that general type. If it cannot do so – if the tax is a special charge introduced for that import alone – then the charge is covered by Article 30 TFEU. Even if the charge is part of the internal system, it must nevertheless be shown to be compatible with Article 110 TFEU – it must be neither discriminatory nor protective.

   See *Commission* v *Denmark* (Case 158/82) [1983] ECR 3573 for an example of violation of Article 30 TFEU; Cases C-367/93–C-377/93 *F.G. Roders BV et al.* v *Inspecteur der Invoerrechten en Accijnzen* [1995] ECR I-2229 on the application of Article 110 TFEU.

FURTHER READING

Danusso, M. and Denton, R., 'Does the European Court of Justice look for a Protectionist Motive under Article 95?' [1990/1] LIEI 67.

Hedemann-Robinson, M., 'Indirect Discrimination: Article 95 EC Back to Front and Inside Out?' (1995) 1 *European Public Law* 439.

SECTION 3: FISCAL HARMONIZATION

The prohibition on discriminatory internal taxation is insufficient to achieve unrestricted free movement of goods in accordance with Article 26 TFEU, p. 244, as the following brief extract from COM (85) 310, the '1992 blueprint', the White Paper on the Completion of the Internal Market, explains.

'Completing the Internal Market', White Paper from the Commission to the European Council

COM (85) 310, 14 June 1985

168. If goods and services and people are to move freely from one member State to another in just the same way as they can move within a member State, it is essential that frontier controls be abolished. Since these are primarily designed to ensure that each member State can collect the revenue in the form of indirect taxation to which it feels entitled, there are clear implications for the indirect taxation policies of individual Member States. Let us be quite clear that we are talking here not in terms of frontier facilitation, i.e., simplifying frontier procedures in the way that the Directive on the Harmonization of Frontier Procedures and the Single Administrative Document aim to do, but in terms of removing the frontiers altogether as only in this way is it possible to achieve the stated objective of free movement of goods and of people.

Harmonization of taxation is extremely complex. A major obstacle is the political symbolism of the power to levy tax. Yet progress has been made, although this is an area which continues to demand delicate negotiation far beyond the end of 1992, the deadline for the completion of the internal market.

As is well known, the pattern chosen for the internal market after the end of 1992 is based on a sharp distinction between private consumers and commercial traders. Private consumers are free to shop in a State other than their own and to take goods back home without having to pay sums representing the difference between the taxes levied in the State of purchase and their home State. The popularity of day-trips from

England to France to buy alcohol is, to the dismay of British brewers, a direct result of this EU initiative; in the area of private consumption there is a 'competition between regulators' in fixing VAT and excise duties (p. 267). A high-taxing State unwilling to accept the shortfall in tax revenues may choose to raise rates, but this risks provoking even higher levels of cross-border shopping. The alternative is a reduction in rates to competitive levels in order to remove the incentive to shop elsewhere. However, in commercial trade the tax differentials which persist between the Member States have led to the introduction of a scheme which requires collection of taxes, although not at physical borders. The scheme, established by Directive 92/12, is now found in Directive 2008/118 [2008] OJ L9/12 (as amended).

Any legal regime which incorporates 'bright lines', such as the crucial distinction between private consumers and commercial trade for the purpose of levying excise duties, tends to provoke litigation. *Commission v France* (Case C-216/11 judgment of 14 March 2013) involved quantitative limits placed on imports, which the Court treated as straightforward disrespect for the rights of private consumers under EU law. *B.F. Joustra* (Case C-5/05 [2006] ECR I-11075) was trickier. The applicant had banded together with 70 or so other private individuals to buy wine from France and have it transported to his home in the Netherlands and then shared out among the participants. It was a club – no profit-making was envisaged. But the Court decided that this fell outwith the scheme envisaged by Directive 92/12 which does not cover products transported on behalf of private consumers. The club therefore had to pay Dutch excise duties. This is hardly a coherent system, but the Court explicitly invited the legislature to clean it up.

Nothing ambitious should be expected, however. The Commission's Single Market Act, published in April 2011, was encountered in the previous Chapter (COM (2011) 206, p. 251). One of its 'twelve levers' to boost growth and strengthen confidence is taxation: 'EU rules on taxation no longer reflect the realities of the Single Market in the 21st century' (page 15). However, the attached 'key action', which the Council and Parliament will be invited to take, is a Review of the Energy Tax Directive (Directive 2003/96) in order to ensure consistent treatment of different sources of energy. Doubtless important in its own right – but far removed from any attempt at comprehensive reform. The Commission's October 2015 Communication 'Upgrading the Single market: more opportunities for people and business' (p. 252) barely mentions taxation.

The technical nature of the subject of tax harmonization precludes exhaustive treatment in this book. However, issues of tax harmonization remain high profile, even though legislative progress has been relatively slow. The method chosen has typically been 'minimum harmonization'. States may not set rates lower than the minimum set by the EU, though they may set higher rates. This reflects the political complexity of the subject – States are not prepared to allow their competence to set tax rates to be totally preempted by the EU and, illuminatingly, unanimous voting in Council remains the rule in the area of taxation even after the entry into force of the Lisbon Treaty in 2009 (see especially Article 113 TFEU). Minimum harmonization yields both a degree of harmonization and, above the minimum rate, a competition between regulators. This is to be observed in relation to value added tax and excise duties. On the latter, some progress was made in a package of Directives adopted in October 1992. Directives 92/79 and 92/80 [1992] OJ L316/8, 10 set minimum rates for cigarettes and other tobacco products respectively, now codified by Directive 2011/64 [2011] OJ L176/24; Directives 92/81 and 92/82 [1992] OJ L316/12, 19 set minimum rates for petroleum products, now replaced by Directive 2003/96 [2003] OJ L283/51; Directives 92/83 and 92/84 [1992] OJ L316/21, 29 cover the harmonization of the structure and of the rates respectively of excise duties on alcoholic beverages. Minimum rates are set for beer, wine, and other defined categories of alcoholic beverage. The text reveals the rather remarkable choice made of the minimum figure for excise rates levied on still and sparkling wine.

COUNCIL DIRECTIVE 92/84/EEC ON THE APPROXIMATION OF THE RATES OF EXCISE DUTY ON ALCOHOL AND ALCOHOLIC BEVERAGES

[1992] OJ L316/29

ARTICLE 1

Not later than 1 January 1993, Member States shall apply minimum rates of excise duty in accordance with the rules laid down in this Directive.

. . .

ARTICLE 5

As from 1 January 1993, the minimum rate of excise duty on wine shall be fixed:

— for still wine at ECU 0, and

— for sparkling wine at ECU 0

per hectolitre of product.

■ QUESTION

Is minimum harmonization of this type worthwhile? What alternatives are available to the EU in developing a tax policy for the internal market?

NOTES

1. The Commission published a report on the rates of excise duty applied on alcohol and alcoholic beverages in 2004, COM (2004) 223, noting that there had been no change since 1992. Change could come only with the unanimous support of the Member States and the Commission wished only to initiate debate. In 2006 it issued a proposal for an amending Directive (COM (2006) 486), which would have adjusted some of the stipulated minimum rates. But it would not have changed Article 5 of the Directive. And in any event the proposal attracted insufficient political support.
2. At a much broader level, in December 1997 the Finance Ministers of the Member States in Council agreed to a package of measures designed to counter 'Harmful Tax Competition'. This was the result of a vigorous Commission initiative (COM (96) 546, COM (97) 564). Binding legislation within the meaning of what is now Article 288 TFEU (p. 27) is not involved. Naturally, the title chosen for this initiative begs the delicate question of what is truly *harmful* competition and what are merely different choices about tax rates and policies. This is closely related to the intriguing issue of reconciling a 'competition between regulators' with the pursuit of a level playing field, introduced at p. 267 and further examined in Chapters 17 and 18. Furthermore, in order to site this new package in its wider legal context, it should be appreciated that tax concessions may in some circumstances fall foul of Article 107 TFEU governing State aids (p. 500). In Joined Cases C-183/02P & C-187/02P *Daewoo Electronics* v *Commission* and Joined Cases C-186/02P & C-188/02P *Ramondin SA* v *Commission* [2004] ECR I-10609, 10653 intriguing though unsuccessful arguments were advanced that the Commission was improperly using its powers to control State aids to achieve tax harmonization. The Commission on 28 April 2009 adopted a Communication entitled 'Promoting Good Governance in Tax Matters' (COM (2009) 201). Again this was not binding legislation but rather encouragement to pursue greater transparency, exchange of information and fair tax competition. For a summary and documents see http://ec.europa.eu/taxation_customs/taxation/company_tax/harmful_tax_practices/index_en.htm.

More generally the economic crisis that has lately swept the world places further pressure on the ability of the EU, and in particular the Commission, to exercise effective control over national responses that risk prioritising pursuit of domestic concerns at the expense of the overall wellbeing of the Union. The Commission first published a communication on a temporary framework for state aid measures to support access to finance in the current financial and economic crisis in January 2009, which has been periodically amended since. Documentation pertinent to this fast-moving area is available *via* http://ec.europa.eu/competition/state_aid/legislation/temporary.html.

NOTE: For additional material and resources see the Online Resource Centre at: www.oxfordtextbooks.co.uk/orc/weatherill12e.

11

Physical and Technical Barriers to Trade: Articles 34–36 TFEU

SECTION 1: THE DEVELOPMENT OF ARTICLE 34

The brevity of Article 34 TFEU is out of all proportion to its immense significance as an instrument for the creation of a market in which the free circulation of goods is ensured.

ARTICLE 34 TFEU

Quantitative restrictions on imports and all measures having equivalent effect shall be prohibited between Member States.

Article 35 applies a similarly worded prohibition to restrictions on exports.

Article 36 permits Member States to advance justifications for obstacles to trade contrary to Articles 34 and 35. Such purported justifications will be closely scrutinized, for they imply lawful trade barriers which handicap the pursuit of an integrated market for the EU.

Here, more than in most areas, it is vital to be unfailingly alert to the horror of renumbering (pp. 10, 19). Articles 34 and 36 TFEU were Articles 28 and 30 EC respectively prior to the entry into force of the Lisbon Treaty in 2009, while, prior to the entry into force of the Amsterdam Treaty in 1999, they were Articles 30 and 36 respectively. So, by odd coincidence, what began life in 1958 as Article 36 (EEC) is today once more Article 36 (TFEU). Remember this when reading the texts in this chapter and the next.

Articles 34 and 35 on the one hand and Article 36 on the other, are provisions which seek to strike a balance between the impetus towards free trade and the acceptance that Member States retain a strictly defined competence lawfully to restrict free trade in order to protect certain important domestic interests. The interpretation and location of this balance is itself an interesting exercise in judicial assessment of competing interests. The chapters which follow will frequently refer to the Court's role as an arbiter. Eventually, however, restrictive national rules which remain justifiable may be replaced by EU rules which set common standards for the Union. This is the process of harmonization. It is designed to secure protection of important interests (as is Article 36), but (unlike Article 36) that protection is achieved within the framework of a Union, not a national, structure, which will permit and stimulate cross-border trade.

The Court defined the 'quantitative restriction' in *Geddo* v *Ente* (Case 2/73) [1973] ECR 865 as 'measures which amount to a total or partial restraint of, according to the circumstances, imports, exports or goods in transit'. But what of the measure 'having equivalent effect' to the quantitative restriction which, according to Article 34, also falls within the scope of the prohibition?

In *Geddo* v *Ente* (Case 2/73), the Court followed its definition of the quantitative restriction by stating briefly that 'measures having equivalent effect not only take the form of restraint described: whatever the description or technique employed, they can also consist of encumbrances having the same effect'.

Further elucidation of the notion may be found in Directive 70/50. Directive 70/50 was formally only of application to the transitional period of the European Community's development, which has long since expired, and the relevant Treaty provisions in this area were repealed by the Treaty of Amsterdam with effect from 1999. Yet its influence as an indication of the Commission's view of the scope of this Article of the Treaty has persisted and the Court continues to refer to it on occasion. The Directive is, then, a useful source of guidance on the nature of the practices which fall foul of the prohibition on 'MEQRs' (measures having equivalent effect to a quantitative restriction).

DIRECTIVE 70/50 EEC ON THE ABOLITION OF MEASURES WHICH HAVE AN EFFECT EQUIVALENT TO THE QUANTITATIVE RESTRICTIONS ON IMPORTS AND ARE NOT COVERED BY OTHER PROVISIONS ADOPTED IN PURSUANCE OF THE EEC TREATY

[1970] OJ (Special Edition) (I), p. 17

ARTICLE 1

The purpose of this Directive is to abolish the measures referred to in Articles 2 and 3, which were operative at the date of entry into force of the EEC Treaty.

ARTICLE 2

1. This Directive covers measures, other than those applicable equally to domestic or imported products, which hinder imports which could otherwise take place, including measures which make importation more difficult or costly than the disposal of domestic production.

2. In particular, it covers measures which make imports or the disposal at any marketing stage, of imported products subject to a condition – other than a formality – which is required in respect of imported products only, or a condition differing from that required for domestic products and more difficult to satisfy. Equally, it covers, in particular, measures which favour domestic products or grant them a preference, other than an aid, to which conditions may or may not be attached.

3. The measures referred to must be taken to include those measures which:
   (a) lay down, for imported products only, minimum or maximum prices below or above which imports are prohibited, reduced or made subject to conditions liable to hinder importation;
   (b) lay down less favourable prices for imported products than for domestic products;
   (c) fix profit margins or any other price components for imported products only or fix these differently for domestic products and for imported products, to the detriment of the latter;
   (d) preclude any increase in the price of the imported product corresponding to the supplementary costs and charges inherent in importation;
   (e) fix the prices of products solely on the basis of the cost price or the quality of domestic products at such a level as to create a hindrance to importation;
   (f) lower the value of an imported product, in particular by causing a reduction in its intrinsic value, or increase its costs;
   (g) make access of imported products to the domestic market conditional upon having an agent or representative in the territory of the importing Member State;
   (h) lay down conditions of payment in respect of imported products only, or subject imported products to conditions which are different from those laid down for domestic products and more difficult to satisfy;
   (i) require, for imports only, the giving of guarantees or making of payments on account;
   (j) subject imported products only to conditions, in respect, in particular of shape, size, weight, composition, presentation, identification or putting up, or subject imported products to conditions which are different from those for domestic products and more difficult to satisfy;

(k) hinder the purchase by private individuals of imported products only, or encourage, require or give preference to the purchase of domestic products only;
(l) totally or partially preclude the use of national facilities or equipment in respect of imported products only, or totally or partially confine the use of such facilities or equipment to domestic products only;
(m) prohibit or limit publicity in respect of imported products only, or totally or partially confine publicity to domestic products only;
(n) prohibit, limit or require stocking in respect of imported products only; totally or partially confine the use of stocking facilities to domestic products only, or make the stocking of imported products subject to conditions which are different from those required for domestic products and more difficult to satisfy;
(o) make importation subject to the granting of reciprocity by one or more Member States;
(p) prescribe that imported products are to conform, totally or partially, to rules other than those of the importing country;
(q) specify time limits for imported products which are insufficient or excessive in relation to the normal course of the various transactions to which these time limits apply;
(r) subject imported products to controls, other than those inherent in the customs clearance procedure, to which domestic products are not subject or which are stricter in respect of imported products than they are in respect of domestic products, without this being necessary in order to ensure equivalent protection;
(s) confine names which are not indicative of origin or source to domestic products only.

ARTICLE 3

This Directive also covers measures governing the marketing of products which deal, in particular, with shape, size, weight, composition, presentation, identification or putting up and which are equally applicable to domestic and imported products, where the restrictive effect of such measures on the free movement of goods exceeds the effects intrinsic to trade rules.

This is the case, in particular, where:

— the restrictive effects on the free movement of goods are out of proportion to their purpose;
— the same objective can be attained by other means which are less of a hindrance to trade.

NOTES

1. The Directive, then, discloses two types of 'MEQR' (measure having equivalent effect to a quantitative restriction), divided according to their application. Article 2 covers national rules which discriminate against imports, which are taken to infringe Article 34; Article 3 covers national rules which apply equally to all goods, which are taken normally to conform to the demands of Article 34.
2. The vigorous work of the Court has transformed Article 34 TFEU into a fundamentally important means of dismantling national barriers to the free movement of goods. The Court was naturally little confined by the explicit terms of the Treaty Article in building its approach, for the provision is of such brevity as to yield almost any interpretation. In its celebrated decision in *Dassonville* (Case 8/74) the Court selected an interpretation of Article 34 which is firmly orientated towards market integration through the abolition of obstructive national rules.

   The Court declared that Article 34 (then 30) prohibits as MEQRs 'all trading rules enacted by Member States which are capable of hindering, directly or indirectly, actually or potentially, intra-Community trade'. Article 34 has, according to Lord Cockfield, the Commissioner responsible for internal market policy in the 1980s, a 'magnificent sweep'.

   On its literal terms, the *Dassonville* formula could even be taken to catch any national measure which circumscribes commercial freedom, even if neither discriminatory against imports nor protective of home production. The Court chose in *Keck and Mithouard* (Joined Cases C-267 and C-268/91) [1993] ECR I-6097 to refine the *Dassonville* formula. The Court stated that 'the application to products from other Member States of national provisions restricting or prohibiting certain selling arrangements is not such as to hinder, directly or indirectly, actually or potentially, trade between Member States, provided that the provisions apply to all affected traders operating within the national territory and provided that they affect in the same manner, in law and in fact, the marketing of domestic products and those from other Member States'. The implications of the cautious Keck ruling, and its requirement of legal or factual inequality as a threshold to the application of Article 34, are examined more fully at p. 329.

At the heart of the Court's declaration in *Dassonville* is the perception that the application of the Article 34 prohibition is dependent on the *effects* of the measure. Article 34 bites where a national rule is shown to have an effect prejudicial to the integration of the markets of the Member States. Article 34 is central to the internal market to which a legal commitment is made by Article 3(3) TEU and Article 26 TFEU.

3. The Court's emphasis differs from that in Directive 70/50. Discrimination is *not* the key. Unequal treatment of domestic and imported goods is likely to violate Article 34 because of the consequential restrictive effect on cross-border trade, but such discrimination is plainly not a pre-condition for the application of Article 34. The essential element is *the restrictive effect on inter-State trade.*

***Procureur du Roi* v *Dassonville* (Case 8/74)**

[1974] ECR 837, Court of Justice of the European Communities

The Court indicated that a Belgian requirement that importers of Scotch whisky possess a British certificate of authentication was incompatible with Article 30 of the EC Treaty (now Article 34 TFEU). The rule favoured direct importers over traders importing Scotch whisky into Belgium from other Member States in which the goods were already in free circulation. The rule 'channelled' trade and distorted the market.

[1] By Judgment of 11 January 1974, received at the Registry of the Court on 8 February 1974, the Tribunal de Première Instance of Brussels referred, under Article 177 of the EEC Treaty, two questions on the interpretation of Articles 30, 31, 32, 33, 36 and 85 of the EEC Treaty, relating to the requirement of an official document issued by the government of the exporting country for products bearing a designation of origin.

[2] By the first question it is asked whether a national provision prohibiting the import of goods bearing a designation of origin where such goods are not accompanied by an official document issued by the government of the exporting country certifying their right to such designation constitutes a measure having an effect equivalent to a quantitative restriction within the meaning of Article 30 of the Treaty.

[3] This question was raised within the context of criminal proceedings instituted in Belgium against traders who duly acquired a consignment of Scotch whisky in free circulation in France and imported it into Belgium without being in possession of a certificate of origin from the British customs authorities, thereby infringing Belgian rules.

[4] It emerges from the file and from the oral proceedings that a trader, wishing to import into Belgium Scotch whisky which is already in free circulation in France, can obtain such a certificate only with great difficulty, unlike the importer who imports directly from the producer country.

[5] All trading rules enacted by Member States which are capable of hindering, directly or indirectly, actually or potentially, intra-Community trade are to be considered as measures having an effect equivalent to quantitative restrictions.

[6] In the absence of a Community system guaranteeing for consumers the authenticity of a product's designation of origin, if a Member State takes measures to prevent unfair practices in this connexion, it is however subject to the condition that these measures should be reasonable and that the means of proof required should not act as a hindrance to trade between Member States and should, in consequence, be accessible to all Community nationals.

[7] Even without having to examine whether or not such measures are covered by Article 36, they must not, in any case, by virtue of the principle expressed in the second sentence of that Article, constitute a means of arbitrary discrimination or a disguised restriction on trade between Member States.

[8] That may be the case with formalities, required by a Member State for the purpose of proving the origin of a product, which only direct importers are really in a position to satisfy without facing serious difficulties.

[9] Consequently, the requirement by a Member State of a certificate of authenticity which is less easily obtainable by importers of an authentic product which has been put into free circulation in a regular manner in another Member State than by importers of the same product coming directly from the country of origin constitutes a measure having an effect equivalent to a quantitative restriction as prohibited by the Treaty.

■ QUESTION

What is meant by the Court's suggestion in para 6 that 'reasonable' measures would not infringe Article 34 (then Article 30)? Could the Belgian authorities have devised an authentication system compatible with Article 34? (The issue of locating the limit to the scope of Article 34 as a means of challenging trade restrictions will be readdressed in the next chapter.)

NOTES

1. The fundamental aim of Article 34 TFEU is to preclude the isolation of national markets and thereby to induce efficient competition irrespective of the existence of national frontiers. Competition yields consumer choice, lower prices, and higher quality. In this way the benefits of the EU's internal market are realized. The economic advantages were discussed more generally in Chapter 9.
2. It is not misleading to view the Court's activism in this area as judicial law making. This integrationist jurisprudence finds little explicit basis in the Treaty or in secondary legislation. Yet implied support exists. The Court has moulded its conception of Article 34 in accordance with the objects of the Treaty. The objective of establishing the internal market provides the inspiration for the development of appropriate substantive rules of law. Just as Part I of this book showed how the Court was not constrained by the absence of explicit instruction in the Treaty from eliciting the constitutional doctrines of supremacy and direct effect as the pillars of the Union's legal order in order to achieve the objectives of the Treaty, so too in the area of substantive law the Court is prepared to construct a body of interpretation which is loosely derived from Article 34, but which, more significantly, is justified as a method of bringing to fruition the Treaty objective of market integration.
3. This approach is certainly distinct from that of the English judges. The traditional English technique is to follow rules laid down with more precision than is the style of the EU Treaties. Judicial development of codified law is less readily acknowledged as either familiar or appropriate in the UK.

R v *Secretary of State, ex parte Bomore*

[1986] 1 CMLR 228, Court of Appeal

> MAY LJ: [The] Court [of Justice] adopts an approach substantially different from that familiar to lawyers in this country . . . the Court of Justice in its decisions on Article 30 [now 34] has sought both to flesh it out and at the same time to limit its apparent generality so as to produce, by a process of judge-made legislation, a developing code of law, founded upon Article 30 [now 34].

■ QUESTIONS

1. Should English judges adopt a more purposive or, perhaps, creative approach (i) in interpreting Union law, (ii) in interpreting domestic law? (Remember the discussion of the implications of *Von Colson* (Case 14/83) and *Pfeiffer and Others* (Joined Cases C-397/01 to C-403/01) in Chapter 5.) You might read Chapter 8 on 'Judicial Creativity' in J. Griffith's *The Politics of the Judiciary* (London: Fontana, 1997), and consider how the debate there presented might be applied to the development of Union law.
2. Can you think of any examples from any area of Union law where the Court of Justice has adopted an unduly activist, creative stance which has failed or may fail to command respect? Are there cases which demonstrate caution about the perils of judicial over-eagerness? Read generally H. Rasmussen, *On Law and Policy in the ECJ* (Dordrecht: Martinus Nijhoff, 1986), K. Alter, *Establishing the Supremacy of European Law* (Oxford: OUP, 2001), M. Everson and J. Eisner, *The Making of a European Constitution* (London: Routledge-Cavendish, 2007), and G. Beck, *The Legal Reasoning of the Court of Justice of the EU* (Oxford: Hart, 2013), and reconsider some of the material in Part One of this book.

SECTION 2: THE APPLICATION OF ARTICLE 34

Examples of the application of Article 34 follow. The consistent theme is the breadth of Article 34 as a prohibition on national measures which have an effect which is restrictive of trade between Member States. In reading these cases, remember that prior to the re-numbering effected by the Lisbon Treaty, what is now Article 34 TFEU was Article 28 EC (and prior to the Amsterdam re-numbering it was, with minor amendment, Article 30); and what is now Article 36 TFEU was Article 30 EC (and pre-Amsterdam, with minor amendment, Article 36).

Schloh v *Auto Controle Technique* (Case 50/85)

[1986] ECR 1855, Court of Justice of the European Communities

Mr Schloh bought a Ford Granada estate car in Germany. He obtained from a Ford dealer in Belgium a certificate of conformity with vehicle types approved in Belgium. In Belgium he was required to submit his car to two roadworthiness tests, for which fees were charged. He challenged the tests on the basis of Article 30 (now 34), the fees on the basis of Article 13 (now deleted: see Chapter 10 on fiscal charges.) The matter reached the Court of Justice by way of a preliminary reference from a Belgian court (see Chapter 7).

THE FIRST ROADWORTHINESS TEST

...

[11] It should be noted first of all that, although Council Directive 77/143/EEC of 29 December 1976 (Official Journal 1977, L 47, p. 47) laid down a number of measures for the harmonization of roadworthiness tests for motor vehicles, the terms of Annex I to the directive make it inapplicable to vehicles in the category to which the plaintiff's vehicle belongs. At this stage in the development of Community law it is therefore for the Member States – provided that they comply with the provisions of the Treaty – to lay down rules for the roadworthiness testing of vehicles in that category in order to ensure road safety.

[12] Under the terms of Article 30 of the Treaty, quantitative restrictions on imports and all measures having equivalent effect are prohibited between Member States. Roadworthiness testing is a formality which makes the registration of imported vehicles more difficult and more onerous and consequently is in the nature of a measure having an effect equivalent to a quantitative restriction.

[13] Nevertheless, Article 36 may justify such a formality on grounds of the protection of human health and life, provided that it is established, first, that the test at issue is necessary for the attainment of that objective and, secondly, that it does not constitute a means of arbitrary discrimination or a disguised restriction on trade between Member States.

[14] As far as the first condition is concerned, it must be acknowledged that roadworthiness testing required prior to the registration of an imported vehicle may, even though the vehicle carries a certificate of conformity to the vehicle types approved in the importing Member State, be regarded as necessary for the protection of human health and life where the vehicle in question has already been put on the road. In such cases roadworthiness testing performs a useful function inasmuch as it makes it possible to check that the vehicle has not been damaged and is in a good state of repair. However, such testing cannot be justified on those grounds where it relates to an imported vehicle carrying a certificate of conformity which has not been placed on the road before being registered in the importing Member State.

[15] As far as the second condition is concerned, it must be stated that the roadworthiness testing of imported vehicles cannot, however, be justified under the second sentence of Article 36 of the Treaty if it is established that such testing is not required in the case of vehicles of national origin presented for registration in the same circumstances. If that were the case it would become apparent that the measure in question was not in fact inspired by a concern for the protection of human health and life but in reality constituted a means of arbitrary discrimination in trade between Member States. It is for the national court to verify that such non-discriminatory treatment is in fact ensured.

[16] It must therefore be stated in reply to the juge de paix of Schaerbeek that Article 30 of the Treaty must be interpreted as meaning that a national measure which requires a roadworthiness test for the purpose of registering an imported vehicle carrying a certificate of its conformity to the vehicle types approved in the importing Member State constitutes a measure having an effect equivalent to a quantitative restriction on imports. Nevertheless, such a measure is justified under Article 36 of the Treaty in so far as it relates to vehicles put on the road before such registration and applies without distinction to vehicles of national origin and imported vehicles.

THE SECOND ROADWORTHINESS TEST

[17] The Commission, which was alone in presenting observations on this point, takes the view that the second test, being imposed for the purpose of exempting the vehicle from regular annual testing for the first four years, constitutes a measure having equivalent effect contrary to Article 30 of the Treaty and not justified by Article 36. In that connection the Commission notes that an exemption from regular annual tests could have been obtained simply by means of a declaration concerning the use of the vehicle made on the occasion of the first roadworthiness test.

[18] It should be pointed out that, as the Court has consistently held, national rules cannot benefit from an exception provided for by Article 36 of the Treaty if the objective pursued by that exception can be as effectively realised by measures which do not restrict intra-Community trade so much.

[19] It must consequently be accepted that Article 36 does not provide justification for roadworthiness testing whose purpose is to obtain from the owner of the imported vehicle a written declaration certifying that the use of the vehicle qualifies it for exemption from annual testing. That purpose may be achieved simply by requiring the owner to supply that written declaration, without its being necessary for the vehicle to be presented to an approved vehicle testing agency.

The Court held the fees unlawful where the test itself violated Article 30 EC (now 34 TFEU), but capable of accommodation within a general system of taxation compatible with Article 95 EC (now 110 TFEU) where the inspection itself was lawful under Article 36 EC (now 36 TFEU).

NOTE: Notice how (para 11) the Court observes that the matter is untouched by the programme of legislative harmonization and that therefore the Treaty alone supplies the basis for judging the permissibility of Member State action. The legal assessment would be different if (as is increasingly common in many sectors) the field had been entered by EU secondary legislation; p. 318.

***International Fruit Company* v *Produktschap voor Groenten en Fruit (No 2)* (Cases 51–54/71)**

[1971] ECR 1107, Court of Justice of the European Communities

The Court was asked to consider whether Article 30 of the EC Treaty (now Article 34 TFEU) applies to 'national legislative provisions prohibiting imports and exports without a licence but which in fact are not applied because exemptions are granted from the prohibition and, where this is not so, because the licence is always issued on request'.

[8] Under Articles 30 and 34(1) of the Treaty quantitative restrictions and measures having equivalent effect are prohibited between Member States both with regard to imports and exports.

[9] Consequently, apart from the exceptions for which provision is made by Community law itself those provisions preclude the application to intra-Community trade of a national provision which requires, even purely as a formality, import or export licences or any other similar procedure.

In *Commission* v *Italy* (Case 159/78) the Court accepted the opportunity to declare its view of the application of Article 30 of the EC Treaty (now Article 34 TFEU) to customs formalities at frontiers which impede inter-state trade in the EU.

***Commission* v *Italy* (Case 159/78)**

[1979] ECR 3247, Court of Justice of the European Communities

[7] As regards intra-Community trade, since all customs duties on imports and exports and all charges having equivalent effect and all quantitative restrictions on imports and exports and measures having equivalent effect had to be abolished, pursuant to Title I of the Treaty, by the end of the transitional period at the latest, it should be emphasised that customs controls properly so-called have lost their raison d'être as regards such trade. Frontier controls remain justified only in so far as they are necessary either for the implementation of the exceptions to free movement referred to in Article 36 of the Treaty; or for the levying of internal taxation within the meaning of Article 95 of the Treaty when the crossing of the frontier may legitimately be assimilated to the situation which, in the case of domestic goods, gives rise to the levying of the tax; or for transit controls; or finally when they are essential in order to obtain reasonably complete and accurate information on movement of goods within the Community. These residuary controls must nevertheless be reduced as far as possible so that trade between Member States can take place in conditions as close as possible to those prevalent on a domestic market.

NOTE: The final sentence is to some extent a statement of the overall objective envisaged by the Treaty.

The completion of the EU's internal market requires the creation of common EU rules to deal with problems of this nature without the need to impose impediments to cross-frontier trade. The realization of Article 26 TFEU's 'area without internal frontiers' demands a deeper intrusion into national competence than is envisaged in the extract. EU legislation of this nature will be discussed further.

Most of the cases considered so far involve controls imposed at frontiers. Such barriers are by definition applicable only to imports and therefore discriminatory. However, there is a further large category of discriminatory measures also caught by Article 34. These are measures which involve discrimination against imports once they have reached the market of the State of destination. The discrimination may apply at a different stage in the marketing chain, but the restrictive effect on inter-State trade is equally apparent.

***Commission* v *Ireland* (Case 113/80)**

[1981] ECR 1625, Court of Justice of the European Communities

[1] By an application lodged at the Court Registry on 28 April 1980, the Commission instituted proceedings under Article 169 of the EEC Treaty [now Article 258 TFEU: see Chapter 4], for a declaration that Ireland had failed to fulfil its obligations under Article 30 of the EEC Treaty [now Article 34 TFEU] by requiring that the imported goods falling within the scope of the Merchandise Marks (Restriction on Sale of Imported Jewellery) Order 1971 (SI No 306, Iris Oifigiúil of 21 November 1971) and the Merchandise Marks (Restriction on Importation of Jewellery) Order 1971 (SI No 307, Iris Oifigiúil of 21 November 1971) bear an indication of origin or the word 'foreign'.

[2] According to the explanatory notes thereto, Statutory Instrument No 306 (hereinafter referred to as 'the Sale Order') prohibits the sale or exposure for sale of imported articles of jewellery depicting motifs or possessing characteristics which suggest that they are souvenirs of Ireland, for example an Irish character, event or scene, wolfhound, round tower, shamrock etc. and Statutory Instrument No 307 (hereinafter referred to as 'the Importation Order') prohibits the importation of such articles unless, in either case, they bear an indication of their country of origin or the word 'foreign'.

[3] The articles concerned are listed in a schedule to each order. However, in order to come within the scope of the orders the article must be made of precious metal or rolled precious metal or of base metal, including polished or plated articles suitable for setting.

[4] In the Commission's opinion, the restrictions on the free movement of the goods covered by the two orders constitute measures having an effect equivalent to quantitative restrictions on imports, contrary to the provisions of Article 30 of the EEC Treaty; it also observes that according to Article 2(3)(f) of Directive 70/50/EEC of 22 December 1969, based on the provisions of Article 33(7) of the Treaty, on the abolition of measures which have an effect equivalent to quantitative restrictions on imports and are not covered by other provisions adopted in pursuance of the EEC Treaty (Official Journal, English Special Edition 1970 (I), p. 17) 'measures which lower the value of an imported product, in particular by causing a reduction in its intrinsic value, or increase its costs' must be regarded as measures having an effect equivalent to quantitative restrictions, contrary to Article 30 of the EEC Treaty.

[5] The Irish Government does not dispute the restrictive effects of these orders on the free movement of goods. However, it contends that the disputed measures are justified in the interests of consumer protection and of fairness in commercial transactions between producers. In this regard, it relies upon Article 36 of the Treaty which provides that Articles 30 to 34 shall not preclude prohibitions or restrictions on imports justified on grounds of public policy or the protection of industrial and commercial property.

[6] The defendant is, however, mistaken in placing reliance on Article 36 of the Treaty as the legal basis for its contention.

[7] In fact, since the Court stated in its judgment of 25 January 1977 in Case 46/76 *Bauhuis* [1977] ECR 5 that Article 36 of the Treaty 'constitutes a derogation from the basic rule that all obstacles to the free movement of goods between Member States shall be eliminated and must be interpreted strictly', the exceptions listed therein cannot be extended to cases other than those specifically laid down.

[8] In view of the fact that neither the protection of consumers nor the fairness of commercial transactions is included amongst the exceptions set out in Article 36, those grounds cannot be relied upon as such in connexion with that article.

[9] However, since the Irish Government describes its recourse to these concepts as 'the central issue in the case', it is necessary to study this argument in connexion with Article 30 and to consider whether it is possible, in reliance on those concepts, to say that the Irish orders are not measures having an effect equivalent to quantitative restrictions on imports within the meaning of that article, bearing in mind that, according to the established case-law of the Court, such measures include 'all trading rules enacted by Member States which are capable of hindering, directly or indirectly, actually or potentially, intra-Community trade' (judgment of 11 July 1974 in Case 8/74 *Dassonville* [1974] ECR 837).

[10] In this respect, the Court has repeatedly affirmed (in the judgments of 20 February 1979 in Case 120/78 *REWE* [1979] ECR 649, 26 June 1980 in Case 788/79 *Gilli and Andres* [1980] ECR 2071, 19 February 1981 in Case 130/80 *Kelderman* [1981] ECR) that 'in the absence of common rules relating to the production and marketing of the product in question it is for Member States to regulate all matters relating to its production, distribution and consumption on their own territory subject, however, to the condition that those rules do not present an obstacle. . .to intra-Community trade' and that 'it is only where national rules, which apply without discrimination to both domestic and imported products, may be justified as being necessary in order to satisfy imperative requirements relating in particular to. . .the fairness of commercial transactions and the defence of the consumer that they may constitute an exception to the requirements arising under Article 30'.

[11] The orders concerned in the present case are not measures which are applicable to domestic products and to imported products without distinction but rather a set of rules which apply only to imported products and are therefore discriminatory in nature, with the result that the measures in issue are not covered by the decisions cited above which relate exclusively to provisions that regulate in a uniform manner the marketing of domestic products and imported products.

[12] The Irish Government recognises that the contested measures apply solely to imported articles and render their importation and sale more difficult than the sale of domestic products. However, it maintains that this difference in the treatment awarded to home-produced articles and to imported articles does not constitute discrimination on the ground that the articles referred to in the contested orders consist mainly of souvenirs; the appeal of such articles lies essentially in the fact of their being manufactured in the place where they are purchased and they bear in themselves an implied indication of their Irish origin, with the result that the purchaser would be misled if the souvenir bought in Ireland was manufactured elsewhere. Consequently, the requirement that all imported 'souvenirs' covered by the two orders must bear an indication of origin is justified

and in no way constitutes discrimination because the articles concerned are different on account of the differences between their essential characteristics.

[13] The Commission rejects this reasoning. In reliance on the judgment of 20 February 1975 in Case 12/74 *Commission* v *Federal Republic of Germany* [1975] ECR 191, it submits that it is unnecessary for a purchaser to know whether or not a product is of a particular origin, unless such origin implies a certain quality, basic materials or process of manufacture or a particular place in the folklore or tradition of the region in question; since none of the articles referred to in the orders display these features, the measures in question cannot be justified and are therefore 'overtly discriminatory'.

[14] It is therefore necessary to consider whether the contested measures are indeed discriminatory or whether they constitute discrimination in appearance only.

[15] The souvenirs referred to in the Sale Order and in the Importation Order are generally articles of ornamentation of little commercial value representing or incorporating a motif or emblem which is reminiscent of an Irish place, object, character or historical event or suggestive of an Irish symbol and their value stems from the fact that the purchaser, more often than not a tourist, buys them on the spot. The essential characteristic of the souvenirs in question is that they constitute a pictorial reminder of the place visited which does not by itself mean that a souvenir, as defined in the orders, must necessarily be manufactured in the country of origin.

[16] Furthermore, leaving aside the point argued by the Commission – with regard to the articles covered by the contested orders – that it would not be enough to require a statement of origin to be affixed to domestic products also, it is important to note that the interests of consumers and fair trading would be adequately safeguarded if it were left to domestic manufacturers to take appropriate steps such as affixing, if they so wished, their mark of origin to their own products or packaging.

[17] Thus by granting souvenirs imported from other Member States access to the domestic market solely on condition that they bear a statement of origin, whilst no such statement is required in the case of domestic products, the provisions contained in the Sale Order and the Importation Order indisputably constitute a discriminatory measure.

[18] The conclusion to be drawn therefore is that by requiring all souvenirs and articles of jewellery imported from other Member States which are covered by the Sale Order and the Importation Order to bear an indication of origin or the word 'foreign', the Irish rules constitute a measure having equivalent effect within the meaning of Article 30 of the EEC Treaty. Ireland has consequently failed to fulfil its obligations under the article.

Commission v *UK* (Case 207/83)

[1985] ECR 1202, Court of Justice of the European Communities

[1] By an application lodged at the Court Registry on 15 September 1983 the Commission of the European Communities brought an action before the Court under Article 169 of the EEC Treaty [now Article 258 TFEU: see Chapter 4] for a declaration that, by prohibiting the retail sale of certain goods imported from other Member States unless they are marked with or accompanied by an indication of origin, the United Kingdom has failed to fulfil an obligation incumbent on it under Article 30 of the EEC Treaty [now Article 34 TFEU].

[2] The national legislation challenged by the Commission is the Trade Descriptions (Origin Marking) (Miscellaneous Goods) Order 1981 (Statutory Instrument 1981 No 121) which entered into force on 1 January 1982.

[3] Article 2 of that Order provides that no person may supply or offer to supply by retail the goods listed in the Schedule to the Order, other than second-hand goods and goods supplied in certain special circumstances, unless the goods are marked with or accompanied by an indication of origin. In a case in which the goods are exposed for supply and the indication of origin would not be conveyed until after delivery, such an indication must also be displayed near the goods. The indication of origin must be clear and legible; it must not in any way be hidden or obscured or reduced in conspicuousness by any other matter, whether pictorial or not.

[4] According to Article 1 of the Order, the 'origin' of goods means 'the country in which the goods were manufactured or produced'.

[5] The Schedule to the Order lists the goods to which the Order applies. Those goods are divided into four categories: clothing and textile goods, domestic electrical appliances, footwear and cutlery.

. . .

[13] The United Kingdom's defence is in substance limited to developing the two arguments which it has already put forward during the procedure prior to the application to the Court. First, it contends that the Order is a national measure which applies to imported and national products alike and the effect of which on trade between Member States is uncertain, if not non-existent. Secondly, it maintains that, in the case of the goods to which the Order applies, the requirements relating to indications of origin meet the requirements of consumer protection since consumers regard the origin of the goods which they buy as an indicator of their quality or true value.

[14] Those two arguments must be examined in turn.

[15] As regards the possible effect of the contested Order on trade, the United Kingdom points out that the requirements laid down in Article 2 of the Order concern the retail sale of all the goods covered by the Order, whether imported or not. Some of those goods, for example woollen knitwear and cutlery, are produced in the United Kingdom in substantial quantities.

[16] It should first be observed, with regard to that argument, that in order to escape the obligations imposed on him by the legislation in question the retailer will tend, as the Commission has rightly pointed out, to ask his wholesalers to supply him with goods which are already origin-marked. That tendency has been confirmed by complaints received by the Commission. Thus, it emerges from the documents before the Court that the *Groupement des industries françaises des appareils déquipement ménager* [French Domestic Appliance Manufacturers' Association] informed the Commission that French manufacturers of domestic appliances who wish to sell their products on the United Kingdom market have had to mark such products systematically in response to pressure brought to bear on them by their distributors. The effects of the contested provisions are therefore liable to spread to the wholesale trade and even to manufacturers.

[17] Secondly, it has to be recognised that the purpose of indications of origin or origin-marking is to enable consumers to distinguish between domestic and imported products and that this enables them to assert any prejudices which they may have against foreign products. As the Court has had occasion to emphasise in various contexts, the Treaty, by establishing a common market and progressively approximating the economic policies of the Member States seeks to unite national markets in a single market having the characteristics of a domestic market. Within such a market, the origin-marking requirement not only makes the marketing in a Member State of goods produced in other Member States in the sectors in question more difficult; it also has the effect of slowing down economic interpenetration in the Community by handicapping the sale of goods produced as the result of a division of labour between Member States.

[18] It follows from those considerations that the United Kingdom provisions in question are liable to have the effect of increasing the production costs of imported goods and making it more difficult to sell them on the United Kingdom market.

[19] The second argument advanced by the United Kingdom is in effect that the contested legislation, applicable without distinction to domestic and imported products, is necessary in order to satisfy imperative requirements relating to consumer protection. It states that a survey carried out amongst United Kingdom consumers has shown that they associate the quality of certain goods with the countries in which they are made. They like to know, for example, whether leather shoes have been made in Italy, woollen knitwear in the United Kingdom, fashion-wear in France and domestic electrical appliances in Germany.

[20] That argument must be rejected. The requirements relating to the indication of origin of goods are applicable without distinction to domestic and imported products only in form because, by their very nature, they are intended to enable the consumer to distinguish between those two categories of products, which may thus prompt him to give his preference to national products.

[21] It must also be observed that the fact that United Kingdom consumers associate a product's quality with its national origin does not appear to have been a consideration which prompted the United Kingdom Government when it suggested to the Commission that, as far as the Member States of the Community were concerned, it was prepared to accept the indication 'Made in the European Community'. Besides, if the national origin of goods brings certain qualities to the minds of consumers, it is in manufacturers' interests to indicate it themselves on the goods or on their packaging and it is not necessary to compel them to do so. In that case, the protection of consumers is sufficiently guaranteed by rules which enable the use of false indications of origin to be prohibited. Such rules are not called in question by the EEC Treaty.

[22] Those considerations lead to the conclusion that Article 2 of the Order constitutes a measure which makes the marketing of goods imported from other Member States more difficult than the marketing of domestically-produced goods and for which Community law does not recognise any ground of justification. That provision therefore falls within the prohibition laid down in Article 30 of the EEC Treaty.

[23] It must therefore be declared that, by prohibiting the retail sale of certain goods imported from other Member States unless they are marked with or accompanied by an indication of origin, the United Kingdom has failed to fulfil an obligation incumbent on it under Article 30 of the EEC Treaty.

NOTE: Notice that para 17 of the judgment in this case envisages a rather extended notion of discrimination.

In *Commission* v *UK* (Case 207/83), the UK had at an earlier stage in its negotiations with the Commission suggested that it would be prepared to amend its law in order to allow a choice between indicating national origin or marking the item 'Made in the European Community'. The Commission was not dissuaded by this suggestion from bringing the matter before the Court. Paragraph 21 of the Court's judgment shows that this concession ultimately weakened the UK's case.

■ QUESTION

Could a Member State require all products marketed in its territory to carry a 'Made in the EU' label?

Commission v *France* (Case 21/84)

[1985] ECR 1356, Court of Justice of the European Communities

The Commission alleged that France had violated Article 30 of the EC Treaty (now Article 34 TFEU) by refusing to approve postal franking machines from other Member States. The action arose out of a complaint to the Commission by a British manufacturer which, despite repeated applications, had failed to secure the approval of the French authorities, even after France had eliminated an earlier law which explicitly envisaged a preference for domestic machines.

[11] The fact that a law or regulation such as that requiring prior approval for the marketing of postal franking machines conforms in formal terms to Article 30 of the EEC Treaty [now Article 34 TFEU] is not sufficient to discharge a Member State of its obligations under that provision. Under the cloak of a general provision permitting the approval of machines imported from other Member States, the administration might very well adopt a systematically unfavourable attitude towards imported machines, either by allowing considerable delay in replying to applications for approval or in carrying out the examination procedure, or by refusing approval on the grounds of various alleged technical faults for which no detailed explanations are given or which prove to be inaccurate.

[12] The prohibition on measures having an effect equivalent to quantitative restrictions would lose much of its useful effect if it did not cover protectionist or discriminatory practices of that type.

[13] It must however be noted that for an administrative practice to constitute a measure prohibited under Article 30 that practice must show a certain degree of consistency and generality. That generality must be assessed differently according to whether the market concerned is one on which there are numerous traders or whether it is a market, such as that in postal franking machines, on which only a few undertakings are active. In the latter case, a national administration's treatment of a single undertaking may constitute a measure incompatible with Article 30.

[14] In the light of those principles it is clear from the facts of the case that the conduct of the French postal administration constitutes an impediment to imports contrary to Article 30 of the EEC Treaty.

NOTE: Read a case note by L. Gormley (1985) 10 EL Rev 449; and see also Case C-489/06 *Commission* v *Greece* [2009] ECR I-1797.

■ QUESTIONS

1. What is a measure, what is a mere isolated act, for the purposes of the application of Article 34? Why did the Court consider the structure of the market relevant in the case of the refusal to authorize postal franking machines (para 13)?
2. Consider whether the following are capable of falling within Article 34:
   (a) The determined policy adopted by an official at Dover as a result of personal prejudice to obstruct wherever possible the importation of goods originating in Greece. Would it make any difference if the officer's superiors turned a blind eye to these practices?
   (b) A party political broadcast on behalf of the Government declaring an intent 'to protect British interests by stopping importers of foodstuffs thinking they can enjoy a free-for-all on the UK marketplace'.

Interventionist governments are fond of price-fixing schemes. As a matter of EU law, such schemes must give the importer an opportunity to benefit from any competitive advantage the imported goods may possess (by setting a lower price than the competing domestic product), or to take account of any disadvantage they may possess (by setting a higher price). Schemes which exclude the importer's ability to achieve such flexibility are capable of violating Article 34 TFEU. These are simply instances of the application of Article 34 to discriminatory practices, but here the discrimination lies in treating imported goods in the same way as domestic goods where such equal treatment is not objectively justified, rather than in treating goods differently when in objective terms they should be treated in the same way.

Criminal Proceedings Against Riccardo Tasca **(Case 65/75)**

[1976] ECR 291, Court of Justice of the European Communities

[13] ... Although a maximum price applicable without distinction to domestic and imported products does not in itself constitute a measure having an effect equivalent to a quantitative restriction, it may have such an effect, however, when it is fixed at a level such that the sale of imported products becomes, if not impossible, more difficult than that of domestic products. A maximum price, in any event in so far as it applies to imported products, constitutes therefore a measure having an effect equivalent to a quantitative restriction, especially when it is fixed at such a low level that, having regard to the general situation of imported products compared to that of domestic products, dealers wishing to import the product in question into the Member State concerned can do so only at a loss.

[14] It is for the national court to decide whether this is so in the present case.

Openbaar Ministerie **v** ***Van Tiggele*** **(Case 82/77)**

[1978] ECR 25, Court of Justice of the European Communities

[16] First a national provision which prohibits without distinction the retail sale of domestic products and imported products at prices below the purchase price paid by the retailer cannot produce effects detrimental to the marketing of imported products alone and consequently cannot constitute a measure having an effect equivalent to a quantitative restriction on imports.

[17] Furthermore the fixing of the minimum profit margin at a specific amount, and not as a percentage of the cost price, applicable without distinction to domestic products and imported products is likewise incapable of producing an adverse effect on imported products which may be cheaper, as in the present case where the amount of the profit margin constitutes a relatively insignificant part of the final retail price.

[18] On the other hand this is not so in the case of a minimum price fixed at a specific amount which, although applicable without distinction to domestic products and imported products, is capable of having an adverse

effect on the marketing of the latter in so far as it prevents their lower cost price from being reflected in the retail selling price.

[19] This is the conclusion which must be drawn even though the competent authority is empowered to grant exemptions from the fixed minimum price and though this power is freely applied to imported products, since the requirement that importers and traders must comply with the administrative formalities inherent in such a system may in itself constitute a measure having an effect equivalent to a quantitative restriction.

[20] The temporary nature of the application of the fixed minimum prices is not a factor capable of justifying such a measure since it is incompatible on other grounds with Article 30 of the Treaty.

[21] The answer to the first question must therefore be that Article 30 of the EEC Treaty must be interpreted to mean that the establishment by a national authority of a minimum retail price fixed at a specific amount and applicable without distinction to domestic products and imported products constitutes, in conditions such as those laid down in the regulation made by the Produktschap voor Gedistilleerde Dranken on 17 December 1975, a measure having an effect equivalent to a quantitative restriction on imports which is prohibited under the said Article 30.

NOTE: In the next case, the Court is astute to maintain a broad approach in defining the 'measure' susceptible to control under Article 34. The dispute related to the alleged passive approach of the French authorities in the face of actions such as the interception of lorries transporting imported fruit and vegetables in France and the destruction of their loads, violence against lorry drivers, and threats against French supermarkets selling imported agricultural products.

Commission v *France* (Case C-265/95)

[1997] ECR I-6959, Court of Justice of the European Communities

[24] In order to determine whether the Commission's action is well founded, it should be stressed from the outset that the free movement of goods is one of the fundamental principles of the Treaty.

[25] Article 3(c) of the EC Treaty provides that, for the purposes set out in Article 2, the activities of the Community are to include an internal market characterized by the abolition, as between Member States, of, *inter alia*, obstacles to the free movement of goods.

[26] Pursuant to the second paragraph of Article 7a of the EC Treaty, the internal market is to comprise an area without internal frontiers in which the free movement of goods is ensured in accordance with the provisions of the Treaty [see now Article 26 TFEU].

[27] That fundamental principle is implemented by Article 30 *et seq.* of the Treaty.

[28] In particular, Article 30 provides that quantitative restrictions on imports and all measures having equivalent effect are prohibited between Member States.

[29] That provision, taken in its context, must be understood as being intended to eliminate all barriers, whether direct or indirect, actual or potential, to flows of imports in intra-Community trade.

[30] As an indispensable instrument for the realisation of a market without internal frontiers, Article 30 therefore does not prohibit solely measures emanating from the State which, in themselves, create restrictions on trade between Member States. It also applies where a Member State abstains from adopting the measures required in order to deal with obstacles to the free movement of goods which are not caused by the State.

[31] The fact that a Member State abstains from taking action or, as the case may be, fails to adopt adequate measures to prevent obstacles to the free movement of goods that are created, in particular, by actions by private individuals on its territory aimed at products originating in other Member States is just as likely to obstruct intra-Community trade as is a positive act.

[32] Article 30 therefore requires the Member States not merely themselves to abstain from adopting measures or engaging in conduct liable to constitute an obstacle to trade but also, when read with Article 5 of the Treaty, to take all necessary and appropriate measures to ensure that that fundamental freedom is respected on their territory.

[33] In the latter context, the Member States, which retain exclusive competence as regards the maintenance of public order and the safeguarding of internal security, unquestionably enjoy a margin of discretion in determining what measures are most appropriate to eliminate barriers to the importation of products in a given situation.

[34] It is therefore not for the Community institutions to act in place of the Member States and to prescribe for them the measures which they must adopt and effectively apply in order to safeguard the free movement of goods on their territories.

[35] However, it falls to the Court, taking due account of the discretion referred to above, to verify, in cases brought before it, whether the Member State concerned has adopted appropriate measures for ensuring the free movement of goods.

The Court proceeded from this statement of legal principle to determine that the violent acts had created obstacles to intra-EU trade; and that France had failed to meet its legal obligations to respond. In reaching this conclusion, the Court referred to:

- the duration of the incidents (which had been occurring regularly for more than 10 years);
- failure of the French police to attend, despite the fact that in certain cases the competent authorities had been warned of the imminence of demonstrations by farmers, or, even if present, to intervene, even where they far outnumbered the perpetrators;
- the fact that although a number of acts of attacks by identifiable individuals were filmed by television cameras, a very small number of persons had been identified and prosecuted.

[52] In the light of all the foregoing factors, the Court, while not discounting the difficulties faced by the competent authorities in dealing with situations of the type in question in this case, cannot but find that, having regard to the frequency and seriousness of the incidents cited by the Commission, the measures adopted by the French Government were manifestly inadequate to ensure freedom of intra-Community trade in agricultural products on its territory by preventing and effectively dissuading the perpetrators of the offences in question from committing and repeating them.

[53] That finding is all the more compelling since the damage and threats to which the Commission refers not only affect the importation into or transit in France of the products directly affected by the violent acts, but are also such as to create a climate of insecurity which has a deterrent effect on trade flows as a whole.

[54] The above finding is in no way affected by the French Government's argument that the situation of French farmers was so difficult that there were reasonable grounds for fearing that more determined action by the competent authorities might provoke violent reactions by those concerned, which would lead to still more serious breaches of public order or even to social conflict.

[55] Apprehension of internal difficulties cannot justify a failure by a Member State to apply Community law correctly (see, to that effect, Case C-52/95 *Commission* v *France* [1995] ECR I-4443, paragraph 38).

[56] It is for the Member State concerned, unless it can show that action on its part would have consequences for public order with which it could not cope by using the means at its disposal, to adopt all appropriate measures to guarantee the full scope and effect of Community law so as to ensure its proper implementation in the interests of all economic operators.

[57] In the present case the French Government has adduced no concrete evidence proving the existence of a danger to public order with which it could not cope.

[58] Moreover, although it is not impossible that the threat of serious disruption to public order may, in appropriate cases, justify non-intervention by the police, that argument can, on any view, be put forward only with respect to a specific incident and not, as in this case, in a general way covering all the incidents cited by the Commission.

The Court concluded by declaring that 'by failing to adopt all necessary and proportionate measures in order to prevent the free movement of fruit and vegetables from being obstructed by actions by private individuals' France was in violation of Article 30 EC (now Article 34 TFEU), in conjunction with Article 5 EC (now, in amended form, Article 4(3) TEU).

NOTES

1. The Court's ruling in this case provided a stimulus to the adoption of Regulation 2679/98 [1998] OJ L337/8 on the functioning of the internal market in relation to the free movement of goods. The Commission is equipped with special powers to act in cases of serious obstacles to free movement, and the Regulation expressly includes inaction by public authorities, not simply action, within its scope for these purposes.
2. Article 2 of Regulation 2679/98 on the functioning of the internal market in relation to the free movement of goods provides that 'This Regulation may not be interpreted as affecting in any way the exercise of fundamental rights as recognised in Member States, including the right or freedom to strike. These rights may also include the right or freedom to take other actions covered by the specific industrial relations systems in Member States.' So where a Member States does not take action to break a lawful strike that is causing an impediment to cross-border trade, it will not fall foul of the Regulation. But would it fall foul of Article 34? How far does the Court's reasoning in Case C-265/95 reach in placing obligations on Member States to suppress private practices such as industrial action or broader forms of public protest that might have an effect hostile to trade integration? The issue is a potential collision between what the Court describes as a 'fundamental freedom' to trade (para 32) and other fundamental freedoms, such as the right to strike or, more generally, the right of assembly or freedom of expression.

Eugen Schmidberger, Internationale Transporte und Planzüge v *Austria* (Case C-112/00)

[2003] ECR I-5659, Court of Justice of the European Communities

The Brenner motorway, a crucial transalpine route, was closed to traffic for almost 30 hours in June 1998. The cause was a demonstration organized by an environmental group. The public authorities in Austria had decided not to ban the demonstration, considering it lawful under Austrian law. Schmidberger's business was transporting timber between Italy and Germany *via* Austria, and it argued the closure of the motorway interfered with trade in breach of EU law, specifically Articles 5 and 30 EC (now, after amendment, Articles 4(3) TEU and 34 TFEU). A preliminary ruling was sought. The Court referred to the 'spirit of cooperation which must prevail in preliminary ruling proceedings' but found no reason to accept Austria's submission that hypothetical or irrelevant questions were at stake (see Chapter 7). The first question for the Court was whether a measure within the meaning of Article 34 had been adopted by the Austrian public authorities. The Court repeated its statement in Case C-265/95 *Commission* v *France* that 'the free movement of goods is one of the fundamental principles of the Community'. And it cited paragraph 30 of that judgment in support of the proposition that Article 34 is apt to apply where a Member State abstains from adopting measures required in order to deal with obstacles to the free movement of goods which are not caused by the State. It stated crisply:

[62] It follows that, in a situation such as that at issue in the main proceedings, where the competent national authorities are faced with restrictions on the effective exercise of a fundamental freedom enshrined in the Treaty, such as the free movement of goods, which result from actions taken by individuals, they are required to take adequate steps to ensure that freedom in the Member State concerned even if, as in the main proceedings, those goods merely pass through Austria en route for Italy or Germany.

[63] It should be added that that obligation of the Member States is all the more important where the case concerns a major transit route such as the Brenner motorway, which is one of the main land links for trade between northern Europe and the north of Italy.

[64] In the light of the foregoing, the fact that the competent authorities of a Member State did not ban a demonstration which resulted in the complete closure of a major transit route such as the Brenner motorway for almost 30 hours on end is capable of restricting intra-Community trade in goods and must, therefore, be regarded as constituting a measure of equivalent effect to a quantitative restriction which is, in principle, incompatible with the Community law obligations arising from Articles 30 and 34 of the Treaty, read together with Article 5 thereof, unless that failure to ban can be objectively justified.

The question whether the State has taken a 'measure' within the scope of Article 34 is logically distinct from the subsequent inquiry into whether any measure is justified. However, the way in which a measure is adopted is relevant to assessing its justifiability. Assessment of possible justification detained the Court only briefly in *Commission* v *France* given the egregious circumstances, but the more sensitive issues raised in *Eugen Schmidberger* demanded a much fuller appraisal of competing claims to fundamental rights. The Court insisted that 'the interests involved must be weighed having regard to all the circumstances of the case in order to determine whether a fair balance was struck' (para 81). The question of justification will be considered in the next chapter (p. 348).

NOTE: The next case also raises the question of what constitutes a measure for the purposes of defining the MEQR caught by Article 34. The decision confirms that even a State's course of conduct which is merely designed to induce discriminatory practices among private individuals can be held in violation of Article 34. Neither the absence of binding character nor the absence of sanctions for refusal to comply with the State's policy necessarily deprive the act of the required quality. The Court avoids a formalistic assessment of the legal status of the act and concentrates instead on its purpose and effect. However, in addition to its interpretation of the concept of a measure, the 'Buy Irish' case has much to commend it as a broader illustration of the scope of what was then Article 30 of the EEC Treaty and is now, after amendment, Article 34 TFEU.

***Commission* v *Ireland* (Case 249/81)**

[1982] ECR 4005, Court of Justice of the European Communities

I – THE SUBJECT-MATTER OF THE APPLICATION

[2] In a reasoned opinion addressed to Ireland on 25 February 1981 concerning the 'Buy Irish' campaign, the Commission noted that in January 1978 the Irish Government had introduced a three-year programme to help to promote Irish products. The campaign was launched on 18 January 1978 in a speech delivered by the Irish Minister for Industry, Commerce and Energy. The Minister declared on that occasion that the aim of the campaign was to achieve 'a switch from imports to Irish products equivalent to 3% of total consumer spending' and that the campaign was 'a carefully thought out set of initiatives that add up to an integrated programme for promoting Irish goods, with specific proposals to involve the producer, distributor and consumer'.

[3] The Irish Government, it was said, had taken and was continuing to take a series of measures designed to promote Irish products in accordance with the terms of that speech. The reasoned opinion cited the following measures:

(a) The organization of a free information service for consumers wishing to know which products in a particular category of goods are made in Ireland and where they may be obtained (the Shoplink Service);
(b) The provision of exhibition facilities, exclusively for exhibiting Irish products, in a large exhibition centre in Dublin run by the Irish Goods Council, which is, it is claimed, a public authority;
(c) The encouragement of the use of the 'Guaranteed Irish' symbol for products made in Ireland together with the organization by the Irish Goods Council of a special system for investigating complaints about products bearing that symbol;
(d) The organization of a big publicity campaign by the Irish Goods Council in favour of Irish products, involving in particular the publication and distribution by that institution of literature encouraging consumers to buy only domestic products.

[4] The Commission notes in the application that the activities connected with the Shoplink Service and the exhibition facilities in Dublin have now been abandoned by the Irish Government. However, the other two activities have continued, even after the expiry of the three-year period for which the campaign was to last. Moreover, the publicity campaign has been gradually extended, in particular by means of widespread advertising in favour of Irish products in the press and on television.

[5] The Irish Government admits that there was a three-year programme in favour of buying Irish products in Ireland. It says that since the Shoplink Service and the exhibition facilities in Dublin were abandoned at the request of the Commission the programme consists merely of an advertising campaign, by means of the press and television, the publication of posters and pamphlets and the use of the 'Guaranteed Irish' symbol, designed to make Irish consumers better acquainted with products made in Ireland and to stimulate awareness in the Irish public of the link between the marketing of such products in Ireland and the unemployment problem in that country.

[6] As far as the advertising campaign is concerned, the Irish Government confirms that it forms part of the activities of the Irish Goods Council. However, that institution cannot be regarded as a public authority; it is merely an arrangement whereby the various industries in Ireland may cooperate for their common good. The activities of the Irish Goods Council are not based on any official enactment and the involvement of the Government consists exclusively of financial aid and moral support.

[7] The Commission maintains that the actions of the Irish Goods Council are unquestionably attributable to the Irish Government. It points out, in particular, that the members of the Management Committee of the Council are appointed, under the Articles of Association of that body, by the Minister for Industry, Commerce and Energy.

[8] The Commission is of the opinion that the campaign to promote the sale and purchase of Irish products in Ireland must be regarded as a measure having an effect equivalent to a quantitative restriction on imports. Ireland contends, first, that the Irish Government has never adopted 'measures' within the meaning of Article 30 of the Treaty and, secondly, that the financial aid given to the Irish Goods Council must be judged in the light of Articles 92 and 93 of the Treaty, and not Article 30.

[9] Before assessing the merits of those arguments the position of the Irish Goods Council must be considered.

II – THE IRISH GOODS COUNCIL

[10] The Irish Goods Council was created on 25 August 1978, a few months after the disputed campaign was launched, in the form of a company limited by guarantee and not having a share capital; it was registered in accordance with Irish company law (Companies Act 1963). The Council is in fact the result of the amalgamation of two bodies, the National Development Council, a company limited by guarantee and registered under the Companies Act, and the Working Group on the Promotion and Sale of Irish Goods.

[11] The Irish Government maintains that the Irish Goods Council was created under the sponsorship of the government in order to encourage Irish industry to overcome its own difficulties. The Council was established for the purpose of creating a framework within which the various industries could come together in order to cooperate for their common good.

[12] The Management Committee of the Irish Goods Council consists, according to the Articles of Association of that institution, of 10 persons appointed in their individual capacities by the Minister for Industry, Commerce and Energy; the same Minister appoints the chairman from among the members of the Management Committee. The members and the chairman are appointed for a period of three years, and their appointments may be renewed. In practice, the members of the Management Committee are selected by the Minister in such a manner as to represent the appropriate sectors of the Irish economy.

[13] It appears from the information supplied by the Irish Government at the request of the Court that the activities of the Irish Goods Council are financed by subsidies paid by the Irish Government and by private industry. The subsidies from the State and from the private sector amounted, respectively to IRL 1 005 000 and IRL 175 000 for the period between August 1978 and December 1979; IRL 940 000 and IRL 194 000 for 1980; and IRL 922 000 and IRL 238 000 for 1981.

[14] The Irish Government has not denied that the activities of the Irish Goods Council consist in particular, after the abandonment of the Shoplink Service and the exhibition facilities offered to Irish manufacturers in

Dublin, in the organization of an advertising campaign in favour of the sale and purchase of Irish products, and in promoting the use of the 'Guaranteed Irish' symbol.

[15] It is thus apparent that the Irish Government appoints the members of the Management Committee of the Irish Goods Council, grants it public subsidies which cover the greater part of its expenses and, finally, defines the aims and the broad outline of the campaign conducted by that institution to promote the sale and purchase of Irish products. In the circumstances the Irish Government cannot rely on the fact that the campaign was conducted by a private company in order to escape any liability it may have under the provisions of the Treaty.

III – THE APPLICABILITY OF ARTICLES 92 AND 93 OF THE TREATY [NOW ARTICLES 107 AND 108 TFEU]

[16] The Irish Government maintains that, even if the purpose or the effect of the campaign was to discourage imports from other Member States, it must be judged on the basis of Articles 92 and 93 of the Treaty, which deal with State aids. The applicability of those provisions excludes the applicability of Article 30 of the Treaty, upon which the Commission has based its case.

[17] The Irish Government states that the campaign has in fact been conducted by the Irish Goods Council and that the role of the government has been restricted to moral support and financial assistance. If, as the Commission maintains, the campaign was liable to hinder the free movement of goods within the Community by promoting domestic products at the expense of imported ones that circumstance is attributable solely to a single government decision, namely the decision to subsidize the Irish Goods Council.

[18] It must be observed, however, that the fact that a substantial part of the campaign is financed by the Irish Government, and that Articles 92 and 93 of the Treaty may be applicable to financing of that kind, does not mean that the campaign itself may escape the prohibitions laid down in Article 30.

[19] In any case, if the Irish Government considered that such financing amounted to aid within the meaning of Articles 92 and 93 it ought to have notified the aid to the Commission in accordance with Article 93(3).

IV – THE APPLICATION OF ARTICLE 30 OF THE TREATY [NOW ARTICLE 34 TFEU]

[20] The Commission maintains that the 'Buy Irish' campaign and the measures taken to prosecute the campaign must be regarded, as a whole, as measures encouraging the purchase of domestic products only. Such measures are said to be contrary to the obligations imposed on the Member States by Article 30. The Commission refers to Article 2(3)(k) of Commission Directive No 70/50/EEC of 22 December 1969, based on the provisions of Article 33(7), on the abolition of measures which have an effect equivalent to quantitative restrictions on imports and are not covered by other provisions adopted in pursuance of the EEC Treaty (Official Journal, English Special Edition 1970 (I), p. 17). According to Article 2(3)(k), measures which encourage the purchase of domestic products only must be regarded as contrary to the prohibitions contained in the Treaty.

[21] The Irish Government maintains that the prohibition against measures having an effect equivalent to quantitative restrictions in Article 30 is concerned only with 'measures', that is to say, binding provisions emanating from a public authority. However, no such provision has been adopted by the Irish Government, which has confined itself to giving moral support and financial aid to the activities pursued by the Irish industries.

[22] The Irish Government goes on to emphasise that the campaign has had no restrictive effect on imports since the proportion of Irish goods to all goods sold on the Irish market fell from 49.2% in 1977 to 43.4% in 1980.

[23] The first observation to be made is that the campaign cannot be likened to advertising by private or public undertakings, or by a group of undertakings, to encourage people to buy goods produced by those undertakings. Regardless of the means used to implement it, the campaign is a reflection of the Irish Government's considered intention to substitute domestic products for imported products on the Irish market and thereby to check the flow of imports from other Member States.

[24] It must be remembered here that a representative of the Irish Government stated when the campaign was launched that it was a carefully thought-out set of initiatives constituting an integrated programme for promoting domestic products; that the Irish Goods Council was set up at the initiative of the Irish Government a few months later; and that the task of implementing the integrated programme as it was envisaged by the government was entrusted, or left, to that Council.

[25] Whilst it may be true that the two elements of the programme which have continued in effect, namely the advertising campaign and the use of the 'Guaranteed Irish' symbol, have not had any significant success in winning over the Irish market to domestic products, it is not possible to overlook the fact that, regardless of their efficacity, those two activities form part of a government programme which is designed to achieve the substitution of domestic products for imported products and is liable to affect the volume of trade between Member States.

[26] The advertising campaign to encourage the sale and purchase of Irish products cannot be divorced from its origin as part of the government programme, or from its connection with the introduction of the 'Guaranteed Irish' symbol and with the organization of a special system for investigating complaints about products bearing that symbol. The establishment of the system for investigating complaints about Irish products provides adequate confirmation of the degree of organization surrounding the 'Buy Irish' campaign and of the discriminatory nature of the campaign.

[27] In the circumstances the two activities in question amount to the establishment of a national practice, introduced by the Irish Government and prosecuted with its assistance, the potential effect of which on imports from other Member States is comparable to that resulting from government measures of a binding nature.

[28] Such a practice cannot escape the prohibition laid down by Article 30 of the Treaty solely because it is not based on decisions which are binding upon undertakings. Even measures adopted by the government of a Member State which do not have binding effect may be capable of influencing the conduct of traders and consumers in that State and thus of frustrating the aims of the Community as set out in Article 2 and enlarged upon in Article 3 of the Treaty.

[29] That is the case where, as in this instance, such a restrictive practice represents the implementation of a programme defined by the government which affects the national economy as a whole and which is intended to check the flow of trade between Member States by encouraging the purchase of domestic products, by means of an advertising campaign on a national scale and the organization of special procedures applicable solely to domestic products, and where those activities are attributable as a whole to the government and are pursued in an organized fashion throughout the national territory.

[30] Ireland has therefore failed to fulfil its obligations under the Treaty by organizing a campaign to promote the sale and purchase of Irish goods within its territory.

NOTE: A delicate but important distinction from the 'Buy Irish' case was made in *Apple and Pear Development Council* v *Lewis* (Case 222/82). The case involved the submission that the fruit promotions undertaken by the Council, a body set up in the UK under statutory instrument, infringed *inter alia* Article 30 of the EC Treaty (now Article 34 TFEU) in so far as they concerned the promotion of varieties typical of English and Welsh production.

Apple and Pear Development Council v *Lewis* (Case 222/82)

[1983] ECR 4083, Court of Justice of the European Communities

[17] As the Court held in its judgment of 24 November 1982 in Case 249/81 (*Commission* v *Ireland* [1982] ECR 4005), a publicity campaign to promote the sale and purchase of domestic products may, in certain circumstances, fall within the prohibition contained in Article 30 of the Treaty, if the campaign is supported by the public authorities. In fact, a body such as the Development Council, which is set up by the government of a Member State and is financed by a charge imposed on growers, cannot under Community law enjoy the same freedom as regards the methods of advertising used as that enjoyed by producers themselves or producers' associations of a voluntary character.

[18] In particular, such a body is under a duty not to engage in any advertising intended to discourage the purchase of products of other Member States or to disparage those products in the eyes of consumers. Nor must it advise consumers to purchase domestic products solely by reason of their national origin.

[19] On the other hand, Article 30 does not prevent such a body from drawing attention, in its publicity, to the specific qualities of fruit grown in the Member State in question or from organizing campaigns to promote

the sale of certain varieties, mentioning their particular properties, even if those varieties are typical of national production.

[20] In the observations which it submitted to the Court, the Commission stated that campaigns to promote certain varieties might result in the exclusion of other varieties from the market and make it necessary, either in the Member State in question or in other Member States which export the latter varieties, to apply the intervention measures provided for in the common organization of the market in relation to those varieties.

[21] Although it is true that such a distortion of the conditions of competition, which would be incompatible with the proper functioning of the common organization of the markets, might occur in a market where the publicity measures related exclusively or essentially to certain varieties to the exclusion of the others, that consideration cannot justify the prohibition of all publicity campaigns whereby an organization such as the Development Council draws attention to the properties of certain varieties and indicates the uses for which those varieties are specifically suitable.

NOTES

1. For subsequent litigation in this area before English courts, see *Meat and Livestock Commission* v *Manchester Wholesale Meat and Poultry Market Ltd* [1997] 2 CMLR 361.
2. The Commission attempted to extract some general principles from these judgments in order to foster predictable application of the law to such practices in the future. It issued guidelines on Member States' Involvement in the Promotion of Agricultural and Fisheries Products for the first time in 1986. The current text dates from 2014.

European union Guidelines for State Aid in the Agriculture and Forestry Sector and in rural areas 2014 to 2020

[2014] OJ C204/01

The principal target of the guidelines is aid provided by public authorities in the Member States to finance the promotion and advertising of products. Aid is subject to supervision pursuant to what are now Articles 107–109 TFEU. The guidelines also briefly (paras 465–466) consider the compatibility with what is now Article 34 TFEU, then Article 28 EC, of the promotion schemes themselves.

The promotion activities ... must not mention any particular undertaking, brand name or origin. ... However ... the origin of the products may be mentioned provided it is secondary in the message. In order to determine whether the reference to origin is secondary, the Commission will take into account the overall amount of text and/or the size of the symbol including images as well as the general presentation referring to the origin as compared with the text and/or symbol referring to the key sales pitch, that is to say, the part of the promotion not focused on the origin of the product.

NOTE: Wherever possible, the Commission wisely has an eye to developing broadly-based interpretation of the law by building on the accidents of litigation. Its predilection for issuing interpretative communications has been encountered in Chapter 9 as part of the exploration of strategies for managing the internal market. By expanding understanding of the reach of Union law, it hopes to improve observance through education. However, in Case C-57/95 *France* v *Commission* [1997] ECR I-1627, the Court was alert to the risk that the Commission might seek in this way improperly to impose new obligations on Member States and annulled a communication on pension funds as a binding act in respect of which the Commission lacked the necessary competence. Accordingly, communications and guidelines must be limited to clarification. Moreover, the Commission has developed a common practice of organizing bilateral meetings with national authorities at which solutions to instances of infringement are sought (see the Annual Reports on monitoring the application of Union law, http://ec.europa.eu/atwork/applying-eu-law/infringements-proceedings/annual-reports/index_en.htm). Reactive, ad hoc litigation can be only one component of supervision. Pursuit of administrative co-operation as a basis for management of the internal market is a prominent feature of the Commission's strategies sketched in Chapter 9.

■ **QUESTION**

Could a campaign which involved the use of a national flag as a campaign logo fall on the lawful side of the line?

NOTE: The basic assumption underpinning the control of national measures pursuant to Article 34 TFEU is that quality, not origin, shall be the primary basis for product differentiation. However, the EU has established its own regime allowing for the registration of protected designations of origin (PDO) and protected geographical indications (PGI). This provides protection under EU law for certain agricultural products and wine and spirits where there is a genuine connection to a particular origin (Regulation 1151/2012 [2012] OJ L343/1). 'Feta' is a not a generic term – it may be applied only to cheese made in Greece.

SECTION 3: THE PERSONAL SCOPE OF ARTICLE 34

In both the 'Buy Irish' and the *Apple and Pear Council* cases (Cases 249/81 and 222/82), the Court examined the character of the body involved in the challenged activities and dismissed arguments that the acts complained of were those of a private body insufficiently closely aligned to the State to fall within the scope of what is now Article 34 TFEU. The clear assumption is that a genuinely private body would *not* be subject to obligations imposed by Article 34. Indeed, this has been the Court's long-standing view (see similarly Case C-325/00 *Commission* v *Germany* [2002] ECR I-9977). On this basis discrimination by a private body on grounds of nationality would not fall foul of Article 34. Consider, for example, a policy decision by a UK supermarket chain to stock only British-made goods; or only French-made goods. The Commission expressed its view on the matter in an answer to a Written Question by a member of the Parliament. It was asked about barriers to imports of foreign beers into Germany. It was told that Germany applied protectionist rules dating from the *Reinheitsgebot* law of 1516; that imported beers had been smeared as 'chemical' beers; and that a member of the Bundestag was alleged to have stated that foreign beers could diminish sexual prowess.

Written Question No 862/83 By Mr Francis Wurtz (COM - F) to the Commission of the European Communities (1 September 1983) [1983] OJ C315/15; Answer given by Mr Narjes on behalf of the Commission (3 October 1983)

The Commission agreed that the German rules were unlawful and explained it had already commenced infringement proceedings against Germany – this is Case 178/84 *Commission v Germany* p. 324. But it also addressed the question of private standards.

3. As regards the problem of standards, it should be pointed out that they are very often drawn up by private bodies and, as such, are not binding. If, however, such standards have been made *de jure* or *de facto* obligatory by the State authorities, their compatibility with the provisions of the Treaty and with the provisions relating to the free movement of goods in particular (Articles 30 to 36) would have to be reviewed. ...

The awkward point is that the Court has not been so reticent in dealing with the personal scope of the Treaty provisions governing the free movement of persons. Articles 45 and 49 TFEU, examined more fully in Chapters 13 and 14, have long been interpreted to impose obligations on private parties acting collectively (e.g. Case C-415/93 *Bosman* [1995] ECR I-4921; Case C-438/05 *Viking Line ABP* [2007] ECR I-10779) and have even on occasion been directed at the activities of a single private party (see Case C-281/98 *Roman Angonese* [2000] ECR I-4139). The Court has explained its approach on the basis that to exclude private parties from the personal scope of these Treaty freedoms would weaken their effective application and, moreover, would create inequality in their application as a result of differences State-by-State in the margin between the public and the private sector. Both considerations hold water. But both apply with equal force to the personal scope of the free movement of goods too. Yet the Court has never explained why the provisions on the free movement of goods should have a narrower personal scope than those on the free movement of persons. Perhaps it will change its mind. The next case is the closest it has got (so far).

Fra.bo sPA (Case C-171/11)

Judgment of 12 July 2012, Court of Justice of the EU

Fra.bo traded in copper fittings used in water and gas pipes. Its certificate was withdrawn by the German certification body, the DVGW. The DVGW was a non-profit body governed by private law set up in 1859, but German law granted a presumption of compliance to products certified by it. Fra.bo argued that the DVGW's withdrawal of the certificate made it virtually impossible for Fra.bo to distribute its products in Germany. But did the scope of Article 28 EC, now Article 34 TFEU, extend as far as a body governed by private law? A preliminary reference gave the Court the chance to clarify the matter. But it did not really do so.

[24] It is common ground that the DVGW is a non-profit, private-law body whose activities are not financed by the Federal Republic of Germany. It is, moreover, uncontested that that Member State has no decisive influence over the DVGW's standardisation and certification activities, although some of its members are public bodies.

[25] The DVGW contends that, accordingly, Article 28 EC is not applicable to it, as it is a private body. The other parties concerned consider that private-law bodies are, in certain circumstances, bound to observe the free movement of goods as guaranteed by Article 28 EC.

[26] It must therefore be determined whether, in the light of inter alia the legislative and regulatory context in which it operates, the activities of a private-law body such as the DVGW has the effect of giving rise to restrictions on the free movement of goods in the same manner as do measures imposed by the State.

[27] In the present case, it should be observed, firstly, that the German legislature has established, in Paragraph 12(4) of the ABVWasserV, that products certified by the DVGW are compliant with national legislation.

[28] Secondly, it is not disputed by the parties to the main proceedings that the DVGW is the only body able to certify the copper fittings at issue in the main proceedings for the purposes of Paragraph 12(4) of the ABVWasserV. In other words, the DVGW offers the only possibility for obtaining a compliance certificate for such products.

[29] The DVGW and the German Government have referred to there being a procedure other than certification by the DVGW, which consists in entrusting an expert with the task of verifying a product's compliance with the recognised rules of technology within the meaning of Paragraph 12(4) of the ABVWasserV. It is apparent, however, from the answers to the written and oral questions put by the Court that the administrative difficulties associated with the absence of specific rules of procedure governing the work of such experts, on the one hand, combined with the additional costs incurred by having an individual expert report drawn up, on the other, make that other procedure of little or no practical use.

[30] Thirdly, the referring court takes the view that, in practice, the lack of certification by the DVGW places a considerable restriction on the marketing of the products concerned on the German market. Although the ABVWasserV merely lays down the general sales conditions as between water supply undertakings and their customers, from which the parties are free to depart, it is apparent from the case-file that, in practice, almost all German consumers purchase copper fittings certified by the DVGW.

[31] In such circumstances, it is clear that a body such as the DVGW, by virtue of its authority to certify the products, in reality holds the power to regulate the entry into the German market of products such as the copper fittings at issue in the main proceedings.

[32] Accordingly, the answer to the first question is that Article 28 EC must be interpreted as meaning that it applies to standardisation and certification activities of a private-law body, where the national legislation considers the products certified by that body to be compliant with national law and that has the effect of restricting the marketing of products which are not certified by that body.

NOTE: This could be interpreted as simple confirmation of the long-standing view of the Commission that private bodies are subject to Article 34 where their standards have been made *de jure* or *de facto* obligatory by the State. This would simply align *Fra.bo* with the 'Buy Irish' and the *Apple and Pear Council* cases (Cases 249/81 and 222/82). Alternatively, *Fra.bo* could be interpreted as embrace of a much broader scope to Article 34, binding private parties more generally, at least where they act in a way apt to fragment the EU internal market along national lines. This would increase the overlap between free movement law and the Treaty rules on competition, Articles 101 and 102 (Chapter 16). The Court's ruling in *Fra.bo* is ambiguous. Probably the judges in Luxembourg are divided. In sum, the personal scope of the Treaty freedoms has not converged – the law currently attributes a narrower personal scope to the provisions on goods than to those on persons – but the case law is dynamic and has probably not completed its evolution.

FURTHER READING ON PERSONAL SCOPE

Caro de Sousa, P., 'Horizontal Expressions of Vertical Desires: Horizontal Effect and the Scope of the EU Fundamental Freedoms' (2013) 2 Camb Jnl Intl Comp Law 1.

Schepel, H., 'Constitutionalising the Market, Marketising the Constitution, and To Tell the Difference: On the Horizontal Application of the Free Movement Provisions in EU Law' (2012) 18 ELJ 177.

Van Harten, H. and Nauta, T., 'Towards Horizontal Direct Effect for the Free Movement of Goods? Comment on Fra.bo' (2013) 38 EL Rev 677.

Verbruggen, P., 'The Impact of Primary EU Law on Private Law Relationships: Horizontal Direct Effect under the Free Movement of Goods and Services' (2014) 22 ERPL 201.

■ QUESTION

What other areas of EU law demand close attention to the extent of State involvement (see p. 123 on the direct effect of Directives)? Are the tests used identical? If not, why not? Read D. Curtin, 'The Province of Government' (1990) 15 EL Rev 195.

SECTION 4: JUSTIFICATION PURSUANT TO ARTICLE 36 TFEU

ARTICLE 36 TFEU

The provisions of Articles 34 and 35 shall not preclude prohibitions or restrictions on imports, exports or goods in transit justified on grounds of public morality, public policy or public security; the protection of health and life of humans, animals or plants; the protection of national treasures possessing artistic, historic or archaeological value; or the protection of industrial and commercial property. Such prohibitions or restrictions shall not, however, constitute a means of arbitrary discrimination or a disguised restriction on trade between Member States.

It is a peculiar coincidence that the Lisbon re-numbering of the Treaty (p. 19) converts what was Article 36 (EEC) in the original Treaty of Rome back into Article 36 (TFEU). From 1999 to 2009 this Article was Article 30 EC as a result of the Amsterdam re-numbering (p. 10).

As a general principle of EU trade law, any derogation from freedom of movement is to be construed strictly, because it is hostile to the aim of achieving an internal market for the EU. This principle can be seen in concrete form in Article 36. In its first sentence, an exhaustive list of possible grounds of derogation is set out. In its second sentence, a caution is issued that reliance on any derogation must be objectively justifiable, not a ruse to protect domestic industry. Moreover, the invocation of Article 36 should be read in the light of Article 26 TFEU's commitment to an area without internal frontiers (p. 244).

The Court, in assessing purported justification under Article 36, consistently requires Member States to show not simply a protectable interest, but also that the means chosen are proportionate to the end in view and the least restrictive of trade available which are necessary to meet that objective. So, for example, in Case 261/81 *Walter Rau* [1982] ECR 3961 it observed that 'If a Member State has a choice between various measures to attain the same objective it should choose the means which least restricts the free movement of goods.'

A: Public morality

R v *Henn and Darby* (Case 34/79)

[1979] ECR 3795, Court of Justice of the European Communities

The defendants were convicted of being 'knowingly concerned in the fraudulent evasion of the prohibition of the importation of indecent or obscene articles' contrary to the Customs Consolidation Act 1876, s.42, and the Customs and Excise Act 1952, s.304. They had shipped pornography into Felixstowe from Rotterdam. Their appeal against conviction was based on the submission that the legal control of pornography restricted the free circulation of goods contrary to Article 30 EC (now Article 34 TFEU). The matter reached the House of Lords which referred questions of interpretation under Article 177 (now Article 267, Chapter 7) to the Court of Justice. The Court first accepts the applicability of Article 30 (now 34) before proceeding to discuss Article 36 (now 36).

[11] The first question asks whether a law of a Member State which prohibits the import into that State of pornographic articles is a measure having equivalent effect to a quantitative restriction on imports within the meaning of Article 30 of the Treaty.

[12] That Article provides that 'quantitative restrictions on imports and all measures having equivalent effect' shall be prohibited between Member States. It is clear that this provision includes a prohibition on imports inasmuch as this is the most extreme form of restriction. The expression used in Article 30 must therefore be understood as being the equivalent of the expression 'prohibitions or restrictions on imports' occurring in Article 36.

[13] The answer to the first question is therefore that a law such as that referred to in this case constitutes a quantitative restriction on imports within the meaning of Article 30 of the Treaty.

SECOND AND THIRD QUESTIONS

[14] The second and third questions are framed in the following terms:

'2. If the answer to Question 1 is in the affirmative, does the first sentence of Article 36 upon its true construction mean that a Member State may lawfully impose prohibitions on the importation of goods from another Member State which are of an indecent or obscene character as understood by the laws of that Member State?

3. In particular:

(i) is the member State entitled to maintain such prohibitions in order to prevent, to guard against or to reduce the likelihood of breaches of the domestic law of all constituent parts of the customs territory of the State?

(ii) is the Member State entitled to maintain such prohibitions having regard to the national standards and characteristics of that State as demonstrated by the domestic laws of the constituent parts of the customs territory of that State including the law imposing the prohibition, notwithstanding variations between the laws of the constituent parts?'

It is convenient to consider these questions together.

[15] Under the terms of Article 36 of the Treaty the provisions relating to the free movement of goods within the Community are not to preclude prohibitions on imports which are justified *inter alia* 'on grounds of public morality'. In principle, it is for each Member State to determine in accordance with its own scale of values and in the form selected by it the requirements of public morality in its territory. In any event, it cannot be disputed that the statutory provisions applied by the United Kingdom in regard to the importation of articles having an indecent or obscene character come within the powers reserved to the Member States by the first sentence of Article 36.

[16] Each Member State is entitled to impose prohibitions on imports justified on grounds of public morality for the whole of its territory, as defined in Article 227 of the Treaty, whatever the structure of its constitution may be and however the powers of legislating in regard to the subject in question may be distributed. The fact that certain differences exist between the laws enforced in the different constituent parts of a Member State does not thereby prevent that State from applying a unitary concept in regard to prohibitions on imports imposed, on grounds of public morality, on trade with other Member States.

[17] The answer to the second and third questions must therefore be that the first sentence of Article 36 upon its true construction means that a Member State may, in principle, lawfully impose prohibitions on the importation from any other Member State of articles which are of an indecent or obscene character as understood by its domestic laws and that such prohibitions may lawfully be applied to the whole of its national territory even if, in regard to the field in question, variations exist between the laws in force in the different constituent parts of the Member State concerned.

FOURTH, FIFTH AND SIXTH QUESTIONS

[18] The fourth, fifth and sixth questions are framed in the following terms:

'4. If a prohibition on the importation of goods is justifiable on grounds of public morality or public policy, and imposed with that purpose, can that prohibition nevertheless amount to a means of arbitrary discrimination or a disguised restriction on trade contrary to Article 36?
5. If the answer to Question 4 is in the affirmative, does the fact that the prohibition imposed on the importation of such goods is different in scope from that imposed by the criminal law upon the possession and publication of such goods within the Member State or any part of it necessarily constitute a means of arbitrary discrimination or a disguised restriction on trade between Member States so as to conflict with the requirements of the second sentence of Article 36?
6. If it be the fact that the prohibition imposed upon importation is, and a prohibition such as is imposed upon possession and publication is not, capable as a matter of administration of being applied by customs officials responsible for examining goods at the point of importation, would that fact have any bearing upon the answer to Question 5?'

[19] In these questions the House of Lords takes account of the appellants' submissions based upon certain differences between, on the one hand, the prohibition on importing the goods in question, which is absolute, and, on the other, the laws in force in the various constituent parts of the United Kingdom, which appear to be less strict in the sense that the mere possession of obscene articles for non-commercial purposes does not constitute a criminal offence anywhere in the United Kingdom and that, even if it is generally forbidden, trade in such articles is subject to certain exceptions, notably those in favour of articles having scientific, literary, artistic or educational interest. Having regard to those differences the question has been raised whether the prohibition on imports might not come within the second sentence of Article 36.

[20] According to the second sentence of Article 36 the restrictions on imports referred to in the first sentence may not 'constitute a means of arbitrary discrimination or a disguised restriction on trade between Member States'.

[21] In order to answer the questions which have been referred to the Court it is appropriate to have regard to the function of this provision, which is designed to prevent restrictions on trade based on the grounds mentioned in the first sentence of Article 36 from being diverted from their proper purpose and used in such a way as either to create discrimination in respect of goods originating in other Member States or indirectly to protect certain national products. That is not the purport of a prohibition, such as that in force in the United Kingdom, on the importation of articles which are of an indecent or obscene character. Whatever may be the differences between the laws on this subject in force in the different constituent parts of the United Kingdom, and notwithstanding the fact that they contain certain exceptions of limited scope, these laws, taken as a whole, have as their purpose the prohibition, or at least, the restraining, of the manufacture and marketing of publications

or articles of an indecent or obscene character. In these circumstances it is permissible to conclude, on a comprehensive view, that there is no lawful trade in such goods in the United Kingdom. A prohibition on imports which may in certain respects be more strict than some of the laws applied within the United Kingdom cannot therefore be regarded as amounting to a measure designed to give indirect protection to some national product or aimed at creating arbitrary discrimination between goods of this type depending on whether they are produced within the national territory or another Member State.

[22] The answer to the fourth question must therefore be that if a prohibition on the importation of goods is justifiable on grounds of public morality and if it is imposed with that purpose the enforcement of that prohibition cannot, in the absence within the Member State concerned of a lawful trade in the same goods, constitute a means of arbitrary discrimination or a disguised restriction on trade contrary to Article 36.

[23] In these circumstances it is not necessary to answer the fifth and sixth questions.

NOTE: Both Articles 30 and 36 of the Treaty (now Articles 34 and 36 TFEU) applied. The convictions were accordingly upheld.

The course of the litigation prior to the Court's decision deserves attention. The decision of the Court of Appeal is an instructive misapplication of Article 30 (now 34): [1978] 1 WLR 1031. The House of Lords' approach to Article 177 (now 267, Chapter 7) is an instructive explanation of the function of that provision: [1980] 2 WLR 597.

Conegate v *Customs and Excise Commissioners* (Case 121/85)

[1986] ECR 1007, Court of Justice of the European Communities

This case also involved the seizure of pornography. Similar arguments were advanced in relation to the lawfulness of the seizure under EU law. There was, however, a different background under the (non-existent, but for these purposes deemed) 'law of the UK'.

[14] ... As the Court held in its judgment of 14 December 1979, cited above [*Henn*] in principle it is for each Member State to determine in accordance with its own scale of values and in the form selected by it the requirements of public morality in its territory.

[15] However, although Community law leaves the Member States free to make their own assessments of the indecent or obscene character of certain articles, it must be pointed out that the fact that goods cause offence cannot be regarded as sufficiently serious to justify restrictions on the free movement of goods where the Member State concerned does not adopt, with respect to the same goods manufactured or marketed within its territory, penal measures or other serious and effective measures intended to prevent the distribution of such goods in its territory.

[16] It follows that a Member State may not rely on grounds of public morality in order to prohibit the importation of goods from other Member States when its legislation contains no prohibition on the manufacture or marketing of the same goods on its territory.

[17] It is not for the Court, within the framework of the powers conferred upon it by Article 177 of the EEC Treaty, to consider whether, and to what extent, the United Kingdom legislation contains such a prohibition. However, the question whether or not such a prohibition exists in a State comprised of different constituent parts which have their own internal legislation, can be resolved only by taking into consideration all the relevant legislation. Although it is not necessary, for the purposes of the application of the above-mentioned rule, that the manufacture and marketing of the products whose importation has been prohibited should be prohibited in the territory of all the constituent parts, it must at least be possible to conclude from the applicable rules, taken as a whole, that their purpose is, in substance, to prohibit the manufacture and marketing of those products.

[18] In this instance, in the actual wording of its first question the High Court took care to define the substance of the national legislation the compatibility of which with Community law is a question which it proposes to determine. Thus it refers to rules in the importing Member State under which the goods in question may be manufactured freely and marketed subject only to certain restrictions, which it sets out explicitly, namely an

absolute prohibition on the transmission of such goods by post, a restriction on their public display and, in certain areas of the Member State concerned, a system of licensing of premises for the sale of those goods to customers aged 18 years and over. Such restrictions cannot however be regarded as equivalent in substance to a prohibition on manufacture and marketing.

[19] At the hearing, the United Kingdom again stressed the fact that at present no articles comparable to those imported by Conegate are manufactured on United Kingdom territory, but that fact, which does not exclude the possibility of manufacturing such articles and which, moreover, was not referred to by the High Court, is not such as to lead to a different assessment of the situation.

[20] In reply to the first question it must therefore be stated that a Member State may not rely on grounds of public morality within the meaning of Article 36 of the Treaty in order to prohibit the importation of certain goods on the grounds that they are indecent or obscene, where the same goods may be manufactured freely on its territory and marketed on its territory subject only to an absolute prohibition on their transmission by post, a restriction on their public display and, in certain regions, a system of licensing of premises for the sale of those goods to customers aged 18 and over.

[21] That conclusion does not preclude the authorities of the Member State concerned from applying to those goods, once imported, the same restrictions on marketing which are applied to similar products manufactured and marketed within the country.

■ QUESTIONS

1. What is presented as the key distinction between these two cases? Explain how the concept of the prohibition on 'arbitrary discrimination' now found in the second sentence of Article 36 TFEU is reflected in the decisions.
2. T. Van Rijn (1988) 25 CML Rev 593, at pp. 608–9 argues as follows:

   > the test in *Conegate* depends on whether the purpose of the internal legislation was, in substance, to prohibit the manufacture and marketing of those products. One may wonder, however, whether that criterion is satisfactory in so far as it refers to prohibitions on marketing. The operation of importation takes place on the same level as the operation of manufacture. Imported products are marketed in the Member State after their importation and are then subject to the same rules as products manufactured in that Member State, as the Court rightly underlined. Control of the marketing of imported indecent products should therefore not take place on the basis of legislation on imports (such as the Customs Consolidation Act), but on the basis of the legislation governing the marketing of nationally manufactured products.

   Do you agree?

   Might it be open to the UK to argue that importation and manufacture are objectively distinct and may therefore be treated differently? The special position of the UK, much (though not all) of which has no land border with another State, may more readily yield justification for controls at the border, on the basis that control there is the most efficient location. Land borders may lose their economic relevance as market integration accelerates; the same may not be true of division by sea. Can such an argument survive the establishment of an internal market in accordance with Articles 3(3) TEU and 26 TFEU?
3. Chapter 14 examines EU trade law's application to the services sector, but the reader should ponder here how Article 36's recognition of permissible variation in standards of morality can be translated into laws capable of effective enforcement in a world of cable and satellite broadcasting and the 'Internet'.
4. Could the UK Government have argued that since the morality laws in question were enforced by criminal sanctions, the area fell within the scope of public policy, which is also a protectable interest under Article 36? See *Criminal proceedings against Karl*

Prantl (Case 16/83) [1984] ECR 1299.Consider also the Court's refusal to interpret Article 36's reference to public policy in such a way as to include the protection of the economic interests of the consumer in *Commission* v *Ireland* (Case 113/80) [1981] ECR 1625, p. 288 and *Kohl* v *Ringelhan* (Case 177/83) [1984] ECR 3651.

5. One of the issues in both *Henn and Darby* (Case 34/79) and *Conegate* (Case 121/85) was the absence of uniformity in the law of the constituent elements of the UK. How did the Court resolve the problem of applying Article 34 TFEU in such circumstances? Is its approach satisfactory? If the sale of an object is banned or severely restricted in Scotland but not in England, what measures could be taken to restrict its importation? Would it matter if importation was into Aberdeen or into Hull? (*Cf* reliance on Article 4(2) TEU in the context of German federalism in Case C-156/13 *Digibet* judgment of 12 June 2014). Would it matter if the law was in practice rarely enforced anyway?

B: The protection of health and life of humans, animals, and plants

Commission v *UK* (Case 40/82)

[1982] ECR 2793, Court of Justice of the European Communities

The UK adopted what amounted in practice to an import ban on poultry meat and eggs from all other Member States except Denmark and Ireland. The stated purpose of the system was to prevent the spread of Newcastle disease, a contagious disease affecting poultry. The Commission considered that the measures adopted went beyond the scope of action permissible under the Treaty. The Court first explained the factual background:

[22] First, there is agreement among the parties that imports of poultry meat and poultry products into the United Kingdom from other Member States showed a remarkable rise in the years preceding the introduction of the 1981 measures. This increase concerned in particular imports of slaughtered whole turkeys; in 1980 imports of whole turkeys from France showed a steep rise as compared with those in 1979.

[23] It is also agreed that by mid-1981 the United Kingdom Government and British producers were gravely concerned by the continuing increase in the importation of turkeys from France, and that British poultry producers made it known that they were troubled about government subsidies which, they asserted, had been made available to French producers. In these circumstances, a certain pressure was put on the United Kingdom Government, by articles in the press and in other ways, to take action in order to reduce imports of poultry products from France.

[24] Secondly, the United Kingdom does not deny that the date chosen for the introduction of the 1981 measures was such as to prevent imports of Christmas turkeys from France into Great Britain for the 1981 season, and that these imports had constituted a very substantial part of the total imports of turkeys in the preceding years.

[25] It is also an established fact that France tried to retain its poultry outlets on the British market by introducing, in September 1981, a policy on Newcastle disease which was broadly similar to the one recently adopted by the United Kingdom. As from 16 September 1981, it prohibited the use of vaccine and instituted a policy of compulsory slaughter in the event of an outbreak of disease. The British authorities refused, however, to admit French poultry products to their territory on the ground that France had not restricted poultry imports from non-member countries, notably from Spain and from some East European countries, where vaccine was still in use. The French Government maintains that it had previously been able to come to arrangements with Switzerland when outbreaks of the disease occurred in France but not in Switzerland, in such a way that French imports into that country could continue, although health controls at the frontier were substantially reinforced.

It then proceeded to examine whether the UK was entitled to act in this manner:

> [36] As the Court has already observed in its judgment of 14 December 1979 in Case 34/79 *Henn and Darby* [1979] ECR 3795, the second sentence of Article 36 is designed to prevent restrictions on trade mentioned in the first sentence of that article from being diverted from their proper purpose and used in such a way as either to create discrimination in respect of goods originating in other Member States or indirectly to protect certain national products.
>
> [37] Certain established facts suggest that the real aim of the 1981 measures was to block, for commercial and economic reasons, imports of poultry products from other Member States, in particular from France. The United Kingdom Government had been subject to pressure from British poultry producers to block these imports. It hurriedly introduced its new policy with the result that French Christmas turkeys were excluded from the British market for the 1981 season. It did not inform the Commission and the Member States concerned in good time, as the letter in which the Commission was informed of the new measures – which took effect on 1 September 1981 – was dated 27 August 1981. It did not find it necessary to discuss the effects of the new measures on imports with the Community institutions, with the Standing Veterinary Committee or with the Member States concerned.
>
> [38] It should be noted, in this context, that when the United Kingdom abandoned, in 1964, the policy of non-vaccination and compulsory slaughter conducted till then in Great Britain, in order to adopt a policy of control of Newcastle disease by vaccination, this change of policy was thoroughly prepared by an elaborate report of a committee of experts, by various studies and by prolonged discussions among veterinary experts. The evidence available in the present case does not suggest that any comparable effort was made before the Government decided, in 1981, to reintroduce the policy which it had applied before 1964. The deduction must be made that the 1981 measures did not form part of a seriously considered health policy.
>
> [39] This conclusion is reinforced by the way in which the United Kingdom dealt with French demands that French poultry products should be readmitted to Great Britain after the French Republic had fulfilled the three conditions laid down by the United Kingdom Government, namely that the exporting country should be totally free from outbreaks of Newcastle disease, should prohibit vaccination and should apply a policy of compulsory slaughter in the event of any future outbreak of the disease. By refusing French imports on the ground that France had not closed its frontiers to poultry imports from non-member countries where vaccine was still in use, the United Kingdom added in fact a fourth condition to the three which it had previously stated in its letter to the Commission of 27 August 1981, and which it still states in its defence in the present case as the only applicable conditions.
>
> [40] Taken together, these facts are sufficient to establish that the 1981 measures constitute a disguised restriction on imports of poultry products from other Member States, in particular from France, unless it can be shown that, for reasons of animal health, the only possibility open to the United Kingdom was to apply the strict measures which are at issue in this case and that, therefore, the methods prescribed by the 1981 measures for obtaining the high standards of animal health which the United Kingdom Government had in mind when it changed its policy with regard to Newcastle disease, were not more restrictive than was necessary for the protection of the health of poultry flocks in Great Britain.
>
> [41] It follows from the information given to the Court during the proceedings that there are less stringent measures for attaining the same result. Thus, the manner in which the Danish authorities deal with imports of poultry products from other Member States – even from those where recent outbreaks of Newcastle disease have been recorded – suggests that it is possible to preserve the highest standard of freedom from Newcastle disease without completely blocking imports from countries where vaccine is still in use.

The UK was accordingly found in breach of Article 30 of the EC Treaty (now Article 34 TFEU).

NOTE: The case reflects the Court's determination to scrutinize closely purported reliance on Article 36. The Court must be satisfied, first, that a genuine threat to one of the interests specified in Article 36 has been established. Then, the Member State must show that the measures taken are apt to achieve protection from the perceived threat and that they are proportionate to the end in view. As an aspect of this rigorous approach to derogation, the State will fail if the Court considers that it was open to the State to achieve protection of a recognized interest through means which are less restrictive of trade.

At the heart of this approach is the key idea expressed in the second sentence of Article 36 TFEU that national measures shall not constitute 'arbitrary discrimination'.

See also, e.g., *Commission* v *France* (Case 42/82) [1983] ECR 1013; *Commission* v *Germany* (Case C-131/93) [1994] ECR I-3303. *Cf* the extract from Case C-265/95 *Commission* v *France*, p. 296.

■ QUESTION

If the UK had instituted a fully considered genuine control of the spread of Newcastle disease, including effective domestic regulation, what type of controls over imports could have been introduced in conformity with Article 34 (and Article 26)?

NOTE: The health risks of many artificial substances are the subject of debate. A Member State may be able to impose controls on products even in the absence of *conclusive* proof of their harmful properties, provided that there is some *objective* reason for doubting the safety of the product. As ever, the State must avoid *arbitrary* discrimination.

***Officier van Justitie* v *Sandoz BV* (Case 174/82)**

[1983] ECR 2445, Court of Justice of the European Communities

Sandoz wished to sell in the Netherlands muesli bars to which vitamins had been added. These bars were freely marketable in Belgium and Germany. Authorization to sell was refused by the Dutch authorities on the basis that the vitamins were dangerous to public health. Questions were referred to Luxembourg. The Court had no doubt that there was a barrier to cross-border trade. It proceeded to examine the relevance of Article 36 EC (now 36 TFEU).

[11] It appears from the file that vitamins are not in themselves harmful substances but on the contrary are recognised by modern science as necessary for the human organism. Nevertheless excessive consumption of them over a prolonged period may have harmful effects, the extent of which varies according to the type of vitamin: there is generally a greater risk with vitamins soluble in fat than with those soluble in water. According to the observations submitted to the Court, however, scientific research does not appear to be sufficiently advanced to be able to determine with certainty the critical quantities and the precise effects.

[12] It is not disputed by the parties who have submitted observations that the concentration of vitamins contained in the foodstuffs of the kind in issue is far from attaining the critical threshold of harmfulness so that even excessive consumption thereof cannot in itself involve a risk to public health. Nevertheless such a risk cannot be excluded in so far as the consumer absorbs with other foods further quantities of vitamins which it is impossible to monitor or foresee.

[13] The addition of vitamins is thus subject to the general policy in relation to food additives, which are already to a limited extent the subject of Community harmonization. Thus in particular the Council Directive of 23 October 1962 on the approximation of the rules of the Member States concerning the colouring matters authorized for use in foodstuffs intended for human consumption (Official Journal, English Special Edition 1959–62, p. 279) and Council Directive No 64/54/EEC of 5 November 1963 on the approximation of the laws of the Member States concerning the preservatives authorized for use in foodstuffs intended for human consumption (Official Journal, English Special Edition 1963–64, p. 99), as amended, require the Member States to authorize only the colouring matters and preservatives set out in the list annexed but leave the Member States free to restrict, in certain circumstances, the use even of the substances listed.

[14] As regards foodstuffs intended for particular nutritional uses there has been some degree of harmonization in Council Directive No 77/94/EEC of 21 December 1976 on the approximation of the laws of the Member States relating to foodstuffs for particular nutritional uses (Official Journal 1977, L 26, p. 55). Article 7 thereof requires the Member States to adopt all the measures necessary to ensure that trade in the said products cannot be impeded by the application of non-harmonized national provisions governing the composition, manufacturing specifications, packaging or labelling of foodstuffs, subject nevertheless to provisions justified on grounds, *inter alia*, of protection of public health.

[15] The abovementioned Community measures clearly show that the Community legislature accepts the principle that it is necessary to restrict the use of food additives to the substances specified, whilst leaving the Member States a certain discretion to adopt stricter rules. The measures thus testify to great prudence regarding the potential harmfulness of additives, the extent of which is still uncertain in respect of each of the various substances, and leave a wide discretion to the Member States in relation to such additives.

[16] As the Court found in its judgment of 17 December 1981 in Case 272/80 (*Frans-Nederlandse Maatschappij voor Biologische Producten* [1981] ECR 3277), in so far as there are uncertainties at the present state of scientific research it is for the Member States, in the absence of harmonization, to decide what degree of protection of the health and life of humans they intend to assure, having regard however for the requirements of the free movement of goods within the Community.

[17] Those principles also apply to substances such as vitamins which are not as a general rule harmful in themselves but may have special harmful effects solely if taken to excess as part of the general nutrition, the composition of which is unforeseeable and cannot be monitored. In view of the uncertainties inherent in the scientific assessment, national rules prohibiting, without prior authorization, the marketing of foodstuffs to which vitamins have been added are justified on principle within the meaning of Article 36 of the Treaty on grounds of the protection of human health.

[18] Nevertheless the principle of proportionality which underlies the last sentence of Article 36 of the Treaty requires that the power of the Member States to prohibit imports of the products in question from other Member States should be restricted to what is necessary to attain the legitimate aim of protecting health. Accordingly, national rules providing for such a prohibition are justified only if authorizations to market are granted when they are compatible with the need to protect health.

[19] Such an assessment is, however, difficult to make in relation to additives such as vitamins the abovementioned characteristics of which exclude the possibility of foreseeing or monitoring the quantities consumed as part of the general nutrition and the degree of harmfulness of which cannot be determined with sufficient certainty. Nevertheless, although in view of the present stage of harmonization of national laws at the Community level a wide discretion must be left to the Member States, they must, in order to observe the principle of proportionality, authorize marketing when the addition of vitamins to foodstuffs meets a real need, especially a technical or nutritional one.

[20] The first question must therefore be answered to the effect that Community law permits national rules prohibiting without prior authorization the marketing of foodstuffs lawfully marketed in another Member State to which vitamins have been added, provided that the marketing is authorized when the addition of vitamins meets a real need, especially a technical or nutritional one.

More recently the Court has adopted the language of the 'precautionary principle' in conceding to Member States the space to maintain rules that restrict trade in goods, especially foodstuffs, on the basis that there is doubt about the effects of particular ingredients on the health of consumers. States enjoy a discretion which is particularly wide where it is shown that uncertainties continue to exist in the current state of scientific research. The Court insists, however, that national authorization procedures shall be targeted at identified risks, rather than applying indiscriminately or in cases of purely hypothetical risk, and that they shall be transparent and open to challenge.

Commission v *Netherlands* (Case C-41/02)

[2004] ECR I-11375, Court of Justice of the European Communities

[49] A decision to prohibit the marketing of a fortified foodstuff, which indeed constitutes the most restrictive obstacle to trade in products lawfully manufactured and marketed in other Member States, can be adopted only if the real risk for public health alleged appears sufficiently established on the basis of the latest scientific data available at the date of the adoption of such decision. In such a context, the object of the risk assessment to be carried out by the Member State is to appraise the degree of probability of harmful effects on human health from the addition of certain nutrients to foodstuffs and the seriousness of those potential effects (see *Commission* v *Denmark* [Case C-192/01], paragraph 48; and *Commission* v *France* [Case C-24/00], paragraph 55).

[50] In assessing the risk in question, it is not only the particular effects of the marketing of an individual product containing a definite quantity of nutrients which are relevant. It could be appropriate to take into consideration the cumulative effect of the presence on the market of several sources, natural or artificial, of a particular nutrient and of the possible existence in the future of additional sources which can reasonably be foreseen (see *Commission* v *Denmark*, paragraph 50).

[51] In a number of cases, the assessment of those factors will demonstrate that there is much uncertainty, in science and in practice, in that regard. Such uncertainty, which is inseparable from the precautionary principle, affects the scope of the Member State's discretion and thus also the manner in which the precautionary principle is applied.

[52] It must therefore be accepted that a Member State may, in accordance with the precautionary principle, take protective measures without having to wait until the existence and gravity of those risks become fully apparent (see, to that effect, *National Farmers' Union* [Case C-157/96], paragraph 63). However, the risk assessment cannot be based on purely hypothetical considerations . . .

This approach may also be found in, e.g., Case C-95/01 *John Greenham* [2004] ECR I-1333, Case C-88/07 *Commission* v *Spain* [2009] ECR I-1353; and see Fisher, E., 'Precaution, Precaution Everywhere: Developing a Common Understanding of the Precautionary Principle in the European Community' (2002) *9 Maastricht Journal of European and Comparative Law* 7; Heyvaert, V., 'Facing the consequences of the precautionary principle in EC law' (2006) 31 EL Rev 185.

NOTE: The circumstances in which a State may impose a health check on products which have already been subjected to a check in the State of origin are closely circumscribed. The key, once again, is the elimination of trade restriction which constitutes 'arbitrary discrimination' within the meaning of the second sentence of Article 36 TFEU.

Frans-Nederlandse Maatschappij voor Biologische Producten (Case 272/80)

[1981] ECR 3277, Court of Justice of the European Communities

The case concerned Dutch checks on plant protection products imported from France where the products had been approved and lawfully marketed.

[13] . . . [I]t is not disputed that the national rules in question are intended to protect public health and that they therefore come within the exception provided for by Article 36. The measures of control applied by the Netherlands authorities, in particular as regards the approval of the product, may not therefore be challenged in principle. However, that leaves open the question whether the detailed procedures governing approvals, as indicated by the national court, may possibly constitute a disguised restriction, within the meaning of the last sentence of Article 36, on trade between Member States, in view, on the one hand, of the dangerous nature of the product and, on the other hand, of the fact that it has been the subject of a procedure for approval in the Member State where it has been lawfully marketed.

[14] Whilst a Member State is free to require a product of the type in question, which has already received approval in another Member State, to undergo a fresh procedure of examination and approval, the authorities of the Member States are nevertheless required to assist in bringing about a relaxation of the controls existing in intra-Community trade. It follows that they are not entitled unnecessarily to require technical or chemical analyses or laboratory tests where those analyses and tests have already been carried out in another Member State and their results are available to those authorities, or may at their request be placed at their disposal.

NOTE: The judgment in *Sandoz* (Case 174/82) (p. 313) indicates that unilateral Member State action in derogation from the basic principle of free movement may be robbed of its legal justification by the introduction of legislation at EU level which secures the protection of the particular interest in issue. Such legislation was not yet sufficiently comprehensive in that case (para 19). This is the 'dual function' of harmonization legislation: a common EU-wide rule which facilitates free trade but on terms which protect the interests which might previously have justified national rules. The EU's work has been particularly intense in the field of health controls. It has sought to establish a system of controls and checks which will allow the dismantling of the existing obstructions of differing rules in each State, because, as recognized in *Biologische Producten* (Case 272/80), it remains lawful to impose 'double checks' in exceptional circumstances where the legitimate concerns of the State of importation are not met by the exporting State.

This has given rise to some difficulty in law in ascertaining the scope of permissible Member State action in areas subject to legislative intervention at EU level.

Rewe-Zentralfinanz Gmbh v *Landwirtschaftskammer* (Case 4/75)

[1975] ECR 843, Court of Justice of the European Communities

The case concerned checks of imported apples by the German authorities. This constituted a clear breach of Article 30 of the EC Treaty (now Article 34 TFEU). Were the checks justifiable? Reliance on Article 36 of the EC Treaty (now Article 36 TFEU) was complicated by the existence of legislation adopted by (what was then) the EC governing the type of controls at issue.

[6] Under the first sentence of Article 36 of the Treaty, the provisions of Articles 30 to 34 are not to preclude restrictions on imports and, therefore, measures having equivalent effect, which are justified for reasons of protection of the health of plants.

Council Directive No 69/466/EEC of 8 December 1969 (OJ 1969, L 323, p. 5) on the control of San José Scale, lays down a series of provisions which are common to all the Member States of the Community.

The purpose of this Directive is to introduce certain minimum measures common to all the Member States by which certain harmful organizms may be controlled 'simultaneously and methodically' throughout the Community and prevented from spreading.

At the same time the Directive, which was adopted under Articles 43 and 100 of the Treaty, forms part of the measures intended to remove obstacles to the free movement of agricultural products within the Common Market.

[7] Its fourth recital shows, however, that the measures laid down are intended to supplement and not to replace the protective measures taken against the introduction of harmful organisms into each Member State.

By authorizing those States to adopt such additional or stricter provisions as may be required to control San José Scale or to prevent it from spreading, Article 11 reserves to them the power to maintain such measures in force to the extent necessary.

In the light of the current Community rules in this matter, a phytosanitary inspection carried out by a Member State on the importation of plant products constitutes, in principle, one of the restrictions on imports which are justified under the first sentence of Article 36 of the Treaty.

[8] However, the restrictions on imports referred to in the first sentence of Article 36 cannot be accepted under the second sentence of that article if they constitute a means of arbitrary discrimination.

The fact that plant products imported from another Member State are subject to a phytosanitary inspection although domestic products are not subject to an equivalent examination when they are despatched within the Member State might constitute arbitrary discrimination within the meaning of the abovementioned provision.

Therefore, the phytosanitary inspection of imported products which are shown to originate in areas other than those referred to in Article 3 of Council Directive No 69/466/EEC may constitute an additional or stricter measure which is not justified by Article 11 of that directive and should be regarded as a means of arbitrary discrimination within the meaning of the second sentence of Article 36 of the Treaty.

The different treatment of imported and domestic products, based on the need to prevent the spread of the harmful organizm could not, however, be regarded as arbitrary discrimination if effective measures are taken in order to prevent the distribution of contaminated domestic products and if there is reason to believe, in particular on the basis of previous experience, that there is a risk of the harmful organism's spreading if no inspection is held on importation.

[9] The reply to the questions put must therefore be that a requirement to submit imports of plant products, such as apples, from another Member State to a phytosanitary inspection at the frontier in order to establish whether such products are carriers of certain organisms harmful to plants constitutes a measure having an effect equivalent to quantitative restrictions within the meaning of Article 30 of the Treaty and is prohibited under that provision, subject to the exceptions laid down in Article 36 of the Treaty.

The additional or stricter provisions which may be required under Article 11 of Council Directive No 69/466/EEC of 8 December 1969 in order to control San José Scale and prevent it from spreading entitle the Member States to make phytosanitary inspections of imported products if effective measures are taken in order to prevent the distribution of contaminated domestic products and if there is reason to believe, in particular on the basis of previous experience, that there is a risk of the harmful organism's spreading if no inspection is held on importation.

***Oberkreisdirektor* v *Moormann* (Case 190/87)**

[1988] ECR 4689, Court of Justice of the European Communities

[10] The Court has consistently held that where . . . Community directives provide for the harmonization of the measures necessary to ensure *inter alia* the protection of animal and human health and establish Community procedures to check that they are observed, recourse to Article 36 is no longer justified and the appropriate checks must be carried out and protective measures adopted within the framework outlined by the harmonizing directive (judgments of 5 October 1977 in 5/77, *Tedeschi* v *Denkavit* ((1977)) ECR 155; 5 April 1979 in Case 148/78, *Ratti* ((1979)) ECR 1629; and 8 November 1979 in Case 251/78, *Denkavit* ((1979)) ECR 3369).

[11] As the Court has already held in its judgment of 6 October 1983 in Joined Cases 2 to 4/82 (Delhaize ((1982)) ECR 2973), Council Directive 71/188/EEC of 15 February 1971 on health problems affecting trade in fresh poultry meat . . . introduced a harmonized system of health inspections. This system of health inspections, harmonized at Community level and based on full inspection of the goods in the exporting State, replaces inspection in the State of destination and is intended to allow the free movement of the goods concerned under the same conditions as those of an internal market.

[12] Consequently, with regard to trade in fresh poultry meat, health inspection carried out systematically on goods when they cross the frontier can no longer be justified on grounds of the protection of health under Article 36 of the Treaty.

[13] Only occasional health inspections carried out by the State of destination are permissible, provided that they are not increased to such an extent as to constitute a disguised restriction on trade between the Member States (see judgment of 6 October 1983, *Delhaize*, cited above).

NOTE: Establishing a balance between the responsibility of the authorities at EU level and those at the national level is perhaps the paramount problem confronting the shapers of the internal market. It is not a problem which miraculously vanished on the last day of 1992! It is deceptively simple to declare that in principle the passage of harmonization legislation by the EU precludes an individual State's reliance on Article 36; and that the interest can be protected in an EU-wide measure which also facilitates free trade. The reality is that in a heterogeneous European Union of 28 Member States a single EU rule cannot encompass all the diffuse interests at work in the structure. So in practice national derogations and differing standards may be judged necessary. Both the two cases just considered illustrate this. The EU has a responsibility to develop a framework in which the objective of free trade will be pursued in accompaniment with the protection of and respect for national diversity and social traditions – see generally in this vein Articles 2, 3(3) and 4(2) TEU. This implies a careful mix between responsibility at EU level and responsibility at national level. In addition, the administration of the law must be allocated to the appropriate level in the structure.

Further discussion of these issues is found at p. 352 and in Chapters 17 and 18.

SECTION 5: ELIMINATING REMAINING BARRIERS TO TRADE

It has been observed that *Sandoz* (Case 174/82) (at p. 313) is a decision which allows national rules to restrict trade pending legislative harmonization by the EU in the pursuit of the protection of public health; *Campus Oil Ltd* v *Minister for Industry and Energy* (Case 72/83) [1984] ECR 2727 provides a parallel example of trade restrictions to protect domestic energy production, permissible in the interest of public security given the inadequacy of existing EU rules guaranteeing energy supplies; *Moormann* (Case 190/87) (at p. 317) demonstrates the interaction of EU rules and national competence, again in the area of health protection.

Are all the heads of justification under Article 36 TFEU susceptible to harmonization, or do they perform different functions calling for different solutions? How could an EU approach to public morality or protection of national treasures be achieved which yields free trade? How will the EU develop? To what extent is a balance between the exclusive competence of the EU and the legitimate concerns of the diverse Member States feasible? This is the very essence of the Union's task.

It falls to be considered how these questions have been addressed in the context of the completion of the internal market in accordance with Article 26 TFEU. As already suggested (in Chapter 9 and subsequently), the problems persist far beyond the target date of the end of 1992, which has in any event been excised from Article 26 TFEU by the amendments made by the Treaty of Lisbon (Chapter 9, p. 244). Articles 100a and 100b were inserted into the Treaty by the Single European Act in 1987 with a view to resolving some of these issues. In practice, much internal market legislation has been based on Article 100a. The Amsterdam Treaty repealed Article 100b, which proved superfluous, but it amended and re-numbered Article 100a. It became Article 95 and is now, post-Lisbon, Article 114 TFEU. Its scope as a basis for harmonization legislation was explored in Chapter 2, in particular in connection with the *Tobacco Advertising judgment* (Case C-376/98) and subsequent rulings. Article 114 TFEU is set out in full at p. 524 in Chapter 17, where harmonization policy is discussed in its wider context.

■ QUESTIONS

Discuss the impact of EU law in the following cases:

1. The French authorities uncover a scandal involving the use of anti-freeze by wine producers. The adulterated wine has already caused several deaths in France. The UK immediately introduces a system whereby all French wine must be inspected and granted a licence before it may be imported. The procedure at the ports can result in the detention of goods for up to one month. A flat rate fee of £1 per case is imposed on all French wine subject to this procedure. How would your answer differ if the French authorities, in an effort to minimize the detrimental effect of the scandal on their wine export trade, had already introduced a similar system of checks on all wine exported from France?
2. Franco exports dairy products from France to Germany. He has always sold his milk in Germany in cartons bearing the French flag. He believes that this is a valuable marketing technique. However, he learns that a new German law prohibits the use of national flags in product promotion. This law is part of a programme introduced by the German Government to make its population more aware of European integration and less likely to exercise national prejudice. Advise Franco.

NOTE: For additional material and resources see the Online Resource Centre at: www.oxfordtextbooks.co.uk/orc/weatherill12e.

12

Beyond Discrimination: Article 34 TFEU

SECTION 1: INDISTINCTLY APPLICABLE RULES: THE *CASSIS DE DIJON* FORMULA

The previous chapter examined a range of rules which discriminated against imports. However, even in the absence of discrimination against imported goods, national rules are capable of impeding the free circulation of goods in the EU. Article 34 TFEU may apply even to national legislation which makes no distinction between domestic and imported goods. The scope and application of EU law in this area is primarily the consequence of the Court's activism, and therefore it is appropriate to allow the leading case to provide the introductory means of explanation. Remember that Article 30, referred to in the judgment, was re-numbered by the Treaty of Amsterdam (as Article 28 EC) and again by the Treaty of Lisbon: it is now Article 34 TFEU.

***Rewe-Zentrale AG* v *Bundesmonopolverwaltung für Branntwein* (Case 120/78)**

[1979] ECR 649, Court of Justice of the European Communities

[1] By order of 28 April 1978, which was received at the Court on 22 May, the Hessisches Finanzgericht referred two questions to the Court under Article 177 of the EEC Treaty [now Article 267 TFEU: Chapter 7] for a preliminary ruling on the interpretation of Articles 30 and 37 of the EEC Treaty, for the purpose of assessing the compatibility with Community law of a provision of the German rules relating to the marketing of alcoholic beverages fixing a minimum alcoholic strength for various categories of alcoholic products.

[2] It appears from the order making the reference that the plaintiff in the main action intends to import a consignment of 'Cassis de Dijon' originating in France for the purpose of marketing it in the Federal Republic of Germany.

The plaintiff applied to the Bundesmonopolverwaltung (Federal Monopoly Administration for Spirits) for authorization to import the product in question and the monopoly administration informed it that because of its insufficient alcoholic strength the said product does not have the characteristics required in order to be marketed within the Federal Republic of Germany.

[3] The monopoly administration's attitude is based on Article 100 of the Branntweinmonopolgesetz and on the rules drawn up by the monopoly administration pursuant to that provision, the effect of which is to fix the minimum alcohol content of specified categories of liqueurs and the potable spirits (Verordnung über den Mindestweingeistgehalt von Trinkbranntweinen of 28 February 1958, Bundesanzeiger No 48 of 11 March 1958).

Those provisions lay down that the marketing of fruit liqueurs, such as 'Cassis de Dijon', is conditional upon a minimum alcohol content of 25%, whereas the alcohol content of the product in question, which is freely marketed as such in France, is between 15 and 20%.

[4] The plaintiff takes the view that the fixing by the German rules of a minimum alcohol content leads to the result that well-known spirits products from other Member States of the Community cannot be sold in the Federal Republic of Germany and that the said provision therefore constitutes a restriction on the free movement of goods between Member States which exceeds the bounds of the trade rules reserved to the latter.

In its view it is a measure having an effect equivalent to a quantitative restriction on imports contrary to Article 30 of the EEC Treaty.

Since, furthermore, it is a measure adopted within the context of the management of the spirits monopoly, the plaintiff considers that there is also an infringement of Article 37, according to which the Member States shall progressively adjust any State monopolies of a commercial character so as to ensure that when the transitional period has ended no discrimination regarding the conditions under which goods are procured or marketed exists between nationals of Member States.

[5] In order to reach a decision on this dispute the Hessisches Finanzgericht has referred two questions to the Court, worded as follows:

1. Must the concept of measures having an effect equivalent to quantitative restrictions on imports contained in Article 30 of the EEC Treaty be understood as meaning that the fixing of a minimum wine-spirit content for potable spirits laid down in the German Branntweinmonopolgesetz, the result of which is that traditional products of other Member States whose wine-spirit content is below the fixed limit cannot be put into circulation in the Federal Republic of Germany, also comes within this concept?
2. May the fixing of such a minimum wine-spirit content come within the concept of 'discrimination regarding the conditions under which goods are procured and marketed . . . between nationals of Member States' contained in Article 37 of the EEC Treaty?

[6] The national court is thereby asking for assistance in the matter of interpretation in order to enable it to assess whether the requirement of a minimum alcohol content may be covered either by the prohibition on all measures having an effect equivalent to quantitative restrictions in trade between Member States contained in Article 30 of the Treaty or by the prohibition on all discrimination regarding the conditions under which goods are procured and marketed between nationals of Member States within the meaning of Article 37.

[7] It should be noted in this connexion that Article 37 relates specifically to State monopolies of a commercial character.

That provision is therefore irrelevant with regard to national provisions which do not concern the exercise by a public monopoly of its specific function – namely, its exclusive right – but apply in a general manner to the production and marketing of alcoholic beverages, whether or not the latter are covered by the monopoly in question.

That being the case, the effect on intra-Community trade of the measure referred to by the national court must be examined solely in relation to the requirements under Article 30, as referred to by the first question.

[8] In the absence of common rules relating to the production and marketing of alcohol – a proposal for a regulation submitted to the Council by the Commission on 7 December 1976 (Official Journal C 309, p. 2) not yet having received the Council's approval – it is for the Member States to regulate all matters relating to the production and marketing of alcohol and alcoholic beverages on their own territory.

Obstacles to movement within the Community resulting from disparities between the national laws relating to the marketing of the products in question must be accepted in so far as those provisions may be recognised as being necessary in order to satisfy mandatory requirements relating in particular to the effectiveness of fiscal supervision, the protection of public health, the fairness of commercial transactions and the defence of the consumer.

[9] The Government of the Federal Republic of Germany, intervening in the proceedings, put forward various arguments which, in its view, justify the application of provisions relating to the minimum alcohol content of alcoholic beverages, adducing considerations relating on the one hand to the protection of public health and on the other to the protection of the consumer against unfair commercial practices.

[10] As regards the protection of public health the German Government states that the purpose of the fixing of minimum alcohol contents by national legislation is to avoid the proliferation of alcoholic beverages on the national market, in particular alcoholic beverages with a low alcohol content, since, in its view, such products may more easily induce a tolerance towards alcohol than more highly alcoholic beverages.

[11] Such considerations are not decisive since the consumer can obtain on the market an extremely wide range of weakly or moderately alcoholic products and furthermore a large proportion of alcoholic beverages with a high alcohol content freely sold on the German market is generally consumed in a diluted form.

[12] The German Government also claims that the fixing of a lower limit for the alcohol content of certain liqueurs is designed to protect the consumer against unfair practices on the part of producers and distributors of alcoholic beverages.

This argument is based on the consideration that the lowering of the alcohol content secures a competitive advantage in relation to beverages with a higher alcohol content, since alcohol constitutes by far the most expensive constituent of beverages by reason of the high rate of tax to which it is subject.

Furthermore, according to the German Government, to allow alcoholic products into free circulation wherever, as regards their alcohol content, they comply with the rules laid down in the country of production would have the effect of imposing as a common standard within the Community the lowest alcohol content permitted in any of the Member States, and even of rendering any requirements in this field inoperative since a lower limit of this nature is foreign to the rules of several Member States.

[13] As the Commission rightly observed, the fixing of limits in relation to the alcohol content of beverages may lead to the standardization of products placed on the market and of their designations, in the interests of a greater transparency of commercial transactions and offers for sale to the public.

However, this line of argument cannot be taken so far as to regard the mandatory fixing of minimum alcohol contents as being an essential guarantee of the fairness of commercial transactions, since it is a simple matter to ensure that suitable information is conveyed to the purchaser by requiring the display of an indication of origin and of the alcohol content on the packaging of products.

[14] It is clear from the foregoing that the requirements relating to the minimum alcohol content of alcoholic beverages do not serve a purpose which is in the general interest and such as to take precedence over the requirements of the free movement of goods, which constitutes one of the fundamental rules of the Community.

In practice, the principal effect of requirements of this nature is to promote alcoholic beverages having a high alcohol content by excluding from the national market products of other Member States which do not answer that description.

It therefore appears that the unilateral requirement imposed by the rules of a Member State of a minimum alcohol content for the purposes of the sale of alcoholic beverages constitutes an obstacle to trade which is incompatible with the provisions of Article 30 of the Treaty.

There is therefore no valid reason why, provided that they have been lawfully produced and marketed in one of the Member States, alcoholic beverages should not be introduced into any other Member State; the sale of such products may not be subject to a legal prohibition on the marketing of beverages with an alcohol content lower than the limit set by the national rules.

[15] Consequently, the first question should be answered to the effect that the concept of 'measures having an effect equivalent to quantitative restrictions on imports' contained in Article 30 of the Treaty is to be understood to mean that the fixing of a minimum alcohol content for alcoholic beverages intended for human consumption by the legislation of a Member State also falls within the prohibition laid down in that provision where the importation of alcoholic beverages lawfully produced and marketed in another Member State is concerned.

NOTE: Notice that such trade restrictions arise simply because national laws are different. Typical French products were excluded from the German market by a rule which on its face made no reference whatsoever to national origin. The result was the isolation of the German market and the protection of the German producer from competition. Such market partitioning subverts the concept of a common market.

P. Cecchini, The European Challenge: 1992, the Benefits of a Single Market

(Aldershot: Wildwood House, 1988), pp. 24–7

DIVERGENCES IN TECHNICAL REGULATIONS AND STANDARDS – COSTS DIFFICULT TO QUANTIFY BUT IMPOSSIBLE TO IGNORE

Rated by companies themselves as one of the most acute problems they face in their European operations. . ., disparities between national technical regulations and standards are a complex and, to the outside observer, an arcane subject. Yet their adverse impact on industry seeking to exploit the full dimension of the EC market, a priority matter for the Community policy-maker as for the businessman, is now widely accepted.

It is not difficult to see why. In an increasing number of sectors, firms will be obliged to survive by selling in quantities much larger than are likely to be absorbed by their share of a single, narrow national market. To compete, they need to produce on a larger scale. To amortize this investment in new plant, and also their spiralling expenditure on research and innovation, they need the larger, European market.

National product regulations and standards, however, impose an entirely contrary logic. They tend, by their differences, to force companies to do what their business strategy tells them is wrong: produce for the national market, innovate for the national market. Manufacturers are thus often constrained either to limit themselves to a sub-optimal market, or to attack new markets *via* a range of sub-optimal plants and narrowly relevant technology. Either option implies extensive costs – the costs of non-Europe.

Adverse effects are thus not limited to restrictions on cross-border trade. They impact on the core functions of business – production and technology. And the costs they incur are often compounded by their use in combination with other obstacles to market entry, notably restrictive public procurement, e.g., telecommunications equipment. . .Among the worst affected by these and related barriers are high tech sectors which are precisely those where market fragmentation has a proven track record in putting Europe at a competitive disadvantage with the US and Japan.

Barriers in this field result from differences between EC countries for three types of arrangement: technical regulations, standards, testing and certification procedures.

Technical regulations lay down legal requirements, enacted by the national legislator mainly in the interests of health, safety and the environment; often these requirements refer to standards.

Standards are not legally binding in themselves, since they are written by private national standardisation bodies like DIN (in Germany), BSI (in Britain) and AFNOR (in France). However, although standards are only voluntary codifications for products and product processes, they often assume a quasi-legal status because of their use as a reference in technical regulations and, for example, in insurance and product liability claims, as well as in calls for tender for public procurement.

Testing and certification procedures are used to check that a product or process complies either with voluntary standards or with statutory regulations. If successfully passed, they result in the issuance of certificates of conformity. However, a typical problem is non-recognition by one EC country of another's certification process, meaning at best additional testing and at worst an absolute market entry barrier.

COSTS: MULTI-SECTOR IMPACT

The costs . . . imposed by these barriers hit manufacturing industries right across the board. But they do so in a manner which is so sector-specific and which, even then, is often inextricably combined with the impact of other barriers, as to make a quantified extrapolation at the general level impossible to undertake. But on an individual industry basis, the story is clear. It is illustrated by the investigations carried out by the research into certain selected industries . . . Their results are in turn corroborated and amplified by company executives themselves in the general survey of manufacturing business conducted for the research.

Telecom equipment, automobiles, foodstuffs, pharmaceuticals and the building products sector are. . . five major EC industries where standards and technical regulations, alone or in combination with other obstacles, inject heavy doses of inefficiency into business operations.

This is most spectacularly the case in the telecom sector. Here the industry's regulators – usually the national PTTs – have traditionally sustained their restrictive procurement practices by demanding observance of narrowly relevant standards reinforced by discriminating certification procedures. The overall cost of these mutually supportive barriers is estimated as high as Ecu 4.8 billion. The experience of telecom equipment, moreover, is to an extent indicative of the massive losses imposed by divergent standards on other high technology sectors, where burgeoning R&D expenditure can only be recouped by manufacturing products to widely marketable standards.

At the other end of industry's product range, foodstuffs and building products have their own experiences to tell. Thus of the total estimated costs of up to Ecu 1 billion attributable to market barriers in the foodstuffs sector, content and ingredient regulations on just four items (chocolates, beer, ice-cream and pasta) contribute over 80% . . . In the building products sector, research shows unequivocally that divergent standards and lengthy certification (whose procedures can last years rather than months) are the primary causes of non-Europe costs estimated in total at around Ecu 2.5 billion. Pharmaceutical companies, meanwhile, face serious problems and significant costs in getting new products authorized and admitted to the market.

Motor manufacturing enjoys a paradoxical but costly situation. It is both the sector where the removal of technical barriers is judged as most necessary by business itself. . .and yet the one where the Community has had most apparent success in harmonising technical regulations. As many as 41 EC harmonisation directives, dealing with specifications for various parts of the automobile, have been adopted over the years. But the key problem is that there remain three further directives which need to be adopted before full EC type approval can be achieved. In the absence of Community type approval (which is being held up on political rather than technical grounds), and thus of a European certification procedure, EC-wide manufacturers are generally being forced into costly duplications.

NOTE: The ruling in *'Cassis de Dijon'* (Case 120/78) is one of the main pillars of the law of the internal market. As already discussed in Chapter 9, the Court has constructed a strategy for judging the permissibility of regulatory diversity between the States in an integrating market. The principles set out by the Court in its ruling in *Gebhard* (Case C-55/94, p. 266), have their roots in the fertile soil of the *'Cassis de Dijon'* ruling.

A further simple example of market partitioning caused by national laws which in effect enshrine a preference for typical national produce is provided by the following case.

***Ministère Public* v *Deserbais* (Case 286/86)**

[1988] ECR 4907, Court of Justice of the European Communities

French legislation restricted the use of the name 'Edam' to cheese with a minimum fat content of 40 per cent. M. Deserbais imported cheese from Germany where it was lawfully produced with a fat content of only 34.3 per cent. When he marketed the cheese in France as 'Edam', he was prosecuted for unlawful use of a trade name. M. Deserbais argued that Article 30 of the EC Treaty (now Article 34 TFEU) provided him with a complete defence to the charge. The matter was referred to the Court under the preliminary reference procedure, found today in Article 267 TFEU (Chapter 7).

[10] [T]he national court starts from the premise that the cheese in question, containing 34% fat, has been lawfully and traditionally produced in the Federal Republic of Germany under the name 'Edam' in accordance with the laws and regulations applicable to it there, and that consumers' attention is adequately drawn to that fact by the labelling.

[11] It must also be stated that at the present stage of development of Community law there are no common rules governing the names of the various types of cheeses in the Community. Accordingly, it cannot be stated in principle that a Member State may not lay down rules making the use by national producers of a name for a cheese subject to the observance of a traditional minimum fat content.

[12] However, it would be incompatible with Article 30 of the Treaty and the objectives of a common market to apply such rules to imported cheeses of the same type where those cheeses have been lawfully produced and marketed in another Member State under the same generic name but with a different minimum fat content. The Member State into which they are imported cannot prevent the importation and marketing of such cheeses where adequate information for the consumer is ensured.

[13] The question may arise whether the same rule must be applied where a product presented under a particular name is so different, as regards its composition or production, from the products generally known by that name in the Community that it cannot be regarded as falling within the same category. However, no situation of that kind arises in the circumstances described by the national court in this case.

The Court's reply to the question referred was accordingly:

Article 30 [now 34] *et seq.* of the Treaty must be interpreted as precluding a Member State from applying national legislation making the right to use the trade name of a type of cheese subject to the observance of a minimum fat content to products of the same type imported from another Member State when those products have been lawfully manufactured and marketed under that name in that Member State and consumers are provided with proper information.

NOTE: There is every reason to insist that Article 34 TFEU is capable of applying to such national rules because of the clear restrictive *effect* on trade between Member States. The *'Cassis de Dijon'* (Case 120/78) approach has this emphasis on effect in common with the *Dassonville* (Case 8/74)

formula (p. 286). This interpretation of Article 34 is crucial to the attack on national protectionism and market division. According to P. Verloren van Themaat (1982) 18 CDE 123, at p. 135:

> La crise économique actuelle augmente sans doute la tentation pour les Etats membres de prendre des mesures qui sont susceptibles d'entraver directement ou indirectement, actuellement ou potentiellement, le commerce intracommunautaire . . .

The Court's application of Article 34 constitutes an important corrective to that persisting temptation. And so deep rooted is the national tendency to maintain technical standards without taking account of the impetus towards cross-border trade that '*Cassis*-type' cases unfailingly form a part of the Court's regular diet today: e.g., Case C-147/04 *de Groot* [2006] ECR I-245; Case C-265/06 *Commission* v *Portugal* [2008] ECR I-2245.

■ QUESTION

To what extent has the Court adopted a more vigorous pro-free trade stance than that envisaged by Article 3 of Directive 70/50 (p. 284)?

NOTES

1. The result of the Court's approach is that goods produced to a standard which entitles access to the market of the Member State of production should normally be recognized as a sufficient standard to deserve access to the market of any other Member State. It is assumed that all Member States have a broadly equivalent approach to basic standards of health and safety, and that they should recognize this in dealing with imports from other Member States. The approach taken in '*Cassis de Dijon*' (Case 120/78) is an important impetus towards market integration. A State can no longer present an importer with a rule book full of technical standards and demand that the importer's goods conform to those standards of manufacture or designation.
2. Only in exceptional circumstances can a State stand on its technical rules to prevent the import of a product from another Member State – when it can show that the rules are necessary to satisfy a mandatory requirement, according to para 8 of the Cassis ruling. There is, then, a strong though not irresistible presumption in favour of free trade inherent in the Court's approach.

Commission v *Germany* (Case 178/84)

[1987] ECR 1227, Court of Justice of the European Communities

This was an infringement procedure against Germany (now Article 258 TFEU, see Chapter 4) alleging breach of Article 30 of the Treaty (now Article 34 TFEU). Germany prohibited the marketing on its territory of beer lawfully produced and marketed in other Member States if the beer failed to comply with the provisions of the *Biersteuergesetz* of 1952. The law applied equally to all beer produced in Germany itself, so there was no question of discrimination against imports. There were two limbs to the *Biersteuergesetz* which the Commission was concerned to challenge. In the first place, the name 'Bier' could be used only for products brewed using malted barley, hops, yeast, and water alone. The use of other ingredients such as maize did not preclude the marketing of the finished product, but it could not be sold as 'Bier'.

> [25] [T]he Commission concedes that as long as harmonisation has not been achieved at Community level the Member States have the power in principle to lay down rules governing the manufacture, the composition and the marketing of beverages. It stresses, however, that rules which, like Article 10 of the Biersteuergesetz, prohibit the use of a generic designation for the marketing of products manufactured partly from raw materials, such as rice and maize, other than those whose use is prescribed in the national territory are contrary to Community law. In any event, such rules go beyond what is necessary in order to protect the German consumer, since that could be done simply by means of labelling or notices. Those rules therefore constitute an impediment to trade contrary to Article 30 of the EEC Treaty.

[26] The German Government has first sought to justify its rules on public-health grounds. It maintains that the use of raw materials other than those permitted by Article 9 of the Biersteuergesetz would inevitably entail the use of additives. However, at the hearing the German Government conceded that Article 10 of the Biersteuergesetz, which is merely a rule on designation, was exclusively intended to protect consumers. In its view, consumers associate the designation 'Bier' with a beverage manufactured from only the raw materials listed in Article 9 of the Biersteuergesetz. Consequently, it is necessary to prevent them from being misled as to the nature of the product by being led to believe that a beverage called 'Bier' complies with the Reinheitsgebot when that is not the case. The German Government maintains that its rules are not protectionist in aim. It stresses in that regard that the raw materials whose use is specified in Article 9(1) and (2) of the Biersteuergesetz are not necessarily of national origin. Any trader marketing products satisfying the prescribed rules is free to use the designation 'Bier' and those rules can readily be complied with outside the Federal Republic of Germany.

[27] According to a consistent line of decisions of the Court (above all, the judgment of 11 July 1974 in Case 8/74 *Procureur du Roi* v *Dassonville* [1974] ECR 837) the prohibition of measures having an effect equivalent to quantitative restrictions under Article 30 of the EEC Treaty covers 'all trading rules enacted by Member States which are capable of hindering, directly or indirectly, actually or potentially, intra-Community trade'.

[28] The Court has also consistently held (in particular in the judgment of 20 February 1979 in Case 120/78 *REWE-Zentrale AG* v *Bundesmonopolverwaltung* [1979] ECR 649, and the judgment of 10 November 1982 in Case 261/81 *Walter Rau Lebensmittelwerke* v *De Smedt* [1982] ECR 3961) that 'in the absence of common rules relating to the marketing of the products concerned, obstacles to free movement within the Community resulting from disparities between the national laws must be accepted in so far as such rules, applicable to domestic and to imported products without distinction, may be recognised as being necessary in order to satisfy mandatory requirements relating *inter alia* to consumer protection. It is also necessary for such rules to be proportionate to the aim in view. If a Member State has a choice between various measures to attain the same objective it should choose the means which least restricts the free movement of goods'.

[29] It is not contested that the application of Article 10 of the Biersteuergesetz to beers from other Member States in whose manufacture raw materials other than malted barley have been lawfully used, in particular rice and maize, is liable to constitute an obstacle to their importation into the Federal Republic of Germany.

[30] Accordingly, it must be established whether the application of that provision may be justified by imperative requirements relating to consumer protection.

[31] The German Government's argument that Article 10 of the Biersteuergesetz is essential in order to protect German consumers because, in their minds, the designation 'Bier' is inseparably linked to the beverage manufactured solely from the ingredients laid down in Article 9 of the Biersteuergesetz must be rejected.

[32] Firstly, consumers' conceptions which vary from one Member State to the other are also likely to evolve in the course of time within a Member State. The establishment of the common market is, it should be added, one of the factors that may play a major contributory role in that development. Whereas rules protecting consumers against misleading practices enable such a development to be taken into account, legislation of the kind contained in Article 10 of the Biersteuergesetz prevents it from taking place. As the Court has already held in another context (judgment of 27 February 1980 in Case 170/78 *Commission* v *United Kingdom* [1980] ECR 417), the legislation of a Member State must not 'crystallize given consumer habits so as to consolidate an advantage acquired by national industries concerned to comply with them'.

[33] Secondly, in the other Member States of the Community the designations corresponding to the German designation 'Bier' are generic designations for a fermented beverage manufactured from malted barley, whether malted barley on its own or with the addition of rice or maize. The same approach is taken in Community law as can be seen from heading No 22.03 of the Common Customs Tariff. The German legislature itself utilizes the designation 'Bier' in that way in Article 9(7) and (8) of the Biersteuergesetz in order to refer to beverages not complying with the manufacturing rules laid down in Article 9(1) and (2).

[34] The German designation 'Bier' and its equivalents in the languages of the other Member States of the Community may therefore not be restricted to beers manufactured in accordance with the rules in force in the Federal Republic of Germany.

[35] It is admittedly legitimate to seek to enable consumers who attribute specific qualities to beers manufactured from particular raw materials to make their choice in the light of that consideration. However, as the Court has already emphasized (judgment of 9 December 1981 in Case 193/80 *Commission* v *Italy* [1981] ECR

3019), that possibility may be ensured by means which do not prevent the importation of products which have been lawfully manufactured and marketed in other Member States and, in particular, 'by the compulsory affixing of suitable labels giving the nature of the product sold'. By indicating the raw materials utilized in the manufacture of beer 'such a course would enable the consumer to make his choice in full knowledge of the facts and would guarantee transparency in trading and in offers to the public'. It must be added that such a system of mandatory consumer information must not entail negative assessments for beers not complying with the requirements of Article 9 of the Biersteuergesetz.

[36] Contrary to the German Government's view, such a system of consumer information may operate perfectly well even in the case of a product which, like beer, is not necessarily supplied to consumers in bottles or in cans capable of bearing the appropriate details. That is borne out, once again, by the German legislation itself.

Article 26(1) and (2) of the aforementioned regulation implementing the Biersteuergesetz provides for a system of consumer information in respect of certain beers, even where those beers are sold on draught, when the requisite information must appear on the casks or the beer taps.

[37] It follows from the foregoing that by applying the rules on designation in Article 10 of the Biersteuergesetz to beers imported from other Member States which were manufactured and marketed lawfully in those States the Federal Republic of Germany has failed to fulfil its obligations under Article 30 of the EEC Treaty.

NOTE: The second limb of the rules involved an absolute ban on the marketing of beers containing additives. This rule also applied to all beers wherever produced; it was not origin specific. Arguments relating to the protection of public health which were rather more powerful than those advanced in relation to the first limb of the *Biersteuergesetz* were advanced.

***Commission* v *Germany* (Case 178/84)**

[1987] ECR 1227, Court of Justice of the European Communities

[39] . . . the German Government considers that in view of the dangers resulting from the utilization of additives whose long-term effects are not yet known and in particular of the risks resulting from the accumulation of additives in the organism and their interaction with other substances, such as alcohol, it is necessary to minimize the quantity of additives ingested. Since beer is a foodstuff of which large quantities are consumed in Germany, the German Government considers that it is particularly desirable to prohibit the use of any additive in its manufacture, especially in so far as the use of additives is not technologically necessary and can be avoided if only the ingredients laid down in the Biersteuergesetz are used. In those circumstances, the German rules on additives in beer are fully justified by the need to safeguard public health and do not infringe the principle of proportionality.

[40] It is not contested that the prohibition on the marketing of beers containing additives constitutes a barrier to the importation from other Member States of beers containing additives authorized in those States, and is to that extent covered by Article 30 of the EEC Treaty. However, it must be ascertained whether it is possible to justify that prohibition under Article 36 of the Treaty on grounds of the protection of human health.

[41] The Court has consistently held (in particular in the judgment of 14 July 1983 in Case 174/82 Sandoz BV [1983] ECR 2445) that 'in so far as there are uncertainties at the present state of scientific research it is for the Member States, in the absence of harmonisation, to decide what degree of protection of the health and life of humans they intend to assure, having regard however to the requirements of the free movement of goods within the Community'.

[42] As may also be seen from the decisions of the Court (and especially the judgment of 14 July 1983 in the Sandoz case, cited above, the judgment of 10 December 1985 in Case 247/84 *Motte* [1985] ECR 3887, and the judgment of 6 May 1986 in Case 304/84 *Ministère public* v *Muller and Others* [1986] ECR 1511), in such circumstances Community law does not preclude the adoption by the Member States of legislation whereby the use of additives is subjected to prior authorization granted by a measure of general application for specific additives, in respect of all products, for certain products only or for certain uses. Such legislation meets a genuine need of health policy, namely that of restricting the uncontrolled consumption of food additives.

[43] However, the application to imported products of prohibitions on marketing products containing additives which are authorized in the Member State of production but prohibited in the Member State of importation is permissible only in so far as it complies with the requirements of Article 36 of the Treaty as it has been interpreted by the Court.

[44] It must be borne in mind, in the first place, that in its judgments in the *Sandoz, Motte* and *Muller* cases, cited above, the Court inferred from the principle of proportionality underlying the last sentence of Article 36 of the Treaty that prohibitions on the marketing of products containing additives authorized in the Member State of production but prohibited in the Member State of importation must be restricted to what is actually necessary to secure the protection of public health. The Court also concluded that the use of a specific additive which is authorized in another Member State must be authorized in the case of a product imported from that Member State where, in view, on the one hand, of the findings of international scientific research, and in particular of the work of the Community's Scientific Committee for Food, the Codex Alimentarius Committee of the Food and Agriculture Organization of the United Nations (FAO) and the World Health Organization, and, on the other hand, of the eating habits prevailing in the importing Member State, the additive in question does not present a risk to public health and meets a real need, especially a technical one.

[45] Secondly, it should be remembered that, as the Court held in its judgment of 6 May 1986 in the *Muller* case, cited above, by virtue of the principle of proportionality, traders must also be able to apply, under a procedure which is easily accessible to them and can be concluded within a reasonable time, for the use of specific additives to be authorized by a measure of general application.

[46] It should be pointed out that it must be open to traders to challenge before the courts an unjustified failure to grant authorization. Without prejudice to the right of the competent national authorities of the importing Member State to ask traders to produce the information in their possession which may be useful for the purpose of assessing the facts, it is for those authorities to demonstrate, as the Court held in its judgment of 6 May 1986 in the *Muller* case, cited above, that the prohibition is justified on grounds relating to the protection of the health of its population.

[47] It must be observed that the German rules on additives applicable to beer result in the exclusion of all the additives authorized in the other Member States and not the exclusion of just some of them for which there is concrete justification by reason of the risks which they involve in view of the eating habits of the German population; moreover those rules do not lay down any procedure whereby traders can obtain authorization for the use of a specific additive in the manufacture of beer by means of a measure of general application.

[48] As regards more specifically the harmfulness of additives, the German Government, citing experts' reports, has referred to the risks inherent in the ingestion of additives in general. It maintains that it is important, for reasons of general preventive health protection, to minimize the quantity of additives ingested, and that it is particularly advisable to prohibit altogether their use in the manufacture of beer, a foodstuff consumed in considerable quantities by the German population.

[49] However, it appears from the tables of additives authorized for use in various foodstuffs submitted by the German Government itself that some of the additives authorized in other Member States for use in the manufacture of beer are also authorized under the German rules, in particular the Regulation on Additives, for use in the manufacture of all, or virtually all, beverages. Mere reference to the potential risks of the ingestion of additives in general and to the fact that beer is a foodstuff consumed in large quantities does not suffice to justify the imposition of stricter rules in the case of beer.

[50] As regards the need, and in particular the technological need, for additives, the German Government argues that there is no need for additives if beer is manufactured in accordance with the requirements of Article 9 of the Biersteuergesetz.

[51] It must be emphasized that mere reference to the fact that beer can be manufactured without additives if it is made from only the raw materials prescribed in the Federal Republic of Germany does not suffice to preclude the possibility that some additives may meet a technological need. Such an interpretation of the concept of technological need, which results in favouring national production methods, constitutes a disguised means of restricting trade between Member States.

[52] The concept of technological need must be assessed in the light of the raw materials utilized and bearing in mind the assessment made by the authorities of the Member State where the product was lawfully

manufactured and marketed. Account must also be taken of the findings of international scientific research and in particular the work of the Community's Scientific Committee for Food, the Codex Alimentarius Committee of the FAO and the World Health Organization.

[53] Consequently, in so far as the German rules on additives in beer entail a general ban on additives, their application to beers imported from other Member States is contrary to the requirements of Community law as laid down in the case law of the Court, since that prohibition is contrary to the principle of proportionality and is therefore not covered by the exception provided for in Article 36 of the EEC Treaty.

■ QUESTIONS

1. Is the beer market so important? Why did the Commission deploy scarce resources pursuing an infringement action in this sector? (The fact that the cutting reproduced below appeared on the front page of the newspaper may assist you in finding an answer.)
2. How is the German brewer likely to react to this judgment (consider Ch. 9 on the nature and purpose of economic integration)? What factors might the German brewer choose to emphasize in launching a campaign in order to maintain customer loyalty now that the protectionist isolation of the domestic beer market has been broken?
3. How is the German consumer likely to react to this judgment?

The following item appeared on p. 1 of *The Guardian* of 13 March 1987, shortly after the judgment.

Anna Tomforde, 'Parts British beers will still not reach'

The Guardian, 13 March 1987

To a chorus of 'Deutschesbier Allein' (German beer only) regulars at Bonn's Haehnchen pub (The Cock) raised their glasses yesterday and vowed to remain true to domestic brews. This is despite a European Court ruling in favour of the import of foreign beers, regarded as impure under Germany's ancient rules.

'The verdict is the best possible advertisement for German beer', said Detlef Haberland, a 40-year-old doctor enjoying a few pints on his afternoon off. 'It will enhance solidarity among German beer drinkers and stir the German national conscience'.

More than 99 per cent of the 94 million hectolitres of beer drunk each year by Europe's thirstiest country, originates in the country's 1,200 breweries. This, according to the top clientele, will not change.

Judging by comments in the pub, the British Brewers' Society's view that there will now be a 'Willkommen' for the British pint amongst the discerning German beer drinkers, is premature and unduly optimistic.

'I drink an English ale once in a while but I miss the froth. I find it tasteless and without charm,' said Mr Hans Pfotenhauer, a vegetable market worker. 'The German beer drinker wants quality'.

This quality, pub-goers believe, is best guaranteed by a 16th century purity law, the 'Reinheitsgebot', which states that German beer must consist only of water, hops, malt and yeast. 'After the Austrian wine scandal and general anxiety over chemicals in our food, at least we know our beer is pure', Dr Haberland said. His friends agreed, ordering another round.

The Luxembourg ruling, given by the court president, Lord Mackenzie Stuart, means that West Germany can no longer exclude foreign beers which do not meet the 471-year-old German beer law, and which contain different ingredients and additives.

'The laws of a member country must not serve to foster consumer habits in the interests of the national industry', the ruling says in a key sentence that marked the end of a five-year legal battle. The case was brought by a French exporter.

The West German Brewers' Association, which stressed yesterday that it would make sure that additives and ingredients of foreign beers are clearly marked on the labels, said it would mount a £415,000 advertising campaign in all West German newspapers this weekend to reassure consumers that Germany's 4,000 domestic brews will continue to be produced according to the purity rules, promulgated by Duke Wilhelm of Bavaria in 1516.

A publicity campaign is also being planned by French and Dutch brewers, as well as the British, in an attempt to penetrate the German market. Behind the outwardly defiant German reaction there is great anxiety that poor Germans will be tempted by cheaper imported beer on supermarket shelves.

'I can well imagine that broad sections of the public will buy the cheaper beer, and that small, family-run pubs and restaurants will be forced to sell it', said the barman at The Cock.

■ QUESTION

How is the German government likely to react to the judgment? Could it introduce labelling requirements relating to ingredients for beers marketed in Germany (see para 35 of the judgment)?

Is the German government obliged to abolish the mandatory purity laws for domestic producers too?

***Nederlandse Bakkerij* v *Edah* (Cases 80 and 159/85)**

[1986] ECR 3359, Court of Justice of the European Communities

[18] It is also impossible to accept Edah BV's argument that such provisions are contrary to Article 30 of the EEC Treaty [now Article 34 TFEU] because they enable imported bread to be sold below the minimum selling price applicable to domestically produced bread when the purchase price is sufficiently low. The purpose of that article is to eliminate obstacles to the importation of goods and not to ensure equal treatment in all cases for goods of national origin and imported goods. Unequal treatment which does not have the effect of hindering imports or making the sale of imported goods more difficult but instead favours them does not fall within the prohibition laid down by that article.

SECTION 2: LOCATING THE OUTER LIMIT OF ARTICLE 34 TFEU

The key to '*Cassis de Dijon*' (Case 120/78) rules is that although they impose burdens on all products irrespective of origin, imported goods feel an extra burden because they have *already* been subject to the technical rules or traditions of the State of origin. In this manner, the '*Cassis de Dijon*' rules protect the domestic economy by subjecting imported goods to *different* technical standards from those to which they have already been exposed in their State of origin. Such rules may be applied to imported goods only provided they are justified. In the cases extracted the national measures were not shown to be justified: the question of the scope of justification is addressed further at p. 341. But the Court has also been obliged to consider rules which *restrict* trade but which do not *protect* the home market. Are these too to be put to the test of justification?

A: The road to *Keck and Mithouard*

For almost a decade the Court was prepared to allow the invocation of Article 30 of the Treaty (now Article 34 TFEU) even where both the application of the rules *and* the consequential burden was felt equally by all goods. However, in its November 1993 ruling in *Keck and Mithouard* (Cases C-267 and 268/91) it changed its mind and set an outer limit to the application of this Article of the Treaty. In order to appreciate the background to the *Keck* ruling, it is appropriate to look first at the notorious 'Sunday trading' litigation.

Torfaen BC v *B&Q plc* (Case 145/88)

[1989] ECR 765, Court of Justice of the European Communities

B&Q was prosecuted for having violated the Shops Act 1950 by allowing its retail premises to be open on Sunday other than for the limited range of transactions permitted under that Act. B&Q argued that the restrictions on 'Sunday trading' depressed sales, including sales of imported products, and that accordingly EU law could be relied on to defeat the prosecution. The Cwmbran Magistrates' Court referred questions on the interpretation of what were then Articles 30–36 EEC (now Articles 34–36 TFEU) to the Court for a preliminary ruling.

[11] The first point which must be made is that national rules prohibiting retailers from opening their premises on Sunday apply to imported and domestic products alike. In principle, the marketing of products imported from other Member States is not therefore made more difficult than the marketing of domestic products.

[12] Next, it must be recalled that in its judgment of 11 July 1985 in Joined Cases 60 and 61/84 (*Cinéthèque SA and Others* v *Fédération Nationale des Cinémas Françaises* ([1985]) ECR 2618) the Court held, with regard to a prohibition of the hiring of video-cassettes applicable to domestic and imported products alike, that such a prohibition was not compatible with the principle of the free movement of goods provided for in the Treaty unless any obstacle to Community trade thereby created did not exceed what was necessary in order to ensure the attainment of the objective in view and unless that objective was justified with regard to Community law.

[13] In those circumstances it is therefore necessary in a case such as this to consider first of all whether rules such as those at issue pursue an aim which is justified with regard to Community law. As far as that question is concerned, the Court has already stated in its judgment of 14 July 1981 in Case 155/80 (Oebel [1981] ECR 1993) that national rules governing the hours of work, delivery and sale in the bread and confectionery industry constitute a legitimate part of economic and social policy, consistent with the objectives of public interest pursued by the Treaty.

[14] The same consideration must apply as regards national rules governing the opening hours of retail premises. Such rules reflect certain political and economic choices in so far as their purpose is to ensure that working and non-working hours are so arranged as to accord with national or regional socio-cultural characteristics, and that, in the present state of Community law, is a matter for the Member States. Furthermore, such rules are not designed to govern the patterns of trade between Member States.

[15] Secondly, it is necessary to ascertain whether the effects of such national rules exceed what is necessary to achieve the aim in view. As is indicated in Article 3 of Commission Directive 70/50/EEC of 22 December 1969 (Official Journal, English Special Edition 1970 (I), p. 17), the prohibition laid down in Article 30 covers national measures governing the marketing of products where the restrictive effect of such measures on the free movement of goods exceeds the effects intrinsic to trade rules.

[16] The question whether the effects of specific national rules do in fact remain within that limit is a question of fact to be determined by the national court.

[17] The reply to the first question must therefore be that Article 30 of the Treaty must be interpreted as meaning that the prohibition which it lays down does not apply to national rules prohibiting retailers from opening their premises on Sunday where the restrictive effects on Community trade which may result therefrom do not exceed the effects intrinsic to rules of that kind.

■ **QUESTION**

Why does the Court choose to refer to Directive 70/50 but not to *Dassonville* (Case 8/74)?

NOTE: This ruling created confusion at national level, where different English and Welsh courts adopted different views of the compatibility of the Sunday trading laws with the Treaty. (See A. Arnull (1991) 16 EL Rev 112.)

In May 1991, a further preliminary reference was made by the House of Lords. This was motivated in part by the Court of Justice's rulings of February 1991 in *Marchandise* (Case C-332/89) [1991] ECR I-1027 and *UDS* v *Conforama* (Case C-312/89) [1991] ECR I-997. These cases, though factually comparable to *Torfaen*, had revealed the Court of Justice much readier explicitly to rule national measures compatible with the Treaty. The second reference yielded a much clearer response from the Court of Justice in December 1992:

***Stoke-on-Trent and Norwich City Councils* v *B&Q* (Case C-169/91)**

[1992] ECR I-6457, Court of Justice of the European Communities

[15] Appraising the proportionality of national rules which pursue a legitimate aim under Community law involves weighing the national interest in attaining that aim against the Community interest in ensuring the free movement of goods. In that regard, in order to verify that the restrictive effects on intra-Community trade of the rules at issue do not exceed what is necessary to achieve the aim in view, it must be considered whether those effects are direct, indirect or purely speculative and whether those effects do not impede the marketing of imported products more than the marketing of national products.

[16] It was on the basis of those considerations that in its judgments in the *Conforama and Marchandise* cases the court ruled that the restrictive effects on trade of national rules prohibiting the employment of workers on Sundays in certain retailing activities were not excessive in relation to the aim pursued. For the same reasons, the court must make the same finding with regard to national rules prohibiting shops from opening on Sundays.

[17] It must therefore be stated in reply to the first question that Article 30 of the Treaty is to be interpreted as meaning that the prohibition which it lays down does not apply to national legislation prohibiting retailers from opening their premises on Sundays.

NOTE: For comment, see R. Rawlings, (1993) 20 *Journal of Law and Society* 309; A. Arnull, (1993) 18 EL Rev 314; and more generally on the strategies involved in this litigation see H. Micklitz, *The Politics of Judicial Co-Operation in the EU* (Cambridge: CUP, 2005), Ch. 2. Eventually, the law in England and Wales was amended, and made more coherent, by the Sunday Trading Act 1994.

■ QUESTION

What do these rulings tell you about the division of function between national and EU courts under Article 267?

NOTE: Lurking beneath this litigation was the point made in para 11 of the ruling in Case 145/88 (p. 330). The Sunday trading rules did not put imported goods at a disadvantage in comparison with domestic goods. All goods were equally affected. Many commentators took the view that free movement law had been pushed beyond its proper scope by the ingenuity of the Sunday traders' lawyers. The search was on for a test which would allow a reorientation towards rules which partitioned national markets rather than general trading rules unconnected with the process of market integration.

B: The ruling in *Keck and Mithouard*

In the period between the two Sunday trading rulings there had already been indications that the Court was ready to rethink its approach in this area. In *Quietlynn Ltd* v *Southend on Sea BC* (Case C-23/89) [1990] ECR I-3059 and in *Sheptonhurst* v *Newham BC* (Case C-350/89) [1991] ECR I-2387, the Court found no effect on inter-State trade adequate to permit the invocation of EU law. Accordingly, questions of justification of national rules simply did not arise, in contrast to the Sunday trading cases. The Court had the chance to provide a bolder formula in *Keck and Mithouard*.

***Bernard Keck and Daniel Mithouard* (Cases C-267 and C-268/91)**

[1993] ECR I-6097, Court of Justice of the European Communities

M.M. Keck and Mithouard had resold goods at a loss. This violated a French law forbidding such practices. Keck and Mithouard submitted that the law restricted the volume of sales of imported goods by depriving them of a method of sales promotion and that it was therefore incompatible with Article 30 of the Treaty (now Article 34 TFEU). Any restrictive effect on trade plainly affected *all* goods, not just imports. *Note* that there is more than one version of this judgment in circulation. This is the official version extracted from the *European Court Reports* and it has some slight textual differences from the version used in the 6th and earlier editions of this book:

[14] In view of the increasing tendency of traders to invoke Article 30 of the Treaty as a means of challenging any rules whose effect is to limit their commercial freedom even where such rules are not aimed at products from other Member States, the Court considers it necessary to re-examine and clarify its case-law on this matter.

[15] It is established by the case-law beginning with 'Cassis de Dijon' (Case 120/78 *Rewe-Zentral* v *Bundesmonopolverwaltung für Branntwein* [1979] ECR 649) that, in the absence of harmonization of legislation, obstacles to free movement of goods which are the consequence of applying, to goods coming from other Member States where they are lawfully manufactured and marketed, rules that lay down requirements to be met by such goods (such as those relating to designation, form, size, weight, composition, presentation, labelling, packaging) constitute measures of equivalent effect prohibited by Article 30. This is so even if those rules apply without distinction to all products unless their application can be justified by a public-interest objective taking precedence over the free movement of goods.

[16] By contrast, contrary to what has previously been decided, the application to products from other Member States of national provisions restricting or prohibiting certain selling arrangements is not such as to hinder directly or indirectly, actually or potentially, trade between Member States within the meaning of the *Dassonville* judgment (Case 8/74 [1974] ECR 837), so long as those provisions apply to all relevant traders operating within the national territory and so long as they affect in the same manner, in law and in fact, the marketing of domestic products and of those from other Member States.

[17] Provided that those conditions are fulfilled, the application of such rules to the sale of products from another Member State meeting the requirements laid down by that State is not by nature such as to prevent their access to the market or to impede access any more than it impedes the access of domestic products. Such rules therefore fall outside the scope of Article 30 of the Treaty.

[18] Accordingly, the reply to be given to the national court is that Article 30 of the EEC Treaty is to be interpreted as not applying to legislation of a Member State imposing a general prohibition on resale at a loss.

■ QUESTION

In 1989, E. White proposed that Article 30, now Article 34, should be interpreted as catching 'the application by a Member State to products legally produced and marketed in another Member State of its national rules relating to the characteristics required of such products on its territory (which therefore prevents this product from benefitting in the importing Member State from the advantages arising out of its production in the different legal and economic environment prevailing in the other Member State' ('In Search of the Limits to Article 30 of the EEC Treaty' (1989) 26 CML Rev 235). Does this proposal conform to the Court's policy in Keck?

NOTE: The Commission declared that in *Keck* 'the Court has completed its case law' ([1993] OJ C353/6). It was plain that in future traders would find it more difficult to employ the Treaty provisions governing free movement of goods to require Member States to justify rules which inhibit commercial freedom. This is well illustrated by the next case, decided by the Court less than seven months after *Keck*, in which a challenge to Dutch rules relating to the compulsory closing of shops at stipulated times was curtly rejected.

Tankstation 't Heukste vof and J.B.E. Boermans (Cases C-401 and C-402/92)

[1994] ECR I-2199, Court of Justice of the European Communities

[12] . . . the application to products from other Member States of national provisions restricting or prohibiting certain selling arrangements is not such as to hinder, directly or indirectly, actually or potentially, trade between Member States within the meaning of the *Dassonville* judgment . . . provided that those provisions apply to all relevant traders operating within the national territory and provided that they affect in the same manner, in law and in fact, the marketing of domestic products and of those from other Member States. Where those conditions are fulfilled, the application of such rules to the sale of products from another Member State meeting the requirements laid down by that State is not by nature such as to prevent their access to the market or to impede access any more than it impedes the access of domestic products. Such rules therefore fall outside the scope of Article 30 of the Treaty (see the judgment in Joined Cases C-267/91 and C-268/91 *Keck and Mithouard* [1993] ECR I-6097, paragraphs 16 and 17).

[13] The conditions laid down in the judgment last cited are fulfilled in the case of rules such as those at issue in the main proceedings.

[14] The rules in question relate to the times and places at which the goods in question may be sold to consumers. However, they apply to all relevant traders without distinguishing between the origin of the products in question and do not affect the marketing of products from other Member States in a manner different from that in which they affect domestic products.

[15] Consequently, the reply to be given to the Gerechtshof is that Article 30 of the Treaty is to be interpreted as not applying to national rules concerning the closing of shops which apply to all traders operating within the national territory and which affect in the same manner, in law and in fact, the marketing of domestic products and of products from other Member States.

NOTE: It was suggested (at p. 323) that the '*Cassis de Dijon*' case law represents the Court's strategy for judging the permissibility of regulatory diversity between the States in an integrating market; *Keck* reflects the Court's concern to establish where regulatory diversity does not affect the integrative process for the purposes of application of Article 34 TFEU and where, accordingly, States remain free to make their own regulatory choices unhindered by the demands of EU trade law. The key jurisdictional point is that where a national measure is excluded from the reach of Article 34 TFEU by virtue of the reasoning found in *Keck* then (in contrast to the 'Sunday Trading' cases) the national regulator does not even fall under an obligation to justify the measure according to standards recognized by the Court. But although *Keck* is, as a general proposition, designed to curtail the reach of the law of the free movement of goods and thereby to immunize certain areas of local market regulation from the threat of challenge based on Article 34 TFEU, the detailed impact of the ruling remains far from settled – not least because ingenious litigants have continued to fight battles over just how much power EU law confers on traders to challenge obstructive national rules of market regulation.

It is instructive to consider cases decided prior to *Keck* in order to determine whether it would now be considered that a sufficient adverse effect on imported products had been shown such as to permit the invocation of Article 34. Consider from this perspective the extracts in *Commission* v *UK* (Case 207/83) at p. 292; *Tasca* (Case 65/75) and *Van Tiggele* (Case 82/77) at p. 295.

Ministère Public v *Buet* (Case 382/87)

[1989] ECR 1235, Court of Justice of the European Communities

A trader was convicted under French law forbidding canvassing at private dwellings for the purpose of selling educational material. It was submitted that the law was incompatible with Article 30 of the EC Treaty (now Article 34 TFEU). The Court found an obstacle to the free movement of goods:

[7] As the Court held in its judgment of 15 December 1982 in Case 286/81 Oosthoek [1982] ECR 4575, the possibility cannot be ruled out that to compel a trader either to adopt advertising or sales promotion schemes which differ from one Member State to another or to discontinue a scheme which he considers to

be particularly effective may constitute an obstacle to imports even if the legislation in question applies to domestic and imported products without distinction.

[8] That finding applies a fortiori when the rules in question deprive the trader concerned of the possibility of using not a means of advertising but a method of marketing whereby he realizes almost all his sales.

[9] Application of a prohibition on canvassing in order to sell foreign-language teaching material from another Member State must therefore be regarded as constituting an obstacle to imports.

The Court then concluded that the French rule was compatible with the Treaty, notwithstanding the obstacle to trade, in view of its contribution to the protection of the consumer.

■ QUESTION

Would the ruling in *Keck* make any difference in such circumstances? Should it?

C: The application of Article 34 TFEU to restrictions on advertising

Cases involving restrictions on marketing methods are among the sternest challenges to the Court's attempt in *Keck* to realign its case law in order to locate a coherent basis for determining the outer limit of Article 34. The next case features distinct approaches taken by the Court and its Advocate-General when confronted by this issue.

***Société d'Importation Edouard Leclerc-Siplec* v *TF1 Publicité SA and M6 Publicité SA* (Case C-412/93)**

[1995] ECR I-179, Court of Justice of the European Communities

TF1 and M6 refused to broadcast an advertisement concerning distribution of fuel in Leclerc supermarkets. The refusal was based on French rules excluding the distribution sector from televised advertising. It was submitted that the rules impeded sales opportunities for imported fuel and that they were therefore susceptible to challenge under Article 30 of the Treaty (now Article 34 TFEU). The *Tribunal de Commerce de Paris* made a preliminary reference to the Court in search of an authoritative interpretation.

[19] A law or regulation such as that at issue in the main proceedings, which prohibits televised advertising in the distribution sector, is not designed to regulate trade in goods between Member States. Moreover, such a prohibition does not prevent distributors from using other forms of advertising.

[20] Such a prohibition may, admittedly, restrict the volume of sales, and hence the volume of sales of products from other Member States, in so far as it deprives distributors of a particular form of advertising their goods. But the question remains whether such a possibility is sufficient to characterise the prohibition in question as a measure having equivalent effect to a quantitative restriction on imports within the meaning of Article 30 of the Treaty.

[21] The application to products from other Member States of national provisions restricting or prohibiting certain selling arrangements it not such as to hinder directly or indirectly, actually or potentially, trade between Member States within the meaning of the *Dassonville* judgment, cited above, so long as those provisions apply to all relevant traders operating within the national territory and so long as they affect in the same manner, in law and in fact, the marketing of domestic products and of those from other Member States. Provided that those conditions are fulfilled, the application of such rules to the sale of products from another Member State meeting the requirements laid down by that State is not by nature such as to prevent their access to the market or to impede access any more than it impedes the access of domestic products. Such rules therefore fall outside the scope of Article 30 of the Treaty (see the judgment in Joined Cases C-267/91 and 268/91 *Keck*

and Mithouard [1993] ECR I-6097, paragraphs 16 and 17, and Case C-292/92 *Hünermund and Others* [1993] ECR I-6787, paragraph 21).

[22] A provision such as that at issue in the main proceedings concerns selling arrangements since it prohibits a particular form of promotion (televised advertising) of a particular method of marketing products (distribution).

[23] Furthermore, those provisions, which apply regardless of the type of product to all traders in the distribution sector, even if they are both producers and distributors, affect the marketing of products from other Member States and that of domestic products in the same manner.

[24] The reply should accordingly be that on a proper construction Article 30 of the Treaty does not apply where a Member State, by statute or by regulation, prohibits the broadcasting of televised advertisements for the distribution sector.

In his Opinion in the case Advocate-General Jacobs embarked on a careful examination of *Keck*. Although his views were not reflected in the Court's ruling, they deserve attention for the light they shed on some of the complexities generated by the Court's refinement of the law in *Keck*. Advocate-General Jacobs stated that he found the Court's reasoning in *Keck* unsatisfactory, although he agreed with the result. He continued (remember that Article 30, to which he refers, was re-numbered Article 28 by the Amsterdam Treaty and is now, post-Lisbon, Article 34 TFEU):

[41] The question then is what test should be applied in order to determine whether a measure falls within the scope of Article 30. There is one guiding principle which seems to provide an appropriate test: that principle is that all undertakings which engage in a legitimate economic activity in a Member State should have unfettered access to the whole of the Community market, unless there is a valid reason for denying them full access to a part of that market. In spite of occasional inconsistencies in the reasoning of certain judgments, that seems to be the underlying principle which has inspired the Court's approach from *Dassonville* through 'Cassis de Dijon' to *Keck*. Virtually all of the cases are, in their result, consistent with the principle, even though some of them appear to be based on different reasoning.

[42] If the principle is that all undertakings should have unfettered access to the whole of the Community market, then the appropriate test in my view is whether there is a substantial restriction on that access. That would of course amount to introducing a *de minimis* test into Article 30. Once it is recognised that there is a need to limit the scope of Article 30 in order to prevent excessive interference in the regulatory powers of the Member States, a test based on the extent to which a measure hinders trade between Member States by restricting market access seems the most obvious solution. Indeed it is perhaps surprising that, in view of the avowed aim of preventing excessive recourse to Article 30, the Court did not opt for such a solution in *Keck*. The reason may be that the Court was concerned lest a *de minimis* test, if applied to all measures affecting trade in goods, might induce national courts, who have primary responsibility for applying Article 30, to exclude too many measures from the scope of the prohibition laid down by that provision. Caution must therefore be exercised and if a *de minimis* test is to be introduced it will be necessary to define carefully the circumstances in which it should apply.

[43] Clearly it would not be appropriate to apply a *de minimis* test to measures which overtly discriminate against goods from other Member States. Such measures are prohibited by Article 30 (unless justified under Article 36) even if their effect on inter-State trade is slight: there is a per se prohibition of overtly discriminatory measures.

[44] Only in relation to measures which are applicable without distinction to domestic goods and goods from other Member States would it be necessary to introduce a requirement that the restriction, actual or potential, on access to the market must be substantial. The impact on access to the market of measures applicable without distinction may vary greatly, depending on the nature of the measure in issue. Where such a measure prohibits the sale of goods lawfully placed on the market in another Member State (as in 'Cassis de Dijon'), it may be presumed to have a substantial impact on access to the market, since the goods are either denied access altogether or can gain access only after being modified in some way; the need to modify goods is itself a substantial barrier to market access.

> [45] Where, on the other hand, a measure applicable without distinction simply restricts certain selling arrangements, by stipulating when, where, how, by whom or at what price goods may be sold, its impact will depend on a number of factors, such as whether it applies to certain goods (as in *Blesgen, Buet* or *Quietlynn*), or to most goods (as in *Torfaen*), or to all goods (as in *Keck*), on the extent to which other selling arrangements remain available, and on whether the effect of the measure is direct or indirect, immediate or remote, or purely speculative[36] and uncertain.[37] Accordingly, the magnitude of the barrier to market access may vary enormously: it may range from the insignificant to a quasi-prohibition. Clearly, this is where a *de minimis* test could perform a useful function. The distinction recognised in *Keck* between a prohibition of the kind in issue in 'Cassis de Dijon' and a mere restriction on certain selling arrangements is therefore valuable: the former inevitably creates a substantial barrier to trade between Member States, whereas the latter may create such a barrier. But it cannot be maintained that the latter type of measure is not capable of hindering trade contrary to Article 30 in the absence of discrimination. It should therefore be recognised that such measures, unless overtly discriminatory, are not automatically caught by Article 30, as are measures of the type at issue in 'Cassis de Dijon', but may be caught if the restriction which they cause on access to the market is substantial.

Advocate-General Jacobs concluded that 'Article 30 [now 34] should be regarded as applying to non-discriminatory measures which are liable substantially to restrict access to the market'. Applying this test to the French measures, he continued:

> [55] . . . The restriction affects only one form of advertising, although the most effective as far as mass consumer goods are concerned; and advertisement of the goods themselves is not affected other than indirectly. As in the case of legislation restricting the opening hours of shops . . . the measure may result in a slight reduction in the total volume of sales of goods, including imports. But it cannot be said to have a substantial impact on access to the market. It therefore falls in my view outside the scope of Article 30.

■ QUESTION

Is the approach advocated by Advocate-General Jacobs likely to breed consistency in the application of (what is now) Article 34 TFEU by national courts? Is it more or less likely to achieve this objective than the Court's own test laid down in *Keck* and repeated in *Société d'Importation Edouard Leclerc-Siplec* v *TF1 Publicité SA and M6 Publicité SA* (Case C-412/93)?

NOTE: The Court continues to be fed a steady diet of cases involving challenge to national rules which limit commercial freedom. *Keck* notwithstanding, there remains scope for argument about the nature of the impediment to market access that must be shown for Article 34 TFEU to come into play where national rules deprive traders of the use of particular practices or require them to adopt practices which they do not favour.

Konsumentombudsmannen v *De Agostini Forlag AB and TV-Shop i Sverige AB* (Joined Cases C-34/95, C-35/95, and C-36/95)

[1997] ECR I-3843, Court of Justice of the European Communities

The background to this case is provided by satellite broadcasting of television programmes, an activity particularly apt for cross-border commerce. The questions referred were prompted by action taken by the Swedish consumer *ombud* to restrain forms of television advertising *inter alia* on the ground that contrary to Swedish law they were targeted at children less than 12 years of age. The Court ruled that Directive 89/552 harmonizing laws governing television broadcasting did not preclude a Member State from taking action to protect consumers in respect of advertisements broadcast from another Member State, provided that this did not prevent retransmission as such. As regards Article 30 of the Treaty (now Article 34 TFEU):

---

36 As in paragraph 15 of the judgment in *Stoke-on-Trent Council* v *B&Q* . . . [p. 331].

37 As in Case C-69/88 Krantz [1990] ECR I-583, paragraph 11 of the judgment.

[39] In paragraph 22 of its judgment in *Leclerc-Siplec*, cited above [Case C-412/93], the Court held that legislation which prohibits television advertising in a particular sector concerns selling arrangements for products belonging to that sector in that it prohibits a particular form of promotion of a particular method of marketing products.

[40] In Joined Cases C-267/91 and C-268/91 *Keck and Mithouard* [1993] ECR I-6097, at paragraph 16, the Court held that national measures restricting or prohibiting certain selling arrangements are not covered by Article 30 of the Treaty, so long as they apply to all traders operating within the national territory and so long as they affect in the same manner, in law and in fact, the marketing of domestic products and of those from other Member States.

[41] The first condition is clearly fulfilled in the cases before the national court.

[42] As regards the second condition, it cannot be excluded that an outright ban, applying in one Member State, of a type of promotion for a product which is lawfully sold there might have a greater impact on products from other Member States.

[43] Although the efficacy of the various types of promotion is a question of fact to be determined in principle by the referring court, it is to be noted that in its observations De Agostini stated that television advertising was the only effective form of promotion enabling it to penetrate the Swedish market since it had no other advertising methods for reaching children and their parents.

[44] Consequently, an outright ban on advertising aimed at children less than 12 years of age and of misleading advertising, as provided for by the Swedish legislation, is not covered by Article 30 of the Treaty, unless it is shown that the ban does not affect in the same way, in fact and in law, the marketing of national products and of products from other Member States.

[45] In the latter case, it is for the national court to determine whether the ban is necessary to satisfy overriding requirements of general public importance or one of the aims listed in Article 36 of the EC Treaty if it is proportionate to that purpose and if those aims or requirements could not have been attained or fulfilled by measures less restrictive of intra-Community trade.

NOTE: The Court proceeded to take a rather different line in response to questions about the impact of Article 59 of the Treaty (now Article 56 TFEU), which concerns the free movement of services (see p. 394).

■ QUESTION

Would a law forbidding retail outlets for widgets from being opened within 10 kilometres of each other be susceptible to challenge under EU law? What about a law forbidding advertising of widgets other than in retail outlets? Or a law forbidding advertising of widgets entirely?

NOTE: The subjection of rules affecting advertising strategies to Article 34 TFEU continues to pose stern tests for the law re-shaped by the Court in Keck. In the next case the Court shows itself receptive to the argument that the dynamic role of advertising in generating the re-structuring of markets should be taken into account in fixing the scope of Article 34.

Konsumentombudsmannen (KO) v *Gourmet International Products AB (GIP)* (Case C-405/98)

[2001] ECR I-1795, Court of Justice of the European Communities

Pursuant to Swedish public health policy, Gourmet International Products AB (hereinafter 'GIP') was restrained from placing advertisements for alcoholic beverages in magazines. It was accepted that the prohibition affected sales of alcoholic beverages there, including those imported from other Member States, since the specific purpose of the Swedish legislation was to reduce the consumption of alcohol.

But advertising was prohibited irrespective of the source of the products. Did this not bring the matter within the '*Keck* formula' – and outwith Article 28 EC, now Article

34 TFEU? In his Opinion Advocate-General Jacobs drew attention to the flaw in this analysis:

> A consumer who is unaware of alternatives to the products he or she is in the habit of purchasing is unlikely to go to any great lengths to discover whether such alternatives exist and is thus likely to continue to purchase the same products. The role of advertising is primordial in launching a new product or in penetrating a new market.

In its judgment the Court did not neglect the crucial point that an advertising ban tends to work to the benefit of the traders currently active in the market.

> [18] It should be pointed out that, according to paragraph 17 of its judgment in *Keck and Mithouard*, if national provisions restricting or prohibiting certain selling arrangements are to avoid being caught by Article 30 of the Treaty, they must not be of such a kind as to prevent access to the market by products from another Member State or to impede access any more than they impede the access of domestic products.
>
> [19] The Court has also held, in paragraph 42 of its judgment in Joined Cases C-34/95 to C-36/95 *De Agostini and TV-Shop* [1997] ECR I-3843, that it cannot be excluded that an outright prohibition, applying in one Member State, of a type of promotion for a product which is lawfully sold there might have a greater impact on products from other Member States.
>
> [20] It is apparent that a prohibition on advertising such as that at issue in the main proceedings not only prohibits a form of marketing a product but in reality prohibits producers and importers from directing any advertising messages at consumers, with a few insignificant exceptions.
>
> [21] Even without its being necessary to carry out a precise analysis of the facts characteristic of the Swedish situation, which it is for the national court to do, the Court is able to conclude that, in the case of products like alcoholic beverages, the consumption of which is linked to traditional social practices and to local habits and customs, a prohibition of all advertising directed at consumers in the form of advertisements in the press, on the radio and on television, the direct mailing of unsolicited material or the placing of posters on the public highway is liable to impede access to the market by products from other Member States more than it impedes access by domestic products, with which consumers are instantly more familiar.

This left only the question of justification. The rules would be permitted 'unless it is apparent that, in the circumstances of law and of fact which characterise the situation in the Member State concerned, the protection of public health against the harmful effects of alcohol can be ensured by measures having less effect on intra-Community trade'.

The Court also considered the matter from the standpoint of the law governing the free movement of services. It concluded that:

> [39] A measure such as the prohibition on advertising at issue in the proceedings before that court, even if it is non-discriminatory, has a particular effect on the cross-border supply of advertising space, given the international nature of the advertising market in the category of products to which the prohibition relates, and thereby constitutes a restriction on the freedom to provide services within the meaning of Article 59 of the Treaty [now Article 56 TFEU] (see, in that regard, *Alpine Investments*, cited above, paragraph 35).

Here too the case accordingly turned on the availability of justification. But, in determining whether Article 34 TFEU catches a national measure, each case must be examined carefully on its facts. In *Herbert Karner GmbH* v *Troostwijk GmbH* (Case C-71/02 [2004] ECR I-3025) the Court concluded that Austrian restrictions on methods of advertising would likely cause a diminution in the volume of sales of goods but that there was no evidence that this would be felt particularly severely by imports or importers. The Court explained that whereas in *Konsumentombudsmannen* v *Gourmet International Products* the total nature of the Swedish ban had been enough to persuade it that trade in imports would be peculiarly disadvantaged, no such factual inequality flowed from the application of the Austrian rule. This had the key jurisdictional consequence that Austria was not required to justify the rule according to standards recognized by EU trade law (though the Court, somewhat illogically, did touch on questions of justification in its ruling; see J. Stuyck, 'Annotation' (2004) 41 CML Rev 1683). In similar vein in Case C-441/04 *A-Punkt Schmuckhandels GmbH* v *Claudia Schmidt* [2006] ECR I-2093 the Court concluded that the information available 'does not allow it to ascertain beyond doubt whether the prohibition on selling in private homes laid down in [an Austrian measure] affects the marketing of products from Member States other than Austria to a greater degree than it affects the marketing of products from that Member State'. It therefore left the matter to the national court which had made the preliminary reference – the assumption being, of course, that only if there *was* such a differential impact would Austria be called on to justify its regulatory choices.

By this time the reader would be forgiven for thinking that the Commission's claim in 1993 that in *Keck* 'the Court has completed its case law' (p. 332) is a joke in poor taste. And yet the cascade of subsequent case law is no surprise. What is at stake is fixing the limits of free movement law's incursion into local regulatory autonomy – put another way, how much power of review of national preferences does Article 34 TFEU hand to the EU's institutions, prompted by self-interested commercial operators? 'Internal discrimination' is not within the reach of Article 34 (*Nederlandse Bakkerij* v *Edah* (Cases 80 and 159/85) p. 329). Nor are rules that apply equally to all products in the sense intended by the *Keck and Mithouard* ruling. But where exactly to draw the line? The debate continues in the next extract.

Alfa Vita Vassilopoulos (formerly Trofo Super-Markets)
(Joined Cases C-158/04 & C-159/04)

Opinion of Advocate General Poiares Maduro, delivered on 30 March 2006

. . . although *Keck and Mithouard* was intended to limit the number of actions and to restrain the excesses which resulted from the application of the principle of free movement of goods, in the end it increases the number of questions about the precise scope of the principle. Yet is there cause to abandon this case-law? I do not think so. However, it is important to clarify it . . . (paras 34–35).

. . . the fundamental objective of the principle of free movement of goods is to ensure that producers are put in a position to benefit, in fact, from the right to carry out their activity at a cross-border level, while consumers are put in a position to access, in practice, products from other Member States in the same conditions as domestic products (para 39).

. . . the task of the Court is not to call into question as a matter of course Member States' economic policies. It is instead responsible for satisfying itself that those States do not adopt measures which, in actual fact, lead to *cross-border situations being treated less favourably than purely national situations* (para 41, emphasis in original).

The Advocate General concluded that the Court's approach focuses on identifying *discrimination against the exercise of freedom of movement* (para 46, emphasis in original). But in its judgment of 14 September 2006 the Court quickly found a barrier to inter-State trade and ignored the deeper questions about the structure of Article 34.

D: The application of Article 34 TFEU to restrictions on use

Litigation dealing with *restrictions on the use of products* offers an opportunity to elucidate the Court's view of the proper reach of Article 34 TFEU. So far the rulings delivered go some way to clarifying what is at stake but without being fully satisfying. Case C-110/05 *Commission* v *Italy* [2009] ECR I-519 was an infringement procedure (Article 258 TFEU: Chapter 4) against Italy for prohibiting the use of motorcycles with a trailer. The Commission took the view that this caused an unlawful barrier to trade in trailers designed to be towed by motorcycles. The *composition* of the product was not affected by the prohibition: the regularity of its use was. The Court's decision in February 2009 is cautious and narrow. It simply finds that the rule suppressed consumer demand for trailers in Italy and, by hindering their importation, fell within the scope of Article 28 EC, now Article 34 TFEU. The analysis goes no deeper and, in particular, even though the judgment reports several submissions made to the Court by the Commission and several Member States about the relevance of *Keck and Mithouard* the findings of the Court make no attempt at all to analyse the matter in the light of that landmark judgment. The Court spends rather longer dealing with the justification of the measure as a contribution to road safety (to which it is favourably disposed).

Aklagaren v *Mickelsson, Roos* (Case C-142/05)

[2009] ECR I-4273, Court of Justice of the European Communities

This is factually similar to *Commission* v *Italy*, the Italian trailers case. It concerns Swedish rules restricting the use of jet-skis on waterways that are not generally navigable. Once again, this is a rule which restricts the use of a product, not its composition. Is Article 30 EC, now Article 34 TFEU, applicable to such a national measure? The Court's answer is that such rules may fall within the scope of the Treaty, but a case-by-case analysis is required.

[26] Even if the national regulations at issue do not have the aim or effect of treating goods coming from other Member States less favourably, which is for the national court to ascertain, the restriction which they impose on the use of a product in the territory of a Member State may, depending on its scope, have a considerable influence on the behaviour of consumers, which may, in turn, affect the access of that product to the market of that Member State (see to that effect, *Commission* v *Italy*, [Case C-110/05], paragraph 56).

[27] Consumers, knowing that the use permitted by such regulations is very limited, have only a limited interest in buying that product (see to that effect, *Commission* v *Italy*, paragraph 57).

[28] In that regard, where the national regulations for the designation of navigable waters and waterways have the effect of preventing users of personal watercraft from using them for the specific and inherent purposes for which they were intended or of greatly restricting their use, which is for the national court to ascertain, such regulations have the effect of hindering the access to the domestic market in question for those goods and therefore constitute, save where there is a justification pursuant to Article 30 EC or there are overriding public interest requirements, measures having equivalent effect to quantitative restrictions on imports prohibited by Article 28 EC.

NOTE: The Court then accepted the relevance of environmental concerns arising in the particular geographical circumstances of the regulating State. The Court leaves Sweden some leeway in choosing how to protect its waterways from aggressive users of jet-skis, but it does not in principle allow the immunization of such regulatory choices from supervision pursuant to Article 28 EC, now Article 34 TFEU. But detailed analysis of *Keck and Mithouard* is missing.

■ QUESTIONS

1. Not all such restrictions on use of products will be caught. The limit of Article 34 TFEU is fixed with reference to whether an influence on consumer behaviour is *considerable* (para 26 of Case C-142/05). How can this be measured? How close is the Court's test to the approach proposed by Advocate General Jacobs in looking for measures which 'are liable substantially to restrict access to the market' (*Société d'Importation Edouard Leclerc-Siplec v TF1 Publicité SA and M6 Publicité SA* (Case C-412/93), p. 334)?
2. If rules preventing resale of products at a loss (the factual issue in Keck) exert a considerable influence on consumer behaviour, is it now correct to conclude that they fall within Article 34 TFEU?
3. In *R (Countryside Alliance)* v *AG* [2008] 2 All ER 95 the House of Lords was asked to decide whether banning (some aspects of) hunting in England and Wales affects the importation of horses from (mainly) Ireland contrary to EU law. Horses are not

banned in the UK, but their use is restricted. The decision of the House of Lords looks forward optimistically to clarification from the 'restrictions on use' cases which were then pending in Luxembourg, and are now decided, but concludes that even if the ban is a barrier to trade within the meaning of (what is now) Article 34 TFEU, it is justified as an expression of local political and moral choice. Is the hunting ban a barrier to trade within the scope of Article 34 TFEU? Should it be?

NOTE: The underlying risk is that the readier the Court is to find the necessary effect on trade apt to bring Article 34 into play, the shallower the reservoir of national regulatory autonomy – and the greater the potential damage to the legitimacy of EU trade law. However, identifying this as the driving tension in the case law does not help to provide a concrete answer to the question as to just where the outer limits of Article 34 TFEU should lie. The Court's case law on 'restrictions on use' raises more questions than it answers. In its control of national regulatory choices plainly EU free movement law reaches beyond a test aimed purely at combating discrimination – but precisely how much further remains elusive.

FURTHER READING

Davies, G., 'Understanding Market Access: Exploring the Economic Rationality of Different Conceptions of Free Movement Law' (2010) 11 *German Law Journal* 671 (www.germanlawjournal.com/).

Enchelmaier, S., 'Moped Trailers, Mickelson & Roos, Gysbrechts: the ECJ's Case Law on Goods Keeps On Moving' (2010) 29 YEL 190.

Gormley, L., Nihoul, P., and Van Nieuwenhuyze, E. (eds), 'What Standard After *Keck*? Free Movement Provisions and National Rules Affecting Consumer Usage or Trade Access', Special Issue of European Journal of Consumer Law 2012/2.

Horsley, T., 'Unearthing Buried Treasure: Article 34 TFEU and the Exclusionary Rules' (2012) 37 EL Rev 734.

Lianos, I., 'In memoriam *Keck*? The Reformation of the EU Law on the Free Movement of Goods' (2015) 40 ELRev 225.

Oliver, P., and Enchelmaier, S., 'Free Movement of Goods: Recent Developments in the Case Law' (2007) 44 CML Rev 649.

Snell, J., 'The Notion of Market Access: a Concept or a Slogan?' (2010) 47 CML Rev 437.

■ QUESTIONS

1. Member State X introduces rules to restrict the use of powerful vehicles that are (according to defined criteria) inefficient in their use of energy. Such vehicles must not be driven on motorways and they may not be driven at all between 6 a.m. and 10 a.m. or 3 p.m. and 7 p.m. These measures make such vehicles less attractive to consumers than other vehicles but the authorities in X insist that the rule applies equally to all products and all producers and that therefore it is not a trade barrier within the meaning of Article 34 TFEU. Zero Cars, based in Member State Y, argues that the measures have the effect of fragmenting the market of the EU along national lines, because the restrictions on use imposed by X make it much less attractive to market such vehicles in X than elsewhere because consumer demand in X is so low. Zero therefore believes that X's rules should be open to challenge under Article 34 TFEU. Does Article 34 TFEU apply in such circumstances?
2. Two decades ago M. Ross identified 'patchwork pragmatism' and an avoidance of long-term commitment to principle in the Court's recent approach in this area ((1995) 20 EL Rev 507, 512). He found this 'disappointing, since the central question to be addressed is simple enough to formulate: what does the notion of a single market require and permit?' Has the case law become more illuminating subsequently? What is the scope for permitting diverse regulatory choices at national level within an internal market as defined in Article 26 TFEU?

NOTE: However the *Keck* ruling may be shaped and re-shaped in future as a method for sheltering national regulatory choices from challenge based on Article 34, it is appropriate to conclude by emphasizing that the Court has not lost its determination to use the '*Cassis de Dijon*' principle to root out measures that segregate national markets and deny consumers choice between goods of different origins.

Verein gegen Unwesen in Handel und Gewerbe Köln v *Mars GmbH* (Case C-470/93)

[1995] ECR I-1923, Court of Justice of the European Communities

Mars ice creams were presented in wrappers marked '10%'. This was part of a Europe-wide publicity campaign during which the quantity of the product was increased by 10 per cent. Proceedings were initiated before a German court to restrain this practice as incompatible with German rules forbidding unfair competition. The question of the impact of Article 30 of the Treaty (now Article 34 TFEU) on such intervention in the market was referred to the Court of Justice. The Court observed:

[11] The first question to be examined is whether a prohibition of the marketing of goods bearing on their packaging a publicity marking such as that in question in the main proceedings constitutes a measure having an effect equivalent to a quantitative restriction within the meaning of Article 30 [now 34] of the Treaty.

[12] According to the case-law of the Court, Article 30 is designed to prohibit any trading rules of Member States which are capable of hindering, directly or indirectly, actually or potentially, intra-Community trade (see the judgment in Case 8/74 *Procureur du Roi* v *Dassonville* [1974] ECR 837, paragraph 5). The Court has held that, in the absence of harmonisation of legislation, obstacles to the free movement of goods that are the consequence of applying, to goods coming from other Member States where they are lawfully manufactured and marketed, rules that lay down requirements to be met by such goods, such as those relating, for example, to their presentation, labelling and packaging, are prohibited by Article 30, even if those rules apply without distinction to national products and to imported products (judgment in Joined Cases C-267/91 and C-268/91 *Keck and Mithouard* [1993] ECR I-6097, paragraph 15).

[13] Although it applies to all products without distinction, a prohibition such as that in question in the main proceedings, which relates to the marketing in a Member State of products bearing the same publicity markings as those lawfully used in other Member States, is by nature such to hinder intra-Community trade. It may compel the importer to adjust the presentation of his products according to the place where they are to be marketed and consequently to incur additional packaging and advertising costs.

[14] Such a prohibition therefore falls within the scope of Article 30 of the Treaty.

Critical to the *Keck* formula is the point that once a law is shown to apply equally in law and in fact, the State is *not* required to justify its law against standards recognized by EU law. By contrast, in this case, the threshold for invocation of Article 28, now 34, was crossed and therefore the State *was* required to show justification for its rules. It was unable to do this to the Court's satisfaction:

THE CONSUMER'S EXPECTATION THAT THE PRICE PREVIOUSLY CHARGED IS BEING MAINTAINED

[17] It is argued that the '10%' marking may lead the consumer to think that the 'new' product is being offered at a price identical to that at which the 'old' product was sold.

[18] As the Advocate-General points out in Paragraphs 39 to 42 of his Opinion, on the assumption that the consumer expects the price to remain the same, the referring court considers that the consumer could be the victim of deception within the meaning of Paragraph 3 of the UWG and that if the price did not increase the offer would meet the consumer's expectation but then a question would arise concerning the application of Paragraph 15 of the GWB, which prohibits manufacturers from imposing prices on retailers.

[19] As regards the first possibility, it must be observed first of all that Mars has not actually profited from the promotional campaign in order to increase its sale prices and that there is no evidence that retailers have themselves increased their prices. In any case, the mere possibility that importers and retailers might increase the price of the goods and that consequently consumers may be deceived is not sufficient to justify a general prohibition which may hinder intra-Community trade. That fact does not prevent the Member States from taking action, by appropriate measures, against duly proved actions which have the effect of misleading consumers.

[20] As regards the second possibility, the principle of freedom of retail trade in the matter of the fixing of prices, provided for by a system of national law, and intended in particular to guarantee the consumer genuine price competition, may not justify an obstacle to intra-Community trade such as that in question in the main proceedings. The constraint imposed on the retailer not to increase his prices is in fact favourable to the consumer. It does not arise from any contractual stipulation and has the effect of protecting the consumer from being misled in any way. It does not prevent retailers from continuing to charge different prices and applies only during the short duration of the publicity campaign in question.

THE VISUAL PRESENTATION OF THE '10%' MARKING AND ITS ALLEGED MISLEADING EFFECT

[21] It is accepted by all the parties that the '10%' marking is accurate in itself.

[22] However, it is contended that the measure in question is justified because a not insignificant number of consumers will be induced into believing, by the band bearing the '10%' marking, which occupies more than 10% of the total surface area of the wrapping, that the increase is larger than that represented.

[23] Such a justification cannot be accepted.

[24] Reasonably circumspect consumers are supposed to know that there is not necessarily a link between the size of publicity markings relating to an increase in a product's quantity and the size of that increase.

[25] The reply to the preliminary question must therefore be that Article 30 of the Treaty is to be interpreted as precluding a national measure from prohibiting the importation and marketing of a product lawfully marketed in another Member State, the quantity of which was increased during a short publicity campaign and the wrapping of which bears the marking '10%',

(a) on the ground that the presentation may induce the consumer into thinking that the price of the goods offered is the same as that at which the goods had previously been sold in their old presentation,
(b) on the ground that the new presentation gives the impression to the consumer that the volume and weight of the product have been considerably increased.

SECTION 3: JUSTIFYING INDISTINCTLY APPLICABLE RULES

The ruling in *Mars* provides a helpful bridge back to the mainstream of '*Cassis de Dijon*' case law. Whether or not a national measure constitutes a trade barrier that requires justification depends on an application of the formula crafted by the Court in *Keck*, which does not disturb the pure stream of *Cassis de Dijon* but rather siphons off the contaminations added by rulings such as the *Sunday Trading* pair (p. 330), in which the Court mistakenly called on the regulating State to justify rules which subjected imports to no greater interference than domestic production. Once it is established that a trade barrier requiring justification is at stake, the *Cassis* formula – the 'mandatory requirements' – applies undisturbed by *Keck*. In '*Cassis de Dijon*' (Case 120/78), the Court indicated that measures 'necessary to satisfy mandatory requirements' are capable of being held compatible with Article 34 despite their restrictive effect on trade. This allows justification in circumstances extending beyond those allowed by Article 36 TFEU, albeit only where there is no discrimination against imported goods. But most cases have been decided against the regulating State – that is, no adequate justification has been shown.

In *Cassis* itself the Court was clearly not satisfied that the German rules on alcohol strength were necessary to satisfy mandatory requirements. In *Commission* v *Germany* (Case 178/84) arguments of justification were similarly dismissed. In both cases no compelling reasons for impeding trade were shown to exist. And *Mars* found the Court in robust mood: 'Reasonably circumspect consumers are supposed to know that there is not necessarily a link between the size of publicity markings relating to an increase in a product's quantity and the size of that increase' (para 24 Case C-470/93). So Germany was 'over-regulating' its market, according to the standards recognized by the Court of Justice. Presumably the interests of German consumers who are *not* reasonably circumspect and who might be confused by the markings on the chocolate bars are judged less important in aggregate than the interests of consumers more generally in participating an integrated, more competitive European market.

The assumption, then, is that consumers benefit from increased cross-border trade in goods. Competition is stimulated; quality should rise while prices fall. This is basic economics – see Chapter 9. The Court's application of Article 34 TFEU in this manner generates deregulation within the territory of the Member State in question. However, the Court does not insist on a 'lowest common denominator' of regulatory protection within the EC (see S. Weatherill, *EU Consumer Law and Policy* (Cheltenham: Edward Elgar, 2013), Ch. 2). As is plain in cases concerning scientific uncertainty about the safety of products (e.g. Case 174/82, p. 313), the application of Article 34 TFEU is not inevitably destructive of national choices. Laws curtailing practices perceived to be 'unfair' were found compatible with Article 34 in *Diensten Groep* v *Beele* (Case 6/81) [1982] ECR 707 and *Buet* (Case 382/87, p. 333) and potentially compatible in *A-Punkt Schmuckhandels* (Case C-441/04, p. 339, see para 29 of the judgment); and see also, in connection with similar issues arising in the services sector under Article 56 TFEU, *Alpine Investments* (Case C-384/93, p. 393).

■ QUESTION

Space for local diversity was acknowledged by the Court in Case C-220/98 *Estee Lauder Cosmetics* [2000] ECR I-117, in which it ruled that in deciding whether a marketing practice forbidden under national rules is 'misleading' – and its suppression therefore potentially justified despite the trade-restrictive effect – 'it is necessary to take into account the presumed expectations of an average consumer who is reasonably well informed and reasonably observant and circumspect', but 'social, cultural or linguistic factors' may justify special local anxiety about particular practices tolerated elsewhere. What might these factors include?

The law of free movement increasingly impinges on matters of wider impact than market economics. The deceptively bland notion that trade restrictions may be 'justified' is capable of becoming very sensitive indeed as its scope becomes more visible.

***Fietje* (Case 27/80)**

[1980] ECR 3839, Court of Justice of the European Communities

> [10] Although the extension to imported products of an obligation to use a certain name on the label does not wholly preclude the importation into the Member State concerned of products originating in other Member States or in free circulation in those States it may none the less make their marketing more difficult, especially in the case of parallel imports. As the Netherlands Government itself admits in its observations, such an extension of that obligation is thus capable of impeding, at least indirectly, trade between Member States. It is therefore necessary to consider whether it may be justified on the ground of the public interest in consumer protection, which, according to the observations of the Netherlands Government and according to the 'Warenwet', underlies the rules in question.

[11] If national rules relating to a given product include the obligation to use a description that is sufficiently precise to inform the purchaser of the nature of the product and to enable it to be distinguished from products with which it might be confused, it may well be necessary, in order to give consumers effective protection, to extend this obligation to imported products also, even in such a way as to make necessary the alteration of the original labels of some of these products. At the level of Community legislation, this possibility is recognised in several directives on the approximation of the laws of the Member States relating to certain foodstuffs . . . [and] labelling . . .

[12] However, there is no longer any need for such protection if the details given on the original label of the imported product have as their content information on the nature of the product and that content includes at least the same information, and is just as capable of being understood by consumers in the importing State, as the description prescribed by the rules of that State. In the context of Article 177 of the EEC Treaty, the making of the findings of fact necessary in order to establish whether there is such equivalence is a matter for the national court.

NOTE: In *Piageme* v *BVBA Peeters* (Case C-369/89) [1991] ECR I-2971, the Court ruled that 'Article 30 of the EEC Treaty [now Article 34 TFEU] and Article 14 of Directive 79/112 preclude a national law from requiring the exclusive use of a specific language for the labelling of foodstuffs, without allowing for the possibility of using another language easily understood by purchasers or of ensuring that the purchaser is informed by other measures'. (See also Case C-85/94 between the same parties, [1995] ECR I-2955; and Case C-33/97 *Colim* v *Biggs* [1999] ECR I-3175; Case C-100/02 *Gerolsteiner Brunnen* v *Putsch* [2004] ECR I-691.) In November 1993, the Commission published a communication concerning the use of languages in the marketing of foodstuffs in the light of Case C-369/89 – COM (93) 532. This is a further example of the Commission's penchant for issuing interpretation of specific Court rulings (*cf* p. 303). The communication observes that 'The grounds of consumer protection which may justify the imposition of the official language(s) of a Member State no longer apply when foreign terms and expressions appearing on product labelling are easily understood and therefore fulfil their informative function.' (On review of rules introduced at EU level, rather than at national level, specifying use of particular languages against the requirements of the Treaty rules governing free movement of goods, see *Meyhui NV* v *Schott Zwiesel Glaswerke AG* (Case C-51/93) [1994] ECR I-3879.)

■ QUESTIONS

1. To what extent is the linguistic competence of consumers relevant to the compatibility of labelling requirements with EU law?
2. Instead of basing justification on the risk of consumer confusion, could one 're-package' and thereby strengthen the defence of a mandatory language rule as a contribution to protecting and promoting local culture? How strong is the argument that language protection is a cultural matter that should not be threatened by Article 34 TFEU?

Cf Article 167 TFEU, especially Article 167(1), (4) TFEU; on preserving and promoting multilingualism see Case C-222/07 *UTECA* [2009] ECR I-1407 and, more broadly, on measures to protect and promote pluralism and cultural diversity, Case C-250/06 *United Pan-Europe Communications Belgium SA* [2007] ECR I-11135; Case C-531/07 *Fachverband/ LIBRO* [2009] ECR I-3717. The EU Charter of Fundamental Rights (the binding status of which is examined in Chapter 2, p. 58) might offer a basis for arguing that the Lisbon Treaty has strengthened the hand of those seeking to justify obstacles to free movement. Article 22 of the Charter directs the Union to respect (inter alia) linguistic diversity and in combination with Article 4(2) TEU on respect for national identities it was cited by the Court in Case C-202/11 *Anton Las* v *PSA Antwerp* judgment of 16 April 2013, a free movement of workers case in which the Court assessed Flemish rules requiring use of Dutch in all employment contracts under an assumption that EU law leaves space for protection and preservation of official languages within a Member State. The same justificatory model, involving citation of both Article 22 Charter and Article 4(2) TEU, is found in Case C-391/09 *Runevič-Vardyn/Runiewicz-Wardyn* [2011] ECR I-3787, concerning Lithuanian restrictions on use of the Polish version of names (see Chapter 15, p. 431). It is, however, not clear that the Charter offers anything *really* new – the Charter was readily cited by the Court in free movement cases even before it was granted binding effect (e.g., Case C-244/06 *Dynamic Medien* [2008] ECR I-505) and, interesting though *Anton Las* and *Runevč-Vardyn/Runiewicz-Wardyn* are, the Court accepted over 25 years ago that in principle such language laws may be justified, e.g., Case C-379/87 *Anita Groener* [1989] ECR I-3967. Read P. Arzoz, 'Accommodating Linguistic Difference: Five Normative Models of Language Rights' (2010) 6 Euro Const Law Review 101; I. Urrutia, 'Approach of the European Court of Justice on the Accommodation of the European Language Diversity in the Internal Market: Overcoming Language Barriers or Fostering Linguistic Diversity?' 18 Columbia J Eur L 243 (2011–12); and, on *Anton Las*, a note by E. Cloots (2014) 51 CMLRev 623.

Imaginative litigants able to exploit (supreme and directly effective) EU law have pushed ever deeper in their quest to challenge national measures which obstruct trade but which exist for reasons which are often only tangentially associated with economic motivations. A powerful example of the range and complexity of issues involved in the Court's process of adjudication is provided by the next case.

***Vereinigte Familiapress Zeitungsverlags- und vertriebs GmbH* v *Heinrich Bauer Verlag* (Case C-368/95)**

[1997] ECR I-3689, Court of Justice of the European Communities

A German publisher fell foul of Austrian law when it tried to market a magazine containing a prize crossword. Such an inducement was lawful in Germany but prohibited in Austria as a means to protect small publishers from damaging competition from bigger rivals with deeper pockets. The rule obstructed cross-border trade but Austria sought to justify it as a means to sustain diversity in media ownership. The Court's ruling exposes the collision of values at stake.

[18] Maintenance of press diversity may constitute an overriding requirement justifying a restriction on free movement of goods. Such diversity helps to safeguard freedom of expression, as protected by Article 10 of the European Convention on Human Rights and Fundamental Freedoms, which is one of the fundamental rights guaranteed by the Community legal order (see Case C-353/89 *Commission* v *Netherlands* [1991] ECR I-4069, paragraph 30, and Case C-148/91 *Vereiniging Veronica Omroep Organisatie* v *Commissariaat voor de Media* [1993] ECR I-487, paragraph 10).

[19] However, the Court has also consistently held (*Cassis de Dijon*, cited above; Case C-238/89 *Pall* [1990] ECR I-4827, paragraph 12, and Case C-470/93 *Mars* [1995] ECR I-1923, paragraph 15) that the provisions of national law in question must be proportionate to the objective pursued and that objective must not be capable of being achieved by measures which are less restrictive of intra-Community trade.

[20] Admittedly, in Case C-275/92 *Schindler* [1994] ECR I-1039, paragraph 61, concerning freedom to provide services, the Court held that the special features of lotteries justify allowing national authorities a sufficient degree of latitude to determine what is required to protect the players and, more generally, in the light of the specific social and cultural features of each Member State, to maintain order in society, as regards the manner in which lotteries are operated, the size of the stakes and the allocation of the profits they yield. The Court therefore considered that it was for the national authorities to assess not only whether it is necessary to restrict the activities of lotteries but also whether they should be prohibited, provided that those restrictions are not discriminatory.

[21] Games such as those at issue in the main proceedings are not, however, comparable to the lotteries the features of which were considered in *Schindler*.

[22] The facts on which that judgment was based were concerned exclusively, as the Court expressly pointed out, with large-scale lotteries in respect of which the discretion enjoyed by national authorities was justified

because of the high risk of crime or fraud, given the amounts which could be staked and the winnings which could be held out to players (paragraphs 50, 51 and 60).

[23] By contrast, such concerns for the maintenance of order in society are not present in this case. The draws in question are organized on a small scale and less is at stake; they do not constitute an economic activity in their own right but are merely one aspect of the editorial content of a magazine; and under Austrian legislation, draws are prohibited only in the press.

[24] Furthermore, it is to be noted that where a Member State relies on overriding requirements to justify rules which are likely to obstruct the exercise of free movement of goods, such justification must also be interpreted in the light of the general principles of law and in particular of fundamental rights (see Case C-260/89 *ERT* [1991] ECR I-2925, paragraph 43).

[25] Those fundamental rights include freedom of expression, as enshrined in Article 10 of the European Convention for the Protection of Human Rights and Fundamental Freedoms (*ERT*, paragraph 44).

[26] A prohibition on selling publications which offer the chance to take part in prize games competitions may detract from freedom of expression. Article 10 of the European Convention for the Protection of Human Rights and Fundamental Freedoms does, however, permit derogations from that freedom for the purposes of maintaining press diversity, in so far as they are prescribed by law and are necessary in a democratic society (see the judgment of the European Court of Human Rights of 24 November 1993 in *Informationsverein Lentia and Others* v *Austria* Series A No 276).

[27] In the light of the considerations set out in paragraphs 19 to 26 of this judgment, it must therefore be determined whether a national prohibition such as that in issue in the main proceedings is proportionate to the aim of maintaining press diversity and whether that objective might not be attained by measures less restrictive of both intra-Community trade and freedom of expression.

[28] To that end, it should be determined, first, whether newspapers which offer the chance of winning a prize in games, puzzles or competitions are in competition with those small press publishers who are deemed to be unable to offer comparable prizes and whom the contested legislation is intended to protect and, second, whether such a prospect of winning constitutes an incentive to purchase capable of bringing about a shift in demand.

[29] It is for the national court to determine whether those conditions are satisfied on the basis of a study of the Austrian press market.

[30] In carrying out that study, it will have to define the market for the product in question and to have regard to the market shares of individual publishers or press groups and the trend thereof.

[31] Moreover, the national court will also have to assess the extent to which, from the consumer's standpoint, the product concerned can be replaced by papers which do not offer prizes, taking into account all the circumstances which may influence the decision to purchase, such as the presence of advertising on the title page referring to the chance of winning a prize, the likelihood of winning, the value of the prize or the extent to which winning depends on a test calling for a measure of ingenuity, skill or knowledge.

[32] The Belgian and Netherlands Governments consider that the Austrian legislature could have adopted measures less restrictive of free movement of goods than an outright prohibition on the distribution of newspapers which afford the chance of winning a prize, such as blacking out or removing the page on which the prize competition appears in copies intended for Austria or a statement that readers in Austria do not qualify for the chance to win a prize.

[33] The documents before the Court suggest that the prohibition in question would not constitute a barrier to the marketing of newspapers where one of the above measures had been taken. If the national court were nevertheless to find that this was the case, the prohibition would be disproportionate.

[34] In the light of the foregoing considerations, the answer to be given to the national court's question must be that Article 30 of the EC Treaty is to be interpreted as not precluding application of legislation of a Member State the effect of which is to prohibit the distribution on its territory by an undertaking established in another Member State of a periodical produced in that latter State containing prize puzzles or competitions which are lawfully organized in that State, provided that that prohibition is proportionate to maintenance of press diversity and that that objective cannot be achieved by less restrictive means. This assumes, *inter alia*, that the

newspapers offering the chance of winning a prize in games, puzzles or competitions are in competition with small newspaper publishers who are deemed to be unable to offer comparable prizes and the prospect of winning is liable to bring about a shift in demand. Furthermore, the national prohibition must not constitute an obstacle to the marketing of newspapers which, albeit containing prize games, puzzles or competitions, do not give readers residing in the Member State concerned the opportunity to win a prize. It is for the national court to determine whether those conditions are satisfied on the basis of a study of the national press market concerned.

The deployment of the language of fundamental rights in the law of free movement is highly significant in showing the permeation of trade law by wider values. But notice that *both* parties in this case are able to play the fundamental rights card. How would you, as a national judge, decide the case in the light of the Court's ruling?

Eugen Schmidberger, Internationale Transporte und Planzüge v *Austria* (Case C-112/00)

[2003] ECR I-5659, Court of Justice of the European Communities

This case was considered in the previous chapter (p. 298) for the light it sheds on the notion of a State 'measure' which is caught by Article 34 TFEU. It was there explained that the Court determined that the decision of the public authorities in Austria not to ban a demonstration by an environmental group could fall within the scope of Article 34 in so far as it led to obstacles to trade for the 30 hours that the Brenner motorway was closed to traffic. The question: was the State's 'hands-off' policy objectively justified? The Court confirmed that fundamental rights form an integral part of the general principles of law the observance of which the Court ensures (para 71). The twist – as in *Vereinigte Familiapress* v *Heinrich Bauer Verlag* – was that fundamental rights assisted both sides of the argument. Schmidberger held a fundamental right to enjoy free movement of goods; the Austrian authorities had a concern to protect the fundamental rights of the demonstrators to freedom of expression and freedom of assembly. None of these rights is regarded as absolute, whether under EU law or the European Convention on Human Rights. The Court of Justice proceeded to balance the rights involved.

[81] . . . the interests involved must be weighed having regard to all the circumstances of the case in order to determine whether a fair balance was struck between those interests.

[82] The competent authorities enjoy a wide margin of discretion in that regard. Nevertheless, it is necessary to determine whether the restrictions placed upon intra-Community trade are proportionate in the light of the legitimate objective pursued, namely, in the present case, the protection of fundamental rights.

[83] As regards the main case, it should be emphasised at the outset that the circumstances characterising it are clearly distinguishable from the situation in the case giving rise to the judgment in *Commission* v *France*, cited above, referred to by Schmidberger as a relevant precedent in the course of its legal action against Austria.

[84] By comparison with the points of fact referred to by the Court at paragraphs 38 to 53 of the judgment in *Commission* v *France*, cited above [summarized at p. 294], it should be noted, first, that the demonstration at issue in the main proceedings took place following a request for authorisation presented on the basis of national law and after the competent authorities had decided not to ban it.

[85] Second, because of the presence of demonstrators on the Brenner motorway, traffic by road was obstructed on a single route, on a single occasion and during a period of almost 30 hours. Furthermore, the obstacle to the free movement of goods resulting from that demonstration was limited by comparison with both the geographic scale and the intrinsic seriousness of the disruption caused in the case giving rise to the judgment in *Commission* v *France*, cited above.

[86] Third, it is not in dispute that by that demonstration, citizens were exercising their fundamental rights by manifesting in public an opinion which they considered to be of importance to society; it is also not in dispute that the purpose of that public demonstration was not to restrict trade in goods of a particular type or from a particular source. By contrast, in *Commission* v *France*, cited above, the objective pursued by the demonstrators was clearly to prevent the movement of particular products originating in Member States other than the French Republic, by not only obstructing the transport of the goods in question, but also destroying those goods in transit to or through France, and even when they had already been put on display in shops in the Member State concerned.

[87] Fourth, in the present case various administrative and supporting measures were taken by the competent authorities in order to limit as far as possible the disruption to road traffic. Thus, in particular, those authorities, including the police, the organisers of the demonstration and various motoring organisations cooperated in order to ensure that the demonstration passed off smoothly. Well before the date on which it was due to take place, an extensive publicity campaign had been launched by the media and the motoring organisations, both in Austria and in neighbouring countries, and various alternative routes had been designated, with the result that the economic operators concerned were duly informed of the traffic restrictions applying on the date and at the site of the proposed demonstration and were in a position timeously to take all steps necessary to obviate those restrictions. Furthermore, security arrangements had been made for the site of the demonstration.

[88] Moreover, it is not in dispute that the isolated incident in question did not give rise to a general climate of insecurity such as to have a dissuasive effect on intra-Community trade flows as a whole, in contrast to the serious and repeated disruptions to public order at issue in the case giving rise to the judgment in *Commission* v *France*, cited above.

[89] Finally, concerning the other possibilities envisaged by Schmidberger with regard to the demonstration in question, taking account of the Member States' wide margin of discretion, in circumstances such as those of the present case the competent national authorities were entitled to consider that an outright ban on the demonstration would have constituted unacceptable interference with the fundamental rights of the demonstrators to gather and express peacefully their opinion in public.

The Court reached the conclusion that in the exercise of the wide discretion permitted by EU law the Austrian authorities were reasonably entitled to consider that the legitimate aim of the demonstration could not be achieved by measures less restrictive of cross-border trade. The decision not to ban it was not incompatible with Article 28, now Article 34. Since there was no breach of the Treaty the Court therefore had no need to rule on further questions which had been referred to it concerning State liability arising from the Austrian measures (Chapter 6).

NOTES

1. Case C-36/02 *Omega Spielhallen* [2004] ECR I-9609 concerned the free movement of services (Art 56 TFEU, Chap 14), not goods (Art 34 TFEU), but reveals a similar acceptance of the State's 'margin of discretion' in circumstances where fundamental rights to trade clash with fundamental rights of a different type, recognized by EU law and embedded within national trade-restrictive rules (in casu, respect for human dignity). In fact, more recent cases bringing different types of fundamental rights into collision have typically arisen outwith the field of the free movement of *goods*: Case C-438/05 *International Transport Workers' Federation* v *Viking Line ABP* [2007] ECR I-10779 concerns the right to trade *versus* assorted rights and freedoms to protect and promote the interests of organized labour. The ruling is placed in context in Chapter 14 (p. 401).
2. The collision of *fundamental* rights which are not *absolute* rights is considered further by Perisin, T., 'Interaction of Fundamental (Human) Rights and Fundamental (Market) Freedoms in the EU' (2006) 2 Croatian YELP 69; and Sweeney, J., 'A Margin of Appreciation in the Internal Market: Lessons from the European Court of Human Rights' (2007) 34 LIEL 27. The capacity of EU law of free movement to absorb the influence of fundamental rights raises intriguing questions about how the EU Charter influences the debate about whether trade barriers are justified, now that it has been elevated to binding status consequent on the entry into force of the Lisbon Treaty: p. 58. This is an area of debate in which one might expect to see the Lisbon Treaty's relegation of the Union's

commitment to undistorted competition from Treaty to Protocol to be deployed as a basis for arguing that 'non-market values' should henceforth be accorded a stronger influence in making balancing calculations between competing types of fundamental rights and freedoms (see Chapter 9, p. 239).

General Reading on the Range of Interests Relevant to the Court's Assessment Whether National Measures that Restrict Trade are Justified

De Vries, S., *Tensions within the Internal Market: The Functioning of the Internal Market and the Development of Horizontal and Flanking Policies* (Groningen: Europa Publishing, 2006).

MacMaolain, C. 'Free Movement of Foodstuffs, Quality Requirements and Consumer Protection: Have the Court and Commission Both Got it Wrong?' (2001) 26 EL Rev 413.

Nic Shuibhne, N., 'Margins of Appreciation: National Values, Fundamental Rights and EC Free Movement Law' (2009) 34 EL Rev 230.

Poiares Maduro, M. 'Striking the Elusive Balance Between Economic Freedom and Social Rights in the EU', Ch. 13 in P. Alston (ed.), *The EU and Human Rights* (Oxford: OUP, 1999).

Semmelmann, C., 'The European Union's Economic Constitution under the Lisbon Treaty: Soul-searching Shifts the Focus to Procedure' (2010) 35 EL Rev 516.

Weatherill, S., 'Protecting the Internal Market from the Charter' in S. De Vries, U. Bernitz, and S. Weatherill (eds), *The EU Charter of Fundamental Rights as a Binding Instrument: Five Years Old and Growing* (Oxford: Hart, 2015).

It is notable that arguments based on the protection of interests that go unrecognized in Article 36 TFEU (Chapter 11, p. 306) were considered available in principle, if rejected on the merits in most of these cases. It will be remembered from the preceding chapter that this had induced both the Irish and the British Governments to defend their origin marking rules as measures of consumer protection (pp. 290 and 292). In both instances the Court held the argument misplaced because both States had established a *discriminatory* system. The element of discrimination against imported goods precluded reliance on the 'mandatory requirements' encompassing, for example, the protection of the economic interests of the consumer. The insistence on the elimination of discrimination is also plain in *Gebhard* (Case C-55/94, p. 266).

Even though the Court ruled against the invocation of the mandatory requirements on the facts of the cases considered ('Cassis', beer purity, *Mars* etc.), the availability of 'defences' not found in Article 36 TFEU indicates a greater willingness to respect national competence to regulate in a manner incompatible with free trade, provided discrimination does not contaminate the system.

Cases concerning environmental protection have provided the sternest challenge to the Court's refusal to permit the 'mandatory requirements' to save discriminatory State measures. In *Commission* v *Belgium* (Case C-2/90) [1992] ECR I-4431 Wallonia (a region of Belgium) prohibited the storage, tipping, or dumping of waste from other Member States or from elsewhere in Belgium. The measure was aimed at protecting Wallonia from becoming the target for waste from areas with tighter regulatory regimes. The Commission challenged the rule. The Court agreed this was a restriction on the importation of goods of commercial value, but found it justified as a measure of environmental protection. The Court observed that '[t]he accumulation of waste . . . constitutes a threat to the environment because of the limited capacity of each region or locality for receiving it'. The oddity in the ruling is that the regime appeared to be discriminatory – Walloon waste was treated in Wallonia, waste from outside could not be. As already explained, discriminatory measures are not justifiable with reference to 'the mandatory requirements' which include environmental protection. The Court expressly confirmed this principle in Case C-2/90, but evaded the problem by finding the Walloon measures to be indistinctly applicable and therefore capable of justification as measures of environmental protection. It drew on the principle expressed in Article 130r(2) of the EC Treaty (now, after amendment, Article 191(2) TFEU) that 'environmental damage should as a priority be rectified at source', which dictates a need to minimize transport of waste. Accordingly, the Court commented that it 'follows that, having regard to the differences between waste produced in one place and that in another and its connection with the place where it is produced, the contested measures cannot be considered to be discriminatory'.

The Court's reasoning that the measure was not discriminatory is not wholly convincing and is contradicted by Advocate-General Jacobs's Opinion in the case. However, the Court's reasoning enabled it to achieve a result in conformity with general Treaty principles on environmental protection. It may be as well not to overestimate the ruling's importance, given that this area is increasingly occupied by legislative initiatives which replace the need to test national initiatives against Articles 34–36 TFEU. Indeed, in Case C-2/90 the Court had also examined Belgian compliance with relevant Directives. At the very least, the decision further demonstrates the sensitivity of litigation which raises the potential collision between national environmental protection and market integration.

Some commentators take these cases as evidence of the Court tacitly changing its mind about its refusal to extend the 'mandatory requirements' to permit justification of discriminatory practices; others would regard environmental cases as quite distinct, in particular because of the impact of the principle that environmental damage be rectified at source (Article 191(2) TFEU) which may be taken to mean that transported waste is simply not the same as local waste and can therefore be treated differently without this being treated as 'discrimination'. In Case C-379/98 *Preussen Elektra* [2001] ECR I-2099 Advocate-General Jacobs called on the Court to improve legal certainty by adopting a unified test that would apply the full spectrum of justifications to all barriers to trade. The presence of discrimination would be relegated to the assessment of whether the national rules should be accepted as proportionate. But the Court was not tempted. The case law is spotted with thoughtful A.G. Opinions pushing in this direction and stubbornly evasive judgments: e.g., Case C-320/03 *Commission* v *Austria* [2005] ECR I-9871 (Geelhoed); Joined Cases C-204/12 to C-208/12 *Essent Belgium* judgment of 11 September 2014 (Bot). In Case C-28/09 *Commission* v *Austria* 21 December 2011 the Court bundled up issues of discrimination into a broader assessment of whether a consistent and systematic scheme had been adopted by the regulating authority. But the judgment remained coyly inconclusive on the point of principle. It is predicted that the Court will eventually accept the invitation of its Advocates-General to declare openly that discrimination plays no role in determining which justifications may be advanced in principle, and that instead it is relevant only to whether in practice a measure is justified.

Notice finally how in '*Cassis de Dijon*' (Case 120/78) and in subsequent cases a key precondition to the application of the Treaty is the absence of legislative measures adopted by the EU in the relevant area. Article 34 TFEU operates pending EU legislative intervention in the field. How might environmental laws be framed in this area in order to remove the barriers to trade caused by divergent national legislation? At what level should the rules be administered and enforced – Union, national, or a combination of both? (See, more generally, Chapters 17 and 18.)

■ QUESTIONS

1. Consider the necessity to satisfy mandatory requirements in '*Cassis de Dijon*' (Case 120/78) and the rule of reason in *Dassonville* (Case 8/74). Do these concepts serve the same *function*; and are they identical in substance? Consider also Article 101 TFEU (pp. 468–78).

2. Joe imports alcoholic drink from the Republic of Ireland into England. However, he has recently become increasingly frustrated due to a variety of British regulations which impede his business. He seeks your advice about the impact of Union law on the following problems he has encountered with his latest consignment:

   (a) British legislation forbids the marketing of whisky above a specified maximum alcohol strength. Joe is therefore unable to sell his 'Super de Luxe Special Irish Whiskey' because it is too strong.

   (b) Joe is unable to sell his beers which are marketed in blue glass bottles, because British legislation reserves the use of blue bottles for medicines.

SECTION 4: WHAT SORT OF MARKET IS BEING MADE? SOME CONSEQUENCES FOR CONSUMER PROTECTION AND BEYOND

The Court's decision in '*Cassis de Dijon*' (Case 120/78) was seized on with enthusiasm by the Commission as a means of advancing the attack on national rules which partition the market.

Commission Communication

[1980] OJ C256/2, 3 October 1980

The following is the text of a letter which has been sent to the member-States; the European Parliament and the Council have also been notified of it.

In the Commission's Communication of 6 November 1978 on 'Safeguarding free trade within the Community', it was emphasised that the free movement of goods is being affected by a growing number of restrictive measures.

The judgment delivered by the Court of Justice on 20 February 1979 in Case 120/78 (the 'Cassis de Dijon' case), and recently reaffirmed in the judgment of 26 June 1980 in Case 788/79, has given the Commission some interpretative guidance enabling it to monitor more strictly the application of the Treaty rules on the free movement of goods, particularly Articles 30 to 36 of the EEC Treaty.

The Court gives a very general definition of the barriers to free trade which are prohibited by the provisions of Article 30 *et seq.* of the EEC Treaty. These are taken to include 'any national measure capable of hindering, directly or indirectly, actually or potentially, intra-Community trade'.

In its judgment of 20 February 1979 the Court indicates the scope of this definition as it applies to technical and commercial rules.

Any product lawfully produced and marketed in one member-State must, in principle, be admitted to the market of any other member-State.

Technical and commercial rules, even those equally applicable to national and imported products, may create barriers to trade only where those rules are necessary to satisfy mandatory requirements and to serve a purpose which is in the general interest and for which they are an essential guarantee. This purpose must be such as to take precedence over the requirements of the free movement of goods, which constitutes one of the fundamental rules of the Community.

The conclusions in terms of policy which the Commission draws from this new guidance are set out below.

— Whereas member-States may, with respect to domestic products and in the absence of relevant Community provisions, regulate the terms on which such products are marketed, the case is different for products imported from other member-States.

  Any product imported from another member-State must in principle be admitted to the territory of the importing member-State if it has been lawfully produced, that is, conforms to rules and processes of manufacture that are customarily and traditionally accepted in the exporting country, and is marketed in the territory of the latter.

> This principle implies that member-States, when drawing up commercial or technical rules liable to affect the free movement of goods, may not take an exclusively national viewpoint and take account only of requirements confined to domestic products. The proper functioning of the common market demands that each member-State also give consideration to the legitimate requirements of the other member-States.
>
> Only under very strict conditions does the Court accept exceptions to this principle; barriers to trade resulting from differences between commercial and technical rules are only admissible:
>
> — if the rules are necessary, that is appropriate and not excessive, in order to satisfy mandatory requirements (public health, protection of consumers or the environment, the fairness of commercial transactions, etc.);
>
> — if the rules serve a purpose in the general interest which is compelling enough to justify an exception to a fundamental rule of the Treaty such as the free movement of goods;
>
> — if the rules are essential for such a purpose to be attained, i.e. are the means which are the most appropriate and at the same time least hinder trade.
>
> The Court's interpretation has induced the Commission to set out a number of guidelines:
>
> — The principles deduced by the Court imply that a member-State may not in principle prohibit the sale in its territory of a product lawfully produced and marketed in another member-State even if the product is produced according to technical or quality requirements which differ from those imposed on its domestic products. Where a product 'suitably and satisfactorily' fulfils the legitimate objective of a member-State's own rules (public safety, protection of the consumer or the environment, etc.), the importing country cannot justify prohibiting its sale in its territory by claiming that the way it fulfils the objective is different from that imposed on domestic products.
>
> In such a case, an absolute prohibition of sale could not be considered 'necessary' to satisfy a 'mandatory requirement' because it would not be an 'essential guarantee' in the sense defined in the Court's judgment.
>
> The Commission will therefore have to tackle a whole body of commercial rules which lay down that products manufactured and marketed in one member-State must fulfil technical or qualitative conditions in order to be admitted to the market of another and specifically in all cases where the trade barriers occasioned by such rules are inadmissible according to the very strict criteria set out by the Court.
>
> The Commission is referring in particular to rules covering the composition, designation, presentation and packaging of products as well as rules requiring compliance with certain technical standards.
>
> — The Commission's work of harmonisation will henceforth have to be directed mainly at national laws having an impact on the functioning of the common market where barriers to trade to be removed arise from national provisions which are admissible under the criteria set by the Court.
>
> The Commission will be concentrating on sectors deserving priority because of their economic relevance to the creation of a single internal market.
>
> To forestall later difficulties, the Commission will be informing member-States of potential objections, under the terms of Community law, to provisions they may be considering introducing which come to the attention of the Commission.
>
> It will be producing suggestions soon on the procedures to be followed in such cases.
>
> The Commission is confident that this approach will secure greater freedom of trade for the Community's manufacturers, so strengthening the industrial base of the Community, while meeting the expectations of consumers.

NOTE: The Commission thus believes that the extension of Article 30 of the Treaty (now Article 34 TFEU) to cover '*Cassis de Dijon*' (Case 120/78)-type rules has reduced the need for harmonization.

■ QUESTION

What would have been the consequence for national diversity and tradition if harmonization at EU level had been required to remove the trade-distortive effect of rules governing the content of fruit liqueurs, the fat levels of Edam cheese, and the designation of beers?

NOTE: The application of Article 34 TFEU stimulates competition. Competition yields consumer choice, lower prices, and higher quality. In this way the benefits of an integrated market are realized. In the 1985 White Paper (p. 240), the Commission located the '*Cassis de Dijon*' (Case 120/78) interpretation of the law governing free movement of goods firmly within the framework of the rules designed to complete the internal market by the end of 1992. The fact that market integration did not stop at the end of 1992, but, as is made plain in Chapter 9, continues to evolve, means that this analysis remains true for the future, subject to the refinements brought about by the ruling in *Keck* (Cases C-267 & C-268/91, p. 329) and subsequently.

Completing the Internal Market, COM (85) 310

White Paper from the Commission to the European Council, 14 June 1985

PART TWO: THE REMOVAL OF TECHNICAL BARRIERS

I. Free movement of goods

60. Whilst the physical barriers dealt with in Part One impede trade flows and add unacceptable administrative costs (ultimately paid by the consumer), barriers created by different national product regulations and standards have a double-edged effect: they not only add extra costs, but they also distort production patterns; increase unit costs; increase stock holding costs; discourage business cooperation, and fundamentally frustrate the creation of a common market for industrial products. Until such barriers are removed, Community manufacturers are forced to focus on national rather than continental markets and are unable to benefit from the economies of scale which a truly unified internal market offers. Failure to achieve a genuine industrial common market becomes increasingly serious since the research, development and commercialisation costs of the new technologies, in order to have a realistic prospect of being internationally competitive, require the background of a home market of continental proportions.

The need for a new strategy

61. The harmonization approach has been the cornerstone of Community action in the first 25 years and has produced unprecedented progress in the creation of common rules on a Community-wide basis. However, over the years, a number of shortcomings have been identified. . .

63. In principle, therefore, given the Council's recognition (Conclusions on Standardization, 16 July 1984) of the essential equivalence of the objectives of national legislation, mutual recognition could be an effective strategy for bringing about a common market in a trading sense. This strategy is supported in particular by Articles 30 to 36 of the EEC Treaty [now Articles 34–36 TFEU], which prohibit national measures which would have excessively and unjustifiably restrictive effects on free movement.

64. But while a strategy based purely on mutual recognition would remove barriers to trade and lead to the creation of a genuine common trading market, it might well prove inadequate for the purposes of the building up of an expanding market based on the competitiveness which a continental-scale uniform market can generate. On the other hand experience has shown that the alternative of relying on a strategy based totally on harmonization would be over-regulatory, would take a long time to implement, would be inflexible and could stifle innovation. What is needed is a strategy that combines the best of both approaches but, above all, allows for progress to be made more quickly than in the past.

The chosen strategy

65. The Commission takes into account the underlying reasons for the existence of barriers to trade, and recognizes the essential equivalence of Member States' legislative objectives in the protection of health and safety, and of the environment. Its harmonization approach is based on the following principles:

— a clear distinction needs to be drawn in future internal market initiatives between what it is essential to harmonize, and what may be left to mutual recognition of national regulations and standards; this implies that, on the occasion of each harmonization initiative, the Commission will determine whether national regulations are excessive in relation to the mandatory requirements pursued and, thus, constitute unjustified barriers to trade according to Article 30 to 36 of the EEC Treaty;

— legislative harmonization ... will in future be restricted to laying down essential health and safety requirements which will be obligatory in all Member States. Conformity with this will entitle a product to free movement;
— harmonization of industrial standards by the elaboration of European standards will be promoted to the maximum extent, but the absence of European Standards should not be allowed to be used as a barrier to free movement. During the waiting period while European Standards are being developed, the mutual acceptance of national standards, with agreed procedures, should be the guiding principle.

NOTES

1. *Cf* p. 284 on the present standing of Directive 70/50.
2. The reaction to the Commission's strategy was mixed.

R. Dehousse, 'Completing the Internal Market: Institutional Constraints and Challenges' in R. Bieber et al. (eds) 1992: One European Market?

(Baden-Baden: Nomos Verlagsgesellschaft, 1988), pp. 311, 324–9

(Footnotes omitted.)

The success of a programme as ambitious as the White Paper depends not only on changes in rules governing decision-making alone but also on the proposed programme itself and the way in which it takes account of the institutional context. The connection between the decision-making procedure and the decisions which eventually emerge is not purely a one-way system. Just as the way in which a decision is taken can largely determine its content, so the way that the decision-making procedure operates can be modified by altering the final product that is expected to emerge. To some extent the means used for a given end condition the feasibility of the undertaking. To give a specific example: basically it would appear simpler to persuade the Twelve [now 28!] to refrain from introducing new provisions that might harm intra-Community trade, rather than to get them to agree on a definition of the technical specifications which a given product must satisfy. Equally it is possible – without tampering with the existing decision-making structures at all – to reduce the degree of consensus needed by cutting down the number of participants involved: all that has to be done is to circumscribe the problem in such a way that only a few Member States are directly concerned. Another possibility is to reduce the bargaining costs by proposing no more than a general agreement which leaves each Member State some room for manoeuvre, either by allowing relative freedom of implementation or by means of exemptions or safeguard clauses. These are some simple ways of getting round the joint-decision trap referred to earlier. Viewed from this angle, a number of recent developments catch the eye.

The broad interpretation given to the notion of 'measures having equivalent effect to quantitative restrictions' in the *Dassonville* and *Cassis de Dijon* cases unquestionably opened up new avenues for the Commission. The Court has stated that a Member State may not in principle prohibit the sale in its territory of a product lawfully produced and marketed in another Member State even if this product is produced according to technical or quality requirements which differ from those imposed on its domestic products. In the absence of Community provisions, only measures covered by article 36 or 'necessary in order to satisfy mandatory requirements' like the effectiveness of fiscal supervision, the protection of public health and of the environment, the fairness of commercial transactions and the defence of the consumer, can take precedence over the requirements of the free movements of goods. By extending the scope of article 30, the Court has rendered possible an emphasis on the removal of technical barriers to trade in areas where it was generally thought that only harmonization of national measures was possible.

The new strategy outlined in the White Paper rests on the implicit premise of this case law, namely the essential equivalence of national legislative objectives concerning the protection of human health and safety, and of the environment. In its conclusions on standardization of July 1984, the Council has explicitly recognised that:

> 'the objectives being pursued by the Member States to protect the safety and health of their people as well as the consumer are equally valid in principle, even if different techniques are used to achieve them.'

The White Paper takes this new situation to a logical conclusion and proposes a theoretical distinction between matters where harmonization is essential and those where it is sufficient for there to be mutual recognition of the equivalence of the various basic requirements laid down under national law. The concept of mutual recognition also appears in several other places in the White Paper: it is referred to in connection with health controls, frontier checks, University degrees and vocational training, and even in such a sensitive matter as financial services.

This approach has many advantages in view of the cumbersome nature of the decision-making process. Unlike harmonization, mutual recognition does not involve the transfer of powers to the Community but, at the very worst, somewhat restricts the freedom of action of the Member States. Furthermore, this emphasis on mutual recognition avoids all the difficulties linked to the necessity of drafting directives so as to suit the substantive concerns of twelve different actors or the specific requirements of their legal system. Thus the lengthy bargaining which tends to accompany harmonization can be reduced to a minimum, with greater reliance being placed on the (politically more neutral) supervision of the Court to ensure that the continued existence of national rules does not constitute a barrier to trade. Both from a political and from a legalistic viewpoint, this new direction should be easier to follow.

. . .

The reliance on mutual recognition is nothing more than the rediscovery of a principle which is fairly common in structures of a federal type – and to which the draft Treaty on European Union gave a prominent place: the principle of subsidiarity. The essence of this principle is very simple: the higher level of government should only intervene when it can provide public goods that lower levels cannot supply. In the Community context, this would imply that Community action should be limited to fields where it is absolutely necessary for market integration, or where it can reach better results than the Member States. As is so often the case, the espousal of this principle seems dictated by a combination of theoretical considerations as to the level at which certain powers would be most fruitfully exercised and more practical considerations of how best to simplify the decision-making process. In this particular case, it is perfectly in line with the Treaty inclination towards negative integration.

NOTE: The extract insists on 'institutional context' in its first sentence, and this remains enduringly important. The distinct functions, and dynamic interaction, of mutual recognition of national practices, on the one hand, and harmonization of laws on the other are elucidated in the following extract.

W. Kerber and R. Van den Bergh, 'Unmasking Mutual Recognition: Current Inconsistencies and Future Chances'

Marburg Papers on Economics, No 11-2207, pp. 20–1

http://www.uni-marburg.de/fb02/makro/forschung/gelbereihe/artikel/2007-11_kerber.pdf

(A version of this paper is also available as 'Mutual Recognition Revisited: Misunderstandings, Inconsistencies, and a Suggested Re-interpretation' (2008) 61 *Kyklos* 447).

The rule of mutual recognition does not lead to a stable allocation of regulatory powers. It either leads to direct or indirect processes of harmonisation and centralisation, or back to the country of destination principle, or to a free internal market for regulations. This is also a consequence of the fact that within a two-level system of regulations only three consistent main options for allocating regulatory powers exist, namely (1) harmonisation, (2) decentralisation of mandatory regulations coupled with the country of destination principle, and (3) decentralisation enabling a free market for regulations with free choice of law as conflict of law rule. These three main solutions can also be combined with each other, as, e.g., minimum harmonisation with a free market for regulations or with stricter standards under the country of destination principle. The rule of mutual recognition does not lead to a consistent solution. However, it cannot be denied that the rule of mutual recognition has played and still plays a very important role in the process of European integration. . . . What kind of role is this? The strategy of 'mutual recognition' can be better understood as the application of a test which breaks up the traditional solution of the sovereign nation state (national regulations combined with the country of destination principle), in order to activate a dynamic process of searching for a superior allocation of regulatory powers. Whereas at the beginning of the European integration process, national regulations only reflected the costs and benefits for the Member States involved, the integration process implies that costs and benefits for the entire population of the EU must be taken into account. Therefore, a new allocation of regulatory powers within the integrated European two-level system of regulations has become necessary. This new solution should solve better the trade off problems between benefits and costs for a single Member State and the costs and benefits for the whole European two-level legal system. Since on the EU level it is difficult to agree to a solution, the strategy of mutual recognition can be used as a pragmatic institutional device to break up the hitherto existing structure of regulatory powers and subject it to a systematic test. In some cases, the continued existence of national regulations 'protected' by the country of destination principle could be defended, but often other solutions have been deemed superior. A reshuffling of regulatory powers within the European two-level system of regulations is ongoing. Testing for mutual recognition leads to decisions about the proper allocation of competences, in other words whether there should be harmonisation or a decentralised solution (coupled with the country of destination principle) or a market solution enabling full regulatory competition (or a combination of them). In our view, the main rationale for the strategy of the application of mutual recognition is that it activates such a dynamic process of reallocation of regulatory powers. In this way, the principle of mutual recognition can play an important role also in the future, e.g., in other regional integration projects and on the global level.

NOTE: So 'mutual recognition' disturbs and is designed to disturb pre-existing allocations of regulatory competence in the EU. Also worth reading in this vein is M. Möstl, 'Preconditions and Limits of Mutual Recognition' (2010) 47 CML Rev 405; P. Caro de Sousa, 'Negative and Positive Integration in EU Economic Law: Between Strategic Denial and Cognitive Dissonance' (2012) 13 *German Law Journal* 979; and A. Saydé, 'One Law, Two Competitions: An Inquiry into the Contradictions of Free Movement Law' (2010–11) 13 Camb Ybk Euro Legal Studies 365.

UK Government, 'Review of the Balance of Competences between the United Kingdom and the European Union: The Single Market' (2013)

https://www.gov.uk/review-of-the-balance-of-competences. Paras 2.59–2.60

(Footnotes omitted.)

The UK government's *Review of the Balance of Competences* finds that the single market is more a matter of free movement. It is a 'bargain' among the Member States (para 1.14). It then surveys the relationship between harmonization and mutual recognition.

Harmonisation may work better where there is a strong need for a single standard, goods are tangible and standards are easily assessed, and the need to maintain consumer confidence is strong. Mutual recognition may be better where there are significant differences between Member States in consumer preference or regulatory regimes. In practice, both processes are used together. There can be a process of regulatory development as economic actors become more comfortable with each others' approaches, with initial EU regulation handled through mutual recognition, before progressing to minimum harmonisation and finally exhaustive harmonisation. Or the two approaches can be used together, with mutual recognition combined with elements of common, positive rules, for example in Directive 2005/36 on the Mutual Recognition of Professional Qualifications. Another alternative is the so-called '28th regime', for example in some EU consumer law, whereby an EU framework exists in parallel, for voluntary use, as well as the national frameworks. In all these processes there is in practice much scope for consultation with stakeholders and for getting the detail of the arrangements right.

NOTE: Some of these issues have already been touched on in Chapter 9. Some, especially those connected with harmonization policy and subsidiarity, will be re-addressed in Chapters 17 and 18. It bears repetition that these are general issues for the evolution of the EU-wide market. They were not suddenly solved at the end of 1992. Nor do any subsequent Treaty revisions, most recently the Lisbon reforms of 2009, seek to provide definitive solutions, for they do not affect the substance of the basic trade law provisions in the Treaty.

An interesting and under-researched question is whether 'mutual recognition' really works in practice. In the Commission's Second Biennial Report on the Application of the Principle of Mutual Recognition in the Single Market, COM (2002) 419 (available *via* http://europa.eu/legislation_summaries/internal_market/internal_market_general_framework/l21001b_en.htm) it is stated in para 5.1 that 'The Commission has always found it very difficult to obtain . . . a clear and reliable picture of how the principle of mutual recognition is actually applied in practice.' This is quite a confession! But mutual recognition continues to play a central role on paper. In 2003 the Commission issued further guidelines: *the interpretative communication on facilitating the access of products to the markets of other Member States: the practical application of mutual recognition* [2003] OJ C265/2, which seeks to elucidate the 'balance' between the fundamental right of free movement and the right of Member States to check the level of protection afforded by the product under scrutiny. The communication places heavy reliance on existing case law, including many decisions considered in this book. A thematic connection should be made to the Commission's use of interpretative guidelines, addressed in Chapter 9 (p. 258) as part of its wider quest for transparent *market management*. The place of mutual recognition in the future management of the single market remains under interrogation. In 2006 the Commission admitted that a process of consultation had revealed that '[a]ccording to some, mutual recognition does not function well, leading to extra administrative controls and tests' (Commission Staff Working Document, *Public Consultation on a Future Single Market Policy: Summary of Responses* (SEC (2006) 1215/2, 30 October 2006, p. 11, available *via* http://ec.europa.eu/internal_market/strategy/index_en.htm. In 2008 a fresh legislative attempt was made to improve the practical management of the internal market. Regulation 764/2008, encountered in Chapter 9 (p. 259), lays down procedures to be followed where national authorities decide to take action against an imported product that has been lawfully marketed in another Member State (OJ 2008 L218/21).

The interaction of the Court and the Commission in shaping the (non-absolute) principle of mutual recognition remains of persisting importance. In Case 45/87 *Commission* v *Ireland* [1988] ECR 4929 the Court found a violation of Article 34 TFEU where the contract specification for a new water supply plant in Dundalk demanded that pipes should be certified as complying with Irish Standard 188: 1975 and where the Irish authorities refused to verify whether those requirements were satisfied where the supplier proposed to use uncertified materials of equivalent standard to those demanded under the Irish Standards system. In Case C-184/96 *Commission* v *France* ('Foie Gras') [1998] ECR I-6197 the Court went further. It agreed with the Commission that it is in breach of Article 34 TFEU to adopt a national rule 'without including in it a mutual recognition clause for products coming from a Member State and complying with the rules laid down by that State'. So a State cannot refuse to consider the possibility that a product made elsewhere according to different rules nevertheless meets the objectives aimed at by its own rules. This is the 'testing for mutual recognition' identified by Kerber and Van den Bergh, p. 354. This, to repeat, is not to say that mutual recognition is absolute. *Cassis de Dijon* establishes a principle of *non-absolute* mutual recognition – as does the Treaty, in Articles 34–36 TFEU. So exceptionally a State may be able to show why products made elsewhere according to different standards do not meet its own requirements. And where a prior authorization requirement is shown to be justified there is no room for the mandatory inclusion of a 'mutual recognition' clause of the type envisaged in the 'Foie Gras' case (Case C-24/00 *Commission* v *France* [2004] ECR I-1277, concerning 'Red Bull').

Many commentators have expressed enthusiasm for the '*Cassis de Dijon*' (Case 120/78) decision as a means of improving the consumer's position. Spurious national rules of consumer protection which were in truth rules of producer protection are exposed as unlawful trade barriers. This opens up the market to competition, which, as far as the consumer is concerned, ought to mean increased choice, lower prices, and higher quality.

Bureau Européen des Unions de Consommateurs

Discussion Document 237/84 on Protectionism and Consumer Protection (1985), p. 3

> . . . [T]he case law of the European Court of Justice . . . serves as a model of how to expose false consumer protection arguments and identify consumers' real interests.

N. Reich, 'European Consumer Law', in Bourgoignie (ed.), *Community Consumer Law* (Brussels: Story-Scienta, 1982), p. 223

> The Court does not denounce consumer policy in general but criticizes false consumer policy. In studying consumer law in the EC Member States on a comparative basis, I have come to the conviction that many regulations which carry the label of consumer protection do not really serve the consumer but instead hinder unwanted competition.

■ QUESTION

Which cases might be cited in support of (or in opposition to) these views?

NOTE: Nevertheless, concern has been expressed about the consequences of the *'Cassis de Dijon'* (Case 120/78) judgment, and particularly the legislative and administrative policy which has developed in its wake. The fears lie essentially in the perception that the judgment is heavily biased towards establishing free trade. Member States wishing to uphold national protection bear a heavy burden of proof that the rules are necessary to satisfy mandatory requirements. The Commission's expressed relief at the reduction in the need for EU-level regulation implies a *negative* rather than a *positive* approach to regulating the EU's internal market. This is capable of depriving the trader of certainty about the terms of inter-State trade, and the consumer of confidence about the safety of products originating in other Member States.

N. Reich, 'Protection of Diffuse Interests in the EEC and the Perspective of Progressively Establishing an Internal Market'
(1988) 11 JCP 395

(References omitted.)

> **'NEGATIVE INTEGRATION'**
>
> The concept of 'integration' defines the central political object of the Community since its coming into existence. Integration looks at Member States' regulations which have an effect on the free circulation of goods, services, persons, and capital transfers as restrictions, whatever their political and legal justifications. The thrust of primary and secondary Community law is directed against member-State regulations. The Community integrates by eliminating member-State law which is in opposition to its functioning. The term 'negative integration'. . . helps to explain this activity of the Community. Pelkmans . . . therefore defines the Community as a free trade zone which has been enlarged by a customs union. Theories of free trade ideas harmonise well with classical liberal and neo-liberal economic thought, which has always been popular in Germany, because it recognises the de-regulatory spirit of Community law. Oppermann . . . has therefore defined as the basic rule of Community law 'European market freedom.'
>
> **Importance of Diffuse Interests**
>
> The second point of this complex triangular relation can be defined by employing the theory of *diffuse interests* . . . It aims at an explanation of the economic and social paradoxes of aggregating and integrating diffuse interests into consumer, environmental, and equal rights protection. From its very beginning the Community did not intend to protect diffuse interests in the quality of life, even though article 2 of the EEC Treaty might be read and has been read in this sense. The Community had primarily allocated right to business, viz., a far-reaching right of market access in the entire common market, in order to achieve economic integration as previously defined. It has only recently tried to develop rights protecting diffuse interests, beginning with article 119 of the EEC Treaty concerning equal treatment of men and women in working conditions [see now Article 157 TFEU]. The social reform movement which had also reached the Community through the Paris declaration of 1972 of the Heads of States and Governments has added separate Community policies in environmental . . . , consumer . . . , health . . . , and workplace protection without formally amending the Treaty. Secondary EEC law, based on broad powers of discretion for the EEC institutions, has been responsive in developing social policies of the EEC to protect diffuse interests. This might be called 'positive integration'. . . The Community is trying to develop its own standards common to all member states and therefore applying to all citizens, and allowing a certain common level in the protection of diffuse interests.

. . .

. . . There is an inherent conflict between market integration, protection of diffuse interests, and the rule of law within the Community. Some trends have turned into a genuine 'acquis communautaire'. Others have been taken up by the Single Act but may not have led to the clear solutions which lawyers are always looking for. The role of law itself becomes a main concern within the Community. It is interesting to note that the autonomy and function of law has been reduced and not increased by the Single Act, quite in contrast to 'post-modern legal theory' which insists on the need for autonomy and reformalisation ('autopoiesis') . . . of law.

The main dilemma of EEC law in the future will be whether the objectives of integration, protection, and rule-of-law can really be balanced and harmonised to an equal extent. Mainstream political and legal thinking in the EEC still has as its starting point a basic right to market access for which law is a mere instrument. Protection enters only through a sort of hidden door, or it is regarded as a restriction to free trade. It is quite revealing to read article 8A in this light [see now Article 26 TFEU]: It comes as no surprise that the free circulation of goods is mentioned before the free circulation of persons! . . .

For a collection of essays grouped around the notion of *diffuse interests* as a means to understand the tensions engaged by the EU's market-making project which are identified in the extract, see L. Krämer, *et al.* (eds), *Law and Diffuse Interests in the European Legal Order: Liber Amicorum Norbert Reich* (Baden Baden: Nomos, 1997). See also the collection of articles grouped around the theme 'Governance in the Internal Market' in (1997) 4 JEPP, Issue 4 (Special Issue) and C. Joerges and R. Dehousse, *Good Governance in Europe's Integrated Market* (Oxford: OUP, 2002). And expect to re-visit these themes in Chapters 17 and 18 of this book.

R. Dehousse, 'Completing the Internal Market: Institutional Constraints and Challenges' in R. Bieber et al. (eds), 1992: One European Market?
(Baden-Baden: Nomos Verlagsgesellschaft, 1988), pp. 334–6

(Footnotes omitted.)

As much as one may approve the White Paper's emphasis on negative integration and the removal of borders, it is clear that market unity will not be possible without a measure of positive integration, even if only in a limited way, for example for the setting up of minimal health and safety requirements or the organization of the cooperation among national customs administrations, which is necessary in order to achieve a real elimination of physical borders. It is likely that the difficulties that traditionally beset Community decision-making will surface again at that level. The Single Act has tried to ease somewhat the taking of decision with a mixture of majority voting and differentiation. The two are closely linked; in a Community of twelve, renewed progress would not be possible without a simplification of decision-making procedures but, at the same time, the latter would have been unthinkable without a measure of flexibility. In substantive terms, additional flexibility is also rendered necessary by the sometimes wide differences which exist between Member States' economies and societal choices. To a certain extent, the impact of these new mechanisms will probably depend on the Commission's ability to maintain a certain degree of momentum in its White Paper programme. At least it will benefit in its quest for an enhanced room for manoeuvre for, as we have seen, the combination of majority voting and derogatory provisions should reinforce the strategic importance of its proposals.

At some point, however, a major challenge will have to be faced, for the objective of market integration itself remains unacceptable, politically speaking, for some Member States if it is not accompanied by a specific effort to improve the social and economic cohesion within the Community. It is worth recalling in this respect that economically weaker countries have been reluctant to accept majority voting, precisely because they are those who might suffer most in the short term from the creation of a single market. Of the many problems linked to the completion of the internal market, this one is perhaps the most difficult: unlike the concerns for a high level of protection for health, consumer safety or the environment, this kind of fear cannot be allayed by derogatory measures alone. A parallel in the Community's allocative and redistributive policies has been strongly advocated by recent studies, both from a theoretical and from a practical viewpoint. The Single Act pledges the Community to reinforce its action in favour of backward areas; it even explicitly states that the completion of the internal market should be pursued taking into account the existence of different levels of development within the Community [see now Article 174 TFEU]. However, it fails to give the Community additional means to reach that end. The crucial point is that, at a given stage, progress towards the single European market might be conditioned by the capacity to tackle the problem of structural imbalances: if the Community does not find a way to offer some compensation to those countries which feel they have more to lose, market integration could be severely hampered. More than institutional pragmatism will be needed in order to cut this Gordian knot.

NOTE: The issues discussed are illustrative of some of the most fundamental which continue to confront the developing European Union. How are the differing demands of national interest groups to be accommodated in a broader structure committed to free trade? The harmonization programme in particular and EU policymaking competence more generally must satisfy many often competing interests. No one doubts that the Union must regulate certain matters in order to achieve genuine integration. Much doubt remains about the nature and scope of that regulation. The rival notions of the 'level playing field' and 'competition between regulators' were introduced at p. 267: the contest between them is enduring.

These are inevitably matters of intense political debate. Yet they are vital for the lawyer too, because the legal rules and institutional structures which emerge and which form the lawyer's working materials will be the product of that political debate.

J. Pelkmans, A Grand Design by the Piece? An Appraisal of the Internal Market Strategy' in R. Bieber *et al. (eds), 1992: One European Market?*
(Baden-Baden: Nomos Verlagsgesellschaft, 1988), p. 371

Finally whether one likes it or not, an Internal Market cutting so deep into the regulatory environment of consumers, traders and producers and limiting even more severely the Member States in their policy instruments *can no longer pretend to be a-political.* In completing the Internal Market by the piece, it becomes more and more artificial to expect conservatives, liberals, progressives, radicals, christian-democrats and socialists to agree, for the mere sake of 'Europe'. The verbal emphasis in the White Paper is, rightly, on fully free and unhindered mutual market access. But it is not very helpful to postulate that the *'positive integration' needed for that, will come forward and be solved, for the good purpose.* As more and more positive integration reduces the national policy autonomy needed to accentuate different positions in domestic politics, the greater the sensitivity to the Community's implicit or explicit political bias. As one begins to touch upon the most deeply entrenched forms of protection and the most cherished state instruments the process of positive integration will become more politicized.

NOTE: Such problems have been deepened by the 'ambiguous compromises' (p. 9) of the Maastricht, Amsterdam, and Nice Treaties. The process continues: the Treaty of Lisbon too contains no decisive choices. In an EU of 28 Member States such choices are close to impossible to make in the absence of a revolutionary jolt.

Dehousse draws attention to questions about the role of redistributive policies at EU level (p. 360); Pelkmans stresses the emerging political nature of the project of integrating markets (p. 361). The gains of economic integration in Europe may be real, as summarized in Chapter 9, but they are not shared equally – between States, between groups in society. In so far as the project is viewed as economically virtuous and yet politically neutral, which has been the understanding which has sustained the plan to complete the internal market up to and long after 'deadline 1992', it enjoys 'output legitimacy': in short, it is legitimate because it works (whereas by contrast 'input legitimacy' focuses on legitimation by democratic process). But the veneer of political neutrality is increasingly thin.

M. Höpner and A. Schäfer (2007), 'A New Phase of European Integration: Organized Capitalisms in Post-Ricardian Europe'

MPifG Discussion Paper 07/4 Max-Planck-Institut für Gesellschaftsforschung, Köln. www.mpifg.de/pu/mpifg_dp/dp07-4.pdf

(Some references and footnotes omitted.)

We have argued that European-level actors have extended the interpretations of the 'four freedoms' to an extent that it becomes increasingly questionable whether the wordings and spirit of the treaties provide (input) legitimacy for the respective liberalization measures. However, one might object, it is so obvious that the member states are deadlocked with immobility and overregulation that the 'neo-liberal bias of the EU, if it exists, is justified by the social welfarist bias of current national policies' [A. Moravcsik, 'In Defence of the Democratic Deficit' (2002) 40 JCMS 603, 618]. We argue that this objection fails to provide (output) legitimacy. The impact of EU legislation differs across member states since Europe consists of various forms of capitalism. . .. Some may benefit from deregulation. For others, however, liberalization could result in a decomposition of the internal logic their production regimes rely on. What has already been shown for the different European welfare regimes holds true. . .: Europeanization has quite different meanings for different member states. Yet if Europe really wants to become the most competitive economic area worldwide, and if the different institutional forms of capitalism differ in their comparative advantages, should not European integration secure the free flow of products, services and capital, but protect the respective internal logics of the member states' economic systems? Would this not imply, in particular, sheltering member states from de-institutionalization? We may, or may not, be right here. But we suggest that the efficiency gains are too uncertain (to say the least) to provide output legitimacy. Deregulating the economy is a genuinely *political* decision that cannot be left to independent agents. Therefore, it requires *input* legitimacy. Whether the member states need a 'neo-liberal' corrective is not for the observer to choose but must be the result of public deliberation and parliamentary decisions – otherwise, the price to pay is a serious democratic deficit. However, instead of a strengthening of input-oriented legitimacy, we witness ongoing – yet increasingly unsuccessful – attempts to de-politicize EU politics. European-level actors transform essentially political matters into apparently technical ones. An extensive interpretation of the 'four freedoms' of the European Treaty allows Commission and Court to enforce liberalization measures juridically. The law shields these attempts from political resistance especially in organized economies. . .The EU has moved beyond the stage of technical harmonization or purely regulatory policies. Boundary redrawing deeply affects the member states' ability to govern the economy, and governments are unable to control further integration: '. . . free circulation and competition policies are the kernel of the atomic engine of the integration process, an engine that is quite difficult, even for the Council, to switch off or even to cool down' [S. Bartolini, *Restructuring Europe* (OUP, 2005) p. 185]. If this is the case, the indirect legitimation of European institutions seems an insufficient democratic basis for economic liberalization. We have suggested that the liberalization attempts of the post-Ricardian phase are either successful or they bring about crises of integration. Failed referendums on the constitutional treaty and considerable Euro-scepticism throughout the Union indicate that the 'permissive consensus' of European integration is dissolving. 'Integration by stealth' [G. Majone, *Dilemmas of European Integration* (OUP, 2005)] has reached its limit because European decisions are in conflict with national welfare traditions or, as we have shown, with European varieties of capitalism.

NOTE: The future shape of the Union, and in particular that of the Eurozone within it, will be governed by the nature of choices about the allocation of responsibility for different functions to different levels of government in the Union – European, national, regional, local. Lately this complex issue has come to be denoted by (less than entirely satisfying) catchphrases such as *subsidiarity* and *flexibility*. These matters are re-visited in Chapters 17 and 18.

NOTE: For additional material and resources see the Online Resource Centre at: www.oxfordtextbooks.co.uk/orc/weatherill12e.

13

The Free Movement of Workers: Article 45 TFEU

ARTICLE 45 TFEU

1. Freedom of movement for workers shall be secured within the Union.

2. Such freedom of movement shall entail the abolition of any discrimination based on nationality between workers of the Member States as regards employment, remuneration and other conditions of work and employment.

3. It shall entail the right, subject to limitations justified on grounds of public policy, public security or public health:
   - (a) to accept offers of employment actually made;
   - (b) to move freely within the territory of Member States for this purpose;
   - (c) to stay in a Member State for the purpose of employment in accordance with the provisions governing the employment of nationals of that State laid down by law, regulation or administrative action;
   - (d) to remain in the territory of a Member State after having been employed in that State, subject to conditions which shall be embodied in implementing regulations to be drawn up by the Commission.

4. The provisions of this Article shall not apply to employment in the public service.

NOTE: The Lisbon Treaty did no more than switch 'Union' for 'Community' in Article 45(1), while also changing the number of this Article. It was Article 39 EC pre-Lisbon and, before the entry into force of the Treaty of Amsterdam in 1999, it was Article 48. As ever, these numerical adjustments must be taken into account when reading older material.

At one level, the Treaty secures the free movement of workers simply as an adjunct to the other freedoms, such as the free movement of goods (Article 34), and services (Article 56). These freedoms all contribute to the realization of mobility within an integrated market. But the free movement of persons has implications beyond the economics of market integration. It concerns human beings. It identifies people as the beneficiaries of the Treaty rules in a more direct sense than any other area of the law of the internal market. The treatment of people in the EU immediately encourages contemplation of the status of Citizenship of the European Union, created at Maastricht and legally articulated in the post-Lisbon Treaty as Articles 20–25 TFEU. But that temptation will be resisted. Citizenship is examined in Chapter 15. In this chapter and the next the predominantly market-focused evolution of the rules on persons and services is examined in the belief that this will allow a clearer appreciation of the possibilities and limitations facing the law of the EU as it gropes beyond the 'market citizen' towards a system that builds fundamental rights and Citizenship.

This chapter explores the scope of the worker's right to free movement. Article 45 TFEU concerns both labour mobility and the rights of the individual. Both the Court and the legislature have developed the scope of the rights conferred upon the migrant worker. These developments mean that, independently of the Maastricht-created notion of

Citizenship, an individual has an extensive range of rights, first, to move freely between Member States to take up employment and, second, to enjoy non-discriminatory access to social protection once installed in the host Member State.

SECTION 1: WHO IS A WORKER?

Levin v *Staatssecretaris van Justitie* (Case 53/81)

[1982] ECR 1035, Court of Justice of the European Communities

Mrs Levin was a British national married to a South African national. She was refused a residence permit by the Dutch authorities because she was not in gainful employment. She challenged the refusal before the Dutch courts. Questions were referred to the Court of Justice. The Court was asked to explain the notion of a 'worker'. The Dutch court was particularly concerned to elucidate the scope of Article 48 of the Treaty (now, after amendment, Article 45 TFEU) where an individual earns an income less than the minimum required for subsistence as defined under national law. The Court observed that no authoritative definition of 'worker' is to be found in the Treaty or secondary legislation. (This remains true today.) It then claimed for itself the job of carrying out that interpretative task.

[11] ... [T]he terms 'worker' and 'activity as an employed person' may not be defined by reference to the national laws of the Member States but have a Community meaning. If that were not the case, the Community rules on freedom of movement for workers would be frustrated, as the meaning of those terms could be fixed and modified unilaterally, without any control by the Community institutions, by national laws which would thus be able to exclude at will certain categories of persons from the benefit of the Treaty.

[12] Such would, in particular, be the case if the enjoyment of the rights conferred by the principle of freedom of movement for workers could be made subject to the criterion of what the legislation of the host State declares to be a minimum wage, so that the field of application *ratione personae* of the Community rules on this subject might vary from one Member State to another. The meaning and the scope of the terms 'worker' and 'activity as an employed person' should thus be clarified in the light of the principles of the legal order of the Community.

[13] In this respect it must be stressed that these concepts define the field of application of one of the fundamental freedoms guaranteed by the Treaty and, as such, may not be interpreted restrictively.

[14] In conformity with this view the recitals in the preamble to Regulation (EEC) No 1612/68 contain a general affirmation of the right of all workers in the Member States to pursue the activity of their choice within the Community, irrespective of whether they are permanent, seasonal or frontier workers or workers who pursue their activities for the purpose of providing services. Furthermore, although Article 4 of Directive 68/360/EEC grants the right of residence to workers upon the mere production of the document on the basis of which they entered the territory and of a confirmation of engagement from the employer or a certificate of employment, it does not subject this right to any condition relating to the kind of employment or to the amount of income derived from it.

[15] An interpretation which reflects the full scope of these concepts is also in conformity with the objectives of the Treaty which include, according to Articles 2 and 3, the abolition, as between Member States, of obstacles to freedom of movement for persons, with the purpose *inter alia* of promoting throughout the Community a harmonious development of economic activities and a raising of the standard of living. Since part-time employment, although it may provide an income lower than what is considered to be the minimum required for subsistence, constitutes for a large number of persons an effective means of improving their living conditions, the effectiveness of Community law would be impaired and the achievement of the objectives of the Treaty would be jeopardized if the enjoyment of rights conferred by the principle of freedom of movement for workers were reserved solely to persons engaged in full-time employment and earning, as a result, a wage at least equivalent to the guaranteed minimum wage in the sector under consideration.

[16] It follows that the concepts of 'worker' and 'activity as an employed person' must be interpreted as meaning that the rules relating to freedom of movement for workers also concern persons who pursue or wish to pursue an activity as an employed person on a part-time basis only and who, by virtue of that fact obtain or would obtain only remuneration lower than the minimum guaranteed remuneration in the sector under consideration. In this regard no distinction may be made between those who wish to make do with their income from such an activity and those who supplement that income with other income, whether the latter is derived from property or from the employment of a member of their family who accompanies them.

[17] It should however be stated that whilst part-time employment is not excluded from the field of application of the rules on freedom of movement for workers, those rules cover only the pursuit of effective and genuine activities, to the exclusion of activities on such a small scale as to be regarded as purely marginal and ancillary. It follows both from the statement of the principle of freedom of movement for workers and from the place occupied by the rules relating to that principle in the system of the Treaty as a whole that those rules guarantee only the free movement of persons who pursue or are desirous of pursuing an economic activity.

[18] The answer to be given to the first and second questions must therefore be that the provisions of Community law relating to freedom of movement for workers also cover a national of a Member State who pursues, within the territory of another Member State, an activity as an employed person which yields an income lower than that which, in the latter State, is considered as the minimum required for subsistence, whether that person supplements the income from his activity as an employed person with other income so as to arrive at that minimum or is satisfied with means of support lower than the said minimum, provided that he pursues an activity as an employed person which is effective and genuine.

[19] The third question essentially seeks to ascertain whether the right to enter and reside in the territory of a Member State may be denied to a worker whose main objectives, pursued by means of his entry and residence, are different from that of the pursuit of an activity as an employed person as defined in the answer to the first and second questions.

[20] Under Article 48(3) of the Treaty the right to move freely within the territory of the Member States is conferred upon workers for the 'purpose' of accepting offers of employment actually made. By virtue of the same provision workers enjoy the right to stay in one of the Member States 'for the purpose' of employment there. Moreover, it is stated in the preamble to Regulation (EEC) No 1612/68 that freedom of movement for workers entails the right of workers to move freely within the Community 'in order to' pursue activities as employed persons, whilst Article 2 of Directive 68/360/EEC requires the Member States to grant workers the right to leave their territory 'in order to' take up activities as employed persons or to pursue them in the territory of another Member State.

[21] However, these formulations merely give expression to the requirement, which is inherent in the very principle of freedom of movement for workers, that the advantages which Community law confers in the name of that freedom may be relied upon only by persons who actually pursue or seriously wish to pursue activities as employed persons. They do not, however, mean that the enjoyment of this freedom may be made to depend upon the aims pursued by a national of a Member State in applying for entry upon and residence in the territory of another Member State, provided that he there pursues or wishes to pursue an activity which meets the criteria specified above, that is to say, an effective and genuine activity as an employed person.

[22] Once this condition is satisfied, the motives which may have prompted the worker to seek employment in the Member State concerned are of no account and must not be taken into consideration.

***Kempf* v *Staatssecretaris van Justitie* (Case 139/85)**

[1986] ECR 1741, [1987] 1 CMLR 764, Court of Justice of the European Communities

The Court took the opportunity in this case to refine further its definition.

[11] As regards, first, the criterion of effective and genuine work as opposed to marginal and ancillary activities not covered by the relevant Community rules, the Netherlands Government expressed doubts at the hearing as to whether the work of a teacher who gives 12 lessons a week may be regarded as constituting in itself effective and genuine work within the terms of the judgment in *Levin*.

[12] There is, however, no need to consider that question since the Raad van State, in the grounds of the judgment making the reference, expressly found that Mr Kempf's work was not on such a small scale as to be purely a marginal and ancillary activity. According to the division of jurisdiction between national courts and the Court of Justice in connection with references for a preliminary ruling, it is for national courts to establish and to evaluate the facts of the case. The question submitted for a preliminary ruling must therefore be examined in the light of the assessment made by the Raad van State.

[13] The Court has consistently held that freedom of movement for workers forms one of the foundations of the Community. The provisions laying down that fundamental freedom and, more particularly, the terms 'worker' and 'activity as an employed person' defining the sphere of application of those freedoms must be given a broad interpretation in that regard, whereas exceptions to and derogations from the principle of freedom of movement for workers must be interpreted strictly.

[14] It follows that the rules on this topic must be interpreted as meaning that a person in effective and genuine part-time employment cannot be excluded from their sphere of application merely because the remuneration he derives from it is below the level of the minimum means of subsistence and he seeks to supplement it by other lawful means of subsistence. In that regard it is irrelevant whether those supplementary means of subsistence are derived from property or from the employment of a member of his family, as was the case in *Levin*, or whether, as in this instance, they are obtained from financial assistance drawn from the public funds of the Member State in which he resides, provided that the effective and genuine nature of his work is established.

NOTE: The Court is plainly concerned in these decisions to establish a broad definition of the worker entitled to rights under the Treaty (see also *Lawrie-Blum* v *Land Baden-Württemberg* (Case 66/85) [1986] ECR 2121; and the noticeably cautious approach to finding 'effective and genuine' work in the case of an individual doing a job specifically designed to rehabilitate drug addicts in *Bettray* v *Staatssecretaris van Justitie* (Case 344/87) [1989] ECR 1621 has subsequently been treated as specific to the unusual circumstances of that case: see *Michel Trojani* (Case C-456/02 [2004] ECR I-7573). A person in part-time employment while a student may be a 'worker' provided the employment activities are effective and genuine, not ancillary and marginal (Case C-46/12 *L.N.* judgment of 21 February 2013). An employed woman who gave up work less than three months before the birth of her child and then returned to work three months after the birth did not lose the status of a 'worker' (Case C-507/12 *Saint Prix* judgment of 19 June 20140. Notice that the notion of worker is held to be a concept of Community (now Union), not national, law in order to preclude the destruction of the integrity of Community (now Union) law through differing national approaches.

It had long been a matter of doubt whether this provision of the Treaty protects an individual who migrates in order to seek work, rather than to take up a job already offered. The Court decided in *R* v *IAT, ex parte Antonissen* (Case C-292/89) that a jobseeker may be a worker, but not indefinitely.

***R* v *IAT, ex parte Antonissen* (Case C-292/89)**

[1991] ECR I-745, Court of Justice of the European Communities

Antonissen, a Belgian, sought to rely on Article 48 of the Treaty (now Article 45 TFEU) to defeat a UK deportation order against him. He had been seeking employment in the UK for more than six months and the Tribunal's view was that he had no rights under the Treaty. *Held* by the Court of Justice:

It is not contrary to the provisions of Community law governing the free movement of workers for the legislation of a Member State to provide that a national of another Member State who entered the first State in order to seek employment may be required to leave the territory of that State (subject to appeal) if he has not found employment there after six months, unless the person concerned provides evidence that he is continuing to seek employment and that he has genuine chances of being engaged.

The equation of genuine jobseeker and 'worker' was confirmed by the Court in *Marìa Martinez Sala* v *Freistaat Bayern* (Case C-85/96) [1998] ECR I-2691 and pursued further in the next case.

***Brian Francis Collins v Secretary of State for Work and Pensions* (Case C-138/02)**
[2004] ECR I-2703, Court of Justice of the European Communities

[36] In the context of freedom of movement for workers, Article 48 of the Treaty [now 45 TFEU] grants nationals of the Member States a right of residence in the territory of other Member States in order to pursue or to seek paid employment (Case C-171/91 *Tsiotras* [1993] ECR I-2925, paragraph 8).

[37] The right of residence which persons seeking employment derive from Article 48 of the Treaty may be limited in time. In the absence of Community provisions prescribing a period during which Community nationals who are seeking employment may stay in their territory, the Member States are entitled to lay down a reasonable period for this purpose. However, if after expiry of that period, the person concerned provides evidence that he is continuing to seek employment and that he has genuine chances of being engaged, he cannot be required to leave the territory of the host Member State (see Case C-292/89 Antonissen [1991] ECR I-745, paragraph 21, and Case C-344/95 *Commission* v *Belgium* [1997] ECR I-1035, paragraph 17).

The *Collins* case primarily concerned the implications of placing a jobseeker within the scope of what is now Article 45 TFEU. Collins, a dual Irish and American national, was claiming a statutory jobseeker's allowance in the United Kingdom, having arrived there in May 1998 for the first time in 17 years (and having previously visited the United Kingdom only briefly as a student and a casual worker). The matter reached the Court of Justice, which drew on what is now Article 18 TFEU and the status of Citizenship of the Union to identify the scope of his entitlement. This will be examined in more depth in Chapter 15: the case is a convenient bridge between matters associated with the personal scope of EU law and the capacity of Citizenship to widen the benefits to be made available on a non-discriminatory basis.

Article 6 of Directive 2004/38 provides that Union citizens are entitled to the right of residence on the territory of another Member State for a period of up to three months without any conditions or any formalities other than the requirement to hold a valid identity card or passport. All Union citizens shall have the right of residence on the territory of another Member State for a period of longer than three months if they are (*inter alia*) workers in the host Member State (Article 7) and the right to reside is retained as long as this condition is met (Article 14). The Union citizen who entered the territory of another Member State in order to seek employment shall not be expelled 'for as long as the Union citizens can provide evidence that they are continuing to seek employment and that they have a genuine chance of being engaged' (Article 14(4)). So the status of the jobseeker is recognized by Directive 2004/38 but the duration of that person's right to keep looking for work is not measured in months or years.

SECTION 2: TO WHAT ADVANTAGES IS THE WORKER ENTITLED?

Directive 68/360 on the Abolition of Restrictions on Movement and Residence within the Community for Workers of Member States and their Families set out more fully than the Treaty the right of entry and residence, and amplified several procedural aspects of the right of free movement.

The legislative framework has been overhauled by Directive 2004/38 of the European Parliament and Council on the right of citizens of the Union and their family members to move and reside freely within the territory of the Member States ([2004] OJ L229/35, corrected version). This Directive is relevant to the material covered in this chapter and the two that follow. It amended, repealed, and replaced a string of older measures.

Directive 2004/38 lays down (a) the conditions governing the exercise of the right of free movement and residence within the territory of the Member States by Union citizens and their family members; (b) the right of permanent residence in the territory of the Member States for Union citizens and their family members; (c) the limits placed on the rights set out in (a) and (b) on grounds of public policy, public security, or public health.

This brings together material relating to persons, and it reflects the Court's sweeping statement that 'Union citizenship is destined to be the fundamental status of nationals of the Member States' (Case C-184/99 *Rudy Grzelczyk*, p. 422, para 31). Nevertheless, Directive 2004/38, which echoes this claim in its Preamble, is not an easy read, because it remains the case that the law has *not* evolved into a general charter of citizen rights, but rather retains features of the emphasis on rights and benefits for particular categories of person, especially the economically active. In fact, the area of law explored in this chapter and the two that follow is not readily subjected to simple explanation.

Chapter II of Directive 2004/38 concerns the right of exit from a Member State (Article 4) and entry to a Member State (Article 5). Chapter III (Articles 6–15) concerns the right of residence.

Article 6 of Directive 2004/38 provides that Union citizens (and certain family members) are entitled to the right of residence on the territory of another Member State for a period of up to three months without any conditions or any formalities other than the requirement to hold a valid identity card or passport. This, however, confers no right to social assistance during this three-month period (Article 24(2)) and the right of residence is anyway lost if the citizen becomes an unreasonable burden on the social assistance system of the host Member State (Article 14(1)).

Article 7 deals with a right of residence for more than three months. This is subdivided according to the category into which the individual falls. Migrant workers or self-employed persons (and certain family members) enjoy the right by virtue of their status. And Article 7(3) protects workers and the self-employed person who lose that status in defined circumstances, including illness or accident, and involuntary unemployment. Others – including the self-funding migrant and students – acquire the right *only* provided they have sufficient resources not to become a burden on the social assistance system of the host Member State and have comprehensive sickness insurance cover in the host Member State. What is visible here is the attempt to craft a general system of rights for Union citizens which nevertheless cannot be detached from the pre-existing focus on special privileged status accorded to the economically active, including the 'worker' within the meaning of Article 45 TFEU (and the self-employed person covered by Article 49 TFEU). In 1990 three Directives were adopted which were designed to extend the protection of the law: Directive 90/364 on a general right of residence ([1990] OJ L180/26), Directive 90/365 on a Right of Residence for employees and self-employed persons who have ceased their occupational activity ([1990] OJ L180/28) and Directive 90/366 on a Right of Residence for Students (annulled by the Court for choice of incorrect legal base in *Parliament* v *Council* (Case C-295/90) [1992] ECR I-4193 but replaced by Directive 93/96, [1993] OJ L317/59). The advances made by these Directives were severely limited by the requirement in each that, according to the Preambles, the 'beneficiaries of the right of residence must not become an unreasonable burden on the public finances of the host Member State'. This considerable limitation, inspired by host State nervousness about the financial implications of unconfined migration and 'welfare tourism', was reflected in the specific provisions of each measure, and though the three Directives were all repealed with effect from 30 April 2006 their replacement by Directive 2004/38 has *not* led to the elimination of these thresholds to acquisition of personal rights. Their significance was vividly confirmed in Case C-333/13 *Elisabeta Dano* judgment of 11 November 2014, in which the Court found that a migrant resident in a host State for more than three months but less than five years who has neither worked nor looked for work may be refused subsistence benefits. Chapter 15 explores the phenomenon of Union citizenship more generally but Article 7 of Directive 2004/38 provides a concrete illustration of the persisting superior status for some purposes of the 'worker' in EU law.

Chapter IV of Directive 2004/38 deals with the right of permanent residence. According to Article 16 the general rule is that Union citizens (and certain family members) who have resided legally for a continuous period of five years in the host Member State shall have the right of permanent residence there. Article 17 provides that the right may accrue before completion of a continuous period of five years of residence to (*inter alia*) particular types of workers or self-employed persons who have reached retirement age or who have stopped working as a result of permanent incapacity to work. The Preamble cites the need for strengthening the feeling of Union citizenship and promoting social cohesion.

Relevant administrative formalities for Union citizens and family members are covered by Articles 8–11 of Directive 2004/38. Rights derive from the Treaty, not from compliance with administrative requirements. Accordingly, failure to comply with registration requirements may render the person concerned liable to proportionate and non-discriminatory sanctions (Articles 8(2), 9(3)). But this could not conceivably encompass deportation (for a good, though now dated, example of the Court's attitude see Case 15/79 *R* v *Pieck* [1980] ECR 2171, which dealt with consequences of failure to acquire a residence permit as foreseen by Directive 68/360: that Directive was replaced by Directive 2004/38 with effect from 30 April 2006, which also abolished the residence permit for EU citizens).

NOTE: Regulation 492/2011, which replaced the long-standing Regulation 1612/68, ensures that the migrant worker, once settled in the host State, shall enjoy non-discriminatory treatment in relation to access to employment and provision of employment-related benefits. These provisions are wide-ranging on their face, but have been taken still further by the Court.

Regulation 492/2011 of the Parliament and Council of 5 April 2011 on freedom of movement for workers within the Union

OJ 2011 L141/1, Articles 1–10.

CHAPTER I

EMPLOYMENT, EQUAL TREATMENT AND WORKERS' FAMILIES

SECTION 1

Eligibility for employment

Article 1

1. Any national of a Member State shall, irrespective of his place of residence, have the right to take up an activity as an employed person, and to pursue such activity, within the territory of another Member State in accordance with the provisions laid down by law, regulation or administrative action governing the employment of nationals of that State.

2. He shall, in particular, have the right to take up available employment in the territory of another Member State with the same priority as nationals of that State.

Article 2

Any national of a Member State and any employer pursuing an activity in the territory of a Member State may exchange their applications for and offers of employment, and may conclude and perform contracts of employment in accordance with the provisions in force laid down by law, regulation or administrative action, without any discrimination resulting therefrom.

Article 3

1. Under this Regulation, provisions laid down by law, regulation or administrative action or administrative practices of a Member State shall not apply:

(a) where they limit application for and offers of employment, or the right of foreign nationals to take up and pursue employment or subject these to conditions not applicable in respect of their own nationals; or

(b) where, though applicable irrespective of nationality, their exclusive or principal aim or effect is to keep nationals of other Member States away from the employment offered.

The first subparagraph shall not apply to conditions relating to linguistic knowledge required by reason of the nature of the post to be filled.

2. There shall be included in particular among the provisions or practices of a Member State referred to in the first subparagraph of paragraph 1 those which:

(a) prescribe a special recruitment procedure for foreign nationals;

(b) limit or restrict the advertising of vacancies in the press or through any other medium or subject it to conditions other than those applicable in respect of employers pursuing their activities in the territory of that Member State;

(c) subject eligibility for employment to conditions of registration with employment offices or impede recruitment of individual workers, where persons who do not reside in the territory of that State are concerned.

Article 4

1. Provisions laid down by law, regulation or administrative action of the Member States which restrict by number or percentage the employment of foreign nationals in any undertaking, branch of activity or region, or at a national level, shall not apply to nationals of the other Member States.

2. When in a Member State the granting of any benefit to undertakings is subject to a minimum percentage of national workers being employed, nationals of the other Member States shall be counted as national workers, subject to Directive 2005/36/EC of the European Parliament and of the Council of 7 September 2005 on the recognition of professional qualifications.

Article 5

A national of a Member State who seeks employment in the territory of another Member State shall receive the same assistance there as that afforded by the employment offices in that State to their own nationals seeking employment.

Article 6

1. The engagement and recruitment of a national of one Member State for a post in another Member State shall not depend on medical, vocational or other criteria which are discriminatory on grounds of nationality by comparison with those applied to nationals of the other Member State who wish to pursue the same activity.

2. A national who holds an offer in his name from an employer in a Member State other than that of which he is a national may have to undergo a vocational test, if the employer expressly requests this when making his offer of employment.

SECTION 2

Employment and equality of treatment

Article 7

1. A worker who is a national of a Member State may not, in the territory of another Member State, be treated differently from national workers by reason of his nationality in respect of any conditions of employment and work, in particular as regards remuneration, dismissal, and, should he become unemployed, reinstatement or re-employment.

2. He shall enjoy the same social and tax advantages as national workers.

3. He shall also, by virtue of the same right and under the same conditions as national workers, have access to training in vocational schools and retraining centres.

4. Any clause of a collective or individual agreement or of any other collective regulation concerning eligibility for employment, remuneration and other conditions of work or dismissal shall be null and void in so far as it lays down or authorises discriminatory conditions in respect of workers who are nationals of the other Member States.

Article 8

A worker who is a national of a Member State and who is employed in the territory of another Member State shall enjoy equality of treatment as regards membership of trade unions and the exercise of rights attaching thereto, including the right to vote and to be eligible for the administration or management posts of a trade union. He may be excluded from taking part in the management of bodies governed by public law and from holding an office governed by public law. Furthermore, he shall have the right of eligibility for workers' representative bodies in the undertaking.

The first paragraph of this Article shall not affect laws or regulations in certain Member States which grant more extensive rights to workers coming from the other Member States.

Article 9

1. A worker who is a national of a Member State and who is employed in the territory of another Member State shall enjoy all the rights and benefits accorded to national workers in matters of housing, including ownership of the housing he needs.

2. A worker referred to in paragraph 1 may, with the same right as nationals, put his name down on the housing lists in the region in which he is employed, where such lists exist, and shall enjoy the resultant benefits and priorities.

If his family has remained in the country whence he came, they shall be considered for this purpose as residing in the said region, where national workers benefit from a similar presumption.

SECTION 3

Workers' families

Article 10

The children of a national of a Member State who is or has been employed in the territory of another Member State shall be admitted to that State's general educational, apprenticeship and vocational training courses under the same conditions as the nationals of that State, if such children are residing in its territory. Member States shall encourage all efforts to enable such children to attend these courses under the best possible conditions.

NOTE: Article 7(2) of the Regulation provides a striking example of a provision which has been developed by the Court in a perhaps unexpectedly broad manner.

Cristini v *SNCF* (Case 32/75)

[1975] ECR 1085, Court of Justice of the European Communities

SNCF, the French railway company, offered a fare reduction for large families. Cristini, an Italian national resident in France and the widow of an Italian national who had worked in France, was refused the reduction card on the basis of nationality. SNCF argued that Article 7(2) of Regulation 1612/68 [now 492/2011] covered only advantages connected with the contract of employment. The Court did not agree.

[12] . . . [T]he reference to 'social advantages' in Article 7(2) cannot be interpreted restrictively.

[13] It therefore follows that, in view of the equality of treatment which the provision seeks to achieve, the substantive area of application must be delineated so as to include all social and tax advantages, whether or not attached to the contract of employment, such as reductions in fares for large families.

[14] It then becomes necessary to examine whether such an advantage must be granted to the widow and children after the death of the migrant worker when the national law provides that, at the request of the head of the family, each member of the family shall be issued with an identity card entitling him or her to the reduction.

[15] If the widow and infant children of a national of the Member State in question are entitled to such cards provided that the request had been made by the father before his death, the same must apply where the deceased father was a migrant worker and a national of another Member State.

[16] It would be contrary to the purpose and the spirit of the Community rules on freedom of movement for workers to deprive the survivors of such a benefit following the death of the worker whilst granting the same benefit to the survivors of a national.

[17] In this respect it is important to note the provisions of Regulation (EEC) No 1251/70 of the Commission on the right of workers to remain in the territory of a Member State after having been employed in that State.

NOTE: Regulation 1251/70 ([1970] OJ (Special Edition) (II) 402), referred to in the judgment, confers rights on the worker to remain in the host State after retirement. This matter is now also dealt with in Chapter IV of Directive 2004/38.

However, there is not a uniform notion of 'worker' for these purposes. In *Brian Francis Collins* v *Secretary of State for Work and Pensions* (Case C-138/02) the Court ruled that persons who have already entered into the employment market in another Member State – and are working or who have worked but are no longer working – are 'workers' who may rely on Article 7(2) of Regulation 492/2011 to claim the same social and tax advantages as national workers. By contrast persons who are merely looking for work in another Member State benefit from the principle of equal treatment only as regards access to employment. Collins, whose previous presence in the United Kingdom was remote in time and wholly unassociated with his new quest for work, fell into the latter category. His entitlement, as perceived by the Court, did not derive from the Regulation, but was still potentially valuable. This is explored in connection with the inquiry into Union Citizenship in Chapter 15. The message is, in the first place, that in claiming equal treatment it is always better to be a 'worker' rather than some other less favoured type of migrant (this theme is traced through the case law by C. O'Brien in 'Social Blind Spots and Monocular Policy Making: the ECJ's Migrant Worker Model' (2009) 46 CML Rev 107; and for a recent example see Case C-46/12 *L.N.* judgment of 21 February 2013) and, more generally, that EU law of persons is in a remarkably dynamic state.

There is a dual focus to the Court's generally broad interpretation of Article 7(2) of Regulation 492/2011. On one level, the Court's actions may be seen as intruding on a State's social welfare system, by guaranteeing the individual 'social and tax advantages' which operate beyond the employment relationship and which affect on the wider sphere of life as a citizen. Yet at another level the conferral of such benefits may be presented as an instrument of market integration. Without the lure of extended equal treatment, labour mobility would in practice prove an illusion. This is a controversial debate both in its substance – *should* the EU touch on welfare laws? – and in its institutional aspects – is this the job of the Court or the EU legislature? This theme, associated with the destabilizing effect of EU law on national social practices, was encountered in Section 4 of Chapter 12, will be seen again in the next chapter and it is readdressed more generally in Chapters 17 and 18 of this book.

Article 7(2) of Regulation 492/2011 ensures non-discrimination. It does not confer an absolute right to a rail concession; it confers a right to such provision on terms which do not discriminate according to nationality. So in principle the migrant worker cannot enjoy rights above the ceiling of national provision. If further rights are to be made available, EU legislation must be passed. This re-opens the controversial debate about the proper scope of EU social legislation.

Article 10 of Regulation 492/2011, on page 369, touches on *Workers' Families*. There would evidently be little labour mobility in Europe were migrant workers unable to bring their families with them. Directive 2004/38 houses the majority of the relevant material. According to Article 2(2) benefits are enjoyed by a 'family member', who acquires relevant rights to free movement and residence if accompanying or joining the migrant Union citizen. This covers:

(a) the spouse;

(b) the partner with whom the Union citizen has contracted a registered partnership, on the basis of the legislation of a Member State, if the legislation of the host Member State treats registered partnerships as equivalent to marriage and in accordance with the conditions laid down in the relevant legislation of the host Member State;

(c) the direct descendants who are under the age of 21 or are dependants and those of the spouse or partner as defined in point (b);

(d) the dependent direct relatives in the ascending line and those of the spouse or partner as defined in point (b).

Article 3(2) adds that:

Without prejudice to any right to free movement and residence the persons concerned may have in their own right, the host Member State shall, in accordance with its national legislation, facilitate entry and residence for the following persons:

(a) any other family members, irrespective of their nationality, not falling under the definition in point 2 of Article 2 who, in the country from which they have come, are dependants or members of the household of the Union citizen having the primary right of residence, or where serious health grounds strictly require the personal care of the family member by the Union citizen;

(b) the partner with whom the Union citizen has a durable relationship, duly attested.

The host Member State shall undertake an extensive examination of the personal circumstances and shall justify any denial of entry or residence to these people.

A detailed reading of Directive 2004/38 is required to understand the precise nature of the rights available to family members *via* a worker. It is notable however that Articles 12 and 13 provide some protection for family members where the Union citizen dies or leaves the host Member State, or where the marriage or registered partnership comes to an end. The Directive's Preamble insists 'on due regard for family life and human dignity' in this matter.

The EU also has legislation on social security provision. These measures are based on perceptions similar to those underlying Regulation 492/2011. They are, however, measures of extraordinary complexity, and are best left for discussion in specialist works.

SECTION 3: EXCEPTIONS

Article 45(3) and (4) TFEU (p. 363) contain derogations from the basic principle of free movement. In common with all provisions which are hostile to free movement, these clauses are to be interpreted narrowly. This approach was confirmed by Directive 64/221 which elaborated the substance and procedure of derogation under the third paragraph.

Directive 64/221 is one of several Directives that were repealed and replaced by Directive 2004/38 with effect from 30 April 2006 (p. 367). This legislative overhaul provided an opportunity to clarify the legal rules governing derogation from free movement, in part by taking account of the Court's case law. The relevant provisions of Directive 2004/38 also take account of other innovations elsewhere in the Directive which did not exist at the time Directive 64/221 was adopted – for example, the status of permanent residence.

Directive 2004/38/EC of the European Parliament and of the Council of 29 April 2004 on the right of citizens of the Union and their family members to move and reside freely within the territory of the Member States amending Regulation (EEC) No 1612/68 and repealing Directives 64/221/EEC, 68/360/EEC, 72/194/EEC, 73/148/EEC, 75/34/EEC, 75/35/EEC, 90/364/EEC, 90/365/EEC and 93/96/EEC [2004] OJ L158/77, corrected version [2004] OJ L229/35

CHAPTER VI (ARTICLES 27–33): RESTRICTIONS ON THE RIGHT OF ENTRY AND THE RIGHT OF RESIDENCE ON GROUNDS OF PUBLIC POLICY, PUBLIC SECURITY OR PUBLIC HEALTH

Article 27: General principles

1. Subject to the provisions of this chapter, Member States may restrict the freedom of movement and residence of Union citizens and their family members, irrespective of nationality, on grounds of public policy, public security or public health. These grounds shall not be invoked to serve economic ends.

2. Measures taken on grounds of public policy or public security shall comply with the principle of proportionality and shall be based exclusively on the personal conduct of the individual concerned. Previous criminal convictions shall not in themselves constitute grounds for taking such measures.

The personal conduct of the individual concerned must represent a genuine, present and sufficiently serious threat affecting one of the fundamental interests of society. Justifications that are isolated from the particulars of the case or that rely on considerations of general prevention shall not be accepted.

3. In order to ascertain whether the person concerned represents a danger for public policy or public security, when issuing the registration certificate or, in the absence of a registration system, not later than three months from the date of arrival of the person concerned on its territory or from the date of reporting his/her presence within the territory, as provided for in Article 5(5), or when issuing the residence card, the host Member State may, should it consider this essential, request the Member State of origin and, if need be, other Member States to provide information concerning any previous police record the person concerned may have. Such enquiries shall not be made as a matter of routine. The Member State consulted shall give its reply within two months.

4. The Member State which issued the passport or identity card shall allow the holder of the document who has been expelled on grounds of public policy, public security, or public health from another Member State to re-enter its territory without any formality even if the document is no longer valid or the nationality of the holder is in dispute.

Article 28: Protection against expulsion

1. Before taking an expulsion decision on grounds of public policy or public security, the host Member State shall take account of considerations such as how long the individual concerned has resided on its territory, his/her age, state of health, family and economic situation, social and cultural integration into the host Member State and the extent of his/her links with the country of origin.

2. The host Member State may not take an expulsion decision against Union citizens or their family members, irrespective of nationality, who have the right of permanent residence on its territory, except on serious grounds of public policy or public security.

3. An expulsion decision may not be taken against Union citizens, except if the decision is based on imperative grounds of public security, as defined by Member States, if they:

(a) have resided in the host Member State for the previous 10 years; or

(b) are a minor, except if the expulsion is necessary for the best interests of the child, as provided for in the United Nations Convention on the Rights of the Child of 20 November 1989.

Article 29:

1. The only diseases justifying measures restricting freedom of movement shall be the diseases with epidemic potential as defined by the relevant instruments of the World Health Organisation and other infectious diseases or contagious parasitic diseases if they are the subject of protection provisions applying to nationals of the host Member State.

2. Diseases occurring after a three-month period from the date of arrival shall not constitute grounds for expulsion from the territory.

3. Where there are serious indications that it is necessary, Member States may, within three months of the date of arrival, require persons entitled to the right of residence to undergo, free of charge, a medical examination to certify that they are not suffering from any of the conditions referred to in paragraph 1. Such medical examinations may not be required as a matter of routine.

Article 30 of the Directive governs the notification of decisions to the persons concerned. Article 31 details relevant procedural safeguards, including judicial and, where appropriate, administrative redress procedures in the host Member State. Article 32 concerns the duration of exclusion orders, and Article 33 places limits on expulsion as a penalty or legal consequence.

NOTE: Article 27(2)'s reference to the controlling effect of the principle of proportionality is an innovation compared with the pre-existing text of Directive 64/221. So too is the second paragraph of Article 27(2). Article 28 was also new. The intent is to confine the scope of recourse to these exceptional restrictions on free movement. This is firmly in line with and inspired by the approach taken by the Court in the past when invited to interpret relevant provisions of Directive 64/221. The older case law remains illuminating, though it is worth considering whether replacement Directive 2004/38 limits even further the scope of State restrictive action against migrants permitted by the Court's reading of Directive 64/221. The following case was one of the earliest involving the UK to reach the Court after accession.

***Van Duyn* v *Home Office* (Case 41/74)**

[1974] ECR 1337, Court of Justice of the European Communities

Ms Van Duyn, a Dutch national, was refused leave to enter the UK to work for the Church of Scientology because the UK Government considered the Church's activities to be socially harmful. Ms Van Duyn's reliance on (what was then) European Community law led to a preliminary reference by the High Court. The Court of Justice first held Article 48 of the Treaty (now, after amendment, Article 45 TFEU) and Article 3(1) of Directive 64/221 directly effective and accordingly enforceable before national courts by private individuals. The Court then turned to the substance of the case.

[17] It is necessary, first, to consider whether association with a body or an organization can in itself constitute personal conduct within the meaning of Article 3 of Directive No 64/221 [*cf.* Art 27(2) Dir. 2004/38]. Although a person's past association cannot in general, justify a decision refusing him the right to move freely within the Community, it is nevertheless the case that present association, which reflects participation in the activities of the body or of the organization as well as identification with its aims and its designs, may be considered a voluntary act of the person concerned and, consequently, as part of his personal conduct within the meaning of the provision cited.

[18] This third question further raises the problem of what importance must be attributed to the fact that the activities of the organization in question, which are considered by the Member State as contrary to the public good are not however prohibited by national law. It should be emphasized that the concept of public policy in the context of the Community and where, in particular, it is used as a justification for derogating from the fundamental principle of freedom of movement for workers, must be interpreted strictly, so that its scope cannot be determined unilaterally by each Member State without being subject to control by the institutions of the Community. Nevertheless the particular circumstances justifying recourse to the concept of public policy may vary from one country to another and from one period to another, and it is therefore necessary in this matter to allow the competent national authorities an area of discretion within the limits imposed by the Treaty.

[19] It follows from the above that where the competent authorities of a Member State have clearly defined their standpoint as regards the activities of a particular organization and where, considering it to be socially harmful, they have taken administrative measures to counteract these activities, the Member State cannot be

required, before it can rely on the concept of public policy, to make such activities unlawful, if recourse to such a measure is not thought appropriate in the circumstances.

[20] The question raises finally the problem of whether a Member State is entitled, on grounds of public policy, to prevent a national of another Member State from taking gainful employment within its territory with a body or organization, it being the case that no similar restriction is placed upon its own nationals.

[21] In this connexion, the Treaty, while enshrining the principle of freedom of movement for workers without any discrimination on grounds of nationality, admits, in Article 48 (3), limitations justified on grounds of public policy, public security or public health to the rights deriving from this principle. Under the terms of the provision cited above, the right to accept offers of employment actually made, the right to move freely within the territory of Member States for this purpose, and the right to stay in a Member State for the purpose of employment are, among others, all subject to such limitations. Consequently, the effect of such limitations, when they apply, is that leave to enter the territory of a Member State and the right to reside there may be refused to a national of another Member State.

[22] Furthermore, it is a principle of international law, which the EEC Treaty cannot be assumed to disregard in the relations between Member States, that a State is precluded from refusing its own nationals the right of entry or residence.

[23] It follows that a Member State, for reasons of public policy, can, where it deems necessary, refuse a national of another Member State the benefit of the principle of freedom of movement for workers in a case where such a national proposes to take up a particular offer of employment even though the Member State does not place a similar restriction upon its own nationals.

NOTE: In both the following decisions, the Court adopted a narrow interpretation of the legitimate scope of Member State action against individual workers.

R v *Bouchereau* (Case 30/77)

[1977] ECR 1999, Court of Justice of the European Communities

Bouchereau, a French national working in England, was convicted of unlawful possession of drugs. He fought proposed deportation. Could the UK authorities show that his case fell within the exception then located in Article 48(3), now Article 45(3) TFEU? The matter reached the Court by way of a preliminary reference. The Court examined the relevance of previous criminal convictions.

[27] The terms of Article 3(2) of the directive [64/221: *cf.* Art 27(2) Dir. 2004/38], which states that 'previous criminal convictions shall not in themselves constitute grounds for the taking of such measures' must be understood as requiring the national authorities to carry out a specific appraisal from the point of view of the interests inherent in protecting the requirements of public policy, which does not necessarily coincide with the appraisals which formed the basis of the criminal conviction.

[28] The existence of a previous criminal conviction can, therefore, only be taken into account in so far as the circumstances which gave rise to that conviction are evidence of personal conduct constituting a present threat to the requirements of public policy.

[29] Although, in general, a finding that such a threat exists implies the existence in the individual concerned of a propensity to act in the same way in the future, it is possible that past conduct alone may constitute such a threat to the requirements of public policy.

The Court then proceeded to consider the notion of 'public policy' mentioned in Article 48(3) (now, after amendment, Article 45(3) TFEU).

[35] In so far as it may justify certain restrictions on the free movement of persons subject to Community law, recourse by a national authority to the concept of public policy presupposes, in any event, the existence, in addition to the perturbation of the social order which any infringement of the law involves, of a genuine and sufficiently serious threat to the requirements of public policy affecting one of the fundamental interests of society.

NOTE: You should now be readily able to spot where the second paragraph of Article 27(2) of Directive 2004/38, p. 375, comes from!

Adoui and Cornuaille v *Belgian State* (Cases 115 & 116/81)

[1982] ECR 1665, Court of Justice of the European Communities

The applicants were French nationals refused permission to reside in Belgium on public policy grounds. The Court delicately described them as waitresses in a Liège bar which was considered 'suspect from the point of view of morals'. It was more direct in the body of the judgment.

[6] Those questions are motivated by the fact that prostitution as such is n[illegible] tion, although the Law does prohibit certain incidental activities, which are particularly ha[illegible] social point of view, such as the exploitation of prostitution by third parties and various forms of incitement to debauchery.

[7] The reservations contained in Articles 48 and 56 of the EEC Treaty permit Member States to adopt, with respect to the nationals of other Member States and on the grounds specified in those provisions, in particular grounds justified by the requirements of public policy, measures which they cannot apply to their own nationals, inasmuch as they have no authority to expel the latter from the national territory or to deny them access thereto. Although that difference of treatment, which bears upon the nature of the measures available, must therefore be allowed, it must nevertheless be stressed that, in a Member State, the authority empowered to adopt such measures must not base the exercise of its powers on assessments of certain conduct which would have the effect of applying an arbitrary distinction to the detriment of nationals of other Member States.

[8] It should be noted in that regard that reliance by a national authority upon the concept of public policy presupposes, as the Court held in its judgment of 27 October 1977 in Case 30/77 Bouchereau [1977] ECR 1999, the existence of 'a genuine and sufficiently serious threat affecting one of the fundamental interests of society'. Although Community law does not impose upon the Member States a uniform scale of values as regards the assessment of conduct which may be considered as contrary to public policy, it should nevertheless be stated that conduct may not be considered as being of a sufficiently serious nature to justify restrictions on the admission to or residence within the territory of a Member State of a national of another Member State in a case where the former Member State does not adopt, with respect to the same conduct on the part of its own nationals repressive measures or other genuine and effective measures intended to combat such conduct.

[9] The answer to Questions 1 to 9, 11 and 12 should therefore be that a Member State may not, by virtue of the reservation relating to public policy contained in Articles 48 and 56 of the Treaty, expel a national of another Member State from its territory or refuse him access to its territory by reason of conduct which, when attributable to the former State's own nationals, does not give rise to repressive measures or other genuine and effective measures intended to combat such conduct.

[10] In the tenth question, the national court asks whether the action taken by a Member State which, 'anxious to remove from its territory prostitutes from a given country because they could promote criminal activities, does so systematically, declaring that their business of prostitution endangers the requirements of public policy and not taking the trouble to consider whether the persons concerned may or may not be suspected of contact with the "underworld" ', constitutes a measure of a general preventive nature within the meaning of Article 3 of Directive No 64/221.

[11] It should be noted that Article 3(1) of the directive provides that measures taken on grounds of public policy or of public security are to be based exclusively on the personal conduct of the individual concerned. In that regard it is sufficient to refer to the judgment of 26 February 1975 in Case 67/74 Bonsignore [1975] ECR 297, in which the Court held that 'measures adopted on grounds of public policy and for the maintenance of public security against the nationals of Member States of the Community cannot be justified on grounds extraneous to the individual case, as is shown in particular by the requirements set out in paragraph (1) that "only" the "personal conduct" of those affected by the measures is to be regarded as determinative'.

■ **QUESTION**

There are two aspects of *Van Duyn* (Case 41/74) (p. 375) which are of particular interest in the present context: (i) its discussion of the nature of 'personal conduct', mentioned in Article 3(1) of Directive 64/221 and taken over into Article 27(2) of Directive 2004/38; (ii) its approach to the competence of Member States to control that conduct, taking account of how nationals behaving in a similar fashion would be treated. Explain how the Court has developed a more rigorous stance since *Van Duyn*.

Donatella Calfa (Case C-348/96)

[1999] ECR I-11, Court of Justice of the European Communities

Ms Calfa, an Italian tourist in Greece, was found guilty of a drugs-related offence. She was sentenced to three months' imprisonment and expelled for life from Greek territory. The case concerned the receipt of services, rather than a worker, and therefore Articles 49–55 EC, now Articles 56–62 TFEU, were relevant (Chapter 14), but the principles of derogation apply *mutatis mutandis* and the Court cited familiar case law concerning workers.

[20] Article 56 [now 52] permits Member States to adopt, with respect to nationals of other Member States, and in particular on the grounds of public policy, measures which they cannot apply to their own nationals, inasmuch as they have no authority to expel the latter from the territory or to deny them access thereto (see Case 41/74 *Van Duyn* v *Home Office* [1974] ECR 1337, paragraphs 22 and 23, Joined Cases 115/81 and 116/81 *Adoui and Cornuaille* v *Belgium* [1982] ECR 1665, paragraph 7 . . .).

[21] Under the Court's case law, the concept of public policy may be relied upon in the event of a genuine and sufficiently serious threat to the requirements of public policy affecting one of the fundamental interests of society (see Case 30/77 *Bouchereau* [1977] ECR 1999, paragraph 35).

[22] In this respect, it must be accepted that a Member State may consider that the use of drugs constitutes a danger for society such as to justify special measures against foreign nationals who contravene its laws on drugs, in order to maintain public order.

[23] However, as the Court has repeatedly stated, the public policy exception, like all derogations from a fundamental principle of the Treaty, must be interpreted restrictively.

[24] In that regard, Directive 64/221, Article 1(1) of which provides that the directive is to apply to *inter alia* any national of a Member State who travels to another Member State as a recipient of services, sets certain limits on the right of Member States to expel foreign nationals on the grounds of public policy. Article 3 of that directive states that measures taken on grounds of public policy or of public security that have the effect of restricting the residence of a national of another Member State must be based exclusively on the personal conduct of the individual concerned. In addition, previous criminal convictions cannot in themselves constitute grounds for the taking of such measures. It follows that the existence of a previous criminal conviction can, therefore, only be taken into account in so far as the circumstances which gave rise to that conviction are evidence of personal conduct constituting a present threat to the requirements of public policy (*Bouchereau*, paragraph 28).

[25] It follows that an expulsion order could be made against a Community national such as Ms Calfa only if, besides her having committed an offence under drugs laws, her personal conduct created a genuine and sufficiently serious threat affecting one of the fundamental interests of society.

[26] In the present case, the legislation at issue in the main proceedings requires nationals of other Member States found guilty, on the national territory in which that legislation applies, of an offence under the drugs laws, to be expelled for life from that territory, unless compelling reasons, in particular family reasons, justify their continued residence in the country. The penalty can be revoked only by a decision taken at the discretion of the Minister for Justice after a period of three years.

[27] Therefore, expulsion for life automatically follows a criminal conviction, without any account being taken of the personal conduct of the offender or of the danger which that person represents for the requirements of public policy.

[28] It follows that the conditions for the application of the public policy exception provided for in Directive 64/221, as interpreted by the Court of Justice, are not fulfilled . . .

Article 28 of Directive 2004/38 (p. 374) now governs expulsion. In the next case the Court carefully explains the limits it places on State autonomy.

***Land Baden-Württemberg* v *Panagiotis Tsakouridis* (Case C-145/09)**

[2010] ECR I-11979, Court of Justice

Tsakouridis was a Greek national who had been convicted of assault and offences associated with illegal drugs. Could he rely on EU law to defend himself against deportation from Germany? A preliminary reference allowed the Court to begin by connecting Directive 2004/38 with its legislative antecedents – including Directive 64/221.

23. . . . Directive 2004/38 aims to facilitate the exercise of the primary and individual right to move and reside freely within the territory of the Member States that is conferred directly on Union citizens by the Treaty, and it aims in particular to strengthen that right, so that Union citizens cannot derive less rights from that directive than from the instruments of secondary legislation which it amends or repeals . . ..

The Court then explained that:

25. . . . Directive 2004/38 . . . establishes a system of protection against expulsion measures which is based on the degree of integration of those persons in the host Member State, so that the greater the degree of integration of Union citizens and their family members in the host Member State, the greater the degree of protection against expulsion should be.

26. In this context, Article 28(1) of that directive provides generally that, before taking an expulsion decision on grounds of public policy or public security, the host Member State must take account in particular of considerations such as how long the individual concerned has resided on its territory, his or her age, state of health, family and economic situation, social and cultural integration into the host Member State and the extent of his or her links with the country of origin.

The Court then proceeded to look more closely at the structure of Article 28 of Directive 2004/38, which sets out separate controls in its second and third paragraphs.

39. . . . the referring court seeks essentially to know whether and to what extent criminal offences in connection with dealing in narcotics as part of an organised group can be covered by the concept of 'imperative grounds of public security', should that court conclude that the Union citizen concerned enjoys the protection of Article 28(3) of Directive 2004/38, or the concept of 'serious grounds of public policy or public security', should it conclude that that citizen enjoys the protection of Article 28(2) of that directive.

40. It follows from the wording and scheme of Article 28 of Directive 2004/38 . . . that by subjecting all expulsion measures in the cases referred to in Article 28(3) of that directive to the existence of 'imperative grounds' of public security, a concept which is considerably stricter than that of 'serious grounds' within the meaning of Article 28(2), the European Union legislature clearly intended to limit measures based on Article 28(3) to 'exceptional circumstances', as set out in recital 24 in the preamble to that directive.

41. The concept of 'imperative grounds of public security' presupposes not only the existence of a threat to public security, but also that such a threat is of a particularly high degree of seriousness, as is reflected by the use of the words 'imperative reasons'.

42. It is in this context that the concept of 'public security' in Article 28(3) of Directive 2004/38 should also be interpreted.

43. As regards public security, the Court has held that this covers both a Member State's internal and its external security . . .

44. The Court has also held that a threat to the functioning of the institutions and essential public services and the survival of the population, as well as the risk of a serious disturbance to foreign relations or to peaceful coexistence of nations, or a risk to military interests, may affect public security. . .

45. It does not follow that objectives such as the fight against crime in connection with dealing in narcotics as part of an organised group are necessarily excluded from that concept.

46. Dealing in narcotics as part of an organised group is a diffuse form of crime with impressive economic and operational resources and frequently with transnational connections. In view of the devastating effects of crimes linked to drug trafficking, Council Framework Decision 2004/757/JHA of 25 October 2004 laying down minimum provisions on the constituent elements of criminal acts and penalties in the field of illicit drug trafficking (OJ 2004 L 335, p. 8) states in recital 1 that illicit drug trafficking poses a threat to health, safety and the quality of life of citizens of the Union, and to the legal economy, stability and security of the Member States.

47. Since drug addiction represents a serious evil for the individual and is fraught with social and economic danger to mankind (see, to that effect, *inter alia*, Case 221/81 *Wolf* [1982] ECR 3681, paragraph 9, and Eur. Court H.R., *Aoulmi v. France*, no. 50278/99, § 86, ECHR 2006-I), trafficking in narcotics as part of an organised group could reach a level of intensity that might directly threaten the calm and physical security of the population as a whole or a large part of it.

48. It should be added that Article 27(2) of Directive 2004/38 emphasises that the conduct of the person concerned must represent a genuine and present threat to a fundamental interest of society or of the Member State concerned, that previous criminal convictions cannot in themselves constitute grounds for taking public policy or public security measures, and that justifications that are isolated from the particulars of the case or that rely on considerations of general prevention cannot be accepted.

49. Consequently, an expulsion measure must be based on an individual examination of the specific case . . . and can be justified on imperative grounds of public security within the meaning of Article 28(3) of Directive 2004/38 only if, having regard to the exceptional seriousness of the threat, such a measure is necessary for the protection of the interests it aims to secure, provided that that objective cannot be attained by less strict means, having regard to the length of residence of the Union citizen in the host Member State and in particular to the serious negative consequences such a measure may have for Union citizens who have become genuinely integrated into the host Member State.

50. In the application of Directive 2004/38, a balance must be struck more particularly between the exceptional nature of the threat to public security as a result of the personal conduct of the person concerned, assessed if necessary at the time when the expulsion decision is to be made (see, *inter alia*, Joined Cases C-482/01 and C-493/01 *Orfanopoulos and Oliveri* [2004] ECR I-5257, paragraphs 77 to 79), by reference in particular to the possible penalties and the sentences imposed, the degree of involvement in the criminal activity, and, if appropriate, the risk of reoffending (see, to that effect, *inter alia*, Case 30/77 *Bouchereau* [1977] ECR 1999, paragraph 29), on the one hand, and, on the other hand, the risk of compromising the social rehabilitation of the Union citizen in the State in which he has become genuinely integrated, which, as the Advocate General observes in point 95 of his Opinion, is not only in his interest but also in that of the European Union in general.

51. The sentence passed must be taken into account as one element in that complex of factors. A sentence of five years' imprisonment cannot lead to an expulsion decision, as provided for in national law, without the factors described in the preceding paragraph being taken into account, which is for the national court to verify.

52. In that assessment, account must be taken of the fundamental rights whose observance the Court ensures, in so far as reasons of public interest may be relied on to justify a national measure which is liable to obstruct the exercise of freedom of movement for persons only if the measure in question takes account of such rights (see, *inter alia*, *Orfanopoulos and Oliveri*, paragraphs 97 to 99), in particular the right to respect for private and family life as set forth in Article 7 of the Charter of Fundamental Rights of the European Union and Article 8 of the European Convention for the Protection of Human Rights and Fundamental Freedoms (see, *inter alia*, Case C-400/10 PPU *McB* [2010] ECR I-0000, paragraph 53, and Eur. Court H.R., *Maslov* v *Austria* [GC], no. 1638/03, § 61 *et seq.*, 23 June 2008).

53. To assess whether the interference contemplated is proportionate to the legitimate aim pursued, in this case the protection of public security, account must be taken in particular of the nature and seriousness of the offence committed, the duration of residence of the person concerned in the host Member State, the period which has passed since the offence was committed and the conduct of the person concerned during that period, and the solidity of the social, cultural and family ties with the host Member State. In the case of a Union citizen who has lawfully spent most or even all of his childhood and youth in the host Member State, very good reasons would have to be put forward to justify the expulsion measure (see, to that effect, in particular, *Maslov v Austria*, §§ 71 to 75).

54. In any event, since the Court has held that a Member State may, in the interests of public policy, consider that the use of drugs constitutes a danger for society such as to justify special measures against foreign nationals who contravene its laws on drugs (see Case C-348/96 *Calfa* [1999] ECR I-11, paragraph 22, and *Orfanopoulos and Oliveri*, paragraph 67), it must follow that dealing in narcotics as part of an organised group is *a fortiori* covered by the concept of 'public policy' for the purposes of Article 28(2) of Directive 2004/38.

55. It is for the referring court to ascertain, taking into consideration all the factors mentioned above, whether Mr Tsakouridis's conduct is covered by 'serious grounds of public policy or public security' within the meaning of Article 28(2) of Directive 2004/38 or 'imperative grounds of public security' within the meaning of Article 28(3) of that directive, and whether the proposed expulsion measure satisfies the conditions referred to above.

NOTE: For an application of these principles to sex-related, rather than drug-related, crimes, see Case C-348/09 *P.I.* judgment of 22 May 2012.

■ QUESTION

Would any of the cases considered at (pp. 375–81) which pre-date the entry into force of Directive 2004/38 be decided differently were they to arise today?

NOTE: It is obscure how the Article 45(3) TFEU derogations can be effectively applied in practice in the light of Article 26 TFEU's commitment to an area without internal frontiers. The intimate relationship between the Treaty rules on free movement and action in common in *inter alia* asylum policy, immigration policy, and police co-operation has a tortured history. The Maastricht Treaty created the 'three pillar' structure which kept apart these areas of activity within the fragmented European Union (p. 9). Partly in consequence of dissatisfaction with the progress made under this structure, the Member States agreed at Amsterdam to adjust the legal framework in favour of increased 'communitiarization' of the material relevant to securing the free movement of persons. Material on visas, asylum, immigration, and other policies related to free movement of persons dedicated to the progressive establishment of 'an area of freedom, security and justice' was brought within the 'first pillar', albeit according to a model that was not orthodox. The Lisbon Treaty did away with the 'three pillar' EU (p. 19) and the TFEU contains not only the provisions on free movement but also, in Title V of Part Three, the cartography of the EU's area of freedom, security, and justice. And yet even today the procedures are not uniform, so in this sense the traces of the pillars are still visible. This is examined in Chapter 15.

Article 45(4) TFEU, the 'public service' exception, has been subjected by the Court to a parallel narrow interpretation.

Commission v *Belgium* (Case 149/79)

[1980] ECR 3881, Court of Justice of the European Communities

The case involved the restriction to Belgians alone of several posts on Belgian railways, including trainee drivers, shunters, and signallers, and also posts with the City of Brussels for, *inter alia*, hospital nurses, plumbers, and electricians. The Court's statements of principle included the following, directed at Article 48(4) of the Treaty (now, after amendment, Article 45(4) TFEU):

[10] That provision removes from the ambit of Article 48(1) to (3) a series of posts which involve direct or indirect participation in the exercise of powers conferred by public law and duties designed to safeguard the general interests of the State or of other public authorities. Such posts in fact presume on the part of those occupying them the existence of a special relationship of allegiance to the State and reciprocity of rights and duties which form the foundation of the bond of nationality.

[11] The scope of the derogation made by Article 48(4) to the principles of freedom of movement and equality of treatment laid down in the first three paragraphs of the article should therefore be determined on the basis of the aim pursued by that article. However, determining the sphere of application of Article 48(4) raises special difficulties since in the various Member States authorities acting under powers conferred by public law have assumed responsibilities of an economic and social nature or are involved in activities which are not identifiable with the functions which are typical of the public service yet which by their nature still come under the sphere of application of the Treaty. In these circumstances the effect of extending the exception contained in Article 48(4) to posts which, whilst coming under the State or other organizations governed by public law, still do not involve any association with tasks belonging to the public service properly so called, would be to remove a considerable number of posts from the ambit of the principles set out in the Treaty and to create inequalities between Member States according to the different ways in which the State and certain sectors of economic life are organized.

[12] Consequently it is appropriate to examine whether the posts covered by the action may be associated with the concept of public service within the meaning of Article 48(4), which requires uniform interpretation and application throughout the Community. It must be acknowledged that the application of the distinguishing criteria indicated above gives rise to problems of appraisal and demarcation in specific cases. It follows from the foregoing that such a classification depends on whether or not the posts in question are typical of the specific activities of the public service in so far as the exercise of powers conferred by public law and responsibility for safeguarding the general interests of the State are vested in it.

NOTE: **The Court felt it had insufficient information to rule in the case itself; the follow-up judgment appears at [1982] ECR 1845. Litigation concerning the scope of this exception is scarce, but for** a more recent treatment see Case C-405/01 *Colegio de Oficiales de la Marina Mercante Española* [2003] ECR I-10391.

NOTE: For additional material and resources see the Online Resource Centre at: www.oxfordtextbooks.co.uk/orc/weatherill12e.

14

Freedom of Establishment and the Free Movement of Services: Articles 49 and 56 TFEU

SECTION 1: THE RIGHTS

Articles 49 and 56 TFEU extend the rights of free movement beyond 'workers' to include the free movement of individuals who are self-employed and wish to establish themselves in another Member State, or to provide services there. These rights are granted not just to the natural person who wishes to migrate, but also to the legal person – i.e., the company.

ARTICLES 49 AND 56 TFEU

ARTICLE 49

Within the framework of the provisions set out below, restrictions on the freedom of establishment of nationals of a Member State in the territory of another Member State shall be prohibited. Such prohibition shall also apply to restrictions on the setting up of agencies, branches or subsidiaries by nationals of any Member State established in the territory of any Member State.

Freedom of establishment shall include the right to take up and pursue activities as self-employed persons and to set up and manage undertakings, in particular companies or firms within the meaning of the second paragraph of Article 54, under the conditions laid down for its own nationals by the law of the country where such establishment is effected, subject to the provisions of the chapter relating to capital.

ARTICLE 56

Within the framework of the provisions set out below, restrictions on freedom to provide services within the Union shall be prohibited in respect of nationals of Member States who are established in a Member State other than that of the person for whom the services are intended.

The European Parliament and the Council, acting in accordance with the ordinary legislative procedure, may extend the provisions of the chapter to nationals of a third country who provide services and who are established within the Union.

NOTES

1. The Lisbon Treaty in 2009 and the Treaty of Amsterdam in 1999 effected merely cosmetic changes to these provisions. On re-numbering (pp. 10, 19), what are now Articles 49 and 56 TFEU replaced what were pre-Lisbon Articles 43 and 49 EC respectively (and pre-Amsterdam Articles 52 and 59 respectively). These numerical games must be borne in mind in reading the material in this chapter.

   The distinction between Article 49, the right of establishment, and Article 56, the right to provide services, is rather artificial. The former envisages a more permanent presence in the host Member State than the latter, but at the margin it may be difficult to select the correct classification (e.g., Case C-215/01 *Bruno Schnitzer* [2003] ECR I-14847). Broadly, however, the problem is unlikely to arise in an acute form, because the Court has wisely recognized the common purpose of the provisions and has shown itself prepared to interpret them in parallel fashion. Article 45 TFEU too joins in this shared purpose; see, e.g., *Procureur du Roi* v *Royer* (Case 48/75) [1976] ECR 497, *Claude Nadin and Nadin-Lux* (Cases C-151/04 & C-152/04) [2005] ECR I-11203.

The rights of the migrating individual to non-discriminatory treatment according to nationality were amplified by Directive 73/148 on the Abolition of Restrictions on Movement and Residence. This measure was analogous to Directive 68/360 applicable to workers. Both Directive 73/148 and Directive 68/360 were repealed with effect from 30 April 2006, the deadline for Member State implementation of replacement Directive 2004/38 (p. 367).

2. Directive 75/34 conferred rights to remain in the host State. It was analogous to Regulation 1251/70, mentioned at p. 372. Here too replacement Directive 2004/38 (Chapter IV) should now be consulted.

   Derogation from the rights is possible in a fashion comparable to Article 45 (p. 373); see Articles 51, 52, and 62 TFEU. This complementarity was encountered in *Donatella Calfa* (Case C-348/96), p. 378.

SECTION 2: NON-DISCRIMINATION

The following case illustrates the application of the principle of non-discrimination.

Thieffry v *Conseil de l'Ordre des Avocats à la Cour de Paris* (Case 71/76)

[1977] ECR 765, Court of Justice of the European Communities

Thieffry, a Belgian advocate, held a Belgian diploma of Doctor of Laws, recognized by a French university as equivalent to the French licenciate's degree in law. Despite this recognition of equivalence, he was refused entry to the Paris Bar because he held no French diploma of the required level. Thieffry's challenge reached the Court *via* the preliminary reference procedure (Chapter 7). The Court cited the General Programme for the abolition of restrictions on freedom of establishment, adopted in 1961, and continued:

[15] ... [F]reedom of establishment, subject to observance of professional rules justified by the general good, is one of the objectives of the Treaty.

[16] In so far as Community law makes no special provision, these objectives may be attained by measures enacted by the Member States, which under Article 5 of the Treaty are bound to take 'all appropriate measures, whether general or particular, to ensure fulfilment of the obligations arising out of this Treaty or resulting from action taken by the institutions of the Community', and to abstain 'from any measure which could jeopardize the attainment of the objectives of this Treaty' [see now Art 4(3) TEU].

[17] Consequently, if the freedom of establishment provided for by Article 52 [now 49] can be ensured in a Member State either under the provisions of the laws and regulations in force, or by virtue of the practices of the public service or of professional bodies, a person subject to Community law cannot be denied the practical benefit of that freedom solely by virtue of the fact that, for a particular profession, the directives provided for by Article 57 of the Treaty have not yet been adopted.

[18] Since the practical enjoyment of freedom of establishment can thus in certain circumstances depend upon national practice or legislation, it is incumbent upon the competent public authorities – including legally recognised professional bodies – to ensure that such practice or legislation is applied in accordance with the objective defined by the provisions of the Treaty relating to freedom of establishment.

[19] In particular, there is an unjustified restriction on that freedom where, in a Member State, admission to a particular profession is refused to a person covered by the Treaty who holds a diploma which has been recognised as an equivalent qualification by the competent authority of the country of establishment and who furthermore has fulfilled the specific conditions regarding professional training in force in that country, solely by reason of the fact that the person concerned does not possess the national diploma corresponding to the diploma which he holds and which has been recognised as an equivalent qualification.

The Court was accordingly able to conclude, in terms obviously favourable to Thieffry:

[27] In these circumstances, the answer to the question referred to the Court should be that when a national of one Member State desirous of exercising a professional activity such as the profession of advocate in another Member State has obtained a diploma in his country of origin which has been recognized as an equivalent qualification by the competent authority under the legislation of the country of establishment and which has thus enabled him to sit and pass the special qualifying examination for the profession in question, the act of demanding the national diploma prescribed by the legislation of the country of establishment constitutes, even in the absence of the directives provided for in Article 57, a restriction incompatible with the freedom of establishment guaranteed by Article 52 of the Treaty.

NOTES

1. A similar approach had been taken in *Reyners* v *Belgian State* (Case 2/74) [1974] ECR 631, where the Court insisted that the principle of non-discrimination had direct effect even in the absence of implementing Directives.
2. The Court has extended the scope of these Treaty Articles in order to accommodate tourists. Tourists are neither self-employed nor providers of services, but they are recipients of services and thus fall within the scope of Article 56 TFEU.

Cowan v *Le Trésor Public* (Case 186/87)

[1986] ECR 195, Court of Justice of the European Communities

Mr Cowan, a British national, was attacked and robbed while visiting Paris as a tourist. He was refused criminal injuries compensation by the French authorities because of his nationality. He challenged this refusal. The matter reached the Court as a preliminary reference. The Court placed great emphasis on the principle of non-discrimination on grounds of nationality under (what was then) Article 7 EEC. It should be noted that this subsequently became Article 6 EC (post-Maastricht), Article 12 (post-Amsterdam) and now it is, in amended form, Article 18 TFEU.

[14] Under Article 7 of the Treaty the prohibition of discrimination applies 'within the scope of application of this Treaty' and 'without prejudice to any special provisions contained therein'. This latter expression refers particularly to other provisions of the Treaty in which the application of the general principle set out in that article is given concrete form in respect of specific situations. Examples of that are the provisions concerning free movement of workers, the right of establishment and the freedom to provide services.

[15] On that last point, in its judgment of 31 January 1984 in Joined Cases 286/82 and 26/83 *Luisi and Carbone* v *Ministero del Tesoro* [1984] ECR 377, the Court held that the freedom to provide services includes the freedom for the recipients of services to go to another Member State in order to receive a service there, without being obstructed by restrictions, and that tourists, among others, must be regarded as recipients of services.

[16] At the hearing the French Government submitted that as Community law now stands a recipient of services may not rely on the prohibition of discrimination to the extent that the national law at issue does not create any barrier to freedom of movement. A provision such as that at issue in the main proceedings, it says, imposes no restrictions in that respect. Furthermore, it concerns a right which is a manifestation of the principle of national solidarity. Such a right presupposes a closer bond with the State than that of a recipient of services, and for that reason it may be restricted to persons who are either nationals of that State or foreign nationals resident on the territory of that State.

[17] That reasoning cannot be accepted. When Community law guarantees a natural person the freedom to go to another Member State the protection of that person from harm in the Member State in question, on the same basis as that of nationals and persons residing there, is a corollary of that freedom of movement. It follows that the prohibition of discrimination is applicable to recipients of services within the meaning of the Treaty as regards protection against the risk of assault and the right to obtain financial compensation provided for by national law when that risk materializes. The fact that the compensation at issue is financed by the Public Treasury cannot alter the rules regarding the protection of the rights guaranteed by the Treaty.

[18] The French Government also submitted that compensation such as that at issue in the main proceedings is not subject to the prohibition of discrimination because it falls within the law of criminal procedure, which is not included within the scope of the Treaty.

[19] Although in principle criminal legislation and the rules of criminal procedure, among which the national provision in issue is to be found, are matters for which the Member States are responsible, the Court has consistently held (see *inter alia* the judgment of 11 November 1981 in Case 203/80 *Casati* [1981] ECR 2595) that Community law sets certain limits to their power. Such legislative provisions may not discriminate against persons to whom Community law gives the right to equal treatment or restrict the fundamental freedoms guaranteed by Community law.

[20] In the light of all the foregoing the answer to the question submitted must be that the prohibition of discrimination laid down in particular in Article 7 of the EEC Treaty must be interpreted as meaning that in respect of persons whose freedom to travel to a Member State, in particular as recipients of services, is guaranteed by Community law that State may not make the award of State compensation for harm caused in that State to the victim of an assault resulting in physical injury subject to the condition that he hold a residence permit or be a national of a country which has entered into a reciprocal agreement with that Member State.

NOTE: Greeting *Cowan* (Case 186/87), F. Mancini congratulated the Court on 'one of its shrewdest judgments' ((1989) 26 CML Rev 595). *Donatella Calfa* (Case C-348/96) (p. 378) was similarly a case concerning a tourist who fell within the scope of application of the Treaty provisions on services.

The scope of the principle of non-discrimination, which as *Cowan* (Case 186/87) indicates derives fundamentally from what is today Article 18 TFEU post-Lisbon, remains unclear. One might suppose that there is no right to equality in all matters, and that the tourist would not be able to use Article 18 TFEU in so extensive a manner as the worker is able to rely on Article 7(2) of Regulation 492/2011 (see cases at p. 371). However, this reading now seems to be challenged by the Court's evolving case law concerning Citizenship. This is addressed at in Chapter 15.

It is also worth noting that each time an enhanced competence is conferred on the Union, as has occurred on periodic Treaty revision at Maastricht, Amsterdam, and (less significantly) at Nice and Lisbon, so the scope of application of *inter alia* Article 18 TFEU is correspondingly widened. The field of education provides a good example of such increasing occupation by requirements drawn from Union law.

■ QUESTION

In its case law, the Court is trying to strike a balance between, on the one hand, applying and extending the principle of non-discrimination already set out in both the Treaty and secondary legislation, and, on the other, acknowledging that some areas are dependent on legislative action to extend the law. Has it gone beyond the scope of due judicial restraint?

SECTION 3: BEYOND DISCRIMINATION

The limits of the non-discrimination approach to market integration are significant. Consider *Thieffry* (Case 71/76) (p. 384). The key to the application of the principle of non-discrimination was the recognition of Thieffry's Belgian degree as sufficient for French purposes. Without recognition, he could have been excluded from the French lawyer's market. There would have been no nationality discrimination; no one could act as *avocat* without a French degree, irrespective of nationality. (See, e.g., *Procureur de la République* v *Bouchoucha* (Case C-61/89) [1990] ECR I-3551.)

This problem is serious for the professional person, who is faced by the need to meet the professional qualification requirements of the host State; in the absence of cross-recognition as in *Thieffry* (Case 71/76), home State qualifications are unlikely to suffice. Similarly, a company may face serious problems in offering services across borders, because it may find that certain regulations are imposed on all firms supplying services in the host State, but with which it, a non-national firm, does not comply. Articles 49(2) and 57(3) TFEU declare that the host State may continue to apply its rules equally to all those active on its market.

A: Challenging and justifying obstructive national measures

It should be immediately apparent that there are potentially close connections with the *'Cassis de Dijon'* case law under Article 34 (Chapter 12). The problem here too arises in relation to national measures which are not discriminatory, but which hinder the exercise of free movement rights. The principles according to which the permissibility of such national measures shall be judged appear to be the same under both Article 34 and Article 56 TFEU, in so far as both enshrine fundamental Treaty freedoms (*cf* Case C-55/94 *Gebhard*, p. 266). However, the Court's scrutiny of regulatory diversity between the Member States in the context of Article 56 has commonly been couched in similar but not identical language to that which occurs under Article 34.

Commission v *Germany* (Case 205/84)

[1986] ECR 3755, Court of Justice of the European Communities

The case involved German law regulating the provision of insurance services on German territory. *All* insurers had to have a permanent establishment in Germany. *All* insurers had to be authorized by the German State. Plainly, insurers from other States wishing to offer services in Germany were impeded by these requirements. The Commission argued that the rules violated Articles 59 and 60 of the Treaty (now, after amendment, Articles 56 and 57 TFEU). The matter reached the Court under Article 169 of the Treaty (now Article 258 TFEU: see Chapter 4). The first extract sets out the Court's approach.

[25] According to the well-established case-law of the Court, Articles 59 and 60 of the EEC Treaty [now Articles 56 and 57 TFEU] became directly applicable on the expiry of the transitional period, and their applicability was not conditional on the harmonisation or the coordination of the laws of the Member States. Those articles require the removal not only of all discrimination against a provider of a service on the grounds of his nationality but also all restrictions on his freedom to provide services imposed by reason of the fact that he is established in a Member State other than that in which the service is to be provided.

[26] Since the German Government and certain other of the governments intervening in its support have referred to the third paragraph of Article 60 as a basis for their contention that the State of the person insured can also apply its supervisory legislation to insurers established in another Member State, it should be added, as the Court made clear in particular in its judgment of 17 December 1981 (Case 279/80 *Webb* [1981] ECR 3305), that the principal aim of that paragraph is to enable the provider of the service to pursue his activities in the Member State where the service is given without suffering discrimination in favour of the nationals of the State. However, it does not follow from that paragraph that all national legislation applicable to nationals of that State and usually applied to the permanent activities of undertakings established therein may be similarly applied in its entirety to the temporary activities of undertakings which are established in other Member States.

[27] The Court has nevertheless accepted, in particular in its judgments of 18 January 1979 (Joined Cases 110 and 111/78 *Ministère public and Another* v *van Wesemael and Others* [1979] ECR 35) and 17 December 1981 (Case 279/80 *Webb*, cited above), that regard being had to the particular nature of certain services, specific requirements imposed on the provider of the services cannot be considered to be incompatible with the Treaty where they have as their purpose the application of rules governing such activities. However, the freedom to provide services, as one of the fundamental principles of the Treaty, may be restricted only by provisions which are justified by the general good and which are applied to all persons or undertakings operating within

the territory of the State in which the service is provided in so far as that interest is not safeguarded by the provisions to which the provider of a service is subject in the Member State of his establishment. In addition, such requirements must be objectively justified by the need to ensure that professional rules of conduct are complied with and that the interests which such rules are designed to safeguard are protected.

[28] It must be stated that the requirements in question in these proceedings, namely that an insurer who is established in another Member State, authorised by the supervisory authority of that State and subject to the supervision of that authority, must have a permanent establishment within the territory of the State in which the service is provided and that he must obtain a separate authorisation from the supervisory authority of that State, constitute restrictions on the freedom to provide services inasmuch as they increase the cost of such services in the State in which they are provided, in particular where the insurer conducts business in that State only occasionally.

[29] It follows that those requirements may be regarded as compatible with Articles 59 and 60 of the EEC Treaty only if it is established that in the field of activity concerned there are imperative reasons relating to the public interest which justify restrictions on the freedom to provide services, that the public interest is not already protected by the rules of the State of establishment and that the same result cannot be obtained by less restrictive rules.

The Court then proceeded to accept the existence of a protectable interest in this area:

[30] ... the insurance sector is a particularly sensitive area from the point of view of the protection of the consumer both as a policy-holder and as an insured person. This is so in particular because of the specific nature of the service provided by the insurer, which is linked to future events, the occurrence of which, or at least the timing of which, is uncertain at the time when the contract is concluded. An insured person who does not obtain payment under a policy following an event giving rise to a claim may find himself in a very precarious position. Similarly, it is as a rule very difficult for a person seeking insurance to judge whether the likely future development of the insurer's financial position and the terms of the contract, usually imposed by the insurer, offer him sufficient guarantees that he will receive payment under the policy if a claimable event occurs.

[31] It must also be borne in mind, as the German Government has pointed out, that in certain fields insurance has become a mass phenomenon. Contracts are concluded by such enormous numbers of policy-holders that the protection of the interests of insured persons and injured third parties affects virtually the whole population.

[32] Those special characteristics, which are peculiar to the insurance sector, have led all the Member States to introduce legislation making insurance undertakings subject to mandatory rules both as regards their financial position and the conditions of insurance which they apply, and to permanent supervision to ensure that those rules are complied with.

[33] It therefore appears that in the field in question there are imperative reasons relating to the public interest which may justify restrictions on the freedom to provide services, provided, however, that the rules of the State of establishment are not adequate in order to achieve the necessary level of protection and that the requirements of the State in which the service is provided do not exceed what is necessary in that respect.

NOTE: After due examination, the Court concluded that the public interest was not adequately protected by the rules of the State of establishment. In the abstract, then, Germany could lawfully restrict trade in order to serve the public interest. It then fell to be determined whether the actual rules enacted could satisfy the requirements of EU law. The Court refused to accept that a blanket requirement of establishment in Germany was compatible with the Treaty. However, it took a rather different view of the necessity to undergo an authorization procedure.

Commission v *Germany* (Case 205/84)

[1986] ECR 3755, Court of Justice of the European Communities

[46] . . . the German Government's argument to the effect that only the requirement of an authorization can provide an effective means of ensuring the supervision which, having regard to the foregoing considerations, is justified on grounds relating to the protection of the consumer both as a policy-holder and as an

insured person, must be accepted. Since a system such as that proposed in the draft for a second directive, which entrusts the operation of the authorization procedure to the Member State in which the undertaking is established, working in close cooperation with the State in which the service is provided, can be set up only by legislation, it must also be acknowledged that, in the present state of Community law, it is for the State in which the service is provided to grant and withdraw that authorization.

[47] It should however be emphasized that the authorization must be granted on request to any undertaking established in another Member State which meets the conditions laid down by the legislation of the State in which the service is provided, that those conditions may not duplicate equivalent statutory conditions which have already been satisfied in the State in which the undertaking is established and that the supervisory authority of the State in which the service is provided must take into account supervision and verifications which have already been carried out in the Member State of establishment. According to the German Government, which has not been contradicted on that point by the Commission, the German authorization procedure conforms fully to those requirements.

[48] It is still necessary to consider whether the requirement of authorization which, under the Insurance Supervision Law, applies to any insurance business other than transport insurance, is justified in all its applications. In that respect it has been pointed out, in particular by the United Kingdom Government, that the free movement of services is of importance principally for commercial insurance and that with regard to that particular type of insurance the grounds relating to the protection of policy-holders relied on by the German Government and the governments intervening in its support do not apply.

[49] It follows from the foregoing that the requirement of authorization may be maintained only in so far as it is justified on the grounds relating to the protection of policy-holders and insured persons relied upon by the German Government. It must also be recognized that those grounds are not equally important in every sector of insurance and that there may be cases where, because of the nature of the risk insured and of the party seeking insurance, there is no need to protect the latter by the application of the mandatory rules of his national law.

[50] However, although it is true that the proposal for a second directive takes account of those considerations by excluding *inter alia* commercial insurance, which is defined in detail, from the scope of the mandatory rules of the State in which the service is provided, it must also be observed that, in the light of the legal and factual arguments which have been presented before it, the Court is not in a position to make such a general distinction and to lay down the limits of that distinction with sufficient precision to determine the individual cases in which the needs of protection, which are characteristic of insurance business in general, do not justify the requirement of an authorization.

[51] It follows from the foregoing that the Commission's first head of claim must be rejected in so far as it is directed against the requirement of authorization.

NOTE: Insurance regulation is increasingly subject to secondary legislation adopted at EU level; and the Commission has a dedicated website containing relevant documentation, http://ec.europa.eu/finance/insurance/index_en.htm. The relevant secondary legislation is of undoubted practical significance, but the principle developed in this ruling that non-discriminatory national rules which have the effect of protecting domestic industry can be challenged under Article 56 TFEU applies across the services sector. Increasingly the market for services has been liberalized through the application of the primary Treaty provisions without the need to resort to harmonization. As suggested at p. 387, there are clear parallels with the Court's approach in *Cassis de Dijon* (Case 120/78, p. 319); see, e.g., the language of para 29 of the judgment in Case 205/84. The issue is similar. One State demands compliance with its rules. *All* firms must adhere, but importers/migrants suffer because they too are subjected to controls in their home State. The next case provides an example. The Commission considered France was in violation of Article 59 of the Treaty (now, after amendment, Article 56 TFEU) by making the provision of services by tourist guides accompanying groups of tourists from another Member State subject to the possession of a licence, itself dependent on possession of a particular qualification. The Court agreed with the Commission.

Commission v *France* (Case C-154/89)

[1991] ECR I-659, Court of Justice of the European Communities

[12] It should further be pointed out that Articles 59 and 60 of the Treaty require not only the abolition of any discrimination against a person providing services on account of his nationality but also the abolition of any restriction on the freedom to provide services imposed on the ground that the person providing a service is established in a Member State other than the one in which the service is provided. In particular, the Member State cannot make the performance of the services in its territory subject to observance of all the conditions required for establishment; were it to do so the provisions securing freedom to provide services would be deprived of all practical effect.

[13] The requirement imposed by the abovementioned provisions of French legislation amount to such a restriction. By making the provision of services by tourist guides accompanying a group of tourists from another Member State subject to possession of a specific qualification, that legislation prevents both tour companies from providing that service with their own staff and self-employed tourist guides from offering their services to those companies for organized tours. It also prevents tourists taking part in such organized tours from availing themselves at will of the services in question.

[14] However, in view of the specific requirements in relation to certain services, the fact that a Member State makes the provision thereof subject to conditions as to the qualifications of the person providing them, pursuant to rules governing such activities within its jurisdiction, cannot be considered incompatible with Articles 59 and 60 of the Treaty. Nevertheless, as one of the fundamental principles of the Treaty the freedom to provide services may be restricted only by rules which are justified in the general interest and are applied to all persons and undertakings operating in the territory of the State where the service is provided, in so far as that interest is not safeguarded by the rules to which the provider of such a service is subject in the Member State where he is established. In addition, such requirements must be objectively justified by the need to ensure that professional rules of conduct are complied with and that the interests which such rules are designed to safeguard are protected (see *inter alia* the judgment in Case 205/84 *Commission* v *Germany* [1986] ECR 3755, at paragraph 27).

[15] Accordingly, those requirements can be regarded as compatible with Articles 59 and 60 of the Treaty only if it is established that with regard to the activity in question there are overriding reasons relating to the public interest which justify restrictions on the freedom to provide services, that the public interest is not already protected by the rules of the State of establishment and that the same result cannot be obtained by less restrictive rules.

[16] The French Government contends that the French legislation in question seeks to ensure the protection of general interests relating to the proper appreciation of places and things of historical interest and the widest possible dissemination of knowledge of the artistic and cultural heritage of the country. According to the French Government, those interests are not adequately safeguarded by the rules to which the provider of the services, in this case the tour company, is subject in the Member State in which it is established. Several States require no occupational qualifications for tourist guides or demand no special knowledge of the historical and cultural heritage of other countries. In the absence of harmonization on that point the French legislation is not, therefore, incompatible with Article 59 of the EEC Treaty.

[17] The general interest in the proper appreciation of places and things of historical interest and the widest possible dissemination of knowledge of the artistic and cultural heritage of a country can constitute an overriding reason justifying a restriction on the freedom to provide services. However, the requirement in question contained in the French legislation goes beyond what is necessary to ensure the safeguarding of that interest inasmuch as it makes the activities of a tourist guide accompanying groups of tourists from another Member State subject to possession of a licence.

[18] The service of accompanying tourists is performed under quite specific conditions. The independent or employed tourist guide travels with the tourists and accompanies them in a closed group; in that group they move temporarily from the Member State of establishment to the Member State to be visited.

[19] In those circumstances a licence requirement imposed by the Member State of destination has the effect of reducing the number of tourist guides qualified to accompany tourists in a closed group, which may lead a tour operator to have recourse instead to local guides employed or established in the Member State in which the service is to be performed. However, that consequence may have the drawback that tourists who are the

recipients of the services in question do not have a guide who is familiar with their language, their interests and their specific expectations.

[20] Moreover, the profitable operation of such group tours depends on the commercial reputation of the operator, who faces competitive pressure from other tour companies; the need to maintain that reputation and the competitive pressure themselves compel companies to be selective in employing tourist guides and exercise some control over the quality of their services. Depending on the specific expectations of the groups of tourists in question, that factor is likely to contribute to the proper appreciation of places and things of historical interest and to the widest possible dissemination of knowledge relating to the artistic and cultural heritage, in the case of conducted tours of places other than museums or historical monuments which may be visited only with a professional guide.

[21] It follows that in view of the scale of the restrictions it imposes, the legislation in issue is disproportionate in relation to the objective pursued, namely to ensure the proper appreciation of places and things of historical interest and the widest dissemination of knowledge of the artistic and cultural heritage of the Member State in which the tour is conducted.

NOTE: In this way a host State's reliance on qualification requirements as a condition of access to its market is put to the test of EU trade law. The preference in para 20 for market rather than regulatory solutions is striking. The Court has subsequently made clear that a State is required actively to assess whether a migrant's qualification is adequate, though different from local requirements. Vlassopoulou was a Greek national and a member of the Athens Bar. She wished to work as a lawyer in Germany. The case was decided in the context of Article 52, which has become Article 49 TFEU post-Lisbon and which sets out the right of establishment, but appears to enshrine a general principle of the law of the internal law.

***Vlassopoulou* v *Ministerium für Justiz, Bundes- und Europaangelegenheiten Baden-Württemberg* (Case C-340/89)**

[1991] ECR I-2357, Court of Justice of the European Communities

[14] [I]t is also clear from the judgment in Case 71/76 *Thieffry* v *Conseil de l'Ordre des Avocats à la Cour de Paris* [1977] ECR 765, at paragraph 16, that, in so far as Community law makes no special provision, the objectives of the Treaty, and in particular freedom of establishment, may be achieved by measures enacted by the Member States, which, under Article 5 of the Treaty, must take 'all appropriate measures, whether general or particular, to ensure fulfilment of the obligations arising out of this Treaty or resulting from action taken by the institutions of the Community' and abstain from 'any measure which could jeopardize the attainment of the objectives of this Treaty' [see now Article 4(3) TEU].

[15] It must be stated in this regard that, even if applied without any discrimination on the basis of nationality, national requirements concerning qualifications may have the effect of hindering nationals of other Member States in the exercise of their right of establishment guaranteed to them by Article 52 of the EEC Treaty. That could be the case if the national rules in question took no account of the knowledge and qualifications already acquired by the person concerned in another Member State.

[16] Consequently, a Member State which receives a request to admit a person to a profession to which access, under national law, depends upon the possession of a diploma or a professional qualification must take into consideration the diplomas, certificates and other evidence of qualifications which the person concerned has acquired in order to exercise the same profession in another Member State by making a comparison between the specialized knowledge and abilities certified by those diplomas and the knowledge and qualifications required by the national rules.

[17] That examination procedure must enable the authorities of the host Member State to assure themselves, on an objective basis, that the foreign diploma certifies that its holder has knowledge and qualifications which are, if not identical, at least equivalent to those certified by the national diploma. That assessment of the equivalence of the foreign diploma must be carried out exclusively in the light of the level of knowledge and qualifications which its holder can be assumed to possess in the light of that diploma, having regard to

the nature and duration of the studies and practical training to which the diploma relates (see the judgment in Case 222/86 *Unectef* v *Heylens* [1987] ECR 4097, paragraph 13).

[18] In the course of that examination, a Member State may, however, take into consideration objective differences relating to both the legal framework of the profession in question in the Member State of origin and to its field of activity. In the case of the profession of lawyer, a Member State may therefore carry out a comparative examination of diplomas, taking account of the differences identified between the national legal systems concerned.

The Court concluded:

[23] Consequently, the answer to the question submitted by the Bundesgerichtshof must be that Article 52 of the EEC Treaty must be interpreted as requiring the national authorities of a Member State to which an application for admission to the profession of lawyer is made by a Community subject who is already admitted to practise as a lawyer in his country of origin and who practises as a legal adviser in the first-mentioned Member State to examine to what extent the knowledge and qualifications attested by the diploma obtained by the person concerned in his country of origin correspond to those required by the rules of the host State; if those diplomas correspond only partially, the national authorities in question are entitled to require the person concerned to prove that he has acquired the knowledge and qualifications which are lacking.

NOTE: This approach was confirmed by the Court in *Gebhard* (Case C-55/94, p. 266) where explicit reference was made to paras 15 and 16 of the ruling in *Vlassopoulou*. In its Twelfth Annual Report on monitoring the application of Community law, the Commission noted that the Dutch *Raad van State* applied the principle illustrated by the ruling in *Vlassopoulou*, although the Court's conclusion was that the relevant Dutch minister had acted properly in withholding recognition of an East German qualification after making comparisons between that qualification and Dutch requirements ([1995] OJ C254/166–7).

Several of the cases in this chapter display the determination of commercial operators to exploit the freedoms found in the Treaty to establish themselves or to provide services in another State. Typically, such parties are anxious to rely on EU law to preclude the host State insisting on conformity with part or all of its regulatory requirements as a pre-condition of market access. Reducing costs by relying on EU law to evade those burdens is commercially attractive and should intensify consumer-friendly competition. As already seen, the Court has developed a formula, inspired by *Cassis de Dijon*, designed to weigh the balance between trade integration and local regulatory concerns. Consider also *Gambelli* (Case C-243/01) [2003] ECR I-13031 (dealing with Italian rules controlling certain types of betting in which the Court noted an Italian policy of expanding other types of betting); *Federico Cipolla, Stefano Macrino* (Joined Cases C-94/04 & C-202/04) [2006] ECR I-11421 (in which the Court did not rule out the possibility that rules setting minimum fees charged by lawyers might be justified by the peculiarly intransparent nature of the Italian market for legal services, even though such rules would clearly restrict competition on price); *United Pan-Europe Communications Belgium SA* (Case C-250/06) [2007] ECR I-11135 (protection of pluralism, cultural diversity and freedom of expression in bilingual Brussels may justify the imposition of 'must carry' obligations on cable broadcasters, though EU law requires use of objective criteria and transparent procedures); *Ladbrokes* (Case C-258/08) [2010] ECR I-4757 (Dutch restrictions on gambling may be justified by reference to 'moral, religious or cultural factors, as well as the morally and financially harmful consequences for the individual and for society', but 'must be suitable for achieving those objectives, inasmuch as they must serve to limit betting activities in a consistent and systematic manner'); and *DKV Belgium SA* v *Association belge des consommateurs Test-Achats ASBL* (Case C-577/11), judgment of 7 March 2013 (a Belgian restriction on increase in insurance premiums payable for particular forms of medical insurance caused out-of-State firms seeking to access the

Belgian market 'to re-think their business policy and strategy', but justification in the name of consumer protection was plausible, given the target of preventing sharp and unexpected increases in insurance premiums).

For an overview see S. Enchelmaier, 'Always at Your Service (Within Limits): The ECJ's Case Law on Article 56 TFEU (2006–2011)' (2011) 36 EL Rev 615; and V. Hatzopoulos, 'The Court's Approach to Services 2006–2012: From Case Law to Case Load' (2013) 50 CML Rev 459. On gambling, S. van den Bogaert and A. Cuyvers, 'Money for Nothing: the Case Law of the EU Court of Justice on the Regulation of Gambling' (2011) 48 CML Rev 1175; and the Commission has produced a Green Paper on on-line gambling, COM (2011) 128, 24 March 2011.

Although there is a strong, deregulatory impulse in this case law, the Court insists that 'the fact that one Member State imposes less strict rules than another Member State does not mean that the latter's rules are disproportionate and hence incompatible with Community law' (e.g., Case C-3/95 *Reiseburo Broede* v *Gerd Sanker* [1996] ECR I-6511; Case C-262/02 *Commission* v *France* [2004] ECR I-6569 ('Loi Evin')). This conforms to the pattern under Articles 34–36 (p. 306). Respect for national regulatory choices is also visible in the next case, in which the Court found itself asked to deal with the question of the permissibility of national measures of market regulation which impede cross-border provision of services in a rather different context.

***Alpine Investments BV* v *Minister van Financiën* (Case C-384/93)**

[1995] ECR I-1141, Court of Justice of the European Communities

Alpine Investments, a provider of financial services, was prevented by Dutch rules from contacting potential customers by telephone without their prior written consent. This ban on 'cold calling' extended to offers made to individuals both inside and outside the Netherlands. The Court ruled that the matter fell within Article 59 of the Treaty (now, after amendment, Article 56 TFEU) by observing that the restriction impeded offers made by a provider in one Member State to a potential recipient established outside that State. But the restriction applied to all Dutch providers, irrespective of the location of their target clients. The UK and Dutch governments argued by analogy with *Keck* (Cases C-267 and 268/91, p. 329) that the rule should be regarded as falling outside the scope of the Treaty rules governing free movement. The Court commented that the ban 'deprives the operators concerned of a rapid and direct technique for marketing and for contacting potential clients in other Member States'. It then stated of the challenged Dutch rules that:

> [36] Such a prohibition is not analogous to the legislation concerning selling arrangements held in *Keck* and *Mithouard* to fall outside the scope of Article 30 [now 34] of the Treaty.
>
> [37] According to that judgment, the application to products from other Member States of national provisions restricting or prohibiting, within the Member State of importation, certain selling arrangements is not such as to hinder trade between Member States so long as, first, those provisions apply to all relevant traders operating within the national territory and, secondly, they affect in the same manner, in law and in fact, the marketing of domestic products and of those from other Member States. The reason is that the application of such provisions is not such as to prevent access by the latter to the market of the Member State of importation or to impede such access more than it impedes access by domestic products.
>
> [38] A prohibition such as that at issue is imposed by the Member State in which the provider of services is established and affects not only offers made by him to addressees who are established in that State or move there in order to receive services but also offers made to potential recipients in another Member State. It therefore directly affects access to the market in services in the other Member States and is thus capable of hindering intra-Community trade in services.

NOTE: The reader should consider whether this finding sheds any light on the task of fixing limits to the scope of EU trade law discussed in connection with *Keck* at p. 329. Is this approach peculiar to cases involving 'export'? The Court's treatment of Swedish restrictions on advertising in *Konsumentombudsmannen* v *De Agostini and TV Shop* (Joined Cases C-34/95, C-35/95, and C-36/95) was considered in the light of (what is now) Article 34 TFEU at p. 336. For the purposes of (what is now) Article 56 TFEU, the Court observed that a restriction on freedom to provide services was imposed where an undertaking established in the broadcasting State was impeded in broadcasting advertisements directed at the public in the receiving State on behalf of advertisers established in that State. It was for the national court to determine whether such trade restrictions were justified (against standards plainly inspired by *Cassis de Dijon*). Articles 34 and 56 TFEU appear to have been handled differently by the Court in this decision, although it is notable that the Court focused on the position of the advertiser in its discussion of Article 34, but on that of the broadcaster in approaching Article 56 (for comment see J. Stuyck (1997) 34 CML Rev 1445). Lurking beneath this analysis is a broader question which asks whether the provisions on free movement in the Treaty *should* be interpreted in a common manner. In his Opinion in *Alfa Vita Vassilopoulos* (*formerly Trofo Super-Markets*), mentioned in Chapter 12 at p. 339, Advocate-General Poiares Maduro pressed for convergence in approach to defining a trade barrier across all the freedoms. The Court, however, has persisted in evading addressing this matter of principle. A rich seam of academic commentary has investigated the case for convergence: see, e.g. Prechal, S. and de Vries, S., 'Seamless Web of Judicial Protection in the Internal Market?' (2009) 34 EL Rev 5; Tryfonidou, A., 'Further Steps on the Road to Convergence among the Market Freedoms' (2010) 35 EL Rev 36; and Connor, T., 'Market Access or Bust? Positioning the Principle within the Jurispridence of Goods, Persons, Services and Capital' (2012) 13 *German Law Journal* 679 (http://www.germanlawjournal.com/). The debate remains open and the Court may not be able to resist making a decision indefinitely.

The finding that the measure in *Alpine Investments* hindered cross-border trade such as to trigger the application of Article 59 of the Treaty (now, after amendment, Article 56 TFEU) then required the Court to examine the justifications advanced in support of the Dutch intervention in the market. The Court was invited to assess various methods of available regulatory techniques in determining whether the Dutch choice was justified.

Alpine Investments BV v *Minister van Financiën* (Case C-384/93)

[1995] ECR I-1141, Court of Justice of the European Communities

[40] The national court's third question asks whether imperative reasons of public interest justify the prohibition of cold calling and whether that prohibition must be considered to be objectively necessary and proportionate to the objective pursued.

[41] The Netherlands Government argues that the prohibition of cold calling in off-market commodities futures trading seeks both to safeguard the reputation of the Netherlands financial markets and to protect the investing public.

[42] Financial markets play an important role in the financing of economic operators and, given the speculative nature and the complexity of commodities futures contracts, the smooth operation of financial markets is largely contingent on the confidence they inspire in investors. That confidence depends in particular on the existence of professional regulations serving to ensure the competence and trustworthiness of the financial intermediaries on whom investors are particularly reliant.

[43] Although the protection of consumers in the other Member States is not, as such, a matter for the Netherlands authorities, the nature and extent of that protection does none the less have a direct effect on the good reputation of Netherlands financial services.

[44] Maintaining the good reputation of the national financial sector may therefore constitute an imperative reason of public interest capable of justifying restrictions on the freedom to provide financial services.

[45] As for the proportionality of the restriction at issue, it is settled case-law that requirements imposed on the providers of services must be appropriate to ensure achievement of the intended aim and must

not go beyond that which is necessary in order to achieve that objective (see Case C-288/89 Collectieve Antennevoorziening *Gouda and Others* v *Commissariaat voor de Media* [1991] ECR I-4007, paragraph 15).

[46] As the Netherlands Government has justifiably submitted, in the case of cold calling the individual, generally caught unawares, is in a position neither to ascertain the risks inherent in the type of transactions offered to him nor to compare the quality and price of the caller's services with competitors' offers. Since the commodities futures market is highly speculative and barely comprehensible for non-expert investors, it was necessary to protect them from the most aggressive selling techniques.

[47] Alpine Investments argues however that the Netherlands Government's prohibition of cold calling is not necessary because the Member State of the provider of services should rely on the controls imposed by the Member State of the recipient.

[48] That argument must be rejected. The Member State from which the telephone call is made is best placed to regulate cold calling. Even if the receiving State wishes to prohibit cold calling or to make it subject to certain conditions, it is not in a position to prevent or control telephone calls from another Member State without the cooperation of the competent authorities of that State.

[49] Consequently, the prohibition of cold calling by the Member State from which the telephone call is made, with a view to protecting investor confidence in the financial markets of that State, cannot be considered to be inappropriate to achieve the objective of securing the integrity of those markets.

[50] Alpine Investments also argues that a general prohibition of telephone canvassing of potential clients is not necessary for the achievement of the objectives pursued by the Netherlands authorities. Requiring broking firms to tape-record unsolicited telephone calls made by them would suffice to protect consumers effectively. Such rules have moreover been adopted in the United Kingdom by the Securities and Futures Authority.

[51] That point of view cannot be accepted. As the Advocate-General correctly states in point 88 of his Opinion, the fact that one Member State imposes less strict rules than another Member State does not mean that the latter's rules are disproportionate and hence incompatible with Community law.

[52] Alpine Investments argues finally that, since it is of a general nature, the prohibition of cold calling does not take into account the conduct of individual undertakings and accordingly imposes an unnecessary burden on undertakings which have never been the subject of complaints by consumers.

[53] That argument must also be rejected. Limiting the prohibition of cold calling to certain undertakings because of their past conduct might not be sufficient to achieve the objective of restoring and maintaining investor confidence in the national securities markets in general.

[54] In any event, the rules at issue are limited in scope. First, they prohibit only the contacting of potential clients by telephone or in person without their prior agreement in writing, while other techniques for making contact are still permitted. Next, the measure affects relations with potential clients but not with existing clients who may still give their written agreement to further calls. Finally, the prohibition of unsolicited telephone calls is limited to the sector in which abuses have been found, namely the commodities futures market.

[55] In the light of the above, the prohibition of cold calling does not appear disproportionate to the objective which it pursues.

[56] The answer to the third question is therefore that Article 59 does not preclude national rules which, in order to protect investor confidence in national financial markets, prohibit the practice of making unsolicited telephone calls to potential clients resident in other Member States to offer them services linked to investment in commodities futures.

NOTE: Telephone selling reflects and advances market integration; it is a medium which renders physical borders irrelevant. At paras 47–49 in its ruling in *Alpine Investments*, the Court shows a shrewd awareness of the limits placed on 'destination State control' in such circumstances. Compare the discussion of problems of enforcing laws that differ from those of other Member States which emerge in an integrating market at p. 310.

■ QUESTIONS

1. Is there an irreconcilability between the Court's acceptance at para 48 that home State control of technologically advanced marketing practices is more effective than destination State control and its comment at para 43 that protection of consumers in other States is not as such a matter for the Dutch authorities? Do you agree that the Netherlands should not be able to export its high standards of consumer protection other than indirectly, as part of a method for securing the high reputation of its own financial services sector (paras 43, 44)?
2. How can the Dutch consumer 'cold-called' from outside the Netherlands be protected? Does this case suggest a need for EU-wide harmonization, or does it display an acceptable level of regulatory diversity within the internal market?

B: Cases dealing with company law

These Treaty provisions have been eagerly exploited by commercial operators seeking advantages in cross-border mobility. This theme is prominent in the next case. It involves a company formed in accordance with the law of one Member State wishing to open a branch in another Member State. This is covered by the right granted by Article 49 TFEU. But the company was not commercially active in the State in which it was formed. It planned to be active in the State in which its branch was to be located.

Centros Ltd v *Erhervs- og Selskabhysstyrelsen* (Case C-212/97)

[1999] ECR I-1459, Court of Justice of the European Communities

Centros Ltd was a private limited company registered in the UK in accordance with English law. Its shares were held by Mr and Mrs Bryde, who were Danish nationals. Centros did not trade in the UK. It planned to trade in Denmark. Its application to register a branch in Denmark was refused by the other party to the proceedings, the Danish Trade and Companies Board, on the ground that Centros was in fact attempting to establish not a branch but a principal establishment in Denmark, which would have involved subjection to Danish regulatory requirements, including the paying-up of minimum share capital, which were far more onerous than those demanded under English law. Centros was, in short, a consumer of competition between (State) regulators (p. xxx); but could it rely on the Treaty to entitle it to act in this way? A preliminary reference seeking an interpretation of Articles 52, 56, and 58 of the Treaty (now, after amendment, Articles 49, 52, and 54 TFEU) was made by a Danish court before which Centros's challenge had been pursued. The Court of Justice treated the refusal to register the branch as an obstacle to the exercise of the freedom of establishment.

[23] According to the Danish authorities, however, Mr and Mrs Bryde cannot rely on those provisions, since the sole purpose of the company formation which they have in mind is to circumvent the application of the national law governing formation of private limited companies and therefore constitutes abuse of the freedom of establishment. In their submission, the Kingdom of Denmark is therefore entitled to take steps to prevent such abuse by refusing to register the branch.

[24] It is true that according to the case-law of the Court a Member State is entitled to take measures designed to prevent certain of its nationals from attempting, under cover of the rights created by the Treaty, improperly to circumvent their national legislation or to prevent individuals from improperly or fraudulently taking advantage of provisions of Community law (see, in particular, regarding freedom to supply services, Case 33/74 *Van Binsbergen* v *Bedrijfsvereniging Metaalnijverheid* [1974] ECR 1299, paragraph 13, Case C-148/91 *Veronica Omroep Organisatie* v *Commissariaat voor de Media* [1993] ECR I-487, paragraph 12, and Case C-23/93 *TV 10*

v *Commissariaat voor de Media* [1994] ECR I-4795, paragraph 21; regarding freedom of establishment, Case 115/78 *Knoors* [1979] ECR 399, paragraph 25, and Case C-61/89 *Bouchoucha* [1990] ECR I-3551, paragraph 14; regarding the free movement of goods, Case 229/83 *Leclerc and Others* v *'Au Blé Vert' and Others* [1985] ECR 1, paragraph 27; regarding social security, Case C-206/94 *Brennet* v *Paletta* [1996] ECR I-2357, *'Paletta II'*, paragraph 24; regarding freedom of movement for workers, Case 39/86 *Lair* v *Universität Hannover* [1988] ECR 3161, paragraph 43; regarding the common agricultural policy, Case C-8/92 *General Milk Products* v *Hauptzollamt Hamburg-Jonas* [1993] ECR I-779, paragraph 21, and regarding company law, Case C-367/96 *Kefalas and Others* v *Greece* [1998] ECR I-2843, paragraph 20).

[25] However, although, in such circumstances, the national courts may, case by case, take account – on the basis of objective evidence – of abuse or fraudulent conduct on the part of the persons concerned in order, where appropriate, to deny them the benefit of the provisions of Community law on which they seek to rely, they must nevertheless assess such conduct in the light of the objectives pursued by those provisions (*Paletta II*, paragraph 25).

[26] In the present case, the provisions of national law, application of which the parties concerned have sought to avoid, are rules governing the formation of companies and not rules concerning the carrying on of certain trades, professions or businesses. The provisions of the Treaty on freedom of establishment are intended specifically to enable companies formed in accordance with the law of a Member State and having their registered office, central administration or principal place of business within the Community to pursue activities in other Member States through an agency, branch or subsidiary.

[27] That being so, the fact that a national of a Member State who wishes to set up a company chooses to form it in the Member State whose rules of company law seem to him the least restrictive and to set up branches in other Member States cannot, in itself, constitute an abuse of the right of establishment. The right to form a company in accordance with the law of a Member State and to set up branches in other Member States is inherent in the exercise, in a single market, of the freedom of establishment guaranteed by the Treaty.

[28] In this connection, the fact that company law is not completely harmonised in the Community is of little consequence. Moreover, it is always open to the Council, on the basis of the powers conferred upon it by Article 54(3)(g) of the EC Treaty [now found in amended form in Article 50 TFEU], to achieve complete harmonisation.

[29] In addition, it is clear from paragraph 16 of *Segers* [Case 79/85 [1986] ECR 2375] that the fact that a company does not conduct any business in the Member State in which it has its registered office and pursues its activities only in the Member State where its branch is established is not sufficient to prove the existence of abuse or fraudulent conduct which would entitle the latter Member State to deny that company the benefit of the provisions of Community law relating to the right of establishment.

[30] Accordingly, the refusal of a Member State to register a branch of a company formed in accordance with the law of another Member State in which it has its registered office on the grounds that the branch is intended to enable the company to carry on all its economic activity in the host State, with the result that the secondary establishment escapes national rules on the provision for and the paying-up of a minimum capital, is incompatible with Articles 52 and 58 of the Treaty, in so far as it prevents any exercise of the right freely to set up a secondary establishment which Articles 52 and 58 are specifically intended to guarantee.

[31] The final question to be considered is whether the national practice in question might not be justified for the reasons put forward by the Danish authorities.

[32] Referring both to Article 56 of the Treaty and to the case-law of the Court on imperative requirements in the general interest, the Board argues that the requirement that private limited companies provide for and pay up a minimum share capital pursues a dual objective: first, to reinforce the financial soundness of those companies in order to protect public creditors against the risk of seeing the public debts owing to them become irrecoverable since, unlike private creditors, they cannot secure those debts by means of guarantees and, second, and more generally, to protect all creditors, whether public or private, by anticipating the risk of fraudulent bankruptcy due to the insolvency of companies whose initial capitalisation was inadequate.

[33] The Board adds that there is no less restrictive means of attaining this dual objective. The other way of protecting creditors, namely by introducing rules making it possible for shareholders to incur personal liability, under certain conditions, would be more restrictive than the requirement to provide for and pay up a minimum share capital.

[34] It should be observed, first, that the reasons put forward do not fall within the ambit of Article 56 of the Treaty. Next, it should be borne in mind that, according to the Court's case-law, national measures liable to hinder or make less attractive the exercise of fundamental freedoms guaranteed by the Treaty must fulfil four conditions: they must be applied in a non-discriminatory manner; they must be justified by imperative requirements in the general interest; they must be suitable for securing the attainment of the objective which they pursue; and they must not go beyond what is necessary in order to attain it (see Case C-19/92 *Kraus* v *Land Baden-Württemberg* [1993] ECR I-1663, paragraph 32, and Case C-55/94 *Gebhard* v *Consiglio dell'Ordine degli Avvocati e Procuratori di Milano* [1995] ECR I-4165, paragraph 37).

[35] Those conditions are not fulfilled in the case in the main proceedings. First, the practice in question is not such as to attain the objective of protecting creditors which it purports to pursue since, if the company concerned had conducted business in the United Kingdom, its branch would have been registered in Denmark, even though Danish creditors might have been equally exposed to risk.

[36] Since the company concerned in the main proceedings holds itself out as a company governed by the law of England and Wales and not as a company governed by Danish law, its creditors are on notice that it is covered by laws different from those which govern the formation of private limited companies in Denmark and they can refer to certain rules of Community law which protect them, such as the Fourth Council Directive 78/660/EEC of 25 July 1978 based on Article 54(3)(g) of the Treaty on the annual accounts of certain types of companies (OJ 1978 L 222, p. 11), and the Eleventh Council Directive 89/666/EEC of 21 December 1989 concerning disclosure requirements in respect of branches opened in a Member State by certain types of company governed by the law of another State (OJ 1989 L 395, p. 36).

[37] Second, contrary to the arguments of the Danish authorities, it is possible to adopt measures which are less restrictive, or which interfere less with fundamental freedoms, by, for example, making it possible in law for public creditors to obtain the necessary guarantees.

[38] Lastly, the fact that a Member State may not refuse to register a branch of a company formed in accordance with the law of another Member State in which it has its registered office does not preclude that first State from adopting any appropriate measure for preventing or penalising fraud, either in relation to the company itself, if need be in cooperation with the Member State in which it was formed, or in relation to its members, where it has been established that they are in fact attempting, by means of the formation of the company, to evade their obligations towards private or public creditors established on the territory of a Member State concerned. In any event, combating fraud cannot justify a practice of refusing to register a branch of a company which has its registered office in another Member State.

[39] The answer to the question referred must therefore be that it is contrary to Articles 52 and 58 of the Treaty for a Member State to refuse to register a branch of a company formed in accordance with the law of another Member State in which it has its registered office but in which it conducts no business where the branch is intended to enable the company in question to carry on its entire business in the State in which that branch is to be created, while avoiding the need to form a company there, thus evading application of the rules governing the formation of companies which, in that State, are more restrictive as regards the paying up of a minimum share capital. That interpretation does not, however, prevent the authorities of the Member State concerned from adopting any appropriate measure for preventing or penalising fraud, either in relation to the company itself, if need be in cooperation with the Member State in which it was formed, or in relation to its members, where it has been established that they are in fact attempting, by means of the formation of a company, to evade their obligations towards private or public creditors established in the territory of the Member State concerned.

NOTE: This ruling does not set aside the ability of Member States to exercise supervision over companies active on their territory in pursuit of economic freedoms guaranteed by the Treaty. Paragraph 34 is familiar territory to the student of EU trade law (*cf* p. 266). However, the ruling confines the scope of permissible public control in cases of strategic choices about company formation. Moreover, it offers possibilities for future exploitation of patterns of interstate regulatory competition by firms seeking what the judgment refers to as the 'least restrictive' regime (para 27). More litigation in these realms was confidently expected (see prognosis by W.-H. Roth (2000) 37 CML Rev 147; P. Calral and P. Cunha (2000) 25 EL Rev 157). The next case is not on precisely the same point as *Centros*, but it adds to the stock of case law to which national company law must adjust.

Überseering BV v *Nordic Construction Company Baumanagement GmbH (NCC)* (C-208/00)

[2002] ECR I-9919, Court of Justice of the European Communities

For the purposes of the preliminary reference, German company law was treated as providing that a company's legal capacity is determined by reference to the law applicable in the place where its actual centre of administration is established ('Sitztheorie' or company seat principle), as opposed to the 'Gründungstheorie' or incorporation principle, by virtue of which legal capacity is determined in accordance with the law of the State in which the company is incorporated. Überseering was a company incorporated under Dutch law that had transferred its actual centre of administration to Germany once its shares had been acquired by two German nationals. So before German courts Überseering, as a Dutch company administered in Germany, was treated as lacking legal capacity. The question was whether this violated Article 43 EC (now Article 49 TFEU). The German rules had the effect of requiring Überseering to reincorporate in Germany in order to sue. This was 'tantamount to outright negation of freedom of establishment' (para 81). Nor could the rules be justified:

[91] The Netherlands and United Kingdom Governments, the Commission and the EFTA Surveillance Authority submit that the restriction in question is not justified. They point out in particular that the aim of protecting creditors was also invoked by the Danish authorities in Centros to justify the refusal to register in Denmark a branch of a company which had been validly incorporated in the United Kingdom and all of whose business was to be carried on in Denmark but which did not meet the requirements of Danish law regarding the provision and paying-up of a minimum amount of share capital. They add that it is not certain that requirements associated with a minimum amount of share capital are an effective way of protecting creditors.

[92] It is not inconceivable that overriding requirements relating to the general interest, such as the protection of the interests of creditors, minority shareholders, employees and even the taxation authorities, may, in certain circumstances and subject to certain conditions, justify restrictions on freedom of establishment.

[93] Such objectives cannot, however, justify denying the legal capacity and, consequently, the capacity to be a party to legal proceedings of a company properly incorporated in another Member State in which it has its registered office. Such a measure is tantamount to an outright negation of the freedom of establishment conferred on companies by Articles 43 EC and 48 EC.

[94] Accordingly, the answer to the first question must be that, where a company formed in accordance with the law of a Member State ('A') in which it has its registered office is deemed, under the law of another Member State ('B'), to have moved its actual centre of administration to Member State B, Articles 43 EC and 48 EC preclude Member State B from denying the company legal capacity and, consequently, the capacity to bring legal proceedings before its national courts for the purpose of enforcing rights under a contract with a company established in Member State B.

Kamer van Koophandel en Fabriekne voor Amsterdam v *Inspire Art Ltd* (Case C-167/01)

[2003] ECR I-10155, Court of Justice of the European Communities

The case law has continued to evolve. The Dutch authorities did not refuse to register Inspire Art's branch – the problem in *Centros* – but they did require it to record in the Dutch commercial register its description as a *formeel buitenlandse vennootschap* (formally foreign company) and to use that description in its business dealings. Moreover, rules governing minimum capital were imposed. Was this a violation of Article 43 (now 49)?

[98] . . . the fact that Inspire Art was formed in the United Kingdom for the purpose of circumventing Netherlands company law which lays down stricter rules with regard in particular to minimum capital and the paying-up of shares does not mean that that company's establishment of a branch in the Netherlands is not

covered by freedom of establishment as provided for by Articles 43 EC and 48 EC. As the Court held in Centros (paragraph 18), the question of the application of those articles is different from the question whether or not a Member State may adopt measures in order to prevent attempts by certain of its nationals improperly to evade domestic legislation by having recourse to the possibilities offered by the Treaty.

This was a barrier to the freedom of establishment, and the Dutch rules could survive only if shown to be justified. They were not.

[135] First, with regard to protection of creditors, and there being no need for the Court to consider whether the rules on minimum share capital constitute in themselves an appropriate protection measure, it is clear that Inspire Art holds itself out as a company governed by the law of England and Wales and not as a Netherlands company. Its potential creditors are put on sufficient notice that it is covered by legislation other than that regulating the formation in the Netherlands of limited liability companies and, in particular, laying down rules in respect of minimum capital and directors' liability. They can also refer, as the Court pointed out in *Centros*, paragraph 36, to certain rules of Community law which protect them, such as the Fourth and Eleventh Directives.

[136] Second, with regard to combating improper recourse to freedom of establishment, it must be borne in mind that a Member State is entitled to take measures designed to prevent certain of its nationals from attempting, under cover of the rights created by the Treaty, improperly to circumvent their national legislation or to prevent individuals from improperly or fraudulently taking advantage of provisions of Community law (*Centros*, paragraph 24, and the decisions cited therein).

[137] However, while in this case Inspire Art was formed under the company law of a Member State, in the case in point the United Kingdom, for the purpose in particular of evading the application of Netherlands company law, which was considered to be more severe, the fact remains that the provisions of the Treaty on freedom of establishment are intended specifically to enable companies formed in accordance with the law of a Member State and having their registered office, central administration or principal place of business within the Community to pursue activities in other Member States through an agency, branch or subsidiary (*Centros*, paragraph 26).

[138] That being so, as the Court confirmed in paragraph 27 of *Centros*, the fact that a national of a Member State who wishes to set up a company can choose to do so in the Member State the company-law rules of which seem to him the least restrictive and then set up branches in other Member States is inherent in the exercise, in a single market, of the freedom of establishment guaranteed by the Treaty.

[139] In addition, it is clear from settled case-law (*Segers*, paragraph 16, and *Centros*, paragraph 29) that the fact that a company does not conduct any business in the Member State in which it has its registered office and pursues its activities only or principally in the Member State where its branch is established is not sufficient to prove the existence of abuse or fraudulent conduct which would entitle the latter Member State to deny that company the benefit of the provisions of Community law relating to the right of establishment.

[140] Last, as regards possible justification of the WFBV on grounds of protection of fairness in business dealings and the efficiency of tax inspections, it is clear that neither the Chamber of Commerce nor the Netherlands Government has adduced any evidence to prove that the measure in question satisfies the criteria of efficacy, proportionality and non-discrimination. . .

NOTE: For analysis see J. Lowry, 'Eliminating Obstacles to Freedom of Establishment: The Competitive Edge of UK Company Law' (2004) 63 Camb LJ 331; and, more generally, P. Schammo, 'Arbitrage and Abuse of Rights in the EC Legal System' (2008) 14 ELJ 351; and W.-G. Ringe, 'Corporate Mobility in the European Union – a Flash in the Pan? An Empirical Study on the Success of Lawmaking and Regulatory Competition' (2013) 10 *European Company and Financial Law Review* 230. In Case C-210/06 *Cartesio* [2008] ECR I-9641 the Court added that moving a company from one Member State to another, i.e., altering the applicable national law, is protected by the Treaty, but moving the seat of the company while keeping the applicable national law unchanged is different, and may lawfully be resisted by the State of incorporation.

Although these cases are of great significance in determining the scope for firms to challenge national restrictions on their commercial opportunities, the choices open to those seeking to convert their companies' operations on to a European scale are not confined to reliance on the Treaty provisions governing free movement to establish branches (Article 49 TFEU) or to providing cross-border services (Article 56 TFEU), nor, for that matter, to setting up distribution agreements or pursuing a merger and acquisition strategy (Chapter 16 provides an overview of competition law). Regulation 2157/2001 on the Statute for a European Company ([2001] OJ L294/1) permits the creation of a *Societas Europea*. The Regulation is accompanied by Directive 2001/86 on the involvement of employees ([2001] OJ L294/22). Employee involvement is a controversial matter, deeply dividing Member State political assumptions about the social role of the company. This long-delayed agreement on the 'SE' and the final pattern agreed in Directive 2001/86 is illuminatingly marked by compromise and options. See on this J. Kenner, 'Worker Involvement in the Societas Europea: Integrating Company and Labour Law in the European Union?' (2005) 24 YEL 223 and on more general trends J. Armour and W.-G. Ringe, 'European Company Law 1999–2010: Renaissance and Crisis' (2011) 48 CML Rev 125.

C: Cases dealing with collective labour action

The cases considered, especially those mentioned at p. 392, provide glimpses of the incursion of EU trade law into national social and cultural choices. In *Omega Spielhallen* (Case C-36/02 [2004] ECR I-9609) the Court dealt with a case pitting the fundamental freedom to trade in services against national rules protecting human dignity – a clash of fundamental but non-absolute rights already observed in the sphere of the free movement of goods (p. 349). The ripples of the case law drift ever wider. In December 2007 the Grand Chamber of the Court of Justice decided two major cases pitting EU free movement law against practices designed to protect the interests of workers harmed by cross-border commercial activity. There is space here to consider only one of the rulings, *International Transport Workers' Federation* v *Viking Line ABP* (Case C-438/05) [2007] ECR I-10779. The other, *Laval un Partneri* (Case C-341/05) [2007] ECR I-11767, is similar but displays some detailed differences (and the sources on the list of *Further Reading* at p. 404 cover both rulings).

International Transport Workers' Federation v *Viking Line ABP* (Case C-438/05)

[2007] ECR I-10779, Court of Justice of the European Communities

Viking Line, a ferry operator, was planning to 'reflag' ships from Finland to Estonia, in order to take advantage of lower labour and regulatory costs in Estonia. Finnish Trade Unions wanted to take action designed to deter this. So this was a commercially and intellectually intriguing mix of EU free movement law and protection of collective labour rights, a matter recognized by national law and European human rights law – and, albeit in ambiguous form, by EU law too. The dispute also reveals an increasingly evident tension within the EU between some newer Member States eager to exploit their comparative advantage in the shape of lower costs and other Member States with relatively high levels of protection for workers.

In litigation before the English courts Viking Line claimed (in effect) that Article 43 EC, which is now Article 49 TFEU, protected it from pressure exerted by trade unions aimed at deterring 're-flagging'. A preliminary reference was made by the English Court of Appeal. The Court of Justice decided that the collective action fell within the scope of Article 43 EC, now Article 49 TFEU. This was probably inescapable given the Court's consistent view that the free movement provisions affecting persons have a binding effect reaching beyond the acts of public authorities (see *URBSFA* v *Bosman* (Case C-415/93) [1995] ECR I-4921, *Roman Angonese* (Case C-281/98) [2000] ECR I-4139), albeit that *Viking Line* increases the anxiety about the absence of rational justification for the Court's refusal to extend this approach to the free movement of *goods* (see Chapter 11,

p. 304, and, examining *Viking Line* itself, in particular Syrpis & Novitz and Wyatt on the *Further Reading* list at p. 404). This, then, was a restriction on free movement and the issues pertaining to rights to take collective action were fed in at the stage of assessing whether the practices were justified. Fundamental rights to trade under EU law clashed with other breeds of fundamental political rights: the Court cited *inter alia* its ruling in *Schmidberger* (Case C-112/00) in which environmental protests impeded the free movement of goods (see Chapter 12, p. 348). It continued:

[75] It is apparent from the case-law of the Court that a restriction on freedom of establishment can be accepted only if it pursues a legitimate aim compatible with the Treaty and is justified by overriding reasons of public interest. But even if that were the case, it would still have to be suitable for securing the attainment of the objective pursued and must not go beyond what is necessary in order to attain it (see, *inter alia*, Case C-55/94 *Gebhard* [1995] ECR I-4165, paragraph 37, and [Case C-415/93] *Bosman*, paragraph 104).

[76] ITF, supported, in particular, by the German Government, Ireland and the Finnish Government, maintains that the restrictions at issue in the main proceedings are justified since they are necessary to ensure the protection of a fundamental right recognised under Community law and their objective is to protect the rights of workers, which constitutes an overriding reason of public interest.

[77] In that regard, it must be observed that the right to take collective action for the protection of workers is a legitimate interest which, in principle, justifies a restriction of one of the fundamental freedoms guaranteed by the Treaty (see, to that effect, *Schmidberger*, paragraph 74) and that the protection of workers is one of the overriding reasons of public interest recognised by the Court (see, *inter alia*, Joined Cases C-369/96 and C-376/96 *Arblade and Others* [1999] ECR I-8453, paragraph 36; Case C-165/98 *Mazzoleni and ISA* [2001] ECR I-2189, paragraph 27; and Joined Cases C-49/98, C-50/98, C-52/98 to C-54/98 and C-68/98 to C-71/98 *Finalarte and Others* [2001] ECR I-7831, paragraph 33).

[78] It must be added that, according to Article 3(1)(c) and (j) EC, the activities of the Community are to include not only an 'internal market characterised by the abolition, as between Member States, of obstacles to the free movement of goods, persons, services and capital', but also 'a policy in the social sphere'. Article 2 EC states that the Community is to have as its task, *inter alia*, the promotion of 'a harmonious, balanced and sustainable development of economic activities' and 'a high level of employment and of social protection'.

[79] Since the Community has thus not only an economic but also a social purpose, the rights under the provisions of the Treaty on the free movement of goods, persons, services and capital must be balanced against the objectives pursued by social policy, which include, as is clear from the first paragraph of Article 136 EC [now 151 TFEU], *inter alia*, improved living and working conditions, so as to make possible their harmonisation while improvement is being maintained, proper social protection and dialogue between management and labour.

[80] In the present case, it is for the national court to ascertain whether the objectives pursued by FSU and ITF by means of the collective action which they initiated concerned the protection of workers.

[81] First, as regards the collective action taken by FSU, even if that action – aimed at protecting the jobs and conditions of employment of the members of that union liable to be adversely affected by the reflagging of the *Rosella* – could reasonably be considered to fall, at first sight, within the objective of protecting workers, such a view would no longer be tenable if it were established that the jobs or conditions of employment at issue were not jeopardised or under serious threat.

[82] This would be the case, in particular, if it transpired that the undertaking referred to by the national court in its 10th question was, from a legal point of view, as binding as the terms of a collective agreement and if it was of such a nature as to provide a guarantee to the workers that the statutory provisions would be complied with and the terms of the collective agreement governing their working relationship maintained.

[83] In so far as the exact legal scope to be attributed to an undertaking such as that referred to in the 10th question is not clear from the order for reference, it is for the national court to determine whether the jobs or conditions of employment of that trade union's members who are liable to be affected by the reflagging of the *Rosella* were jeopardised or under serious threat.

[84] If, following that examination, the national court came to the conclusion that, in the case before it, the jobs or conditions of employment of the FSU's members liable to be adversely affected by the reflagging of the *Rosella* are in fact jeopardised or under serious threat, it would then have to ascertain whether the

collective action initiated by FSU is suitable for ensuring the achievement of the objective pursued and does not go beyond what is necessary to attain that objective.

[85] In that regard, it must be pointed out that, even if it is ultimately for the national court, which has sole jurisdiction to assess the facts and interpret the national legislation, to determine whether and to what extent such collective action meets those requirements, the Court of Justice, which is called on to provide answers of use to the national court, may provide guidance, based on the file in the main proceedings and on the written and oral observations which have been submitted to it, in order to enable the national court to give judgment in the particular case before it.

[86] As regards the appropriateness of the action taken by FSU for attaining the objectives pursued in the case in the main proceedings, it should be borne in mind that it is common ground that collective action, like collective negotiations and collective agreements, may, in the particular circumstances of a case, be one of the main ways in which trade unions protect the interests of their members (European Court of Human Rights, *Syndicat national de la police belge* v *Belgium*, of 27 October 1975, Series A, No 19, and *Wilson, National Union of Journalists and Others* v *United Kingdom* of 2 July 2002, 2002-V, § 44).

[87] As regards the question of whether or not the collective action at issue in the main proceedings goes beyond what is necessary to achieve the objective pursued, it is for the national court to examine, in particular, on the one hand, whether, under the national rules and collective agreement law applicable to that action, FSU did not have other means at its disposal which were less restrictive of freedom of establishment in order to bring to a successful conclusion the collective negotiations entered into with Viking, and, on the other, whether that trade union had exhausted those means before initiating such action.

[88] Secondly, in relation to the collective action seeking to ensure the implementation of the policy in question pursued by ITF, it must be emphasised that, to the extent that that policy results in shipowners being prevented from registering their vessels in a State other than that of which the beneficial owners of those vessels are nationals, the restrictions on freedom of establishment resulting from such action cannot be objectively justified. Nevertheless, as the national court points out, the objective of that policy is also to protect and improve seafarers' terms and conditions of employment.

[89] However, as is apparent from the file submitted to the Court, in the context of its policy of combating the use of flags of convenience, ITF is required, when asked by one of its members, to initiate solidarity action against the beneficial owner of a vessel which is registered in a State other than that of which that owner is a national, irrespective of whether or not that owner's exercise of its right of freedom of establishment is liable to have a harmful effect on the work or conditions of employment of its employees. Therefore, as Viking argued during the hearing without being contradicted by ITF in that regard, the policy of reserving the right of collective negotiations to trade unions of the State of which the beneficial owner of a vessel is a national is also applicable where the vessel is registered in a State which guarantees workers a higher level of social protection than they would enjoy in the first State.

[90] In the light of those considerations, the answer to the third to tenth questions must be that Article 43 EC is to be interpreted to the effect that collective action such as that at issue in the main proceedings, which seeks to induce an undertaking whose registered office is in a given Member State to enter into a collective work agreement with a trade union established in that State and to apply the terms set out in that agreement to the employees of a subsidiary of that undertaking established in another Member State, constitutes a restriction within the meaning of that article. That restriction may, in principle, be justified by an overriding reason of public interest, such as the protection of workers, provided that it is established that the restriction is suitable for ensuring the attainment of the legitimate objective pursued and does not go beyond what is necessary to achieve that objective.

NOTE: The Court's approach in *Viking Line* is thematically consistent with its anxiety in *Schmidberger* to craft a free movement law that is sensitive to the importance of issues that transcend narrowly economic calculation and which are protected under national law and recognized at European level. Free movement law is not only about free movement. The ruling leaves the ultimate decision on whether *this* action was justified in the hands of the referring court, in accordance with the orthodox approach under the preliminary reference procedure (Chapter 7). But *Viking Line* will offer no further insight. The case was settled out of court soon after the Court of Justice's ruling.

Those wishing to protect the muscle of organized labour from the control of EU trade law would be encouraged by acceptance that the right to take collective action for the protection of workers is a legitimate interest which, in principle, justifies a restriction on free movement (para 77) and, more grandly still, by identification of an economic and a social purpose to the whole system (para 79; repeated in para 105 of *Laval* (Case C-341/05) and subsequently in para 58 of Case C-319/07P *3F* v *Commission* [2009] ECR I-5963). On the other hand, collective action which restricts inter-State trade may be taken only on condition that it meets standards recognized by EU law. This is, at best, a source of unpredictability for trade unions. It will be especially hard to decide whether action goes beyond what is necessary to achieve its objective, and violations of the Treaty may result not only in litigation designed to put an end to unlawful action but also conceivably to actions for damages brought by traders (see Chapter 6, and K. Apps, 'Damages Claims Against Trade Unions after *Viking* and *Laval*' (2009) 34 EL Rev 141; and on an award made by Swedish courts pursuant to *Laval* see U. Bernitz and N. Reich, 'Annotation' (2011) 48 CML Rev 603). At worst, the Court has mapped a route to subordination of collective action by labour to commercial exploitation of competition between cost bases across the 28 Member States of the Union. Paragraph 81 of *Viking Line* appears to exclude from the permissible scope of justified practices action taken where jobs or conditions of employment are not jeopardized or under serious threat. So collective action which lacks an intimate connection with the nuts and bolts of a particular labour dispute and which instead has a more long-term strategic and/or political objective would appear to be unjustifiable in so far as it impedes cross-border commercial activity.

■ QUESTION

Why should EU law, and the Court of Justice in particular, dictate to organized labour what falls within its permissible range of interests? Is 'because this will promote the interests of workers in Member States where costs are lower' an adequate answer?

NOTE: The right to strike is explicitly excluded from the scope of EU legislative competence in the social policy field (now by Article 153(5) TFEU), yet the matter is subject to the free movement provisions as interpreted by the Court. As seen in Chapter 2, 'negative law' reaches further than 'positive law' under the Treaty: all the more so in so far as horizontal effect is accorded to the relevant Treaty freedoms. The risk has already been discussed in Chapter 12, pp. 352–62: the Court may act beyond the mandate granted by the Treaty in so far as it weighs matters of social and political freedom against economic considerations, thereby destabilizing national preferences. This is to question not simply the content of the test of justification chosen by the Court in *Viking Line*, which limits the scope of labour unions' autonomy, but to question the very legitimacy of the EU in becoming involved in such affairs in the name of advancing the internal market. The reforms of the Lisbon Treaty, especially adjustment to the profile of the commitment to undistorted competition and the grant of binding effect to the Charter which refers to the right of workers to take collective action in Article 28, have prompted two Advocates General (Cruz Villalón in Case C-515/08 *Santos Palhota* and Trstenjak in Case C-271/08 *Commission v Germany*) to invite the Court to reconsider the balance of priorities it has chosen (see further p. 239). It has not done so, and for the time being this ruling offers a vivid demonstration of the sensitivity of the adjudicative role assumed by the Court in free movement cases. And the powerful role of the Court is further emphasized by appreciation that an attempt to find a *political* reconciliation of the competing priorities proved impossible because of blockages in the legislative process caused by deeply divergent views among Member States, the Parliament, and, using the procedures created by the Lisbon Treaty (Chapter 18, p. 568), the national Parliaments. (This story is told by F. Fabbrini and K. Granat, 'Yellow Card but No Foul: The Role of the National Parliaments under the Subsidiarity Protocol and the Commission Proposal for an EU Regulation on the Right to Strike' (2013) 50 CML Rev 115).

FURTHER READING

Ashiagbor, D., 'Unravelling the Embedded Liberal Bargain: Labour and Social Welfare Law in the Context of EU Market Integration' (2013) 19 ELJ 303.

Azoulai, L., 'The Court of Justice and the Social Market Economy: The Emergence of an Ideal and the Conditions for its Realisation' (2008) 45 CML Rev 1335.

Barnard, C., 'A Proportionate Response to Proportionality in the Field of Collective Action' (2012) 37 EL Rev 117.

Barnard, C., 'British Jobs for British Workers: The Lindsey Oil Refinery Dispute and the Future of Local Labour Clauses in an Integrated EU Market' (2009) 38 ILJ 245.

Davies, A., 'One Step Forward, Two Steps Back?' (2008) 37 ILJ 126.

Hinarejos, A., 'Laval and Viking: The Right to Collective Action versus EU Fundamental Freedoms' (2008) 8 Human Rights Law Review 714.

Joerges, C. and Rödl, F., 'Informal Politics, Formalised Law and the "Social Deficit" of European Integration: Reflections after the Judgments of the ECJ in *Viking* and *Laval*' (2009) 15 ELJ 1.

Nicol, D., 'Europe's Lochner Moment' [2011] Public Law 308.

NicShuibhne, N., 'Settling Dust? Reflections on the Judgments in *Viking* and *Laval*' [2010] Euro Bus Law Rev 681.

Syrpis, P. and Novitz, T., 'Economic and Social Rights in Conflict: Political and Judicial Approaches to their Reconciliation' (2008) 33 EL Rev 411.

Wyatt, D., 'Horizontal Effect of Fundamental Freedoms and the Right to Equality after Viking and Mangold, and the Implications for Community Competence' (2008) 4 *Croatian Yearbook of European Law and Policy* 1.

D: Cases dealing with health care provision

The law of free movement has evidently moved far beyond blackcurrant liqueur. Ever broader and more important national interests seek reconciliation with the process of economic integration. The next case considers the extent to which the provision of health care services may be subjected to market competition. The potential impact on national welfare provision as an element in securing social cohesion makes this litigation unavoidably sensitive. Legitimacy is once again at stake. The Court is not deterred. It sanctions a form of inter-State competition in the provision of medical care, and it also takes the opportunity to demonstrate its awareness that the effective application of the EU rules is heavily dependent on ensuring that national decisions are taken on a transparent basis.

B.S.M. Geraets-Smits v *Stichting Ziekenfonds VGZ, H.T.M. Peerbooms* v *Stichting CZ Groep Zorgverzekeringen* (Case C-157/99)

[2001] ECR I-5473, Court of Justice of the European Communities

Mrs Geraets-Smits, a Dutch national, suffered from Parkinson's disease. She had been treated in Germany and sought reimbursement of the costs of care from the Dutch sickness insurance scheme. Mr Peerbooms had fallen into a coma following a road accident. He was taken to hospital in the Netherlands and then transferred in a vegetative state to a clinic in Innsbruck in Austria. His neurologist sought payment of the costs of treatment from the Dutch scheme (ZFW). Both applications were rejected, for reasons explained in the Court's summary of the questions referred to it by a Dutch court under the preliminary reference procedure (Chapter 7).

[43] By its two questions, which fall to be dealt with together, the national court is asking essentially whether Articles 59 and 60 [now 56 and 57 TFEU] of the Treaty are to be interpreted as precluding legislation of a Member State, such as the legislation at issue in the main proceedings, which makes the assumption of the costs of care provided in a hospital establishment in another Member State conditional upon prior authorisation by the sickness insurance fund with which the insured person is registered, that authorisation being granted only in so far as the following two conditions are satisfied. First, the proposed treatment must be among the benefits for which the sickness insurance scheme of the first Member State assumes responsibility, which means that the treatment must be regarded as 'normal in the professional circles concerned'. Second, the treatment abroad must be necessary in terms of the medical condition of the person concerned, which supposes that adequate care cannot be provided without undue delay by a care provider which has entered into an agreement with a sickness insurance fund in the first Member State.

The Court first addressed the question of the competence of the EU to intrude on national social security systems. It offered a classic statement of the 'spillover' effect of trade law.

[44] . . . it should be remembered at the outset that, according to settled case-law, Community law does not detract from the power of the Member States to organise their social security systems (Case 238/82 *Duphar and Others* [1984] ECR 523, paragraph 16, Case C-70/95 *Sodemare and Others* [1997] ECR I-3395, paragraph 27, and Case C-158/96 *Kohll* [1998] ECR I-1931, paragraph 17).

[45] In the absence of harmonisation at Community level, it is therefore for the legislation of each Member State to determine, first, the conditions concerning the right or duty to be insured with a social security scheme (. . . *Kohll*, paragraph 18) and, second, the conditions for entitlement to benefits (. . . *Kohll*, paragraph 18).

[46] Nevertheless, the Member States must comply with Community law when exercising that power.

So the absence of a general legislative competence in the field of social security (Chapter 2) did not preclude *national* social security rules falling within the scope of application of the law of free movement. This compares to the subjection of collective labour action to free movement law in *Viking Line* (Case C-438/05, p. 401). The next objection faced by the Court was that Article 60 EC, now Article 57 TFEU, provides that services are subject to the Treaty rules 'where they are normally provided for remuneration'. Does this cover hospital services where the patient receives care without having to pay for it where all or part of the cost is reimbursed?

[55] With regard more particularly to the argument that hospital services provided in the context of a sickness insurance scheme providing benefits in kind, such as that governed by the ZFW, should not be classified as services within the meaning of Article 60 [now 57] of the Treaty, it should be noted that, far from falling under such a scheme, the medical treatment at issue in the main proceedings, which was provided in Member States other than those in which the persons concerned were insured, did lead to the establishments providing the treatment being paid directly by the patients. It must be accepted that a medical service provided in one Member State and paid for by the patient should not cease to fall within the scope of the freedom to provide services guaranteed by the Treaty merely because reimbursement of the costs of the treatment involved is applied for under another Member State's sickness insurance legislation which is essentially of the type which provides for benefits in kind.

[56] Furthermore, the fact that hospital medical treatment is financed directly by the sickness insurance funds on the basis of agreements and pre-set scales of fees is not in any event such as to remove such treatment from the sphere of services within the meaning of Article 60 of the Treaty.

[57] First, it should be borne in mind that Article 60 of the Treaty does not require that the service be paid for by those for whom it is performed (Case 352/85 *Bond van Adverteerders and Others* [1988] ECR 2085, paragraph 16, and Joined Cases C-51/96 and C-191/97 *Deliège* [2000] ECR I-2549, paragraph 56).

[58] Second, Article 60 of the Treaty states that it applies to services normally provided for remuneration and it has been held that, for the purposes of that provision, the essential characteristic of remuneration lies in the fact that it constitutes consideration for the service in question (Humbel, paragraph 17). In the present cases, the payments made by the sickness insurance funds under the contractual arrangements provided for by the ZFW, albeit set at a flat rate, are indeed the consideration for the hospital services and unquestionably represent remuneration for the hospital which receives them and which is engaged in an activity of an economic character.

The Court turned to consider whether there was a restriction on freedom to provide services where the costs of treatment provided in a hospital in another Member State was reimbursed by the local sickness insurance scheme provided that the insured person complied with rules laid down by the Dutch scheme.

[61] According to settled case-law, Article 59 of the Treaty precludes the application of any national rules which have the effect of making the provision of services between Member States more difficult than the provision of services purely within one Member State (Case C-381/93 *Commission* v *France* [1994] ECR I-5145, paragraph 17, and *Kohll*, paragraph 33).

[62] In the present case, while the ZFW does not deprive insured persons of the possibility of using a provider of services established in another Member State, it does nevertheless make reimbursement of the costs

incurred in another Member State subject to prior authorisation and provides for such reimbursement to be refused where the two requirements referred to in paragraph 60 above are not satisfied.

[63] As regards the first of those requirements, namely that the proposed treatment must be treatment covered by the ZFW, in other words treatment which can be regarded as 'normal in the professional circles concerned', it is sufficient to point out that by its very essence such a condition is liable to lead to refusals of authorisation. It is only the precise frequency with which authorisation is refused, not refusal itself, that will be determined by the interpretation of 'normal' treatment and 'the professional circles concerned'.

[64] As regards the second requirement, namely that provision of hospital treatment in another Member State must be a medical necessity, which will be the case only if adequate treatment cannot be obtained without undue delay in contracted hospitals in the Member State in which the person seeking treatment is insured, this requirement by its very nature will severely limit the circumstances in which such authorisation can be obtained.

Were the rules justified? This drew the Court into assessment of the nature and purpose of a State's social security system.

[71] In that regard, it is first necessary to determine whether there are overriding reasons which can be accepted as justifying barriers to freedom to provide medical services supplied in the context of a hospital infrastructure, then to determine whether the prior authorisation principle is justifiable in the light of such overriding needs and last to consider whether the conditions governing the grant of prior authorisation can themselves be justified.

Overriding considerations which may be relied on to justify barriers to the exercise of freedom to provide services in the sphere of hospital treatment

[72] As all the governments which have submitted observations to the Court have pointed out, the Court has held that it cannot be excluded that the possible risk of seriously undermining a social security system's financial balance may constitute an overriding reason in the general interest capable of justifying a barrier to the principle of freedom to provide services (*Kohll*, paragraph 41).

[73] The Court has likewise recognised that, as regards the objective of maintaining a balanced medical and hospital service open to all, that objective, even if intrinsically linked to the method of financing the social security system, may also fall within the derogations on grounds of public health under Article 56 of the EC Treaty (now, after amendment, Article 46 EC), in so far as it contributes to the attainment of a high level of health protection (*Kohll*, paragraph 50).

[74] The Court has further held that Article 56 of the Treaty permits Member States to restrict the freedom to provide medical and hospital services in so far as the maintenance of treatment capacity or medical competence on national territory is essential for the public health, and even the survival of, the population (*Kohll*, paragraph 51).

[75] It is therefore necessary to determine whether the national rules at issue in the main proceedings can actually be justified in the light of such overriding reasons and, in such a case, in accordance with settled case-law, to make sure that they do not exceed what is objectively necessary for that purpose and that the same result cannot be achieved by less restrictive rules (Case 205/84 *Commission* v *Germany* [1986] ECR 3755, paragraphs 27 and 29; Case C-180/89 *Commission* v *Italy* [1991] ECR I-709, paragraphs 17 and 18; and Case C-106/91 *Ramrath* [1992] ECR I-3351, paragraphs 30 and 31).

The prior authorisation requirement

[76] As regards the prior authorisation requirement to which the ZFW subjects the assumption of the costs of treatment provided in another Member State by a non-contracted care provider, the Court accepts, as all the governments which have submitted observations have argued, that, by comparison with medical services provided by practitioners in their surgeries or at the patient's home, medical services provided in a hospital take place within an infrastructure with, undoubtedly, certain very distinct characteristics. It is thus well known that the number of hospitals, their geographical distribution, the mode of their organisation and the equipment with which they are provided, and even the nature of the medical services which they are able to offer, are all matters for which planning must be possible.

[77] As may be seen, in particular, from the contracting system involved in the main proceedings, this kind of planning therefore broadly meets a variety of concerns.

[78] For one thing, it seeks to achieve the aim of ensuring that there is sufficient and permanent access to a balanced range of high-quality hospital treatment in the State concerned.

[79] For another thing, it assists in meeting a desire to control costs and to prevent, as far as possible, any wastage of financial, technical and human resources. Such wastage is all the more damaging because it is generally recognised that the hospital care sector generates considerable costs and must satisfy increasing needs, while the financial resources which may be made available for health care are not unlimited, whatever the mode of funding applied.

[80] From both those perspectives, a requirement that the assumption of costs, under a national social security system, of hospital treatment provided in another Member State must be subject to prior authorisation appears to be a measure which is both necessary and reasonable.

[81] Looking at the system set up by the ZFW, it is clear that, if insured persons were at liberty, regardless of the circumstances, to use the services of hospitals with which their sickness insurance fund had no contractual arrangements, whether they were situated in the Netherlands or in another Member State, all the planning which goes into the contractual system in an effort to guarantee a rationalised, stable, balanced and accessible supply of hospital services would be jeopardised at a stroke.

[82] Although, for the considerations set out above, Community law does not in principle preclude a system of prior authorisation, the conditions attached to the grant of such authorisation must none the less be justified with regard to the overriding considerations examined and must satisfy the requirement of proportionality referred to in paragraph 75 above.

A prior authorization system may be justified. But was this one? The Court had already conceded that it is for the legislation of each Member State to organize its national social security system, which includes a competence to fix limits on entitlement to benefits and access to medical treatment paid for by the social security scheme (paras 44–46). Equally the law of the EU's internal market cannot be disregarded.

[90] It likewise follows from settled case-law that a scheme of prior authorisation cannot legitimise discretionary decisions taken by the national authorities which are liable to negate the effectiveness of provisions of Community law, in particular those relating to a fundamental freedom such as that at issue in the main proceedings … Therefore, in order for a prior administrative authorisation scheme to be justified even though it derogates from such a fundamental freedom, it must, in any event, be based on objective, non-discriminatory criteria which are known in advance, in such a way as to circumscribe the exercise of the national authorities' discretion, so that it is not used arbitrarily (Analir and Others, paragraph 38). Such a prior administrative authorisation scheme must likewise be based on a procedural system which is easily accessible and capable of ensuring that a request for authorisation will be dealt with objectively and impartially within a reasonable time and refusals to grant authorisation must also be capable of being challenged in judicial or quasi-judicial proceedings.

After examining the Dutch scheme the Court observed that:

[95] It follows from the those requirements that the institution of a system such as that at issue in the main proceedings, under which the authorisation decision needed to undergo hospital treatment in another Member State is entrusted to the sickness insurance funds, means that the criteria which those funds must apply in reaching that decision must be objective and independent where the providers of treatment are established.

[96] To allow only treatment habitually carried out on national territory and scientific views prevailing in national medical circles to determine what is or is not normal will not offer those guarantees and will make it likely that Netherlands providers of treatment will always be preferred in practice.

[97] If, on the other hand, the condition that treatment must be regarded as 'normal' is extended in such a way that, where treatment is sufficiently tried and tested by international medical science, the authorisation sought under the ZFW cannot be refused on that ground, such a condition, which is objective and applies without distinction to treatment provided in the Netherlands and to treatment provided abroad, is justifiable in view of the need to maintain an adequate, balanced and permanent supply of hospital care on national territory and to ensure the financial stability of the sickness insurance system, so that the restriction of the freedom to provide services of hospitals situated in other Member States which might result from the application of that condition does not infringe Article 59 of the Treaty.

[98] Further, where, as in the present case, a Member State decides that medical or hospital treatment must be sufficiently tried and tested before its cost will be assumed under its social security system, the national authorities called on to decide, for authorisation purposes, whether hospital treatment provided in another Member States satisfies that criterion must take into consideration all the relevant available information, including, in particular, existing scientific literature and studies, the authorised opinions of specialists and the fact that the proposed treatment is covered or not covered by the sickness insurance system of the Member State in which the treatment is provided.

. . .

The condition concerning the necessity of the proposed treatment

[103] In view of what is stated in paragraph 90 above, it can be concluded that the condition concerning the necessity of the treatment, laid down by the rules at issue in the main proceedings, can be justified under Article 59 of the Treaty, provided that the condition is construed to the effect that authorisation to receive treatment in another Member State may be refused on that ground only if the same or equally effective treatment can be obtained without undue delay from an establishment with which the insured person's sickness insurance fund has contractual arrangements.

[104] Furthermore, in order to determine whether equally effective treatment can be obtained without undue delay from an establishment having contractual arrangements with the insured person's fund, the national authorities are required to have regard to all the circumstances of each specific case and to take due account not only of the patient's medical condition at the time when authorisation is sought but also of his past record.

[105] Such a condition can allow an adequate, balanced and permanent supply of high-quality hospital treatment to be maintained on the national territory and the financial stability of the sickness insurance system to be assured.

The Court concluded:

[108] In view of all the foregoing considerations, the answer to be given to the national court must be that Articles 59 and 60 of the Treaty do not preclude legislation of a Member State, such as that at issue in the main proceedings, which makes the assumption of the costs of treatment provided in a hospital located in another Member State subject to prior authorisation from the insured person's sickness insurance fund and the grant of such authorisation subject to the condition that (i) the treatment must be regarded as 'normal in the professional circles concerned', a criterion also applied in determining whether hospital treatment provided on national territory is covered, and (ii) the insured person's medical treatment must require that treatment. However, that applies only in so far as:

— the requirement that the treatment must be regarded as 'normal' is construed to the effect that authorisation cannot be refused on that ground where it appears that the treatment concerned is sufficiently tried and tested by international medical science, and
— authorisation can be refused on the ground of lack of medical necessity only if the same or equally effective treatment can be obtained without undue delay at an establishment having a contractual arrangement with the insured person's sickness insurance fund.

The interest in the 'health care cases' has been advanced by subsequent judgments.

Müller-Fauré and van Riet (Case C-385/99)

[2003] ECR I-4509, Court of Justice of the European Communities

The Court confirmed that a requirement of prior authorization imposed where care is to be provided in another Member State may be justified. It also accepted that high levels of mobility which upset the system's financial balance and endanger the overall level of public health protection within a Member State might justify restrictions. There was no such justification available on the evidence presented in the case. A prominent issue is evidently the desire of patients to circumvent waiting lists and the preference of suppliers to use waiting lists to manage demand patterns. The Court added that:

> [92] . . . a refusal to grant prior authorisation which is based not on fear of wastage resulting from hospital overcapacity but solely on the ground that there are waiting lists on national territory for the hospital treatment concerned, without account being taken of the specific circumstances attaching to the patient's medical condition, cannot amount to a properly justified restriction on freedom to provide services. It is not clear from the arguments submitted to the Court that such waiting times are necessary, apart from considerations of a purely economic nature which cannot as such justify a restriction on the fundamental principle of freedom to provide services, for the purpose of safeguarding the protection of public health. On the contrary, a waiting time which is too long or abnormal would be more likely to restrict access to balanced, high-quality hospital care.

The Court also took the view that on the evidence presented restrictions on non-hospital treatment could not be justified.

> [95] However, the documents before the Court do not indicate that removal of the requirement for prior authorisation for that type of care would give rise to patients travelling to other countries in such large numbers, despite linguistic barriers, geographic distance, the cost of staying abroad and lack of information about the kind of care provided there, that the financial balance of the Netherlands social security system would be seriously upset and that, as a result, the overall level of public-health protection would be jeopardised – which might constitute proper justification for a barrier to the fundamental principle of freedom to provide services.

The tension between patients' (understandable) desire to receive speedy treatment and suppliers' (understandable) concern to use waiting lists as a device to control spending is visible in the next case too.

R v *Bedford Primary Care Trust and the Secretary of State for Health, ex parte Yvonne Watts* (Case C-372/04)

[2006] ECR I-4325, Court of Justice of the European Communities

Mrs Watts suffered from arthritis of the hips and was in constant pain. She was at first told she would have to wait a year for surgery, but, after her condition worsened, this was reduced to three or four months. She had asked her local health authority in Bedford to authorize her to receive surgery abroad, but it refused on both occasions, taking the view that she could be treated at home 'without undue delay' in accordance with governmental guidelines. She went to France and paid some £3900 for a hip replacement operation and then sought reimbursement. The Court of Appeal, relying on both the above-extracted Court of Justice judgments, accepted that the refusal could be justified by the need to maintain a balanced medical and hospital service available to everyone, and that such justification is excluded where it would result in undue delay in the provision of treatment to the patient. It considered that the case law did not clearly explain the concept of 'undue delay' or the relevance of budgetary considerations. The matter was referred to the Court of Justice. The Court confirmed the possibility to justify requirements of prior authorization, but repeated the requirement for an impartial and transparent procedure that is amenable to review (for one that was not, see Case C-169/07 *Hartlauer Handelsgesellschaft* [2009] ECR I-1721). It then addressed the link between delay suffered by patients and the control exercised over spending by providers of health services in the context of reliance on Article 49 EC, now Article 56 TFEU, by Mrs Watts.

> [119] . . . a refusal to grant prior authorisation cannot be based merely on the existence of waiting lists enabling the supply of hospital care to be planned and managed on the basis of predetermined general clinical priorities, without carrying out in the individual case in question an objective medical assessment of the patient's medical condition, the history and probable course of his illness, the degree of pain he is in and/or the nature of his disability at the time when the request for authorisation was made or renewed.
>
> [120] It follows that, where the delay arising from such waiting lists appears to exceed in the individual case concerned an acceptable period having regard to an objective medical assessment of all the circumstances of the situation and the clinical needs of the person concerned, the competent institution may not refuse the authorisation sought on the grounds of the existence of those waiting lists, an alleged distortion of the normal order of priorities linked to the relative urgency of the cases to be treated, the fact that the hospital treatment provided under the national system in question is free of charge, the duty to make available specific funds to reimburse the cost of treatment provided in another Member State and/or a comparison between the cost of that treatment and that of equivalent treatment in the competent Member State.

NOTE: By recognizing the relevance of the health care system's financial stability in judging the permissibility of prior authorization requirements, the Court has not thrown the provision of medical care on to the mercy of the market at the expense of State involvement. However, it has adjusted the 'balance of power' between the patient's freedom to receive services and the State's competence to define the terms of the provisions of health care. As the Court put it in *Müller-Fauré* (Case C-385/99), 'achievement of the fundamental freedoms guaranteed by the Treaty inevitably requires Member States to make some adjustments to their national systems of social security' (para 102), an observation which it repeated in para 121 of *ex parte Watts* (Case C-372/04). EU free movement law puts national systems to the test. The Court's case law nudges our assumptions about the discharge of a State's responsibility to its citizens in an era of transnational economic growth.

■ QUESTION

One person's delayed treatment is another person's access to treatment. Does the Court's approach provide a reliable guide for health authorities when they have to choose which patient comes first?

NOTE: The Services Directive, Directive 2006/123 (p. 558) excludes health care services from its scope, which ensures that Article 56 TFEU – and the Court! – remains centrally important. In line with a phenomenon observed on several occasions (e.g., pp. 303, 345, 358) the Commission attempted to clarify the law by issuing a non-binding Communication on 'A Community framework on the application of patients' rights in cross-border healthcare' (COM (2008) 415, available *via* http://ec.europa.eu/health/cross_border_care/policy/index_en.htm). Eventually a binding text was agreed, Directive 2011/24 on the application of patients' rights in cross-border healthcare (OJ [2011] L88/45), but this is no innovation, rather it is 'intended to achieve a more general, and also effective, application of principles developed by the Court of Justice on a case-by-case basis' (Recital 8). So once again the Court's pivotal role is not displaced.

FURTHER READING

Dougan, M. and Stalford H. (eds), Special Issue on 'The Impact of Migration on Healthcare Systems in the EU' 14 MJ 3 (2007).

Greer, S. and Sokol, T., 'Rules for Rights: European Law, Health Care and Social Citizenship' (2014) 20 ELJ 66.

Hervey, T. and Trubek, L., 'Freedom to Provide Health Care Services in the EU: An Opportunity for Hybrid Governance?' (2007) 13 Columbia Jnl Euro Law 623.

Newdick, C. 'Citizenship, Free Movement and Health Care: Cementing Individual Rights by Corroding Social Solidarity' (2006) 43 CML Rev 1645.

■ **QUESTION**

Could one employ the reasoning used in the 'health care cases' to claim a right to seek reimbursement for the costs of education which one prefers to obtain in another Member State?

***Society for the Protection of Unborn Children Ireland Ltd (SPUC) v Grogan* (Case C-159/90)**

[1991] ECR I-4685, Court of Justice of the European Communities

The litigation arose against the background of the right to life of the unborn under the Irish Constitution. Thousands of Irish women travel annually to London to receive abortion services because they are unable to receive such services in Ireland. A Students' Union in Dublin provided information about services lawfully available in London. This practice was challenged before the Irish courts by SPUC. The Students' Union claimed that as a matter of (what was then) Community law it was entitled to distribute such information, relying on Articles 59–66 of the EC Treaty (now, after amendment, Articles 56–62 TFEU).

The Court of Justice accepted that abortion was a commercial service within the meaning of then Article 60 of the Treaty (now, after amendment, Article 57 TFEU). It then observed that the Students' Union did not in any way cooperate with the clinics whose addresses were published. It declared that:

> [26] The information to which the national court's questions refer is not distributed on behalf of an economic operator established in another Member State. On the contrary, the information constitutes a manifestation of freedom of expression and of the freedom to impart and receive information which is independent of the economic activity carried on by clinics established in another Member State.
>
> [27] It follows that, in any event, a prohibition of the distribution of information in circumstances such as those which are the subject of the main proceedings cannot be regarded as a restriction within the meaning of Article 59 of the Treaty.

This perception that there was no economic motivation in the case allowed the Court to conclude that:

> It is not contrary to Community law for a Member State in which medical termination of pregnancy is forbidden to prohibit students associations from distributing information about the identity and location of clinics in another Member State where voluntary termination of pregnancy is lawfully carried out and the means of communicating with those clinics, where the clinics in question have no involvement in the distribution of the said information.

NOTE: The Court thus sidestepped the need to make an assessment which Advocate-General van Gerven had characterized in his Opinion as a balancing exercise.

> The question remains whether it is consonant with the general principles of Community law with regard to fundamental rights and freedoms for a Member State to prohibit the provision and receipt of information by way of assistance about abortions lawfully carried out in other Member States, thereby infringing individuals' freedom of expression. It is a question here of balancing two fundamental rights, on the one hand the right to life as defined and declared to be applicable to unborn life by a Member State, and on the other the freedom of expression, which is one of the general principles of Community law on the basis of the constitutional traditions of the Member States and the European and international treaties and declarations on fundamental rights, in particular Article 10 of the European Convention on Human Rights.

The Advocate-General, in contrast to the Court, explored these difficult issues. He concluded his Opinion by proposing that the following answer should be given to the referring court:

The Treaty provisions with regard to the freedom to provide services do not prevent a Member State where the protection of unborn life is recognised in the Constitution and in its legislation as a fundamental principle from imposing a general prohibition, applying to everyone regardless of their nationality or place of establishment, on the provision of assistance to pregnant women, regardless of their nationality, with a view to the termination of their pregnancy, more specifically through the distribution of information as to the identity and location of and method of communication with clinics located in another Member State where abortions are carried out, even though the services of medical termination of pregnancy and the information relating thereto are provided in accordance with the law in force in that second Member State.

The final clause of the Court's ruling clearly indicated the potential for future litigation where the required commercial link is shown to exist. A Protocol annexed to the Maastricht Treaty on European Union declared that nothing therein 'shall affect the application in Ireland' of the relevant provision of the Irish Constitution. The protection which that Protocol afforded Ireland against further litigation was soon seen to be a mixed blessing as a combination of domestic and European pressures led to reconsideration of the nature of the Constitutional guarantees (see R. Pearce, 'Abortion and the Right to Life under the Irish Constitution' [1993] JSWFL 396).

Looking beyond the specific problem of abortion and Irish law, the litigation strikingly illustrates the potential depth of the intrusion of EU law into national life and the potential of the Court of Justice to assume a controversial adjudicative role far beyond the economic sphere as narrowly understood. The following articles draw broader conclusions from the process of the litigation in *SPUC* v *Grogan* (Case C-159/90):

de Búrca, G., 'Fundamental Human Rights and the Reach of EC Law' (1993) 13 OJLS 283.

Hervey, T., 'Buy Baby: The European Union and Regulation of Human Reproduction' (1998) 18 OJLS 207.

O'Leary, S., 'The Court of Justice as a Reluctant Constitutional Adjudicator' (1992) 71 EL Rev 138.

Spalin, E., 'Abortion, Speech and the European Community' (1992) Journal of Social Welfare and Family Law 17.

■ QUESTION

'[R]ights to travel or freedom of information are rights with which men [rather than women] can more easily identify. By focussing on matters which are peripheral to the abortion issue itself, the media, in common with politicians, have sought refuge in the discourse of liberal legalism which more easily accommodates rights to travel or information than rights to abortion' (M. Fox and T. Murphy, 'Irish Abortion: Seeking Refuge in a Jurisprudence of Doubt and Delegation' (1992) 19 Journal of Law and Society 454, 457). Might this criticism be fairly extended to apply to the structure of European Union law?

NOTE: The most striking theme which binds together the Court's most sensitive case law is how matters where the EU has little or no *legislative* competence – collective labour rights, health care, abortion – are nevertheless subjected to free movement law in so far as an effect on the internal market is found. The Court's 'testing' of such practices draws it into difficult areas of calculation, measurement and balance. As considered at pp. 352–62 after similar sensitivities were observed in the area of the free movement of goods in Chapter 12, the legitimacy of EU law is placed under strain as the Court decides how much respect to show for national autonomy both by determining what constitutes a barrier to trade that requires justification and in making that assessment of justification. (Read in this vein F. De Witte, 'Sex, Drugs and EU Law: The Recognition of Moral and Ethical Diversity in EU Law' (2013) 50 CMLRev 1545). This is another area in which one might anticipate the Lisbon Treaty's relegation of the Union's commitment to undistorted competition from Treaty to Protocol being exploited to strengthen the case for a more cautious application of free movement law (see Chapter 9, p. 239, Chapter 12, p. 350). One might envisage the Court being pressed to accept that *Viking Line* (Case C-438/05) or *Watts* (Case C-372/04) were driven by a thirst for undistorted competition which is no longer so constitutionally pressing. The (binding) Charter of Fundamental Rights may play a role – e.g., Article 28 provides *inter alia* that workers have the right to take collective action to defend their interests, including strike action - and the Treaty now commits the Union to *inter alia* a 'social market' in Article 3(3) TEU. Moreover, Article 4(2) TEU contains a much strengthened version of the pre-existing commitment to respect the national identities of the Member States, which is apt for deployment in defence of socially sensitive practices which happen also to impede cross-border trade (see further Chapter 15, 'Citizenship and Constitutional Identity', p. 429). However, even though such Lisbon alterations alter the tone of the Treaty, the Member States were not able to agree definitively to change the heartland of the law of the internal market. The Treaty provisions on free movement themselves have not been changed. Fidelity to 'undistorted competition' is a commitment found now only in a Protocol, but a Protocol is legally binding. Although there is scope for the Court to adopt an adjusted interpretation of the free movement rules which gives greater weight to justification of practices that tend to inhibit cross-border commercial activity, the Lisbon reforms are too legally 'soft' to *require* that outcome. What is at stake is a possible re-balancing of priorities with consequences sympathetic to social protection but such an impact is far from guaranteed. Much will depend on the process of adjudication. (See C. Semmelmann, 'The European Union's Economic Constitution under the Lisbon Treaty: Soul-searching Shifts the Focus to Procedure' (2010) 35 EL Rev 516; N. Nic Shuibhne, 'Margins of Appreciation: National Values, Fundamental Rights and EC Free Movement Law' (2009) 34 EL Rev 230; A. Von Bogdandy and S. Schill, 'Overcoming Absolute Primacy: Respect for National Identity under the Lisbon Treaty' (2011) 48 CML Rev 1417; and D. Damjanovic, 'The EU Market Rules as Social Market Rules: Why the EU Can Be a Social Market Economy' (2013) 50 CML Rev 1685.)

SECTION 4: HARMONIZATION

The Court, in its judgments discussed in the previous section, recognizes, as it did in *'Cassis de Dijon'* (p. 319), that where a genuine interest is the subject of protection, national restrictive rules may remain compatible with the Treaty provided they comply with the principle of proportionality. So professional qualifications, designed to maintain standards and integrity, obstruct free movement but may be lawful. So, too, rules protecting the consumer or the investor, or the reputation of financial markets. Here lie the limits of the Court's role. This suggests a role for legislative harmonization.

Harmonization requires all professionals to meet common standards, wherever qualified. There is then no obstruction to free movement (see, e.g., *Auer* v *Ministère Public* (Case 271/82) [1983] ECR 2727). Yet achieving such harmonization proved extremely difficult. Profession by profession, progress has been painfully slow, doubtless because vested interests, many of them perfectly legitimate, are at stake. A 'New Approach' has been initiated. This sets broad common standards which must be met, but avoids the detailed, laborious approach of old. Again, an analogy with the free movement of goods is appropriate, for in that field, too, it has been recognized that the inclusion of excessive detail in legislative measures adopted at EU level is counterproductive (see p. 526).

The first measure which adopted the 'New Approach' to harmonization in this field was Directive 89/48 on a General System for the Recognition of Higher Education Diplomas [1989] OJ L19/16. The regime applicable to recognition of professional qualifications was subsequently consolidated by Directive 2005/36 on the recognition of professional qualifications ([2005] OJ L255/22, frequently amended). This brings together into a single text the General Directives on recognition of qualifications and some sector-specific Directives, including those covering doctors, nurses, and architects.

For lawyers, then, as for other professions, cross-border competition should become a reality. The barriers created by long-standing professional requirements should fall. The migrant lawyer must demonstrate a basic ability, but is not to be subjected to the full period of professional training normal in the host State. (Primary law already plays a role; note that the dispute in Case C-340/89 *Vlassopoulou* (p. 391) pre-dated the entry into force of Directive 89/48. See also Case C-55/94 *Gebhard* (p. 266). UK lawyers can expect to face developing competition from outside the UK; but the process is two-way, and UK lawyers can also look to expand their own activities beyond traditional frontiers. Strictly, the Directive is not of purely internal effect. It is concerned with migration. Yet the Directive has served to supplement the many factors operative as catalysts in the reform of the English legal profession. The market for legal services had undergone further adjustment as a result of Directive 98/5 [1998] OJ L77/36, which provided for lawyers to be entitled to pursue specified activities on a permanent basis in another Member State while using their home-State professional title. Moreover, a lawyer so practising who has 'effectively and regularly' pursued an activity in the host State in that State's law or EU law for at least three years is exempted from the conditions of Article 4(1)(b) of Directive 89/48, now transplanted to Article 14 of Directive 2005/36, with regard to gaining admission to the profession of lawyer in the host State.

Similar initiatives aim to remove trade barriers resulting from divergent company law and other regulatory regimes, which hinder the free movement of services provided by companies. Financial Services markets have been the subject of vigorous legislative initiatives designed to promote EU-wide structures: the sector is too detailed for further exploration here. These issues are considered further in Chapter 17, which discusses some of the policy implications of the new style of harmonization.

The legislative agenda in the services sector has lately been driven with considerable energy. This is fuelled by a perception, mentioned in Chapter 9, that integration of services markets in the EU is much further from completion than integration of goods markets, and that economic benefits are being squandered as a result of the inadequate legal framework. The Directive on unfair business-to-consumer commercial practices in the internal market, Directive 2005/29 ([2005] OJ L149/22), was adopted with precisely this objective in mind. It was accepted that diverse national approaches to the regulation of unfair commercial practices constituted barriers to inter-State trade and that therefore there was a need for a common regime at EU level. The Directive stipulates that all Member States must suppress unfair practices, which are practices which contrary to 'professional diligence' 'materially distort the economic behaviour' of an average consumer (Article 5). The Directive amplifies two particular types of outlawed practice – the 'misleading' and the 'aggressive' practice (Articles 6–9). As a corollary, traders are entitled to employ any practice which is not unfair within the meaning of the Directive. Member States are therefore forbidden from preventing the use of strategies which meet the requirements of fairness established by the Directive. In this sense Directive 2005/29 is a measure of 'maximum' harmonization. Accordingly, a presumption of unlawfulness attached by Belgian law to a particular marketing strategy which was stricter than the requirements laid down by the Directive could no longer be applied (Case C-261/07 *VTB-VAB NV* [2009] ECR I-2949). The same was true of a German rule against combining participation in a prize competition with the purchase of goods which took no account of the specific circumstances of individual cases (Case C-304/08 *Plus Warenhandelsgesellschaft* [2010] ECR I-217). A much more ambitious legislative initiative ran into trouble when it followed this 'maximum' model. The 'Services Directive' was designed as a broad measure of 'horizontal harmonisation', applicable across the whole of the services sector and designed to sweep away fragmented national rules in favour of a common EU-wide system of regulation. This, it was argued by the Commission, would shake up the services sector, promote integration and deliver economic benefits. It was too much for the Member States to swallow. The original Commission proposal, which would have applied a model of maximum harmonization (COM(2004) 2), did not attract sufficient political support in the Council or Parliament. A watered-down version was adopted in 2006 – Directive 2006/123 of the Parliament and the Council on services in the internal market ([2006] OJ L376/36). This is much more limited in its material scope than the 2004 proposal (see, e.g., Articles 1, 2, 3, 17 of Directive 2006/123: health care services, affected by Article 49 EC, now Article 45 TFEU, in Case C-372/04 *ex parte Watts* and other cases at pp. 405–12, are not affected by the Services Directive; the same is true of restrictions on gambling, see Case C-258/08 *Ladbrokes* at p. 392). And it acquiesces in national rules which are stricter than the EU standard for the quality of services and which therefore may constitute persisting barriers to inter-State trade (e.g., Articles 15, 16, 18). It is a heavily – and instructively – politicized question how far, if at all, Member States should be able to impose stricter requirements than a harmonized EU rule as a pre-condition of access to their market. Chapter 17 will address the sensitivity of harmonization policy more generally.

NOTE: For additional material and resources see the Online Resource Centre at: www.oxfordtextbooks.co.uk/orc/weatherill12e.

15

European Citizenship Within an Area of Freedom, Security, and Justice

SECTION 1: INTRODUCTION

The case law and legislation examined in the previous two chapters is straining to break the bounds of economics. The law governing the free movement of persons and services is rooted in Treaty Articles which are squeezed in between provisions dealing with the free movement of goods, agriculture, and the free movement of capital. This is trade law. Persons and services are treated as factors of production, and their enhanced mobility is a means to improve competition and economic performance. But this is only part of the story. The mobility of people implicates more than simply economics. It concerns individual human beings.

This has always been true. But the growth of the scope of activities of the European Union has generated new momentum in the quest to devise a coherent law of persons for the EU that is not confined to economic performance. Part of this new dimension is directed at ensuring that the economic law provisions are interpreted with due respect for the dignity of the person. Part of it is more ambitious, and is directed at shaping a case for the treatment of people in the European Union that is distinct from market economics.

This is law and policy in flux. There is a profound lack of agreement about what should be the scope of the EU's relationship with the peoples of Europe. Policy-making is at times awkward and tentative, at others vigorous and demanding.

The next case represents a powerful assertion by the Court that once a matter is shown to fall within the scope of application of the EU's rules on the free movement of persons, the range of legal sources that become relevant in influencing the legal protection afforded by what is nominally 'trade law' is broad indeed. But it is a ruling which in some respects is hard to fathom. That is why it is chosen. It captures the enduringly dynamic nature of this area of law.

***Mary Carpenter* v *Secretary of State for the Home Department* (Case C-60/00)**

[2002] ECR I-6279, Court of Justice of the European Communities

Mrs Carpenter, a national of the Philippines, had entered the UK on a six months' visa, stayed after its expiry without receiving any extension, and then married Peter Carpenter, a UK national. She was subsequently served with a deportation order, against which she appealed. Points of law were referred to Luxembourg by the Immigration Appeal Tribunal.

As a third country national, Mrs Carpenter's rights under EU law, if any, were not free-standing but rather derived from her husband. But he was a national of the UK living in the UK. In *Morson* v *State of the Netherlands* (Cases 35 and 36/82) [1982] ECR 3723 the Court held that Dutch nationals working in the Netherlands had no rights under Article 48 of the EC Treaty (now, after amendment, Article 45 TFEU) and therefore could not rely on the secondary legislation to protect their Surinamese mothers who wished to join them. By contrast, in *R* v *IAT and Singh, ex parte Secretary of State* (Case C-370/90) [1992] ECR I-4265 a British national was able to rely on EU law to protect an Indian spouse when returning to the UK after working in Germany.

Mr Carpenter ran a business selling advertising space in medical and scientific journals and offering various administrative and publishing services to the editors of those journals. The business was established in the UK, but a significant proportion of the business was conducted with advertisers established in other Member States. Mr Carpenter on occasion travelled to other Member States for the purpose of his business. It was argued that his wife's deportation would require him to go to live with her in the Philippines or separate the members of the family unit if he remained in the United Kingdom. In both cases his business would be affected.

Mr Carpenter seemed to be more mobile than Morson but less mobile than Singh.

[28] ... the provisions of the Treaty relating to the freedom to provide services, and the rules adopted for their implementation, are not applicable to situations which do not present any link to any of the situations envisaged by Community law ...

[29] ... a significant proportion of Mr Carpenter's business consists of providing services, for remuneration, to advertisers established in other Member States. Such services come within the meaning of 'services' in Article 49 EC both in so far as the provider travels for that purpose to the Member State of the recipient and in so far as he provides cross-border services without leaving the Member State in which he is established (see, in respect of 'cold-calling', Case C-384/93 *Alpine Investments* [1995] ECR I-1141, paragraphs 15 and 20 to 22).

[30] Mr Carpenter is therefore availing himself of the right freely to provide services guaranteed by Article 49 EC. Moreover, as the Court has frequently held, that right may be relied on by a provider as against the State in which he is established if the services are provided for persons established in another Member State (see, among others, *Alpine Investments*, cited above, paragraph 30).

The Court was remarkably quick to find the case fell within the scope of the Treaty. Would someone moving to *receive* services also be protected? If so, is it rational to leave out of the scope of protection the few people who doggedly never move across a border? And wouldn't even they be protected as long as they occasionally use the Internet to buy from another Member State?

Directive 73/148 on the abolition of restrictions on movement and residence for nationals of Member States with regard to establishment and the provision of services was of no assistance to the Carpenters. It applies to cases where nationals of Member States leave their Member State of origin and move to another Member State, not to cases concerning the right of residence of members of the family in the home State of the right-holder. And the same is true of Directive 2004/38, which replaced Directive 73/148 with effect from 30 April 2006, met at p. 367 and examined more fully at p. 427. So the matter fell for resolution in the light of general principles.

[38] In that context it should be remembered that the Community legislature has recognised the importance of ensuring the protection of the family life of nationals of the Member States in order to eliminate obstacles to the exercise of the fundamental freedoms guaranteed by the Treaty, as is particularly apparent from the provisions of the Council regulations and directives on the freedom of movement of employed and self-employed workers within the Community (see, for example, Article 10 of Council Regulation (EEC) No 1612/68 of 15 October 1968 on freedom of movement for workers within the Community ...; Articles 1 and 4 of Council Directive 68/360/EEC of 15 October 1968 on the abolition of restrictions on movement and residence within the Community for workers of Member States and their families ..., and Articles 1(1)(c) and 4 of the Directive).

[39] It is clear that the separation of Mr and Mrs Carpenter would be detrimental to their family life and, therefore, to the conditions under which Mr Carpenter exercises a fundamental freedom. That freedom could not be fully effective if Mr Carpenter were to be deterred from exercising it by obstacles raised in his country of origin to the entry and residence of his spouse (see, to that effect, *Singh*, cited above, paragraph 23).

[40] A Member State may invoke reasons of public interest to justify a national measure which is likely to obstruct the exercise of the freedom to provide services only if that measure is compatible with the fundamental rights whose observance the Court ensures (see, to that effect, Case C-260/89 ERT [1991] ECR I-2925, paragraph 43, and Case C-368/95 *Familiapress* [1997] ECR I-3689, paragraph 24).

[41] The decision to deport Mrs Carpenter constitutes an interference with the exercise by Mr Carpenter of his right to respect for his family life within the meaning of Article 8 of the Convention for the Protection of Human Rights and Fundamental Freedoms, signed at Rome on 4 November 1950 (hereinafter 'the Convention'), which is among the fundamental rights which, according to the Court's settled case-law, restated by the Preamble to the Single European Act and by Article 6(2) EU, are protected in Community law.

[42] Even though no right of an alien to enter or to reside in a particular country is as such guaranteed by the Convention, the removal of a person from a country where close members of his family are living may amount to an infringement of the right to respect for family life as guaranteed by Article 8(1) of the Convention. Such an interference will infringe the Convention if it does not meet the requirements of paragraph 2 of that article, that is unless it is 'in accordance with the law', motivated by one or more of the legitimate aims under that paragraph and 'necessary in a democratic society', that is to say justified by a pressing social need and, in particular, proportionate to the legitimate aim pursued (see, in particular, *Boultif* v *Switzerland*, no 54273/00, §§ 39, 41 and 46, ECHR 2001-IX).

[43] A decision to deport Mrs Carpenter taken in circumstances such as those in the main proceedings, does not strike a fair balance between the competing interests, that is, on the one hand, the right of Mr Carpenter to respect for his family life, and, on the other hand, the maintenance of public order and public safety.

[44] Although, in the main proceedings, Mr Carpenter's spouse has infringed the immigration laws of the United Kingdom by not leaving the country prior to the expiry of her leave to remain as a visitor, her conduct, since her arrival in the United Kingdom in September 1994, has not been the subject of any other complaint that could give cause to fear that she might in the future constitute a danger to public order or public safety. Moreover, it is clear that Mr and Mrs Carpenter's marriage, which was celebrated in the United Kingdom in 1996, is genuine and that Mrs Carpenter continues to lead a true family life there, in particular by looking after her husband's children from a previous marriage.

[45] In those circumstances, the decision to deport Mrs Carpenter constitutes an infringement which is not proportionate to the objective pursued.

[46] In view of all the foregoing, the answer to the question referred to the Court is that Article 49 EC, read in the light of the fundamental right to respect for family life, is to be interpreted as precluding, in circumstances such as those in the main proceedings, a refusal, by the Member State of origin of a provider of services established in that Member State who provides services to recipients established in other Member States, of the right to reside in its territory to that provider's spouse, who is a national of a third country.

NOTE: It is striking how easy the Court finds it to establish a connection between the threatened deportation and the perceived impediment to trade. If EU trade law can achieve a result as remarkable as this, what is the need for any extra level of fundamental rights protection? The Court's practice makes plain that a *wider* scope for EU free movement law means a correspondingly *wider* scope for affording individuals the protection of fundamental rights recognized by the EU legal order. It widens the scope of its own adjudicative function too. But it also means a correspondingly *narrower* scope for national rule-making which is sheltered from the need to show compliance with standards demanded by EU free movement law. In this sense a connection may usefully be made with discussion elsewhere about the legitimate limits of EU law's review of national regulatory choices. The issues raised by the Court's shaping of the scope of Article 49 EC, now Article 56 TFEU, in *Carpenter* are thematically linked to those relevant to Article 34 TFEU addressed in *Keck and Mithouard* (Chapter 12, p. 329) and also encountered in Chapter 14 (p. 394). But *Carpenter* has none of the feel of caution about over-extension of EU trade law which is so conspicuous in *Keck and Mithouard*.

So in turning to consider the status of Citizenship of the Union it is important to remember that EU free movement law already grants generous protection to nationals of the Member States and members of their family.

SECTION 2: CITIZENSHIP OF THE UNION

Since the entry into force of the Maastricht Treaty in 1993 there exists the status of Citizenship of the EU. A shiny label – but what might change, what has changed? The rights enjoyed by natural and legal persons discussed in the two preceding chapters are grouped around two distinct types: those concerning the basic entitlement to free movement between Member States and those involving non-discriminatory treatment once installed in the host Member State – which might involve access to social protection and/or a right to be accompanied by family, and so on. In line with the constitutional fundamental principle of conferral under EU law, such rights are not available to everyone. The matter must fall within the scope of the Treaty – that concerns both the personal scope of the Treaty and its material scope. Questions of personal scope are straightforward where cross-border economic activity is plainly involved. The worker, the provider or the recipient of services, the natural or legal person seeking to establish him-, her- or itself are within the scope of the Treaty. *Carpenter* shows how easily the required cross-border element may be found. And questions of material scope are usually readily decided in favour of the application of EU law, especially by virtue of Article 7 of Regulation 492/2011, which has been broadly interpreted by the Court (p. 371). But have the limits of free movement law, already stretched close to breaking point, now been set aside entirely? Does the status of Citizenship (plus Directive 2004/38) now mean everyone is covered, provided they are an EU national? This asks whether an economic link is any longer required when an individual has moved from one Member State to another: and it asks whether a cross-border element is even required. It also asks whether there are limits on the material scope of entitlement on a non-discriminatory basis. And these are questions that as yet attract incomplete answers.

A: Citizenship defined, citizenship limited

The Maastricht Treaty introduced provisions on 'Citizenship of the Union', comprising Articles 8–8e EC. These were adjusted by the Treaty of Amsterdam, albeit in rather minor ways, becoming Articles 17–22 EC on re-numbering. The Treaty of Nice adjusted Article 18 alone among these provisions. The Lisbon Treaty made only minor modifications to the wording of the provisions, but they are now situated as Articles 20–25 TFEU, joined to Articles 18 and 19 TFEU (formerly Articles 12 and 13 EC) in Part Two of the TFEU, which is entitled *Non-Discrimination and Citizenship of the Union*. The post-Lisbon text reads as follows.

ARTICLE 18

Within the scope of application of the Treaties, and without prejudice to any special provisions contained therein, any discrimination on grounds of nationality shall be prohibited.

The European Parliament and the Council, acting in accordance with the ordinary legislative procedure, may adopt rules designed to prohibit such discrimination.

ARTICLE 19

1. Without prejudice to the other provisions of the Treaties and within the limits of the powers conferred by them upon the Union, the Council, acting unanimously in accordance with a special legislative procedure and after obtaining the consent of the European Parliament, may take appropriate action to combat discrimination based on sex, racial or ethnic origin, religion or belief, disability, age or sexual orientation.

2. By way of derogation from paragraph 1, the European Parliament and the Council, acting in accordance with the ordinary legislative procedure, may adopt the basic principles of Union incentive measures, excluding any harmonisation of the laws and regulations of the Member States, to support action taken by the Member States in order to contribute to the achievement of the objectives referred to in paragraph 1.

ARTICLE 20

1. Citizenship of the Union is hereby established. Every person holding the nationality of a Member State shall be a citizen of the Union. Citizenship of the Union shall be additional to and not replace national citizenship.

2. Citizens of the Union shall enjoy the rights and be subject to the duties provided for in the Treaties. They shall have, *inter alia*:

(a) the right to move and reside freely within the territory of the Member States;
(b) the right to vote and to stand as candidates in elections to the European Parliament and in municipal elections in their Member State of residence, under the same conditions as nationals of that State;
(c) the right to enjoy, in the territory of a third country in which the Member State of which they are nationals is not represented, the protection of the diplomatic and consular authorities of any Member State on the same conditions as the nationals of that State;
(d) the right to petition the European Parliament, to apply to the European Ombudsman, and to address the institutions and advisory bodies of the Union in any of the Treaty languages and to obtain a reply in the same language.

These rights shall be exercised in accordance with the conditions and limits defined by the Treaties and by the measures adopted thereunder.

ARTICLE 21

1. Every citizen of the Union shall have the right to move and reside freely within the territory of the Member States, subject to the limitations and conditions laid down in the Treaties and by the measures adopted to give them effect.

2. If action by the Union should prove necessary to attain this objective and the Treaties have not provided the necessary powers, the European Parliament and the Council, acting in accordance with the ordinary legislative procedure, may adopt provisions with a view to facilitating the exercise of the rights referred to in paragraph 1.

3. For the same purposes as those referred to in paragraph 1 and if the Treaties have not provided the necessary powers, the Council, acting in accordance with a special legislative procedure, may adopt measures concerning social security or social protection. The Council shall act unanimously after consulting the European Parliament.

ARTICLE 22

1. Every citizen of the Union residing in a Member State of which he is not a national shall have the right to vote and to stand as a candidate at municipal elections in the Member State in which he resides, under the same conditions as nationals of that State. This right shall be exercised subject to detailed arrangements adopted by the Council, acting unanimously in accordance with a special legislative procedure and after consulting the European Parliament; these arrangements may provide for derogations where warranted by problems specific to a Member State.

2. Without prejudice to Article 223(1) and to the provisions adopted for its implementation, every citizen of the Union residing in a Member State of which he is not a national shall have the right to vote and to stand as a candidate in elections to the European Parliament in the Member State in which he resides, under the same conditions as nationals of that State. This right shall be exercised subject to detailed arrangements adopted by the Council, acting unanimously in accordance with a special legislative procedure and after consulting the European Parliament; these arrangements may provide for derogations where warranted by problems specific to a Member State.

ARTICLE 23

Every citizen of the Union shall, in the territory of a third country in which the Member State of which he is a national is not represented, be entitled to protection by the diplomatic or consular authorities of any Member State, on the same conditions as the nationals of that State. Member States shall adopt the necessary provisions and start the international negotiations required to secure this protection.

The Council, acting in accordance with a special legislative procedure and after consulting the European Parliament, may adopt Directives establishing the coordination and cooperation measures necessary to facilitate such protection.

ARTICLE 24

The European Parliament and the Council, acting by means of regulations in accordance with the ordinary legislative procedure, shall adopt the provisions for the procedures and conditions required for a citizens' initiative within the meaning of Article 11 of the Treaty on European Union, including the minimum number of Member States from which such citizens must come.

Every citizen of the Union shall have the right to petition the European Parliament in accordance with Article 227.

Every citizen of the Union may apply to the Ombudsman established in accordance with Article 228.

Every citizen of the Union may write to any of the institutions, bodies, offices or agencies referred to in this Article or in Article 13 of the Treaty on European Union in one of the languages mentioned in Article 55(1) of the Treaty on European Union and have an answer in the same language.

ARTICLE 25

The Commission shall report to the European Parliament, to the Council and to the Economic and Social Committee every three years on the application of the provisions of this Part. This report shall take account of the development of the Union.

On this basis, and without prejudice to the other provisions of the Treaties, the Council, acting unanimously in accordance with a special legislative procedure and after obtaining the consent of the European Parliament, may adopt provisions to strengthen or to add to the rights listed in Article 20(2). These provisions shall enter into force after their approval by the Member States in accordance with their respective constitutional requirements.

There is sweeping ambition here – and there are limits too. These provisions are an exercise in glorious evasion. Article 18 forbids any discrimination on grounds of nationality – but only within the scope of application of the Treaties. Article 20 establishes 'Citizenship of the Union' and lists a set of rights, with 'the right to move and reside freely within the territory of the Member States' first on the list followed by others of varying and peculiar shape, subject to legislative amplification as envisaged in the Treaty provisions that follow – only to conclude that they 'shall be exercised in accordance with the conditions and *limits* defined by the Treaties and by the measures adopted thereunder' (emphasis added). Similarly, Article 21 confers on Citizens of the Union a right to move and reside freely within the territory of the Member States – but 'subject to the limitations and conditions laid down in the Treaties and by the measures adopted to give them effect'.

The Court too has played this evasive game.

***Rudy Grzelczyk* v *Centre public d'aide sociale d'Ottignies-Louvain-la-Neuve* (Case C-184/99)**

[2001] ECR I-6193, Court of Justice of the European Communities

[31] Union citizenship is destined to be the fundamental status of nationals of the Member States, enabling those who find themselves in the same situation to enjoy the same treatment in law irrespective of their nationality, subject to such exceptions as are expressly provided for.

A grand destiny – yet one subject to exceptions! We already saw in *Collins* (Case C-138/02), considered in Chapter 13 (p. 367), that there are different types of 'worker', distinguished by the varying scope of entitlement to equal access to benefits. Citizenship adds in yet more awkward such distinctions – again driven by a tension between true equality and the stretched budgets of Member States asked to provide resources for migrant non-nationals. There is a persistent ambiguity at the heart of the status of Citizenship of the Union: nationals of one Member State are entitled to be treated by another Member State as if they were nationals of that second Member State . . . up to a point. Yet that 'point' is ill-defined.

Directive 2004/38 of the European Parliament and Council on the right of citizens of the Union and their family members to move and reside freely within the territory of the Member States has, as its title shows, a wide sweep. It establishes common standards in a number of matters such as rights of exit and entry, rights of residence and applicable restrictions. So, for example, in the matter of expulsion from a host Member State *Tsakouridis* (Case C-145/09) was encountered in Chapter 13 (p. 379). He had worked in Germany, but the Court's analysis of the conditions governing his expulsion is not at all limited to his status as a worker. Accordingly, in a number of important respects Directive 2004/38 is the governing measure for all citizens of the Union, irrespective of their economic status.

However, it is not possible simply to assume that EU law's preferred status for the economically active migrant has been eliminated in favour of a general non-hierarchical 'law of persons'. The Directive distinguishes between types of migrants for the purposes of both a right of residence and the scope of the principle of equal treatment. Reference to two of the Articles in the Directive is enough to elucidate the tensions:

Directive 2004/38 of the European Parliament and Council on the right of citizens of the Union and their family members to move and reside freely within the territory of the Member States

ARTICLE 7

Right of residence for more than three months

1. All Union citizens shall have the right of residence on the territory of another Member State for a period of longer than three months if they:
   (a) are workers or self-employed persons in the host Member State; or
   (b) have sufficient resources for themselves and their family members not to become a burden on the social assistance system of the host Member State during their period of residence and have comprehensive sickness insurance cover in the host Member State; or
   (c) – are enrolled at a private or public establishment, accredited or financed by the host Member State on the basis of its legislation or administrative practice, for the principal purpose of following a course of study, including vocational training; and
   – have comprehensive sickness insurance cover in the host Member State and assure the relevant national authority, by means of a declaration or by such equivalent means as They may choose, that they have sufficient resources for themselves and their family members not to become a burden on the social assistance system of the host Member State during their period of residence; or
   (d) are family members accompanying or joining a Union citizen who satisfies the conditions referred to in points (a), (b) or (c).

2. The right of residence provided for in paragraph 1 shall extend to family members who are not nationals of a Member State, accompanying or joining the Union citizen in the host Member State, provided that such Union citizen satisfies the conditions referred to in paragraph 1(a), (b) or (c).

3. For the purposes of paragraph 1(a), a Union citizen who is no longer a worker or self-employed person shall retain the status of worker or self-employed person in the following circumstances:
   (a) he/she is temporarily unable to work as the result of an illness or accident;
   (b) he/she is in duly recorded involuntary unemployment after having been employed for more than one year and has registered as a job-seeker with the relevant employment office;

(c) he/she is in duly recorded involuntary unemployment after completing a fixed-term employment contract of less than a year or after having become involuntarily unemployed during the first twelve months and has registered as a job-seeker with the relevant employment office. In this case, the status of worker shall be retained for no less than six months;

(d) he/she embarks on vocational training. Unless he/she is involuntarily unemployed, the retention of the status of worker shall require the training to be related to the previous employment.

4. By way of derogation from paragraphs 1(d) and 2 above, only the spouse, the registered partner provided for in Article 2(2)(b) and dependent children shall have the right of residence as family members of a Union citizen meeting the conditions under 1(c) above. Article 3(2) shall apply to his/her dependent direct relatives in the ascending lines and those of his/her spouse or registered partner.

ARTICLE 24

Equal treatment

1. Subject to such specific provisions as are expressly provided for in the Treaty and secondary law, all Union citizens residing on the basis of this Directive in the territory of the host Member State shall enjoy equal treatment with the nationals of that Member State within the scope of the Treaty. The benefit of this right shall be extended to family members who are not nationals of a Member State and who have the right of residence or permanent residence.

2. By way of derogation from paragraph 1, the host Member State shall not be obliged to confer entitlement to social assistance during the first three months of residence or, where appropriate, the longer period provided for in Article 14(4)(b), nor shall it be obliged, prior to acquisition of the right of permanent residence, to grant maintenance aid for studies, including vocational training, consisting in student grants or student loans to persons other than workers, self-employed persons, persons who retain such status and members of their families.

There is a visible legislative nervousness about extending equal rights to *all* EU nationals. According to this text the economically active are still in a superior position to those who are not. The Court's ruling on the economically *inactive* migrant in *Elisabeta Dano* (Case C-333/13, p. 368) provides a vivid example. And yet even these provisions of the Directive present conundrums. Were the Court to conclude that the Treaty grants a right in circumstances excluded by the Directive, then, as a matter of constitutional hierarchy, the Treaty would prevail. Moreover, there are situations which lie beyond the scope of application of the Directive, yet which have been found to fall within the scope of the Treaty, most prominently cases concerning the right of residence of members of the family in the *home* State of the EU national. Formally the Directive's limitations cannot apply here, for it is not itself engaged. Here too the question is what level of protection the Court will afford in the name of free movement (as in *Carpenter*) or 'Citizenship' (*Dereci*, p. 428). In fact, as so often in the shaping of EU law, a great deal of autonomy is permitted to the Court to determine the scope of rights.

B: Citizenship and the derivative rights of third country nationals (TCNs)

Carpenter was treated by the Court as a case of economic free movement, but the purpose of using EU law was to protect a third country national spouse. And in fact an increasing number of cases involve attempts to rely on EU law to secure a derivative right for a third country national ('TCN'). Where EU law bites the result is that the competence of Member States to decide their policy towards admission and residence of third country nationals is subject to compliance with any requirements of EU law which may arise. The awkward questions then surround the precise scope of EU law's intervention, given that the limits are fixed not by precise and exhaustive wording in the Treaty nor in secondary legislation but rather according to the case law that happens to reach the Court. And the case law is proving extraordinarily dynamic.

In *Akrich* (Case C-109/01) [2003] ECR I-9607 Akrich, a Moroccan national, was deported from the UK in 1991 and 1992. He clandestinely returned to the UK and in 1996, while he was residing unlawfully in the UK, he married a British national. He was deported in 1997 to Ireland, in accordance with his wishes because his spouse had also moved to Ireland shortly before. She decided to return to the UK and the question then arose whether he could claim a right under EU law to enter the UK as her spouse. If the answer is 'yes' the vigour of EU law's ability to subvert a Member State's policy on admission of third country nationals would be highlighted. But in *Akrich* the answer was not 'yes'. The Court concluded that the benefits of Regulation 1612/68, now Regulation 492/2011, would be available only where the 'TCN' is lawfully resident in a Member State when he moves to another Member State to which the citizen of the Union is migrating or has migrated.

The Court was evidently concerned to craft a formula that will balance on the one hand protection of the migrant EU national and, derivatively, his or her spouse and, on the other, the prerogatives enjoyed by Member States in determining who they will admit to their territory. To this end it draws a line: only the third country national equipped with a right of prior lawful residence may enjoy protection. But such delicate balances, which are not based on unambiguous legislative texts, are durable only until the Court reconsiders. And five years later it did reconsider.

Blaise Baheten Metock (Case C-127/08)

[2008] ECR I-6241, Court of Justice of the European Communities

Mr Metock was a national of Cameroon. He arrived in Ireland where he applied for asylum. He then married a British national who was working in Ireland, with whom he had a pre-existing relationship. His application for asylum in Ireland was refused and he was also refused recognition of rights as a spouse of an EU national on the basis that he had no prior lawful residence in another EU Member State. The Court was asked whether this was compatible with EU law. It considered the matter from the perspective of Directive 2004/38 (p. 423), which amended Regulation 1612/68 which had been at stake in *Akrich*. But the legislation did not bring about change: rather, the Court's interpretation of it involved a reconsideration of *Akrich*.

[54] Directive 2004/38 must be interpreted as applying to all nationals of non-member countries who are family members of a Union citizen within the meaning of point 2 of Article 2 of that directive and accompany or join the Union citizen in a Member State other than that of which he is a national, and as conferring on them rights of entry and residence in that Member State, without distinguishing according to whether or not the national of a non-member country has already resided lawfully in another Member State.

[55] That interpretation is supported by the Court's case-law on the instruments of secondary law concerning freedom of movement for persons adopted before Directive 2004/38.

[56] Even before the adoption of Directive 2004/38, the Community legislature recognised the importance of ensuring the protection of the family life of nationals of the Member States in order to eliminate obstacles to the exercise of the fundamental freedoms guaranteed by the EC Treaty (Case C-60/00 Carpenter [2002] ECR I-6279, paragraph 38; Case C-459/99 MRAX [2002] ECR I-6591, paragraph 53; Case C-157/03 *Commission* v *Spain* [2005] ECR I-2911, paragraph 26; Case C-503/03 *Commission* v *Spain* [2006] ECR I-1097, paragraph 41; Case C-441/02 *Commission* v *Germany* [2006] ECR I-3449, paragraph 109; and Case C-291/05 Eind [2007] ECR I-0000, paragraph 44).

[57] To that end, the Community legislature has considerably expanded, in Regulation No 1612/68 and in the directives on freedom of movement for persons adopted before Directive 2004/38, the application of Community law on entry into and residence in the territory of the Member States to nationals of non-member

countries who are spouses of nationals of Member States (see, to that effect, Case C-503/03 *Commission* v *Spain*, paragraph 41).

[58] It is true that the Court held in paragraphs 50 and 51 of Akrich that, in order to benefit from the rights provided for in Article 10 of Regulation No 1612/68, the national of a non-member country who is the spouse of a Union citizen must be lawfully resident in a Member State when he moves to another Member State to which the citizen of the Union is migrating or has migrated. However, that conclusion must be reconsidered. The benefit of such rights cannot depend on the prior lawful residence of such a spouse in another Member State (see, to that effect, MRAX, paragraph 59, and Case C-157/03 *Commission* v *Spain*, paragraph 28).

[59] The same interpretation must be adopted a fortiori with respect to Directive 2004/38, which amended Regulation No 1612/68 and repealed the earlier directives on freedom of movement for persons. As is apparent from recital 3 in the preamble to Directive 2004/38, it aims in particular to 'strengthen the right of free movement and residence of all Union citizens', so that Union citizens cannot derive less rights from that directive than from the instruments of secondary legislation which it amends or repeals.

[60] In the second place, the above interpretation of Directive 2004/38 is consistent with the division of competences between the Member States and the Community.

[61] It is common ground that the Community derives from Articles 18(2) EC, 40 EC, 44 EC and 52 EC – on the basis of which Directive 2004/38 inter alia was adopted – competence to enact the necessary measures to bring about freedom of movement for Union citizens.

[62] As already pointed out in paragraph 56 above, if Union citizens were not allowed to lead a normal family life in the host Member State, the exercise of the freedoms they are guaranteed by the Treaty would be seriously obstructed.

[63] Consequently, within the competence conferred on it by those articles of the Treaty, the Community legislature can regulate the conditions of entry and residence of the family members of a Union citizen in the territory of the Member States, where the fact that it is impossible for the Union citizen to be accompanied or joined by his family in the host Member State would be such as to interfere with his freedom of movement by discouraging him from exercising his rights of entry into and residence in that Member State.

[64] The refusal of the host Member State to grant rights of entry and residence to the family members of a Union citizen is such as to discourage that citizen from moving to or residing in that Member State, even if his family members are not already lawfully resident in the territory of another Member State.

[65] It follows that the Community legislature has competence to regulate, as it did by Directive 2004/38, the entry and residence of nationals of non-member countries who are family members of a Union citizen in the Member State in which that citizen has exercised his right of freedom of movement, including where the family members were not already lawfully resident in another Member State.

NOTE: For analysis of *Metock* see C. Costello, (2009) 46 CML Rev 587; S. Currie, (2009) 34 EL Rev 310. This ruling significantly circumscribes national autonomy in the treatment of third country nationals. Several Member States intervened in vain to urge the Court not to adopt this interpretation and in consequence of the judgment the Court attracted some criticism. Here is not the place to pursue analysis of the Court's choices in more detail. The point is only that the dynamic logic of free movement law is that it intrudes profoundly and sometimes unpredictably into national practices which seem remote from economic affairs.

But there clearly was cross-border movement in these cases. Is 'Citizenship of the Union' an enlarged notion which allows a national of an EU Member State to rely on EU law even against his or her *own* State, which he or she has not left, in circumstances when a third country national relative is faced with deportation? The Treaty does not say this. What of the Court?

In Cases C-64/96 and C-65/96 *Land Nordrhein-Westfalen* v *Uecker, Jacquet* [1997] ECR I-3171 the Court ruled that the insertion of the Citizenship provisions is not intended to extend the material scope of the Treaty to internal situations with no link to EU law. In 2011 the Court delivered three judgments which did not contradict this principle – but which revealed that the category of 'internal situations with no link to EU law' is smaller than previously thought, and that accordingly the reach of EU law is correspondingly – and unexpectedly – wider.

Case C-34/09 *Ruiz Zambrano* [2011] ECR I-1177 concerned a Colombian national in Belgium with dependent children who held Belgian nationality. The question was whether the Colombian acquired a right of residence in Belgium under EU law. Directive 2004/38 requires a Union citizen to have moved between Member States so it did not apply. The Treaty alone determined the outcome. The Court held that Article 20 TFEU 'precludes national measures which have the effect of depriving citizens of the Union of the genuine enjoyment of the substance of the rights conferred by virtue of their status as citizens of the Union' (para 42). And since refusal to grant a right of residence to the Colombian would mean the children, citizens of the Union, would have to leave the territory of the Union, as a result they would be unable to exercise the substance of the rights conferred on them by virtue of their status as citizens of the Union. EU law applied even though the EU nationals had never left their home State, Belgium.

The judgment is especially gnomic, because the Court acknowledged that it had had pressed on it the absence of any cross-border element to the case and consequently the inapplicability of the free movement provisions – see para 37 of the judgment – but then it completely ignored the objection, and asserted the matter to fall within the scope of EU law.

The Court treated this as a national measure which deprived an individual of 'genuine enjoyment of the substance of the rights conferred by virtue of their status as citizens of the Union'. But it seemed possible to interpret this as tantamount to allowing EU law to apply even in a purely internal situation.

Two months later the Court decided Case C-434/09 *Shirley McCarthy* [2011] ECR I-3375. McCarthy was a dual Irish/UK national but she was born and had always lived in the UK. She married a third country national – a Jamaican – who had no leave to remain in the UK. Once again Directive 2004/38 did not apply, for want of cross-border movement. Nor did Article 21 TFEU apply, because the Court considered that there was no deprivation of genuine enjoyment of the substance of rights conferred by the status of citizenship. 'By contrast' (para 50) with *Ruiz Zambrano* the UK measure did not oblige her to leave the territory of the EU.

There is no right to family reunification per se. The Court has decided that the central issue is whether what is at stake is deprivation of 'genuine enjoyment of the substance of the rights' conferred by virtue of the status of citizenship. Some apparently internal situations are controlled under EU law: where, in short, the substance of rights is damaged, as in *Ruiz Zambrano*. In others – such as *McCarthy* –we see the last remnants of State autonomy untouched by EU law.

This creates a great deal of uncertainty. What if McCarthy had argued that she would be forced to move to Jamaica unless a right of residence were granted to her husband? Is parents-plus-children (*Ruiz Zambrano*) a family unit recognized by EU law as more deserving of protection than spouse-plus-spouse (*McCarthy*)? Hailbronner and Thym (Annotation, 2011 48 CML Rev 1253) explain that the Court has taken a leap forward – which stops half way! The 'purely internal' situation is curtailed – but not abandoned. And in troublingly uncertain circumstances. They lament that 'A Supreme Court should behave more responsibly' (p. 1259).

Late in 2011 the Court felt constrained to return to the fray in order to clarify the extent to which the Treaty provisions on Citizenship allow incursion into what we might previously have assumed to be a situation internal to one Member State and so excluded from the scope of application of EU law.

Case C-256/11 *Murat Dereci, Vishaka Heiml, Alban Kokollari, Izunna Emmanuel Maduike, Dragica Stevic* v *Bundesministerium für Inneres*

[2011] ECR I-11315

The applicants were all third country nationals who had been refused permission to live with family members who were European Union citizens resident in and nationals of Austria. The EU citizens concerned had never exercised their right to free movement. So the fact pattern has much in common with *Ruiz Zambrano* and *McCarthy* and, as in those rulings, Directive 2004/38 does not apply, so it is the Treaty provisions on Citizenship that count. The EU citizens are, however, not maintained by the 'TCNs' – unlike in *Ruiz Zambrano*.

This is a ruling of the Grand Chamber of the Court and is plainly intended to clean up this area of the law.

[60] . . . it must be borne in mind that the Treaty rules governing freedom of movement for persons and the measures adopted to implement them cannot be applied to situations which have no factor linking them with any of the situations governed by European Union law and which are confined in all relevant respects within a single Member State (see, to that effect, Case C-212/06 *Government of the French Community and Walloon Government* [2008] ECR I-1683, paragraph 33; *Metock and Others*, paragraph 77 and, *McCarthy*, paragraph 45).

[61] However, the situation of a Union citizen who, like each of the citizens who are family members of the applicants in the main proceedings, has not made use of the right to freedom of movement cannot, for that reason alone, be assimilated to a purely internal situation (see Case C-403/03 *Schempp* [2005] ECR I-6421, paragraph 22, and *McCarthy*, paragraph 46).

[62] Indeed, the Court has stated several times that citizenship of the Union is intended to be the fundamental status of nationals of the Member States (see *Ruiz Zambrano*, paragraph 41, and the case-law cited).

[63] As nationals of a Member State, family members of the applicants in the main proceedings enjoy the status of Union citizens under Article 20(1) TFEU and may therefore rely on the rights pertaining to that status, including against their Member State of origin (see *McCarthy*, paragraph 48).

[64] On this basis, the Court has held that Article 20 TFEU precludes national measures which have the effect of depriving Union citizens of the genuine enjoyment of the substance of the rights conferred by virtue of that status (see *Ruiz Zambrano*, paragraph 42).

[65] Indeed, in the case leading to that judgment, the question arose as to whether a refusal to grant a right of residence to a third country national with dependent minor children in the Member State where those children are nationals and reside and a refusal to grant such a person a work permit have such an effect. The Court considered in particular that such a refusal would lead to a situation where those children, who are citizens of the Union, would have to leave the territory of the Union in order to accompany their parents. In those circumstances, those citizens of the Union would, in fact, be unable to exercise the substance of the rights conferred on them by virtue of their status as citizens of the Union (see *Ruiz Zambrano*, paragraphs 43 and 44).

[66] It follows that the criterion relating to the denial of the genuine enjoyment of the substance of the rights conferred by virtue of European Union citizen status refers to situations in which the Union citizen has, in fact, to leave not only the territory of the Member State of which he is a national but also the territory of the Union as a whole.

[67] That criterion is specific in character inasmuch as it relates to situations in which, although subordinate legislation on the right of residence of third country nationals is not applicable, a right of residence may not, exceptionally, be refused to a third country national, who is a family member of a Member State national, as the effectiveness of Union citizenship enjoyed by that national would otherwise be undermined.

[68] Consequently, the mere fact that it might appear desirable to a national of a Member State, for economic reasons or in order to keep his family together in the territory of the Union, for the members of his family who do not have the nationality of a Member State to be able to reside with him in the territory of the Union, is not sufficient in itself to support the view that the Union citizen will be forced to leave Union territory if such a right is not granted.

NOTE: Here then are the limits of EU law – though not necessarily the limits of legal protection. The Court added:

> [72] . . . if the referring court considers, in the light of the circumstances of the disputes in the main proceedings, that the situation of the applicants in the main proceedings is covered by European Union law, it must examine whether the refusal of their right of residence undermines the right to respect for private and family life provided for in Article 7 of the Charter. On the other hand, if it takes the view that that situation is not covered by European Union law, it must undertake that examination in the light of Article 8(1) of the ECHR.
>
> [73] All the Member States are, after all, parties to the ECHR which enshrines the right to respect for private and family life in Article 8.

NOTE: *Dereci* (Case C-256/11) has become the Court's primary point of reference in determining when an EU national who has not left his or her home State may rely on EU law to protect 'TCN' family members. In Case C-40/11 *Iida* judgment of 8 November 2012 the TCN did *not* get a derivative right under EU law (to remain in Germany) because on the facts there was no inhibition or deterrence of free movement by the EU citizen (to whom he was married). In Cases C-356/11 and C-357/11 *O, S & L* judgment of 6 December 2012 the Court cautiously left it to the referring Finnish court to apply the test of whether excluding the TCN 'entails, for the Union citizens concerned, a denial of the genuine enjoyment of the substance of the rights conferred by their status', but ruled that blood relationship between the TCN and the child who is an EU national – missing in the case – is *not* necessary. But dependency of the child on the TCN is significant. Case C-87/12 *Ymeraga* judgment of 8 May 2013 concerns a Luxembourg national who has never exercised a right of free movement and TCN family members (from Kosovo). The *Dereci* formula is cited, but it seems that here there is simply a desire to achieve family re-unification and, when that is refused by the Luxembourg authorities, there is no denial of genuine enjoyment of the substance of the right conferred by EU law. (And this is not a matter of implementing EU law, so the Charter does not apply.) In *Alokpa* (Case C-86/12 judgment of 10 October 2013) the Court went out of its way to confirm what it had already declared in *Dereci* – that protection arises only 'exceptionally' (para 33).

■ QUESTIONS

1. How does one judge whether a Union citizen 'has to leave' the territory of the Union as a whole (para 66 *Dereci*)? Is this based on a subjective or objective inquiry?
2. Why doesn't the Court bite the bullet, and insist that protection of the fundamental rights recognized by the EU Treaty applies in all circumstances arising on the territory of the EU?

FURTHER READING

Kochenov, D. and Plender, R., 'EU Citizenship: From an Incipient Form to an Incipient Substance? The Discovery of the Treaty Text' (2012) 37 EL Rev 369.

Nic Shuibhne, N., '(Some of) The Kids Are All Right: Comment on McCarthy and Dereci' (2012) 49 CML Rev 349.

Strumia, F., 'Looking for Substance at the Boundaries: European Citizenship and Mutual Recognition of Belonging' (2013) 32 YEL 432.

Tryfonidou, A., 'Redefining the Outer Boundaries of EU Law: The Zambrano, McCarthy and Dereci Trilogy' (2012) 18 European Public Law 493.

C: Citizenship and constitutional identity

We have seen how the rights conferred by the Treaty provisions on Citizenship have been treated as apt to curtail the 'internal situation' in which Member State autonomy is protected from EU law. Member State competence to regulate the admission of TCNs is correspondingly limited. In other circumstances the Citizenship provisions are apt to achieve less innovative, yet still significant, consequences. In the next case the cross-border element is plain, and the interest lies in the way that the Court aligns free movement rights enjoyed by Citizens with the economic free movement rights explored in earlier chapters.

Case C-208/09 *Ilonka Sayn-Wittgenstein* v *Landeshauptmann von Wien*

[2010] ECR I-13693

Austria has a 1919 law abolishing the nobility which *inter alia* does away with titles, whereas Germany has a 1919 law which does away with privileges but allows parts of the noble title to be retained in the surname. Ilonka was adopted in Germany by Lothar Fürst von Sayn-Wittgenstein. In Germany she was known as Ilonka Fürstin von Sayn-Wittgenstein. In Austria she was advised she must be registered instead as Ilonka Sayn-Wittgenstein.

> [54] ... obliging a person who has exercised his right to move and reside freely in the territory of another Member State to use a surname, in the Member State of which he a national, which is different from that already conferred and registered in the Member State of birth and residence is liable to hamper the exercise of the right, established in Article 21 TFEU, to move and reside freely within the territory of the Member States (*Grunkin and Paul*, paragraphs 21 and 22).
>
> [55] In Case C-148/02 *Garcia Avello* [2003] ECR I-11613, the Court held legislation of a Member State which obliged a person to use different family names in different Member States to be incompatible with Articles 12 EC and 17 EC. In that context the Court held, as regards children with the nationality of two Member States, that a discrepancy in surnames is liable to cause serious inconvenience for those concerned at both professional and private levels resulting from, inter alia, difficulties in benefiting, in the Member State of which they are nationals, from the legal effects of diplomas or documents drawn up in the name recognised in another Member State of which they are also nationals. The person concerned may also encounter difficulties linked inter alia to the drawing up of certificates or diplomas which clearly reveal a name that differs from his surname. That fact may give rise to doubts as to the person's identity, the authenticity of the documents submitted or the veracity of their content (see, to that effect, *Garcia Avello*, paragraph 36).
>
> [56] The Court held in paragraph 24 of *Grunkin and Paul* that such serious inconvenience may likewise arise where the child concerned holds the nationality of only one Member State, but that State of origin refuses to recognise the family name acquired by the child in the State of birth and residence.

The Court accepted that Sayn-Wittgenstein was so *inconvenienced* by the Austrian rules, and that accordingly she was the victim of a restriction within the meaning of Article 21 TFEU. So was there a sufficient justification?

> [81] In accordance with settled case-law, an obstacle to the freedom of movement of persons can be justified only where it is based on objective considerations and is proportionate to the legitimate objective of the national provisions ...
>
> [82] According to the referring court and the governments which submitted observations to the Court, an objective consideration could be invoked as a justification in the main proceedings in conjunction with the Law on the abolition of the nobility, which has constitutional status and implements the principle of equal treatment in this field, and with the case-law of the Verfassungsgerichtshof dating from 2003.
>
> [83] In that regard, it must be accepted that, in the context of Austrian constitutional history, the Law on the abolition of the nobility, as an element of national identity, may be taken into consideration when a balance is struck between legitimate interests and the right of free movement of persons recognised under European Union law.
>
> [84] The justification relied upon by the Austrian Government by reference to the Austrian constitutional situation is to be interpreted as reliance on public policy.

[85] Objective considerations relating to public policy are capable of justifying, in a Member State, a refusal to recognise the surname of one of its nationals, as accorded in another Member State (see, to that effect, *Grunkin and Paul*, paragraph 38).

[86] The Court has repeatedly noted that the concept of public policy as justification for a derogation from a fundamental freedom must be interpreted strictly, so that its scope cannot be determined unilaterally by each Member State without any control by the European Union institutions (see Case C-36/02 *Omega* [2004] ECR I-9609, paragraph 30, and Case C-33/07 *Jipa* [2008] ECR I-5157, paragraph 23). Thus, public policy may be relied on only if there is a genuine and sufficiently serious threat to a fundamental interest of society (see *Omega*, paragraph 30 and the case-law cited).

[87] The fact remains, however, that the specific circumstances which may justify recourse to the concept of public policy may vary from one Member State to another and from one era to another. The competent national authorities must therefore be allowed a margin of discretion within the limits imposed by the Treaty (see *Omega*, paragraph 31 and the case-law cited).

[88] In the context of the main proceedings, the Austrian Government has stated that the Law on the abolition of the nobility constitutes implementation of the more general principle of equality before the law of all Austrian citizens.

[89] The European Union legal system undeniably seeks to ensure the observance of the principle of equal treatment as a general principle of law. That principle is also enshrined in Article 20 of the Charter of Fundamental Rights. There can therefore be no doubt that the objective of observing the principle of equal treatment is compatible with European Union law.

[90] Measures which restrict a fundamental freedom may be justified on public policy grounds only if they are necessary for the protection of the interests which they are intended to secure and only in so far as those objectives cannot be attained by less restrictive measures (see *Omega*, paragraph 36, and *Jipa*, paragraph 29).

[91] The Court has already explained in that regard that it is not indispensable for the restrictive measure issued by the authorities of a Member State to correspond to a conception shared by all Member States as regards the precise way in which the fundamental right or legitimate interest in question is to be protected and that, on the contrary, the need for, and proportionality of, the provisions adopted are not excluded merely because one Member State has chosen a system of protection different from that adopted by another State (see *Omega*, paragraphs 37 and 38).

[92] It must also be noted that, in accordance with Article 4(2) TEU, the European Union is to respect the national identities of its Member States, which include the status of the State as a Republic.

[93] In the present case, it does not appear disproportionate for a Member State to seek to attain the objective of protecting the principle of equal treatment by prohibiting any acquisition, possession or use, by its nationals, of titles of nobility or noble elements which may create the impression that the bearer of the name is holder of such a rank. By refusing to recognise the noble elements of a name such as that of the applicant in the main proceedings, the Austrian authorities responsible for civil status matters do not appear to have gone further than is necessary in order to ensure the attainment of the fundamental constitutional objective pursued by them.

[94] In those circumstances, the refusal, by the authorities of a Member State, to recognise all the elements of the surname of a national of that State, as determined in another Member State – in which that national resides – at the time of his or her adoption as an adult by a national of that other Member State, where that surname includes a title of nobility which is not permitted in the first Member State under its constitutional law cannot be regarded as a measure unjustifiably undermining the freedom to move and reside enjoyed by citizens of the Union.

NOTE: The ruling in Case C-391/09 *Runevič-Vardyn/Runiewicz-Wardyn* [2011] ECR I-3787 follows a similar line. The litigation concerned practices in Lithuania which prevented individuals using the Polish version of their names on civil (birth, marriage) certificates. It was for the national court to determine which practices constituted restrictions within the meaning of Article 21 TFEU. The Court then turned to justifications. It drew on Article 22 of the Charter of Fundamental Rights: the Union must respect its rich cultural and linguistic diversity. It also drew on Article 4(2) EU: the Union must respect the national identity of its Member States, which includes protection of a State's official national language. The objective pursued by the Lithuanian rules was in principle a legitimate objective capable of justifying restrictions on the rights of freedom of movement and residence'. Ultimately the factual assessment belonged with the national court.

These decisions look remarkably similar *in structure* to many familiar economic free movement cases. As one would expect: this is the model of *Gebhard* (p. 266) and *Cassis de Dijon* (p. 319), where laws which differ State by State damage the position of the migrant, asked to adapt to local regulatory conditions. In fact, as the Court observed in the judgment, Sayn-Wittgenstein could have relied also on Article 56 TFEU, for the inconvenience affected both her private and her professional life. The sensitivity of the task of adjudication which the Court here assumes in assessing justification for national practices should be considered alongside cases involving the interaction of fundamental rights in Chapters 12 (eg *Schmidberger* p. 348) and 14 (*Ladbrokes, Omega, Viking Line*, pp. 349, 392, 401 respectively). To repeat: 'Free movement law is not only about free movement' (*cf* p. 403).

One might plausibly identify a difference between the approach adopted in *Sayn-Wittgenstein* and that found in *Omega*. Instead of converting a national constitutional concern into an EU constitutional concern, which is the technique employed in *Omega* (p. 401), the Court here uses Article 4(2) TEU to show concern to respect a specifically *Austrian* concern. One might find a hint here that Article 4(2) TEU is a route to soften the deregulatory cutting-edge of free movement law yet further – although admittedly the outcome is on the facts the same: free movement law yields to justified national measures. In Chapter 19 it will be further explored whether the Court is developing a more overt concern to 'open up' EU law to national constitutional concerns while still laying formal claim to the supremacy of EU law over national law, in balance with the concern of national legal orders (inspired especially by the *Bundesverfassungsgericht*) to open up national law to EU law, while still placing limits on its subjection to EU law in the name of, *inter alia*, defence of constitutional identity.

FURTHER READING

Dobbs, M., 'Sovereignty, Article 492) TEU and Respect of National Identities' (2014) 33 YEL 298.

Guastaferro, B., 'Beyond the Exceptionalism of Constitutional Conflicts: The Ordinary Functions of the Identity Clause' (2012) 31 YEL 263.

Van der Schyff, G., 'The Constitutional Relationship between the European Union and its Member States: The Role of National Identity in Article 4(2) TEU' (2012) 37 EL Rev 563.

Von Bogdandy, A. and Schill, S., 'Overcoming Absolute Primacy: Respect for National Identity under the Lisbon Treaty' (2011) 48 CML Rev 1417.

D. The material scope of the rights of the citizen

The previous sub-sections disclose how the Treaty provisions on Citizenship are treated as cautiously transformative by the Court. In particular, the 'purely internal' situation, which escapes the scope of application of EU law, is curtailed. What of the material scope of a citizen's entitlement to equal access to benefits in the host State? This is another area left incomplete by the Treaty and the secondary legislation and consequently offers another fertile field for the Court. In *Maria Martinez Sala* v *Freistaat Bayern* (Case C-85/96) [1998] ECR I-2691 the Court ruled that a national of a Member State lawfully residing in the territory of another Member State falls within the personal scope of the Treaty provisions on European Citizenship. This triggered a right to, *inter alia*, protection from discrimination on grounds of nationality within the material scope of application of the Treaty. In *Martinez Sala* this allowed the applicant access to benefits which, one might previously have supposed, would have been available to her only had she held a more active economic status than mere lawful residence in the host State. *Martinez Sala* was greeted as a potential bridge between the orthodoxy of economic rights for economic migrants and new horizons lit up by comprehensive rights to equal treatment for Union citizens. See S. Fries and J. Shaw, 'Citizenship of the Union: First Steps in the Court of Justice' (1998) 4 *European Public Law* 533; S. O'Leary, 'Putting Flesh on the Bones of European Union Citizenship' (1999) 24 EL Rev 68. But what if the applicant had *not* been lawfully resident in Germany? Would the Treaty provisions on citizenship secure that right, even for individuals falling outwith the scope of the familiar economically-focused Treaty provisions and the package of secondary legislation adopted in 1990 and updated in Directive 2004/38 (p. 423)? *Martinez Sala* does not answer this question. But even at the time of the creation of the status of Citizenship such questions were being asked:

C. Closa, 'The Concept of Citizenship in the Treaty on European Union'

(1992) 29 CML Rev 1137, 1162

. . . the character of the union citizenship is determined by the progressive acquisition of rights stemming from the dynamic development of the Union. That is, the gradual acquisition by the European citizen of specific rights in new policy-areas transferred to the Union . . ..

The institutional role for the development of the dynamic character of citizenship will be the determinant factor to produce a qualitative leap forward.

And, as so often in EU law, it is to the Court that we must look for such dynamism. We already met Grzelczyk at p. 422: remember that 'Union citizenship is destined to be the fundamental status of nationals of the Member States'. Here now is the ruling in its proper context, developing *Martinez Sala*.

***Rudy Grzelczyk* v *Centre public d'aide sociale d'Ottignies-Louvain-la-Neuve* (Case C-184/99)**

[2001] ECR I-6193, Court of Justice of the European Communities

The applicant, a French national studying in Belgium, had been denied the 'minimex', a minimum subsistence allowance paid in Belgium. Previous case law established that the minimex was a social advantage within the meaning of Regulation 1612/68, now Regulation 492/2011, p. 369. But the Regulation concerns workers. Grzelczyk was not a worker. He was a student.

[29] It is clear from the documents before the Court that a student of Belgian nationality, though not a worker within the meaning of Regulation No 1612/68, who found himself in exactly the same circumstances as Mr Grzelczyk would satisfy the conditions for obtaining the minimex. The fact that Mr Grzelczyk is not of Belgian nationality is the only bar to its being granted to him. It is not therefore in dispute that the case is one of discrimination solely on the ground of nationality.

[30] Within the sphere of application of the Treaty, such discrimination is, in principle, prohibited by Article 6 [now 18 TFEU]. In the present case, Article 6 [now 18 TFEU] must be read in conjunction with the provisions of the Treaty concerning citizenship of the Union in order to determine its sphere of application.

[31] Union citizenship is destined to be the fundamental status of nationals of the Member States, enabling those who find themselves in the same situation to enjoy the same treatment in law irrespective of their nationality, subject to such exceptions as are expressly provided for.

[32] As the Court held in paragraph 63 of its judgment in *Martínez Sala*, cited above, a citizen of the European Union, lawfully resident in the territory of a host Member State, can rely on Article 6 of the Treaty in all situations which fall within the scope ratione materiae of Community law.

[33] Those situations include those involving the exercise of the fundamental freedoms guaranteed by the Treaty and those involving the exercise of the right to move and reside freely in another Member State, as conferred by Article 8a of the Treaty (see Case C-274/96 *Bickel and Franz* [1998] ECR I-7637, paragraphs 15 and 16).

[34] It is true that, in paragraph 18 of its judgment in Case 197/86 *Brown* [1988] ECR 3205, the Court held that, at that stage in the development of Community law, assistance given to students for maintenance and training fell in principle outside the scope of the EEC Treaty for the purposes of Article 7 thereof (later Article 6 of the EC Treaty [and now Article 18]).

[35] However, since *Brown*, the Treaty on European Union has introduced citizenship of the European Union into the EC Treaty and added to Title VIII of Part Three a new chapter 3 devoted to education and vocational training. There is nothing in the amended text of the Treaty to suggest that students who are citizens of the Union, when they move to another Member State to study there, lose the rights which the Treaty confers on citizens of the Union. Furthermore, since *Brown*, the Council has also adopted Directive 93/96, which provides that the Member States must grant right of residence to student nationals of a Member State who satisfy certain requirements.

[36] The fact that a Union citizen pursues university studies in a Member State other than the State of which he is a national cannot, of itself, deprive him of the possibility of relying on the prohibition of all discrimination on grounds of nationality laid down in Article 6 of the Treaty.

[37] As pointed out in paragraph 30 above, in the present case that prohibition must be read in conjunction with Article 8a(1) of the Treaty, which proclaims 'the right to move and reside freely within the territory of the Member States, subject to the limitations and conditions laid down in this Treaty and by the measures adopted to give it effect'.

NOTE: The Court agreed that Directive 93/96, mentioned in para 35 and replaced by Directive 2004/38 with effect from 30 April 2006 (p. 423), envisages that a host State may require migrant students to have means to support themselves without falling back on the host State's system of social assistance as a precondition for enjoying rights of residence under the Directive. A student may lose the right of residence under the Directive if incapable of self-support. But this was no basis for excusing the discrimination practised by Belgium.

It was commented at p. 422 that the scope of Article 18 TFEU is enhanced each time that Treaty revision extends the scope of Union competence. But something different is at stake here. Once the individual's case is shown to have a connection with EU law there then arises an entitlement to equal treatment with a home State national by virtue of Article 18 read with the Citizenship provisions. The Court's vivid insistence that 'Union citizenship is destined to be the fundamental status of nationals of the Member States' pleads for a single basis for entitlements. Once the applicant had squeezed inside the personal scope of Treaty-conferred competence – as a lawful resident of Belgium – the pull of Citizenship plus Article 18 took over, and secured him the same treatment as a Belgian student. This gives a strong appearance of case law moving away from the grant of particular rights to particular groups of (economic) actors and instead embracing a powerful mission of protection of individual rights. The gap in legal protection between the migrant economic actor and the Citizen of the Union gets ever smaller.

Brian Francis Collins v *Secretary of State for Work and Pensions* (Case C-138/02)

[2004] ECR I-2703, Court of Justice of the European Communities

Grzelczyk was a student; Collins was a jobseeker. As explained in Chapter 13 (p. 367) the Court agreed that what is now Article 45 TFEU covers jobseekers, but it concluded that since Collins had not already entered the employment market of the host Member State (*in casu*, the UK) he, like Grzelczyk, was excluded from the right to rely on Article 7(2) of Regulation 1612/68, now 492/2011, to claim equality in social advantages with national workers. His claim for a jobseekers' allowance under relevant 1996 regulations had been refused by the British authorities on the ground that he was not habitually resident in the United Kingdom. The matter reached the Court of Justice by way of the preliminary reference procedure. Collins, as a jobseeker, was within the personal scope of the Treaty. The Court addressed the scope of the rule against nationality discrimination in Article 6 of the Treaty (which is now located in Article 18 TFEU).

[61] As the Court has held on a number of occasions, citizens of the Union lawfully resident in the territory of a host Member State can rely on Article 6 of the Treaty in all situations which fall within the scope *ratione materiae* of Community law. Citizenship of the Union is destined to be the fundamental status of nationals of

the Member States, enabling those who find themselves in the same situation to enjoy the same treatment in law irrespective of their nationality, subject to such exceptions as are expressly provided for (see, in particular, *Grzelczyk*, cited above, paragraphs 31 and 32, and Case C-148/02 *Garcia Avello* [2003] ECR I-0000, paragraphs 22 and 23).

[62] It is to be noted that the Court has held, in relation to a student who is a citizen of the Union, that entitlement to a non-contributory social benefit, such as the Belgian minimum subsistence allowance ('minimex'), falls within the scope of the prohibition of discrimination on grounds of nationality and that, therefore, Articles 6 and 8 of the Treaty preclude eligibility for that benefit from being subject to conditions which are liable to constitute discrimination on grounds of nationality (*Grzelczyk*, paragraph 46).

[63] In view of the establishment of citizenship of the Union and the interpretation in the case-law of the right to equal treatment enjoyed by citizens of the Union, it is no longer possible to exclude from the scope of Article 48(2) of the Treaty – which expresses the fundamental principle of equal treatment, guaranteed by Article 6 of the Treaty – a benefit of a financial nature intended to facilitate access to employment in the labour market of a Member State.

So Collins was able to rely on the principle of equal treatment to challenge the qualifying criterion that a jobseeker's habitual residence must be in the United Kingdom, which placed migrants at a disadvantage. But this did not necessarily mean he would succeed.

[66] A residence requirement of that kind can be justified only if it is based on objective considerations that are independent of the nationality of the persons concerned and proportionate to the legitimate aim of the national provisions (Case C-274/96 *Bickel and Franz* [1998] ECR I-7637, paragraph 27).

[67] The Court has already held that it is legitimate for the national legislature to wish to ensure that there is a genuine link between an applicant for an allowance in the nature of a social advantage within the meaning of Article 7(2) of Regulation No 1612/68 and the geographic employment market in question (see, in the context of the grant of tideover allowances to young persons seeking their first job, *D'Hoop*, cited above [Case C-224/98], paragraph 38).

[68] The jobseeker's allowance introduced by the 1995 Act is a social security benefit which replaced unemployment benefit and income support, and requires in particular the claimant to be available for and actively seeking employment and not to have income exceeding the applicable amount or capital exceeding a specified amount.

[69] It may be regarded as legitimate for a Member State to grant such an allowance only after it has been possible to establish that a genuine link exists between the person seeking work and the employment market of that State.

[70] The existence of such a link may be determined, in particular, by establishing that the person concerned has, for a reasonable period, in fact genuinely sought work in the Member State in question.

[71] The United Kingdom is thus able to require a connection between persons who claim entitlement to such an allowance and its employment market.

[72] However, while a residence requirement is, in principle, appropriate for the purpose of ensuring such a connection, if it is to be proportionate it cannot go beyond what is necessary in order to attain that objective. More specifically, its application by the national authorities must rest on clear criteria known in advance and provision must be made for the possibility of a means of redress of a judicial nature. In any event, if compliance with the requirement demands a period of residence, the period must not exceed what is necessary in order for the national authorities to be able to satisfy themselves that the person concerned is genuinely seeking work in the employment market of the host Member State.

[73] The answer to the third question must therefore be that the right to equal treatment laid down in Article 48(2) of the Treaty, read in conjunction with Articles 6 and 8 of the Treaty, does not preclude national legislation which makes entitlement to a jobseeker's allowance conditional on a residence requirement, in so far as that requirement may be justified on the basis of objective considerations that are independent of the nationality of the persons concerned and proportionate to the legitimate aim of the national provisions.

Like Martinez Sala and Grzelczyk, Collins was lawfully resident in the host Member State and claiming a benefit that fell within the material scope of EU law. But the concluding extract demonstrates that equal treatment with nationals of the host State does not follow automatically.

A residence requirement may be objectively justified (para 66 of *Collins*); a 'genuine link' between applicant and the employment market in question may be demanded by the host State as a pre-condition to grant of the claimed benefit (paras 67, 69).

So the Court permits the migrant to rely on relevant provisions of the Treaty, in particular what are now Articles 18 and 20 TFEU, to claim equality in access to benefits in circumstances which transcend the limitations of the secondary legislation. But it then re-introduces a degree of protection for the host Member State by allowing a restriction to be imposed in the absence of the necessary 'genuine link'.

The use of the Citizenship provisions coupled to the rule of non-discrimination on grounds of nationality reduces the significance of the dividing line between true 'workers' and individuals such as jobseekers and students, whereas the 'genuine link' test reasserts it. It is clearly always desirable for an applicant to be treated as a true worker for these purposes. The importance of the Court's case law on Citizenship is that even where the individual does not fall within one of the favoured categories of economically active migrant recognized by the Treaty, the assistance of EU law is not exhausted. However, much will depend on exactly how far the host Member State may go in denying benefits on the basis that a 'genuine link' is missing. What constitutes objective justification for refusal to grant a benefit that falls within the material scope of EU law to an EU national lawfully resident in the host Member State?

The next cases take us back to students, rather than jobseekers, but they share with *Collins* an evident concern to allow the migrant to challenge discriminatory practices while conceding to the host State the possibility to show an objective justification for them.

In *Grzelczyk* (Case C-184/99) it was explained that in *Brown* (Case C-197/86) the Court had found assistance to students for maintenance to lie outwith the Treaty for the purposes of a claim to non-discriminatory treatment under what is now Article 18 TFEU (para 34, p. 433) – but that EU law had moved on (para 35, p. 434). Case C-197/86 *Brown* harks back to the happy days when UK students received maintenance grants while studying at university. A migrant student was, however, not held not entitled to equal access to grants because such assistance was a matter of educational policy (which was not at the time a matter for the EU) and also a matter of social policy (which fell within the competence of the Member States in so far as not covered by specific provisions of the Treaty).

Student grants are long gone, replaced by student loans. Are migrant students today able to claim equal access to such assistance?

Dany Bidar (Case C-209/03)

[2005] ECR I-2119, Court of Justice of the European Communities

Bidar was a French national who had moved with his mother to the UK, where he completed his secondary education. In September 2001 he started a course in economics at University College London. He received assistance with tuition fees, but his application for a student loan to help him cover his maintenance costs was refused on the ground that he was not 'settled' in the United Kingdom. Bidar contended that this requirement violated Article 12 EC, now after amendment Article 18 TFEU. Although since *Brown* grants had been replaced by loans, the UK argued that the same principles should apply – that the provision of assistance for maintenance lies beyond the scope of Article 12 EC. The matter was evidently financially sensitive, but the Court was not

deterred by the implications of allowing students who were not UK nationals access to such advantages in the name of EU Citizenship.

[31] To assess the scope of application of the Treaty within the meaning of Article 12 EC [now Article 18 TFEU], that article must be read in conjunction with the provisions of the Treaty on citizenship of the Union. Citizenship of the Union is destined to be the fundamental status of nationals of the Member States, enabling those who find themselves in the same situation to receive the same treatment in law irrespective of their nationality, subject to such exceptions as are expressly provided for (Case C-184/99 *Grzelczyk* [2001] ECR I-6193, paragraphs 30 and 31, and Case C-148/02 *Garcia Avello* [2003] ECR I-11613, paragraphs 22 and 23).

[32] According to settled case-law, a citizen of the European Union lawfully resident in the territory of the host Member State can rely on Article 12 EC in all situations which fall within the scope *ratione materiae* of Community law (Case C-85/96 *Martínez Sala* [1998] ECR I-2691, paragraph 63, and *Grzelczyk*, paragraph 32).

[33] Those situations include those involving the exercise of the fundamental freedoms guaranteed by the Treaty and those involving the exercise of the right to move and reside within the territory of the Member States, as conferred by Article 18 EC (see Case C-274/96 *Bickel and Franz* [1998] ECR I-7637, paragraphs 15 and 16, *Grzelczyk*, paragraph 33, and *Garcia Avello*, paragraph 24).

[34] Moreover, there is nothing in the text of the Treaty to suggest that students who are citizens of the Union, when they move to another Member State to study there, lose the rights which the Treaty confers on citizens of the Union (*Grzelczyk*, paragraph 35).

[35] As is apparent from Case C-224/98 *D'Hoop* [2002] ECR I-6191, paragraphs 29 to 34, a national of a Member State who goes to another Member State and pursues secondary education there exercises the freedom to move guaranteed by Article 18 EC.

[36] Furthermore, a national of a Member State who, like the claimant in the main proceedings, lives in another Member State where he pursues and completes his secondary education, without it being objected that he does not have sufficient resources or sickness insurance, enjoys a right of residence on the basis of Article 18 EC and Directive 90/364.

[37] With regard to social assistance benefits, the Court held in Case C-456/02 *Trojani* [2004] ECR I-0000, paragraph 43, that a citizen of the Union who is not economically active may rely on the first paragraph of Article 12 EC where he has been lawfully resident in the host Member State for a certain time or possesses a residence permit.

[38] It is true that the Court held in *Lair* and *Brown* (paragraphs 15 and 18 respectively) that 'at the present stage of development of Community law assistance given to students for maintenance and for training falls in principle outside the scope of the EEC Treaty for the purposes of Article 7 thereof [later Article 6 of the EC Treaty, now, after amendment, Article 12 EC]'. In those judgments the Court considered that such assistance was, on the one hand, a matter of education policy, which was not as such included in the spheres entrusted to the Community institutions, and, on the other, a matter of social policy, which fell within the competence of the Member States in so far as it was not covered by specific provisions of the EEC Treaty.

[39] However, since judgment was given in *Lair* and *Brown*, the Treaty on European Union has introduced citizenship of the Union into the EC Treaty and added to Title VIII (now Title XI) of Part Three a Chapter 3 devoted inter alia to education and vocational training (*Grzelczyk*, paragraph 35).

[40] Thus Article 149(1) EC [see now Art 165 TFEU] gives the Community the task of contributing to the development of quality education by encouraging cooperation between Member States and, if necessary, by supporting and supplementing their action, while fully respecting the responsibility of those States for the content of teaching and the organisation of education systems and their cultural and linguistic diversity.

[41] Under paragraphs 2 and 4 of that article, the Council may adopt incentive measures, excluding any harmonisation of the laws and regulations of the Member States, and recommendations aimed in particular at encouraging the mobility of students and teachers (see *D'Hoop*, paragraph 32).

[42] In view of those developments since the judgments in *Lair* and *Brown*, it must be considered that the situation of a citizen of the Union who is lawfully resident in another Member State falls within the scope of application of the Treaty within the meaning of the first paragraph of Article 12 EC for the purposes of

obtaining assistance for students, whether in the form of a subsidised loan or a grant, intended to cover his maintenance costs.

[43] That development of Community law is confirmed by Article 24 of Directive 2004/38, which states in paragraph 1 that all Union citizens residing in the territory of another Member State on the basis of that directive are to enjoy equal treatment 'within the scope of the Treaty'. In that the Community legislature, in paragraph 2 of that article, defined the content of paragraph 1 in more detail, by providing that a Member State may in the case of persons other than workers, self-employed persons, persons who retain such status and members of their families restrict the grant of maintenance aid in the form of grants or loans in respect of students who have not acquired a right of permanent residence, it took the view that the grant of such aid is a matter which, in accordance with Article 24(1), now falls within the scope of the Treaty.

[44] That interpretation is not invalidated by the argument put forward by the governments which have submitted observations and by the Commission concerning the limitations and conditions referred to in Article 18 EC. Those governments and the Commission observe that, while citizenship of the Union enables nationals of the Member States to rely on the first paragraph of Article 12 EC when they exercise the right to move and reside within the territory of those States, their situation falls within the scope of application of the Treaty within the meaning of Article 12 EC only, in accordance with Article 18(1) EC, subject to the limitations and conditions laid down in the Treaty and by the measures adopted to give it effect, which include those laid down by Directive 93/96. Since Article 3 of that directive excludes the right to payment of maintenance grants on the part of students benefiting from the right of residence, those grants are still outside the scope of the Treaty.

[45] In this respect, it is indeed the case that students who go to another Member State to start or pursue higher education there and enjoy a right of residence there for that purpose under Directive 93/96 cannot base any right to payment of maintenance assistance on that directive.

[46] However, Article 3 of Directive 93/96 does not preclude a national of a Member State who, by virtue of Article 18 EC and Directive 90/364, is lawfully resident in the territory of another Member State where he intends to start or pursue higher education from relying during that residence on the fundamental principle of equal treatment enshrined in the first paragraph of Article 12 EC.

NOTE: The question then was whether the UK's rules requiring the applicant student to be 'settled' in the UK, which clearly had an effect that discriminated against nationals of other Member States, were justified.

[54] Such a difference in treatment can be justified only if it is based on objective considerations independent of the nationality of the persons concerned and is proportionate to the legitimate aim of the national provisions (see *Bickel and Franz*, paragraph 27, *D'Hoop*, paragraph 36, and *Garcia Avello*, paragraph 31).

[55] According to the United Kingdom Government, it is legitimate for a Member State to ensure that the contribution made by parents or students through taxation is or will be sufficient to justify the provision of subsidised loans. It is also legitimate to require a genuine link between the student claiming assistance to cover his maintenance costs and the employment market of the host Member State.

[56] On this point, it must be observed that, although the Member States must, in the organisation and application of their social assistance systems, show a certain degree of financial solidarity with nationals of other Member States (see *Grzelczyk*, paragraph 44), it is permissible for a Member State to ensure that the grant of assistance to cover the maintenance costs of students from other Member States does not become an unreasonable burden which could have consequences for the overall level of assistance which may be granted by that State.

[57] In the case of assistance covering the maintenance costs of students, it is thus legitimate for a Member State to grant such assistance only to students who have demonstrated a certain degree of integration into the society of that State.

[58] In this context, a Member State cannot, however, require the students concerned to establish a link with its employment market. Since the knowledge acquired by a student in the course of his higher education does not in general assign him to a particular geographical employment market, the situation of a student who applies for assistance to cover his maintenance costs is not comparable to that of an applicant for a tideover allowance granted to young persons seeking their first job or for a jobseeker's allowance . . ..

NOTE: The Court concluded that this 'certain degree of integration' into the host State's society (para 57) could be assessed by reference to the student's residence in the host Member State for a certain length of time. A requirement that the student be settled in the host State might similarly serve to demonstrate the necessary degree of integration. But the UK's rules precluded any possibility of a national of another Member State obtaining settled status as a student. So a student from another Member State with a genuine link with UK society still could not qualify for a loan on the same terms as a UK national. This was not compatible with EU law.

The door is, however, open to Member States to protect their budgets through adoption of more sophisticated schemes than the one attacked in *Bidar*.

Jacqueline Förster (Case C-158/07)

[2008] ECR I-8507, Court of Justice of the European Communities

The applicant was a German national studying in the Netherlands. She was refused a maintenance grant because the host State imposed a prior residence requirement of five years on nationals of other Member States. The Court was asked whether this was compatible with Article 12 EC, now Article 18 TFEU.

[36] It is settled case-law that a citizen of the European Union lawfully resident in the territory of the host Member State can rely on Article 12 EC in all situations which fall within the scope *ratione materiae* of Community law (Case C-85/96 *Martínez Sala* [1998] ECR I-2691, paragraph 63, and *Bidar* [Case C-209/03], paragraph 32).

[37] Those situations include those involving the exercise of the fundamental freedoms guaranteed by the Treaty and those involving the exercise of the right to move and reside within the territory of the Member States conferred by Article 18 EC (see Case C-148/02 *Garcia Avello* [2003] ECR I-11613, paragraph 24, and Case C-403/03 *Schempp* [2005] ECR I-6421, paragraph 18).

[38] In this connection, the Court has already held that a national of a Member State who goes to another Member State and pursues secondary education there exercises the freedom to move guaranteed by Article 18 EC (see Case C-224/98 *D'Hoop* [2002] ECR I-6191, paragraphs 29 to 34, and *Bidar*, paragraph 35).

[39] With regard to social assistance benefits, the Court has held that a citizen of the Union who is not economically active may rely on the first paragraph of Article 12 EC where he or she has been lawfully resident in the host Member State for a certain time (*Bidar*, paragraph 37).

[40] A student who travels to another Member State to start or pursue education can benefit from a right of residence on the basis of Article 18 EC and Directive 93/96 when he or she fulfils the conditions set out in Article 1 of that directive as regards having sufficient resources and sickness insurance and being enrolled in a recognised educational establishment for the principal purpose of following a vocational training course.

[41] The situation of a student who is lawfully resident in another Member State thereby falls within the scope of application of the Treaty within the meaning of the first paragraph of Article 12 EC for the purposes of obtaining a maintenance grant (see *Bidar*, paragraph 42).

[42] Admittedly, in accordance with Article 3 of Directive 93/96, that does not establish any entitlement to the payment of maintenance grants by the host Member State on the part of students benefiting from the right of residence.

[43] However, that provision does not preclude a national of a Member State who, by virtue of Article 18 EC and the provisions adopted to implement that article, is lawfully resident in the territory of another Member State where he or she intends to start or pursue education from relying during that residence on the fundamental principle of equal treatment enshrined in the first paragraph of Article 12 EC (see, to that effect, *Bidar*, paragraph 46).

[44] For that purpose, the fact that Ms Förster came to the Netherlands principally in order to study there is irrelevant.

[45] Moreover, pursuant to the Policy rule of 9 May 2005, a student who is a national of a Member State of the European Union may be eligible for a maintenance grant if, prior to the application, he or she has been lawfully resident in the Netherlands for an uninterrupted period of at least five years. Since that requirement concerning the duration of residence is not applicable to students of Netherlands nationality, the issue is raised of what restrictions may be imposed on the right of students who are nationals of other Member States to a maintenance grant without the different treatment of those students in comparison to national students which may result being considered discriminatory and, consequently, prohibited under the first paragraph of Article 12 EC.

[46] That issue was examined by the Court in *Bidar*.

[47] Unlike the present case, the *Bidar* case concerned national legislation which, in addition to imposing a residence requirement, required students from other Member States claiming assistance to cover their maintenance expenses to be established in the host Member State. In so far as the legislation at issue in the main proceedings in that case made it impossible for a national of another Member State to acquire, as a student, the status of established person, that legislation placed such nationals, whatever their actual degree of integration into the society of the host Member State, in a position in which they could not satisfy that condition, and consequently could not enjoy the right to assistance to cover their maintenance costs.

[48] In *Bidar*, the Court observed that, although the Member States must, in the organisation and application of their social assistance systems, show a certain degree of financial solidarity with nationals of other Member States, it is permissible for a Member State to ensure that the grant of assistance to cover the maintenance costs of students from other Member States does not become an unreasonable burden which could have consequences for the overall level of assistance which may be granted by that State (see *Bidar*, paragraph 56).

[49] The Court also pointed out that it is legitimate for a Member State to grant assistance covering maintenance costs only to students who have demonstrated a certain degree of integration into the society of that State (*Bidar*, paragraph 57).

[50] On the basis of those considerations, the Court held that the existence of a certain degree of integration may be regarded as established by a finding that the student in question has resided in the host Member State for a certain length of time (*Bidar*, paragraph 59).

[51] As regards, specifically, the compatibility with Community law of a condition of five years' uninterrupted residence, as required by the national legislation at issue in the main proceedings, it is necessary to examine whether such a requirement can be justified by the objective, for the host Member State, of ensuring that students who are nationals of other Member States have to a certain degree integrated into its society.

[52] In the present case, such a condition of five years' uninterrupted residence is appropriate for the purpose of guaranteeing that the applicant for the maintenance grant at issue is integrated into the society of the host Member State.

[53] That requirement must also be proportionate to the legitimate objective pursued by the national law in order to be justified in the light of Community law. It may not go beyond what is necessary in order to attain that objective.

[54] A condition of five years' continuous residence cannot be held to be excessive having regard, inter alia, to the requirements put forward with respect to the degree of integration of non-nationals in the host Member State.

[55] In that connection, Directive 2004/38, although not applicable to the facts in the main proceedings, provides in Article 24(2) that, in the case of persons other than workers, self-employed persons, persons who retain such status and members of their families, the host Member State is not obliged to grant maintenance assistance for studies, including vocational training, consisting in student grants or student loans, to students who have not acquired the right of permanent residence, while also providing, in Article 16(1), that Union citizens will have a right of permanent residence in the territory of a host Member State where they have resided legally for a continuous period of five years.

[56] The Court has also stated that, in order to be proportionate, a residence requirement must be applied by the national authorities on the basis of clear criteria known in advance (see Case C-138/02 Collins [2004] ECR I-2703, paragraph 72).

[57] By enabling those concerned to know, without any ambiguity, what their rights and obligations are, the residence requirement laid down by the Policy rule of 9 May 2005 is, by its very existence, such as to guarantee a significant level of legal certainty and transparency in the context of the award of maintenance grants to students.

[58] It must therefore be stated that a residence requirement of five years, such as that laid down in the national legislation at issue in the main proceedings, does not go beyond what is necessary to attain the objective of ensuring that students from other Member States are to a certain degree integrated into the society of the host Member State.

NOTE: Remember, as is thematically familiar, a *worker* who then undertakes a course of education would be better treated – Regulation 492/2011 p. 369. So in Case C-46/12 *L.N.* judgment of 21 February 2013 the applicant was entitled to access to a maintenance grant to support his education provided he was engaged in genuine and effective, albeit part-time, employment. The legislative contribution is referred to in passing in para 55 of *Förster.* The relevant provision, Article 24 of Directive 2004/38, was already encountered in this chapter at p. 424 as a demonstration of the EU legislature's concern to place limits on the scope of entitlements of individuals who lie beyond the favoured categories of workers and the self-employed. Anxiety about public finances lies beneath such legislative caution.

Joined Cases C-22/08 & C-23/08 *Vatsouras et al.* [2009] ECR I-4585 discussed the withdrawal of benefits from jobseekers. Article 39(2) EC, now Article 45(2) TFEU, covers benefits intended to facilitate access to the labour market, though a limit may be imposed to ensure the case is genuine, as is clear from *Collins*. The Court in *Vatsouras* then held that the derogation in Article 24(2) of Directive 2004/38 must be interpreted in accordance with Article 39(2) EC/ 45(2) TFEU, so benefits intended to facilitate access to the labour market cannot be 'social assistance' within Article 24(2) of the Directive. In future much will depend on precisely where the line is drawn between those benefits covered by Article 39(2) EC/ 45(2) TFEU and those subject to derogation from the principle of equal treatment by virtue of Article 24(2) of Directive 2004/38.

It is constitutionally conceivable that the Court might decide that the limits envisaged by Article 24(2) of Directive 2004/38 are overridden by reliance on the Treaty provisions themselves. After all, a Directive cannot take away rights granted by the Treaty. And in cases that fall outside the scope of Directive 2004/38 its limitations are anyway not formally relevant. *Vatsouras* and *Förster*, however, suggest that the Court has so far chosen to interpret the scope of the Treaty in a way that aligns it with the restrictive legislative choice made in Article 24(2) of the Directive. Moreover, in Case C-456/12 *O, B* judgment of 12 March 2014 it dealt with a case beyond the scope of the Directive by relying by analogy on its terms. None of this is not *formally* inconsistent with the Court's buoyant insistence in *Metock* (Case C-127/08 p. 425) that Directive 2004/38 aims to strengthen the right of free movement and residence of all Union citizens, but it reveals a more cautious judicial tone in Luxembourg – one that reflects a preference not to interpret the scope of obligations imposed by the Treaty in such a way as to undermine the limits written by the EU legislature into Directive 2004/38.

More generally, outwith the particular circumstances covered by Article 24(2) of the Directive, the future promises plenty more case law in which the Court is invited to elucidate the notion of the 'genuine link' that may be required by a host State as a precondition to access to benefits claimed by an individual such as a jobseeker or student who is not in the charmed circle of the economically active migrant fully favoured by the Treaty. Put another way, how is it determined when a migrant has achieved a sufficient integration into the host society to deserve access to its financial largesse? Conversely, the situation may arise where a migrant *leaves* his or her Member State only to find that he or she is then cut off from benefits payable to those resident in the State he or she has quit. When is this permitted?

Examples of the growing case law include:

- Case C-192/05 *Tas-Hagen* [2006] ECR I-10451: Dutch nationals resident in Spain were refused payments due to civilian war victims. The Court treated the refusal as a consequence of exercise of the right granted by Article 18(1) EC, now Article 21(1) TFEU, to move and reside freely within the EU and therefore a breach of EU law unless objectively justified. Such payments may properly be confined to those who had links with the population of the Netherlands during and after the war, but a blanket Dutch residence requirement could not be objectively justified.
- Case C-499/06 *Halina Nerkowska* [2008] ECR I-3993: a disability pension was payable only if the applicant was resident in Poland. That clearly acted as a restriction on the mobility of a Pole choosing to reside in another Member State, and it could not be justified by the need to carry out checks on the status and health of the recipient because the residence requirement was disproportionately burdensome.
- Case C-103/08 *Arthur Gottwald* [2009] ECR I-9117: Austrian motorway tolls were not payable by disabled persons resident in Austria. Article 12 EC, now Article 18 TFEU, applies in all cases falling within the material scope of EU law (*Martinez Sala* p. 430), so Gottwald, a disabled German on holiday in Austria, could challenge the Austrian measure, and the question was only whether it was objectively justified. The measure is designed to promote the mobility and social integration of disabled persons: the residence requirement reflects the integration of the recipient of free travel into Austrian society. The measure is lawful if proportionate, and the wide margin of appreciation enjoyed by the Member State is emphasized.
- Case C-135/08 *Janko Rottman* [2010] ECR I-1449: Rottman, an Austrian, had acquired German nationality by deception, having failed to disclose material information about his past. Acquisition of German nationality had the effect of removing his Austrian nationality, and Germany now proposed to revoke his German nationality, rendering him stateless. It is for Member States, not the EU, to fix rules on the grant and loss of nationality, but Rottman was faced with loss of the status conferred by Article 17 EC, now Article 20 TFEU, and so EU law was relevant, and requires that withdrawal of nationality observe the principle of proportionality.
- Case C-220/12 *Thiele Meneses* v *Region Hannover* judgment of 24 October 2013: a German national resident in Turkey found that a grant to study in the Netherlands was available only to those permanently resident in Germany. The Court agreed that Germany may impose requirements associated with the integration of the applicant into its society – a 'genuine link' (para 36) – but found a bare requirement of permanent residence an inadequately nuanced basis. Assessment should be open to other elements representative of the level of connection between applicant and Member State, such as family, employment, language skills, or other social and economic factors (para 38).
- Case C-359/13 *Martens v Minsiter van Onderwijs* judgment of 26 February 2015: the Court agreed that integration into Dutch society was a legitimate pre-condition for access to an educational grant to support study in another Member State, but held that requiring three years' residence in the Netherlands out of the last six was an unjustifiably inflexible measure of that integration.

The case law is driven by varying features – different types of migrant, different types of benefit, different types of devices chosen by Member States to check the existence of a 'genuine link' for these purposes. Fact-rich, it resists systematic treatment. However, it is at least possible to argue that the overall shape of the case law on citizenship could be reduced to a model that is familiar, indeed orthodox, in EU trade law: first, is there a restriction on cross-border mobility? If so, is it justified? Something functionally analogous to the 'mandatory requirements' (Chapter 12) can be invoked by a Member State in order to restrict the right of residence found in Article 21(1) TFEU and, more broadly, the right to equal treatment found in Article 18 TFEU. In this vein, you might consider whether *Mary Carpenter* (Case C-60/00 p. 417), *Metock* (Case C-127/08 p. 425), *Dereci* (Case C-256/11 p. 428), and *Sayn-Wittgenstein* (C-208/09 p. 430) disclose functional similarities to the cases in this sub-section which confer rights on Citizens of the Union at the expense of national legislative autonomy. See also J. Borgmann-Prebil, 'The Rule of Reason in European Citizenship' (2008) 14 ELJ 328.

E: Reflecting on the nature of Citizenship of the Union

The precise nature of Citizenship of the Union required elaboration when it was introduced at Maastricht and it still requires elaboration today. For the German Federal Constitutional Court in its *Maastricht* decision, Union citizenship represents 'a lasting legal tie . . . knotted between the nationals of the individual Member States' (p. 591). Nevertheless, even today it remains unclear *precisely* how far in practical terms citizenship of the Union transcends the pre-existing law, which already conferred on migrants a bundle of rights which *de facto* created a form of citizenship. As a label, Union citizenship hints at a step beyond the largely economic focus of the history of EU law applied to persons. But closer inspection of the text is less encouraging to the proponent of a more overtly political connection between the Union and nationals of the Member States. To this extent one cannot be immediately confident that the Citizen of the Union is qualitatively different from the migrant economic actor. Moreover, as already explained, secondary legislation persists in granting more generous rights to Union citizens who are workers or self-employed than to others who are less overtly 'economic' (Dir. 2004/38, p. 367), and the Court's case law is similarly riven by hierarchies of entitlement. Citizens of the Union are not equal.

Plainly European Citizenship does not at all imply a transfer of status from State to European level. Indeed, Article 20(1) TFEU provides that Citizenship of the Union 'shall be additional to and not replace national citizenship'. But the very language of *Citizenship* suggests an attempt to convey something of the shifting sands of allegiance and legitimacy that flow from the deepening role of the European Union, and to add a (supplementary) European level of democratic legitimacy. It has not done very well on this score. But it could. In so far as it involves the construction of a sense of European identity which is, first, in supplement to and not in replacement for national loyalties and, second, built around social values not ethnicity or nationhood, then European Citizenship has some potential for developing an appealingly inclusive notion of political belonging. One may therefore argue for a distinct form of European identity-formation built around shared constitutional values. (Consider in this vein J. Habermas, *The Inclusion of the Other: Studies in Political Theory* (London: Polity Press, 1999); N. MacCormick, 'Democracy, Subsidiarity and Citizenship in the European Commonwealth' (1997) 16 *Law and Philosophy* 331.) This would not be a static notion but would be susceptible to development and, in particular, to widening. This could begin to help to underpin multiple sites of political authority with a degree of social legitimacy and begin to challenge approaches that too readily assume that membership of a single political community is descriptively and normatively orthodox. So one cannot sensibly attempt to get to grips with the nature of citizenship without considering what it is in the EU that people are classified as citizens *of.* Chapter 19 will present a more general discussion of what the Union is and might become.

For the time being, the status of Citizenship of the Union offers more questions than answers, more promise than fulfilment.

H.U. Jessurun D'Oliveira, 'Union Citizenship: Pie in the Sky?' in A. Rosas and E. Antola (eds), *A Citizen's Europe*
(London: Sage Publications, 1995), pp. 82–4

(Footnotes omitted.)

Up till now, as far as citizenship is concerned, the European market is a 'futures' market. Citizenship is, in other words, nearly exclusively a symbolic plaything without substantive content, and in the Maastricht Treaty very little is added to the existing status of nationals of Member States. It is worth noting that, whereas in the Member States the notion of citizenship historically accrued around the *political* rights of the individual, it is around the freedom of movement that the notion of Union citizenship is crystallising.

It is unclear which rights and duties together are connected with Union citizenship because there is no cohesive notion of this new citizenship, and because the political dimension of citizenship here is underdeveloped. The instruments for participation in the public life of the Union are lacking as this public life itself, as distinguished from public life in the Member States, is virtually non-existent: a weak Parliament, next to no direct access to the European Courts, and so on.

Furthermore, the rights and obligations of the European citizen as granted by the Maastricht Treaty do differentiate only very partially between citizens and non-citizens. Several rights, such as the freedom of movement, are granted to large categories of non-nationals, such as nationals of the EFTA countries, or even to 'everyone', or normally to those legally resident in the territory of one of the Member States. Thus, European citizenship is not only severely underdeveloped, but also insufficiently distinctive between those who 'belong' and those who do not. In this situation, and also for policy reasons, it is better to forge a Union citizenship not only for nationais of Member States, but for resident aliens as part of the population of the Member States of the Union as well. This would increase rationality and cohesiveness of such a larger concept, and would reinforce democratic access to participation in the cultural, political and economic life of the Union and Community of the resident population of the Member States.

One must not forget, after all, that the creation, albeit in an as yet very rudimentary form, of a concept of citizenship which is related to a community of states, marks a significant departure from the traditional link between nationality and citizenship in the nation-state. It represents a loosening of the metaphysical ties between persons and a state, and forms a symptom of cosmopolitisation of citizenship. The rising concept of European citizenship is not the concept of national citizenship writ large: its quality has changed in that it does not presuppose any more a large set of common or shared values. It is a clear indication of a phenomenon which is also to be observed in the component parts of the European Community: that the Member States have to a large extent become multicultural and multi-ethnic societies which may be bound together not in the first place by a set of common values, but by a developing competence of persons to deal with differences in their dealing with others who do not necessarily share the same values and with redefined institutions. It is this competence to deal with differences which may be the nucleus of modern active citizenship, and European citizenship may be useful as a laboratory for this procedural concept of proto-cosmopolitan citizenship.

As it stands, Union citizenship is misleading in that it suggests that the Union is a state-like entity.. . .Nobody in his or her right mind would use the word citizen to describe the relationship between people and international organisations like GATT or the Hague Conference for private international law. To indicate the position of people under the Maastricht Treaty as citizenship is nearly as gross a misnomer. The populations of the Member States have not asked for citizenship; it has graciously been bestowed upon them as a cover-up for the still existing democratic deficit. As an alibi it may please Brussels; whether it changes anything in the sceptical attitude and weak position of the populations of the Member States is, in my view, rather improbable.

N. Nic Shuibhne, 'The Resilience of EU Market Citizenship'
(2010) 47 CML Rev 1597, 1599–600

(Footnotes omitted.)

The language of citizenship is essentially one of membership (and, conversely, of non-membership or exclusion). It draws from discourse on democracy, participation and contribution; politics and constitutionalism; rights or entitlements; and reciprocal obligations or duties. There is an unsettled question about whether or not it also has an emotional dimension, moving the language of citizenship into (self-)perception, loyalty, and belonging (not far removed from the concept of nationality) .... The relationship between and proportional importance attached to these elements is typically contested, however; there is no universal definition and citizenship is inevitably contextualized – in other words, there can be *versions* of citizenship, within which different elements are highlighted, configured or emphasized in different ways, to explain different social and historical contexts, or to fit different ideological or philosophical perspectives. Through this manoeuvring, the concept of citizenship acquires not just contexts, but also a series of framing adjectives – market citizenship, political citizenship, cultural citizenship, social citizenship, and so on. The selection and attachment of adjectives can be loaded with meaning, preference and expectation – and can also bring about negative associations.

Our experience and expectations of contemporary citizenship have emerged mainly through centuries of citizenship practice within the paradigm of States. But that polity connection is circumstantial. It has been essential, of course; but it is neither necessarily nor irrevocably written into citizenship's genetic code. Whether it was an attempt to capture or manufacture a relationship between the EU and Member State nationals, the choice of "citizenship" at Maastricht as the centre of gravity for Articles 20–25 TFEU brought with it State-citizenship's primeval narrative of meaning, ideology, and expectation – though, again, it would be more accurate to say meanings, ideologies and expectations. A perennial question in the EU context is whether a legitimate or accepted form of citizenship can be re-imagined in the context of a non-State polity.

J. Shaw, 'Citizenship: Contrasting Dynamics at the Interface of Integration and Constitutionalism' in P. Craig and G. De Búrca (eds), *The Evolution of EU Law*
(Oxford: OUP, 2011), pp. 575–609, 608–9

(Footnotes omitted.)

While citizenship as a thin transnational concept sits comfortably within the 'old' constitutional norms of the constitutionalised legal order based on the Treaties as interpreted by the Court of Justice, it has not been taken forward in a coherent manner in the context of the various processes of constitution-building (Charters, Conventions, Treaties, and ratification processes) of the 2000s. On the contrary, 'citizenship' has rather been invoked to contest rather than to confirm the legitimacy of the EU, through rejectionist referendums in particular. Inevitably – in declaring that Citizenship of the Union is destined to be the fundamental status of the nationals of the Member States – the Court has not paid equal attention to the construction of a defensible and legitimate concept of citizenship at the EU level as it has to hollowing out, sometimes at an alarming rate, national competences which ostensibly exist in relation to citizenship rights (e.g. welfare issues) and – most recently – citizenship status definition (in the *Rottman* case [p. 440]). Thus, in most respects, citizenship has had integrative rather than constitutive effects, despite the symbolic power of the membership concept. But this is a dangerous and unsustainable status quo, not least because it demands, as the Court has itself recognized, a 'certain degree of solidarity between the Member States' [cf para 56 of *Bidar* (Case C-209/03) p. 434, para 48 of *Förster* (Case C-158/07) p. 437]. And while the Treaty of Lisbon does slowly begin to invest more political content into the citizenship provisions, the challenge of simultaneously thinking about what kind of membership is appropriate for a polity emerging *beyond* but not *without* the state has yet to be taken up.

NOTE: Detailed rules elaborate the rights accruing to the Citizen of the Union envisaged by Articles 18–25 TFEU (p. 420), such as Directives 93/109 and 94/80 laying down arrangements whereby nationals residing in a Member State other than their own may vote and stand as a candidate in European Parliament and municipal elections respectively. In its periodic reports, the Commission has claimed that the insertion of the Citizenship provisions into the Treaty has elevated the status of the people to a new constitutional plane in the EU's legal order. (See, for example, COM (93)

702, COM (97) 230, COM (2008) 85.) Even if there is truth in this ambition claim, practical issues of misapplication of the several provisions, in both primary and secondary EU law, that make up the legal underpinning of EU Citizenship dog the visibility of the project. As the Commission's fifth report (COM (2008) 85) put it, 'the multitude of national authorities which are susceptible to limit the effective exercise of such rights (from border guards to immigration authorities to local councils) means that the implementation of EC law is often uneven across the EU' (page 9). In this vein the Commission's EU citizenship report of 27 October 2010 is aptly entitled 'Dismantling the obstacles to EU citizens' rights', COM (2010) 603. The Commission's *EU Citizenship Report 2013* insists that 'Citizens are and must be at the heart of European integration' (p. 3) and puts forward 12 new actions in six key areas 'to further remove obstacles standing in the way of citizens' enjoyment of their EU rights' (p. 5). For up-to-date information on developments see: http://europa.eu/legislation_summaries/justice_freedom_security/citizenship_of_the_union/index_en.htm; and remember how Chapter 9 addressed comparable issues of practical 'market management'.

It is also possible to understand the citizenship rights conferred on migrants as a way to induce adaptation of a model based solely on *national* solidarity, while leaving scope for Member States to show why in particular circumstances fidelity to the national model is nonetheless justified (see e.g., A. Somek, 'Solidarity Decomposed: Being and Time in European Citizenship' (2007) 32 EL Rev 787). This is part of a broader narrative which depicts the EU and its legal order as a transformative medium, capable of promoting collaboration and tolerance, rather than conflict, among European States (see further Chapter 19).

FURTHER READING

Hoogenboom, A., 'Mind the Gap: Mobile Students and their Access to Study Grants and Loans in the EU' 22 MJ 1 (2015) 96.

Kostakopoulou, D., 'Ideas, Norms and European Citizenship: Explaining Institutional Change' (2005) 68 MLR 233.

NicShuibhne, N., 'Limits Rising, Duties Ascending: The Changing Legal Shape of Union Citizenship' (2015) 52 CMLRev 889.

O'Brien, C., 'I Trade, Therefore I Am: Legal Personhood in the European Union' (2013) 50 CML Rev 1643.

O'Leary, S., 'Equal Treatment and EU Citizens: A New Chapter on Cross-border Educational Mobility and Access to Student Financial Assistance' (2009) 34 EL Rev 612.

Skovgaard-Petersen, H., 'There and Back Again: Portability of Student Loans, Grants and Fee Support in a Free Movement Perspective' (2013) 38 EL Rev 783.

Spaventa, E., 'Seeing the Wood despite the Trees? On the Scope of Union Citizenship and its Constitutional Effects' (2008) 45 CML Rev 13.

Wollenschläger, F., 'A New Fundamental Freedom beyond Market Integration: Union Citizenship and its Dynamics for Shifting the Economic Paradigm of European Integration' (2011) 17 ELJ 1.

■ QUESTIONS

1. Wilkinson asserts that 'this mythical European citizen might, to paraphrase Mark Twain, complain that rumours of his or her birth have been greatly exaggerated' ((1995) 1 *European Public Law* 417). Do you agree? To what extent have things changed since 1995?
2. 'Citizenship is part of the political development of the EU. As such, it is likely to evolve in the classic Union fashion: gradually and eliptically, with gaps and inconsistencies, as opportunities, agents and sponsors can be found. In that fascinating struggle, "European" citizenship will move beyond its formally frozen condition, but in a direction and to an extent that it would be foolhardy to predict' (A. Warleigh, 'Purposeful Opportunists? EU Institutions and the Struggle over European Citizenship' in R. Bellamy and A. Warleigh (eds), *Citizenship and Governance in the EU* (London: Continuum, 2001), pp. 34–5). Discuss.

SECTION 3: FREE MOVEMENT OF PERSONS WITHIN AN AREA OF FREEDOM, SECURITY, AND JUSTICE

The removal of internal frontiers within the EU at the end of 1992 was discussed in Chapter 9. The 1992 project suggested that date as a 'Big Bang' in the historical evolution of the Union. For consumers, there was certainly a very specific advantage to be enjoyed at the turn of the year 1992. It became possible to buy goods for private consumption in another Member State and to return home with those goods without the need to pay any duties to the home State. However, frontier controls did not vanish at the end of 1992; '1992' was not legally unambiguous.

In December 1992, the European Council meeting in Edinburgh concluded that:

> The European Council has had to take note of the fact that free movement of persons within the Community, in accordance with Article 8a of the Treaty of Rome [now found in amended form as Article 26 TFEU], cannot be completely assured on 1 January 1993. The work necessary to achieve this result without creating dangers for public security and compromising the fight against illegal immigration, although having progressed, is still under way. Further progress is needed in particular to complete the ratification process of the Dublin Asylum Convention, to conclude the External Frontiers Convention and to complete negotiations on a Convention on the European Information System.

The view of the European Council is constitutionally not the final word within the system. The authoritative source of interpretation of the law is the Court of Justice. In Case C-378/97 *Florius Ariel Wijsenbeek* [1999] ECR I-6207, decided in the light of the law of the post-Maastricht, pre-Amsterdam period, the Court accepted that a Member State was entitled to require a person crossing an internal EU frontier to establish his or her nationality. The expiry of the 1992 deadline had not altered this. The Court referred to the need for, and absence of, common rules governing, in particular, the crossing of the external frontiers of the EU as a precondition to elimination of internal frontiers. Article 14 EC had no automatic effect, and the same is doubtless true of the current Treaty provision defining the internal market, Article 26 TFEU, from which specific references to 1992 were deleted by the Lisbon Treaty. The Treaty provisions on European Citizenship (p. 420) were also considered insufficient to deprive the Member States of the legal right to perform border checks.

The 'flanking measures', the adoption of which the European Council in 1992 regarded as necessary preconditions for securing the free movement of persons in accordance with the Treaty, were not envisaged as creatures of the EC legal order which had been initiated in the 1950s. They were primarily the province of co-operation between the Member States in Justice in Home Affairs, the so-called 'third pillar' of the EU created at Maastricht (p. 9). However, negligible progress having been made by this route, the Treaty of Amsterdam altered the structure by substantially re-working the provisions governing the free movement of persons, in particular by modifying some of the relevant material from the 'third pillar' created at Maastricht (Justice and Home Affairs) and transferring it to the first, EC, pillar. As already suggested at p. 10, this 'communitiarization' suggests that Amsterdam saw a triumph of EC institutional and constitutional method over the species of intergovernmentalism found in the non-EC EU, albeit that the relevant provisions did not follow exactly the orthodoxy of the EC model. There was still something 'special' about the area of freedom, security, and justice.

The basic issue was and remains how to manage co-operation between the Member States in sensitive matters concerning asylum, security, and immigration. Now we live in a world altered by the Treaty of Lisbon, and the old three pillar structure of the EU has been abandoned. But even so the marks of history have not vanished. It is helpful here to have an awareness of the staggered development of the EU's law governing the area of freedom, security, and justice, because even though all the relevant material has now been absorbed into the TFEU it nevertheless still retains some features which separate it from the orthodox pattern of lawmaking on, for example, goods or services or agriculture or transport.

Title IV of the TFEU post-Lisbon is entitled *Area of Freedom, Security and Justice* and it is here that the consolidation of the former third pillar with the first pillar treatment of matters pertaining to persons is housed. Title IV of the TFEU comprises five chapters: general provisions; policies on border checks, asylum and immigration; judicial co-operation in civil matters; judicial co-operation in criminal matters; and police co-operation. As was already the case under the EC Treaty amended at Amsterdam, there are *some* aspects of these TFEU provisions which depart from the orthodoxy of what used to be labelled the 'Community method' – now, post-Lisbon, we note absence of general reliance on the 'ordinary legislative procedure' (p. 20). The right of legislative initiative is not enjoyed exclusively by the Commission. Article 76 TFEU makes clear that acts adopted under Chapters 4 and 5 (plus the special niche case of Article 74 TFEU) shall be adopted either on a Commission proposal or on the initiative of a quarter of the Member States. The withholding of the Commission's cherished exclusive right of initiative reveals a desire among the Member States to retain a degree of involvement in the setting of the legislative agenda. Moreover, suggesting similar motivation, there are pockets of decision-making where unanimity in Council is still required. Article 276 TFEU excludes the Court from exercising jurisdiction to review the validity or proportionality of police or law enforcement activities of Member States, or activities relevant to the maintenance of law and order, when exercising its powers under Chapters 4 and 5 of Title IV. Moreover, the fragmentation of uniformity that has characterized this area of EU policymaking ever since the inception of the three pillar structure at Maastricht (p. 9) endures, but in hideously complicated fashion. There is a five-year transitional period retaining (in effect) the character of the third pillar; and there are some special arrangements ('opt-outs') affecting Denmark, the UK, and Ireland.

One might regret this uneven pattern. Indeed, the notion that the area of freedom, security, and justice within which the Citizen of the European Union moves is not one in which equality prevails may seem deeply incongruous. However, the reality today is that a great deal of EU activity is fragmented in some way or other. Chapter 18 offers reflection on these increasingly prominent patterns of *flexibility*. They are perhaps inevitable in a Union of 28 Member States stretching from the Atlantic to the Black Sea. They also call into question the feasibility and desirability of core assumptions of EU law and policymaking such as equality and uniformity of application.

Generally, however, in inspecting the state of the *area of freedom, security and justice* post-Lisbon it is fair to reflect that the oddities are less significant than the principal narrative – which is that the 'ordinary legislative procedure' has become dominant if not ubiquitous even in the sensitive context of the building of an area of freedom, security, and justice. So methods of law- and policymaking under Title IV TFEU are not the *same* as under the other Titles in the TFEU but they are *similar.* And the Lisbon Treaty has significantly increased the similarities.

What of the *content* of the law governing the area of freedom, security, and justice? It is necessary either to embark on a detailed examination of the law and practice that is shaping the EU's area of freedom, security, and justice or to content oneself with a brisk overview, and for reasons of space this book is constrained to prefer the latter course.

Prior to the entry into force of the Lisbon Treaty a large number of legislative acts had been adopted by the EU, under either Title IV of the EC Treaty or Title VI of the EU Treaty. The method of lawmaking is changed by the Lisbon Treaty but the breadth of subject matter is not significantly altered. Existing measures cover immigration and asylum, the control of external borders and visa policy. So, for example, the basic law of free movement may create derivative rights for third country nationals in the particular case where they are members of a migrant EU national's family and that this may affect Member States' competence to decide whether to admit such third country nationals on to their territory. Here, however, is the possibility for the adoption of a much wider range of EU legislative measures dealing with the treatment of third country nationals in a range of different situations. EU measures touch organized crime, drug smuggling, judicial co-operation between national courts, both in civil and criminal matters, co-operation between national customs and police forces, fundamental rights, Citizenship of the European Union, co-operation with third countries and international organizations, as well as matters associated with free movement within the EU. The legislative material may be found collected at http://ec.europa.eu/justice/index_en.htm.

The Tampere European Council of October 1999 was significant in accelerating the momentum towards adding legislative meat to the area of freedom, security, and justice. The perceived threat of illegal immigration was a factor in promoting recourse to these procedures; so too the distinct issue of asylum. The bloody events of 11 September 2001 hastened the speed at which the legislative programme has been agreed (for good or ill). The Tampere work programme was declared completed in 2004, and the European Council agreed a new five-year programme for EU Action, the so-called 'Hague Programme', to cover the period 2005–10. The Commission placed renewed emphasis on implementation at national level. It issued 'Scoreboards' designed to encourage better compliance by Member States. This strategy had been pioneered in the management of the internal market and has already been encountered in that context in Chapter 9 (p. 255).

The EU's follow-up 'Stockholm Programme' took as its title 'An open and secure Europe serving and protecting citizens'. It covered the period 2010–14 (OJ 2010 C115). Its priority areas: Europe of rights; Europe of justice; Europe that protects; Access to Europe; Europe of solidarity; and Europe in a globalised world. This has now been replaced by strategic guidelines for justice and home affairs for the period 2015–20, which focus *inter alia* on the fight against terrorism, combating serious organized crime, and cybersecurity.

So far, so uncritical. But there is much critical bite in the current debate. The very name of the enterprise, an Area of Freedom, Security and Justice, suggests a tension between priorities, and the very first provision of the Title, Article 67(1) TFEU, accentuates the unease: 'The Union shall constitute an area of freedom, security and justice with respect for fundamental rights and the different legal systems and traditions of the Member States.' But can we have it all? 'Security' suggests a concern for repressive public measures, which is not readily reconcilable with 'freedom', while 'justice', though potentially the underlying value which will bridge the gap, depends in its legislative manifestations on the procedures and institutions which give it concrete shape. Fundamental rights must do more than legitimate the evolving processes on paper – they must be embedded in practice and fidelity to their function must be open to inspection. The issue, then, is priorities and institutional design, including accountability.

The internal market is built on a mix of mutual recognition of national practices and common EU-level standards. Is this a suitable model for the area of freedom, security, and justice too? Mutual recognition of civil and criminal judgments is stipulated as a principle (Articles 81(1), 82(1) TFEU). However, one should be wary of simple analogy. Mutual recognition of, say, the validity of technical standards applicable to manufactured goods leads to freedom of trade between Member States. Mutual recognition of judgments in criminal matters leads to free movement of measures that may *deprive* a person of freedom.

Clearly this debate must remain vigorous as the procedures initiated by the Lisbon Treaty are put into practice and take shape. Exploration and critique of the balance the EU is attempting to hold between the potentially competing notions of freedom, security, and justice, and the values which underpin its evolving legislative acquis, is a vast and vital task. This chapter ends with just one illustration of the complexity and sensitivity of the programme.

N.S. v *Secretary of State* (Case C-411/10)

Court of Justice, Judgment of 21 December 2011

Regulation 343/2003, successor to the Dublin Asylum Convention (p. 447), determines which Member State is responsible for examining an asylum application. In the case the applicant was seeking to resist transfer by the British authorities to Greece, the responsible State under the Regulation, arguing that Greece, faced by large numbers of applicants for asylum, was operating to inadequate standards. The Court was quick to capture the magnitude of the issues:

> [83] At issue here is the raison d'être of the European Union and the creation of an area of freedom, security and justice and, in particular, the Common European Asylum System, based on mutual confidence and a presumption of compliance, by other Member States, with European Union law and, in particular, fundamental rights.

Before the Court the UK Secretary of State contended that the scheme of Regulation 343/2003 was such that Greece should be *conclusively* presumed to comply with its obligations under EU law. The Court disagreed.

> [100] . . . were Regulation No 343/2003 to require a conclusive presumption of compliance with fundamental rights, it could itself be regarded as undermining the safeguards which are intended to ensure compliance with fundamental rights by the European Union and its Member States.
>
> [101] That would be the case, inter alia, with regard to a provision which laid down that certain States are 'safe countries' with regard to compliance with fundamental rights, if that provision had to be interpreted as constituting a conclusive presumption, not admitting of any evidence to the contrary.
>
> [102] In that regard, it should be pointed out that Article 36 of Directive 2005/85, concerning the safe third country concept, provides, in paragraph 2(a) and (c), that a third country can only be considered as a 'safe third country' where not only has it ratified the Geneva Convention and the ECHR but it also observes the provisions thereof.
>
> [103] Such wording indicates that the mere ratification of conventions by a Member State cannot result in the application of a conclusive presumption that that State observes those conventions. The same principle is applicable both to Member States and third countries.
>
> [104] In those circumstances, the presumption underlying the relevant legislation . . . that asylum seekers will be treated in a way which complies with fundamental rights, must be regarded as rebuttable.

The Court's conclusion was therefore that:

> [106] Article 4 of the Charter of Fundamental Rights of the European Union must be interpreted as meaning that the Member States, including the national courts, may not transfer an asylum seeker to the 'Member State responsible' within the meaning of Regulation No 343/2003 where they cannot be unaware that systemic deficiencies in the asylum procedure and in the reception conditions of asylum seekers in that Member State amount to substantial grounds for believing that the asylum seeker would face a real risk of being subjected to inhuman or degrading treatment within the meaning of that provision.

This formula, carefully crafted but abstract, will doubtless provoke many more preliminary references seeking amplification. So, for example, in *Zuheyr Frayeh Halaf* (Case C-528/11 judgment of 30 May 2013) the Court held the Member State in which the asylum seeker is present is not obliged during the process of determining the Member State responsible to request the UNHCR to present its views. However, documents from the UNHCR are among the instruments properly drawn on by the Member State to assess the functioning of the asylum system in the Member State indicated as responsible by Regulation 343/2003 in order to check whether risks of the type set out in *N.S.* are present. In the summer of 2015 the system of allocation of responsibility envisaged by the Regulation broke down under pressure of numbers, and it remains to be seen whether it will be re-instated or replaced.

FURTHER READING

Douglas-Scott, S., 'The Rule of Law in the European Union – Putting the Security into the Area of Freedom, Security and Justice' (2004) 29 EL Rev 219.

Hinarejos, A., 'Integration in Criminal Matters and the Role of the Court of Justice' (2011) 36 EL Rev 420.

Peers, S., 'Mission Accomplished? EU Justice and Home Affairs Law after the Treaty of Lisbon' (2011) 48 CML Rev 661.

Rijken, C., 'Re-Balancing Security and Justice: Protection of Fundamental Rights in Police and Judicial Co-operation in Criminal Matters' (2010) 47 CML Rev 1455.

See also in a broader context, Dauvergne, C., 'Sovereignty, Migration and the Rule of Law in Global Times' (2004) 67 MLR 588.

NOTE: For additional material and resources see the Online Resource Centre at: www.oxfordtextbooks.co.uk/orc/weatherill12e.

16

Competition Law and Policy

SECTION 1: THE SCHEME OF EU COMPETITION LAW AND POLICY

The author holds the conviction that no student of EU law can afford to be unfamiliar with the mainstream of competition law. Equally, however, there is a great deal of complex and fast-moving material in the field that can be safely left aside by the student looking at the big picture. The purpose of this chapter is to chart the general structure of the law without delving deeply into sector-specific issues or obscure economists' wrangles.

The competition law provisions of the Treaty are probably the most important of all from the perspective of the commercial lawyer or business person. Nothing could illustrate this more vividly than the fines, occasionally well in excess of 10 million euros, which have been imposed on firms by the Commission, which is responsible for the administration of these rules, subject to judicial supervision (initially, by the General Court, known as the Court of First Instance before the entry into force of the Lisbon Treaty in December 2009).

There are two principal Treaty provisions: Article 101 TFEU, which deals with bilateral and multilateral practices, and Article 102 TFEU, the principal concern of which is dominant economic power held by a single firm. What is now Article 101 TFEU was Article 81 EC pre-Lisbon, and it was Article 85 before the entry into force of the Amsterdam Treaty in 1999. What is now Article 102 TFEU was Article 82 EC pre- Lisbon, and it was Article 86 before the entry into force of the Amsterdam Treaty. This numerical juggling must be borne in mind when reading the material collected in this chapter.

Articles 101 and 102 need to read in combination. The former deals with agreements between firms, the latter with practices of economically dominant firms. But they share an objective.

***Continental Can* v *Commission* (Case 6/72)**

[1973] ECR 215, Court of Justice of the European Communities

Articles 85 and 86 [now 101 and 102] seek to achieve the same aim on different levels, viz. the maintenance of effective competition within the common [now internal] market . . .

The function of the competition rules was summarized by the Court in the following dictum:

***Metro-SB-Grossmärkte GmbH & Co. KG* v *Commission* (Case 26/76)**

[1977] ECR 1875, Court of Justice of the European Communities

The requirement contained in Articles 3 and 85 of the EEC Treaty that competition shall not be distorted implies the existence on the market of workable competition, that is to say the degree of competition necessary to ensure the observance of the basic requirements and attainment of the objectives of the Treaty, in particular the creation of a single market achieving conditions similar to those of a domestic market.

NOTE: Two ringing phrases may be extracted from that dictum: *workable competition* and a *single market*.

The first, the notion that the Treaty competition rules are concerned to promote *workable competition*, reflects a kind of economic pragmatism. 'Perfect' competition, where producers respond instantly and inevitably to consumer demand and where the efficient allocation of resources is ensured, is in practice an illusion. 'Workable' competition is concerned to achieve the most efficient resource allocation available, given the constraints of a modern economy where consumer choice cannot be perfectly expressed. So EU competition law controls cartels under Article 101, because such arrangements tend to suppress improvements normally stimulated by competition and to reduce consumer choice. Yet some cartels yield benefits, for example, through the ability of firms to specialize; this is reflected in Article 101(3), which allows exemption from prohibition for economically desirable cartels. EU law accepts that monopolies – 'dominant positions' in the terminology of the Treaty – exist and may yield inefficient results. So it uses Article 102 to prohibit abuse of that position of economic strength.

The second idea, that of the *single market*, is a familiar one. Here we see the special role of competition law in an integrated market. The establishing of the competition rules necessary for the functioning of the internal market is a competence held exclusively by the EU according to Article 3 TFEU, and Articles 101 and 102 are concerned with market integration as well as with suppressing anti-competitive conduct. In fact, Articles 101 and 102 have much in common with Articles 30, 34, 45, etc., which aim to eliminate State barriers to trade and to convert a fragmented market into an integrated market. Articles 101 and 102 perform a similar role but they operate in the private sector. It will be seen that firms which agree to carve up the EU's internal market along national lines are targets for severe penalties under EU competition law.

Moreover, the Court of Justice itself is not shy in emphasizing the central role of the Treaty competition rules.

Eco Swiss China Time Ltd v *Benetton International NV* (Case C-126/97)

[1999] ECR I-3055, Court of Justice of the European Communities

[36] ... according to Article 3(g) of the EC Treaty (now, after amendment, Article 3(1)(g) EC), Article 81 EC (ex Article 85) constitutes a fundamental provision which is essential for the accomplishment of the tasks entrusted to the Community and, in particular, for the functioning of the internal market. The importance of such a provision led the framers of the Treaty to provide expressly, in Article 81(2) EC (ex Article 85(2)), that any agreements or decisions prohibited pursuant to that article are to be automatically void.

NOTE: this extract needs to be read with a qualification since the entry into force of the Lisbon Treaty. As explained in Chapter 9 (p. 239), Article 3(1)(g) EC, on which the Court relies in this extract from *Eco Swiss*, provided that the activities of the EC shall include 'a system ensuring that competition in the internal market is not distorted,' but this was deleted by the Lisbon Treaty.

Instead a Protocol on the Internal Market and Competition attached to both the EU Treaty and the TFEU states that the internal market referred to in Article 2 EU 'includes a system ensuring that competition is not distorted'. Although formally Protocols carry the same legal force as the Treaty itself, and although the concern to root out 'distortion' is still found within Article 101 TFEU, it is at least possible that it will be argued that the fundamental status of the Treaty competition rules has been compromised by the Lisbon alteration. What this may mean in practice will be addressed in this chapter (p. 477) and has been considered earlier (pp. 239, 350, 413).

ARTICLE 101 TFEU

1. The following shall be prohibited as incompatible with the internal market: all agreements between undertakings, decisions by associations of undertakings and concerted practices which may affect trade between Member States and which have as their object or effect the prevention, restriction or distortion of competition within the internal market, and in particular those which:

(a) directly or indirectly fix purchase or selling prices or any other trading conditions;
(b) limit or control production, markets, technical development, or investment;

(c) share markets or sources of supply;
(d) apply dissimilar conditions to equivalent transactions with other trading parties, thereby placing them at a competitive disadvantage;
(e) make the conclusion of contracts subject to acceptance by the other parties of supplementary obligations which, by their nature or according to commercial usage, have no connection with the subject of such contracts.

2. Any agreements or decisions prohibited pursuant to this Article shall be automatically void.

3. The provisions of paragraph 1 may, however, be declared inapplicable in the case of:

— any agreement or category of agreements between undertakings;
— any decision or category of decisions by associations of undertakings;
— any concerted practice or category of concerted practices;

which contributes to improving the production or distribution of goods or to promoting technical or economic progress, while allowing consumers a fair share of the resulting benefit, and which does not:

(a) impose on the undertakings concerned restrictions which are not indispensable to the attainment of these objectives;
(b) afford such undertakings the possibility of eliminating competition in respect of a substantial part of the products in question.

NOTE: The text of this provision was untouched by the Lisbon Treaty, save only for the alteration of 'common market' in the first paragraph to 'internal market'. This is not a change of substance. Remember that Article 101 TFEU was Article 81 EC pre-Lisbon (and Article 85 pre-Amsterdam).

ARTICLE 102 TFEU

Any abuse by one or more undertakings of a dominant position within the internal market or in a substantial part of it shall be prohibited as incompatible with the internal market in so far as it may affect trade between Member States.

Such abuse may, in particular, consist in:

(a) directly or indirectly imposing unfair purchase or selling prices or other unfair trading conditions;
(b) limiting production, markets or technical development to the prejudice of consumers;
(c) applying dissimilar conditions to equivalent transactions with other trading parties, thereby placing them at a competitive disadvantage;
(d) making the conclusion of contracts subject to acceptance by the other parties of supplementary obligations which, by their nature or according to commercial usage, have no connection with the subject of such contracts.

NOTE: This text was untouched by the Lisbon Treaty, save only for the alteration of 'common market' to 'internal market' twice in the first sentence. This is not a change of substance. Remember that Article 102 TFEU was Article 82 EC pre-Lisbon (and Article 86 pre-Amsterdam).

Several elements of Articles 101 and 102 run in common.

First, both require an understanding of the notion of an 'undertaking'. A consistently broad approach has been taken. An 'undertaking' within the meaning of EU competition law is any entity that is engaged in an economic activity, regardless of the legal status of that entity and the way in which it is financed (e.g. Case C-41/90 *Höfner and Elser* [1991] ECR I-1979; Joined Cases C-264/01, C-306/01, C-354/01, and C-355/01 *AOK-Bundesverband and Others* [2004] ECR I-2493; Case C-205/ 03P *FENIN* v *Commission* [2006] ECR I-6295). Occasional awkward questions have arisen at the margins, where it has been necessary to consider whether entities performing public services should be regarded as 'undertakings' for these purposes. So, for example, in Case C-364/92 *SAT* v *Eurocontrol* [1994] ECR I-43 Eurocontrol's function was to establish and collect charges levied on users of air navigation services in accordance with an international agreement. The Court found its activities to be 'connected with the exercise of powers relating to the control and supervision of air space which are typically those of a public authority' (para 30). They were not of an economic nature such as to fall within the Treaty's competition rules. A similar result was reached in Case C-138/11 *Compass Datenbank GmbH* v *Republic Oesterreich* judgment of 12 July 2012: a public authority that stored data which undertakings were obliged to report on the basis of statutory obligations was not itself an 'undertaking'. But the mainstream of practice readily brings commercial operators within the scope of the Treaty competition rules as 'undertakings'.

Both Article 101 and Article 102 catch only practices which 'may affect trade between Member States'. This is a jurisdictional requirement which serves in particular to demarcate EU competition law from national competition law. A practice that exerts a solely domestic impact lies beyond the reach of the Treaty. Such isolated practices are however rare – all the more so as the project of market integration in the EU deepens. An illuminating insight into practice may be obtained from the Commission's 'Guidelines on the effect on trade concept contained in Articles 81 and 82 of the Treaty' ([2004] OJ C101/81, also available *via* http://ec.europa.eu/competition/index_en.html). But the Court has for a long time accepted that a deal apparently internal to one Member State is capable of falling within the scope of the Treaty competition rules.

***Cooperative Stremsel- en Kleurselfabriek* v *Commission* (Case 61/80)**

[1981] ECR 851, Court of Justice of the European Communities

A cooperative of producers in the dairy sector required all its members to buy exclusively from each other. All the members were Dutch. They accounted for more than 90 per cent of Dutch cheese output. The Commission held that an effect on inter-State trade had been established. The Court agreed, for the following reasons:

> [14] In order to determine whether the agreement is contrary to Article 85(1) [now 101(1)] it is also necessary to consider whether it is liable to affect trade between Member States, that is to say whether, according to the consistent case-law of the Court, it is possible to foresee with a sufficient degree of probability that it may have an influence, direct or indirect, actual or potential, on the pattern of trade between Member States, thus rendering more difficult the interpenetration of trade which the Treaty is intended to create.
>
> [15] It emerges from information supplied by the Commission that there is already trade in animal rennet and colouring agents between Member States and no mention has been made of technical or economic difficulties standing in the way of the expansion of such trade. On the other hand, bearing in mind the economic context to which they belong, the obligations contained in the rules of the Cooperative are precisely of such a nature as to reinforce the partitioning of markets on a national basis, thereby holding up the economic interpenetration which the Treaty is designed to bring about.

NOTE: Notice how the stress on preventing the isolation of national markets has much in common with the rationale of the *'Cassis de Dijon'* (Case 120/78) line of authority under Article 34 TFEU. It can also be identified in *Keck* (Cases C-267 and 268/91) (p. 329). This is the law of market integration rather than a set of individual Treaty provisions.

Clearly, despite their similarities, there are important features which differentiate Articles 101 and 102. What is meant by the 'agreement' or 'concerted practice' to which Article 101 is directed? What is the 'dominant position' which is fundamental to the scope of Article 102? And what scope is there for justification of practices – Article 101 contains a specific exemption procedure in Article 101(3), whereas Article 102 has no specific window of justification and instead places reliance on the interpretation in particular cases of its prohibition on 'abuse'. These issues are examined in this chapter. However, at a general level both provisions are intimately linked by their aim of controlling practices which are exposed as incompatible with the competitive structures mapped out for the EU's internal market by the Treaty.

But even if Articles 101 and 102 'seek to achieve the same aim' which is 'the maintenance of effective competition' (Case 6/72 *Continental Can*, p. 452) there are gaps in their coverage. And there are intended to be gaps. Article 101's preoccupation is with collaboration between two or more firms. Article 102 addresses the entity possessing a position of economic dominance on the market. The unilateral practices of a single firm which is not dominant are not touched. The limits of the Treaty regime are explicitly recognized in the next decision.

***Viho Europe BV* v *Commission* (Case C-73/95P)**

[1996] ECR I-5457, Court of Justice of the European Communities

The applicant, Viho, had attempted unsuccessfully to persuade the Parker Pen Company to enter into a business relationship with it. It then complained to the Commission that Parker Pen was guilty of anti-competitive practices, involving in particular banning its distributors from exporting products across borders with the result that the EU market was fragmented along national lines. This is quite common: complaining of a breach of EU competition law might sometimes be a useful commercial strategy. However, the Commission declined to proceed with Viho's complaint. It took the view that the arrangements involved Parker Pen and its wholly-owned subsidiaries. This was the conduct of a single firm, and therefore outwith the reach of what is now Article 101, then Article 85. What is now Article 102, then Article 86, would apply if Parker Pen were economically dominant, but there was no suggestion that it enjoyed such power. As far as the Commission was concerned, Parker Pen was *commercially* entitled to refrain from dealing with Viho without fearing *legal* reproach under the Treaty competition rules. The Commission's stance was challenged unsuccessfully before what is now the General Court, then the Court of First Instance (Case T-102/92 *Viho* v *Commission* [1995] ECR II-17). Viho appealed, but again had no success.

The Court of Justice first recorded the core of the CFI's ruling:

> . . . where there is no agreement between economically independent entities, relations within an economic unit cannot amount to an agreement or concerted practice between undertakings which restricts competition within the meaning of Article 85(1) of the Treaty. Where, as in this case, the subsidiary, although having a separate legal personality, does not freely determine its conduct on the market but carries out the instructions given to it directly or indirectly by the parent company by which it is wholly controlled, Article 85(1) does not apply to the relationship between the subsidiary and the parent company with which it forms an economic unit.
>
> While, admittedly, it cannot be excluded that the distribution policy applied by Parker, which consists of prohibiting its subsidiaries from supplying Parker products to customers established in Member States other than that of the subsidiary, may contribute to preserving and partitioning the various national markets and, in so doing, thwart one of the fundamental objectives to be achieved by the common market, it nevertheless follows from the abovementioned case-law that such a policy, followed by an economic unit such as the Parker group within which the subsidiaries do not enjoy any freedom to determine their conduct in the market, does not fall within the scope of Article 85(1) of the Treaty.

The Court then approved this approach, which rejects the suggestion that a broad concern for market integration should override the textual limitations of the Treaty.

> [16] Parker and its subsidiaries. . .form a single economic unit within which the subsidiaries do not enjoy real autonomy in determining their course of action in the market, but carry out the instructions issued to them by the parent company controlling them (Case 48/69 *ICI* v *Commission* [1972] ECR 619, paragraphs 133 and

134; Case 15/74 *Centrafarm* v *Sterling Drug* [1974] ECR 1147, paragraph 41; Case 16/74 *Centrafarm* v *Winthrop* [1974] ECR 1183, paragraph 32; Case 30/87 *Bodson* v *Pompes Funèbres* [1988] ECR 2479, paragraph 19; and Case 66/86 *Ahmed Saeed Flugreisen and Others* v *Zentrale zur Bekaempfung Unlauteren Wettbewerbs* [1989] ECR 803, paragraph 35).

[17] In those circumstances, the fact that Parker' s policy of referral, which consists essentially in dividing various national markets between its subsidiaries, might produce effects outside the ambit of the Parker group which are capable of affecting the competitive position of third parties cannot make Article 85(1) applicable, even when it is read in conjunction with Article 2 and Article 3(c) and (g) of the Treaty. On the other hand, such unilateral conduct could fall under Article 86 of the Treaty if the conditions for its application, as laid down in that article, were fulfilled.

This means that the unilateral practices of a firm that is not in a position of economic dominance are immune from control under the Treaty competition rules. That in turn means, first, that it will be crucially important to determine the margin between unilateral action and bilateral or multilateral co-ordination – for that margin defines the scope of Article 101. Second, it means that identifying economic dominance is crucially important – for that is the threshold for subjection to the obligations not to act abusively contained in Article 102. Only once it is established that a particular commercial practice is capable of falling within the scope of either Article 101 or Article 102 is it necessary to proceed to consider whether it is compatible with the requirements of those Treaty provisions. This chapter is structured to examine first Article 101 and then Article 102 in order to discover the type of practice which falls within their net and then to discover the circumstances in which practices will stand condemned by them. Thereafter, to conclude the chapter, the matter of enforcement of the competition rules is addressed.

SECTION 2: ARTICLE 101 TFEU

A: The objective of Article 101

No case better illustrates the nature and purpose of Article 101 than the following:

Établissements Consten SA and Grundig GmbH v _Commission_ (Cases 56 and 58/64)

[1966] ECR 299, Court of Justice of the European Communities

Consten, a French firm, agreed to handle only German-made Grundig electrical products in France. Grundig agreed to supply only Consten in France and to ensure that its customers outside France were restrained from delivering the goods into France. This was an 'exclusive distribution' deal which conferred 'absolute territorial protection' in France on Consten. The Commission found the agreement unlawful and the parties applied to the Court for annulment of that decision. The Court's ruling deserves close attention. Remember that Article 85 is now, post-Lisbon, Article 101.

The applicants submit that the prohibition in Article 85(1) applies only to so-called horizontal agreements. The Italian Government submits furthermore that sole distributorship contracts do not constitute 'agreements between undertakings' within the meaning of that provision, since the parties are not on a footing of equality. With regard to these contracts, freedom of competition may only be protected by virtue of Article 86 of the Treaty.

Neither the wording of Article 85 nor that of Article 86 gives any ground for holding that distinct areas of application are to be assigned to each of the two Articles according to the level in the economy at which the contracting parties operate. Article 85 refers in a general way to all agreements which distort competition within the Common Market and does not lay down any distinction between those agreements based on whether they are made between competitors operating at the same level in the economic process or between non-competing persons operating at different levels. In principle, no distinction can be made where the Treaty does not make any distinction.

Furthermore, the possible application of Article 85 to a sole distributorship contract cannot be excluded merely because the grantor and the concessionnaire are not competitors *inter se* and not on a footing of equality. Competition may be distorted within the meaning of Article 85(1) not only by agreements which limit it as between the parties, but also by agreements which prevent or restrict the competition which might take place between one of them and third parties. For this purpose, it is irrelevant whether the parties to the agreement are or are not on a footing of equality as regards their position and function in the economy. This applies all the more, since, by such an agreement, the parties might seek, by preventing or limiting the competition of third parties in respect of the products, to create or guarantee for their benefit an unjustified advantage at the expense of the consumer or user, contrary to the general aims of Article 85.

It is thus possible that, without involving an abuse of a dominant position, an agreement between economic operators at different levels may affect trade between Member States and at the same time have as its object or effect the prevention, restriction or distortion of competition, thus falling under the prohibition of Article 85(1).

In addition, it is pointless to compare on the one hand the situation, to which Article 85 applies, of a producer bound by a sole distributorship agreement to the distributor of his products with on the other hand that of a producer who includes within his undertaking the distribution of his own products by some means, for example, by commercial representatives, to which Article 85 does not apply. These situations are distinct in law and, moreover, need to be assessed differently, since two marketing organizations, one of which is integrated into the manufacturer's undertaking whilst the other is not, may not necessarily have the same efficiency. The wording of Article 85 causes the prohibition to apply, provided that the other conditions are met, to an agreement between several undertakings. Thus it does not apply where a sole undertaking integrates its own distribution network into its business organization. It does not thereby follow, however, that the contractual situation based on an agreement between a manufacturing and a distributing undertaking is rendered legally acceptable by a simple process of economic analogy – which is in any case incomplete and in contradiction with the said Article. Furthermore, although in the first case the Treaty intended in Article 85 to leave untouched the internal organization of an undertaking and to render it liable to be called in question, by means of Article 86, only in cases where it reaches such a degree of seriousness as to amount to an abuse of a dominant position, the same reservation could not apply when the impediments to competition result from agreement between two different undertakings which then as a general rule simply require to be prohibited.

Finally, an agreement between producer and distributor which might tend to restore the national divisions in trade between Member States might be such as to frustrate the most fundamental object of the Community. The Treaty, whose preamble and content aim at abolishing the barriers between States, and which in several provisions gives evidence of a stern attitude with regard to their reappearance, could not allow undertakings to reconstruct such barriers. Article 85(1) is designed to pursue this aim, even in the case of agreements between undertakings placed at different levels in the economic process.

The submissions set out above are consequently unfounded . . .

The complaints relating to the concept of 'agreements . . . which may affect trade between member states'

The applicants and the German Government maintain that the Commission has relied on a mistaken interpretation of the concept of an agreement which may affect trade between Member States and has not shown that such trade would have been greater without the agreement in dispute.

The defendant replies that this requirement in Article 85(1) is fulfilled once trade between Member States develops, as a result of the agreement, differently from the way in which it would have done without the restriction resulting from the agreement, and once the influence of the agreement on market conditions reaches a certain degree. Such is the case here, according to the defendant, particularly in view of the impediments resulting within the Common Market from the disputed agreement as regards the exporting and importing of Grundig products to and from France.

The concept of an agreement 'which may affect trade between Member States' is intended to define, in the law governing cartels, the boundary between the areas respectively covered by Community law and national law. It is only to the extent to which the agreement may affect trade between Member States that the deterioration in competition caused by the agreement falls under the prohibition of Community law contained in Article 85; otherwise it escapes the prohibition.

In this connexion, what is particularly important is whether the agreement is capable of constituting a threat, either direct or indirect, actual or potential, to freedom of trade between Member States in a manner which might harm the attainment of the objectives of a single market between States. Thus the fact that an agreement encourages an increase, even a large one, in the volume of trade between States is not sufficient to exclude the possibility that the agreement may 'affect' such trade in the abovementioned manner. In the present case, the contract between Grundig and Consten, on the one hand by preventing undertakings other than Consten from importing Grundig products into France, and on the other hand by prohibiting Consten from re-exporting those products to other countries of the Common Market, indisputably affects trade between Member States. These limitations on the freedom of trade, as well as those which might ensue for third parties from the registration in France by Consten of the GINT trade mark, which Grundig places on all its products, are enough to satisfy the requirement in question.

Consequently, the complaints raised in this respect must be dismissed.

The complaints concerning the criterion of restriction on competition

The applicants and the German Government maintain that since the Commission restricted its examination solely to Grundig products the decision was based upon a false concept of competition and of the rules on prohibition contained in Article 85(1), since this concept applies particularly to competition between similar products of different makes; the Commission, before declaring Article 85(1) to be applicable, should, by basing itself upon the 'rule of reason', have considered the economic effects of the disputed contract upon competition between the different makes. There is a presumption that vertical sole distributorship agreements are not harmful to competition and in the present case there is nothing to invalidate that presumption. On the contrary, the contract in question has increased the competition between similar products of different makes.

The principle of freedom of competition concerns the various stages and manifestations of competition. Although competition between producers is generally more noticeable than that between distributors of products of the same make, it does not thereby follow that an agreement tending to restrict the latter kind of competition should escape the prohibition of Article 85(1) merely because it might increase the former.

Besides, for the purpose of applying Article 85(1), there is no need to take account of the concrete effects of an agreement once it appears that it has as its object the prevention, restriction or distortion of competition.

Therefore the absence in the contested decision of any analysis of the effects of the agreement on competition between similar products of different makes does not, of itself, constitute a defect in the decision.

It thus remains to consider whether the contested decision was right in founding the prohibition of the disputed agreement under Article 85(1) on the restriction on competition created by the agreement in the sphere of the distribution of Grundig products alone. The infringement which was found to exist by the contested decision results from the absolute territorial protection created by the said contract in favour of Consten on the basis of French law. The applicants thus wished to eliminate any possibility of competition at the wholesale level in Grundig products in the territory specified in the contract essentially by two methods.

First, Grundig undertook not to deliver even indirectly to third parties products intended for the area covered by the contract. The restrictive nature of that undertaking is obvious if it is considered in the light of the prohibition on exporting which was imposed not only on Consten but also on all the other sole concessionnaires of Grundig, as well as the German wholesalers. Secondly, the registration in France by Consten of the GINT trade mark, which Grundig affixes to all its products, is intended to increase the protection inherent in the disputed agreement, against the risk of parallel imports into France of Grundig products, by adding the protection deriving from the law on industrial property rights. Thus no third party could import Grundig products from other Member States of the Community for resale in France without running serious risks.

The defendant properly took into account the whole distribution system thus set up by Grundig. In order to arrive at a true representation of the contractual position the contract must be placed in the economic and legal context in the light of which it was concluded by the parties. Such a procedure is not to be regarded as an unwarrantable interference in legal transactions or circumstances which were not the subject of the proceedings before the Commission.

The situation as ascertained above results in the isolation of the French market and makes it possible to charge for the products in question prices which are sheltered from all effective competition. In addition, the more producers succeed in their efforts to render their own makes of product individually distinct in the eyes of the consumer, the more the effectiveness of competition between producers tends to diminish. Because of the considerable impact of distribution costs on the aggregate cost price, it seems important that competition between dealers should also be stimulated. The efforts of the dealer are stimulated by competition between distributors of products of the same make. Since the agreement thus aims at isolating the French market for Grundig products and maintaining artificially, for products of a very well-known brand, separate national markets within the Community, it is therefore such as to distort competition in the Common Market.

It was therefore proper for the contested decision to hold that the agreement constitutes an infringement of Article 85(1). No further considerations, whether of economic data (price differences between France and Germany, representative character of the type of appliance considered, level of overheads borne by Consten) or of the corrections of the criteria upon which the Commission relied in its comparisons between the situations of the French and German markets, and no possible favourable effects of the agreement in other respects, can in any way lead, in the face of above mentioned restrictions, to a different solution under Article 85(1).

NOTE: Was this an *anti-competitive* deal? In one sense it was, because Grundig goods were available in France from just one source, Consten. But did it really matter? After all, if Consten had sold Grundig goods at unreasonably high prices, consumers would simply have bought the electrical products of other manufacturers. Competition between different brands of the goods would restrain Consten.

So, adopting this perspective, the US Supreme Court declared in *Continental TV* v *Sylvania* 433 US 36 (1977) that:

Interbrand competition . . . is the primary concern of antitrust law . . . When interbrand competition exists . . . it provides a significant check on the exploitation of intrabrand market power because of the ability of consumers to substitute a different brand of the same product.

■ QUESTION

Explain how and why this perception went largely ignored in *Consten* (Cases 56 and 58/64). Notice the Court's concern to preserve 'parallel trade'; cross-border intrabrand competition must be secured, whatever the interbrand competitive situation may be.

NOTE: So EU competition law has special objectives. It aims to further *market integration*. It is different from US law, and, for that matter, from UK or German law. *Consten* (Cases 56 and 58/64), then, has caused us to ask some important questions about the *purpose* of competition law. It seems that EU law may have suspicions about 'vertical' deals which improve product distribution which would not be entertained by other competition law systems which are not designed to help market integration.

But *should* it? Is interventionism of this type, even in markets shown to be characterized by interbrand competition, truly justified or is market integration but a shibboleth? Even if such an approach *was* so justified in 1966, can it remain so in the climate of today's internal market? Or – to approach the matter from a quite different perspective – does the enlargement of the EU into Central and Eastern Europe provide a reason for maintaining or even strengthening the emphasis on promoting market integration in the interpretation of Article 101 as a means to lock the new economies into the existing bloc? These questions about the shape of EU competition policy were among those that prompted a review of the application of Article 101 to vertical restraints (those between traders at different points in the supply chain), including distribution agreements of the *Consten and Grundig* type. This review led to reform, and today Regulation 330/2010 governs vertical restraints. It is mentioned at p. 479, after the structure of Article 101 has been placed in its full context. More generally the inquiry into the proper shape of a 'modernized' EU competition law and policy will recur in this chapter – and it will conclude it too (p. 518).

B: The 'agreement' and the 'concerted practice'

The 'agreement' which may be caught by Article 101 goes beyond the formal contract. Article 101 is aimed at the parties' intent, not the form in which that may be expressed. It covers informal agreements, claimed to be non-binding, secret cartels, and even imposed agreements. The next case involves the uncovering of the multi-faceted 'Quinine Cartel'.

ACF Chemiefarma v *Commission* (Cases 41, 44, and 45/69)

[1970] ECR 661, Court of Justice of the European Communities

[106] The applicant complains that the Commission considered that the export agreement relating to trade with third countries and the gentlemen's agreement governing the conduct of its members in the Common Market constituted an indivisible entity as far as Article 85 [now Article 101 TFEU] was concerned.

[107] The applicant states that the gentlemen's agreement, unlike the export agreement, did not constitute an agreement within the meaning of Article 85(1) and in any event it definitively ceased to exist from the end of October 1962.

[108] The conduct of the parties to the export agreement does not in the applicant's view indicate that they continued the restrictions on competition which were originally provided for in the gentlemen's agreement.

[109] The opposite conclusions reached by the contested decision are therefore alleged to be vitiated because they are based on incorrect findings.

[110] The gentlemen's agreement, which the applicant admits existed until the end of October 1962, had as its object the restriction of competition within the Common Market.

[111] The parties to the export agreement mutually declared themselves willing to abide by the gentlemen's agreement and concede that they did so until the end of October 1962.

[112] This document thus amounted to the faithful expression of the joint intention of the parties to the agreement with regard to their conduct in the Common Market.

[113] Furthermore it contained a provision to the effect that infringement of the gentlemen's agreement would ipso facto constitute an infringement of the export agreement.

[114] In those circumstances account must be taken of this connexion in assessing the effects of the gentlemen's agreement with regard to the categories of acts prohibited by Article 85(1).

[115] The defendant bases its view that the gentlemen's agreement was continued until February 1965 on documents and declarations emanating from the parties to the agreement the tenor of which is indistinct and indeed contradictory so that it is impossible to conclude whether those undertakings intended to terminate the gentlemen's agreement at their meeting on 29 October 1962.

[116] The conduct of the undertakings in the Common Market after 29 October 1962 must therefore be considered in relation to the following four points: sharing out of domestic markets, fixing of common prices, determination of sales quotas and prohibition against manufacturing synthetic quinidine.

[117] The gentlemen's agreement guaranteed protection of each domestic market for the producers in the various Member States.

[118] After October 1962 when significant supplies were delivered on one of those markets by producers who were not nationals, as for example in the case of sales of quinine and quinidine in France, there was a substantial alignment of prices conforming to French domestic prices which were higher than the export prices to third countries.

[119] It does not appear that there were alterations in the insignificant volume of trade between the other Member States referred to by the clause relating to domestic protection in spite of considerable differences in the prices prevailing in each of those States.

[120] The divergences between the domestic legislation of those States cannot by itself explain those differences in price or the substantial absence of trade.

[121] Obstacles which might arise in the trade in quinine and quinidine from differences between national legislation governing pharmaceutical products under trade-mark cannot relevantly be invoked to explain those facts.

[122] The correspondence exchanged in October and November 1963 between the parties to the export agreement with regard to the protection of domestic markets merely confirmed the intention of those undertakings to allow this state of affairs to remain unchanged.

[123] This intention was subsequently confirmed by Nedchem during the meeting of the undertakings concerned in Brussels on 14 March 1964.

[124] From those circumstances it is clear that with regard to the restriction on competition arising from the protection of the producers' domestic markets the producers continued after the meeting on 29 October 1962 to abide by the gentlemen's agreement of 1960 and confirmed their common intention to do so.

NOTE: For an indication that covert cartels involving market-sharing and price-fixing are far from things of the past see Decision 2003/2 *Vitamins* [2003] OJ L6/1 (which, as is typical given the size of fines in such cases, provoked further litigation: e.g., Case T-15/02 *BASF* v *Commission* [2006] ECR II-497).

Even arrangements which are less formal than an agreement are caught by Article 101 if they constitute a 'concerted practice'. In fact, because both the agreement and the concerted practice fall within Article 101, there may be little point distinguishing between them. However, it remains crucial to differentiate collusion, whether agreement or concerted practice, from mere parallel behaviour, for the latter remains perfectly lawful. The next case illustrates the notion of the concerted practice and raises complex questions about the reach of Article 101. It is concerned with the dyestuffs industry and is commonly referred to as the 'Dyestuffs' case. Remember: Article 85, referred to in this extract, is now Article 101 TFEU.

***ICI* v *Commission* (Case 48/69)**

[1972] ECR 619, Court of Justice of the European Communities

The Court first examined the concept of a concerted practice.

[64] Article 85 draws a distinction between the concept of 'concerted practices' and that of 'agreements between undertakings' or of 'decisions by associations of undertakings'; the object is to bring within the prohibition of that article a form of coordination between undertakings which, without having reached the stage where an agreement properly so-called has been concluded, knowingly substitutes practical cooperation between them for the risks of competition.

[65] By its very nature, then, a concerted practice does not have all the elements of a contract but may *inter alia* arise out of coordination which becomes apparent from the behaviour of the participants.

[66] Although parallel behaviour may not by itself be identified with a concerted practice, it may however amount to strong evidence of such a practice if it leads to conditions of competition which do not correspond to the normal conditions of the market, having regard to the nature of the products, the size and number of the undertakings, and the volume of the said market.

[67] This is especially the case if the parallel conduct is such as to enable those concerned to attempt to stabilize prices at a level different from that to which competition would have led, and to consolidate established positions to the detriment of effective freedom of movement of the products in the Common Market and of the freedom of consumers to choose their suppliers.

[68] Therefore the question whether there was a concerted action in this case can only be correctly determined if the evidence upon which the contested decision is based is considered, not in isolation, but as a whole, account being taken of the specific features of the market in the products in question.

The Court then proceeded to explore the nature of the dyestuffs market.

[69] The market in dyestuffs is characterised by the fact that 80% of the market is supplied by about ten producers, very large ones in the main, which often manufacture these products together with other chemical products or pharmaceutical specialities.

[70] The production patterns and therefore the cost structures of these manufacturers are very different, and this makes it difficult to ascertain competing manufacturers' costs.

[71] The total number of dyestuffs is very high, each undertaking producing more than a thousand.

[72] The average extent to which these products can be replaced by others is considered relatively good for standard dyes, but it can be very low or even non-existent for speciality dyes.

[73] As regards speciality products, the market tends in certain cases towards an oligopolistic situation.

[74] Since the price of dyestuffs forms a relatively small part of the price of the final product of the user undertaking, there is little elasticity of demand for dyestuffs on the market as a whole and this encourages price increases in the short term.

[75] Another factor is that the total demand for dyestuffs is constantly increasing, and this tends to induce producers to adopt a policy enabling them to take advantage of this increase.

[76] In the territory of the Community, the market in dyestuffs in fact consists of five separate national markets with different price levels which cannot be explained by differences in costs and charges affecting producers in those countries.

[77] Thus the establishment of the Common Market would not appear to have had any effect on this situation, since the differences between national price levels have scarcely decreased.

[78] On the contrary, it is clear that each of the national markets has the characteristics of an oligopoly and that in most of them price levels are established under the influence of a 'priceleader', who in some cases is the largest producer in the country concerned, and in other cases is a producer in another Member State or a third State, acting through a subsidiary.

[79] According to the experts this dividing-up of the market is due to the need to supply local technical assistance to users and to ensure immediate delivery, generally in small quantities, since, apart from exceptional cases, producers supply their subsidiaries established in the different Member States and maintain a network of agents and depots to ensure that user undertakings receive specific assistance and supplies.

[80] It appears from the data produced during the course of the proceedings that even in cases where a producer establishes direct contact with an important user in another Member State, prices are usually fixed in relation to the place where the user is established and tend to follow the level of prices on the national market.

[81] Although the foremost reason why producers have acted in this way is in order to adapt themselves to the special features of the market in dyestuffs and to the needs of their customers, the fact remains that the dividing-up of the market which results tends, by fragmenting the effects of competition, to isolate users in their national market, and to prevent a general confrontation between producers throughout the Common Market.

[82] It is in this context, which is peculiar to the way in which the dyestuffs market works, that the facts of the case should be considered.

The increases of 1964, 1965 and 1967

[83] The increases of 1964, 1965 and 1967 covered by the contested decision are interconnected.

[84] The increase of 15% in the prices of most aniline dyes in Germany on 1 January 1965 was in reality nothing more than the extension to another national market of the increase applied in January 1964 in Italy, the Netherlands, Belgium and Luxembourg.

[85] The increase in the prices of certain dyes and pigments introduced on 1 January 1965 in all the Member States, except France, applied to all the products which had been excluded from the first increase.

[86] The reason why the price increase of 8% introduced in the autumn of 1967 was raised to 12% for France was that there was a wish to make up for the increases of 1964 and 1965 in which that market had not taken part because of the price control system.

[87] Therefore the three increases cannot be isolated from one another, even though they did not take place under identical conditions.

[88] In 1964 all the undertakings in question announced their increases and immediately put them into effect, the initiative coming from Ciba-Italy which, on 7 January 1964, following instructions from Ciba-Switzerland,

announced and immediately introduced an increase of 15%. This initiative was followed by the other producers on the Italian market within two or three days.

[89] On 9 January ICI Holland took the initiative in introducing the same increase in the Netherlands, whilst on the same day Bayer took the same initiative on the Belgo-Luxembourg market.

[90] With minor differences, particularly between the price increases by the German undertakings on the one hand and the Swiss and United Kingdom undertakings on the other, these increases concerned the same range of products for the various producers and markets, namely, most aniline dyes other than pigments, food colourings and cosmetics.

[91] As regards the increase of 1965 certain undertakings announced in advance price increases amounting, for the German market, to an increase of 15% for products whose prices had already been similarly increased on the other markets, and to 10% for products whose prices had not yet been increased. These announcements were spread over the period between 14 October and 28 December 1964.

[92] The first announcement was made by BASF, on 14 October 1964, followed by an announcement by Bayer on 30 October and by Casella on 5 November.

[93] These increases were simultaneously applied on 1 January 1965 on all the markets except for the French market because of the price freeze in that State, and the Italian market where, as a result of the refusal by the principal Italian producer, ACNA, to increase its prices on the said market, the other producers also decided not to increase theirs.

[94] ACNA also refrained from putting its prices up by 10% on the German market.

[95] Otherwise the increase was general, was simultaneously introduced by all the producers mentioned in the contested decision, and was applied without any differences concerning the range of products.

[96] As regards the increase of 1967, during a meeting held at Basel on 19 August 1967, which was attended by all the producers mentioned in the contested decision except ACNA, the Geigy undertaking announced its intention to increase its selling prices by 8% with effect from 16 October 1967.

[97] On that same occasion the representatives of Bayer and Francolor stated that their undertakings were also considering an increase.

[98] From mid-September all the undertakings mentioned in the contested decision announced a price increase of 8%, raised to 12% for France, to take effect on 16 October in all the countries except Italy, where ACNA again refused to increase its prices, although it was willing to follow the movement in prices on two other markets, albeit on dates other than 16 October.

[99] Viewed as a whole, the three consecutive increases reveal progressive cooperation between the undertakings concerned.

[100] In fact, after the experience of 1964, when the announcement of the increases and their application coincided, although with minor differences as regards the range of products affected, the increases of 1965 and 1967 indicate a different mode of operation. Here, the undertakings taking the initiative, BASF and Geigy respectively, announced their intentions of making an increase some time in advance, which allowed the undertakings to observe each other's reactions on the different markets, and to adapt themselves accordingly.

[101] By means of these advance announcements the various undertakings eliminated all uncertainty between them as to their future conduct and, in doing so, also eliminated a large part of the risk usually inherent in any independent change of conduct on one or several markets.

[102] This was all the more the case since these announcements, which led to the fixing of general and equal increases in prices for the markets in dyestuffs, rendered the market transparent as regard the percentage rates of increase.

[103] Therefore, by the way in which they acted, the undertakings in question temporarily eliminated with respect to prices some of the preconditions for competition on the market which stood in the way of the achievement of parallel uniformity of conduct.

[104] The fact that this conduct was not spontaneous is corroborated by an examination of other aspects of the market.

[105] In fact, from the number of producers concerned it is not possible to say that the European market in dyestuffs is, in the strict sense, an oligopoly in which price competition could no longer play a substantial role.

[106] These producers are sufficiently powerful and numerous to create a considerable risk that in times of rising prices some of them might not follow the general movement but might instead try to increase their share of the market by behaving in an individual way.

[107] Furthermore, the dividing-up of the Common Market into five national markets with different price levels and structures makes it improbable that a spontaneous and equal price increase would occur on all the national markets.

[108] Although a general, spontaneous increase on each of the national markets is just conceivable, these increases might be expected to differ according to the particular characteristics of the different national markets.

[109] Therefore, although parallel conduct in respect of prices may well have been an attractive and risk-free objective for the undertakings concerned, it is hardly conceivable that the same action could be taken spontaneously at the same time, on the same national markets and for the same range of products.

[110] Nor is it any more plausible that the increases of January 1964, introduced on the Italian market and copied on the Netherlands and Belgo-Luxembourg markets, which have little in common with each other either as regards the level of prices or the pattern of competition, could have been brought into effect within a period of two to three days without prior concertation.

[111] As regards the increases of 1965 and 1967 concertation took place openly, since all the announcements of the intention to increase prices with effect from a certain date and for a certain range of products made it possible for producers to decide on their conduct regarding the special cases of France and Italy.

[112] In proceeding in this way, the undertakings mutually eliminated in advance any uncertainties concerning their reciprocal behaviour on the different markets and thereby also eliminated a large part of the risk inherent in any independent change of conduct on those markets.

[113] The general and uniform increase on those different markets can only be explained by a common intention on the part of those undertakings, first, to adjust the level of prices and the situation resulting from competition in the form of discounts, and secondly, to avoid the risk, which is inherent in any price increase, of changing the conditions of competition.

NOTE: The key point about the 'Dyestuffs' case is that the Court decided that there was no oligopoly. There must, the Court deduced, have been a concerted practice which explained the absence of effective competition. Proof of concertation is problematic. You should carefully examine the 'Dyestuffs' judgment and the *Commission's decision* ([1969] CMLR D23) in order to determine which pieces of evidence you may take into account in locating a concerted practice.

The development of the law has been distorted because procedural irregularities have led to the annulment of some Commission Decisions which have found the existence of concerted practices. The Commission's Decision concerning the 'Woodpulp Cartel' was largely annulled. However, the Court provided important comment on proof of concertation. It said that parallel conduct is not proof of concertation unless concertation represents the only plausible explanation for such conduct. It then applied this principle to the producers' quarterly price announcements which the Commission had used as evidence of concertation:

Ahlström O Sakyhtio v *Commission* (Cases C-89, 104, 114, 116–17, 125–29/85)

[1993] ECR I-1307, Court of Justice of the European Communities

[126] . . . [I]t must be stated that, in this case, concertation is not the only plausible explanation for the parallel conduct. To begin with, the system of price announcements may be regarded as constituting a rational response to the fact that the pulp market constituted a long-term market and to the need felt by both buyers and sellers to limit commercial risks. Further, the similarity in the dates of price announcements may be regarded as a direct result of the high degree of market transparency, which does not have to be described as

artificial. Finally, the parallelism of prices and the price trends may be satisfactorily explained by the oligopolistic tendencies of the market and by the specific circumstances prevailing in certain periods. Accordingly, the parallel conduct established by the Commission does not constitute evidence of concertation.

[127] In the absence of a firm, precise and consistent body of evidence, it must be held that concertation regarding announced prices has not been established by the Commission. Article 1(1) of the contested decision must therefore be annulled.

NOTE: See comment by A. Jones, (1993) 14 ECLR 273; G. Cumming, [1994] JBL 165; C. Osti, [1994] ECLR 176.

Consider also *John Deere* v *Commission* (Case T-35/92) [1994] ECR II-957, for a case in which information exchange was found to violate what is now Article 101 TFEU, in part because of the confidential nature of the data exchanged. Residual market competition was inhibited by the reduced uncertainty about strategies planned by rival firms. By contrast there is unlikely to be a violation of Article 101 where information exchange occurs in a market which is not highly concentrated and where the identity of individual commercial operators is not revealed (e.g., Case C-238/05 *Asnef-Equifax* [2006] ECR I-11125). Case C-8/08 *T-Mobile Netherlands* [2009] ECR I-4529 examines the law on information exchange.

Where a true oligopoly exists (which in the view of both Court and Commission was not the case in 'Dyestuffs'), firms may make parallel decisions without colluding. Yet the observable result on the market would be more or less the same as if they had colluded. The inadequacies of the collusion-based Article 101 as a method for controlling true oligopolies have tempted the Commission to move in the direction of treating firms in an oligopoly as collectively dominant and subject to control under Article 102. But the Commission has suffered economic and legal setbacks in developing this notion, which is one of profound complexity and escapes exploration in this chapter. See R. Whish and D. Bailey, *Competition Law* (8th ed., Oxford: OUP, 2015), Ch. 14.

Whether 'horizontal' practices (i.e., those involving firms at the same level in the market, as in the 'Dyestuffs' case) or 'vertical' practices (involving an upstream and a downstream participant, e.g. in a supply or distribution chain) are involved it should be plain that meticulous attention must be paid to the evidence. In *Viho Europe BV* v *Commission* (Case C-73/95P, p. 456) it was concluded that Parker Pen's arrangements fell outwith Article 101 because they were pursued within a single economic unit. But even practice under a genuinely bilateral distribution arrangement does not inevitably fall within Article 101 unless there is a true 'agreement'. So for example in Case C-74/04P *Commission* v *Volkswagen* [2006] ECR I-6585 the Court accepted that 'in order to constitute an agreement within the meaning of Article 81(1) EC [now Article 101(1) TFEU], it is sufficient that an act or conduct which is apparently unilateral be the expression of the concurrence of wills of at least two parties, the form in which that concurrence is expressed not being by itself decisive (para 37); the will of the parties may result from both the clauses of the dealership agreement in question and from the conduct of the parties, and in particular from the possibility of there being tacit acquiescence by the dealers in a call from the manufacturer' (para 39). But the mere fact that two independent parties within a vertical distribution system follow an apparently compatible course of action does not *of itself* mean that the ingredients of Article 101 are present. There must be a concurrence of wills pertaining to the particular impugned conduct, rather than simple unilateral dictation of terms by a supplier.

■ QUESTION

You are asked to advise Alpha, a producer in a market which contains only three other producers. Would the following be caught by Article 101?

(a) Alpha's announcement of a 10 per cent price rise, communicated 14 days in advance through a statement in the trade's leading journal;

(b) Alpha's Christmas card, sent to the other three producers, which adds to seasonal greetings the comment: 'Life would be so much easier if we simply followed each other's prices! But of course we'd never get away with it'. Alpha's 5 per cent price rise on 1 January is followed by the other three producers on 10 January;

(c) the establishment of a trade association of which all four producers are members.

C: The restriction or distortion of competition

The deal, having satisfied the preceding requirements, must have as its 'object or effect the prevention, restriction or distortion of competition within the internal market'. Each word in this phrase has some independent relevance, but the classic broad statement of the requirements of this test was supplied in *Société Technique Minière* v *Maschinenbau Ulm* (Case 56/65) [1966] ECR 235:

> It must be possible to foresee with a sufficient degree of probability on the basis of a set of objective factors of law or fact that the agreement in question may have an influence, direct or indirect, actual or potential, on the pattern of trade between Member States.

Often this is not a difficult test to satisfy. In *Consten* (Cases 56 and 58/64), the contract distorted normal competitive conditions. In *Cooperatieve Stremsel* (Case 61/80), the Court explained how the arrangement distorted patterns of trade between the Netherlands and the rest of the EU market. But we have already seen the problems associated with an over-extensive interpretation of EU trade law in connection with Article 34 TFEU (Chapter 12) and some comparable sensitivities are at stake in determining the scope of Article 101(1) TFEU.

A balance needs to be struck in the legal control of agreements which may contain terms seemingly restrictive of competition, yet which also may serve to promote market integration and product distribution. The next case examines whether the required element of market distortion may be found in an agreement which contributes to furthering competition and distribution in circumstances where both were previously lacking.

Nungesser v _Commission_ (Case 258/78)

[1982] ECR 2015, Court of Justice of the European Communities

There is considerable technical expertise involved in the development of new types of seeds. The case involves techniques of cultivating new types of maize varieties. These skills are passed between plant breeders and are valuable. An agreement which may be subject to Article 101 TFEU is concluded where technical knowledge is transferred between traders in different Member States. The transfer in this case conferred exclusive rights for Germany on Nungesser. The Court was asked to annul the Commission's decision relating to the lawfulness of the agreement.

> [44] ... [T]he applicants criticize the Commission for wrongly taking the view that an exclusive licence of breeders' rights must by its very nature be treated as an agreement prohibited by Article 85(1) of the Treaty [now Article 101(1) TFEU]. They submit that the Commission's opinion in that respect is unfounded in so far as the exclusive licence constitutes the sole means, as regards seeds which have been recently developed in a Member State and which have not yet penetrated the market of another Member State, of promoting competition between the new product and comparable products in that other Member State; indeed, no grower or trader would take the risk of launching the new product on a new market if he were not protected against direct competition from the holder of the breeders' rights and from his other licensees.

The Court went on to examine the nature of the licences at issue; there were two distinct types.

> [53] ... The first case concerns a so-called open exclusive licence or assignment and the exclusivity of the licence relates solely to the contractual relationship between the owner of the right and the licensee, whereby the owner merely undertakes not to grant other licences in respect of the same territory and not to compete

himself with the licensee on that territory. On the other hand, the second case involves an exclusive licence or assignment with absolute territorial protection, under which the parties to the contract propose, as regards the products and the territory in question, to eliminate all competition from third parties, such as parallel importers or licensees for other territories.

[54] That point having been clarified, it is necessary to examine whether, in the present case, the exclusive nature of the licence, in so far as it is an open licence, has the effect of preventing or distorting competition within the meaning of Article 85(1) of the Treaty.

[55] In that respect the Government of the Federal Republic of Germany emphasized that the protection of agricultural innovations by means of breeders' rights constitutes a means of encouraging such innovations and the grant of exclusive rights for a limited period, is capable of providing a further incentive to innovative efforts.

From that it infers that a total prohibition of every exclusive licence, even an open one, would cause the interest of undertakings in licences to fall away, which would be prejudicial to the dissemination of knowledge and techniques in the Community.

[56] The exclusive licence which forms the subject-matter of the contested decision concerns the cultivation and marketing of hybrid maize seeds which were developed by INRA after years of research and experimentation and were unknown to German farmers at the time when the cooperation between INRA and the applicants was taking shape. For that reason the concern shown by the interveners as regards the protection of new technology is justified.

[57] In fact, in the case of a licence of breeders' rights over hybrid maize seeds newly developed in one Member State, an undertaking established in another Member State which was not certain that it would not encounter competition from other licensees for the territory granted to it, or from the owner of the right himself, might be deterred from accepting the risk of cultivating and marketing that product; such a result would be damaging to the dissemination of a new technology and would prejudice competition in the Community between the new product and similar existing products.

[58] Having regard to the specific nature of the products in question, the Court concludes that, in a case such as the present, the grant of an open exclusive licence, that is to say a licence which does not affect the position of third parties such as parallel importers and licensees for other territories, is not in itself incompatible with Article 85(1) of the Treaty.

[59] Part B of the third submission is thus justified to the extent to which it concerns that aspect of the exclusive nature of the licence.

[60] As regard to the position of third parties, the Commission in essence criticizes the parties to the contract for having extended the definition of exclusivity to importers who are not bound to the contract, in particular parallel importers. Parallel importers or exporters, such as Louis David KG in Germany and Robert Bomberault in France who offered INRA seed for sale to German buyers, had found themselves subjected to pressure and legal proceedings by INRA, Frasema and the applicants, the purpose of which was to maintain the exclusive position of the applicants on the German market.

[61] The Court has consistently held (*cf.* Joined Cases 56 and 58/64 *Consten and Grundig* v *Commission* [1966] ECR 299) that absolute territorial protection granted to a licensee in order to enable parallel imports to be controlled and prevented results in the artificial maintenance of separate national markets, contrary to the Treaty.

NOTE: The Court is prepared to accept that some apparent restrictions on trade are immune from control under what is now Article 101(1) TFEU, provided that they are necessary as part of a package for securing the conclusion of a deal. Put another way, one should consider the state of the market *in the absence of the agreement*. Yet a balance must be struck: only reasonable restraints are permitted to escape Article 101. Unduly tight or lengthy restrictions will not escape the prohibition in this way. So in *Nungesser* (Case 258/78) the Court would not countenance a licence which suppressed parallel trade (paras 53, 61). And in *Consten* (Cases 56 and 58/64) itself (p. 457), a deal which enhanced product distribution was held incompatible with the Treaty because of the extra clause which forbade parallel trade.

J. Peeters, 'The Rule of Reason Revisited: Prohibition on Restraints of Competition in the Sherman Act and the EEC Treaty'

(1989) 37 *American Journal of Comparative Law* 521, 550–7, 568–70

(Footnotes omitted.)

Under the traditional analysis, such an open exclusive license is restrictive of competition within the meaning of Article 85(1) since the licensor undertakes to license no one else for the licensed territory, a restriction on the freedom of action of the parties to the agreement having a perceptible effect on third parties. The Court's holding [in *Nungesser*] that such a license is not in itself incompatible with Article 85(1) is, however, in no way based on a balancing of the restrictions imposed on intra-brand competition with the enhancement of inter-brand competition. Rather, the Court refers to the need to protect the licensee against competition from licensees for the same territory or the licensor himself to induce him to make the necessary investments in a new technology being licensed. Only 'in a case such as the present' will an open exclusive license not be incompatible with Article 85(1), implying that the Court has probably applied the doctrine of market opening. This doctrine starts from the premise that introducing a new product in the territory granted to the licensee, implies that the product itself was not yet available in that area, meaning no intrabrand competition could be restricted but inter brand competition will be created. Although one can argue that under such type of analysis the Court should not have objected to absolute territorial protection, including protection against parallel importers, such an argument tends to forget the goal of market integration and should therefore be rejected.

NOTE: In the following case the Court considered the application of Article 85 of the EC Treaty (now Article 101 TFEU) to franchising agreements. Once again, it accepted that some apparent restraints on competition are simply part of a wider deal and therefore unaffected by the Treaty.

***Pronuptia de Paris GmbH* v *Pronuptia de Paris Irmgaard Schillgalis* (Case 161/84)**

[1986] ECR 353, Court of Justice of the European Communities

[27] ...

(1) The compatibility of franchise agreements for the distribution of goods with Article 85(1) depends on the provisions contained therein and on their economic context.

(2) Provisions which are strictly necessary in order to ensure that the know-how and assistance provided by the franchisor do not benefit competitors do not constitute restrictions of competition for the purposes of Article 85(1).

(3) Provisions which establish the control strictly necessary for maintaining the identity and reputation of the network identified by the common name or symbol do not constitute restrictions of competition for the purposes of Article 85(1).

(4) Provisions which share markets between the franchisor and the franchisee or between franchisees constitute restrictions of competition for the purposes of Article 85(1).

(5) The fact that the franchisor makes price recommendations to the franchisee does not constitute a restriction of competition, so long as there is no concerted practice between the franchisor and the franchisees or between the franchisees themselves for the actual application of such prices.

(6) Franchise agreements for the distribution of goods which contain provisions sharing markets between the franchisor and the franchisees or between franchisees are capable of affecting trade between Member States.

NOTE: In relation to several types of agreement, including distribution and franchising agreements, it has long ago been decided that the uncertainty which surrounds the application of Article 101 can best be allayed by the introduction of Block Exemption Regulations. These constitute, more or less, lists of permissible and impermissible clauses, and are of immense practical importance to the commercial lawyer. Regulation 330/2010 now governs vertical restraints (see p. 479).

The use of this so-called 'rule of reason' approach as a means to cut down the scope of application of the basic prohibition against restrictions on competition is well established in US antitrust law. There are, however, reasons for doubting whether the US analogy can usefully be transplanted into EU law. Under the Sherman Act in the US the case for a cautiously narrow interpretation of the prohibition is strengthened by the absence of any statutory exemption for practices judged restrictive of competition yet beneficial. By contrast in Europe, the prohibition in Article 101(1) is accompanied by the exemption provision of Article 101(3) (p. 454). So, one may argue, a wide interpretation of the basic prohibition, and a rejection of its curtailment by a 'rule of reason', is a proper consequence of the choice made under the EU system to assess costs and benefits pursuant to Article 101(3) which is unavailable in the US. Whether this structural difference is sufficient to *justify* a refusal to transplant a 'rule of reason' from the US to the EU as a softening of Article 101(1) remains controversial. But it is, undoubtedly, a difference. In policy terms, restricting the reach of Article 101(1) would doubtless permit greater commercial freedom, while also curtailing the heavy emphasis on the role of exemption under Article 101(3). The reader should be aware that an extra motivation for advocating this shift has long been the Commission's monopoly over the grant of exemption pursuant to Article 101(3). The Commission's inability to deal efficiently with the workload imposed by this monopoly prompted many frustrated commentators to urge a narrower reading of Article 101(1) as a means to liberate firms from dependence on the Commission. From 1 May 2004 the Commission's exclusive grip on Article 101(3) was lifted by Regulation 1/2003, p. 505. The force of the case against a European 'rule of reason' that is driven by administrative concerns is therefore diminished. The EU's new regime applicable to *vertical restraints*, considered at p. 479, should be assessed with awareness of this debate.

In the next case the Court of First Instance (now the General Court) directly addresses the status of a 'rule of reason'. Notice that the rulings in both *Nungesser* (Case 258/78) and *Pronuptia* (Case 161/84) are cited.

***Métropole télévision (M6), Suez-Lyonnaise des eaux, France Télécom* v *Télévision française 1 SA (TF1)* (Case T-112/99)**

[2001] ECR II-2159, Court of First Instance of the European Communities

[74] Article 85 of the Treaty expressly provides, in its third paragraph, for the possibility of exempting agreements that restrict competition where they satisfy a number of conditions, in particular where they are indispensable to the attainment of certain objectives and do not afford undertakings the possibility of eliminating competition in respect of a substantial part of the products in question. It is only in the precise framework of that provision that the pro and anti-competitive aspects of a restriction may be weighed (see, to that effect, Case 161/84 Pronuptia [1986] ECR 353, paragraph 24, and Case T-17/93 *Matra Hachette* v *Commission* [1994] ECR II-595, paragraph 48, and *European Night Services and Others* v *Commission*, cited in paragraph 34 above, [Cases T-374/94 et al] paragraph 136). Article 85(3) of the Treaty would lose much of its effectiveness if such an examination had to be carried out already under Article 85(1) of the Treaty.

[75] It is true that in a number of judgments the Court of Justice and the Court of First Instance have favoured a more flexible interpretation of the prohibition laid down in Article 85(1) of the Treaty (see, in particular, *Société technique minière and Oude Luttikhuis and Others* [Case C-399/93], cited in paragraph 70 above, *Nungesser and Eisele* v *Commission* and *Coditel* v *Ciné-Vog Films* [Case 262/81], cited in paragraph 68 above, *Pronuptia*, cited in paragraph 74 above, and *European Night Services and Others* v *Commission*, cited in paragraph 34 above, as well as the judgment in Case C-250/92 DLG [1994] ECR I-5641, paragraphs 31 to 35).

[76] Those judgments cannot, however, be interpreted as establishing the existence of a rule of reason in Community competition law. They are, rather, part of a broader trend in the case-law according to which it is not necessary to hold, wholly abstractly and without drawing any distinction, that any agreement restricting the freedom of action of one or more of the parties is necessarily caught by the prohibition laid down in Article 85(1) of the Treaty. In assessing the applicability of Article 85(1) to an agreement, account should be taken of the actual conditions in which it functions, in particular the economic context in which the undertakings operate, the products or services covered by the agreement and the actual structure of the market concerned (see, in particular, *European Night Services and Others* v *Commission*, cited in paragraph 34 above,

paragraph 136, *Oude Luttikhuis*, cited in paragraph 70 above, paragraph 10, and *VGB and Others* v *Commission*, cited in paragraph 70 above, [Case T-77/94] paragraph 140, as well as the judgment in Case C-234/89 *Delimitis* [1991] ECR I-935, paragraph 31).

[77] That interpretation, while observing the substantive scheme of Article 85 of the Treaty and, in particular, preserving the effectiveness of Article 85(3), makes it possible to prevent the prohibition in Article 85(1) from extending wholly abstractly and without distinction to all agreements whose effect is to restrict the freedom of action of one or more of the parties. It must, however, be emphasised that such an approach does not mean that it is necessary to weigh the pro and anti-competitive effects of an agreement when determining whether the prohibition laid down in Article 85(1) of the Treaty applies.

NOTE: For insight into Commission practice, read the (misleadingly narrowly titled) 'Guidelines on the application of Article 81(3) of the Treaty' ([2004] OJ C101/97, also available *via* http://ec.europa.eu/competition/index_en.html).

Some agreements have an insignificant economic impact. In such circumstances the market distortion threshold is not crossed. The Court accepted the validity of this analysis in *Volk* v *Verwaecke* (Case 5/69) [1969] ECR 295. Article 101 is not applicable where the impact of the agreement on intra-Union trade or on competition is not appreciable. The Commission has sought to bring clarity to its scope by issuing an explanatory Notice on agreements of minor importance which do not appreciably restrict competition ('de minimis'). Such a Notice is not legislation, but its terms are influential, particularly in respect of Commission enforcement practice. The current version dates from 2014 ([2014] OJ C291/1) and is at http://ec.europa.eu/competition/index_en.html.

NOTE: In assessing the economic impact of an agreement, its wider context must be appraised. An apparently minor agreement may fall foul of Article 101 if in reality it forms part of a network of similar agreements. The point is made in the 'de minimis' Notice. Point 8 of the Notice envisages that there is no appreciable restriction of competition if the aggregate market share held by the parties to the agreement does not exceed 10 per cent on any of the affected markets (where the parties are actual or potential competitors) or where it does not exceed 15 per cent (where the parties are not actual or potential competitors). But point 10 is more cautious where a network is involved:

10. Where, in a relevant market, competition is restricted by the cumulative effect of agreements for the sale of goods or services entered into by different suppliers or distributors (cumulative foreclosure effect of parallel networks of agreements having similar effects on the market), the market share thresholds set out in point 8 and 9 are reduced to 5 %, both for agreements between competitors and for agreements between non-competitors. Individual suppliers or distributors with a market share not exceeding 5 %, are in general not considered to contribute significantly to a cumulative foreclosure effect. [1] A cumulative foreclosure effect is unlikely to exist if less than 30 % of the relevant market is covered by parallel (networks of) agreements having similar effects.

This insistence on a realistic assessment of the economic impact of agreements is embedded in the Court's case law.

***Stergios Delimitis* v *Henninger Brau* (Case C-234/89)**

[1991] ECR I-935, Court of Justice of the European Communities

[14] In its judgment in Case 23/67 *Brasserie De Haecht* v *Wilkin* [1967] ECR 407, the Court held that the effects of such an agreement had to be assessed in the context in which they occur and where they might combine with others to have a cumulative effect on competition. It also follows from that judgment that the cumulative

1 See also the Guidelines on Vertical Restraints OJ C130 19.5.2010 p. 1, in particular points 76, 134, and 179. While in the Guidelines on Vertical Restraints in relation to certain restrictions reference is made not only to the total but also to the tied market share of a particular supplier or buyer, in this Notice all market share thresholds refer to total market shares.

effect of several similar agreements constitutes one factor amongst others in ascertaining whether, by way of a possible alteration of competition, trade between Member States is capable of being affected.

[15] Consequently, in the present case it is necessary to analyse the effects of a beer supply agreement, taken together with other contracts of the same type, on the opportunities of national competitors or those from other Member States, to gain access to the market for beer consumption or to increase their market share and, accordingly, the effects on the range of products offered to consumers.

[16] In making that analysis, the relevant market must first be determined. The relevant market is primarily defined on the basis of the nature of the economic activity in question, in this case the sale of beer. Beer is sold through both retail channels and premises for the sale and consumption of drinks. From the consumer's point of view, the latter sector, comprising in particular public houses and restaurants, may be distinguished from the retail sector on the grounds that the sale of beer in public houses does not solely consist of the purchase of a product but is also linked with the provision of services, and that beer consumption in public houses is not essentially dependent on economic considerations. The specific nature of the public house trade is borne out by the fact that the breweries organize specific distribution systems for this sector which require special installations, and that the prices charged in that sector are generally higher than retail prices.

[17] It follows that in the present case the reference market is that for the distribution of beer in premises for the sale and consumption of drinks. That finding is not affected by the fact that there is a certain overlap between the two distribution networks, namely inasmuch as retail sales allow new competitors to make their brands known and to use their reputation in order to gain access to the market constituted by premises for the sale and consumption of drinks.

[18] Secondly, the relevant market is delimited from a geographical point of view. It should be noted that most beer supply agreements are still entered into at a national level. It follows that, in applying the Community competition rules, account is to be taken of the national market for beer distribution in premises for the sale and consumption of drinks.

[19] In order to assess whether the existence of several beer supply agreements impedes access to the market as so defined, it is further necessary to examine the nature and extent of those agreements in their totality, comprising all similar contracts tying a large number of points of sale to several national producers (judgment in Case 43/69 *Bilger* v *Jehle* [1970] ECR 127). The effect of those networks of contracts on access to the market depends specifically on the number of outlets thus tied to national producers in relation to the number of public houses which are not so tied, the duration of the commitments entered into, the quantities of beer to which those commitments relate, and on the proportion between those quantities and the quantities sold by free distributors.

[20] The existence of a bundle of similar contracts, even if it has a considerable effect on the opportunities for gaining access to the market, is not, however, sufficient in itself to support a finding that the relevant market is inaccessible, inasmuch as it is only one factor, amongst others, pertaining to the economic and legal context in which an agreement must be appraised (Case 23/67 Brasserie De Haecht, cited above). The other factors to be taken into account are, in the first instance, those also relating to opportunities for access.

[21] In that connection it is necessary to examine whether there are real concrete possibilities for a new competitor to penetrate the bundle of contracts by acquiring a brewery already established on the market together with its network of sales outlets, or to circumvent the bundle of contracts by opening new public houses. For that purpose it is necessary to have regard to the legal rules and agreements on the acquisition of companies and the establishment of outlets, and to the minimum number of outlets necessary for the economic operation of a distribution system. The presence of beer wholesalers not tied to producers who are active on the market is also a factor capable of facilitating a new producer's access to that market since he can make use of those wholesalers' sales networks to distribute his own beer.

[22] Secondly, account must be taken of the conditions under which competitive forces operate on the relevant market. In that connection it is necessary to know not only the number and the size of producers present on the market, but also the degree of saturation of that market and customer fidelity to existing brands, for it is generally more difficult to penetrate a saturated market in which customers are loyal to a small number of large producers than a market in full expansion in which a large number of small producers are operating without any strong brand names. The trend in beer sales in the retail trade provides useful information on the development of demand and thus an indication of the degree of saturation of the beer market as a whole. The analysis of that trend is, moreover, of interest in evaluating brand loyalty. A steady increase in sales of beer

under new brand names may confer on the owners of those brand names a reputation which they may turn to account in gaining access to the public-house market.

[23] If an examination of all similar contracts entered into on the relevant market and the other factors relevant to the economic and legal context in which the contract must be examined shows that those agreements do not have the cumulative effect of denying access to that market to new national and foreign competitors, the individual agreements comprising the bundle of agreements cannot be held to restrict competition within the meaning of Article 85(1) of the Treaty. They do not, therefore, fall under the prohibition laid down in that provision.

[24] If, on the other hand, such examination reveals that it is difficult to gain access to the relevant market, it is necessary to assess the extent to which the agreements entered into by the brewery in question contribute to the cumulative effect produced in that respect by the totality of the similar contracts found on that market. Under the Community rules on competition, responsibility for such an effect of closing off the market must be attributed to the breweries which make an appreciable contribution thereto. Beer supply agreements entered into by breweries whose contribution to the cumulative effect is insignificant do not therefore fall under the prohibition under Article 85(1).

[25] In order to assess the extent of the contribution of the beer supply agreements entered into by a brewery to the cumulative sealing-off effect mentioned above, the market position of the contracting parties must be taken into consideration. That position is not determined solely by the market share held by the brewery and any group to which it may belong, but also by the number of outlets tied to it or to its group, in relation to the total number of premises for the sale and consumption of drinks found in the relevant market.

[26] The contribution of the individual contracts entered into by a brewery to the sealing-off of that market also depends on their duration. If the duration is manifestly excessive in relation to the average duration of beer supply agreements generally entered into on the relevant market, the individual contract falls under the prohibition under Article 85(1). A brewery with a relatively small market share which ties its sales outlets for many years may make as significant a contribution to a sealing-off of the market as a brewery in a relatively strong market position which regularly releases sales outlets at shorter intervals.

[27] The reply to be given to the first three questions is therefore that a beer supply agreement is prohibited by Article 85(1) of the EEC Treaty, if two cumulative conditions are met. The first is that, having regard to the economic and legal context of the agreement at issue, it is difficult for competitors who could enter the market or increase their market share to gain access to the national market for the distribution of beer in premises for the sale and consumption of drinks. The fact that, in that market, the agreement in issue is one of a number of similar agreements having a cumulative effect on competition constitutes only one factor amongst others in assessing whether access to that market is indeed difficult. The second condition is that the agreement in question must make a significant contribution to the sealing-off effect brought about by the totality of those agreements in their economic and legal context. The extent of the contribution made by the individual agreement depends on the position of the contracting parties in the relevant market and on the duration of the agreement.

NOTES

1. The Commission's view of the implications of the *Delimitis* ruling for beer supply agreements was set out in a Notice published at [1992] OJ C121/2. This is a further example of the Commission's work in developing policy from the accidents of litigation, *cf* pp. 303, 345, and 411. More generally see now Regulation 330/2010 on vertical agreements, p. 479.
2. For another example of the Court's insistence on appraising the pattern of contractual relationships in their true economic and legal context, see Case C-214/99 *Neste Markkinointi Oy* [2000] ECR I-11121 (in which the length of notice periods in the relevant contracts was regarded as relevant to assessment of the degree of foreclosure caused by the network of agreements).

D: Assessing a 'restriction of competition' in its full context

Nungesser and *Pronuptia* reveal the Court's concern to examine apparent restrictions on competition in their full economic and legal context for the purposes of application of Article 101(1). *Delimitis*, which is mentioned in para 76 of *M6* (Case T-112/99 p. 470), demonstrates a comparable concern. One may disagree with the Court's conclusions on the particular facts of the cases, but the point of principle is that a mechanical assumption that any contractual or other restriction on freedom inevitably falls within the scope of Article 101(1) is false. Article 101(1) is not so broad. But what issues are contextually relevant for the purposes of this inquiry?

***Wouters, J.W. Savelbergh, Price Waterhouse Belastingadviseurs BV* v *Algemene Raad van de Nederlandse Orde van Advocaten* (Case C-309/99)**

[2002] ECR I-1577, Court of Justice of the European Communities

The Court was asked to rule on the application of Article 85 EC, now Article 101 TFEU, in the context of Dutch rules prohibiting multi-disciplinary partnerships between members of the Bar and accountants.

[86] It appears to the Court that the national legislation in issue in the main proceedings has an adverse effect on competition and may affect trade between Member States.

[87] As regards the adverse effect on competition, the areas of expertise of members of the Bar and of accountants may be complementary. Since legal services, especially in business law, more and more frequently require recourse to an accountant, a multi-disciplinary partnership of members of the Bar and accountants would make it possible to offer a wider range of services, and indeed to propose new ones. Clients would thus be able to turn to a single structure for a large part of the services necessary for the organisation, management and operation of their business (the 'one-stop shop' advantage).

[88] Furthermore, a multi-disciplinary partnership of members of the Bar and accountants would be capable of satisfying the needs created by the increasing interpenetration of national markets and the consequent necessity for continuous adaptation to national and international legislation.

[89] Nor, finally, is it inconceivable that the economies of scale resulting from such multi-disciplinary partnerships might have positive effects on the cost of services.

[90] A prohibition of multi-disciplinary partnerships of members of the Bar and accountants, such as that laid down in the 1993 Regulation, is therefore liable to limit production and technical development within the meaning of Article 85(1)(b) of the Treaty . . ..

[95] . . . As regards the question whether intra-Community trade is affected, it is sufficient to observe that an agreement, decision or concerted practice extending over the whole of the territory of a Member State has, by its very nature, the effect of reinforcing the partitioning of markets on a national basis, thereby holding up the economic interpenetration which the Treaty is designed to bring about (Case 8/72 *Vereeniging van Cementhandelaren* v *Commission* [1972] ECR 977, paragraph 29; Case 42/84 *Remia and Others* v *Commission* [1985] ECR 2545, paragraph 22; and *CNSD*, paragraph 48).

[96] That effect is all the more appreciable in the present case because the 1993 Regulation applies equally to visiting lawyers who are registered members of the Bar of another Member State, because economic and commercial law more and more frequently regulates transnational transactions and, lastly, because the firms of accountants looking for lawyers as partners are generally international groups present in several Member States.

[97] However, not every agreement between undertakings or every decision of an association of undertakings which restricts the freedom of action of the parties or of one of them necessarily falls within the prohibition laid down in Article 85(1) of the Treaty. For the purposes of application of that provision to a particular case, account must first of all be taken of the overall context in which the decision of the association of undertakings was taken or produces its effects. More particularly, account must be taken of its objectives, which are here connected with the need to make rules relating to organisation, qualifications, professional ethics, supervision and liability, in order to ensure that the ultimate consumers of legal services and the sound administration of justice are provided with the necessary guarantees in relation to integrity and experience (see, to that effect, Case C-3/95 *Reisebüro Broede* [1996] ECR I-6511, paragraph 38). It has then to be considered whether the consequential effects restrictive of competition are inherent in the pursuit of those objectives.

[98] Account must be taken of the legal framework applicable in the Netherlands, on the one hand, to members of the Bar and to the Bar of the Netherlands, which comprises all the registered members of the Bar in that Member State, and on the other hand, to accountants.

[99] As regards members of the Bar, it has consistently been held that, in the absence of specific Community rules in the field, each Member State is in principle free to regulate the exercise of the legal profession in its territory (Case 107/83 *Klopp* [1984] ECR 2971, paragraph 17, and *Reisebüro*, paragraph 37). For that reason, the rules applicable to that profession may differ greatly from one Member State to another.

[100] The current approach of the Netherlands, where Article 28 of the Advocatenwet entrusts the Bar of the Netherlands with responsibility for adopting regulations designed to ensure the proper practice of the profession, is that the essential rules adopted for that purpose are, in particular, the duty to act for clients in complete independence and in their sole interest, the duty, mentioned above, to avoid all risk of conflict of interest and the duty to observe strict professional secrecy.

[101] Those obligations of professional conduct have not inconsiderable implications for the structure of the market in legal services, and more particularly for the possibilities for the practice of law jointly with other liberal professions which are active on that market.

[102] Thus, they require of members of the Bar that they should be in a situation of independence *vis-à-vis* the public authorities, other operators and third parties, by whom they must never be influenced. They must furnish, in that respect, guarantees that all steps taken in a case are taken in the sole interest of the client.

[103] By contrast, the profession of accountant is not subject, in general, and more particularly, in the Netherlands, to comparable requirements of professional conduct.

[104] As the Advocate-General has rightly pointed out in paragraphs 185 and 186 of his Opinion, there may be a degree of incompatibility between the 'advisory' activities carried out by a member of the Bar and the 'supervisory' activities carried out by an accountant. The written observations submitted by the respondent in the main proceedings show that accountants in the Netherlands perform a task of certification of accounts. They undertake an objective examination and audit of their clients' accounts, so as to be able to impart to interested third parties their personal opinion concerning the reliability of those accounts. It follows that in the Member State concerned accountants are not bound by a rule of professional secrecy comparable to that of members of the Bar, unlike the position under German law, for example.

[105] The aim of the 1993 Regulation is therefore to ensure that, in the Member State concerned, the rules of professional conduct for members of the Bar are complied with, having regard to the prevailing perceptions of the profession in that State. The Bar of the Netherlands was entitled to consider that members of the Bar might no longer be in a position to advise and represent their clients independently and in the observance of strict professional secrecy if they belonged to an organisation which is also responsible for producing an account of the financial results of the transactions in respect of which their services were called upon and for certifying those accounts.

[106] Moreover, the concurrent pursuit of the activities of statutory auditor and of adviser, in particular legal adviser, also raises questions within the accountancy profession itself, as may be seen from the Commission Green Paper 96/C/321/01 'The role, the position and the liability of the statutory auditor within the European Union' (OJ 1996 C 321, p. 1; see, in particular, paragraphs 4.12 to 4.14).

[107] A regulation such as the 1993 Regulation could therefore reasonably be considered to be necessary in order to ensure the proper practice of the legal profession, as it is organised in the Member State concerned.

[108] Furthermore, the fact that different rules may be applicable in another Member State does not mean that the rules in force in the former State are incompatible with Community law (see, to that effect, Case C-108/96 *Mac Quen and Others* [2001] ECR I-837, paragraph 33). Even if multi-disciplinary partnerships of lawyers and accountants are allowed in some Member States, the Bar of the Netherlands is entitled to consider that the objectives pursued by the 1993 Regulation cannot, having regard in particular to the legal regimes by which members of the Bar and accountants are respectively governed in the Netherlands, be attained by less restrictive means (see, to that effect, with regard to a law reserving judicial debt-recovery activity to lawyers, *Reisebüro*, paragraph 41).

[109] In light of those considerations, it does not appear that the effects restrictive of competition such as those resulting for members of the Bar practising in the Netherlands from a regulation such as the 1993 Regulation go beyond what is necessary in order to ensure the proper practice of the legal profession (see, to that effect, Case C-250/92 *DLG* [1994] ECR I-5641, paragraph 35).

[110] Having regard to all the foregoing considerations, the answer to be given to the second question must be that a national regulation such as the 1993 Regulation adopted by a body such as the Bar of the Netherlands does not infringe Article 85(1) of the Treaty, since that body could reasonably have considered that that regulation, despite the effects restrictive of competition that are inherent in it, is necessary for the proper practice of the legal profession, as organised in the Member State concerned.

NOTE: The Court does not deny that the Dutch rules constitute a restriction of competition, viewed in the abstract. But it takes account of the contribution of the rules to the sound administration of justice. This is part of the relevant context within which to assess the reach of Article 101(1). In Case C-519/04 *Meca-Medina and Majcen* v *Commission* [2006] ECR I-6991 the Court, citing its ruling in *Wouters*, held that anti-doping rules limited athletes' freedom of action but that they do not 'necessarily constitute a restriction of competition incompatible with the common market, within the meaning of Article 81 EC [now Article 101 TFEU], since they are justified by a legitimate objective. Such a limitation is inherent in the organization and proper conduct of competitive sport and its very purpose is to ensure healthy rivalry between athletes' (para 45). The next case is further demonstration of the Court's broad understanding of the context within which to locate legal interpretation of the Article 101(1) prohibition.

Albany International v *Stichting Bedrijfspensioenfonds Textielindustrie* (Case C-67/96)

[1999] ECR I-5751, Court of Justice of the European Communities

As foreseen under Dutch legislation, management and labour had jointly requested the public authorities to make affiliation to a sectoral pension fund compulsory. But did this collective agreement struck between both sides of industry constitute an agreement within the meaning of Article 85(1) EC, now Article 101 TFEU? After all, it envisaged the exclusion from the market of pension providers outside the system that was to be made compulsory. It was argued that this would damage competition and, ultimately, consumer choice.

[54] . . . it is important to bear in mind that, under Article 3(g) and (i) of the EC Treaty (now, after amendment, Article 3(1)(g) and (j) EC), the activities of the Community are to include not only a 'system ensuring that competition in the internal market is not distorted' but also 'a policy in the social sphere'. Article 2 of the EC Treaty (now, after amendment, Article 2 EC) provides that a particular task of the Community is 'to promote throughout the Community a harmonious and balanced development of economic activities' and 'a high level of employment and of social protection'.

[55] In that connection, Article 118 of the EC Treaty (Articles 117 to 120 of the EC Treaty have been replaced by Articles 136 EC to 143 EC [see now Articles 151–161 TFEU]) provides that the Commission is to promote close cooperation between Member States in the social field, particularly in matters relating to the right of association and collective bargaining between employers and workers.

[56] Article 118b of the EC Treaty (Articles 117 to 120 of the EC Treaty having been replaced by Articles 136 EC to 143 EC [see now Articles 151–161 TFEU]) adds that the Commission is to endeavour to develop the dialogue between management and labour at European level which could, if the two sides consider it desirable, lead to relations based on agreement.

[57] Moreover, Article 1 of the Agreement on social policy (OJ 1992 C 191, p. 91) states that the objectives to be pursued by the Community and the Member States include improved living and working conditions, proper social protection, dialogue between management and labour, the development of human resources with a view to lasting high employment and the combatting of exclusion.

[58] Under Article 4(1) and (2) of the Agreement, the dialogue between management and labour at Community level may lead, if they so desire, to contractual relations, including agreements, which will be implemented either in accordance with the procedures and practices specific to management and labour and the Member States, or, at the joint request of the signatory parties, by a Council decision on a proposal from the Commission.

[59] It is beyond question that certain restrictions of competition are inherent in collective agreements between organisations representing employers and workers. However, the social policy objectives pursued by such agreements would be seriously undermined if management and labour were subject to Article 85(1) of the Treaty when seeking jointly to adopt measures to improve conditions of work and employment.

[60] It therefore follows from an interpretation of the provisions of the Treaty as a whole which is both effective and consistent that agreements concluded in the context of collective negotiations between management and labour in pursuit of such objectives must, by virtue of their nature and purpose, be regarded as falling outside the scope of Article 85(1) of the Treaty.

NOTE: In the light of this statement the Court proceeded to examine the particular arrangements at issue in the case. The vital point, however, is that, as in *Wouters* (Case C-309/99, p. 474), the Court in *Albany International* did not deny that the rules restricted competition. But it placed its investigation into the scope of Article 101(1) in a wider context. The Treaty competition rules are porous: the very scope of Article 101(1) is influenced by policy objectives located elsewhere in the framework of EU law and policy. As mentioned (Chapter 9, p. 239, and in this chapter at p. 453) the Lisbon Treaty has adjusted and arguably downgraded the commitment to undistorted competition mentioned in para 54 of the judgment in *Albany International* but since the Court here even pre-Lisbon was receptive to interpreting the competition rules with reference to social policy concerns it does not seem likely that the Lisbon adjustment will have practical significance.

It is worth recalling that both Articles 34 and 56 TFEU on the free movement of goods and services respectively offer similar insight into the way in which the Court interprets EU trade law in a manner that seeks to avoid trampling other regulatory objectives underfoot. In fact, an apparent convergence between the assumptions of EU law of free movement and EU competition law emerges from the ruling in *Wouters*. The Dutch rules prohibiting multi-disciplinary partnerships between members of the Bar and accountants were not only attacked as violations of Article 101 TFEU, then Article 85 EC, but also as violations of Article 56 TFEU, then Article 59 EC concerning the free movement of services (Chapter 13). The Court was curt.

***Wouters, J.W. Savelbergh, Price Waterhouse Belastingadviseurs BV* v *Algemene Raad van de Nederlandse Orde van Advocaten* (Case C-309/99)**

[2002] ECR I-1577, Court of Justice of the European Communities

[120] It should be observed at the outset that compliance with Articles 52 and 59 of the Treaty is also required in the case of rules which are not public in nature but which are designed to regulate, collectively, self-employment and the provision of services. The abolition, as between Member States, of obstacles to freedom of movement for persons would be compromised if the abolition of State barriers could be neutralised by obstacles resulting from the exercise of their legal autonomy by associations or organisations not governed by public law (Case 36/74 *Walrave and Koch* [1974] ECR 1405, paragraphs 17, 23 and 24; Case 13/76 *Donà* [1976] ECR 1333, paragraphs 17 and 18; Case C-415/93 *Bosman* [1995] ECR I-4921, paragraphs 83 and 84, and Case C-281/98 *Angonese* [2000] ECR I-4139, paragraph 32).

[121] In those circumstances, the Court may be called upon to determine whether the Treaty provisions concerning the right of establishment and freedom to provide services are applicable to a regulation such as the 1993 Regulation.

[122] On the assumption that the provisions concerning the right of establishment and/or freedom to provide services are applicable to a prohibition of any multi-disciplinary partnerships between members of the Bar and accountants such as that laid down in the 1993 Regulation and that that regulation constitutes a restriction on one or both of those freedoms, that restriction would in any event appear to be justified for the reasons set out in paragraphs 97 to 109 above.

■ **QUESTION**

The key to this case law seems to be a refusal explicitly to accommodate a 'rule of reason' within EU competition law but a readiness to use the interpretative rule that restrictions on competition be seen in their full legal and economic context as a basis for permitting

Article 101(1)'s scope to be affected by a range of (loosely stated) public interest considerations. Is this approach sufficiently reliable and predictable as a basis for the regulation of commerce under a regime which includes the possibility of the imposition of heavy fines? If not, what improvements would you advocate for this regime?

FURTHER READING

Monti, G., 'Article 81 EC and Public Policy' (2002) 39 CML Rev 1057.

Mortelmans, K., 'Towards Convergence in the Application of the Rules on Free Movement and on Competition?' (2001) 38 CML Rev 613.

Parret, L., 'Shouldn't We Know What We Are Protecting? Yes We Should! A Plea for a Solid and Comprehensive Debate about the Objectives of EU Competition Law and Policy' (2010) 6 Eur Comp Jnl 339.

Nazzini, R., 'Article 81 EC Between Time Present and Time Past: A Normative Critique of Restriction of Competition in EU Law' (2006) 43 CML Rev 497.

Townley, C., *Article 81 EC and Public Policy* (Oxford: Hart, 2009); for review and critique see Odudu, O., 'The Wider Concerns of Competition Law' (2010) 30 OxJLS 599.

Van Cleynenbreugel, P., 'Article 101 TFEU and the EU Courts: Adapting legal form to the realities of modernization?' (2014) 51 CMLRev 1381.

Witt, A., 'Public Policy Goals under EU Competition Law–Now is the Time to Set the House in Order' (2012) 8 Eur Comp Jnl 443.

E: Exemption

Article 101(3) permits exemption of agreements falling within Article 101(1). It is set out at p. 454. It implies a cost-benefit assessment, whereby the advantages of collaboration are balanced against the disadvantages of impeded competition. However, the terms of Article 101(3) are rather more specific than general economic cost-benefit. The provision contains four elements; two positive conditions and two negative conditions. All must be satisfied. The two positive conditions demand a yield of economic progress, a fair share of which must percolate to the consumer; the two negative conditions forbid unnecessary extra restraints and the elimination of competition. Article 101(3) provides a specific framework for weighing the pro- and the anti-competitive features of a restriction (Case T-112/99 *M6* para 74, p. 470).

Typically, a Commission Decision relating to Article 101(3) will appraise the general economic context of an agreement and then proceed to apply these four elements. Despite this step-by-step approach, all four elements are inter-linked. The following Decision illustrates the types of argument relevant under Article 101(3) and the application of the conditions, two positive, two negative.

Prym-Werke

[1973] CMLR D250; [1973] OJ L296/24, Commission Decision 73/323

Prym agreed to give up making needles. It agreed to buy its needle needs from Beka. Beka agreed to supply Prym. Beka could then specialize in needle production. The Commission decided to exempt the agreement after the following analysis.

> ... [T]he concentration of manufacturing agreed on by Prym and Beka has, from the point of view of the improvement of production, favourable effects analogous to those of specialisation; it causes an increase of at least 50 per cent in the quantity of needles to be manufactured in the Eupen factory, which makes it possible to make more intensive use of the existing plant and to introduce production-line manufacture.

This rationalisation of production has in particular made it possible to reduce the very large proportion of labour costs in the producer's cost price. The producer's cost price of 'Standard' quality needles, which fell by some 20 per cent in 1970 after the concentration of production at Eupen, was still lower at the end of 1972 than in 1969 in spite of the increases in wages and in the cost of raw materials which had occurred during those four years. The introduction of mechanised production-line manufacture with increased productive capacity also makes it possible to manufacture articles of a more even quality.

The agreement allows consumers a fair share of the benefit resulting from it, as it must be supposed that because of the pressure of competition existing on the needle market the advantages resulting from rationalisation will be passed on to consumers.

The agreement does not contain restrictions which are not indispensable to the attainment of the said advantages. The favourable effects of the agreement are due essentially to the improvement in productivity resulting from a more intensive utilisation of productive capacity, and that more intensive utilisation is only possible if the quantities of needles to be manufactured are, and are to remain, considerably larger than before. That being so, it is essential that Prym should enter into a commitment for a long period, not only to cease manufacture, but also to purchase all its requirements of needles for domestic sewing machines from Beka, so as to provide a guarantee for an increased output by the latter.

The long-term commitments by Prym to obtain its supplies exclusively from Beka thus represents an indispensable restriction if the favourable effects of the agreement are to be achieved and, moreover, maintained. That commitment, moreover, does not go beyond what is strictly necessary, since it allows Prym the possibility, in the event of Beka being unable to meet its commitments, of buying from other sources and since, in any case, Prym gets the benefit of preferential prices.

The agreement does not afford the parties the possibility of eliminating competition in respect of a substantial part of the products in question. In the amended version in force since 10 October 1972 the agreement no longer prevents Beka and Prym from competing with each other on any EEC market, whether geographic or sectoral. Both undertakings rest exposed to the keen competition from other, sometimes larger, producers who appear as sellers within the EEC.

All the conditions necessary for the application of Article 85(3) of the Treaty [now Article 101(3)] are thus fulfilled.

■ QUESTION

Why was exemption unavailable to the Consten/Grundig deal (p. 457)? After all, it improved product distribution; German goods were available in France. Consider each of the four elements of Article 101(3) TFEU.

NOTE: It is relatively uncommon for an agreement to be denied exemption due to failure to satisfy one element only. *WANO Schwarzpulver* [1978] OJ L322/26 offers an example of a Commission Decision which finds several reasons for refusal and illustrates how the four elements of Article 101(3) are connected. The Commission has helpfully released 'Guidelines on the application of Article 81(3) of the Treaty' ([2004] OJ C101/97, also available *via* http://ec.europa.eu/competition/index_en.html).

The four elements of Article 101(3) find practical expression in Block Exemption Regulations. These measures apply the criteria for exemption to particular types of collaboration. As charters for lawful agreements, they assist in the practical administration of the competition rules by the Commission; and in commercial planning by firms. Twenty years ago there were several Block Exemption Regulations in force. They covered several types of agreement – exclusive distribution, franchising, and so on. Some regulations dealt with agreements of a vertical type (those between traders at different points in the supply chain). Others covered agreements more typically struck on a horizontal basis (between traders at the same point on the supply chain). But the Commission radically overhauled its approach as part of its campaign to 'modernize' EU competition law. Regulation 2790/1999 altered the law by adjusting the conditions for exempting vertical deals (as defined) from prohibition. Regulation 2790/1999 expired in 2010 and was replaced by the similarly structured Regulation 330/2010. The Commission has also 'modernized' its treatment of horizontal restraints. There are Block Exemption Regulations on the application of Article 101(3) to categories of specialization agreements (now found in Regulation 1218/2010) and research and development agreements (Regulation 1217/2010), supplemented by Guidelines on the applicability of Article 101 to horizontal co-operation agreements ([2011] OJ C11/1). Here too the Commission wishes to free

both itself and commercial actors of burdens associated with supervision of deals that are insignificant in competition terms in order to target resources more efficiently on more serious cases. A more flexible regime is the result.

SECTION 3: ARTICLE 102 TFEU

The text of Article 102 TFEU is set out at p. 454. It stands alongside Article 101 TFEU as the second of the twin pillars of the EU's competition law system. Like Article 101, it controls undertakings, depends on an effect on trade between Member States, and has as its objective the control of market distortion. However, unlike Article 101, it controls the conduct of an economically dominant firm, rather than bilateral or multilateral practices involving firms. Articles 101 and 102 complement each other and should be read together as a competition law regime, not as two independent provisions.

The rationale for controlling the conduct of a single firm is found in the damage which it can wreak on the market. The firm may charge high prices, or it may refuse to supply customers. None of this matters in a competitive market. Our firm will simply lose business. But where our firm is economically powerful, it may be able to distort the market without fear of effective competition. The result may be inefficiency as a result of mismatch between the influence of supply and demand. The law, then, has reason to control the conduct of a single firm, but only where the firm has passed a threshold of economic power. English law has called that threshold the monopoly; Article 102 refers to it as the dominant position.

But it is not the dominant position that is condemned. It is the *abuse* of a dominant position, not its existence, which is unlawful. Article 102, set out at p. 454, supplies an illustrative list of the type of practice which may be held abusive.

Logically, there are two elements to an analysis under Article 102. First, is the firm in a dominant position? If so, secondly, has it abused that *dominant position*? The discussion uses as its framework the Court's decision in *United Brands* v *Commission* (Case 27/76), a famous case which touches on many of the issues of law and policy in this area.

A: The dominant position: defining the market

The question 'Is this firm in a dominant position?' is simply answered: 'It depends!' And it depends on exactly what it is that the firm is alleged to be dominating. The producer of 80 per cent of a nation's ox liver dominates the ox liver market. But there is no lack of competition if the consumer will freely switch preference to lamb's liver in the event of the ox liver producer raising prices. The breadth of the market, then, has to be defined accurately before one can logically accuse a firm of dominance on that market, and before one can claim a rationale for intervention to control dominance.

***United Brands* v *Commission* (Case 27/76)**

[1978] ECR 207, Court of Justice of the European Communities

The United Brands Company (UBC) was found by the Commission to have abused a dominant position in the banana market. The firm sought annulment of that Decision before the Court. The following extract involves assessment of the market, defined according to product.

[12] As far as the product market is concerned it is first of all necessary to ascertain whether, as the applicant maintains, bananas are an integral part of the fresh fruit market, because they are reasonably interchangeable by consumers with other kinds of fresh fruit such as apples, oranges, grapes, peaches, strawberries, etc. or whether the relevant market consists solely of the banana market which includes both branded bananas and unlabelled bananas and is a market sufficiently homogeneous and distinct from the market of other fresh fruit.

[13] The applicant submits in support of its argument that bananas compete with other fresh fruit in the same shops, on the same shelves, at prices which can be compared, satisfying the same needs: consumption as a dessert or between meals.

[14] The statistics produced show that consumer expenditure on the purchase of bananas is at its lowest between June and December when there is a plentiful supply of domestic fresh fruit on the market.

[15] Studies carried out by the Food and Agriculture Organization (FAO) (especially in 1975) confirm that banana prices are relatively weak during the summer months and that the price of apples for example has a statistically appreciable impact on the consumption of bananas in the Federal Republic of Germany.

[16] Again according to these studies some easing of prices is noticeable at the end of the year during the 'orange season'.

[17] The seasonal peak periods when there is a plentiful supply of other fresh fruit exert an influence not only on the prices but also on the volume of sales of bananas and consequently on the volume of imports thereof.

[18] The applicant concludes from these findings that bananas and other fresh fruit form only one market and that UBC's operations should have been examined in this context for the purpose of any application of Article 86 of the Treaty.

[19] The Commission maintains that there is a demand for bananas which is distinct from the demand for other fresh fruit especially as the banana is a very important part of the diet of certain sections of the community.

[20] The specific qualities of the banana influence customer preference and induce him not to readily accept other fruits as a substitute.

[21] The Commission draws the conclusion from the studies quoted by the applicant that the influence of the prices and availabilities of other types of fruit on the prices and availabilities of bananas on the relevant market is very ineffective and that these effects are too brief and too spasmodic for such other fruit to be regarded as forming part of the same market as bananas or as a substitute therefore.

[22] For the banana to be regarded as forming a market which is sufficiently differentiated from other fruit markets it must be possible for it to be singled out by such special features distinguishing it from other fruits that it is only to a limited extent interchangeable with them and is only exposed to their competition in a way that is hardly perceptible.

[23] The ripening of bananas takes place the whole year round without any season having to be taken into account.

[24] Throughout the year production exceeds demand and can satisfy it at any time.

[25] Owing to this particular feature the banana is a privileged fruit and its production and marketing can be adapted to the seasonal fluctuations of other fresh fruit which are known and can be computed.

[26] There is no unavoidable seasonal substitution since the consumer can obtain this fruit all the year round.

[27] Since the banana is a fruit which is always available in sufficient quantities the question whether it can be replaced by other fruits must be determined over the whole of the year for the purpose of ascertaining the degree of competition between it and other fresh fruit.

[28] The studies of the banana market on the Court's file show that on the latter market there is no significant long term cross-elasticity any more than – as has been mentioned – there is any seasonal substitutability in general between the banana and all the seasonal fruits, as this only exists between the banana and two fruits (peaches and table grapes) in one of the countries (West Germany) of the relevant geographic market.

[29] As far as concerns the two fruits available throughout the year (oranges and apples) the first are not interchangeable and in the case of the second there is only a relative degree of substitutability.

[30] This small degree of substitutability is accounted for by the specific features of the banana and all the factors which influence consumer choice.

[31] The banana has certain characteristics, appearance, taste, softness, seedlessness, easy handling, a constant level of production which enable it to satisfy the constant needs of an important section of the population consisting of the very young, the old and the sick.

[32] As far as prices are concerned two FAO studies show that the banana is only affected by the prices – falling prices – of other fruits (and only of peaches and table grapes) during the summer months and mainly in July and then by an amount not exceeding 20%.

[33] Although it cannot be denied that during these months and some weeks at the end of the year this product is exposed to competition from other fruits, the flexible way in which the volume of imports and their marketing on the relevant geographic market is adjusted means that the conditions of competition are extremely limited and that its price adapts without any serious difficulties to this situation where supplies of fruit are plentiful.

[34] It follows from all these considerations that a very large number of consumers having a constant need for bananas are not noticeably or even appreciably enticed away from the consumption of this product by the arrival of other fresh fruit on the market and that even the personal peak periods only affect it for a limited period of time and to a very limited extent from the point of view of substitutability.

[35] Consequently the banana market is a market which is sufficiently distinct from the other fresh fruit markets.

NOTE: The Commission had adopted a narrower market definition than that advocated by United Brands. The narrower the definition, the more likely that dominance will be established. Disagreement between Commission and undertaking in this fashion is a common feature of Article 102 cases.

Markets may also be defined by reference to their territorial scope. Even if consumers will not switch from ox liver to other types of liver, the single national ox liver producer is not dominant if producers of ox liver in other States can import their produce as competition.

United Brands v *Commission* (Case 27/76)

[1978] ECR 207, Court of Justice of the European Communities

The Commission had analysed UBC's conduct in a market comprising Germany, Ireland, Denmark, Belgium, the Netherlands, and Luxembourg, but excluding the other three Member States at that time, the UK, France, and Italy. UBC argued that the geographic market 'should only comprise areas where the conditions of competition are homogeneous' and that this test was not satisfied by the Commission's chosen market. The Court, however, agreed with the Commission:

[44] The conditions for the application of Article 86 [now 102] to an undertaking in a dominant position presuppose the clear delimitation of the substantial part of the Common Market in which it may be able to engage in abuses which hinder effective competition and this is an area where the objective conditions of competition applying to the product in question must be the same for all traders.

[45] The Community has not established a common organization of the agricultural market in bananas.

[46] Consequently import arrangements vary considerably from one Member State to another and reflect a specific commercial policy peculiar to the States concerned.

[47] This explains why for example the French market owing to its national organization is restricted upstream by a particular import arrangement and obstructed downstream by a retail price monitored by the Administration.

[48] This market, in addition to adopting certain measures relating to a 'target price' ('prix objectif') fixed each year and to packaging and grading standards and the minimum qualities required, reserves about two thirds of the market for the production of the overseas departments and one third to that of certain countries enjoying preferential relations with France (Ivory Coast, Madagascar, Cameroon) the bananas whereof are imported duty-free, and it includes a system the running of which is entrusted to the 'Comité interprofessionnel bananier' ('CIB').

[49] The United Kingdom market enjoys 'Commonwealth preferences', a system of which the main feature is the maintenance of a level of production favouring the developing countries of the Commonwealth and of a price paid to the associations of producers directly linked to the selling price of the green banana charged in the United Kingdom.

[50] On the Italian market, since the abolition in 1965 of the State Monopoly responsible for marketing bananas, a national system of quota restrictions has been introduced, the Ministry for Shipping and the Exchange Control Office supervising the imports and the charterparties relating to the foreign ships which carry the bananas.

[51] The effect of the national organization of these three markets is that the applicant's bananas do not compete on equal terms with the other bananas sold in these States which benefit from a preferential system and the Commission was right to exclude these three national markets from the geographic market under consideration.

[52] On the other hand the six other States are markets which are completely free, although the applicable tariff provisions and transport costs are of necessity different but not discriminatory, and in which the conditions of competition are the same for all.

[53] From the standpoint of being able to engage in free competition these six States form an area which is sufficiently homogeneous to be considered in its entirety.

[54] UBC has arranged for its subsidiary in Rotterdam – UBCBV – to market its products. UBCBV is for this purpose a single centre for the whole of this part of the Community.

[55] Transport costs do not in fact stand in the way of the distribution policy chosen by UBC which consists in selling f.o.r. Rotterdam and Bremerhaven, the two ports where the bananas are unloaded.

[56] These are factors which go to make relevant market a single market.

[57] It follows from all these considerations that the geographic market as determined by the Commission which constitutes a substantial part of the common market must be regarded as the relevant market for the purpose of determining whether the applicant may be in a dominant position.

The defined market, then, was internally more or less homogeneous and distinct in material respects from the wider market, defined by product and by territory. The next question was whether United Brands dominated that market. The Court established its test:

[65] The dominant position referred to in this article relates to a position of economic strength enjoyed by an undertaking which enables it to prevent effective competition being maintained on the relevant market by giving it the power to behave to an appreciable extent independently of its competitors, customers and ultimately of its consumers.

[66] In general a dominant position derives from a combination of several factors which, taken separately, are not necessarily determinative.

The first set of factors then analysed relate to the structure of UBC.

[69] It is advisable to examine in turn UBC's resources for and methods of producing, packaging, transporting, selling and displaying its product.

[70] UBC is an undertaking vertically integrated to a high degree.

[71] This integration is evident at each of the stages from the plantation to the loading on wagons or lorries in the ports of delivery and after those stages, as far as ripening and sale prices are concerned, UBC even extends its control to ripener/distributors and wholesalers by setting up a complete network of agents.

[72] At the production stage UBC owns large plantations in Central and South America.

[73] In so far as UBC's own production does not meet its requirements it can obtain supplies without any difficulty from independent planters since it is an established fact that unless circumstances are exceptional there is a production surplus.

[74] Furthermore several independent producers have links with UBC through contracts for the growing of bananas which have caused them to grow the varieties of bananas which UBC has advised them to adopt.

[75] The effects of natural disasters which could jeopardize supplies are greatly reduced by the fact that the plantations are spread over a wide geographic area and by the selection of varieties not very susceptible to diseases.

[76] This situation was born out by the way in which UBC was able to react to the consequences of hurricane 'Fifi' in 1974.

[77] At the production stage UBC therefore knows that it can comply with all the requests which it receives.

[78] At the stage of packaging and presentation on its premises UBC has at its disposal factories, manpower, plant and material which enable it to handle the goods independently.

[79] The bananas are carried from the place of production to the port of shipment by its own means of transport including railways.

[80] At the carriage by sea stage it has been acknowledged that UBC is the only undertaking of its kind which is capable of carrying two thirds of its exports by means of its own banana fleet.

[81] Thus UBC knows that it is able to transport regularly, without running the risk of its own ships not being used and whatever the market situation may be, two thirds of its average volume of sales and is alone able to ensure that three regular consignments reach Europe each week, and all this guarantees it commercial stability and well being.

[82] In the field of technical knowledge and as a result of continual research UBC keeps on improving the productivity and yield of its plantations by improving the draining system, making good soil deficiencies and combating effectively plant disease.

[83] It has perfected new ripening methods in which its technicians instruct the distributor/ripeners of the Chiquita banana.

[84] That is another factor to be borne in mind when considering UBC's position since competing firms cannot develop research at a comparable level and are in this respect at a disadvantage compared with the applicant.

[85] It is acknowledged that at the stage where the goods are given the final finish and undergo quality control UBC not only controls the distributor/ripeners which are direct customers but also those who work for the account of its important customers such as the Scipio group.

[86] Even if the object of the clause prohibiting the sale of green bananas was only strict quality control, it in fact gives UBC absolute control of all trade in its goods so long as they are marketable wholesale, that is to say before the ripening process begins which makes an immediate sale unavoidable.

[87] This general quality control of a homogeneous product makes the advertising of the brand name effective.

[88] Since 1967 UBC has based its general policy in the relevant market on the quality of its Chiquita brand banana.

[89] There is no doubt that this policy gives UBC control over the transformation of the product into bananas for consumption even though most of this product no longer belongs to it.

[90] This policy has been based on a thorough reorganization of the arrangements for production, packaging, carriage, ripening (new plant with ventilation and a cooling system) and sale (a network of agents).

[91] UBC has made this product distinctive by large-scale repeated advertising and promotion campaigns which have induced the consumer to show a preference for it in spite of the difference between the price of labelled and unlabelled bananas (in the region of 30 to 40%) and also of Chiquita bananas and those which have been labelled with another brand name (in the region of 7 to 10%).

[92] It was the first to take full advantage of the opportunities presented by labelling in the tropics for the purpose of large-scale advertising and this, to use UBC's own words, has 'revolutionized the commercial exploitation of the banana' (Annex II (a) to the application, p. 10).

[93] It has thus attained a privileged position by making Chiquita the premier banana brand name on the relevant market with the result that the distributor cannot afford not to offer it to the consumer.

[94] At the selling stage this distinguishing factor – justified by the unchanging quality of the banana bearing this label – ensures that it has regular customers and consolidates its economic strength.

[95] The effect of its sales networks only covering a limited number of customers, large groups or distributor/ripeners, is a simplification of its supply policy and economies of scale.

[96] Since UBC's supply policy consists – in spite of the production surplus – in only meeting the requests for Chiquita bananas parsimoniously and sometimes incompletely UBC is in a position of strength at the selling stage.

The Court went on to examine the competitive situation on the market. UBC was by no means the only active trader. The Court declared that 'an undertaking does not have to have eliminated all opportunity for competition in order to be in a dominant position'; and it observed that UBC's market share, fixed by the Court at 40–45 per cent, was several times greater than its nearest rival. Limited price wars had not altered market shares. The Court came to the conclusion that:

[121] UBC's economic strength has thus enabled it to adopt a flexible overall strategy directed against new competitors establishing themselves on the whole of the relevant market.

[122] The particular barriers to competitors entering the market are the exceptionally large capital investments required for the creation and running of banana plantations, the need to increase sources of supply in order to avoid the effects of fruit diseases and bad weather (hurricanes, floods), the introduction of an essential system of logistics which the distribution of a very perishable product makes necessary, economies of scale from which newcomers to the market cannot derive any immediate benefit and the actual cost of entry made up *inter alia* of all the general expenses incurred in penetrating the market such as the setting up of an adequate commercial network, the mounting of very large-scale advertising campaigns, all those financial risks, the costs of which are irrecoverable if the attempt fails.

[123] Thus, although, as UBC has pointed out, it is true that competitors are able to use the same methods of production and distribution as the applicant, they come up against almost insuperable practical and financial obstacles.

[124] That is another factor peculiar to a dominant position.

[125] However UBC takes into account the losses which its banana division made from 1971 to 1976 – whereas during this period its competitors made profits – for the purpose of inferring that, since dominance is in essence the power to fix prices, making losses is inconsistent with the existence of a dominant position.

[126] An undertaking's economic strength is not measured by its profitability; a reduced profit margin or even losses for a time are not incompatible with a dominant position, just as large profits may be compatible with a situation where there is effective competition.

[127] The fact that UBC's profitability is for a time moderate or non-existent must be considered in the light of the whole of its operations.

[128] The finding that, whatever losses UBC may make, the customers continue to buy more goods from UBC which is the dearest vendor, is more significant and this fact is a particular feature of the dominant position and its verification is determinative in this case.

[129] The cumulative effect of all the advantages enjoyed by UBC thus ensures that it has a dominant position on the relevant market.

NOTE: Of course, the bigger the market share, the more likely that dominance is established. But *United Brands* (Case 27/76) emphasizes that each market requires special attention and must be judged according to its own peculiarities.

In 1997, the Commission sought to make its approach to market definition more transparent. In reading this text, remember it is a pre-Amsterdam document. So references to Articles 85 and 86 now need to be understood as references to Articles 101 and 102 TFEU respectively. Textually the provisions have not been materially altered by revision of the Treaty.

COMMISSION NOTICE ON THE DEFINITION OF THE RELEVANT MARKET FOR THE PURPOSES OF COMMUNITY COMPETITION LAW, CHAPTERS I AND II

[1997] OJ C372/5, available *via* http://ec.europa.eu/competition/index_en.html

I. INTRODUCTION

1. The purpose of this notice is to provide guidance as to how the Commission applies the concept of relevant product and geographic market in its ongoing enforcement of Community competition law, in particular the application of Council Regulation No 17 and (EEC) No 4064/89, their equivalents in other sectoral applications such as transport, coal and steel, and agriculture, and the relevant provisions of the EEA Agreement.[1] Throughout this notice, references to Articles 85 and 86 of the Treaty and to merger control are to be understood as referring to the equivalent provisions in the EEA Agreement and the ECSC Treaty.

2. Market definition is a tool to identify and define the boundaries of competition between firms. It serves to establish the framework within which competition policy is applied by the Commission. The main purpose of market definition is to identify in a systematic way the competitive constraints that the undertakings involved[2] face. The objective of defining a market in both its product and geographic dimension is to identify those actual competitors of the undertakings involved that are capable of constraining those undertakings' behaviour and of preventing them from behaving independently of effective competitive pressure. It is from this perspective that the market definition makes it possible *inter alia* to calculate market shares that would convey meaningful information regarding market power for the purposes of assessing dominance or for the purposes of applying Article 85.

3. It follows from point 2 that the concept of 'relevant market' is different from other definitions of market often used in other contexts. For instance, companies often use the term 'market' to refer to the area where it sells its products or to refer broadly to the industry or sector where it belongs.

4. The definition of the relevant market in both its product and its geographic dimensions often has a decisive influence on the assessment of a competition case. By rendering public the procedures which the Commission follows when considering market definition and by indicating the criteria and evidence on which it relies to reach a decision, the Commission expects to increase the transparency of its policy and decision-making in the area of competition policy.

5. Increased transparency will also result in companies and their advisers being able to better anticipate the possibility that the Commission may raise competition concerns in an individual case. Companies could,

1 The focus of assessment in State aid cases is the aid recipient and the industry/sector concerned rather than identification of competitive constraints faced by the aid recipient. When consideration of market power and therefore of the relevant market are raised in any particular case, elements of the approach outlined here might serve as a basis for the assessment of State aid cases.

2 For the purposes of this notice, the undertakings involved will be, in the case of a concentration, the parties to the concentration; in investigations within the meaning of Article 86 of the Treaty, the undertaking being investigated or the complainants; for investigations within the meaning of Article 85, the parties to the Agreement.

therefore, take such a possibility into account in their own internal decision-making when contemplating, for instance, acquisitions, the creation of joint ventures, or the establishment of certain agreements. It is also intended that companies should be in a better position to understand what sort of information the Commission considers relevant for the purposes of market definition.

6. The Commission's interpretation of 'relevant market' is without prejudice to the interpretation which may be given by the Court of Justice or the Court of First Instance of the European Communities.

II. DEFINITION OF RELEVANT MARKET

Definition of relevant product market and relevant geographic market

7. The Regulations based on Articles 85 and 86 of the Treaty, in particular in section 6 of Form A/B with respect to Regulation No 17, as well as in section 6 of Form CO with respect to Regulation (EEC) No 4064/89 on the control of concentrations having a Community dimension have laid down the following definitions. 'Relevant product markets' are defined as follows:

'A relevant product market comprises all those products and/or services which are regarded as interchangeable or substitutable by the consumer, by reason of the products' characteristics, their prices and their intended use'.

8. Relevant geographic markets' are defined as follows:

'The relevant geographic market comprises the area in which the undertakings concerned are involved in the supply and demand of products or services, in which the conditions of competition are sufficiently homogeneous and which can be distinguished from neighbouring areas because the conditions of competition are appreciably different in those areas'.

9. The relevant market within which to assess a given competition issue is therefore established by the combination of the product and geographic markets. The Commission interprets the definitions in paragraphs 7 and 8 (which reflect the case-law of the Court of Justice and the Court of First Instance as well as its own decision-making practice) according to the orientations defined in this notice.

Concept of relevant market and objectives of Community competition policy

10. The concept of relevant market is closely related to the objectives pursued under Community competition policy. For example, under the Community's merger control, the objective in controlling structural changes in the supply of a product/service is to prevent the creation or reinforcement of a dominant position as a result of which effective competition would be significantly impeded in a substantial part of the common market. Under the Community's competition rules, a dominant position is such that a firm or group of firms would be in a position to behave to an appreciable extent independently of its competitors, customers and ultimately of its consumers.[3] Such a position would usually arise when a firm or group of firms accounted for a large share of the supply in any given market, provided that other factors analysed in the assessment (such as entry barriers, customers' capacity to react, etc.) point in the same direction.

11. The same approach is followed by the Commission in its application of Article 86 of the Treaty to firms that enjoy a single or collective dominant position. Within the meaning of Regulation No 17, the Commission has the power to investigate and bring to an end abuses of such a dominant position, which must also be defined by reference to the relevant market. Markets may also need to be defined in the application of Article 85 of the Treaty, in particular, in determining whether an appreciable restriction of competition exists or in establishing if the condition pursuant to Article 85(3)(b) for an exemption from the application of Article 85(1) is met.

12. The criteria for defining the relevant market are applied generally for the analysis of certain types of behaviour in the market and for the analysis of structural changes in the supply of products. This methodology, though, might lead to different results depending on the nature of the competition issue being examined. For instance, the scope of the geographic market might be different when analysing a concentration, where the analysis is essentially prospective, from an analysis of past behaviour. The different time horizon considered in each case might lead to the result that different geographic markets are defined for the same products depending on whether the Commission is examining a change in the structure of supply, such as a concentration or a cooperative joint venture, or examining issues relating to certain past behaviour.

3 Definition given by the Court of Justice in its judgment of 13 February 1979 in Case 85/76, *Hoffmann-La Roche* [1979] ECR 461, and confirmed in subsequent judgments.

Basic principles for market definition

Competitive constraints

13. Firms are subject to three main sources or competitive constraints: demand substitutability, supply substitutability and potential competition. From an economic point of view, for the definition of the relevant market, demand substitution constitutes the most immediate and effective disciplinary force on the suppliers of a given product, in particular in relation to their pricing decisions. A firm or a group of firms cannot have a significant impact on the prevailing conditions of sale, such as prices, if its customers are in a position to switch easily to available substitute products or to suppliers located elsewhere. Basically, the exercise of market definition consists in identifying the effective alternative sources of supply for the customers of the undertakings involved, in terms both of products/services and of geographic location of suppliers.

14. The competitive constraints arising from supply side substitutability other than those described in paragraphs 20 to 23 and from potential competition are in general less immediate and in any case require an analysis of additional factors. As a result such constraints are taken into account at the assessment stage of competition analysis.

Demand substitution

15. The assessment of demand substitution entails a determination of the range of products which are viewed as substitutes by the consumer. One way of making this determination can be viewed as a speculative experiment, postulating a hypothetical small, lasting change in relative prices and evaluating the likely reactions of customers to that increase. The exercise of market definition focuses on prices for operational and practical purposes, and more precisely on demand substitution arising from small, permanent changes in relative prices. This concept can provide clear indications as to the evidence that is relevant in defining markets.

16. Conceptually, this approach means that, starting from the type of products that the undertakings involved sell and the area in which they sell them, additional products and areas will be included in, or excluded from, the market definition depending on whether competition from these other products and areas affect or restrain sufficiently the pricing of the parties' products in the short term.

17. The question to be answered is whether the parties' customers would switch to readily available substitutes or to suppliers located elsewhere in response to a hypothetical small (in the range 5% to 10%) but permanent relative price increase in the products and areas being considered. If substitution were enough to make the price increase unprofitable because of the resulting loss of sales, additional substitutes and areas are included in the relevant market. This would be done until the set of products and geographical areas is such that small, permanent increases in relative prices would be profitable. The equivalent analysis is applicable in cases concerning the concentration of buying power, where the starting point would then be the supplier and the price test serves to identify the alternative distribution channels or outlets for the supplier's products. In the application of these principles, careful account should be taken of certain particular situations as described within paragraphs 56 and 58.

18. A practical example of this test can be provided by its application to a merger of, for instance, soft-drink bottlers. An issue to examine in such a case would be to decide whether different flavours of soft drinks belong to the same market. In practice, the question to address would be whether consumers of flavour A would switch to other flavours when confronted with a permanent price increase of 5% to 10% for flavour A. If a sufficient number of consumers would switch to, say, flavour B, to such an extent that the price increase for flavour A would not be profitable owing to the resulting loss of sales, then the market would comprise at least flavours A and B. The process would have to be extended in addition to other available flavours until a set of products is identified for which a price rise would not induce a sufficient substitution in demand.

19. Generally, and in particular for the analysis of merger cases, the price to take into account will be the prevailing market price. This may not be the case where the prevailing price has been determined in the absence of sufficient competition. In particular for the investigation of abuses of dominant positions, the fact that the prevailing price might already have been substantially increased will be taken into account.

Supply substitution

20. Supply-side substitutability may also be taken into account when defining markets in those situations in which its effects are equivalent to those of demand substitution in terms of effectiveness and immediacy. This means that suppliers are able to switch production to the relevant products and market them in the short term[4]

4 That is such a period that does not entail a significant adjustment of existing tangible and intangible assets (see paragraph 23).

without incurring significant additional costs or risks in response to small and permanent changes in relative prices. When these conditions are met, the additional production that is put on the market will have a disciplinary effect on the competitive behaviour of the companies involved. Such an impact in terms of effectiveness and immediacy is equivalent to the demand substitution effect.

21. These situations typically arise when companies market a wide range of qualities or grades of one product; even if, for a given final customer or group of consumers, the different qualities are not substitutable, the different qualities will be grouped into one product market, provided that most of the suppliers are able to offer and sell the various qualities immediately and without the significant increases in costs described above. In such cases, the relevant product market will encompass all products that are substitutable in demand and supply, and the current sales of those products will be aggregated so as to give the total value or volume of the market. The same reasoning may lead to group different geographic areas.

22. A practical example of the approach to supply-side substitutability when defining product markets is to be found in the case of paper. Paper is usually supplied in a range of different qualities, from standard writing paper to high quality papers to be used, for instance, to publish art books. From a demand point of view, different qualities of paper cannot be used for any given use, i.e., an art book or a high quality publication cannot be based on lower quality papers. However, paper plants are prepared to manufacture the different qualities, and production can be adjusted with negligible costs and in a short time-frame. In the absence of particular difficulties in distribution, paper manufacturers are able therefore, to compete for orders of the various qualities, in particular if orders are placed with sufficient lead time to allow for modification of production plans. Under such circumstances, the Commission would not define a separate market for each quality of paper and its respective use. The various qualities of paper are included in the relevant market, and their sales added up to estimate total market value and volume.

23. When supply-side substitutability would entail the need to adjust significantly existing tangible and intangible assets, additional investments, strategic decisions or time delays, it will not be considered at the stage of market definition. Examples where supply-side substitution did not induce the Commission to enlarge the market are offered in the area of consumer products, in particular for branded beverages. Although bottling plants may in principle bottle different beverages, there are costs and lead times involved (in terms of advertising, product testing and distribution) before the products can actually be sold. In these cases, the effects of supply-side substitutability and other forms of potential competition would then be examined at a later stage.

Potential competition

24. The third source of competitive constraint, potential competition, is not taken into account when defining markets, since the conditions under which potential competition will actually represent an effective competitive constraint depend on the analysis of specific factors and circumstances related to the conditions of entry. If required, this analysis is only carried out at a subsequent stage, in general once the position of the companies involved in the relevant market has already been ascertained, and when such position gives rise to concerns from a competition point of view.

Having set out the guiding principles governing practice in this area in Parts I and II of the Notice, the Commission continues to provide practical amplification of the way it assembles evidence relevant to market definition. In Part III it emphasizes that the evidence relied on to define relevant markets does not follow a rigid hierarchy of different sources of information or types of evidence. The Commission will consider *inter alia* evidence of patterns of product substitution or of geographical trends in the recent past, the views of customers and competitors, consumer preferences, and barriers and costs associated with switching demand to potential substitutes. Part IV of the Notice briefly explains how market share is calculated. The full text of the Notice, which runs to 58 paragraphs, is available *via* http://ec.europa.eu/competition/index_en.html.

NOTE: It is constitutionally plain that the Court, not the Commission, serves as the authoritative source of interpretation of Union law. This is made explicit in para 6 of the Notice. However, the Commission's dominant role in the practical administration of competition policy ensures that this Notice enjoys considerable influence in the treatment of cases. A test for determining substitutability based on customer reaction to a 'small [5–10 per cent], non-transitory change in relative prices' (paras 15, 17) is not to be found in such terms in judgments delivered by the Court of Justice, but is instead drawn directly from North American practice. An illustration of the application of this test is provided by Commission Decision 2000/12 1998 *Football World Cup* [2000] OJ L5/55. The market for match tickets for the tournament stood alone from the perspective of the consumer.

It should be obvious from the approach taken in *United Brands* (Case 27/76), that defining a market involves a calculation of the barriers which surround that market (see para 122). Over-estimation of entry barriers leads to unduly narrow market definition, which leads to unnecessary intervention in markets which would correct themselves. At one extreme, even 100 per cent occupation of a market is not a cause for concern where any other firm is able freely to enter that market. Potential competition controls the liberty of the firm in occupation. (See the annulment of an economically inadequate Commission Decision in *Continental Can* v *Commission* (Case 6/72) [1973] ECR 215.) However, the Commission's Notice prefers to treat this not as a matter of market definition, but rather as a (logically subsequent) matter of market power (para 24). In a well-functioning competition law system the stage at which the role of potential competition is taken into account in the analysis should not be of any practical significance to the outcome.

Other classic cases which deserve attention for their approach to market definition include: *Hoffman la Roche* v *Commission* (Case 85/76) [1979] ECR 461; *Michelin* v *Commission* (Case 322/81) [1983] ECR 3461; *Continental Can* v *Commission* (Case 6/72), p. 453; Case T-219/99 *British Airways* v *Commission* [2003] ECR II-5917, from which an appeal was unsuccessful in Case C-95/04P *British Airways* v *Commission* [2007] ECR I-2331.

Comparable issues arise in EU merger control which, since 21 September 1990, has been dealt with under the 'Merger Regulation', the current version of which is Regulation 139/2004 ([2004] OJ L24/1). Like Article 102 TFEU, merger control is motivated by the need to keep a check on market power and the specialized merger regime has many features in common with Article 102. This is evident from the cross-references in the Commission's Notice on Definition of the Relevant Market, p. 486. Article 2(3) of the Merger Regulation provides that:

> A concentration which would significantly impede effective competition, in the common market or in a substantial part of it, in particular as a result of the creation or strengthening of a dominant position, shall be declared incompatible with the common market.

The Commission Decision in M053 *Aerospatiale Alenia/De Havilland* [1991] OJ L334/42, [1992] 4 CMLR M2, provides a good example of the process of market definition under (an earlier version of) the Regulation, covering matters such as substitutability and the impact of governmental regulation of airlines. Once the market was defined to cover specific types of short haul commuter aircraft the merger was blocked as incompatible with the Regulation.

■ QUESTION

Are the EU's institutions consistent in these cases in their approach to the role of potential competition brought about by adaptation of existing techniques? Are they too ready to permit intervention in the market?

B: Abuse

Dominance is not unlawful. Once the firm has been held dominant, it is necessary to decide whether it has abused that dominance. Again, *United Brands* (Case 27/76) provides an example of the types of conduct subject to control.

***United Brands* v *Commission* (Case 27/76)**

[1978] ECR 207, Court of Justice of the European Communities

First, UBC forbade its distributors from reselling bananas when still green. The Commission considered this an abusive tactic, because it effectively prohibited cross-border trade in green bananas. UBC also routinely undersupplied in response to orders so as to force distributors to sell locally rather than seek to penetrate new markets. UBC was controlling the structure of the market.

Secondly, UBC cut off supply of Chiquita bananas to Olesen, a Danish distributor, in response to Olesen's participation in a promotion of Dole bananas, a rival brand.

The third practice condemned by the Commission related to UBC's selling prices, which differed dependent on the customer's Member State. These price differences were imposed at the banana's port of entry into the EU, before any supplement based on transport costs within the EU might have caused such discrepancy.

Finally, the Commission accused UBC of charging unfair prices; prices 'excessive in relation to the economic value of the product supplied'.

[157] [In response to the first practice.] To impose on the ripener the obligation not to resell bananas so long as he has not had them ripened and to cut down the operations of such a ripener to contacts only with retailers is a restriction of competition.

[158] Although it is commendable and lawful to pursue a policy of quality, especially by choosing sellers according to objective criteria relating to the qualifications of the seller, his staff and his facilities, such a practice can only be justified if it does not raise obstacles, the effect of which goes beyond the objective to be attained.

[159] In this case, although these conditions for selection have been laid down in a way which is objective and not discriminatory, the prohibition on resale imposed upon duly appointed Chiquita ripeners and the prohibition of the resale of unbranded bananas – even if the perishable nature of the banana in practice restricted the opportunities of reselling to the duration of a specific period of time – when without any doubt an abuse of the dominant position since they limit markets to the prejudice of consumers and affects trade between Member States, in particular by partitioning national markets.

[160] Thus UBC's organization of the market confined the ripeners to the role of suppliers of the local market and prevented them from developing their capacity to trade *vis-à-vis* UBC, which moreover tightened its economic hold on them by supplying less goods than they ordered.

[161] It follows from all these considerations that the clause at issue forbidding the sale of green bananas infringes Article 86 of the Treaty.

...

[182] [In response to the second practice.] ... [I]t is advisable to assert positively from the outset that an undertaking in a dominant position for the purpose of marketing a product – which cashes in on the reputation of a brand name known to and valued by the consumers – cannot stop supplying a long standing customer who abides by regular commercial practice, if the orders placed by that customer are in no way out of the ordinary.

[183] Such conduct is inconsistent with the objectives laid down in Article 3(f) of the Treaty, which are set out in detail in Article 86, especially in paragraphs (b) and (c), since the refusal to sell would limit markets to the prejudice of consumers and would amount to discrimination which might in the end eliminate a trading party from the relevant market.

[184] It is therefore necessary to ascertain whether the discontinuance of supplies by UBC in October 1973 was justified.

[185] The reason given is in the applicant's letter of 11 October 1973 in which it upbraided Olesen in no uncertain manner for having participated in an advertising campaign for one of its competitors.

[186] Later on UBC added to this reason a number of complaints, for example, that Olesen was the exclusive representative of its main competitor on the Danish market.

[187] This was not a new situation since it goes back to 1969 and was not in any case inconsistent with fair trade practices.

[188] Finally UBC has not put forward any relevant argument to justify the refusal of supplies.

[189] Although it is true, as the applicant points out, that the fact that an undertaking is in a dominant position cannot disentitle it from protecting its own commercial interests if they are attacked, and that such an undertaking must be conceded the right to take such reasonable steps as it deems appropriate to protect its said interests, such behaviour cannot be countenanced if its actual purpose is to strengthen this dominant position and abuse it.

[190] Even if the possibility of a counter-attack is acceptable that attack must still be proportionate to the threat taking into account the economic strength of the undertakings confronting each other.

[191] The sanction consisting of a refusal to supply by an undertaking in a dominant position was in excess of what might, if such a situation were to arise, reasonably be contemplated as a sanction for conduct similar to that for which UBC blamed Olesen.

[192] In fact UBC could not be unaware of that fact that by acting in this way it would discourage its other ripener/distributors from supporting the advertising of other brand names and that the deterrent effect of the sanction imposed upon one of them would make its position of strength on the relevant market that much more effective.

[193] Such a course of conduct amounts therefore to a serious interference with the independence of small and medium sized firms in their commercial relations with the undertaking in a dominant position and this independence implies the right to give preference to competitors' goods.

[194] In this case the adoption of such a course of conduct is designed to have a serious adverse effect on competition on the relevant banana market by only allowing firms dependant upon the dominant undertaking to stay in business.

. . .

[227] [In response to the third practice.] Although the responsibility for establishing the single banana market does not lie with the applicant, it can only endeavour to take 'what the market can bear' provided that it complies with the rules for the regulation and coordination of the market laid down by the Treaty.

[228] Once it can be grasped that differences in transport costs, taxation, customs duties, the wages of the labour force, the conditions of marketing, the differences in the parity of currencies, the density of competition may eventually culminate in different retail selling price levels according to the Member States, then it follows those differences are factors which UBC only has to take into account to a limited extent since it sells a product which is always the same and at the same place to ripener/distributors who – alone – bear the risks of the consumers' market.

[229] The interplay of supply and demand should, owing to its nature, only be applied to each stage where it is really manifest.

[230] The mechanisms of the market are adversely affected if the price is calculated by leaving out one stage of the market and taking into account the law of supply and demand as between the vendor and the ultimate consumer and not as between the vendor (UBC) and the purchaser (the ripener/ distributors).

[231] Thus, by reason of its dominant position UBC, fed with information by its local representatives, was in fact able to impose its selling price on the intermediate purchaser. This price and also the 'weekly quota allocated' is only fixed and notified to the customer four days before the vessel carrying the bananas berths.

[232] These discriminatory prices, which varied according to the circumstances of the Member States, were just so many obstacles to the free movement of goods and their effect was intensified by the clause forbidding the resale of bananas while still green and by reducing the deliveries of the quantities ordered.

[233] A rigid partitioning of national markets was thus created at price levels, which were artificially different, placing certain distributor/ripeners at a competitive disadvantage, since compared with what it should have been competition had thereby been distorted.

[234] Consequently the policy of differing prices enabling UBC to apply dissimilar conditions to equivalent transactions with other trading parties, thereby placing them at a competitive disadvantage, was an abuse of a dominant position.

. . .

[248] [In response to the last practice.] The imposition by an undertaking in a dominant position directly or indirectly of unfair purchase or selling prices is an abuse to which exception can be taken under Article 86 of the Treaty.

[249] It is advisable therefore to ascertain whether the dominant undertaking has made use of the opportunities arising out of its dominant position in such a way as to reap trading benefits which it would not have reaped if there had been normal and sufficiently effective competition.

[250] In this case charging a price which is excessive because it has no reasonable relation to the economic value of the product supplied would be such an abuse.

[251] This excess could, *inter alia*, be determined objectively if it were possible for it to be calculated by making a comparison between the selling price of the product in question and its cost of production, which would disclose the amount of the profit margin; however the Commission has not done this since it has not analysed UBC's costs structure.

[252] The questions therefore to be determined are whether the difference between the costs actually incurred and the price actually charged is excessive, and, if the answer to this question is in the affirmative, whether a price has been imposed which is either unfair in itself or when compared to competing products.

The Court decided that the Commission had not proved this last allegation and annulled this part of the Decision.

NOTE: Unfairness in pricing is obviously hard to pin down. For discussion see R. Whish and D. Bailey, *Competition Law* (Oxford: OUP, 2015), Ch. 18.

■ QUESTION

Consider which aspects of United Brands' policy were likely to exploit consumers directly; and which were more indirect in that they served to reduce or suppress competition. Article 102 TFEU is broad enough to cover both types of practice.

NOTE: One of the several matters considered in *United Brands* (Case 27/76) was the conduct of a dominant firm towards the supply of its customers. The circumstances in which this may involve an 'abuse' offers a helpful insight into the nature and purpose of Article 102. The Court accepts that the dominant firm is precluded from arbitrary conduct (paras 182–189). The precise nature of the control exercised in this area depends on the nature of the market in issue. The next case is an important decision on abusive refusal to supply.

***Istituto Chemicoterapico Italiano SpA and Commercial Solvents Corporation* v *Commission* (Cases 6 and 7/73)**

[1974] ECR 223, Court of Justice of the European Communities

Commercial Solvents (CSC) stopped supplying Zoja with aminobutanol, a raw material used in the production of ethambutol. The Commission held CSC dominant in the market for aminobutanol. The firm challenged the subsequent finding that it had abused that dominance by refusing to continue supplies to Zoja.

[23] The applicants state that they ought not to be held responsible for stopping supplies of aminobutanol to Zoja for this was due to the fact that in the spring of 1970 Zoja itself informed Istituto that it was cancelling the purchase of large quantities of aminobutanol which had been provided for in a contract then in force between Istituto and Zoja. When at the end of 1970 Zoja again contacted Istituto to obtain this product, the latter was obliged to reply, after consulting CSC, that in the meantime CSC had changed its commercial

policy and that the product was no longer available. The change of policy by CSC was, they claim, inspired by a legitimate consideration of the advantage that would accrue to it of expanding its production to include the manufacture of finished products and not limiting itself to that of raw material or intermediate products. In pursuance of this policy it decided to improve its product and no longer to supply aminobutanol save in respect of commitments already entered into by its distributors.

[24] It appears from the documents and from the hearing that the suppliers of raw material are limited, as regards the EEC, to Istituto, which, as stated in the claim by CSC, started in 1968 to develop its own specialities based on ethambutol, and in November 1969 obtained the approval of the Italian government necessary for the manufacture and in 1970 started manufacturing its own specialities. When Zoja sought to obtain further supplies of aminobutanol, it received a negative reply. CSC had decided to limit, if not completely to cease, the supply of nitropropane and aminobutanol to certain parties in order to facilitate its own access to the market for the derivatives.

[25] However, an undertaking being in a dominant position as regards the production of raw material and therefore able to control the supply to manufacturers of derivatives, cannot, just because it decides to start manufacturing these derivatives (in competition with its former customers) act in such a way as to eliminate their competition which in the case in question, would amount to eliminating one of the principal manufacturers of ethambutol in the Common Market. Since such conduct is contrary to the objectives expressed in Article 3(f) of the Treaty and set out in greater detail in Articles 85 and 86, it follows that an undertaking which has a dominant position in the market in raw materials and which, with the object of reserving such raw material for manufacturing its own derivatives, refuses to supply a customer, which is itself a manufacturer of these derivatives, and therefore risks eliminating all competition on the part of this customer, is abusing its dominant position within the meaning of Article 86. In this context it does not matter that the undertaking ceased to supply in the spring of 1970 because of the cancellation of the purchases by Zoja, because it appears from the applicants' own statement that, when the supplies provided for in the contract had been completed, the sale of aminobutanol would have stopped in any case.

[26] It is also unnecessary to examine, as the applicants have asked, whether Zoja had an urgent need for aminobutanol in 1970 and 1971 or whether this company still had large quantities of this product which would enable it to reorganize its production in good time, since that question is not relevant to the consideration of the conduct of the applicants.

The Court upheld the finding of abuse.

NOTE: A different market yielded a different result in the next case.

BP v *Commission* (Case 77/77)

[1978] ECR 1511, Court of Justice of the European Communities

The Commission found abusive BP's reduction in supply of oil to ABG, a Dutch customer, during the oil crisis of the early 1970s. The Court disagreed.

[28] It emerges from the contested decision that the fact that BP in November 1972 terminated its commercial relations with ABG was connected with the regrouping of BP's operational activities which was made necessary by the nationalization of a large part of that company's interests in the production sector and by the participation of the producer countries in its extracting activities and is thus explained by considerations which have nothing to do with its relations with ABG.

[29] It therefore follows that at the time of the crisis and even from November 1972, ABG's position in relation to BP was no longer, as regards the supply of motor spirit, that of a contractual customer but that of an occasional customer.

[30] The principle laid down by the contested decision that reductions in supplies ought to have been carried out on the basis of a reference period fixed in the year before the crisis, although it may be explicable in cases in which a continued supply relationship has been maintained, during that period, between seller and purchaser, cannot be applied when the supplier ceased during the course of that same period to carry on such relations with its customer, regard being had in particular to the fact that the plans of any undertaking are normally based on reasonable forecasts.

[31] Moreover, the advances in petrol against crude oil agreed to by BP in pursuance of the processing agreement, as they occur within the context of an agreement whose purpose was solely the refining of crude oil supplied by ABG and not the supplying of ABG with motor spirit, cannot serve as a valid argument to compare ABG's position in this case in relation to BP with that of a traditional customer of BP during the above-mentioned reference period.

[32] For all these reasons, since ABG's position in relation to BP had been, for several months before the crisis occurred, that of an occasional customer, BP cannot be accused of having applied to it during the crisis less favourable treatment than that which it reserved for its traditional customers.

NOTE: Broadly, this type of intervention can be justified as an attempt to preserve vestiges of competition and to curb potential inefficiencies flowing from the dominator's tactics. However, the concept of 'abuse' is slippery. The cases have, not surprisingly, aroused concern about the nature of the policy pursued and the depth of intervention asserted, especially into practices that tend to exclude potential competition. In the next case the Court upheld the Commission's extension of control to cover a refusal to supply a first-time customer.

***Radio Téléfis Eireann and Independent Television Publications* v *Commission* (Cases C-241/91P, C-242/91P)**

[1995] ECR I-801, Court of Justice of the European Communities

Three British and Irish television companies, RTE, BBC, and ITP, held copyright over programme listings. Each produced a guide to its own programmes, but they did not produce a single guide available to Irish consumers containing the combined listings. Third party publishers were unable to produce a comprehensive guide, because the companies refused to license use of the copyright-protected material. The Court of First Instance (now the General Court) rejected an application for the annulment of the Commission Decision that the companies were abusing their dominant position (Case T-69/89 [1991] ECR II-485). The companies' appeal to the Court of Justice was also unsuccessful. In reading this extract from the judgment remember that Article 86 should be read with post-Lisbon eyes as Article 102.

[52] Among the circumstances taken into account by the Court of First Instance in concluding that such conduct was abusive was, first, the fact that there was, according to the findings of the Court of First Instance, no actual or potential substitute for a weekly television guide offering information on the programmes for the week ahead. On this point, the Court of First Instance confirmed the Commission's finding that the complete lists of programmes for a 24-hour period – and for a 48-hour period at weekends and before public holidays – published in certain daily and Sunday newspapers, and the television sections of certain magazines covering, in addition, 'highlights' of the week's programmes, were only to a limited extent substitutable for advance information to viewers on all the week's programmes. Only weekly television guides containing comprehensive listings for the week ahead would enable users to decide in advance which programmes they wished to follow and arrange their leisure activities for the week accordingly. The Court of First Instance also established that there was a specific, constant and regular potential demand on the part of consumers (see the *RTE* judgment, paragraph 62, and the *ITP* judgment, paragraph 48).

[53] Thus the appellants – who were, by force of circumstances, the only sources of the basic information on programme scheduling which is the indispensable raw material for compiling a weekly television guide – gave viewers wishing to obtain information on the choice of programmes for the week ahead no choice but to buy the weekly guides for each station and draw from each of them the information they needed to make comparisons.

[54] The appellants' refusal to provide basic information by relying on national copyright provisions thus prevented the appearance of a new product, a comprehensive weekly guide to television programmes, which the appellants did not offer and for which there was a potential consumer demand. Such refusal constitutes an abuse under heading (b) of the second paragraph of Article 86 of the Treaty.

[55] Second, there was no justification for such refusal either in the activity of television broadcasting or in that of publishing television magazines (*RTE* judgment, paragraph 73, and *ITP* judgment, paragraph 58).

[56] Third, and finally, as the Court of First Instance also held, the appellants, by their conduct, reserved to themselves the secondary market of weekly television guides by excluding all competition on that market (see the judgment in Joined Cases 6/73 and 7/73 *Commercial Solvents* v *Commission* [1974] ECR 223, paragraph 25) since they denied access to the basic information which is the raw material indispensable for the compilation of such a guide.

[57] In the light of all those circumstances, the Court of First Instance did not err in law in holding that the appellants' conduct was an abuse of a dominant position within the meaning of Article 86 of the Treaty.

NOTE: The decision is remarkable for its assertion of control of the firms' exercise of exclusive rights under national copyright law. P. Crowther comments that '[t]aken literally, the court's pronouncement on the fact that the copyright was used to restrict competition on a derivative market leaves the owner of an intellectual property right in a very precarious position . . . the upshot . . . is that owners of intellectual property rights, controlling "indispensable raw materials", might think twice about launching expensive R[esearch] & D[evelopment] programmes' ((1995) 20 EL Rev 521, 528).

■ QUESTION

Did the Court establish a satisfactory balance between the consumer interest in a market that is currently competitive and the consumer interest in a market which encourages innovators by rewarding them through shelter from competition?

NOTE: The economic circumstances prevailing in the market for television guides were unusual: supply was essential to the third party and the refusal prevented the introduction of a new product subject to consumer demand. Imposition of an obligation to contract on the dominant firm is exceptional, as the next case reveals.

Oscar Bronner GmbH & Co. KG v *Mediaprint* (Case C-7/97)

[1998] ECR I-7791, Court of Justice of the European Communities

This was a preliminary reference made by an Austrian court. Mediaprint, a publisher, had established a nationwide home-delivery scheme for newspapers. No competing facility existed in Austria. Oscar Bronner claimed that Mediaprint was acting in breach of the Treaty by refusing to include Bronner's newspaper, *Der Standard*, in the delivery service (for which Bronner was prepared to pay). Mediaprint pointed to the considerable investment it had made in developing the service and submitted that even though it held considerable market power in the Austrian daily newspaper market, it was not obliged to assist competing companies by allowing access to its facility. The Court agreed with Mediaprint.

[32] In examining whether an undertaking holds a dominant position within the meaning of Article 86 [now 102] of the Treaty, it is of fundamental importance, as the Court has emphasised many times, to define the market in question and to define the substantial part of the common market in which the undertaking may be able to engage in abuses which hinder effective competition (Case C-242/95 *GT-Link* v *DSB* [1997] ECR I-4449, paragraph 36).

[33] It is settled case-law that, for the purposes of applying Article 86 of the Treaty, the market for the product or service in question comprises all the products or services which in view of their characteristics are particularly suited to satisfy constant needs and are only to a limited extent interchangeable with other products or services (Case 31/80 *L'Oréal* v *De Nieuwe AMCK* [1980] ECR 3775, paragraph 25; Case C-62/86 *AKZO* v *Commission* [1991] ECR I-3359, paragraph 51).

[34] As regards the definition of the market at issue in the main proceedings, it is therefore for the national court to determine, *inter alia*, whether home-delivery schemes constitute a separate market, or whether other methods of distributing daily newspapers, such as sale in shops or at kiosks or delivery by post, are sufficiently interchangeable with them to have to be taken into account also. In deciding whether there is a dominant position the court must also take account, as the Commission has emphasised, of the possible existence of regional home-delivery schemes.

[35] If that examination leads the national court to conclude that a separate market in home-delivery schemes does exist, and that there is an insufficient degree of interchangeability between Mediaprint's nationwide scheme and other, regional, schemes, it must hold that Mediaprint, which according to the information in the order for reference operates the only nationwide home-delivery service in Austria, is de facto in a monopoly situation in the market thus defined, and thus holds a dominant position in it.

[36] In that event, the national court would also have to find that Mediaprint holds a dominant position in a substantial part of the common market, since the case-law indicates that the territory of a Member State over which a dominant position extends is capable of constituting a substantial part of the common market (see, to that effect, Case 322/81 *Michelin* v *Commission* [1983] ECR 3461, paragraph 28; Case C-323/93 *Centre d'Insémination de la Crespelle* [1994] ECR I-5077, paragraph 17).

[37] Finally, it would need to be determined whether the refusal by the owner of the only nationwide home-delivery scheme in the territory of a Member State, which uses that scheme to distribute its own daily newspapers, to allow the publisher of a rival daily newspaper access to it constitutes an abuse of a dominant position within the meaning of Article 86 of the Treaty, on the ground that such refusal deprives that competitor of a means of distribution judged essential for the sale of its newspaper.

[38] Although in *Commercial Solvents* v *Commission* [Cases 6 & 7/73 p. 491] and *CBEM* v *CLT and IPB* [Case 311/84 [1985] ECR 3261] cited above, the Court of Justice held the refusal by an undertaking holding a dominant position in a given market to supply an undertaking with which it was in competition in a neighbouring market with raw materials (*Commercial Solvents* v *Commission*, paragraph 25) and services (*CBEM*, paragraph 26) respectively, which were indispensable to carrying on the rival's business, to constitute an abuse, it should be noted, first, that the Court did so to the extent that the conduct in question was likely to eliminate all competition on the part of that undertaking.

[39] Secondly, in *Magill* [Cases C-241/91P, C-242/91P *RTE and ITP* v *Commission*], at paragraphs 49 and 50, the Court held that refusal by the owner of an intellectual property right to grant a licence, even if it is the act of an undertaking holding a dominant position, cannot in itself constitute abuse of a dominant position, but that the exercise of an exclusive right by the proprietor may, in exceptional circumstances, involve an abuse.

[40] In *Magill*, the Court found such exceptional circumstances in the fact that the refusal in question concerned a product (information on the weekly schedules of certain television channels) the supply of which was indispensable for carrying on the business in question (the publishing of a general television guide), in that, without that information, the person wishing to produce such a guide would find it impossible to publish it and offer it for sale (paragraph 53), the fact that such refusal prevented the appearance of a new product for which there was a potential consumer demand (paragraph 54), the fact that it was not justified by objective considerations (paragraph 55), and that it was likely to exclude all competition in the secondary market of television guides (paragraph 56).

[41] Therefore, even if that case-law on the exercise of an intellectual property right were applicable to the exercise of any property right whatever, it would still be necessary, for the *Magill* judgment to be effectively relied upon in order to plead the existence of an abuse within the meaning of Article 86 of the Treaty in a situation such as that which forms the subject-matter of the first question, not only that the refusal of the service comprised in home delivery be likely to eliminate all competition in the daily newspaper market on the part of the person requesting the service and that such refusal be incapable of being objectively justified, but also that the service in itself be indispensable to carrying on that person's business, inasmuch as there is no actual or potential substitute in existence for that home-delivery scheme.

[42] That is certainly not the case even if, as in the case which is the subject of the main proceedings, there is only one nationwide home-delivery scheme in the territory of a Member State and, moreover, the owner of that scheme holds a dominant position in the market for services constituted by that scheme or of which it forms part.

[43] In the first place, it is undisputed that other methods of distributing daily newspapers, such as by post and through sale in shops and at kiosks, even though they may be less advantageous for the distribution of certain newspapers, exist and are used by the publishers of those daily newspapers.

[44] Moreover, it does not appear that there are any technical, legal or even economic obstacles capable of making it impossible, or even unreasonably difficult, for any other publisher of daily newspapers to establish, alone or in cooperation with other publishers, its own nationwide home-delivery scheme and use it to distribute its own daily newspapers.

[45] It should be emphasised in that respect that, in order to demonstrate that the creation of such a system is not a realistic potential alternative and that access to the existing system is therefore indispensable, it is not enough to argue that it is not economically viable by reason of the small circulation of the daily newspaper or newspapers to be distributed.

[46] For such access to be capable of being regarded as indispensable, it would be necessary at the very least to establish, as the Advocate General has pointed out at point 68 of his Opinion, that it is not economically viable to create a second home-delivery scheme for the distribution of daily newspapers with a circulation comparable to that of the daily newspapers distributed by the existing scheme.

[47] In the light of the foregoing considerations, the answer to the first question must be that the refusal by a press undertaking which holds a very large share of the daily newspaper market in a Member State and operates the only nationwide newspaper home-delivery scheme in that Member State to allow the publisher of a rival newspaper, which by reason of its small circulation is unable either alone or in cooperation with other publishers to set up and operate its own home-delivery scheme in economically reasonable conditions, to have access to that scheme for appropriate remuneration does not constitute abuse of a dominant position within the meaning of Article 86 of the Treaty.

In the next case the Court took a further opportunity to confirm that the intervention of what is now Article 102 TFEU into intellectual property rights which it authorized in *RTE* and *ITP* (Cases C-241/91P, C-242/91P) is to be treated as exceptional. It reviewed its decision in *Oscar Bronner* (Case C-7/97) and then set out the conditions that must be satisfied before abusive conduct within the meaning of Article 102 TFEU may be found in a refusal to supply by an owner of intellectual property.

IMS Health GmbH (Case C-418/01)

[2004] ECR I-5039, Court of Justice of the European Communities

[52] . . . the refusal by an undertaking which holds a dominant position and owns an intellectual property right in a brick structure indispensable to the presentation of regional sales data on pharmaceutical products in a Member State to grant a licence to use that structure to another undertaking which also wishes to provide such data in the same Member State, constitutes an abuse of a dominant position within the meaning of Article 82 EC where the following conditions are fulfilled:

- the undertaking which requested the licence intends to offer, on the market for the supply of the data in question, new products or services not offered by the owner of the intellectual property right and for which there is a potential consumer demand;
- the refusal is not justified by objective considerations;
- the refusal is such as to reserve to the owner of the intellectual property right the market for the supply of data on sales of pharmaceutical products in the Member State concerned by eliminating all competition on that market.

NOTE: The Commission has fined Microsoft for violation of what is now Article 102 TFEU for (*inter alia*) its refusal to supply interoperability information concerning its programmes. This is another example of exclusionary tactics employed by a dominant firm – and also another example of how intervention may be criticized for its dissuasive effect on incentives to innovate. Extended litigation was pursued: see in particular Case T-201/04 *Microsoft* v *Commission* [2007] ECR II-3601 and Case T-167/08 *Microsoft* v *Commission* judgment of 27 June 2012.

Article 101 TFEU has been 'modernized' – *inter alia* by the release of the Commission's exclusive grip over Article 101(3) exemption (Regulation 1/2003) and by reform of the law governing vertical restraints (Regulations 2790/1999 and now 330/2010). The Commission then turned to reform of Article 102 TFEU in order to provide a more predictable and clear regime. A long-standing criticism of Commission practice has been the perception that it has used this Treaty provision to protect not only consumers but also small rivals of the dominant firm (see e.g. A. Pathak, 'Vertical Restraints in EEC Competition Law' [1988/2] LIEI 15). Without explicitly conceding past sins, the Commission has committed itself in future to an application of Article 102 to practices that exclude competition which will be informed by identification of harm to the interests of consumers and the competitive process, but which will not be designed to protect actual or potential competitors as such. The logic of this is that it is open to dominant firms to show that practices which tend to exclude rivals are efficient: the consequence in law of such economic analysis would be that there is no 'abuse' within the meaning of Article 102 TFEU. Guidance on Commission enforcement priorities in cases of exclusionary conduct by dominant firms was published in February 2009, [2009] OJ C45/7. The relevant Commission documentation is available *via* http://ec.europa.eu/competition/index_en.html and for comment see P. Akman, (2010) 73 MLR 605; A. Witt, (2010) 35 EL Rev 214.

Determination to consider refusal to supply in the particular economic context in which it occurs is not a current preoccupation of the Commission alone. In *Sot. Lelos kai Sia* (Joined Cases C-468/06 to C-478/06) [2008] ECR I-7139, which concerns the market for pharmaceuticals, the Court agreed that a dominant firm could in some circumstances refuse to meet orders likely to fuel parallel trade. The generally favourable attitude of EU competition to parallel trade as a motor for the integration of markets in the EU was acknowledged (paras 37, 65–6; and see p. 468), but the context of individual markets must be taken into account. Here the distortive effect of state price regulation in pharmaceutical markets made parallel trade attractive to importers, but the Court was persuaded that the consequent risk that suppliers would simply prefer not to operate in markets where prices are particularly low for fear of losing profits in other markets was not in the consumer interest. So a dominant seller can take reasonable and proportionate measures to protect its commercial interests, which might include refusing orders that are out of the ordinary and/or go beyond what is needed for the target market. This is a worryingly unpredictable test (Kingston, S., 'Annotation' (2009) 46 CML Rev 683) but the general message is that the Court will not pursue market integration as a non-negotiable priority.

■ QUESTION

Alpha plc is the sole UK manufacturer of Brillyarn, and its output of Brillyarn constitutes 50 per cent of production of the fibre in the EU. There are only two other EU producers: Heinz, a German firm responsible for 30 per cent of the EU output; and Ventoux, a French firm responsible for the remaining 20 per cent of EU production.

Brillyarn cannot be manufactured without the constituent material, 'Coralfoam'. The only supplier of 'Coralfoam' presently active in the EU is an Italian firm, Donadoni, although several American companies also produce 'Coralfoam', but have not attempted to enter the European market due to the costs of transporting 'Coralfoam' across the Atlantic.

Donadoni has supplied Alpha with 'Coralfoam' for six years, since the discovery of the process for manufacturing Brillyarn. However, when Alpha orders an increase in supplies of 'Coralfoam' as part of an expansion programme, Donadoni rejects the order and informs Alpha that it no longer intends to do business with it. Donadoni explains that it has concluded an exclusive dealing contract with Heinz, designed to permit Heinz to purchase all Donadoni's supplies of 'Coralfoam' with a view to rapid expansion.

Alpha seeks your advice as to whether any infringements of the EU Treaty have been committed.

Advise Alpha.

How, if at all, would your answer differ if Donadoni had agreed to continue supplying Alpha but had insisted on an immediate 50 per cent price increase?

SECTION 4: STATE INVOLVEMENT

What if the State is involved in the practice which causes market distortion? The approach of EU law depends on the precise nature of State participation. If the State is simply pursuing a commercial activity in, perhaps, the guise of a nationalized industry, then Articles 101 and 102 may apply in the normal way (e.g., *Aluminium Products* [1985] OJ L92/1). If the body is a public undertaking or an undertaking to which the State grants special or exclusive rights, Article 106 TFEU applies. Article 106 requires conformity with the requirements of Articles 101 and 102, but offers exception in its second paragraph where this is necessary to enable the entity to perform its assigned tasks. This is a narrow exception. Where the State obstructs cross-border trade in goods by legislative or administrative action, Article 34 applies (Chapter 10). So the price-fixing cases such as *Tasca* (Case 65/75) (discussed at p. 295) involve obligations imposed on private firms to set prices within certain bands, but the measure caught by EU law is the State compulsion which falls within the definition of Article 34's prohibition on MEQRs. The State which subsidizes domestic industry is liable to distort the market. Article 107 TFEU controls State aids.

Where the State legislates to permit or encourage a breach of the competition rules, then not only do the parties to the agreement act in breach of the Treaty, but also the State has violated its duty to co-operate in the pursuit of the objectives of the EU. It may be in breach of what was Article 10 EC pre-Lisbon, Article 5 pre-Amsterdam, and now, in amended form, Article 4(3) TEU, applied in conjunction with the Treaty competition provisions. In the next case, the issue arose in relation to State approval of airline fare structures.

Ahmed Saeed Flugreisen v Zentrale zur Bekämpfung unlauteren Wettbewerbs (Case 66/86)

[1989] ECR 803, Court of Justice of the European Communities

[48] ... [I]t should be borne in mind in the first place that, as the Court has consistently held, while it is true that the competition rules set out in Articles 85 and 86 [now 101 and 102] concern the conduct of undertakings and not measures of the authorities in the Member States, Article 5 of the Treaty [now in amended form 4(3) TEU] nevertheless imposes a duty on those authorities not to adopt or maintain in force any measure which could deprive those competition rules of their effectiveness. That would be the case, in particular, if a Member State were to require or favour the adoption of agreements, decisions or concerted practices contrary to Article 85 or reinforce their effects ...

[49] It must be concluded as a result that the approval by the aeronautical authorities of tariff agreements contrary to Article 85(1) is not compatible with Community law and in particular with Article 5 of the Treaty. It also follows that the aeronautical authorities must refrain from taking any measure which might be construed as encouraging airlines to conclude tariff agreements contrary to the Treaty.

[50] In the specific case of tariffs for scheduled flights that interpretation of the Treaty is borne out by Article 90(1) of the Treaty [now 106 TFEU], which provides that in the case of undertakings to which Member States grant special or exclusive rights – such as rights to operate on an air route alone or with one or two other undertakings – Member States must not enact or maintain in force any measure contrary to the competition rules laid down in Articles 85 and 86. Moreover, it is stated in the preambles to Council Regulations Nos 3975 and 3976/87 that those regulations do not prejudge the application of Article 90 of the Treaty.

[51] Admittedly, in the preamble to Regulation No 3976/87 the Council expressed a desire to increase competition in air transport services between Member States gradually so as to provide time for the sector concerned to adapt to a system different from the present system of establishing a network of agreements between Member States and air carriers. However, that concern can be respected only within the limits laid down by the provisions of the Treaty.

[52] Whilst, as a result, the new rules laid down by the Council and the Commission leave the Community institutions and the authorities in the Member States free to encourage the airlines to organize mutual consultations on the tariffs to be applied on certain routes served by scheduled flights, such as the consultations provided for in Directive 87/601/EEC, the Treaty nevertheless strictly prohibits them from giving encouragement, in any form whatsoever, to the adoption of agreements or concerted practices with regard to tariffs contrary to Article 85(1) or Article 86, as the case may be.

[53] The national court also refers to Article 90(3), but that provision appears to be of no relevance for the purpose of resolving the problems raised by this case. That provision places the Commission under a duty to ensure the application of the provisions of Article 90 and to address, where necessary, appropriate directives or decisions to Member States; it does not, however, preclude the application of paragraphs (1) and (2) of that article where the Commission fails to act.

[54] In contrast, Article 90(2) might entail consequences for decisions by the aeronautical authorities with regard to the approval of tariffs. That provision provides *inter alia* that undertakings entrusted with the operation of services of general economic interest are to be subject to the competition rules contained in the Treaty, in so far however as the application of such rules does not obstruct the performance of the particular tasks assigned to them.

[55] That provision may be applied to carriers who may be obliged, by the public authorities, to operate on routes which are not commercially viable but which it is necessary to operate for reasons of the general interest. It is necessary in each case for the competent national administrative or judicial authorities to establish whether the airline in question has actually been entrusted with the task of operating on such routes by an act of the public authority (judgment of 27 March 1974 in Case 127/73 *Belgische Radio en Televisie* v *Sabam* (*'BRT-II'*) [1974] ECR 313).

[56] However, for it to be possible for the effect of the competition rules to be restricted pursuant to Article 90(2) by needs arising from performance of a task of general interest, the national authorities responsible for the approval of tariffs and the courts to which disputes relating thereto are submitted must be able to determine the exact nature of the needs in question and their impact on the structure of the tariffs applied by the airlines in question.

[57] Indeed, where there is no effective transparency of the tariff structure it is difficult, if not impossible, to assess the influence of the task of general interest on the application of the competition rules in the field of tariffs. It is for the national court to make the necessary findings of fact in that connection.

[58] It follows from the foregoing considerations that it should be stated in reply to the third question submitted by the national court that Articles 5 and 90 of the EEC Treaty must be interpreted as:

- (i) prohibiting the national authorities from encouraging the conclusion of agreements on tariffs contrary to Article 85(1) or Article 86 of the Treaty, as the case may be;
- (ii) precluding the approval by those authorities of tariffs resulting from such agreements;
- (iii) not precluding a limitation of the effects of the competition rules in so far as it is indispensable for the performance of a task of general interest which air carriers are required to carry out, provided that the nature of that task and its impact on the tariff structure are clearly established.

NOTE: German legislation which restricted the growth of a market in employment procurement services was at issue in the next case. The Court made it clear that a State which nurtures an uncompetitive market may violate the Treaty rules. The result of the application of the Treaty rules is market liberalization.

Höfner v *Macrotron* (Case C-41/90)

[1991] ECR I-1979, Court of Justice of the European Communities

> [34] . . . [A] public employment agency engaged in employment procurement activities is subject to the prohibition contained in Article 86 of the Treaty [now Article 102], so long as the application of that provision does not obstruct the performance of the particular task assigned to it. A Member State which has conferred an exclusive right to carry on that activity upon the public employment agency is in breach of Article 90(1) of the Treaty [now Article 106(1) TFEU] where it creates a situation in which that agency cannot avoid infringing Article 86 of the Treaty [now Article 102]. That is the case, in particular, where the following conditions are satisfied:
>
> — the exclusive right extends to executive recruitment activities;
> — the public employment agency is manifestly incapable of satisfying demand prevailing on the market for such activities;
> — the actual pursuit of those activities by private recruitment consultants is rendered impossible by the maintenance in force of a statutory provision under which such activities are prohibited and non-observance of that prohibition renders the contracts concerned void;
> — the activities in question may extend to the nationals or to the territory of other Member States.

NOTE: The EU's supervision of (allegedly) anticompetitive State laws has given rise to challenges to long-standing national monopolies in areas important to the citizen such as energy supply and telecommunications. It is beyond the scope of this book to provide extended coverage. Its purpose is simply to alert the reader to the shape of the law and, in particular, to the wide scope of EU trade law, which is capable of being used to challenge national assumptions about the way in which services are delivered to the public. A good source of further reading is Sauter, W., *Public Services in EU Law* (Cambridge: CUP, 2014). Nevertheless, the Court does not assert a general power to supervise all State intervention in the market. It is necessary to establish the application of one or more specific Treaty provisions. In the next case the Court picks its way carefully through the Treaty provisions to which reference is made by the national court and concludes that none prevents the application of the Italian rules in question.

DIP SpA v *Comune di Bassano del Grappa* (Case C-140/94), *LIDL Italia SrL* v *Comune di Chioggia* (Case C-141/94), *Lingral SrL* v *Comune di Chioggia* (Case C-142/94)

[1995] ECR I-3257, Court of Justice of the European Communities

The three applicants had been refused licences to open retail premises. Under the relevant Italian legislation, opening a new shop is subject to the issue of a licence by the local mayor on the opinion of a municipal committee, taking into account the criteria laid down in a commercial development plan drawn up by each municipality after consulting the committee. The committee membership is determined by law and its precise composition differs depending whether the municipality has more or fewer than 50,000 inhabitants. However, in either instance, members include public officials, an urban planning expert and traffic expert appointed by the town council, experts on distribution problems appointed with the involvement of trade and consumer representative organizations, and, finally, workers' representatives. The Court first considered whether the State could be held in violation of Article 5 read with Articles 85 and 86 of the EC Treaty (now in amended form Article 4(3) TEU read with Articles 101 and

102 TFEU) by introducing or maintaining in force measures which may render ineffective the competition rules applicable to undertakings. It stated that:

[15] The Court has held that Articles 5 and 85 are infringed where a Member State requires or favours the adoption of agreements, decisions or concerted practices contrary to Article 85 or reinforces their effects, or where it deprives its own rules of the character of legislation by delegating to private economic operators responsibility for taking decisions affecting the economic sphere.

The Court continued:

[17] As regards rules such as those contained in the Italian Law, it should first be pointed out that members appointed or nominated by traders' organisations are in a minority on the municipal committees, side by side with workers' representatives, representatives of public authorities and experts appointed by the latter.

[18] Moreover, as expressly indicated in that law, the members appointed or nominated by traders' organisations are present as experts on distribution problems and not in order to represent their own business interests, and in drawing up its opinions the municipal committee is to observe the public interest.

[19] It follows from the foregoing considerations that in a trading licence system such as that established by the Italian Law, the opinions adopted by the municipal committee cannot be regarded as agreements between traders which the public authorities have required or favoured or the effects of which they have reinforced.

[20] It must next be considered . . . whether the public authorities have delegated their powers in the matter of trading licences to private economic operators.

[21] The Italian Law provides that licences are to be issued by the mayor of the municipality concerned, taking into account the criteria laid down in the municipal commercial development plan. The purpose of that plan is to provide the best possible service for consumers and the best possible balance between permanent trading establishments and foreseeable demand from the population.

[22] Furthermore, the municipal committee is called on to give the mayor merely an opinion on individual licenses. It is only where the municipality does not yet have an approved commercial development plan that licences may not be issued unless the committee's opinion is favourable.

[23] It follows from the foregoing considerations that, in a system such as that established by the Italian Law, the public authorities have not delegated their powers to private economic operators.

[24] Articles 3(g), 5 and 86 of the Treaty could apply to rules such as those contained in the Italian Law only if it were proved that that law creates a position of economic strength for an undertaking which enables it to prevent effective competition being maintained on the relevant market by affording it the power to behave to an appreciable extent independently of its competitors, its customers and, ultimately, the consumers (judgment in Case 85/76 *Hoffmann-La Roche* v *Commission* [1979] ECR 461, paragraph 38).

[25] The Court has held that Article 86 of the Treaty prohibits abusive practices resulting from the exploitation, by one or more undertakings, of a dominant position on the common market or in a substantial part of it, in so far as those practices may affect trade between Member States (judgment in Case C-393/92 *Almelo and Others* v *Energiebedriff IJsselmij* [1994] ECR I-1477, paragraph 40).

[26] In order to find that a collective dominant position exists, the undertakings in question must be linked in such a way that they adopt the same conduct on the market (judgment in Almelo, paragraph 42).

[27] National rules which require a licence to be obtained before a new shop can be opened and limit the number of shops in the municipality in order to achieve a balance between supply and demand cannot be considered to put individual traders in dominant positions or all the traders established in a municipality in a collective dominant position, a salient feature of which would be that traders did not compete against one another.

[28] It follows that Articles 85 and 86, in conjunction with Articles 3(g) and 5, of the Treaty do not preclude rules such as those contained in the Italian Law.

The Court then completed its exploration of EU trade law by adding reference to Article 30 of the EC Treaty (now, after amendment, Article 34 TFEU: Chapters 11 and 12):

> [29] On this point, it is sufficient to observe that rules such as those contained in the Italian Law make no distinction according to the origin of the goods distributed by the business concerned, that their purpose is not to regulate trade in goods with other Member States and that the restrictive effects which they might have on the free movement of goods are too uncertain and indirect for the obligation which they impose to be regarded as being capable of hindering trade between Member States (judgment in Case C-379/92 *Peralta* [1994] ECR I-3453, paragraph 24, and the decisions cited above).
>
> [30] Article 30 does not therefore preclude legislation such as the Italian Law.

■ **QUESTIONS**

1. The referring national court did not ask about the potential application of Articles 52 or 59 of the EC Treaty (now, after amendment, Articles 49 and 56 TFEU respectively), which govern establishment and provision of services respectively. What would be the relevance of those Treaty provisions in such circumstances?
2. Laws such as that in issue in this decision place barriers to entry on to the market by potential new suppliers. Where a licence is refused, this may forestall a widening of consumer choice and may allow existing operators to cushion themselves from (potentially price-cutting) competitors. So is the Court of Justice well advised to decline to take a stand on the permissibility of such a rule?

NOTE: See also Case C-38/97 *Autotrasporti Librandi Snc di Librandi F & C* [1998] ECR I-5955. The market regulation in question is treated by the Court as a matter of national competence untouched by EU trade law. The decision should be read in conjunction with earlier discussion of the outer limits to EU trade law (pp. 329, 394). In adopting a relatively narrow focus, the Court has here declined the temptation to create a general economic constitutional law for the Union (see P. Davies, 'Market Integration and Social Policy' (1995) 25 ILJ 49; H. Schepel, 'Delegation of Regulatory Powers to Private Parties under EC Competition Law: Towards a Procedural Public Interest Test' (2002) 39 CML Rev 31; S. Prechal and S. de Vries, 'Seamless Web of Judicial Protection in the Internal Market?' (2009) 34 EL Rev 5).

SECTION 5: THE ENFORCEMENT OF THE COMPETITION RULES

Enforcement at two levels – 'dual vigilance' – is a familiar feature of the EU legal order. In the event of violation of the law, action may be taken both by the Commission at EU level and by private individuals relying on the direct effect of EU law before national courts. The competition rules are in this structural respect no different from Treaty provisions such as Articles 34 and 56. Much of the material in Part One of this book dealing with patterns of enforcement is largely applicable also to the competition rules. There are, however, some special features which apply exclusively in the area of competition law, most of all concerning the special powers of investigation and sanction which are enjoyed by the Commission. It will be necessary for the reader to turn to specialist works to explore the details of the matter. This section offers an overview.

A: Enforcement by the Commission

The Council is empowered to adopt measures to give effect to the principles contained in Articles 101 and 102 TFEU. The relevant provision post-Lisbon is Article 103 TFEU.

The system of enforcement was first established by Regulation 17/62 and subsequently elaborated in case law. With effect from 2004 it is contained in Council Regulation 1/2003, based on Article 83 EC, predecessor to Article 103 TFEU.

The regime established by Regulation 1/2003 is not written on a clean slate, for some of the pre-existing practice and case law remains influential in so far as aspects of the long-standing scheme of Regulation 17/62 have been retained, albeit in the new form provided by Regulation 1/2003. For example, the structure of the Commission's powers of investigation into suspected infringements of the competition rules has been largely retained. Accordingly, the case law that has developed governing procedural protection for firms subject to Commission inquiry has an enduring significance. However, other aspects of previous practice were consigned to history. A dominant feature of the regime established by Regulation 17/62 was the conferral on the Commission of exclusive competence to grant exemption pursuant to what is now Article 101(3) TFEU. Firms were expected to notify agreements and await Commission approval. This helped to secure uniformity in the interpretation and application of the exemption procedure, but it also made a bottleneck of the Commission. The beginning of the Regulation's Preamble is helpful in setting out the principal motivations for 'modernization' of the regime.

Council Regulation (EC) No 1/2003 of 16 December 2002 on the Implementation of the Rules on Competition Laid Down in Articles 81 and 82 of the Treaty [Now Articles 101 and 102 TFEU] (Text With EEA Relevance)

[2003] OJ L/1/1, Preamble

(1) In order to establish a system which ensures that competition in the common market is not distorted, Articles 81 and 82 [now 101 and 102] of the Treaty must be applied effectively and uniformly in the Community. Council Regulation No 17 of 6 February 1962, First Regulation implementing Articles 81 and 82(4) of the Treaty, has allowed a Community competition policy to develop that has helped to disseminate a competition culture within the Community. In the light of experience, however, that Regulation should now be replaced by legislation designed to meet the challenges of an integrated market and a future enlargement of the Community.

(2) In particular, there is a need to rethink the arrangements for applying the exception from the prohibition on agreements, which restrict competition, laid down in Article 81(3) of the Treaty. Under Article 83(2)(b) of the Treaty, account must be taken in this regard of the need to ensure effective supervision, on the one hand, and to simplify administration to the greatest possible extent, on the other.

(3) The centralised scheme set up by Regulation No 17 no longer secures a balance between those two objectives. It hampers application of the Community competition rules by the courts and competition authorities of the Member States, and the system of notification it involves prevents the Commission from concentrating its resources on curbing the most serious infringements. It also imposes considerable costs on undertakings.

(4) The present system should therefore be replaced by a directly applicable exception system in which the competition authorities and courts of the Member States have the power to apply not only Article 81(1) and Article 82 of the Treaty, which have direct applicability by virtue of the case-law of the Court of Justice of the European Communities, but also Article 81(3) of the Treaty.

NOTE: Chapter 1 of Regulation 1/2003 provides for the pattern of application advocated by the fourth recital. The abandonment of the system of notification of agreements falling within Article 101(1) and the lifting of the Commission's exclusive grip over the grant of exemption pursuant to Article 101(3) represented a profound adjustment in the very structure of competition law enforcement.

■ QUESTION

Is it surprising that this decentralization occurred shortly before enlargement into Central and Eastern Europe? Is the 'competition culture' mentioned in the first recital sufficiently well entrenched to guard against the risk that divergent decisions among the newly empowered courts and competition authorities of the Member States will imperil the uniform application of EU competition law across the territory of the Union?

It is not possible here to explore the whole of Regulation 1/2003. The following extracts are chosen to convey the breadth of the power conferred on the Commission to root out anti-competitive practices perpetrated in the EU market. They cover decision-making power (Articles 7 and 8), power of inspection (Articles 20–22) and the power to impose fines and/or penalty payments on those engaged in anti-competitive practices (Articles 23 and 24).

Council Regulation (EC) NO 1/2003 of 16 December 2002 on the Implementation of the Rules on Competition Laid Down in Articles 81 and 82 of the Treaty ([Now Articles 101 and 102 TFEU] Text With EEA Relevance)

[2003] OJ l/1/1

Article 7: Finding and termination of infringement

1. Where the Commission, acting on a complaint or on its own initiative, finds that there is an infringement of Article 81 or of Article 82 of the Treaty, it may by decision require the undertakings and associations of undertakings concerned to bring such infringement to an end. For this purpose, it may impose on them any behavioural or structural remedies which are proportionate to the infringement committed and necessary to bring the infringement effectively to an end. Structural remedies can only be imposed either where there is no equally effective behavioural remedy or where any equally effective behavioural remedy would be more burdensome for the undertaking concerned than the structural remedy. If the Commission has a legitimate interest in doing so, it may also find that an infringement has been committed in the past.

2. Those entitled to lodge a complaint for the purposes of paragraph 1 are natural or legal persons who can show a legitimate interest and Member States.

Article 8: Interim measures

1. In cases of urgency due to the risk of serious and irreparable damage to competition, the Commission, acting on its own initiative may by decision, on the basis of a prima facie finding of infringement, order interim measures.

2. A decision under paragraph 1 shall apply for a specified period of time and may be renewed in so far this is necessary and appropriate.

. . .

Article 20: The Commission's powers of inspection

1. In order to carry out the duties assigned to it by this Regulation, the Commission may conduct all necessary inspections of undertakings and associations of undertakings.

2. The officials and other accompanying persons authorised by the Commission to conduct an inspection are empowered:

(a) to enter any premises, land and means of transport of undertakings and associations of undertakings;
(b) to examine the books and other records related to the business, irrespective of the medium on which they are stored;
(c) to take or obtain in any form copies of or extracts from such books or records;
(d) to seal any business premises and books or records for the period and to the extent necessary for the inspection;
(e) to ask any representative or member of staff of the undertaking or association of undertakings for explanations on facts or documents relating to the subject-matter and purpose of the inspection and to record the answers.

3. The officials and other accompanying persons authorised by the Commission to conduct an inspection shall exercise their powers upon production of a written authorisation specifying the subject matter and purpose of the inspection and the penalties provided for in Article 23 in case the production of the required books or other records related to the business is incomplete or where the answers to questions asked under

paragraph 2 of the present Article are incorrect or misleading. In good time before the inspection, the Commission shall give notice of the inspection to the competition authority of the Member State in whose territory it is to be conducted.

4. Undertakings and associations of undertakings are required to submit to inspections ordered by decision of the Commission. The decision shall specify the subject matter and purpose of the inspection, appoint the date on which it is to begin and indicate the penalties provided for in Articles 23 and 24 and the right to have the decision reviewed by the Court of Justice. The Commission shall take such decisions after consulting the competition authority of the Member State in whose territory the inspection is to be conducted.

5. Officials of as well as those authorised or appointed by the competition authority of the Member State in whose territory the inspection is to be conducted shall, at the request of that authority or of the Commission, actively assist the officials and other accompanying persons authorised by the Commission. To this end, they shall enjoy the powers specified in paragraph 2.

6. Where the officials and other accompanying persons authorised by the Commission find that an undertaking opposes an inspection ordered pursuant to this Article, the Member State concerned shall afford them the necessary assistance, requesting where appropriate the assistance of the police or of an equivalent enforcement authority, so as to enable them to conduct their inspection.

7. If the assistance provided for in paragraph 6 requires authorisation from a judicial authority according to national rules, such authorisation shall be applied for. Such authorisation may also be applied for as a precautionary measure.

8. Where authorisation as referred to in paragraph 7 is applied for, the national judicial authority shall control that the Commission decision is authentic and that the coercive measures envisaged are neither arbitrary nor excessive having regard to the subject matter of the inspection. In its control of the proportionality of the coercive measures, the national judicial authority may ask the Commission, directly or through the Member State competition authority, for detailed explanations in particular on the grounds the Commission has for suspecting infringement of Articles 81 and 82 of the Treaty, as well as on the seriousness of the suspected infringement and on the nature of the involvement of the undertaking concerned. However, the national judicial authority may not call into question the necessity for the inspection nor demand that it be provided with the information in the Commission's file. The lawfulness of the Commission decision shall be subject to review only by the Court of Justice.

Article 21: Inspection of other premises

1. If a reasonable suspicion exists that books or other records related to the business and to the subject-matter of the inspection, which may be relevant to prove a serious violation of Article 81 or Article 82 of the Treaty, are being kept in any other premises, land and means of transport, including the homes of directors, managers and other members of staff of the undertakings and associations of undertakings concerned, the Commission can by decision order an inspection to be conducted in such other premises, land and means of transport.

2. The decision shall specify the subject matter and purpose of the inspection, appoint the date on which it is to begin and indicate the right to have the decision reviewed by the Court of Justice. It shall in particular state the reasons that have led the Commission to conclude that a suspicion in the sense of paragraph 1 exists. The Commission shall take such decisions after consulting the competition authority of the Member State in whose territory the inspection is to be conducted.

3. A decision adopted pursuant to paragraph 1 cannot be executed without prior authorisation from the national judicial authority of the Member State concerned. The national judicial authority shall control that the Commission decision is authentic and that the coercive measures envisaged are neither arbitrary nor excessive having regard in particular to the seriousness of the suspected infringement, to the importance of the evidence sought, to the involvement of the undertaking concerned and to the reasonable likelihood that business books and records relating to the subject matter of the inspection are kept in the premises for which the authorisation is requested. The national judicial authority may ask the Commission, directly or through the Member State competition authority, for detailed explanations on those elements which are necessary to allow its control of the proportionality of the coercive measures envisaged.

However, the national judicial authority may not call into question the necessity for the inspection nor demand that it be provided with information in the Commission's file. The lawfulness of the Commission decision shall be subject to review only by the Court of Justice.

4. The officials and other accompanying persons authorised by the Commission to conduct an inspection ordered in accordance with paragraph 1 of this Article shall have the powers set out in Article 20(2)(a), (b) and (c). Article 20(5) and (6) shall apply mutatis mutandis.

Article 22: Investigations by competition authorities of Member States

1. The competition authority of a Member State may in its own territory carry out any inspection or other fact-finding measure under its national law on behalf and for the account of the competition authority of another Member State in order to establish whether there has been an infringement of Article 81 or Article 82 of the Treaty. Any exchange and use of the information collected shall be carried out in accordance with Article 12.

2. At the request of the Commission, the competition authorities of the Member States shall undertake the inspections which the Commission considers to be necessary under Article 20(1) or which it has ordered by decision pursuant to Article 20(4). The officials of the competition authorities of the Member States who are responsible for conducting these inspections as well as those authorised or appointed by them shall exercise their powers in accordance with their national law. If so requested by the Commission or by the competition authority of the Member State in whose territory the inspection is to be conducted, officials and other accompanying persons authorised by the Commission may assist the officials of the authority concerned.

CHAPTER VI: PENALTIES

Article 23: Fines

1. The Commission may by decision impose on undertakings and associations of undertakings fines not exceeding 1% of the total turnover in the preceding business year where, intentionally or negligently:

(a) they supply incorrect or misleading information in response to a request made pursuant to Article 17 or Article 18(2);
(b) in response to a request made by decision adopted pursuant to Article 17 or Article 18(3), they supply incorrect, incomplete or misleading information or do not supply information within the required time-limit;
(c) they produce the required books or other records related to the business in incomplete form during inspections under Article 20 or refuse to submit to inspections ordered by a decision adopted pursuant to Article 20(4);
(d) in response to a question asked in accordance with Article 20(2)(e),

— they give an incorrect or misleading answer,
— they fail to rectify within a time-limit set by the Commission an incorrect, incomplete or misleading answer given by a member of staff, or
— they fail or refuse to provide a complete answer on facts relating to the subject-matter and purpose of an inspection ordered by a decision adopted pursuant to Article 20(4);

(e) seals affixed in accordance with Article 20(2)(d) by officials or other accompanying persons authorised by the Commission have been broken.

2. The Commission may by decision impose fines on undertakings and associations of undertakings where, either intentionally or negligently:

(a) they infringe Article 81 or Article 82 of the Treaty; or
(b) they contravene a decision ordering interim measures under Article 8; or
(c) they fail to comply with a commitment made binding by a decision pursuant to Article 9.For each undertaking and association of undertakings participating in the infringement, the fine shall not exceed 10% of its total turnover in the preceding business year. Where the infringement of an association relates to the activities of its members, the fine shall not exceed 10% of the sum of the total turnover of each member active on the market affected by the infringement of the association.

3. In fixing the amount of the fine, regard shall be had both to the gravity and to the duration of the infringement.

4. When a fine is imposed on an association of undertakings taking account of the turnover of its members and the association is not solvent, the association is obliged to call for contributions from its members to cover the amount of the fine. Where such contributions have not been made to the association within a time-limit fixed by the Commission, the Commission may require payment of the fine directly by any of the undertakings whose representatives were members of the decision-making bodies concerned of the association.

After the Commission has required payment under the second subparagraph, where necessary to ensure full payment of the fine, the Commission may require payment of the balance by any of the members of the association which were active on the market on which the infringement occurred.

However, the Commission shall not require payment under the second or the third subparagraph from undertakings which show that they have not implemented the infringing decision of the association and either were not aware of its existence or have actively distanced themselves from it before the Commission started investigating the case. The financial liability of each undertaking in respect of the payment of the fine shall not exceed 10% of its total turnover in the preceding business year.

5. Decisions taken pursuant to paragraphs 1 and 2 shall not be of a criminal law nature.

Article 24: Periodic penalty payments

1. The Commission may, by decision, impose on undertakings or associations of undertakings periodic penalty payments not exceeding 5% of the average daily turnover in the preceding business year per day and calculated from the date appointed by the decision, in order to compel them:

(a) to put an end to an infringement of Article 81 or Article 82 of the Treaty, in accordance with a decision taken pursuant to Article 7;
(b) to comply with a decision ordering interim measures taken pursuant to Article 8;
(c) to comply with a commitment made binding by a decision pursuant to Article 9;
(d) to supply complete and correct information which it has requested by decision taken pursuant to Article 17 or Article 18(3);
(e) to submit to an inspection which it has ordered by decision taken pursuant to Article 20(4).

2. Where the undertakings or associations of undertakings have satisfied the obligation which the periodic penalty payment was intended to enforce, the Commission may fix the definitive amount of the periodic penalty payment at a figure lower than that which would arise under the original decision. Article 23(4) shall apply correspondingly.

NOTE: Both EU level – the Commission – and national level – the competition authorities and the courts – are involved in the effective enforcement of EU competition law. The Commission's exclusive grip over Article 101(3) is eliminated. The Commission is able to re-allocate resources from the notification process to more intense investigation of covert anti-competitive practices which in the past would certainly not have been notified by the participants. The risk is plainly that these benefits will come at a cost, largely paid in the currency of diverse approaches to the availability of (in particular) Article 101(3) exemption taken by national authorities and courts. In response to this peril, Chapter IV of the Regulation in particular is directed at the establishment of an effective system of co-operation between the several bodies charged with the responsibility of applying the Treaty provisions. The aim is to minimize the risk of the law being applied in different ways in different States. The Commission has published guidelines which are designed to address this issue: on co-operation within the Network of Competition Authorities (the 'European Competition Network', [2004] OJ C101/43, which works to share best practice, see http://ec.europa.eu/competition/ecn/index_en.html) and on co-operation with national courts ([2004] OJ C101/54). Research is needed to reveal the extent to which this process of modernization, built on decentralization, can be prevented from generating damaging unevenness in the application of the Treaty rules governing competition law across the territory of the Union. In April 2009 the Commission issued its own report (COM (2009) 206). This is short and largely descriptive, but the Commission lauds its ability 'to become more proactive, tackling weaknesses in the competiveness of key sectors of the economy in a focused way'. Its ten-year review of the operation of Regulation 1/2003 (COM (2014) 453) is similarly short but positive about improved patterns of enforcement. Both documents are at http://ec.europa.eu/competition/antitrust/legislation/regulations.html.

To place the risk of divergent application of EU competition law in context, it is worth recalling that the system created by Regulation 1/2003 is comparable to the system of enforcement according to the pattern of 'dual vigilance' that applies to Union law generally. As Chapter 4 of this book demonstrates, enforcement generally is placed in the hands of both EU and national-level bodies, with a corresponding risk of diversity in practice. After all, both Article 36 TFEU and the Court's 'mandatory requirements' invented in *Cassis de Dijon* (Case 120/78), which offer the possibility of justifying national measures that restrict inter-State trade in goods, are capable of application by national courts. There is no reservation of competence to the Commission. To this extent one may choose to regard the old system of Commission exclusivity over exemption pursuant to Article 101(3) as abnormal, and Regulation 1/2003 as a transfer of the practice of competition law enforcement back to the mainstream of EU law.

■ QUESTION

The substantive alignment of national competition law with the EU model has been a feature of recent years. To what extent will this serve to diminish the risk of misunderstanding of EU practice by the national courts and administrators empowered by Regulation 1/2003?

NOTE: Achieving a balance between the needs of effective enforcement of the competition rules and the protection of firms subject to the rules is a difficult but vital issue. See Article 20, the Commission's powers of investigation, and Article 21, inspection of other premises. They are especially sensitive. They govern the so-called 'dawn raids' of premises, which, since the Commission prefers to find buildings open, tend not to happen at dawn. The procedure assumes a Commission Decision with which a firm must comply but, in the event of non-compliance, recourse to national procedures to secure compliance is envisaged. Equipping the Commission with tough powers of this type is plainly important in creating an effective regime that will be capable of uncovering secret cartels, which are likely to be the most pernicious of all. Equally firms subject to such intrusion have a proper concern for protection from undue or unfair administrative interference.

Article 14 of Regulation 17/62 contained a procedure that is recognizably the precursor of the set of powers now found in Chapter V of Regulation 1/2003. However, the provisions of Regulation 1/2003 represent a significant adjustment of the pre-existing regime. Article 21 of Regulation 1/2003 constitutes a significant widening of the scope of the power to search. And the provisions of Regulation 1/2003 absorb the important decisions handed down in this area by the Court. The exercise of these powers of the Commission has been the subject of regular challenges which have permitted the Court to elaborate its own view of the appropriate scope of procedural protection for natural or legal persons subject to investigation. It is worth briefly setting out the key components of decisions of the Court dealing with Regulation 17/62, both in order to expose the source of some of the wording found in the Articles contained in Chapter V of Regulation 1/2003 and also to identify the source of inspiration of the Court in developing these legal principles. The latter point is of more general importance. The Court's cases in this area are important in competition law, but they also reflect the development of EU notions of fundamental rights (p. 54).

The General Court now exercises jurisdiction in this area. However, the following decision of the Court of Justice remains highly significant.

Hoechst v *Commission* (Case 46/87)

[1989] ECR 2859, Court of Justice of the European Communities

The Commission suspected Hoechst was implicated in a cartel. Seeking information, it arrived unannounced at Hoechst's premises, as it was entitled to do under Article 14 of Regulation 17/62 (the precursor of Article 20 of Regulation 1/2003, albeit that the latter is a much more elaborate provision). Hoechst refused to admit the Commission officials and argued that it was entitled to exclude them until a search warrant had been obtained through national procedures. The Commission eventually obtained access using this route, but imposed financial penalties on Hoechst for refusal to comply with the original decision under Article 14. Hoechst sought the annulment of that decision before the Court.

[12] It should be noted, before the nature and scope of the Commission's powers of investigation under Article 14 of Regulation No 17 are examined, that that article cannot be interpreted in such a way as to give rise to results which are incompatible with the general principles of Community law and in particular with fundamental rights.

[13] The Court has consistently held that fundamental rights are an integral part of the general principles of law the observance of which the Court ensures, in accordance with constitutional traditions common to the

Member States, and the international treaties on which the Member States have collaborated or of which they are signatories (see, in particular, the judgment of 14 May 1974 in Case 4/73 *Nold* v *Commission* [1974] ECR 491). The European Convention for the Protection of Human Rights and Fundamental Freedoms of 4 November 1950 (hereinafter referred to as 'the European Convention on Human Rights') is of particular significance in that regard (see, in particular, the judgment of 15 May 1986 in Case 222/84 *Johnston* v *Chief Constable of the Royal Ulster Constabulary* [1986] ECR 1651).

[14] In interpreting Article 14 of Regulation No 17, regard must be had in particular to the rights of the defence, a principle whose fundamental nature has been stressed on numerous occasions in the Court's decisions (see, in particular, the judgment of 9 November 1983 in Case 322/81 *Michelin* v *Commission* [1983] ECR 3461, paragraph 7).

[15] In that judgment, the Court pointed out that the rights of the defence must be observed in administrative procedures which may lead to the imposition of penalties. But it is also necessary to prevent those rights from being irremediably impaired during preliminary inquiry procedures including, in particular, investigations which may be decisive in providing evidence of the unlawful nature of conduct engaged in by undertakings for which they may be liable.

[16] Consequently, although certain rights of the defence relate only to the contentious proceedings which follow the delivery of the statement of objections, other rights, such as the right to legal representation and the privileged nature of correspondence between lawyer and client (recognised by the Court in the judgment of 18 May 1982 in Case 155/79 *AM & S* v *Commission* [1982] ECR 1575) must be respected as from the preliminary-inquiry stage.

[17] Since the applicant has also relied on the requirements stemming from the fundamental right to the inviolability of the home, it should be observed that, although the existence of such a right must be recognised in the Community legal order as a principle common to the laws of the Member States in regard to the private dwellings of natural persons, the same is not true in regard to undertakings, because there are not inconsiderable divergences between the legal systems of the Member States in regard to the nature and degree of protection afforded to business premises against intervention by the public authorities.

[18] No other inference is to be drawn from Article 8(1) of the European Convention on Human Rights which provides that: 'Everyone has the right to respect for his private and family life, his home and his correspondence'. The protective scope of that article is concerned with the development of man's personal freedom and may not therefore be extended to business premises. Furthermore, it should be noted that there is no case law of the European Court of Human Rights on that subject.

[19] None the less, in all the legal systems of the Member States, any intervention by the public authorities in the sphere of private activities of any person, whether natural or legal, must have a legal basis and be justified on the grounds laid down by law, and, consequently, those systems provide, albeit in different forms, protection against arbitrary or disproportionate intervention. The need for such protection must be recognised as a general principle of Community law. In that regard, it should be pointed out that the Court has held that it has the power to determine whether measures of investigation taken by the Commission under the ECSC Treaty are excessive (judgment of 14 December 1962 in Joined Cases 5 to 11 and 13 to 15/62 *San Michele and Others* v *Commission* [1962] ECR 449).

These statements of principle echo the discussion of fundamental rights within EU law in Chapter 2 (p. 54). The Court then turned to consider the nature and scope of Article 14 of Regulation 17/62 in detail. The entry into force of Regulation 1/2003 on 1 May 2004 removes the practical value of pursuing a close examination of this aspect of the judgment, but the Court's conclusion that in the case itself there was no violation by the Commission of these requirements deserves reading to acquire a flavour of the basis for judicial review.

[41] As has been stated above, the Commission's obligation to specify the subject-matter and purpose of the investigation constitutes a fundamental guarantee of the rights of the defence of the undertakings concerned. It follows that the scope of the obligation to state the reasons on which decisions ordering investigations are based cannot be restricted on the basis of considerations concerning the effectiveness of the

investigation. Although the Commission is not required to communicate to the addressee of a decision ordering an investigation all the information at its disposal concerning the presumed infringements, or to make a precise legal analysis of those infringements, it must none the less clearly indicate the presumed facts which it intends to investigate.

[42] Although the statement of the reasons on which the contested decision is based is drawn up in very general terms which might well have been made more precise, and is therefore open to criticism in that respect, it none the less contains the essential indications prescribed by Article 14(3) of Regulation No 17. The decision at issue refers in particular to information suggesting the existence and application of agreements or concerted practices between certain producers and suppliers of PVC and polyethylene (including, but not limited to, LdPE) in the EEC, concerning prices, quantities or sales targets for those products. It states that those agreements and practices may constitute a serious infringement of Article 85(1) of the Treaty. According to Article 1 of the decision in question, the applicant 'is required to submit to an investigation concerning its possible participation' in those agreements or concerted practices and, consequently, to give the Commission's officials access to its premises and to produce or allow copies to be made for the purpose of inspection of business documents 'related to the subject-matter of the investigation'.

[43] In those circumstances, the submission alleging that the statement of reasons is insufficient must be rejected.

***Roquette Frères S A* v *Directeur général de la concurrence, de la consommation et de la répression des frauds* (Case C-94/00)**

[2002] ECR I-9011, Court of Justice of the European Communities

The Commission adopted a decision pursuant to Article 14 of Regulation 17/62 requiring Roquette Frères to submit to an investigation. The Commission requested the French Government to take the necessary steps to ensure that, in the event of opposition by Roquette Frères, the national authorities would provide assistance of the type envisaged by Article 14 of Regulation 17/62. The competent French administrative authorities duly sought a court order providing authorization to enter the premises of Roquette Frères and seize documents. The application before the French court consisted in essence of a copy of the Commission decision and the text of the judgment in *Hoechst*. The order was granted and Roquette Frères co-operated, but then appealed against the authorization order. The company asserted that it was not open to the French judge to order entry onto private premises without first determining that there were indeed reasonable grounds for suspecting the existence of anti-competitive practices such as to justify the grant of coercive powers. This determination had not been made, nor did the Commission decision disclose any relevant information explaining its briefly stated view that the company was engaging in practices contrary to the Treaty. The matter was referred to the Court of Justice under the preliminary reference procedure (Chapter 7), and the Court was invited to consider the development of the law since *Hoechst*.

[27] . . . in paragraph 19 of the judgment in Hoechst, the Court recognised that the need for protection against arbitrary or disproportionate intervention by public authorities in the sphere of the private activities of any person, whether natural or legal, constitutes a general principle of Community law.

[28] The Court has likewise stated that the competent authorities of the Member States are required to respect that general principle when they are called upon to act in response to a request for assistance made by the Commission pursuant to Article 14(6) of Regulation No 17 (see *Hoechst*, paragraphs 19 and 33).

[29] For the purposes of determining the scope of that principle in relation to the protection of business premises, regard must be had to the case-law of the European Court of Human Rights subsequent to the judgment in Hoechst. According to that case-law, first, the protection of the home provided for in Article 8 of the ECHR may in certain circumstances be extended to cover such premises (see, in particular, the judgment of 16 April 2002 in *Colas Est and Others* v *France*, not yet published in the Reports of Judgments and Decisions,

§ 41) and, second, the right of interference established by Article 8(2) of the ECHR 'might well be more far-reaching where professional or business activities or premises were involved than would otherwise be the case' (*Niemietz* v *Germany*, cited above, § 31).

As in *Hoechst*, so in *Roquette Frères* – the material in Chapter 2 dealing with the infusion of EU law by rules protecting fundamental rights should be recalled (p. 54). The Court proceeded to consider the more detailed questions concerning the position of a national court called on to issue an order in support of a Commission Decision authorizing an inspection of premises. It provided a detailed set of requirements.

And these have inspired and been absorbed by (in particular) Articles 20(8) and 21(3) of Regulation 1/2003. Remember also the Commission's guidelines on co-operation with national courts ([2004] OJ C101/54, mentioned at p. 509).

■ QUESTION

How successful is the Court's balance between the interests of the Commission and of the firm under investigation?

NOTE: Important secondary legislation amplifies the procedural protection to which firms under scrutiny are entitled. In particular Regulation 773/2004 ([2004] OJ L123/18) concerns the conduct of proceedings by the Commission pursuant to what are now Articles 101 and 102 TFEU and covers (*inter alia*) complaint-handling and hearings.

Having obtained the necessary information, and respected the requirements of Regulation 773/2004, the Commission is in a position to conclude the matter. Article 23 of Regulation 1/2003, p. 508, confers the power to fine on the Commission. Article 24 supplements this with the power to impose periodic penalty payments. As a deterrent, these powers are key elements in an effective system. Hunting secret cartels is a difficult job, and the Commission uses the lure of partial or even total immunity from fines to encourage participants to own up. The latest version of the Commission's 'leniency notice' on immunity from fines and reduction of fines in cartel cases was published in 2006 ([2006] OJ C298/17, as amended [2015] OJ C256). The use of explanatory Notices conforms with practice visible elsewhere in the competition field, e.g., in relation to market definition (p. 486).

The power to investigate, decide and impose sanctions adds up to a striking concentration of power in the hands of the Commission. The availability of vigorous judicial review is important not only to safeguard affected parties in individual cases, but also to resist allegations that the EU system violates fundamental rights standards. In the next case, decided in 2013, the Court of Justice sets out its view of this matter. Remember Chapter 2 – it should be no surprise that the EU Charter of Fundamental Rights is prominent in the Court's reasoning.

***Schindler* v *Commission* (Case C-501/11P)**

Judgment of 18 July 2013, Court of Justice of the EU

[33] . . . the fact that decisions imposing fines in competition matters are adopted by the Commission is not in itself contrary to Article 6 of the ECHR as interpreted by the European Court of Human Rights. It is to be noted in this connection that, in its judgment in *A. Menarini Diagnostics v. Italy*, relating to a penalty imposed by the Italian competition authority for anti-competitive practices similar to those of which the appellants were accused, the European Court of Human Rights considered that, given that the fine imposed was high, the penalty, because of its severity, fell within the criminal sphere.

[34] It pointed out, however, in paragraph 58 of that judgment, that, entrusting the prosecution and punishment of breaches of the competition rules to administrative authorities is not inconsistent with the ECHR in so far as the person concerned has an opportunity to challenge any decision made against him before a tribunal that offers the guarantees provided for in Article 6 of the ECHR.

[35] In paragraph 59 of its judgment in *A. Menarini Diagnostics v. Italy*, the European Court of Human Rights explained that, in administrative proceedings, the obligation to comply with Article 6 of the ECHR does not preclude a 'penalty' from being imposed by an administrative authority in the first instance. For this to be possible, however, decisions taken by administrative authorities which do not themselves satisfy the requirements laid down in Article 6(1) of the ECHR must be subject to subsequent review by a judicial body that has full jurisdiction. The characteristics of such a body include the power to quash in all respects, on questions of fact and law, the decision of the body. The judicial body must in particular have jurisdiction to examine all questions of fact and law relevant to the dispute before it.

[36] Ruling on the principle of effective judicial protection, a general principle of European Union law to which expression is now given by Article 47 of the Charter and which corresponds, in European Union law, to Article 6(1) of the ECHR, the Court of Justice has held that, in addition to the review of legality provided for by the FEU Treaty, the European Union judicature has the unlimited jurisdiction which it is afforded by Article 31 of Regulation No 1/2003, in accordance with Article 261 TFEU, and which empowers it to substitute its own appraisal for the Commission's and, consequently, to cancel, reduce or increase the fine or periodic penalty payment imposed (*Chalkor* v *Commission*, paragraph 63).

[37] As regards the review of legality, the Court has pointed out that the European Union judicature must carry it out on the basis of the evidence adduced by the applicant in support of the pleas in law put forward and that it cannot use the Commission's margin of discretion – either as regards the choice of factors taken into account in the application of the criteria mentioned in the 1998 Guidelines or as regards the assessment of those factors – as a basis for dispensing with the conduct of an in-depth review of the law and of the facts (*Chalkor* v *Commission*, paragraph 62).

[38] As the review provided for by the Treaties involves review by the European Union judicature of both the law and the facts, and means that it has the power to assess the evidence, to annul the contested decision and to alter the amount of a fine, the Court has concluded that the review of legality provided for under Article 263 TFEU, supplemented by the unlimited jurisdiction in respect of the amount of the fine, provided for under Article 31 of Regulation No 1/2003, is not contrary to the requirements of the principle of effective judicial protection which is currently set out in Article 47 of the Charter (*Chalkor* v *Commission*, paragraph 67).

B: Enforcement at national level

So much for enforcement by the Commission. Action may also be taken by private individuals relying on EU law before national courts. The competition rules are in this respect no different from the provisions on free movement considered elsewhere in this book. And, on the entry into force of Regulation 1/2003 on 1 May 2004, the alignment was enhanced. The pre-existing exclusive competence to grant exemption vested in the Commission was lifted, and national competition authorities and courts are empowered to apply Article 101(3) as well as Articles 101(1), 101(2), and 102. In the wake of this 'decentralization' of enforcement practice much of the material in Part 1 of this book dealing with patterns of enforcement is largely applicable also to the competition rules. Moreover, since all relevant Treaty provisions can now be applied by all relevant institutions at EU and at national level, the awkward question of which issues fall to be considered under Article 101(1) and which are reserved to Article 101(3), examined at p. 477 in connection with the 'rule of reason', is of much less practical relevance. The demarcation still has significance (e.g. in connection with the burden of proof, see Art 2 Reg 1/2003), but much less than in the days before Regulation 1/2003 when matters relevant to Article 101(3), but not Article 101(1), were none of a national court's business. The Commission is eager that this reform will bring about much more vigorous domestic enforcement of the competition rules, as a means to generate better compliance rates.

In this vein, the rules of State liability discussed in Chapter 6 deserve consideration in the context of competition law. A victim of anti-competitive conduct may be interested not merely in putting an end to the practice by securing a court order but also in claiming compensation for loss suffered. Article 6 of Regulation 1/2003 provides simply that 'National courts shall have the power to apply Articles 81 and 82 of the Treaty'. The question of remedies is not addressed. But the case law is already more ambitious. In the preliminary reference in *H. Banks & Co. Ltd* v *British Coal Corporation* (Case C-128/92) [1994] ECR I-1209 Advocate-General Van Gerven had analysed *Francovich* liability as part of the general system of (what was then) Community law and, in pursuit of effective protection of Community law rights against both public and private sector defendants, he favoured its application to violations by private parties. However, the Court, in a cautious ruling carefully confined to the Coal and Steel Treaty, held that an action for damages before a national court could not be pursued in the absence of a Commission finding of violation. But the next case revealed the Court's approach to the availability of compensation for breach of the competition rules.

Courage Ltd v *Bernard Crehan* (Case C-453/99)

[2001] ECR I-6297, Court of Justice of the European Communities

Crehan was not a third-party victim of an anti-competitive practice. He was party to an agreement that was susceptible to challenge as a violation of what was then Article 81 EC, now Article 101 TFEU. He was a tenant of a public house who had been sued for money due under a contract obliging him to buy his beer from Courage, the brewer. His defence to the claim was that the 'beer tie' violated Article 81, that he was therefore not liable to pay and he also counter-claimed for damages for loss suffered as a result of the illegality. The English courts were minded to treat him as a participant in an anti-competitive practice, not a victim of one, and to deny in principle his claim for compensation. A preliminary reference was made to Luxembourg, asking for guidance.

[19] It should be borne in mind, first of all, that the Treaty has created its own legal order, which is integrated into the legal systems of the Member States and which their courts are bound to apply. The subjects of that legal order are not only the Member States but also their nationals. Just as it imposes burdens on individuals, Community law is also intended to give rise to rights which become part of their legal assets. Those rights arise not only where they are expressly granted by the Treaty but also by virtue of obligations which the Treaty imposes in a clearly defined manner both on individuals and on the Member States and the Community institutions (see the judgments in Case 26/62 *Van Gend en Loos* [1963] ECR 1, Case 6/64 *Costa* [1964] ECR 585 and Joined Cases C-6/90 and C-9/90 *Francovich and Others* [1991] ECR I-5357, paragraph 31).

[20] Secondly, according to Article 3(g) of the EC Treaty (now, after amendment, Article 3(1)(g) EC), Article 85 of the Treaty constitutes a fundamental provision which is essential for the accomplishment of the tasks entrusted to the Community and, in particular, for the functioning of the internal market (judgment in Case C-126/97 Eco Swiss [1999] ECR I-3055, paragraph 36).

[21] Indeed, the importance of such a provision led the framers of the Treaty to provide expressly, in Article 85(2) of the Treaty, that any agreements or decisions prohibited pursuant to that article are to be automatically void (judgment in *Eco Swiss*, cited above, paragraph 36).

[22] That principle of automatic nullity can be relied on by anyone, and the courts are bound by it once the condi tions for the application of Article 85(1) are met and so long as the agreement concerned does not justify the grant of an exemption under Article 85(3) of the Treaty (on the latter point, see *inter alia* Case 10/69 *Portelange* [1969] ECR 309, paragraph 10). Since the nullity referred to in Article 85(2) is absolute, an agreement which is null and void by virtue of this provision has no effect as between the contracting parties and cannot be set up against third parties (see the judgment in Case 22/71 *Béguelin* [1971] ECR 949, paragraph 29). Moreover, it is capable of having a bearing on all the effects, either past or future, of the agreement or decision concerned (see the judgment in Case 48/72 *Brasserie de Haecht II* [1973] ECR 77, paragraph 26).

[23] Thirdly, it should be borne in mind that the Court has held that Article 85(1) of the Treaty and Article 86 of the EC Treaty (now Article 82 EC) produce direct effects in relations between individuals and create rights for the individuals concerned which the national courts must safeguard (judgments in Case 127/73 *BRT and*

SABAM [1974] ECR 51, paragraph 16, ('*BRT I*') and Case C-282/95P *Guérin Automobiles* v *Commission* [1997] ECR I-1503, paragraph 39).

[24] It follows from the foregoing considerations that any individual can rely on a breach of Article 85(1) of the Treaty before a national court even where he is a party to a contract that is liable to restrict or distort competition within the meaning of that provision.

[25] As regards the possibility of seeking compensation for loss caused by a contract or by conduct liable to restrict or distort competition, it should be remembered from the outset that, in accordance with settled case-law, the national courts whose task it is to apply the provisions of Community law in areas within their jurisdiction must ensure that those rules take full effect and must protect the rights which they confer on individuals (see *inter alia* the judgments in Case 106/77 *Simmenthal* [1978] ECR 629, paragraph 16, and in Case C-213/89 *Factortame* [1990] ECR I-2433, paragraph 19).

[26] The full effectiveness of Article 85 of the Treaty and, in particular, the practical effect of the prohibition laid down in Article 85(1) would be put at risk if it were not open to any individual to claim damages for loss caused to him by a contract or by conduct liable to restrict or distort competition.

[27] Indeed, the existence of such a right strengthens the working of the Community competition rules and discourages agreements or practices, which are frequently covert, which are liable to restrict or distort competition. From that point of view, actions for damages before the national courts can make a significant contribution to the maintenance of effective competition in the Community.

[28] There should not therefore be any absolute bar to such an action being brought by a party to a contract which would be held to violate the competition rules.

[29] However, in the absence of Community rules governing the matter, it is for the domestic legal system of each Member State to designate the courts and tribunals having jurisdiction and to lay down the detailed procedural rules governing actions for safeguarding rights which individuals derive directly from Community law, provided that such rules are not less favourable than those governing similar domestic actions (principle of equivalence) and that they do not render practically impossible or excessively difficult the exercise of rights conferred by Community law (principle of effectiveness) (see Case C-261/95 *Palmisani* [1997] ECR I-4025, paragraph 27).

[30] In that regard, the Court has held that Community law does not prevent national courts from taking steps to ensure that the protection of the rights guaranteed by Community law does not entail the unjust enrichment of those who enjoy them . . ..

[31] Similarly, provided that the principles of equivalence and effectiveness are respected (see *Palmisani*, cited above, paragraph 27), Community law does not preclude national law from denying a party who is found to bear significant responsibility for the distortion of competition the right to obtain damages from the other contracting party. Under a principle which is recognised in most of the legal systems of the Member States and which the Court has applied in the past (see Case 39/72 *Commission* v *Italy* [1973] ECR 101, paragraph 10), a litigant should not profit from his own unlawful conduct, where this is proven.

[32] In that regard, the matters to be taken into account by the competent national court include the economic and legal context in which the parties find themselves and, as the United Kingdom Government rightly points out, the respective bargaining power and conduct of the two parties to the contract.

[33] In particular, it is for the national court to ascertain whether the party who claims to have suffered loss through concluding a contract that is liable to restrict or distort competition found himself in a markedly weaker position than the other party, such as seriously to compromise or even eliminate his freedom to negotiate the terms of the contract and his capacity to avoid the loss or reduce its extent, in particular by availing himself in good time of all the legal remedies available to him.

[34] Referring to the judgments in Case 23/67 *Brasserie de Haecht* [1967] ECR 127 and Case C-234/89 *Delimitis* [1991] ECR I-935, paragraphs 14 to 26, the Commission and the United Kingdom Government also rightly point out that a contract might prove to be contrary to Article 85(1) of the Treaty for the sole reason that it is part of a network of similar contracts which have a cumulative effect on competition. In such a case, the party contracting with the person controlling the network cannot bear significant responsibility for the breach of Article 85, particularly where in practice the terms of the contract were imposed on him by the party controlling the network.

[35] Contrary to the submission of Courage, making a distinction as to the extent of the parties' liability does not conflict with the case-law of the Court to the effect that it does not matter, for the purposes of the application of Article 85 of the Treaty, whether the parties to an agreement are on an equal footing as regards their economic position and function (see *inter alia* Joined Cases 56/64 and 58/64 *Consten and Grundig* v *Commission* [1966] ECR 382). That case-law concerns the conditions for application of Article 85 of the Treaty while the questions put before the Court in the present case concern certain consequences in civil law of a breach of that provision.

[36] Having regard to all the foregoing considerations, the questions referred are to be answered as follows:

— a party to a contract liable to restrict or distort competition within the meaning of Article 85 of the Treaty can rely on the breach of that article to obtain relief from the other contracting party;
— Article 85 of the Treaty precludes a rule of national law under which a party to a contract liable to restrict or distort competition within the meaning of that provision is barred from claiming damages for loss caused by performance of that contract on the sole ground that the claimant is a party to that contract;
— Community law does not preclude a rule of national law barring a party to a contract liable to restrict or distort competition from relying on his own unlawful actions to obtain damages where it is established that that party bears significant responsibility for the distortion of competition.

NOTE: The anxiety to promote the *effectiveness* of private enforcement is prominent in this ruling (paras 26 and 27). This tool of legal reasoning has been encountered elsewhere in comparable circumstances in which the Court delivers a ruling that, in so far as it improves methods for policing the rules of the Treaty, is likely to be welcomed by the Commission (*cf*, e.g., p. 258). Subsequently, however, Crehan was denied damages in the English courts when the House of Lords concluded that after all he had not been the victim of a practice contrary to the Treaty (*Crehan* v *Inntrepreneur Pub Co* [2006] 4 All ER 465, annotated by Hanley (2007) 44 CML Rev 817).

So far private enforcement of the competition rules seems a good deal more appealing in theory than in practice. There is enormous diversity between legal orders in the Member States in the approach taken to private enforcement and in practice a very low level of such litigation. The Commission, motivated by the desire to secure private litigants as its reliable allies in the fight against anti-competitive practices, has tried to 'modernize' this area too. A 2005 Green Paper (COM (2005) 672) was followed by a White Paper on damages actions in competition cases published in 2008. This made suggestions about how to improve access to redress for victims of violation of the competition rules: COM (2008) 165. One may legitimately wonder whether the almost total dearth of private litigation over several decades tells a revealing story of profound disincentives to bring such matters before a court. Eventually the Commission succeeded in persuading the Council and Parliament to legislate. . Directive 2014/104 [2014] OJ L349 is designed to establish certain common standards in national proceedings, although it is not comprehensive in its scope. For documentation see http://ec.europa.eu/competition/antitrust/actionsdamages/index.html.

FURTHER READING ON PATTERNS OF PRIVATE ENFORCEMENT

Camilleri, E., 'A Decade of EU Antitrust Private Enforcement: Chronicle of a Failure Foretold?' [2013] ECLR 531.

Nebbia, P., 'Damages Actions for the Infringement of EC Competition Law: Compensation or Deterrence?' (2008) 33 EL Rev 23.

Reich, N., 'Horizontal Liability in EC law: Hybridization of Remedies for Compensation in Case of Breaches of EC Rights' (2007) 44 CML Rev 705.

Tzakas, D.-P., 'Effective Collective Redress in Antitrust and Consumer Protection Matters: a Panacea or a Chimera?' (2011) 48 CML Rev 1125.

Wardhaugh, B., 'Bogeymen, Lunatics and Fanatics: Collective Actions and the Private Enforcement of European Competition Law' (2014) 34 Legal Studies 1.

Wils, W., 'The Relationship between Public Antitrust Enforcement and Private Actions for Damages' (2009) 32 World Competition 3.

NOTE: How 'modern' has the EU's system of competition law and policy really become?

A. Albors-Llorens, 'Competition Policy and the Shaping of the Single Market',
Ch. 12 in C. Barnard and J. Scott (eds), *The Law of the Single European Market: Unpacking the Premises*
(Oxford: Hart Publishing, 2002), pp. 330–1

(Footnotes omitted.)

Has the time come for the single market objective to play a less prominent role in the context of competition policy? After all, it could be argued that the 31 December 1992 deadline has long expired and that competition policy should move into a more economically based terrain. This idea infused the debate on vertical restraints and culminated in the adoption of the new block exemption regulations on vertical and horizontal agreements [p. xxx]. In the context of that debate some authors and the Commission itself have already argued that it might be too early to relax the importance of that goal given the price differentials still subsisting between the Member States, the minimum impact of cross-border purchasing groups, and the prospective further enlargement of the Union. Furthermore, two additional factors may have a decisive influence on the way the single market objective is deployed in the interpretation of Articles 81 and 82 EC [now Articles 101 and 102 TFEU]. First, the fully decentralised system for the enforcement of these provisions envisaged by the Commission in its 1999 White Paper is likely to have an impact on this area [see now Reg 1/2003 p. 506]. While it is true that the Commission will continue to play a pivotal role in directing competition policy in the new system, it remains to be seen whether national competition authorities and national courts will be as motivated as the Commission is by the goal of market integration. Second, the growing trend towards economic globalisation, which is progressively leading to the international integration of markets, may also have a diluting effect on the single market aim.

■ **QUESTION**

In the light of these trends and pressures, which direction do you expect EU competition law to take? Which direction should it take?

NOTE: For additional material and resources see the Online Resource Centre at: www.oxfordtextbooks.co.uk/orc/weatherill12e.

PART III

Policy-Making, Governance, and the Constitutional Debate

17

Harmonization and Common Policy-Making

SECTION 1: INTRODUCTION

Much – perhaps too much – of this book has concentrated on the *negative* aspects of the European Union's substantive law. Articles 30, 34, 45, and 110 TFEU, for example, all forbid the maintenance of national rules which restrict free movement. The suppression by law of trade barriers assists in market integration. Yet the development of the Union is also dependent on a *positive* contribution by the law. An integrated market can only be fully realized by common policy-making; by creating positive EU rules. Article 3(3) TEU, set out at p. 236, insists on the importance of both negative and positive action. The positive elements of Union policy-making assume many forms and may be adopted under a wide range of Treaty provisions. This chapter is by no means an exhaustive survey of EU policy-making. Instead, it selects particular areas as illustrations and endeavours to extract and illuminate key themes and endemic problems in the shaping of EU policies. The Lisbon Treaty has made small, mostly cosmetic, adjustments to the material under examination in this chapter, but it has not addressed, still less solved, any of the deep-rooted questions.

The first extract presents a useful overview of the issues. It reintroduces some aspects already touched on in Chapter 9. It is also well over two decades old. Deliberately so. These are not simply today's issues. These are yesterday's issues and they are tomorrow's issues too.

J. Lodge, *The European Community and the Challenge of the Future*
(London: Pinter Publishers, 1989), pp. 83–5

(Footnote omitted.)

The 1990s are clearly going to be preoccupied with issues arising out of the attempt to realize the Single European Market (SEM). An artificial distinction can be made between what might loosely be defined as 'internal' and 'external' policies. However, it must be remembered that internal policies have external effects and the idea of an impenetrable barrier separating the two is misleading. By 'internal' policies, we mean that group of policies whose goals are directly related to the accomplishment of targets within the EC: they are inner-directed; they seek to modify in some way policy activities within the domestic settings of the EC and its member states. 'External policies' are outer-directed and aim at producing a degree of agreement and/or consensual policies . . . towards non-EC, often known as 'third', states . . .

However, 'domestic' policies like the C[ommon] A[gricultural] P[olicy], attempts to manage difficult sectoral areas (like steel and textiles) and to advance EC monetary integration, fiscal harmonization and capital and labour mobility as well as new efforts in the environmental and information technology as well (IT) trade spheres spill-out into the external arena. As a result, the EC's own arrangements for initiating, managing and executing policies in those sectors become stressed by the absence of appropriate mechanisms to manage effectively external effects of domestic policies that are often highly sensitive. Moreover, the goal of achieving a common market (as in the 1950s) and now a SEM inadvertently encourages policymakers at all levels from the EC itself through national government down to local government to focus on internal problems and on the difficulties associated with member states having to adjust to new policy environments and conditions. Since the effects of policies are largely unknown at the outset, and since subsequent wrangling is likely to result from unpalatable effects within certain sectors or member states, it is to be expected that policymakers will not necessarily anticipate possibly deleterious external effects. Moreover, in dealing with them (as in the case of Mediterranean enlargement), they have to adopt some means of prioritizing the claims of those who feel that their interests (usually trade interests) have been harmed as a result. The criteria they choose will almost always be contested.

It is obvious that neither a common market nor the SEM can be established without often unwelcome consequences for third states. The mere establishment of a Common External Tariff demands adjustments both by members of the bloc applying that tariff and by those who export to the bloc. Various forms of protectionism and market support also have trade diversifying effects. The year 1992 has become shorthand for the completion of the SEM. While its consolidation will extend beyond the 1990s, many third states and commercial interests within them are operating as if the SEM will assume concrete shape by 1992. This is especially true of the EC's major trading partners, including the rump EFTA. . . Third states are forced to adapt to the EC's policies and its anticipated effects. EC rim states seem to be following parallel actions, at a minimum, to minimize anticipated difficulties from the SEM's establishment.

While such effects are largely an unknown quantity, they are recognized. Predicting and managing them is, however, difficult. Equally, the internal consequences of a limited range of inner-directed policies are often overlooked, or insufficient resources are set aside to encourage appropriate supranational-led action. Economic and political considerations explain this. Certainly this has been the EC's experience. The accent on the removal of obstacles to trade within the EC led, for example, to the EC being castigated as a 'rich man's club'. The SEM has been similarly construed as a commercial ploy whose uncertain benefits would gravitate towards already rich centres – the Golden Triangle – wealthy elites and powerful companies already in a position to benefit from the hypothesized economies of scale consequent upon the SEM . . .. Whereas the Rome Treaty establishing the EEC made some provisions to assist poorer sectors, it did not 'flag' them in the way in which Commission President Delors did.

The qualitative difference to European integration in the 1990s inheres not simply in the modifications to the Rome Treaty introduced through the Single European Act, but in the way in which they have been interpreted in the public domain. The politico-economic context in which the SEA unfurled partly accounts for this. The era of Green parties on mainland Europe and generalized high unemployment with its attendant social problems meant that something more than mere lip-service had to be paid to sectors that clearly were high on the Member States' domestic political agenda. Equally important, however, was M. Delors's intention to define the EC's *raison d'être*. Since its inception, this issue had been side-stepped. . . . The Monnet-Schuman visions and methods stressed the establishment of concrete achievements to create real solidarity and to realise the common good. However, the goal of European Union had been obfuscated by the process. Gradualism reigned supreme: indeed, had to assume centre stage at a time when national sovereignty was not only sorely tried but was still being slowly granted to the new West German state by its Western allies.

The phrase 'an ever closer union' disguised or hid the likely extensive implications of the creation of a common market for thirty years. National governments occasionally protested loudly at steps likely to augment the authority and competence of the EC's institutions. Such protestations seemed to reflect anxiety over an inability to make others in the EC follow a line prescribed by one state's national interest. A well thought-out understanding of what the various sectoral policy measures to advance integration implied in the longer term for both the Member States' and the EC's capacity to deliver the goods proved elusive. No matter how serious and protracted disagreements among the Member States, it was clear that the EC was not only an acceptable forum for the pursuit of goals but one which soon attracted more members. The effect on the EC of many states using it instrumentally to advance national interests was, paradoxically and contrary to the assumptions implicit in many integration theories, to reinforce and consolidate rather than weaken it. Many appreciated that the political implications of the processes of economic integration could not be forever ignored. Few appreciated that greater political integration would have consequences for macro and microeconomic sectoral integration.

It was comparatively easy in the early stages of European integration to deride and dismiss the future visions as 'federalist rantings'. By the 1980s, as Mrs Thatcher was to learn, this ceased to be the case. Many still abhor 'federalism' (often without understanding what it implies). But it is also clear that the EC's *raison d'être* needs some clarification. Public and elite expectations of what it can deliver exceed its capacity. The notion that the EC is a political animal is accepted. M. Delors tried to set out some parameters and to project a vision of a future EC. The precise details of the vision are less important than the fact that the vision makes clear that domestic and external policy sectors are irrevocably intertwined; that any benefits from economic integration must be shared in the name of social justice and its disadvantages offset. While the 'Social Europe' package was disappointing, the highlighting of different tranches of the SEM has imprinted a socialist element firmly on the EC.

A faint socialist watermark is clear in the Rome Treaty. Conscience calls for measures to deal with the negative effects of integration. Some incentives exist for labour mobility. By and large, however, the 'social' aspects of integration have played a secondary role. Attention has focused on removing barriers to trade and other forms of economic discrimination that might adversely affect intra-EC trade. The creation of the SEM and an industrial base for the EC remains frustrated by weaknesses in the EC's policy processes, the absence of consensus over macroeconomic goals and the continuing wrangling among the Twelve over the locus of authority.

Problems also inhere in the piecemeal approach to policymaking, the identification and implementation of sectoral policy goals that require a horizontal rather than a vertical approach to ensure rational and optimal outcomes. Moreover, the domestic organization and funding of agencies and departments charged with implementing and enforcing EC policy varies so greatly as to further frustrate rational and approximately common outcomes. Moreover, the EC lacks an overall economic plan (the SEM only partly disguises this). Instead of coherent over-arching economic policy, the EC has a series of economic instruments, often designed to prevent national actions that will distort competition (such as non-tariff and technical barriers to trade, state aids, export premiums, preferential energy and freight rates for exports, for example) or that unfairly give or allow companies to abuse a dominant position . . .

NOTE: To repeat Professor Lodge's words – 'Many appreciated that the political implications of the processes of economic integration could not be forever ignored' . . . 'it is also clear that the EC's *raison d'être* needs some clarification'. And how! The reader who has reached this stage of the book will have no difficulty in identifying how these comments may be extended beyond the SEM project to *inter alia* the prospects for Economic and Monetary Union, the role of the Charter on Fundamental Rights, the construction of an 'area of freedom, security and justice' and the rise of the status of Citizenship of the Union, Enlargement to embrace 28 Member States today and the path *via* the Convention on the 'Future of Europe' to the downfall of the Treaty establishing a Constitution and the uncelebrated, almost apologetic, entry into force of the Lisbon Treaty in December 2009.

SECTION 2: HARMONIZATION POLICY

Even at the simple level of the quest for market access, it is obvious that not just *negative* but also *positive* rule making is required. Articles 34 and 45 TFEU, for example, do not forbid all national rules which partition the market. There are derogations in Article 36 and Article 45(3) TFEU which envisage the maintenance of lawful trade barriers. Moreover, the *Cassis de Dijon* principle introduced a principle of mutual recognition that was qualified by the admission that a regulating State is entitled to show a justification in the public interest for its rules even if they impede inter-State trade (see Chapter 12 dealing with Article 34 TFEU, Chapter 14 dealing with Article 56 TFEU). Article 110 TFEU forbids discriminatory internal taxation, but the tax systems of the Member States remain different, and consequently trade barriers may remain justified in order to allow the collection of taxes. A *positive* set of rules is needed to remove such lawful trade barriers. This explains the need for the European Union's harmonization programme.

THE COMMISSION'S SECOND BIENNIAL REPORT ON THE APPLICATION OF THE PRINCIPLE OF MUTUAL RECOGNITION IN THE SINGLE MARKET

COM (2002) 419, Para 3

Mutual recognition is not always a miracle solution for ensuring the free movement of goods in the single market. Harmonisation or further harmonisation remains without doubt one of the most effective instruments, both for economic operators and for the national administrations.

Harmonization sets common EU standards of, for example, health or consumer protection, which deprive States of the ability to take unilateral action in defence of such interests which would inhibit free trade.

A: Harmonization as an introduction to the wider debate

The Treaty has always contained a legal base authorizing legislative harmonization. It has been used for a wide variety of harmonization Directives connected with the process of building the internal market, stretching from, for example, procedures for the award of public works and supply contracts (Dir. 2004/18 [2004] OJ L134/114) to unfair terms in consumer contracts (Dir. 93/13 [1993] OJ L95/29) to the regulation of unfair business-to-consumer commercial practices (Dir. 2005/29 [2005] OJ L149/22, encountered in Chapter 14). Today the most important provision is Article 114 TFEU. This was Article 100a before the entry into force of the Amsterdam Treaty, it was then amended and re-numbered Article 95 EC, before finally becoming Article 114 TFEU in December 2009 as a result of the entry into force of the Lisbon Treaty, which made minor adjustments to the text which are of no material significance to the law. Article 114 TFEU has been encountered before in this book (pp. 33, 318) but its text deserves repetition.

ARTICLE 114 TFEU

ARTICLE 114

1. Save where otherwise provided in the Treaties, the following provisions shall apply for the achievement of the objectives set out in Article 26. The European Parliament and the Council shall, acting in accordance with the ordinary legislative procedure and after consulting the Economic and Social Committee, adopt the measures for the approximation of the provisions laid down by law, regulation or administrative action in Member States which have as their object the establishment and functioning of the internal market.

2. Paragraph 1 shall not apply to fiscal provisions, to those relating to the free movement of persons nor to those relating to the rights and interests of employed persons.

3. The Commission, in its proposals envisaged in paragraph 1 concerning health, safety, environmental protection and consumer protection, will take as a base a high level of protection, taking account in particular of any new development based on scientific facts. Within their respective powers, the European Parliament and the Council will also seek to achieve this objective.

4. If, after the adoption of a harmonisation measure by the European Parliament and the Council, by the Council or by the Commission, a Member State deems it necessary to maintain national provisions on grounds of major needs referred to in Article 36, or relating to the protection of the environment or the working environment, it shall notify the Commission of these provisions as well as the grounds for maintaining them.

5. Moreover, without prejudice to paragraph 4, if, after the adoption of a harmonisation measure by the European Parliament and the Council, by the Council or by the Commission, a Member State deems it necessary to introduce national provisions based on new scientific evidence relating to the protection of the environment or the working environment on grounds of a problem specific to that Member State arising after the adoption of the harmonisation measure, it shall notify the Commission of the envisaged provisions as well as the grounds for introducing them.

6. The Commission shall, within six months of the notifications as referred to in paragraphs 4 and 5, approve or reject the national provisions involved after having verified whether or not they are a means of arbitrary discrimination or a disguised restriction on trade between Member States and whether or not they shall constitute an obstacle to the functioning of the internal market.

In the absence of a decision by the Commission within this period the national provisions referred to in paragraphs 4 and 5 shall be deemed to have been approved.

When justified by the complexity of the matter and in the absence of danger for human health, the Commission may notify the Member State concerned that the period referred to in this paragraph maybe extended for a further period of up to six months.

7. When, pursuant to paragraph 6, a Member State is authorised to maintain or introduce national provisions derogating from a harmonisation measure, the Commission shall immediately examine whether to propose an adaptation to that measure.

8. When a Member State raises a specific problem on public health in a field which has been the subject of prior harmonisation measures, it shall bring it to the attention of the Commission which shall immediately examine whether to propose appropriate measures to the Council.

9. By way of derogation from the procedure laid down in Articles 258 and 259, the Commission and any Member State may bring the matter directly before the Court of Justice of the European Union if it considers that another Member State is making improper use of the powers provided for in this Article.

10. The harmonisation measures referred to above shall, in appropriate cases, include a safeguard clause authorising the Member States to take, for one or more of the non-economic reasons referred to in Article 36, provisional measures subject to a Union control procedure.

NOTE: It was established in Chapter 2 that Article 114 TFEU does not confer an open-ended competence on the Union legislature to approximate or to harmonize laws. The 'Tobacco Advertising' case (Case C-376/98 *Germany* v *European Parliament and Council of the European Union* [2000] ECR I-8419), examined at p. 33, insists on the demonstration of an adequate link between the measure of harmonization and the process of market-making in Europe. This, at bottom, reflects the constitutionally vital principle of conferral found in Article 5 TEU.

ARTICLE 5(1), (2) TEU

1. The limits of Union competences are governed by the principle of conferral. The use of Union competences is governed by the principles of subsidiarity and proportionality.

2. Under the principle of conferral, the Union shall act only within the limits of the competences conferred upon it by the Member States in the Treaties to attain the objectives set out therein. Competences not conferred upon the Union in the Treaties remain with the Member State.

NOTE: The principle of conferral represents the formal constitutional dimension of a much deeper set of policy questions. These may be grouped around the general inquiry – *how much Europe*? Or more precisely, *how much European Union*? 'Tobacco Advertising' emphasizes the Court's readiness to police the limits of the powers granted to the EU by the Treaty, but there are broader normative questions about what *should be* the nature of the relationship between the Union and its Member States. It is undisputed that in some areas action in common is required in order to achieve the objectives of the Union. Member States have agreed that they will surrender aspects of local autonomy in favour of a centralized decision-making competence. But how much action in common? Across how many fields? Professor Lodge's sketch (p. 521) reveals some of the tensions associated with the expansion of Union activity, and this is a process that has evolved according to ever more complex patterns as the experiment has continued. The fact that each successive round of Treaty revision has tended to add new competences to the Union's list, combined with the steady enlargement of the Union, once six States, now 28, has deepened the scope of action in common. Moreover, many EU competences are capable of exercise by Qualified Majority Vote in Council according to the ordinary legislative procedure found in Article 294 TFEU. This is true of Article 114 TFEU. The release of State veto power in Council accentuates the impression of a Union which possesses a degree of self-momentum– or at least a Union in which majoritarian practices hold sway. And so the hubbub of debate has grown louder – has the European Union been tipped too far in favour of centralized decision-making authority to the detriment of local autonomy?

This chapter explores the contours of the debate: *how much Europe, how much European Union?* Harmonization pursuant to Article 114 TFEU offers a helpfully illuminating introduction to the investigation. There are important policy issues which emerge from the harmonization programme. Harmonization is designed to protect interests such as public health in the framework of an integrating Union in which the advantages of free trade will be secured. Harmonization, then, has a dual aim: protection of the citizen and facilitation of free trade. The difficulty of achieving both objectives was discussed in the context of the free movement of goods in the several extracts presented at pp. 352–62. The problems of fiscal harmonization were discussed at p. 379.

Harmonization, as a process of replacing diverse national rules with common rules for a common market, is a perfect example of the triumph of centralized rule-making over local autonomy. Market integration seems to demand such a transfer of regulatory authority, but the functional and geographical expansion of the Union increasingly reveals that harmonization cannot be treated merely as a technical process. It is capable of affecting important national interests. In Article 114 itself, the tensions involved in attempting to satisfy all interests affected by harmonization emerge in the procedure found in paras (4) *et seq*. This demonstrates that 'levelling the playing field' is not of itself a strong enough rationale to persuade States to surrender all regulatory leeway in a harmonized field. And Article 114(3) suggests anxiety about the *quality* of the regime to be introduced as the harmonized basis for regulating the market.

At least two arguments may be advanced to question the feasibility and desirability of harmonization:

(a) Harmonization of this nature tends to be conservative. The standard is fixed until such time as the legislator is able to alter it – a laborious process, especially at EU level. The inflexible, rigid standard hinders innovation (e.g., in respect of cheaper or safer devices), and is consequently inefficient.

(b) Harmonization of this nature suppresses national tradition. Why should one single EU rule replace national preference? Is free trade a goal which overrides the capacity of individual States to retain higher standards of, say, environmental and consumer protection?

B: The New Approach to harmonization policy

The difficulties in achieving the harmonization of technical rules relating to products led in the 1980s to a new impetus in harmonization policy. The problems of old style harmonization are well explained in the following extract.

J. Pelkmans, 'The New Approach to Technical Harmonization and Standardization' (1986–87) 25 JCMS 249, 251–3

(Footnote omitted.)

THE 'TRADITIONAL' APPROACH OF THE POLICY REGIME

For more than one and a half decades the European Commission has tried to pursue an ambitious harmonization programme. Following a few ad hoc cases, and a prudent first step towards the harmonization of the national regulations concerning pharmaceutical products, in March 1968, the Commission proposed a General Programme. From that time until the so-called Mutual Information Directive 83/189/EEC [now replaced by Directive 98/34: pp. 126, 258], an incredible amount of energy on the part of civil servants and experts had been devoted to the production of an extremely limited number of Council Directives. Many of these directives focus on specific technical *aspects* of products and they therefore fail to solve all the problems of access in product markets. During these fifteen years the EC has adopted on average only a little over ten technical directives a year.

It is doubtful, to say the least, whether such a slow speed can actually bring about a net reduction in the technical barriers to trade in the Community in view of the simultaneous accretion of regulations in Member States. To put it more strongly, given the increase in bureaucratic regulatory capacity in recent decades in all Member States and the greater societal preference for environmental and consumer protection, it can safely be presumed that the tempo of national regulation has, for many years, exceeded by far that of the annual output of 'aspect-directives' at EC level with respect to a rather limited group of products. Apart from being *inefficient* – due to extensive and drawn out consultations on technical specifications – the method was *ineffective* as well: a general improvement of mutual market access was not achieved, at best there was only a slowing down of the rate of increase of technical barriers.

Nor did the wider European standardization processes proceed smoothly. The history of CEN (European Standardization Committee) shows clearly that, without some connection with the EC's own harmonization policy, progress at the wider European level tends to be exceedingly difficult. A serious drawback of the functioning of CEN is that no long-term programmes are being developed to remove the trade-impeding effects of different national standards (notwithstanding their private and voluntary character) . . .

DRAWBACKS OF THE 'TRADITIONAL' APPROACH

In earlier work I have analyzed extensively the considerable disadvantages and shortcomings of the traditional strategy of technical harmonization (and standardization) of the Community. Briefly these consist of:

1. time-consuming and cumbersome procedures
2. excessive uniformity
3. unanimity (ex Art. 100, EEC) [now 115 TFEU]
4. the failure, except rarely, to develop a linkage between the harmonization of technical regulations and European standardization, leading to wasteful duplication, useless inconsistencies and time lost
5. the slowness of European harmonization and standardization relative to national regulation and standardization
6. a neglect of the problems of certification and testing
7. the incapacity to solve the third country problem
8. implementation problems in Member States
9. a lack of political interest by the Ministers.

It is not surprising that by the early 1980s the question of the removal of technical barriers to trade in the EC had led to profound feelings of frustration and disappointment.

The policy climate in which the elimination of technical barriers to trade in the EC had to be realized was such that the individual protectionist was thriving whereas the dynamic exporter, attempting to encroach upon other markets, was hampered. Of course, the opposite climate should characterize European market integration for the benefit of the Community's economy at large.

NOTE: Consequently, the Council adopted in 1985 a Resolution approving a *New Approach* to technical harmonization.

COUNCIL RESOLUTION OF 7 MAY 1985 ON A NEW APPROACH TO TECHNICAL HARMONIZATION AND STANDARDS [1985] OJ C136/1; ANNEX, 'GUIDELINES FOR A NEW APPROACH TO TECHNICAL HARMONIZATION AND STANDARDS'

The following are the four fundamental principals [sic] on which the new approach is based:

(i) legislative harmonization is limited to the adoption, by means of Directives based on Article 100 of the EEC Treaty, of the essential safety requirements (or other requirements in the general interest) with which products put on the market must conform, and which should therefore enjoy free movement throughout the Community.
(ii) the task of drawing up the technical specifications needed for the production and placing on the market of products conforming to the essential requirements established by the Directives, while taking into account the current stage of technology, is entrusted to organizations competent in the standardization area,
(iii) these technical specifications are not mandatory and maintain their status of voluntary standards,
(iv) but at the same time national authorities are obliged to recognise that products manufactured in conformity with harmonized standards (or, provisionally, with national standards) are presumed to conform to the 'essential requirements' established by the Directive. (This signifies that the producer has the choice of not manufacturing in conformity with the standards but that in this event he has an obligation to prove that his products conform to the essential requirements of the Directive).

In order that this system may operate it is necessary:

(i) on the one hand that the standards offer a guarantee of quality with regard to the 'essential requirements' established by the Directives.
(ii) on the other hand that the public authorities keep intact their responsibility for the protection of safety (or other requirements envisaged) on their territory.

The quality of harmonized standards must be ensured by standardization mandates, conferred by the Commission, the execution of which must conform to the general guidelines which have been the subject of agreement between the Commission and the European standardization organizations. In so far as national standards are concerned their quality must be verified by a procedure at Community level managed by the Commission, assisted by a standing committee composed of officials from national administrations.

At the same time safeguard procedures must be provided for, under the management of the Commission assisted by the same committee, in order to allow the competent public authorities the possibility of contesting the conformity of a product, the validity of a certificate or the quality of a standard.

In following this system of legislative harmonization in each area in which it is feasible, the Commission intends to be able to halt the proliferation of excessively technical separate Directives for each product. The scope of Directives according to the 'general reference to standards' formula should encompass wide product categories and types of risk.

The Community could on the one hand, therefore, complete the extremely complex undertaking of harmonizing technical legislation and on the other hand promote the development and application of European standards. These are essential conditions for the improvement of the competitiveness of its industry.

NOTE: Accordingly, Directives conforming to the New Approach need not include detailed specifications. They instead set broad performance standards. Products meeting those standards are entitled to access to the markets of all the Member States. See, for example, Directive 2001/95, the Directive on General Product Safety [2002] OJ L11/4.

The advantages of the New Approach are manifold.

J. Pelkmans, 'The New Approach to Technical Harmonization and Standardization' (1986–7) 25 JCMS 249, 257

(Footnotes omitted.)

ADVANTAGES OF THE 'NEW APPROACH'

The most important potential advantages of the 'new approach' are (i) greater coherence between the policy regime and the legal regime to eliminate technical barriers, and (ii) the better conveyance between European harmonization of technical regulations and European standardization. As stated earlier, the Council will have to assume the task of reaching a 'European doctrine' in the fields of safety, health, etc., so that the technical barriers to intra-EC free movement can disappear. The new approach is a serious attempt to achieve this coherence by combining *total harmonization* of the objectives at issue (safety, etc.) with a *flexible approach* of the means (standardization). It also improves the scope for a timely interchange of information so that national draft-standards and technical draft-regulations can be altered or converted into European ones before formally taking effect.

These advantages are commendable and may explain the willingness in Member States and in various circles to view the new approach with a 'prejugé favourable'. They are however *potential* advantages because a great deal depends on the actual results, both in the Council, with respect to the total harmonization of objectives of health, safety, etc., and also from the standardization processes in the CEN/CENELEC framework.

NOTE: Successful standards-making is by no means a merely technical matter – in this paper Pelkmans concludes that 'European industry lacks these standards and, thereby, a necessary condition for maintaining and improving its world competitive position (p. 261). Many of the perceived economic advantages of the New Approach should be familiar from the material found in Chapter 9. See also G. Bermann, 'The Single European Act: A New Constitution for the Community?' (1989) 27 *Columbia Journal of Transnational Law* 529; D. Waelbroeck, 'L'harmonisation des règles et normes téchniques dans la CEE' (1988) CDE 243.

C: Questioning the New Approach

Nonetheless, fears have been expressed on several levels about the desirability of the New Approach. First, it has been alleged that the New Approach is liable to reduce effective protection of the citizen by diminishing the explicit detailed commitment to social protection. A connection should here be made with the discussion at p. 352 of the arguably related shift in balance in favour of free trade achieved by the '*Cassis de Dijon*' (Case 120/78) judgment and its subsequent interpretation. The following extract discusses the matter in connection with the free movement of foodstuffs.

O. Brouwer, 'Free Movement of Foodstuffs and Quality Requirements; Has the Commission Got it Wrong?'

(1988) 25 CML Rev 237, 248–52

(Some footnotes omitted.)

4. CRITICAL REMARKS

The Commission's rejection of detailed recipes in Community legislation can be qualified as a minimalist approach; the Commission leaves quality policy with regard to foodstuffs to the Member States and leaves the enforcement and further realisation of the free movement of foodstuffs in this respect to the judiciary. A minimalist approach is not necessarily a bad one; however, in the present case, the foundations for the adoption of this approach are shaky, for the reasons discussed below.

4.1 The borderline between quality requirements and public health requirements

It must first of all be noted that, in general, the composition or manufacturing characteristics of a foodstuff cannot be isolated from matters which are covered by public health requirements. The use of certain ingredients may have as a corollary the use of certain pesticides or additives (the German beer case provides a striking example in this respect [p. 324]), or the prescription of a certain manufacturing process or treatment which is regulated by law to protect public health (e.g., a biotechnological process). In consequence, the mutual recognition of quality requirements is often only one aspect when the question arises whether a foodstuff, which is lawfully manufactured and marketed in one Member State, may be marketed in another Member State. In any event, it seems inevitable that the free movement of foodstuffs within the Community will remain dependent on the harmonisation of public health requirements (and methods of inspection, analysis and sampling) and the further development and coordination of a public health policy with regard to foodstuffs at Community level.

However, the point at issue is that difficulties may arise as to the borderline between quality requirements and issues of public health even with regard to recipe laws as such. The Commission rightly admits in its Communication that it may be necessary, in the interest of public health, to define in law the nature and composition of a foodstuff, even if the purchaser is adequately informed, by a label, of these elements. The fear then arises that the new legislative approach of the Commission, as set out in its Communication, may partly be jeopardised; after all, who is going to establish whether a given composition of a foodstuff, despite the fact that it may have been lawfully produced and marketed in the exporting Member State, may be undesirable from the point of view of public health in the Member State of import? It must be borne clearly in mind that the Court has in this respect consistently held that the eating habits in the Member State of import comprise one of the elements which may be taken into account when considering potential dangers for public health.

The Commission's viewpoint seems to indicate that it is the task of national courts and the Court of Justice to assess this matter. In fact, the judiciary has been able in a number of cases to dismiss the plea of public health when manifestly ill-founded or when the national legislation in question was clearly disproportionate.[29] However, apart from these situations, the general problem arises to what extent the judiciary is equipped to assess whether products are or may be positively harmful to health. Often scientists, who have been called as expert witnesses in legal proceedings, do not agree, or, findings of scientific research show that uncertainties remain. If one adds to this difficulty the fact that the Court has consistently held that, insofar as scientific uncertainties remain, it is in principle for the Member States, in the absence of harmonisation, to decide what degree of protection of public health they intend to assure,[30] it seems justified to conclude that the judiciary may often not be in a position to overrule the view of the national legislator.

29 The German beer case is a clear example in this respect [Case 178/84, p. 324].

30 See in particular Case 174/82, *Sandoz*, [1983] ECR 2445 [p. 313; and note accompanying discussion there of the 'precautionary principle'].

4.2 Is the Commission's approach desirable?

Apart from the preceding observations, it is submitted that the rigorousness of the Commission's new approach is not desirable. The absolute priority accorded to the principle of free movement of goods, and the abandonment, as a matter of principle, of further harmonisation, is undesirable for several reasons.

4.2.1 The protection of the consumer

4.2.1.1 Foodstuffs which lack essential characteristics

It is not my intention to rehearse once again the frequent criticism that the *Cassis de Dijon* ruling will automatically lead to a general reduction in quality, since the most liberal national rule will become general practice. This question has already been discussed *in extenso* on many occasions and the Commission is probably right to reject this criticism in general. The Commission is equally right to reject the similar criticism that a lack of Community compositional rules will automatically lead to a general reduction in quality.

However, the question which seems more appropriate in the context of its Communication and which the Commission does not discuss, is whether the Commission should, as a matter of principle, abandon the introduction of any Community legislation in this field. It may turn out in the end to be highly undesirable with regard to the protection of the consumer to abandon such legislation. In particular, if foodstuffs are brought on the market which lack essential characteristics and are nutritionally inferior, the argument that the choice should be left to the consumer comes across as a bromide. Such situations do not necessarily stem from the disparity in national recipe laws, but may stem from the fact that a foodstuff is not subject to any regulation in the exporting Member State or has been exempted therefrom.

The food laws of the Member States provide numerous exemptions for the manufacturing of foodstuffs which are intended for export. An illustration of this can be found again in the Italian pasta cases: the mandatory use of durum wheat meal is not prescribed for pasta intended for export. Moreover, it may be noted that a number of Member States have exempted products which are intended for export from the official inspections which are prescribed by national legislation with regard to foodstuffs, to ensure protection against public health risks and fraud. But apparently, even if there is no such exemption, the competent authorities of Member States do often, in practice, not carry out any inspections with regard to foodstuffs intended for export.

NOTE: Also worth reading in this vein are H.-C. Von Heydebrand u.d. Lasa, 'Free Movement of Foodstuffs, Consumer Protection and Food Standards in the European Community: has the Court of Justice got it wrong?' (1991) 16 EL Rev 391; C. MacMaolain, 'Free movement of foodstuffs, quality requirements and consumer protection: have the Court and Commission both got it wrong?' (2001) 26 EL Rev 413.

Concern has also been expressed about what has been seen as the privatization of the standards-making process under the New Approach. The next extract addresses some questions about the democratic accountability of aspects of the legislative process which emerges from the New Approach's shift in emphasis.

R. Dehousse, '1992 and Beyond: the Institutional Dimension of the Internal Market Programme'

[1989/1] LIEI 109, 125–7

(Footnotes omitted.)

A. DELEGATION OF POWERS: EFFICIENCY V DEMOCRACY?

We have seen that the internal market programme was framed under the assumption that no major alteration to the key principle of decision-making by consensus was likely to take place in the near future. In spite of the long-term effects they might possibly have, the modifications contained in the Single Act did not fundamentally change the nature of the problem. If a leap forward is to be realised, it is therefore necessary to think of alternative ways of avoiding the protracted bargaining to which decision-making by consensus amounts most of the time.

One such way is of course to reduce the legislative agenda, which is as we saw one of the main advantages of the principle of mutual recognition. Another way is to limit the Council's work-load by delegating more decision-making powers to other bodies. This latter way has been more actively explored at Community level in recent years, be it in the field of standardisation or through an increase in the Commission's powers as regards the implementation of Community legislation. Although these two techniques involve different kinds of problems, they raise similar political issues.

The new strategy defined by the Commission in the wake of *Cassis de Dijon* not only limits the extent to which harmonisation is necessary, but also involves a new approach to ways of harmonisation. The basic feature of this new line is the distinction drawn between essential safety requirements, which must be adopted at Community level, and technical specifications, the defining of which can be entrusted to private standardisation bodies. This new approach was defined by the Council even before the White Paper on the internal market was finalised. Later on, the 'Model directive' on technical harmonisation made it clear that although standards defined by European bodies like CEN or CENELEC – or, in their absence, by national bodies – were to retain their non-mandatory character, products manufactured according to these technical specifications were to be regarded as conforming to the essential requirements laid down by the directives.

One of the reasons used to justify this mechanism is that since harmonisation is of direct interest to the industry and industrialists have a more direct knowledge of the technical problems involved, it would be unwise to give this task to an already overburdened Community legislator. It is clear that the reference to standards can also ease the updating of technical regulations, which is often a delicate matter. But this search for greater efficiency cannot ignore the basic requirements of the Commission legal system. It has been stressed that since compliance with standards entitles a product to free movement, the reference to standards in directives amounts to a delegation of competence from the Council to private bodies. It can therefore only be made in accordance with the general principles laid down by the Court of Justice: delegated powers must be of a clearly defined executive nature and subject to the same conditions as those imposed on the delegating institution, such as the duty to state reasons and the necessary [sic] of judicial control [*Meroni* (Case 9/56)]. These requirements are in a way the transportation in legal terms of more general concerns. If reference to standards is to become a permanent feature of Community regulatory policy, the transparency of this process must be ensured so as to guarantee that the interests of all parties concerned (the industry, of course, but consumers as well, for instance) are duly taken into account. In other words, a balance must be struck between public and private concerns.

How could the requirements laid down by the Court be satisfied? It has been suggested that standards could be published as an annex to which harmonisation directives will refer, in order to make judicial control possible. To some extent, the difficulty was also anticipated by the Model Directive. The need to assign clear limits to the delegated powers surfaces in the description which is given of the essential requirements to be covered by harmonisation directives:

> 'The essential safety requirements. . . shall be worded precisely enough in order to create, on transposition into national law, legally binding obligations which can be enforced. They should be so formulated as to enable the certifications straight away to certify products as being in conformity, having regard to those requirements in the absence of standards.'

While this line of conduct is probably able to reconcile the somewhat contradictory requirements of legitimacy and efficiency, the practical difficulties should not be underestimated: whereas too much discretion given to private bodies could be regarded as incompatible with the guidelines given by the Court, a too detailed directive would amount to no less than a return to the 'old approach'. The implementation of the new approach will therefore be no easy task.

■ QUESTION

P. Birkenshaw, I. Harden, and N. Lewis, in *Government by Moonlight* (London: Unwin, 1990), conclude a survey of the implications for democratic accountability of privatization in the UK context as follows:

> It would be a fine irony if British citizens were to get a bill of rights only to find that the 'public' authorities against which the rights might be impleaded had largely been replaced by 'private' bodies, which can be rendered accountable only through private law mechanisms.

To what extent do you think that the privatizing trend of the New Approach yields a parallel (and perhaps greater) democratic deficit at EU level?

NOTES

1. The general issue is how to assess the efficiency and legitimacy of the harmonization programme as a basis for managing the market created pursuant to the rules of the Treaty. As the extracts demonstrate, this is not a narrow technical matter. And it is an enduring area of interest. For more recent debate in related areas, see C. Hodges, *European Regulation of Consumer Product Safety* (Oxford: OUP, 2005); H. Schepel, *The Constitution of Private Governance* (Oxford: Hart Publishing, 2005); and M. de Visser, *Network-based Governance in EC Law – The example of EC Competition and EC Communications Law* (Oxford: Hart Publishing, 2009).

   In conclusion, it should be pointed out that the New Approach, although now firmly embedded within the EU's regulatory strategy, is not seen as appropriate for *all* future harmonization. The realization of economies of scale within the wider market will sometimes be dependent on effective EU-wide harmonization. In the absence of uniformity, as H. von Sydow has observed (in R. Bieber et al., at p. 239), 'it will be possible to buy an electrical appliance in any part of the Community and to take it across the border without restriction, but, once at home, it may still prove impossible to plug it into the wall socket'.
2. The second important component in the shift of emphasis in the Commission's harmonization programme was the change in voting rules introduced by the Single European Act in 1987. In what was then Article 100a, an important move towards qualified majority voting in Council in place of unanimity was made. This is now found in Article 114 TFEU. Yet States still retain some protection against the risk that their standards would be lowered by the harmonized rule. This is the purpose of Article 114(3) and (4) *et seq*. See p. 524 for the text: as already suggested, these provisions show the sensitivity of trying to introduce a common rule into a system characterized by the diversity that is a feature (and strength) of Europe. This is the thematic issue that holds together the material traversed in this chapter.

SECTION 3: METHODS OF HARMONIZATION

A: Harmonization and the allocation of competence between the EU and the Member States

When the EU adopts secondary legislation, what is the impact on the competence of Member States in the area covered by the EU measure? Some provisions of the Treaty that authorize the adoption of secondary legislation explicitly address this question. Others do not.

Articles 12 and 169 TFEU deal with consumer protection. The Union is authorized to legislate in order to promote the interests of consumers and to ensure a high level of consumer protection. It shall do so by adopting measures pursuant to Article 114 in the context of the completion of the internal market (Article 169(2)(a)) and also by adopting measures which support, supplement, and monitor the policy pursued by the Member States (Article 169(2)(b)). In the latter case it is explicitly provided that such measures 'shall not prevent any Member State from maintaining or introducing more stringent protective measures. Such measures must be compatible with the Treaties. The Commission shall be notified of them.' This is Article 169(4) TFEU.

A similar formula governs the impact of EU action on national competence to legislate in the field of environmental protection. Article 192 TFEU provides a base for the adoption of EU measures to protect the environment. Article 193 then declares that 'The protective measures adopted pursuant to Article 192 shall not prevent any Member State from maintaining or introducing more stringent protective measures. Such measures must be compatible with the Treaties. They shall be notified to the Commission.'

Accordingly, Union legislation governing consumer protection adopted under Article 169 and environmental protection adopted under Article 192 does not displace national competence to act. The Member States must comply with the rules adopted at Union level but, if they so choose, they can also go further to protect the consumer and the environment. So, for example, in *Commission* v *Belgium* (Case C-100/08 [2009] ECR I-140) Regulation 338/97 on protection of species, adopted pursuant to the Treaty provisions on environmental protection, did *not* preclude Belgium from choosing to apply its own stricter rules of bird conservation (though such rules had to comply with the requirements of the law of free movement of goods) The Union's rules operate as a *minimum* standard.

In December 1992, the Edinburgh European Council concluded that:

> . . . where it is necessary to set standards at Community level, consideration should be given to setting minimum standards, with freedom for Member States to set higher standards, not only in the areas where the Treaty so requires . . . but also in other areas where this would not conflict with the objectives of the proposed measure or with the Treaty.

What of harmonization? In contrast to Articles 169 and 192 the Treaty provisions governing harmonization do not make clear what shall be the effect of EU legislation on national competence. Article 115 TFEU is completely silent on the issue. Article 114 TFEU contains within it only the strictly limited derogation foreseen by Article 114(4) *et seq*. Article 114 is set out in full at p. 524 but the relevant paragraphs deserve repetition.

ARTICLE 114(4)–(5)

> 4. If, after the adoption of a harmonisation measure by the European Parliament and the Council, by the Council or by the Commission, a Member State deems it necessary to maintain national provisions on grounds of major needs referred to in Article 36, or relating to the protection of the environment or the working environment, it shall notify the Commission of these provisions as well as the grounds for maintaining them.
>
> 5. Moreover, without prejudice to paragraph 4, if, after the adoption of a harmonisation measure by the European Parliament and the Council, by the Council or by the Commission, a Member State deems it necessary to introduce national provisions based on new scientific evidence relating to the protection of the environment or the working environment on grounds of a problem specific to that Member State arising after the adoption of the harmonisation measure, it shall notify the Commission of the envisaged provisions as well as the grounds for introducing them.

The paragraphs that follow within Article 114 map out the manner in which the Commission shall manage this procedure.

The first question asks how this procedure is handled. The second question is a more general one – if the procedure set out in Article 114(4) *et seq* is not invoked, what competence (if any) do Member States retain to legislate in areas covered by a measure of harmonization? Is *minimum harmonization* permitted?

B: The management of Article 114(4) *et seq*

On the first question: in the next case the Court decided that a narrow interpretation should be placed on these provisions, for they challenge the attainment of a fundamental Treaty objective, the integration of the market for goods.

France v *Commission* (Case C-41/93)

[1994] ECR I-1829, Court of Justice of the European Communities

[23] . . . if the conditions which Article 100a(4) [now 114(4)] lays down are fulfilled, that provision allows a Member State to apply rules derogating from a harmonisation measure adopted in accordance with the procedure laid down in Paragraph 1.

[24] As this possibility constitutes a derogation from a common measure aimed at attaining one of the fundamental objectives of the Treaty, namely the abolition of obstacles to the free movement of goods between Member States, Article 100a(4) makes it subject to review by the Commission and the Court of Justice.

[25] It is in the light of those considerations that it is necessary to examine the procedure according to which the Commission must review and, where appropriate, confirm the national provisions of which it is notified by a Member State.

[26] In the first place, where, after the expiry of the time allowed for transposing, or after the entry into force of, a harmonisation measure mentioned in Article 100a(1), a Member State intends, as in this case, to continue to apply national provisions derogating from the measure, it is required to notify the Commission of those provisions.

[27] The Commission must then satisfy itself that all the conditions for a Member State to be able to rely on the exception provided for by Article 100a(4) are fulfilled. In particular, it must establish whether the provisions in question are justified on grounds of the major needs mentioned in the first subparagraph of Article 100a(4) and are not a means of arbitrary discrimination or a disguised restriction on trade between Member States.

[28] The procedure laid down by that provision is intended to ensure that no Member State may apply national rules derogating from the harmonised rules without obtaining confirmation from the Commission.

[29] Measures for the approximation of the provisions laid down by law, regulation or administrative action in Member States which are such as to hinder intra-Community trade would be rendered ineffective if the Member States retained the right to apply unilaterally national rules derogating from those measures.

[30] A Member State is not, therefore, authorised to apply the national provisions notified by it until after it has obtained a decision from the Commission confirming them.

NOTE: The Court adopted the same narrow approach to the interpretation of this device in Case C-319/97 *Antoine Kortas* [1999] ECR I-3143. (It should be noted *en passant* that the details of the procedure were significantly amended and made more sophisticated by the Amsterdam Treaty and the fact pattern of *Kortas* could not recur.)

But the procedure offers at least the possibility of a departure from harmonized orthodoxy – provided Commission authorization is forthcoming.

Denmark v *Commission* (Case C-3/00)

[2003] ECR I-2643, Court of Justice of the European Communities

Denmark had notified the Commission of more restrictive rules governing food additives than were laid down in the relevant harmonization Directive. The Commission found the measures excessive and refused to authorize them. In a Danish challenge to the Commission Decision, the Court insisted on the (admittedly limited) degree of respect for diversity which is the hallmark of the procedure in what is now Article 114(4) TFEU *et seq*.

[63] The applicant Member State may, in order to justify maintaining such derogating national provisions, put forward the fact that its assessment of the risk to public health is different from that made by the Community legislature in the harmonisation measure. In the light of the uncertainty inherent in assessing the public health risks posed by, *inter alia*, the use of food additives, divergent assessments of those risks can legitimately be made, without necessarily being based on new or different scientific evidence.

[64] A Member State may base an application to maintain its already existing national provisions on an assessment of the risk to public health different from that accepted by the Community legislature when it adopted the harmonisation measure from which the national provisions derogate. To that end, it falls to the applicant Member State to prove that those national provisions ensure a level of health protection which is higher than the Community harmonisation measure and that they do not go beyond what is necessary to attain that objective.

The Court found the Commission's assessment of the relevant evidence to be flawed and it annulled the Decision. A report of the Scientific Committee for Food had made a 'highly critical evaluation' of the maximum amounts for additives set by the Directive (para 110), but the Court considered the Commission had failed to take sufficient account of this opinion in rejecting the Danish application. However, it is plain that derogation of this type will not be lightly permitted.

Commission practice follows suit. It is not readily persuaded of the need to depart from the agreed EU standard for fear of damage to what in a communication on the procedure released in 2002 it chose to describe as 'the unity of the internal market' (COM (2002) 760, para 4). Information on the treatment of applications for derogations from harmonization measures pursuant to this procedure is routinely provided in the Annual Reports on Monitoring the Application of Community, now Union, Law, currently available *via* http://ec.europa.eu/atwork/applying-eu-law/infringements-proceedings/annual-reports/index_en.htm.

The next case is simply an illustration.

DECISION 2001/571/EC COMMISSION DECISION OF 18 JULY 2001 ON THE NATIONAL PROVISIONS NOTIFIED BY GERMANY IN THE FIELD OF PHARMACOVIGILANCE

[2001] OJ L202/46

The aim of Directive 2000/38/EC was to remodel pharmacovigilance systems, previously primarily paper-based and organized at national level, into an EU-wide electronic data system. The obligation imposed on a trader to report adverse reactions to a medicinal product under German law (the 'AMG') differed from the obligation under the Directive in two respects. First, German law required notification of an adverse reaction irrespective of whether the suspected case occurred inside or outside Germany, whereas the Directive required only notification to the competent authority of the Member State in which the adverse reaction took place. Second, adverse reactions occurring outside the EU had to be notified pursuant to the Directive only if unexpected, whereas German law contained no such restriction. Germany applied under what was then Article 95(4) EC, now Article 114(4) TFEU, for authorization to maintain its pre-existing regime.

[17] The Commission can only approve a notification pursuant to Article 95(4) of the EC Treaty if all of the conditions listed in Article 95 of the EC Treaty are met. In particular, maintaining the national provisions must be justified on grounds of major needs referred to in Article 30 of the EC Treaty, or relating to protection of the environment or the working environment (Article 95(4) of the EC Treaty). In addition the national provisions may neither be a means of arbitrary discrimination or a disguised restriction on trade between Member States; neither can they constitute an obstacle to the functioning of the internal market (Article 95(6) of the EC Treaty).

[18] When examining whether the national measures notified under Article 95(4) are justified by major needs, the Commission has to take as a basis 'the grounds' put forward by the Member State to justify the maintenance of its national provisions. This means that, according to the provisions of the Treaty, the responsibility for proving that these measures are justified lies with the requesting Member State. Given the procedural framework established by Article 95 of the EC Treaty, in principle the Commission has to limit itself to examining the relevance of the elements which are submitted by the requesting Member State, without itself having to seek possible grounds of justification.

[19] Germany invokes major needs to protect the health and life of humans and consequently one of the circumstances referred to in Article 30 of the EC Treaty. Maintaining the obligations to report as provided for in the current provisions of sentences 2 to 8 of Section 95(1) AMG would attain the highest possible level of health protection for the population in their use of medicinal products. This high national level of protection was endangered by Directive 2000/38/EC since, firstly, adverse reactions will in future only be reported to the Member state in which they take place and, secondly, adverse reactions which take place in a non-member country are only covered by the obligation to report when they are 'unexpected'.

The Commission examined the detail of the matter, and was not convinced by Germany's submission. On the first point, it ruled that the system of information sharing foreseen by Directive 2000/38 would adequately protect health.

[24] ... no major needs within the meaning of Article 30 of the EC Treaty [now Article 36 TFEU] can be recognised which could justify maintaining the obligation to report adverse reactions from other Member States. Rather the restriction contained in the new version of Article 29d(2) [of the Directive] represents a logical conclusion to the establishment of the new data network. This will make the same information available to the Member States as previously, but presentation will be improved. Maintaining the previous obligations to report would place an unnecessary and unjustifiable burden on the respective marketing authorisation holders.

Neither did the Commission accept Germany's second point, which was directed against the Directive's limitation to notification of *unexpected* reactions in the case of events occurring outside the EU.

[27] ... any expected adverse reactions have to be taken into account during the testing and authorisation of a product, while obviously this is not possible when these are unexpected, During the subsequent monitoring of a medicinal product in the framework of pharmacovigilance, special significance is thus attached to unexpected as opposed to expected adverse reactions. For this reason, the general reporting and evaluation of adverse reactions, even when they occur outside the Community, appears necessary only when these are unexpected.

[28] This conclusion is based on scientific evidence acquired in recent years relating to the medicinal products approved as part of the centralized Community procedure pursuant to Regulation (EEC) 2309/93. This procedure is obligatory for certain products of the biotechnology and high technology industries, which are regarded as particularly complex and sensitive. None the less the second subparagraph of Article 22(1) of Regulation (EEC) 2309/93 restricts the obligation to report the adverse reactions of such medicinal products which occur in non-member countries to those which are unexpected. Analyses and evaluations of the information on adverse reactions generated from centrally authorised medicinal products have confirmed that it is also not necessary to report and evaluate information on expected adverse reactions from non-member countries.

[29] This assessment is further supported by the fact that the Federal Republic of Germany is the only Member State which does not restrict the obligation to report adverse reactions occurring in non-member countries to those which are unexpected, but extends this obligation to adverse reactions which are expected. This highlights the fact that none of the other Member States considers it necessary, in order to protect the health and life of humans, to include reports of suspected serious expected adverse reactions from non-member countries in the pharmacovigilance systems.

[30] Consequently, in maintaining an obligation to report suspected serious expected adverse reactions from non-member countries, Germany is not able to invoke major needs within the meaning of Article 30 of the EC Treaty. The provision of the new version of Article 29d(4) applies new scientific evidence without prejudicing the high level of health protection in the Community.

The Commission rejected the application. Notice the concern for burdens imposed on traders (para 24) and the relevance of choices made by other Member States (para 29). A connection should be made with the broader discussion of the scope allowed to States to justify trade barriers under Article 34 (pp. 307, 344) and Article 56 (p. 393). A helpful contrast with Decision 2001/571 is provided by Decision 2004/1 concerning Dutch provisions on use of short-chain chlorinated paraffins ([2004] OJ L1/20). The Commission approved the notified stricter rules for a limited period pending further scientific inquiry, citing the 'precautionary principle' relevant to environmental protection (*cf* pp. 313–15).

In Joined Cases T-366/03 & T-235/04 *Land Oberösterreich* v *Commission* [2005] ECR I-4005 the CFI (which post-Lisbon is known as the General Court) took the opportunity to consider the difference in treatment under Article 114 of new and existing national provisions. New measures are more likely to jeopardize harmonization (para 62). On the facts there was no problem specific to Austria on which the applicants sought to rely in their desire to set stricter rules on genetically modified organisms than were envisaged by a relevant measure of harmonisation. So the action for annulment of the Commission Decision which had rejected the Austrian application failed. The CFI decision was upheld by the Court of Justice on appeal (Joined Cases C-439/05P & C-454/05P *Land Oberösterreich* v *Commission* [2007] ECR I-7141).

C: Harmonization, competence, and the scope for minimum rules

The second question posed at p. 533 is a more general one – if the procedure set out in Article 114(4) *et seq* is not invoked, what competence (if any) do Member States retain to legislate in areas covered by a measure of harmonization?

The legal aspects of this issue under Articles 34–36 TFEU were discussed in *Rewe* (Case 4/75) and *Moormann* (Case 190/87), at p. 316. It was there demonstrated that action taken to harmonize national laws by the EU's legislature may have the effect of depriving Member States of the competence to resort to Article 36 to justify obstructive trading rules in the field covered by the Directive. The relevant jargon holds that the EU has 'occupied the field'; it has 'pre-empted' national competence. Free trade proceeds on the basis of a rule which is identical throughout the Union and States are deprived of the ability to set standards which diverge from the agreed EU norm. In the next case the Court's interpretation of Directive 76/756 in 'Dim Dip' follows this resolutely pro-integrative line. The UK is held to have acted in breach of the Treaty by imposing a requirement not included in the exhaustive list of requirements permissible under the relevant Directive. It prohibited the use of motor vehicles not equipped with dim dip lighting.

Commission v *UK* (Case 60/86)

[1988] ECR 3921, Court of Justice of the European Communities

[10] It is clear from the documents before the Court that the reason for which dim-dip devices were not included in the provisions, even as optional devices, is that the technical committee of national experts did not consider them acceptable given the state of technical progress at the time. In addition, it was not considered appropriate to adapt Directive 76/756/EEC, after its entry into force, so as to take account of technical progress in accordance with the procedure laid down in Article 13 of Directive 70/156/EEC and Article 5 of Directive 76/756/EEC, by bringing dim-dip devices within the scope of the latter directive.

[11] Such an interpretation of the exhaustive nature of the list of lighting and light-signalling devices set out in Annex I to the directive is consistent with the purpose of Directive 70/156/EEC which is to reduce, and even eliminate, hindrances to trade within the Community resulting from the fact that mandatory technical requirements differ from one Member State to another (see the first and second recitals in the preamble to Directive 70/156/EEC). In the context of Directive 76/756/EEC that objective is reflected in the obligation imposed on the Member States to adopt the same requirements 'either in addition to or in place of their existing rules' (second recital).

[12] It follows that the Member States cannot unilaterally require manufacturers who have complied with the harmonized technical requirements set out in Directive 76/756/EEC to comply with a requirement which

is not imposed by that directive, since motor vehicles complying with the technical requirements laid down therein must be able to move freely within the common market.

[13] It must therefore be declared that, by prohibiting, in breach of Council Directive 76/756/EEC of 27 July 1976, the use of motor vehicles manufactured after 1 October 1986 and put into service after 1 April 1987 which are not equipped with a dim-dip device, the United Kingdom has failed to fulfil its obligations under Community law.

NOTE: The approach taken in *Commission* v *UK* (Case 60/86) is obviously potentially of relevance beyond its facts. The same approach might be taken, for example, to the effect of rules relating to the quality of goods or the qualifications which a migrant professional must possess.

The Court's interpretative approach in this case is based on the purpose of the Directive. It is not rooted in the Treaty provision on which the Directive was based. As mentioned, neither Article 114 nor Article 115 TFEU make explicit what should be the impact of EU legislation on residual national competence. Articles 169 and 192 TFEU, by contrast, stipulate that Union legislation adopted under those provisions governing consumer and environmental protection respectively establish *minimum* rules only. One may assume that the minimum formula is appropriate in the fields of environmental and consumer protection because the dominant purpose of the relevant Treaty provisions is to pursue the objectives of those policies and not explicitly to integrate markets, whereas, by contrast, one might choose to argue that Articles 114 and 115, as foundation stones of market building, should always pre-empt national competence to act in the occupied field. Were it otherwise, there would loom the possibility of an uneven 'playing field' for traders in so far as States choose to set rules above the EU minimum.

But the Court's case law is not so neat. In the next case the Court rejected a submission that a Directive should be interpreted as setting both floor and ceiling (total or maximum harmonization). It found instead that it fixed a floor only (minimum harmonization). Stricter State rules were therefore not pre-empted by the Directive.

Hans Hönig v *StadtStockach* (Case C-128/94)

[1995] ECR I-3389, Court of Justice of the European Communities

Directive 88/166 established standards for the protection of laying hens kept in battery cages. German rules required larger cages than were provided for under the Directive. Hönig, a German farmer, submitted that to allow a State to set a stricter rule would frustrate the Directive's capacity to achieve uniform conditions of competition in the EU. The Directive's legal base was Article 43 EC (now, in amended form, Article 43 TFEU), governing the common organization of agricultural markets. (Where EU legislation concerns the production and marketing of agricultural products and contributes to the achievement of one or more of the aims of the objectives of the common agricultural policy, this Treaty provision applies; the Treaty provisions governing harmonization cannot be relied upon as a ground for restricting its scope, see e.g., Case C-269/97 *Commission* v *Council* [2000] ECR I-2257.) *Via* the preliminary reference procedure, a German court sought the Court of Justice's interpretation of the leeway permitted to Member States under the Directive.

[9] As the Court has emphasised in its decisions, it is necessary in interpreting a provision of Community law to consider not only its wording but also the context in which it occurs and the objects of the rules of which it is part (judgment in Case 292/82 *Merck* v *Hauptzollamt Hamburg-Jonas* [1983] ECR 3781, paragraph 12, and in Case 337/82 *St Nikolaus Brennerei* v *Hauptzollamt Krefeld* [1984] ECR 1051, paragraph 10).

[10] As regards in the first place the wording of the directive, Article 3(1)(a) of the Annex provides as follows: Member States shall ensure that from 1 January 1988:

— all newly built cages for use within the Community,
— all cages brought into use for the first time,

at least comply with the following requirements:

(a) at least 450cm^2 of cage area . . . shall be provided for each laying hen . . .

[11] On the wording of the provision, therefore, the Member States may not lay down a minimum surface area of less than 450cm^2 per cage, but may lay down a minimum cage area per hen greater than that provided for; that is shown, moreover, by the title of the directive and Article 1 thereof, which provides that 'this directive lays down the minimum standards for the protection of laying hens kept in battery cages'.

[12] The minimum standards contained in the directive were laid down as a consequence of the Council Resolution of 22 July 1980 on the protection of laying hens in cages (OJ 1980 C 196, p. 1) and in Council Decision 78/923/EEC of 19 June 1978 approving the European Convention for the Protection of Animals kept for Farming Purposes (OJ 1978 L 323, p. 12).

[13] Next, the purpose of the directive must be considered.

[14] As the Advocate General pointed out in paragraph 13 of his Opinion, the directive seeks first to provide protection for animals kept for farming purposes and secondly to reduce the disparities in conditions of competition as between Member States on the market in eggs and poultry.

[15] The Community legislature therefore sought to reconcile the interests of the proper functioning of the organisation of the market in eggs and poultry with those of animal protection by laying down, according to the third recital in the preamble to the directive, common minimum requirements applicable to all intensive housing systems, including those for laying hens kept in battery cages.

[16] Lastly, the use of the words 'as a first step' in the third recital, and the content of the fourth recital in the preamble to the directive, indicate that the latter seeks only a certain degree of harmonisation in the protection of hens by means of provisions laying down minimum standards.

[17] Admittedly, that interpretation of the directive's provisions may lead, as the plaintiff in the main action has pointed out, to battery hen farmers in one Member State receiving less favourable treatment than those in other Member States, thus allowing some inequalities in competition to persist. However, those are the consequences of the level of harmonisation sought by those provisions, which lay down minimum standards.

NOTE: Inspection of the Directive's text and its purpose led the Court to its conclusion. These were minimum rules only, so a degree of local regulatory autonomy remained, unsuppressed by centralized rule-making.

However, this understanding of 'minimum harmonization' appears to be challenged by the Court's ruling in the *Tobacco Advertising* case, more properly *Germany* v *Parliament and Council*, examined at length in Chapter 2 (p. 33). This reveals that the presence in a Directive of a clause which permits a Member State to introduce stricter rules that impede imports complying with the requirements of the harmonization Directive may be relevant in determining whether valid use has been made of what was then Article 95 EC, now Article 114 TFEU.

***Germany* v *European Parliament and Council of the European Union* (Case C-376/98)**

[2000] ECR I-8419, Court of Justice of the European Communities

The Court annulled Directive 98/43, which imposed severe restrictions on the advertising of tobacco products. It was based on Article 100a, now, after amendment, Article 114 TFEU (and on relevant Treaty provisions governing the services sector). But it did not sufficiently contribute to market-making. Among the Court's objections to the Directive was that:

[101] . . . the Directive does not ensure free movement of products which are in conformity with its provisions.

[102] Contrary to the contentions of the Parliament and Council, Article 3(2) of the Directive, relating to diversification products, cannot be construed as meaning that, where the conditions laid down in the Directive are fulfilled, products of that kind in which trade is allowed in one Member State may move freely in the other Member States, including those where such products are prohibited.

[103] Under Article 5 of the Directive, Member States retain the right to lay down, in accordance with the Treaty, such stricter requirements concerning the advertising or sponsorship of tobacco products as they deem necessary to guarantee the health protection of individuals.

[104] Furthermore, the Directive contains no provision ensuring the free movement of products which conform to its provisions, in contrast to other directives allowing Member States to adopt stricter measures for the protection of a general interest (see, in particular, Article 7(1) of Council Directive 90/239/EEC of 17 May 1990 on the approximation of the laws, regulations and administrative provisions of the Member States concerning the maximum tar yield of cigarettes (OJ 1990 L 137, p. 36) and Article 8(1) of Council Directive 89/622/EEC of 13 November 1989 on the approximation of the laws, regulations and administrative provisions of the Member States concerning the labelling of tobacco products (OJ 1989 L 359, p. 1).

[105] In those circumstances, it must be held that the Community legislature cannot rely on the need to eliminate obstacles to the free movement of advertising media and the freedom to provide services in order to adopt the Directive on the basis of Articles 100a, 57(2) and 66 of Treaty.

NOTE: Chapter 2 also considered the unsuccessful legal challenge to the validity of Directive 2001/37 on tobacco labelling (p. 38). It was based on Article 95 EC, today Article 114 TFEU, and, in view of its impact on external trade, Article 133 EC, today Article 207 TFEU. It contained a clause requiring Member States to accept on to their market goods complying with the terms of the Directive; put another way, it prohibited the application of stricter rules. This was an element in the Court's finding that the Directive was valid.

***R* v *Secretary of State for Health, ex parte British American Tobacco(Investments) Ltd and Imperial Tobacco Ltd* (Case C-491/01)**

[2002] ECR I-11453, Court of Justice of the European Communities

[74] It must be added that, unlike the directive at issue in the case giving rise to the tobacco advertising judgment, the Directive contains a provision, Article 13(1), which guarantees the free movement of products which comply with its requirements. By forbidding the Member States to prevent, on grounds relating to the matters harmonised by the Directive, the import, sale or consumption of tobacco products which do comply, that provision gives the Directive its full effect in relation to its object of improving the conditions for the functioning of the internal market.

[75] It follows that the Directive genuinely has as its object the improvement of the conditions for the functioning of the internal market and that it was, therefore, possible for it to be adopted on the basis of Article 95 EC, and it is no bar that the protection of public health was a decisive factor in the choices involved in the harmonising measures which it defines.

NOTE: Comparable approval of a provision guaranteeing free movement of complying products appears in the Court's judgment in Case C-380/03 *Germany* v *Parliament and Council* [2006] ECR I-11573 (paras 73–74), in which the Court found Directive 2003/33, which replaced the annulled 'Tobacco Advertising' Directive, to be validly based on Article 95 EC, now Article 114 TFEU (Chapter 2, p. 40).

Minimum harmonization therefore seems to be treated as a contradiction in terms. A measure of harmonization adopted on the basis of Article 114 or 115 takes as one of its constitutional rationales the suppression of local regulatory competence to maintain or introduce stricter rules that impede the access to the local market of goods or services from other Member States that comply with the harmonized standard. A State wishing to demand higher standards of imports has available to it only the procedure set out in Article 114(4) *et seq.*

This, however, is inconsistent with legislative practice. It is not hard to find individual Directives formally adopted as measures of harmonization designed to advance the building of an integrated market which contain a minimum clause. This is especially common in the batch of measures harmonizing the legal protection of the economic interests of consumers. Directive 85/577 governing 'Doorstep Selling', adopted under Article 100 (now 115 TFEU), provides an example. (It was, you may remember, the Directive at stake in *Dori* (Case C-91/92), in which the Court rejected the horizontal direct effect of Directives: Chapter 5, p. 122.)

DIRECTIVE 85/577 ON THE PROTECTION OF THE CONSUMER IN RESPECT OF CONTRACTS NEGOTIATED AWAY FROM BUSINESS PREMISES

[1985] OJ L372/31

ARTICLE 8

This Directive shall not prevent Member States from adopting or maintaining more favourable provisions to protect consumers in the field which it covers.

NOTE: The Directive has now been replaced by Directive 2011/83 on Consumer Rights ([2011] OJ L304/64), which abandons the minimum clause. But the change is policy driven (see p. 552) and not the result of constitutional anxiety. It was the presence of this minimum clause that allowed the Court in *Ministère Public* v *Buet* (Case 382/87 [1989] ECR 1235, encountered in Chapter 11 (p. 333) to treat a French decision to ban doorstep selling of certain materials as *not* pre-empted by Directive 85/577, which governs exactly that marketing practice and which requires only that the consumer be given a seven-day cooling off period after concluding such a contract. Because the Directive explicitly envisaged Member States applying stricter measures more favourable to the consumer even where they obstruct imported goods, the French ban stood provided only that it was justified (which the Court thought it could be, given its function of protecting vulnerable consumers, as explained at p. 333).

The Court's willingness in *Buet* to entertain justification for rules stricter than those laid down in Directive 85/577 might seem incompatible with the rulings in the 'Tobacco' cases of 2000, 2002, and 2006. And Directive 85/577's concession that 'This Directive shall not prevent Member States from adopting or maintaining more favourable provisions to protect consumers in the field which it covers' might in this vein seem *either* fatal to the Directive's validity as a measure of harmonization *or else*, less savagely, properly interpreted to allow the application of more favourable rules only to domestic goods, and not to imports. Nonetheless, subsequently in *Doc Morris* (Case C-322/01 [2003] ECR I-14887), *Herbert Karner* v *Troostwijk* (Case C-71/02 [2004] ECR I-3025), *A-Punkt Schmuckhandels GmbH* v *Claudia Schmidt* (Case C-441/04 [2006] ECR I-2093) and *Jyske Bank Gibraltar* (Case C-212/11 judgment of 25 April 2013) the Court seemed to revert to the assumption already found in *Buet* that States may be able to justify rules above the harmonized norm provided the Directive expressly authorizes this possibility, although it did not mention *Tobacco Advertising* at all. *Tobacco Advertising* is best interpreted narrowly – the Court's remarks were probably directed at the (in)validity of that particular measure of harmonization and were not an assault on the *general* constitutional viability of minimum harmonization.

FURTHER READING

de Cecco, F., 'Room to Move? Minimum Harmonisation and Fundamental Rights' (2006) 43 CML Rev 9.

Dougan, M., 'Minimum Harmonisation and the Internal Market' (2000) 37 CML Rev 853.

Schütze, R., 'Supremacy without Pre-Emption? The Very Slowly Emergent Doctrine of Community Pre-emption' (2006) 43 CML Rev 1023.

SECTION 4: THE EXAMPLE OF CONSUMER LAW

The field of consumer law deserves attention as a case study in choice of patterns of harmonization. The key to understanding the apparent paradox of a measure of harmonization, designed to build an integrated market, which includes a 'minimum clause' permitting States to introduce (doubtless varying) stricter rules lies in the enduringly important issue of choosing a legal base in the Treaty that authorizes the adoption of secondary legislation. Directive 85/577 on 'Doorstep Selling' in fact had little to do with market-building, even though it was adopted as a measure of harmonization on the basis of Article 100, now Article 115 TFEU. The Directive reflected unanimous political preference for the development of a legislative programme of consumer protection at a time when the Treaty conferred no relevant competence in that field. (What is now) Article 169 TFEU governing consumer protection was inserted into the Treaty only with effect from 1993, when the Maastricht Treaty entered into force. In fact, a number of Directives dealing with the harmonization of laws protecting the economic interests of consumers include the minimum formula. Examples include Directive 93/13 on unfair terms in consumer contracts and Directive 90/314 on package travel [1993] OJ L95/29 and [1990] OJ L158/59 respectively; see further S. Weatherill, *EU Consumer Law and Policy* (Cheltenham: Edward Elgar, 2013).

A: Minimum harmonization

The next extract, from an article published in 1988, is written against the background of this history. It sets out the appeal of minimum harmonization.

K. Mortelmans, 'Minimum Harmonization and Consumer Law'
[1988] ECLJ 2, 5–7

(Footnotes omitted.)

The double objective of harmonization, i.e., the establishment of a Common Market and the protection of the interests of the consumer, may be related to the technique of minimum harmonization. Free movement is facilitated as the harmonization of legislation removes distortions in competition; but, since consumer legislation in a number of Member States provides more stringent safeguards, such Member States regard harmonization as a minimum and, on the basis of a provision in the directive, they are authorized to introduce more stringent national measures . . .

The provisions for minimum harmonization arise primarily in directives aimed specifically at the protection of the consumer, the environment or other justified interests and where the abolition of obstacles to free movement of goods comes in second place. In such cases the public interest, in this context in terms of consumer protection, acquires relative precedence over the free movement of goods. More stringent national measures most often arise when scholarly or legal doubts obtain in respect of the protection required for certain specific situations, persons or geographical areas. This then leads to national legislation with different levels of protection.

The technique of minimum harmonization is consequently [a more] than honourable means of reconciling the common market with consumer interests . . .

NOTE: At a descriptive level, the concluding comment now comfortably fits Article 169 TFEU, but it fits Article 114 TFEU only provided the 'narrow' interpretation of '*Tobacco Advertising*' (Case C-376/98) is accepted.

■ QUESTION

To what extent is the Court's approach in Case C-376/98 (p. 539) and Case C-491/01 (p. 540) to the place of 'minimum clauses' in measures of legislative harmonization vulnerable to the accusation that it represents an undue emphasis on market integration promoted by centralized rule-making at the expense of local regulatory preferences?

NOTE: The next section concerns a Directive concerned with the harmonization of civil liability rules. Once again, the policy issue relates to the accommodation of diverse aspirations within a regime devoted to free trade.

B: The Product Liability Directive

Directive 85/374 [1985] OJ L210/29 as amended by Directive 99/34 [1999] L141/20 harmonizes the rules on liability for injury caused by defective consumer products. It was adopted on the basis of Article 100 (now 115). Article 1 provides that 'The producer shall be liable for damage caused by a defect in his product.' The Directive is a classic 'dual aim' harmonization measure.

R. Merkin, *A Guide to the Consumer Protection Act 1987*
(London: Financial Training Publications, 1987), pp. 4–5

. . . REASONS FOR THE DIRECTIVE

The introduction of a uniform code of product liability within the European Community is perceived by the Community authorities as being necessary to bring about two broad sets of objectives: consumer protection objectives and market unity objectives.

The importance of consumer protection is recognised by the second recital of the product liability Directive, which states that:

> . . . liability without fault on the part of the producer is the sole means of adequately solving the problem, peculiar to our age of increasing technicality, of a fair apportionment of the risks inherent in modern technological production.

This broad statement encompasses a number of distinct arguments in favour of strict liability:

(a) The general desire to spread loss throughout society rather than to allow it to fall on individual consumers.
(b) The belief that producers can insure against third-party risks at a lower cost than individual consumers could insure against first-party risks, so that strict liability is the cheapest form of risk-spreading.
(c) The possibility that strict liability will provide manufacturers with the incentive to increase safety and standards generally, an incentive which is not diminished by the probable existence of liability insurance, given the dangers of premium-rating and of adverse publicity.
(d) The illogicality and expense of maintaining a fault-based system.

The market unity arguments for strict liability are rather more subtle. The first recital of the Directive asserts that:

> . . . the existing divergences [between the laws of Member States] may distort competition and affect the movement of goods within the common market and entail a differing degree of protection of the consumer.

Two distinct issues are at stake here:

(a) The principle that goods must be allowed to move freely between Member States, enshrined in articles 30 to 36 [now 34–36] of the Treaty of Rome, is overriden by mandatory consumer protection laws which prevent the sale of dangerous goods, imported or otherwise. By imposing strict liability, standards will improve and goods will be permitted to circulate more freely as between Member States.
(b) if the laws of one Member State are less generous to manufacturers than the laws of other Member States, by the imposition of strict liability, those manufacturers subject to strict liability will be at a competitive disadvantage when exporting to Member States offering a lesser degree of consumer protection. This is so because their products will be more expensive, either as a result of the costs of higher safety standards or as a result of the price of the goods containing an element representing domestic liability insurance premiums. Failure to implement strict liability is thus seen as a form of indirect protectionism.

■ QUESTION

That the Directive promotes consumer protection is plain. But it is a harmonization measure based on Article 100 (now 115). Are the 'market unity' arguments strong enough to secure the Directive against allegations that it is inadequately closely tied to the process of market-making to constitute a valid measure of harmonization? See Chapter 2, p. 33 for discussion in this vein of Case C-376/98 '*Tobacco Advertising*'.

NOTE: Two distinct issues associated with the effect of the Directive on national competence arise. The first concerns the scope for local choice expressly allowed within the scope of application of the Directive. The second concerns 'pre-emption' – does the Directive leave any scope for national rules governing product liability that are more generous to the consumer than those mandated by the Directive?

On the first issue, one might suppose that a measure of harmonization should exclude a menu of options from which Member States could select. Yet it was not possible to achieve unanimity in drafting a final version of the Directive which would apply without derogation to all Member States.

R. Merkin, *A Guide to the Consumer Protection Act 1987*
(London: Financial Training Publications, 1987), pp. 6–7

One interesting feature of the Directive is that it permits three 'derogations', i.e., matters in respect of which each Member State is free to determine whether or not it wishes to follow the terms of the Directive. The derogations are as follows:

(a) Agricultural products and game. Article 1 of the Directive provides that there is to be no strict liability upon the producers of these products, although Article 15.1(a) permits Member States to impose such liability if they so wish . . .
(b) A 'development risks' defence. The Directive contains, in Article 7(e), a defence open to a manufacturer to the effect that the state of scientific and technical knowledge was not such as to enable the defect to be discovered when the product was put into circulation. However, Article 15.1(b) allows Member States to extend strict liability to cover development risks of this nature. It would appear that the majority of Member States intend to avail themselves of the derogation, but the UK has again opted to follow the Directive and to retain the defence . . . [In fact, it emerged that most Member States permit the defence; COM (2006) 496, the Commission's third report on the Directive, relates that only Finland and Luxembourg exclude it].
(c) Maximum liability. Article 16 allows the imposition of a maximum liability in respect of individual claims or in respect of aggregate claims arising out of a particular defect in a product, of some £40 million. The UK did not think it necessary to limit liability in this way . . .

The operation of these three derogations is to be assessed in July 1995 to determine whether they should be abandoned or made mandatory . . . [In fact the only modification has brought agricultural products and game (point (a)) within the liability regime as a result of amending Directive 99/34, introduced 'in the aftermath of the mad cow crisis', COM (00) 893, p. 6.]

NOTE: A major stumbling block was the argument over whether or not to include the 'development risks' defence; derogation (b) in the preceding extract. Its absence would, it was alleged, lead, *inter alia*, to undesirable inhibition of technical innovation.

R. Merkin, *A Guide to the Consumer Protection Act 1987*
(London: Financial Training Publications, 1987), pp. 35–6

. . . The most important justification of the development risks defence is that it encourages research into new products. The argument runs that a producer facing absolute liability for unforeseeable defects will simply not risk marketing new products, to the ultimate detriment of all consumers, because of the cost of potential liability from doing so and because of the danger of damage to reputation resulting from widely publicised successful proceedings.

The validity of the cost approach rests upon two assumptions. First, it presupposes that insurance will not be available for development risk liability. The preliminary view of the Association of British Insurers is, as already noted, that premiums will not be increased significantly by the imposition of strict liability as long as the development risks defence is available, but that there will be a substantial rise if absolute liability is imposed. Given, however, that insurance is available – albeit at a price – the question becomes whether it is proper to allow loss by development risks to fall upon individuals, or whether it is more desirable to require all consumers to contribute to the costs of insurance when making their purchases.

The underlying assumption of product liability is that the latter option is the most desirable. It might also be questioned whether premiums would in fact have to rise as steeply as has been predicted by the Association of British Insurers: most of the calculations were done by assessing the American experience, although the high levels of damages there awarded and the contingency fee system may both render any comparison with the UK misleading.

The second assumption is that producers will not face development risk liability if a development risks defence is included. This, however, is not the case. First, an exporter to other Member States of the EEC may, depending upon the conflict of laws rules prevailing in those States, face absolute liability. Secondly, the original producer may face liability in the UK under the Sale of Goods Act 1979, where a chain action is commenced. Finally, there is always the possibility that, following expensive litigation, the defence cannot be made out. Consequently, it would appear that UK suppliers would be unwise not to carry development risk cover irrespective of the position under the Consumer Protection Act 1987.

The reputation argument would not appear to be significant. In the absence of a development risks defence there would appear not to be a need for litigation, and all manufacturers would in any event face the same liability, so that there ought not be a fear of competitive disadvantage. In addition, reputation may be lost as much in successfully defending litigation as in accepting liability quietly.

NOTE: The existence of the development risk defence has been criticized as a severe curtailment of the ability of the measure to provide effective consumer protection. For example, a modern parallel to the thalidomide tragedy would probably still go uncompensated in the UK because of the producer's ability to rely on the defence. See Cmnd. 7054 (1978), para 1259, *Report of the Pearson Commission on Civil Liability and Compensation for Personal Injury*. See also C. Newdick, 'The Future of Negligence in Product Liability' (1987) 103 LQR 288 and, more broadly, M. Reimann, 'Liability for Defective Products at the Beginning of the Twenty-First Century: Emergence of a Worldwide Standard?' (2003) 51 AJCL 751. In 2004 the Commission published a report on the economic effect of the defence (http://ec.europa.eu/growth/single-market/goods/free-movement-sectors/liability-defective-products/index_en.htm). The report is favourably disposed to what it describes as the 'balance' achieved by the inclusion of the defence. The Commission's third report on the Directive, published in 2006 (COM (2006) 496), reported 'no clear and consistent call from within the EU for significant reform of the Directive' (p. 6). It knows of only one example of successful reliance on the development risk defence, by a Dutch supplier of contaminated blood able to show the absence of any reliable method for screening the product in advance. The Commission's fourth report is equally resistant to reform, depicting the Directive 'as achieving a balance between consumer protection and the producers' interests' (COM (2011) 547, p. 11).

Furthermore, the nature of the defence and its implementation in the UK has provoked controversy; Article 7(e) of Directive 85/374 provides that 'the producer shall not be liable as result of this Directive if he proves that the state of scientific and technical knowledge at the time when he put the product into circulation was not such as to enable the existence of the defect to be discovered'. The UK's implementing Consumer Protection Act 1987, s.4(1)(e), provides that it is a defence to show 'that the state of scientific and technical knowledge at the relevant time was not such that a producer of products of the same description as the product in question might be expected to have discovered the defect if it had existed in his products while they were under his control'. For a challenging argument that the UK's implementation is in fact correct, notwithstanding the textual discrepancy, see C. Newdick, 'The Development Risk Defence of the Consumer Protection Act 1987' (1988) 47 CLJ 455 and 'Risk, Uncertainty and "Knowledge" in the Development Risk Defence' [1991] Anglo-Amer LR 127. The Court was provided with the opportunity to clarify the position by Commission infringement proceedings brought against the United Kingdom under Article 169 EC (now 258 TFEU: Chapter 4), but the Court's ruling did not entirely resolve the matters of substance.

Commission v *United Kingdom* (Case C-300/95)

[1997] ECR I-2649, Court of Justice of the European Communities

The core of the Commission's complaint is summarized as follows:

[16] In its application, the Commission argues that the United Kingdom legislature has broadened the defence under Article 7(e) of the Directive to a considerable degree and converted the strict liability imposed by Article 1 of the Directive into mere liability for negligence.

[17] The Commission submits that the test in Article 7(e) of the Directive is objective in that it refers to a state of knowledge, and not to the capacity of the producer of the product in question, or to that of another producer of a product of the same description, to discover the defect. However, by its use of the words 'a producer of products of the same description as the product in question [who] might be expected to have discovered the defect', section 4(1)(e) of the Act presupposes a subjective assessment based on the behaviour of a reasonable producer. It is easier for the producer of a defective product to demonstrate, under section 4(1)(e), that neither he nor a producer of similar products could have identified the defect at the material time, provided that the standard precautions in the particular industry were taken and there was no negligence, than to show, under Article 7(e), that the state of scientific and technical knowledge was such that no-one would have been able to discover the defect.

The Court proceeded to reject the Commission's application:

[23] In order to determine whether the national implementing provision at issue is clearly contrary to Article 7(e) as the Commission argues, the scope of the Community provision which it purports to implement must first be considered.

[24] In order for a producer to incur liability for defective products under Article 4 of the Directive, the victim must prove the damage, the defect and the causal relationship between defect and damage, but not that the producer was at fault. However, in accordance with the principle of fair apportionment of risk between the injured person and the producer set forth in the seventh recital in the preamble to the Directive, Article 7 provides that the producer has a defence if he can prove certain facts exonerating him from liability, including 'that the state of scientific and technical knowledge at the time when he put the product into circulation was not such as to enable the existence of the defect to be discovered' (Article 7(e)).

[25] Certain general observations can be made as to the wording of Article 7(e) of the Directive.

[26] First, as the Advocate General rightly observes in paragraph 20 of his Opinion, since that provision refers to 'scientific and technical knowledge at the time when [the producer] put the product into circulation', Article 7(e) is not specifically directed at the practices and safety standards in use in the industrial sector in which the producer is operating, but, unreservedly, at the state of scientific and technical knowledge, including the most advanced level of such knowledge, at the time when the product in question was put into circulation.

[27] Second, the clause providing for the defence in question does not contemplate the state of knowledge of which the producer in question actually or subjectively was or could have been apprised, but the objective state of scientific and technical knowledge of which the producer is presumed to have been informed.

[28] However, it is implicit in the wording of Article 7(e) that the relevant scientific and technical knowledge must have been accessible at the time when the product in question was put into circulation.

[29] It follows that, in order to have a defence under Article 7(e) of the Directive, the producer of a defective product must prove that the objective state of scientific and technical knowledge, including the most advanced level of such knowledge, at the time when the product in question was put into circulation was not such as to enable the existence of the defect to be discovered. Further, in order for the relevant scientific and technical knowledge to be successfully pleaded against the producer, that knowledge must have been accessible at the time when the product in question was put into circulation. On this last point, contrary to what the Commission seems to consider, Article 7(e) of the Directive raises difficulties of interpretation which, in the event of litigation, the national courts will have to resolve having recourse, if necessary, to Article 177 of the EC Treaty.

[30] For the present, it is the heads of claim raised by the Commission in support of its application that have to be considered.

[31] In proceedings brought under Article 169 of the Treaty the Commission is required to prove the alleged infringement. The Commission must provide the Court with the material necessary for it to determine whether the infringement is made out and may not rely on any presumption (see, in particular, Case C-62/89 *Commission* v *France* [1990] ECR I-925, paragraph 37).

[32] The Commission takes the view that inasmuch as section 4(1)(e) of the Act refers to what may be expected of a producer of products of the same description as the product in question, its wording clearly conflicts with Article 7(e) of the Directive in that it permits account to be taken of the subjective knowledge of a producer taking reasonable care, having regard to the standard precautions taken in the industrial sector in question.

[33] That argument must be rejected in so far as it selectively stresses particular terms used in section 4(1)(e) without demonstrating that the general legal context of the provision at issue fails effectively to secure full application of the Directive. Taking that context into account, the Commission has failed to make out its claim that the result intended by Article 7(e) of the Directive would clearly not be achieved in the domestic legal order.

[34] First, section 4(1)(e) of the Act places the burden of proof on the producer wishing to rely on the defence, as Article 7 of the Directive requires.

[35] Second, section 4(1)(e) places no restriction on the state and degree of scientific and technical knowledge at the material time which is to be taken into account.

[36] Third, its wording as such does not suggest, as the Commission alleges that the availability of the defence depends on the subjective knowledge of a producer taking reasonable care in the light of the standard precautions taken in the industrial sector in question.

[37] Fourth, the Court has consistently held that the scope of national laws, regulations or administrative provisions must be assessed in the light of the interpretation given to them by national courts (see, in particular, Case C-382/92 *Commission* v *United Kingdom* [1994] ECR I-2435, paragraph 36). Yet in this case the Commission has not referred in support of its application to any national judicial decision which, in its view, interprets the domestic provision at issue inconsistently with the Directive.

[38] Lastly, there is nothing in the material produced to the Court to suggest that the courts in the United Kingdom, if called upon to interpret section 4(1)(e), would not do so in the light of the wording and the purpose of the Directive so as to achieve the result which it has in view and thereby comply with the third paragraph of Article 189 of the Treaty (see, in particular, Case C-91/92 *Faccini Dori* v *Recreb* [1994] ECR I-3325, paragraph 26). Moreover, section 1(1) of the Act expressly imposes such an obligation on the national courts.

[39] It follows that the Commission has failed to make out its allegation that, having regard to its general legal context and especially section 1(1) of the Act, section 4(1)(e) clearly conflicts with Article 7(e) of the Directive. As a result, the application must be dismissed.

■ QUESTION

How does one determine when knowledge is 'accessible'? Is such an issue apt for preliminary reference to the Court of Justice, as suggested in para 29 of the ruling?

C: Uniform application of EU consumer law

For our purposes the central question must be whether the existence of the options in the Directive tracked in the previous sub-section represents a satisfactory compromise between the demands of free trade and consumer protection. But there is another question inextricably associated with this inquiry, and it is introduced in the next extract.

G. Howells, 'Implications of the Implementation and Non-Implementation of the EC Products Liability Directive'
(1990) 41 NILQ 22, 25–7

(Footnotes omitted.)

THE THREAT TO HARMONISATION

... The options resulted, of course, from compromises which had to be reached in order for the Directive to be acceptable to all the Member States in the first place. Article 15(2) does provide a partial safeguard, in that it provides that a Member State wishing to derogate from Article 7(e) (the development risks defence) must communicate the proposed text to the Commission, who must then inform the other Member States. In general, however, the problem of not knowing how other Member States will decide on the optional provisions has been a disincentive to Member States to provide more than a minimalist level of consumer protection . . . with so many rumours abounding about the form which implementing legislation would take across the Community, it is easy to understand the confusion . . .

There also seems to be a more subtle threat to harmonisation implicit in the Directive's definition of 'defect' as including a product which does not provide 'the safety which a person is entitled to expect'. Although the same test will be applied in each Member State, will the answer vary between them? One might wonder, for example, whether a Greek consumer has the same expectations as a West German?

NOTE: The final paragraph of this extract raises a connected point of great significance. Beyond the existence of options, one can legitimately question whether the terms of the Directive are sufficiently clear and precise to lead to effective harmonization. (*cf* Brouwer's discussion of food law, at p. 529.) Of course Article 267 TFEU is the channel of communication between national courts and the Court of Justice established by the Treaty for the purposes of securing uniform interpretation of EU law (see Chapter 7). But how 'uniform' can one realistically expect the application of such broad notions to be? The field of private law remains illuminating – from tort/delict, to contract law.

COMMUNICATION FROM THE COMMISSION TO THE COUNCIL AND THE EUROPEAN PARLIAMENT ON EUROPEAN CONTRACT LAW

[2001] OJ C255/1, http://ec.europa.eu/justice/contract/document/index_en.htm

The Commission's 2001 Communication was designed to prompt debate about the role of the EU in the development of contract law. Thus far its role had mainly been concerned with the adoption of harmonization measures affecting consumer contract law – Directive 85/577 on Doorstep Selling and Directive 93/13 on unfair terms in consumer contracts have been encountered. Four options were floated for the future:

(i) No EC action – based on the perception that markets have a capacity to achieve self-correction that should not be underestimated;
(ii) The promotion of the development of common contract law principles leading to greater convergence of national laws;
(iii) Improving the quality of legislation already in place;
(iv) The adoption of new comprehensive legislation at EC level – an idea that is floated conspicuously cautiously.

One question is whether the EU is even legally competent to pursue these ambitions. In paras 23–33 of the Communication on Contract Law the Commission calls explicitly for information on whether diversity between national contract laws 'directly or indirectly obstructs the functioning of the internal market, and if so to what extent', with a view to considering appropriate action by the EU's institutions. To what extent do you think this is inspired by awareness of the limits of what was then Article 95 EC, now Article 114 TFEU, revealed by the Court's judgment in '*Tobacco Advertising*' (Case C-376/98), p. 33?

The Commission also addresses the issue of uniformity. This extract offers a salutary reminder that 'harmonization' is a long-term process, rather than a one-off act.

(Some footnotes omitted.)

3.3. UNIFORM APPLICATION OF COMMUNITY LAW

[34] The European Community legislator must ensure consistency in the drafting of Community legislation as well as in its implementation and application in the Member States. The measures adopted by the European Community must be consistent with each other, interpreted in the same manner and produce the same effects in all Member States. The Court of Justice of the European Communities . . . has stated that 'the need for uniform application of Community law and the principle of equality require that the terms of a provision of Community law which makes no express reference to the law of the Member States for the purpose

of determining its meaning and scope must normally be given an autonomous and uniform interpretation throughout the Community.[16]

[35] In the area of contract law the European legislator has taken a 'piecemeal' approach to harmonisation. This approach combined with unforeseen market developments, could lead to inconsistencies in the application of Community law. For example, under certain circumstances it is possible to apply both the doorstep selling Directive and the timeshare Directive. Both Directives give the consumer a right of withdrawal; however the time period during which the consumer can exercise this right is different. Although such cases of conflicts between rules are exceptional, the Commission would welcome information on problems resulting from possible inconsistencies between Community rules.

[36] Using abstract terms in Community law can also cause problems for implementing and applying Community law and national measures in a non-uniform way. Abstract terms may represent a legal concept for which there are different rules in each national body of law.[18]

[37] In general, differences between provisions in directives can be explained by differences in the problems which those directives seek to solve. One cannot, therefore, require that a term used to solve one problem is interpreted and applied in precisely the same manner in a different context. However, differences in terms and concepts that cannot be explained by differences in the problems being addressed should be eliminated.

[38] In addition, domestic legislation adopted by Member States to implement Community directives refers to domestic concepts of these abstract terms. These concepts vary significantly from one Member State to another. The absence of a uniform understanding in Community law of general terms and concepts (at least in specific or linked areas) may lead to different results in commercial and legal practice in different Member States.[20]

[39] This kind of problem does not only apply to horizontal questions concerning general terms of contract law as mentioned above. It is also relevant to specific economic sectors.

[40] The Commission is reflecting whether, in order to avoid the kind of problems described above, the necessary consistency could be ensured through the continuation of the existing approach or should be improved through other means. The Commission is therefore interested in receiving information on practical problems relating to contract law resulting from the way that Community rules are applied and implemented in the Member States.

NOTE: A follow-up to the 2001 Communication was published in February 2003: the Action Plan on a more coherent European Contract Law, COM (2003) 68. A third in the series of documents setting out options in the field of contract law was published in October 2004.

COMMUNICATION FROM THE COMMISSION TO THE EUROPEAN PARLIAMENT AND COUNCIL: EUROPEAN CONTRACT LAW AND THE REVISION OF THE ACQUIS: THE WAY FORWARD

COM (2004) 651; available *via* http://ec.europa.eu/justice/contract/document/index_en.htm

The 2004 Communication, like that of 2001, nods cautiously to the awkward question of competence to act in this field in the wake of the *'Tobacco Advertising'* judgment.

16 Case C-357/98 *The Queen* v *Secretary of State for the Home Department ex parte Nana Yaa Konadu Yiadom* [2000] ECR-9265, at paragraph 26. See also Case C-287/98 *Luxemburg* v *Linster* [2000] ECR-6917, at paragraph 43; Case C-387/97 *Commission* v *Greece* [2000] ECR-5047; Case C-327/82 *Ekro* v *Produktschap voor Vee en Vlees* [1984] ECR I-107, at paragraph 11. The principle of uniform application also applies in the area of private law see CaseC-373/97 *Dionisios Diamantis* v *Elliniko Dimosio (Greek State), Organismos Ikonomikis Anasinkrotisis Epikhiriseon AE (OAE)* [2000] ECR I-1705, at paragraph 34; Case C-441/93 *Pafitis and Others* v *TKE and Others* [1996] ECR I-1347, at paragraphs 68 to 70.

18 These matters have recently been examined by a European Parliament study, drafted by a team of high ranking independent legal experts. It states with regard to the example of the term 'damage' that 'The European laws governing liability do not yet have even a reasonably uniform idea of what damage is or how it can be defined, which naturally threatens to frustrate any efforts to develop European directives in this field'; European Parliament, DG for Research: 'Study of the systems of private law in the EU with regard to discrimination and the creation of a European civil code' (PE 168.511, p.56). Some Directives (Article 9 of Directive 85/374/EEC, Article 17 of Directive 86/653/EEC) contain differing definitions of the term 'damage'. Each definition, however, is intended solely for the purpose of each respective Directive. Other Directives (Article 5 of Directive 90/314/EEC) use the term without defining it.

20 The Commission has emphasized for example in its report on the application of the commercial agents Directive (COM (1996) 364 final of 23 July 1996) that the application of the system of compensation for damage foreseen in the Directive concerning the same factual situation produces completely different practical results in France and the UK due to different methods of calculation for the quantum of compensation.

It also maintains an emphasis on the need to secure greater uniformity in application. The 2001 'menu' (p. 548) has been trimmed, in the light of consultation. Options (i) and (iv), respectively the least and the most ambitious, are dropped. The 2004 Communication instead builds on three measures suggested by the 2003 Action Plan and uses them to map the 'Way Forward' for European Contract Law.

> Measure I: Improving the present and future *acquis*
> Measure II: promoting the use of EU-wide standard terms and conditions
> Measure III: an 'optional instrument' in European contract law

Measure I, improving the present and future *acquis*, is to be driven by the elaboration of a Common Frame of Reference (CFR). This is presented as a new method for improving uniformity of application of the EC rules.

> ***2.1.1 The main role of the CFR***
>
> The [2003] Action Plan identified different categories of problems of the *acquis*. The main ones were:
>
> - Use of abstract legal terms in directives which are either not defined or too broadly defined
> - Areas where the application of directives does not solve the problems in practice
> - Differences between national implementing laws deriving from the use of minimum harmonisation
> - Inconsistencies in EC contract law legislation
>
> First a policy choice must be made on the need to modify the existing directives in order to address these problems. If so, the Commission will use the CFR as a toolbox, where appropriate, when presenting proposals to improve the quality and coherence of the existing *acquis* and future legal instruments in the area of contract law. At the same time, it will serve the purpose of simplifying the *acquis*. The CFR will provide clear definitions of legal terms, fundamental principles and coherent model rules of contract law, drawing on the EC *acquis* and on best solutions found in Member States' legal orders . . .
>
> It would also be desirable that the Council and the EP could use the CFR when tabling amendments to Commission proposals. Such use of the CFR would be consistent with the shared goal of achieving high quality EU legislation and the commitment of the European institutions to promote simplicity, clarity and consistency of the EU legislation.
>
> ***2.1.2 Other possible roles of the CFR***
>
> National legislators could use the CFR when transposing EU directives in the area of contract law into national legislation. They could also draw on the CFR when enacting legislation on areas of contract law which are not regulated at Community level . . .
>
> . . . the CFR, based on the EC *acquis* and on best solutions identified as common to Member States contract laws, could inspire the European Court of Justice when interpreting the *acquis* on contract law.

In February 2007 the Commission published a *Green Paper on the Review of the Consumer Acquis* (COM (2006) 744. This summarizes the Commission's initial findings on the problems associated with the current legislation in the area of consumer protection. It lists the main options for reform aimed at creating a better regulatory environment for the internal market.

The Green Paper identifies two damaging types of fragmentation – first, that which flows from the prevalent model of minimum harmonization, in so far as Member States have chosen to set stricter rules of consumer protection, and second, that which flows from inconsistent treatment between the Directives, or from failure to address a particular matter. Fragmentation is costly.

> . . . There are a number of issues which are common to all directives forming part of the consumer *acquis*. Definitions of basic notions such as *consumer* and *professional*, the length of cooling-off periods and the modalities for the exercise of the right of withdrawal are examples of issues that are of relevance in the context of several directives. These common issues could be extracted from the existing directives and regulated in a systematic fashion in a horizontal instrument (p. 8).

Read L. Miller, 'After the Unfair Contract Terms Directive: Recent European Directives and English Law' (2007) 3 Euro Rev Contract Law 88 and E. Van Schagen, 'More Consistency and Legal Certainty in the Private Law Acquis: A Plea for Better Justification for the Harmonization of Private Law' 19 MJ 1 (2012) 37 for insight into the practical reality of divergent application. The preparation of the Common Frame of Reference (the 'CFR') was the task of expert researchers funded by the Commission. A supporting network of stakeholder experts ('CFR-net') was also assembled. The CFR has the potential to improve the coherent interpretation and application of EU rules, both at EU and at national level. The text of the CFR which was finalized in 2008 was published as *Principles, Definitions and Model Rules of European Private Law: draft Common Frame of Reference* (Munich: Sellier, 2009). It goes far beyond the Commission's focus on the legislative *acquis* affecting *consumer* contract law in particular, and indeed far beyond the plausible scope of EU legislative competence. The Commission chose to treat this as the 'academic CFR' and proceeded to consider how to take the project forward on the political level. It established an Expert Group on a Common Frame of Reference in the area of European Contract Law, Dec 2010/233 OJ 2010 L105/109, which used the draft CFR as a starting point. In May 2011 this Expert Group published its (coyly labelled) 'Feasibility Study' on a draft instrument of European contract law, under the title 'A European contract law for consumers and businesses'. Next, the 'Feasibility Study' was presented as a 'toolbox' which in October 2011 the Commission integrated into a *Proposal for a Regulation of the Parliament and the Council on a Common European Sales Law*, ('CESL', COM (2011) 635). The Explanatory Memorandum begins by asserting that 'Differences in contract law between Member States hinder traders and consumers who want to engage in cross-border trade within the internal market', but the intention behind the proposal is not to harmonize national laws, but rather to create an 'optional instrument': a uniform EU regime of sales law which would exist as a second regime in each Member State, available for parties concluding cross-border contracts but only if they choose to use it. This is controversial because it assumes that 'choice' is realistic when frequently an economically weak party has little choice (see e.g. J. Cartwright, 'Choice is good. Really?' (2011) 7 ERCL 335); and controversial too for the Commission's assumption that Article 114 TFEU is a valid legal base for an EU measure which creates a new EU regime rather than harmonizing national rules (see e.g., M. Heidemann, 'European Private Law at the Crossroads: The Proposed European Sales Law' (2012) 20 Euro Rev Private Law 1119). The draft 'CESL' was attacked by (*inter alia*) national parliaments for violation of the subsidiarity principle (COM (2012) 373, and see Chapter 18 on subsidiarity) and in its Work Programme for 2015 the Commission announced it had withdrawn the proposal. This review of EU contract law, now extending over a decade and a half, plainly remains dynamic and without any agreed destination.

Relevant documentation may be inspected *via* http://ec.europa.eu/justice/contract/document/index_en.htm.

■ QUESTION

'The Common Frame of Reference heralds departure from orthodox notions of legislative harmonization and judicial interpretation as the route to uniformity in the application of EU law. This is a fresh attempt to find methods for achieving the uniform application of EU law which seeks to involve a much wider range of affected interests.' Discuss.

NOTE: The CFR and its ilk offer one route to reducing fragmentation in EU law. There is also a more orthodox legislative route. In October 2008, as a result of its review of the Consumer *Acquis*, the Commission adopted a proposal for a Directive on Consumer Rights, COM (2008) 614, which would *replace* Directive 85/577 on doorstep selling, Directive 97/7 on distance selling, Directive 93/13 on unfair terms and Directive 99/44 on consumer sales with a 'horizontal instrument' which, moreover, would abandon minimum harmonization in favour of full or maximum harmonization, in order to reduce inter-State fragmentation in the application of consumer law.

Oddly, however, the Commission failed to make any link in its proposal with the possible role of the CFR. In any event the proposal proved politically unacceptable. The Commission revised its proposal. In 2011 Directive 2011/83 on consumer rights (OJ 2011 OJ L304/64) was adopted, based on Article 114 TFEU. It is a measure of maximum harmonisation, but it replaces only two of the four Directives, Directives 85/577 and 97/7, leaving the much more important pair of minimum measures, Directives 93/13 and 99/44, largely untouched. This reveals the political sensitivity associated with the Commission's policy preference for maximum harmonization: see S. Weatherill, 'The Consumer Rights Directive: How and Why a Quest for "Coherence" Has (Largely) Failed' (2012) 49 CML Rev 1279.

■ QUESTION

The Commission's 2007 Green Paper (p. 550) declares that 'At the end of the exercise it should, ideally, be possible to say to EU consumers "wherever you are in the EU or wherever you buy from it makes no difference: your essential rights are the same" ' (p. 3). Is this realistic? Is the EU competent to adopt the measures necessary to achieve this objective?

FURTHER READING ON EUROPEAN CONTRACT LAW

Collins, H., 'Why Europe Needs a Civil Code' (2013) 21 Euro Rev Private Law 907.

Eidenmüller, H., et al., 'Towards a Revision of the Consumer *Acquis*' (2011) 48 CML Rev 1077.

Micklitz, H.-W., 'The Expulsion of the Concept of Protection from the Consumer Law and the Return of Social Elements in the Civil Law: a Bittersweet Polemic' (2012) 35 JCP 283.

Rutgers, J. and Sefton-Green, R. 'Revising the Consumer Acquis: (Half) Opening the Doors of the Trojan Horse' [2008] ERPL 427.

Van Gerven, W., 'Harmonization of Private law: Do We Need It?' (2004) 41 CML Rev 505.

Vogenauer, S. and Weatherill, S. (eds), *The Harmonisation of European Contract Law: Implications for European Private Laws, Business and Legal Practice* (Oxford: Hart, 2006).

■ QUESTION

The development risk defence under the Product Liability Directive is an example of optional differentiated integration within a measure of harmonization. It also allows appreciation of the problems in securing a uniform interpretation and application of notionally 'harmonized' terms. Might one see failure to implement Directives in the national legal order as a further means of choosing differentiated integration? How effective are the EU rules on the direct and indirect effect of Directives (see Chapter 5) as controls over inadequate national implementation of Directives? What might be the impact of the ruling in *Francovich* (Cases C-6, C-9/90), p. 143?

D: The Product Liability Directive and pre-emption

The earlier inquiry concentrates on derogations and options expressly foreseen by the Product Liability Directive, and on its uniform interpretation. What of the *pre-emptive effect* of Directive 85/374? Are different national liability systems to be tolerated? Article 13 provides that 'This Directive shall not affect any rights which an injured person may have according to the rules of the law of contractual or non-contractual liability or a special liability system existing at the moment when this Directive is notified'. The meaning of this provision was elucidated in the next case.

María Victoria González Sánchez v Medicina Asturiana SA (Case C-183/00)

[2002] ECR I-3901, Court of Justice of the European Communities

Ms González Sánchez sued Medicina Asturiana for compensation for injury allegedly caused on their premises belonging to Medicina Asturiana in the course of a blood transfusion. She claimed to have been infected by the Hepatitis C virus. The Spanish court concluded that the rights afforded to consumers under pre-existing Spanish law were more extensive than those available under the rules introduced to transpose Directive 85/374 into domestic law. The Court of Justice was asked for a preliminary ruling on the question whether Article 13 of the Directive should be interpreted as precluding the restriction or limitation, as a result of transposition of the Directive, of rights granted to consumers under the legislation of the Member State.

[22] By its question the referring court is essentially seeking to ascertain whether Article 13 of the Directive must be interpreted as meaning that the rights conferred under the legislation of a Member State on victims of damage caused by a defective product may be limited or restricted as a result of the Directive's transposition into the domestic law of that State.

[23] It should be noted that the Directive was adopted by the Council by unanimity under Article 100 of the EEC Treaty (amended to Article 100 of the EC Treaty, now Article 94 EC [now Article 115 TFEU]) concerning the approximation of such laws, regulations or administrative provisions of the Member States as directly affect the establishment or functioning of the common market. Unlike Article 100a of the EC Treaty (now, after amendment, Article 95 EC [now Article 114 TFEU]), which was inserted into the Treaty after the adoption of the Directive and allows for certain derogations, [see Art 114(4) *et seq* p. 531] that legal basis provides no possibility for the Member States to maintain or establish provisions departing from Community harmonising measures.

[24] Nor can Article 153 EC [now Article 169 TFEU], likewise inserted into the Treaty after the adoption of the Directive, be relied on in order to justify interpreting the directive as seeking a minimum harmonisation of the laws of the Member States which could not preclude one of them from retaining or adopting protective measures stricter than the Community measures. In fact, the competence conferred in that respect on the Member States by Article 153(5) EC concerns only the measures mentioned at paragraph 3(b) of that article, that is to say measures supporting, supplementing and monitoring the policy pursued by the Member States. That competence does not extend to the measures referred to in paragraph 3(a) of Article 153 EC, that is to say the measures adoptedpursuant to Article 95 EC in the context of attainment of the internal market with which in that respect the measures adopted under Article 94 EC must be equated. Furthermore, as the Advocate General noted at point 43 of his Opinion, Article 153 EC is worded in the form of an instruction addressed to the Community concerning its future policy and cannot permit the Member States, owing to the direct risk that would pose for the *acquis communautaire*, autonomously to adopt measures contrary to the Community law contained in the directives already adopted at the time of entry into force of that law.

[25] Accordingly, the margin of discretion available to the Member States in order to make provision for product liability is entirely determined by the Directive itself and must be inferred from its wording, purpose and structure.

[26] In that connection it should be pointed out first that, as is clear from the first recital thereto, the purpose of the Directive in establishing a harmonised system of civil liability on the part of producers in respect of damage caused by defective products is to ensure undistorted competition between traders, to facilitate the free movement of goods and to avoid differences in levels of consumer protection.

[27] Secondly, it is important to note that unlike, for example, Council Directive 93/13/EEC of 5 April 1993 on unfair terms in consumer contracts (OJ 1993 L 95, p. 29), the Directive contains no provision expressly authorising the Member States to adopt or to maintain more stringent provisions in matters in respect of which it makes provision, in order to secure a higher level of consumer protection.

[28] Thirdly, the fact that the Directive provides for certain derogations or refers in certain cases to national law does not mean that in regard to the matters which it regulates harmonisation is not complete.

[29] Although Articles 15(1)(a) and (b) and 16 of the Directive permit the Member States to depart from the rules laid down therein, the possibility of derogation applies only in regard to the matters exhaustively specified and it is narrowly defined. Moreover, it is subject *inter alia* to conditions as to assessment with a view to further harmonisation, to which the penultimate recital in the preamble expressly refers. An illustration of progressive harmonisation of that kind is afforded by Directive 1999/34/EC of the European Parliament and of the Council of 10 May 1999 amending Council Directive 85/374/EEC (OJ 1999 L 141, p. 20), which by bringing agricultural products within the scope of the Directive removes the option afforded by Article 15(1)(a) thereof.

[30] In those circumstances Article 13 of the Directive cannot be interpreted as giving the Member States the possibility of maintaining a general system of product liability different from that provided for in the Directive.

[31] The reference in Article 13 of the Directive to the rights which an injured person may rely on under the rules of the law of contractual or non-contractual liability must be interpreted as meaning that the system of rules put in place by the Directive, which in Article 4 enables the victim to seek compensation where he proves damage, the defect in the product and the causal link between that defect and the damage, does not preclude the application of other systems of contractual or non-contractual liability based on other grounds, such as fault or a warranty in respect of latent defects.

[32] Likewise the reference in Article 13 to the rights which an injured person may rely on under a special liability system existing at the time when the Directive was notified must be construed, as is clear from the third clause of the 13th recital thereto, as referring to a specific scheme limited to a given sector of production (see judgments of today in Case C-52/00 *Commission* v *France* [2002] ECR I-3827, paragraphs 13 to 23, and Case C-154/00 *Commission* v *Greece* [2002] ECR I-3879, paragraphs 9 to 19).

[33] Conversely, a system of producer liability founded on the same basis as that put in place by the Directive and not limited to a given sector of production does not come within any of the systems of liability referred to in Article 13 of the Directive. That provision cannot therefore be relied on in such a case in order to justify the maintenance in force of national provisions affording greater protection than those of the Directive.

[34] The reply to the question raised must therefore be that Article 13 of the Directive must be interpreted as meaning that the rights conferred under the legislation of a Member State on the victims of damage caused by a defective product under a general system of liability having the same basis as that put in place by the Directive may be limited or restricted as a result of the Directive's transposition into the domestic law of that State.

NOTE: The same identification of a 'complete' system of harmonization (para 28) emerges from the Court's two other rulings of the same day dealing with Directive 85/374: Case C-52/00 *Commission* v *France*, Case C-154/00 *Commission* v *Greece* mentioned in para 32. This ruling fits into the pattern of *inter alia* that in '*Tobacco Advertising*' (Case C-376/98) in its thematic insistence on legislative harmonization as an instrument for building an internal market.

■ QUESTION

Para 27 of this judgment refers briefly to the inclusion in Directive 93/13 on unfair terms in consumer contracts of a provision expressly authorizing the Member States to adopt or to maintain more stringent provisions in order to secure a higher level of consumer protection. This was also referred to at p. 542. But Directive 93/13 was adopted under Article 100a EC (now, after amendment, Article 114 TFEU): what is the status today of such a 'minimum clause' in a measure of harmonization?

NOTE: The Court's interpretation of Article 13 of the Directive is vulnerable to the criticism that it locates competence in this field exclusively in the hands of the EU legislature and that it accordingly precludes the expression of local diversity and regulatory innovation. The troubling implications of this prompted the Council to adopt the following Resolution.

COUNCIL RESOLUTION OF 19 DECEMBER 2002 ON AMENDMENT OF THE LIABILITY FOR DEFECTIVE PRODUCTS DIRECTIVE

[2003] OJ C26/02

THE COUNCIL OF THE EUROPEAN UNION, RECALLING THAT:

[1] Council Directive 85/374/EEC of 25 July 1985 on the approximation of the laws, regulations and administrative provisions of the Member States concerning liability for defective products (OJ 1985 L210), as amended by European Parliament and Council Directive 1999/34/EC of 10 May 1999 (OJ 1999 L141), seeks to achieve an approximation of the laws of the Member States concerning the liability of the producer for damage caused by the defectiveness of his products because the existing divergences may distort competition and affect the movement of goods within the common market and entail a differing degree of protection of the consumer against damage caused by a defective product to his health or property. To provide an adequate solution to the problem, peculiar to our age of increasing technicality, of a fair apportionment of the risks inherent in modern technological production, the Directive imposes liability on the producer without fault on his part for damage caused by the defectiveness of his products.

[2] The producer is considered to be the manufacturer of a finished product, the producer of any raw material or the manufacturer of a component part and any person who, by putting his name, trade mark or other distinguishing feature on the product, presents himself as the producer, cf. Article 3(1) of the Directive. Without prejudice to the liability of the producer, any person who imports into the Community a product for sale, hire, leasing or any form of distribution in the course of his business shall be deemed to be a producer and shall be responsible as a producer, cf. Article 3(2) of the Directive.

[3] Where the producer or the importer of the product cannot be identified, each supplier of the product shall be treated as its producer unless he informs the injured person, within a reasonable time, of the identity of the producer or the importer or of the person who supplied him with the product, cf. Article 3(3) of the Directive. Apart from this specific Article the Directive contains no provisions concerning the liability of the supplier.

[4] At the time of the adoption of the Directive (Session 1025 of the Council, 25 July 1985), the following joint statement of the Council and the Commission concerning the scope of the Directive was inserted in the Council minutes: 'With regard to the interpretation of Articles 3 and 12, the Council and the Commission are in agreement that there is nothing to prevent individual Member States from laying down in their national legislation rules regarding liability for intermediaries, since intermediary liability is not covered by the Directive. There is further agreement that under the Directive the Member States may determine rules on the final mutual apportionment of liability among several liable producers (see Article 3) and intermediaries.' At the same time the following statement was inserted in the Council minutes concerning the understanding of Article 3(3): 'The Council notes that the word "supplier" within the meaning of Article 3(3) means the person who operates in the chain of distribution.'

[5] In a judgment of 25 April 2002 (Case C-52/00) the Court of Justice of the European Communities established that the Directive seeks to achieve, in the matters regulated by it, complete harmonisation of the laws, regulations and administrative provisions of the Member States (see also judgments of the same date in cases C-154/00 and C-183/00). Furthermore, the Court of Justice also established in case C-52/00 that a national legislation providing that the supplier of a defective product is to be liable in all cases and on the same basis as the producer constitutes a violation of the Directive.

[6] Thus, it seems that Member States may no longer lay down rules on liability of suppliers, i.e., persons who operate in the chain of distribution, based on the same ground as the liability system in the Directive concerning liability of producers. Except for cases provided for in Article 3(3) a system of liability of suppliers based on strict liability therefore seems to be precluded.

[7] This legal situation gives rise to concern, since as pointed out in paragraph 3 the Directive does not, apart from Article 3(3), contain provisions concerning the liability of the supplier.

[8] The possibility to lay down rules on liability of suppliers, including rules on strict liability, could involve benefits to the consumers, regardless of whether these rules are laid down at national or Community level. In relevant cases the consumer would then be able to raise his claim against the producer, subsequent suppliers, including the seller of the product, or them all. This could improve consumer's possibility of actually obtaining

compensation. The Council also recalls that one of the general objectives of the Community is to promote consumer interests and ensure a high level of consumer protection, cf. Articles 95 and 153 of the Treaty.

[9] THE COUNCIL CONSIDERS that against this background there is a need to assess whether Directive 85/374/EEC, as amended by Directive 1999/34/EC, should be modified in such a way as to allow for national rules on liability of suppliers based on the same ground as the liability system in the Directive concerning liability of producers.

■ **QUESTION**

What does this tell you about the perils of 'complete harmonization'? What does this tell you about the perils of adding statements to Council minutes that are not carried through in the formal text of adopted legislation?

The Council's Resolution has not provoked the Commission to propose legislative reform. But the Resolution has not gone unnoticed.

***Sko* v *and Bilka* (Case C-402/03)**

[2006] ECR I-199, Court of Justice of the European Communities

Under Danish law a supplier is fully responsible for the liability which the Directive imposes on the producer. As para 8 of the Council Resolution suggests, this seems consumer-friendly in that it allows a choice of targets to sue in case of harm caused by a defective product (*in casu* eggs leading to salmonella poisoning). But the Court was asked whether this generous Danish rule was excluded by the liability regime envisaged by Directive 85/374. It was.

[39] On this point, it should be recalled that in *Commission* v *France*, paragraph 21, *Commission* v *Greece*, paragraph 17, and *González Sánchez*, paragraph 30, the Court held, after analysing the wording, purpose and structure of the Directive, that Article 13 could not be interpreted as leaving it open to the Member States to maintain a general system of product liability different from that provided for in the Directive.

[40] The Danish Government wants that case-law to be reconsidered in the light of the statement on Articles 3 and 13 in point 2 of the minutes of the meeting of the Council of Ministers of 25 July 1985, according to which those articles do not prevent each Member State from laying down in its national legislation rules regarding liability for intermediaries.

[41] To defend maintaining the national rule that the supplier is answerable for the liability of the producer, which was developed by the case-law before the Directive entered into force and was merely confirmed by the law transposing the Directive, the Danish Government also relies on the statement in point 16 of those minutes, in which the Council expressed 'the wish that Member States which currently apply provisions relating to consumer protection which are more favourable than those under the Directive [might] not rely on the options afforded by the Directive to reduce that level of protection'.

[42] On this point, first, it must be recalled that, where a statement recorded in Council minutes is not referred to in the wording of a provision of secondary legislation, it cannot be used for the purpose of interpreting that provision (see, in particular, Case C-292/89 *Antonissen* [1991] ECR I-745, paragraph 18, and Case C-375/98 *Epson Europe* [2000] ECR I-4243, paragraph 26).

[43] Second, the two statements referred to by the Danish Government cannot justify altering, in contradiction of the wording and structure of the measure, the class of persons liable defined by the Directive. In particular, they cannot be relied on to allow the Member States to transfer to the supplier, beyond the cases listed exhaustively in Article 3(3), the burden of the liability established by the Directive and imposed by it on the producer.

[44] As regards the Danish Government's argument that that interpretation of the Directive is liable to lower the level of consumer protection in Denmark, it must be stated that any extension to suppliers of the liability established by the Directive falls within the competence of the Community legislature, for whom it is to amend, if appropriate, the provisions concerned.

Did this damage consumer protection? Perhaps – but imposing unconditional liability on suppliers forces them to buy extra insurance beyond that required to cope with the Directive's more focused ascription of legal responsibility. That could lead to higher prices to the detriment of the consumer. The Court acknowledges the need for a cost/benefit analysis, but the tart constitutional point which it makes in para 44 of its ruling is that this legislative choice belongs at *EU* level, and its interpretation of the Directive precludes the system being undermined by diverse national choices. The Directive has *centralized* the site of legislative authority in the EU.

The Court did however accept that Danish rules under which the supplier is fully responsible for the *fault*-based liability of the producer in such circumstances are not affected by the Product Liability Directive. Citing para 31 of the ruling in *Gonzalez Sanchez* (Case C-183/00) it accepted that Article 13 of the Directive does not preclude the application of systems of contractual or non-contractual liability based on grounds *other* than those envisaged by the Directive, such as fault. The result is doubtless a rather uncomfortable co-existence for domestic and EU-derived law governing defective products.

The Commission's Third Report on the Product Liability Directive, published in 2006 (COM (2006) 496), did not ignore the Council Resolution. It stated that 'if the Resolution were given effect, this would mark a departure from the objective of harmonization of product liability laws under the Directive' (p. 11). The Commission is visibly protective of the existing model. The field of contract law also provides fertile material for this debate. The Commission's October 2004 communication (p. 549) explicitly promises review of Directives which harmonize consumer contract laws 'in particular in the light of the minimum harmonisation clauses they contain'. This conforms to the general concerns expressed by the Commission about the fragmenting effect of a model of minimum rule-making and its corresponding intention to press for maximum harmonization in order to drive forward market integration more vigorously. Its 2007 *Green Paper on the Review of the Consumer Acquis*, mentioned at p. 550, did not even offer maintenance of the current model of minimum harmonization as an option (COM (2006) 744, p. 15). Instead it offered only choice between different varieties of maximum rule-making and mutual recognition. So the Court's case law constitutes a constitutional challenge to the viability of minimum harmonization (Case C-376/98 p. 539); and the Commission's policy preferences are hostile to minimum rule-making because of a perception that it cannot provide the uniform regulatory environment needed to construct a viable internal market. A connection should be made with the discussion at the end of Chapter 14 (p. 415). It was there explained that Directive 2005/29 on unfair business-to-consumer commercial practices in the internal market was adopted under Article 95 EC (now Article 114 TFEU) as a measure of 'maximum harmonization'. That means Member States may not suppress the use of strategies which meet the requirements of fairness established by the Directive. But the Commission's preference to use this same maximum model for the 'Services Directive' proved politically unacceptable. The finally adopted version yields scope for national measures that restrict trade in services by setting protective standards above those mandated by the EU's measure: Directive 2006/123 on services in the internal market.

The Commission's commitment to press ahead with a preference for maximum harmonization in the re-thinking of European contract law adds fresh fuel to this debate about the proper relationship between the Union and the Member States in the regulation of the internal market. Harmonization policy, as an exercise in distributing competences to regulate the market between the EU and its Member States, is an intensely sensitive legal and political matter. It is illuminating that the October 2008 Commission proposal for a Directive on Consumer Rights, COM (2008) 614 (p. 551) met fierce political resistance largely because of its intended maximum character, which would have disabled national competence to set rules more generous to the consumer. Instead Directive 2011/83 on consumer rights (OJ 2011 OJ L304/64) was adopted, based on Article 114 TFEU. It is a measure of maximum harmonization, but, as mentioned (p. 552), much less ambitious in scope.

FURTHER READING ON THE POLICY ISSUES ASSOCIATED WITH THE DEBATE ABOUT MINIMUM AND MAXIMUM HARMONIZATION

Boeger, N., 'Minimum Harmonization, Free Movement and Proportionality' in P. Syrpis (ed), *The Judiciary, the Legislature and the EU Internal Market* (Cambridge: CUP, 2012).

Gomez, F. and Ganuza, J., 'An Economic Analysis of Harmonization Régimes: Full Harmonization, Minimum Harmonization or Optional Instrument?' (2011) 7 ERCL 275.

Mak, V., 'Review of the Consumer Acquis: Towards Maximum Harmonisation?' [2009] Euro Rev Private Law 55.

Weatherill, S., 'Maximum versus Minimum Harmonization: Choosing between Unity and Diversity in the Search for the Soul of the Internal Market' in N. Nic Shuibhne and L. Gormley (eds), *From Single Market to Economic Union: Essays in Memory of John A Usher* (Oxford: OUP, 2012).

For contrasting views of the choice of a maximum model in Directive 2005/29 on unfair commercial practices see G. Howells (unfavourable), 'Unfair Commercial Practices Directive – a missed opportunity?' Ch. 6 in S. Weatherill and U. Bernitz (eds), *The Regulation of Unfair Commercial Practices under EC Directive 2005/29* (Oxford: Hart Publishing, 2007) and G. Abbamonte (favourable), 'The Unfair Commercial Practices Directive and its General Prohibition', Ch. 1 ibid.

NOTE: For additional material and resources see the Online Resource Centre at: www.oxfordtextbooks.co.uk/orc/weatherill12e.

18

Subsidiarity, Flexibility, and New Forms of Governance

Chapter 17 explored the extent to which EU rule-making need not result in an all-or-nothing transfer of competence from Member States to the Union. Minimum harmonization in the fields of consumer and environmental protection provides a good example of the rise of a system of 'multi-level governance', within which both State and Union authorities are active as regulators. Sub-national and regional actors within the States may be involved too – so might international bodies. There are layers of legal authority in today's interdependent world. However, the process of harmonization as a basis for constructing an internal market carries a different emphasis. Derogations within the scope of a Directive are possible, as the case of the Product Liability Directive illustrates (p. 544). But some recent trends are motivated by the perceived need to establish the agreed EU rule as the basis for cross-border trade, and to exclude the possibility of Member States treating the harmonized rule as a minimum. Chapter 17 concludes by showing how this has become the Commission's preference in proposing legislation directed at the functioning of the internal market, which in turn has generated some, but not consistent, political resistance to maximum harmonization in the legislative process.

But there is much more to consider in appreciating the sweep of the EU's regulatory strategy and, in particular, the extent to which the pressure for centralized decision-making is softened by respect for local autonomy and diversity.

The next issue asks: even if the EU is, as a general observation, competent to act, should it exercise that competence in a particular case, or should it instead leave the matter in the hands of the Member States? This is Subsidiarity, and it is treated in Section 1 of this chapter.

Then, to what extent is it desirable to establish systems for decision-making in common which do not implicate all the Member States? This is not a derogation of the detailed type of which the Product Liability Directive offers an illustration, nor even an individual opt-out. It is more fundamental. It suggests a European Union of varying intensities of integration, within which States may choose the depth of their commitment to available common projects. Section 2 covers this.

A further question of governance relates to the instruments to be used. Can the relationship between central and local legal and political authority be better managed by using 'softer' instruments of law- and policy-making that are more conducive to local preferences and regulatory reform than binding instruments such as Regulations and Directives envisaged by Article 288 TFEU? This is the terrain covered in Section 3.

SECTION 1: SUBSIDIARITY

Neither the Treaty of Rome nor the Single European Act contained explicit reference to the principle of subsidiarity. Its essence appears, however, in (what was) Article 130r(4), a provision inserted by the Single European Act with effect from 1987.

> 4. The Community shall take action relating to the environment to the extent to which the objectives referred to in paragraph 1 *can be attained better at Community level than at the level of the individual Member States.* [emphasis added]

NOTE: The Maastricht Treaty introduced a broader formulation of the principle of subsidiarity. It was Article 3b EC, which became in unamended form Article 5(2) EC. It is now found in Article 5 TEU, which was first encountered in examining the principle of conferral in Chapter 2, p. 29.

ARTICLE 5(1) TEU

> The limits of Union competences are governed by the principle of conferral. The use of Union competences is governed by the principles of subsidiarity and proportionality.

NOTE: Article 5(1) TEU contains the principle of conferral, which dictates that the Union shall act only within the limits of the competences conferred upon it by the Member States in the Treaties (Article 5(2) TEU, p. 29). The *exercise* of such conferred competence is then subjected to two preconditions: that it shall comply with the principle of proportionality, as set out in Article 5(4) TEU and examined at p. 48, and the principle of subsidiarity, which is defined in Article 5(3) TEU.

ARTICLE 5(3) TEU

> Under the principle of subsidiarity, in areas which do not fall within its exclusive competence, the Union shall act only if and in so far as the objectives of the proposed action cannot be sufficiently achieved by the Member States, either at central level or at regional and local level, but can rather, by reason of the scale or effects of the proposed action, be better achieved at Union level. The institutions of the Union shall apply the principle of subsidiarity as laid down in the Protocol on the application of the principles of subsidiarity and proportionality. National Parliaments ensure compliance with the principle of subsidiarity in accordance with the procedure set out in that Protocol.

NOTE: The Lisbon Treaty changed the numbers of the relevant provisions, which must be borne in mind in reading the older material contained in this chapter, and it adjusted the text, but not in a way that altered the core meaning or purpose of these provisions. Lisbon added an extra device for monitoring the application of the subsidiarity principle – the involvement of the national Parliaments, mentioned in the final sentence of Article 5(3) TEU. It is also covered in Article 12 TEU:

ARTICLE 12 TEU

> National Parliaments contribute actively to the good functioning of the Union:
>
> (a) through being informed by the institutions of the Union and having draft legislative acts of the Union forwarded to them in accordance with the Protocol on the role of national Parliaments in the European Union;
>
> (b) by seeing to it that the principle of subsidiarity is respected in accordance with the procedures provided for in the Protocol on the application of the principles of subsidiarity and proportionality . . .

NOTES

1. The role of national Parliaments, and the reason for their insertion into the Treaties as a result of the Lisbon amendments, will be considered at p. 568, once the development of the principle of subsidiarity in EU law has been put into context.
2. The principle of subsidiarity has been cited in connection with the withdrawal of a number of legislative proposals in recent years. The Product Liability Directive (85/374) was examined in the preceding chapter. The Commission proposed that this liability system for the supply of defective goods should be complemented by a Directive governing liability for supply of defective services (COM (90) 482). In the Commission's report submitted to the Edinburgh European Council

in December 1992, which reviewed existing and proposed legislation in the light of the subsidiarity principle, the Commission included the draft Directive in its list of excessively detailed instruments which required revision. It became plain that there was an absence of political will behind the proposed Directive. Eventually, in a Communication on new directions on the liability of suppliers of services (COM (94) 260), the Commission concluded that its 'proposal stands no chance of being adopted without sweeping changes which would risk voiding it of much of its substance'. It therefore withdrew it. Lately the Commission has tended to situate withdrawal of legislative proposals in the broader context of its commitment to 'Better Regulation' (see e.g., comment on 78 withdrawn proposals in 2006 in its 'Report on Better Lawmaking 2006' COM (2007) 286 para 1.1.6).

3. 'Subsidiarity' has commonly been employed as a slogan for challenging the expansion of Union activity. Yet the wording of Article 5(3) TEU is directed at identification of the appropriate level at which action should be taken. It is not based on any entrenched preconception in favour of State action at the expense of the Union. The next extract was written at an early stage of the EU's 'subsidiarity mood', and it sets the scene.

M. Wilke and H. Wallace, 'Subsidiarity: Approaches to Power-Sharing in the European Community'

RIIA Discussion Paper No 27 (1990) pp. 21, 30–3

(Some footnotes omitted.)

The current British political debate links the principle of subsidiarity exclusively to the debate about the European Community. Policy-makers and academics are attempting to develop new definitions of the concept, recognizing that Roman Catholic sources have supplied the basic foundations. It is not surprising, however, given that British experience is different from Dutch or German, that a considerable confusion persists when it comes to 'pinning down' the principle of subsidiarity.

In February 1990, the Legal Adviser of the Select Committee on European Legislation of the House of Commons was asked to produce a note on subsidiarity.[23] Mentioning the Madrid European Council and the different interventions on the subject made by Jacques Delors, the note states that, in absence of a 'precise identity', it is time 'to start with . . . a clean sheet of paper' as 'the concept of subsidiarity is assigned a major constitutional role'. This last assumption necessitates a clarification of the subsidiarity concept, which is 'clearly established as a manufactured term; and accordingly there is ample scope for argument about the meaning to be ascribed to it today'.

The note attempts to clarify the political function of the principle of subsidiarity. The concept might facilitate more efficient and productive policy-making and implementation, thus following the exhortation given by the House of Lords Select Committee on the EC, in its *Report on the Community Social Charter*, which stated that 'the Community should act only where objectives can be attained better at Community level than at the level of the individual Member States'?[26] If so, 'the Commission is likely to take a more generous view of the benefits of Community action and of its own capability than Member States may be disposed to do'. Does the principle of subsidiarity serve the common interest, as mentioned the Commission's Programme for 1989? Is the principle to add to democratic accountability, as Leon Brittan suggested in his speech of 13 July 1989? If so, stated the note, 'little would be appropriate for Community action because ordinarily Member States will be much closer to the people affected'. Or is it Francis Maude's definition of subsidiarity that should stand, namely 'that things should not be done at Community level unless they cannot be done at national level'? This definition, the note concludes, 'would raise substantially the barrier which the Community must cross'. Its author believed, however, that the definition given by House of Lords Select Committee on the EC, using the wording 'attained better', would 'command the greatest measure of support'.

The issue which justifies these speculations, and which 'is in the air' remains: whether to incorporate the principle of subsidiarity into the EC Treaties. 'Any such suggestion', states the note 'would be received with alarm by lawyers brought up in the common law tradition. For if written in as a pure statement of principle, it would serve no purpose. And if written in as something more, it could do great harm'.

. . .

---

23 See the House of Commons Foreign Affairs Committee, *The Operation of the Single European Act: Minutes of Evidence*, 17 January 1990, Select Committee on European Legislation, House of Commons, Session 1989–1990, pp.68–72.

26 House of Lords Select Committee of the European Communities, *Report on a Community Social Charter*, House of Lords Paper 6 (1989–90), 5 December 1989, p.26.

Subsidiarity has thus been introduced into the debate about EC institutions and policies. Its wide ranging character has not, however, been derived from a concrete formulation of the principle. The Commission has over the last two years attempted to clarify, define and explore how it might help to identify the appropriate level of policy competence. But so far each case for its application has rested on a separate analysis, in relation to criteria of efficiency, proportionality and judicial soundness.

Jacques Delors has become the leading exponent of the principle of subsidiarity. His political, philosophical and social background suggests some familiarity with the concept. Through his readings of Emmanuel Mounier, Jacques Delors acquired a specific perception of the individual in society. Mounier, born in Grenoble in 1905 and founder of the prestigious review *Esprit*, became a major spokesman for the so-called *personalisme* movement, which sought to reconcile Christianity and socialism.

Jacques Delors was inspired by the idea that a global approach rather than particular solutions was needed to define the proper place of the individual in society. As a member of a community, the individual was enabled to participate in the creation of a growing socio-economical world. Finding and implementing the 'difficile équilibre entre la nécessaire affirmation de la volonté collective par l'Etat et le libre jeu de tous les centres de décisions' became a leading objective of Jacques Delors' political career. Any member of society is to be allocated a considerable autonomy in his activities, an idea cherished by Jacques Delors since his earliest participation in the semi-religious movement *Vie Nouvelle*. These thoughts were further elaborated during his first encounters with socialism, which focused on the development of the so-called 'communautés de base', as an alternative to the omnipresent state...

... Leon Brittan, in his Granada lecture of November 1989, stated that it was 'impossible to set down in advance clear guidelines as to when the subsidiarity principle should apply'. Nevertheless if the EC is to prove a liberating influence and not a centralizing and corporatist one, we must further develop and apply the principle that decisions should be taken at the lowest appropriate level: as close as possible, that is, to the people who are affected by them.

There is a challenge involved here, Brittan believed, as we should ask ourselves, particularly in the social domain, is this really a decision that needs to be taken at Community level? If it is not, the Community would be wise to set out the general objective, but leave it to the individual Member State to achieve that as they wish, according to their own traditions and their own laws.

Leon Brittan, a lawyer himself, argued that subsidiarity 'should not be seen as something for the theologians of Community law, but as something intensely practical: where to draw the dividing line between what is best done by the Community and what is best done by national governments'. Subsidiarity 'needs to be developed and applied with much more vigour in practice'.

NOTE: The frequently observed British tendency to view European federalism as a centralizing process may be corrected by a fuller understanding of the implications of the principle of subsidiarity. Indeed, far from leading inevitably to centralization, the development of the Union may have quite the reverse effect.

M. Wilke and H. Wallace, 'Subsidiarity: Approaches to Power-Sharing in the European Community'

RIIA Discussion Paper No 27 (1990), p. 8

In addition it should be borne in mind that the concern of the German Länder is not about the balance of powers between the Community and the Member States, but about the impact on the regional level of government for a country with a federal constitution. The logic of their complaint is that the EC should not be empowered to make EC legislation in areas of Länder competence, unless the Länder themselves have endorsed the measure. One can envisage similar arguments being made in Belgium, Italy or Spain. To follow this logic would be enormously to complicate the EC process and would also set a model which could become an issue in other Member States with rather different internal arrangements. Thus within the UK one could envisage the supporters of Scottish devolution, who in any event can also plead differences between Scottish and English law, rushing to exploit the precedent.

■ QUESTION

'... the chief advantage of [subsidiarity] seems to be its capacity to mean all things to all interested parties – simultaneously' (Mary Robinson [when President of Ireland],

'Constitutional Shifts in Europe and the US: Learning from Each Other' (1996) 32 Stanford Jnl Int L 1, 10). Is this a good thing or a bad thing? Is this law or politics?

NOTE: The general issue of competence allocation and identification of the appropriate respective contributions of the Union and the Member States to the evolution of the Union is quite fundamental to any perspective on the future of Europe. Subsidiarity has acted as a catchphrase for that debate (and not always helpfully, as the quote from Mary Robinson suggests). Its high profile is accordingly hardly surprising. The quest to imbue the subsidiarity principle with a degree of operational value in determining whether or not the EU should act prompted the attachment of a Protocol on the application of the principles of subsidiarity and proportionality to the Treaty by the Treaty of Amsterdam. This was replaced by a new version by the Treaty of Lisbon, which includes the novel procedures for involving national Parliaments (p. 568). Does this Protocol help you to grasp the intended impact of subsidiarity on the EU's institutional culture?

PROTOCOL ON THE APPLICATION OF THE PRINCIPLES OF SUBSIDIARITY AND PROPORTIONALITY

THE HIGH CONTRACTING PARTIES

WISHING to ensure that decisions are taken as closely as possible to the citizens of the Union,

RESOLVED to establish the conditions for the application of the principles of subsidiarity and proportionality, as laid down in Article 5 of the Treaty on European Union, and to establish a system for monitoring the application of those principles,

HAVE AGREED UPON the following provisions, which shall be annexed to the Treaty on European Union and to the Treaty on the Functioning of the European Union:

ARTICLE 1

Each institution shall ensure constant respect for the principles of subsidiarity and proportionality, as laid down in Article 5 of the Treaty on European Union.

ARTICLE 2

Before proposing legislative acts, the Commission shall consult widely. Such consultations shall, where appropriate, take into account the regional and local dimension of the action envisaged. In cases of exceptional urgency, the Commission shall not conduct such consultations. It shall give reasons for its decision in its proposal.

ARTICLE 3

For the purposes of this Protocol, 'draft legislative acts' shall mean proposals from the Commission, initiatives from a group of Member States, initiatives from the European Parliament, requests from the Court of Justice, recommendations from the European Central Bank and requests from the European Investment Bank for the adoption of a legislative act.

ARTICLE 4

The Commission shall forward its draft legislative acts and its amended drafts to national Parliaments at the same time as to the Union legislator.

The European Parliament shall forward its draft legislative acts and its amended drafts to national Parliaments.

The Council shall forward draft legislative acts originating from a group of Member States, the Court of Justice, the European Central Bank or the European Investment Bank and amended drafts to national Parliaments.

Upon adoption, legislative resolutions of the European Parliament and positions of the Council shall be forwarded by them to national Parliaments.

ARTICLE 5

Draft legislative acts shall be justified with regard to the principles of subsidiarity and proportionality.

Any draft legislative act should contain a detailed statement making it possible to appraise compliance with the principles of subsidiarity and proportionality. This statement should contain some assessment of the proposal's financial impact and, in the case of a directive, of its implications for the rules to be put in place by Member States, including, where necessary, the regional legislation. The reasons for concluding that a Union objective can be better achieved at Union level shall be substantiated by qualitative and, wherever possible, quantitative indicators. Draft legislative acts shall take account of the need for any burden, whether financial or administrative, falling upon the Union, national governments, regional or local authorities, economic operators and citizens, to be minimised and commensurate with the objective to be achieved.

ARTICLE 6

Any national Parliament or any chamber of a national Parliament may, within eight weeks from the date of transmission of a draft legislative act, in the official languages of the Union, send to the Presidents of the European Parliament, the Council and the Commission a reasoned opinion stating why it considers that the draft in question does not comply with the principle of subsidiarity. It will be for each national Parliament or each chamber of a national Parliament to consult, where appropriate, regional parliaments with legislative powers.

If the draft legislative act originates from a group of Member States, the President of the Council shall forward the opinion to the governments of those Member States.

If the draft legislative act originates from the Court of Justice, the European Central Bank or the European Investment Bank, the President of the Council shall forward the opinion to the institution or body concerned.

ARTICLE 7

1. The European Parliament, the Council and the Commission, and, where appropriate, the group of Member States, the Court of Justice, the European Central Bank or the European Investment Bank, if the draft legislative act originates from them, shall take account of the reasoned opinions issued by national Parliaments or by a chamber of a national Parliament.

Each national Parliament shall have two votes, shared out on the basis of the national Parliamentary system. In the case of a bicameral Parliamentary system, each of the two chambers shall have one vote.

2. Where reasoned opinions on a draft legislative act's non-compliance with the principle of subsidiarity represent at least one third of all the votes allocated to the national Parliaments in accordance with the second subparagraph of paragraph 1, the draft must be reviewed. This threshold shall be a quarter in the case of a draft legislative act submitted on the basis of Article 76 of the Treaty on the Functioning of the European Union on the area of freedom, security and justice.

After such review, the Commission or, where appropriate, the group of Member States, the European Parliament, the Court of Justice, the European Central Bank or the European Investment Bank, if the draft legislative act originates from them, may decide to maintain, amend or withdraw the draft. Reasons must be given for this decision.

3. Furthermore, under the ordinary legislative procedure, where reasoned opinions on the noncompliance of a proposal for a legislative act with the principle of subsidiarity represent at least a simple majority of the votes allocated to the national Parliaments in accordance with the second subparagraph of paragraph 1, the proposal must be reviewed. After such review, the Commission may decide to maintain, amend or withdraw the proposal. If it chooses to maintain the proposal, the Commission will have, in a reasoned opinion, to justify why it considers that the proposal complies with the principle of subsidiarity. This reasoned opinion, as well as the reasoned opinions of the national Parliaments, will have to be submitted to the Union legislator, for consideration in the procedure:

(a) before concluding the first reading, the legislator (the European Parliament and the Council) shall consider whether the legislative proposal is compatible with the principle of subsidiarity, taking particular account of the reasons expressed and shared by the majority of national Parliaments as well as the reasoned opinion of the Commission;

(b) if, by a majority of 55 % of the members of the Council or a majority of the votes cast in the European Parliament, the legislator is of the opinion that the proposal is not compatible with the principle of subsidiarity, the legislative proposal shall not be given further consideration.

ARTICLE 8

The Court of Justice of the European Union shall have jurisdiction in actions on grounds of infringement of the principle of subsidiarity by a legislative act, brought in accordance with the rules laid down in Article 263 of the Treaty on the Functioning of the European Union by Member States, or notified by them in accordance with their legal order on behalf of their national Parliament or a chamber thereof.

In accordance with the rules laid down in the said Article, the Committee of the Regions may also bring such actions against legislative acts for the adoption of which the Treaty on the Functioning of the European Union provides that it be consulted.

ARTICLE 9

The Commission shall submit each year to the European Council, the European Parliament, the Council and national Parliaments a report on the application of Article 5 of the Treaty on European Union. This annual report shall also be forwarded to the Economic and Social Committee and the Committee of the Regions.

NOTE: The several Programmes for creating an area of freedom, security, and justice were encountered in Chapter 15. As part of the drive against money laundering the Council in 2006 adopted a 'third pillar' Framework Decision, 2006/783 on the application of the principle of mutual recognition to confiscation orders ([2006] OJ L328/59). In Recital [9] it was stated that co-operation between Member States presupposes confidence that decisions to be recognized and executed 'will always be taken in compliance with the principles of legality, subsidiarity and proportionality'. But nowhere else in the 20-page text is subsidiarity mentioned. What does this suggest about the possibilities for making the role of subsidiarity in the EU's institutional culture more precise and consistent?

■ QUESTION

The idea of subsidiarity, if not the word, has been familiar for decades in the EU. Consider, for example, how you might use subsidiarity to analyse:

(a) The division of function between national and EU courts under the Article 267 preliminary reference procedure (Chapter 7).

(b) The distinction between the Regulation and the Directive under Article 288; p. 27).

(c) The scope of Article 34, as illuminated by the rulings of the Court of Justice in *Torfaen* v *B & Q plc* (Case 145/88); *Stoke-on-Trent and Norwich City Councils* v *B & Q* (Case C-169/91); and *Keck and Mithouard* (Joined Cases C-267 and C-268/91) (Chapter 12).

(d) The scope of Article 101 (which is explicitly considered from the perspective of subsidiarity in Case T-168/01 *Glaxo Smith Kline* [2006] ECR II-2969, paras 201–202).

(e) The enforcement of competition law envisaged by Regulation 1/2003 (p. 506).

Do you agree with the Commission's view that 'subsidiarity cannot be reduced to a set of procedural rules; it is primarily a state of mind' (COM (93) 545)? What, then, of the Protocol? You might also consider the Commission's tart comment in its first annual report on the subsidiarity principle that 'one cannot help observing that principle and practice are often far apart with Member States meeting within the Council often adopting positions on individual cases at variance with their respect in principle for Article 3b [now 5 TEU]' (COM (94) 533). The Commission is regularly quick to insist that, in line with Article 1 of the Protocol, the application of the subsidiarity principle is not its responsibility alone but also that of the other political institutions, in particular the Council and the Parliament (e.g., 'Better Lawmaking 2005' (COM (2006) 289), pp. 6–9, 'Better Lawmaking 2009' (COM (2010) 547, p. 3).

NOTE: The Court's approach to the subsidiarity principle as a specifically legal rule took some time to become clear. Article 8 of the Protocol envisages judicial review of EU acts for compliance with the subsidiarity principle, but this is already obvious and, in any event, tells us nothing about the *basis* of such review. The next far-sighted extract explains how the changing patterns of governance in the EU made it inevitable that the Court would eventually find itself invited to explore the nature of subsidiarity in the context of a legal challenge to adopted legislation.

W. Robinson, 'The Court of Justice after Maastricht' in D. O'Keeffe and P. Twomey (eds), *Legal Issues of the Maastricht Treaty*
(Chichester: Chancery Law Publishing, 1994), 187–9

The principle of subsidiarity has been described as a 'national precedence',[43] a 'best level' test,[44] 'an anti-competitive arrangement among executive branches',[45] 'an elementary principle of good government'[46] and 'a principle of social organisation developed to be used in combination with other principles of collective and individual action'[47]. Any definition of 'subsidiarity' will therefore include an ideological underpinning. [. . .]

Whilst it is clear therefore that all parties accept the binding nature of Article 3b EC [now Article 5 TEU], their purposes for such acceptance are markedly different. The political motivations range the *Länder's* fear of the extension of Community responsibility into areas within their exclusive competence under the *Grundgesetz*, through the UK's desire to preserve 'sovereignty' at a national level to the introduction of subsidiarity as an acceptance of federalism. Article 3b has enabled national politicians to claim that the Treaty of European Union, and Community law, will serve their requirements. Clearly, the uniformity of interpretation which will arise from the Court of Justice's jurisprudence on the principle will not enable the expectations of all the Member States to be met. Professor Curtin's statement that 'subsidiarity is presented in terms capable of papering over any number of cracks and crevices in the structure of the Maastricht Treaty'[48] reflects the difference between the political and legal implications of the principle.

The Treaty on European Union has increased the use of qualified majority voting in the Council. This follows the precedent set by the Single European Act. The combination of varying political perceptions of the principle of subsidiarity and the increase in qualified majority voting is likely to result in litigation. Member States who argued, unsuccessfully, within the Council that the Community should not act on a particular matter may challenge the adopted legislation before the Court on the principle of subsidiarity. The Court of Justice will, seemingly inevitably, be drawn into political dispute resolution which has arisen within one institution, rather than between institutions. This may be regarded as the first significant difference from the Court's existing constitutional jurisprudence.

Secondly, the Court of Justice has determined the majority of its constitutional cases on the interpretation of the aim and content of the particular legislative act, as seen above, the text and spirit of the Treaties and the general principles of law. Challenges by Member States to enacted legislation on the principle of subsidiarity will not, however, seek to annul legislation on the determination of the aim and content of the measure itself, but upon the question whether those aims should be pursued at a Community level at all. Put another way, should those aims exist at all at the Community level within Community legislation?

The way a particular act is phrased will suggest that the Community is indeed both competent in that area and should enact legislation. The adopted act must state the reasons for its adoption. These will have been drafted in order to give effect to the wishes of the majority. The reasons for Community action will therefore be stated on the face of the act. The arguments of the dissenting voices will not appear. The content and aim of the act is therefore unlikely to assist the Court. The Court would consider the Treaty provisions upon which basis the act was adopted. Unless the act is *ultra vires*, the provision will provide jurisdiction for the Community to act, albeit concurrently with Member States. This is unlikely to provide guidance for the level of action. Similarly, the spirit of the Treaty has been interpreted, to date, as integrating action at a Community level in the pursuit of an 'ever closer union among the peoples of Europe'. The existing *acquis communautaire* and the drafting of the disputed act are unlikely to assist the Court. The applicants would, however, argue that the Community should not have acted at all. The general principle of subsidiarity will require the Court to 'step back' from the particular act and the existing *acquis communautaire* to consider the level at which the measure should have been adopted. This is an almost unprecedented task, which requires the Court to place constraints upon its methods of interpretation and to consider arguments based on a general principle against an adopted act and the spirit of the Treaty itself.

NOTE: William Robinson accurately predicts the emergence of ***subsidiarity*** in challenges to the validity of adopted legislation before the Court. The lack of clarity in the early litigation was

43 Major, speech to the Conservative Group for Europe, 22 April 1993.

44 Brittan, 'Institutional Developments of the European Community' (1992) Public Law, 567–579 at 574.

45 Allott, 'Europe after Maastricht: Interim Report', First Report from the foreign Affairs Committee, HC 205, 1992–93, Ev at 51.

46 MacKenzie-Stuart, 'Assessment of the view expressed and introduction to a panel discussion' in *Subsidiarity: the Challenge of Change* (1991), European Institute of Public Administration at 38.

47 Wilke and Wallace, *Subsidiarity: Approaches to Power-Sharing in the European Community* (1990) at 11.

48 Curtin, *The Irish Times*, 16 October 1992 at 16.

instructive. In Case C-84/94 *UK* v *Council* [1996] ECR I-5755, the almost entirely unsuccessful challenge to the 'Working Time' Directive mentioned at p. 33, the Court felt able to reject the argument based on subsidiarity 'at the outset'. Advocate-General Leger was more blunt: the UK 'created some confusion by regularly invoking the principle of subsidiarity in the course of the proceedings – without, however, relying on it as a ground of annulment – and seemingly equating it with the principle of proportionality'. The applicant was also unsuccessful in Case C-223/94 *Germany* v *Parliament and Council* [1997] ECR I-2304.

But – by no means for the first time in this book! – the search for insight takes us to the Court's rulings in Case C-376/98 *Germany* v *European Parliament and Council of the European Union* [2000] ECR I-8419 (*'Tobacco Advertising'*, at p. 33) and in Case C-491/01 *R* v *Secretary of State, ex parte BAT and Imperial Tobacco* [2002] ECR I-11453, p. 38.

Subsidiarity was not mentioned by the Court in its judgment in the *'Tobacco Advertising'* case, other than simply to acknowledge that Germany had invoked its violation as one of the bases for its application for annulment. There is a perfectly logical explanation for the Court's silence. Once the challenged Directive had been shown to lie beyond the EU's legislative competence, it fell to be annulled and its conformity with the subsidiarity principle was irrelevant. In this sense, the first hurdle that a disputed EU act must cross is that presented by the first sentence of Article 5(1) TEU, p. 560, the principle of conferral. Only if that hurdle is crossed does the second sentence of Article 5(1) TEU, the subsidiarity and proportionality principles, come into play as a basis for judicial review.

The *'Tobacco Advertising'* judgment is therefore hugely significant for its reminder that the relationship between Member State and Union competences is in the first place fixed by the principle of conferral. Subsidiarity is then relevant – and sensitive – in determining whether a competence once established should be exercised in a particular sector. After the annulment of Directive 98/43 in *'Tobacco Advertising'* (Case C-376/98) on the ground that it fell outside the EU's competence, an outstanding question was how the subsidiarity principle would be used to check the validity of a measure of harmonization that did fall within the scope of competence conferred by the Treaty. This in turn demanded an answer to the question whether Article 95 EC, now Article 114 TFEU, falls within an area of exclusive competence enjoyed by the Community, now Union – if so, then according to the explicit terms of Article 5(3) TEU (p. 560), subsidiarity has no role to play. In *'Tobacco Advertising'* Advocate-General Fennelly expressed the opinion that Article 95 EC, now Article 114 TFEU, is a matter of exclusive competence and that accordingly review of an adopted act against the requirements of the subsidiarity principle was excluded. The Court did not address the issue in that case, but in the next case it did: and it took the opposite view from Mr Fennelly.

R v *Secretary of State, ex parte BAT and Imperial Tobacco* (Case C-491/01)

[2002] ECR I-11453, Court of Justice of the European Communities

[177] The principle of subsidiarity is set out in the second paragraph of Article 5 EC [now Article 5 TEU], according to which, in areas which do not fall within its exclusive competence, the Community is to take action only if and in so far as the objectives of the proposed action cannot be sufficiently achieved by the Member States and can therefore, by reason of the scale or effects of the proposed action, be better achieved at Community level.

[178] Article 3 of the protocol on the application of the principles of subsidiarity and proportionality, annexed to the Treaty establishing the European Community, states that the principle of subsidiarity does not call into question the powers conferred on the Community by the Treaty as interpreted by the court.

[179] It is to be noted, as a preliminary, that the principle of subsidiarity applies where the Community legislature makes use of Article 95 EC, inasmuch as that provision does not give it exclusive competence to regulate

economic activity on the internal market, but only a certain competence for the purpose of improving the conditions for its establishment and functioning, by eliminating barriers to the free movement of goods and the freedom to provide services or by removing distortions of competition (see, to that effect, the tobacco advertising judgment, paragraphs 83 and 95).

[180] As regards the question whether the Directive was adopted in keeping with the principle of subsidiarity, it must first be considered whether the objective of the proposed action could be better achieved at Community level.

[181] As the Court has stated in paragraph 124 above, the Directive's objective is to eliminate the barriers raised by the differences which still exist between the Member States' laws, regulations and administrative provisions on the manufacture, presentation and sale of tobacco products, while ensuring a high level of health protection, in accordance with Article 95(3) EC.

[182] Such an objective cannot be sufficiently achieved by the Member States individually and calls for action at Community level, as demonstrated by the multifarious development of national laws in this case (see paragraph 61 above).

[183] It follows that, in the case of the Directive, the objective of the proposed action could be better achieved at Community level.

[184] Second, the intensity of the action undertaken by the Community in this instance was also in keeping with the requirements of the principle of subsidiarity in that, as paragraphs 122 to 141 above make clear, it did not go beyond what was necessary to achieve the objective pursued.

[185] It follows from the foregoing conclusions concerning Question 1(f) that the Directive is not invalid by reason of infringement of the principle of subsidiarity.

NOTE: See in similarly cautious vein Case C-103/01 *Commission* v *Germany* [2003] ECR I-5369 para 47; Cases C-154/04 & C-155/04 *Alliance for Natural Health* [2005] ECR I-6451 paras 99–108; Case C-58/08 *Vodafone*, O2 [2010] ECR I-4999, paras 72–80; and (not concerning Art 114) Case C-539/09 *Commission* v *Germany* judgment of 15 November 2011, para 84.

■ QUESTION

Can you envisage a measure of harmonization that would be validly adopted pursuant to Article 114 TFEU yet ruled invalid for violation of the subsidiarity principle in Article 5 TEU? Can you imagine *any* common rule adopted at EU level that would violate the principle of subsidiarity as interpreted by the Court?

A *better division and definition of competence in the European Union* was one of the agenda items identified for the Convention on the Future of Europe by the Laeken Declaration (p. 14). As both Wilke and Wallace (p. 561) and Robinson (p. 566) mention, the German Länder have been especially agitated by the anxiety that an expansion in EU law- and policy-making tends to undermine their historically protected sphere of influence within Germany's internal federal allocation of powers.

The fresh procedures introduced by the Lisbon Treaty involve the recasting of the provisions on EU competence in more intelligible form in Article 5 TEU and Articles 2–6 TFEU (Chapter 2, p. 30) plus monitoring by national Parliaments, as detailed in the Protocol, extracted at p. 563. The scrutiny performed by national Parliaments is not designed to replace judicial review of EU measures for compliance with the subsidiarity principle. It is quite separate. The new procedures reveal the concern to strengthen the *political* debate about whether the EU should act. The 'reasoned opinion' issued by a national Parliament (which may also be issued in relation to use of Article 352 TFEU: Chapter 2, p. 32) offers the opportunity for dialogue about the worth of EU legislative action. And, as Article 7 of the Protocol details, formal consequences follow intervention by a sufficiently large coalition of national Parliaments. They do not have the formal power to require that a legislative proposal be abandoned but presumably the louder the collective protesting voice, the harder it will be politically to ignore.

The involvement of national Parliaments in this way had been proposed by the Convention on the Future of Europe (p. 18), albeit that participants varied in the strength of their criticism (see S. Weatherill, 'Competence Creep and Competence Control' (2005) 24 YEL 1). It formed part of the now extinct Treaty establishing a Constitution (p. 18). The finally adopted Procotol is functionally similar to what had been planned, though there are alterations of detail (e.g., the eight-week period mentioned in Article 6 of the Protocol was previously six weeks). The Commission had already been actively practising such co-operation with national Parliaments even in advance of the entry into force of the Lisbon Treaty and it reported that by the end of 2007 it had received 168 opinions from national Parliaments, although not all were concerned with matters of subsidiarity (COM (2008) 237, 6 May 2008). A comparable picture is visible 'post-Lisbon'. The Commission's annual reports on subsidiarity and proportionality are available at http://ec.europa.eu/smart-regulation/better_regulation/reports_en.htm. There were 64 reasoned opinions from National Parliaments in 2011, relating to 28 different proposals, but the threshold for yellow and orange cards was not approached. One of the target proposals, receiving five reasoned opinions, was that for a Regulation on a Common European Sales Law, met in Chapter 17 (p. 551). The annual report concedes a visible overlap between political dialogue and subsidiarity review 'proper'. In 2012 there were 70 reasoned opinions, on 23 different proposals, and again a stretching in the scope of subsidiarity review practised by national Parliaments is noted. The first 'yellow card' was issued in 2012. This was in connection with the so-called 'Monti II' legislative proposal of the Commission aimed at clarifying the consequences of the Court's rulings on labour law and free movement of companies in Case C-438/05 *Viking Line* and Case C-341/05 *Laval*, met in Chapter 14. The Commission withdrew this proposal, but it did not admit to violation of the subsidiarity principle and instead simply cited absence of adequate political support (see F. Fabbrini and K. Granat, 'Yellow Card but no Foul: the role of the national parliaments under the subsidiarity protocol and the Commission proposal for an EU regulation on the right to strike' (2013) 50 CMLRev 115). The second yellow card, issued in the autumn of 2013, concerned the Proposal for a Council Regulation on the establishment of the European Public Prosecutor's Office. The Commission has not abandoned this proposal, but it has not been adopted.. In 2013 there were 88 reasoned opinions, on 36 different proposals, while in 2014 the numbers dropped (21 reasoned opinions on 15 different proposals), though the Commission explains this with reference to the decrease in the number of legislative proposals it has made, not to any diminution in national Parliaments' interest (COM (2015) 315, paras. 2.2, 4). National Parliaments' opinions may be tracked via IPEX, http://www.ipex.eu/IPEXL-WEB/search.do, and on the basis of these first two 'yellow cards' it appears they are able to convert the modest role granted by the Lisbon Treaty reforms into something close in practice to a political veto. The new procedures' importance may also be gauged by the reliance placed on them by the *Bundesverfassungsgericht*, the German Constitutional Court, in concluding that ratification of the Lisbon Treaty was compatible with the German constitution – see *Lisbon* p. 596.

■ QUESTION

In issuing the 'reasoned opinion' envisaged by the Protocol, should national Parliaments be confined to the approach to the subsidiarity principle employed by the Court in Case C-491/01 *ex parte BAT* (p. 567)? How effective is the procedure likely to be in increasing the attention paid to the demands of the subsidiarity principle in EU lawmaking? What more might be done?

FURTHER READING ON THE PRINCIPLE OF SUBSIDIARITY AND ITS MONITORING

Bertrand, B., 'Un principe politique saisi par le droit. La justiciabilité du principe de subsidiarité en droit de l'Union européenne' (2012) 48 RTDE 329.

Breyer, S., 'Does Federalism Make a Difference?' [1999] *Public Law* 651.

Craig, P., 'Subsidiarity: A Political and Legal Analysis' (2012) 50 JCMS 72.

Cygan, A., 'The Parliamentarisation of EU Decision-Making? The Impact of the Treaty of Lisbon on National Parliaments' (2011) 36 EL Rev 480.

Davies, G., 'Subsidiarity: the Wrong Idea, in the Wrong Place, at the Wrong Time' (2006) 43 CML Rev 63.

Emerson, M., 'Proportionality Needed in the Subsidiarity Debate in the EU – Appraisal of the British and Dutch Initiatives' CEPS Essay 11, April 2014, https://www.ceps.eu/book-series/ceps-essays.

Jančić, D., 'The Game of Cards: National Parliaments in the EU and the Future of the Early Warning Mechanism and the Political Dialogue' (2015) 52 CMLRev 939.

Kiiver, P., 'The Early-Warning System for the Principle of Subsidiarity: the National Parliament as a *Conseil d'Etat* for Europe' (2011) 36 EL Rev 98.

■ QUESTION

'The federalist structure of the United States Constitution was designed in part to gain the States' acceptance of a stronger central government by assuring meaningful residual state sovereignty', S. Day O'Connor, 'Altered States: Federalism and Devolution at the Real Turn of the Millennium' (2001) 60 CLJ 493, 507. To what extent is a comparable bargain being struck today in the European Union? How reliable are the instruments for weighing the claims of centralization against local autonomy?

Comparisons between the USA and Europe must pay heed to the different historical and political context, but, if treated with due caution, such investigation is potentially fascinating; see K. Nicolaidis and R. Howse, *The Federal Vision: Legitimacy and Levels of Governance in the United States and the European Union* (Oxford: OUP, 2001); D. Halberstam, 'Of Power and Responsibility: The Political Morality of Federal Systems' (2004) 90 Virginia Law Rev 731; E. Fahey and D. Curtin (eds), *A Transatlantic Community of Law* (Cambridge: CUP, 2015). It is also worth noting that not only in the EU but also in the US disputes about the validity of centralizing legislation spill over into the judicial arena: 'We enforce the outer limits of Congress' Commerce Clause authority not for their own sake, but to protect historic spheres of state sovereignty from excessive federal encroachment and thereby to maintain the distribution of power fundamental to our federalist system of government', O'Connor, J. (*dissenting* in the decision of the US Supreme Court in *Gonzalez* v *Raich* 545 U.S. (2005) (find *via* http://www.supremecourt.gov/, and compare with the case law on what was Article 95 EC, now Article 114 TFEU, with which you are familiar from Chapter 2 in particular).

SECTION 2: VARIABLE INTEGRATION AND FLEXIBILITY

The discussion so far in this chapter has taken account of the pressures caused by an expansion in EU competence. The extent to which legislative action by the EU preempts national competence has been considered. The criteria that govern the exercise of a Union competence have been discussed, under the catchphrase 'subsidiarity'. This represents an inquiry into the tension between centralized rule-making and preservation of local diversity. A further element in this volatile debate relates to the question of whether a majority decision among the Member States in favour of pursuit of a particular common policy should bind all participants, or whether dissentient States can be permitted to 'opt out' (and thereby to 'compete' against the standards chosen by the majority). This raises the prospect of the 'two (or more)-speed Europe', or patterns of 'variable' or 'differentiated' integration. As already mentioned in Chapter 9, pressures in this direction have increased as the Union enlarges. The next extract was written in 1992 at a time when the issue first came to prominence.

J. Harrop, *The Political Economy of Integration in the EC*
(2nd ed., Aldershot: Edward Elgar Publishing, 1992), pp. 262–7

B DIFFERENTIATED AND FLEXIBLE INTEGRATION

Enlargement is likely to accelerate the more pragmatic and flexible approach to integration. However, a range of basic common policies have formed the building blocks of the Community. Countries have to conform to the Treaties and to the ongoing legislation from Community institutions. The basic foundations of the EC, such as the principle of non-discrimination against its members, have to be respected and countries cannot reimpose trading barriers against other members of the Community. Unless these principles are applied, the EC cannot operate effectively and will be undermined. Nevertheless, a pursuit of excessive common standardisation and an attempt to impose uniformity for its own sake is undesirable and certainly less practicable for a Community of twelve different countries. The Community has acknowledged this, using various instruments such as gradual and phased directives, plus some derogations, and some national discretion in how measures are to be applied . . .

The Community is likely to be confined to core policies, though there is no consensus over what they should be; for example, R. Dahrendorf's list in a Europe à la carte included foreign policy, trade, monetary policy and overseas development. France approved a variable-geometry Community in the 1970's, particularly in industrial and technological policy. The *'acquis communautaire'* applies to core policies, but in other areas countries may choose whether to participate or not. Even some non-members of the EC have participated in the EUREKA project and projects of nuclear fusion, such as the Joint European Torus (JET).

The new Community of twelve cannot be optimal for all activities. It has striven hard to obtain basic agreement in key areas and indeed it is surprising in some respects that the Community has been able to make as much progress as it has, given the differences and at times the unco-operativeness of new members. A much looser pattern of integration seems inevitable in the future and the UK may look back wistfully on why it could not attain flexibility to a greater extent in the first place in sectors such as agriculture. A more variegated pattern of integration enables the more dynamic countries to press on ahead, acting as catalysts to new policy areas.. . .

NOTES

1. This extract floats the idea that there are core areas where a rule of action in common cannot be abandoned but also areas in which looser patterns of involvement may be tolerated, even encouraged. This is a fine line to tread. 'Flexibility', to which Harrop refers, is an appealing, even irresistible, word, yet what can it really mean in a *single* market and a European *Union*? The question whether the emerging structure of a two (or more)-speed Europe represents a fragmentation or an evolution in the entity's endeavours already deserves the reader's attention. 'Flexibility' as a catchphrase encompasses not only constructive but also perilous trends for the Union.
2. Social policy has provided one battleground. There are fundamentally important questions about the extent to which the EU should develop common policies designed to regulate the market in the wake of the process of integration. The administrations in the UK of Margaret Thatcher (1979–90) and John Major (1990–7) were marked by stubborn resistance to new legislative measures in the social policy field. Only in the limited areas where the Council could act by qualified majority vote was advancing the social policy agenda possible: this is the background to the legal wrangle over the 'legal base' of the 'Working Time' Directive in Case C-84/94 *UK* v *Council*, mentioned in Chapter 2 (p. 33). At Maastricht the other Member States were determined to amend the Treaty to extend the possibilities for social policy-making. The UK was implacably opposed. A novel deal was struck, widely described as the UK's 'opt-out' from deeper social policy-making, although a strict reading might have labelled it as an 'opt-in' by the other Member States. Whichever formulation is preferred, the structure envisaged the uneven development of social policy among the Member States. The Maastricht Protocol was more

symbol than reality. Little legislation was in fact adopted under its provisions. And after the Labour Government took power in May 1997, the political climate changed so that agreement at Amsterdam led to that Treaty eliminating even the possibility of a separate stream of social policy legislation applying to all Member States save the UK. Accordingly, the modestly ambitious social policy arrangements found in the Protocol were amalgamated with the existing, and in part modified, long-standing provisions on social policy found in the Treaty 'proper'. They are now found in Title X on *Social Policy*, Articles 151–161 TFEU. In this sphere, 'variable integration' is for the time being at an end.

But the symbol was vivid. The critical questions for the future were the extent to which willingness in the social policy sphere to allow a dissenting minority to opt out of common policy-making would and should become a model for resolving disagreements about the path the Union should follow. In times of geographic and functional expansion, there is a probability that consensus will be increasingly elusive. The temptation for a majority to push ahead, without waiting to persuade a reluctant minority, will be powerful. Yet, for some, such variable integration undermines the traditional foundations of the European project initiated in the 1950s.

At stake is the identification of the proper and achievable scope of EU intervention into the market. There is a fierce debate about the extent to which the EU should combine a commitment to market liberalization with a readiness to establish a common basis for the regulation of the market. As mentioned in Chapter 9 (p. 267), this is reducible (with a risk of over-simplification) to the battle between a 'competition between regulators' (which favours a basic rule of mutual market access against a background of regulatory diversity which breeds competition and releases comparative advantage) and the 'level playing field' (which prefers a greater degree of rule-making in common in order to equalize competitive conditions and deepen interdependence between the Member States). This is a choice that must be confronted by the EU's legislature, although the scope of its action is confined by the dictates of the principle of conferral set out in Article 5 TEU, which denies the EU any general regulatory competence. Moreover, choices made by the Court about the reach of free movement law have implications for the possibility of legislative solutions: the intervention into collective labour law in the name of free movement examined in Chapter 14 (p. 401) offers an especially vivid example of how the Court can use EU law to unsettle existing balances without any incursion by legislative act.

The debate is being conducted in many sectors. For example, in the social policy field, anxiety is frequently expressed that inadequate common rules will release a market for regulation in which firms will relocate to jurisdictions offering them the cheapest regime, thereby driving down social standards in Europe. From another perspective, this is precisely the sort of competition that will equip European firms with the efficiency required to succeed in global markets, thereby enhancing job creation. For discussion, see C. Barnard, *EU Employment Law* (Oxford: OUP, 4th ed., 2012). In another sector: to what extent should the liberalization of the market for financial services be accompanied by the fixing of standards that must be met before a provider may claim access to the integrated market? And should any EU standards that are set be minimum standards only? See Chapter 14; and for a comprehensive investigation, see N. Moloney, *EU Securities and Financial Markets Regulation* (Oxford: OUP, 3rd ed., 2014).

■ QUESTION

'. . . competition processes among jurisdictions . . . up until now . . . are not seen as being an integral part of the process of European integration. . . It seems rather that advocates of European integration have a hostile attitude toward the idea of competition among jurisdictions . . . The core of the problem is that simultaneous realization of mobility and decentralization logically implies the existence of competition among jurisdictions', '. . . if we want simultaneous mobility and decentralisation, then we must accept interjurisdictional competition and we must think about ways to make competition processes workable', W. Kerber, 'Interjurisdictional Competition within the European Union' (2000) 23 Fordham Intl Law Jnl S217, S221, S249. Discuss. Do we want decentralization? How much decentralization?

The significance of developments in the social policy sphere is that the Member States at Maastricht were prepared to abandon the search for an agreed common path through this policy maze. One State, the UK, was allowed to opt out; one State, the UK, was allowed to maintain regulatory diversity and compete with its partners by offering firms a lighter regulatory regime. Elsewhere, in relation to the third stage of Economic and Monetary Union, two States, Denmark and the UK, were allowed to choose whether or not to proceed, whereas all other Member States are committed according to the Treaty, even if some have not met specified economic pre-conditions for participation. Moreover, as observed in Chapter 15, the arrangements for creating an area of freedom, security, and justice in the EU are subject to special provision made to cater for British, Irish, and Danish concerns.

Such variable integration – or 'flexibility' – raises questions of the highest significance in judging the future institutional and constitutional shaping of the Union. Is it possible to permit a degree of 'flexibility' but to subject it to pre-conditions that would ensure that such arrangements were permitted only provided they did not imperil the achievement of the Union's mission? A pragmatic concern is that any attempt to maintain the 'purity' of an all-or-nothing approach to participation in activities conducted under the Union umbrella is not likely to persuade groupings of States wishing to develop co-operation mechanisms in fields unattractive to some of their partners to abandon their plans if unable to secure unanimous support. Rather it would likely provoke those States to deepen co-operation outwith the EU's relatively well-developed institutional and constitutional apparatus. In the negotiations leading up to agreement on a revised Treaty at Amsterdam in the 1990s, the anxiety to craft a workable system for variable integration, which had become regarded as a necessary element of the EU system, was driven by a desire to fashion a model that would be objectively justifiable and comprehensible as a new feature of the Union's *constitutionalized* structure. The Maastricht social policy arrangements, underpinned by nothing other than political intransigence, were treated as an *ad hoc* aberration.

The two brief extracts that follow draw attention to the key point that 'flexibility' is likely to be tolerable within the EU only provided it does not infect core areas of action in common. The section then concludes with the provisions introduced by the Treaty of Amsterdam, now in their post-Lisbon form, which were designed to provide a general framework for integration at different speeds – so-called 'enhanced cooperation', p. 577.

D. Curtin, 'The Shaping of a European Constitution and the 1996 IGC'
(1995) 50 *Aussenwirtschaft* 237, 244–9

4. TOWARDS A SYSTEMATISATION OF 'FLEXIBILITY'

In many respects the EC has always been a multi-speed phenomenon and multiple speed integration in this almost classic sense can be defined as integration whereby the policy objective is the same for all the Member States and has been agreed to by all of them: it is only the speed at which it is achieved which varies.[23] Generally such differentiation must be capable of objective justification and be temporary in nature. The reason for the

---

23 See the House of Commons Foreign Affairs Committee, *The Operation of the Single European Act: Minutes of Evidence*, 17 January 1990, Select Committee on European Legislation, House of Commons, Session 1989–1990, pp. 68–72.

introduction of this type of divergence which is mainly to be found in the application of secondary Community law is to account for internal (social or economic) difficulties of one or several Member States which are expected to be overcome during the period of exception.[24] Nevertheless the underlying legislative act (often a harmonising directive) is based on the principle of unanimous will of all the Member States including the declared intention of the excluded Member State(s) to introduce the harmonised standard at the agreed and fixed date. The ultimate aim is clearly a *uniform rule* for a fully integrated market.[25]

The transition to the third stage of EMU as regulated in the TEU is another example of multiple speed integration more or less in the classic sense, albeit regulated *via* a Treaty amendment: it does not undermine the Community legal order as such nor arguably impair the cohesion of the internal market. Rather it enables a leading group of Member States to proceed with further cooperation and integration on the basis of objectively defined criteria with the intention that the other Member States will in principle, in the ripeness of time, join this leading group in the path ahead which has been forged. The controversial point is the inevitable creation of two classes of membership without adequate provision for common action to enable weaker economies to catch up and earn their membership of the common currency regime.

In the EMU system, the possibility of a leading group is explicitly accepted by all the EU Member States in the TEU, including the UK and Denmark, although they have secured an opt-out for themselves. It can be argued however that the emergence of an EMU leading group is not only compatible with the internal market but enables additional profit to be obtained from it.[26] The quibble one can have with the opt-out's which Denmark and the UK obtained in Maastricht and Edinburgh regarding the move to the final stage of the EMU is that they provide the possibility of *permanently* 'opting out' of the provisions laid down in the Treaty on the third stage of the EMU (in the sense of an indefinite period as opposed to a merely undefined period) and that they were obtained for purely political reasons (as opposed to social and economic factors which were the only objective justification in the classic approach[27]). To this extent one can indeed claim that the opt-outs do in fact contribute to the undermining of the Community legal order.

The bottom line in a multiple (or two) speed approach such as that encapsulated in the EMU is that it probably is possible to a considerable extent to maintain the principle of the single institutional framework as enshrined in article C of the Treaty [now Preamble, TEU] on the assumption that, although temporary derogations or special arrangements might be granted, 'all those who are party to the single institutional framework share the same framework and are ready in time to conform to the same system'.[28]

However another different form of graduated integration may also be distinguished and this is one which gives rise to more serious problems. *Variable geometry* is quite different from variable speeds in the sense that the group of Member States deciding to proceed with closer integration actually agree *among themselves* their policy objectives as well as the tempo for their realisation.[29]

In this construction those left 'behind' are not at all involved and simply 'opt out' of any agreement as to the policy objectives. So it is not only the speed but also the specific policy objectives and the means of achieving these which varies for different groups of countries.

It is submitted that this (disintegrative) formula should not be applied to the so-called 'hard core' of Community law and in particular not to those policy areas which might impair the cohesion of the internal market. The same is arguably also true with regard to the organisation of the Union's external economic relations as well as solidarity within the Union.[30]

The substantive *hard core* of the Union can be tentatively defined for present purposes as the rules and obligations entailed in the establishment of the internal market including the necessary harmonisation of legislation, the five freedoms and the common competition, agriculture, transport and trade policies as well as certain aspects of the EMU which constitute a necessary addition to the internal market.[31] This definition does not

---

24 See further, Feenstra and Mortelmans, 33–34. See too, Article 35 of the European Parliaments Draft Treaty on European Union, 1984 which accepted the idea of the differentiated application of Community rules provided that such differentiation was limited in time, being 'designed to facilitate the subsequent application of all the provisions of the law to all of its addressees'. See further, Louis, 'Europese Unie en gedifferentieerde integratie', SEW 6 (1985) 410.

25 Feenstra and Mortelmans, *op. cit.* 33.

26 House of Lords Select Committee of the European Communities, *Report on a Community Social Charter*, House of Lords Paper 6 (1989–90), 5 December 1989, p. 26.

27 See, in general Ehlermann, 'How flexible is Community law? An unusual approach to the concept of "two speeds"' in (1984) *Michigan Law Review*, 136, 151.

28 Ludlow, *Beyond Maastricht*, Brussels, 1993, p. 70.

29 See, in general, Maillet and Velo (eds.), *Europe a geometrie variable. Transition vers l'integration* (Paris, 1994).

30 See, Maillet and Velo, *op. cit.*, 125.

31 See further, the interesting discussion by Verloren van Themaat. 'Epiloog, De horizon 2000', in Kapteyn, Verloren van Themaat et al., *Jnleiding tot het Recht van de Europese Gemeenschappen*, 5th ed., 1995 . . ..

necessarily exclude the right for small groups of countries to take more *far-reaching measures* in certain areas of 'supplementary policy' which essentially seek to establish *minimum* norms (for example, environmental policy, social policy, research and technological policy, etc).[32]

For the internal market and the foundations of the Community system (the substantive 'hard core' and the institutional core *acquis*), it is mandatory, at least from the perspective of the *acquis communautaire*, that the Community decision making procedure as such is followed and that all Member States participate (albeit with the possibility of different speeds, see *supra*) with regard to Community policy. Moreover, when action is envisaged in the so-called 'hard core' of the Community then the principle of institutional unity and balance as envisaged in the Treaty itself must be respected. Finally, the fundamental rule is that of the equality of the Member States, thereby prohibiting the exclusion of one or more Member States from a particular policy area. These are the three fundamental rules mandated by the *acquis communautaire* with regard to the substantive 'hard core' of the Community.[33]

R. Harmsen, 'A European Union of Variable Geometry: Problems and Perspectives'
(1994) 45 NILQ 109, 129–33

IV. THE LIMITS OF VARIABILITY

If 'variable geometry' corresponds to deep-seated political trends, it nonetheless also poses significant problems with respect to both the maintenance of system legitimacy and the practical functioning of institutions. As regards the legitimacy of the politico-legal system, extensive recourse to variable institutional structures risks undermining the minimal sense of 'community' necessary for the creation or maintenance of a cohesive political unit. At a more practical level, problems are presented by the coexistence of parallel legal orders as well as by the need to redesign common political institutions in a way which corresponds to jurisdictional variations. Straddling the line between abstract considerations of legitimacy and more practical problems of institutional design, the overall level of systemic complexity further gives cause for concern.

. . . considerations of legitimacy and practicality overlap. In part, as suggested by the preceding discussion of institutional mechanics, the limits of variability are set by the practical capacity of a legal or political system to cope with complexity. However, beyond the internal manageability of the system, attention must be paid to its external intelligibility. Simply put, institutional variability, though it may correspond to very real political necessity, also renders the politico-legal system as a whole exceptionally opaque. For the European Union, already sharply criticised for a relatively low degree of intelligibility, there is a very real danger that further moves down the path of 'variable geometry' will render still more difficult its legitimation in the eyes of often sceptical national publics.

CONCLUSION

It has clearly emerged in the preceding sections that multiple forms of both 'structural' and 'jurisdictional' variability have been accepted within the European Union and that these variable institutional structures correspond to deeply embedded political imperatives. It is equally clear, however, that such differentiated institutional structures pose significant problems, potentially even calling into question basic precepts of the entire integration project. More than most problems of institutional design, there is no readily apparent way of resolving this tension between strong demands for diversity and an equally compelling logic of uniformity. Nevertheless, a promising path forward has been sketched out by the Court of Justice, with its tentative acceptance of a notion of 'supraconstitutionality' at the supranational level.

Although essentially unknown in the common-law world, the idea of 'supraconstitutionality' has been a staple of post-war public-law theory in much of continental Western Europe.[71] As the term implies, 'supraconstitutionality' refers to the existence of principles or positive law norms which are logically prior to and therefore in some sense 'above' the written constitution. It follows that these principles or norms must be respected by every governmental and legislative act, including constitutional amendment. Most simply, one notes the prohibition on the abolition of the Republican form of government contained in both the French and the Italian Constitutions;

32 See, Dutch government policy document on enlargement, *op. cit* where it suggests the test in each case whether the differentiation of norms and policy in this way will gradually undermine the level playing field of the internal market.

33 See further, Feenstra and Mortelmans, *op. cit*.

71 The doctrinal background is discussed in Stéphane Rials. 'Supraconstitutionnalité et systématicité du droit' [1986] 31 *Archives de Philosophie du Droit* 57. A somewhat more empirical survey may be found in Arne. 'Existe-t-ildes normes supraconstitutionnelles? Contribution à l'étude des fondamentaux et de la constitutionnalité' (1993) 205 *Revue du Droit public* 459.

'Republicanism' is defined as a prior value which even the constitutional legislator must respect.[72] In a more elaborate fashion, Article 79(3) of the German Basic Law enumerates a number of 'unrevisable' provisions, placing certain basic individual rights and the federal character of the State beyond the realm of constitutional amendment. In each case, while one may question the practical effectiveness of such provisions, they unquestionably make explicit the core or constitutive values of the regime.

In the Community context, the Court of Justice broached the idea of supraconstitutionality in its first decision concerning the EEA Agreement, handed down on 14 December 1991.[73] Specifically, the Commission asked the Court to rule on whether any incompatibilities found to exist between the judicial mechanism provided for in the EEA Agreement and the EC founding treaties might be resolved by way of amendment to the Treaty of Rome. The Commission envisaged a simple amendment to Article 238, permitting the establishment of the court system agreed. The Court of Justice, in response, ruled that even Treaty amendment would 'not cure the incompatibility', as the proposed system of courts (functionally integrating the CJEC and the Court of First Instance into EEA courts for EEA purposes) conflicted 'with the very foundations of the Community.'[74] In other words, the autonomy and integrity of the Community legal system has been held by the Court of Justice to constitute a 'prior' or 'supraconstitutional' value of the Community order, which even Treaty amendment should not be allowed to violate.

Relative to the present concern with 'variable geometry', the CJEC's decision crucially underlines the need for variable or asymmetrical structures to be conceived with reference to a Community 'core'.[75] Simply put, increased institutional variability must inevitably call forward a stronger and more explicit conception of which principles, values, and policies integrally define the Community. Although the exact parameters of such a core can emerge only gradually, its constituent elements must reasonably include the basic precepts of the common market, the underlying principles of the legal order, and some sense of a common political destiny (parallelling, at the supranational level, Renan's classic definition of a nation in terms of a *vouloir vivre ensemble*).

At the same time, the limits of a Community-level reliance on the notion of supraconstitutionality must also be underlined. First, concerning the substantive definition of a Community core, it is essential that the *noyau communautaire* not be confused with the *acquis communautaire*. The core, by definition, must include only those principles which are constitutive of the Community order, not the sum total of all policies and practices which might have developed under the Community rubric. Second, at a procedural level, the part played by the Court of Justice in defining this supraconstitutional core must be carefully limited relative to the role of political actors. In this regard, it should be borne in mind that a Community supraconstitutionality lacks the inherent legitimacy of its national counterparts, as it refers only to fairly abstract concepts of 'order', rather than to basic human rights or founding principles of liberal democracy.

In sum, a logic of supraconstitutionality would appear to offer a conceptual framework within which an increasing variability of institutional structures might be reconciled with the need to preserve the basic tenets of the Union as an economic, legal, and political order. Nevertheless, whether through the adoption of such a framework or through another means, it is clear that an increasing structural and jurisdictional variability must be accompanied by a more explicit definition of the Union's invariable core. Therein lies a task, whatever their initial differences, which would seem singularly well suited to a co-operative effort on the part of lawyers and political scientists.

■ QUESTION

Do you find attractive the attempt in these two extracts to identify a 'hard core' of obligations of membership? What machinery could be used to define the content and to secure the inviolability of such a hard core? Does the Court's Opinion 2/13 on accession to the ECHR, in which it defended the 'autonomy' of EU law (Chapter 2, p. 65), illuminate this debate?

NOTE: One of the more innovative amendments made by the Treaty of Amsterdam with effect from 1999 was the introduction of new provisions designed to permit 'enhanced' or 'closer' co-operation, through which some, but not all, Member States may choose to deepen their mutual

---

72 Article 89 of the Constitution of the French Fifth Republic: Article 139 of the present Italian Constitution.

73 *Re The Draft Treaty on a European Economic Area*. Opinion 1/91. [1992] 1 CMLR 245.

74 Opinion 1/91 at 275.

75 It may be argued that the European Convention on Human Rights already has such a core, in so far as contracting States may not derogate, even in time of emergency, from specified central Articles (*viz* 2, 3, 4/1, and 7). See Arné, *op cit*, p. 466.

interdependence. These provisions are by no means exhaustive of the models of 'flexibility' available to the Member States, but they represent an illuminating attempt to chart a course in the Treaty for forms of action that may be thought to carry a disturbing momentum towards fragmentation of the unity of the legal order. Rigorous criteria must be satisfied before 'enhanced cooperation' is permitted. The governing provisions are now contained in Title IV TEU, *Provisions on Enhanced Co-Operation*, which is Article 20 TEU, and in Title III of Part Six TFEU, *Enhanced Co-Operation*, which contains Articles 326–334 TFEU.

ARTICLE 20 TEU

1. Member States which wish to establish enhanced cooperation between themselves within the framework of the Union's non-exclusive competences may make use of its institutions and exercise those competences by applying the relevant provisions of the Treaties, subject to the limits and in accordance with the detailed arrangements laid down in this Article and in Articles 326 to 334 of the Treaty on the Functioning of the European Union.

Enhanced cooperation shall aim to further the objectives of the Union, protect its interests and reinforce its integration process. Such cooperation shall be open at any time to all Member States, in accordance with Article 328 of the Treaty on the Functioning of the European Union.

2. The decision authorising enhanced cooperation shall be adopted by the Council as a last resort, when it has established that the objectives of such cooperation cannot be attained within a reasonable period by the Union as a whole, and provided that at least nine Member States participate in it. The Council shall act in accordance with the procedure laid down in Article 329 of the Treaty on the Functioning of the European Union.

3. All members of the Council may participate in its deliberations, but only members of the Council representing the Member States participating in enhanced cooperation shall take part in the vote. The voting rules are set out in Article 330 of the Treaty on the Functioning of the European Union.

4. Acts adopted in the framework of enhanced cooperation shall bind only participating Member States. They shall not be regarded as part of the *acquis* which has to be accepted by candidate States for accession to the Union.

Articles 326–334 TFEU

ARTICLE 326

Any enhanced cooperation shall comply with the Treaties and Union law. Such cooperation shall not undermine the internal market or economic, social and territorial cohesion. It shall not constitute a barrier to or discrimination in trade between Member States, nor shall it distort competition between them.

ARTICLE 327

Any enhanced cooperation shall respect the competences, rights and obligations of those Member States which do not participate in it. Those Member States shall not impede its implementation by the participating Member States.

ARTICLE 328

1. When enhanced cooperation is being established, it shall be open to all Member States, subject to compliance with any conditions of participation laid down by the authorising decision. It shall also be open to them at any other time, subject to compliance with the acts already adopted within that framework, in addition to those conditions.

The Commission and the Member States participating in enhanced cooperation shall ensure that they promote participation by as many Member States as possible.

2. The Commission and, where appropriate, the High Representative of the Union for Foreign Affairs and Security Policy shall keep the European Parliament and the Council regularly informed regarding developments in enhanced cooperation.

ARTICLE 329

1. Member States which wish to establish enhanced cooperation between themselves in one of the areas covered by the Treaties, with the exception of fields of exclusive competence and the common foreign and security policy, shall address a request to the Commission, specifying the scope and objectives of the enhanced cooperation proposed. The Commission may submit a proposal to the Council to that effect. In the event of the Commission not submitting a proposal, it shall inform the Member States concerned of the reasons for not doing so.

Authorisation to proceed with the enhanced cooperation referred to in the first subparagraph shall be granted by the Council, on a proposal from the Commission and after obtaining the consent of the European Parliament.

2. The request of the Member States which wish to establish enhanced cooperation between themselves within the framework of the common foreign and security policy shall be addressed to the Council. It shall be forwarded to the High Representative of the Union for Foreign Affairs and Security Policy, who shall give an opinion on whether the enhanced cooperation proposed is consistent with the Union's common foreign and security policy, and to the Commission, which shall give its opinion in particular on whether the enhanced cooperation proposed is consistent with other Union policies. It shall also be forwarded to the European Parliament for information. Authorisation to proceed with enhanced cooperation shall be granted by a decision of the Council acting unanimously.

ARTICLE 330

All members of the Council may participate in its deliberations, but only members of the Council representing the Member States participating in enhanced cooperation shall take part in the vote. Unanimity shall be constituted by the votes of the representatives of the participating Member States only. A qualified majority shall be defined in accordance with Article 238(3).

ARTICLE 331

1. Any Member State which wishes to participate in enhanced cooperation in progress in one of the areas referred to in Article 329(1) shall notify its intention to the Council and the Commission.

The Commission shall, within four months of the date of receipt of the notification, confirm the participation of the Member State concerned. It shall note where necessary that the conditions of participation have been fulfilled and shall adopt any transitional measures necessary with regard to the application of the acts already adopted within the framework of enhanced cooperation.

However, if the Commission considers that the conditions of participation have not been fulfilled, it shall indicate the arrangements to be adopted to fulfil those conditions and shall set a deadline for re-examining the request. On the expiry of that deadline, it shall re-examine the request, in accordance with the procedure set out in the second subparagraph. If the Commission considers that the conditions of participation have still not been met, the Member State concerned may refer the matter to the Council, which shall decide on the request. The Council shall act in accordance with Article 330. It may also adopt the transitional measures referred to in the second subparagraph on a proposal from the Commission.

2. Any Member State which wishes to participate in enhanced cooperation in progress in the framework of the common foreign and security policy shall notify its intention to the Council, the High Representative of the Union for Foreign Affairs and Security Policy and the Commission. The Council shall confirm the participation of the Member State concerned, after consulting the High Representative of the Union for Foreign Affairs and Security Policy and after noting, where necessary, that the conditions of participation have been fulfilled. The Council, on a proposal from the High Representative, may also adopt any transitional measures necessary with regard to the application of the acts already adopted within the framework of enhanced cooperation. However, if the Council considers that the conditions of participation have not been fulfilled, it shall indicate the arrangements to be adopted to fulfil those conditions and shall set a deadline for re-examining the request for participation.

For the purposes of this paragraph, the Council shall act unanimously and in accordance with Article 330.

ARTICLE 332

Expenditure resulting from implementation of enhanced cooperation, other than administrative costs entailed for the institutions, shall be borne by the participating Member States, unless all members of the Council, acting unanimously after consulting the European Parliament, decide otherwise.

ARTICLE 333

1. Where a provision of the Treaties which may be applied in the context of enhanced cooperation stipulates that the Council shall act unanimously, the Council, acting unanimously in accordance with the arrangements laid down in Article 330, may adopt a decision stipulating that it will act by a qualified majority.

2. Where a provision of the Treaties which may be applied in the context of enhanced cooperation stipulates that the Council shall adopt acts under a special legislative procedure, the Council, acting unanimously in accordance with the arrangements laid down in Article 330, may adopt a decision stipulating that it will act under the ordinary legislative procedure. The Council shall act after consulting the European Parliament.

3. Paragraphs 1 and 2 shall not apply to decisions having military or defence implications.

ARTICLE 334

The Council and the Commission shall ensure the consistency of activities undertaken in the context of enhanced cooperation and the consistency of such activities with the policies of the Union, and shall cooperate to that end.

NOTES

1. Special rules apply to enhanced co-operation in judicial co-operation in criminal matters and in police co-operation, pursuant to Chapters 4 and 5 of Title V of the TFEU. As seen in Chapter 15, these provisions, governing the area of freedom, security, and justice, are distinct from the orthodoxy of Union law.
2. Intriguing though the Treaty provisions on enhanced co-operation are as a window on the tension between allowing acceleration beyond the speed of the slowest member and the damage done by fragmentation, they remain as yet a source of only marginal interest in practice. It was as late as 2010 before they were formally invoked for the first time. This was Decision 2010/405 (OJ 2010 L189/2) which, with delicious appropriateness, authorized enhanced co-operation in the law applicable to divorce; and then in 2011 Decision 2011/167 (OJ 2011 L76/53) authorized enhanced co-operation in the creation of unitary patent protection. Both Decisions are striking for how brief is the explanation of how and why the Treaty pre-conditions are met.

The use of the enhanced co-operation procedures to authorize rules on unitary patent protection was challenged before the Court by non-participating Member States. The application failed, and the Court's attitude is of crucial significance in mapping the potential for and likelihood of future resort to enhanced co-operation.

***Spain and Italy* v *Council* (Joined Cases C-274/11 and C-295/11)**

Judgment of 16 April 2013, Court of Justice of the European Union

The Court readily found the matter (intellectual property rights within Article 118 TFEU) to be a shared competence, and so open in principle to enhanced co-operation (Article 20(1) TEU, Article 329(1) TFEU). It readily approved the Council's view that resort to enhanced co-operation was a last resort (Article 20(2) TEU). It then turned to the substantive controls associated with protection of the internal market (Article 326 TFEU).

[66] It is apparent from the first paragraph of Article 326 TFEU that the exercise, within the ambit of enhanced cooperation, of any competence conferred on the Union must comply with, among other provisions of the Treaties, that which confers that competence. The enhanced cooperation to which these actions relate must, therefore, be consistent with Article 118 TFEU.

[67] Having regard to this duty to ensure accordance with Article 118 TFEU, the enhanced cooperation in question must establish measures for the creation of European intellectual property rights to provide uniform protection of intellectual property rights.

[68] With regard, on the other hand, to the expressions 'throughout the Union' and 'Union-wide' used in Article 118 TFEU, it must be held that it is inherent in the fact that the competence conferred by that article is, in this instance, exercised within the ambit of enhanced cooperation that the European intellectual property

right so created, the uniform protection given by it and the arrangements attaching to it will be in force, not in the Union in its entirety, but only in the territory of the participating Member States. Far from amounting to infringement of Article 118 TFEU, that consequence necessarily follows from Article 20(4) TEU, which states: 'Acts adopted in the framework of enhanced cooperation shall bind only participating Member States.'

[69] Consequently, the arguments alleging infringement of Article 118 TFEU are unfounded.

The alleged infringement of the second paragraph of Article 326 TFEU

– Arguments of the parties

[70] The Kingdom of Spain and the Italian Republic recall the wording of the second paragraph of Article 326 TFEU, according to which enhanced cooperation 'shall not undermine the internal market or economic, social and territorial cohesion [and] shall not constitute a barrier to or discrimination in trade between Member States, nor shall it distort competition between them.'

[71] The enhanced cooperation in question would, in their opinion, jeopardise all those principles and objectives. Creating uniform protection for innovation in one part only of the Union would encourage activities relating to innovatory products to be drawn to that part of the Union, to the detriment of the non-participating Member States.

[72] In addition, they claim that the enhanced cooperation in question would be the source of distortion of competition and of discrimination between undertakings by reason of the fact that trade in innovatory products will be, according to the language arrangements provided for in recital 7 of the preamble to the contested decision, made easier for undertakings working in English, French or German. The enhanced cooperation contemplated would, moreover, reduce the mobility of researchers from Member States not taking part in this cooperation or from Member States whose official language is not English, French or German, for the language arrangements provided for by the decision will make access to information on the scope of the patents difficult for those researchers.

[73] Economic, social and territorial cohesion in the Union too would be damaged, they argue, in that the enhanced cooperation would prevent the coherent development of industrial policy and increase the differences between Member States from the technological point of view.

[74] The Council and the parties intervening in its support take the view that this plea in law is based on premises in the realm of speculation. Furthermore, the origin of the fragmentation of the market is to be found, not in the contested decision, but in the present situation, in which the protection offered by European patents is national. What is more, inasmuch as the applicants base their arguments on the language arrangements contemplated, their actions are inadmissible, the definitive features of those language arrangements not being fixed by the contested decision.

– Findings of the Court

[75] For the same reason as that set out in paragraph 68, it cannot validly be maintained that, by having it in view to create a unitary patent applicable in the participating Member States and not in the Union, the contested decision damages the internal market or the economic, social and territorial cohesion of the Union.

[76] In so far as, in order to demonstrate such damage to the internal market and discrimination and distortion of competition as well, the applicants also make reference to the language arrangements considered in recital 7 in the preamble to the contested decision, it must be declared that the compatibility of those arrangements with Union law may not be examined in these actions.

[77] As is stated in recital 7, the language arrangements there described do no more than correspond to a proposal by the Commission with the addition of certain elements of compromise proposed by the Member State presiding over the Council of the Union at the time the requests for enhanced cooperation were made. The language arrangements as set out in that recital were, therefore, only at a preparatory stage when the contested decision was adopted and do not form a component part of the latter.

[78] It follows that the arguments alleging infringement of Article 326 TFEU are in part unfounded and in part inadmissible.

NOTE: The Court assesses uniformity with reference to what is occurring within the bloc of participating States only (paras 68, 75). That, it finds, is the very nature of enhanced co-operation. The Court's approach in effect largely insulates the political decision to pursue enhanced co-operation from allegations that it violates the Treaty pre-conditions pertaining to the integrity of the internal market. A similar pattern is plain in the subsequent equally unsuccessful challenge to Regulation 1257/2012, which implemented the authorization to pursue enhanced co-operation (Case C-146/13 *Spain v Council and Parliament* judgment of 5 May 2015).

■ QUESTION

Will this endorsement of enhanced co-operation in fact lead to its diminished use because of its inducement to an objecting minority of Member States to seek legislative compromise among all 28 Member States rather than pursue fruitless constitutional challenges to splinter groups of enhanced co-operators?

NOTE: There is value in comparing the Court's cautious attitude to review of the design of enhanced co-operation to its artfully reticent attitude to subsidiarity review (C-491/01, p. 567). Its judgment in *Pringle* (Case C-370/12 judgment of 27 November 2012) is also revealing. In a sense *Pringle* comes from the opposite direction – it involves review of arrangements struck by a group of Member States but not according to the Treaty's blueprint for enhanced co-operation but rather pursuant to a free-standing international Treaty, the European Stability Mechanism (ESM) Treaty. This is permissible only provided it does not compromise existing obligations under EU law which one might have thought a high hurdle given the density of existing EU competences on monetary policy. But, as in the matter of unitary patent protection, an apparently high hurdle was found to be crossed with some ease. The theme – judicial disinclination to cut across majoritarian political preferences.

■ QUESTIONS

1. Would a two-speed model of social policy of the type invented at Maastricht (and abandoned at Amsterdam, p. 572) comply with the Treaty provisions controlling the establishment of a framework for enhanced co-operation between some, but not all, Member States? Would the pattern for securing an Area of Freedom, Security, and Justice, which, as explained in Chapter 14, includes opt-outs for some Member States comply?
2. Review the provisions on enhanced co-operation in the light of the two extracts, pp. 573–6. Are the anxieties and suggestions expounded by Curtin and Harmsen reflected in these provisions?

FURTHER READING

Avbelj, M., 'Revisiting Flexible Integration in Times of Post-Enlargement and the Lustration of EU Constitutionalism' (2008) 4 Croatian YEL&P 131.

Bieber, R., 'On the Mutual Completion of Overlapping Legal Systems: the Case of the European Communities and the National Legal Orders' (1988) 13 EL Rev 147.

de Búrca, G. and Scott, J. (eds), *Constitutional Change in the EU: From Uniformity to Flexibility?* (Oxford: Hart Publishing, 2000).

Ehlermann, C.D., 'How Flexible is Community Law? An Unusual Approach to the Concept of "Two Speeds" ' (1984) 82 Michigan Law Rev 1274.

Fabbrini, F., 'Enhanced Co-Operation under Scrutiny: Revisiting the Law and Practice of Multi-Speed Integration in Light of the First Involvement of the EU Judiciary' (2013) 40 LIEI 197.

Kuipers, J.-J., 'The Law Applicable to Divorce as Test Ground for Enhanced Co-Operation' (2012) 18 ELJ 201.

Majone, G., 'Unity in Diversity: European Integration and the Enlargement Process' (2008) 33 EL Rev 457.

Schimmelfennig, F. and Winzen, T., 'Instrumental and Constitutional Differentiation in the European Union' (2014) 52 JCMS 354.

Thym, D., 'The Political Character of Supranational Differentiation' (2006) 31 EL Rev 781.

SECTION 3: INSTRUMENTS OF GOVERNANCE

How should the Union go about achieving its tasks? Can the relationship between central and local legal and political authority be better managed by using 'softer' instruments of law and policy-making that are more conducive to respect for local preferences and pursuit of effective regulatory reform than binding instruments such as Regulations and Directives envisaged by Article 288 TFEU?

In March 2000 the European Council held a special meeting in Lisbon at which a new strategic goal for the next decade was agreed.

Presidency Conclusions, Lisbon European Council, March 23 and 24 2000

5. The Union has today set itself a *new strategic goal* for the next decade: *to become the most competitive and dynamic knowledge-based economy in the world, capable of sustainable economic growth with more and better jobs and greater social cohesion.* Achieving this goal requires an *overall strategy* aimed at:

— preparing the transition to a knowledge-based economy and society by better policies for the information society and R&D, as well as by stepping up the process of structural reform for competitiveness and innovation and by completing the internal market;
— modernising the European social model, investing in people and combating social exclusion;
— sustaining the healthy economic outlook and favourable growth prospects by applying an appropriate macro-economic policy mix.

6. This strategy is designed to enable the Union to regain the conditions for full employment, and to strengthen regional cohesion in the European Union. The European Council needs to set a goal for full employment in Europe in an emerging new society which is more adapted to the personal choices of women and men. If the measures set out below are implemented against a sound macro-economic background, an average economic growth rate of around 3% should be a realistic prospect for the coming years.

7. Implementing this strategy will be achieved by improving the existing processes, introducing a *new open method of coordination* at all levels, coupled with a stronger guiding and coordinating role for the European Council to ensure more coherent strategic direction and effective monitoring of progress. A meeting of the European Council to be held every Spring will define the relevant mandates and ensure that they are followed up.

NOTE: It is readily apparent that the quest to advance economic integration, even if taken to include a generous spillover into choices about social policy, is treated as but part of a much broader readiness to identify social matters as an arena for co-operation under the European Union umbrella. Five years later the Heads of State and Government sheepishly confessed that the results of the Lisbon Strategy were 'mixed', with 'shortcomings and obvious delays' (Presidency Conclusions, European Council, Brussels, 22 and 23 March 2005, p. 3). A relaunch was announced, to 're-focus priorities on growth and employment' (p. 4). A year later the same group of politicians asserted the persisting importance of providing the Union with the means necessary 'to carry through its policies, including those contributing to an effective implementation of the renewed Lisbon Strategy' (Presidency Conclusions, European Council, Brussels, 23 and 24 March 2006, p. 3). The ten-year process initiated at Lisbon expired in 2010 and the later stages were buffeted by the global economic crisis. A new strategy emerged under the headline 'Europe 2020' (http://ec.europa.eu/europe2020/index_en.htm). This set out a strategy for growth in the EU over the next decade for the EU to become 'a smart, sustainable and inclusive economy'. Five objectives were chosen concerning employment, innovation, education, social inclusion, and climate/energy.

It is difficult to plan ahead with confidence when economic conditions are unstable, and a sense of uncertainty is readily identifiable in the next extract.

COMMUNICATION FROM THE COMMISSION TO THE EUROPEAN PARLIAMENT, THE COUNCIL, THE EUROPEAN CENTRAL BANK, THE EUROPEAN ECONOMIC AND SOCIAL COMMITTEE AND THE COMMITTEE OF THE REGIONS: 'ENHANCING ECONOMIC POLICY COORDINATION FOR STABILITY, GROWTH AND JOBS – TOOLS FOR STRONGER EU ECONOMIC GOVERNANCE'

COM (2010) 367, p. 2

Europe has learned many lessons from the recent financial and economic crisis. We see very clearly now that in a highly integrated Union, and even more so in a monetary union, our economies and our successes are linked. Although the EU has a number of instruments for the co-ordination of economic policy the crisis has shown that they have not been used to the full and that there are gaps in the current governance system. There is broad political agreement that this has to change and that the EU needs to be equipped with a broader and more effective set of policy instruments to ensure its future prosperity and standards of living.

The EU has taken bold, comprehensive and consistent measures to overcome the crisis and draw lessons for the future. The launch of the European Economic Recovery Programme in 2008 helped cushion the shock of the downturn on our economies. Coordinated support was provided to EU Member States that needed it and to safeguard the stability of the Economic and Monetary Union. A set of measures to strengthen the supervision and regulation of the financial system is under negotiation, in the EU and beyond. Now that the framework of the Europe 2020 Strategy is in place, a series of initiatives will follow, designed to unlock the EU's potential to boost growth and create jobs.

What the EU needs is a well defined policy approach that supports economic recovery, puts public finances back on a sound footing and actively promotes sustainable growth and jobs. This is the policy vision set out in the Europe 2020 strategy that has just been endorsed by the European Council. All relevant instruments need to be brought together to ensure that future policy decisions are coherent, serve these goals and, once decided, are implemented and enforced. By strengthening its economic policy co-ordination the EU can deliver a new and sustainable growth agenda for its citizens.

The ambitions embraced at Lisbon in 2000 have not been realized and now look little short of hubristic. However, the questions of 'governance' at stake have enduring salience. The binding legal acts put at the Union's disposal by what is now Article 288 TFEU are not even mentioned by the European Council. Paragraph 7 of the Lisbon Conclusions refers to a new open method of co-ordination at all levels. The intent is helpfully amplified by returning to the Lisbon Presidency Conclusions.

37. Implementation of the strategic goal will be facilitated by applying a new open method of coordination as the means of spreading best practice and achieving greater convergence towards the main EU goals. This method, which is designed to help Member States to progressively develop their own policies, involves:

- fixing guidelines for the Union combined with specific timetables for achieving the goals which they set in the short, medium and long terms;
- establishing, where appropriate, quantitative and qualitative indicators and benchmarks against the best in the world and tailored to the needs of different Member States and sectors as a means of comparing best practice;
- translating these European guidelines into national and regional policies by setting specific targets and adopting measures, taking into account national and regional differences;
- periodic monitoring, evaluation and peer review organised as mutual learning processes.

38. A fully decentralised approach will be applied in line with the principle of subsidiarity in which the Union, the Member States, the regional and local levels, as well as the social partners and civil society, will be actively involved, using variable forms of partnership. A method of benchmarking best practices on managing change will be devised by the European Commission networking with different providers and users, namely the social partners, companies and NGOs.

D. Hodson and I. Maher, 'The Open Method as a New Mode of Governance: the Case of Soft Economic Policy Co-Ordination'
(2001) 39 JCMS 719, 721–2

There are three reasons why the open method may be seen as a new mode of governance. First, taking developments in economic policy as our case study, the open method emerged to deal with the specific issue of factor (capital and labour) and product market flexibility under EMU. Within the current paradigm of sound money and sound finance, national responses in the framework of commonly agreed parameters to this issue are deemed superior to either unco-ordinated national action or action *via* the traditional and more legally structured Community method. Second, as EU policy-making moves into politically sensitive areas such as immigration, defence and taxation, the centralisation of policy formation encapsulated in the Monnet method is more problematic due to difficulties in achieving policy convergence and popular dissatisfaction with the Union. This has prompted the development of new methods of governance that facilitate further Europeanization outside existing institutional forms. Third, the open method provides a pragmatic rather than principled answer to the Achilles' heel of the EU – legitimacy. Legitimation is presumed for policy formed at the national level and, even if contested, arguments are framed in national rather than EU terms and hence are unlikely to call into question fundamentally the role of the EU in facilitating co-ordination. It is, however, debatable whether the open method transcends the usual criticisms of governance in the EU, notably elitism and opacity.

Whether the open method is merely a transitional method governance is answered in part by Dyson's view that it is intended to bring about a convergence in policy-makers' attitudes towards specific issues. '*Benchmarking* can be a factor in reframing domestic discourse and shifting the distribution of power over ideas and agenda setting' [K. Dyson, *The Politics of the Eurozone: Stability or Breakdown* (OUP, 2000), p. 5]. This suggests that the sound money, sound finance paradigm is currently seen as a necessary truth, although such truths can become contingent in the presence of a changing conceptual paradigm. For example, the view that the heterogenous nature of national economies made monetary union impossible was prevalent in many states in the years before EMU. Once member governments accepted the sound money, sound finance paradigm for monetary policy, other pre-existing barriers, such as diversity in national economies, were surmounted. Arguably, as common values begin to grow (through the open method), the possibility of a transfer in competence to the EU level could increase. If this happens, the open method would be transitional and its novelty as a mode of governance would diminish.

Hodson and Maher proceed to reflect on the Open Method in the light of other trends and techniques explored in this chapter.

First, subsidiarity (p. 559):

[Subsidiarity] now forms an important part of the cultural frame within which policy formation takes place and is a tool in deciding whether or not particular action should be taken by the EU . . . The open method seems entirely consistent with the principle, with its emphasis on policy learning among different levels of government. The Lisbon Conclusions themselves note that a fully decentralized approach will be applied in line with the principle (. . . para 38). Arguably, the open method goes further and radicalises subsidiarity; this is a static principle with its focus on what level of government at a particular time of rule formation in the policy process and with a continuing emphasis on hierarchy of structures. The open method, being focused on horizontal learning processes and peer pressure where individual action runs counter to broadly accepted principles, is dynamic in nature, heterarchical, decentered as a *modus operandi* and without any particular rule or single policy objective as an objective . . .

And then 'flexibility' (pp. 570–81):

The open method can also be seen as a form of 'soft' flexibility in contrast to that found under Art. 11EC and Art. 40–43 EU [enhanced co-operation: for the post-Lisbon versions see p. 577] These provisions allow for closer co-operation between states aspiring to greater integration than is currently envisaged under the treaties, by setting down specific steps that have to be taken in order to protect the interests of non-participants and the *acquis* . . . Even with reform, the provisions form a legal straitjacket determining how much further co-operation can take place and reflect an anxiety about the ability of the EU to control outcomes. This can be contrasted with the open method that occurs in a space devoid of formal legal norms apart from the Treaty provisions themselves and the decisions establishing the relevant committees. There is no formal attempt to control outcomes (outside of fiscal policy of course), and process is determined by a system of benchmarking and lesson-drawing, emphasising state competence and the voluntary alignment of policies. Thus the open method provides real flexibility and marks a further maturation of the integration process. The desire of the EC to control outcomes, as manifest in the directive as the rule of choice in the single market, with its emphasis on common outcomes if not methods, is overcome by recognition of the importance of diversity at the national level in relation to policy formation, legal frameworks, ideational references and popular perceptions and reactions to either the European project generally or the specific policy being co-ordinated.

NOTE: The desire to craft a European Union that is enriched by a constructive relationship with its Member States, and not simply seen as an elite-driven, 'top-down' project is plain here, and it binds together much of the material collected in this chapter. Rigid hierarchies may make the European Union seem aloof. And yet Hodson and Maher, discussing the Open Method, identify a real problem already remarked upon by Harmsen in examining 'variable geometry'. The more complex the system becomes, the more intransparent and alienating it becomes. Hierarchical structures are at least intelligible. The Union is grappling with some dauntingly difficult dilemmas here.

In fact, a great deal of vigorous re-thinking is accompanying the debate about methods of governance for a functionally and geographically enlarged Union. The so-called *Community method* – or the *Monnet method* referred to by Hodson and Maher and sketched in Chapter 1 of this book – is increasingly regarded as inapt to provide an effective basis for advancing the rich variety of policy objectives that have been embedded within the system. At the same time there is a genuine anxiety that departures from it may heedlessly abandon the very core of the 'constitutionalized' legal order that has contributed so much to stabilizing the successes of the integration experiment achieved so far. Can there be adaptation without fragmentation? It is a debate that first emerged in a vigorous fashion at the time of the creation of the European Union by the Treaty of Maastricht, when the deliberate crafting of the two non-EC pillars of the EU under arrangements that were institutionally and constitutionally distinct from – and less sophisticated than – those reigning in the EC attracted criticism for its perceived undermining of *Community method* (p. 9). Since then other features of the EU's evolution have presented themselves as further candidates for the sceptic, anxious lest cherished features of the long-established style of governance be diluted.

In July 2001 the Commission published a White Paper on Governance. Its anxieties are still pressing today. It defines *governance* to mean 'rules, processes and behaviour that affect the way in which powers are exercised at European level, particularly as regards openness, participation, accountability, effectiveness and coherence' (p. 8).

European Governance: A White Paper

COM (2001) 428, pp. 7–9

I. WHY REFORM EUROPEAN GOVERNANCE?

European integration has delivered fifty years of stability, peace and economic prosperity. It has helped to raise standards of living, built an internal market and strengthened the Union's voice in the world. It has achieved results which would not have been possible by individual Member States acting on their own. It has attracted a succession of applications for membership and in a few years time it will expand on a continental scale. It has also served as a model for regional integration across the world.

These results have been achieved by democratic means. The Union is built on the rule of law; it can draw on the Charter of fundamental rights, and it has a double democratic mandate through a Parliament representing EU citizens and a Council representing the elected governments of the Member States. Yet despite its achievements, many Europeans feel alienated from the Union's work. This feeling is not confined to the European Institutions. It affects politics and political institutions around the globe. But for the Union, it reflects particular tensions and uncertainty about what the Union is and what it aspires to become, about its geographical boundaries, its political objectives and the way these powers are shared with the Member States. The decreasing turnout in the European Parliament elections and the Irish 'No' vote also serve to show the widening gulf between the European Union and the people it serves:

- There is a perceived inability of the Union to act effectively where a clear case exists, for instance, unemployment, food safety scares, crime, the conflicts on the EU's borders and its role in the world.
- Where the Union does act effectively, it rarely gets proper credit for its actions. People do not see that improvements in their rights and quality of life actually come from European rather than national decisions. But at the same time, they expect the Union to act as effectively and visibly as their national governments.
- By the same token, Member States do not communicate well about what the Union is doing and what they are doing in the Union. 'Brussels' is too easily blamed by Member States for difficult decisions that they themselves have agreed or even requested.
- Finally, many people do not know the difference between the Institutions. They do not understand who takes the decisions that affect them and do not feel the Institutions act as an effective channel for their views and concerns. People do not necessarily feel less European. They still expect Europe-wide action in many domains, but they no longer trust the complex system to deliver what they want. In other words, people have disappointed expectations, but expectations nevertheless.

NOTE: That a document published in 2001 can refer to 'the widening gulf between the European Union and the people it serves' with reference to 'the Irish "No" vote' – 'no' to Nice, p. 12 – suggests an alarming circularity in the history of the EU, as well as reason for anxiety that the second Irish 'No' vote – 'no' to Lisbon, p. 19 – reveals that few, if any, of these flaws have been successfully tackled. The White Paper on Governance is plainly part of the general process of introspection that has lately dominated the European Union.

The next extract pursues the debate on a more specifically legal plane. The authors define new governance as any major departure from 'Classic Community method' ('CCM'), covering departures within CCM and alternatives to it. They then identify the following dimensions as characteristic of new forms of governance:

J. Scott and D. Trubek, 'Mind the Gap: Law and New Approaches to Governance in the European Union'
(2002) 8 ELJ 1, 5–6

A Participation and Power-Sharing

Many of the new governance approaches involve novel ways to expand participation by elements of civil society in policy making. And some entail a greater degree of power sharing than traditional legislation or regulation. This in some cases, policy making may be seen not as something to be done by autonomous regulators but rather as a process of mutual problem-solving among stakeholders from government and the private sector, and from different levels of government.

B Multi-level integration

New governance tends to accept the necessity for coordination of action and actors at many levels of government, as well as between government and private actors. This means that new governance mechanisms may include machinery that brings actors from various levels of government (localities, sub-national regions, national, European) together in ways that facilitate dialogue and coordination.

C Diversity and Decentralisation

New governance, unlike much EU legislation and regulation, accepts the possibility of coordinated diversity and the advantages of leaving final policy making to the lowest possible level when this is feasible. To that end, several new governance mechanisms are designed more to support and coordinate Member State policies than to create uniformity across the Union.

D Deliberation

Many of the new governance mechanisms are designed to foster extended deliberation among stakeholders over the nature of problems, the best way to solve them, and the challenge of carrying out solutions within the widely differing contexts of the fifteen Member States. Deliberation serves both to improve problem-solving capabilities and possibly provide some degree of democratic legitimation.

E Flexibility and Revisability

Many of the approaches emerging in the area of 'new governance', including some that are carried through the Community method, rely less on formal rules and 'hard law' than on open-ended standards, flexible and revisable guidelines, and other forms of 'soft law'. In this way, these mechanisms can adopt to diversity, tolerate alternative approaches to problem solving, and make it easier to revise strategies and standards in light of evolving knowledge.

F Experimentation and Knowledge Creation

Some new governance mechanisms facilitate experimentation and the creation of new knowledge. New knowledge may come from deliberative processes, from combining local experimentation with multilateral surveillance, and from formal and informal ways of exchanging results, benchmarking performance, and sharing best practices.

This was rich fare for the Convention on the 'Future of Europe' (p. 18). The Open Method of Co-ordination and wider issues of governance were firmly on the agenda as the path to Treaty reform was debated in the first half of the 2000s.

Paper 6/2003 Constitutionalising the Open Method of Coordination By Gráinne de Búrca (European University Institute/Columbia Law School) and Jonathan Zeitlin (European Union Center, University of Wisconsin-Madison)

Thinking Outside the Box Editorial Series, Paper 6/2003: JURIST EU

Within the Convention process, the final reports of no less than four separate working groups – those on Simplification, Complementary Competences, Economic Governance and Social Europe respectively – have come out in favour of including the 'Open Method of Coordination' (OMC) within the Constitutional Treaty. The reasons for this relatively broad agreement, as expressed in the various reports, stem from an apparently widespread recognition of the usefulness, efficiency, and flexibility of this new form of national policy coordination for dealing jointly with issues of common interest to the Member States. Several of the reports point out that in addition to the two Treaty-based coordination mechanisms in employment and economic policy launched during the 1990s, the Lisbon European Council authorised the extension of this method to a broad range of other policy domains, such as information society, enterprise policy, research and development, education and training, combating social exclusion and modernising social protection. Since then, significant OMC processes have been developed in a number of these fields, especially social protection (inclusion, pensions, health care), while new ones have begun to emerge in other areas like immigration and asylum, as well as industrial policy, youth policy and disability policy . . .

We argue that the value of the OMC lies not simply in its general usefulness, efficiency, and flexibility as an instrument of EU policymaking. Rather, because the OMC encourages convergence of national objectives, performance and policy approaches rather than specific institutions, rules and programs, this mechanism is particularly well suited to identifying and advancing the common concerns and interests of the Member States while simultaneously respecting their autonomy and diversity. It is neither strictly a supranational nor an intergovernmental method of governance, but one which is genuinely joint and multilevel in its operation. By committing the Member States to share information, compare themselves to one another, and reassess current policies against their relative performance, the OMC is also proving to be a valuable tool for promoting deliberative problem-solving and cross national learning across the EU. It is for precisely these reasons that the OMC has so rapidly become a virtual template for Community policymaking in complex, domestically sensitive areas where diversity among the Member States precludes harmonisation but inaction is politically unacceptable, and where widespread strategic uncertainty recommends mutual learning at the national as well as the European level.

The authors recommended that the Open Method be admitted to the Treaty. It should be applicable to the existing co-ordination processes in employment and economic policy, added to the social policy field and, moreover, 'a flexible generic enabling OMC provision should be introduced for areas other than these three'. The OMC should not be used in a way which would undermine or weaken the existing EU acquis, nor as a permanent substitute for Union legislative action. However, this advice was not taken. The Treaty establishing a Constitution did not make any attempt to provide a general 'constitutionalized' framework for the operation of emergent softer forms of EU governance, and the Lisbon Treaty is similarly barren. This, one may readily suppose, will not halt the rise of such patterns, but a chance was evidently missed to grant a firmer shape to the institutional arrangements. Perhaps it is no surprise that the ambiguities of new governance have been left to evolve. And perhaps it is wise, since there is no single model of policy co-ordination within the EU, but rather many forms, mutating over time. As the extracts reveal the advantages of softer forms of governance are also their disadvantages. The bright side is flexibility and adaptability, within which respect may be paid to State autonomy. The dark side is intransparency and unenforceability, allowing room for States to act selfishly and to shift blame. Moreover, the rise of 'soft law' in these guises may tempt an unchecked outward drift in the scope of EU action, disempowering (*inter alia*) national political processes and deepening the sense of alienation from the EU in a way that no 'relaunch' can adequately address. The debate about governance in general and the Open Method in particular continues.

NOTE: The choice of the preferred governance model(s) for 'Europe 2020' (p. 582) offers an interesting case study, although the intricate detail of the evolving design cannot be traced here. However, as the next extract shows, there are profound questions about governance and priorities that present enduring challenges.

Christian Schweiger, 'Beyond Growth and Jobs? Perspectives for the EU Single Market Policy Framework'

(2009) 5 *Journal of Contemporary European Research* 521, 534–5

> Due to the lack of consensus between member states on the elements of a common European social agenda, the Commission also seems to be determined to widen the OMC approach to further areas, and to deepen its remit by enhancing the input of citizens and stakeholders through better information and dialogue with the aim 'to help build consensus on single market issues' (European Commission 2009b: 4). It remains to be seen if this softer, and more inclusive, approach can indeed create a new consensus between citizens, national policy-makers and the Commission on the future shape of the Single Market, and its role in the global economy. Such a consensus will inevitably depend on the establishment of a shared set of values and integrated standards in the social area, which prevents the SEM from remaining on the level of a borderless free trade area with an increasing diversity of national regulations in the area of employment, welfare, education and training. The current economic crisis shows that the Single Market is hardly likely to function efficiently on the basis of 'race to the bottom' competition for low regulatory standards between member states. As national policy-makers and citizens are struggling to come to terms with the knock-on effects of the global economic crisis on their domestic economies, they have become more defensive over their national regulatory powers and are unlikely to support further intrusion of Single Market legislation in this area. This is mainly the result of the fact that the European integration process has made the inefficiencies of domestic employment and welfare systems to fulfil their traditional functions of preventing mass unemployment and providing citizens with essential welfare provision in the face of globalisation and demographic change more obvious . . . As a result, national policy-makers and citizens show a tendency to, at least partially, blame the EU for the increasing lack of employment and welfare security.

■ QUESTION

'The OMC is a uniquely different form of economic governance. It seeks to establish a set of autonomous national decision-making arenas, coordinated by jointly produced best practice models. It attempts the best of all worlds: combining decentralisation of policy formulation and decision-making with re-integration at the EU level' (E. Szyszczak, 'Experimental Governance: The Open Method of Coordination' (2006) 12 ELJ 486, 488). Can OMC deliver the best of all worlds?

FURTHER READING ON ASPECTS OF 'NEW GOVERNANCE'

Armstrong, K., 'The Character of EU Law and Governance: From 'Community Method' to New Modes of Governance' (2011) 64 Current Legal Problems 179.

Borras, S. and Radaelli, C. (eds), 'The Politics of the Lisbon Agenda: Governance Architectures and Domestic Usages of Europe'. Special Issue of JEPP, (2011) 18/4.

Dawson, M., 'The Ambiguity of Social Europe in the Open Method of Co-ordination' (2009) 34 EL Rev 55.

De Sadeleer, 'The New Architecture of the European Economic Governance: A Leviathan or a Flat-Footed Colossus' (2012) 19 MJ 354.

Joerges, C., 'Integration through De-legalisation?' (2008) 33 EL Rev 291.

Maher, I., 'Regulating Markets and Social Europe: New Governance in the EU' Special Issue (2009) 15/2 ELJ.

Möllers, C., 'European Governance: Meaning and Value of a Concept' (2006) 43 CML Rev 313.

Sabel, C. and Zeitlin, J., 'Learning from Difference: the New Architecture of Experimentalist Governance in the EU' (2008) 14 ELJ 271.

Schäfer, A. 'Resolving Deadlock: Why International Organisations Introduce Soft Law' (2006) 12 ELJ 194.

Senden, L., 'Soft Post-Legislative Rulemaking: A Time for More Stringent Control' (2013) 19 ELJ 57.

Smismans, S., 'From Harmonization to Co-ordination? EU Law in the Lisbon Governance Architecture' (2011) 18 JEPP 504.

Terpan, F., 'Soft Law in the European Union – The Changing Nature of EU Law' (2015) 21 ELJ 68.

Case C-27/04 *Commission* v *Council* [2004] ECR I-6649 – the so-called Stability Pact case – deserves attention for insight into the Court's role in policing the operation of one aspect of what may loosely be called new forms of governance. For comment see Hodson D. and Maher, I., 'Soft Law and Sanctions: Economic Policy Co-ordination and Reform of the Stability and Growth Pact' (2004) 11 Journal of European Public Policy 798.

■ QUESTIONS

1. Norbert Reich has commented that 'the more competences the Community is acquiring, the less exclusive will be its jurisdiction' ((1992) 29 CML Rev 861, 895). What are the manifestations of this development? Is it desirable?
2. Article I-8 of the Treaty establishing a Constitution for Europe declared that the motto of the Union shall be *United in diversity*. That Treaty is now dead (p. 18) but the motto need not be forgotten. How is this reflected in the legal system, if at all? What is the relationship between unity and uniformity?

NOTE: For additional material and resources see the Online Resource Centre at: www.oxfordtextbooks.co.uk/orc/weatherill12e.

19

What Sort of 'Europe'?

Chapters 17 and, in particular, 18 were by no means designed to show that the core assumptions of the nature and purpose of EU policy-making are now outmoded, but they were designed to show the widening variety of methods of governance that now contribute to the workings of the Union. The remarkable tale of the 'constitutionalization' of the Treaties provided the binding thread for the material in Part One of this book. That story was built on a legal order for the EU that is supreme: a 'new legal order' according to the Court of Justice. This chapter is designed to survey some of the challenges to the Court's portrayal of the nature of EU law, while also inquiring more generally into how discourse surrounding democracy and legitimacy in and for the European Union might be assessed. As with Chapters 17 and 18, so with Chapter 19: the intent is not at all to suggest received wisdom about the nature and purpose of the Union is flawed, but rather to suggest that the geographical and functional growth of the system has generated a much wider dynamic debate about the ramifications of what is and should be done in the name of European integration.

One of the notions lurking in the previous chapter was that of legitimacy. It also surfaced in Chapter 1 (pp. 12, 13) and in both Chapters 12 and 14 (pp. 348, 401). This is a notion that carries heavy weight.

With hindsight one of the most remarkable features of the early years of the Union's development was the small amount of attention paid to the fundamental constitutional questions of what really was being created. A new legal order, that was supreme over the laws of the Member States. Was this State-building? State-*replacing*?

SECTION 1: THE CHALLENGE OF NATIONAL CONSTITUTIONAL COURTS

Denmark ratified the Maastricht Treaty in 1993 after a popular referendum voted in favour of ratification. But this was the second bite of the cherry. In 1992 the Danes had voted 'No'. Discontent had been reduced from majority to minority sentiment in the period between the first and second referendum, but the jolt to assumptions about the popular appeal of the European integration process was profound. Nor was Denmark alone in ratifying the Maastricht Treaty only after considerable internal difficulty. It was mentioned in Chapter 1 (at p. 9) that Germany was the last State to ratify the Maastricht Treaty and that it did so only after its Constitutional Court (*Bundesverfassungsgericht*) approved ratification. The German Court rejected an individual's constitutional complaint, but the ruling is remarkable for observations about the Treaty-defined limits of competence and the inapplicability of acts of the EU's institutions which trespass on areas of exclusive national competence.

The ruling is by no means the inevitable starting point in any debate about the true nature of the European Union and its relationship with its Member States. But it is nevertheless worthy of attention. After decades of assumptions that European integration was a project handled by elites, the rocky road to ratification of the Maastricht Treaty changed perceptions.

The Danish 'No' must be taken as an expression of popular disquiet. But it is hard to draw clear lessons from the result of a single-issue, single-answer referendum, not least because of the tiny majorities involved in both votes. By contrast the intervention of the German *Bundesverfassungsgericht* provides us with more tangible bases for understanding what is at stake.

In the following extract the German Federal Constitutional Court considers its perception of the nature of the European Union, both generally and in the light of Germany's 'Basic Law':

Ruling of the Federal Constitutional Court, Second Division

12 October 1993, 2 BvR 2134/92, 2 BvR 2159/92 (*Brunner* v *European Union Treaty*)

. . . b 1) The European Union is, in accordance with its understanding of itself as a union of the peoples of Europe (Art. A para 2 Union Treaty), a confederation of allied democratic states whose objectives include dynamic development (see, e.g., Arts. B para 1 last indent and C para 1, Union Treaty). If the Union carries out its sovereign duties and thereby exercises sovereign powers, it is in the first place the nationals of the Member States through their national parliaments who have to legitimise this democratically.

At the same time, with the development of the functions and powers of the Community it becomes increasingly necessary to allow the democratic legitimation and influence provided by way of national parliaments to be accompanied by a representation of the nationals of a Member State through a European Parliament as the source of a supplementary democratic support for the policies of the European Union. With the establishment of union citizenship by the Maastricht Treaty, a lasting legal tie is knotted between the nationals of the individual Member States which, though not as strong as the common nationality of a single state, provides a legally binding expression of the degree of *de facto* community already in existence (see especially Art. 8b paras. 1 and 2, EC Treaty). The influence extending from the citizens of the Union can eventually become a part of the democratic legitimation of the European institutions, to the extent that the peoples of the European Union fulfill the necessary preconditions for such.

Democracy, if it is not to remain as merely a formal principle of accountability, is dependent on the existence of certain pre-legal conditions, such as a continuous free debate between opposing social forces, interests, and ideas, in which political goals become clarified and change course (see 5 BVerfGE 85 at 135, 198 and 205; 69 BVerfGE 315 at 344 *et seq*) and out of which a public opinion emerges which starts to shape a political will. This also means that the decision-making processes of the organs exercising sovereign powers and the various political objectives pursued can be generally perceived and understood, and therefore that citizens entitled to vote can communicate, in their own language, with the sovereign authority to which they are subject.

Such factual conditions, to the extent that they do not yet exist, can develop in the course of time within the institutional framework of the European Union. Such development to no small extent is dependent on a process for imparting the objectives of the Community institutions and the effects of their decisions to the member nations. Parties, associations, the press and the broadcasting services are as much a medium as a factor of this process, out of which a European public opinion may come into being (see Art. 138a, EC Treaty). The European Council is also eager for more openness and transparency in the European decision-making process (see Birmingham Declaration: A Community close to its citizens nos, 2, 3, BullBReg. No 115 of 23 Oct. 1992, p. 1058; Final Conclusions of the European Council Presidency in Edinburgh, 11/12 Dec. 1992, part A, sect. 7, and annex 3 BullBReg. No 140 of 28 Dec. 1992, pp. 1278, 1284 *et seq*.

b 2) In the confederation of allied states formed by the European Union, therefore, democratic legitimation necessarily comes about through the feed-back of the actions of the European institutions into the parliaments of the Member States; within the institutional structure of the Union there is the additional factor (which increases as European nations grow closer together) of the provision of democratic legitimation by means of the European Parliament which is elected by the citizens of the Member States. Already at the present stage of development the legitimation of the European Parliament has a supporting function, which could become stronger were it to be elected by uniform voting rules in all the Member States in accordance with Art. 138 para 3 of the EC Treaty and if its influence on the policies and legislation of the European Community were to increase. What is decisive is that the democratic bases of the European Union are built up in step with integration, and that as integration proceeds a thriving democracy is also maintained in the Member States. Excessive functions and powers within the sphere of responsibility of the European confederation of states would effectively weaken democracy at the national level, so that the parliaments of the Member States could no longer adequately provide the legitimation for the sovereign power exercised by the Union.

If, as at present, the peoples of the individual states provide democratic legitimation through their national parliaments, limits to the extension of the European Communities' functions and powers are then set by virtue of the democratic principle. Each of the peoples of the individual states is the starting point for the public authority relating to that people. The states need sufficiently important spheres of activity of their own in which the peoples of each can develop and articulate in a process of political will – formation which it legitimates and controls, in order to give legal expression to what – relatively homogeneously – binds the people spiritually, socially, and politically together (see H. Heller, *Politische Demokratie and soziale Homogenität, Gesammelte Schriften*, Vol. 2 (1971), p. 421 at 427 *et seq*).

From all that it follows that functions and powers of substantial importance must remain for the German *Bundestag*.

c) The exercise of sovereign power through a confederation of allied states such as the European Union is based on authorisations from states which remain sovereign and which in international matters generally act through their governments and thereby control the integration process. It is therefore primarily governmentally determined. If such a community power is to rest on the political will-formation which is supplied by the people of each individual state, and is to that extent democratic, it presupposes that the power is exercised by an entity made up of representatives sent by Member States' governments, which in turn are subject to democratic control. The issue of European legal regulations may – without prejudice to the need for democratic control of the government – as well lie with an institution composed of representatives of Member States' governments, i.e., an executive organ, to a greater extent than would be constitutionally acceptable at national level.

3. As the German voter essentially exercises his right to participate in the democratic legitimation of the institutions and agencies entrusted with sovereign powers by means of the elections for the German *Bundestag*, the *Bundestag* must also decide on German membership in the European Union and on its continuation and development.

Article 38 of the Basic Law is accordingly breached if a law that opens up the German legal system to the direct validity and application of the law of the – supranational – European Communities does not establish with adequate certainty what powers are transferred and the intended program of integration (see 58 BVerfGE 1 at 37). When it is unclear to what extent and degree the German legislature has assented to the transfer of the exercise of sovereign powers, then the European Communities may possibly claim functions and powers that were not specified. That would be equivalent to a general authorisation, and therefore would be a relinquishment of powers, against which Art. 38 of the Basic Law provides protection.

In view of the fact that the text of an international treaty must be negotiated by the treaty parties, the certainty and tightness of the treaty provisions cannot be set in the same way as for a law under parliamentary jurisdiction (see 77 BVerfGE 170 at 231 *et seq*). What is decisive is that Germany's membership and the pendant rights and duties – especially the immediately binding legal effect of the Communities' actions within the national sphere – have been defined in the Treaty so as to be predictable for the legislature and are enacted by it in the Law on Accession with sufficient certainty (see 58 BVerfGE 1 at 37; 68 BVerfGE 1 at 98 *et seq*). At the same time that means that subsequent important changes to the integration program set up in the Union Treaty and to the Union's powers of action are no longer covered by the Law on Accession to the present Treaty (see *ibid*; Mosler in *Handbuch des Staatsrechts*, Vol. VII, 1992, sec. 175, n. 60). Thus, if European institutions or agencies were to treat or develop the Union Treaty in a way that was no longer covered by the Treaty in the form that is the basis for the Law on Accession, the resulting legislative instruments would not be legally binding within the sphere of German sovereignty. The German state organs would be prevented, for constitutional reasons, from applying them in Germany. Accordingly, the Federal Constitutional Court reviews legal instruments of European institutions and organs to see whether they remain within the limits of the sovereign rights conferred on them or whether they transgress those limits (see 58 BVerfGE 1 at 30 *et seq*; 75 BVerfGE 223 at 235, 242) . . .

The German court concluded that the Union Treaty measured up to these standards, thereby clearing the way for German ratification of the Maastricht Treaty. However, in the later stages of the ruling it reaffirmed its sensitivity to the location of the outer limits of EU competence:

. . . Inasmuch as the Treaties establishing the European Communities on the one hand in limited circumstances confer sovereign rights, and on the other hand regulate Treaty amendments – through a normal and also in a simplified procedure – does this distinction take on meaning for the future treatment of the

> individual powers. Whereas a dynamic extension of the existing Treaties has been supported so far on the basis of a broad treatment of Art. 235 of the EEC Treaty [now Art. 352 TFEU, p. 31] in the sense of a 'lacuna-filling competence' (*Vertragsabrundungskompetenz*) and on the basis of considerations relating to the implied powers of the Communities and of Treaty interpretation as allowing maximum exploitation of Community powers of 'effect utile' (see Zuleeg in: von der Groeben/Thiesing/Ehlermann, *EWG-Vertrag*, 4th ed. 1991, Art 2, note 3), in future the interpretation of enabling provisions by institutions and agencies of the Community will have to consider that the Union Treaty basically distinguishes between the exercise of a conferred limited sovereign power and the amendment of the Treaty, thus the interpretation will not result in an extension of the Treaty: such an interpretation of enabling provisions would not have a binding effect for Germany . . .

The *Bundesverfassungsgericht's* parting shot was:

> The Maastricht Treaty – especially by the extension of EC competences and the inclusion of monetary policy – confers further essential functions and powers on European organs – which at Treaty level are not yet supported by a corresponding strengthening and extension of the democratic bases. It sets up a new stage of European unification, which according to the stated intentions of the Contracting Parties is to enhance further the democratic and efficient functioning of the institutions (fifth considérant of the Preamble). Democracy and efficiency are here not to be separated; it is also expected that the strengthening of the democratic principle will improve work at the Community level in all its organs. At the same time, in accordance with Art. F para 1 of the Union Treaty [now Art. 4(2) TEU], the Union will respect the national identities of its Member States, the governmental systems of which are based on democratic principles. To that extent the Union preserves the democratic bases already existing in the Member States and builds on them.
>
> Any further development of the European Union cannot evade the conceptual framework set out above. The constitution-amending legislature had in connection with this Treaty taken that into account when they inserted Art. 23 into the Basic Law, as there the development of the European Union is expressly mentioned, subject to the principles of democracy and the rule of law, social and federal principles, and the subsidiarity principle. It is decisive, therefore, from the point of view of both the Treaties and of constitutional law, that the democratic bases of the Union will be built in step with integration, and also as integration progresses a living democracy will be maintained in the Member States.

It is hard to read these observations other than as warnings for the future. Note that they are addressed to *all* the Community/Union institutions. H. Hauser and A. Müller summarize the Court's view in the following terms ((1995) 50 *Aussenwirtschaft* 17, 30):

> EU institutions provide no primary source for democratic legitimisation. The democratic systems of the Member States are the primary source for democratic legitimisation of EU legislation. Because citizen participation is only guaranteed on the national and not on the European level, democratic legitimisation needs clearly defined restrictions on the transfer of sovereignty. National constitutional courts should have the ultimate interpretation whether EU legislation corresponds to the principle of specific delegation of power.

It is important to realize that the German Court is, in effect, threatening to deprive the Court of Justice of exclusive competence to determine the limits of EU competence, but that it is doing so out of a declared perception based on the need to secure effective democratic control of political decision-making. Nevertheless, there is much to be said for the view that the *Bundesverfassungsgericht's* concerns are not prompted by the pattern of the Maastricht Treaty itself, but rather by a belated recognition of expansionist trends in the evolution of EU law and policy through legislative and judicial activism over an extended period (the subject matter of this book!). J. Weiler suggests that for the *Bundesverfassungsgericht* 'the only way out was to legitimate the past by . . . weak notions of Member State democratic mediation, and put the polity on notice that German constitutionalism will not be caught napping again' ('Does Europe need a Constitution? Reflections on Demos, Telos, and the German Maastricht Decision') (1995) 1 *European Law Journal* 219, 237). It has been suggested at several points in this book that a post-Maastricht sensitivity affects the EU institutions when they are invited to act at the outer limits of Treaty-conferred competence; and that this is in part attributable to an awareness that the EU system, built on willing and active co-operation between EU and national bodies, can survive only if negative reactions at national level are absorbed and answered at EU level. Examples might include *Dori* (Case C-91/92, p. 122) and *Tobacco Advertising* (Case C-376/98, p. 33) – although there are counter-examples too, where deep incursion into national practice is visible even where the Treaty's authorization is tenuous, such as *Mangold* (Case C-144/04, p. 71) *Viking Line* (Case C-438/05, p. 401) and some of the cases on Citizenship such as *Dereci* (Case C-256/11) considered in Chapter 15. It is, of course, in the interest of the Court of Justice to maintain the loyal support of national courts, for the evolution of the EU legal system and its practical enforcement depend heavily on the inter-penetration of Union law and national law. Coercive measures are not available to the Court of Justice, so it must seek to persuade.

In fact, this is a two-way process of dialogue. The harsh tone of the *Maastricht* judgment should be contrasted with the more emollient expressions of a subsequent ruling of the *Bundesverfassungsgericht*.

BANANAS, ORDER OF THE SECOND SENATE OF 7 JUNE 2000 – 2 BVL 1/97

I

Submissions of cases to the Federal Constitutional Court for constitutional review under Article 100(1) GG which refer to rules that are part of secondary European Community law are only admissible if their grounds show in detail that the present evolution of law concerning the protection of fundamental rights in European Community law, especially in case law of the Court of Justice of the European Communities, does not generally ensure the protection of fundamental rights required unconditionally the protection in the respective case. Certainly the submitting court has, in a way which meets the requirements under Article 80 (2), sentence 1 of the BVerfGG [*Bundesverfassungsgerichtsgesetz – Federal Constitutional Court Act*] set forth its conviction that, and for what reasons, it regards the application of the submitted legal rules as unconstitutional (*cf.* BVerfGE [*Bundesverfassungsgerichtsentscheidungen – Decisions of the Federal Constitutional Court*] 37, 328 <333 *et seq*>; 66, 265 <269 *et seq*>; 84, 160 <165>; 86, 52 <57>). Its opinion that the decision it must take depends on the decision on the issue submitted is clearly stated in the decision for submission (*cf.* BVerfGE 97, 49 <60>, 98, 169 <199>). However, the submitting court's position that the rules of Articles 17–19 and Article 21 (2) of Regulation (EEC) No 404/93 as well as other secondary rules of Community law to which it objects may be submitted to the Federal Constitutional Court for constitutional review under Article 100(1) GG cannot be supported.

II

1. In its decision of 29 May 1974 – 2 BvL 52/71 (BVerfGE 37, 271 – 'As long as. . . Decision' [*Solange* I]), the competent Senate of the Federal Constitutional Court had, with reference to actual jurisdiction, come to the result that the integration process of the Community had not progressed so far that Community law also contained a codified catalogue of fundamental rights decided on by a Parliament and of settled validity, which was adequate in comparison with the catalogue of fundamental rights contained in the Basic Law. For this reason, the Senate regarded the reference by a court of the Federal Republic of Germany to the Federal Constitutional Court in constitutional review proceedings, following the obtaining of a ruling of the Court of Justice of the European Communities under Article 177 of the EEC Treaty, which was required at that time, as admissible and necessary if the German court regards the rule of Community law that is relevant to its decision as inapplicable in the interpretation given by the Court of Justice of the European Communities because and in so far as it conflicts with one of the fundamental rights of the Basic Law (BVerfGE 37, 271 <285>).

2 a) In its decision of 22 October 1986 – 2 BvR 197/83 (BVerfGE 73, 339 – [*Solange II*]), the Senate holds that a measure of protection of fundamental rights has been established in the meantime within the sovereign jurisdiction of the European Community which in its conception, substance and manner of implementation is essentially comparable with the standards of fundamental rights provided in the Basic Law, and that there are no decisive factors to lead one to conclude that the standard of fundamental rights which has been achieved under Community law is not adequately consolidated and only of a transitory nature (BVerfGE 73, 339 <378>).

On the basis of individual decisions of the Court of Justice of the European Communities, the Senate made statements concerning the standard of fundamental rights, and holds that this standard, particularly through the decisions of the Court of Justice of the European Communities, has been formulated in content, consolidated and adequately guaranteed (BVerfGE 73, 339 <378–381>). In this context, the Senate commented on the decisions of the Court of Justice of the European Communities concerning the fundamental rights and freedoms relating to economic activities, such as the right to property and the freedom to pursue economic activities (above, p. 380), but also on the freedom of association, on the general principle of equal treatment and the prohibition of arbitrary acts, religious freedom and the protection of the family, as well as on the principles, which follow from the rule of law, of the prohibition of excessive action and of proportionality as general legal principles in achieving a balance between the common interest objectives of the Community legal system, and on the safeguarding of the essential content of fundamental rights (above, p. 380).

In summary, the Senate made the following statement: As long as the European Communities, in particular European case law, generally ensure effective protection of fundamental rights as against the sovereign powers of the Communities which is to be regarded as substantially similar to the protection of fundamental rights required unconditionally by the Basic Law, and in so far as they generally safeguard the essential content of fundamental rights, the Federal Constitutional Court will no longer exercise its jurisdiction to decide on the applicability of secondary Community legislation cited as the legal basis for any acts of German courts or authorities within the sovereign jurisdiction of the Federal Republic of Germany, and it will no longer review such legislation by the standard of fundamental rights contained in the Basic Law. References (of rules of secondary Community law to the Federal Constitutional Court) under Article 100(1) GG are therefore inadmissible (BVerfGE 73, 339 <387>).

b) In its Maastricht Decision (BVerfGE 89, 155), the Senate maintained this view. In this decision, the Senate stressed that the Federal Constitutional Court, through its jurisdiction, guarantees, in co-operation with the Court of Justice of the European Communities, that effective protection of fundamental rights for the residents of Germany will also be secured against the sovereign powers of the Communities and is generally to be regarded as substantially similar to the protection of fundamental rights required unconditionally by the Basic Law, and that in particular the Court provides a general safeguard of the essential contents of the fundamental rights. The Federal Constitutional Court thus guarantees this essential content against the sovereign powers of the Community as well (BVerfGE 89, 155 <174–175>, with reference to BVerfGE 37, 271 <280 *et seq*> and 73, 339 <376–377, 386>). Under the preconditions the Senate has formulated in BVerfGE 73, 339 – 'Solange II' –, the Court of Justice of the European Communities is also competent for the protection of the fundamental rights of the citizens of the Federal Republic of Germany against acts done by the national (German) public authority on account of secondary Community law. The Federal Constitutional Court will only become active again in the framework of its jurisdiction should the Court of Justice of the European Communities depart from the standard of fundamental rights stated by the Senate in BVerfGE 73, 339 (378–381).

c) Article 23 (1), sentence 1 GG (inserted pursuant to the Law amending the Basic Law of 21 December 1992 – BGBl I, p. 2086 –) confirms this ruling. Pursuant to this law, the Federal Republic of Germany shall participate, with a view to establishing a united Europe, in the development of the European Union that is committed to democratic, social, and federal principles, to the rule of law, and to the principle of subsidiarity, and that guarantees a level of protection of fundamental rights essentially comparable to that afforded by the Basic Law. An identical protection in the different areas of fundamental rights afforded by European Community law and by the rulings of the Court of Justice of the European Communities, which are based on Community law, is not called for. The constitutional requirements are satisfied in accordance with the preconditions mentioned in BVerfGE 73, 339 (340, 387) if the rulings of the Court of Justice of the European Communities generally ensure effective protection of fundamental rights as against the sovereign powers of the Communities which is to be regarded as substantially similar to the protection of fundamental rights required unconditionally by the Basic Law, and in so far as they generally safeguard the essential content of fundamental rights.

d) Thus, constitutional complaints and submissions by courts are, also pursuant to the Senate decision in BVerfG 89, 155, inadmissible from the outset if their grounds do not state that the evolution of European law, including the rulings of the Court of Justice of the European Communities, has resulted in a decline below the required standard of fundamental rights after the 'Solange II' decision (BVerfGE 73, 339 <378–381>). Therefore, the grounds for a submission by a national court of justice or of a constitutional complaint which puts forward an infringement by secondary European Community Law of the fundamental rights guaranteed in the Basic Law must state in detail that the protection of fundamental rights required unconditionally by the Basic Law is not generally assured in the respective case. This requires a comparison of the protection of fundamental rights on the national and on the Community level similar to the one made by the Federal Constitutional Court in BVerfGE 73, 339 (378–381).

NOTE: Such a statement of detail was found to be lacking in the case. Concluding that 'the judicial protection of fundamental rights by national courts of justice and Community courts of justice interlock on the European level', the *Bundesverfassungsgericht* found the application inadmissible.

Bananas concerns review of acts for compliance with fundamental rights; *Maastricht* concerned alleged trespass beyond the outer limits of Treaty-conferred competence. But the pivotal issue was the same – what competence did a national court enjoy when faced with a plea that an EU act was invalid according to domestic constitutional standards? The pure logic of supremacy insists that the EU act must prevail; and the Court of Justice's view is that that act can be set aside only by the Court of Justice itself applying the rules of the EU legal order (Case 314/85 *Foto-Frost*, p. 222). But this is not what the *Bundesverfassungsgericht* decides. The *Bundesverfassungsgericht* does not concede to the Court of Justice an exclusive jurisdiction to decide on the validity of EU law. The ruling in *Bananas* is stated to be consistent with that in the *Maastricht* case, and indeed it is. It maintains an ultimate review competence vested in the German court in the event that review of EU acts against the standards of fundamental rights by the Court of Justice is shown to be deficient judged by German constitutional standards. But it places a heavy burden on the applicant seeking to demonstrate such deficiency. This ruling is strikingly more concerned than *Maastricht* to assert the extreme improbability that the German court would rule in favour of the disapplication of an EU act on German territory. In form this is not compatible with the Court of Justice's insistence that it and it alone is competent to rule on the validity of Union legislative acts. But in practice the disagreement matters little, at least while the German courts remain content with the steering role played by the Court of Justice.

The *Bundesverfassungsgericht* rejoined the debate in 2009 when invited to consider whether German ratification of the Lisbon Treaty was compatible with German constitutional law. The Lisbon judgment has much in common with its Maastricht predecessor in that the *Bundesverfassungsgericht* took the opportunity to explain at some length its understanding of the nature of the EU and Germany's relationship with it, while ultimately giving the green light to German ratification of the Lisbon Treaty.

LISBON, JUDGMENT OF THE SECOND SENATE OF 30 JUNE 2009 – 2 BVE 2/08

(Available *via* http://www.bundesverfassungsgericht.de/EN/Homepage/home_node.html : the fact that an English-language version was quickly made available is doubtless because of concern to exert the widest possible influence).

The judgment places heavy emphasis on the role of what we know, post-Lisbon, as the 'principle of conferral' (Article 5 TEU, pp. 29, 560):

[231] . . . The empowerment to transfer sovereign powers to the European Union or other intergovernmental institution permits a shift of political rule to international organisations. The empowerment to exercise supranational competences comes, however, from the Member States of such an institution. They therefore permanently remain the masters of the Treaties. In a functional sense, the source of Community authority, and of the European constitution that constitutes it, are the peoples of Europe with their democratic constitutions in their states. The 'Constitution of Europe', the law of international agreements or primary law, remains a derived fundamental order. It establishes a supranational autonomy which is quite far-reaching in political everyday life but is always limited factually. Here, autonomy can only be understood - as is usual regarding the law of self-government - as an autonomy to rule which is independent but derived, i.e. is accorded by other legal entities . . ..

[234] . . . the principle of conferral under European law and the duty, under European law, to respect identity, are the expression of the foundation of Union authority in the constitutional law of the Member States.

This means that:

[239] It is therefore constitutionally required not to agree dynamic treaty provisions with a blanket character or if they can still be interpreted in a manner that respects the national responsibility for integration, to establish, at any rate, suitable national safeguards for the effective exercise of such responsibility. Accordingly, the Act approving an international agreement and the national accompanying laws must therefore be such that

European integration continues to take place according to the principle of conferral without the possibility for the European Union of taking possession of *Kompetenz-Kompetenz* or to violate the Member States' constitutional identity which is not amenable to integration. . . .

The judgment insists on the 'the guarantee of national constitutional identity' (para 240), and declares that 'The *ultra vires* review as well as the identity review can result in Community law or Union law being declared inapplicable in Germany (para 241).

The judgment is rich and complex. The feature that may prove to be the most fertile source of debate is the Court's identification of what must be protected as a matter of German constitutional law. In particular, what is this 'identity review'?

[244] . . . The shape of the European Union must comply with democratic principles as regards the nature and the extent of the transfer of sovereign powers and also as regards the organisational and procedural elaboration of the Union authority acting autonomously (Article 23.1, Article 20.1 and 20.2 in conjunction with Article 79.3 of the Basic Law). European integration may neither result in the system of democratic rule in Germany being undermined (a) nor may the supranational public authority as such fail to fulfil fundamental democratic requirements (b).

NOTE: The question then is what precisely the Court means by the notion that 'the system of democratic rule in Germany' must not be undermined, and by the requirement that the supranational public authority shall not 'fail to fulfil fundamental democratic requirements'.

[245] a) A permanent responsibility for integration is incumbent upon the German constitutional bodies. It is aimed at ensuring, as regards the transfer of sovereign powers and the elaboration of the European decision-making procedures, that in an overall view, the political system of the Federal Republic of Germany as well as that of the European Union comply with democratic principles within the meaning of Article 20.1 and 20.2 in conjunction with Article 79.3 of the Basic Law.

[246] The election of the Members of the German *Bundestag* by the people only fulfils its central role in the system of the federal and supranational intertwining of power if the German *Bundestag*, which represents the people, and the Federal Government borne by it, retain a formative influence on the political development in Germany. This is the case if the German *Bundestag* retains responsibilities and competences of its own of substantial political importance or if the Federal Government, which is answerable to it politically, is in a position to exert a decisive influence on European decision-making procedures (see BVerfGE 89, 155 <207>).

[247] aa) Inward federalisation and outward supranationalisation can open up new possibilities of civic participation. An increased cohesion of smaller or larger units and better chances of a peaceful balancing of interests between regions and states grow from them. Federal or supranational intertwining creates possibilities of action which otherwise would encounter practical or territorial limits, and they make the peaceful balancing of interests easier. At the same time, they make it more difficult to create a will of the majority that can be asserted and that directly goes back to the people (Article 20.2 sentence 1 of the Basic Law). The transparency of the assignment of decisions to specific responsible actors decreases, with the result that the citizens can hardly take any tangible contexts of responsibility as an orientation for their vote. The principle of democracy therefore sets content-related limits to the transfer of sovereign powers, limits which do not result already from the inalienability of the constituent power and of state sovereignty.

[248] bb) The safeguarding of sovereignty, demanded by the principle of democracy in the valid constitutional system, in the manner prescribed by the Basic Law, i.e. in a manner that is open to integration and to international law, does not mean per se that a number of sovereign powers which can be determined from the outset or specific types of sovereign powers must remain in the hands of the state. The participation of Germany in the development of the European Union, which is permitted by Article 23.1 sentence 1 of the Basic Law, comprises, apart from the formation of an economic and monetary union, also a political union. Political union means the joint exercise of public authority, including the legislative authority, which even reaches into the traditional core areas of the state's area of competence. This is rooted in the European idea of peace and unification especially where it deals with the coordination of cross-border aspects of life and with guaranteeing a single economic area and area of justice in which citizens of the Union can freely develop (Article 3.2 TEU Lisbon).

[249] cc) European unification on the basis of a union of sovereign states under the Treaties may, however, not be realised in such a way that the Member States do not retain sufficient space for the political formation of the economic, cultural and social circumstances of life. This applies in particular to areas which shape the citizens' circumstances of life, in particular the private space of their own responsibility and of political and social security, which is protected by the fundamental rights, and to political decisions that particularly depend on previous understanding as regards culture, history and language and which unfold in discourses in the space of a political public that is organised by party politics and Parliament. Essential areas of democratic formative action comprise, *inter alia*, citizenship, the civil and the military monopoly on the use of force, revenue and expenditure including external financing and all elements of encroachment that are decisive for the realisation of fundamental rights, above all as regards intensive encroachments on fundamental rights such as the deprivation of liberty in the administration of criminal law or the placement in an institution. These important areas also include cultural issues such as the disposition of language, the shaping of circumstances concerning the family and education, the ordering of the freedom of opinion, of the press and of association and the dealing with the profession of faith or ideology.

[250] dd) Democracy not only means respecting formal principles of organisation (see BVerfGE 89, 155 <185>) and not only a cooperative involvement of interest groups. Democracy first and foremost lives on, and in, a viable public opinion that concentrates on central acts of determination of political direction and the periodic allocation of highest-ranking political offices in the competition of government and opposition. Only this public opinion makes visible the alternatives for elections and other votes and continually calls them to mind also as regards decisions relating to individual issues so that they may remain continuously present and effective in the political opinion-formation of the people *via* the parties, which are open to participation for all citizens, and in the public space of information. To this extent, Article 38 and Article 20.1 and 20.2 of the Basic Law also protect the connection between political decisions on facts and the will of the majority that has been constituted by elections, and the dualism between government and opposition that results from it, in a system of a variety of competing parties and of the observing and controlling formation of public opinion.

[251] Even if due to the great successes of European integration, a joint European public that engages in an issue-related cooperation in the rooms of resonance of their respective states is evidently growing (see on this already BVerfGE 89, 155 <185>; *Trenz, Europa in den Medien. Die europäische Integration im Spiegel nationaler Öffentlichkeit*, 2005), it cannot be overlooked, however, that the public perception of factual issues and of political leaders remains connected to a considerable extent to patterns of identification which are related to the nation-state, language, history and culture. The principle of democracy as well as the principle of subsidiarity, which is structurally demanded by Article 23.1 sentence 1 of the Basic Law as well, therefore require to factually restrict the transfer and exercise of sovereign powers to the European Union in a predictable manner particularly in central political areas of the space of personal development and the shaping of the circumstances of life by social policy. In these areas, it particularly suggests itself to draw the limit where the coordination of circumstances with a cross-border dimension is factually required.

[252] What has always been deemed especially sensitive for the ability of a constitutional state to democratically shape itself are decisions on substantive and formal criminal law (1), on the disposition of the police monopoly on the use of force towards the interior and of the military monopoly on the use of force towards the exterior (2), the fundamental fiscal decisions on public revenue and public expenditure, with the latter being particularly motivated, *inter alia*, by social-policy considerations (3), decisions on the shaping of circumstances of life in a social state (4) and decisions which are of particular importance culturally, for instance as regards family law, the school and education system and dealing with religious communities (5).

The judgment then tests the Lisbon Treaty at length, and concludes that the exacting standards laid down are met, provided that certain adjustments are made domestically to allow firmer political supervision of decisions to be taken at EU level, in particular those pursuant to Article 352 TEU (p. 31). Germany may ratify the Lisbon Treaty.

[298] As regards its competences and its exercising these competences, the European Union, as a supranational organisation, must comply as before with the principle of conferral that is exercised in a restricted and controlled manner. Especially after the failure of the project of a Constitution for Europe, the Treaty of Lisbon has shown sufficiently clearly that this principle remains valid. The Member States remain the masters of the Treaties. In spite of a further expansion of competences, the principle of conferral is retained. The provisions of the Treaty can be interpreted in such a way that the constitutional and political identity of the fully democratically organised Member States is safeguarded, as well as their responsibility for the fundamental direction and elaboration of Union policy. Even after the entry into force of the Treaty of Lisbon, the Federal Republic

of Germany will remain a sovereign state and thus a subject of international law. The substance of German state authority, including the constituent power, is protected (aa), the German state territory remains assigned only to the Federal Republic of Germany (bb), there are no doubts concerning the continued existence of the German state people (cc).

Lisbon is comparable to *Maastricht* in some matters of detail. For example, the concern that the scope of competence conferred on the Union shall be 'defined in the Treaty so as to be predictable' appears in *Maastricht* (p. 591) and is echoed at para [251] and visible in para [298] of *Lisbon*. And the judgments share a concern to examine in depth Germany's constitutional relationship with the EU, while ultimately acquiescing in the political desire to ratify the Lisbon Treaty. Like *Bananas, Lisbon* stresses that only exceptionally could one imagine non-compliance: *Lisbon* refers to the 'openness' of the German Constitution to EU law ('Europarechtsfreundlichkeit'). The *Bundesverfassungsgericht* may be developing a reputation as a court that barks but does not bite. The title of an analysis of the judgment by D. Doukas is deftly chosen – 'Not guilty, but don't do it again!' (2009) 34 EL Rev 866 – but the *Maastricht* judgment 16 years earlier was at the time similarly treated as a final warning! Even so, once again parts of the judgment are apt to be interpreted as instructions for the future about what may *not* be done. In particular, safeguarding the system of democratic rule (para 244) and 'the constitutional and political identity of the fully democratically organised Member States' (para 298) is a job loaded with ambiguous meaning but it represents the *Bunderverfassungsgericht's* ill-defined view of where the EU may not go. And, in rooting restraining power in national constitutional law, *Lisbon* shares with *Maastricht* and *Bananas* an understanding of the relationship between EU law and national law which is different from that held by the Court of Justice.

Several questions emerge. What kind of unstable legal order is this? How can we truly bask in the successful remaking of the EU legal order as an independent source of law which is, moreover, supreme over conflicting national laws when such audacious claims are so readily challenged by a national court? Has the Court of Justice been exposed as the Walter Mitty of European legal hierarchies?

And yet the quest to hammer out an answer to the question 'who is boss?' should not be lightly undertaken by Europeans. History reveals what happens when one group seeks to impose its views on others. Is acquiescence in 'constitutional plurality' feasible in Europe?

Miguel Poiares Maduro, 'Europe and the Constitution: What if this is As Good As It Gets?' Constitutionalism Web-Papers (University of Manchester) http://papers.ssrn.com/sol3/papers.cfm?abstract_id=1576085

WHO DECIDES WHO DECIDES?

Constitutional law has usually been considered as the higher degree and ultimate source of legitimacy of the legal system and its rules. Independently of ones conception of constitutional law as a 'grundnorm', a set of rules of recognition, positivized natural law, an higher command of a sovereign supported by an habit of obedience, or other, constitutional law has always been conceived as the higher law of the legal system, criterion of legitimacy and validity of other sources of the law. European integration 'attacks' this hierarchical understanding of the law. In reality, both national and European constitutional law assume in the internal logic of their respective legal systems the role of higher law. According to the internal conception of the EU legal order developed by the European Court of Justice, Community primary law will be the 'higher law' of the Union, the criterion of validity of secondary rules and decisions as well as that of all national legal rules and decisions within its scope. Moreover, the Court of Justice is the higher court of this legal system. However, a different perspective is taken by national legal orders and national constitutions. Here, Community Law owes its supremacy to its reception by a higher national law (normally constitutions). The higher law remains, in the national legal orders, the national constitution and the ultimate power of legal adjudication belongs to national constitutional courts. In this way, the question of who decides who decides has different answers in the European and the national legal orders[42] and when viewed from a perspective outside both national and Community legal orders requires a conception of the law which is no longer dependent upon an hierarchical construction. Such form of legal pluralism has already been convincingly argued by Neil MacCormick.[43] However, the Maastricht Decision of the German Constitutional Court and the possibility of this Court striking down a Community legal act on its decision on the Bananas regulation,[44] have again raised fears of actual conflicts between national courts and the ECJ disrupting the European Union legal order and ultimately the process of European integration. In my view, the question of 'who decides who decides' has long been present within constitutionalism. It is a normal consequence of the divided powers system inherent in constitutionalism. In fact, it can be considered as an expected result of the Madisonian view of separation of powers as creating a mechanism of checks and balances. The conflicts surrounding the exercise of judicial review, for example, are linked to this question: when a Court strikes down a piece of legislation according to its interpretation of a constitutional norm which could be object of different interpretations two opposing positions can be argued: one, arguing that the Court has done nothing else but apply the higher law; another, arguing that the Court has overstepped its role since the indeterminacy of the constitutional norm meant that it was for the legislator to choose one among several possible interpretations of that norm. Of course, in the operation of national constitutions and where constitutional judicial review exists it is expected for the legislator to accept the Court's decision and therefore it is stated that it is the later that has the 'right to decide who decides'. But that is a more a result of the historical development of separation of powers than a logical conclusion to be derived from the foundations of constitutionalism. Moreover, the reality is that the political system can still impact upon the judiciary (for example by changing the members of the constitutional court)[45] and, in this way, still has an important share of the power 'to decide who decides'. I am not going to address the complex questions involved in judicial review and separation of powers. What I want to stress is that the paradox of 'who decides who decides' is inherent to the values of constitutionalism as one of its guarantees of limited power. If the question of 'who decides who decides' was constitutionally allocated to a single institution all the mechanisms of countervailing powers and checks and balances would be easily undermined. Therefore, in a multi-level or federal system it is the vertical or federal conception of constitutionalism (as a form of limited government at the State and federal level) that requires for the decision on 'who decides who decides' to be left unresolved. The open question should be left open. What then, are conflicts unavoidable? Should the conflicts between EU law and national constitutional law be subject to a primus inter pares (for example, international law[46] or a new Constitutional Court composed of EU and National constitutional judges[47])? Can't different legal orders coexist in the same sphere of application under different claims of legitimacy?[48] And if they can, how can conflicts be avoided or dealt with?

The general tendency may be for national courts to comply with the 'European Constitution' but there is still on the part of several national high courts a challenge to the absolute supremacy of EU law. This is visible either in the description that national constitutionalism makes of itself or in the dependence of EU law effectiveness upon national law and national courts. National law still holds a veto power over national law[49] and that is important even when not used. It is well known that many developments in EU law can be explained by the European Court of Justice perception of the possible reactions by national courts. A hierarchical alternative imposing a monist authority of European law and its judicial institutions over national law would be difficult to impose in practical

42 Rossa Phelan has made a detailed analysis of the different viewpoints on the relationship between national and the European legal order depending on whether it is observed from the perspective of EC law, national constitutional law or even public international law. See D. Rossa *Phelan, Revolt or Revolution: The Constitutional Boundaries of the European Community,* Dublin: Sweet & Maxwell, 1997.

43 N. MacCormick, 'Beyond the Sovereign State', (1993) 56 *Modern Law Review* 1.

44 See, for example, M. Kumm, 'Who Is the Final Arbiter of Constitutionality in Europe?', Harvard Jean Monnet Chair Working Papers 10/98. Among other relevant issues (mainly, the direct effect of the GATT rules in the German legal order), the argument is made by some German Companies which traditionally imported Bananas from Latin-American countries that the EC Regulation discriminates against those importers in favor of intra-EC Bananas producers (mainly from Canarias and Madeira) and importers from ACP countries.

45 An exemplary case, is Roosevelt's 're-packaging' of the American Supreme Court to change the classical economic due process interpretation of the American Constitution.

46 N. MacCormack, 'Risking Constitutional Collision in Europe?', (1998) 18 *Oxford Journal of Legal Studies* 517. Although MacCormick suggests subjecting such conflicts to the arbitration of international law as a possible direction, he does not really take that path [and] prefers to remain faithful to a totally legal pluralistic solution where the question of conflict is left open.

47 J. Weiler, 'The European Union Belongs to Its Citizens: Three Immodest Proposals', (1997) 22 *European Law Review* 150.

48 Rossa Phelan, above n.42, for example, argues that 'revolt or revolution' is unavoidable unless Community law partly redraws its claim of supremacy over national law. For a critical review of Rossa Phelan's position see MacCormick, above n.46 and Poiares Maduro, 'The Heteronyms of European Law', (1999) 5 *European Law Journal, Annual Review of Books, Weiler and Poiares Maduro* (eds.), at 160.

49 See D. Chalmers, 'Judicial Preferences and the Community Legal Order', (1997) 60 *Modern Law Review* 164 at 180.

terms and could undermine the legitimacy basis on which European law has developed.[50] Though the grammar used by EU lawyers in describing the process of constitutionalisation may assume a top-down approach, the reality is that the legitimacy of European constitutionalism as developed in close co-operation with national courts and national legal communities which have an increasing bottom-up effect on the nature of the European legal order.[51]

We have to start reasoning in the realm of what could be called counterpunctual law. Counterpoint is the musical method of harmonising different melodies that are not in a hierarchical relationship among them. The discovery that different melodies could be heard at the same time in an harmonic manner was one of the greatest developments in musical history and greatly enhanced the pleasure and art of music. In law we too have to learn how to manage the non-hierarchical relationship between different legal orders and institutions and to discover how to gain from the diversity and choices that offer us without generating conflicts that ultimately will destroy those legal orders and the values they sustain. There is much to be gained from a pluralist conception of the EU legal order. In a world where problems and interests have no boundaries, it is a mistake to concentrate the ultimate authority and normative monopoly in a single source. Legal pluralism constitutes a form of checks and balances in the organisation of power in the European and national polities and, in this sense, it is an expression of constitutionalism and its paradoxes. But, to take full advantage of this legal pluralism we need to conceive forms of reducing or managing the potential conflicts between legal orders while promoting exchanges between them and requiring courts to conceive their decisions and the conflicts of interests at hand in the light of a broader European context. This will also highlight the trans-national character of much of these conflicts which is often ignored by national constitutional law. Catherine Richmond has proposed an attractive framework for the 'legal indeterminacy' entailed in the non- hierarchical relationship between national and European legal orders. She argues that each legal order has its own viewpoint over the same set of norms[52] and that each is to take into account the changes in that set of norms arising from the other legal orders: 'each time a norm is created or amended in one particular legal order, the cognitive arrangement of norms must, from our one particular viewpoint, be shuffled around in order to accommodate the change'.[53] However, no legal order should be forced to abandon its own viewpoint (or, if you prefer, its own cognitive framework). In her own words: 'A state of legal indeterminacy is only stable, however, as long as no *normative* challenge is made to it which challenges the political basis of the cognitive model adopted (. . .). Therefore it is in all parties' interest to preserve the indeterminacy in the Community, enabling each to latch on to the model of legal authority that is politically most comfortable'.[54] Identity is lost if it is not self-determined. On the other hand, such self-determination should not dispute the self-determined identity of the other legal orders. In my view, one of the consequences ought to be that each time a legal order changes the set of norms shared with the broader European legal community it ought to do it in a manner that can be accommodated by the other legal orders (a good example being the introduction of fundamental rights protection in the Community legal order). The EU legal order should be conceived as integrating both the claims of validity of national and EU constitutional law. Any judicial body (national or European) would be obliged to reason and justify its decisions in the context of a coherent and integrated EU legal order. In this way, I do not share the view that the best form of safeguarding legal pluralism is to recognise, pragmatically and normatively, the possibility for national constitutional authorities to derogate from EU law so long as that would not itself be recognised by EU law and will be valid under national constitutional law but not EU law. For Kumm, who has powerfully argued in favour of such a view,[55] the fact that the deviations will take place under national law and not EU law will mean that the integrity and uniformity of EU law would be safeguarded. But this will be so from a purely formal perspective. Further, the fact that the deviations would be legitimised on purely national grounds and 'not affect' EU law may promote the use and abuse of that national constitutional exceptions without any form of EU control. Ultimately, it could lead to a 'race to the bottom' between national courts in the uniform application of EU law. I argue that national deviations can still be possible but they need to be argued in 'universal' terms, safeguarding the coherence and integrity of the EU legal order. The idea is to promote the universalisability of national decisions on EU law and integrate them into a coherent system of interpretation of EU law by national courts. In other words, national decisions on EU law should not be seen as separated national interpretations and

50 In the words of Chalmers, 'the regime is able to develop provided it does not significantly disrupt the egalitarian relations enjoyed between national courts and the Court of Justice', ibidem.

51 Kamiel Mortelmans, 'Community Law: More than a Functional Area of Law, Less than a Legal System', *Legal Issues of European Integration*, 1996/1, 23, at 42–43.

52 In the suggestive expression of Jo Shaw: 'each national constitution creates a different "gateway" for the EU legal order'. Postnational Constitutionalism, n.2.

53 Catherine Richmond, 'Preserving the Identity Crisis: Autonomy, System and Sovereignty in European Law', (1997) 16 *Law and Philosophy* 377 at 417.

54 *Ibid.*

55 Kumm, above n.44.

applications of EU law but as decisions to be integrated in a system of law requiring compatibility and coherence. This may raise fears of corrosion of EU law since it appears to promote and multiply national deviations from the European rule of law. However, this assumption must be confronted with the dynamics of law and legal reasoning. If a national constitutional court is aware that the decision that it will take becomes part of European law as interpreted by the 'community' of national courts, it will internalise in its decisions the consequences in future cases and the system as a whole. This will prevent national courts from using the autonomy of their legal system as a form of evasion and free-riding and will engage the different national courts and the ECJ in a true discourse and coherent construction of the EU pluralist legal order. At the same time, we should improve European legal pluralism by raising in each legal order the awareness of the constitutional boundaries of the other legal orders. And, in here, an important role is to be played by the changes in constitutional thinking which I have been arguing for, particularly the abandoning of single constitutionalism which has dominated the conceptions of national constitutionalism. The conception of European legal pluralism or contrapunctual law argued for in here safeguards the constitutional value of the paradox of who decides who decides by preserving the identity of each legal order while at the same time promoting its inclusiveness through what, following Luhmann's and Teubner's autopoeisis, could be described as a process of reflexivity. It is not only identity but also communication that needs to be fostered between national and European legal orders. In this case, 'the fact that we define our identity by exclusion from the other does not ultimately exclude because there is no way of knowing where the next redefinition will go'.[56] This discourse between different legal orders and different institutions resulting from the emerging European polity is a further promotion of constitutionalism, broadening its deliberative elements beyond the exclusive deliberative communities involved in each national institution.

What future for this 'deliberative constitutionalism'? It is necessary to keep watching the process as it develops, which implies a need for forbiddingly wide and deep knowledge of judicial practice in Europe. In Case C-303/05 *Advocaten voor de wereld* [2007] ECR I-3633 the Court of Justice upheld the validity of Framework Decision 2002/584 on the European Arrest Warrant ([2002] OJ L190/1), a device, adopted under what was pre-Lisbon Article 34 EU (i.e., it is an old 'third pillar' measure – see Chapter 1, p. 9, and Chapter 15) which is designed to promote mutual recognition in criminal matters by replacing lengthy extradition procedures with quicker procedures for surrender of individuals across borders. In particular, the Court found no violation of the general principles of the EU legal order. However, several national courts had expressed serious concerns about the compatibility of the EU measure and/or national implementing measures with fundamental rights standards. It is not possible here to provide an account of the large amount of litigation at national and EU level concerning the European Arrest Warrant (see e.g., E. Herlin-Karnell, 'From Mutual Trust to the Full Effectiveness of EU Law: Ten Years of the European Arrest Warrant' (2013) 38 EL Rev 79: the list includes *Stefano Melloni* (Case C-399/11, judgment of 26 February 2013), met in Chapter 3).

The point is simply that this is the type of flashpoint, which one may suppose will arise more frequently given the expansion of the Court's jurisdiction in the area of freedom, security, and justice consequent on the Lisbon reforms (Chapter 15), which risks translating the differences *in principle* between the Court of Justice and national judges' views on the source of ultimate legal authority into differences that have real practical consequences for the viability of the EU legal order. As mentioned, the *Bundesverfassungsgericht* so far barks but does not bite. If any national court does 'bite' – most obviously by refusing to accept the authority of a particular ruling of the Court of Justice – then the model of 'legal pluralism' will be damaged, perhaps irreparably. But – and this is a further element in some of the pluralist scholarship – the courts involved *know* of these risks and have incentives to behave in such a way as to minimize them.

56 Z. Bankowski and E. Christodoulidis, 'The European Union as an Essentially Contested Project', (1998) 4 European Law Journal 341 at 351–2.

Pollicino, O., 'European Arrest Warrant and Constitutional Principles of the Member States: a Case law-based Outline in the Attempt to Strike the Right Balance between Interacting Legal Systems'
(2008) 9 German Law Journal 1313, 1351

> . . . it is plausible to state . . . that constitutional judges' concern 'to have the last word' reflect a questionable methodological approach, i.e. an 'old fashion' expression of the pursuit of the 'final power', or even 'Kompetenz-Kompetenz.' Such a concept which lead back to old-fashioned struggles for unity and the attainment of an exclusive centre of gravity is destined to give way instead to a network of complex, 'multi-centered' relations amongst courts, fuelled by the principle of loyal cooperation between Community and constitutional judges, and reluctant, by definition, to favour any sort of hierarchal process whatsoever.

De Witte, B., 'Direct Effect, Primacy and the Nature of the Legal Order' Ch. 12 in P. Craig and G. de Búrca, *The Evolution of EU Law*
(Oxford: OUP, 2nd ed., 2011), pp. 356–7

> . . . a 'pluralist' reading of the relation between EU law and national law . . . insist[s] on the need for an open attitude both on the side of the European Court (and the EU law doctrine) and on that of national Constitutional Courts (and constitutional law doctrine), whereby the values and interests of the 'other side' are taken seriously, and are seen to be taken seriously. In order to do this, those courts should engage in a structured dialogue, whereby national supreme and constitutional courts are prepared to submit controversial issues to the ECJ rather than solve them solely according to their own preferences, and whereby the European Court of Justice in turn shows willingness to listen to the constitutional concerns of its national interlocutors.

Whether or not one finds the vision sketched by Pollicino and by De Witte appealing, the next question is: but will this happen? So centrally important have been the contributions made to this debate by the German judiciary that the last words in this sub-section should belong with them. Extra-judicial comments made by the President of the *Bundesverfassungsgericht* offer an intriguing insight.

A Vosskuhle, 'Multilevel Cooperation of the European Constitutional Courts'
(2010) 6 European Constitutional Law Review 175, 195–6

(Some footnotes omitted.)

Vosskuhle explains that 'The Federal Constitutional Court has recognised the primacy of Union law from the perspective of national constitutional law' (p. 190); 'such primacy is neither absolute nor based on Union law, but anchored in national constitutional law, and therefore also limited by it (p. 191). This is evidently not in line with the view of the Court of Justice. On the other hand, the risk of such disagreement having practical significance is minimized by 'the principle of openness towards European law (*Europarechtsfreundlichkeit*), which not only permits Germany's participation in European integration but, as has been emphasized by the Federal Constitutional Court in its *Lisbon* decision, even requires it as a constitutional obligation' (pp. 179–80). He therefore finds a 'triangle of jurisdiction between Karlsruhe, Luxembourg and Strasbourg as part of . . . a multilevel cooperation of the European constitutional courts' (p. 178). And he makes plain what this co-operation should and does involve:

> It must, however, be noted that in the seventeen years that have passed since the pronouncement of the *Maastricht* judgment, the two Senates of the Federal Constitutional Court have never seen themselves compelled to establish that a legal act transgressed the boundaries of the sovereign powers accorded to the European institutions

and bodies by way of conferral. All actors involved have made their contribution to achieving this harmony. The German legislative bodies have promptly and duly implemented the rulings of the court in Luxembourg . . . The Court of Justice, for its part, has contributed to constructive co-existence by showing the first signs of a change in the image that it has of itself. This change sometimes becomes apparent in a more restrictive interpretation of Union competences[86] and more fundamentally in the area of direct and indirect taxation,[87] where the court's approach is more cautious than in earlier case-law. The same applies to the realisation of the fundamental freedoms in the subject areas that are the competence of the member states, such as health policy.[89] Finally, the Court of Justice has on several occasions shown consideration for the member states' identities, their particular traditions and important structural principles of their legal systems. By way of example, I would like to mention the recognition of member states' decisions restricting fundamental Union freedoms by giving priority to the protection of human dignity,[90] concerns of freedom of assembly and of opinion,[91] the protection of national culture or the combating of crime related to games of chance.

Some of these rulings which Vosskuhle cites as evidence of greater sensitivity in Luxembourg are familiar from earlier in this book – *Tobacco Advertising I* (p. 33), *Omega* (p. 401), and *Schmidberger* (p. 348) – and the narrative of 'willing and active cooperation between EU and national bodies' was already met earlier in this chapter. Were he writing now he might add reference to the potential for using Article 4(2) TEU to shelter national measures from the blast of EU law suggested by the Court in *Ilonka Sayn-Wittgenstein* (Case C-208/09, p. 430) and *Runevič-Vardyn / Runiewicz-Wardyn* (Case C-391/09, p. 431). One could readily see the Court of Justice's approach in these cases as a means to open up EU law to national constitutional concerns while still laying formal claim to the supremacy of EU law over national law, in balance with the *Bundesverfassungsgericht*'s concern to open up German law to EU law, while still placing limits on its subjection to EU law in the name of, *inter alia*, defence of constitutional identity.

However, Vosskuhle's account is selective. *Tobacco Advertising I* looks less compelling as a constraint on abuse of EU legislative competence now than it did at the time – Vosskuhle mentions *Tobacco Advertising II* and there are other cases in which the Court has given a cheerful green light to legislative harmonization (see Chapter 2, pp. 38–41) And a decision such as *Mangold* (Case C-144/04) sits uneasily in a narrative emphasizing the Court of Justice's caution – although the *Bundesverfassungsgericht* in 2010 refused to treat *Mangold* as a judgment lying beyond the competence of the EU (*Honeywell* 6 July 2010, 2 BvR 2661/06). The line of case law initiated by *Francovich (*Cases C-6, C-9/90 p. 143) is a long-standing example of judicial boldness in Luxembourg – which has, moreover, attracted constitutional objections from Germany (p. 157). Vosskuhle is, of course, perfectly aware of rulings which suggest that judicial restraint in Luxembourg is only patchy. His selectivity is deliberate – and that of itself is revealing of a desire to promote a culture of co-operation among Europe's leading courts.

The latest and as yet incomplete chapter in this story has the financial crisis and in particular EU monetary policy at its heart. A challenge was brought before the German courts to a scheme devised by the European Central Bank (ECB) to buy government bonds issued by States in the Eurozone. These came to be known as Outright Monetary Transactions (OMTs) and they were intended to promote confidence in the durability of the Euro as a single currency. The *Bundesverfassungsgericht* doubted that the programme

86 For instance ECJ, Case C-376/98, *Germany* v. *European Parliament and Council of the European Union* ('Tobacco Advertising Directive I'), *ECR* 2000, I-8419, marginal nos. 76 *et seq*.; differently, however, ECJ, Case C-380/03, *Germany* v. *European Parliament and Council of the European Union* ('Tobacco Advertising Directive II'), *ECR* 2006, I-11573, marginal nos. 36 *et seq* . . . .

87 *Cf.* e.g., ECJ, Case C-376/03, *D* v. *Inspecteur van de Belastingdienst*, *ECR* 2005, I-5821; ECJ, Case C- 513/04, *Kerckhaert and Morres* v. *Belgium*, *ECR* 2006, I-10967; ECJ, Case C-184/05, *Twoh International BV*, *ECR* 2007, I-7897; ECJ, Case C-284/06, *Burda*, *ECR* 2008, I-4571.

89 ECJ, Case C-171/07, *Doc Morris* . . ., Case C-141/07, *Commission* v. *German y*. . . .

90 ECJ, Case C-36/02, *Omega* v. *Bonn*, *ECR* 2004, I-9609 (*Laserdrome*).

91 ECJ, Case C-112/00, Schmidberger, *ECR* 2003, I-5659 (*Brenner motorway closure*).

fell within the scope of the powers conferred on the ECB by the Treaty and it also thought it violated the prohibition on financing found in Article 123(1) TFEU. In the 2010 ruling in *Honeywell*, mentioned already (p. 604), it had promised that in such a case it would involve the Court of Justice in the process. It now did so. The *Bundesverfassungsgericht* made its first ever preliminary reference to the Court of Justice in Luxembourg. This manifests a co-operative attitude. But the content of the questions was different in tone. At stake was suspicion of ultra vires action, though, as the Opinion of Advocate General Cruz Villalón explains, the material submitted by the *Bundesverfassungsgericht* stated that there were also consequences for German constitutional identity. In the questions it referred, the German court aggressively set out its view of the limited conditions on which it considered the scheme could possibly comply with EU law.

Case C-62/14 Peter Gauweiler

Judgment of 16 June 2015, Court of Justice of the EU

Advocate General Cruz Villalón supplied a brilliant summary of the sensitivities involved.

> 59 . . . it seems to me an all but impossible task to preserve *this* Union, as we know it today, if it is to be made subject to an absolute reservation, ill-defined and virtually at the discretion of each of the Member States, which takes the form of a category described as 'constitutional identity'. That is particularly the case if that 'constitutional identity' is stated to be different from the 'national identity' referred to in Article 4(2) TEU.
>
> 60. Such a 'reservation of identity', independently formed and interpreted by the competent — often judicial — bodies of the Member States (of which, it need hardly be recalled, there are currently 28) would very probably leave the EU legal order in a subordinate position, at least in qualitative terms. Without going into details, and without seeking to pass judgment, I think that the characteristics of the case before us may provide a good illustration of the scenario I have just outlined.

The Court, in its ruling, found a way to treat the scheme as compatible with EU law, depending on how it was administered. The *Bundesverfassungsgericht* BVerfG has not yet ruled on the final resolution of the case.

■ **QUESTION**

'Constitutional pluralism is widely regarded as presenting a paradigm shift; however, absent agreement on whether this shift is for better or for worse. The sceptics have blamed constitutional pluralists for justifying national constitutional courts' diversions from the clear and precise requirements of European Union law, assisting them in turning the 'real world into a fable'. The opposite side reacted that the so-called 'real world' has, perhaps, never been what it was thought to be and that it is only now with the help of constitutional pluralism that we are pulling our heads out of the sand' (Introduction, p. 9, M. Avbelj and J. Komarek (eds), *Constitutional Pluralism in the European Union and Beyond* (Oxford, Hart, 2012). Discuss. Is the shift for better or for worse?

FURTHER READING ON THE IMPLICATIONS OF THE JUDICIAL DIALOGUE ABOUT THE NATURE OF THE EUROPEAN LEGAL ORDER

Special Issue, The Federal Constitutional Court's Lisbon Case, German Law Journal Vol 10 Issue 8, August 2009.

Albi, A., 'From the Banana Saga to a Sugar Saga and Beyond: Could the Post-Communist Constitutional Courts Teach the EU a Lesson in the Rule of Law?' (2010) 47 CML Rev 791.

Baquero Cruz, J., 'The Legacy of the Maastricht-Urteil and the Pluralist Movement' (2008) 14 ELJ 389.

Everson, M. and Eisner, J., *The Making of a European Constitution: Judges and Law beyond Constitutive Power* (London: Routledge, 2007).

Guastaferro, B., 'Beyond the Exceptionalism of Constitutional Conflicts: The Ordinary Functions of the Identity Clause' (2012) 31 YEL 263.

Mayer, F., 'Rashomon in Karlsruhe – A Reflection on Democracy and Identity in the European Union', 05/10 Jean Monnet Working Paper, http://jeanmonnetprogram.org/papers/paper-serie/2010/.

Payandeh, M., 'Constitutional Review of EU Law after *Honeywell*: Contextualising the Relationship between the German Constitutional Court and the EU Court of Justice' (2011) 48 CML Rev 9.

Piqani, D., 'Arguments for a Holistic Approach in European Constitutionalism: What Role for National Institutions in Avoiding Constitutional Conflicts between National Constitutions and EU Law' (2012) 8 Euro Const Law Rev 493.

Sabel, C. and Gerstenberg, O., 'Constitutionalising an Overlapping Consensus: the ECJ and the Emergence of a Coordinate Constitutional Order' (2010) 16 ELJ 511.

Slaughter, A.-M., Stone Sweet, A., and Weiler, J.H.H. (eds), *The European Courts and National Courts: Doctrine and Jurisprudence* (Oxford: Hart Publishing, 1997).

Theil, S., 'What Red Lines, if any, do the Lisbon Judgments of European Constitutional Courts Draw for Future EU Integration?' (2014) 15 German Law Jnl 599.

Thym, D., 'In the Name of Sovereign Statehood: a Critical Introduction to the Lisbon Judgment of the German Constitutional Court' (2009) 46 CML Rev 1795.

Von Bogdandy, A. and Schill, S., 'Overcoming Absolute Primacy: Respect for National Identity under the Lisbon Treaty' (2011) 48 CML Rev 1417.

You might also read P. Kirchhof, 'The Balance of Powers between National and European Institutions' (1999) 5 ELJ 225; the author was a member of the *Bundesverfassungsgericht* and widely supposed to have exerted significant influence over the drafting of its 'Maastricht' judgment. It is of interest that his discussion includes explicit reference to judicial anxieties expressed in other Member States (pp. 240–1), which suggests *inter alia* that Vosskuhle's 'triangle of jurisdiction between Karlsruhe, Luxembourg and Strasbourg' (p. 603) needs a still wider geographical and jurisdictional shape.

■ QUESTION

In Chapter 3 a question was raised which, it was suggested (at p. 77), could usefully be re-addressed later. Now is the moment. The Treaty establishing a Constitution for Europe would have brought the principle of supremacy within the text of the Treaty for the first time.

ARTICLE I-6, UNION LAW

> The Constitution and law adopted by the institutions of the Union in exercising competences conferred on it shall have primacy over the law of the Member States.

Would this have changed anything – (i) from the perspective of the EU legal order, (ii) from the perspective of national legal orders? (You might read G. Beck, 'The Problem of *Kompetenz Kompetenz*: a Conflict Between Right and Right in which There Is No *Praetor*' (2005) 30 EL Rev 42.)

The Lisbon Treaty took a less radical course. It merely added a non-binding Declaration to the Treaty which recalls the Court's case law on supremacy (or primacy). Attached as an annex to the Declaration is an opinion of the Council Legal Service on primacy, stating that:

> The fact that the principle of primacy will not be included in the future treaty shall not in any way change the existence of the principle and the existing case-law of the Court of Justice.

Is it wise to try to change anything in this contested area?

SECTION 2: STATES AND BEYOND: MULTI-LEVEL GOVERNANCE AND CONSTITUTIONALISM

This complex layering of multi-level legal authority, which seems to resist reduction to a simple hierarchy, finds an echo in the even wider phenomenon of the political character of the Union itself. Is it a State or is it not a State? And whose benchmark do we employ to measure what it really is? In fact, these kinds of 'simple questions' are exactly the numbingly pedestrian questions that preclude necessary leaps of imagination. The European Union need not be a State – on some accounts, *should* not be a State – and yet may accomplish its mission. At the core of the debate is the question of where lies the legitimate source of authority? And, as with the search to locate the 'constitutional right answer' on whose law should prevail, there is much to be said for an approach which respects the different and differently motivated voices of claimants instead of demanding that one win, and others lose.

The following two extracts build beyond the 'Maastricht ruling' of the *Bundesverfassungsgericht* to discuss the present and future shaping of the Union.

H. Hauser and A. Müller, 'Legitimacy: The Missing Link for Explaining EU-Institution Building' (1995) 50 *Aussenwirtschaft* 17, 18–22

(Footnotes omitted, small linguistic alterations made with the copyright holder's permission.)

1.1. FROM INTERGOVERNMENTAL TO SUPRANATIONAL

The EU is an institution 'sui generis' with no historical precedent. Accordingly, it is difficult to describe the institution in traditional terms. . . . The institutional structure goes far beyond an international agreement between sovereign states, even beyond a confederation between sovereign states with unlimited veto power. On the other hand, the EU clearly lacks main features of a federal state. Until now the European Union was qualified as a supranational co-operation, but this organisation never achieved the quality of a state. The Preamble speaks about the growing union of the peoples of Europe. It is difficult to qualify the nature of the European Union, e.g., the German Constitutional Court in the judgment of Maastricht talks about a 'parent organisation' . . . and other new qualifications. Similarly, when the German Constitutional Court talks about the future of Europe, it explains itself very carefully, 'stateconnection' . . . and 'growing union of the peoples of Europe' . . . are expressions which reveal its fear of becoming more concrete. The Court describes the European Union not as no state, not even a 'federal' one . . ., but as a process of integration of its own nature as an 'interstate establishment'. . . . The complex structure of supranational and intergovernmental elements in institutions and decision making processes must be at the core of a theoretical discussion of EU institutional development . . .

To summarise: Institutional tensions in the EU can best be explained by the weak correspondence between the distribution of power to regulate and the institutional structure of decision making. With regard to the separation of power in the field of economic regulation, the EU comes very close to a federation: within the broad competences of the Maastricht Treaty, EU institutions decide on the separation of power (with the restriction of unanimity vote in some areas), the European Court of Justice has the right for authoritative interpretation, in areas of majority voting Member States have lost control over future regulation. Institutional structures do not follow these developments. The separation of power within the EU does not correspond to requirements of a democratic state: EU legislation is in the hands of members of the executive of Member States, the executive function in the EU is a shared responsibility of the Commission and the Council, the exclusive right to initiatives gives the Commission an important role in the legislative process, members of the Commission and of the European Court of Justice are delegated by national governments and not appointed by the legislator.

The tension between the regulative power of a federation and the weak institutional structure which does not meet basic requirements of a democratic state is at the heart of most critical voices in the academic and political debate. . . . Complaints about democratic deficits, weak accountability of EU institutions, inefficient decision procedures, or over-centralisation are the symptoms. Reforms to either better restrict EU competences or to develop democratic EU institutions are proposals to ease the underlying tensions . . .

NOTE: The reader would profit at this point from re-visiting some of the material contained in Chapter 1 of this book. In particular, consider the extent to which the *Laeken Declaration* (p. 14) fits the authors' descriptive and prescriptive summary in the concluding two paragraphs of this extract. And then consider the extent to which the two routes suggested in the final sentence help in mapping the choices made in the Lisbon Treaty and, more generally, whether they offer a normative basis for re-thinking patterns of reform in the EU. Also of interest is Opinion 2/13 on accession to the ECHR, met in Chapter 2 (p. 65), in which the Court declared that 'the EU is, under international law, precluded by its very nature from being considered a State' (para. 56).

J. Habermas, 'Remarks on Dieter Grimm's "Does Europe Need a Constitution?" '

(1995) 1 *European Law Journal* 303–7

THE DIAGNOSIS

From a constitutional perspective, one may discern a contradiction in the European Union's present situation. On the one hand, the EU is a supranational organisation established by international treaties and without a constitution of its own. In this respect it is not a state (in the modern sense of a constitutional state characterised by a monopoly on violence and a domestically and internationally recognised sovereignty). On the other hand, Community institutions create European law that binds the Member States – thus the EU exercises a supreme authority previously claimed only by individual states. From this results the oft-bemoaned democratic deficit. Commission and Council pronouncements, as well as decisions by the European Court, are intervening ever more profoundly into the Member States' internal affairs. Within the framework of the rights conferred upon the Union, the European Executive may enforce its pronouncements over and against the opposition of the national governments. At the same time, as long as the European Parliament is equipped with only weak competences, these pronouncements and enactments lack direct democratic legitimation. The executive institutions of the community derive their legitimacy from that of the member governments. They are not institutions of a state that is itself constituted by the act of will on the part of the united citizens of Europe. The European passport is not as yet associated with rights constitutive for democratic citizenship.

POLITICAL CONCLUSION

In contrast with the Federalists, who recommend a democratic pattern for the EU, Grimm warns [in an article to be found in the same issue of the *European Law Journal*] against any further European-law induced eroding of national competences. The democratic deficit would not be effectively filled by a 'statist shortcut' to the problem, but rather deepened. New political institutions such as a European Parliament with the usual powers, a government formed out of the Commission, a Second Chamber replacing the Council, and a European Court of Justice with expanded competences, as such offer no solutions. If they are not filled with life, they will instead accelerate tendencies already apparent within the national frameworks, tendencies towards autonomisation of bureaucratised politics. The real prerequisites for a European-wide integration of citizen will-formation have been absent up to now. Constitutional Euroscepticism thus amounts to the empirically-based argument that runs as such: as long as there is not a European people which is sufficiently 'homogenous' to form a democratic will, there should be no constitution.

THE DISCUSSION

My reflections are directed against (a) the insufficient account of alternative courses and (b) the not entirely unambiguous normative underpinnings of the functional requirements for democratic will-formation.

(a) Grimm sets before us the undesired consequences that would result from the transition of the European Community to a democratically-constituted, federal state should the new institutions not take root. So long as a European-networked civil society, a European-wide political public sphere and a common political culture are lacking, the supranational decision processes would become increasingly independent of the still nationally organised opinion- and will-formation processes. This dangerous prognosis is plausible as far as I am concerned. However what is the alternative? Grimm's option seems to suggest that the constitutional status quo can at least freeze the extant democratic deficit. Completely independent of constitutional innovations however this deficit expands day by day because the economic and social dynamics even within the existing institutional framework perpetuate the erosion of national powers through European law. As Grimm himself acknowledges: 'The democratic principle is valid for the Member States whose own decision capabilities are however diminishing: decisional capability is accruing to the European Community where the democracy principle is developing only weakly.' But if the gap is steadily widening between the European authorities' expanding scope and the inadequate legitimation of the proliferating European regulations, then decisively adhering to an exclusively nation-state mode of legitimation does not necessarily mean opting for the lesser evil. The Federalists at least face the foreseeable – and perhaps avoidable – risk of the autonomisation of supranational organisations as a challenge. The Eurosceptics have, from the start, acquiesced in the supposedly irresistible erosion of democratic substance so that they do not have to leave what appears as the reliable shelter of the nation-state.

In fact the shelter is becoming increasingly less comfortable. The debates on national economic competitiveness and the international division of labour in which we are engaged make us aware of quite another gap – a gap between the nation state's increasingly limited maneuverability, and the imperatives of modes of production interwoven worldwide. Modern revenue-states profit from their respective economies only so long as there are 'national economies' that can still be influenced by political means. With the denationalisation of the economy, especially of the financial markets and of industrial production itself, national governments today are increasingly compelled to accept permanently high unemployment and the marginalisation of a growing minority for the sake of international competitiveness. If there is to be at least some substantive maintaining of the welfare state and some avoiding the further segmentation of an underclass, then institutions capable of acting supranationally must be formed. Only regionally comprehensive regimes like the European Community can still affect the global system in line with a coordinated world domestic policy.

In Grimm's account, the EU appears as an institution to be *put up with*, and with whose abstractions we must live. The reasons why we should *want* it politically are not presented. I would submit that the greater danger is posed by the autonomisation of globalised networks and markets which simultaneously contribute to the fragmentation of public consciousness. If these systemic pressures are not met by politically capable institutions then the crippling fatalism of the Old Empires will grow again in the midst of a highly mobile economic modernity. The decisive elements of this future scenario would be the postindustrial misery of the 'surplus' population produced by the surplus society – the Third world within the First – and an accompanying moral erosion of community. *This* future-present would in retrospect view itself as the future of a past illusion – the democratic illusion according to which societies could still determine their own destinies through political will and consciousness.

(b) *Apropos* the second problem. Naturally any assessment of the chances for a European-wide democracy depends in the first place upon empirically grounded arguments. But we first have to determine the functional requirements; and for that the normative perspective in which the former are supposed to fit is crucial.

Grimm rejects a European constitution 'because there is as yet no European people'. This would on first glance seem founded upon the same premise that informed the tenor of the German Constitutional Court's Maastricht judgment: namely, the view that the basis of the state's democratic legitimation requires a certain homogeneity of the state-constituting people. However Grimm immediately distances himself from a Schmittian kind of definition of *völkischen* homogeneity: 'The presuppositions for democracy are developed here not of the people, but from the society that wants to constitute itself as a political unit. But this presumes a collective identity, if it wants to settle its conflicts without violence, accept majority rule and practice solidarity.' This formulation leaves open the question of how the called-for collective identity is to be understood. I see the nub of republicanism in the fact that the forms and procedures of the constitutional state together with the democratic mode of legitimation simultaneously forge a new level of social integration. Democratic citizenship establishes an abstract, legally mediated solidarity among strangers. This form of social integration which first emerges with the nation-state is realised in the form of a politically socialising *communicative* context. Indeed this is dependent upon the satisfaction of certain important functional requirements that cannot be fulfilled by administrative means. To these belong conditions in which an ethical political self-understanding of citizens can communicatively develop and likewise be reproduced – but in no way a collective identity that is *independent of the democratic process itself* and as such existing prior to that process. What unites a nation of citizens as opposed to a *Volksnation* is not some primordial substrate but rather an intersubjectively shared context of possible understanding.

It is therefore crucial in this context whether one uses the term 'people', in the juristically neutral sense of 'state-constituting people', or whether one associates the term with notions of identity of some other kind. In Grimm's view the identity of a nation of citizens 'need not' be 'rooted in ethnic origin, but may also have other bases'. I think on the contrary that it *must* have another basis if the democratic process is to finally guarantee the social integration of a differentiated – and today increasingly differentiating – society. This burden must not be shifted from the levels of political will-formation to pre-political, pre-supposed substrates because the constitutional state guarantees that it will foster necessary social integration in the legally abstract form of political participation and that it will actually secure the status of citizenship in democratic ways. The examples of culturally and ideologically pluralistic societies only serve to emphasise this normative point. The multicultural self-understanding of the nations of citizens formed in classical countries of immigration like the USA is more instructive in this respect than that derived from the assimilationist French model. If in the same democratic political community various cultural, religious and ethnic forms of life are to exist among and with each other then the majority culture must be sufficiently detached from its traditional fusion with the political culture shared by all citizens.

To be sure, a politically constituted context of solidarity among citizens who despite remaining strangers to one another are supposed to stand up for each other is a communicative context *rich in prerequisites*. In this point there is no dissent. The core is formed by a political public sphere which enables citizens to take positions at the same time on the same topics of the same relevance. This public sphere must be deformed neither through external nor internal coercion. It must be embedded in the context of a freedom-valuing political culture and be supported by a liberal associational structure of a civil society. Socially relevant experience from still-intact private spheres must flow into such a civil society so that they may be processed there for public treatment. The political parties – not state-dependent – must remain rooted in this complex so as to mediate between the spheres of informal public communication, on the one hand, and the institutionalised deliberation and decision processes, on the other. Accordingly, from a normative perspective, there can be no European Federal state worthy of the name of a democratic Europe unless a European-wide, integrated public sphere develops in the ambit of a common political culture: a civil society with interest associations; nongovernmental organisations; citizens' movements etc.; and naturally a party system appropriate to a European arena. In short, this entails public communication that transcends the boundaries of the until now limited national public spheres.

Certainly, the ambitious functional requirements of democratic will-formation can scarcely be fulfilled in the nation-state framework; this is all the more true for Europe. What concerns me, however, is the perspective from which these functional prerequisites are normatively justified; for this, as it were, prejudices the empirical evaluation of the present difficulties. These must, for the time being, seem insuperable if a pre-political collective identity is regarded as necessary, that is an independent cultural substrate which is *articulated only* in the fulfilment of the said functional requirements. But a communications-theoretical understanding of democracy, one that Grimm also seems to favour, can no longer rest upon such a concretistic understanding of 'the people'. This notion falsely pretends homogeneity, where in fact something still quite heterogeneous is met.

The ethical-political self-understanding of citizens in a democratic community must not be taken as an historical-cultural a *priori* that makes democratic will-formation possible, but rather as the flowing contents of a circulatory process that is generated through the legal institutionalisation of citizens' communication. This is precisely how national identities were formed in modern Europe. Therefore it is to be expected that the political institutions to be created by a European constitution would have an inducing effect. Europe has been integrating economically, socially and administratively for some time and in addition can base itself on a common cultural background and the shared historical experience of having happily overcome nationalism. Given the political will, there is no a priori reason why it cannot subsequently create the politically necessary communicative context as soon as it is constitutionally *prepared* to do so. Even the requirement of a common language – English as a second first language – ought not be an insurmountable obstacle with the existing level of formal schooling. European identity can in any case mean nothing other than unity in national diversity. And perhaps German Federalism, as it developed after Prussia was shattered and the confessional division overcome, might not be the worst model.

■ QUESTION

How can democratic participation best be secured within the EU? Insofar as the EU is a response to the inadequacies of a system based on the nation-State, is it helpful to look to the national level as a model for the future institutional and constitutional development of the EU?

The diminished capacity of the nation-State to provide a 'reliable shelter', to which Habermas refers at p. 609, continues to attract differing views on what could and should be put in its place, or at least what could and should supplement it. Habermas and Grimm themselves continue to be regular sparring partners: for their latest bout see (2015) 21 ELJ 460 and 546. It is not simply a question of the weakening of State power in modern economic and political conditions. Habermas also perceives 'the *democratic illusion* according to which societies could still determine their own destinies through political will and consciousness' (p. 609, emphasis added). In similar vein Christian Joerges asserts that 'nationally organised constitutional states are becoming increasingly incapable of acting democratically. This is because they cannot include all those Europeans who will be affected by their decisions in the electoral processes, and – vice versa – citizens cannot influence the behaviour of those political actors who are taking decisions on their behalf. In other words, we should be prepared to shift our awareness of democracy deficits from the European to the national level of governance' (Joerges, C., 'What is Left of the European Economic Constitution?' (2005) 30 EL Rev 461, 488). This insight is central to imagining what we want 'Europe' to deliver seventy years after the end of the Second World War and more than two decades after the collapse of the Soviet empire. Europe today is built on a multi-level system of governance. In this vein Pernice treats the European Union as a divided power system, and sees 'a progressive constitution of legitimate institutions and powers at the European level, which are complementary to the national constitutions and designed to meet the challenges of an evolving global society' (I. Pernice, 'Multi-level Constitutionalism and the Treaty of Amsterdam: European Constitution-Making Revisited' (1999) 36 CML Rev 703; see also Special Issue on 'The Constitutional Adulthood of Multi-Level Governance', 21 MJ 2 (2014)).

Bohman, J., 'From Demos to Demoi: Democracy across borders' (2005)
18 *Ratio Juris* 293, 312

Should we be optimistic about the potential for democratisation under current conditions of globalization? The world that we live in is now more complex and interdependent and highly uneven than ever with regard to the distribution of power and resources. For the last two centuries from the Chartist movement for universal suffrage forward, democracy has been seen as a means to achieve more justice. Under current conditions, it can do so only if it is organised transnationally, as a democracy of many *demoi* that crosses the borders between them and organises inquiry and deliberation into the conditions for ongoing cooperation and collaborative problem solving.

■ **QUESTION**

How, if at all, does Bohman's notion of democracy organized transnationally fit with the *Bundesverfassungsgericht's* depiction of 'the constitutional and political identity of the fully democratically organised Member States' (para 298 *Lisbon*, p. 596)? Which is the more convincing approach?

This is an unsettlingly ambiguous environment. It envisages arenas for problem-solving (which might involve problem-avoiding) within an overall system which emphasizes the necessary interconnection of national and European constitutional legal orders. In so far as it is an attempt to provide an arena within which national and transnational law and politics can co-exist it is inevitably characterized in Europe by a certain imprecision for, after all, what is at stake is nothing less than a challenge to the hegemony of national constitutional law and the development of a legal order that involves a re-distribution of power. In fact, as already investigated in the context of the interventions of the *Bundesverfassungsgericht*, the system works (for the time being) precisely because each participant can rest its consent to involvement on different bases which may be constitutionally irreconcilable in a purely formal sense but which do not cause any practical need to choose. It would be problematic only if there was some attempt to find the 'correct' answer – that is, to adjudicate who is the winner and who the loser – the either/or question. So 'Multi-level governance' acts as a rather neat shorthand for describing the way in which Europe (and not only Europe) is the subject of many layers of intersecting legal and political authority, some territorially defined, others sectorally defined, not necessarily capable of subjection to a single, internally consistent rule of authority, yet working more or less successfully because of adaptation along the way and the vested interest of participants in avoiding conflict.

SECTION 3: LEGITIMACY AND DEMOCRACY

Multi-level constitutionalism possesses the singular attraction that it frees us from the trap that treats the increase in private economic power in supra-State domains as a basis for shifting extra public power to that same level, which would in turn draw demands for greater institutional accountability to be transplanted to that level, a process which is then seen to impoverish the domestic political sphere. This is a self-defeating prognosis. Instead a multi-level approach argues for the importance of different levels of governance in dealing with the growth of transnational economic activity.

What does this mean from the perspective of *legitimacy*?

A. Menon and S. Weatherill, 'Legitimacy, Accountability and Delegation in the European Union', Ch. 7 in A. Arnull and D. Wincott (eds), *Accountability and Legitimacy in the European Union* (Oxford: OUP, 2002), pp. 115–16, 129–31

LEGITIMACY AND THE EUROPEAN UNION

Fritz Scharpf has drawn a distinction between input and output legitimacy in assessing the European Union. Democratic self-determination, he insists, requires that choices made by the given political system be driven by the authentic preferences of citizens. This suggests a chain of accountability linking those governing to those governed. It is input legitimation, or government by the people. But democratic self-determination also demands that those exercising political power are able to achieve a high degree of effectiveness in meeting the expectations of the governed. The democratic process is, for Scharpf, an 'empty ritual' without such delivery – output legitimacy, or government for the people. Scharpf argues vigorously and persuasively that although the Union is regularly and (to some extent) justifiably criticised for deficiencies in input legitimacy, too little attention is paid to the inadequacies of States when judged from the standpoint of output legitimacy. This tends to breed an inflated assumption of the claim of States to legitimacy. Scharpf's key point is that in at least some policy areas it may be possible to conceive of the EU as capable of legitimation by reference to its output, even if input legitimation is lacking.

In a similar vein, Giandomenico Majone famously describes the EU as a 'regulatory State', drawing attention to the remarkable gulf between the Union (and especially the Community's) extensive rule-making capacity and its negligible administrative infrastructure.[1] Policy-implementation is heavily reliant on the Member States' own legal and administrative agencies. Majone draws normative conclusions. He finds a ready legitimation of the EU through its outputs provided that its activities are confined to securing efficient outcomes. This suggests a temptingly clean-cut model according to which to define the proper limits of regulatory activity 'above' the State. It makes the important claim that legitimation may require assessment in different ways in different policy sectors.

The insights of Scharpf and Majone carry great weight in guiding our understanding of the problems associated with the growth of regulatory activity 'above' the State. They are especially valuable in emphasising the value that is properly attached to output legitimacy. This is especially important in the light of the effect that membership of the EU exerts in confining policy options available to Member States while not recreating equal opportunities for rule-making at transnational level. Under such arrangements, orthodox assumptions about securing input legitimacy for decisions by public bodies are undermined. A response based on reversion to unilateral, bilateral or ad hoc multilateral State action will be confronted by limitations in achieving effective problem-solving. A response based on re-creating State structures at transnational level, in order to re-locate sites of input legitimacy, raises all manner of awkward problems associated with the disinclination of citizens simply to shift their sense of allegiance. As Fritz Scharpf puts it:

> Given the historical, linguistic, cultural, ethnic and institutional diversity of its member states, there is no question that the Union is very far from having achieved the 'thick' collective identity that we have come to take for granted in national democracies – and in its absence, institutional reforms will not greatly increase the input-oriented legitimacy of decisions taken by majority rule.[2]

---

1 *Regulating Europe* (London, Routledge, 1996).

2 F. Scharpf *Governing in Europe: Effective and Democratic*? (Oxford, OUP 1998), p.9.

Consequently, input legitimacy must be seen as one important element in assessing the legitimacy of the European Union, but it should be assessed in combination with an unavoidable appreciation of the virtues of output legitimacy. It is in the very nature of the Union that it invites such nuanced examination. And it is therefore quite proper to identify a road to legitimacy paved by the ability of the Union to deliver responses to problems that would be insoluble or even simply less effectively solved by individual States. . . .

CONCLUSION

. . . The 'problem with States' is not merely that they may be incapable of effective problem-solving. The rise of transnational economies also tends to accentuate the extent to which State decisions may be driven by the orthodox pressures of national-level representative democracy and yet impose costs on actors who are intimately affected by those decisions yet who are not represented or only inadequately represented in the State's political processes. The juxtaposition of State political decision-making and burgeoning transnational economic activity allows or even induces States to externalise costs and a method is required for reducing, if not eliminating, the ability of the State to take decisions which are neglectful of costs imposed on parties who are not able to gain (adequate) access to the (domestic) market for votes. A supranational legal order is capable of achieving this, and exploration of its legitimacy should encompass respect for this capacity.

Assessing problems of legitimacy by extending emphasis on European-level governance can always be criticised for its illegitimacy by those who assume the pre-eminence of national-level political structures. It is the specious but primitively compelling 'loss of sovereignty' argument, but such debates cannot sensibly be conducted pending liberation from (frequently unwitting) preconceptions about sites of legitimacy. So solutions must be pragmatic, incremental and cautious. They must identify the different strands of legitimacy and be aware that tweaking one tweaks all. A starting point might have been that output legitimacy is a Union strength while input legitimacy is a State strength but in fact the interconnections are decidedly more sophisticated than such a model will allow. The least ambitious case made by this paper is that it is wrong to make assumptions about which element to privilege. The more ambitious, and as yet relatively tentative, claim is that we can have it all – provided that all elements are cherished and treated as mutually reinforcing aspects of a broad and multi-level conception of European constitutionalism.[3] That is, a legitimacy test insisting on both input and output legitimacy may be failed both by States and the EU, though in respect of different criteria and/or by different degrees, but taken together, the combination passes. In so far as this represents the essence of transnational governance, it should be seen as a necessarily dynamic and creative process.

There is not the space here to draw out fully the implications of this analysis. One important, though by no means the only such issue concerns the appropriate scope of EU action. Both Majone and Scharpf argue that the EU should remain somewhat restricted in scope because of the necessary 'strong' (input) legitimation that must underpin many areas of public policy and which the EC lacks.[4] Such preferences should be expressed, if at all, only by Member States. Yet at a time when the EU is embarking on its experiment with a single currency, such arguments seem curiously anachronistic. It may well be that the Union is confronted with the stark choice between on the one hand risking its potential to deliver effective outputs by controlling monetary policy in the euro zone without an effective fiscal policy to redress regional disparities and, on the other, venturing into larger scale redistributive policies that surpass its capacity to muster input legitimacy. There are no easy solutions to such dilemmas. The most that we can hope to have achieved here is to suggest that by looking at the structure of the multilevel European constitutional system as a whole, rather than performing misleading 'legitimacy tests' based on standards developed for nation states upon the EU alone, we may have suggested a more appropriate and effective way of beginning the task of thinking about the legitimacy of the Union.

NOTE: The reader is invited to add these arguments to reflection on the suggestion advanced by Hauser and Müller that 'Reforms to either better restrict EU competences or to develop democratic EU institutions are proposals to ease the underlying tensions' (p. 607), and to re-visit both the vista presented by the *Laeken Declaration* (p. 14) and the eventually agreed shape of the system after the entry into force of the Lisbon Treaty (p. 19). There is also ample scope for reconsidering the extensive use made by the Court of the free movement provisions in testing national laws and practices. Is legitimacy achievable in Europe? And what of democracy?

---

3 Similarly Maduro [extract, p. 599].

4 Scharpf talks of the need for EU policies to satisfy the conditions of low visibility and being confl ict minimising, whilst Majone insists on the need for the Union to steer clear of redistributive policies. Fritz Scharpf, *Governing in Europe*, pp. 21–25; G. Majone, *Regulating Europe* (London, Routledge, 1996).

T. Kostakopoulou, 'Democracy-talk in the European Union: the Need for a Reflexive Approach'

(2003) 9(3) *Columbia Journal of European Law* 411

(Some footnotes omitted.)

III. THE CENTRALITY OF ANTINOMIC CO-OPERATION IN EUROPEAN GOVERNANCE

The European Union is a complex and unique edifice. Good theorising about democracy in the European Union needs to address its distinctive features. For example, the Community's founding Treaties (ECSC, Euratom and EEC) do not represent the crystallisation of a unified and homogeneous constituent political will. Although the Community has its origins in international law, the founding of a 'Community', that is, the inauguration of a framework of co-operation among states and peoples, did not represent a way of 'doing that it comes naturally'. Its architects took 'a leap in the dark'[32] and proposed a framework for integration that transcended the traditional framework of interdependence.

Anchored in the memory of war, the urgent need for post-war economic reconstruction, and against a background of popular movements championing federalist ideas, the European Community, in its early days, represented the organisation of industrial sector communities setting up integration in limited, but vital, economic fields (i.e., coal and steel). The avowed objectives of the founders of the European Coal and Steel Community[33] included the prospect of a 'European federation'. The political dimensions of the integrationist framework featured in the Schuman Plan (1950): closer co operation between France and Germany would furnish a 'broader and deeper community among peoples long divided by bloody conflicts'.[34] Ensuring peace and prosperity in Europe through a supranationalist experiment with no historical precedent has been a 'master ideal' of the Community,[36] alongside ensuring undistorted competition in a barrier-free market, raising the standard of living, promoting social cohesion and so on.

Although European integration is oriented to the realisation of these ideals,[37] the Community lacks a set of generalised shared beliefs concerning how to go about realising these ideals, a clear conception of its development and the scope of its competences, a settled constitutional structure and so on. The Treaties make no reference to a shared political end, the ultimate telos of European integration. Questions about the nature and the end of European integration and the role and future of the state are thus the primary source of disagreement. Europe is a contested polity.[38]

In this contested polity of crosscutting levels of decision-making, Community law does not reflect the consensus of competing constituencies. Instead, it delineates an evolving and ambiguous system of relationships. Both the incremental development of the human rights policy and the evolving constitutional framework in relation to the vertical division of powers attest to this. This rules out the application of a Rawlsian approach to the EU whereby we would have to assume that the European legislative process does not involve fundamental disagreements about matters of principle, for these have been settled at an earlier stage.[39] Nor can it be argued that an agreement about the norms of deliberation is what binds the Community together. Moments of crisis in the European integration process, such as the failure of the European Defence Community or the Empty Chair Crisis in 1965 highlight the fact that the norms of deliberation themselves can be the subject of much contention thereby leading to a renegotiation of the rules of the game.

If I am correct on this, then the European Community cannot be analysed as a community like any other. Its operation disproves Hayek's argument that democracy can only work in the long run if the great majority has in

32 J. Monnet, *Memoirs* (Collins, 1978), 305.

33 ECSC [18 April 1951] 25 July 1952.

34 See the preamble to the Treaty of Paris, 18 April 1951.

36 The term is borrowed from Philip Selznick, 'Sociology and Natural Law', (1961) *Natural Law Forum* pp. 84–108. For a critical discussion of the ideals of the Community, see J. Weiler, 'Fin de Siecle Europe', in R. Dehousse (ed.), *Europe After Maastricht: An Ever Closer Union* (Beck, 1994), pp. 203–216.

37 One could see the 'master ideals' of the Community as signposts or road maps. On this, see Z. Bankowski and E. Christodoulidis, 'The European Union as an Essentially Contested Project', (1998) 4(4) *European Law Journal* pp. 341–354 at p. 342. On the member states' divergent preferences over the institutional structure of the Coal and Steel Community, see B. Rittberger, 'Which Institutions for Europe? Explaining the Birth of a Unique Institutional Structure', Paper presented at the ECSA *7th Biennial International Conference*, May 31-June 2, Madison, USA. Weiler argues that the European Union suffers from a 'crisis of ideals'; Weiler, *The Constitution of Europe, op. cit.*, 238–245, 259–262.

38 Z. Bankowski and E. Christodoulidis, 'The European Union as an Essentially Contested Project'; T. Banchoff and M. P. Smith (eds.), *Legitimacy and the European Union: the contested polity* (Routledge, 1999).

39 For a critique, see J. Waldron, *The Dignity of Legislation* (Cambridge University Press, 1999), 71.

common at least a general conception of the type of society desired.[40] The master ideals of the Community form a 'fuzzy' presuppositional framework within which the actors declare their willingness to engage in a process of devising the rules and terms of their interaction without presupposing commonalities, common interests, shared beliefs about the common good and shared dispositions. The European Community is not a complete, homogeneous and unified body governed by a set of closed, coherent and definite rules. Although Monnet was correct to state that the union of Europe cannot be based on goodwill alone and that nothing lasts without institutions,[41] it is interesting that both the scope and nature of these rules continue to be the subject of debate. For example, national constitutional courts have not unconditionally accepted the principle of the supremacy of the Community law.[42] The debates concerning the meaning and justiciability of the principle of subsidiarity in post-Maastricht Europe and on the meaning and implications of flexibility in post-Amsterdam Europe also confirm this.[43] The grammar of the Community legal order thus remains incomplete, contested and unsettled.

The European Court of Justice has made a vital contribution to furnishing the basic tenets of this grammar. In *Van Gend Loos* it pronounced that the Community constitutes a new legal order of international law, and subsequently it held that the Treaty constitutes the constitutional charter of a Community based on the rule of law.[44] The ECJ has also adjudicated the numerous inter-institutional conflicts and helped delineate the powers and prerogatives of the institutions on the basis of the principle of institutional balance. In the *Isoglucose* cases, the Court established the European Parliament's participation in the legislative process through consultation,[45] and in the *Chernobyl* case[46] it gave the EP standing to challenge the acts of the other institutions under Article 230 EC in order to protect its prerogatives, thereby reversing its earlier position.[47] All this disproves the argument that democratic politics can be deeply satisfactory only to the extent that fairly clear normative standards are accepted by the participants at the outset, just as overarching rules are required to enjoy playing games.[48]

Additionally, unlike modern liberal communities, the Community is neither a community of shared ends nor a community of destiny.[49] European integration is a process and an adventure. It is akin to a conversation that evolves endlessly as the parties engage in a collective quest for community. And although the conversation does not mean the same thing for everyone at the same time, since domestic constraints inform state preferences and shape the various interpretations of the European output, it is, nevertheless, shared. As Preuss has put it, 'the dynamic character and the openness of the European Union require a constitutional framework which does not fix boundaries to the evolution and self-transformation of the Union – boundaries of objectives and of competences – but provides appropriate institutional schemes with the help of which the deliberations about the next step of the political transformation can be performed and the changes, if considered necessary and desirable, can be accomplished'.[50] The ongoing and open-ended European conversation,[51] however, has to be conducted within the context of a culturally heterogeneous political community that is open to disagreements, to critique, to new ideas and cultural collisions.

It is true that strong disagreements and dissent often put pressure on the delicate institutional balances of the Community, and conflicts on the policies of the EU often take the form of conflicts on the EU itself in national

40 F. Hayek, *The Constitution of Liberty* (Routledge and Kegan Paul, 1960).

41 Jean Monnet, *Memoirs, op. cit.*

42 See Case 11/70, *Internationale Handelsgesellshaft mbH* v *Einfuhr* [1970] ECR 1125, [1972] CMLR 255; *Internationale Handelsgesellshaft mbH* v *Einfuhr* [1972] CMLR 177; *Raul Georges Nicolo* [1990] 1 CMLR 173; *Brunner* v *The European Union Treaty* [1994] 1 CMLR 57; *Frontini* v *Ministero delle Finanze* [1974] 2 CMLR 372.

43 On subsidiarity, see A. G. Toth, 'A Legal Analysis of Subsidiarity', in D. O'Keeffe and P. Twomey (eds), *Legal Issues of the Maastricht Treaty* (Wiley, 1994); J. Steiner, 'Subsidiarity under the Maastricht Treaty', in *Legal Issues of the Maastricht Treaty*; N. Emiliou, 'Subsidiarity: An Effective Barrier Against the "Enterprises of Ambition"?', in *Legal Issues of the Maastricht Treaty.* On flexibility, see C. D. Ehlermann, *Differentiation, Flexibility, Closer Co-operation: The New Provisions of the Amsterdam Treaty* (European University Institute, 1998); J. Shaw, 'The Treaty of Amsterdam: Challenges of Flexibility and Legitimacy', (1998) 4(1) *European Law Journal* pp. 63–86; N. Walker, 'Theoretical Reflections on Flexibility and Europe's Future', in G. de Burca and J. Scott (eds), *Constitutional Change in the EU: From Uniformity to Flexibility*? (Hart Publishing, 2000).

44 Case 26/62 *Van Gend Loos* [1963] ECR 1, [1963] CMLR 105; Case 294/83 *Parti Ecologiste 'Les Verts'* v *European Parliament* [1986] ECR 1339, [1987] 2 CMLR 343; Opinion 1/91 [1991] (Draft Treaty on a European Economic Area) ECR I-6079, [1992] 1 CMLR 245.

45 Case 138/79 *Roquette Freres* v *Council* [1980] ECR 3333; Case 139/79 *Maizena* v *Council* [1980] ECR 3393.

46 C-70/88 *European Parliament* v *Council* (Chernobyl) [1990] ECR I-2041.

47 Case 302/87 *European Parliament* v *Council* [1988] ECR 5616.

48 See J. Elster, 1986.

49 P. Howe, 'A Community of Europeans: The Requisite Underpinnings', (1995) 33(1) *Journal of Common Market Studies* pp. 27–46; 'Insiders and Outsiders in a Community of Europeans: A Reply to Kostakopoulou', (1997) 35(2) *Journal of Common Market Studies* pp. 309–14.

50 U. Preuss, 'The Constitution of a European Democracy and the Role of the Nation-State', (1999) 12(4) *Ratio Juris* pp. 417–28, at p. 427.

51 J. Shaw, 'Postnational Constitutionalism in the European Union', (1999) 6(4) *Journal of European Public Policy* pp. 579–97.

arenas. Intergovernmental reflexes have also exercised a strong hold on the trend towards supranationalism in the 1990s. In addition, the forthcoming enlargement is bound to accentuate pressures for differentiated and asymmetrical solutions. But at the same time, however, the constituent units demonstrate a deep commitment to continued co-operation and to the joint creation of common, albeit contested, institutional realities. The absence of either some kind of consensus over the final shape of the Union, or an agreement over a common set of determinate values[52] is counterbalanced by a strong commitment on behalf of the constituent units to co-operation, in the sense that 'we are all in this together and we will collectively shape this process by designing appropriate institutions and common rules'.[53] The European political community is a community of concern and engagement.[54] It is perhaps the member states' awareness of the indispensability of their involvement in the European collective adventure – and not their conviction that 'Europe' will produce answers or solutions on which all will agree,[55] that leads them to comply with even those European norms that conflict with conventional understandings and settled traditions in domestic arenas.

The delicate balance between co-operation and antinomy (antinomic co-operation) can be seen in the following table, which outlines the prospects for democratic governance.

Cooperation ⇒ Antinomy ⇓	Intensive	Relaxed
Weak	Low	Low
Strong	Low	High

The opportunities for democratic governance are higher when co-operation is relaxed and antinomy is strong. Too much emphasis on co-operation will lead to the obliteration of antinomy and will thus undermine the maintenance of a democratic community. On the other hand, enhanced voice must be accompanied with the awareness that the parties have embarked upon a common journey or a common quest for understanding and the design of institutions that accommodate conflicting interests and meet common as well as distinct needs – rather than for a 'common weal' or a common good'. It is precisely this awareness that binds the units together and makes outside options unappealing. In sum, the art of European association requires antinomic co-operation.

A prominent and rather permanent feature of the incipient political culture of the EU is the politics of 'becoming'. Unlike its constituent units, the member states, the European Community is a community of multifarious minorities whose perspectives, interests and opinions are equally legitimate. The process of collective collaboration of diverse political communities cannot but induce fundamental changes and facilitate an awareness of both the contestability and relativity of their own positions, assumptions and beliefs. For the same reason, European institutions are characterised by conditionality and reflexivity; they recognise their cognitive and coercive limits, seek to accommodate multiple and often contending visions even within a single provision or a legislative instrument and, more importantly, their output is open to review and renegotiation. Contestation is thus as much as a discursive process as an institutional fact. Disagreements and conflicts do not have a fleeting quality; they do not evaporate when Treaty amendments are agreed or secondary legislation is published in the Official Journal. Rather, they continue as much as after deliberation as during and before it. And European Community law serves as a surface for the inscription of disagreement and strife as well as a medium for the (co-ordinated) management and maintenance of dissent and antinomy. But this does not make the European Community democratically

52 P. Lehning, 'European Citizenship: A Mirage?', in P. Lehning and A. Weale (eds), *Citizenship, Democracy and Justice in the New Europe* (Routledge, 1997), 175–99. But compare Siedentop's argument for the need of a 'moral con- sensus' or a common 'culture of consent' in the European Union.

53 T. Kostakopoulou, 'Towards a Theory of Constructive Citizenship in Europe', (1996) 4(4) *Journal of Political Philosophy* pp. 337–358.

54 T. Kostakopoulou, *Citizenship, Identity and Immigration in the European Union: Between Past and Future* (Manchester University Press, 2001).

55 Walker has argued that the present pattern of differentiated integration has evolved as a result of a series of strategic compromises and gambits, of policy-driven sectoral initiatives, and of accommodations of new geopolitical forces; N. Walker, 'Sovereignty and Differentiated Integration in the European Union, (1998) 4(4) *European Law Journal* pp. 355–388, at p. 374.

unstable or disorderly. On the contrary, it makes it precisely what it is; namely, a community of antinomic co-operation and a site for reflexive governance.

V. CONCLUSION

If we are to take the task of democratising the European Union seriously, be it in the sense of strengthening recent institutional reforms, or perfecting and deepening democracy in certain areas, or making the transition to democracy in other areas, then we need to reflect on the models of democracy we use in order to theorise and measure democracy at the European level. Quite often lens-shaped problems either create an 'apparent democratic deficit effect' or magnify or even conceal crucial deficiencies of democracy in institutional design and practice. The main rationale of this paper has been to show that the European democracy question cannot be addressed adequately without first addressing the suitability of existing models of national democracy for the European polity in formation, and perhaps without radically transforming these models. Premised on the ideals of consensus and stability such models are ill equipped to capture the process of the formation of a community at the European level in which there are strong disagreements about the type of community desired and its scope, divergent interpretations of civic values, an incomplete legal grammar and contested rules. The European political community has been created and is being sustained through practices of antinomic co-operation. Such practices of antinomic co-operation presuppose neither the presence of a constituent European people, nor the existence of a relatively stable background of settled cultural-cum-political norms. Although it has long been assumed that the latter are necessary conditions of democracy, the process of European integration has shown that democratic processes and institutional design do not need consensus, be it over a set of meanings, or a set of principles or the rules of the game, in order to advance.

But they do need a more serious effort on the part of European institutional actors to engage critically with the national-statist frames of reference they use, to reflect seriously on the models of democracy they employ at the European setting and their tensions, competing demands and incoherences, and to direct their focus towards the search for avenues for democratisation in the EU, rather than insisting on a particular notion of democracy or blending several notions of it.

Essential as they are, solving the 'paradox of democracy' and shifting the focus from the inherited models of democracy to democratisation are not the only relevant criteria for devising a complex model of democracy beyond the nation-state. Ensuring fairness in representation, rethinking the model of representative democracy itself, introducing mechanisms to improve the responsiveness of the system, searching for institutional devices that improve the citizens' inclusion in the policy process, including their ability to initiate legislation and Europe-wide referenda, are equally important. Nothing I have said in this paper should be taken to imply that the search for a postnational model of democracy that is suited to the evolving European experimental community is an easy task.[76] However, it seems to me that two ingredients are necessary for any significant advance. First, we need to identify problems, to understand the bias of our frames, to search for solutions beyond the confines of existing models of national democracy and to be more imaginative in the design of mechanisms to control political power and to enhance citizen participation. Secondly, it would be wise to abandon the logic of the 'eclipsing binaries' of the EU and the state, and to embrace the democratisation of institutions and sociopolitical life both vertically, that is, at all levels of governance, and horizontally.

Moravcsik, A., 'The European Constitutional Compromise and the Neofunctionalist Legacy' (2005) 12(2) *Journal of European Public Policy* 349, 376

The multi-level governance system of the EU is the only distinctively new form of state organisation to emerge and prosper since the rise of the democratic social welfare state at the turn of the twentieth century. Recent events suggest that it may now have reached, through a characteristically incremental process, a stable political equilibrium. This 'constitutional compromise' is unlikely to be upset by major functional challenges, autonomous institutional evolution, or demands for democratic accountability. There is, moreover, an undeniable normative attraction to a system that preserves national democratic politics for those issues most salient in the minds of citizens, but delegates to more indirect democratic forms those issues that are of less concern, or on which there is an administrative or legal consensus. Contrary to what Haas and Monnet believed, the EU does not (or no longer

76 See E. Grande, 'Postnational Democracy in Europe', in M. T. Greven and L. W. Pauly (eds), Democracy Beyond the Nation-State (Rowman and Littlefield, 2000).

needs to) move forward to consolidate its current benefits. This is good news for those who admire the European project. When a constitutional system no longer needs to expand and deepen in order to assure its own continued existence, it is truly stable. It is a mark of constitutional maturity.

■ **QUESTION**

To what extent are the 'two ingredients' identified by Kostakopoulou at the end of the extract visible in the reforms made by, and the process leading to the ratification of, the Treaty of Lisbon (p. 19)? Does the diagnosis of constitutional maturity offered by Moravcsik in 2005 still appear persuasive today?

Menéndez, A.J., 'The European Democratic Challenge: the Forging of a Supranational Volonté Générale'
(2009) 15 ELJ 277, 308

On the one hand, the Laeken Treaty amendment process was framed as an exercise in revolutionary constitution making, which revealed itself as too much to swallow in one shot. In the absence of stable channels of cross-European political communication, and of a genuine proposal of constitutional change, any process which presents itself as 'constitutional' is bound to fail. On the other hand, Lisbon was presented as a grand diplomatic bargain. But European leaders were oblivious to the fact that the Laeken Treaty amendment process was a ratification failure that revealed to all Europeans the constitutional nature of the Union. As a result, we are well beyond the point at which citizens will tolerate an enlightened constitutionalism that excludes them. What the EU urgently needed was thus an intermediate step in constitutional clarification, which would have rendered explicit how the Union was *constituted*, and would have facilitated the later articulation of an agenda of constitutional reform. It seems to me that the Charter of Fundamental Rights held much promise as a vehicle of constitution making. But it may well be that the EU has missed its last constitutional train, and that only a political act of refoundation led by the Members of Euroland could rescue the Union.

FURTHER READING ON THE DEBATE ABOUT LEGITIMACY, DEMOCRACY, AND CONSTITUTIONS

Special Issue on Constructing Legal Systems: ' "European Union" in Legal Theory' (1997) 163/4 Law and Philosophy.

Avbelj, M., 'Questioning EU Constitutionalisms' (2008) 9 German Law Journal 1.

Eleftheriadis, P., 'The Idea of a European Constitution' (2007) 27 OxJLS 1.

Krisch, N., 'Europe's Constitutional Monstrosity' (2005) 25 OxJLS 321.

Nicolaïdis, K., 'European Democracy and its Crisis' (2013) 51 JCMS 359.

Poiares Maduro, M., 'The Importance of Being Called a Constitution: Constitutional Authority and the Authority of Constitutionalism' (2005) 3 Int J Constitutional Law 332.

Shaw, J., 'Postnational Constitutionalism in the European Union' (1999) 6 JEPP 579.

Somek, A., 'Delegation and Authority: Authoritarian Liberalism Today' (2015) 21 ELJ 340.

Von Bogdandy, A., 'Pluralism, direct effect and the ultimate say: on the relationship between international and domestic constitutional law' (2008) 6 Intl J Constitutional Law 397.

Walker, N., 'Europe's Constitutional Engagement' (2005) 18 Ratio Juris 387.

The several electronic sources provided in Chapter 1 (p. 22) are likely to offer up-to-date reflection.

■ **QUESTION**

'. . . the EU illustrates the spirit of a contemporary constitutionalism which sees conflict on the basis of rules as a source of civic education and legitimation. The Union does not limit its participants to reflecting on the normative basis of a given political order. Instead, it demonstrates how a constitution can both frame democratic deliberation and be the object of it' (Lord, C. and Magnette, P., 'E Pluribus Unum? Creative Disagreement about Legitimacy in the EU' (2004) 42 JCMS 183, 199). Is this convincing? Why isn't the EU more popular?

SECTION 4: EUROPE'S TRUE SOUL

And where is 'Europe's true soul'? The next and final extract finds it in the principle of 'constitutional tolerance'.

J. Weiler, 'The Function and Future of European Law' in V. Heiskanen and K. Kulovesi (eds), *Function and Future of European Law* (Helsinki, 1999), pp. 12–16

There are, it seems to me, two basic human strategies of dealing with the alien and these two strategies have played a decisive role in Western civilisation. One strategy is to remove the boundaries. It is the spirit of 'come, be one of us'. It is noble since it involves, of course, elimination of prejudice, of the notion that there are boundaries that cannot be eradicated. But the 'be one of us,' however well intentioned, is often an invitation to the alien to be one of us, by being us. *Vis-à-vis* the alien, it risks robbing him of his identity. *Vis-à-vis* one's self, it may be a subtle manifestation of intolerance. If I cannot tolerate the alien, one way of resolving the dilemma is to make him like me, no longer an alien. This is, of course, infinitely better than the physical annihilation. But it is still a form of dangerous internal and external intolerance.

The alternative strategy is to acknowledge the validity of certain forms of bounded identity but simultaneously to reach across boundaries. We acknowledge and respect difference (and what is special and unique about ourselves as individuals and groups) and yet we reach across differences in recognition of our essential humanity. I never tire of referring to Hermann Cohen (1842–1918), the great neo-Kantian philosopher of religion, in an exquisite modern interpretation of the Mosaic law on this subject which captures its deep meaning in a way which retains its vitality even in today's ever closer union. It can be summarised as follows: The law of shielding the alien from all wrong is of vital significance. The alien was to be protected, not because he was a member of one's family, clan, religious community or people; but because he was a human being. In the alien, therefore, man discovered the idea of humanity. What is significant in this are the two elements I have mentioned. On the one hand, the identity of the alien, as such, is maintained. One is not invited to go out and, for example, 'save him' by inviting him to be one of you. One is not invited to recast the boundary. On the other hand, despite the boundaries which are maintained, and constitute the I and the Alien, one is commanded to reach over the boundary and love him, in his alienship, as oneself. The alien is accorded human dignity. The soul of the I is tended to not by eliminating the temptation to oppress but by maintaining it and overcoming it.

Europe represents this alternative, civilising strategy of dealing with the 'other'. This is, more than peace and prosperity, Europe's true soul. The constitutional expression of this strategy is the principle of Constitutional Tolerance and it is encapsulated in that most basic articulation of its meta-political objective in the Preamble of the EC Treaty:

> Determined to lay the foundations of an ever closer union among the peoples of Europe.

No matter how close the Union, it is to remain among distinct peoples. An ever closer union could be achieved by an amalgam of distinct peoples into one nation – which is both the ideal and/or the de facto experience of most federal and non federal states. The rejection by Europe of that one nation ideal, or destiny, is usually understood as intended to preserve the rich diversity – cultural and other – of the distinct European peoples as well as to respect their political self-determination. But 'the European choice' has an even deeper spiritual meaning.

An ever closer union is altogether more easy if differences among the components are eliminated, if they come to resemble each other, if they aspire to become one. The more identical the 'Other's' identity is to my own, the easier it is for me to identify with him and accept him. It demands less of me to accept another if he is very much like me. It is altogether more difficult to attain an ever closer Union if the components of that Union preserve their distinct identities, if they retain their 'otherness' vis-à-vis each other, if they do not become 'one flesh,' politically speaking.

Herein resides the principle of Constitutional Tolerance. Inevitably I define my distinct identity by a boundary which differentiates me from those who are unlike me. My continued existence as a distinct identity depends, ontologically, on that boundary and, psychologically and sociologically, on preserving that sentiment of otherness. The call to bond with those very others in an ever closer union demands an internalisation (individual and societal) of a very high degree of toleration. The Leviticus imperative to love thy neighbour as oneself is so difficult and hence civilising because that neighbour is not like myself. Living the Kantian categorical imperative is most meaningful when it is extended to those who are unlike me.

It is in legal terms that the principle of Constitutional Tolerance finds its deepest and most remarkable expression. The European *Courts* of Justice – in Luxembourg and the various Member States – have enjoined us to accept European law as the supreme law of the land. This, despite the fact that at face value this law defies the normal premise of democracy. Normally in democracy, we demand democratic discipline, i.e., accepting the authority of the majority over the minority only within a polity which understands itself as being constituted of one people, however defined. A majority demanding obedience from a minority which does not regard itself as belonging to the same people is usually regarded as subjugation. And yet, in the Community, through the doctrines of direct effect and supremacy we subject the European peoples to the discipline of democracy even though the European polity is composed of distinct peoples. It is a remarkable instance of Constitutional Tolerance to accept to be bound of course, infinitely, better than the physical annihilation. But it is still a form of dangerous internal and external intolerance. The alternative strategy is to acknowledge the validity of certain forms of bounded identity but simultaneously by a decision not by 'my people' but by a majority among peoples which are precisely not mine – a people, if you wish, of 'others'. I compromise my self-determination in this fashion as an expression of this kind of internal (towards myself) and external (towards others) Constitutional Tolerance.

However – and there is a big 'however' at this point. This, the Union's most fundamental principle, that of Constitutional Tolerance, becomes a travesty if the norms I follow, if the democratic discipline I obey is not adopted by others, my fellow European citizens, with whom I do not share the bonds of peoplehood but instead the bonds of a community of values and a new civic and political culture of transnational tolerance, but by a technocratic bureaucracy over which I have little control – presided over in the unreachable supranational Olympus of the European Council (and even European Parliament) and within the infranational netherworld of comitology. A non-democratic Europe extinguishes the principle of Constitutional Tolerance just as a statal or a one nation Europe would.

And that exactly is the weakness of the European Court of Justice ('ECJ') and some of its national counterparts. Their scant regard for, and weak sensibility to, the democratic processes by which the norms of which they demand supreme loyalty are enacted. It was evident in the Court's historic decisions such as *Van Gend en Loos* [see Chapter 3] where the Court said:

> The objective of the EEC Treaty, which is to establish a Common Market, the functioning of which is of direct concern to interested parties in the Community, implies that this Treaty is more than an agreement which merely creates mutual obligations between the contracting states. This view is confirmed by the preamble to the Treaty which refers not only to governments but to peoples. It is also confirmed more specifically by the establishment of institutions endowed with sovereign rights, the exercise of which affects Member States and also their citizens. *Furthermore, it must be noted that the nationals of the states brought together in the Community are called upon to cooperate in the functioning of this Community through the intermediary of the European Parliament and the Economic and Social Committee'* (Recital 10, emphasis added)

There is something deeply unsettling to present the European Parliament and the Economic and Social Committee as a chamber that can be said to express a meaningful democratic notion of citizen cooperation in governance and justify rendering laws coming out of the Community process an obligatory nature binding upon States and individuals:

> Independently of the legislation of Member States. (Recital 12)

This original sin of the Court and its acceptance by national jurisdictions may have been justified at the time when the international legal nature of the Community was strong and ratification of the EC Treaty in national parliaments could have been considered as an effective means for democratic legitimacy. But in today's incredibly complex and wide ranging Community when national ratification after each Inter-Governmental Conference ('IGC') is an impossible take-it-or-leave-it pact, reminiscent of the worst plebiscites in authoritarian regimes and nothing more than a formal act rather than a civic exercise of democracy, the continued indifference of the Court to the weak democratic basis of many of the norms which it upholds – notably in those coming out of the comitology process is more than unsettling – it is an act of Constitutional abdication.

The late Judge Mancini was right [see Vol. 4 ELJ (1998)]: The Court assumes that – respectable democracy – which is not there.

NOTE: And where next? And how? The phrase 'ever closer Union' to which Weiler refers was omitted from the Preamble to the Treaty establishing a Constitution for Europe, but after that text's demise and the switch to the Treaty of Lisbon the phrase remains unscathed in the Preamble to both TEU and TFEU. The significance of the principle of Constitutional Tolerance is enduring. So too are Weiler's reservations about 'respectable democracy'.

This is plainly an enormous debate. It is of the most profound importance. If this chapter in particular, and this book in general, has left you with the impression that if only someone can put their hands on the 'right answer' then the mysteries of European integration can be resolved in a simple Treaty text, then the author has failed miserably in his endeavours and offers humble apologies. European integration is an evolving process with no defined end in view.

■ QUESTIONS

1. '. . . [S]tates in the European Union are being melded gently into a multilevel polity by their leaders and by the actions of numerous subnational and supranational actors. State-centric theorists are right when they argue that states are extremely powerful institutions that are capable of crushing direct threats to their existence. The organizational form of the state emerged because it proved a particularly effective means of systematically wielding violence, and it is difficult to imagine any generalized challenge along these lines. But this is not the only, nor even the most important, issue facing the institution of the state. One does not have to argue that states are on the verge of political extinction to believe that their control of those living in their territories has significantly weakened' (L. Hooghe and G. Marks, 'Contending Models of Governance in the European Union', in A. Cafruny and C. Lankowski (eds), *Europe's Ambiguous Unity: Conflict and Consensus in the Post-Maastricht Era* (Boulder: Rienner, 1997), Ch. 1, p. 38).

   Assess the contribution of the European Union (i) to the weakening of State power and (ii) to offering a secure basis for subjecting power dispersed from States to transnational actors and markets to effective and democratically legitimate supervision.

2. '. . . it could be argued that an ideal democracy, as conceived by accepted standards, is neither a purely popular democracy nor a purely constitutionalist one [that is, one in which majoritarianism is confined by e.g., a Bill of Rights, judicial control, territorial or functional devolution], but rather a system able to realize a satisfactory equilibrium between the two . . . to conform to the principles at the basis of its constitution, any ideal democracy should seek to balance one element with the other, taking great care that none of the components offsets the other. If this analysis is correct, it can be argued that the growing dissatisfaction with democracy, particularly in Europe, is the result of the continuing expansion of the constitutional pillar to the detriment of the popular one. Democratic citizens have the feeling that their votes matter less and less' (Y. Mény, 'De la démocratie en Europe: Old Concepts and New Challenges' (2002) 41 JCMS 1). Is this accurate? If so, what can be done?

NOTE: For additional material and resources see the Online Resource Centre at: www.oxfordtextbooks.co.uk/orc/weatherill12e

FINAL QUESTIONS

1. 'E[U] law represents, more evidently perhaps than most other academic subjects, an intricate web of politics, economics and law. It virtually calls out to be understood by means of a political economy of law or from an interdisciplinary, contextual or critical approach. Nevertheless, it has often been regarded. . .simply as a highly technical set of rules, a dense doctrinal thicket where only the ignorant or the foolish would jump in and scratch out their eyes. . .' (F. Snyder, *New Directions in European Community Law* (London: Weidenfeld and Nicolson, 1990) p. 9.) Discuss.
2. '. . . [T]here are two vital differences between the formal structure of traditional international law and that of European [Union] law. These differences represent a particularly strong limitation upon State sovereignty and justify the common description of the [Union] as "supranational" rather than an international entity. First, even viewed from the limited perspective of the traditional subjects of international law – the sovereign Member States – the formal structure of European [Union] law displays those features that characterize a well-developed legal system as opposed to a simple set of primary rules. Second, [Union] law and the [Union] legal system penetrate deeply and pervasively into the Member States. This penetration is manifested in particular by the direct and indirect modification of the legal position of individuals – the traditional subjects of municipal law.' (M. Jones, 'The Legal Nature of the European Community: A Jurisprudential Analysis using H.L.A. Hart's Model of Law and a Legal System' (1984) 17 *Cornell International Law Journal* 1, 15–16.) Discuss.
3. 'There is no motivation for European unification that is surpassed by the desire for peace.' Discuss.

SELECTED BIBLIOGRAPHY

This bibliography is by no means exhaustive. However, in it the student should find enough sources to assist in deeper exploration of EU law. Books published before the entry into force of the Lisbon Treaty in December 2009 are retained here where they have value as explorations of broad themes: the detail needs to be considered with 'post-Lisbon' eyes.

Concentrating on substantive law

Barnard, C., *The Substantive Law of the EU*, 4th ed. (Oxford: OUP, 2013).

Barnard, C. and Scott, J., *The Law of the Single European Market: Unpacking the Premises* (Oxford: Hart Publishing, 2002).

Caro de Sousa, P., *The European Fundamental Freedoms: A Contextual Approach* (Oxford: OUP, 2015).

Nic Shuibhne, N., *The Coherence of EU Free Movement Law: Constitutional Responsibility and the Court of Justice* (Oxford: OUP, 2015).

Oliver, P., *Free Movement of Goods in the EU*, 5th ed. (Oxford: Hart, 2010).

Concentrating on institutional and constitutional law and practice

Alter, K., *The European Court's Political Power* (Oxford: OUP, 2009).

Hix, S. and Høyland, B., *The Political System of the European Union*, 3rd ed. (Basingstoke: Palgrave Macmillan, 2011).

Lenaerts, K. and Van Nuffel, P., *European Union Law*, 3rd ed. (London: Sweet and Maxwell, 2011).

Schũtze, R., *European Constitutional Law* (Cambridge: CUP, 2012).

Von Bogdandy, A. and Bast, J., *Principles of European Constitutional Law*, 2nd ed. (Munich: Beck, Oxford: Hart, 2010).

Weiler, J.H.H., *The Constitution of Europe: Do the New Clothes Have an Emperor?* (Cambridge: CUP, 1999).

Covering all or most aspects of the Union legal order

Arnull, A. and Chalmers, D., *The Oxford Handbook of European Union Law* (Oxford: OUP, 2015).

Barnard, C. and Peers, S., *European Union Law* (Oxford: OUP, 2014).

Chalmers, D., Davies, G., and Monti, G., *European Union Law* 3rd ed. (Cambridge: CUP, 2014).

Craig, P. and de Búrca, G., *The Evolution of EU Law*, 2nd ed. (Oxford: OUP, 2010).

Craig, P. and de Búrca, G., *EU Law*, 6th ed. (Oxford: OUP, 2015).

Mathijsen, P. and Dyrberg, A., *Mathijsen's Guide to European Union Law*, 11th ed. (London: Sweet & Maxwell, 2014).

Schütze, R., *European Union Law* (Cambridge: CUP, 2015).

Wyatt, D. and Dashwood, A., *European Union Law*, 6th ed. (Oxford: Hart, 2011).

INDEX